# Visual Basic™ 4.0 Power Toolkit

## Cutting-Edge Tools & Techniques for Programmers

[redacted]

# Visual Basic™ 4.0 Power Toolkit

## Cutting-Edge Tools & Techniques for Programmers

Richard Mansfield
&
Evangelos Petroutsos

VENTANA

**Visual Basic 4.0 Power Toolkit: Cutting-Edge Tools & Techniques for Programmers**



Library of Congress Cataloging-in-Publication Data

Mansfield, Richard.
Visual Basic 4.0 power toolkit : cutting-edge tools & techniques for programmers / Richard Mansfield and Evangelos Petroutsos. -- 1st ed.
p. cm.
Includes index.
ISBN 1-56604-321-2
1. BASIC (Computer program language) 2. Microsoft Visual BASIC.
I. Petroutsos, Evangelos. II. Title.
QA76.73.B3M3648 1995
005.265--dc20 95-38805

Book design: Marcia Webb
Cover illustration: Jeff Brice

Acquisitions Editor: Sherri Morningstar
Art Director: Marcia Webb
Design staff: Bradley King, Charles Overbeck, Dawne Sherman
Developmental Editor: Tim C. Mattson
Editorial staff: Angela Anderson, Amy Moyers, Beth Snowberger
Managing Editor: Pam Richardson
Print Department: Kristen De Quattro, Dan Koeller
Production Manager: John Cotterman
Production staff: Patrick Berry, Scott Hosa, Jaimie Livingston
Project Editor: Lynn Jaluvka
Technical Director: Dan Brown

Index service: Dianne Bertsch, Answers Plus
Proofreader: Angela Anderson
Technical review: Charles Brannon

First Edition 9 8 7 6 5 4 3 2 1
Printed in the United States of America

Ventana Communications Group, Inc.
P.O. Box 13964
Research Triangle Park, NC 27709-3964
919/544-9404
FAX 919/544-9472

## Trademarks

## About the Authors

Richard Mansfield's books have sold more than 300,000 copies worldwide. He was editor-in-chief of *Compute* magazine for seven years. His published work includes columns on computer topics, magazine articles and several short stories. He is co-author of *The Windows 95 Book* (Ventana). He is author of *Machine Language for Beginners* (Compute Press) and *The Visual Guide to Visual Basic for Windows* (Ventana), and 12 other computer books.

Evangelos Petroutsos received his master's degree in Computer Engineering from the University of California in 1982. He was a computer analyst at the California Institute of Technology for five years, before becoming an independent programming consultant for various companies including MCI and Infonet. He is currently involved in a research project funded by the European Community.

## Acknowledgments

Our thanks to Lynn Jaluvka for her watchful, excellent editing. Thanks also to Charles Brannon who provided a close, helpful technical edit. Special gratitude goes to the acquisitions committee at Ventana who backed this project, believing, as do the authors, that a clear, understandable book about advanced Visual Basic programming would have wide appeal. Last, but not least, we would like to thank Pam Richardson for handling every minor and major crisis in her usual, graceful way.

# Dedication

Richard Mansfield dedicates this book
to David Lee Roach.

Evangelos Petroutsos dedicates this book
to his parents, Efi and Spiros.

# Contents

# Introduction

We had a specific goal when writing this book. We wanted to cover sophisticated, advanced topics, but explain them so simply and clearly that anyone who programs in Visual Basic can easily add these impressive techniques to their own applications.

Our goal was to explain advanced programming techniques for the average VB programmer, and our book is essentially version-independent. All the techniques we present can be used with both Visual Basic 3.0 (VB3) and Visual Basic 4.0 (VB4). Because the implementation of our examples may differ, however, we provide two versions of our applications on the CD—one for VB3 and another for VB4 users.

CD-ROM

In addition, wherever there are differences between the two versions of the language, we mention them in the text.We believe that a number of VB users will not switch immediately to VB4, and we don't want to leave them out. Moreover, our explanations and the dual examples should help ease your transition from VB3 to VB4.

## WHAT'S IN THIS BOOK?

We selected topics that we think are inherently useful in Visual Basic programming, and also inherently interesting. Beyond that, we chose some—like ergonomic Forms design, creating fractals, and encryption—because they've either been ignored or only superficially described elsewhere. Others were chosen because they are on the cutting edge of computing, such as multimedia effects, workgroup networking and the design of mail-aware applications.

The CD-ROM bound into this book includes everything we thought you might find useful. First, it has all of the book's text, programming examples and applications. It also has demos and sample applications from commercial products that we think are valuable to VB programmers. Rounding out the CD are fractal animations, a collection of images and sounds, demos of commercial applications, and a few very useful shareware applications.

CD-ROM

## WHAT YOU'LL LEARN

Here are some of the topics and tools explored in this book:

***Visual Transitions***. Everyone knows how important transitions are in writing, music and other creative activities. But little thought has been given to transitions in the user interface of computer applications. When you make a transition from one Form to another, or change the contents of a Text Box or Picture Box, it's sometimes desirable to borrow from the techniques used in TV and movies.

We've included dozens of visual transitions in this book. These *wipes*, as they're called, replace one image (or piece of text) with another by sliding the new one over the old one, by dissolving one into another, or with venetian blind and other effects. They're very fast and visually far more professional-looking than simply slapping the new element on top of the old one. You'll find them in Chapter 9 and several related techniques in Chapter 8.

***Image Processing Techniques***. With graphics programs like CorelDRAW!, many of us have used image processing techniques like mosaic, sharpening and diffusion without knowing how they were done. Chapter 6 shows you exactly how to transform graphics in VB. We demonstrate how to manipulate graphics every which way—through sharpening, diffusing, mosaic, embossing, engraving, blurring, neon, inversion, and conversion from color to monochrome. What's more, the same programming that sharpens a picture can also be used to "sharpen" the tone of *sound* (like turning up the treble control on a HiFi). So we show how to do that, too.

***Fractals***. We explain why fractals—which make complicated mathematical ideas visible—are important in mathematics, and we show how to program and even animate them in VB. There are many books about fractals, filled with impressive images. But as far as we know, nowhere outside this book will you find simple, clear, easy-to-follow instructions telling you how to create these often stunning images. Chapter 14 also explains the math behind fractals in a way that is understandable to most anyone, regardless of your math background.

***Optimizing Program Execution***. In Chapter 1, we cover all the ways you can speed up program execution. Chapter 2 explains how to manage data efficiently. If that's not enough, Chapter 15 shows how to create high-speed dynamic link libraries (DLLs) in VB-like Turbo Pascal and Delphi, and demonstrates how easy it is to use DLLs in computation-intensive sections of your VB programs. You'll see exactly what DLLs can do for you when you want to turbo-charge a VB program.

***Looking Good***. Few topics have been more universally ignored than how a computer application *looks*. Computing is a young technology and, as with early automobiles, the focus has been on how they run. But with GUIs and increasingly powerful computer video, the time has come to consider the appearance, the visual design, of your applications along with their speed and reliability. Chapter 7 provides guidelines that can both improve the ergonomics of your programs and make them look more professional.

***API Routines***. When the more than 500 commands available in VB can't accomplish something you want to do, or can't accomplish it fast enough, you can turn to the built-in Windows library of routines called the API (Application Programming Interface). In Chapter 8, you'll find what we believe to be all the most useful API routines. These dozens of techniques are explained in depth with complete, understandable working examples—such as capturing any part of the screen, checking system resources, and adding special effects like auto-scrolling to Text Boxes and graphics.

***Database Programming.*** Database programming with VB is already popular, and it will become more so in the future. However, it's new to many VB programmers. In Chapters 3 and 4 we help you make the transition from elementary flat-file databases to relational databases and true database programming. Both chapters cover the principles of database programming and concentrate on the design of front-end applications. Visual Basic 4.0 provides many additional features for database management, and we cover both versions of the language in two separate chapters. If you are using VB3 for database programming, read Chapter 3. If you are using VB4, or would like to learn about the new database management capabilities of VB4, read Chapter 4. The two chapters overlap in many areas, but we decided we would best serve the needs of our readers by providing two separate chapters. (A rather unorthodox approach, but we want to address the needs of all users of Visual Basic.)

***OLE Automation***. In Chapter 10, we cover the cutting-edge technique called OLE Automation. With it you can do two new and very valuable things. First, you can directly employ any of the tools in an OLE-capable application (heightening contrast in a photo, sending email or whatever tasks that application performs). You can employ those tools from within a separate application. Second, you can have these services performed *automatically* between applications.

***New Directions***. A new macro language called Visual Basic, Applications Edition (VBA), has been added to most of Microsoft's applications, except Word. VBA/Excel incorporates much from VB, but goes beyond VB, adding 59 new commands to the Basic language. We predict that many of these commands will eventually become part of Visual Basic and even Windows itself. In Chapter 11, we cover each generic command's uses and techniques and provide real-world examples.

***Multimedia Programming***. In Chapter 9, we demonstrate the nuts and bolts of multimedia technology. You'll find out how sounds are stored and processed in computers. You'll see how to add echo and reverberation effects, and discover interesting similarities between sounds and images. We also include a proofreader program that audibly reads out the numbers in a spreadsheet. (If you've ever transferred numbers from paper to a spreadsheet application, you'll understand why VBReader can save many hours of tedious proofing.)

***Adding Animation***. You'll also find out how to add animation to your applications. We'll give you the tools to create animated fractals, and explain how you can plug the real power of the Windows multimedia capabilities into your Visual Basic applications.

***Workgroup Computing***. For many years programmers were busy perfecting the single-user environment. We are taking our first tentative steps toward what could end up being one global "computer," with outlets (hardware) all over the world. One such step is a new generation of applications that's making news in the computer press. This software deals not only with the individual user, but also with a group of users that share common resources and goals. In Chapter 13 we demonstrate how to make good use of the Windows electronic mail engine—to establish communication not only between users, but also between applications. We'll cover mail-enabled and mail-aware applications, and show how to write applications that send, receive and process mail messages automatically.

***Recursion***. Chapter 12 attempts to demystify recursive programming—demonstrating how to put it to good use, and providing both simple and advanced examples. Some programming problems, like the file-managing utility we construct, are best solved with recursion. For the adventurous, we'll also write a math parser—a program that understands, manipulates and visually displays numeric expressions. Among other things, you'll discover why parsing is best programmed recursively.

***Data Security—and a $1,000 Prize***. Finally, we look at data security in Chapter 16—how you can encode a text file (or any other kind of file, for that matter) so intruders can't break the code. We explore various approaches to computer encryption, describe some weaknesses in currently popular schemes and then present a detailed explanation (including the source code and a complete encoder/decoder application) of an encryption algorithm that we've designed. We're convinced of its security—so convinced, in fact, that we give you a chance to win $1,000 by cracking the coded message at the end of Chapter 16, according to the contest rules also provided there. Nearly a year after its publication in *Visual Basic Power Toolkit*, no one has cracked it. (Unfortunately, this chapter cannot be published outside the U.S. for legal reasons.)

# Chapter 1

# Optimizing Your Programs

Much of the time you can take it fast and loose while writing Visual Basic programs. You don't have to worry about conserving memory, nor do you have to think about increasing your program's speed. You don't have to think about screen resolution, color settings, Windows messages, display arcana, the mysteries of DIBs and twips and all the rest.

One reason that VB is the most popular Windows programming language is that it takes care of so many tiresome, niggling details. It's the easiest way by far to program in Windows. However, there will be times that you will want to fiddle with your VB program. Make it run faster.

There are a variety of ways to reduce memory usage and increase execution speed.

Often you can locate a bottleneck, a section where the program slows down because it is repeatedly calculating (often it's a loop like For...Next or While...Wend). One way to improve speed in these cases is to write your own DLL (see Chapter 15). In other cases you can simply change a line of programming, use a particular type of variable or adjust the way you are displaying graphics. In this chapter we will explore these and other techniques that can make your programs run more swiftly.

### Why Are Some Languages Easier to Program?

Before we start looking at speed optimization techniques, let's consider a related question. Computer languages are created for the convenience of programmers. All programming languages are translated, ultimately, into machine language—the only language the computer speaks. Why, then, are some computer languages, like VB, relatively intuitive and easy for humans to use, while others, like C, are sometimes counterintuitive? Why aren't all programming languages designed to be as natural, as English-like, as possible? Wouldn't this make programmers more productive?

Programming languages fall into two primary categories: those that produce faster-running programs and those that are easier to use. Although these two qualities are not completely mutually exclusive, execution speed versus programming convenience is the main trade-off when you pick a language. If your program displays rich graphics more quickly than other programs, or sorts huge amounts of information more rapidly, extra effort on your part is worthwhile. It's like choosing a stick shift: you work harder while driving, but are more intimately in touch with the machine. Race cars don't have automatic transmissions.

VB gives you the convenience of an automatic, with the option to exert the control of a stick shift when you need it.

## OPTIMIZING FOR SPEED

At times, though, you will want to get down closer to the machine's core—to find ways to improve the speed of execution. There are a number of tips and techniques you may find useful. The first and most important technique is to use integers whenever possible. Remember that VB considers all variables to be of the default Variant type. Unless you specify otherwise, everything, text and numeric, will be a Variant.

### Use Integers Whenever Possible

With Variants, VB makes its own decisions about variable typing.

Consider, as one of many possible proofs of its human-friendliness, VB's Variant variable. It's up to VB to figure out the variable type of a Variant based on its context. Like a good, intelligent butler, VB says to itself, "Master is trying to print something, so we'll make this a string at this time." But later in the program, it says, "Master is adding this to a number, so we have to treat it now as an Integer variable. This a mathematical maneuver, so we must change the variable type."

No other language allows you to ignore the type of data that you are working with.

### A 50-Million-Loop Time Test

Here is a brief program that counts 50 million times. Note that in the speed trial that follows, the test computer we used was a 486/100, with a Diamond Stealth 64 video card running VB4/32-bits under Windows 95. Most of the speed tests in this book were conducted with a 486/66. However, many factors are involved when you measure speed in a computer—even the same test run repeatedly on the same computer can produce varying results because of caching and other factors. Therefore, you should consider the speed results in this book useful only as relative indicators. In other words, it's worth knowing that Integer variable types will always be faster than Floating Point types on any PC, but absolutely how much faster depends on many variables.

VB ran the following tests in under a minute. If you want to try these timing tests on a 386 computer, you may want to substitute For i = 1 To 20000 instead of the For i = 1 To 200000 below.

```
Private Sub Form_Load()

Dim i As Long, j As Byte
Dim start As Double, Elapse As Double
Show
start = Timer
For i = 1 To 200000
   For j = 1 To 254
   Next j
Next i
Elapse = Timer - start
Print Elapse

End Sub
```

When this Form loads, the inner loop counter *j* is defined as a Byte variable type for the first test. The starting and ending times are held in the variables start and Elapse. We make them Double (a capacious Floating Point type) so they will permit great precision (large fractions are used in VB to store time information). Then we begin with start = Timer to get the current time. We use the Timer function in VB (unrelated to Timer Controls). It provides elapsed time since midnight each day, then resets. Then we start running the nested loop. When the loop finishes, we subtract the starting time from the current (Timer) time and print the results on the Form.

To test each variable type, all we have to do is change the type of *j* in the first line of the program: Dim j as Integer, Dim j as Long, and so forth.

Table 1-1 shows the results (in elapsed seconds, rounded off):

| | |
|---|---|
| Integer | 36 |
| Byte | 39 |
| Long | 35 |
| Currency | 48 |
| Variant | 56 |
| Single Precision Floating Point | 60 |
| Double Precision Floating Point | 63 |

Table 1-1: The difference in speed between variable types.

In some computers, using the Integer variable type makes a program run 25 times faster.

As you can see, it does matter what kind of variable you use. The Integer variable type runs quite a bit faster than the Floating Point types. The Variant—considering that it must analyze context and requires more storage in memory than any other type—runs surprisingly fast. However, you can gain about 40 percent in speed by simply using an Integer instead of the default Variant. (These results differ under different operating systems and different versions of VB. For example, with VB3 under Windows 3.x, Currency is the slowest type by quite a margin. The Long type was fastest in this test because, in a 32-bit environment, Long doesn't require offsetting at the register.) However, in any context, Floating Point tends to be slower than Integer types, with the Variant somewhere in between.

Traditionally, Basic used the Single Precision Floating Point type as the default. For this reason, and because until recently computers had no math coprocessors, most Basic programmers changed the default variable to Integer. They did so by placing the following line at the top of each program (VB programmers put it in the General Declarations section at the top of the programming for each Form):

```
DefInt a-z
```

This command causes all undeclared variables to default to Integers, the quickest type. In computers without math coprocessors, this simple step typically causes loops like the one in our test program above to run 25 times faster. So the old habit of putting DefInt a-z into the General Declarations section of each of your Forms and Modules is still worth doing if you need to speed up a program's execution.

Clearly, you can't use integers in all your programs, everywhere. Calculations requiring greater precision (a result including a fraction) must be made with Floating Point variable types (Single or Double). Calculations requiring a large range cannot be made with integers (which can manipulate only the numbers between –32768 and 32767). In that case, you have to resort to "long integers" (Long), Floating Point (Single or Double) or Currency data types.

### Using Integers Instead of Floating Point

However, in some situations you might think you can't, but you actually can, employ integers. For example, if you are working with a matrix of 60,000 elements, you can ignore the minus sign and work within the –32768 to 32767 range that integers permit. You can also ignore the decimal point as you might have done when figuring your checkbook balance on a calculator: to add $33.55 and $12 you would just tap in 3355+1200 and then remember that the last two digits are pennies. Even better, you could just follow the advice of the IRS and round off pennies—eliminating the whole problem of decimals and the thereby obligatory and messy floating-point data types. The fastest, easiest way to round decimal numbers is to merely assign them to an integer variable:

```
Z = 4.7
Y% = Z
X% = 4.2
Print Y%, X%
```

This results in:

```
5    4
```

### When to Use the New Byte

There is a new *Byte* data type in VB4, which holds a single byte (it can hold numbers between 0 and 255). As you can see in Table 1-1 above, using a Byte type doesn't improve on the speed of the Integer type. However, there is a special situation where the Byte type will speed up your programs. Until now, you had to use the Integer type when pulling data in from a disk file (an Integer works with 2-byte chunks) or use a string defined as a single-byte character if your goal was to work with individual bytes.

Assuming that you wanted to work with numeric data in single-byte chunks, you had a problem. The Integer type required that you read or write a disk file in 2-byte chunks. The alternative, bringing in a single byte from a disk file *as a character* (String data type), required that you translate the string into a numeric variable type—wasting time during the translation. Here's an example:

```
Open "C:\WINDOWS\WIN.INI" For Binary As #1
X$ = String$(1," ") 'This creates a single-byte string
Get #1, X$
A% = Val(X$) 'translate
```

This is a rather indirect way to read or write single-byte numeric data to disk. VB4 solves the Byte type problem. However, VB4 32-bit introduces a new kink in data storage (there's no free lunch). OLE and Windows 95 and NT require that text characters be stored as 2-byte ("Unicode") units. This permits languages like Chinese to be accommodated (the ANSI code from 0 to 255 couldn't hope to cope with the world's languages). However, many people have written programs based on the assumption that text characters are single-byte-sized. This shift to Unicode breaks these older programs. For more about the efficiencies of the Byte type, see Chapter 6.

## ANIMATION

VB can create dramatic visual effects such as the "wipes" discussed in Chapter 9. Let's make a skeleton dance across a Form 9 and then see how to speed it up.

To measure the elapsed time in this and the rest of the examples in this chapter, we'll want to modify our Elapse routine. The following Function will be triggered at the start and end of the programming whose duration we want to measure:

```
Function Elapse ()

Static c As Integer, Start As Double, Done As Double

c = c + 1

If c = 1 Then
   Start = Timer
Else
   Done = Timer - Start
   MsgBox "Time Elapsed: " & Done
```

```
End If
End Function
```

We use the Static command to force our variables to retain their values during those times when the Function is not active. (Static preserves local variables when you exit from a procedure. Normally, a local variable resets to zero or empty when you leave the function or sub in which the variable is located.) The variable *c* is used as a counter. The first time we use this Function, we put the value of the Timer into the variable Start. The second time (after our programming has finished executing), we calculate the duration and display it in a Message Box.

If you want to measure various execution times, type the Elapse Function into a Module. Then, simply call it just before and just after the lines of programming that you want to measure (see the next programming example).

## The Dancing Skeleton

This next example illustrates what happens if you are animating something. Unlike the empty loop in the example above, this program actually does something.

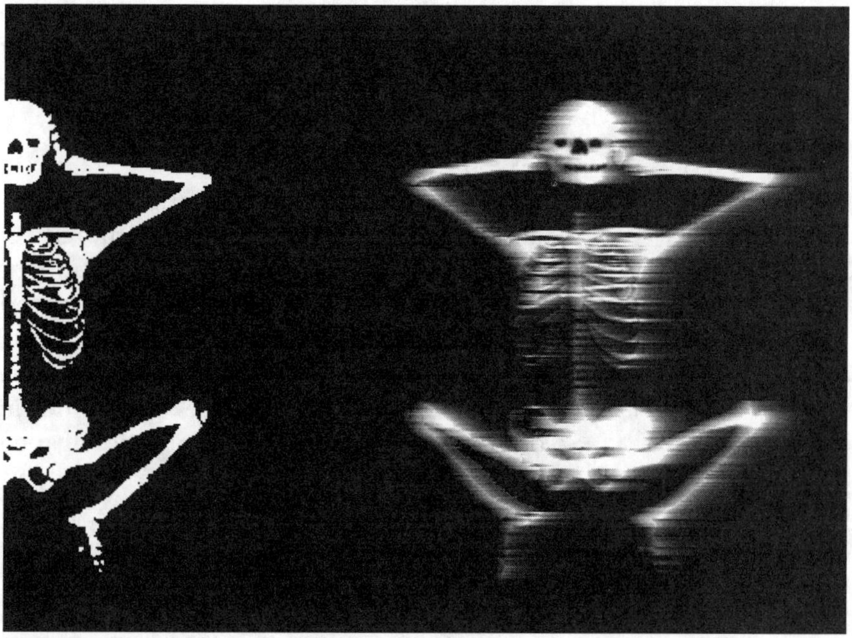

Figure 1-1: Increasing the step value accelerates this animation.

Here's the program that animates the skeleton:

```
Sub Form_Load ()

Dim i As Integer
picture1.Left = Left + width
Show
x = elapse()
For i = 1 To 1500
   picture1.Left = picture1.Left –10
Next i
x = elapse()

End Sub
```

The primary speed improvements in this example come from changing the following line.

```
picture1.Left = picture1.Left –10
```

If you move the Picture Box in steps of 10, our test results show that it takes the skeleton 22.41 seconds to move across the Form. If you change the line to

```
picture1.Left = picture1.Left –30
```

the animation takes 12 seconds. Change it to Left - 60, and it takes 7 seconds. It makes little difference whether you use a Variant or Integer for the variable *i*.

## Image Boxes Are Faster

Another way to speed up animation is to use an Image Box rather than a Picture Box (which has many more Events, thus keeping VB busy checking to see if something has happened to the Picture Box). Tests show a 15 percent improvement in speed (using integers and a step of 10) when you replace a Picture Box with an Image Box.

Find the best trade-off between smooth animation and a step size that will speed your loops.

But in the real world, a 15 percent improvement is often barely noticeable to the viewer. People don't notice minor changes in speed. So our concern is not pure computational speed, but the observed, or perceived, speed. The amount of jerkiness you believe the user will tolerate should determine the step size. You could move this skeleton in three steps by changing this line to

```
picture1.Left = picture1.Left – 500
```

but it would look crude. (All these effects depend, too, on the user's video card. A fast video card will make things look smoother than a slow one.) Try a step size of –500 to see the abrupt changes. For smooth animation, you obviously want a step size lower than –500.

The lower the step size, the better and smoother the animation. Is there a way to use a low step size like 10, but have the skeleton fly gracefully and liquidly across the form?

## A 2100% Improvement

What if we rearrange the programming a little?

```
Sub Form_Load ()
Dim i As Integer
picture1.Left = left + width
Show
x = elapse()

For i = 1 To 1500 Step 10
   picture1.Left = picture1.Left –i
Next i

x = elapse()

End Sub
```

When we add a Step command to the For statement and then subtract the resulting value of i (instead of picture1.left –10), our elapsed time function reports that the routine finishes in .9921 seconds (vs. the previous 22.41 seconds).

Always see if you can reduce calculations with a loop.

What we have done here is reduce the number of For...Next statements by adding the Step command. Instead of 1,500 iterations, the For...Next command loops only 150 times.

The following structure reduces the time somewhat less (to 3.24 seconds), but is still far faster than the 1,500-loop example at 22.41 seconds:

```
For i = 1 To 1500 Step 10
   picture1.Left = picture1.Left - 100
Next i
```

The moral of this story: If you are looping, see if you can decrease the number of iterations in the loop.

## Creating a Ride

Since our goal is to increase the speed of calculations, wouldn't the fastest calculations be those that we do before even running the routine? In other words, let's say that we want to bounce an object up and down a few times on a Form. Most programmers would just create a set of loops that would repeatedly calculate the object's position as it moves up and down.

Some speed improvements result if you plot a path during program design, rather than during execution.

But what if we gather the data beforehand? Then we would merely feed VB a series of known absolute positions for the bouncing picture, rather than calculating each change in position. Instead of a bus trip where the driver must constantly correct the position of the bus on the road, we've built a ride like a roller coaster. Our bouncing image will move along an already existing "track" of positions because these positions have been calculated before our program even runs. This, in essence, is also the reason that compiled computer programs can run faster than interpreted programs.

Let's try it.

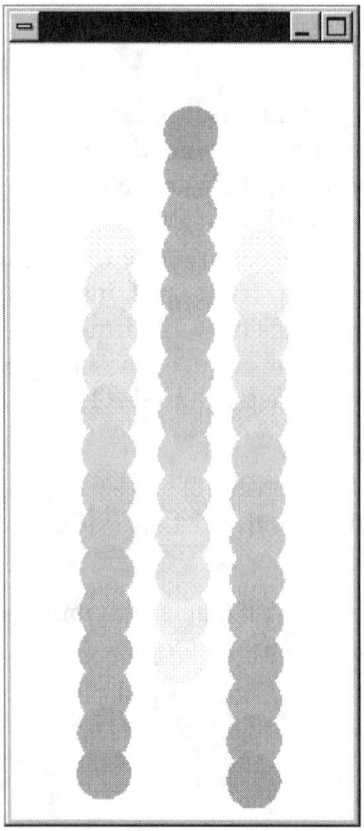

Figure 1-2: This ball is bouncing on a precalculated "track."

First, recall that Visual Basic has eliminated the Data...Read command. The theory as to why it was taken out of Basic is that the program will run more quickly if you hard-code the data in-line, like this

```
A(1) = 100
A(2) = 300
A(3) = 400
A(4) = 700
```

rather than this

```
DATA 100, 300, 400, 700
For I = 1 to 4
READ A(I)
NEXT I
```

(Fortunately, Data...Read has been revived, albeit in disguise. In Visual Basic for Applications there is a new command called Array, which does what Data...Read did. The Array command is now available in VB4.)

To test the bouncing ball animation, put a Shape Control on a Form. Set its FillStyle Property to Solid and its FillColor to gray or some other color. Now type this into the Form_Load Event:

```
Sub Form_Load ()
Dim i As Integer, j As Integer
shape1.Top = Top
Show
x = elapse()
For j = 1 To 25
 For i = 1 To 10
    shape1.Top = shape1.Top + 400
 Next i
 For i = 1 To 10
    shape1.Top = shape1.Top - 400
 Next i
Next j
x = elapse()
End Sub
```

This is a standard, run-time-calculated trajectory for our animated bouncing ball. The elapsed time is 2.91 seconds. (See the listing for the Elapse function under "Animation" earlier in this chapter.)

## USE A LITERAL PATH FOR ANIMATION

Now we'll replace the calculations with data specifying the literal position of the ball at each stage of the animation. We find out that the Top of the Form (the starting point) is 1,215. (To get this value, put a breakpoint on the second line, shape1.Top = Top, and then highlight Top and press F9. Or temporarily insert a Msgbox into the code.) For convenience, we'll use a starting point of 1,200. So our data will be multiples of 400, added to 1,200. Replace the inner loops (For i) with this:

```
For j = 1 To 25
   shape1.Top = 1600
   shape1.Top = 2000
   shape1.Top = 2400
   shape1.Top = 2800
   shape1.Top = 3200
   shape1.Top = 3600
   shape1.Top = 4000
   shape1.Top = 4400
   shape1.Top = 4800
   shape1.Top = 5200

   shape1.Top = 4800
   shape1.Top = 4400
   shape1.Top = 4000
   shape1.Top = 3600
   shape1.Top = 3200
   shape1.Top = 2800
   shape1.Top = 2400
   shape1.Top = 2000
Next j
```

The result is 2.64 seconds, an improvement of 10 percent. One reason it's not *much* faster is that the calculations use simple addition. More complex calculations could be considerably faster when replaced by constants. Replacing calculated with known values sometimes results in greater speed improvements. Compare, for instance, the time required to load a finished bitmap of a fractal or ray-traced image from disk against the time required to calculate the image in a running program. Likewise, precalculations involving the equations for planetary motion would greatly speed up an astronomy application. For large amounts of data, consider precalculating the data and storing it in arrays, or even on disk, rather than doing it while the user sits and waits.

## Background Calculation

Hide delays from the user by calculating during idle time.

You might also consider background calculation—that is, doing your calculations while the program loads or while it is idle. This won't speed up the actual calculations, but it will make the program seem faster to the user. In a calendar application, for instance, the dates of several special days, including Easter, vary according to formulas (such as the third Thursday in the month). Since you can assume that the user will most often stay within the current year, have your program fill an array with these moveable dates for the current year while the program loads. Then, when the user switches to April, the program won't have to pause to figure out Easter.

# GRAPHICS SPEED

Adjusting your visuals can also speed things up. One of the most time-consuming tasks is loading high-resolution pictures. This isn't just a VB phenomenon—any program has to pause for high-res graphics to load from disk because graphics take lots of room. A large, color .BMP file can get up into the megabytes. In the following speed tests, we use the Elapse Function described under "Animation" earlier in this chapter.

Note that this next test, and others, seem to reveal small differences in elapsed time. However, if you are loading, say, 10 graphic objects, 5 Forms, or large amounts of data, it makes a considerable difference to the user if your program takes 1 second or 5 seconds to start running. Even seemingly small speed improvements in your program can, cumulatively, make the difference between the user's perception of a slick or a sluggish application.

```
Sub Form_Load ()
x = elapse()
   Show
   x = elapse()
End Sub
```

Figure 1-3: A textured background can slow a VB program (this one adds 1.1 seconds).

In the Picture Property for the Form in Figure 1-3 we specified that the marble .BMP file should appear as a background to whatever Controls we will put on the Form. Backgrounds are attractive, but they exact a speed penalty. Loading this Form takes more than three times longer with the graphic than without (.16 vs. .05 seconds). (For a solution to this problem, see "BitBlt: Instant Tiled Wallpaper on Forms" in Chapter 8.)

The result is the same, .16 seconds, if you put the marble background into a Picture Box or Image Control (instead of the Picture Property of the Form). Likewise, there is no significant difference between the elapsed time measured while running a program in the VB design environment versus running it as an .EXE file directly under Windows.

The marble background is 811,078 bytes. What if we use a high-resolution grayscale image of more than 4 million bytes? The graphic in Figure 1-4 adds almost 2 seconds to the time required to Load the Form (1.93 seconds). And in a computer with 4mb or even 8mb of RAM, the computer must struggle for a much longer time to display a 4mb image. Disk paging can become severe.

Figure 1-4: This 4mb high-resolution picture takes 2 seconds to Load (if the computer has enough RAM).

## LoadPicture, RLE & WMF

Load optional images dynamically.

What are the benefits of loading a graphic only when it's needed (as opposed to embedding it in a Form so that it always loads with the Form)? The VB command LoadPicture allows you to bring in files from the disk dynamically, while a program is running. Clearly this would be of no value for our marble background graphic—that should be part of the Form. However, for optional graphics, things the user might or might not need to see, LoadPicture can permit the program to run at top speed until LoadPicture is activated.

But if we load the marble graphic shown in Figure 1-3 again for the sake of comparison, using the following technique, it takes 10 times longer to display—1.6 versus .16 seconds—than when the graphic is embedded (described in the Picture Property):

```
Sub Form_Load ()
x = elapse()
Show
Picture1.Picture = LoadPicture("C:\NEW-1.BMP")
x = elapse()
End Sub
```

However, moving the Show command below LoadPicture in the program reduces the load time to .6 seconds:

```
Sub Form_Load ()
x = elapse()
Picture1.Picture = LoadPicture("C:\NEW-1.BMP")
Show
x = elapse()
End Sub
```

And eliminating the Show command entirely reduces the time further, to .4 seconds.

One alternative to .BMP files is the .WMF (Windows MetaFile) format. This is not, however, a "photographic" type—it is not stored as a point-for-point copy of an image (as are .BMP, .TIF and various other graphics files). Instead a .WMF image is stored as a mathematical description of colors, fills and shapes called *vector graphics*. No matter how detailed the description, though, .WMF images always look like drawings. By contrast, .BMP images can look like photographs. Because .BMP images contain more information than comparably sized .WMF files, .BMP files take longer to load and to display. However, if your application can benefit from the less realistic .WMF graphics, you'll speed things up by using them instead of photographic .BMP files. One example would be the classic "starfield" illustration—a background of black with various white dots simulating the view out a spaceship porthole. You could create this image as a .BMP file, but since there is relatively little real data, it would be better to create it in a drawing program like CorelDRAW! or Adobe Illustrator and save it as a .WMF file.

## .WMF Images Are Scalable

Note also that .WMF images can be freely resized. So if you want to avoid a calculation speed penalty, resize your .WMF drawing to the same size as you'll want to display it in VB (all graphics programs have a resizing feature, sometimes called "scale," or "resample"). Then load the .WMF file into an Image Control with its Stretch Property set to False (so the Image Control won't resize itself to fit the size of your file).

Figure 1-5: The horse is a .WMF (drawing); the woman is a .BMP (copy).

## RLE

RLE is a way of compressing, or squeezing, a file down so it takes up less space on disk. VB can load and use RLE-encoded files. However, a compressed file has to be decompressed before it can be displayed. Let's see if it makes any difference in the timing.

Figure 1-6: Loading the pharaoh into VB via BMP, RLE and DIB graphics file formats.

A DIB graphic exacts a speed penalty.

It takes 1.62 seconds to load Figure 1-6 into an Image Control as a .BMP image, and 1.76 seconds to load it as an RLE. The RLE uses up about half as much space on the disk (721k vs. 1421k) as the uncompressed .BMP file. Another format which VB can read—DIB, or Device Independent Bitmap—is designed to work with anything: screens, plotters, printers and so on. However, this file requires 4.44 seconds to load, so there's a speed penalty for the file's ability to serve so many different output devices. Most of the popular graphics programs do not load or save files in the DIB or RLE format (only HiJaak, Photoshop and PaintShop do). And note that the RLE format is really a type of .BMP and should be saved with the .BMP extension.

Interestingly, if you load the same picture twice into a VB program, the second time takes about one-third as long (1.8 seconds down to .6). This effect is computer-dependent because it relies on disk caching, if any. Another technique that can improve speed is useful when you are loading the same graphic into several Picture Boxes or Image Controls. Load it into one of them, then copy it to the others by setting the Picture Property of the other Controls to match the original. Here's how.

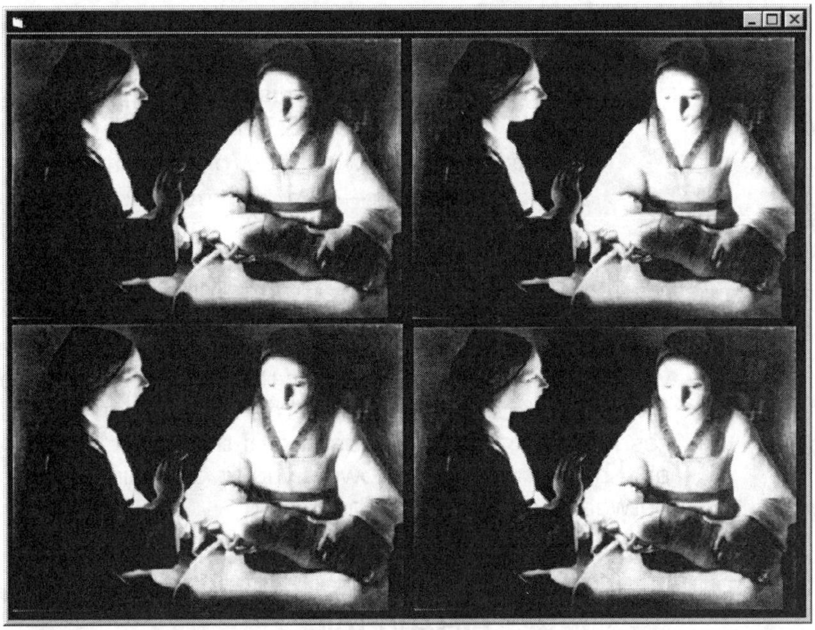

Figure 1-7: Copying the paintings with Properties is five times faster than loading each one.

It takes 1.05 seconds to load the image four times:

```
Sub Form_Load ()
x = elapse()
image1.Picture = LoadPicture("C:\GRAPHICS\MADONNA.BMP")
image2.Picture = LoadPicture("C:\GRAPHICS\MADONNA.BMP")
image3.Picture = LoadPicture("C:\GRAPHICS\MADONNA.BMP")
image4.Picture = LoadPicture("C:\GRAPHICS\MADONNA.BMP")
Show
x = elapse()
End Sub
```

Copying the Picture Property takes .21 seconds:

```
Sub Form_Load ()
x = elapse()
Image1.Picture = LoadPicture("C:\GRAPHICS\MADONNA.BMP")
image2.Picture = Image1.Picture
image3.Picture = Image1.Picture
image4.Picture = Image1.Picture
Show
x = elapse()
End Sub
```

There are several uses for invisible Controls.

To speed things up, you might consider using an invisible Image Box. If a graphic isn't needed right away, load it into an Image Control while your program is starting up. But set the Image Control's Visible Property to False. When the graphic is needed you can reset the Visible Property to True (or you can copy the Picture Property—the actual graphic—from the Image Control to other Image Controls or Picture Boxes).

Invisible Controls can also be useful when you want to sort something. For example, you can use a List Box to maintain a sorted list without ever showing the user the Box. Or you can place invisible Shape Controls on a Form to mark a position regardless of screen resolution or any other resizing of the Form. These Controls can anchor line drawing, allowing you to draw lines and "frames" between points on the Form.

## LINE DRAWING

If you are creating simple geometric graphics on a Form, use the Line and Circle commands (or the Shape Control) rather than PSet. PSet draws a dot on a Form, Picture Box or the Printer. Even using an integer as a counter, the following example takes 5.8 seconds to draw the simple rectangle shown in Figure 1-8:

```
Sub Form_Load ()
Dim i As Integer
Show
x = elapse()
For i = 2000 To 6000
   PSet (i, 1000), QBColor(0)
   PSet (i, 5000), QBColor(0)
Next i
For i = 1000 To 5000
   PSet (2000, i), QBColor(0)
   PSet (6000, i), QBColor(0)
Next i
x = elapse()
End Sub
```

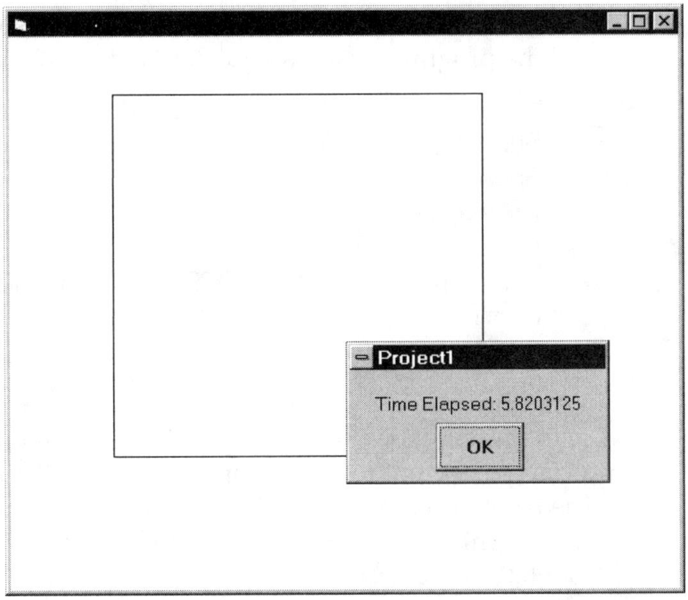


Figure 1-8: This rectangle draws extremely slowly with the PSet command.

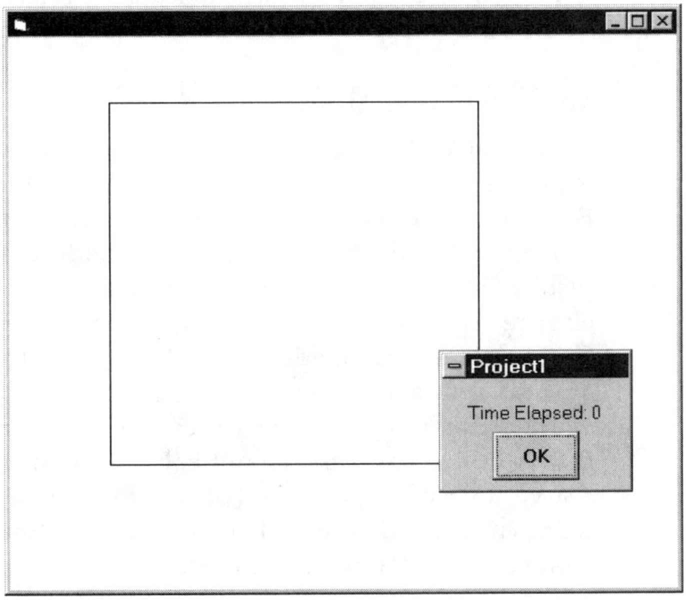


Figure 1-9: Using the Line command, the elapsed time is too quick to measure.

Substitute the VB Line command (which also draws rectangles), and the program draws so quickly that the elapsed time is reported to be zero:

```
Sub Form_Load ()
Show
x = elapse()
for I = 1 to 10
   Line (2000,1000)-(6000,5000),Qbcolor(0),B
next I
x = elapse()
End Sub
```

To measure the actual time the Line command takes to draw this rectangle, we put it into a loop which drew the rectangle 100 times. The result: each rectangle draws in .0005 seconds. You can also create line graphics with the Line or Shape Controls. They will delay things about .05 seconds.

Since there isn't much of a penalty for using the Line or Shape Controls, why bother with the Line command? The answer is that you can efficiently create sophisticated special effects, particularly frames, only with the Line command (see "Frames" in Chapter 7 ).

## AUTOREDRAW

By default VB handles graphics in two fundamental ways. One way is to make the visual a part of the Form, as if it were carved into the Form. The other is to redraw the visual each time the Form is moved, resized or covered by another Form (window). All Controls, bitmap pictures imported into a Picture or Image Box, and most everything else are "carved." However, images or designs created with the Line, Circle or PSet commands, and text created with the Print command, are redrawn as necessary.

The AutoRedraw Property is available only for a Form or a Picture Box. AutoRedraw is by default False. Set it to True, and VB will "carve" everything into the Form or Picture Box. Nothing will be redrawn on the fly. VB will keep a copy, a bitmap picture, of the entire Form or Picture Box in memory.

## Repaint Forms Twice as Fast

In most cases, put drawing commands within the Paint Event.

When AutoRedraw is turned off, a Form repaints at least twice as fast. Many Windows activities—such as pressing Alt+Tab to display a different application, putting a Form on top of the current Form, resizing and minimizing—will erase your images. To repair whatever is erased, you may either set AutoRedraw to True or put your drawing or printing commands within the Paint Event. (Microsoft suggests that all drawing/printing programming be placed within the Paint Event.)

If your drawing activity takes a long time to complete, set AutoRedraw to False. Otherwise, VB will wait for the code to finish before updating a Control or Form.

The Paint Event is triggered when VB needs to repaint a window (Form). VB automatically repaints such things as Button Controls, the frame around the Form and so on. However, if you are printing or drawing on a Form or Picture Box, you must either put your printing/drawing commands within the Paint Event of the Form or Picture Box or let VB do it for you by setting AutoRedraw to True.

Here's a test which compares the two techniques:

```
Sub Form_Load ()
Show
For i = 1 To 1000 Step 100
   Line (2000 + i, 1000 + i)-(6000 + i, 5000 + i), QBColor(0), B
Next i
x = elapse()
For i = 1 To 50
   Refresh
Next i
x = elapse()
End Sub
```

When we put the above into the Form_Load Event, we must turn on the Form's AutoRedraw Property. If we don't, the graphic displayed in Figure 1-10 will disappear after the Refresh command is executed. (Refresh forces a Paint Event to execute, destroying any drawn or printed images.) With AutoRedraw on, the above example takes 2.86 seconds.

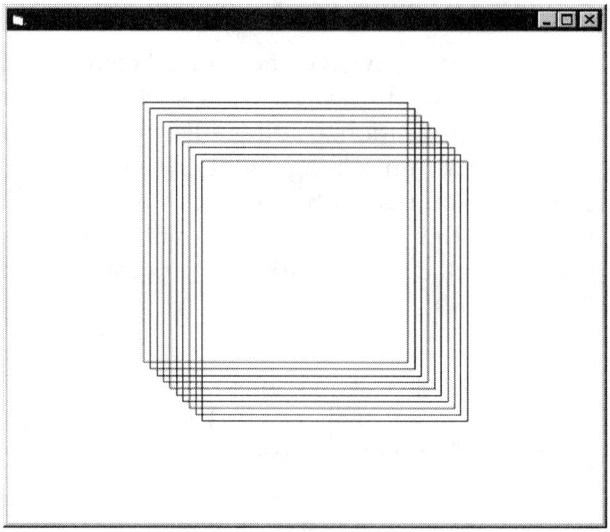

Figure 1-10: This dynamically drawn graphic requires either AutoRedraw (2.86 seconds) or a Paint Event (.597 seconds).

Now let's test the same repeatedly recalculated and redisplayed graphic using the Paint Event. Set AutoRedraw to False, and then type this into the Paint Event:

```
Sub Form_Paint ()
For i = 1 To 1000 Step 100
   Line (2000 + i, 1000 + i)-(6000 + i, 5000 + i), QBColor(0), B
Next i
End Sub
```

And leave this in the Form_Load Event:

```
Sub Form_Load ()
Show
x = elapse()
For i = 1 To 50
   Refresh
Next i
x = elapse()
End Sub
```

This repeated Paint Event triggering approach goes almost five times faster (.597 seconds). But AutoRedraw is convenient.

When AutoRedraw is False, the Print, Line, Circle or PSet commands create text or drawings that are impermanent. If the Form is minimized, or another Form covers, then uncovers, your Form, the drawings or text will be erased.

## CLIPCONTROLS

Like AutoRedraw, the ClipControls Property of a Form, Frame Control or Picture Box tells VB how you want drawn images (Line, Circle and PSet) or printed text (Print) handled. ClipControls defaults to True. However, you'll usually want to set it to False.

### Windows Has Two Repaint Options

When something covers up a Form, or part of a Form (when it's minimized, resized, another window is moved on top of it, etc.), VB must repaint the Form when the intruder is removed. When VB repaints a Form (a window) in your program, it has two options. It can simply repaint the entire window en masse, or it can repaint only the areas that need to be repainted.

Most visual elements are an inherent part of a Form.

As you know, most objects on a Form are carved into that Form and are merely slapped onto the screen—VB doesn't have to repaint them at all because they are an inherent part of the Form. All Controls, bitmap pictures, icons, etc., are part of the Form. They are not superimposed, "written," on the Form each time it is refreshed.

But the temporary, fragile things on the surface of the Form—the lines, circles, PSet images and printed text—are redone each time the Form is refreshed. So you have to decide what to do with them. If you want them to disappear, print or draw them in an Event other than the Paint Event or set the AutoRedraw Property to False, and they will disappear when the host Form is covered or made invisible. (For interesting effects, try playing around with this fragility of painted objects and the CLS command. For more on this technique, see Chapter 5.)

ClipControls, when True, tells VB to repaint the background around the stable, carved elements of the Form. It says, forget about painting the background under these elements; just paint the objects that are "transparent," like printed text (where the background must be painted because it shows through). This selective background-repainting obviously involves a map, geometric calculations, etc. It takes time and slows things up—unless there are things that need redrawing. So if you have not used the Print, PSet, Circle or Line commands with a Form, change the ClipControls Property to False (the default is True).

It's odd that VB defaults ClipControls to True. Forms that would benefit from ClipControls—Forms that feature programmed line drawings or Printed text—are relatively rare in VB programming. So if you want a really quick way of speeding up repainting, remember to set ClipControls to False.

If you leave ClipControls set to True, the following test of 100 repaintings takes 151.16 seconds, or two-and-a-half minutes. With ClipControls set to False, it takes 1.8 seconds.

Put a Picture Box on a Form. Put a picture in the Box with the Picture Property. Make a Control Array by setting the Picture Box's Index Property to 0.

```
Sub Form_Load ()
Show
Rows = 5
Columns = 5
Movedown = Picture1(0).Height
Moveacross = Picture1(0).Width
Picture1(0).Visible = False

For i = 0 To Rows - 1
 For J = 0 To Columns - 1
     x = x + 1
     Load Picture1(x)
     Picture1(x).Top = Movedown * i
     Picture1(x).Left = Moveacross * J
     Picture1(x).Visible = True
 Next J
Next i

x = elapse()
For i = 1 To 100
 Refresh
Next i
x = elapse()

End Sub
```

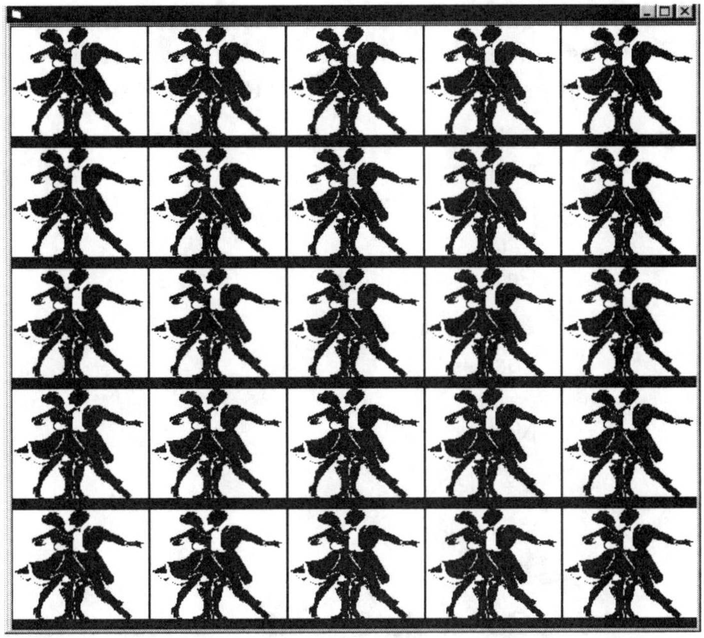

Figure 1-11: When there are no drawn or printed graphics, set ClipControls to False.

What is the time savings if you have a few Controls along with printed or drawn elements? The whole point of having a ClipControls option is that, when True, ClipControls does save time when you've combined drawn with carved images on a Form.

Figure 1-12: When you combine Printing with Controls on a Form, leave ClipControls set to the default True.

Figure 1-12 illustrates a fair speed test of ClipControls, combining as it does both printed text and a variety of Controls. Here is the test program (the Form's AutoRedraw Property is set to True):

```
Sub Form_Load ()
Show
FontSize = 38
Print
Print "     Bibliographic Engine"

x = elapse()
For i = 1 To 50
   Refresh
Next i

x = elapse()

End Sub
```

## ClipControls Speeds Up Repainting

ClipControls improved our test program's efficiency by more than 300%.

When you set ClipControls to False, VB draws the entire background, then superimposes the Controls (the various Command Buttons, a Picture Box, etc.). This wastes time, and the test takes 7.08 seconds. With ClipControls set to True—so that VB paints only the background around and between the Controls—the test takes 2.26 seconds.

Note, also, that drawing/printing will be superimposed on Controls if ClipControls is set to False. (See Figure 1-13.)

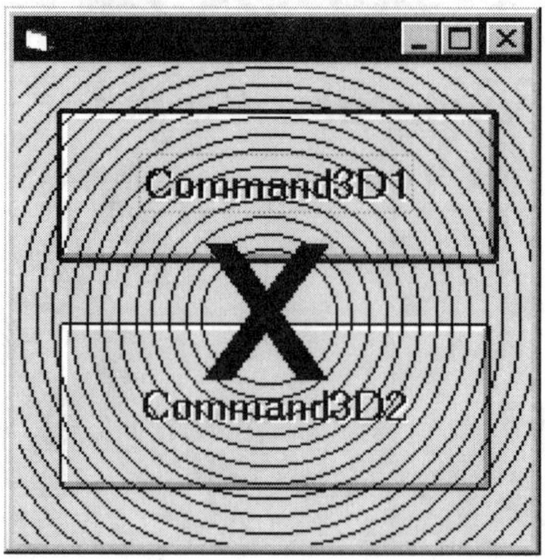


Figure 1-13: ClipControls also determines whether Controls can be overprinted, as here.

The effect in Figure 1-13 was created by turning off the Form's ClipControls (set to False), and then running the following program:

```
Sub Form_Click ()
Dim i As Integer
For i = 400 To 2000 Step 100
   Circle (1500, 1500), i
Next i
Currentx = 1100: currenty = 500
Fontsize = 78
Fontname = "Arial"
Print "x"
End Sub
```

## COMMON SENSE

Most of the time you'll notice if your VB program is running too slowly. When testing the program, figure out what kind of computer—what speed, processor and memory size—is likely to host your application. (Be sure to try it out on a slow computer with less memory than you're used to, and try turning off the turbo button if your machine is so equipped.) Then note which operations take too much time, seem sluggish or otherwise appear to make the program seem inept. Is it the graphics redraws? Is it a major time-consumer like sorting? Is it disk access?

Proceed through the program and make adjustments where necessary. Some techniques you might have used in the past won't work with VB (but common sense always works). In the old days, people used to speed up disk access and printer access by going through low-level routines. For instance, you could send or retrieve whole chunks of text from the disk, or you could manipulate the printer directly by sending strings of codes it understood.

### A Higher-Level Operating System

The Windows environment is certainly more complex than DOS. Windows rightly wants to handle many optimizations for you. Windows so increases the distance between the programmer and peripherals that it's now getting difficult to create a "misbehaved" application. You simply cannot pervert the intentions of the Windows API from within Visual Basic. The intention, the goal, of VB and Windows is that you consider things to be objects. You send messages to these objects and get messages back from them, but you don't fiddle with most of the mechanisms inside the objects.

However, some common-sense rules apply when you are moving masses of data around. For example, reading a disk file character by character, or even line by line, is obviously less efficient than using the Input command to take in the whole chunk of text.

Remember, too, that you should avoid repetitive updating of a Control. In the next example, the speed penalties of continuously updating a Text box are far greater than those of reading a file using the wrong Input technique. The following character-by-character reading of SYSTEM.INI (1896 bytes large) takes about three minutes (176.48 seconds):

```
Sub Form_Load ()
Show
x = Elapse()
Open "C:\WINDOWS\SYSTEM.INI" For Input As #1
Do While Not EOF(1)
   a$ = Input(1, 1)
   text1.Text = text1.Text + a$
Loop
Close 1
x = Elapse()
End Sub
```

This line-by-line read of SYSTEM.INI takes 9.44 seconds:

```
Sub Form_Load ()
Show
x = Elapse ()
Open "C:\WINDOWS\SYSTEM.INI" For Input As #1
Do While Not EOF(1)
   Input #1, a$
   text1.Text = text1.Text + a$
Loop
Close 1
x = Elapse ()
End Sub
```

The fastest way—reading the whole file first, then moving it into the Text Box—takes only ⅕ second (.22).

```
Private Sub Form_Load()

Show

Open "C:\WINDOWS\SYSTEM.INI" For Input As #1
Do While Not EOF(1)
   Input #1, a$
   t$ = t$ & a$
Loop
Close 1

Text1.Text = t$

End Sub
```

Changing a character-by-character input to a line-by-line input speeds things up about six times. But the main reason for the extreme speed differences in the examples above is that the Text Box is being repeatedly updated visually as the data comes in from the disk. We've incorrectly placed Text1.Text within our loop. You can greatly improve the performance of even the first example above by merely avoiding the constant updating of the Text Box.

Change the line

```
Text1.Text = Text1.Text + a$
```

to

```
t$ = t$ + a$
```

In this way the Text Box is left alone while the loop is pulling in text. Then, when the loop has finished, assign a$ to the Text Property:

```
Loop
Text1.Text = a$
Close 1
```

## MOVING ON

In the next chapter we'll see how to manage data efficiently. We'll look at the various file types and find out which are best to use in various situations to optimize disk-intensive applications. We'll also present efficient strategies for the common tasks of searching and sorting data.

# Chapter 2

# Storing, Searching & Sorting

One of the most important aspects of every computer language is its ability to handle files. Nearly every application must be able to store data in files. And as the volume of data to be processed increases, your application must be able to handle data directly from disk, simply because any computer will eventually run out of memory for storing information.

Visual Basic has its own commands for working with files, and these are no different from the commands found in older versions of Basic. However, Visual Basic also offers new tools that can facilitate the handling of files. These new tools are the subject of this chapter and the following chapter. In this chapter, we'll start with a review of the VB file types. Then we'll cover ways to keep data sorted.

---

You are probably aware of a Control introduced in Visual Basic 3.0, the Data Control, which was designed specifically for handling databases. Then why aren't we using it? If you have used this Control in the past and feel that this is all you need, then by all means use it. But in many applications, this Control is seriously limited. It is very difficult for users to position themselves in a database with VCR-style buttons, and even more difficult to develop a file management application without the VB programmer writing some serious coding "underneath" the Data Control. Besides, simple applications like the ones of this chapter are easier to distribute than applications developed with VB's Data Access Objects.

---

Fancy tools aren't always the best.

In the next chapter we will examine in depth Visual Basic's professional tools for database design, including the Data Control. But try not to complicate your code unnecessarily. Simple but very functional applications, like those in this chapter, can be implemented efficiently with less exotic techniques. Besides, the better you can handle simple files, the more prepared you will be to tackle the topic of database design.

## VISUAL BASIC'S FILE TYPES

Before getting down to algorithms, let's take a brief tour of VB's file types. Visual Basic supports three different file types: sequential, binary and random access. The next few paragraphs compare the different types and discuss their potential and drawbacks. We assume that the reader has a working knowledge of the various file types.

### Sequential Files

Sequential files are mostly text files (those that can be displayed on the DOS screen with the TYPE command). If you open a sequential file, you can write to it everything you could display on the screen with the Print Method. One of the commands to send output to a sequential file is even named Print.

A sequential file, as the name implies, is written to or read from the beginning to the end. Once you have read a line of text, you cannot go back. Although a sequential file can be either read or written to, you cannot read and write to it at the same time. If your application must read and write sequential data at the same time—to process an entire file, for example, and write the processed information back—you must open two sequential files, one for reading and one for writing. Although they were used a lot in the first days of personal computing, sequential files are the least-used file type today. That shouldn't, of course, stop you from using them if you feel they are appropriate for your application. Like prevailing winds, prevailing wisdom changes.

### Random Access Files

Most of the time you will be working with random access files, which offer the most efficient ways to locate information. Random access files could be called simply "random files" because this is how data are stored in them. (An even better name, reflecting the ease of access they provide, would be "immediate access" files.)

If your data are organized in well-defined units, or if you must access information in a nonsequential manner, random access files are probably preferable to sequential files. Random access files are organized in records, and you can simultaneously read and write records in the file. A record is a unit of information with a fixed length that you specify ahead of time. If you are writing an application for maintaining a list of customers, you can't afford to read all the names from the beginning of the file until you reach the desired name. Since every record (or unit of information) has a predefined length, it is easy to locate the desired record in the file and read it. After processing it, you can write it back to the file, replacing the old one. Because records have the same length, there is no chance of overwriting the adjacent ones.

Random access files are like two-dimensional arrays on disk. They are made up of rows (records) and columns (fields).

Another good reason for using random access files is their similarity to arrays. Each record of a random access file can be viewed as an element of a user-defined array. The difference is that the records of a file don't have to reside in memory and therefore will never cause memory problems. In most applications you need not manipulate more than one record at a time, so it makes perfect sense to grab the record you need from the disk, process it in memory and then return it to disk when you no longer need it.

Random access files do have some inefficiencies. First of all, they are rarely sorted. The user works most naturally when data are sorted by some meaningful key. Quite often, we need to see our data sorted in different ways in a single session.

Another problem with random access files is that they are not "disk-aware." The basic assumption you make when you work with random access files is that disk space is inexpensive, and you are willing to trade it for speed. This is true in many cases (especially when you can't do otherwise), but there are cases where you may wish to conserve disk space. Binary files are not as convenient as random access files, but they don't waste a single byte. We will see how we can combine both types of files to optimize disk-based applications.

## Binary Files

Binary files are very much like sequential files, but they are meant for storing binary digits. For example, an EXE file is stored as a binary file. An image is also a binary file.

Binary files can be described as sequences of bytes thrown on the disk. In binary files, unlike sequential files, Visual Basic does not insert special codes to mark the end of each variable or line of text. The bytes of a binary file may represent characters, numbers, sounds—just about anything you can create with your computer. It is the programmer's responsibility to extract information from a binary file.

Binary files are as simple as sequential files.

Binary files do have a major advantage over sequential files, though: like random access files, they can be open for reading and writing at the same time. Binary files are sequential in nature, but with some extra programming effort you can handle them as random access files. The section "Combining Multiple File Types" contains an example of using binary files as random access files.

## A SIMPLE APPLICATION

CD-ROM

Let's start with a very simple example, which is shown in Figure 2-1. This application is called PRICELST, and you can find it in the 2\APPS\PRICELST directory on the CD.

### EXAMPLE: PRICELST

Here we have a Price List maintenance application based on a few simple Controls: a List Box, in which the price list is displayed, three Text Boxes for editing a particular record, and a few Command Buttons. The items are stored in a random access file in the order the user enters them, but when they are read into the List, they are always sorted simply because the List's Sorted Property is set to True. As you know, many VB Controls have built-in intelligence. A List Box knows how to sort. In this case, we can borrow this functionality without writing a sorting routine of our own.

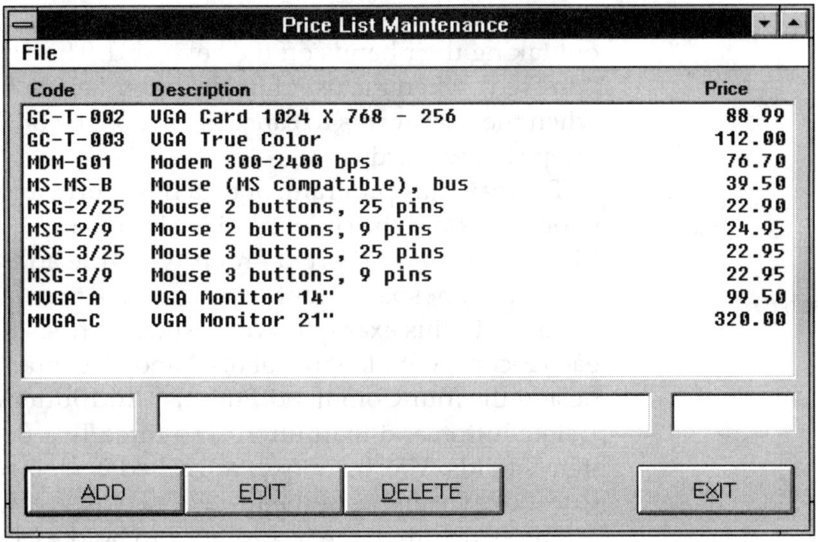


Figure 2-1: A simple application for maintaining price lists.

Each item of the List corresponds to a different product and consists of three fields: a code, description and price.

The List Control does not allow the direct entry of data. To add a new item, the user types its fields in the appropriate Text Boxes and then clicks on the Add Button.

To edit or delete an item, the user first selects it and then clicks on the Edit or Delete Button. The line is removed from the List. If the operation was Edit, its fields are copied to the three Text Boxes, where they can be edited and added back to the List with the Add Button. If the user clicks on the Delete Button, the program simply removes the line from the List without confirmation from the user. The application is very simple, and owes much of its functionality to the Sorted Property of the List. Because the lines are sorted by the code field, the user can easily locate an item with the help of the vertical scroll bar.

## Keep the Interface Simple

This example demonstrates another aspect of Visual Basic: simplicity. The Command Buttons at the bottom of the screen allow you to enter, modify or delete data. There are no buttons to confirm or abort an operation (the usual OK/Cancel Buttons), but stop and ask yourself: are these buttons really needed? In a simple application like this one, probably not. It is best to let users enter new items as fast as they can. Actually, if we make the Add Button the default Control on the Form (by setting its Default Property to True), users can enter items without taking their hands off the keyboard. The default button is "pressed" when the user hits the Enter key. In the few occasions when the user wants to cancel an action, he or she will merely have to retype a few words.

Try to incorporate the intelligence of VB's Controls in your application.

To create this program, open a new Form and draw a List large enough to hold the code, the description and the price of each item. Make sure that the Sorted Property is True and the FontName Property is a monospaced font (like Courier), to facilitate the alignment of the data. In this example, we use three strings for storing the fields of each record, with lengths of 8, 40 and 10 characters respectively. Next, design the four Command Buttons (AddButton, EditButton, DeleteButton and ExitButton) and three Text Boxes for entering each item's fields. The Text Boxes are called CodeBox, DescriptionBox and PriceBox. The name of the List is PriceList.

The structure of the record used to hold each entry in the list is shown here:

```
Type ItemRecord
    PrCode As String * 8
    PrDescr As String * 40
    PrPrice As Double
End Type
```

CD-ROM

To get some data in the List, the user must open a file with the File/Open command. (The data you see in Figure 2-1 are stored in the file PRLIST.DAT in directory 2\APPS\PRICELST of the CD.) Here is how the data are loaded from a file into the List Control:

```
Sub FileOpen_Click ()
Dim Item As ItemRecord
Dim PrString As String * 10

    CMDialog1.Filter = "DATA FILES|*.DAT"
    CMDialog1.InitDir = app.Path
    CMDialog1.Action = 1
    PRFILENAME = CMDialog1.FILENAME
    If PRFILENAME = "" Then Exit Sub

    PriceList.Clear      ' Clear data from list

    ' Open file and load records onto List
    PRFILENUMBER = FreeFile
    Open PRFILENAME For Random As #PRFILENUMBER →
    Len = Len(Item)
```

```
    TotRecs = FileLen(PRFILENAME) / Len(Item)
    ' Now read all records, format fields and add them to List
    For i = 1 To TotRecs
        Get #PRFILENUMBER, i, Item
        RSet PrString = Format$(Item.PrPrice, "#######.00")
        ItemLine$ = Item.PrCode + "  " + Item.PrDescr + "  " →
        + PrString
        PriceList.AddItem ItemLine$
        Next

    Close #PRFILENUMBER

End Sub
```

FileOpen is the name of the File menu's Open command. The code is straightforward, except perhaps for the RSet command. RSet right-justifies the price in a 10-character string, filling unused characters with spaces. The PRFILENAME and PRFILENUMBER, two global variables defined in the application's module, are the name of the file with the data and its number.

The code below for saving the records to file is quite similar to the listing we just saw above:

```
Sub FileSave_Click ()
Dim Item As ItemRecord

    If PRFILENAME = "" Then
        Beep
        Exit Sub
    End If

    PRFILENUMBER = FreeFile
    Kill PRFILENAME
    Open PRFILENAME For Random As #PRFILENUMBER →
    Len = Len(Item)
    For i = 0 To PriceList.ListCount - 1
        Item.PrCode = Trim$(Left$(PriceList.List(i), 8))
        Item.PrDescr = Trim$(RTrim$(Mid$(PriceList.List(i), →
        9, 30)))
        Item.PrPrice = Val(Right$(PriceList.List(i), 10))
        Put #1, , Item
    Next
    Close #PRFILENUMBER

End Sub
```

A random access file can only grow in size. A record can be overwritten, but not removed.

Why do we first delete the file from disk (Kill PRFILENAME) and then open it again? Random access files can't be made any shorter, no matter how many records you write to them or what you put in the records. Every time you append a new record to a random access file, it gets larger by one record's length. Since there are no commands to physically remove a record, the size of the file will never shrink.

The only way to get rid of unwanted records in a random access file is to delete the entire file and then open it again. This new version of the file is initially empty, and we can write in it the Price List's items. (If you experience a power failure during the creation of the new file, all the data will be lost. Before you delete the original file, copy it to another name. This way, you will still have the old data.)

The two Subroutines we just presented move the data from the file to the application and vice versa. (The Save As Subroutine is quite similar to the Save Subroutine, and we will not present it here.) This is the way most people used Basic's random access files: for storing data. The real processing took place after the records were moved from disk into memory.

## Adding, Editing & Deleting Records

Let's look at the code behind the Command Buttons. The Add Button transfers the data from the three Text Boxes to the List, and here is its implementation:

```
Sub AddButton_Click ()

Dim Str1 As String * 8
Dim Str2 As String * 40
Dim Str3 As String * 10

' Check for missing code
    If CodeBox.Text = "" Then
        i = MsgBox("Missing Code !", 32, "Price List: →
        Operator error")
        Exit Sub
    End If
' check for missing price
    If PriceBox.Text = "" Then
        i = MsgBox("Missing Price", 32, "Price List: Operator →
        error")
        Exit Sub
    End If
' Is price too large?
```

```
    If Val(PriceBox.Text) > 9999999 Then
        i = MsgBox("Price can not exceed 9,999,999", 32, →
        "Price List: Operator Error")
        Exit Sub
    End If
' Prepare List's line
    LSet Str1 = CodeBox.Text
    LSet Str2 = DescriptionBox.Text
    StrPr$ = Format$(Val(PriceBox.Text), "#######.00")
    RSet Str3 = StrPr$
    Item$ = Str1 + Space$(2) + Str2 + Space$(2) + Str3
' and add it to the list
    PriceList.AddItem Item$

' Prepare for next entry
    ClearFields
    CodeBox.SetFocus
    EditButton.Enabled = True
    DeleteButton.Enabled = True

End Sub
```

The Add Button assumes that the new entry's fields have been typed into the three Text Boxes. It reads the Text Property of each box and then forms a new item and adds it to the List. The first half of the code makes sure that the Text Boxes contain valid codes and prices before adding the new line to the List. The remaining code does nothing more than justify the fields of the line. The LSet command copies the contents of the Text Boxes to a string variable and pads the string variable to the right with spaces. This forces all code and all description fields to be of the same length.

Vertically aligning the fields in the List Box is simply a matter of concatenating the individual strings. This technique is very simple and works only with monospaced fonts. Finally, the price field is formatted with seven integer and two decimal digits. Notice also that each new item is added to the proper place in the List Box without any programming effort because the Box's Sorted Property was set to True. Before exiting, the ADDButton_Click Subroutine clears the Text Boxes in preparation for the next entry. If they were not cleared, the user could accidentally add the same line more than once by clicking on the Add button.

The code for editing a line is simpler, since much of the work is performed by the Add Button:

```
Sub EditButton_Click ()
Dim ItemIndex As Integer

    ItemIndex = PriceList.ListIndex
    If ItemIndex < 0 Then
        i = MsgBox("Select a Line to Edit", 32, "Price List: →
        Operator error")
        Exit Sub
    Else
        CodeBox.Text = RTrim$(Left$(PriceList.Text, 10))
        DescriptionBox.Text = →
LTrim$(RTrim$(Mid$(PriceList.Text, 11, 40)))
        Price = Val(Right$(PriceList.Text, 10))
        PriceBox.Text = Format$(Price, "#######.00")
    End If
    PriceList.RemoveItem PriceList.ListIndex
    EditButton.Enabled = False
    DeleteButton.Enabled = False

End Sub
```

This Subroutine extracts the three fields of a line, copies them to the appropriate Text Boxes and removes the corresponding entry from the List. The user can edit the three fields. When done, he can click on the Add button to add the modified line to the List with the AddItem Method, effectively replacing the old line. Notice that the Subroutine checks first to make sure that a line has been selected (property ListIndex). If no line has been selected, it displays a warning and exits.

The Subroutine for deleting a line is even simpler:

```
Sub DeleteButton_Click ()
ItemIndex = PriceList.ListIndex

If ItemIndex < 0 Then
    i = MsgBox("Select a Line to Delete", 32, "Price List: →
    Operator error")
Else
    PriceList.RemoveItem ItemIndex
    ClearFields
End If

End Sub
```

The DeleteButton_Click() Subroutine makes sure that a line has been selected and, if so, it removes it from the List Box. It also clears the contents of the Text Boxes to ready them for the next Add or Edit operation.

Lists are visual arrays.

We used the List just like an array because that's what it is in its simplest form. It has many properties and can add a new dimension to an application. But, like the random access file, it really is an array in disguise.

The Price List example is a good demonstration of what Visual Basic can do for you. The code is kept to the bare minimum needed for a functional application. The application is not only functional, but user-friendly too. And as you can see, we didn't try very hard to incorporate user-friendliness in our code. It's there because Visual Basic provides it.

### The List's Limitations

However, the Price List application has a serious limitation: the amount of data a List Box Control can hold. This limitation is a real problem with VB3 because a List Box Control can't hold more than 64,000 characters. Based on the record size we have defined, our Price List application can't hold more than 64,000/58, or approximately 1,000 products. In many situations this might be adequate, but you would have a hard time selling this program. And what if you wanted to use a List Box to maintain a personal mailing list? Assuming 200 characters per entry, you wouldn't be able to fit more than 300 names in the List.

VB4 List Boxes can hold up to 32,000 items, regardless of each entry's length. This is not a real restriction for more practical situations, but why keep all that information in memory? Keeping data in files and accessing them as needed is much more efficient and practical.

Another disadvantage of our List Box approach is the fact that it doesn't exploit the very nature of disk files. The disk was meant for permanent and safe storage of data. When working with files, we should transfer our data to disk as frequently as possible. If we wait too long—as we do in the List Box-based application—we increase the chances of aggravating the user.

Imagine you have entered data in the Price List application all morning long. You switch to another application. Then Windows crashes. You have to restart your computer without having a chance to save your work. If you are a good-natured person, you will probably at least return the program and ask for your money. When you work with files, send the data to disk as frequently as possible.

### Using List Boxes Effectively

To overcome the first limitation, let's recall why we used a List Control in the first place. The List keeps our data sorted, allowing the user to locate information quickly by means of some key field (the product code, in our example). Therefore, there is no need to store all of our data, all the time, in the List Box. We can store the product codes of the previous example in a List Control, and display the rest of the fields in Text Boxes. Fields that are used to navigate through a set of data are called *key fields*, or *index fields*. (For more on key fields, indices and other database concepts, see Chapter 3 if you are using VB3, or Chapter 4 if you are using VB4.)

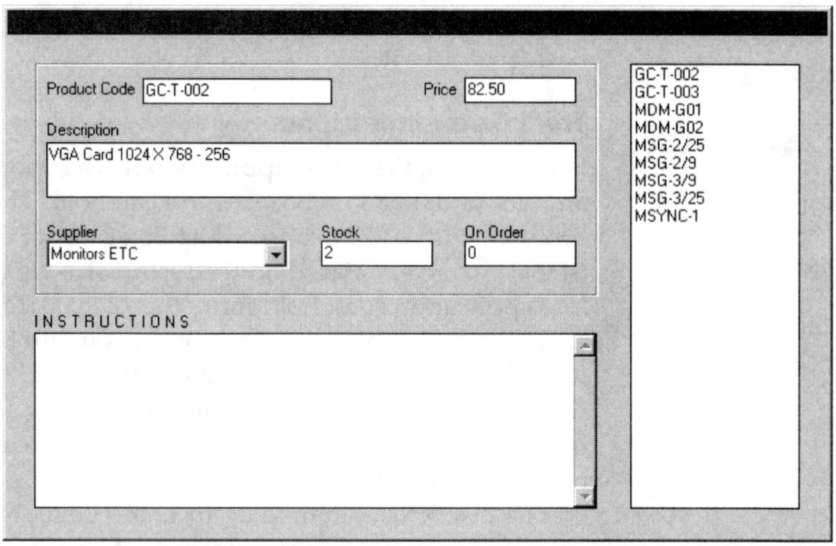


Figure 2-2: This time the List Box is used to maintain a sorted list of key fields, rather than entire records.

Figure 2-2 demonstrates this approach. Every time the user clicks on a product code in the List Box, the program displays the corresponding fields in separate Text Boxes. The key fields (product codes, in this case) are kept in a sorted List Box. The remaining fields can be kept in an array or on a disk file. For this scheme to work, we must maintain links between the List Box's entries and the elements of the array or the records of the disk file. These links (or pointers) are just integers that point to the proper elements of the array.

### Record Indexing Made Simple With List Boxes

The approach we just described is not unique to Visual Basic. If you have used database management systems (such as dBASE or Clipper), you are familiar with the concept of indexing. The entries of the List Box are simply the indices to our file. Each line of the List Box functions as a pointer to the random access file. The records need not be stored in any specific order in the file, but they are always in some order in the List Box. Moreover, you can change this order by loading a different field into the List Box, or you can maintain multiple sorted List Boxes that are based on different fields.

Indexing is a way to access a file's records in a specific order, regardless of their physical order on the disk. The user selects a name or product code. The program then does its magic and displays the entire record. Of course, no real magic is involved. All we need is a link between the List Box's entry and the corresponding record of the file. This link is called—you guessed it—ItemData. When you load the data, just assign the record number to the ItemData Property of the corresponding item in the List Box. Then, every time the user selects an item from the List, the program retrieves the record pointed to by the ItemData Property of the specific item. The process of reading a record from a random access file is very fast, and no noticeable delays are introduced. That's all there is to it. The records can be sorted according to any field (or combination of fields) you see fit for your application.

Moreover, they will remain indexed after you modify or delete them, and even after you add new records.

Indexing is an efficient shortcut to sorting.

This link between the List Box's items and the records on disk automatically solves our second problem too! We no longer have to read all data in the memory at once. Every time the user selects a new name in the List Box, we simply read the corresponding record from the disk and display its fields. Similarly, every time the user modifies a record, we write the record over the old one. Our file is always up-to-date, and the user can never lose more than one record, no matter what the disaster. That's good news for users and developers.

## INDEXED RANDOM ACCESS FILES

CD-ROM

Our next example demonstrates the principles of indexed random access files. This time we are going to use the mailing list application shown in Figure 2-3. This application is called MLIST, and you can find it in the 2\APPS\MLIST subdirectory of the CD.

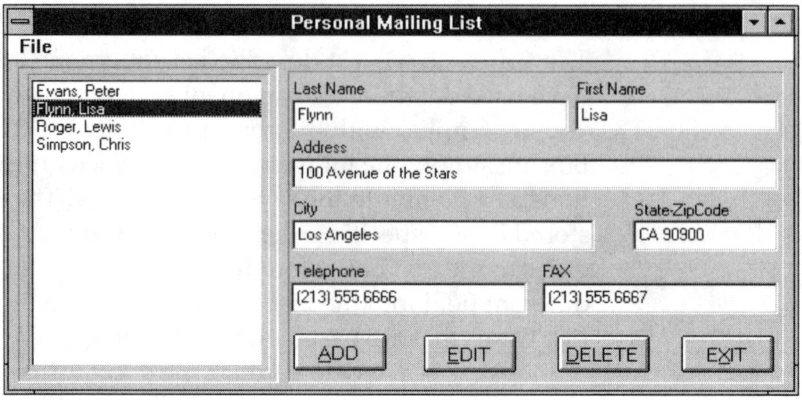


Figure 2-3: A mailing list application.

## Example: Personal Mailing List

The Personal Mailing List maintains a list of names and addresses, each stored in its own record. We will use a random access file, and here is the structure of its records. (*Note:* In the actual module of the application you will also find some global definitions; we'll discuss these later.)

```
Type person
    LName As String * 20
    FName As String * 12
    Address As String * 40
    Tel As String * 20
    Fax As String * 20
    City As String * 20
    State As String * 10   ' includes ZIP
    Deleted As Integer
End Type
```

Random access files can't be reduced in size.

The fields are self-explanatory except for Deleted, which is False unless the record has been deleted. Why do we have to store this information? As noted earlier, there are no commands for removing records from a random access file. The only way to physically remove a record is to move all following records up by one place. But this approach will make our application unacceptably slow, so we prefer to mark the deleted records and leave them in place. We can get rid of the deleted records when saving the file, as in the previous example.

Our application will check the Deleted field of each record and will never recall records that have been marked as deleted. As far as the user is concerned, it will seem as if the application has physically removed the deleted records from the file. Similarly, all new records will be appended after the last record in the file.

## Using the Application

Let's describe the application. When first executed, all Text Boxes are empty and the Command Buttons at the bottom of the Form are disabled. The user must create a new file (with the File/New command) or open an existing one (with the File/Open command). Once a file is open, the names are loaded into the list, the first record is displayed, and the Add, Edit, Delete and Exit buttons are enabled. Then the user can browse, add, edit or delete records.

To locate a record, the user may use the scrollbars on the List Control or the navigational keys. Typing the first character of the name (the key field of the record the user wishes to view) brings the user to the first name that begins with that character. The Home key goes to the very first item, and the End key goes to the last item. Every time the user makes a new selection, the corresponding record's fields appear in the Text Boxes. The record's fields are read from the disk as needed. Later in this chapter, you'll see how to move to a specific List item by typing the first few characters of the name.

## Programming the Application

Now let's look at the application from a programmer's point of view. To delete a record, we simply set its Deleted field to True and write the record back to the file. To edit it, we copy its fields to the appropriate Text Boxes and let the user modify them. When the user clicks the Edit Command Button, we disable all Command Buttons and display two new ones, OK and Cancel. When the user clicks the Add Button, we then clear the Text Boxes and display the OK and Cancel Buttons. The user either confirms changes with the OK Button or reverts to the original record with the Cancel Button.

This application has two more or less independent sections: the loading of the key fields from the disk file and the processing of individual records. The key fields are loaded using a loop that scans the entire file and reads each record but extracts only two fields to copy onto the List. Here is the code that opens the file and loads the key fields (ListOfNames is the Name of the List Control):

```
Private Sub FileOpen_Click()
Dim Entry As person

    Close
    CMDialog1.Filter = "DATA FILE|*.LST"
    CMDialog1.InitDir = App.Path
    CMDialog1.DefaultExt = "*.LST"
    CMDialog1.Action = 1
    DATAFILE = CMDialog1.filename
    If DATAFILE = "" Then Exit Sub

    DataFileNum = FreeFile
    Open DATAFILE For Random As #DataFileNum Len = →
    Len(Entry)

    ListOfNames.Clear
    NumRecs = LOF(DataFileNum) / Len(Entry)
    For i = 1 To NumRecs
        Get #DataFileNum, i, Entry
        If Not Entry.Deleted Then
            S$ = Trim$(Entry.LName) + ", " + Trim$(Entry.FName)
            ListOfNames.AddItem S$
            ListOfNames.ItemData(ListOfNames.NewIndex) = i
        End If
    Next
    ShowButtons
    Panel3D4.Visible = False
    If ListOfNames.ListCount > 0 Then ListOfNames.ListIndex = 0

End Sub
```

Use the List Box's ItemData Property to index records in a random access file.

In effect, this Subroutine builds the file's index based on a combination of fields. It reads one record at a time, extracts the first two fields (last and first name), concatenates them with a comma in between, and inserts them into the List Box using the AddItem Method. Because the Sorted Property of the List Box is True, each new item is inserted in the proper place.

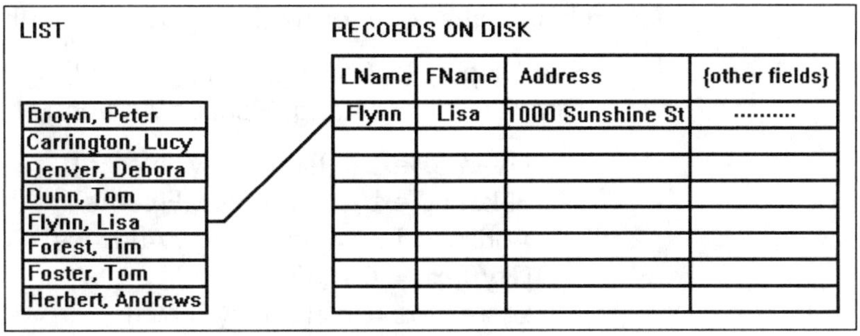


Figure 2-4: The link between a Sorted List's items and a file's record numbers is called the *index*.

At the same time, the Subroutine assigns the current record number to the new item's ItemData Property. Remember that the new item's index in the List Box is supplied by the List's NewIndex Property. This is taken care of by the line:

```
ListOfNames.ItemData(ListOfNames.NewIndex) = i
```

Reading the records and transferring key fields to the List Box takes a few seconds (depending on the number of records), but this happens only when we load a file. At all other times our application accesses one record at a time, so the only noticeable delay takes place before the user starts doing some real work. The ShowButtons Subroutine displays the Add, Edit, Delete and Exit Buttons.

### Keeping the List & Text Boxes Synchronized

Once the file is loaded, it's as if all the data are in memory. There will be no noticeable delays for the user. To guarantee smooth operation of the program, we must make sure that every time the user makes a new selection in the List Box, the corresponding fields are displayed in the Text Boxes. The routine DisplayRecord, which is called from within the List's Click Event, synchronizes the List and Text Box Controls:

```
Sub ListOfNames_Click ()
Dim Entry As Person

    RecNum = ListOfNames.ItemData(ListOfNames.ListIndex)
    Get #DATAFILENUM, RecNum, Entry
    Call DisplayRecord(Entry)

End Sub
```

And here is the code for the DisplayRecord Subroutine:

```
Sub DisplayRecord (Entry As Person)
Dim RecPos As Long, RecLen As Long

    LName.Text = Trim(Entry.LName)
    FName.Text = Trim(Entry.FName)
    Address.Text = Trim(Entry.Address)
    City.Text = Trim(Entry.City)
    State.Text = Trim(Entry.State)
    Tel.Text = Trim(Entry.Tel)
    Fax.Text = Trim(Entry.Fax)

End Sub
```

The code of the Add and Edit Buttons is shown next:

```
Sub AddButton_Click ()

    Call ClearFields
    Call HideButtons
    EDITMODE = False
    LName.SetFocus

End Sub

Private Sub EditButton_Click()

   If ListOfNames.ListIndex < 0 Then   ' No item, no EDIT
      Beep
      Exit Sub
   End If
   Call HideButtons            ' Display OK/CANCEL Buttons
   EDITMODE = True              ' in EDIT mode
   EditRecordNumber   →
    =ListOfNames.ItemData(ListOfNames.ListIndex)

End Sub
```

The Add Button clears the fields (Subroutine ClearFields), hides the normal editing buttons, displays the OK and Cancel buttons and lets the user enter data by moving the focus to the first Text Box (Last Name). Later in the code, the global variable EDITMODE will be used to differentiate between the two actions (addition of a new entry and editing of an existing one). The Edit Button doesn't display the record's fields in the Text Boxes because that was done when the user selected the record from the List Box. The EditRecordNumber is a global variable, holding the current record's position in the List. If the user cancels the edit operation by pressing Esc (or clicking on the Cancel Button), the program uses this variable to restore the original contents of the record. See the implementation of the Cancel Button to understand how the program uses the EditRecordNumber variable.

### One Button, Two Jobs

The most interesting routine in this application is in the OK Button's Click Event. The Click Event signifies the end of two different operations, the addition and editing of a record:

```
Private Sub OKButton_Click()
Dim Entry As person
Dim RecordNumber As Integer

   If EDITMODE Then     ' Got here with EDIT Button
      RecordNumber = EditRecordNumber
      ListOfNames.RemoveItem ListOfNames.ListIndex
   Else                 ' Got here with ADD Button
      RecordNumber = LOF(DataFileNum) / Len(Entry) + 1
   End If
' Make key, add it to List and set its ItemData Property
   Call UpdateIndex(RecordNumber)
' Make record and save it to file
   Call MakeRecord(Entry)
   Put #DataFileNum, RecordNumber, Entry
' Finally select newly added row in List
   ListOfNames.ListIndex = ListOfNames.NewIndex
   Call ShowButtons            ' out of EDIT/ADD mode,

End Sub
```

The EDITMODE global variable differentiates the actions of adding and editing a record.

When the user confirms his action by clicking on the OK Button, the program first removes the original key field from the List Box. It then adds the key field of the new (or modified) entry to the List Box. The addition of the new entry to the List Box is done by the UpdateIndex Subroutine:

```
Private Sub UpdateIndex(RecNum As Integer)

   EntryKey$ = LName.TEXT + ", " + FName.TEXT
   ListOfNames.AddItem EntryKey$
   ListOfNames.ItemData(ListOfNames.NewIndex) = RecNum

End Sub
```

Notice how the Subroutine uses the EDITMODE global variable to establish whether the current record was being added or modified. In the first case, it must append a new record to the file; in the second, it writes over the record being modified. Then it displays the normal editing Buttons and hides the OK/Cancel Buttons.

The MakeRecord Subroutine simply extracts the entries from the Text Boxes and places them in the record's fields:

```
Sub MakeRecord (Entry As Person)

    Entry.LName = LName.Text
    Entry.FName = FName.Text
    Entry.Address = Address.Text
    Entry.City = City.Text
    Entry.State = State.Text
    Entry.Tel = Tel.Text
    Entry.Fax = Fax.Text
    Entry.Deleted = False

End Sub
```

To cancel an Add or Edit operation, we need only display the fields of the last selected item in the List Box (or clear the fields, if it was an Add operation):

```
Sub CancelButton_Click ()

' If user was EDITing a record, simply cause a click event
' in the list, to force the re-display of original data
    If EDITMODE Then
        ListOfNames_Click
    Else
        ClearFields
    End If
    ShowButtons   ' out of EDIT/ADD mode,

End Sub
```

### Intercepting Keystrokes

One last remark about the application's operation. What will stop the user from entering information in the Text Boxes at inappropriate times? Suppose, for example, that the user attempts to modify a record without first clicking on the Edit button. The Text Boxes' default behavior is to accept the input. Somehow, we must disable the user's keystrokes in the Form's Text Boxes when he or she is not adding or editing a record. This can be accomplished from within each Text Box's KeyPress Event or from the Form's KeyPress Event. The Form's KeyPress Event can be used to intercept any keystroke, even if it was intended for a Control, as long as the Form's KeyPreview Property was set to True. Set the Form's KeyPreview Property to True and the List's Tag Property to "SEARCHSTRING". Then enter the following lines in the Form's KeyPress Event:

The KeyPreview Property lets you preview any keystroke before it is passed to a Control.

```
Sub Form_KeyPress (KeyAscii As Integer)

' If user is entering a key, exit
    If ActiveControl.Tag = "SEARCHSTRING" Then Exit Sub
    If Not OKButton.Visible Then
        KeyAscii = 0
        Beep
    End If

End Sub
```

Although many Visual Basic programmers ignore this simple technique, it is probably among the most useful features introduced with Visual Basic 3.0. The Form's KeyPreview Property gives you centralized control over the user's keyboard input. You can use this Property in similar cases to trap keystrokes before they reach any of the Controls. If you run the application, you will be able to move the focus to the Text Boxes, but you will be able to enter text only when you are editing or adding a record. (To determine the mode, the application checks the OK Button, which is visible only when you are adding or editing a record.)

If you thought that displaying a message would be a better idea, remember that your application's interface should be simple. Don't force the user to click buttons and acknowledge any trivial mistake. The first If clause in the previous Subroutine makes sure that the user can type a new selection in the List Box at all times. Keystrokes intended for the List Box are not intercepted by this Subroutine.

### Purging Deleted Records

Eventually, you will have to purge deleted records, which may cause the file to grow quite large. A utility that simply reads the file's records and copies the nondeleted ones to another file is fairly simple, so we're not going to cover it here. You can find the appropriate code in the Save As Subroutine of the application on the CD.

CD-ROM

## COMBINING MULTIPLE FILE TYPES

Random access files are convenient for storing and recalling well-defined units of information, but they are not especially efficient in terms of disk usage. Each record must have the same length, regardless of the information stored. In other words, each field must be long enough to accommodate the longest possible piece of information to be stored. The longest last name we can store in the previous example may not exceed 20 characters. While this is adequate for American names, you may have to adjust it to do business in India. If you attempt to store a longer name in the field, it will be truncated.

In our day and age, hard disks are relatively inexpensive. We can afford to trade some space for speed. But there is a limit to this trade-off. In Figure 2-5 you can see a variation of the previous example. The new application is called MLIST2 and can be found in the CD's 2\APPS\MLIST2 subdirectory. The new mailing list Form contains a Text Box for storing comments. But how can we estimate the length of the comments? What if we may have to store up to 1k characters in this field for certain records, while others contain no comments at all? We could allow for a few kilobytes per record, but that could waste anywhere from a few hundred kilobytes to a megabyte of disk space. It seems that a binary file would be a better choice, but do we want to give up the benefits of random access files?

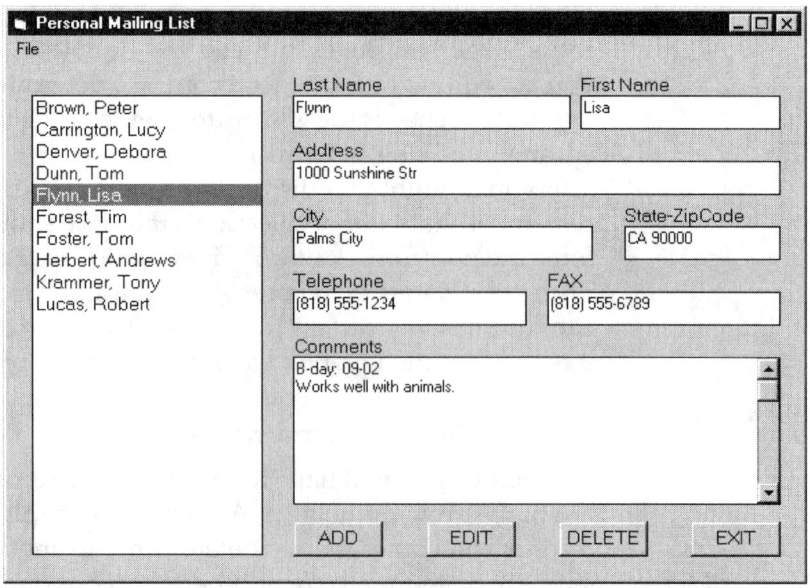


Figure 2-5: The Personal Mailing List application with an added Comments field, which may not be used at all in some records, but may grow quite large in others.

The answer is to combine file types. We can use a random access file to store the names, addresses and telephone numbers (the entries that fit easily in fixed-length fields). For the comments, we can use a binary file. The two files must be linked somehow so that when we move to a new record in the random access file, we can quickly locate the comments in the binary file. Don't let the name fool you. Binary files are the simplest files, even simpler than sequential files. They need not contain code or any other form of unintelligible data. Characters are binary numbers, after all.

To accommodate the comments, we must slightly modify our record structure. The new record contains two extra fields:

```
Type person
    LName As String * 20
    FName As String * 12
    Address As String * 40
    Tel As String * 20
    Fax As String * 20
    City As String * 20
    State As String * 10 ' includes zip code
    Deleted As Integer
    RecordsComments As Long
    CommentsLength As Long
End Type
```

The RecordsComments field is a pointer to the location of the binary file, where the record's comments begin (a number that points to the first byte of the comments in the binary file). Since the binary file is not structured with lines or records, we must know how many bytes to read from it. The number of characters making up the comments is stored in the CommentsLength field. Both new fields of the record are long integers, to accommodate any number of records and comments of any length (although limiting the size of the comments wouldn't be a bad idea).

This application differs from the previous one only in the sections where we display the comments or store them on disk. When a new record is entered, we extract the comments from the Text Box into a string variable, which then is appended to the binary file. The length of the string is stored in the CommentsLength field, and its location in the binary file is stored in the RecordsComments field. This location is simply 1 byte after the file's last character:

```
EOF(#FileNumber)+1
```

To recall the comments, we extract CommentsLength characters from the binary file, starting at the RecordsComments position. We move to the byte indicated by RecordsComments with the Seek command. In this segment of code, we read as many consecutive bytes as indicated by the CommentsLength field:

```
RecPos = Entry.RecordsComments
reclen = Entry.CommentsLength
If RecPos > 0 Then
    Seek #CommentsFileNum, RecPos
    Comments$ = Input$(reclen, #CommentsFileNum)
    CommentsBox.TEXT = Comments$
Else
    CommentsBox.TEXT = ""
End If
```

Finally, we must add the following lines to the OK button's Click Subroutine:

```
Comments$ = Trim$(Form1!CommentsBox.TEXT)
If Len(Trim(Comments$)) > 0 Then
    Put #CommentsFileNum, Entry.RecordsComments,  →
    Comments$
End If
```

These lines append the comments to the binary file. To look at the rest of the code, load the project MLIST2, located in 2\MLIST2 on the CD, to Visual Basic.

### Make Sure Both Files Are Present

A drawback of this approach is that we must use two different files. To simplify matters, you can use the same file name with two different extensions (.NAM and .COM, for example). When you display the File Open dialog, show only the .NAM files (no need to confuse the user). Of course, there is always the danger that the user of your application might delete the auxiliary file. Your application should be prepared for that (it shouldn't attempt to create a new auxiliary file). Display a message and let the user cope with the problem. If you want to be more protective, change the file's attributes to read-only or hidden when your application is done with it.

There is one more thing you can do to protect the user. Check the date and time of the two files. If you see that they differ by more than a minute or two, display a warning that the two files may be out of sync.

If you want to be extremely professional, you can incorporate a way to rescue information if one of the files becomes corrupt. The files are linked from the random access file to the binary file, but not vice versa. If you add two integers in front of each comment, you can provide a back-link from the comments' file to the file with the names. These two integers would be the record number to which the comments belong and the length of the comments, and they would make it possible for you to rescue data if the files got out of sync. At this point, however, the code becomes so complicated that it would be a good point to consider the Data Access Objects described in the next two chapters.

## Multiple Indices

Many applications may require multiple key fields. In Figure 2-6 you see the main Form of an application that small businesses might use to recall accounting information for specific customers.

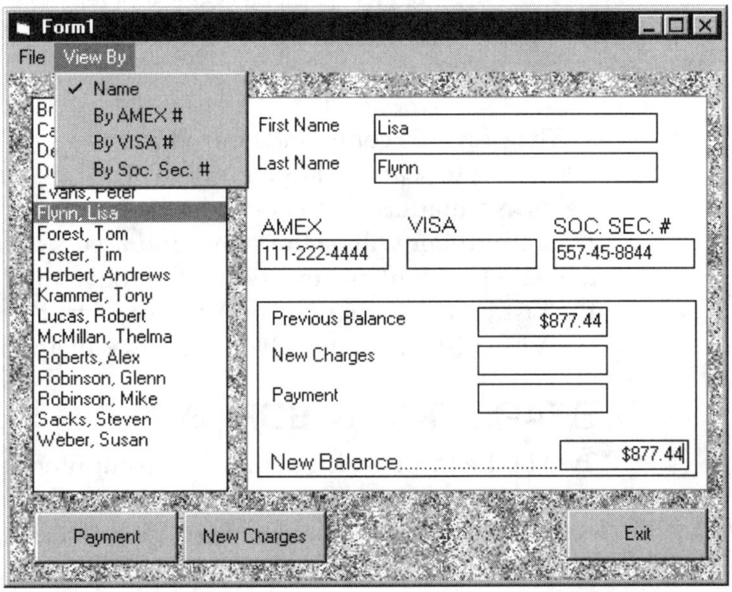


Figure 2-6: To locate a record using a different key field, select a different index from the View menu.

Use more than one List Box to maintain multiple indices.

The information at hand may not always be the name of a customer, but the customer's credit card number or Social Security number. To locate a customer's balance using a key field other than the name, select one of the View menu's options. This application maintains four different Sorted Lists, one for each key field. Every time you add a new entry or delete an existing one, you must update four Lists instead of one. The code for updating the Lists should be something like this:

```
NameList.AddItem NameKey$
NameList.ItemData(NameList.NewIndex) = RecordNumber
If AMEXNumber$ <> "" Then
    AMEXList.AddItem AMEXNumber$
    AMEXList.ItemData(AMEXList.NewIndex) = RecordNumber
End If
If VISANumber$ <> "" Then
    VISAList.AddItem VISANumber$
    VISAList.ItemData(VISAList.NewIndex) = RecordNumber
End If
If SocSecNumber$ <> "" Then
    SocSecList.AddItem SocSecNumber$
    SocSecList.ItemData(SocSecList.NewIndex) = →
    RecordNumber

End If
```

The previous commands introduce no significant delay, yet they allow you to search a large random access file using multiple key fields. No matter which key field the user selects, the corresponding record number will be the same, and access to the record is immediate. The If statements make sure that only valid entries are added to the List. If a customer has no VISA card, he cannot be looked up in the VISAList. However, all customers will appear in the NameList.

## SEARCHING & SORTING

Two of the most basic operations a computer can perform are sorting lists of data and searching a list for a specific piece of information. Searching and sorting techniques, therefore, have received enormous attention since the early days of computing.

So far we have been able to maintain our data sorted and provide the user with simple tools for locating the desired information, without any need for sorting or searching functions (the List Box Control took care of both). This is usually the right way to work with Visual

Basic—or any other language, for that matter. If it's been done for you, use it. Occasionally, though, you may need your own searching or sorting function. Let's look at two simple and efficient algorithms.

Let's start with a searching algorithm, because it is simpler. And, given the flexibility of the Sorted List Box, in most cases you will be searching for data rather than sorting them.

## Searching a List

Scroll bars or navigational keys can help the user locate the desired item in a List Box, provided that its Sorted Property is set to True. But some users might find it easier to type in the item they want to move to. If you type a character while the List Control has the focus, Visual Basic moves to the first line in the List Box that begins with that character. However, it does not allow you to specify more than one character. Visual Basic provides no method for searching a List Box for a specific element.

Navigational keys are fun, but ask a seasoned data entry operator what he or she thinks about the mouse.

Fortunately, this feature can be implemented easily. In Figure 2-7 you see a Form with a Sorted List Box. Above the List Control there is a small Text Box where the user can type the string he or she is looking for (or part of it). When the user types a character, the program displays the first item that matches the current contents of the Text Box. (If you have used the search feature of Windows's Help system, this arrangement should be familiar to you.) The List's entries are random strings generated when the Form is loaded.

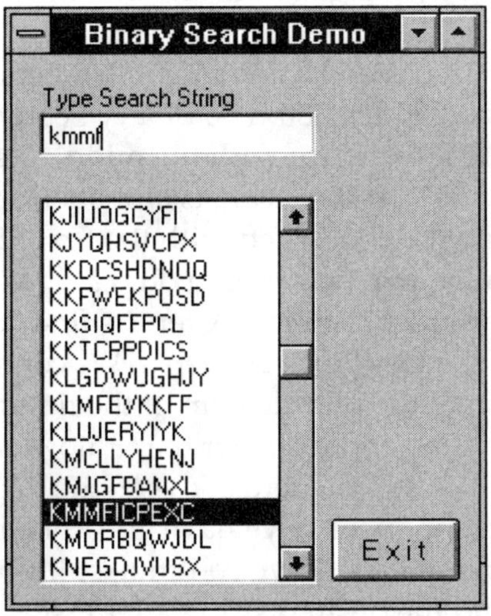


Figure 2-7: If you don't want to scroll to an item in the List Box, just type it in the Text Box.

To implement this real-time search feature, we must insert some code in the Text Box's Change Event. This Event is invoked every time the user types a character in the Text Box, so the List Box will be searched every time the user updates the Text Box. Here is the code of the Text Box's Change Event (SearchText is the name of the Text Box):

```
Sub SearchText_Change ()

ItemIndex = BSearch()
If ItemIndex = -1 Then
    Beep
Else
    ListOfNames.ListIndex = ItemIndex
End If

End Sub
```

As you can guess, the BSearch function locates the string of the Text Box in the List Box and returns its index. If it's negative, the string was not found and the program simply beeps. If the string was found, the program selects the corresponding line in the List Box by setting its ListIndex Property to the value returned by BSearch.

### Binary Search

All the work is done by the BSearch Function, which is named for Binary Search, the fastest searching algorithm. The Binary Search algorithm takes advantage of the fact that the List Box's lines are sorted to rapidly locate the desired item.

Binary Search is a powerful algorithm based on a simple idea.

Let's assume that the List contains 1,024 items, and the one we are looking for has the index 380. The Binary Search algorithm compares the string we are looking for with the middle item in the List Box (the item with index 512). If the string is alphabetically greater than this item, we need not be concerned with the first 512 items of the List Box. If it is smaller, which is true in our case, we repeat the same process with the first 512 items. After the first comparison we have rejected half of the List Box's elements. We continue by comparing the search string to the middle item of the first half of the list (the item with index 256) and discover that it now belongs to the upper half of the new list, somewhere between the items with index 256 and 512. With two comparisons, we have already eliminated three quarters of the list's elements. If we continue splitting the list in half, we are bound to find the desired string after just a few comparisons. Figure 2-8 shows the Binary Search algorithm at work, locating the number 53 in a 16-item list.

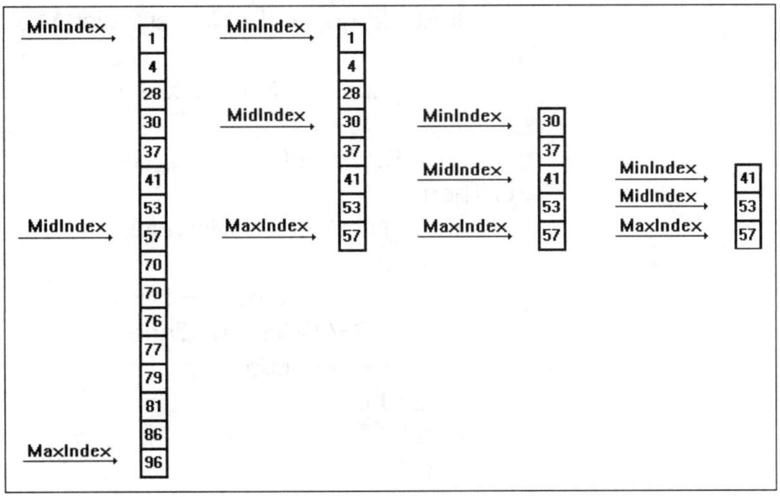


Figure 2-8: Illustration of a successful search using the Binary Search algorithm.

The Binary Search algorithm cuts the list in half at every iteration. After $\log_2(N)$ iterations it is left with one item, which should be the one we are looking for. If it is not, we know the search string does not belong to the list. Why $\log_2(N)$? Consider that we begin with a list that has one line only and that we keep doubling the number of lines: 1 - 2 - 4 - 8 - 16 . . . . This sequence of numbers may be familiar to you. After n steps, the size of the list, N, will be $2^n$. If you start with N items, you must halve the size of the list n times (or $\log_2(N)$ times) to be left with just one item.

Here is the implementation of the BSearch Function:

```
Private Function BSEARCH() As Integer
Dim MidIndex As Integer
Dim MinIndex As Integer
Dim MaxIndex As Integer

    MinIndex = 0
    MaxIndex = List1.ListCount - 1
    s$ = Trim$(Text1.TEXT)
    While 1
        MidIndex = (MinIndex + MaxIndex) / 2
        If MaxIndex < MinIndex Then
            BSEARCH = -1
            Exit Function
        End If
```

```
        If StrComp(s$, Left$(List1.List(MidIndex), Len(s$)), 1) > 0
Then
            MinIndex = MidIndex + 1
        Else
            If StrComp(s$, Left$(List1.List(MidIndex), Len(s$)), 1)
< 0 Then
                MaxIndex = MidIndex - 1
            Else
                List1.ListIndex = MidIndex
                BSEARCH = MidIndex
                Exit Function
            End If
        End If
    Wend

End Function
```

The Binary Search algorithm works like 20 Questions, rejecting half the possibilities at each step.

The variables MinIndex and MaxIndex are the indices of the first and last items of each new sublist. MidIndex marks the item at the middle of the sublist. With each repetition we reject one half of the list's items and make either the MinIndex or the MaxIndex variable equal to MidIndex (depending on whether we rejected the lower or the upper half of the list). If the search string is located in the second half of the list, we set MinIndex to the middle index of the list (MinIndex = MidIndex + 1) and leave the upper limit as is. If the string is located in the first half of the list, we set MaxIndex to the middle index of the list (MaxIndex = MidIndex - 1). This process ends when MaxIndex becomes less than MinIndex.

The application we used to create Figure 2-7 is called BSEARCH, and you can find it in the 2\APPS\BSEARCH subdirectory of the CD. This feature is also implemented in the MLIST2 application, so that you can locate names by just typing the first few characters of the last name.

CD-ROM

### Speed Considerations

The Binary Search algorithm is extremely fast. It will locate a string in a List of 1,024 items with just 10 comparisons, and will not make more than 12 comparisons to locate a string in a List of 4,096 items.

You can get a good feel for the power of this algorithm by running the Personal Mailing List application. Every time you press a new key, the program selects a different name in the List. Moreover, as soon as you form a string that does not exist in the List, it beeps to warn you. In other words, this little tool locates a string as fast as you can type its characters, and that should be fast enough for nearly all of your everyday needs.

The BSearch function picks up the search string from the Text Box Control. To modify the function to search for any other string, assign the search string to the variable s$. If you like, substitute the List items with array elements to search sorted arrays as well.

The Binary Search algorithm is as useful as it is simple. If you are using long Lists in an application, it is a good practice to provide the Text Box alternative for locating an item. (We will explore an even simpler implementation of the Binary Search algorithm in Chapter 12.)

## Sorting

The Binary Search algorithm performs very well, but it does require sorted data. At times, you may have to sort the data on your own. If you are dealing with arithmetic data, for example, the List Box can't be used. The List Control was not designed to hold arithmetic data, so the string "2" will be placed after the string "11111." You can always convert the numbers to strings that are padded with zeros to the left before adding them to the List Box. But this is time-consuming and will probably offset any benefits of the List Box's Sorted Property. Although List Boxes will take care of data-sorting chores most of the time, in some cases you have to provide your own sorting function.

The sorting algorithm presented here is called ShellSort. It is a fairly efficient one and among the easiest to understand.

The less often data are swapped, the faster they are sorted.

The basic task for any sorting algorithm is to successively compare elements and swap them if they are not in order. The fewer comparisons your code makes, the sooner it sorts the data. Moreover, not all comparisons lead to swapping of data. Swapping takes much more time than comparing two values, so the fewer data swapped, the faster the program.

### Sorting Is a Painstaking Process

We assume that you are familiar with the notorious Bubble Sort algorithm, which is extremely simple to understand but, alas, terribly slow. The Bubble Sort algorithm picks an element in an array and compares it to each of the elements that follow, swapping them if they are out of order. The first element of the array will be compared to each one following. When the sorting is done, the smallest element (the one that is arithmetically least, or first in the alphabet) will be on top of the array. We must then repeat the process, comparing the second element to the N – 2 following ones, then the third element to the N – 3 following ones, and so on. Smaller elements slowly make their way to the top, like bubbles in a glass of soda, while larger ones sink gradually to the bottom of the array.

## ShellSort

The ShellSort algorithm is based on the same idea as the Bubble Sort, but it compares elements that are far from each other. For this reason, many values that are out of place move more quickly to their proper place. It performs fewer comparisons, and many of the comparisons require no data swapping. The ShellSort algorithm, named for its inventor Donald Shell, is much more efficient than the Bubble Sort. In Figure 2-9 you can see how the ShellSort algorithm sorts an array of 16 elements. In the first pass, the algorithm compares elements that are N/2 places apart. It compares (and swaps when needed) the pairs (0, 8), (1, 9), (2, 10), (3, 11), (6, 12) and so on. After the first pass, the element 0 need not be compared again with 8, element 1 need not be compared again with element 9, and so on. In the second pass, the algorithm compares elements that are N/4, or 4 places apart: (0, 4), (1, 5), (2, 6), . . . (11, 15). In the third step, it compares elements that are N/8, or 2 places apart, and in the last pass it compares consecutive elements (i.e., elements that are one place apart). After this last pass, all elements are sorted.

ORIGINAL ARRAY

| Index | 0 | 1 | 2 | 3 | 4 | 5 | 6 | 7 | 8 | 9 | 10 | 11 | 12 | 13 | 14 | 15 |
|---|---|---|---|---|---|---|---|---|---|---|---|---|---|---|---|---|
| Element | 70 | 53 | 57 | 28 | 30 | 77 | 1 | 76 | 81 | 70 | 4 | 41 | 86 | 79 | 37 | 96 |
| 1st Pass | 70 | 53 | 4 | 28 | 30 | 77 | 1 | 76 | 81 | 70 | 57 | 41 | 86 | 79 | 37 | 96 |
| 2nd Pass | 30 | 53 | 1 | 28 | 70 | 70 | 4 | 41 | 81 | 77 | 37 | 76 | 86 | 79 | 57 | 96 |
| 3rd Pass | 1 | 28 | 4 | 41 | 30 | 53 | 37 | 70 | 57 | 76 | 70 | 77 | 81 | 79 | 86 | 96 |
| 4th Pass | 1 | 4 | 28 | 30 | 37 | 41 | 53 | 57 | 70 | 70 | 76 | 77 | 79 | 81 | 86 | 96 |

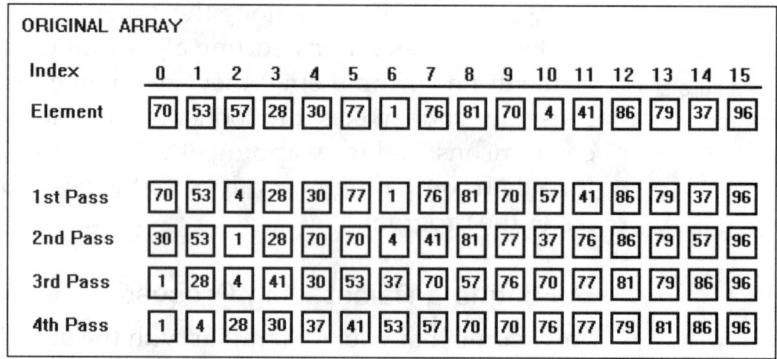

Figure 2-9: Using the ShellSort algorithm to sort 16 elements. With each pass, the distance between elements being compared is reduced.

Here is a Visual Basic function that implements the ShellSort algorithm:

```
Private Function SHELSORT(N As Integer) As Integer
Dim gap As Integer, i As Integer, j As Integer
Dim temp As Double

On Error GoTo FAILED
    gap = N / 2' Initial distance between successive comparisons
    While (gap > 0)
        For i = gap To N - 1     ' Compare each element
            j = i - gap
            Do While ((j >= 0)) ' ... with the one gap elements →
            apart
                If ddata(j) < ddata(j + gap) Then Exit Do     ' and →
                swap if needed
                temp = ddata(j)
                ddata(j) = ddata(j + gap)
                ddata(j + gap) = temp
                j = j - gap
            Loop
        Next
        gap = gap / 2   ' Halve distance
    Wend                 ' and continue
    SHELSORT = 1         ' Ended successfully
    Exit Function
FAILED:
    SHELSORT = -1
    Exit Function

End Function
```

The array a() can be of any type and must be declared in one of the application's modules, with the Option Base 0. (If you change the array's start, you must modify the ending condition of the While...Wend loops in the code.)

CD-ROM

The application SHELSORT in the 2\APPS\SHELSORT directory of the CD uses the ShellSort algorithm to sort numeric arrays. You can extract the ShellSort Subroutine and use it in your own projects.

In Chapter 12 we'll look at the QuickSort algorithm. It performs far better than the ShellSort algorithm, but it has one paradoxical weakness: the more ordered (sorted) the data are when QuickSort starts working, the more slowly it does the job. The ShellSort algorithm, however, is adequate for sorting moderately sized arrays (those of a

Sort only if you can't avoid it. And Visual Basic has many ways to help you avoid it.

few hundred records). If you have a large number of data to sort, then you must resort to a more powerful routine, such as the QuickSort algorithm.

As the volume of data increases, any sorting function becomes less and less efficient. However, if you find yourself trying to sort several thousand names, you are probably doing something wrong. Programs should not be spending their time sorting. The data originate somewhere, most likely from a disk file, and they are associated with other data too. For example, customer names are linked to invoices, which in turn are linked to inventories, and so on. In an application of this complexity, you just don't sort your data to display them. You decide how to display data when you design the application, and you provide the mechanisms to keep them sorted at all times. Then, when you need the data, they already will be sorted.

When possible, avoid writing special code that will sort things. As our examples illustrate, you can often rely on Visual Basic's List Box Control to do it for you. When this is not feasible, use the "Jet Engine" (the engine beneath Microsoft's Access database application, which is included in VB and described in Chapter 3, for VB3, and Chapter 4, for VB4). Use a sorting routine that you construct only as a last resort, after you've rejected the alternatives.

## MOVING ON

Chapter 3 covers VB3's built-in mechanisms for handling databases, and Chapter 4 covers the same topics from VB4's point of view. If you don't know how to use VB's Data Access Objects—or if you don't feel comfortable with such terms and concepts as SQL, Tables and DynaSets—these chapters are for you. We will endeavor to describe the database management features of the language in a way that is understandable to any Basic programmer.

# Chapter 3

# Working With Databases (Visual Basic 3.0)

*This chapter and Chapter 4 both explore the techniques and capabilities of relational databases. When revising the* Visual Basic Power Toolkit *to include new features of VB4, we realized that database programming had changed so significantly from VB3 to VB4 that it would be awkward at best to attempt to cover both versions in a single chapter.*

*For one thing, the sample databases we use for the examples have different structures. One of them takes advantage of the new features of VB4. Also, the term* Recordset *has a slightly different meaning in the two versions of Visual Basic. In fact, the differences between the two versions of the language are not limited to a few commands; they permeate the language itself. We felt that an attempt to cover both versions of the Jet Engine in a single chapter would probably confuse, rather than help, the reader.*

*Both chapters are similarly structured and contain, in places, identical information–Chapter 4 is a revision of Chapter 3, but we didn't want to eliminate Chapter 3 and thereby abandon VB3 programmers. So we took this rather unorthodox approach of including parallel chapters rather than attempting to blend the tutorials into a single chapter. If you are interested in database programming in VB3, read this chapter. If you are working with VB4, skip to Chapter 4.*

*If you have a choice, we suggest that you use VB4 to develop database applications. The new version of the Jet Engine incorporates features like referential integrity (which permits the design of true relational databases), a powerful utility for designing databases and new data-bound Controls. VB4 also provides improved connectivity features for connecting to remote databases and a faster SQL engine.*

## DATABASE PROGRAMMING IN VB3

Visual Basic offers an impressive array of commands for managing databases. In fact, Visual Basic includes the Jet Engine, the extensive Database Management System that powers Microsoft Access. To the Visual Basic programmer, database management is like a whole other language embedded within VB itself.

The purpose of this chapter is to explore the techniques and capabilities of relational databases, which are new to many Visual Basic programmers.

Microsoft's VB manuals, however, are written for people who *are* acquainted with relational databases. We will endeavor to clearly explain and illustrate terms such as *Table*, *Dynaset*, *SQL*, *Index* and all the rest of database terminology needed to understand and exploit Visual Basic's extensive and powerful database management capabilities.

You'll find practical examples here that should prepare you to tackle everyday situations. For most programmers the material in this chapter will be adequate for a wide range of applications. Those of you who wish to write highly specialized applications that, for instance, combine data from different servers, or access external databases (Paradox, other SQL servers, etc.), should supplement the information in this chapter with a more specific book on the subject.

This chapter relies on many short examples, especially on the topic of SQL (Structured Query Language, a way to get information from your database using all kinds of wild cards and complex queries such as "Every author who's written more than three books and who lives in Vermont, but hasn't written a book in the last five years").

The goal in this chapter is to present in simple, nontechnical language the basic concepts and mechanisms you will need to use Visual Basic to handle databases. We also try to make this chapter equally attractive and interesting to both Visual Basic programmers who haven't had any experience with databases, as well as newcomers to Visual Basic who've developed database applications with other DOS- or Windows-based products (like dBASE, Clipper, etc.).

# DATABASE MANAGEMENT SYSTEMS

Computers manage information. As information stored in a computer increases, so does the need for efficient tools for its management. There comes a time when simple "flat" (one-dimensionally organized) files are no longer a practical solution.

As with every other area of computing, programmers can rely on specialized mechanisms for handling large collections of files. These specialized mechanisms are called Database Management Systems, and they free the programmer from the drudgery of trivial (and mostly uninteresting and noncreative) low-level tasks that deal with files. Just as the Multimedia Control Interface provides all the low-level services on the multimedia devices and allows your applications to "play" a sound or an animation file, Database Management Systems allow your applications to concentrate on managing information, rather than the specifics of storing and retrieving data in files and maintaining links among them.

## What Is a Database?

A database is a collection of information, organized for easy processing and retrieval. Of course, you could say the same thing about a hard drive, or of a computer in general. But the essence of a database is that it is more *organized*, more structured than the collection of files and applications on a typical computer's hard drive.

At the highest level, a database is composed of *tables*, which are similar to random access files. A table is a collection of related data. The rows of the table contain identically structured pieces of information. The table's rows are the equivalent of a random access file's records. The table's columns are the fields. For an in-depth explanation of these terms, see Chapter 2.

Rows and columns do not describe a file's physical structure on disk. Instead, they describe a way of organizing data, which is completely independent of the way data are actually stored in files. When working with databases, we can't open a specific file. We open the *database*, and then we specify the tables we want to work with. The Database Management System not only handles the low-level functions, but it also hides them from the programmer. How the computer actually stores the data is irrelevant and not our job.

In a database, each table holds a collection of information, usually a *category* or subset of the data in the entire database. For example, a business might use a database for all of its accounting. Within this database, there might be a table containing all of the customers. Another table might contain the inventory, and so on. By maintaining our data in separate large-scale units (tables), we can manage them more easily. Moreover, we avoid unnecessary duplication of data. If we were storing the customer information along with each invoice, then every time a customer changed address or phone number, we would have to update possibly thousands of records in several tables. By keeping our data in well-defined, separate tables, we only have to change one record: the record for the specific customer in the customers table.

Tables are assisted by *indices*, which dictate the order in which data should be retrieved. Data aren't maintained within a database in any particular order. (They're actually stored in the order in which they were entered, but this is hardly ever meaningful.) With the help of an index, though, we can make the data seem to the user to be sorted in a meaningful way. In the MLIST example in Chapter 2 we showed how to sort data with the help of a sorted List Box. The records were not sorted in any way on the disk. When we placed them in a List Box, however, they appeared sorted. Then, the ItemData Property of the List Box was used as a pointer to the record's location in the file. The first name in the List Box (which is the alphabetically first record) might, in fact, be the 16th record as physically stored in the file. By setting the ItemData Property of the List Box's first item to 16, we were able to locate the (alphabetically) first record very quickly. The collection of the ItemData Properties of all the items in the List Box was actually an index. In that example (using ordinary random access files) we had to keep track of the ItemData Properties and update them. In a database, the indexing of the entries is maintained automatically for us by the database "engine." Moreover, we can specify as many indices as we need.

Once the data have been divided into tables and indexed according to our application's needs, we must create and maintain some links among the tables, so that we can access information. The customer ID (basically a number) appears in the customer table as well as in each invoice, so that we can find the customer for whom the invoice was issued, or list all the invoices issued to a specific customer. This link is called a *relation*. The tables are related by some value. In this example, the value that relates (connects) the two tables is the customer ID.

The organizational model we just described is called *relational*, because it makes use of relations between tables. Unlike a flat file, or other database types, a relational database keeps the information in smaller, more manageable units (tables), and maintains the information via relations among tables. The fields that are used to establish relations are called *keys*. The key fields relate the tables to each other, so that we can find the customer to whom an invoice was issued, or the descriptions of the items listed in the invoice (or even the products sold to a specific state). Each of these "lists"—customer, invoice, details—would be kept in separate tables.

Figure 3-1 is a pictorial representation of a simple sales database. The customers, invoices and invoice details are kept in three separate files. The lines indicate relations between fields. The fields that are connected by lines have the same value on both tables, and they are called keys.

TABLE: Customers

| CUSTOMER | ID |
|---|---|
| Sunshine Oranges | 11 |
| Fish ETC | 12 |

TABLE: Invoices

| ID | DATE | TOTAL | ID |
|---|---|---|---|
| 12 | 10/10/94 | 54.19 | 20 |
| 11 | 10/10/94 | 21.66 | 21 |

TABLE: Details

| ID | PRCODE | QTY |
|---|---|---|
| 20 | BVRG010 | 12 |
| 20 | BVRG07 | 12 |
| 21 | BVRG07 | 3 |
| 21 | BVRG014 | 4 |
| 21 | BVRG202 | 10 |

Figure 3-1: A simple relational database for maintaining sales data.

A database created with Visual Basic is stored in a single file, with the extension MDB. (Visual Basic creates another file, with the extension LDB, but you can't access this file directly.) Visual Basic and Access use the same format and they can both operate on the same database. The single database file contains all the tables and indices. You can't see them and you can't access them individually. The index isn't a file anymore. It is stored somehow in the database, and it could even be stored along with the table's data. A Database Management System introduces a new level of abstraction, enabling us to concentrate on what we want to do, and not the nuts and bolts of how to do it. There is another benefit, perhaps less obvious. The Database Management System protects the database against errors too. For example, if you specified that the customer name is an index, so that the customers appear sorted according to their names, the Database Management System will not let you enter a customer without a name. Likewise, if you specified that the customer's ID is unique, you will be protected from accidentally assigning the same customer ID to more than one customer.

# TWO SAMPLE DATABASES

Let's take a closer look at two specific databases. In this chapter we will be using two databases for our examples. BIBLIO.MDB, which comes with Visual Basic, is a database of titles, authors and publishers. It is a simple database that can be used to demonstrate most kinds of operations performed on a database, but it falls short when it comes to demonstrating some of the most useful database operations, which deal with numeric data.

To illustrate manipulation of numeric data, we've designed another database, called VBINC.MDB, for storing customers, products and invoices. It is an elementary database for business applications, but it's important to keep the complexity of the code in our examples to a minimum. Our goal is to explain the concepts behind database programming and how Visual Basic is used in this capacity, and to show you how to write data-entry or decision-support applications. Once you understood the concepts, employing Visual Basic to write complete applications should be fairly easy.

## The BIBLIO Database

In Figure 3-2 you can see the structure of the BIBLIO database. Tables are represented as boxes. The lines that connect certain fields between tables show the relations between the tables. The first thing you'll notice is that the Titles table doesn't contain author and publisher names. Instead, it contains two fields called Au_ID and PubID. These fields "point" to the appropriate entries in the other two tables.

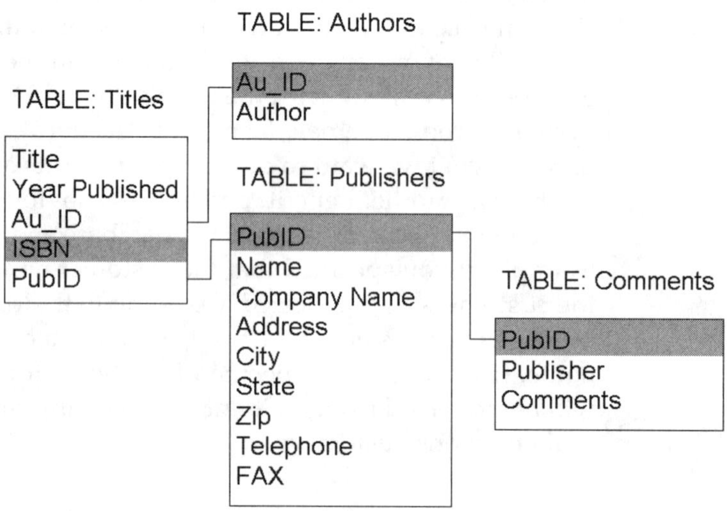


Figure 3-2: The structure of the BIBLIO database. The key fields are grayed.

A publisher will have more than one title. It wouldn't make sense to repeat the publisher's name in every row of the Titles table. There are several reasons why this repetition isn't a good practice, but we'll mention just one. It would take some programming effort to ensure that all publisher names in the Titles table are spelled identically, so that we can recall information reliably. By keeping the titles separated from the publishers, each publisher's name appears only once in the database. You can even change the publisher's name and the titles will still point to the correct publisher.

The same is true for authors. Since an author may write more than a single book, why repeat his name in the Titles table?

## Keys, Primary & Foreign

The fields Au_ID and PubID are called *keys*. The Au_ID field of the Authors table is called a *primary key*, meaning that it is the field by which we look up entries in the Authors table. The entries of the Authors table are indexed by the primary key (this index is maintained for us by the system), so that we can locate a specific entry based on its primary key very quickly. The Au_ID field of the Titles table is a *foreign key*. The titles need not be sorted by their Au_ID field, but this field does allow us to connect each title to its author. Similarly, the PubID field of the Titles table relates each title to its publisher and is a foreign key for the Titles table. The PubID field of the Publishers table, however, is the primary key of that table.

The primary and foreign keys in the BIBLIO database have identical field names. This is not a restriction imposed by the Data Manager application or Visual Basic. They could be different, but in most cases it makes sense that they have the same names, because they refer to the same physical entity. The field names must be unique within a table, but not across the database.

A primary key field is determined by which index you define as the *primary index* within a given table. To make a primary key, define a primary index based on that key. A table may contain several indices, so that it can be sorted according to more than one field. Only one of the indices, however, can be the primary one. The key on which the primary index is based is the primary key.

Foreign keys are not defined in the database. Any field can be a foreign key, as long as it points to another table's primary key. To understand the purpose of the primary and foreign keys, consider what you would be doing with the BIBLIO database. The most basic operation would be to look up titles. Along with the titles, you would like to be able to look at authors and publishers. To find out the author of a title, you would read the title's Au_ID field, and then use it to find the row of the Authors table whose Au_ID field has the same value. If the Authors table wasn't sorted according to its Au_ID field, you would have to scan the entire table, row after row, until you find the row with the matching Au_ID field. However, because the Authors table is sorted according to the Au_ID field, locating a specific value is extremely fast. Similarly, you can quickly locate a title's publisher in the Publishers table.

## The VBINC Database

Now let's look at the structure of the VBINC database, which is shown in Figure 3-3. The VBINC database is made up of four tables: Customers, Products, Invoices and Invdetails. Similar to the BIBLIO database, VBINC's tables are linked with keys. The invoices do not contain the customer name. Instead, they are linked by a number (an ID) to the customer they belong to. The table contains the invoice headers (the invoice number, customer ID, date and total). The lines of the invoices (items sold) are kept in a separate table, called Invdetails. The INV_ID field of the Invoices table links the invoice header to the invoice lines. All the rows of the Invdetails table whose INVDET_ID value is 21 belong to the invoice whose INV_ID is 21.

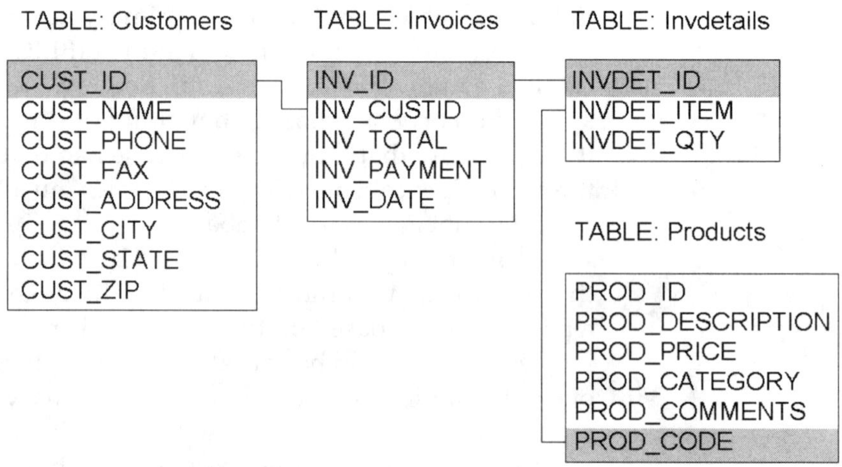


Figure 3-3: The structure of the VBINC database.

## DESIGNING DATABASES WITH VB

Designing a database is no simple task. If the database is not designed properly, it will not be easy to extract the information you need. There are rules for designing databases, but they are beyond the scope of this book. Do, though, bear in mind two basic rules:

- ❒ Do not duplicate information.
- ❒ Make sure the information you need can be easily extracted.

The first rule says that if information is repeated in more than one place in a table in the database, that table must be broken into two or more smaller tables. The second rule says that the tables must be linked to each other in ways that will later on facilitate the retrieval of information from multiple tables. If the invoice file is not linked to the customers file, you will not be able to know what each customer has purchased. Many of the flaws in the design of a database will become obvious as you start writing applications to store and retrieve the data.

Visual Basic's tool for designing databases is called Data Manager. Unfortunately, it's a rather primitive tool for database design, but it's the only way you can design databases in the Visual Basic environment—short of writing a program that does it for you. (If you have Microsoft Access installed on your computer, then you should be using Access to design the database. Just make sure that the version of the database is 1.1, because Visual Basic 3.0 can't understand the databases created by Access version 2.0.)

Microsoft intended Visual Basic to be used for the design of front-end applications—applications that act upon the data of existing databases designed with more professional tools, such as Microsoft Access or Microsoft FoxPro, or even third-party programs, such as Borland's Paradox and dBASE. The inadequacy of VB's Data Manager strongly suggests that Microsoft isn't encouraging the design and implementation of database applications with Visual Basic 3.0. This situation has changed with VB4. The latest version of the Data Manager, which comes with VB4, is described in the next chapter.

The Data Manager application lets you specify the tables in the database and their indices. Tables are defined similarly to records of random access files. Each field in the record has its own type (integer, long, text, etc.). Once you've defined the fields, you can specify the indices for each table. An index determines how the rows of a table will be sorted. The table's rows are not *physically* sorted. Visual Basic simply presents them to you in a different order, depending on the index. That's why you can specify more than one index for a table. Sometimes, you may want to display the invoices sorted according to date, and other times according to the customer's ID. You can specify two different indices and use the appropriate one each time. Use the Data Manager application to look at the two sample databases, BIBLIO and VBINC. Look at the definitions of the fields and their indices. You can even browse through the tables and add new data.

There is one point worth mentioning here. Among the various data types a field can have (the types you see in a Combo Box when you design the database), there is one called *counter*. A counter is a long integer that the system automatically increases each time a new record is created. Counter fields are used as keys. Visual Basic makes sure that they take on unique values, but their actual value is of no interest to the user. In other words, you can use a counter field to connect two tables (as in "list all the titles whose PubID fields match the PubID field of publisher 'Ventana' in the publishers table"). The actual values in this field are completely irrelevant, as long as they provide the necessary links among tables. All fields that include the string "ID" in their field names, in both databases, are counters.

In the following sections of the chapter we are going to present Visual Basic's tools for handling databases, starting with the simplest one, the Data Control.

## USING THE DATA CONTROL

We've seen the structure of two databases and discussed the organization of the data in them. Now let's see what we can do with this data. In Figure 3-4 you see a simple Form that lets you browse the publishers of the BIBLIO database. This application is called PUBLSHRS, and you can find it on the 3\APPS\PUBLSHRS subdirectory of the CD. The PUBLSHRS application is based on the Data Control, the horizontal scroll bar at the bottom of the Form. The buttons at the two ends of the scroll bar (triangle symbol with line) take you to the first and last records in the Publishers table. The inner two buttons (triangle only), move you to the previous and next publisher. To use more correct terms, the arrows at the two ends of the Control move you to the first and last rows of the table. The other two move you to the previous and next rows.

CD-ROM

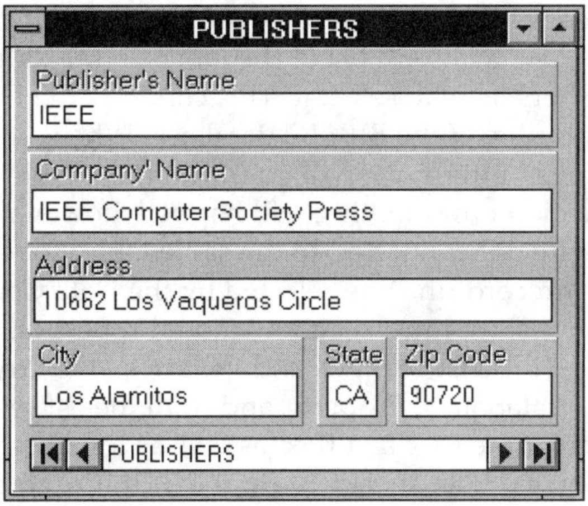


Figure 3-4: This data-browsing application was built entirely around the Data Control. It doesn't contain a single line of code.

Moving to the first, last, next or previous record within a database isn't terribly impressive; you can easily program the same maneuvers as the front end for data contained within an ordinary random access file. However, this application doesn't contain a single line of code. Instead, it was built by assigning the proper values to certain Properties of the VB Data Control.

Design a Form similar to that in Figure 3-4. Place all the Text Boxes on the Form and draw a Data Control at the bottom of the Form. Then select the Data1 Data Control with the mouse and press F4 to see the Properties Window. Click on the DatabaseName Property and a File Open window will be displayed. From this window locate the BIBLIO database on your hard disk and open it. The name BIBLIO.MDB will appear in the DatabaseName Property's setting.

CD-ROM

If you have copied the PUBLSHRS application of this book's CD onto a subdirectory of your hard disk and have problems running it, make sure the Data Control can "see" the database. You can either copy the VBINC database in your \VB directory and make sure this directory is on the path, or change the Data Control's DatabaseName Property so that it points to wherever you've stored the VBINC database on your disk.

Then select the RecordSource Property and click on the down arrow. You will see a list of the tables in the database. Click on the Publishers table to select it. This connects the Data Control to a specific table of the BIBLIO database. When we click on the Data Control's buttons, we will go through the table's rows. If you run the application now, nothing will happen, however, because the Text Boxes are not connected to the same table. To force the fields of the current record (the one selected by the Data Control) to appear in the Text Boxes, we must set a few more Properties.

Select the first Text Box and then open the Properties window. Click on the DataSource Property, and from the list select Data1. The source of data for the first Text Box (as well as for all others) is the Data Control: the Publishers table in the BIBLIO database. Then select the Property DataField, and then open the drop-down list in the Properties window. You will see a list of all fields in the Publishers table. Select the Name field. Repeat the same process for all Text Boxes. Assign the value Data1 to their RecordSource Properties and the corresponding field to their DataField Properties. The DataField Properties of the Text Boxes are Name, Company Name, Address, City, State and Zip. Then run the application and browse through the publishers. As you click on the buttons of the Data Control, you are moved to another row of the table and another publisher's data are displayed.

Writing a functional database-browsing application (even a very simple one) without any programming is no small feat. And it's all made possible thanks to Visual Basic's Data Control and the so-called Data Bound Controls. The Data Control connects your application to a specific table of a database. The Data Bound Controls can be bound (connected, or linked) to the Data Control. As the Data Control moves through the rows (records) of a table, the Data Bound Text Boxes see one column (field) of the specific row and they display it.

Data Bound Controls display the current value of a specific field in the current row.

Change the state field of the current publisher. Then move to the next record and then back to the previous record. The changes you made have taken effect already. But when? You didn't see the usual OK and Cancel buttons and you weren't asked to either confirm or cancel the operation. This is how the Data Control works. Every time you move to another record, contents of the Data Bound Controls are moved back into the database on disk. This probably isn't what you'd expect from a data-entry application, and it sure isn't appropriate for a seasoned data-entry operator. However, all the actions performed by the Data Control are available to you as Methods and you can modify the behavior of the Data Control to suit your needs. We'll see how this is done in a bit, but first let's talk more about the Data Bound Controls.

## Data Bound Controls

As you saw in the previous example, the Text Box is a Data Bound Control, because it can be connected to a specific field of a table and follow its changes. The field changes value because we moved to a new record, and the Text Box's Text is updated to reflect the new value. You change the value of the Text Box, then the field changes value accordingly. Other than that, the Data Bound Text Box is a regular Text Box.

The Text Box isn't the only Data Bound Control. There's also the Label, the Check Box and the Picture and Image Boxes. The Professional Edition of VB adds three more Data Bound Controls: the Masked Edit, the 3D Panel and the 3D Check Box. The Label and 3D Panel Controls work just like the Text Box, but the user can't change the value of the field, because you can't type into them. The Check Box can be connected to True/False fields, and its Value Property determines whether the field's value is True or False. Finally, the Picture Box and the Image Box can be connected to special fields of the table that contain images (their type is LongBinary).

Our example application, PUBLSHRS, doesn't employ the best data-entry methods—it doesn't give the user a chance to confirm or cancel the operation. Although it can't be used very effectively for data entry, it is a functional data-browsing tool. If you want to make sure that the user can't inadvertently modify the contents of the database, change all the Text Boxes to Labels or Panels. This way, the fields' values can be displayed, but not modified. The Data Control (and its Data Bound Controls) doesn't allow you to enter new records. You have to write some code to add new records. The same is true for deleting records. Soon, we'll see how to design data-entry screens, but first we must briefly mention the Data Control's Validate Event. This event is invoked every time the Control is ready to make changes to the database. Using the Validate Event, you can check the user's changes before committing them to the database. Every time the user clicks on one of the Control's navigational buttons, the Validate Event is triggered. With the appropriate code you can prompt the user to confirm his or her intentions to update the data, or discard the changes and revert to the original data.

The Validate Event lets you validate the values of Data Bound Controls before they are committed to the database.

The Validate Event is triggered every time the Data Control is about to send new data to the table. By placing a few additional lines of code in this event's subroutine, we can validate the user's input before the Data Control commits it to the database. The Validate subroutine accepts two arguments:

```
Sub Data1_Validate (Action As Integer, Save As Integer)
```

The Action argument describes the action that triggered the Validate Event. It's 1 if it was triggered because the user clicked on the Button that moves to the first record (MoveFirst), 2 if the user clicked on the button that moves to the previous record, 11 if the Form received an Unload message, and so on. As you will see shortly, there are many other actions that can trigger the Validate Event, such as the addition or deletion of a record, etc. The Save argument is True if the Data Bound Controls connected to the Data1 Control have changed, and False otherwise. You can also set the value of the Save argument. If you set this argument to False from within the Data1_Validate subroutine, the data will not be saved to the database.

Now let's see how to use Methods to manage the Data Control under our program's control. This will enable us to take advantage of the functionality built into the Data Control and at the same time work around its limitations.

## PROGRAMMING THE DATA CONTROL

Now it's time to take a plunge into the real world of database programming, and see how we can "write" data-entry applications. Before we do so, however, we must discuss a fundamental concept in Visual Basic's database capabilities: the Recordset.

A *Recordset* is a group of records (rows) in a database. The recordset can be an entire table, such as the Publishers table, which contains all the publishers' names, or part of a table, such as the publishers in the New York area (the rows of the Publishers table in which the State field has the value NY). (Programmatically you can access more than one table in a single recordset. We will see how to do this later in the chapter.) So far, we have seen how to connect a Data Control to an entire table by assigning the name of a table to its RecordSource Property. We will see other ways to define Recordsets in the rest of the chapter.

As soon as the execution of the PUBLSHRS application starts, Visual Basic creates a set of records, which are all the records of the Publishers table. This collection of records is accessed through the Data Control. All references to the selected records must use the following construct:

```
Data1.Recordset
```

The Recordset is not a Property of the Data Control. A Recordset is an independent entity—an object. Perhaps the easiest way to explain recordsets is to describe how they're used. The Data Control has its own Properties, like any other Control. It has all the usual Properties, like Caption, Width, Height, Tag, etc. It also has some unique Properties that make it suitable for working with databases (DatabaseName and RecordSource).

The purpose of the Data Control is to give us access to Recordsets. Therefore, there must be a way to address the Recordset itself through the Data Control. All the Properties and Methods of the Recordset are addressed through the object Data1.Recordset (or MyDataControl.Recordset, or whatever the name of the Data Control is). For example, to find out if we have reached the last row of the Recordset, we must examine the EOF Property of the Recordset, with an If statement like this:

```
If Data1.Recordset.EOF Then
...
End If
```

The Data Control itself doesn't have an EOF Property, and there is no such thing a Data1.EOF. Similarly, to delete the current row of the Recordset we must issue this command:

```
Data1.Recordset.Delete
```

This command won't work:

```
Data1.Delete
```

The Recordset, therefore, is not a Property of the Data Control. Data1.Recordset is an object. It is the set of all rows in the table that we can act upon through the Data1 Data Control.

## Navigating Through the Recordset

How do you "move" through the data (change the current record)? Table 3-1 lists the four Methods for navigating through the Recordset:

| | |
|---|---|
| MoveFirst | Moves to the first record in the recordset. |
| MovePrevious | Moves to the previous record in the recordset. |
| MoveLast | Moves to the last record in the recordset. |
| MoveNext | Moves to the next record in the recordset. |

Table 3-1: Four Methods for navigating the Recordset.

These Methods allow you to move from one record to another, similarly to clicking on the VCR-style buttons of the Data Control, and they refer to the Control's Recordset Property. (The Data Control is always pointing to a particular record, called the *current* record.) Their syntax, therefore, would be as follows:

```
Data1.Recordset.MoveFirst
```

The Move Methods let you select the Data Control's current record from within your application.

It is very easy, therefore, to emulate the actions caused by clicking on the Data Control's buttons. When using the navigational Methods of the Data Control to position ourselves in the recordset (to move among the rows), we always take into consideration the Properties EOF and BOF, which become True when we are at the last or first record in the recordset respectively. There is no next record after the last one (when EOF = True), or previous record before the first one (when BOF = True). You would expect the Data Control not to react to MovePrevious and MoveNext Methods when you are already in the first or last record respectively, but it *does*. We'll get into this later in "Designing Data-Entry Applications."

There is one more Property that is used in conjunction with the navigational Methods: the Bookmark Property. This Property is a string that holds the position of the current row in the Recordset. The Bookmark Property allows you to "mark" the current record, and return to it instantly from any place in the recordset. A Bookmark is not a record number, and it can't be used in any calculations. You can't find the distance between two records by subtracting two Bookmarks; neither can you use it to move to the next or previous record from a Bookmark by adding or subtracting one. It's simply a string that indicates the current row in the recordset.

You can assign the value of the Bookmark Property to a string variable, and then return instantly to this record by assigning the value of the variable to the Bookmark Property. The following command stores the position of the current row:

```
ReturnToThisRecord = Data1.Recordset.Bookmark
```

Even if new rows are added to, or existing rows are deleted from, the Recordset, the Bookmark Property of a record doesn't change. To return to the same record after moving away from it, use this command:

```
Data1.Recordset.Bookmark = ReturnToThisRecord
```

(Provided, of course, that the record hasn't been deleted.)

## Accessing a Field in the Recordset

How do you access a particular piece of data? Now that we've seen how to move among records, we should consider how to get to a particular field within a given record.

There are many ways to programmatically access the fields in a table through a Data Control—enough to be confusing at first. The simplest way is to use the Field Property of the Recordset object. To read the value of the Title field in the Titles table of the BIBLIO database, use the following line:

```
BookTitle$ = Data1.Recordset.Fields("Title")
```

The current record's fields can be accessed either by name or by their order in the record.

This is the lengthiest syntax for the Fields Property, but it is unambiguous, and the easiest to read. The same field can be referenced via its order in the record. In other words, you can use the following command to obtain the value of the Title field of the current record, because it is the first field in the table:

```
BookTitle$ = Data1.Recordset.Fields(0)
```

Fields in Recordsets have the same order as they do in the underlying tables. The order of the fields in a table is the one you see in the Data Manager application, when you design the corresponding table. The name of the field, or its order in the table's definition, can be substituted with variables too:

```
fname$ = "Title"
BookTitle$ = Data1.Recordset.Fields(fname$)
```

Or you could also use the following:

```
n = 0
BookTitle$ = Data1.Recordset.Fields(n)
```

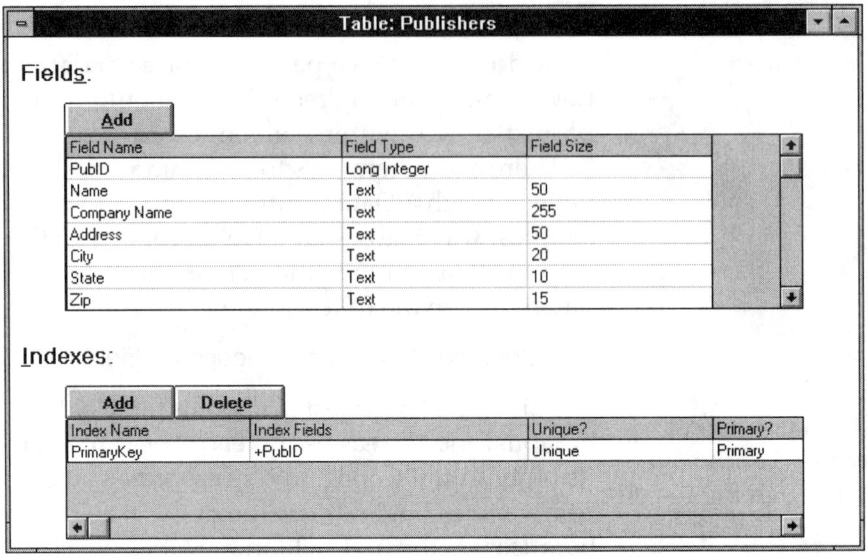


Figure 3-5: The order of a table's fields is determined by the order in which they appear in the table's definition.

The Fields Property also happens to be the default Property of the Recordset object, so you can omit it from the previous expressions. You can write either of the following:

```
BookTitle$ = Data1.Recordset("Title")
BookTitle$ = Data1.Recordset(0)
```

Keep in mind that field names are not case-sensitive. You could refer to the same field as "TITLE" or "title."

In the rest of the chapter, we are going to use the lengthiest notation (that is, identify fields by their names) to increase the readability of the code. Of course, there are cases where this can't be done. For example, if we don't know the structure of the recordset, we can still access its fields by their order.

The order of the field may not be as clear as its name, but it comes in handy when reading many rows of the table. Let's say we want to read an entire table in a Grid Control (provided the table's contents do not exceed the capacity of a Grid). The number of columns (fields) in the table is given by the Property Data1.Recordset.Fields.Count. Similarly, the number of rows (records) in the table is given by the Property Data1.Recordset.RecordCount.

Start the PUBLSHRS application, then stop it and move to the Debug Window and type the following lines:

```
Print Data1.Recordset.Fields.Count
9
Print Data1.Recordset.RecordCount
30
```

The first number is the number of columns (fields) in the Publishers table and the second number is the number of rows (records) in the same table.

Now you can scan the entire Recordset with two nested loops, as if it were a two-dimensional array. The outer loop will scan the rows of the Recordset (from 1 to Data1.Recordset.RecordCount) and the inner loop will scan the columns (from 1 to Data1.Recordset.Fields.Count).

### Example: Reading a Recordset in a Grid Control

Let's put together some of the Properties and Methods of the Recordset object to build the application in Figure 3-6. The DAGRID application loads all the titles stored in the Titles table of the BIBLIO database, along with their ISBN numbers, on a Grid Control. Our Form this time contains a Data Control and a Grid Control. (Note: The Grid Control is not Data Bound.) There is no simple way to automatically load all the titles on a Grid Control, and we will have to do it with a loop through the Recordset, one title at a time.

| | Book Title | ISBN |
|---|---|---|
| 01 | The database experts' guide to SQL | 0070390061 |
| 02 | Database system concepts | 0070447527 |
| 03 | Database design | 007070130X |
| 04 | Using SQL | 007881524X |
| 05 | Visual Basic for Windows inside & out | 0078819318 |
| 06 | Conceptual schema and relational database | 0131672630 |
| 07 | Fundamental concepts of information modeling | 0133355896 |
| 08 | Visual basic [programming] | 0134892879 |
| 09 | Practical data design | 0136908276 |
| 10 | A practical guide to data base design | 0136909671 |
| 11 | Relational database design with | 0137718411 |
| 12 | Strategic information planning methodologies | 0138505381 |
| 13 | Fundamentals of data normalization | 0201066459 |
| 14 | Database: a primer | 0201113589 |

Figure 3-6: The DAGRID application loads the titles on a Grid Control.

You can exploit the Data Control's functionality through its Methods and Properties.

In this application, we have made the Data Control invisible at run time. All the titles appear in the Grid. The user can click on the vertical scroll bar of the Grid Control to move through the titles. Set the DatabaseName Property of the Data Control to BIBLIO and its RecordSource Property to Titles. Then enter the following code in the Form's Load Event:

```
Sub Form_Load ( )

    Data1.Refresh ' sets the object
' The next few lines size the Grid Control
        Grid1.Height = 3600
        Grid1.ColWidth(1) = TextWidth("This is the longest →
        title the first column can hold")
        Grid1.ColWidth(2) = TextWidth("333-333-333-333")
        Grid1.Width = Grid1.ColWidth(0) + Grid1.ColWidth(1) →
        + Grid1.ColWidth(2) + 325
        Form1.Width = Grid1.Width + 320
        Form1.Height = Grid1.Top + Grid1.Height + 550
        Data1.Visible = False
        Grid1.Row = 0

' Get the number of rows
    Data1.Recordset.MoveLast
    TotRows% = Data1.Recordset.RecordCount
    Grid1.Rows = TotRows% + 1
    Grid1.Row = 0
    Grid1.Col = 1
    Grid1.Text = "Book Title"
    Grid1.Col = 2
    Grid1.Text = "ISBN"
' steps through the rows of recordset
    Data1.Recordset.MoveFirst
    For i = 1 To TotRows%
        Grid1.Row = Grid1.Row + 1
        Grid1.Col = 0
        Grid1.Text = Format$(i, "00")
        Grid1.Col = 1
        Grid1.Text = Data1.Recordset.Fields("Title")
        Grid1.Col = 2
        Grid1.Text = Data1.Recordset.Fields("ISBN")
        Data1.Recordset.MoveNext
    Next
```

```
        Grid1.Row = 1
        Grid1.Col = 1

    End Sub
```

The first line creates the Recordset. If you omit it, Visual Basic will generate an error message stating that the "Object is not Set." The Data Control's Recordset is created the first time the user clicks on one of its buttons. Since no user action is involved here, we must create the Recordset ourselves, with the Refresh Method. The Refresh Method copies all the records from the table, in effect creating a new Recordset.

The following lines in the listing simply size the Grid Control and the Form. Notice that the Data1 Control is made invisible with this line (this is a Property of the Data Control and not its Recordset):

```
    Data1.Visible = False
```

Then we get the number of rows (Data1.Recordset.RecordCount), but not before we move to the last row with the MoveLast Method. The RecordCount Property of the Recordset is the number of records that have been actually accessed by your application. Therefore, executing the MoveLast Method causes the value of this Property to be set to the number of records in the Recordset. (The RecordCount Property will not be decremented if we move to another record. The only way to decrement the value of RecordCount is by deleting a record.)

Then we loop through the Recordset, extract the values of the fields "Title" and "ISBN," and append them to the Grid. The code for the DAGRID application is rather lengthy, but most commands deal with the Grid and not the Recordset itself.

## Editing the Recordset

Now let's look at Methods that allow us to perform operations not possible with the Data Control: adding, editing and deleting records. Table 3-2 lists the three Methods for manipulating data in the database's tables:

| | |
|---|---|
| AddNew | Adds a new record. |
| Delete | Deletes the current record. |
| Edit | Edits the current record. |

Table 3-2: Methods for manipulating a database's tables.

The AddNew Method appends a new blank record at the end of the recordset and positions you there. *This record is not yet committed to the database.* After assigning values to its fields, you can either commit the changes to the database with the Update Method, or cancel the AddNew operation with the Refresh Method.

The Refresh Method re-creates the Recordset by getting the data from disk.

Recall that the Refresh Method creates a Recordset from the table. The temporary record hasn't become part of the table, and when the Recordset is read again from the table it will not be there. This seems like overkill, having to read all the records from the table just to eliminate one record, but it is the only way to remove the temporary record. It's not a slow process, because Visual Basic doesn't really go to the disk to read all the records making up the Recordset. It rebuilds the Recordset with data that are already in memory.

The Delete Method simply removes the current record from the table, without any confirmation from the user. The Edit Method prepares the record for editing. The changes will be committed to the table with the Update Method, as with the AddNew Method. To cancel the changes, call the Refresh Method.

How exactly is a record prepared for editing? Nothing really happens to the record or the table. The Edit Method stores the original record and gives your program permission to change the values of the current record's fields. Here is the common sequence of commands for updating a record's values:

```
Data1.Recordset.Edit
Data1.Recordset.Fields(0)= UCase$(Data1.Recordset.Fields(0))
Data1.Recordset.Update
```

Use the Update Method to commit changes to the database.

If you attempt to change the value of a field while not in Edit mode, Visual Basic will generate the error message "Update without AddNew or Edit" and will not accept the changes.

To abort the changes, call the Refresh Method. If you move to another record without committing the edits with the Update Method, Visual Basic will ignore them and restore the fields you have already changed to their original values. Another way to discard the changes made to some fields is to move to the next (or previous) record and then back to the one you were editing.

The following command prepares the current record for editing:

```
Data1.Recordset.Edit
```

Next, change the value of a field:

```
Data1.Recordset.Fields(0) =
UCase$(Data1.Recordset.Fields(0))
```

Then reject the changes with these commands:

```
Data1.Recordset.MoveNext
Data1.Recordset.MovePrevious
```

If you look at the value of the first field with the following command, you will find out that it hasn't changed:

```
Debug.Print Data1.Recordset.Fields(0)
```

This simple experiment indicates that you must make sure that the user of your application has no way to move to another record before either committing or discarding the changes made to the current record. The best way to do this is to disable the navigational keys in your application.

## Designing Data-Entry Applications

We have seen how to gain access to the Data Control's capabilities through the Methods and Properties of the Recordset object. Now we're ready to build a data-entry application that has all the functionality of the Data Control, but none of its shortcomings. The VBCUST application (subdirectory 3\APPS\VBCUST on the CD), shown in Figure 3-7, is a data-entry application for the Customers table of the VBINC database. The Form in Figure 3-7 looks much more like a data-entry screen, and any data-entry operator would prefer it over the scroll bar with the VCR-style buttons of the Data Control.

CD-ROM

A data-entry application must provide options for confirming or aborting any changes.

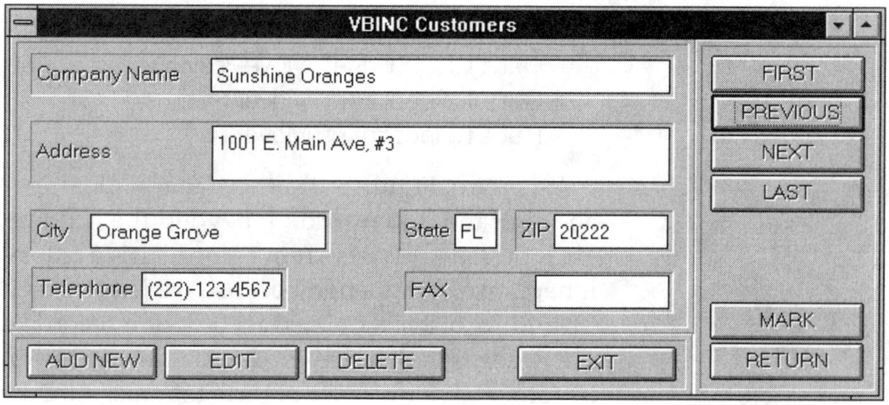


Figure 3-7: A familiar data-entry screen based on Visual Basic's Data Control.

Figure 3-8 shows the application in the design phase. The Form contains a few more buttons (OK and Cancel), which become visible during the operations of adding and editing a record, and a Data Control, which remains hidden at run time.

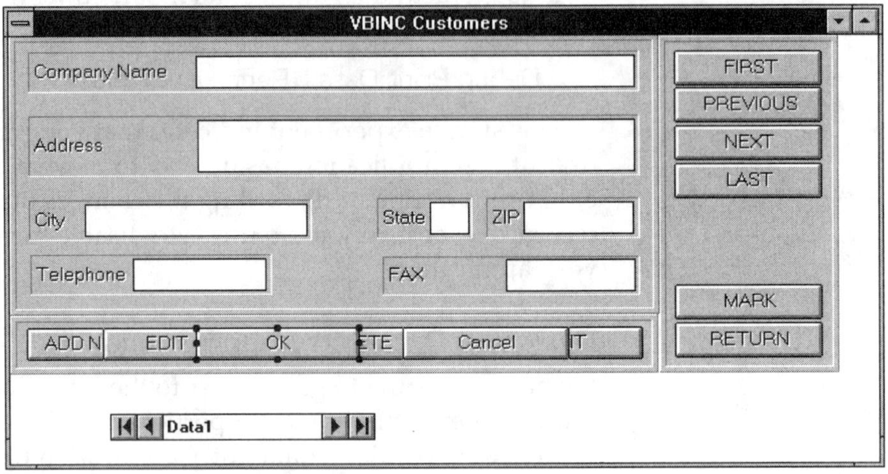


Figure 3-8: The Form shown in Figure 3-7 during the design phase.

Let's see how the navigational Methods work by implementing the code for the First, Previous, Next and Last Command Buttons. If you didn't know better, you would be tempted to insert these lines in the subroutines of the respective navigational Buttons:

```
Data1.Recordset.MoveFirst
Data1.Recordset.MovePrevious
Data1.Recordset.MoveNext
Data1.Recordset.MoveLast
```

If you do, Figure 3-9 shows what will happen. An attempt to move ahead of the first record, or beyond the last one, will result in the error message "No current record." It's a trappable error, but why did it happen? It happened because we landed on an invalid record. An invalid record is a deleted record, or a record beyond either end of the Recordset. Since it's possible to move beyond the two ends of the Recordset, we must write code to make sure that this doesn't happen.

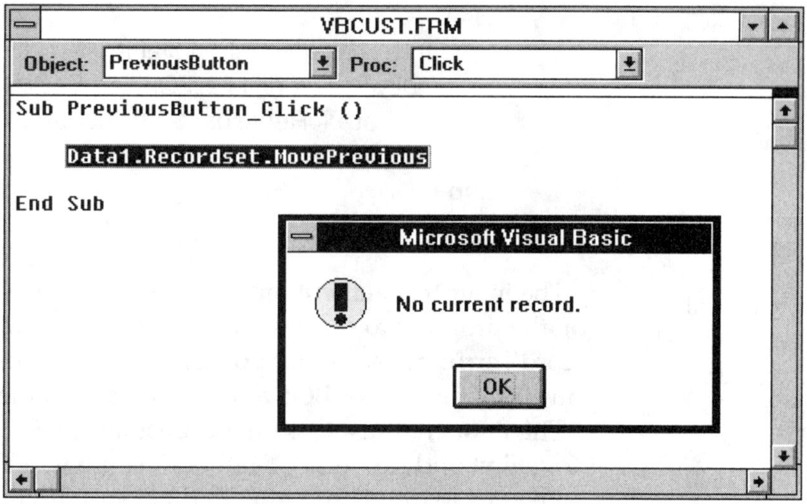


Figure 3-9: The MovePrevious and MoveNext Methods unchecked can take you ahead of the first record or beyond the last record in the Recordset.

In the Next Command Button's code we must check the EOF Property, to make sure that we'll never attempt to move beyond the last record. Similarly, in the Previous Command Button's code we must check the BOF Property, to make sure that we'll never attempt to move beyond the first record. Here's one way to avoid this situation:

```
Sub PreviousButton_Click ( )

    If Data1.Recordset.BOF Then
        Beep
        Data1.Recordset.MoveFirst
    Else
        Data1.Recordset.MovePrevious
        If Data1.Recordset.BOF Then
            Data1.Recordset.MoveFirst
        End If
    End If

End Sub

Sub NextButton_Click ( )

    If Data1.Recordset.EOF Then
        Beep
        Data1.Recordset.MoveLast
```

```
        Else
            Data1.Recordset.MoveNext
            If Data1.Recordset.EOF Then
                Data1.Recordset.MoveLast
            End If
        End If
    End Sub
```

The MoveNext and MovePrevious Methods can take you past the table's ends.

The inner If statement may not be very clear. Comment it out and run the program to see what will happen. You won't get a "No current record" error message, but you *will* land on a blank record. That's why you check for EOF or BOF after each move in the Recordset.

The First and Last Command Buttons are implemented with the MoveFirst and MoveLast Methods. There will always be a first and a last record to move to, right? Perhaps not. If you delete all the records, there will be neither first nor last records. *Any* record you are currently at will be invalid. The simplest way to cope with this situation is to disable all four navigational buttons after a deletion, if the deleted record was the last one in the Recordset. Then the user cannot click on those buttons. In this case, both the EOF and BOF Properties will become True. We are not dealing with this situation here, but your applications should of course try to foresee and forestall all kinds of mishaps. Here is the code for the First and Last Buttons:

```
Sub FirstButton_Click ( )

    Data1.Recordset.MoveFirst

End Sub

Sub LastButton_Click ( )

    Data1.Recordset.MoveLast

End Sub
```

To add a new record, use the AddNew Method. The Data Control will take you to an empty record, where you can type the values of the fields. Then you can either commit the new record to the database with the Update Method, or cancel the operation and delete the temporary record with the Refresh Method. The Update Method commits the new record to the database. The Refresh Method rebuilds the recordset, in effect removing the temporary record. The code behind the Add Command Button is as follows:

```
Sub AddButton_Click ( )

    Call HideButtons

    Data1.Recordset.AddNew

End Sub
```

The HideButtons subroutine hides (makes invisible) all the buttons on the bottom of the Form and displays two new ones—the OK and Cancel Buttons.

Here's the line that does all the work:

```
Data1.Recordset.AddNew
```

The user can enter values in the Text Boxes, and when done, click either on the OK Button to commit the new record, or on the Cancel Button to remove the temporary record. Here is the code behind the OK and Cancel Buttons:

```
Sub OKButton_Click ( )

On Error GoTo NoUpdate
    If Trim(Text1.Text) = "" Then
        MsgBox "Record must have a valid Company Name"
    Else
        Data1.Recordset.Update
        Call ShowButtons
    End If
    Exit Sub

NoUpdate:
    MsgBox Error
    Exit Sub

End Sub

Sub CancelButton_Click ( )

    Call ShowButtons
    Data1.Refresh

End Sub
```

Again, two Methods are all you need:

```
Data1.Recordset.Update
Data1.Recordset.Refresh
```

The Update Method commits the new record to the database, and Refresh deletes the temporary record and makes no changes to the database.

The If clause in the OKButton_Click subroutine requires some explanation. Before committing a new record to the database, we must make sure that the new record is a valid one. Visual Basic will check the fields against their types in the definition of the table, and if they do not conform to the type of the table's fields it will generate an error message. If you type a string in a numeric field, for instance, the message will be "Type mismatch." If you exceed the length of a text field, you will get the error message "Couldn't insert or paste; data too long for field." As you see, Visual Basic will not even ignore the extra characters in order to make the string fit into the field's length. It is imperative that the program validate the user's data before sending them to the database. This is why we are writing data-entry screens in the first place.

The Update Method commits both modified and new records to the database.

The fields must not only conform to the table's definition, but in most cases they must maintain referential integrity. *Referential integrity* means that links between data mustn't be broken. For example, if you let the user enter a publisher ID in the Titles table and there is no corresponding publisher ID in the Publishers table, this violates the referential integrity of the database. It will cause a reference (a link) to a nonexistent publisher. Similarly, if you issue an invoice to a nonexistent customer, the integrity of the database will be seriously impaired. Entering information that doesn't correspond to a real-world entity violates the integrity of the database and leads to incorrect results when the database is queried. Visual Basic 3.0 does not enforce referential integrity. It is your responsibility in your programming to maintain valid references among the fields in the database.

The Jet Engine itself doesn't enforce the database's referential integrity. It will accept any data you enter, as long as they conform to the definition of the corresponding fields. Toward the end of this chapter, we will present the VBINV application, which prepares invoices for the VBINC database. The VBINV application enforces referential integrity, as it will not allow you to issue an invoice to a nonexistent customer, or sell items that have not been entered in the database. This requires some additional programming effort, of course, but you can't avoid it. (VB4 supports referential integrity, which greatly simplifies the design of database applications.)

You can include all types of error checking and data validation in the OK Button's subroutine. Even so, you can never be sure that all errors are caught. In this example we don't perform any serious error checking, since error checking is such an application-specific process. However, we do display any error message Visual Basic may generate in the process of updating the database and give the user a chance to correct the mistake. Your applications should do more than just display Visual Basic's generic error message in similar cases.

The code of the OKButton is executed when a record is edited as well, since the Update Method commits both new and modified records to the database. Here is the code behind the Edit Button:

```
Sub EditButton_Click ( )

    Call HideButtons
    If Data1.Recordset.EOF Or Data1.Recordset.BOF Then
        MsgBox "No record to edit"
    Else
        Data1.Recordset.Edit
    End If

End Sub
```

This code makes sure that the current record is valid, and if so it allows editing of the record. When the user is done, he or she can click on the OK Button to commit the changes to the database, or on the Cancel Button to revert to the original record.

The Mark and Return Buttons let the user mark a record and return to the last marked record quickly. They use the Bookmark Property of the Recordset, but will not present their implementation here.

CD-ROM

On the CD you'll find an application similar to the VBCUST one. It is called VBPROD, and it is a data-entry program for the Products table. Use these applications to populate the Customers and Products tables of the VBINC database. In "Preparing Invoices" later in the chapter, we will present the VBINV application, which operates on both tables to prepare invoices.

CD-ROM

The VBCUST and VBPROD applications operate on the VBINC database located in the 3\APPS\VBINC subdirectory of the CD. To use the applications, copy them from the CD's directory on your hard disk and make sure that the database is on the current path. Do not duplicate the database in the current subdirectory. Other applications that use the same database will not find it there. Of course, you can copy all the applications of Chapter 3 into the same subdirectory, along with the VBINC database, allthough this isn't the best approach, especially if you want to write additional applications. When copying a database, make sure you copy both the MDB and LDB files.

So far we have explored the most basic mechanisms of the Data Control: how to navigate through the Recordset and how to add/edit/delete records. You know how to use a Data Control to browse and update your databases. In the next sections we will look at some more advanced, and highly useful, operations, such as searching for data and combining multiple tables.

## Searching the Recordset

One of most basic operations we perform on databases is locating specific records. Visual Basic offers many ways of locating the desired records. Let's start with the Methods for locating records in a Recordset. Visual Basic offers four different Find Methods (shown in Table 3-3), which are appropriately named:

| | |
|---|---|
| FindFirst | Locates the first record meeting certain criteria. |
| FindNext | Locates the next record meeting certain criteria. |
| FindPrevious | Locates the previous record meeting certain criteria. |
| FindLast | Locates the last record meeting certain criteria. |

Table 3-3: VB's Find Methods.

The Find Methods can locate any record in the Recordset, based on any specified criteria. The FindFirst and FindLast Methods locate the very first and very last record that meets the criteria you specify. The FindNext and FindPrevious Methods locate the first record matching the criteria after or before the current record. In other words, the FindFirst starts searching from the start of the recordset toward the end. FindLast starts at the end of the recordset and moves toward the beginning. FindNext and FindPrevious start at the current record and move toward the end or the beginning of the recordset.

Here is the syntax of the FindFirst Method:

```
FindFirst criteria
```

The Find Methods scan the entire table and check each record to see if it meets the search criteria.

The syntax is the same for the other three Find Methods.

The criteria argument is a regular VB expression specifying a relationship between field values and constants, expressed as a string. The following expression specifies the first author from the Authors table (in the BIBLIO database) whose name begins with *N*:

```
"Author > 'N'"
```

If no such author exists, the Find Method will return the first author whose name begins with O, and so on.

The criteria argument is a string that involves field names and relational operators. The following string would indicate all products whose category is DAIRY:

```
"PROD_CATEGORY = 'DAIRY'"
```

Notice that the single quotes are used to indicate literals within the string. (As you'll see later in the chapter, the same notation is used with SQL statements as well.)

To select all the invoices issued after 04/01/94, you would use this argument:

```
"INVDATE => '04/01/94'"
```

You can build more complicated expressions by combining relational and logical operators. The following expression will locate the first publisher in the Publishers table who is located in New York or California:

```
Data1.Recordset.FindFirst "State = 'NY' Or State = 'CA'"
```

Besides the usual relational operators of Visual Basic, you can also use the LIKE operator, which lets you locate records using wildcard characters. To find the first title that contains the word "DATABASE" in its title, use the following command:

```
Data1.Recordset.FindFirst "Title LIKE '*DATABASE*'"
```

This expression will look for records in the Titles table whose Title field contains the string "DATABASE." The asterisks in front and after the string indicate that any other string (text) may appear in front of the desired string, and any other string may follow it. In other words, titles like "The Database Expert's Guide to SQL" and "Database System Concepts" will be located.

When used with the LIKE operator, the asterisk means "any string," even if it's an empty string. Another character that appears frequently with the LIKE operator is the question mark (?), which stands for a single character (it can be any character, but only one).

The LIKE operator accepts wildcard characters, just like the file selection commands.

The searches performed by the Find Methods are by default case-insensitive. This means that the string "database" will match titles that contain the words "Database" or "DATABASE." To change the default behavior of Visual Basic, you can use the Option Compare statement in the application's module, or in a Form. Just as the Option Base statement lets you change the default array indexing scheme, Option Compare specifies how the searches will be performed. The following command makes the comparisons case-insensitive:

```
Option Compare Text
```

This command makes the comparisons case-sensitive:

```
Option Compare Binary
```

(Text and Binary are literals, not constants.)

At the time of this writing, we haven't been able to test the Option Compare statement, because it appears not to work as expected.

The Find Methods are always used in conjunction with the NoMatch Property, which is True if no record matches the specified criteria. If a matching record was found, then you can issue the FindNext (and/or FindPrevious) Method to move through the found records in the same way you would move in a Recordset.

After calling one of the Find Methods, we always test the NoMatch Property. If it's False, the Find Method has located a record matching the criteria. If not, there are no more matching records in the direction of the search. Here's how the Find Methods usually appear in a program:

```
Data1.Recordset.FindFirst expression
If Data1.Recordset.NoMatch Then
    MsgBox "No such record found"
End If
```

There is no Else clause in this code segment, because the Data Control moves automatically to the newly found record—no need for any special action.

The Find Methods are also useful when you need to locate fields with Null values (fields that contain no value). For example, it's likely to be an error in a database if you have a record that contains an address, phone number, etc., but an empty name field. Similarly, an Author field in a record in our Authors table shouldn't be Null. To make sure that no records contain Null values in the Author field, use the Find Methods with the following argument:

```
criteria = "IsNull(Data1.Recordset.Fields('Author')"
```

Then find the matching records with a loop like this:

```
Data1.FindFirst criteria
Do Until Data1.NoMatch
    {process the record}
    Data1.Recordset.FindNext
Loop
```

This code segment assumes that the Data1 Data Control is connected to the Authors table of the BIBLIO database.

As an example of the Find Method, we will explain the implementation of the Find Publisher and Find Next Command Buttons of the FINDPUBL application.

### EXAMPLE: FINDING PUBLISHERS BY NAME

CD-ROM

Now let's look at the Find Methods with an application very similar to PUBLSHRS. The FINDPUBL application (in the subdirectory 3\APPS\FINDPUBL on the CD) is identical to the PUBLSHRS application we presented earlier in the chapter, with one exception. It contains two Command Buttons at the bottom of the Form, which allow the user to search for specific publishers. When the user clicks on the Find Publisher Button, the program prompts him or her for the name of the publisher to search for. Then it uses the user's response to build the argument of the FindFirst Method. The criteria argument for the search is as follows:

```
criteria = "Name LIKE'" & PubName$ & "'"
```

PubName$ is the string the user typed in the InputBox. We use the relational operator LIKE for the comparison, because the user may not know the publisher's full and exact name. If the user knows the name of the publisher and types "Ventana" in the InputBox, the expression will become

```
"Name LIKE 'Ventana'"
```

This expression, however, will not match any record, if the publisher's full name is "Ventana Press." The user can also enter a string like "Ventana*" to locate publishers whose name begins with the string "Ventana", followed by any other character(s).

This string is used with the FindFirst Method on the Data1.Recordset (Publishers), to find the first matching publisher. Here's the routine that locates publishers by name:

```
Sub FindPublisher_Click ( )

    PubName$ = InputBox("Enter Publisher's name →
    to search for")
    If PubName$ = "" Then
        Exit Sub
```

```
    Else
        criteria = "Name LIKE'" & PubName$ & "'"
        Data1.Recordset.FindFirst criteria
        If Data1.Recordset.NoMatch Then
            MsgBox "No such Publisher in the database"
            Exit Sub
        Else
            NextButton.Enabled = True
        End If
    End If

End Sub
```

If the FindFirst Method is successful, we enable the Find Next Button, which will locate more publisher names meeting the same criteria. The code of the Find Next Button is much simpler, because the criteria argument has been defined already (it is a global variable). The Find Next Button's subroutine simply calls the FindNext Method with the already prepared argument:

```
Sub NextButton_Click ( )

    Data1.Recordset.FindNext criteria

    If Data1.Recordset.NoMatch Then
        MsgBox "No more matching records found!"
        NextButton.Enabled = False
    Else
        NextButton.Enabled = True
    End If

End Sub
```

We have seen how to use the Data Control, how to manipulate a table with the Recordset's Properties and Methods, but we are still scratching the surface of Visual Basic's powerful database handling capabilities. Now it's time for some more heavy-duty database programming.

## Working With Multiple Tables

Now we will move a level up in the complexity of our examples, toward a real-life situation. An application that looks at just publishers or just customers is of rather limited practical value. In most practical cases, you will have to combine data from multiple tables. An application like the one shown in Figure 3-10, which displays the titles along with the author's and the publisher's names, is much more likely to be required in a real-world situation. The application in Figure 3-10 is called BOOKS, and it can be found in the 3\APPS\BOOKS subdirectory of the CD.

CD-ROM

Figure 3-10: The BOOKS application combines fields from three different tables to display each title.

The most useful and common database operations involve multiple tables.

Let's gang the tables of the BIBLIO database together, so that when the user moves to a different title, the author and publisher of the new title will be displayed as well. The frames that contain the fields are Labels, so that they can't be changed by the user. This application contains two more Data Controls. The one that allows the user to navigate through the Titles is called Data1. The other two remain invisible at run time. The Data1 Data Control is tied to the Titles table of the database, and it serves the Labels that display the book's title and the year of publication. The Author's Label is tied to the second Data Control (Data2) which is connected to the Authors table, and the Publisher's Label accepts the Name field of the Publishers table, through the third Data Control (Data3). In Figure 3-11 you see the BOOKS application at the design phase, including the two invisible Controls.

Figure 3-11: The BOOKS application during the design phase. The Data2 and Data3 Data Controls are invisible at run time.

Every time the user clicks on the Data Control, the application displays the Title and the Publication Year fields from the Titles table, because the DataSource and DataField Properties of these two Labels were set properly at the design phase. If you were to run the application at this stage, you would see all the titles in the table, but the author's and publisher's names wouldn't change. (What you will see is the first author in the Authors table and the first publisher in the Publishers table.) Each Data Control is completely independent from any other. You can make all Data Controls visible at run time and see for yourself that they operate independently from each other and you can display any title, along with any publisher and any author on the Form.

### Connecting the Tables

To connect the fields of the various tables, we must do some programming. There is no simple way to specify a restriction like "Whenever the Data1 Data Control changes, cause the Data2 Data Control to move to the record whose Au_ID field is the same as the Au_ID field of the current record in the Titles table." Fortunately, we don't need to write more than a few lines of code, because much of the functionality we are after has already been built into the language.

In order to display the appropriate author and publisher names, we must set the RecordSource Properties of the two Data Controls to the appropriate fields of the Authors and Publishers tables. In other words, the RecordSource Property of the Data2 should not be the entire Authors table, but the row whose Au_ID field matches the Au_ID field of the current title. Similarly, the RecordSource Property of Data3 should not be the entire Publishers table, but the row of the table whose PubID field matches the PubID Field of the selected title. The Data Control need not see an entire table. It is possible to specify only a range of records, selected according to our application's requirements. And the way to do this is, logically enough, by changing the setting of the RecordSource Property of the Control.

You can change a Data Control's RecordSource Property at run time to select a different recordset.

How do we change the RecordSource Property at run time so that it points to a specific row (record) of the table? The answer is what you were probably afraid of: With an SQL statement. Although SQL statements will be presented in detail later in this chapter, we will use a few simple SQL statements here to complete our example.

The SQL statement for the Data2 (Authors) Data Control should be as follows:

```
SELECT Author FROM Authors WHERE Au_ID = N
```

This statement simply tells Visual Basic to select the Author field (which is the author's name) from the Authors table, such that the Au_ID field of the selected row is N. Presumably, N must be the value of the Au_ID field of the record pointed to by the Data1 Data Control. Because the value of N will be different for each author, we can't just type the previous statement in the RecordSource Property setting at design time. We must form the appropriate string at run time and assign it to the RecordSource Property of the Control. This is accomplished with a single line:

```
Data2.RecordSource = "SELECT Author FROM Authors →
WHERE Au_ID = " & Data1.RecordSet.Fields("Au_ID")
```

A Recordset need not be an entire table. You can use an SQL command to select the records you are interested in.

Data1.Recordset.Fields("Au_ID") is the value of the Au_ID field of the current record of the table pointed to by the Data1 Data Control.

The Data1 Data Control points to a record in the Titles table. The author of the current title (the one whose fields are displayed on the Form) is identified by the Au_ID field. What the previous statement does is to look into the Authors table and find the row in which the Au_ID field has the same value as the Au_ID field in the current row of the Titles table. Because an author ID uniquely identifies the author, the Recordset of the Data2 Data Control will contain one record only.

The equivalent line for the Data3 Data Control looks like this:

```
Data3.RecordSource = "SELECT Name FROM Publishers →
WHERE PubID = " & Data1.Recordset.Fields("PubID")
```

This SQL statement searches the Publishers table for a row in which the PubID field matches the value of the PubID field of the selected row in the Titles table. The fact that the matching fields have the same names is coincidental—although this will be the case in most databases. Why use different names for fields that serve the same purpose?

The changes we make in the RecordSource Property of the Data Control will not take effect immediately. To force the new Properties to take effect, we must execute the Refresh Method for each Control:

```
Data2.Refresh
Data3.Refresh
```

Notice how it is possible to redirect the RecordSource Property of a Data Control at run time, and moreover, force a Data Control to see not an entire table, but a single record. Technically, the SQL statement does not return a single record. It returns a collection of records (Recordset). In our case, however, because the Au_ID and PubID fields have unique values (this is how they were designed), the Recordset is bound to contain a single record.

Where do we insert the previous lines? If you look at the Data Control's Events, you will find an Event called Reposition. The Reposition Event is invoked every time the user moves to another record by clicking on one of the Control's buttons. Here is the complete code of the Data1 Data Control's Reposition Event:

```
Sub Data1_Reposition ( )
Dim PubNum As Long, Authnum As Long

    Data2.RecordSource = "SELECT Author FROM Authors →
    WHERE Au_ID=" & Data1.Recordset.Fields("Au_ID")
    Data2.Refresh
    Data3.RecordSource = "SELECT Name FROM Publishers →
    WHERE PubID=" & Data1.Recordset.Fields("PubID")
    Data3.Refresh

Exit Sub
```

SQL statements are a great way to locate items in a database. However, they require a certain amount of overhead. SQL statements are not executed directly by Visual Basic. They are passed to the underlying database management system, which executes them. We will not get into any deep technical details regarding the execution of SQL commands, but it wouldn't be a bad idea to time our program. The GetCurrentTime( ) function (see Chapter 8 for more on this API call), returns the current time in milliseconds. Its declaration is in the Module of the application. If we call this function before and after the execution of the previous commands, the difference of the two values will be the time required for the execution of the commands that connect the three Data Controls. Insert the following line at the beginning of the Data1_Reposition( ) subroutine:

```
t1# = GetCurrentTime( )
```

And these lines right before End Sub (these lines exist in the BOOKS application, but they are commented out):

```
t2# = GetCurrentTime( )
Debug.Print t2# - t1#
```

Then run the application, and move from one title to the other with the Data Control. On our 486/66 system, the execution time of the Reposition subroutine varied from 55 to 220 milliseconds (nearly a fifth of a second). Considering the size of the database, a fifth of a second is a considerable amount of time.

Can we do any better? The answer is yes, and we will return to this application to make it faster, but only after first looking more closely at recordsets.

## BEYOND THE DATA CONTROL

A database is a (potentially) huge collection of data. Some databases may contain tables a user will never look at, either because they aren't needed, or because the user isn't allowed to look at them. If you're making purchasing decisions, you probably don't care about customers. You don't really need to know where the items were sold. Instead, you want to know about your suppliers—who delivers on time, how much they charge, etc. In other situations, you may not be allowed to look at certain tables. For example, many of the employee data may be available to anyone who has access to your company's main database, but to look at their salaries, or other personal data, you must have special privileges.

In practice, we never work with an entire database at once. Usually, we isolate the data we need and work with them. The set of data we are interested in is called a *Recordset*. We have seen how to use the RecordSource Property of the Data Control to specify a table, or part of a table. This is the Data Control's Recordset. Now let's explore other kinds of Recordsets, how they are defined, and how to create and manage Recordsets without using the Data Control at all.

So far, we have used the term Recordset to describe an object, which contains a part of database, which we access through a Data Control. From now on, we will use the term Recordset in a different context. A Recordset refers to a group of objects used in database programming, and the Data Control is not involved.

## More Recordsets: Tables, Dynasets & Snapshots

There are three different types of Recordsets: Tables, Dynasets and Snapshots. As we will see shortly, Tables, Dynasets and Snapshots are objects. To access the contents of a table in the Database without the help of the Data Control (as we were doing so far), we must create a variable with the type Table and assign to it the contents of a table in the database. That may be confusing at the beginning. To make reading this section easier, we will use *Table* to refer to objects (variables), and the *table* (lowercase) to refer to tables in the database.

A Table is an object that contains all the rows of an actual table. If you want to access a database directly, without the Data Control, you must create a Table variable and then assign to it the actual contents of a table. Creating a Table variable is as simple as declaring it with the Dim statement and then using it. As we mentioned in the chapter introduction, you can't access the database directly. To use a table's data, you must create a variable of Table type and then ask Visual Basic to assign it the contents of the table. This is the level of abstraction we talked about in the introduction to this chapter. What you see is the model of the database: a collection of related tables. How the data are actually stored in the database, or how Visual Basic handles them, is completely transparent to you and your application. You ask for the data you need, and Visual Basic provides them. Recordsets are the objects that contain the data Visual Basic extracts from the database according to your commands.

A *Dynaset* is a set of records of one or more tables and it may contain selected items only. A Dynaset may be a collection of tables, or just a few records from one or more tables. The difference between Tables and Dynasets is that a Table can't contain anything less or anything more than its entire contents. A Snapshot, finally, is similar to a Dynaset, but a Snapshot cannot be modified. Let's see why there are three different types of Recordsets and when to use them.

After creating a new database, you will probably have to enter lots of data (customer names, product codes, publishers, book titles, etc.). This is when you use a Table Recordset. You just fill the whole thing up with new data.

Changes made to the database are immediately reflected in a Table variable.

If you want to make massive updates to your data, such as adding a prefix to all records in a certain field, or changing a date throughout a table, then you must open a Table Recordset. In other words, we open a Table Recordset when we need access to the latest data, even if other users are modifying them at the same time.

Dynasets can combine data from more than one table, and a Dynaset need not be as long as the table it references. A Dynaset may contain the new book titles and the corresponding publisher (for example, books published in 1994), or the items that have been sold to customers in California. The Dynaset could be significantly smaller than any of the tables involved, which in turn will make the program run faster.

A very important distinction between Tables and Dynasets is the fact that Dynasets are not refreshed automatically. In other words, if another user adds a new title in the BIBLIO database after our Dynaset is created, that title will not show up in the Dynaset. The Dynaset is a partial image of the database, an image of the state of the database at the moment the Dynaset was created. This is not true with Tables, which are always synchronized with the database. In Microsoft's terminology this is called "membership." Records that became part of the Recordset when it was created are *members* of the Recordset. If the type of the Recordset is Table, the membership can change. If the type of the Recordset is Dynaset or Snapshot, the membership can't change. However, changes made to a Dynaset can be written back to the database if the programmer uses the Update Method.

The third type of Recordset, the Snapshot, is, as the name implies, a "snapshot" of the database. When you create a Snapshot, Visual Basic goes to the database, picks up the records you requested and never looks at the database again for as long as you work with the Snapshot. Moreover, you can't change the database through a Snapshot.

Snapshots are the most restrictive type of Recordset, but they should be used most often in decision-support applications—applications that *analyze* data need not update the database. By using Snapshots, not only do you make the programs run faster, but you protect a user from accidentally overwriting original data with the results of possible "what-if" scenarios.

Unlike Table and Dynaset variables, Snapshots can't modify the database.

From a programmer's point of view, the most important distinction among the three types of Recordsets is the fact that Dynasets and Snapshots can be the results of queries. A Dynaset, for example, may contain the titles which were published in 1994. A Snapshot may contain the invoices issued to customers with State = "CA." A Table, however, is an entity of the database that can't be broken down, and therefore can't be the result of a query. As you will see shortly, Tables are "opened," while Dynasets and Snapshots are "created."

In this chapter we will use the term *recordset* (lowercase *r*) when we refer to Properties or Methods that apply to Tables, Dynasets or Snapshots. For example, the recordset Property EOF is set to True when we reach the last record in any type of recordset. The RecordCount Property returns the number of records in all three types of recordsets. The Updatable Property indicates whether a recordset can be updated or not, and obviously it is always False for Snapshots.

What type of recordset does the Data Control create? It sure isn't a Snapshot, because it allows you to change the database's contents. It is either a Table or a Dynaset, depending on how you defined it. If you assigned the name of a table to the RecordSource Property, it will be a Table. If you assigned an SQL statement to the same Property, then it will be a Dynaset.

## Programming Recordsets

Let's leave the Data Control now and see how we can handle databases with Visual Basic commands. In this section, we'll open a database, create and manipulate all types of recordsets and perform operations that can't be performed with the Data Control. If the previous section left some questions about the various types of recordsets, things should become very clear now, as we see how the recordsets are created and used.

Visual Basic's Data Control is probably not the tool you would choose to build a professional database application. The no-programming approach to databases is a short-lived illusion. It can come in handy in simple situations, but you shouldn't rely on it as a way of manipulating and navigating large volumes of data. Visual Basic itself, however, is widely used for writing database applications, especially for front-end applications. You must merely abandon the Data Control in favor of using the powerful collection of VB database programming commands.

### Opening a Database

To open a database programmatically, you must first dimension a variable of the Database type and use the OpenDatabase command to open an existing database:

```
Dim DB As Database
Set DB = OpenDatabase(db_name)
```

Here db_name is the name of an existing database, such as "C:\VB\BIBLIO.MDB" or the FileName Property of the File Open Common Dialog. You can also specify certain options when you open a database. Here is the complete syntax of the OpenDatabase command:

```
OpenDatabase(db_name[, exclusive[, readonly[, connect]]])
```

In this statement, *exclusive* and *readonly* are either True or False. If you open a database as exclusive, no one else can use it until you close it. Certain operations, such as repairing a database, require that it be open in exclusive mode. If you only need to look up data in the database and make no changes, then open it as readonly, with a command like this:

```
Set DB = OpenDatabase("C:\VB\BIBLIO.MDB", False, True)
```

The last argument in the complete OpenDatabase command syntax, *connect*, is a string, which is used only if you want to connect to databases created with programs other than Visual Basic or Access. For example, to connect to the DB.DBF database, created with dBASE III, use the string "dBASE III." You can connect to a variety of external databases, but in this chapter we will deal with native, Visual Basic and Access (1.1) databases only. They are the databases created by the Data Manager application or by Access, and they have the extension MDB.

We must mention that it is possible to create new databases with Visual Basic commands, but we are not going to cover this topic here.

### Creating Recordsets

Once the database has been opened, you need a way to look at its contents. You can't access the contents of the database directly. First, you must decide what part of the database you need and then create a recordset (Table, Dynaset or Snapshot) that contains this information. To be exact, you can't *create* a table—you just open it. The other two types of recordsets must be created, however.

Recordsets are accessed through variables of the appropriate type: Table, Dynaset and Snapshot variables.

There are three Methods for opening or creating a recordset, and they all apply to the database object. Assuming you have opened a database with the OpenDatabase command, you can open a Table with the OpenTable Method, create a Dynaset with the CreateDynaset Method and a Snapshot with the CreateSnapshot Method. First, however, you must dimension accordingly the variables that will hold the recordset.

To create a Table variable, use these commands:

```
Dim DB As Database, TBLTitles As Table
Set DB = OpenDatabase("C:\VB\BIBLIO.MDB")
Set TBLTitles = DB.OpenTable("Titles")
```

The argument of the OpenTable Method must be a valid table name. The OpenTable returns all the rows of the table.

TBLTitles is a Table variable, not the table itself. TBLTitles contains the rows of the Titles table, but it is a new, distinct object. In a multi-user environment, another user may be accessing the same table through a different Table variable.

To create a Dynaset variable, use the CreateDynaset Method. When creating Dynaset variables, you can specify either the name of a table, or an SQL statement that specifies which records will be retrieved from the database. Here are the commands that open the BIBLIO database and create a Dynaset variable based on the Publishers table:

```
Dim DB As Database, DYNAPubs As Dynaset
Set DB = OpenDatabase("C:\VB\BIBLIO.MDB")
Set DYNAPubs = DB.CreateDynaset("Publishers")
```

If you want to look at the Publishers table but not make any changes, create a Snapshot instead. Use the same sequence of commands, but replace the CreateDynaset Method with the CreateSnapshot Method:

```
Dim DB As Database, SNAPPubs As Snapshot
Set DB = OpenDatabase("C:\VB\BIBLIO.MDB")
Set SNAPPubs = DB.CreateSnapshot("Publishers")
```

*Note:* In this book we are using the prefixes TBL, DYNA and SNAP to indicate recordsets of the corresponding type.

Dynasets and Snapshots are more flexible than Table variables because they can accept the results of SQL statements. Instead of the table name in the corresponding Method, use an SQL statement. (SQL statements will be discussed in detail shortly.) Here are the commands that create a Dynaset with the titles, their authors and their publishers:

```
Dim DB As Database
Dim DYNATitles As Dynaset

SQL$ = "SELECT Titles.Title, Authors.Author, Publishers.Name"
SQL$ = SQL$ & "FROM Titles, Authors, Publishers"
```

```
SQL$ = SQL$ & "WHERE Titles.Au_ID = Authors.Au_ID"
SQL$ = SQL$ & "AND Titles.PubID = Publishers.PubID"

Set DYNATitles = DB.CreateDynaset(SQL$)
```

Most of the Data Control's Properties and Methods apply to Tables, Dynasets and Snapshots.

A Dynaset is a recordset. All the Properties of a Recordset object of a Data Control apply to Dynasets (and Snapshots) as well. The references to the object Data1.Recordset must be replaced with references to a recordset variable. The following command assigns to the TotRows variable the number of rows in the Recordset of the Data1 Data Control:

```
TotRows = Data1.Recordset.RecordCount
```

This command assigns the number of rows in the DYNATitles Dynaset to the same variable:

```
TotRows = DYNATitles.RecordCount
```

To access the first field of the current record in the Data1.Recordset, you would write a line like this:

```
Print Data1.Recordset.Fields(0)
```

You can print the value of the first field of the current record in a Table variable with the following command:

```
Print TBLTitles.Fields(0)
```

If the recordset was a Dynaset, you'd have to use this command:

```
Print DYNATitles.Fields(0)
```

To navigate through a recordset's records, use the MoveFirst, MoveLast, MovePrevious and MoveNext Methods. With the Data Control you would write this:

```
Data1.Recordset.MoveNext
```

But you can write this to move to the next row of a Dynaset:

```
DYNATitles.MoveNext
```

Or you can write this to move to the next row of a Table variable:

```
TBLTitles.MoveNext
```

Manipulating the records of a Table, Dynaset or Snapshot variable is no different than before. The AddNew, Edit, Update and Refresh Methods apply to both Tables and Dynasets. As you can see, the Data Control is a camouflaged recordset. It gives you easy access to the tables of a database, by hiding all the details we presented in this section. However, to be able to manipulate databases in any way you like, you must be able to use recordsets.

A recordset can be compared to the *data type* of a regular variable. To assign an integer to a variable, you can first dimension an Integer-type variable. Similarly, to assign the contents of a table to a variable, you first dimension that variable as Table, Dynaset or Snapshot. Visual Basic doesn't enforce the declaration of regular variables (integers, singles, etc.)—it even offers the Variant data type. But database-related variables are much more complicated than regular variables, and therefore are required to be dimensioned before they are used. Just as an integer variable can hold an integer, a Table variable can hold records. Integer variables are processed with mathematical operations. Table variables are processed with recordset Methods (like the ones we presented for the Data Control).

### Ordering Records

All three types of recordsets get the data from the specified table(s) in the order in which the data were entered into the database. In most cases, when you open a recordset variable the records appear in a seemingly random order, because this is how they are usually entered. There are ways, however, to present the data sorted in any fashion you like.

The Order Property of a recordset object lets you order the data in any way you like.

There are two different ways to sort data. A Table variable's data can be sorted according to one of the table's indices. To specify the index by which the data will be sorted, use the Table's Index Property. This Property must be set only after the Table has been opened. If you don't specify an Index value, the Table variable will be sorted according to the table's primary key.

Here is an example of the Index Property:

```
Dim DB As Database
Dim TBLProd As Table

Set DB = OpenDatabase("VBINC.MDB")
Set TBLProd = DB.OpenTable("PRODUCTS")
Debug.Print TBLProd.Fields("PROD_CODE"), →
TBLProd.Fields("PROD_DESCRIPTION")
TBLProd.Index = "PRODUCTBYCATEGORY"
Debug.Print TBLProd.Fields("PROD_CODE"), →
TBLProd.Fields("PROD_DESCRIPTION")
```

This program segment opens the Products table of the VBINC database as a Table variable, and prints the fields PROD_CODE and PROD_DESCRIPTION of the first product. The product printed is the first one entered in the Products table. Then, it sets the table's Index Property to "PRODUCTBYCATEGORY", which is the product's category, and again prints the same fields. The second time, a new product is printed, which is the product with the smallest category.

Here's what you will get if you execute the previous lines:

```
BVRG301  Chan's Regular Beer
BVRG310  Cold Dark Beer
```

The rows of a Table variable can be sorted only according to one of the table's indices.

The first field of the Table variable is different according to the current index.

Table variables can be sorted only according to one of the indices defined in the database. You can't create new indices at run time; neither can you sort a table according to any field that is not an index. If you realize that an application calls for more indices than you have designed, you can always add new ones from within the Data Manager application.

Dynaset and Snapshot variables can be sorted in any way you like. If the variable was created with an SQL statement, the order of the records can be determined by the SQL statement itself. If you don't want to specify the order of the records from within the SQL statement, you can use the Sort Property of the Dynaset or Snapshot variable. (Table variables have an Index Property only—no Sort Property.) Here is how the Sort Property is used:

```
Dim DB As Database
Dim SNAPAuthors As Snapshot

Set DB = OpenDatabase("BIBLIO.MDB")
Set SNAPAuthors = DB.CreateSnapshot("AUTHORS")
Debug.Print SNAPAuthors.Fields("Author")
SNAPAuthors.Sort = "Author"
Set SNAPAuthors = SNAPAuthors.CreateSnapshot( )
Debug.Print SNAPAuthors.Fields("Author")
```

The first Print command prints the name of the author that was entered first in the database:

```
Flavin, Matt.
```

After sorting the records according to the Name field, this becomes the first name in the Snapshot variable:

```
Atre, Shaku.
```

Notice also in the previous code segment that the Sort Property can be set only after the Snapshot variable has been created. Moreover, it doesn't take effect immediately. Instead, we must rebuild the Snapshot with the new value of the Sort Property. To rebuild the Snapshot, we simply use the CreateSnapshot Method on the SNAPAuthors variable, this time without arguments.

The Sort Property is much more flexible than the Table variable's Index Property, but it's slower as well. Every time you set the Sort Property's value, the data are actually sorted. This introduces some delay, which can become significant for large amounts of data. The Index Property introduces no delays because it already exists in the database. Visual Basic doesn't have to sort the data. It simply looks up the index and presents the data in the corresponding order.

### Filtering Recordsets

The Filter Property of the recordset allows us to further limit the selected records. The Filter Property can be set to a string containing any Visual Basic expression, similar to the argument of the Find Method. To read all the dairy products into a Dynaset variable, first create the Dynaset and then set its Filter Property:

```
Dim DB As Database
Dim DYNAProds As Dynaset

Set DB = OpenDatabase("VBINC.MDB")
Set DYNAProds = DB.CreateDynaset("PRODUCTS")
DYNAProds.Filter = "PROD_CATEGORY = 'DAIRY' "
Set DYNAProds = DYNAProds.CreateDynaset( )
```

This code segment creates a Dynaset variable (DYNAProds) that contains all the rows of the PRODUCTS table, and whose PROD_CATEGORY field is "DAIRY." You can't set the Filter Property on a nonexistent Dynaset. That's why we first create it, set its Filter Property and then "refresh" it. The second time we call the CreateDynaset Method, we don't have to specify the arguments again. Notice that the second CreateDynaset Method applies to the Dynaset and not to the database.

## Seeking Records in Tables

We have seen the Find Methods for locating records in the Data Control's Recordset. The same Methods apply to Table, Dynaset and Snapshot variables too. When it comes to Table variables, though, Visual Basic provides a much faster Method for locating records: the Seek Method.

The Seek Method locates records in a table using the current index (which is either the primary index, or the one you specified with the Index Property). The syntax of the Seek command is as follows:

Unlike the Find Methods, the Seek Method uses an index to locate records instantly.

```
Seek operator, key1, key2, ...
```

In this statement, operator is one of the relational operators shown in Table 3-4:

| | |
|---|---|
| = | Equal |
| > | Greater than |
| < | Less than |
| >= | Greater or equal |
| <= | Less or equal |

Table 3-4: Relational operators.

The key1, key2, etc., are the values to be compared to the key fields of the index. If the index is made up of a single key, you only need one argument following the comparison operator. The following commands open the Titles table of the BIBLIO database and look for the title whose ISBN number is "0070447527":

```
Dim DB As Database
Dim TBL As Table
Set DB = OpenDatabase("BIBLIO.MDB")
Set TBL = DB.OpenTable("Titles")
ISBNNum = "0070447527"
TBL.Seek "=", ISBNNum
```

If such a record exists, the NoMatch Property of the TBL variable will be set to False, and the found record will become the current record.

Normally, we supply a value for each key in the index. Let's say that the index of a customer table is the state, followed by the city. To locate customers in California, we can use a statement like this:

```
TBL.Seek "=", "CA"
```

In other words, we can omit the second key field. To locate customers in Santa Barbara, CA, we must use a statement like this:

```
TBL.Seek "=", "CA", "Santa Barbara"
```

The state value can't be omitted, because the state is the first field in the index.

To summarize, the Seek Method is much faster, and is the preferred Method when possible. The Find Method may not be as fast, but its facilities are much more generic, and can be used to perform searches on any field, or combination of fields, of the table. The following example is a demonstration of the Seek Method.

### EXAMPLE: POPULATING LISTS FROM MULTIPLE TABLES

Our next example is an application that demonstrates how to combine data from multiple tables using the Seek Method. In Figure 3-12 you see the PUBTITLS application. The List on the left contains the names of all publishers. Every time the user double-clicks on a publisher name, the titles published by that publisher, along with the names of the authors, are displayed in the second List. Every time a publisher name is double-clicked, the List on the right is populated from scratch. This application shows how to create Snapshots using the Sort Property and how to use their contents to populate Lists. It also makes use of the Seek Method to quickly locate each title's author.

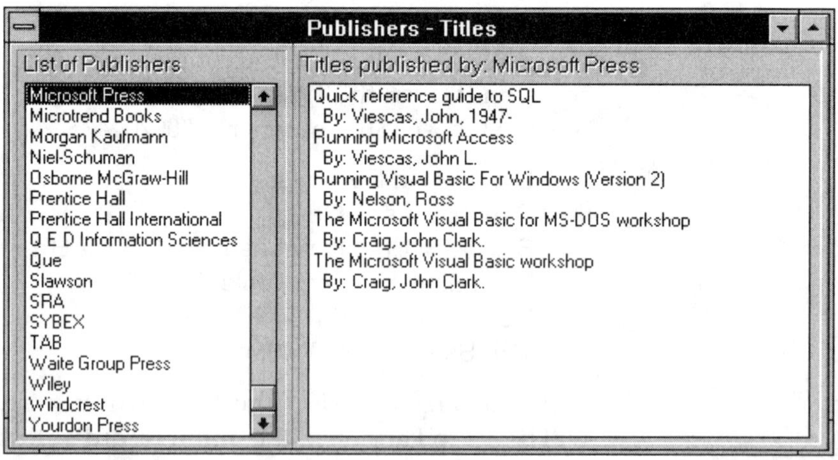


Figure 3-12: Combining data from multiple tables.

When the program starts, the list of publishers is created as a Snapshot variable that contains all the rows of the Publishers table. Then we scan each element in the Snapshot and append the Name field (the publisher's name) to the List. At the same time, we assign the PubID field's value to the ItemData Property of the corresponding item in the List. Later on, we want to be able to retrieve the titles published by a specific publisher. The Titles and Publishers tables are connected through the publisher's ID (the PubID field) and not the publisher's name. We need, therefore, to keep track of the publishers' IDs, and what better place to store them than the List's ItemData Property? Here is the code that populates the first List:

```
Sub Form_Load ( )
Dim SNAPPublishers As snapshot

    Set DB = OpenDatabase("biblio.mdb")
    Set SNAPPublishers = DB.CreateSnapshot("Publishers")
    SNAPPublishers.Sort = "Name"
    Set SNAPPublishers = SNAPPublishers.CreateSnapshot( )
    Print SNAPPublishers.Fields.Count
    While Not SNAPPublishers.EOF
        LstLine$ = SNAPPublishers.Fields("Name")
        List1.AddItem LstLine$
        List1.ItemData(List1.NewIndex) = →
SNAPPublishers.Fields("PubID")
        SNAPPublishers.MoveNext
    Wend

End Sub
```

The List is populated when the program starts. Notice that we first create the SNAPPublishers Snapshot variable and then we sort it according to the Name field. When an entry in the first List is double-clicked upon, we must clear the second List and add all the books published by the selected publisher. In the Double_Click( ) subroutine of the second List, we create another Snapshot variable, consisting of all the entries in the Titles table whose PubID field matches the ID of the selected publisher. This ID has been stored in the ItemData Property of the selected item in the first List.

You can combine the Find and Seek Methods to locate data across tables.

Also, for each title in the Snapshot, the program locates the author's name in the Authors table. Notice that we have the author's ID from the Snapshot of the Titles table. Locating the author's record is a matter of seeking for known ID in the Authors table with the Seek Method. Here is the code that creates the Snapshot and then populates with it the second List:

```
Sub List1_DblClick ( )
Dim SNAPTitles As snapshot
Dim TBLAuthors As table

    List2.Clear
    Panel3D2.Caption = "Titles published by: " + List1.Text
    Set SNAPTitles = DB.CreateSnapshot("Titles")
    SNAPTitles.Sort = "Title"
    SNAPTitles.Filter = "[PubID]=" & →
Str$(Trim(List1.ItemData(List1.ListIndex)))
    Set SNAPTitles = SNAPTitles.CreateSnapshot( )
    Set TBLAuthors = DB.OpenTable("Authors")
    TBLAuthors.Index = "PrimaryKey"

    While Not SNAPTitles.EOF
        LstLine$ = SNAPTitles.Fields("Title")
        List2.AddItem LstLine$
        TBLAuthors.Seek "=", SNAPTitles.Fields("Au_ID")
        LstLine$ = " By: " + TBLAuthors.Fields("Author")
        List2.AddItem LstLine$
        SNAPTitles.MoveNext
    Wend

End Sub
```

The DB variable is dimensioned in the Form's declaration section, because it is used by both subroutines. Here is its declaration:

```
Dim DB As database
```

This is a very short program given the complexity of the operations it performs. Just consider for a moment all the housekeeping you would have to do if you had to provide a similar solution with flat, random access files.

This example application is of rather limited interest. However, the same approach would apply to many different applications. Instead of publishers and titles you could have a list of customers and invoices. By clicking on a customer name you would see all the invoices issued to the specific customer in the last month. Then by clicking on an individual invoice header, you could see all the details (lines) of the selected invoice. You could also apply more restrictions to the Snapshot. For example, you could display only customers that have not paid an invoice within 60 days after the date on the invoice. And so on, and so forth.

The Data Bound Controls are good for designing data-entry and very simple browsing applications. For more advanced and practical applications, you'll be using unbound Controls, which you will have to populate yourself. In an example below, SQLGRID, you'll see how to extract the data contained in a recordset and display them on a Grid Control, without any prior knowledge of the recordset's contents.

## The BOOKS Application Revisited

Earlier in the chapter (in the "Working With Multiple Tables" section) we saw the BOOKS application, which displayed data from three different tables with the help of the Data Control's RecordSource Property and SQL statements. We promised you then to improve the application. Now that we've explored the concepts of Table and Dynaset variables and you know how to manipulate them, we'll see a better way of connecting multiple tables in an application.

Let's try to take advantage of the fact that the Au_ID and PubID fields are also the primary keys for their tables. This time we'll use the Seek command to move instantly to the matching records in the Authors and Publishers tables. (The modified application is called BOOKSEEK and can be found in the 3\APPS\BOOKSEEK subdirectory of the CD.)

CD-ROM

As you recall from our previous discussion, the Seek Method can only be used with indexed tables. This means that we can't use the Data2 and Data3 Controls any more. Instead, we will create two Table variables, TBLAuthors and TBLPublishers. Then, each time the user moves to another title with the Data1 Control, we'll use the Au_ID and PubID fields to locate the corresponding author and publisher in the two tables. The two Table variables are indexed on these two keys (the default indices for both tables), and we'll use the Seek Method on both. Here's the new Data1_Reposition subroutine:

```
Sub Data1_Reposition ( )
Dim PubNum As Long, Authnum As Long

' t1# = GetCurrentTime( )
    PubNum = Data1.Recordset.Fields("PubID")
```

```
        TBLPublishers.Seek "=", PubNum
        If TBLPublishers.NoMatch Then
            BookPublisher.Caption = "Unknown Publisher"
        Else
            BookPublisher.Caption = TBLPublishers.Fields("Name")
        End If

        Authnum = Data1.Recordset.Fields("Au_ID")
        TBLAuthors.Seek "=", Authnum
        If TBLAuthors.NoMatch Then
            BookAuthor.Caption = "Unknown Author"
        Else
            BookAuthor.Caption = TBLAuthors.Fields("Author")
        End If

    ' t2# = GetCurrentTime( )
    ' Debug.Print t2# - t1#

    End Sub
```

The Seek Method is faster than the Find Methods or SQL statements.

Now we're ready to time our new approach with the GetCurrentTime( ) function (the commands for timing the subroutine are commented out in the listing). Although this time there are significantly more lines in the subroutine, they are all executed faster than before. On the same 486/66 system, the execution times for the new Reposition subroutine varied from 0 to 110 milliseconds. After moving back and forth in the tables for a while, the execution time was constantly less than 55 milliseconds, because many of the needed data were already in the cache. (You shouldn't count on such luck, however, because a real application will be handling much larger databases). Even with a small database like BIBLIO, the Seek Method is on average at least four times faster than the previous technique. This gain in speed will become even more important with larger databases. (Note: Part of the gain is also due to the fact that we have eliminated the overhead of the two Data Controls. Now we are going directly to the source—the tables—extracting the data and placing them on the Labels.)

The BOOKSEEK application contains a few Command Buttons to locate records with the Find Method. The "Find by Author" and "Find by Publisher" Command Buttons work in very similar ways. When you look for titles by author, the program prompts you with an InputBox to enter the name of the author you are looking for. Then it locates the author with the desired name in the Authors table (if any), and extracts the Author's ID (field AU_ID). This field is then used to perform another search, in the Titles table, to locate titles of books written by the author. If a title is found, the program displays it and enables the "Find Next" Command Button. The programming involved is fairly straightforward, so we won't cover it here. If you want, load the application into VB and look at the code. It's essentially self-explanatory.

Being able to programmatically manipulate the database object through recordset variables offers not only more flexibility than the Data Control, but results in faster programs too.

## STRUCTURED QUERY LANGUAGE

Now we will move away from data manipulating commands and look at ways to extract information from databases. The Seek and Find Methods of the Recordset object are good for connecting records of one table to records of another table, or doing simple searches, but decision making calls for complicated queries. To efficiently use the information stored in a database, we must be able to recall data in many different ways, combine data from multiple tables, with various restrictions, and finally summarize large volumes of data in a few meaningful numbers. The Find and Seek Methods would be very limiting to a manager, not to mention that he or she would have to have a small program for each type of data-retrieval operation that may be needed. The most flexible way to recall information from databases is through the use of a special language called Structured Query Language, or SQL.

You are certainly aware that Visual Basic 3.0 supports SQL statements for locating records, and you may be wondering why we haven't mentioned them so far. SQL statements are indeed much more flexible than the Find and Seek Methods, but they are more complicated as well. If you want to make optimal use of your database, though, you need to master this language.

SQL is a universal language for database manipulation.

SQL is a language for manipulating databases, and a rather old one. Unlike VB, SQL is a nonprocedural language. In other words, there are no procedures (subs or functions), and it operates at a much higher level than VB. A nonprocedural language is one that is told what to do, but not how to do it. For example, you can issue an SQL command to ask for all invoices issued to customers in California in the first quarter of 1994. How the computer does it is not your concern. The mechanism that performs the query and reports the results is a complicated one, but fortunately SQL hides it from you.

Another advantage of the SQL language is that it is universal. All database manufacturers implement the language in their products, and the developer need not be concerned with the specifics. Once you've learned SQL, you can program any database that provides an SQL interface. (The truth of the matter is that not all manufacturers conform to the exact same SQL standard. Some introduce additional commands, others use a slightly different syntax. But for the most part, SQL is a universal language for database manipulation. Or at least as universal as one can expect in the computer industry.)

SQL provides many commands, for all types of operations you'd want to perform on a database. Covering the entire range of SQL is beyond the scope of this book. There are many books on SQL in the market, and if you are going to use it intensely you should have at least a good reference book on your desk. In this chapter we will cover the basic SQL commands for retrieving data from databases, because this is what Visual Basic programmers will mostly use it for. We'll also look at some of the commands that perform massive updates in a database, which will come in handy at one time or another. The examples of this chapter are relatively simple. They are the type of commands you will be using most of the time. SQL, however, can become quite complicated and sometimes you may have to resort to some really sophisticated SQL commands. As you become more and more experienced with the SQL syntax, however, you'll realize that many of the commands that may seem frightening now are not that complicated after all. Moreover, if you can't figure out the SQL command for a certain task, you always have the option to perform it with a sequence of Visual Basic commands. Your code may not be as compact or as efficient, but it'll get the job done.

Select queries retrieve data. Action queries manipulate data.

An SQL command's job is to carry out a query. Some queries let you retrieve data from databases. These are called select queries. Others let you carry out certain actions on the database, and they are called action queries. We'll look first at the set of select query commands, which are also referred to as DQL (Data Query Language) or data retrieval statements. These commands obtain data from the tables of a database in many different ways and determine how the selected data will be furnished to the application (sorted, grouped, etc.).

## Experimenting With SQL Statements

CD-ROM

Here's a small program that lets you enter and execute SQL statements and then displays the results. The SQLGRID application (in the 3\APPS\SQLGRID subdirectory of the CD) consists of three Forms. The SQL Query Definition Form contains a Text Box where you enter an SQL statement. To execute the statement, click on the Execute Command Button. As soon as the results become available, they will be displayed in a Grid on the SQL Query Results Form.

To execute another SQL statement, type it in the SQL Query Definition Form's Text Box and click on the Execute Command Button again. The results of the new query will overwrite the previous contents of the Grid. The Clear SQL Button simply clears the Text Box with the SQL statement.

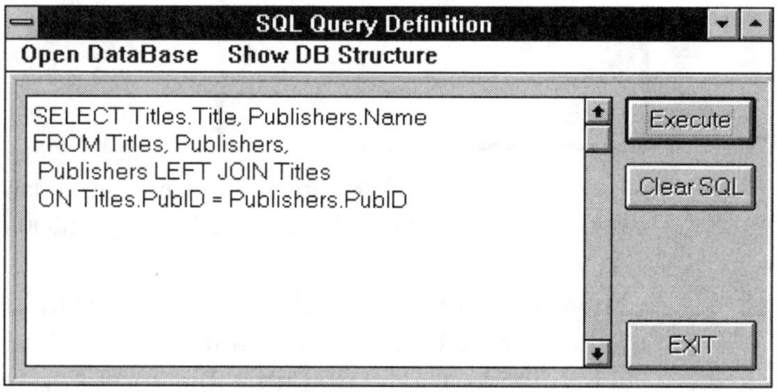


Figure 3-13: The SQLGRID application will help you explore SQL statements, by displaying their results on a Grid Control.

The SQL Query Definition Form also contains two menu options. The Open Database command lets you open a new database. Before executing an SQL statement, make sure that you've opened the appropriate database. The other menu option, Show DB Structure, displays the Database Structure Map, shown in Figure 3-14, which contains the structure of the database. (It's an interesting application, and we'll look at it in "Database Definitions" later in the chapter. We included it as a separate Form in the SQLGRID application so that you can look up the fields of any table in a database from within SQLGRID, without having to switch to the Data Manager application.)

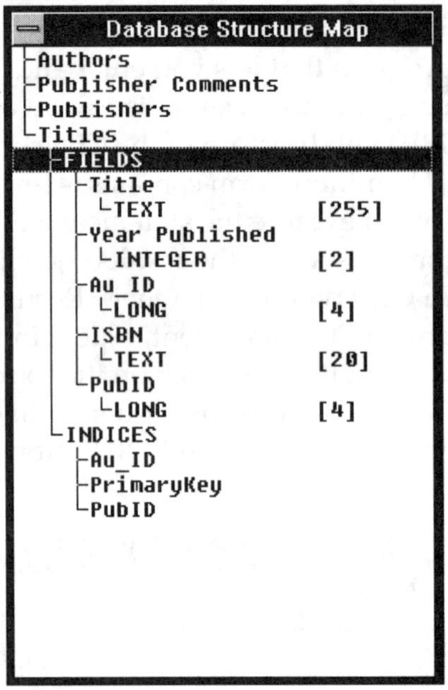


Figure 3-14: The Database Structure Map lets you view the structure of the current database from within the SQLGRID application.

If you want to look at the tables and/or fields of a database, click on the Show DB Structure Command, and the Form shown in Figure 3-14 will appear. The first time this Form appears on the screen, it contains a list of the tables in the database. Click on the line in front of the table you're interested in, and you'll see two headings underneath the name of the table: FIELDS and INDICES. Click on either heading to see the list of the field names in the table or the list of indices. Then click on a field name to see its data type, or on an index name to see the definition of the index. If you want to hide a list of fields or indices, click on the table name or index name.

Later on we're going to look at the programming behind the SQLGRID application. For now, you can use it to familiarize yourself with the SQL language.

Notice that with Visual Basic comes a similar application, called VISDATA, which lets you enter SQL statements and displays the results. The VISDATA application does much more than that, however, and the programming involved is much too complicated to be presented here. SQLGRID is a simple application that focuses on Dynasets created with SQL statements, and we'll be able to explain its operation in this book.

## Select Queries

The purpose of a select query is to extract information from a database and put it into a recordset. The recordset can be a Dynaset or a Snapshot variable (but not a Table variable). The contents of the recordset are defined in the SQL statement and may contain any combination of fields, from any table in the database. User-defined constraints determine which rows will appear in the recordset.

An SQL select statement starts with the verb SELECT followed by a list of fields on which the verb acts. The keyword FROM specifies the table(s) to which the fields belong, and a number of keywords, which we'll explain shortly. Here is the simplest form of a select query:

Select queries begin with the verb SELECT.

```
SELECT selection_list
FROM table_list
```

*selection_list* is a list of fields, and *table_list* the list of the tables to which the specified fields belong.

Selection queries are used in building recordsets, either with the RecordSource Property of the Data Control, or with the CreateDynaset and CreateSnapshot Methods. The following SQL statement selects the author names from the Authors table:

```
SELECT Author
FROM Authors
```

To create a recordset that contains all the author names, first assign the previous SQL statement to a string variable:

```
SQL$ = "SELECT Author FROM Authors"
```

Then assign it to the Data Control's RecordSource Property:

```
Data1.Recordset.RecordSource = SQL$
```

The Data1.Recordset now contains the author names from the Authors table.

To create a Dynaset variable with the same contents, use these commands:

```
Dim DB As Database
Dim DYNAAuthors As Dynaset

Set DB = OpenDatabase("BIBLIO.MDB")
Set DYNAAuthors = DB.CreateDynaset("SELECT Author FROM
Authors")
```

Similarly, you can use the same SQL statement to create a Snapshot. The SQL statement takes the place of the table name in the CreateDynaset and CreateSnapshot Methods. At the end of this section, you'll find more ways of using SQL statements in your application. Next, we are going to present the most common SQL statements and their options through examples.

The general form of a select query looks like this:

```
SELECT selection_list
FROM table_list
WHERE criteria
```

*criteria* is an expression that specifies some selection criteria. Only the records that meet the criteria will be returned. One of the simplest select queries is as follows:

```
SELECT Author
FROM Authors
```

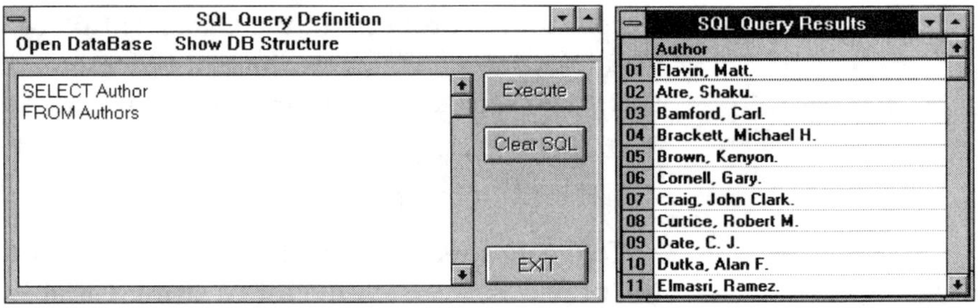


Figure 3-15: This is the simplest query: it returns an entire column (field) from a table.

This query selects all author names from the Authors table and returns them to the application. "Author" is the field name we are interested in and "Authors" is the table it belongs to. In effect, this statement returns the Author column of the table.

Use the * symbol to select all columns in a table.

Multiple field names in the selection_list are separated by commas. If you want to select all the rows of the tables in the table_list, use the asterisk (*). The following SQL statement returns all the rows and all columns of the Authors table:

```
SELECT *
FROM Authors
```

SQL statements are indented too, as if they were a small program. As statements become longer, indentation improves readability, but in this book we will follow a simple rule: each new clause of the statement will begin on a new line, and only long lines will be indented. In your programs you will be typing them on a single line.

Also, SQL is not case-sensitive, but for clarity's sake we'll be using uppercase for SQL reserved keywords and lowercase for everything else. In your programs you can use lowercase and uppercase as you wish.

The WHERE keyword limits the scope of the search to the rows of the table that meet the search criteria. The following statement returns the names of the publishers located in New York:

```
SELECT Name
FROM Publishers
WHERE State = 'NY'
```

Notice that literals are enclosed in single quotes. This makes it easy for programmers to prepare strings with SQL statements. To assign the previous SQL statement to a string variable before passing it to a command, you would have written this:

```
criteria$ = "SELECT Name FROM Publishers WHERE State =
'NY'"
```

If the state is stored in a variable, you can write this:

```
criteria$ = "SELECT Name FROM Publishers WHERE State = '"
& StateVar & "'"
```

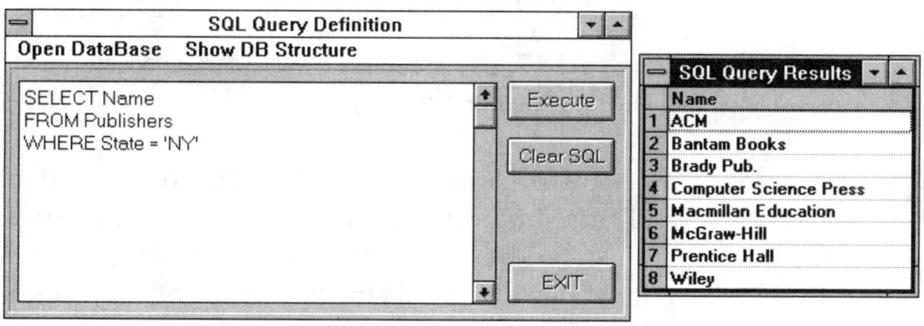


Figure 3-16: The WHERE clause limits the range of the resulting recordset.

Field names, however, are not enclosed in quotes. This poses a small problem, because Visual Basic allows for spaces in field names. Most programmers simply don't use spaces in the field names. If you have a field name consisting of more than one word, enclose the field in square brackets [], like [Company Name] or [State Tax].

### The LIKE Operator

Like Visual Basic, SQL provides a LIKE operator to recall data with wild card characters.

The criterion State = 'NY' specifies exact matching. You can also use the regular relational operators like <, >, <>, <=, etc., just as you would use them with Visual Basic. In addition, SQL offers the LIKE operator, which lets you recall data with wild card characters. (Wild card characters are the asterisk, which can replace any string, and the question mark, which can replace any single character. Every DOS user is familiar with those two wild card characters.)

If you want to recall the record(s) of the author whose name is "Flavin," use the following statement:

```
SELECT Author
FROM Authors
WHERE Author LIKE "*Flavin*"
```

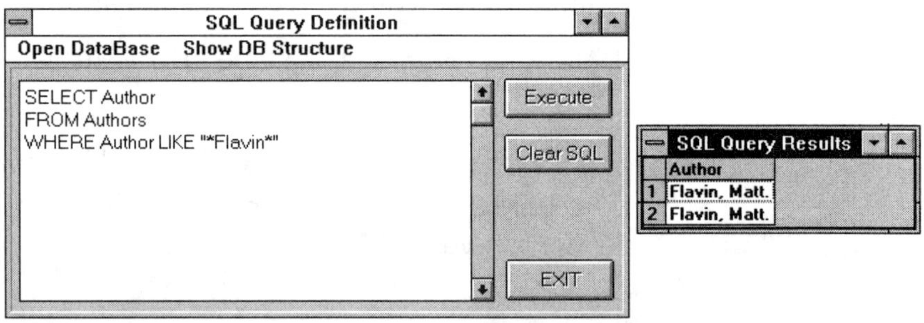


Figure 3-17: Use asterisks as wild card characters in SQL, just as you do to display file names in DOS.

This statement returns two authors with the name "Flavin, Matt." (There shouldn't be two authors with the same name in the Authors table, but this is a demonstration database.) In string matching, you must use the equals (=) operator only if you know how the full name is stored in the database.

Let's open the VBINC database and recall the Code and Description fields of all products that contain the word "juice" in their description. Open the VBINC database with the Open Database command and then issue the following SQL statement:

```
SELECT Prod_Code, Prod_Description
FROM Products
WHERE Prod_Description LIKE "*juice*"
```

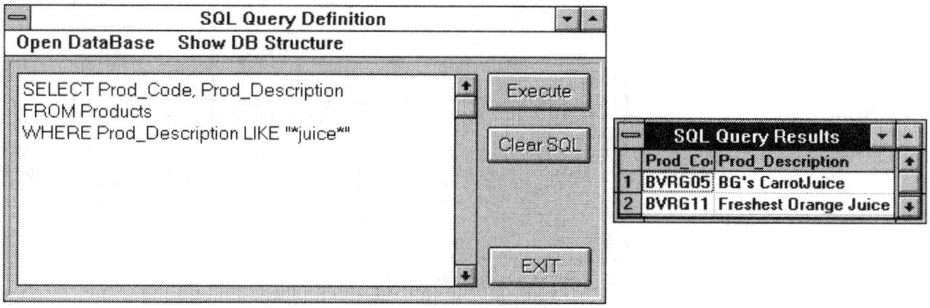


Figure 3-18: SQL string matching is case-insensitive.

This statement retrieves and displays on the Grid the product codes and descriptions of all products that have the string "juice" in their description. Notice that string matching with SQL statements is case-insensitive, as it is with the Find Method.

### Retrieving Data From Multiple Tables

SQL statements are not limited to single tables. You can just as easily recall data from multiple tables. In most cases we are interested in combining data from two, or even more, tables. For example, we can recall all the titles in the BIBLIO database, but what about their authors? A statement like this would return the titles along with a number, which is the ID of the author:

```
SELECT Titles, Au_ID
FROM Titles
```

But the actual name of the author resides in a different table. To make a query from two tables, we must ask for the Title field in the Titles table and the Name field in the Authors table. To select fields from multiple tables, the field names must be prefixed by the name of the tables they belong to. To make sure that each title will be displayed along with its author, we must impose the restriction that the author ID be the same in both rows:

```
SELECT Titles.Title, Authors.Author
FROM Titles, Authors
WHERE Title.Au_ID = Authors.Au_ID
```

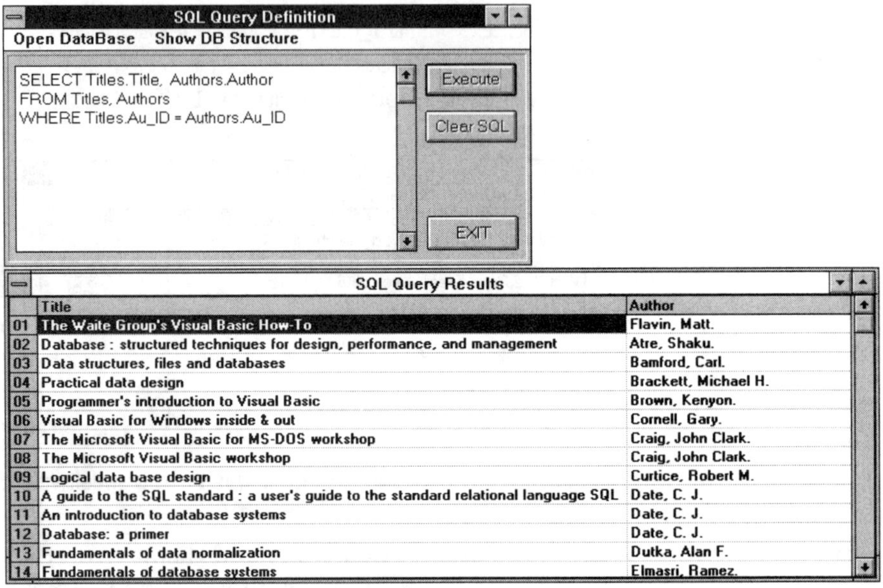


Figure 3-19: Pairing data from two different tables.

If the names of the fields are unique in the specified tables, they need not be prefixed by the table's name. In the previous statement, we could have written Titles.Title as Title and Authors.Author as Author. But the Au_ID field is common to both tables, and the prefix becomes mandatory—or else Visual Basic wouldn't know which field to use. In the rest of the chapter we will be prefixing the field names with the corresponding table names, to make the statements easier to read.

This statement recalls all the rows of the Titles table and the records of the Authors table whose Au_ID fields match. The result of the query is a recordset with two columns and as many rows as there are titles. If some titles were entered without an author, these titles would not be displayed.

The previous operation is called an *Inner-Join*. Inner-Joins allow us to combine two tables on the basis of the value of fields that are common to both tables. Inner-Joins are so common that SQL provides the keyword INNER JOIN for that purpose:

```
SELECT Titles.Title, Authors.Author
FROM Titles, Authors,
Titles INNER JOIN Authors
ON Titles.Au_ID = Authors.Au_ID
```

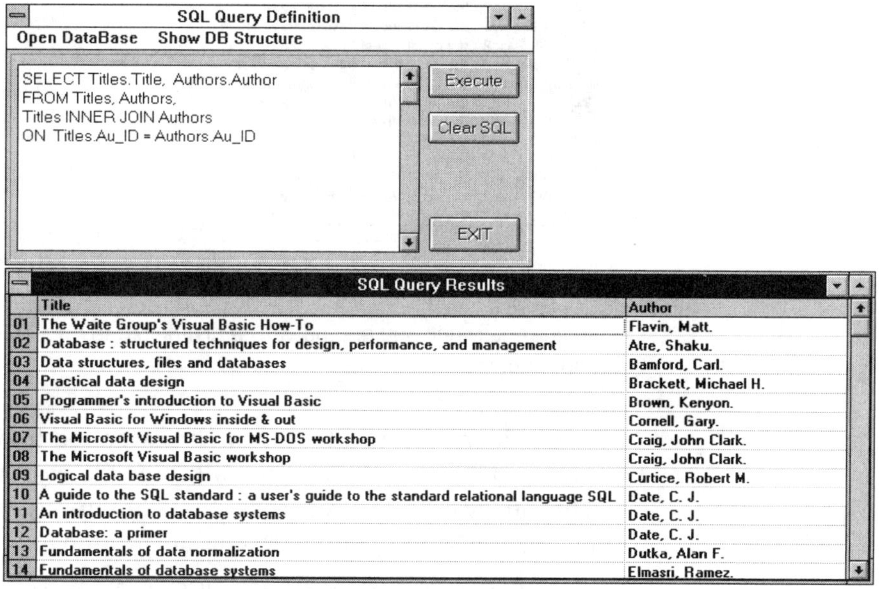


Figure 3-20: The Titles-Authors collection as an Inner-Join.

When you execute this statement, the Titles and Authors tables are joined by the Au_ID column of both tables. The INNER JOIN keyword appears between the names of the two tables to be joined. Following the name of the second table is the keyword ON, which specifies the fields to be used for joining the tables and their relationship. The ON clause is identical to the WHERE clause of the last example.

If you omit the INNER JOIN clause in the previous SQL statement, the recordset will contain all possible combinations of titles and authors! This is called a cross-join, and it's very unlikely that you will ever need a cross-join in a real-life application. The number of rows in the result is the product of all authors (46) times the number of all titles (50), which is 2300 (imagine the size of a cross-join in a large database).

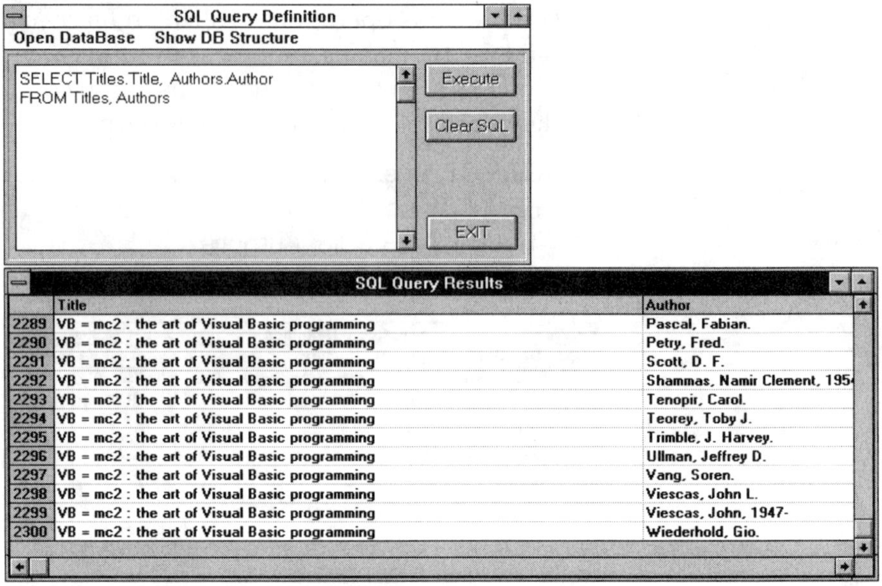


Figure 3-21: Omit the INNER JOIN or the WHERE clause in a multiple-table select query and you end up with a cross-join (all possible combinations of titles and authors).

The idea of joined tables can be extended to more than two tables. The next statement combines all three tables of the BIBLIO database. This query creates a recordset that contains all titles, along with the book's ISBN, the publisher's name and the author's name:

```
SELECT Titles.Title, Titles.ISBN, Authors.Author,
Publishers.Name
FROM Titles, Authors, Publishers,
    Publishers INNER JOIN Titles
    ON Publishers.PubID = Titles.PubID,
        Titles INNER JOIN Authors
        ON Titles.Au_ID = Authors.Au_ID
```

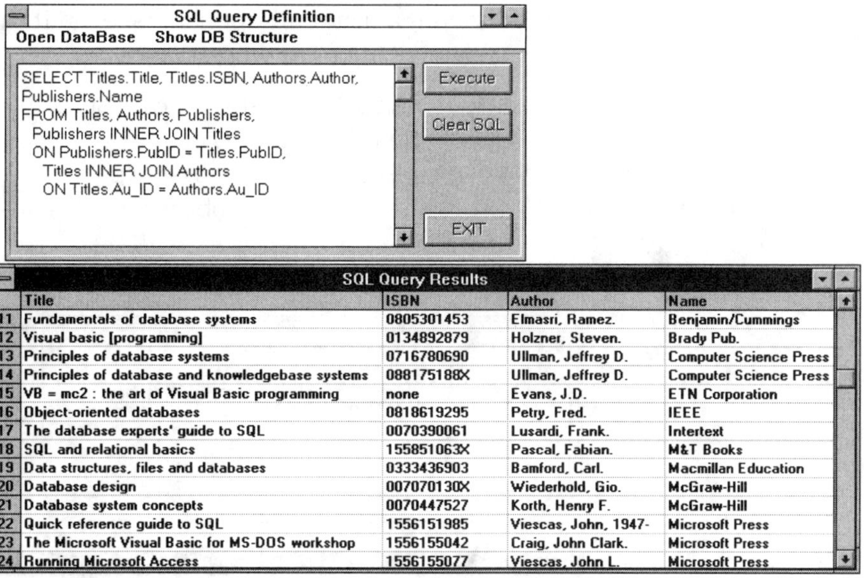


Figure 3-22: Combine data from multiple tables with successive Inner-Joins.

This statement creates an Inner-Join between the Publishers and Titles tables—that is, it creates a table with all the book titles that have a valid publisher, along with each book's publisher. Then, it joins this table with the table of authors, by matching the Au_ID field of the Titles table to the Au_ID field of the Authors table.

Here's the equivalent SQL statement with a WHERE clause:

```
SELECT Titles.Title, Titles.ISBN, Authors.Author,
Publishers.Name
FROM Titles, Authors, Publishers
WHERE Publishers.PubID = Titles.PubID
    AND Titles.Au_ID = Authors.Au_ID
```

In general, the WHERE clause is simpler to use. The INNER JOIN is used frequently, though, for reasons of consistency, along with the two other types of joins we're exploring next.

## Left- & Right-Joins

Besides the INNER JOIN, you can create Left-Joins and Right-Joins. The INNER JOIN operation combines records from two tables whenever there are matching values in a field common to both tables. The RIGHT JOIN includes all the records from the second (right-hand) table, even if there are no matching values in the first (left-hand) table.

If you want a list of all publishers, even if they have no titles in the Titles table, use the following statement:

```
SELECT Titles.Title, Publishers.Name
FROM Titles, Publishers,
    Titles RIGHT JOIN Publishers
    ON Titles.PubID = Publishers.PubID
```

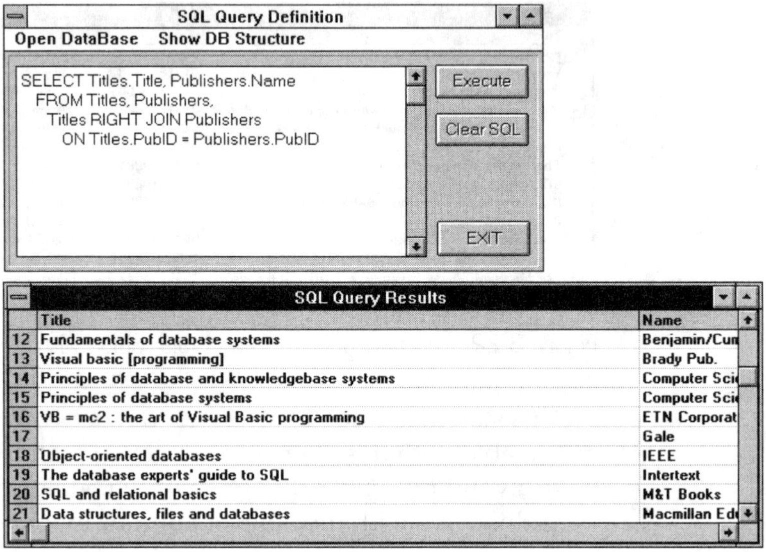


Figure 3-23: Right-Joins include all the records from the right-hand table, and only the matching records of the left-hand table.

This statement returns all rows of the Publishers table and the titles they have published from the Titles table. The INNER JOIN would not have returned the publishers that don't have a matching value in the Titles table.

The LEFT JOIN includes all the records (rows) from the first of the two tables (the one appearing on the left), even if there are no matching values for records in the other table (the one on the right). If you create a Left-Join on the Titles and Publishers tables of the BIBLIO database, the resulting recordset will contain some publishers without any titles:

```
SELECT Titles.Title, Publishers.Name
FROM Titles, Publishers,
    Publishers LEFT JOIN Titles
    ON Titles.PubID = Publishers.PubID
```

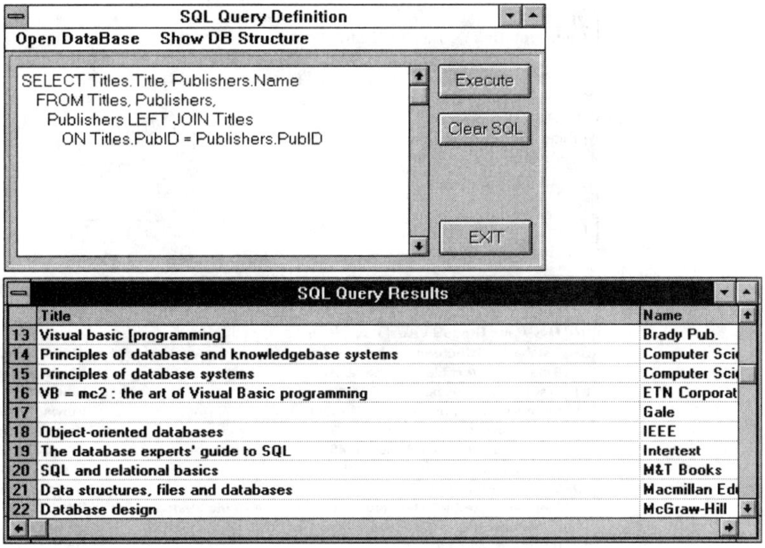


Figure 3-24: Left-Joins return all the records from the left-hand table, and only the matching records of the right-hand table.

Both statements returned the same recordset—notice the similarity between the Left- and Right-Joins. Apart from differing in the LEFT (RIGHT) keyword, the names of the tables joined are inverted.

## The AS Option

As you may have noticed, the title of each column of the recordset returned by an SQL statement is identical to the field name as you typed it in the SQL statement. That's why the heading for the author's name is always "Author." (You could have typed **AUTHOR** as well. Field names are not case-sensitive, and this poses no problem to Visual Basic.)

A column's title is by default the field's name, but you can change it with the AS keyword.

But what if you wanted to use a different heading, like "By" or "Author's Name"? The keyword AS lets you specify the column title for each field in the resulting recordset. Here is an SQL statement with different headings for each column of the recordset:

```
SELECT Titles.Title AS [BOOK'S TITLE], Authors.Author AS
[BOOK'S AUTHOR]
FROM Titles, Authors,
     Titles INNER JOIN Authors
     ON Titles.Au_ID = Authors.Au_ID
```

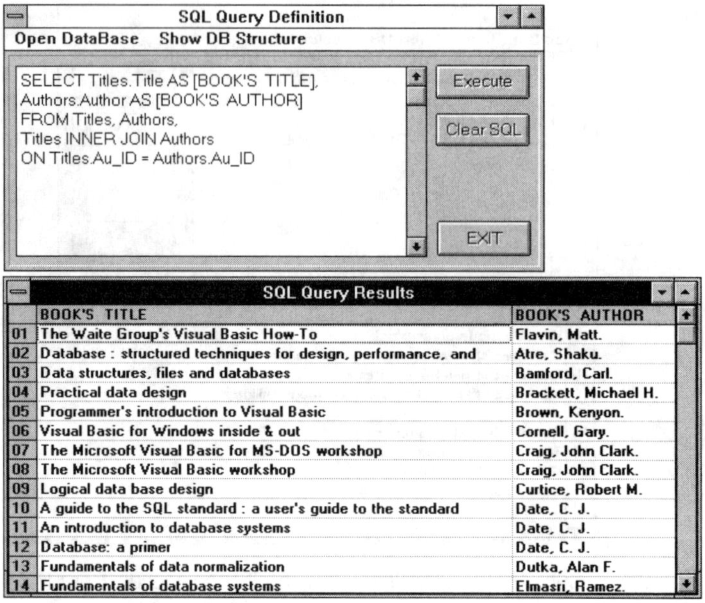


Figure 3-25: Use the AS option to define headings for the recordset's columns.

## The ORDER BY Option

Another noticeable problem with many of our example queries is the order of the recordset's rows. The data don't seem to be sorted in any specific way. To rearrange them, use the ORDER BY keywords, followed by the name of the field on whose value you wish to order the table.

The statement displays all the authors in alphabetical order:

```
SELECT Au_ID, Author
FROM Authors
ORDER BY Author
```

The Au_ID field is displayed so that you can see that the order the records are displayed in is different than the order they were entered (reflected by the Au_ID field, which is a counter).

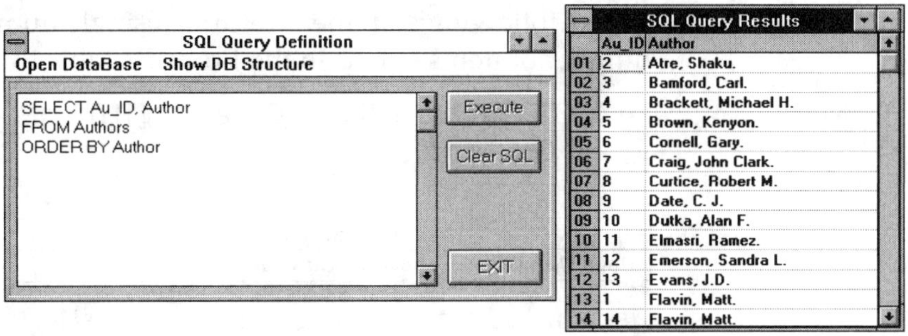


Figure 3-26: To order the rows of the recordset in a particular sequence, use the ORDER BY option.

## Using Aggregate Functions in SQL Statements

The list of fields following the SELECT keyword can also contain functions. SQL supports five aggregate functions, shown in Table 3-5:

| Function | Description |
|---|---|
| COUNT(field_name) | Returns the number of rows in which field_name is not NULL. A field is NULL if it has not been initialized—an empty field is not NULL. If you specify COUNT(*), the total number of rows will be returned, regardless of whether some of their fields are NULL or not. |
| MAX(field_name) | Returns the largest value of field_name in the recordset. |
| MIN(field_name) | Returns the smallest value of field_name in the recordset. |
| SUM(field_name) | Returns the sum of the values of field_name in the recordset. |
| AVG(field_name) | Returns the average (mean) of the values of field_name in the recordset. |

Table 3-5: Aggregate functions supported by SQL.

Access SQL supports a few more functions, such as FIRST( ), LAST( ) and STDEV( ), but we will not discuss them here. Let's look at some examples of using aggregate functions with the VBINC database.

The following statement returns a single number, which is the total number of items stored in the Products table of the VBINC database:

```
SELECT COUNT(Prod_Code) AS [TOTAL]
FROM Products
```

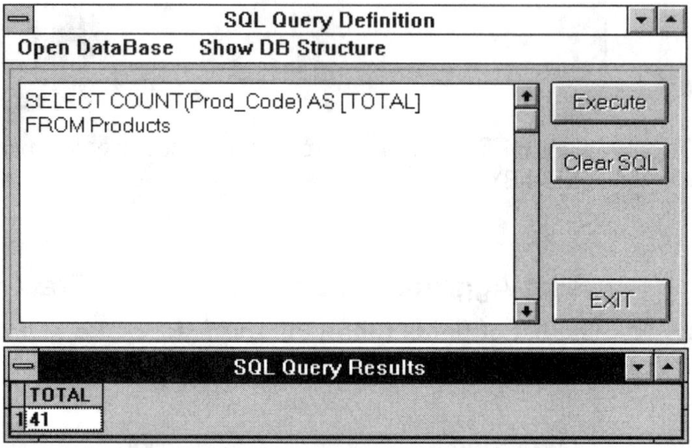


Figure 3-27: It is possible for an SQL statement to return a single number.

## Grouping the Query's Results

It would probably make more sense to break down the total into categories. The following statement returns the number of items in the Products table for each product category:

```
SELECT Prod_Category AS CATEGORY, COUNT(Prod_Category)
AS Items
FROM Products
GROUP BY Prod_Category
```

The results of aggregate functions are usually grouped by some field with the GROUP BY option.

When you want to break down the aggregate functions according to some classification scheme, you must specify the GROUP BY option. GROUP BY is a new keyword that is used with aggregate functions to specify the classification scheme. In our example, it groups the totals (the numbers returned by the COUNT function) according to their category.

Let's say you want to keep track of the lowest, highest and average price of the products in each category. Here is the SQL statement that does exactly that:

```
SELECT Prod_Category AS CATEGORY, COUNT(Prod_Category)
AS Items,
        MIN(Prod_Price) AS Min,
        MAX(Prod_Price) AS Max,
        AVG(Prod_Price) AS AVRG
FROM Products
GROUP BY Prod_Category
```

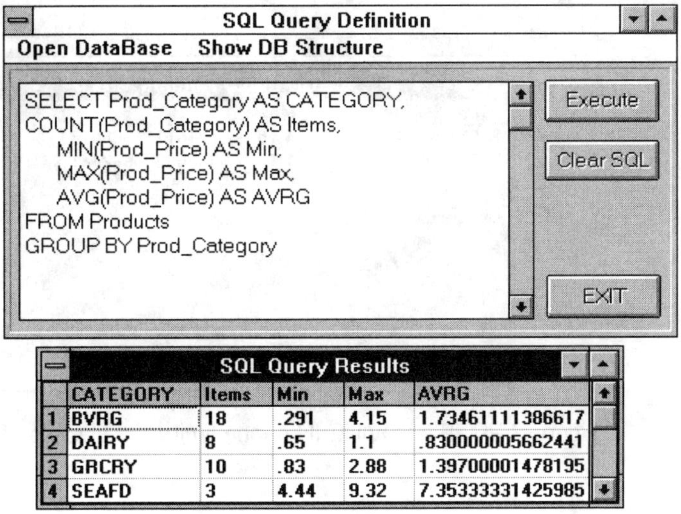


Figure 3-28: The GROUP BY option groups the results of an SQL query according to the value of a field.

If you want to limit the scope of the SQL statement to certain categories, you can't use the WHERE clause. The WHERE clause applies to the entire table. Instead, you can follow the GROUP BY clause with the HAVING keyword. HAVING is similar to a WHERE clause, but it applies to the results of the query. Here is the same query, only this time applied to products of the DAIRY and BVRG categories:

```
SELECT Prod_Category AS CATEGORY, COUNT(Prod_Category)
AS Items,
    MIN(Prod_Price) AS Min,
    MAX(Prod_Price) AS Max,
    AVG(Prod_Price) AS AVRG
FROM Products
GROUP BY Prod_Category
HAVING Prod_Category IN ("DAIRY", "BVRG")
```

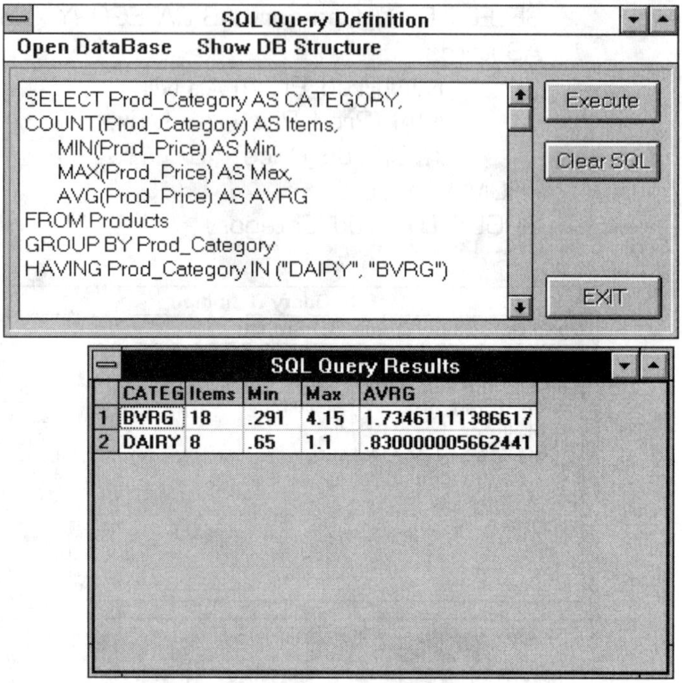


Figure 3-29: The HAVING IN option limits the classes of the GROUP BY option.

### Formatting Numeric Results

If you look at the results of the last two queries, you'll realize that there is something wrong with their formatting. The AVG function returns a double-precision number (which is fine for calculations, but you don't really need all that accuracy for printing the average dollar prices), and the integers are not aligned. To fix the appearance of the results on the Grid, we can use the FORMAT command, which is identical to Visual Basic's Format$( ) function. You can rewrite the previous SQL statement as follows, to format and align the numeric columns:

```
SELECT Prod_Category,
    FORMAT(COUNT(Prod_Category), "000") AS Items,
    FORMAT(MIN(Prod_Price), "$0.00") AS Min,
    FORMAT(MAX(Prod_Price), "$0.00") AS Max,
    FORMAT(AVG(Prod_Price), "$0.00") AS AVRG
FROM Products
GROUP BY Prod_Category
```

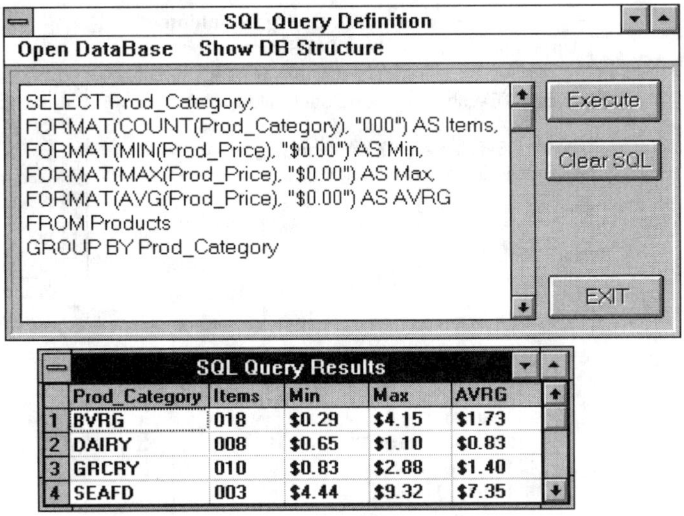


Figure 3-30: SQL's FORMAT function is the same as Visual Basic's Format$( ) function.

All we did in the previous statement was include the aggregate functions as arguments to the FORMAT function.

### More Examples of Aggregate Functions

Let's look at some examples of the COUNT function involving data from more than one table. The following examples are based on the BIBLIO database, and if you are using the SQLGRID application to follow the examples, don't forget to open the BIBLIO database.

We'll start by displaying the authors and the number of titles their names appears on. Here is the SQL statement:

```
SELECT Authors.Author, Count(Titles.Title)
FROM Authors, Titles
WHERE Titles.Au_ID = Authors.Au_ID
GROUP BY Authors.Author
```

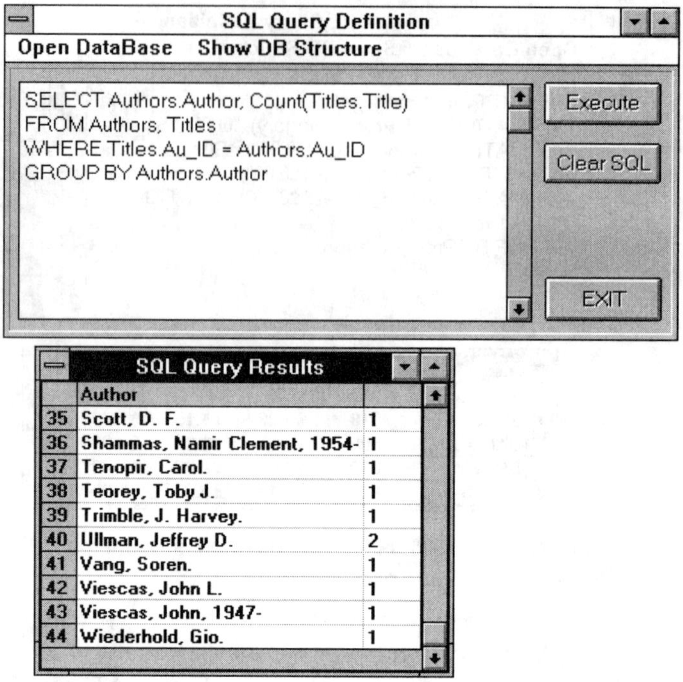


Figure 3-31: The number of titles per author.

This query returns all the authors, along with the number of books per author. The result of the query is a recordset with 44 records. We know there are 50 titles in the table, therefore there must be 6 titles written by authors who have written at least one other book. To verify this, we can select only the authors who have written more than one book:

```
SELECT Authors.Author, COUNT(Titles.Title)
FROM Authors, Titles
WHERE Authors.Au_ID = Titles.Au_ID
GROUP BY Authors.Author
HAVING Count(Titles.Title)>1
```

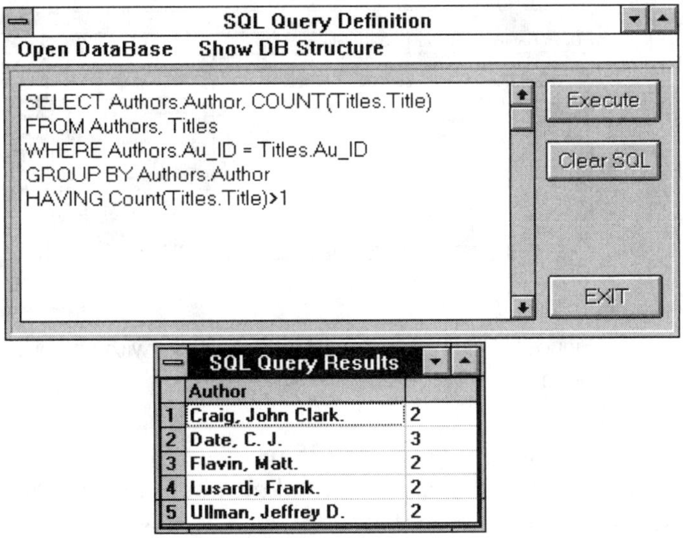


Figure 3-32: There are five authors in the Authors table with more than one title.

This query returns five records. Each author in this recordset has two or more titles. There are six titles written by authors with at least one other title, so if you add 6 to 44 (the result of the previous query) the result is the total number of titles in the database (50).

As another example, consider creating a list of all publishers whose names appear in one (possibly more) titles in the Titles table. This time, we'll count the number of books published by each publisher, and our query will not include the names of publishers without any titles in the Titles table:

```
SELECT Publishers.Name, COUNT (Titles.Title)
FROM Publishers, Titles
WHERE Titles.PubID = Publishers.PubID
GROUP BY Publishers.Name
```

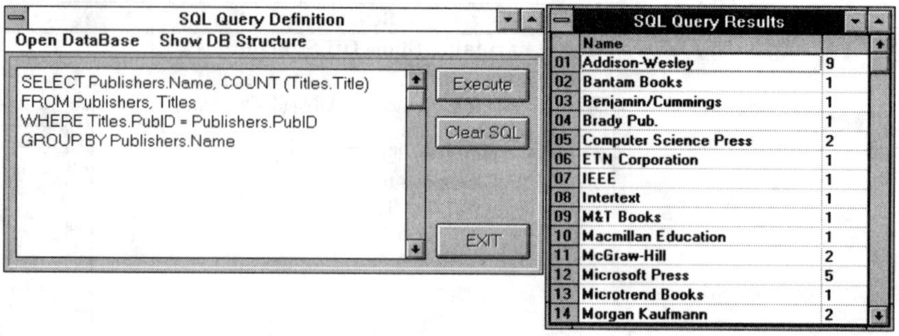


Figure 3-33: This is the list of publishers with one or more titles in the Titles table.

This query returns 25 records—there are 25 publishers with titles in our database. The total number of titles per publisher varies from one to nine books.

One detail you should notice in this example is the fact that the field on which the grouping is based is different than the field specified in the aggregate function. However, the field following the GROUP BY option must appear in the selection list.

You could obtain the same result with a RIGHT JOIN too:

```
SELECT Publishers.Name, COUNT (Titles.Title)
FROM Publishers, Titles,
Publishers RIGHT JOIN Titles
    ON Titles.PubID = Publishers.PubID
GROUP BY Publishers.Name
```

As a reminder, the RIGHT JOIN includes all the records from the right-hand table, but only those records of the left-hand table that have matching values. Therefore, publishers without one or more titles in the Titles table will not appear in the query's result.

Now change the RIGHT JOIN to LEFT JOIN:

```
SELECT Publishers.Name, COUNT (Titles.Title)
FROM Publishers, Titles,
Publishers LEFT JOIN Titles
    ON Titles.PubID = Publishers.PubID
GROUP BY Publishers.Name
```

You'll get a complete list of publishers, even the ones who have no titles published (a total of 30 publisher names). Some of them have no titles in the Titles table, yet they appear in the query.

### The DISTINCT Keyword

The DISTINCT keyword omits records that contain duplicate data in the selected fields. In other words, if a query result contains the same field value in more than one row, the DISTINCT keyword will eliminate all duplicates after the first one. Let's say you want to see the list of all publishers who have at least one title in the database (some publishers appear in the Publishers table, but no rows in the Titles table point to them). A statement that involved a single table (Publishers) wouldn't work. It would return all the publisher names, regardless of whether they have a title in the Titles table or not.

Use the DISTINCT keyword to eliminate duplicate fields.

The following query would return the names of all 30 publishers:

```
SELECT Name FROM Publishers
```

Let's try to get the list of publishers who have at least one title in the Titles table. This query returns a recordset with 50 rows, which is the number of books in the Titles table (it's an INNER JOIN):

```
SELECT Publishers.Name
FROM Publishers, Titles
WHERE Publishers.PubID = Titles.PubID
```

To reject all duplicates, we can use the DISTINCT keyword in the last SQL statement:

```
SELECT DISTINCT Publishers.Name
FROM Publishers, Titles
WHERE Publishers.PubID = Titles.PubID
```

This time the query returns 25 publisher names, which are all unique. They are the publishers that appear in one or more entries in the Titles table.

## Action Queries

Now we will turn our attention from the select queries to the action queries. SQL provides a few options for performing certain actions on the database. The two most common and useful action queries are UPDATE and DELETE.

Action queries do not return any recordset. They act on the data in the database.

Action queries do not create (or return) recordsets. They simply change selected records in one or more tables and return control to the program. Action queries are especially useful when updating more than one table en masse. For example, you would use an action query to increase the value of all products in a certain category by some percentage, or to remove all of the invoices issued last year that have been paid for. Performing similar actions on a record-by-record basis is not only time-consuming, it's error-prone too.

CD-ROM

If you are using a database to experiment with action queries, especially if you are going to use the DELETE action query, be sure to first make a copy of the database. If you accidentally destroy data from a database, you can copy the VBINC database from the CD. The BIBLIO database must be copied from Visual Basic's distribution diskettes.

The SQLGRID application can't be used with action queries. Where select queries can be used to build recordsets, action queries do not report any results. Where selection queries are usually used as arguments in building recordsets, action queries must be executed with the Execute Method. The Execute Method applies to the database object and its syntax is as follows:

```
DB.Execute SQL_statement
```

DB is a properly dimensioned Database variable and SQL_statement is an action query. The following commands open the BIBLIO database and delete all the titles containing the string "SQL":

```
Dim DB As Database
Set DB = OpenDatabase("BIBLIO.MDB")
DB.Execute = "DELETE FROM Titles WHERE Title LIKE '*SQL*' "
```

Action queries must be executed with the Execute Method.

If you attempt to use an action query in the way you would use a select query (as we have been doing so far) Visual Basic will generate an error message. Do not execute any of the following examples in the SQLGRID application. To execute any of the action query examples below, create a string (text enclosed in quotes) with the SQL statement and use it as argument of the Execute Method of the database.

### Updating Records

The UPDATE verb lets you specify an action query to update a large number of records in a single step. Let's say you want to increase the price of the dairy products in the VBINC database by three percent. You can start the VBPRODS application and change each price individually. Or, you can issue a single SQL statement that increases the price of all products whose PROD_CATEGORY field equals "DAIRY." The UPDATE verb is even more useful when we want to change data in multiple tables.

The syntax of the UPDATE verb is very similar to that of SELECT, only this time you must use the keyword SET to specify the changes that will take place. The following statement increases the price of all dairy products by three percent:

```
UPDATE Prod_Price
FROM Products
SET Prod_Price = 1.03 * Prod_Price
WHERE Prod_Category = "DAIRY"
```

The UPDATE verb performs an action, and it doesn't return any records. The SET option specifies the action that will take place.

### Deleting Records

Another action you can specify with SQL is the deletion of certain records. The DELETE verb's syntax is similar to that of UPDATE, without the SET keyword. You can't delete specific fields from a table, only entire rows (records). The FROM word lets you specify the table(s) from which data will be deleted, and the WHERE option specifies the criteria. All rows meeting the criteria are deleted.

If your company hires students during the summer, you can delete their names from the employees database when the fall semester begins with a single statement (assuming that the database with the employee data is called Employees and the Title field contains the value "Trainee" for all students):

```
DELETE FROM Employees
WHERE Title = "Trainee"
```

Similarly, if the owner of the VBINC company decides that dairy products don't sell well, he can remove all the items from the Products table that have the value "DAIRY" in their PROD_CATEGORY field:

```
DELETE FROM Products
WHERE Prod_Category = "DAIRY"
```

Before deleting rows from one or more tables, create the equivalent recordset to see the rows you are about to delete.

Let's look at a more complicated deletion process. This time we'll delete from the BIBLIO database all publishers that do not appear in a title—in other words, all publishers that happen to be in the database, but that are not connected to any title. As you may have guessed, we will create an Inner-Join between publishers and titles. To be on the safe side, we will first create a recordset with the rows that will be removed with a SELECT statement:

```
SELECT Publishers.PubID, Publishers.Name
FROM Publishers
INNER JOIN Titles
    ON Publishers.PubID <> Titles.PubID
```

Or we could use the following SELECT statement, which is even simpler:

```
SELECT Publishers.PubID, Publishers.Name
FROM Publishers
WHERE Publishers.PubID <> Titles.PubID
```

The recordset returned by this query will contain the names of the publishers without any titles—that is, the publishers we wish to delete. Even if you are not familiar with the database, you will easily spot any mistakes—the wrong recordset will probably contain too many rows. If the recordset contains the entries you want to delete, then you can use the WHERE clause with a DELETE statement:

```
DELETE FROM Publishers
WHERE Publishers.PubID <> Titles.PubID
```

The SQL DELETE statement is identical to the SELECT statement, with the exception that you don't have to specify any fields. All fields in the selected rows will be deleted. You can also delete entries in multiple tables, by creating Inner-Joins. The two databases we are using for the examples of this chapter do not lend themselves to this type of operation, so let's return to our hypothetical employee database example. If the trainee names appear also in the company's payroll, when removing their names from the Employees table, you should also remove them from the Payroll table. Here is the SQL statement that removes all employees with a title of "Trainee" from both the Employees and the Payroll tables (where EmployeeID is the common field between the two tables):

```
DELETE
FROM Employees, Payroll,
Employees INNER JOIN Payroll
    ON Employees.EmployeeID = Payroll.EmployeeID
WHERE Title = 'Trainee'
```

## Defining Query Objects

In the previous section, we discussed the topic of SQL, and you saw how to retrieve the data you want from the database. The most common use of SQL statements is in creating recordsets (Dynasets and Snapshots). The SQLGRID application shows how to create Dynasets with SQL statements and how to manipulate their data. SQL statements can also be used as values for the RecordSource Property of the Data Control, to limit the number of records the Data Control can access. In the discussion of the BOOKS example, we used selection queries to limit the scope of the Data Controls. Doing so let the Data Controls "see" only the part of the database we were interested in.

The queries you use most often can be named and attached to the database itself, so that you can call them by name.

Queries are so common when working with databases that they can become part of the database. In other words, you can create queries and store them in the database along with the tables and indices. Then you can use them again and again. If you are using the same query with some frequency, you can attach it to the database and have it at your disposal each time you need it. You can even specify parameters, so that the scope of the statement can be altered each time the query is executed.

To create a query and attach it to the database, you must first dimension a new variable of type QueryDef:

```
Dim QUERYCust As QueryDef
```

Then create the new variable with the CreateQueryDef Method:

```
Set QUERYCust = DB.CreateQueryDef("CACustomers")
```

"CACustomers" is the name of the query and DB is a properly initialized Database variable. From now on, you will be using the name "CACustomers" to refer to the query. To complete the definition, assign the desired SQL statement to the variable's SQL Property:

```
QUERYCust.SQL = "SELECT * FROM Customers WHERE
CUST_STATE = 'CA' "
```

This query recalls all the customers from California. To create a Dynaset based on the QUERYCust query, use the CreateDynaset Method on the QueryDef object (where DYNACust has been dimensioned as a Dynaset variable):

```
Set DYNACust = QUERYCust.CreateDynaset( )
```

You can also create and define a query in one step, by supplying both the name of the query and its SQL statement as arguments to the CreateQueryDef Method:

```
Set QUERYCust = DB.CreateQueryDef("CACustomers", →
"SELECT * FROM Customers WHERE CUST_ID = 'CA' ")
```

Similar to the CreateQueryDef Method, which attaches new query definitions to the database, Visual Basic provides the DeleteQueryDef Method for removing existing QueryDef objects from the database. The following line removes the CACustomers query from the database:

```
DB.DeleteQueryDef "CACustomers"
```

Note: QUERYCust is only the name of a variable that was used to create the QueryDef object. Once the query has been attached to the database, you can't use the QUERYCust name to refer to it. You must use the QueryDef object's name ("CACustomers").

Before using a query, you must open it, just like any other object stored in the database. Similar to the OpenTable Method, use the OpenQueryDef Method to open an existing QueryDef:

```
Dim QUERY As QueryDef
Set QUERY = DB.OpenQueryDef("CACustomers")
```

Then use the QUERY object to create Dynasets or Snapshots. If it's an action query, use the Execute Method of the QueryDef object. Let's define an action query that deletes all the products in the SEAFD category (table Products of the VBINC database):

```
Dim DELQUERY As QueryDef
Set QUERY = DB.CreateQueryDef("Delete", "DELETE FROM →
Products WHERE PROD_CATEGORY = 'SEAFD' "
```

These lines create the query "Delete," and attach it to the database. To delete the products in the SEAFD category, you must first open the QueryDef object:

```
DIM DELQUERY As QueryDef
Set DELQUERY = DB.OpenQueryDef("Delete")
```

Then you must execute it:

```
DB.Execute DELQUERY
```

## Parameter Queries

Finally, you can define queries with parameters, which are specified when the query is executed. The PARAMETERS option, which determines the parameters, must always appear first in an SQL statement, followed by the parameter names and their types. Here is the syntax of the PARAMETERS option:

```
PARAMETERS parametertext parametertype;
```

The semicolon at the end is mandatory. The *parametertext* argument is the name of the parameter. It can be a single word, like "Value" or "Month," or an entire sentence, such as "[Please enter the value"]. Note that if the parametertext argument contains spaces, then it must be enclosed in braces.

The parametertype argument is the data type of the parameter (Text, Date, Currency, etc.). You can also specify more than one parameter, as long as you separate them with commas:

```
PARAMETERS parametertext parametertype, parametertext →
parametertype;
```

Here is an SQL statement that recalls the invoices with a total that exceeds a user-specified value (parameter) and displays the name of the customer to whom the invoice was issued, along with the invoice's total:

```
PARAMETERS [InvTot] Currency;
SELECT Customers.Cust_Name, Invoices.Inv_Total
FROM Customers, Invoices
WHERE Invoices.Inv_CustID = Customers.Cust_ID
    AND Invoices.Inv_Total > [InvTot]
```

You can't execute this statement with SQLGRID. You must first attach it to the database and then execute it with the Execute Method of the database. Let's follow the steps.

First append this query to the VBINC database. Start a new project and enter the following lines in a Command Button's Click Event:

```
Sub Command1_Click ( )
Dim DB As Database
Dim QUERYInv As QueryDef

    Set DB = OpenDatabase("C:\VB\VBINC.MDB")
    Set QUERYInv = DB.CreateQueryDef("InvTotals")

    QSQL = "PARAMETERS [InvTot] Currency; "
    QSQL = QSQL + "SELECT Customers.Cust_Name, →
```

```
Invoices.Inv_Total "
    QSQL = QSQL + "FROM Customers, Invoices "
    QSQL = QSQL + "WHERE Invoices.Inv_CustID = →
Customers.Cust_ID "
    QSQL = QSQL + " AND Invoices.Inv_Total > [InvTot]"
    QUERYInv.SQL = QSQL

    QUERYInv.Close
    DB.Close

End Sub
```

Note that you may have to change the full name of the database if it is stored in a different location in your computer.

First, we create the QUERYInv object (of type QueryDef) and attach it to the database with the following line:

Queries attached to a database can contain parameters, which are assigned values when they are executed.

```
Set QUERYInv = DB.CreateQueryDef("InvTotals")
```

Then we create a string variable (QSQL) that contains the previous SQL statement, and assign it to the QUERYInv object's SQL Property. The "InvTotals" QueryDef object has been attached to the database.

To use this query we must create a QueryDef variable. As soon as this variable is assigned the "InvTotals" query from the VBINC database, the names of the query's parameters can be accessed through the QUERYInv object. Let's examine the following code segment that makes use of the "InvTotals" query:

```
Sub Command2_Click ( )
Dim DB As Database
Dim QUERYInv As QueryDef
Dim SNAPInv As Snapshot

    Set DB = OpenDatabase("C:\VB\VBINC.MDB")
    Set QUERYInv = DB.OpenQueryDef("InvTotals")
    QUERYInv!InvTot = 50
    Set SNAPInv = QUERYInv.CreateSnapshot( )
    Print SNAPInv.Fields(0), SNAPInv.Fields(1)
    SNAPInv.MoveNext
    Print SNAPInv.Fields(0), SNAPInv.Fields(1)

End Sub
```

First, we open the database and assign the "InvTotals" query to a QueryDef object (which is the QUERYInv variable). Then, we use the QUERYInv!InvTot expression to assign a value to the query's parameter:

```
QUERYInv!InvTot = 50
```

As you can see, the parameter name we used in the definition of the SQL statement becomes a "property" of a QueryDef object. (Actually it's not a real Property, because if you use the period in the place of the exclamation mark, Visual Basic will generate the error message "Property Not Found.")

Then, we can use the query to create a Snapshot with the following command:

```
Set SNAPInv = QUERYInv.CreateSnapshot( )
```

Notice that the CreateSnapshot Method is applied to the QueryDef object, and not to the database.

Finally, to test the results of the parameter query, we print the first two rows of the resulting recordset.

This concludes our presentation of the SQL statements. In the next section, we will present the actual code of the SQLGRID application. The SQLGRID application will help you understand how select queries are used in programs and how you can access the recordsets they return.

## Example: The SQLGRID Application

Now we can look at the code of the SQLGRID application. The SQL statement the user types in the Text Box is used to build a Dynaset variable (DYNA). Then we use the recordset Methods and Properties to read all the data in the Grid. The core of the SQLGRID application is similar to the DAGRID application we presented earlier in the chapter. Each SQL statement is used to create a Dynaset variable (called DYNA). This variable is an array, with DYNA.RecordCount rows and DYNA.Fields.Count columns. These two numbers are used to set up a Grid of the appropriate dimensions. Then, we loop through each row of the DYNA variable (with the MoveNext Method) and transfer all the fields from the Dynaset variable to the Grid. Here is the code of the Execute Command Button:

```
Sub ExecuteButton_Click ( )
Dim Books As Database
Dim DYNA As Dynaset

    SQLline$ = Trim(Text1.Text)
    cr = Chr$(10) + Chr$(13)
    If DataBaseName = "" Then
        MsgBox "You must first open a database"
```

```
        Exit Sub
    End If
    Screen.MousePointer = 11
    Form1.Caption = "Building Dynaset..."

On Error GoTo DBError
    Set Books = OpenDatabase(DataBaseName)
On Error GoTo SETError
    Set DYNA = Books.CreateDynaset(SQLline$)
    DYNA.MoveLast
On Error GoTo GridError
    Form2.Grid1.Rows = 1
    Form2.Grid1.Cols = 1
    Form2.Grid1.Rows = DYNA.RecordCount + 1
    Form2.Grid1.Cols = DYNA.Fields.Count + 1
    Form2.Grid1.FixedRows = 1
    Form2.Grid1.FixedCols = 1
    NumberGrid (DYNA.RecordCount)
    For i = 0 To DYNA.Fields.Count - 1
        DYNA.MoveFirst
        Form2.Grid1.Col = i + 1
        Form2.Grid1.Row = 0
        Form2.Grid1.Text = DYNA.Fields(i).Name
        For j = 0 To DYNA.RecordCount - 1
            Form2.Grid1.Row = j + 1
            If Not IsNull(DYNA.Fields(i)) Then
                Form2.Grid1.Text = DYNA.Fields(i)
                If TextWidth(DYNA.Fields(i)) > →
Form2.Grid1.ColWidth(i + 1) Then Form2.Grid1.ColWidth →
(i + 1) = TextWidth(DYNA.Fields(i) + " ")
            End If
            DYNA.MoveNext
        Next
    Next

    Form1.Caption = "SQL Query Definition"
    Screen.MousePointer = 0
    Form2.Grid1.Row = 1
    Form2.Grid1.Col = 1
    Form2.Show
    Books.Close    ' Close database
    Exit Sub
```

```
DBError:
    Form1.Caption = "SQL Query Definition"
    Screen.MousePointer = 0
    Exit Sub

SETError:
    ErrorMsg$ = "Couldn't create Dynaset" + cr + Error
    MsgBox ErrorMsg$
    Form1.Caption = "SQL Query Definition"
    Screen.MousePointer = 0
    Exit Sub

GridError:
    ErrorMsg$ = "Couldn't fill the Grid" + cr + "VB Error →
    Message: " + Error
    ErrorMsg$ = ErrorMsg$ + cr + "Query result probably →
    a cross-join"
    MsgBox ErrorMsg$
    Form1.Caption = "SQL Query Definition"
    Screen.MousePointer = 0
    Exit Sub

End Sub
```

The DataBaseName variable is defined in the application's module as a global variable, so that all modules can access it. The Show DB Structure command leads to the MAPDB application, which will be explained near the end of this chapter.

One item worth discussing in the previous code is the use of the IsNull function. If a certain field in a row hasn't been assigned a value, it contains a NULL "value." A NULL value is just that: no value. It is not an empty string (""); neither is it zero (for numeric fields). Visual Basic initializes all fields of a record to NULL values. NULL values, however, can't be assigned to Properties. If you attempt to assign a NULL value to the Grid's Text Property, Visual Basic will generate the error message "Invalid Use of Null."

Always check fields for Null values before you use them in an operation.

Of course, the same will happen if you assign a NULL value to the Text Property of a Text Box, the Caption Property of a Label, and so on. The NULL value can't be used in operations; neither can it be assigned to variables. That's why it is necessary to always check for NULL values and skip them, or take some other action.

Notice also the number of error trapping statements. There are many distinct things that can go wrong in this application. The user may attempt to execute an SQL statement before opening a database with the Open Database command. The most common error is an incorrect SQL statement. In that case we display the error message generated by Visual Basic and exit. An SQL statement that creates a cross-join can easily overflow the Grid. If that happens, the program exits again.

## TRANSACTION PROCESSING

We have seen how to handle databases in many ways: How to navigate through a recordset's rows, how to combine multiple recordsets, how to recall information in any way we see fit and how to change and update the information in the database. There is one very practical situation we have been avoiding so far: How to update multiple recordsets. If you think about it, in most databases we don't add new publishers and titles, or customers and products. The most common operation performed on a database is a *transaction*. A transaction is a series of operations that must be performed at once. When you use your bank's ATM to transfer funds from your checking account to your savings account, you perform a transaction that involves two steps: Removing money from your checking account (decreasing the balance) and adding the same amount to your savings account (increasing the balance). If these two operations aren't performed together, some money will be lost. Either you or the bank will be unhappy about it.

Transactions are very common in everyday business life. Issuing an invoice is a transaction. The customer is debited, the company's accounts are credited and the inventory is decreased accordingly. Like an ATM transaction, all these actions must be performed at once. If you credit your company's accounts, but something goes wrong and the program stops before the invoice has been issued, the transaction can't be considered complete.

If even a single step in a transaction fails, the entire transaction must be aborted.

If the transaction is interrupted for some reason, the computer should be able to undo the changes. In database terminology, this is called *rollback*. If the transaction can't complete, the computer must roll back to the last known "good" state. By good state we mean the last state before the database's integrity was impaired. And this state is the state of the database right before the transaction started.

To handle transactions, Visual Basic keeps track of all changes in a log file. If the transaction completes successfully, it commits the changes to the database. If the transaction fails for some reason, then it rolls back (it "undoes" the changes in the database). This isn't exactly what goes on, but we needn't be concerned with the mechanics of the process.

What can go wrong in a transaction? Everything that can go wrong in a program. A transaction involves several steps, such as checking a customer's current balance, subtracting items sold from inventory, etc. Any of these steps may fail. Even a programming bug can cause a transaction to fail. Even more things can go wrong in a multi-user environment (another user has locked the record you want to update, you lost your connection to a server, and so on). With Visual Basic's transactional capabilities, however, no matter what happens to the program, the database will not become corrupted.

Visual Basic provides three statements for handling transactions, shown in Table 3-6:

| | |
|---|---|
| BeginTrans | Begins the transaction. |
| CommitTrans | Commits a successful transaction (commits all the changes made to the database since the last BeginTrans statement). |
| Rollback | Rolls back all changes made since the last BeginTrans statement. |

Table 3-6: VB's transaction-handling statements.

Here is a sequence of commands that shows how these statements are used:

```
On Error Goto RollBackLabel
BeginTrans
{perform the transaction}

{use the Update Method for the changes to take effect}

CommitTrans
{program continues}
On Error Goto 0

RollBackLabel:
    RollBack
    Exit Sub
```

Let's explain this sequence of commands. First we issue an On Error Goto RollBackLabel command. Should an error happen during the transaction, we simply roll it back and exit. By default, when Visual Basic detects an error, it displays an error message and stops the execution of the program. This certainly isn't what we want to happen. While in another situations you might attempt to remedy the situation that caused the problem, in transaction processing it is imperative that we roll back the transaction to protect the database.

If the Update statement is successful, then the CommitTrans Statement will be executed and the procedure will exit normally. If not, the On Error statement will send the program to the RollBackLabel line and the changes will be undone with the RollBack statement.

Notice that the On Error Goto RollBackLabel statement appears right in front of the commands that take care of the transaction. The program above should use its own error trapping routines. Moreover, as soon as the transaction is committed to the database, the On Error statement must change. Any error that may occur after the successful completion of a transaction shouldn't be handled by the RollBack statement. Besides, you can't execute a RollBack after a CommitTrans. The CommitTrans Method commits the changes to the database irreversibly.

Every BeginTrans statement in a procedure must have a matching CommitTrans or Rollback statement.

Notice that you can have nested transactions too—up to five levels. We won't discuss this possibility any further here, but if you nest multiple transactions, make sure that they are all committed (or rolled back) in the same subroutine. Also, if you begin a transaction, you must either complete it or roll it back. If you forget to, then the transactions will accumulate and eventually Visual Basic will generate an error message. An error message will also be generated if you attempt to close the database while any transactions are pending.

### Example: Preparing Invoices

To demonstrate the topics of this section we will implement the application shown in Figure 3-34. This is an invoice-issuing application based on a Grid Control. This program may not be suited for your needs, but we decided to demonstrate an alternative (and very interesting) approach. The Grid Control contains all the items in the Products table, and the user can select the desired item and type the quantity—as opposed to many invoicing applications that require that the user types the item's code as well.

As you know, the Grid Control doesn't accept input. We therefore must program the Control's KeyPress Event to fake user input on the Grid. This program accepts only numeric digits and lets you edit an entry with the Backspace key only. If you like the idea of preparing invoices with a Grid Control, your best bet would be to buy a Grid Control that accepts user input, such as FarPoint's Spread/VBX. We decided to use the standard Grid Control in our application so that all readers can follow the example on their computers. It's not as flexible as it should be, but our goal is to demonstrate the transaction processing mechanism of Visual Basic and not to present a complete invoicing application.

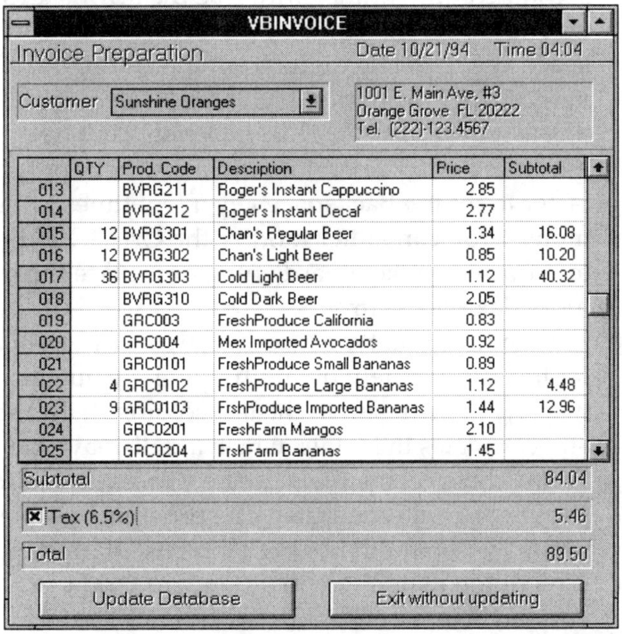


Figure 3-34: The VBINV application uses a Grid Control to prepare invoices.

To use this application, familiarize yourself with the VBINC database. You can open the database with the Data Manager application to see the contents of the tables, or use the VBCUST and VBPROD data-entry applications to browse through the database's customers and products, and possibly add new entries.

CD-ROM

The VBINV application (located in the 3\APPS\VBINV subdirectory of the CD) is a standalone application that lets you prepare one invoice only. Normally, you would call a similar Form from another application's menu. To prepare an invoice you must select a customer's name from the combo box in the upper section of the Form. The customers' names are placed in the combo box when the program starts, and you can only specify a valid customer name. The customer's data will be displayed on the Panel next to the name, to help you make sure that you have indeed selected the correct name.

With a few lines of code in its KeyPress Event you can use the Grid Control for simple data entry too.

Then you can click on any line of the Grid and type the quantity for the selected item. The numbers you type always appear in the second column of the Grid. Use the arrow keys or the mouse to move up and down the Grid. To correct an entry you must press the Backspace key to delete digits from the end of the number and then type new digits. For example, you can't select the entire number and delete it or replace it. This, however, isn't a serious limitation, since most data-entry operators use a few keys only, and it is so much faster to hit the Backspace key a few times rather than reach for the mouse. You can either modify the Grid's KeyPress Event's subroutine to improve the keyboard entry, or replace the standard Grid with a more flexible Control.

Each time you type a new digit, the program updates the subtotal for the selected item by multiplying the quantity by the price and displaying the result in the last column. It also scans the entire Grid and calculates the totals, which are displayed at the bottom of the Form. These calculations can be very easily performed between keystrokes on a 386 computer. The program's response time would be seriously impaired by a very long list of products, but then again you can't fit too many lines in a standard Grid Control. The VBINV application can be used efficiently with small product lists, but if the list of products grows large, you must resort to a different type of interface.

When you're done, you can click on the Update Database Command Button to update the database, or on the Exit without updating Button to discard the invoice. Let's see what happens when you update the database. Either action will end the program. VBINV is the type of program you call from within a larger application, not a standalone application.

First, the program must add an entry to the INVOICES table of the VBINC database. The INV_CUSTID field of the invoice will be set to the CUST_ID field of the CUSTOMERS table so that the invoice will be linked to its customer. The INVDATE field will be also set to the current date, so that you can later recall invoices on the base of their dates. Finally, the INV_TOTAL must be set to the invoice's total amount.

Then, the program must scan the entire Grid, and for each entry that has a nonzero quantity, it must add a new line to the INVDETAILS table. This table holds the individual lines of the invoices. For each row we add to the INVDETAILS table, we must set its INVDET_ID field equal to the value of the INV_ID field of the invoice, its INVDET_ITEM to the product's code, and the INVDET_QTY field to the quantity entered in the Grid.

Next we list the code behind the Update Database Command Button. Notice the use of the BeginTrans, CommitTrans and Rollback statements, along with the On Error Goto RollBackLabel statement.

```
Sub UpdateButton_Click ( )

Dim TBLInvoices As Table
Dim TBLInvDetail As Table
Dim InvNumber As Long
Dim ProdCode As String * 12

    If Combo1.Text = "" Then
        MsgBox "Invalid customer name. Please select a →
         customer from dropdown list"
        Exit Sub
    End If

    On Error GoTo RollBackLabel
    Set TBLInvoices = DB.OpenTable("INVOICES")
    BeginTrans
    TBLInvoices.AddNew
    TBLInvoices.Fields("INV_TOTAL") = Val(Panel3D6.Caption) →
    TBLInvoices.Fields("INV_CUSTID") = →
    SNAPCust.Fields("CUST_ID")
    TBLInvoices.Fields("INVDATE") = Date
    TBLInvoices.Update
    TBLInvoices.MoveLast
    InvNumber = TBLInvoices.Fields("INV_ID")

    Set TBLInvDetail = DB.OpenTable("INVDETAILS")
    For i = 1 To Grid1.Rows - 1
        Grid1.Row = i
        Grid1.Col = 1
        If Val(Grid1.Text) > 0 Then
```

```
                TBLInvDetail.AddNew
                TBLInvDetail.Fields("INVDET_ID") = InvNumber
                Grid1.Col = 2
                TBLProds.Seek "=", Trim(Grid1.Text)
                ProdCode = TBLProds.Fields("PROD_CODE")
                TBLInvDetail.Fields("INVDET_ITEM") = ProdCode
                Grid1.Col = 1
                TBLInvDetail.Fields("INVDET_QTY") = Grid1.Text
                TBLInvDetail.Update
            End If
        Next
        CommitTrans
        MsgBox "Invoice saved OK"
        End

    RollBackLabel:
        MsgBox "Could not write to database. Program ends"
        Rollback
        End

    End Sub
```

The following lines add a new record to the INVOICES table and assign the proper values to its fields:

```
    TBLInvoices.AddNew
    TBLInvoices.Fields("INV_TOTAL") = Val(Panel3D6.Caption)
    TBLInvoices.Fields("INV_CUSTID") = SNAPCust.Fields("CUST_ID")
    TBLInvoices.Fields("INVDATE") = Date
    TBLInvoices.Update
    TBLInvoices.MoveLast
    InvNumber = TBLInvoices.Fields("INV_ID")
```

The values for the INV_TOTAL and INVDATE fields are readily available. The Customer's ID must be looked up in the Customer's Snapshot (created earlier). The last two lines read the invoice's ID, so that it can be used later in the INVDETAILS table. The invoice's ID is not assigned by the program. It's a long number (Counter) assigned to each new invoice automatically by Visual Basic. That's why we must go to the end of the table (where the new line is added) and read it.

Then, we scan the Grid, and for each row with a nonzero quantity we append another record to the INVDETAILS table.

Run the application and see how it works. Prepare an invoice, and before you update the database switch to the Data Manager application and delete one of the products you have included in the invoice. Then switch back to the VBINV application and try to update the database. Predictably, the program will fail to add a line for the product you deleted to the INVDETAILS table and will abort the operation. No changes will be made to the database.

The Rollback statement protects your database's integrity, no matter what has gone wrong.

If you do the same with a customer's name, the program will update the database. What happened this time? The customer's names are kept in a Snapshot. Deleting a customer entry from the actual table has no effect on the Snapshot. That's why the program doesn't fail to update the database (it makes no changes to the CUSTOMERS table). In a practical situation, you must either make sure that the customer's ID is valid at the moment the invoice is issued, or (most likely) prevent users from deleting records for no reason at all, while other users rely on these records.

Before we end this discussion we'll show the Grid's KeyPress subroutine:

```
Sub Grid1_KeyPress (KeyAscii As Integer)
Dim QTY As Integer, PRICE As Single, SUBTOT As Single

    If KeyAscii >= 48 And KeyAscii <= 57 Then
        Grid1.Col = 1
        Grid1.Text = Grid1.Text + Chr$(KeyAscii)
    ElseIf KeyAscii = 8 Then
        Grid1.Col = 1
        If Len(Grid1.Text) > 0 Then
            Grid1.Text = Left$(Grid1.Text, Len(Grid1.Text) - 1)
        End If
    End If

    QTY = Val(Grid1.Text)
    Grid1.Col = 4
    PRICE = Val(Grid1.Text)
    SUBTOT = QTY * PRICE
    Grid1.Col = 5
    Grid1.Text = Format$(SUBTOT, "0.00") + " "
    Call ShowTotals

End Sub
```

This subroutine responds only to numeric digits and the Backspace key. Every time a digit is typed, it is appended to current contents of the cell. When the user presses the Backspace key, the last character of the same cell is removed. Then the program proceeds with the calculation of the subtotal for the current item, and finally it calls the ShowTotals subroutine to update the invoice's totals at the bottom of the Form.

You can load the project in Visual Basic's editor and look at the ShowTotals subroutine. You can also see the code that is executed when the program starts, which transfers the names of the customers to the Combo Box and the descriptions and prices of the products to the Grid Control. We've seen similar pieces of code earlier in the chapter and we need not repeat them here.

## DATABASE DEFINITIONS

To conclude the chapter on databases, we're going to look into the structure of databases and see how the definition of the database itself is stored in the MDB file. You don't need to know how the description of a database is stored in an MDB file in order to use the database, and you can skip this section if you aren't interested in this information. Knowing where and how these descriptions are stored, however, will enable you to write programs that open databases and manipulate them, and even create new databases without the Data Manager tool. The information presented in this chapter will be used shortly to build the MAPDB application, which you have already seen in action in the SQLGRID application. MAPDB reads the description of the database from the MDB file and displays its complete structure in an Outline Control.

A database consists of tables, each one having its own collection of fields. Each field in turn has a type. Moreover, each table can be indexed in more than one way (though it may not be indexed at all). Visual Basic must therefore maintain lists of all tables and indices in a database.

TableDefs describes all the tables in the database and is a list of TableDef objects, one for each table.

The description of a database is stored in an object called TableDefs. TableDefs is a list of all tables making up the database and its elements can be accessed with the Name Property or an index value, similar to the ListIndex Property of a List Control. The total number of tables in the database is returned by the Count Property of the TableDefs object. Here is how you can read the names of all tables in the database and put them in a List (assuming that DB is a Database object, set to an actual database):

```
For i% = 0 To DB.TableDefs.Count - 1
    LstLine$ = DB.TableDefs(i%).Name
    List1.AddItem LstLine$
Next
```

For each table in the database, there is a TableDef object, which describes the corresponding table. Strictly speaking, TableDefs is a collection of objects, specifically, the TableDef objects for each table.

TableDef is also a collection of objects, called Fields. Fields in turn have Properties, the most common of which are shown in Table 3-7 below:

| Property | Description |
|---|---|
| Count | The number of fields in the table. |
| Name | The field's name. |
| Type | The field's type. |
| Size | The field's maximum size. |

Table 3-7: Some common Properties of Fields.

Here is how you can add the fields of the first table of the DB database in a separate List, along with their definitions (data type and size):

```
For i% = 0 To DB.TableDefs(0).Fields.Count
    LstLine$ = DB.TableDefs(0).Fields(i%).Name + "("
    LstLine$ = LstLine$ + DB.TableDefs(0).Fields(i%).Type + ",)"
    LstLine$ = LstLine$ + DB.TableDefs(0).Fields(i%).Size
    List2.AddItem LstLine$
Next
```

Besides fields, each table contains indices, which are stored in Index objects. All the Index objects of a TableDef form another collection, called the Indexes collection. As you may expect, the Index objects contain information describing the table's indices, and their basic Properties (shown in Table 3-8) are appropriately named:

| Property | Description |
|---|---|
| Count | The number of indexes in the table |
| Name | The name of the index. |
| Fields | The fields used in the index. |
| Unique | True if the index is unique, false otherwise. |
| Primary | True if it's the primary index, false otherwise. |

Table 3-8: Properties of Index objects.

The previous Properties are straightforward, except for the Fields Property, which is the name of the field(s) used in the index. An index can use multiple fields. Moreover, their order can be different. Some may be in ascending order, others in descending order. The Fields Property is made up of the name(s) of the fields used in the index, with the symbols + and - in front of each name, depending on whether the corresponding field is used in ascending, or descending order. Multiple fields are separated with semicolons.

An index that sorts addresses according to state, and within each state according to the city, has the following form:

```
+State;+City
```

When you create this index with the Data Manager application, you don't have to type the previous expression. You select the State and City fields and move them to the Fields In Index Box by clicking on the "Add (Asc)" Command Button. Data Manager creates the index and stores its description in the database definition.

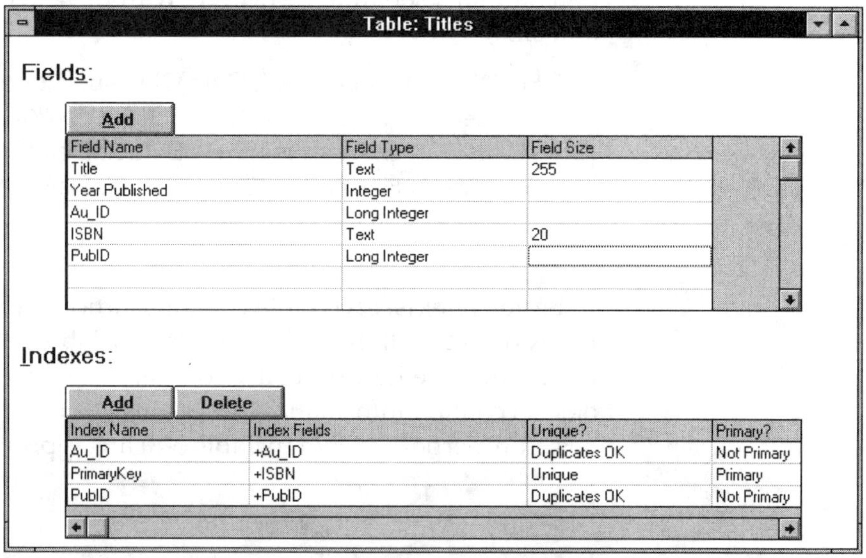


Figure 3-35: Looking at the descriptions of a table's indices with the Data Manager.

The following lines place all the indexes of the first table of the DB database in a List:

```
For i% = 1 To DB.TableDef(0).Indexes.Count
    LstLine$ = DB.TableDefs(0).Indexes(i%).Fields
    If DB.TableDefs(0).Indexes(i%).Unique Then
        LstLine$ = LstLine$ + " U"
    End If
    If DB.TableDefs(0).Indexes(i%).Primary Then
        LstLine$ = LstLine$ + " P"
    End If
    List3.AddItem LstLine$
Next
```

Notice the similarity among the last three code segments (the one that reads the database's table names, the one that reads a table's field names and the one that reads a database's indices). The last program is somewhat different because it prints the characters *U* and *P* only if the corresponding index is unique or primary.

### Example: Mapping A Database

Let's put all of the information we've presented here together to build a useful example. What you see in Figure 3-36 is an Outline Control for displaying the structure of a database. If you don't know how the Outline Control works, it's like a List. We add items with the AddItem Method. Unlike the List Control, however, the Outline Control provides various expandable levels, like the directory structure of the Windows File Manager. When you first open the File Manager, you see the root's subdirectories. By clicking on a directory name, you see the names of the subdirectories of that directory. With the Outline Control, the user can view the information he or she is interested in by expanding a given item, and keep the irrelevant information out of sight by collapsing all other items. When you don't need all the information on the Control, click on the expanded item again to collapse it.

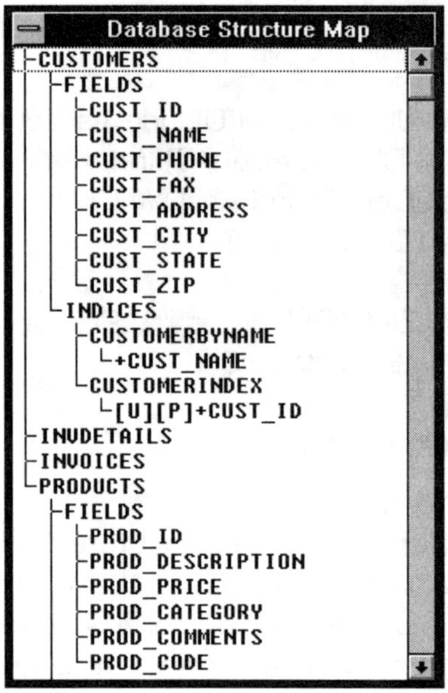


Figure 3-36: The MAPDB application displays the structure of any database.

In the first level you see the names of the tables in the database. When you click on a table name, two more items will appear: FIELDS and INDICES. Click on FIELDS to see the list of the fields, or on the INDICES to see the list of Indexes for the specific table. Once the field names appear, you can click on a field name to see its type. Similarly, you can click on an index name to see the structure of the index. An index is made up of one or more fields, in ascending or descending order, indicated by the + or - sign in front of the field's name. Consecutive fields are separated by a semicolon. If an index is Unique, or Primary, the corresponding indication appears in front of the first field's name.

The code that implements the MAPDB application is entered in the Click Event of the Show DB Structure Command Button.

```
Sub OpenDB_Click ( )

    CMDialog1.Filter = "Databases|*.MDB"
    CMDialog1.InitDir = App.Path
    CMDialog1.Action = 1
    If CMDialog1.Filename = "" Then Exit Sub
    Set DB = OpenDatabase(CMDialog1.Filename)
    Outline1.Clear
    Tables% = DB.TableDefs.Count          ' number of tables
```

```
For itables = 0 To Tables% - 1          ' scans each table
    If (DB.TableDefs(itables).Attributes And →
    DB_SYSTEMOBJECT) = 0 Then
        Outline1.AddItem DB.TableDefs(itables).Name
        Outline1.Indent(item) = 1
        item = item + 1
        Set FldDef = DB.TableDefs
        Set Fld = FldDef(itables).Fields
        Fields% = Fld.Count      ' Number of fields
        If Fields% > 0 Then
            Outline1.AddItem "FIELDS"' Add literal FIELDS
            Outline1.Indent(item) = 2
            item = item + 1
            For ifield = 0 To Fields% - 1
            ' Add each field to the list
                FLine = Fld(ifield).Name
                FldDesc = TypeNames(Fld(ifield).Type) + "[" →
                +  Format$(Fld(ifield).Size, "####") + "]"
                Outline1.AddItem FLine
                Outline1.Indent(item) = 3
                item = item + 1
                Outline1.AddItem FldDesc
                Outline1.Indent(item) = 4
                item = item + 1
            Next
        End If
        Set Idx = FldDef(itables).Indexes
        Indices% = Idx.Count              ' number of indices
        If Indices% > 0 Then
            Outline1.AddItem "INDICES"
            Outline1.Indent(item) = 2
            item = item + 1
            For iindex = 0 To Indices% - 1 ' Add each index
                IndxName = Idx(iindex).Name
                Outline1.AddItem IndxName
                Outline1.Indent(item) = 3
                item = item + 1
                indxStr = ""
                If Idx(iindex).Unique Then indxStr = "[U]"
                If Idx(iindex).Primary Then indxStr = →
                indxStr + "[P]"
                indxStr = indxStr + Idx(iindex).Fields
```

```
                        Outline1.AddItem indxStr
                        Outline1.Indent(item) = 4
                        item = item + 1
                    Next
                End If
            End If
        Next
    End Sub
```

If you haven't programmed an Outline Control before, you can think of the lines that refer to the Outline1 Control as adding items to a regular List. An Outline Control is very similar to a List, with the exception that it accepts various levels of indentation. Each item is placed on the Outline Control with the proper indentation, and from there on the Control takes over. Expanding and collapsing its contents is done simply by clicking on the line in front of each item.

The databases you create contain a few system tables in addition to the ones you specified.

There is one item worth discussing in this application. When a new database is built, along with the tables you define, some extra tables are stored in the same MDB file. These tables are used by the system and you never see them with the Data Manager application, but their definitions are present in the TableDefs object. The first If statement in the For...Next loop checks the attributes of each table and skips it if it's a system table:

```
If (DB.TableDefs(itables).Attributes And DB_SYSTEMOBJECT) →
= 0 Then
{it's a regular table, process it ... }
```

For other uses of the Attributes Property, see the documentation of the Professional Edition of Visual Basic. DB_SYSTEMOBJECT is a constant defined in the DATACON.TXT file.

The variables DB, FldDef, Fld and Idx are Form-wide variables, defined in the Form's declarations section as follows:

```
Dim DB As database
Dim FldDef As TableDefs
Dim Fld As Fields
Dim item As Integer
Dim Idx As Indexes
```

The MAPDB application works with any database and is a handy development tool. If you need quick access to names of tables and fields in a database (as when writing SQL statements) you can add this Form to your application. The SQLGRID application incorporates the MAPDB application in a separate Form.

## MOVING ON

If you've read this chapter, you'll probably want to skip Chapter 4. To maintain clarity, we've included what are essentially two versions of Chapter 3. Chapter 3 covers VB3 database programming, and Chapter 4 is a revision of Chapter 3 covering the considerably changed techniques of database programming in VB4. The Jet Engine is now much more powerful; there are new data-bound Controls; and most significantly, VB4 has a referential integrity feature that makes VB capable of creating a truly professional Database Management System.

# Chapter 4

# Working With Databases (Visual Basic 4.0)

*This chapter and Chapter 3 both explore the techniques and capabilities of relational databases. When revising the* Visual Basic Power Toolkit *to include the many new features of VB4, we decided that it would be awkward at best to attempt to cover both versions in a single chapter. Therefore, if you are interested in database programming in VB3, read Chapter 3. If you are working with VB4, read this chapter.*

*Both chapters are similarly structured and contain, in places, identical information. The examples are essentially the same, but their implementation is different. If you are familiar with VB3's database management capabilities and you are making the transition to the new Jet Engine, you may find it helpful to look at the old and new examples and examine their differences.*

Visual Basic 4.0 offers an impressive array of commands for managing databases. In fact, Visual Basic includes the Jet Engine, the extensive Database Management System that powers Microsoft Access. To the Visual Basic programmer, database management is like a whole other language embedded within VB itself.

The purpose of this chapter is to explore the techniques and capabilities of relational databases, which are new to many Visual Basic programmers. We will endeavor to clearly explain and illustrate terms such as Recordsets, Tables, Dynasets, SQL, Index and all the rest of database terminology needed to understand and exploit Visual Basic's extensive and powerful database management capabilities.

You'll find practical examples here that should prepare you to tackle everyday situations. For most programmers the material in this chapter will be adequate for a wide range of applications. Those of you who wish to write highly specialized applications that, for instance, combine data from different servers or access external databases (Paradox, other SQL servers, etc.), should supplement the information in this chapter with a more specific book on the subject.

This chapter relies on many short examples, especially on the topic of Structured Query Language (SQL). SQL is a data access language that lets you get information from your database using all kinds of wild cards and complex queries such as "Every author who's written more than three books and who lives in Vermont, but hasn't written a book in the last five years."

Our goal here is to present in simple, nontechnical language the basic concepts and techniques you will need to use VB4 to handle databases. We also try to make this chapter equally attractive and interesting to both Visual Basic programmers who haven't had any experience with databases, as well as newcomers to Visual Basic who've developed database applications with other DOS- or Windows-based products (like dBASE, Clipper, etc.).

## DATABASE MANAGEMENT SYSTEMS

Computers manage information. As information stored in a computer increases, so does the need for efficient tools for its management. There comes a time when simple "flat" (one-dimensionally organized) files are no longer a practical solution.

As with every other area of computing, programmers can rely on specialized mechanisms for handling large collections of files. These specialized mechanisms are called *Database Management Systems*, and they free the programmer from the drudgery of trivial (and mostly uninteresting and noncreative) low-level tasks that deal with files. Just as the Multimedia Control Interface provides all the low-level services on the multimedia devices and allows your applications to "play" a sound or an animation file, Database Management Systems allow your applications to concentrate on managing information, rather than the specifics of storing and retrieving data in files and maintaining links among them.

## What Is a Database?

A database is a collection of information, organized for easy processing and retrieval. Of course, you could say the same thing about a hard drive, or of a computer in general. But the essence of a database is that it is more organized, more structured than the collection of files and applications on a typical computer's hard drive.

At the highest level, a database is composed of *Tables*, which are similar to random access files. A Table is a collection of related data. The rows of the Table contain identically structured pieces of information. The Table's rows are the equivalent of a random access file's records. The Table's columns are the fields.

Rows and columns do not describe a file's physical structure on disk. Instead, they describe a way of organizing data that is completely independent of the way data are actually stored in files. This is the way *we see* the database. When working with databases, we can't open a specific file. We open the database, and then we specify the Tables we want to work with. The Database Management System not only handles the low-level functions but also hides them from the programmer. How the computer actually stores the data is irrelevant and not our job.

In a database, each Table holds a collection of information, usually a category or subset of the data in the entire database. For example, a business might use a database for all of its accounting. Within this database, there might be a Table containing all of the customers. Another Table might contain the inventory, and so on. By maintaining our data in separate units (Tables), we can manage them more easily. Moreover, we avoid unnecessary duplication of data. If we were storing the customer information along with each invoice, then every time a customer changed address or phone number, we would have to update possibly thousands of records in the invoices Table. By keeping our data in well-defined, separate Tables, we have to change only one record: the record for the specific customer in the Customers Table.

Tables are assisted by indices, which dictate the order in which data should be retrieved. Data aren't maintained within a database in any particular order. (They're actually stored in the order in which they were entered, but this is hardly ever meaningful.) With the help of an index, though, we can make the data seem to the user to be sorted in a meaningful way. In the MLIST example in Chapter 2, we showed how to sort data with the help of a sorted List Box. The records were not sorted in any way on the disk. When we placed them in a List Box, however, they appeared sorted. Then, the ItemData Property of the List Box was used as a pointer to a specific location in the file. The first name in the List Box (which is the alphabetically first record) might, in fact, be the 16th record as physically stored in the file. By setting the ItemData Property of the List Box's first item to 16, we were able to locate the (alphabetically) first record very quickly. The collection of the ItemData Properties of all the items in the List Box was actually an index. In that example (using ordinary random access files), we had to keep track of the ItemData Properties and update them. In a database, the indexing of the entries is maintained automatically for us by the database "engine." Moreover, we can specify as many indices as we need.

Once the data have been divided into Tables and indexed according to our application's needs, we must create and maintain some links among the Tables so that we can access the information. The customer ID (basically a number) appears in the Customers Table as well as in each invoice, so we can find the customer for whom the invoice was issued or list all the invoices issued to a specific customer. This link is called a *relation*. The Tables are related by some common value. In this example, the value that relates (connects) the two Tables is the customer ID.

The organizational model we just described is called *relational* because it makes use of relations between Tables. Unlike a flat file or other database types, a relational database keeps the information in smaller, more manageable units (Tables) and maintains the information via relations among Tables. The fields that are used to establish relations are called *keys*. The key fields relate the Tables to each other so that we can find the customer to whom an invoice was issued, or the descriptions of the items listed in the invoice (or even the products sold to a specific state). Each of these "lists"—customer, invoice, details—would be kept in separate Tables.

Each relation involves two keys: the *primary* and the *foreign* key. They are fields of the same type (usually numeric fields) in different Tables. Pairs of records (one in each Table) with matching primary and foreign keys are related. The role of primary and foreign keys in database operations is explored later in this chapter in the section "Keys, Primary & Foreign." We will also see how pairs of primary and foreign keys are used to define relations in the section "Maintaining Referential Integrity."

Figure 4-1 is a pictorial representation of a simple sales database. The customers, invoices and invoice details are kept in three separate

Tables. The lines indicate relations between fields. The fields that are connected by lines have the same value on both Tables, and are called the key fields.

TABLE: Customers

| CUSTOMER | ID |
|---|---|
| Sunshine Oranges | 11 |
| Fish Etc | 12 |

TABLE: Invoices

| ID | DATE | TOTAL | ID |
|---|---|---|---|
| 12 | 10/10/94 | 54.19 | 20 |
| 11 | 10/10/94 | 21.66 | 21 |

TABLE: Details

| ID | PR. CODE | QTY |
|---|---|---|
| 20 | BVRG010 | 12 |
| 20 | BVRG07 | 12 |
| 21 | BVRG07 | 3 |
| 21 | BVRG014 | 4 |
| 21 | BVRG202 | 10 |

Figure 4-1: A simple relational database for maintaining sales data.

A database created with Visual Basic is stored in a single file with the extension MDB. (Visual Basic creates another file, with the extension LDB, but you can't access this file directly.) Visual Basic and Access use the same format, and they can both operate on the same database. The single database file contains all the Tables and indices. You can't see them, and you can't access them individually. The index isn't a file anymore. It is stored somehow in the database, and it could even be stored along with the Table's data. A Database Management System introduces a new level of abstraction, enabling us to concentrate on what we want to do, and not the nuts and bolts of how to do it. There is another benefit, perhaps less obvious. The Database Management System protects the database against errors too. For example, if you specified that the customer name is an index, so that the customers appear sorted according to their names, the Database Management System will not let you enter a customer without a name. Likewise, if you specified that the customer's ID is unique, you will be protected from accidentally assigning the same customer ID to more than one customer.

## TWO SAMPLE DATABASES

Let's take a closer look at two specific databases. In this chapter we use two databases for our examples. BIBLIO.MDB, which comes with VB4, is a database of titles, authors and publishers. It is a simple database that can be used to demonstrate most kinds of operations performed on a database, but it falls short when it comes to demonstrating some of the most useful database operations, which deal with numeric data. (The BIBLIO database that ships with VB4 is substantially different from the BIBLIO database of VB3. The examples of this chapter will not work with the BIBLIO database of VB3.)

To illustrate the manipulation of numeric data, we've designed another database, called VBINC.MDB, for storing customers, products and invoices. It is an elementary database for business applications, but it's important to keep the complexity of the code in our examples to a minimum. Our goal is to explain the concepts behind database programming and how Visual Basic is used in this capacity, and to show you how to write data entry or decision-support applications. Once you understand the concepts, employing Visual Basic to write complete applications should be fairly easy.

## The BIBLIO Database

In Figure 4-2 you can see the structure of the BIBLIO database. Tables are represented as boxes. The lines that connect certain fields between Tables show the relations between them. The first thing you'll notice is that the Titles Table doesn't contain author and publisher names. The relation to publisher data is defined by the field called PubID, which "points" to the appropriate entry in the Publishers Table. The relation to author data is defined by the field called ISBN, which points to the corresponding entry in the Title Author Table.

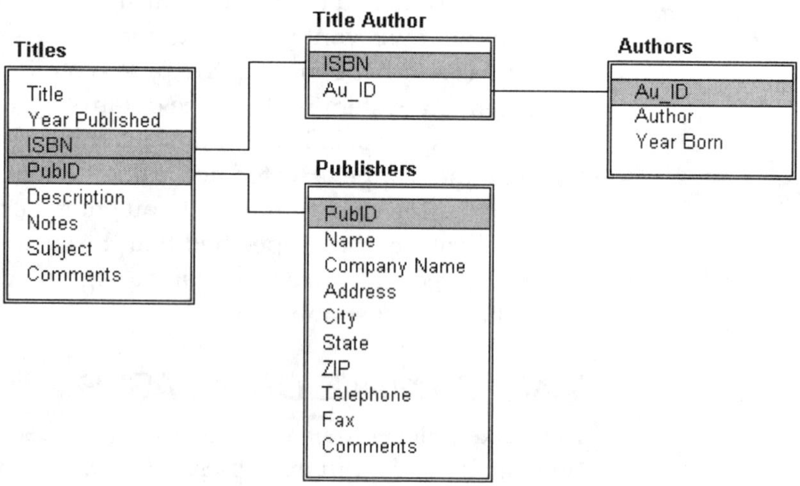


Figure 4-2: The structure of the BIBLIO database. The primary key fields are grayed.

A publisher will have more than one title. It wouldn't make sense to repeat the publisher's name in every row of the Titles Table. There are several reasons why this repetition isn't a good practice, but we'll mention just one. It would take a significant programming effort to ensure that all publisher names in the Titles Table are spelled identically so that we can recall information reliably. By keeping the titles separated from the publishers, we ensure that each publisher's name appears only once in the database. We can even change the publisher's name, and the titles will still point to the correct publisher.

The same is true for authors. The name of the author shouldn't appear on the same record as the title, for the reasons we stated earlier. But there is no "pointer" to the Authors Table. Instead, there's an additional Table, called Title Author, which contains ISBN numbers and Author IDs. Why aren't we using a similar approach for authors, as we did for publishers? Each book is uniquely identified by its ISBN, and each author by his or her Au_ID field. Instead of storing each author's name along with the book, we maintain a separate Table, the Title Author Table, which contains pairs of ISBNs and author IDs. If an author's name appears in multiple books, we use a title-author pair in this Table, instead of replicating the author's name in every title.

This scheme solves another problem. How do we store multiple author names in a single title? Should we provide several fields in each title record, one for each author? Most books have a single author. Once in a while, though, you run into a book with five, or maybe more, authors. By separating the authors from the titles, we can add as many authors to a title as necessary, yet keep our Tables compact and flexible. That's why the authors are linked to the titles with the help of the ISBN field, and not via the author's ID, as we did for publishers (since a book has only one publisher). For every author, we add an ISBN/Au_ID pair in the [Title Author] Table. With this scheme, we can locate all the authors of a specific title or all the titles with a specific author. Yet, no information is duplicated.

### Keys, Primary & Foreign

The fields Au_ID and PubID are called keys. The Au_ID field of the Authors Table is called a primary key, meaning that it is the field by which we look up entries in the Authors Table. The entries of the Authors Table are indexed by the primary key (this index is maintained for us by the system) so that we can locate a specific entry based on its primary key very quickly. The PubID field of the Publishers Table is also a primary key. The titles, however, need not be sorted by their PubID, or Au_ID fields. These two fields in the Titles

Table are foreign keys. The PubID field, for example, lets us connect each title to its publisher. First we locate a title and then we use the PubID field to look up the publisher's name in the Publishers Table. The PubID field of the Titles Table relates each title to its publisher and is a foreign key for the Titles Table. The PubID field of the Publishers Table, however, is the primary key of that Table.

The primary and foreign keys in the BIBLIO database have identical field names. This is not a restriction imposed by the Jet Engine or by Visual Basic. The keys' field names could be different, but in most cases it makes sense that they are the same because they refer to the same physical entity. The field names must be unique within a Table, but not across the database.

To understand the purpose of the primary and foreign keys, consider what you would do with the BIBLIO database. The most basic operation would be to look up titles. Along with the titles, you should be able to see author and publisher names, instead of their IDs, which are listed in the database. To find out the author of a title, you would read the title's ISBN field, use it to find the matching rows of the [Title Author] Table, pick up the Au_ID fields of the matching records and then look up their names in the Authors Table. If the Authors Table wasn't sorted according to its Au_ID field, you would have to scan the entire Table, row after row, until you found the row with the matching Au_ID field. However, because the Authors Table is indexed according to the Au_ID field, you can locate a specific value extremely quickly. Similarly, you can quickly locate a title's publisher in the Publishers Table with the help of the PubID field.

## The VBINC Database

Now let's look at the structure of the VBINC database, which is shown in Figure 4-3. The VBINC database is made up of four Tables: Customers, Products, Invoices and Invoice Details. Similar to the BIBLIO database, VBINC's Tables are linked with keys. The invoices do not contain the customer name. Instead, they are linked by a number (an ID) to the customer they belong to. The Invoices Table contains the invoice headers (the invoice number, customer ID, date and total). The lines of the invoices (items sold) are kept in a separate Table called Invoice Details. The Inv_ID field of the Invoices Table links the invoice header to the invoice lines. All the rows of the Invoice Details Table whose InvDet_ID value is 21 belong to the invoice whose Inv_ID is 21.

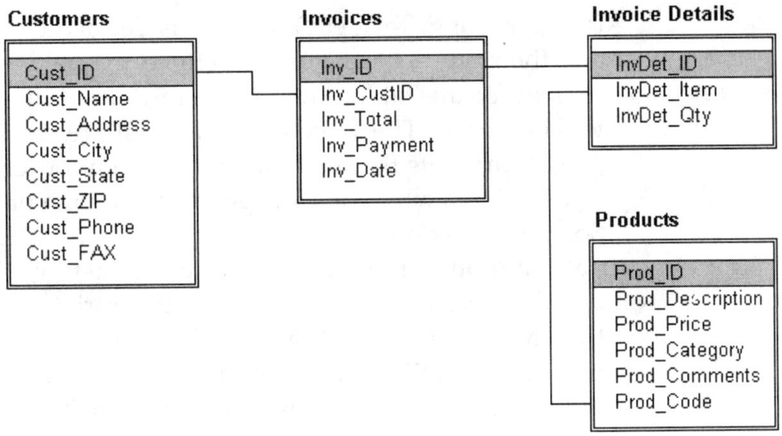


Figure 4-3: The structure of the VBINC database.

## DESIGNING DATABASES WITH VB

Designing a database is no simple task. If the database is not designed properly, it will not be easy to extract the information you need. There are rules for designing databases, but they are beyond the scope of this book. Do, though, bear in mind two basic rules:

- Do not duplicate information.
- Make sure the information you need can be easily extracted.

The first rule says that if information is repeated in more than one place in a Table in the database, that Table must be broken into two or more smaller Tables. The second rule says that the Tables must be linked to one another in ways that will later facilitate the retrieval of information from multiple Tables. If the Invoices file is not linked to the Customers file, you won't be able to tell what each customer has purchased. Many of the flaws in a database's design will become obvious as you start writing applications to store and retrieve the data.

Visual Basic's tool for designing databases is called *Data Manager*. Data Manager was a rather primitive tool for database design until version 4.0. The new Data Manager is a much more functional tool that actually helps you design databases. Yet, it's not the ultimate tool, and once you exhaust its capabilities, you may wish to look for other, more advanced tools for database design.

The Data Manager application lets you specify the Tables in the database and their indices. Tables are defined similarly to the records of random access files. Each field in the record has its own type

(Integer, Long, Text, etc.). A Table is defined by declaring its fields and their types. Once you've defined the fields, you can specify the indices for the Table. An index determines how the rows of a Table will be sorted. The Table's rows are not physically sorted. Visual Basic simply presents them to you in a different order, depending on the index. That's why you can specify more than one index for a Table. Sometimes, you may want to display the invoices sorted according to date, and other times according to the customer's ID. You can specify two different indices and use the appropriate one each time. Use the Data Manager application to look at the two sample databases, BIBLIO and VBINC. Look at the definitions of the fields and their indices. You can even browse through the Tables and add new data.

There is one point worth mentioning here. Among the various data types a field can have (the types you see in a Combo Box when you design the database), there is one called *counter*. A counter is a long integer that the system automatically increases each time a new record is created. Counter fields are often used as keys. Visual Basic makes sure that they take on unique values, but their actual value is of no interest to the user. You can use a counter field to connect two Tables (for example, since the PubID field is a counter, it will help you create a query to "list all the titles whose PubID fields match the PubID field of publisher 'Ventana' in the publishers Table"). The actual values in this field are completely irrelevant, as long as they provide the necessary links among Tables. All fields of the VBINC Tables that include the string "ID" in their field names, in both databases, are counters.

## Using the Data Manager

Data Manager is a simple, almost intuitive program for designing simple databases. As an example, we will go through the steps of designing the VBINC database with Data Manager. (If you wish, you can simply follow the steps by opening the VBINC database and looking at the various Table and index definitions). If you are familiar with the Data Manager tool, you can skip this section and move to "Maintaining Referential Integrity" for a discussion of referential integrity, the most important aspect of database design.

Although Data Manager is a stand-alone application that can be started from the desktop (with the File/Run menu command), it is also available from within the Visual Basic environment, as an add-in. Follow these steps to create a new database or look at the structure of an existing one:

1. Start the Data Manager application by selecting Data Manager from the Add-Ins menu in the Visual Basic Editor.
2. Select New Database (or Open Database) from Data Manager's File menu. You will be prompted to enter a name for the new database (or select an existing database). Choose a name other than VBINC.MDB, or make a copy of the database in a different subdirectory. (If you overwrite VBINC by mistake, you can always copy it from the CD-ROM onto your hard disk. Just remember to change the Read-Only property of the files VBINC.MDB and VBINC.LDB.)
3. If you opened an existing database, you should see a list of the Tables in the database. If you created a new database and the list is empty, click on New to create the first Table.
4. Enter the Table's name (Customers) in the appropriate Box, and then define each field by typing its name in the Field Name Box, selecting its type from the Data Type Combo Box and finally setting the length of the field. Numeric fields have fixed lengths, and you needn't define them. Assign lengths to Text fields only.
5. Click on the right arrow to add the newly defined field into the Table's list of fields. After you have defined all the fields in the Customers Table, the Add Table window of Data Manager should look like the one in Figure 4-4.

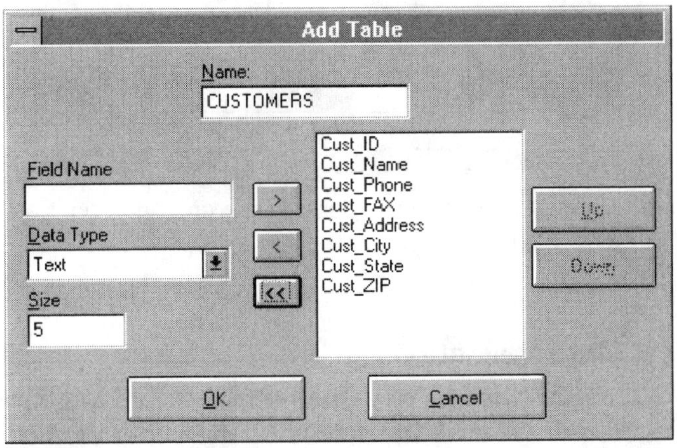


Figure 4-4: Data Manager: Adding fields to a new Table.

The remaining Tables (Products, Invoices and Invoice Details) can be defined in a similar manner.

We mentioned earlier that most key fields are counter fields (Long Integers that are assigned values by the Jet Engine itself each time a new record is created and that never change value). Yet, this field type wasn't part of the Data Type Combo Box. Counter fields are declared as Long Integers. Then, you can specify that they are to be treated as counters from the Edit window. Let's declare the counter fields of our Tables:

1. Select the Customers Table and click on Design. What you now see onscreen is the Table Editor window, where you can modify the structure of the Table as well as further refine your design.
2. Select the Cust_ID field by clicking on its name and then click on Edit. The Edit Field window, which is shown in Figure 4-5, contains the specifications of the selected field, as well some additional properties.
3. Click on the Counter Check Box to make the Cust_ID field a counter. You will never have to assign value to this field, neither will you be able to change it.

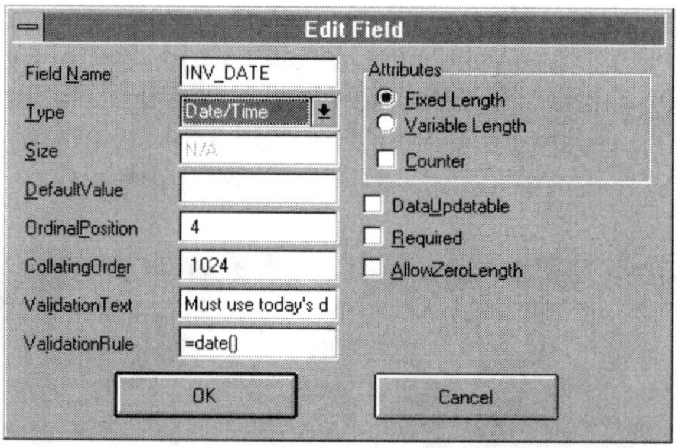


Figure 4-5: Setting additional field properties from Data Manager's Edit Field window.

## Data Validation

The last two Boxes, Validation Text and Validation Rule, let you specify some basic data validation operations to be performed when new data are entered. Again, the data validation rules will apply to all records of the Table and will be performed by the Jet Engine itself, regardless of how you enter their field values (through the Data Manager, or an application of your own). Before commiting the record to the database, the Jet Engine will validate this field's value according to the rule you specified. If the field doesn't meet the specified requirements, the Jet Engine will abort the operation and will display an error message with the text you have entered in the Validation Text Box.

Let's apply a validation rule to our database. Close this window and open the Invoices Table in design mode. Then select the field Inv_Date to edit. Enter the string **Must use today's date** in the Validation Text Box and the expression **=date( )** in the Validation Rule Box, as shown in Figure 4-5. If the date used for the invoice isn't the current date, the record will be aborted.

Another validation rule we can use in our example database is that all quantities must be positive numbers. Open the Invoice Details Table in design mode and enter the string **Please enter a positive quantity** in the Validation Text and the expression **>0** in the Validation Rule Boxes. You can use similar validation rules for the Prod_Price field of the Products Table.

The validation rules you can incorporate in the database itself are rather simple ones, but they can save significant programming effort should you have to implement them in your data entry routines. Moreover, you need not remember which validation rules apply to each field, since you may update the same Tables from various places in your programs. Having the most important validation rules become part of the database and be handled by the database engine itself allows you to concentrate on the design of your application and the more meaningful operations, rather than dealing with trivial, and error-prone, details.

What other validation rules can you use in the design of a database? Usually we specify comparisons in the form they appear in the WHERE clause of an SQL statement, without the WHERE keyword. If you are not familiar with SQL, we cover this topic in detail under "Structured Query Language" later in the chapter. In the meantime, here's an example.

Let's say we want to recall all the invoices issued on the current date. The SQL statement we must use is

```
SELECT * FROM Invoices WHERE Inv_Date = Date()
```

where Date( ) is an SQL Function that returns the current date (the asterisk denotes all fields). The expression Inv_Date = Date() is a validation rule. However, since the validation rule applies to the field we are editing, we needn't include the field's name in the Validation Rule Box. That's why the rule entered in the Validation Rule Box is =Date().

Similarly, to recall all invoice lines with a quantity larger than 10, we must use this statement:

```
SELECT * FROM InvDetails WHERE InvDet_QTY > 10
```

Again, the equivalent validation rule for the InvDet_QTY field is >10 (the field name is implied). After you become familiar with SQL statements, you will be able to incorporate more complicated validation rules into the database. Keep in mind, though, that the validation rule must be a simple expression. You can't use a VB function that performs complicated validation steps. In some cases you'll have to write your own validation routines in VB to achieve the desired results.

Now you can open one of the Tables for which you have defined validation rules by double-clicking on its name. Enter data that violate the validation rules, and see how the Jet Engine handles them.

### Index for Speed

So far, we have defined the structure of our database—the Tables in which the data will be stored. The fields we have defined are the columns of the Tables. The data will be added later on, one row at a time. In other words, what we have so far are the headings of the columns. Before we can start adding data to our Tables, we must define the indices.

Let's start with the Customers Table. We make the Cust_ID field the primary index for this Table so that we can quickly locate customers by their IDs, which appear on the invoices. However, when we display the list of customers, we want them to appear sorted according to their names. To define indices, take these steps:

1. Open the Customers Table in Design mode and click on the Indexes Button.
2. Click on the Add Button, and the Add Index window will appear. Type the name of the Index (PrimaryIndex) in the appropriate Box and then select the Cust_ID field to add to the List of Index Fields.
3. Click on Add again to create the second index. Call it CustomerByName and, this time, define the Cust_Name as the index field.

Similarly, the primary index of the Products Table (PrimaryIndex) is based on the Prod_ID field. We have defined another index, based on the product's category (field Prod_Category), to locate easily the products in a given category.

The Invoices Table has three indices. The primary one is based on the Inv_ID field. The InvoiceByCustomer index (field Inv_CustID) allows us to locate (and sort) invoices by customer ID, and the InvoiceByDate index (field Inv_Date) allows us to locate (and sort) invoices by date.

Finally, the Invoice Details Table has a single index based on the InvDet_ID field. Usually we look up the lines of a given invoice, and we never have to find out the invoice to which a line belongs. That's why we haven't defined additional indices for the Invoice Details Table.

We have completed the definition of the database's structure. We know where to enter our data and how to display our Tables according to their index fields. So, are we ready to populate the database? Not quite. We must also define the relations among the various fields of the database.

## Referential Integrity: Keeping Your Data in Good Shape

We have seen how Tables relate to one another with the help of primary and foreign keys. However, these relations are meaningful only if the foreign keys refer to valid records in another Table. If a record in the primary Table is deleted, any relations based on this record are no longer valid. Modern database management systems make sure the relations between Tables can't be destroyed, using a mechanism called *referential integrity*.

Let's return for a moment to the VBINC database (see Figure 4-3). Each invoice contains a pointer to the Customers Table. The Inv_CustID is a number identifying the customer to whom the invoice was issued. Every time a new invoice is issued, your program must make sure that it is issued to an existing customer.

After issuing an invoice, though, we must make sure that the Inv_CustID reference is still valid. In other words, we shouldn't open the Customers Table and remove the customer to whom the invoice was just issued. With VB3, it is very easy to open the database and delete any entry from any Table. Suppose we have issued an invoice to a customer whose ID is 100. What happens if we now remove customer 100 from the Customers Table? If we scan all customers and calculate the totals of their invoices, the grand total will not include the invoices issued to this customer. If we sum the totals of all invoices in the Invoices Table, we do come up with the actual grand total, but a different one. This condition is clearly unacceptable. To use proper database terminology, the integrity of our database has been violated.

A modern database management system should protect the integrity of the data by enforcing referential integrity. Records referred to by at least one record in another Table should not be deleted. Some database management systems pass the responsibility of maintaining referential integrity to the programmer. With VB4, though, you don't have to write complicated code to detect this situation. The Jet Engine itself will catch operations that threaten the integrity of the database and refuse to carry them out. But how does the Jet Engine know which references are crucial, and which ones aren't? Deleting an entire invoice, for example, doesn't threaten the integrity of our database (though it will ruin your company's data). Deleting a product that has never been sold (and therefore doesn't appear in any invoice) doesn't violate the integrity of the database either. Deleting a product that appears in one or more invoices gravely violates the integrity of the database.

VB4 (or the Jet Engine, to be exact) doesn't know anything about the crucial relations in your database. You have to tell it which relations are important and should therefore be protected against errors. Let's return to the Data Manager screen and this time add the necessary information for establishing referential integrity. All we have to do is define the relations (the pair of primary and foreign key fields in two Tables) and tell the Jet Engine to enforce these relations.

Open the BIBLIO database, select the Publishers Table and then click on the Relations Button. What you see now (Figure 4-6) are the relations of the Publishers Table (there's just one). The Publishers Table is related to the Titles Table, with a one-to-many relation. This means one publisher can appear in multiple titles, and many titles can have the same publisher. The Publishers Table is on the "one" side of the relation, and the titles are on the "many" side. The primary key field of the Publishers Table is equal to the foreign key of the Titles Table. They have the same name (PubID), but they are different fields in two different Tables.

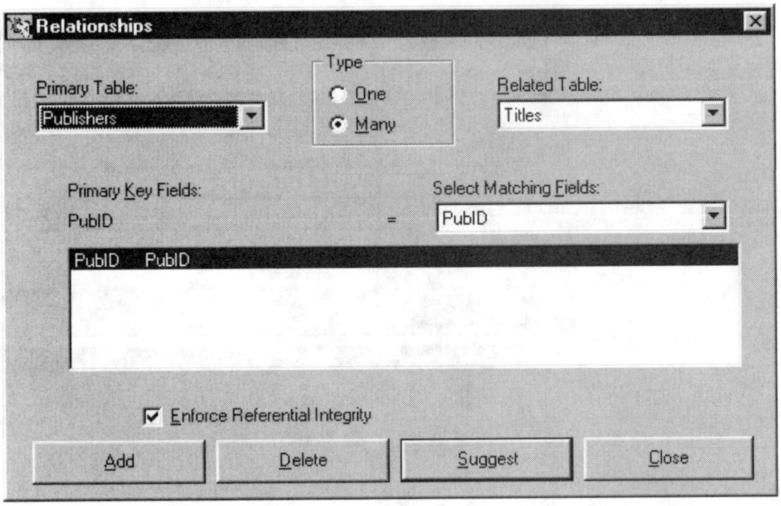


Figure 4-6: Establishing the rules for referential integerity with Data Manager.

The equals sign between them says that there must be a pair of matching fields. Each PubID in the Titles Table must have a corresponding PubID field in the Publishers Table. Notice the Enforce Referential Integrity Check Box. By checking this box, you ask the Jet Engine to enforce this relation. In other words, it will not allow the user to enter a title with a nonexistent publisher or delete a publisher as long as the publisher's ID is associated with a title.

Let's see how the Jet Engine enforces referential integrity. First, make a copy of the BIBLIO database (copy the files BIBLIO.MDB and BIBLIO.LDB to another subdirectory). Close the Design window and open the Titles Table. Select a record and change its PubID field to a value that doesn't exist in the Publishers Table (set it to a very large value). Then try to commit the changes to the database by clicking on the Update Button. The Jet Engine will detect this attempt to violate the referential integrity of the database and will abort the operation, displaying the error message you see in Figure 4-7.

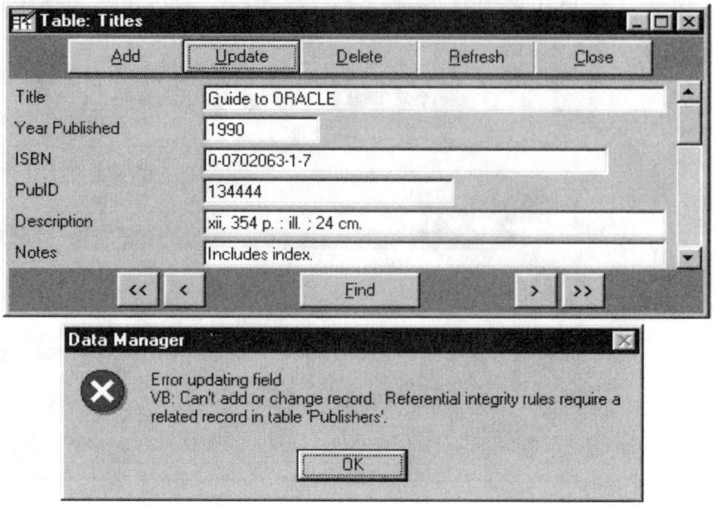


Figure 4-7: The Jet Engine will not let you enter data that violate the database's referential integrity.

Let's attempt to violate the integrity of our database by deleting a publisher. Open the Publishers Table by clicking on the Open Button. Select a record and click on the Delete Button. The Jet Engine will abort this operation, too, and will explain why with the same error message. It knows that related records exist in the Titles Table and that they would be left without a publisher should this entry be removed from the Publishers Table.

Now we'll see when it *is* allowable to delete a record from the Publishers Table. If a publisher doesn't appear in any title, then the integrity of the database will not be violated by removing the specific publisher. Open the Titles Table again and delete all the records with a specific publisher. You can either scan the entire Table and delete the records with a specific PubID (since the Table is very small) or Find all records with the specific PubID and delete them. After deleting all the titles of a specific publisher, you should be able to delete the Publisher too.

Open the Publishers Table now and Find the publisher. Click on the Delete Button, and you'll be moved to the next record. The publisher you wished to delete was removed, and you weren't even asked to confirm the operation. Because there are no longer any records referring to this publisher, removing the corresponding record from the Publishers Table doesn't affect the referential integrity of the database.

The conclusion from these experiments is that the Jet Engine knows exactly what goes on in the database, knows when to enforce referential integrity and when not to. Whether you are casually browsing through a database or developing applications, the enforcement of referential integrity is an extremely handy feature. If the database management system couldn't enforce referential integrity, you'd have to do from within your code—and it wouldn't be simple.

### VBINC's Referential Integrity

Let's turn our attention to VBINC and apply the referential integrity rules for this database.

The first relation is between customers and invoices:

1. Select Customers as the Primary Table and Invoices as the Related Table.
2. Click on the Many Option Button to declare that this is a one-to-many relation (one customer may appear in multiple invoices, but each invoice is issued to a single customer). The Data Manager will suggest the primary index key for the Customers Table.
3. Select the Inv_CustID field from the Invoices Table.
4. Since this relation is crucial for the integrity of the database, click on the Enforce Referential Integrity Check Box and then on the Add Button. This relation has been added to the database definition, and the Jet Engine will make sure that its integrity is maintained.

Another crucial relation in our database is between invoices and invoice details. Each invoice is made up of a number of lines, which are stored in the Invoice Details Table. We know which invoice each detail (line) belongs to because they share a common field. Use the Relations Window of Data Manager to enforce another relation, this time between the Inv_ID field of the Invoices Table and the InvDet_ID field of the Invoice Details Table.

There's one last relation in our database, between invoice details and products. Deleting records from the Products Table will result in invoices referring to nonexistent products. Select the Products Table as the Primary Table and the Invoice Details as the related Table. Data Manager will again suggest the fields to be matched, and they are Prod_Code and InvDet_Item. This means you can't add a line in an invoice if the corresponding product code (field InvDet_Item) doesn't exist in the Products Table (field Prod_Code). Likewise, you will not be allowed to remove a record from the Products Table if there are still invoices referring to this item.

At this point, you have completed the design of the VBINC database, and you can experiment with it. Try to delete records from the Products or Customers Tables, enter invoice details with negative amounts, issue invoices to nonexistent customers and create invoice lines referring to nonexistent products (you can do it directly from within Data Manager, or from the VBCUST application we will present later in the chapter). Jet Engine itself will protect the integrity of the database against malicious or inadvertent mistakes. Of course, it will do so only to the extent defined by the relations incorporated in the database design. If you omit some relations that are critical for the proper operation of the database, the Jet Engine can't possibly figure them out for you.

If you examine the relations in the BIBLIO database with Data Manager, you'll discover that some relations are not enforced. Then why are they there? The Jet Engine will use these relations to speed up SQL queries, so it always a good idea to define them. At the very least, you are documenting your database this way, in case you forgot why a specific key field was defined.

In the following sections of the chapter, we present Visual Basic's tools for handling databases, starting with the simplest one, the Data Control.

## USING THE DATA CONTROL

We've seen the structure of two databases and discussed the organization of the data in them. Now let's see what we can do with this data. In Figure 4-8 you see a simple Form that lets you browse the publishers of the BIBLIO database. This application is called PUBLSHRS, and you can find it on the 4\APPS\PUBLSHRS subdirectory of the CD. The PUBLSHRS application is based on the Data Control, the horizontal scroll bar at the bottom of the Form. The buttons at the two ends of the scroll bar (triangle symbol with a line) take you to the first and last records in the Publishers Table. The inner two buttons (triangle only), move you to the previous and next publishers. To use more correct terms, the arrows at the two ends of the Control move you to the first and last rows of the Table. The other two move you to the previous and next rows.

CD-ROM

Figure 4-8: This data-browsing application was built entirely around the Data Control. It doesn't contain a single line of code.

### Example: The Simplest Data Browser

Moving to the first, last, next or previous record within a database isn't terribly impressive; you can easily program the same maneuvers as the front end for data contained within an ordinary random access file. However, this application doesn't contain a single line of code. Instead, it was built by assigning the proper values to certain Properties of the VB4 Data Control.

Design a Form similar to that in Figure 4-8. Place all the Text Boxes on the Form and draw a Data Control at the bottom of the Form. Then select the Data1 Data Control with the mouse and press F4 to display the Properties Window. We'll set some Properties that will connect the Controls to the database, and every time we move to a different record with the Data Control, another publisher's data will be displayed on the Text Boxes:

1. Click on the DatabaseName Property, and a File Open window is displayed. From this window locate the BIBLIO database on your hard disk and open it. The path name of the BIBLIO database appears in the DatabaseName Property's setting. If you have copied the PUBLSHRS application of this book's CD into a subdirectory on your hard disk and have problems running it, make sure the Data Control can "see" the database. You can copy the VBINC database into a subdirectory on your hard disk and change the Data Control's DatabaseName Property so that it points to the location of the VBINC database.

2. Select the RecordSource Property and click on the down arrow. You will see a list of the Tables in the database. Click on the Publishers Table to select it. This connects the Data Control to a specific Table of the BIBLIO database. When you click on the Data Control's buttons, you will go through the Table's rows. If you run the application now, nothing will happen, however, because the Text Boxes are not connected to the same Table. To force the fields of the current record (the one selected by the Data Control) to appear in the Text Boxes, we must set a few more Properties.
3. Select the first Text Box and then open the Properties window. Click on the DataSource Property, and from the list, select Data1. The source of data for the first Text Box (as well as all others) is the Data Control: the Publishers Table in the BIBLIO database. Then select the Property DataField, and open the drop-down list in the Properties window. You will see a list of all fields in the Publishers Table. Select the Name field.
4. Repeat Step 3 for all Text Boxes. Assign the value Data1 to their RecordSource Properties and the corresponding field to their DataField Properties. The DataField Properties of the Text Boxes are Name, Company Name, Address, City, State and ZIP.
5. Run the application and browse through the publishers. As you click on the buttons of the Data Control, you are moved to another row of the Table, where another publisher's data are displayed.

Writing a functional database-browsing application (even a very simple one) without any programming is no small feat. And it's all made possible thanks to VB4's Data Control and the so-called Data Bound Controls. The Data Control connects your application to a specific Table of a database. The Data Bound Controls are *bound* (connected, or linked) to the Data Control, and they see the database through the Data Control. The Data Control can move through the rows (records) of a Table. The Data Bound Text Boxes see one column (field) in the specific row and display it. The row of the Table pointed to by the Data Control is the current record.

Another interesting thing about this no-code database-browsing application is that it's also a data entry application. If you change the value of a Text Box, the new value will be written to the database. Try this: Change the State field of the current publisher. Then move to the next record and back. The change you made has taken effect already.

But when? You didn't see the usual OK and Cancel buttons, and you weren't asked to either confirm or cancel the operation. This is how the Data Control works. Every time you move to another record, contents of the Data Bound Controls are moved back into the database on disk. This probably isn't what you'd expect from a data entry application, and it sure isn't appropriate for a seasoned data entry operator. However, all the actions performed by the Data Control are available to you as Methods, and you can modify the behavior of the Data Control to suit your needs. We'll see how this is done in a bit, but first let's talk more about the Data Bound Controls.

## Data Bound Controls

Data Bound Controls display the current value of a specific field in the current row.

As you saw in the previous example, the Text Box is a Data Bound Control because it can be connected to a specific field of a Table, and it's Text is tied directly to the actual value in the database. You change the value of the Text Box, and the field changes value accordingly. Other than that, the Data Bound Text Box is a regular Text Box.

The Text Box isn't the only Data Bound Control. There's also the Label, the Check Box and the Picture and Image Boxes. The latest version of VB adds three more Data Bound Controls: the Masked Edit, the 3D Panel and the 3D Check Box. The Label and 3D Panel Controls work just like the Text Box, but the user can't type into the field and therefore can't change its value. The Check Box can be connected to True/False fields, and its Value Property determines whether the field's value is True or False. Finally, the Picture Box and the Image Box can be connected to special fields of the Table that contain images (their type is LongBinary). VB4 contains three more Data Bound Controls: the DBGrid, the DBList and the DBCombo Box Controls, which include all the functionality of the equivalent nonbound Controls, as well as Properties to connect them to a Data Control.

Our example application, PUBLSHRS, doesn't employ the best data entry methods—it doesn't give the user a chance to confirm or cancel the operation. Although it can't be used very effectively for data entry, it is a functional data-browsing tool. If you want to keep users from inadvertently modifying the contents of the database, change all the Text Boxes to Labels or Panels. This way, the fields' values can be displayed but not modified.

The Data Control (and its Data Bound Controls) also allows you to enter new records. Select the Data Control and press F4 to see its Properties window. You'll find a Property called EOFAction, which determines the action taken by the Control when it reaches the last record in the Table. It is set to Move Last. In other words, if the user attempts to move past the end of the Table, the Data Control stays on the last record and grays the next arrow button. Another setting for this Property is Add New. If you set the EOFAction Property to Add New, every time the user goes past the end of the Table, a new, empty record is presented for data entry. This is convenient if you want to continuously append records to a Table, but once you've landed on a new record, there's no way to cancel the action. You must enter some valid data.

Another disadvantage of this approach is that you can't delete a record. To develop useful, functional data entry applications, you have to write some code. Soon, we'll see how to design data entry screens, but first we must briefly mention the Data Control's Validate Event. This event is invoked every time the Control is ready to make changes to the database. Using the Validate Event, you can check the user's changes before committing them to the database. Every time the user clicks on one of the Control's navigational buttons, the Validate Event is triggered. With the appropriate code, you can prompt the user to confirm his or her intentions to either update the data or revert to the original data. You can also display your own OK/Cancel Dialog Box from within the Validate Event. The user can then confirm or abort any changes to the current record.

The Validate Event lets you validate the values of Data Bound Controls before they are committed to the database.

The Validate Event is triggered every time the Data Control is about to send new data to the Table. By placing a few lines of code in this event's subroutine, we can validate the user's input before the Data Control commits it to the database. The Validate Subroutine accepts two arguments:

```
Sub Data1_Validate (Action As Integer, Save As Integer)
```

The Action argument describes the action that triggered the Validate Event. It's 1 if it was triggered because the user clicked on the Button that moves to the first record (MoveFirst); it's 2 if the user clicked on the button that moves to the previous record; it's 11 if the Form received an Unload message; and so on. As you will see shortly, there are many other actions that can trigger the Validate Event, such as the addition or deletion of a record. The Save argument is True if the Data Bound Controls connected to the Data1 Control have changed, and False otherwise. If it's False, you don't have to perform any validation because the data hasn't changed. If the data has been edited, you can display a Dialog Box in which the user will either confirm the edits or abort them.

You can also set the value of the Save argument. If you set this argument to False from within the Data1_Validate subroutine, the data will not be saved to the database. Bear in mind that the validation rules you have incorporated in the database itself are always applied by the Jet Engine, and you needn't be concerned with them in the Validate Event.

In the following section we'll see how to use Methods to manage the Data Control under our program's control. This will let us take advantage of the functionality built into the Data Control and, at the same time, work around its limitations.

## PROGRAMMING THE DATA CONTROL

Now it's time to take a plunge into the real world of database programming and see how we can "write" data entry applications. Before we do so, however, we must discuss a fundamental concept in Visual Basic's database capabilities: the Recordset.

A *Recordset* is a group of records (rows) in a database. The Recordset can be an entire Table, such as the Publishers Table, which contains all the publishers' names, or part of a Table, such as the publishers in the New York area (the rows of the Publishers Table in which the State field has the value NY). So far, we have seen how to connect a Data Control to an entire Table by assigning the name of a Table to its RecordSource Property. We will see other ways to define Recordsets, even how to combine data from multiple Tables, in the rest of the chapter.

As soon as the PUBLSHRS application starts executing, Visual Basic creates a set of records that contains all the records of the Publishers Table. This collection of records is accessed through the Data Control. All references to the selected records must use the following construct:

```
Data1.Recordset
```

The Recordset is not a Property of the Data Control. A Recordset is an independent entity—an object. Perhaps the easiest way to explain Recordsets is to describe how they're used.The Data Control has its own Properties, like any other Control. It has all the usual Properties, like Caption, Width, Height, Tag and so on. It also has some unique Properties that make it suitable for working with databases (DatabaseName and RecordSource). The purpose of the Data Control is to give us access to the Recordset itself.

You refer to a Recordset using the syntax

```
data_control.Recordset
```

where *data_control* is the name of the Data Control associated with the Recordset. All the Properties and Methods of the Recordset are addressed through the object *data_control.Recordset*. For example, to find out if we have reached the last row of the Recordset associated with the Data1 Data Control, we must examine the EOF Property of the Recordset with an If statement like this:

```
If Data1.Recordset.EOF Then
...
End If
```

The Data Control itself doesn't have an EOF Property, and there is no such thing as Data1.EOF. Similarly, to delete the current row of the Recordset we must issue this command:

```
Data1.Recordset.Delete
```

This command won't work:

```
Data1.Delete
```

The Recordset, therefore, is not a Property of the Data Control. Data1.Recordset is an object. It is the set of all rows in the Table that we can act upon through the Data1 Data Control.

## Navigating Through the Recordset

How do you "move" through the data (change the current record)? Table 4-1 lists the four Methods for navigating through the Recordset.

| | |
|---|---|
| MovePrevious | Moves to the previous record in the Recordset. |
| MoveFirst | Moves to the first record in the Recordset. |
| MovePrevious | Moves to the previous record in the Recordset. |
| MoveLast | Moves to the last record in the Recordset. |
| MoveNext | Moves to the next record in the Recordset. |

Table 4-1: Four Methods for navigating the Recordset.

These Methods allow you to move from one record to another, as you might click on the VCR-style buttons of the Data Control, and they refer to the Control's Recordset Property. (The Data Control is always pointing to a particular record, called the *current* record.) The Methods' syntax, therefore, would be as follows:

```
Data1.Recordset.MoveFirst
```

It is very easy, therefore, to emulate the actions caused by clicking on the Data Control's buttons. When using the navigational Methods of the Data Control to position ourselves in the Recordset (to move among the rows), we always take into consideration the Properties EOF and BOF, which become True when we are at the last or first record in the Recordset respectively. There is no next record after the last one (when EOF = True), nor is there a previous record before the first one (when BOF = True). You would expect the Data Control not to react to MovePrevious and MoveNext Methods when you are already in the first or last record respectively, but it does. We'll get into this later in "Designing Data Entry Applications."

The Move Methods let you select the Data Control's current record from within your application.

There is one more Property that is used in conjunction with the navigational Methods: the Bookmark Property. This Property is a string that holds the position of the current row in the Recordset. The Bookmark Property allows you to "mark" the current record and return to it instantly from any place in the Recordset. A Bookmark is not a record number, and it can't be used in calculations. You can't find the distance between two records by subtracting two Bookmarks; neither can you use it to move to the next or previous record by adding or subtracting one. It's simply a string that indicates the current row in the Recordset.

You can assign the value of the Bookmark Property to a string variable, and then return instantly to this record by assigning the value of the variable to the Bookmark Property. The following command stores the position of the current row:

```
ReturnToThisRecord = Data1.Recordset.Bookmark
```

Even if new rows are added to, or existing rows are deleted from, the Recordset, the Bookmark Property of a record doesn't change. To return to the same record after moving away from it, use this command:

```
Data1.Recordset.Bookmark = ReturnToThisRecord
```

(Provided, of course, that the record hasn't been deleted.)

## Accessing Fields in the Recordset

How do you access a particular piece of data? Now that we've seen how to move among records, we should consider how to get to a particular field within a given record.

There are many ways to programmatically access the fields in a Table through a Data Control—enough to be confusing at first. The simplest way is to use the Field Property of the Recordset object. To read the value of the Title field in the Titles Table of the BIBLIO database, use the following line:

```
BookTitle$ = Data1.Recordset.Fields("Title")
```

The current record's fields can be accessed either by name or by their order in the record.

This is the lengthiest syntax for the Fields Property, but it is unambiguous and the easiest to read. The same field can be referenced via its order in the record. In other words, you can use the following command to obtain the value of the Title field of the current record, because it is the first field in the Table:

```
BookTitle$ = Data1.Recordset.Fields(0)
```

Fields in Recordsets have the same order as they do in the underlying Tables. The order of the fields in a Table is the one you see in the Data Manager application when you design the corresponding Table. The name of the field, or its order in the Table's definition, can be substituted with variables too:

```
fname$ = "Title"
BookTitle$ = Data1.Recordset.Fields(fname$)
```

Or you could use the following:

```
n = 0
BookTitle$ = Data1.Recordset.Fields(n)
```

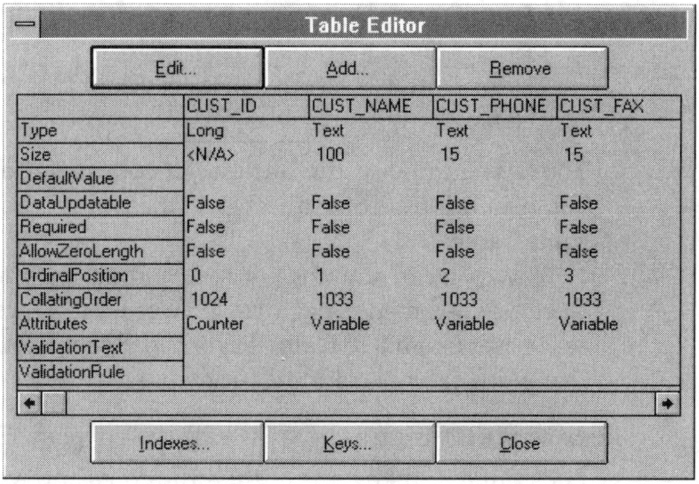

Table Editor
Edit...
Add...
Remove
CUST_ID
CUST_NAME
CUST_PHONE
CUST_FAX
Type
Long
Text
Text
Text
Size
<N/A>
100
15
15
DefaultValue
DataUpdatable
False
False
False
False
Required
False
False
False
False
AllowZeroLength
False
False
False
False
OrdinalPosition
0
1
2
3
CollatingOrder
1024
1033
1033
1033
Attributes
Counter
Variable
Variable
Variable
ValidationText
ValidationRule
Indexes...
Keys...
Close


Figure 4-9: The order of a Table's fields is determined by the order in which they appear in the Table's definition.

The Fields Property also happens to be the default Property of the Recordset object, so you can omit it from the previous expressions. You can write either of the following:

```
BookTitle$ = Data1.Recordset("Title")
BookTitle$ = Data1.Recordset(0)
```

Keep in mind that field names are not case-sensitive. You could refer to the same field as "TITLE" or "title."

In the rest of the chapter, we'll use the lengthiest notation (that is, identify fields by their names) to increase the readability of the code. Of course, there are cases where this can't be done. For example, if we don't know the structure of the Recordset, we can still access its fields by their order. You will see examples of this technique in the SQLGRID example later in this chapter.

The order of the field may not be as clear as its name, but it comes in handy when reading many rows of the Table. Let's say we want to read an entire Table in a Grid Control (provided the Table's contents do not exceed the capacity of a Grid). The number of columns (fields) in the Table is given by the Property Data1.Recordset.Fields.Count. Similarly, the number of rows (records) in the Table is given by the Property Data1.Recordset.RecordCount.

Start the PUBLSHRS application, then stop it and move to the Debug Window. Type the following lines:

```
Print Data1.Recordset.Fields.Count
9
Print Data1.Recordset.RecordCount
30
```

The first number is the number of columns (fields) in the Publishers Table, and the second number is the number of rows (records) in the same Table.

Now you can scan the entire Recordset with two nested loops, as if it were a two-dimensional array. The outer loop will scan the rows of the Recordset (from 0 to Data1.Recordset.RecordCount –1), and the inner loop will scan the columns (from 0 to Data1.Recordset.Fields.Count –1).

### Example: Reading a Recordset in a Grid Control

Let's put together some of the Properties and Methods of the Recordset object to build the application in Figure 4-10. The DAGRID application loads all the titles stored in the Titles Table of the BIBLIO database, along with their ISBN numbers, on a Grid Control. Our Form this time contains a Data Control and a Grid Control. (*Note:* The Grid Control is not Data Bound; it's a simple Grid Control.) There is no simple way to automatically load all the titles on a Grid Control, and we will have to do it with a loop through the Recordset, one title at a time.

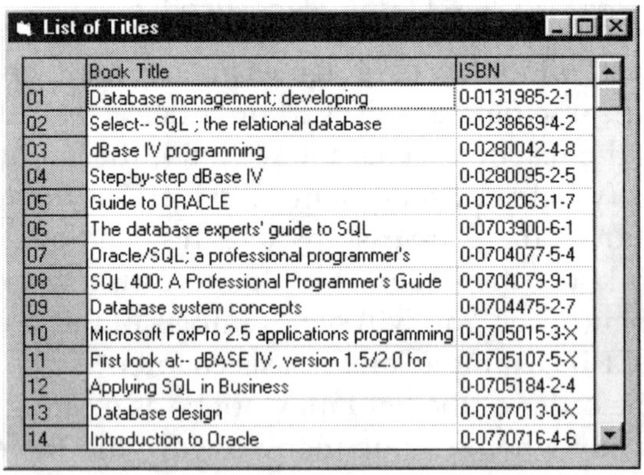


| | Book Title | ISBN |
|---|---|---|
| 01 | Database management; developing | 0-0131985-2-1 |
| 02 | Select-- SQL ; the relational database | 0-0238669-4-2 |
| 03 | dBase IV programming | 0-0280042-4-8 |
| 04 | Step-by-step dBase IV | 0-0280095-2-5 |
| 05 | Guide to ORACLE | 0-0702063-1-7 |
| 06 | The database experts' guide to SQL | 0-0703900-6-1 |
| 07 | Oracle/SQL; a professional programmer's | 0-0704077-5-4 |
| 08 | SQL 400: A Professional Programmer's Guide | 0-0704079-9-1 |
| 09 | Database system concepts | 0-0704475-2-7 |
| 10 | Microsoft FoxPro 2.5 applications programming | 0-0705015-3-X |
| 11 | First look at-- dBASE IV, version 1.5/2.0 for | 0-0705107-5-X |
| 12 | Applying SQL in Business | 0-0705184-2-4 |
| 13 | Database design | 0-0707013-0-X |
| 14 | Introduction to Oracle | 0-0770716-4-6 |

Figure 4-10: The DAGRID application loads the titles on a Grid Control.

You can exploit the Data Control's functionality through its Methods and Properties.

In this application, we have made the Data Control invisible at run time. All the titles appear in the Grid. The user can click on the vertical scroll bar of the Grid Control to move through the titles. Set the DatabaseName Property of the Data Control to BIBLIO, and its RecordSource Property to Titles. Then enter the following code in the Form's Load Event:

```
Private Sub Form_Load ( )
    Data1.Refresh ' sets the object
' The next few lines size the Grid Control
        Grid1.Height = 3600
        Grid1.ColWidth(1) = TextWidth("This is the longest →
        title the first column can hold")
        Grid1.ColWidth(2) = TextWidth("333-333-333-333")
        Grid1.Width = Grid1.ColWidth(0) + Grid1.ColWidth(1) →
        + Grid1.ColWidth(2) + 325
        Form1.Width = Grid1.Width + 320
        Form1.Height = Grid1.Top + Grid1.Height + 550
        Data1.Visible = False
        Grid1.Row = 0
' Get the number of rows
    Data1.Recordset.MoveLast
    TotRows% = Data1.Recordset.RecordCount
    Grid1.Rows = TotRows% + 1
    Grid1.Row = 0
    Grid1.Col = 1
    Grid1.Text = "Book Title"
    Grid1.Col = 2
    Grid1.Text = "ISBN"
' steps through the rows of recordset
    Data1.Recordset.MoveFirst
    For i = 1 To TotRows%
        Grid1.Row = Grid1.Row + 1
        Grid1.Col = 0
        Grid1.Text = Format$(i, "00")
        Grid1.Col = 1
        Grid1.Text = Data1.Recordset.Fields("Title")
        Grid1.Col = 2
        Grid1.Text = Data1.Recordset.Fields("ISBN")
        Data1.Recordset.MoveNext
    Next
    Grid1.Row = 1
    Grid1.Col = 1
End Sub
```

The first line creates the Recordset. If you omit it, VB4 will generate an error message stating that the "Object is not Set." The Data Control's Recordset is created the first time the user clicks on one of its buttons. Since no user action is involved here, we must create the

Recordset ourselves with the Refresh Method. The Refresh Method copies all the records from the Table, in effect creating a new Recordset.

The following lines in the listing simply size the Grid Control and the Form. Notice that the Data1 Control is made invisible with this line (this is a Property of the Data Control and not its Recordset):

```
Data1.Visible = False
```

Next, we get the number of rows (Data1.Recordset.RecordCount), but not before we move to the last row with the MoveLast Method. The RecordCount Property of the Recordset is the number of records that actually have been accessed by your application. Therefore, executing the MoveLast Method causes the value of this Property to be set to the number of records in the Recordset. (The RecordCount Property will not be decremented if we move to another record. The only way to decrement the value of RecordCount is by deleting a record.)

We loop through the Recordset, extract the values of the fields "Title" and "ISBN," and append these values to the Grid. The code for the DAGRID application is rather lengthy, but most commands deal with the Grid and not the Recordset itself.

The DAGRID example demonstrates how we access a Recordset's fields. To load some data on a Grid Control, you can use the Data Bound Grid Control. The Data Bound Grid, introduced with VB4, is similar to the regular Grid Control, except that it can be populated automatically and permits editing of the displayed data. However, we suggest that you use it to display data and not as a data entry tool.

## Editing the Recordset

Now let's look at Methods that allow us to perform operations not possible with the Data Control: adding, editing and deleting records. Table 4-2 lists the three Methods for manipulating data in the database's Tables:

| Method | Description |
|---|---|
| AddNew | Adds a new record. |
| Delete | Deletes the current record. |
| Edit | Edits the current record. |

Table 4-2: Methods for manipulating a database's Tables.

The AddNew Method appends a new blank record at the end of the Recordset and positions you there. This record is not yet committed to the database. After assigning values to its fields, you can either commit the changes to the database with the Update Method or cancel the AddNew operation with the Refresh Method.

The Refresh Method recreates the Recordset by getting the data from disk.

Recall that the Refresh Method recreates the corresponding Recordset. The temporary record hasn't become part of the Table, and when the Recordset is read again from the Table, it will not be there. This seems like overkill, having to read all the records from the Table just to eliminate one record, but it is the only way to remove the temporary record. It's not a slow process, because Visual Basic doesn't really go to the disk to read all the records making up the Recordset. It rebuilds the Recordset with data that are already in memory.

The Delete Method simply removes the current record from the Table, without any confirmation from the user. The Edit Method prepares the record for editing. The changes will be committed to the Table with the Update Method, as with the AddNew Method. To cancel the changes, call the Refresh Method.

How exactly is a record prepared for editing? Nothing really happens to the record or the Table. The Edit Method stores the original record and gives your program permission to change the values of the current record's fields. Here is the common sequence of commands for updating a record's values:

```
Data1.Recordset.Edit
Data1.Recordset.Fields(0)= UCase$(Data1.Recordset.Fields(0))
Data1.Recordset.Update
```

Use the Update Method to commit changes to the database.

If you attempt to change the value of a field while not in Edit mode, Visual Basic will generate the error message "Update without AddNew or Edit" and will not accept the changes.

To abort the changes, call the Refresh Method. If you move to another record without committing the edits with the Update Method, Visual Basic will ignore them and restore the fields you have already changed to their original values. Another way to discard the changes made to some fields is to move to the next (or previous) record and then back to the one you were editing.

The following command prepares the current record for editing:

```
Data1.Recordset.Edit
```

Next, change the value of a field:

```
Data1.Recordset.Fields(0) = UCase$(Data1.Recordset.Fields(0))
```

And then reject the changes with these commands:

```
Data1.Recordset.MoveNext
Data1.Recordset.MovePrevious
```

If you look at the value of the first field with the following command, you will find out that it hasn't changed:

```
Debug.Print Data1.Recordset.Fields(0)
```

This simple experiment indicates that you must make sure the user of your application has no way to move to another record before either committing or discarding the changes made to the current record. The best way to do this is to disable the navigational keys in your application.

## Designing Data Entry Applications

We have seen how to gain access to the Data Control's capabilities through the Methods and Properties of the Recordset object. Now we're ready to build a data entry application that has all the functionality of the Data Control but none of its shortcomings. The VBCUST application (subdirectory 4\APPS\VBCUST on the CD), shown in Figure 4-11, is a data entry application for the Customers Table of the VBINC database. The Form in Figure 4-11 looks much more like a data entry screen, and any data entry operator would prefer it over the scroll bar with the VCR-style buttons of the Data Control.

CD-ROM

A data-entry application must provide options for confirming or aborting any changes.

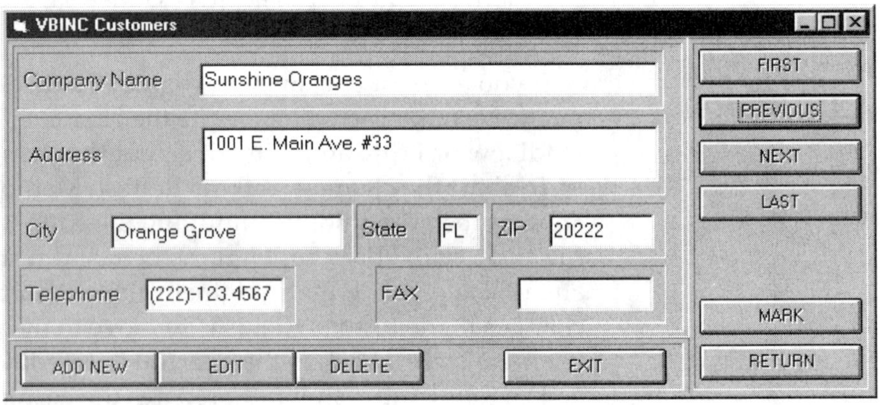


Figure 4-11: A familiar data entry screen based on Visual Basic's Data Control.

## Example: A More Familiar Data Entry Application

Figure 4-12 shows the application in the design phase. The Form contains a few more buttons (OK and Cancel), which become visible during the operations of adding and editing a record, and a Data Control, which remains hidden at run time.

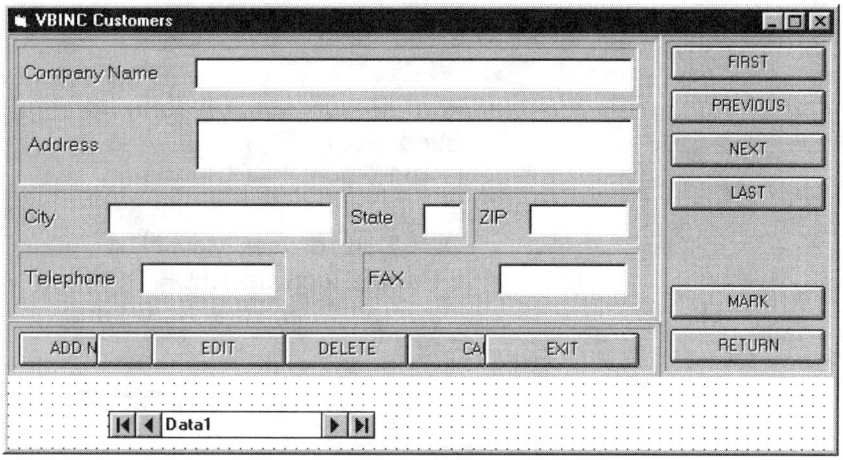


Figure 4-12: The Form shown in Figure 4-11 during the design phase.

Let's see how the navigational Methods work by implementing the code for the First, Previous, Next and Last Command Buttons. If you didn't know better, you would be tempted to insert these lines in the subroutines of the respective navigational Buttons:

```
Data1.Recordset.MoveFirst
Data1.Recordset.MovePrevious
Data1.Recordset.MoveNext
Data1.Recordset.MoveLast
```

If you implement the navigational Buttons with the Move Methods, there's a chance the user will try to move past the end of the Recordset by clicking on the Next Button. This will result in the following error message:

```
"No current record"
```

It's a trappable error, but why is it generated? This error message is generated every time we land on an "invalid record." An invalid record is a deleted record or a record beyond either end of the Recordset. Since it's possible to move beyond the two ends of the Recordset, we must write code to make sure this doesn't happen in our application.

In the code for the Next Command Button, we must check the EOF Property to make sure that we'll never move beyond the last record. Similarly, in the code for the Previous Command Button, we must check the BOF (Beginning Of File) Property to make sure we'll never attempt to move beyond the first record. Here's one way to avoid this situation:

```
Private Sub NextButton_Click()

    If Data1.Recordset.EOF Then
        Beep
        Data1.Recordset.MoveLast
    Else
        Data1.Recordset.MoveNext
        If Data1.Recordset.EOF Then
            Data1.Recordset.MoveLast
        End If
    End If

End Sub

Private Sub PreviousButton_Click()

    If Data1.Recordset.BOF Then
        Beep
        Data1.Recordset.MoveFirst
    Else
        Data1.Recordset.MovePrevious
        If Data1.Recordset.BOF Then
            Data1.Recordset.MoveFirst
        End If
    End If

End Sub
```

The inner If statement may not be very clear. Comment it out and run the program to see what will happen. You won't get a "No current record" error message, but you *will* land on a blank record. That's why we check for EOF or BOF after each move in the Recordset.

The MoveNext and MovePrevious Methods can take you past the Table's end.

The First and Last Command Buttons are implemented with the MoveFirst and MoveLast Methods. There will always be a first and a last record to move to, right? Perhaps not. If the user deletes all records, there will be neither a first nor last record. Any record he's currently at will be invalid. The simplest way to cope with this situation is to disable all four navigational buttons after a deletion if the deleted record was the last one in the Recordset. Then the user cannot click on those buttons. In this case, both the EOF and BOF Properties will become True. We are not dealing with this situation here, but your applications should of course try to foresee and forestall all kinds of mishaps.

To add a new record, use the AddNew Method. The Data Control will take you to an empty record, where you can type the values of the fields. Then you can either commit the new record to the database with the Update Method, or cancel the operation and delete the temporary record with the Refresh Method. The Update Method commits the new record to the database. The Refresh Method rebuilds the Recordset, in effect removing the temporary record. The code behind the Add Command Button is as follows:

```
Private Sub AddButton_Click ( )
    Call HideButtons
    Data1.Recordset.AddNew
End Sub
```

The HideButtons subroutine hides (makes invisible) all the Buttons on the bottom of the Form and displays two new ones, the OK and Cancel Buttons.

Here's the line that does all the work:

```
Data1.Recordset.AddNew
```

The user can enter values in the Text Boxes, and when done, click on either the OK Button to commit the new record, or the Cancel Button to remove the temporary record. Here is the code behind the OK and Cancel Buttons:

```
Private Sub OKButton_Click ( )

On Error GoTo NoUpdate
    If Trim(Text1.Text) = "" Then
        MsgBox "Record must have a valid Company Name"
    Else
        Data1.Recordset.Update
        Call ShowButtons
    End If
    Exit Sub
```

```
NoUpdate:
    MsgBox Error
    Exit Sub

End Sub

Private Sub CancelButton_Click ( )

Call ShowButtons
    Data1.Refresh

End Sub
```

Again, two Methods are all you need:

```
Data1.Recordset.Update
Data1.Recordset.Refresh
```

The Update Method commits the new record to the database, and Refresh deletes the temporary record and makes no changes to the database.

The If clause in the OKButton_Click Subroutine requires some explanation. Before committing a new record to the database, we must make sure that the new record is a valid one. Visual Basic will check the fields against their types in the definition of the Table, and if they don't conform to the type of the Table's fields, it will generate an error message. If you type a string in a numeric field, for instance, the message will be "Type mismatch." If you exceed the length of a text field, you will get the error message "Couldn't insert or paste; data too long for field." As you see, Visual Basic will not even ignore the extra characters in order to make the string fit into the field's length. Any validation rules you have incorporated in the database design will be applied as well. It is imperative that the program validate the user's data before sending them to the database. This is why we are writing data entry screens in the first place. Just consider how many lines of code you'd have to insert in this subroutine if Visual Basic did not enforce referential integrity.

The Update Method commits both modified and new records to the database.

You can include all types of error checking and data validation in the OK Button's subroutine. Even so, you can never be sure that all errors will be caught. In this example, we don't perform any serious error checking, since error checking is such an application-specific process. However, we do display any error message Visual Basic may generate in the process of updating the database and give the user a chance to correct the mistake. Your applications should do more than just display Visual Basic's generic error message in similar cases.

The code of the OK Button is executed when a record is edited, as well, since the Update Method commits both new and modified records to the database. Here is the code behind the Edit Button:

```
Private Sub EditButton_Click ( )

    Call HideButtons
    If Data1.Recordset.EOF Or Data1.Recordset.BOF Then
        MsgBox "No record to edit"
    Else
        Data1.Recordset.Edit
    End If

End Sub
```

This code makes sure that the current record is valid, and if so, it allows editing of the record. When the user is done, he or she can click on the OK Button to commit the changes to the database or on the Cancel Button to revert to the original record.

The Mark and Return Buttons let the user mark a record and return to the last marked record quickly. These two Buttons use the Bookmark Property of the Recordset, but we will not present their implementation here.

CD-ROM

On the CD you'll find an application similar to VBCUST. It is called VBPRODS, and it is a data entry program for the Products Table. Use VBCUST and VBPRODS to populate the Customers and Products Tables, respectively, of the VBINC database. In the section "Preparing Invoices" later in the chapter, we will present the VBINV application that operates on both Tables to prepare invoices.

The VBCUST and VBPRODS applications operate on the VBINC database located in the 4\APPS\VBINC subdirectory of the CD. To use the applications, copy them from the CD's directory on your hard disk and make sure that the database is on the current path. Do not duplicate the database in the current subdirectory. Other applications that use the same database will not find it there. Of course, you can copy all the applications of Chapter 4 into the same subdirectory, along with the VBINC database, although this isn't the best approach, especially if you want to write additional applications. When copying a database, make sure you copy both the MDB and LDB files and clear their Read Only Properties.

So far we have explored the most basic mechanisms of the Data Control: how to navigate through the Recordset and how to add, edit and delete records. In the following sections we will look at some more advanced, and highly useful, operations, such as searching for data and combining multiple Tables.

## Searching the Recordset

One of most basic operations we perform on databases is locating specific records. Visual Basic offers many ways of locating the desired records. Let's start with the Methods for locating records in a Recordset. Visual Basic offers four different Find Methods (shown in Table 4-3), which are appropriately named.

| Method | Description |
|---|---|
| FindFirst | Locates the first record meeting specified criteria. |
| FindNext | Locates the next record meeting specified criteria. |
| FindPrevious | Locates the previous record meeting specified criteria. |
| FindLast | Locates the last record meeting specified criteria. |

Table 4-3: VB's Find Methods.

The Find Methods can locate any record in the Recordset, based on any specified criteria. The FindFirst and FindLast Methods locate the very first and very last record that meet the criteria you specify. The FindNext and FindPrevious Methods locate the first record matching the criteria after or before the current record. In other words, FindFirst starts searching from the start of the Recordset toward the end. FindLast starts at the end of the Recordset and moves toward the beginning. FindNext and FindPrevious start at the current record and move toward the end or the beginning of the Recordset.

Here is the syntax of the FindFirst Method:

```
FindFirst criteria
```

The syntax is the same for the other three Find Methods.

The Find Methods scan the entire Table and check each record to see if it meets the search criteria.

The criteria argument is a regular VB expression specifying a relationship between field values and constants, expressed as a string. The following expression specifies the first author from the Authors Table (in the BIBLIO database) whose name begins with N:

```
"Author > 'N'"
```

If no such author exists, the Find Method will return the first author whose name begins with O, and so on.

The criteria argument is a string that involves field names and relational operators. The following string would indicate all products whose category is DAIRY:

```
"Prod_Category = 'DAIRY'"
```

Notice that the single quotes are used to indicate literals within the string. (As you'll see later in the chapter, the same notation is used with SQL statements.)

To select all the invoices issued on or after 04/01/94, you would use this argument:

```
"Inv_Date => '04/01/94'"
```

Notice the single quotes surrounding the date. You can build more complicated expressions by combining relational and logical operators. The following expression will locate the first publisher in the Publishers Table that is located in New York or California:

```
Data1.Recordset.FindFirst "State = 'NY' Or State = 'CA'"
```

Besides the usual relational operators of Visual Basic, you also can use the LIKE operator, which lets you locate records using wild card characters. To find the first title that contains the word "DATABASE" in its title, use the following command:

```
Data1.Recordset.FindFirst "Title LIKE '*DATABASE*'"
```

This expression will look for records in the Titles Table whose Title field contains the string "DATABASE." The asterisks before and after the string indicate that any other string (text) may appear in front of the desired string, and any other string may follow it. In other words, titles like "The Database Expert's Guide to SQL" and "Database System Concepts" will be located.

The LIKE operator accepts wildcard characters, just like the file selection commands.

When used with the LIKE operator, the asterisk means "any string," even if it's an empty string. Another character that appears frequently with the LIKE operator is the question mark (?), which stands for a single character (it can be any character, but only one).

The searches performed by the Find Methods are by default case-insensitive. This means that the string "database" will match titles that contain *Database* or *DATABASE*. To change the default behavior of Visual Basic, you can use the Option Compare statement in the application's module or in a Form. Just as the Option Base statement lets you change the default array indexing scheme, Option Compare specifies how the searches will be performed. The following command makes the comparisons case-insensitive:

```
Option Compare Text
```

And this command makes the comparisons case-sensitive:

```
Option Compare Binary
```

(Text and Binary are literals, not constants.)

The Find Methods are always used in conjunction with the NoMatch Property, which is True if no record matches the specified criteria. If a matching record was found, then you can issue the FindNext (and/or FindPrevious) Method to move through the found records in the same way you would move in a Recordset.

After calling one of the Find Methods, we always test the NoMatch Property. If it's False, the Find Method has located a record matching the criteria. If not, there are no more matching records in the direction of the search. Here's how the Find Methods usually appear in a program:

```
Data1.Recordset.FindFirst expression
If Data1.Recordset.NoMatch Then
    MsgBox "No such record found"
End If
```

There is no Else clause in this code segment because the Data Control moves automatically to the newly found record—no need for any special action.

The Find Methods are also useful when you need to locate fields with Null values (fields that contain no value). For example, it's likely to be an error in a database if you have a record that contains an address, phone number, etc., but an empty name field. Similarly, an Author field in a record in our Authors Table shouldn't be Null. To make sure that no records contain Null values in the Author field, use the Find Methods with the following argument:

```
criteria = "IsNull(Data1.Recordset.Fields('Author')"
```

Then find the matching records with a loop like this:

```
Data1.FindFirst criteria
Do Until Data1.NoMatch
    {process the record}
    Data1.Recordset.FindNext
Loop
```

This code segment assumes that the Data1 Data Control is connected to the Authors Table of the BIBLIO database.

As an example of the Find Method, we will explain the implementation of the Find Publisher and Find Next Command Buttons of the FINDPUBL application.

### EXAMPLE: FINDING PUBLISHERS BY NAME

Now let's look at the Find Methods with an application very similar to PUBLSHRS. The FINDPUBL application (located in subdirectory 4\APPS\FINDPUBL on the CD) is identical to the PUBLSHRS application we presented earlier in the chapter, with one exception. It contains two Command Buttons at the bottom of the Form that allow the user to search for specific publishers, as shown in Figure 4-13.

Figure 4-13: The FINDPUBL application lets you specify the name of a publisher to search for.

When the user clicks on the Find Publisher Button, the program prompts him or her with an Input Box for the name of the publisher to search for. Then it uses the user's response to build the argument of the FindFirst Method. The criteria argument for the search is as follows:

```
criteria = "Name LIKE'" & PubName$ & "'"
```

PubName$ is the string the user typed into the Input Box. We use the relational operator LIKE for the comparison because the user may not know the publisher's full and exact name. If the user knows the name of the publisher and types **Ventana** into the Input Box, the expression will become

```
"Name LIKE 'Ventana'"
```

This expression, however, will not match any record if the publisher's full name is "Ventana Press." The user can also enter a string like **Ventana*** to locate publishers whose name begins with the string Ventana, followed by any other character(s).

This string is used with the FindFirst Method on the Data1.Recordset (Publishers) to find the first matching publisher. Here's the routine that locates publishers by name:

```
Private Sub FindPublisher_Click ( )

PubName$ = InputBox("Enter Publisher's name →
to search for")
    If PubName$ = "" Then
        Exit Sub
    Else
        criteria = "Name LIKE'" & PubName$ & "'"
        Data1.Recordset.FindFirst criteria
        If Data1.Recordset.NoMatch Then
            MsgBox "No such Publisher in the database"
            Exit Sub
        Else
            NextButton.Enabled = True
        End If
    End If

End Sub
```

If the FindFirst Method is successful, the Find Next Button, which will locate more publisher names meeting the same criteria, is enabled. The code of the Find Next Button is much simpler because the criteria argument has been defined already (it is a global variable). The Find Next Button's Subroutine simply calls the FindNext Method with the already prepared argument:

```
Private Sub NextButton_Click ( )

    Data1.Recordset.FindNext criteria
    If Data1.Recordset.NoMatch Then
```

```
        MsgBox "No more matching records found!"
        NextButton.Enabled = False
    Else
        NextButton.Enabled = True
    End If

End Sub
```

We have seen how to use the Data Control and how to manipulate a Table with the Recordset's Properties and Methods, but we are still scratching the surface of Visual Basic's powerful database handling capabilities. Now it's time for some more heavy-duty database programming.

## Working With Multiple Tables

Now we'll move up a level in the complexity of our examples, toward a real-life situation. An application that looks at just publishers or just customers is of rather limited practical value. In most practical cases, you will have to combine data from multiple Tables. An application like the one shown in Figure 4-14, which displays the titles along with the publishers' names, is much more likely to be required in a real-world situation.

### Example: The BOOKS Application

CD-ROM

The application in Figure 4-14 is called BOOKS, and it can be found in the 4\APPS\BOOKS subdirectory on the CD.

Figure 4-14: The BOOKS application combines fields from three different Tables to display each title.

Let's gang the Tables of the BIBLIO database together so that when the user moves to a different title, the publisher of the new title will be displayed as well. The frames that contain the fields are Labels, so they can't be changed by the user. This application contains an extra Data Control. The one that allows the user to navigate through the Titles is called Data1. The other one, which is linked to the Publishers Table, remains invisible at run time. The Data1 Data Control is tied to the Titles Table of the database, and it serves the Labels that display the book's title and the year of publication. The Publisher Label accepts the Name field of the Publishers Table, through the second Data Control, Data2. In Figure 4-15 you see the BOOKS application at the design phase, including the invisible Control.

The most useful and common database operations involve multiple Tables.

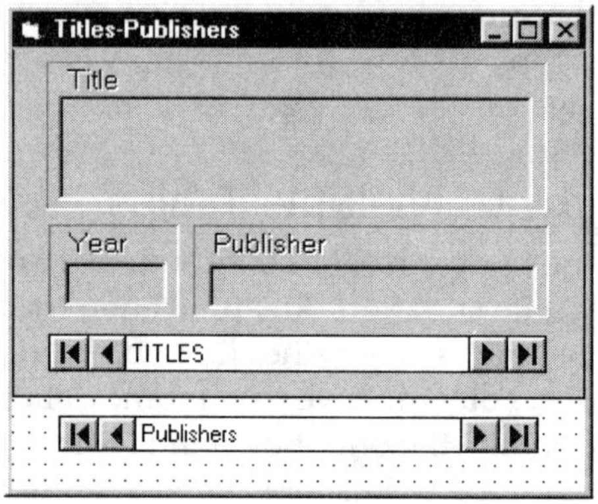


Figure 4-15: The BOOKS application during the design phase. The Data2 Data Control, which is tied to the Publishers Table, remains invisible at run time.

Every time the user clicks on the Data Control, the application displays the Title and the Publication Year fields from the Titles Table—this happens because the DataSource and DataField Properties of these two Labels were set properly at the design phase. If you were to run the application at this stage, you would see all the titles in the Table, but the publishers' names wouldn't change. (What you will see is the first publisher in the Publishers Table.) Each Data Control is completely independent from any other. You can make all Data Controls visible at run time and see for yourself that they operate independently from one another and you can display any title, along with any publisher, on the Form.

### Connecting the Tables

To connect the fields of the various Tables, we must do some programming. There is no simple way to specify a restriction like "Whenever the Data1 Data Control changes, cause the Data2 Data Control to move to the record whose PubID field is the same as the PubID field of the current record in the Titles Table." Fortunately, we don't need to write more than a few lines of code because much of the functionality we are after has already been built into the language.

In order to display the appropriate publisher name, we must set the RecordSource Property of the Data2 Data Controls to the appropriate field of the Publishers Table. In other words, the RecordSource Property of the Data2 should not be the entire Publishers Table, but only the row whose PubID field matches the PubID field of the current title. The invisible Data Control need not see the entire Table. It is possible to specify only a range of records, selected according to our application's requirements. And the way to do this, logically enough, is by changing the setting of the RecordSource Property of the Control.

You can change a Data Control's RecordSource Property at run time to select a different Recordset.

How do we change the RecordSource Property at run time so that it points to a specific row (record) of the Table? The answer is what you were probably afraid of: with an SQL statement. Although SQL statements will be presented in detail later in this chapter, we will use a few simple SQL statements here to complete our example.

The SQL statement for the Data2 (Publishers) Data Control should be as follows:

```
Data2.RecordSource = "SELECT * FROM Publishers →
WHERE PubID= " & Data1.Recordset.Fields("PubID")
```

This SQL statement searches the Publishers Table for a row in which the PubID field matches the value of the PubID field of the selected row in the Titles Table. The Jet Engine locates the matching publisher's record instantly because the PubID field is the primary key in the Publishers Table. The fact that the matching fields have the same names is coincidental—although this will be the case in most databases. Why use different names for fields that serve the same purpose?

A Recordset need not be an entire Table. You can use an SQL command to select the records you're interested in.

Notice that the RecordSetType Property of the Data2 Control must be 2 (Snapshot). A Table Recordset can't be defined with an SQL statement, and can't be anything less, or anything more, than a database Table. (Snapshots and other types of Recordsets are explained in the next section.) Also make sure that the SQL statements are typed exactly as shown here. If you make a typing error, you will get the wrong result but no error message. For more information on SQL statements, see the section "Structured Query Language" later in this chapter.

The changes we make in the RecordSource Property of the Data Control will not take effect immediately. To force the new Properties to take effect, we must execute the Refresh Method for the second Control:

```
Data2.Refresh
```

Where do we insert the previous lines? If you look at the Data Control's Events, you'll find an Event called Reposition. The Reposition Event is invoked every time the user moves to another record by clicking on one of the Control's buttons. Here is the complete code of the Data1 Data Control's Reposition Event:

```
Private Sub Data1_Reposition ( )

    Data2.RecordSource = "SELECT Name FROM Publishers →
    WHERE PubID=" & Data1.Recordset.Fields("PubID")
    Data2.Refresh

Exit Sub
```

SQL statements are a great way to locate items in a database. However, they require a certain amount of overhead. SQL statements are not executed directly by Visual Basic. They are passed to the underlying database management system, which executes them. We won't get into any deep technical details regarding the execution of SQL commands, but it wouldn't be a bad idea to time our program. Insert the following line at the beginning of the Data1_Reposition( ) Subroutine:

```
t1# = Timer
```

And insert these lines right before End Sub (these lines exist in the BOOKS application, but they are commented out):

```
t2# = Timer
Debug.Print t2# - t1#
```

Then run the application, and move from one title to the other with the Data Control. On our 486/66 system, the execution time of the Reposition subroutine is approximately 330 milliseconds (nearly a third of a second). Considering the size of the database, a third of a second is a considerable amount of time.

Can we do any better? The answer is yes, and we will return to this application to make it faster, but only after looking more closely at Recordsets.

# BEYOND THE DATA CONTROL

A database is a (potentially) huge collection of data. Some databases may contain Tables that users will never look at, either because they don't need them or aren't allowed to look at them. If you're making purchasing decisions, you probably don't care about customers. You don't really need to know where items were sold. Instead, you want to know about your suppliers—which ones deliver on time, how much they charge, etc. In other situations, you may not be allowed to look at certain Tables. For example, much of the employee data may be available to anyone who has access to your company's main database, but to look at salaries or other personal data, you must have special privileges.

In practice, we never work with an entire database at once. Usually, we isolate the data we need and work with them. The set of data we are interested in is called a Recordset. We have seen how to use the RecordSource Property of the Data Control to specify a Table or part of a Table. This is the Data Control's Recordset. So far, we used the term *Recordset* to describe the collection of records we can access (and manipulate) through the Data Control. Now let's explore the various types of Recordsets, how they are defined and how to create and manage Recordsets without using the Data Control at all.

## Tables, Dynasets & Snapshots

The Data Control lets you see part of the database through the Recordset object. In other words, the Recordset is the object that contains the data Visual Basic extracts from the database according to your commands. If you look at the settings of the RecordsetType Property of a Data Control, you'll see that there are three different types of Recordsets: Tables, Dynasets and Snapshots. To access the contents of one of these objects in a database without the help of the Data Control (as we were doing so far), we must create a variable with the type Recordset and assign to it the contents of the Recordset object we want to access. Let's explore the three different types of Recordsets and when to use them.

A Table is an object that contains all the rows of an actual Table. If you want to access a database Table directly, without the Data Control, you must create a Table-type Recordset variable and then assign to it the actual contents of a Table. Creating a Recordset variable is as simple as declaring it with the Dim statement and then using it.

A Dynaset is a set of records from one or more Tables, and it may contain selected items only. The difference between Tables and

Changes made to the database are immediately reflected in a Table-type Recordset.

Dynasets is that a Table can't contain anything less or anything more than the entire contents of a database Table. A Snapshot, finally, is similar to a Dynaset, but a Snapshot cannot be modified. Let's see why there are three different types of Recordsets and when to use each type.

After creating a new database, you will probably have to enter lots of data (customer names, product codes, publishers, book titles, etc.). This is when you use a *Table-type* Recordset. You just fill the whole thing up with new data. Also, if you want to make massive updates to your data, such as adding a prefix to all records in a certain field or changing a date throughout a Table, then you must open a Table-type Recordset. In other words, we open a Table-type Recordset when we need access to every record in a table.

Dynasets can combine data from more than one Table, and a Dynaset need not be as long as the Table it references. A Dynaset-type Recordset may contain the new book titles and the corresponding publisher (for example, books published in 1994), or the items that have been sold to customers in California. The Dynaset-type Recordset could be significantly smaller than any of the Tables involved, which in turn will make the program run faster.

A very important distinction between Tables and Dynasets is the fact that Dynasets are not refreshed automatically. In other words, if another user adds a new title in the BIBLIO database after our Dynaset is created, that title will not show up in the Dynaset. The Dynaset is a partial image of the database, an image of the state of the database at the moment the Dynaset was created. This is not true with Tables, which are always synchronized with the database. In Microsoft's terminology, this is called *membership*. If the Recordset's type is Table, the membership changes dynamically; if the Recordset's type is Dynaset, the membership can't change unless you refresh that Recordset explicitly. Changes made to a Dynaset-type Recordset can be written back to the database if the programmer uses the Update Method.

The third type of Recordset, the Snapshot, is, as the name implies, a "snapshot" of the database. When you create a Snapshot-type Recordset, Visual Basic goes to the database, picks up the records you requested and never looks at the database again for as long as you work with the Recordset. Moreover, you can't change the database through a Snapshot-type Recordset. If you are writing an invoicing application, like the VBINV application we present toward the end of this chapter, you can store the customer names in a Snapshot-type Recordset because you need only to look up customers, not enter new ones.

Snapshots are the most restrictive type of Recordset, but they should be used most often in decision-support applications—applications that analyze data and need not update the database. By using Snapshots, not only do you make the programs run faster, but you also protect a user from accidentally overwriting original data with the results of possible "what-if" scenarios (provided you're interested in trends, and not the most up-to-date data).

Unlike Tables and Dynaset variables, Snapshots can't modify the database.

From a programmer's point of view, the most important distinction among the three types of Recordsets is the fact that Dynaset- and Snapshot-type Recordsets can be the results of queries. A Dynaset-type Recordset, for example, may contain the titles that were published in 1994. A Snapshot-type Recordset may contain the invoices issued to customers with State = "CA." A Table, however, is an entity of the database that can't be broken down, and therefore can't be the result of a query.

## Programming Recordsets

Let's move beyond the Data Control and see how we can handle databases with Visual Basic commands. In this section, we'll open a database, create and manipulate all types of Recordsets and perform operations that can't be performed with the Data Control. If the previous section left some questions about the various types of Recordsets, things should become very clear now, as we see how the Recordsets are created and used.

Visual Basic's Data Control is probably not the tool you would choose to build a professional database application. The no-programming approach to databases is a short-lived illusion. It can come in handy in simple situations, but you shouldn't rely on it as a way of manipulating and navigating large volumes of data. Visual Basic itself, however, is widely used for writing database applications, especially front-end applications. You must merely abandon the Data Control in favor of using the powerful collection of VB database programming commands.

### Opening a Database

To open a database programmatically, you must first dimension a variable of the Database type and use the OpenDatabase command:

```
Dim DB As Database
Set DB = OpenDatabase(db_name)
```

Here, db_name is the name of an existing database, such as "C:\VB\BIBLIO.MDB", or the FileName Property of the File Open Common Dialog. You can also specify certain options when you open a database. Here is the complete syntax of the OpenDatabase command:

```
OpenDatabase(db_name[, exclusive[, readonly[, connect]]])
```

In this statement, *exclusive* and *readonly* are either True or False. If you open a database as exclusive, no one else can use it until you close it. Certain operations, such as repairing a database, require that it be open in exclusive mode. If you need only to look up data in the database and make no changes, then open it as readonly, with a command like this:

```
Set DB = OpenDatabase("C:\VB\BIBLIO.MDB", False, True)
```

The last argument in the complete OpenDatabase command syntax, *connect*, is a string, which is used only if you want to connect to databases created with programs other than Visual Basic or Access. For example, to connect to a database created with dBASE III, use the string "dBASE III." You can connect to a variety of external databases, but in this chapter we will deal with native, Visual Basic and Access databases only. They are the databases created by the Data Manager application or by Access, and they have the extension MDB.

### Creating Recordsets

Once the database has been opened, you need a way to look at its contents. You can't access the contents of the database directly. First, you must decide what part of the database you need and then create a Recordset (of Table, Dynaset or Snapshot type) that contains this information.

The Method for creating the various Recordset types is called OpenRecordset, and its syntax is

Recordsets are accessed through Recordset variables.

```
Set <variable> = database.OpenRecordset(source[, type[, →
options]])
```

where <variable> is a variable defined as Recordset. *source* is the database where the data will come from, and it can be a Table name, a query name or an SQL statement that returns records. For a Table-type Recordset, the source can only be a Table name.

The *type* argument determines the Recordset's type and may have one of the following values:

| | |
|---|---|
| dbOpenTable | For a Table-type Recordset object. |
| dbOpenDynaset | For a Dynaset-type Recordset object. |
| dbOpenSnapshot | For a Snapshot-type Recordset object. |

When opening a new Recordset, you can also set a number of options with the *option* argument. Table 4-4 lists the most common options, which you can combine with the OR operator.

| | |
|---|---|
| dbDenyWrite | Other users can't modify or add records. |
| dbDenyRead | Other users can't view records (Table-type Recordset only). |
| dbReadOnly | You can only view records; other users can modify them. |
| dbAppendOnly | You can only append new records (Dynaset-type Recordset only). |
| dbInconsistent | Inconsistent updates are allowed (Dynaset-type Recordset only). |
| dbConsistent | Only consistent updates are allowed (Dynaset-type Recordset only). |
| dbSeeChanges | Generate a run-time error if another user is changing data you are editing. |

Table 4-4: The most common Recordset options.

For example, to open a Table-type Recordset that accepts new records and other users can't modify, use the following argument:

```
option = dbDenyRead OR dbAppendOnly
```

VB3 provided three different Methods for creating Recordsets: OpenTable, CreateDynaset and CreateSnapshot. The names of these Methods also reflected the nature of the Recordsets. Tables can only be "opened," but Dynasets and Snapshots must be "created." These Methods are supported in VB4 for compatibility reasons, but all types of Recordsets are created with the OpenRecordset Method.

To create a Table-type Recordset, use these commands:

```
Dim DB As Database, TBLTitles As Recordset
Set DB = OpenDatabase("C:\VB\BIBLIO.MDB")
Set TBLTitles = DB.OpenRecordset("Titles", dbOpenTable)
```

The Recordset returned by this OpenRecordset Method contains all the rows of the Table. TBLTitles is a Table-type Recordset, not the Table itself. TBLTitles contains the rows of the Titles Table, but it is a new, distinct object. In a multiuser environment, another user may be accessing the same Table through a different variable.

To create a Dynaset variable, use the OpenRecordset Method with the dbOpenDynaset argument. When creating Dynaset-type Recordsets, you can specify either the name of a Table, or an SQL statement that specifies which records will be retrieved from the database. Here are the commands that open the BIBLIO database and create a Dynaset-type Recordset based on the Publishers Table:

```
Dim DB As Database, DYNAPubs As Recordset
Set DB = OpenDatabase("C:\VB\BIBLIO.MDB")
Set DYNAPubs = DB.OpenRecordset("Publishers", →
dbOpenDynaset)
```

If you want to look at the Publishers Table but not make any changes, create a Snapshot-type Recordset instead. Use the same sequence of commands, but replace the dbOpenDynaset argument with dbOpenSnapshot:

```
Dim DB As Database, SNAPPubs As Recordset
Set DB = OpenDatabase("C:\VB\BIBLIO.MDB")
Set SNAPPubs = DB.OpenRecordset("Publishers", →
dbOpenSnapshot)
```

*Note:* In this book we are using the prefixes TBL, DYNA and SNAP to indicate Recordsets of the corresponding type.

Dynasets and Snapshots are more flexible than Table Recordset because they can accept the results of SQL statements. Instead of the Table name in the corresponding Method, use an SQL statement. (SQL statements will be discussed in detail shortly.) Here are the commands that create a Dynaset with the titles and their publishers:

```
Dim DB As Database
Dim DYNATitles As Recordset
SQL$ = "SELECT Titles.Title, Authors.Author, Publishers.Name"
SQL$ = SQL$ & "FROM Titles, Authors, Publishers"
SQL$ = SQL$ & "WHERE Titles.PubID = Publishers.PubID"
Set DYNATitles = DB.OpenRecordset(SQL$, dbOpenDynaset)
```

Most of the Data Control's Properties and Methods apply to Recordset variables as well.

All the Properties of the Recordset object of a Data Control apply to Table-, Dynaset- and Snapshot-type Recordsets as well. The references to the object Data1.Recordset must be replaced with references to a Recordset variable. The following command assigns to the TotRows variable the number of rows in the Recordset of the Data1 Data Control:

```
TotRows = Data1.Recordset.RecordCount
```

This command assigns the number of rows in the DYNATitles Recordset to the same variable:

```
TotRows = DYNATitles.RecordCount
```

To access the first field of the current record in the Data1.Recordset, you would write a line like this:

```
Print Data1.Recordset.Fields(0)
```

You can print the value of the first field of the current record in a Table-type Recordset with the following command:

```
Print TBLTitles.Fields(0)
```

If the Recordset was a Dynaset, you'd have to use this command:

```
Print DYNATitles.Fields(0)
```

To navigate through a Recordset's records, use the MoveFirst, MoveLast, MovePrevious and MoveNext Methods. With the Data Control you would write this:

```
Data1.Recordset.MoveNext
```

But you can write this to move to the next row of a Dynaset-type Recordset:

```
DYNATitles.MoveNext
```

Or you can write this to move to the next row of a Table-type Recordset:

```
TBLTitles.MoveNext
```

Manipulating the records of a Table-, Dynaset- or Snapshot-type Recordset is no different than before. The AddNew, Edit, Update and Refresh Methods apply to both Table- and Dynaset-type Recordsets. As you can see, the Data Control is a camouflaged Recordset. It gives you easy access to the Tables of a database by hiding all the details we presented in this section. However, to be able to manipulate databases in any way you like, you must be able to use Recordsets.

## Ordering Records

All three types of Recordsets get the data from the specified Table(s) in the order in which the data were entered into the database. In most cases, when you open a Recordset variable, the records appear in a seemingly random order because this is how they are usually entered. There are ways, however, to present the data sorted in any fashion you like.

The Order Property of a Recordset object lets you order the data any way you like.

There are two different ways to sort data. A Table-type Recordset's data can be sorted according to one of the Table's indices. To specify the index by which the data will be sorted, use the Table's Index Property. This Property must be set only after the Table has been opened. If you don't specify an Index value, the Table variable will be sorted according to the Table's primary key.

Here is an example of the Index Property:

```
Dim DB As Database
Dim TBLProds As Recordset

Set DB = OpenDatabase("VBINC.MDB")
Set TBLProds = DB.OpenRecordset("PRODUCTS", dbOpenTable)
Debug.Print TBLProds.Fields("PROD_CODE"), →
TBLProds.Fields("PROD_DESCRIPTION") →
TBLProds.Index = "PRODUCTBYCATEGORY"
Debug.Print TBLProds.Fields("PROD_CODE"), →
TBLProds.Fields("PROD_DESCRIPTION")
```

This program segment opens the Products Table of the VBINC database as a Table-type Recordset and prints the fields PROD_CODE and PROD_DESCRIPTION of the first product. The product printed is the first one entered in the Products Table. Then, the program sets the Table's Index Property to "PRODUCTBYCATEGORY", which is the product's category, and again prints the same fields. The second time, a new product is printed, which is the product with the smallest category.

Here's what you will get if you execute the previous lines:

```
BVRG301  Chan's Regular Beer
BVRG310  Cold Dark Beer
```

The first field of the Table-type Recordset is different according to the current index.

The rows of a Table-type Recordset can be ordered only according to one of the Table's indices.

Table-type Recordsets can be sorted only according to one of the indices defined in the database. You can't create new indices at run time; neither can you sort a Table according to any field that is not an index. If you realize that an application calls for more indices than you have designed, you can always add new ones from within the Data Manager application.

Dynaset- and Snapshot-type Recordsets can be sorted in any way you like. If the variable was created with an SQL statement, the order of the records can be determined by the SQL statement itself. If you don't want to specify the order of the records from within the SQL statement, you can use the Sort Property of the Recordset variable. (Table-type Recordsets have an Index Property only—no Sort Property.) Here is how the Sort Property is used:

```
Dim DB As Database
Dim SNAPProds As Recordset

Set DB = OpenDatabase("VBINC.MDB")
Set SNAPProds = DB.OpenRecordset("PRODUCTS", →
dbOpenSnapshot)
Debug.Print SNAPProds.Fields("PROD_CODE")
SNAPProds.Sort = "PROD_CODE"
Set SNAPProds = SNAPProds.OpenRecordset( )
Debug.Print SNAPProds.Fields("PROD_CODE")
```

Here's the output of this short program:

```
BVRG301
BVRG010
```

Notice also in the previous code segment that the Sort Property can be set only after the Snapshot variable has been created. Moreover, it doesn't take effect immediately. Instead, we must rebuild the Snapshot with the new value of the Sort Property. To rebuild the Snapshot, we simply use the OpenRecordset Method on the SNAPProds variable, this time without arguments.

The Sort Property is much more flexible than the Table variable's Index Property, but it's slower as well. Every time you set the Sort Property's value, the data are actually sorted. This introduces some delay, which can become significant for large amounts of data. The Index Property introduces no delays because it already exists in the database. Visual Basic doesn't have to sort the data. It simply looks up the index and presents the data in the corresponding order.

### Filtering Recordsets

The Filter Property of the Recordset allows us to further limit the selected records. The Filter Property can be set to a string containing any Visual Basic expression, similar to the argument of the Find Method. To read all the dairy products into a Dynaset-type Recordset, first create the Recordset and then set its Filter Property:

```
Dim DB As Database
Dim DYNAProds As Recordset
Set DB = OpenDatabase("VBINC.MDB")
Set DYNAProds = DB.OpenRecordset("PRODUCTS")
DYNAProds.Filter = "PROD_CATEGORY = 'DAIRY' "
Set DYNAProds = DYNAProds.OpenRecordset( )
```

This code segment creates a Dynaset-type Recordset (DYNAProds) that contains all the rows of the PRODUCTS Table, and whose PROD_CATEGORY field is "DAIRY." You can't set the Filter Property on a nonexistent Dynaset. That's why we first create it, then set its Filter Property and "refresh" it. The second time we call the OpenRecordset Method, we don't have to specify the arguments again.

### Seeking Records in Tables

We have seen the Find Methods for locating records in the Data Control's Recordset. The same Methods apply to all types of Recordsets. When it comes to Table-type Recordsets, though, Visual Basic provides a much faster Method for locating records: the Seek Method.

The Seek Method locates records in a Table using the current index (which is either the primary index or the one you specified with the Index Property). The syntax of the Seek command is as follows:

```
Seek operator, key1, key2, ...
```

Unlike the Find Methods, the Seek Method uses an index to locate records instantly.

In this statement, operator is one of the relational operators shown in Table 4-5.

| | |
|---|---|
| = | Equal |
| > | Greater than |
| < | Less than |
| >= | Greater or equal |
| <= | Less or equal |

Table 4-5: The relational operators used with the Seek Method.

The key1, key2, etc., are the values to be compared to the key fields of the index. If the index is made up of a single key, you need only one argument following the comparison operator. The following commands open the Titles Table of the BIBLIO database and look for the title whose ISBN number is "1-0070447-527-X":

```
Dim DB As Database
Dim TBL As Recordset
Set DB = OpenDatabase("BIBLIO.MDB")
Set TBL = DB.OpenRecordset("Titles", dbOpenTable)
ISBNNum = "1-0070447-527-X"
TBL.Seek "=", ISBNNum
```

If such a record exists, the NoMatch Property of the TBL variable will be set to False, and the found record will become the current record.

Normally, we supply a value for each key in the index. Let's say that the index of a customer Table is the state, followed by the city. To locate customers in California, we can use a statement like this:

```
TBL.Seek "=", "CA"
```

In other words, we can omit the second key field. To locate customers in Santa Barbara, CA, we must use a statement like this:

```
TBL.Seek "=", "CA", "Santa Barbara"
```

The state value can't be omitted because the state is the first field in the index.

To summarize, the Seek Method is much faster, and is the preferred Method when possible. The Find Method may not be as fast, but its facilities are much more generic and can be used to perform searches on any field, or combination of fields, of the Recordset. The following example is a demonstration of the Seek Method.

### EXAMPLE: POPULATING LISTS FROM MULTIPLE TABLES

Our next example is an application that demonstrates how to combine data from multiple Tables using the Seek Method. In Figure 4-16 you see the PUBTITLS application. The List on the left contains the names of all publishers. Every time the user double-clicks on a publisher name, the titles published by that publisher, along with the names of the authors, are displayed in the second List. This application shows how to create Snapshots using the Sort Property and how to use their contents to populate Lists. It also makes use of the Seek Method to quickly locate each title's author.

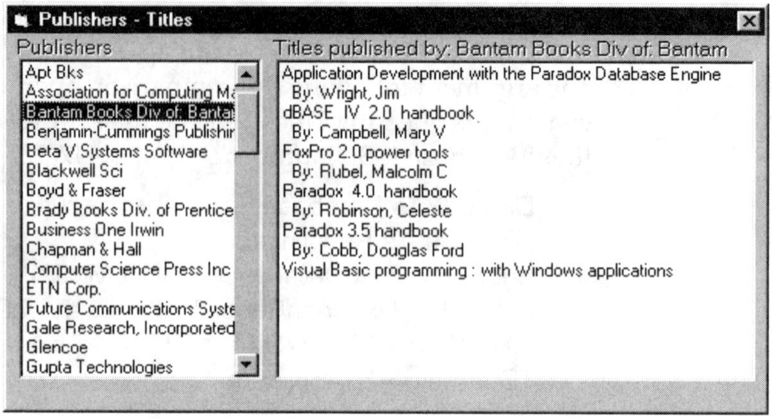


Figure 4-16: Combining data from multiple Tables with the List Box Control.

You can combine the Find and Seek Methods to locate data across Tables.

When the program starts, the list of publishers is created as a Snapshot-type Recordset that contains all the rows of the Publishers Table. Then we scan each element in the Snapshot and append the [Company Name] field (the publisher's name) to the List. At the same time, we assign the PubID field's value to the ItemData Property of the corresponding item in the List. Later on, we want to be able to retrieve the titles published by a specific publisher. The Titles and Publishers Tables are connected through the publisher's ID (the PubID field) and not the publisher's name. We need, therefore, to keep track of the publishers' IDs, and what better place to store them than the List's ItemData Property? Here is the code that populates the left List:

```
Private Sub Form_Load()
Dim SNAPPublishers As Recordset

On Error GoTo NoDatabase
    Set DB = OpenDatabase("c:\vb\biblio.mdb")
    Set SNAPPublishers = DB.OpenRecordset("Publishers", →
    dbOpenSnapshot)
    SNAPPublishers.Sort = "[Company Name]"
    Set SNAPPublishers = SNAPPublishers.OpenRecordset()
    While Not SNAPPublishers.EOF
        LstLine$ = SNAPPublishers.Fields("Company Name")
        List1.AddItem LstLine$
        List1.ItemData(List1.NewIndex) = →
        SNAPPublishers.Fields("PubID")
        SNAPPublishers.MoveNext
    Wend
```

```
    Exit Sub

NoDatabase:
    MsgBox "Couldn't create Recordset. Please make sure →
    the BIBLIO database in the current directory"
    End

End Sub
```

The List is populated when the program starts. Notice that we first create the SNAPPublishers Recordset and then sort it according to the [Company Name] field. When an entry in the first List is double-clicked upon, we must clear the second List and add all the books published by the selected publisher. In the Double_Click( ) Subroutine of the left List, we create another Snapshot-type Recordset, consisting of all the entries in the Titles Table whose PubID field matches the ID of the selected publisher. This ID has been stored in the ItemData Property of the selected item in the first List.

Also, for each title in the Snapshot, the program locates the author's name in the Authors Table. Notice that we have the book's ISBN, which we use as a pointer to the [Title Author] Table. There, we locate the author's ID, which is then used to look up the author's name in the Authors Table. Locating the author's record is a matter of seeking for a known ID in the Authors Table with the Seek Method. Here is the code that creates the Snapshot-type Recordset and then populates with it the second List:

```
Private Sub List1_DblClick()
Dim SNAPTitles As Recordset
Dim TBLISBNAuthor  As Recordset
Dim TBLAuthors As Recordset

    List2.Clear
    SSPanel2.Caption = "  Titles published by: " + List1.TEXT
    Set SNAPTitles = DB.OpenRecordset("Titles",   →
    dbOpenSnapshot)
    SNAPTitles.Sort = "Title"
    SNAPTitles.Filter = "[PubID]=" &   →
    Str$(Trim(List1.ItemData(List1.ListIndex)))
    Set SNAPTitles = SNAPTitles.OpenRecordset()
    Set TBLISBNAuthor = DB.OpenTable("Title Author")
    TBLISBNAuthor.Index = "ISBN"
```

```
        Set TBLAuthors = DB.OpenRecordset("Authors",  →
        dbOpenTable)
        TBLAuthors.Index = "PrimaryKey"

        While Not SNAPTitles.EOF
            LstLine$ = SNAPTitles.Fields("Title")
            List2.AddItem LstLine$
            TBLISBNAuthor.Seek "=", SNAPTitles.Fields("ISBN")
            If Not TBLISBNAuthor.NoMatch Then
                TBLAuthors.Seek "=", TBLISBNAuthor.Fields("Au_ID")
                If Not TBLAuthors.NoMatch Then
                    LstLine$ = "   By: " + TBLAuthors.Fields("Author")
                    List2.AddItem LstLine$
                Else
                    LstLine$ = "   Author Not Listed"
                    List2.AddItem LstLine$
                End If
            End If
            SNAPTitles.MoveNext
        Wend

    End Sub
```

The DB variable is dimensioned in the Form's declaration section because it is used by both Subroutines. Here is its declaration:

```
    Dim DB As database
```

This is a very short program, given the complexity of the operations it performs. Just consider for a moment all the housekeeping you would do if you had to provide a similar solution with flat, random access files.

This example application is of rather limited interest. However, the same approach would apply to many situations. Instead of publishers and titles, you could have a list of customers and invoices. By clicking on a customer name, you would see all the invoices issued to the specific customer in the last month. Then by clicking on an individual invoice header, you could see all the details (lines) of the selected invoice. You could also apply more restrictions to the Snapshot. For example, you could display only customers that have not paid an invoice within 60 days after the date on the invoice. And so on and so forth.

The Data Bound Controls are good for designing data entry and very simple browsing applications. For more advanced and practical applications, you'll be using unbound Controls, which you have to populate yourself. In an example below, SQLGRID, you'll see how to extract the data contained in a Recordset and display them on a Grid Control, without any prior knowledge of the Recordset's contents.

## The BOOKS Application Revisited

Earlier in the chapter (in the "Working With Multiple Tables" section) we saw the BOOKS application, which displayed data from different Tables with the help of the Data Control's RecordSource Property and SQL statements. We promised you then to improve the application. Now that we've explored the concepts of Recordsets and the Seek Method, we'll see a better way of connecting multiple Tables in an application.

Let's take advantage of the fact that the Au_ID and PubID fields are the primary keys for their Tables. This time we'll use the Seek command to move instantly to the matching records in the Authors and Publishers Tables. (The modified application, BOOKSEEK, is shown in Figure 4-17, and can be found in the 4\APPS\BOOKSEEK subdirectory on the CD.)

CD-ROM

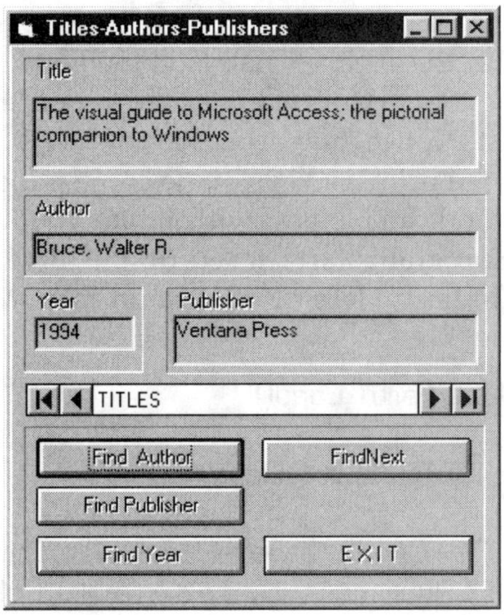


Figure 4-17:The BOOKSEEK application combines data from multiple Tables with the Seek Method.

### Example: The BOOKSEEK Application

As you recall from our previous discussion, the Seek Method can be used only with indexed Tables. This means that we can't use the Data Control any more. Instead, we will create three Table-type Recordsets, TBLTitleAuthor, TBLAuthors and TBLPublishers. Then, each time the user moves to another title with the Data1 Control, we'll use the ISBN, Au_ID and PubID fields to locate the corresponding author and publisher in the other two Tables. The two Recordsets are indexed on the appropriate keys (the default indices for both Tables), and we'll use the Seek Method on both. Before we present the actual code, let's describe what happens each time the user moves to a new title by clicking on the Data Control's arrows.

The book's title and publication year are automatically displayed because the corresponding Data Bound Controls are linked to the Data1 Data Control. Then we read the Pub_ID field of the current record and use it to locate and display the matching record in the Publishers Table (TBLPublishers Recordset). We also read the current title's ISBN field and use it to locate the matching record in the [Title Author] Recordset. Once the record is found, we have the current title's author ID. This number is then used to locate the matching record in the Authors Table (TBLAuthors Recordset). At this point, we can display the author's name on the Form.

All searches are performed with the Seek Method, and they are extremely fast. Notice, however, that this is possible because the search fields are primary keys of the corresponding Tables. Moreover, the Seek Method can be used with Table-type Recordsets only.

When the program starts, it sets up the three Recordsets and their appropriate indices. Here's initializaton code in the Form's Load Event:

```
Private Sub Form_Load()

On Error GoTo NoDataBase

    Set DB = OpenDatabase("c:\vb\BIBLIO.MDB")
    Set TBLPublishers = DB.OpenTable("Publishers")
    Set TBLAuthors = DB.OpenTable("Authors")
    Set TBLTitleAuthor = DB.OpenTable("Title Author")

    TBLPublishers.Index = "PrimaryKey"
    TBLAuthors.Index = "PrimaryKey"
    TBLTitleAuthor.Index = "ISBN"
```

```
    FindNextButton.Enabled = False
    Exit Sub

NoDataBase:
    MsgBox Error + Chr$(10) + " Program will end"
    End

End Sub
```

After the Recordsets have been set, they can be used from within the Data Control's Reposition Event to perform the necessary searches:

```
Private Sub Data1_Reposition()
Dim PubNum As Long, Authnum As Long, ISBNNum As String

 ' t1# = Timer
    PubNum = Data1.Recordset.Fields("PubID")
    TBLPublishers.Seek "=", PubNum
    If TBLAuthors.NoMatch Then
        BookPublisher.Caption = "Unknown Publisher"
    Else
        BookPublisher.Caption = TBLPublishers.Fields("Company →
        Name")
    End If

    ISBNNum = Data1.Recordset.Fields("ISBN")
    TBLTitleAuthor.Seek "=", ISBNNum
    If TBLTitleAuthor.NoMatch Then
        BookAuthor.Caption = "UNKNOWN AUTHOR"
        Exit Sub
     End If

    Authnum = TBLTitleAuthor.Fields("Au_ID")
    TBLAuthors.Seek "=", Authnum
    If TBLAuthors.NoMatch Then
        BookAuthor.Caption = "UNKNOWN AUTHOR"
    Else
        BookAuthor.Caption = TBLAuthors.Fields("Author")
    End If
 ' t2# = Timer()
 ' Debug.Print t2# - t1#

End Sub
```

The Seek Method is faster than both the Find Methods and SQL statements.

Now we're ready to time our new approach (the commands for timing the Subroutine are commented out in the listing). Although this time there are significantly more lines in the Subroutine, they are all executed faster than before. On the same 486/66 system, the execution times for the new Reposition Subroutine varied from 0 to 330 milliseconds. After moving back and forth in the Tables for a while, the execution time was consistently less than 55 milliseconds because many of the needed data were already in the cache. (You shouldn't count on such luck, however, because a real application will be handling much larger databases.) Even with a small database like BIBLIO, the Seek Method is on average at least four times faster than the previous technique. This gain in speed will become even more important with larger databases. (*Note:* Part of the gain is due to the fact that we have eliminated the overhead of the two Data Controls. Now we are going directly to the source, the Tables, extracting the data and placing them on the Labels.)

The BOOKSEEK application contains a few Command Buttons to locate records with the Find Method. The Find by Author and Find by Publisher Command Buttons use additional Data Controls to locate any author and publisher respectively. When you look for titles by author, the program prompts you with an Input Box to enter the name of the author you are looking for. Then it locates the author with the desired name in the Authors Table (if any), and extracts the Author's ID (field AU_ID). This field is then used to perform another search, in the [Title Author] Table, to locate the ISBN numbers of the titles written by the author. Then the ISBN number is used to locate the author's books in the Titles Table. If a title is found, the program displays it and enables the Find Next Command Button. The Find Buttons are examples of using the Find Methods across multiple Tables. The programming involved is fairly straightforward, so we won't cover it here. If you want, load the application into VB and look at the code.

## STRUCTURED QUERY LANGUAGE

Now we will move away from data manipulation commands and look at ways to extract information from databases in more complicated ways. The Seek and Find Methods of the Recordset object are good for connecting records of one Table to records of another Table, or doing simple searches, but decision making calls for complicated queries. To efficiently use the information stored in a database, we must be able to recall data in many different ways; combine data from multiple Tables, applying various restrictions; and finally summarize large volumes of data in a few meaningful numbers. The Find and Seek Methods would be very limiting to a manager, not to mention that he or she would need a small program for each type of data-retrieval operation required. The most flexible way to recall information from databases is through the use of a special language called Structured Query Language, or SQL.

You are certainly aware that Visual Basic supports SQL statements for locating records, and you may be wondering why we haven't mentioned them so far. SQL statements are indeed much more flexible than the Find and Seek Methods, but they are more complicated as well. If you want to make optimal use of your database, though, you need to master this language.

SQL is a universal language for database manipulation.

SQL is a language for manipulating databases, and a rather old one. Unlike most programming languages, SQL is a nonprocedural language. In other words, there are no procedures (subs or functions), and it operates at a much higher level than VB. A nonprocedural language is one that is told what to do, but not how to do it. For example, you can issue an SQL command to ask for all invoices issued to customers in California in the first quarter of 1995. How the computer does it is not your concern. The mechanism that performs the query and reports the results is a complicated one, but fortunately SQL hides it from you. (The database model we have used so far is called *navigational* because it makes use of the positions of the records in the Tables. Now we are switching to the *relational* model, which makes use of the relations between Tables.)

Another advantage of the SQL language is that it is universal. All database manufacturers implement the language in their products, and the developer need not be concerned with the specifics. Once you've learned SQL, you can program any database that provides an SQL interface. (The truth of the matter is that not all manufacturers conform to the exact same SQL standard. Some introduce additional commands; others use a slightly different syntax. But for the most part, SQL is a universal language for database manipulation—or at least as universal as one can expect in the computer industry.)

SQL provides many commands, for all types of operations you'd want to perform on a database. Covering the entire range of SQL is beyond the scope of this book. There are many books on SQL in the market, and if you are going to use it routinely you should have at least a good reference book on your desk. In this chapter we will cover the basic SQL commands for retrieving data from databases because this is what Visual Basic programmers will use it for most. We'll also look at some of the commands that perform massive updates in a database, which will come in handy at one time or another. The examples of this chapter are relatively simple. They are the type of commands you will be using most of the time. But SQL can become quite complicated, and you may have to resort at times to some really sophisticated SQL commands. As you become more and more experienced with the SQL syntax, however, you'll realize that many of the commands that may seem frightening now are not that complicated after all. Moreover, if you can't figure out the SQL command for a certain task, you always have the option to perform it with a sequence of Visual Basic commands. Or you can combine SQL statements with database manipulation commands. For example, you can first create a Recordset with the appropriate SQL statement and then manipulate the Recordset's contents with the Find and Seek Methods. Your code may not be as compact or as efficient, but it'll get the job done.

Select queries retrieve data. Action queries manipulate data.

An SQL command's job is to carry out a query. Some queries let you retrieve data from databases. These are called *select queries*. Others let you carry out certain actions on the database, and they are called *action queries*. We'll look first at the set of select query commands, which are also referred to as *Data Query Language (DQL)* or *data retrieval statements*. These commands obtain data from the Tables of a database in many different ways and determine how the selected data will be furnished to the application (sorted, grouped, etc.).

## Experimenting With SQL Statements

CD-ROM

Here's a small program that lets you enter and execute SQL statements and then displays the results. The SQLGRID application (in the 4\APPS\SQLGRID subdirectory of the CD) consists of three Forms. The SQL Query Definition Form (Figure 4-18) contains a Text Box where you enter an SQL statement. To execute the statement, click on the Execute Command Button. As soon as the results become available, they will be displayed in a Grid on the SQL Query Results Form.

To execute another SQL statement, type it in the SQL Query Definition Form's Text Box and click on the Execute Command Button again. The results of the new query will overwrite the previous contents of the Grid. The Clear SQL Button simply clears the Text Box with the SQL statement.

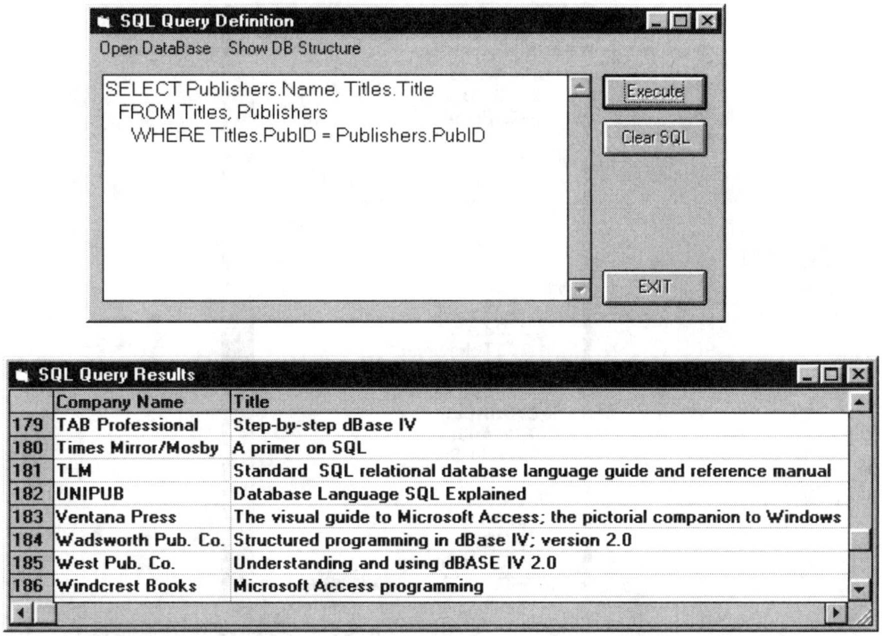


Figure 4-18: The SQLGRID application will help you explore SQL statements, by displaying their results on a Grid Control.

The SQL Query Definition Form also contains two menu options. The Open Database command lets you open a new database. Before executing an SQL statement, make sure that you've opened the appropriate database. The other menu option, Show DB Structure, displays the Database Structure Map, shown in Figure 4-19, which contains the structure of the database (Tables, their fields and indices). It's an interesting application, and we'll look at it in the section "Database Definitions" later in the chapter. We included it as a separate Form in the SQLGRID application so that you can look up the fields of any Table in a database from within SQLGRID, without having to switch to the Data Manager application.

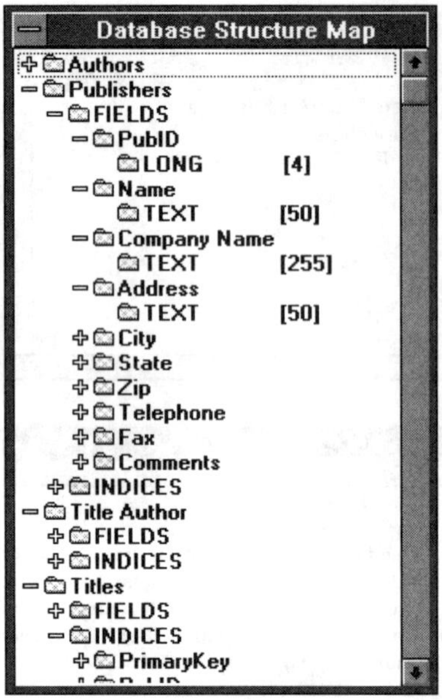


Figure 4-19: The Database Structure Map lets you view the structure of the current database from within the SQLGRID application.

If you want to look at the Tables and/or fields of a database, click on the Show DB Structure Command, and the Form shown in Figure 4-19 will appear. The first time this Form appears on the screen, it contains a list of the Tables in the database. Click on the plus sign in front of the Table you're interested in, and you'll see two headings underneath the name of the Table: FIELDS and INDICES. Click on either heading to see the list of the field names in the Table or the list of indices. Then click on a field name to see its data type, or on an index name to see the definition of the index. If you want to hide a list of fields or indices, click on the Table name or index name.

Later we'll look at the programming behind the SQLGRID application. For now, you can use it to familiarize yourself with the SQL language.

Notice that with Visual Basic comes a similar application, called VISDATA, which lets you enter SQL statements and displays the results. The VISDATA application does much more than that, however, and the programming involved is much too complicated to be presented here. SQLGRID is a simple application that focuses on Dynasets created with SQL statements, and we'll be able to explain its operation in this book.

## Select Queries

The purpose of a select query is to extract information from a database and put it into a Recordset. The Recordset can be a Dynaset or a Snapshot variable (but not a Table variable). The contents of the Recordset are defined in the SQL statement and may contain any combination of fields, from any Table in the database. User-defined constraints determine which rows will appear in the Recordset.

An SQL select statement starts with the verb SELECT followed by a list of fields on which the verb acts. The keyword FROM specifies the Table(s) to which the fields belong and a number of keywords, which we'll explain shortly. Here is the simplest form of a select query:

Select queries begin with the verb SELECT.

```
SELECT selection_list
FROM Table_list
```

selection_list is a list of fields, and Table_list the list of the Tables to which the specified fields belong. Here is a simple select query:

```
SELECT Author
FROM Authors
```

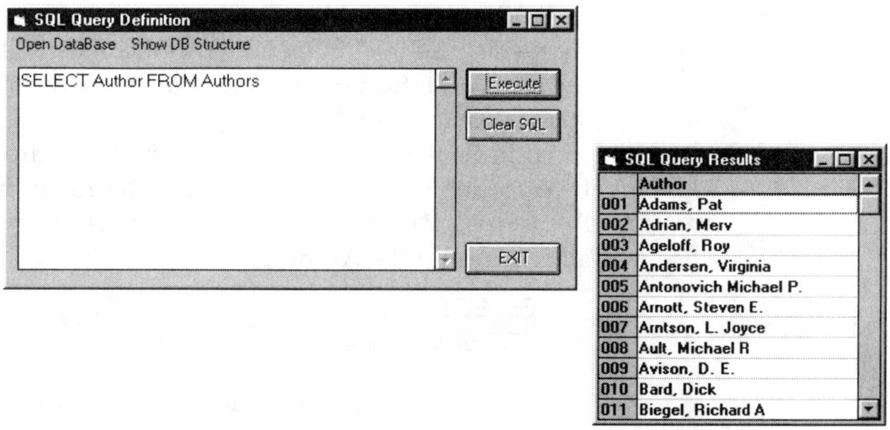


Figure 4-20: This is the simplest query: it returns an entire column (field) from a Table.

This query selects all author names from the Authors Table and returns them. "Author" is the field name we are interested in, and "Authors" is the Table it belongs to. In effect, this statement returns the Author column of the Authors Table.

Selection queries are used in building Recordsets, either with the RecordSource Property of the Data Control or with the OpenRecordset Method.

To create a Recordset that contains all the author names, first assign the previous SQL statement to a string variable:

```
SQL$ = "SELECT Author FROM Authors"
```

Then assign it to the Data Control's RecordSource Property:

```
Data1.Recordset.RecordSource = SQL$
```

The Data1.Recordset now contains the author names from the Authors Table.

To create a Dynaset variable with the same contents, use these commands:

```
Dim DB As Database
Dim DYNAAuthors As Dynaset
Set DB = OpenDatabase("BIBLIO.MDB")
Set DYNAAuthors = DB.OpenRecordset("SELECT Author →
FROM Authors", dbOpenDynaset)
```

Similarly, you can use the same SQL statement to create a Snapshot—just use the dbOpenSnapshot constant. At the end of this section, you'll find more ways of using SQL statements in your application.

Multiple field names in the selection_list are separated by commas. If you want to select all the rows of the Tables in the Table_list, use the asterisk (*). The following SQL statement returns all the rows and all columns of the Authors Table:

Use the * symbol to select all columns in a Table.

```
SELECT *
FROM Authors
```

SQL statements are indented, too, as if they were a small program. As statements become longer, indentation improves readability. In your programs, you'll type SQL statements on a single line. Also, SQL is not case-sensitive, but for clarity's sake we'll be using uppercase for SQL reserved keywords and lowercase for everything else. In your programs, you can use lowercase and uppercase as you wish.

The WHERE keyword limits the scope of the search to the rows of the Table that meet the search criteria. The general form of a select query with a WHERE clause looks like this:

```
SELECT selection_list
FROM Table_list
WHERE criteria
```

*criteria* is an expression that specifies some selection criteria. Only the records that meet the criteria will be returned.

The following statement returns the names of the publishers located in New York:

```
SELECT Name
FROM Publishers
WHERE State = 'NY'
```

Notice that literals are enclosed in single quotes. This makes it easy for programmers to prepare strings with SQL statements. To assign the previous SQL statement to a string variable before passing it to a command, you would have written this:

```
criteria$ = "SELECT Name FROM Publishers WHERE State = 'NY'"
```

If the state is stored in a variable, you can write this:

```
criteria$ = "SELECT Name FROM Publishers WHERE State = →
"'" & StateVar & "'"
```

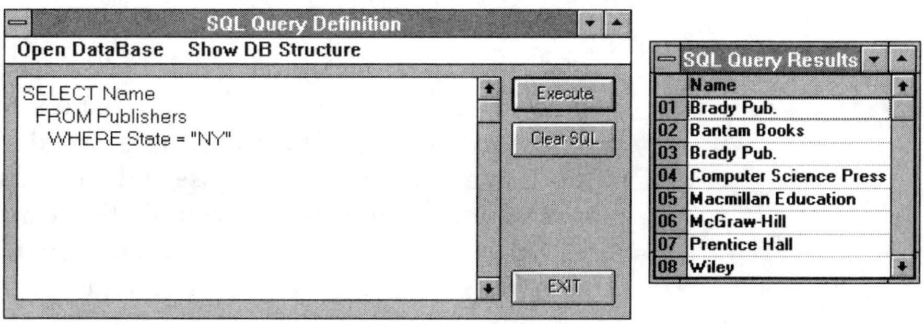


Figure 4-21: The WHERE clause limits the range of the resulting Recordset.

Field names, however, are not enclosed in quotes. This poses a small problem because Visual Basic allows for spaces in field names. Most programmers simply don't use spaces in the field names. If you have a field name consisting of more than one word, enclose the field in square brackets [], like [Company Name] or [State Tax].

Like Visual Basic, SQL provides a LIKE operator to recall data with wildcard characters.

### The LIKE Operator

The criterion State = 'NY' specifies exact matching. You can also use the regular relational operators like <, >, <>, <=, etc., just as you would use them with Visual Basic. In addition, SQL offers the LIKE operator, which lets you recall data with wild card characters. (Wild card characters are the asterisk, which can replace any string, and the question mark, which can replace any single character. Every DOS user is familiar with those two wild card characters.)

If you want to recall the record(s) of the author whose name begins with F, use the following statement:

```
SELECT Author
FROM Authors
WHERE Author LIKE "F*"
```

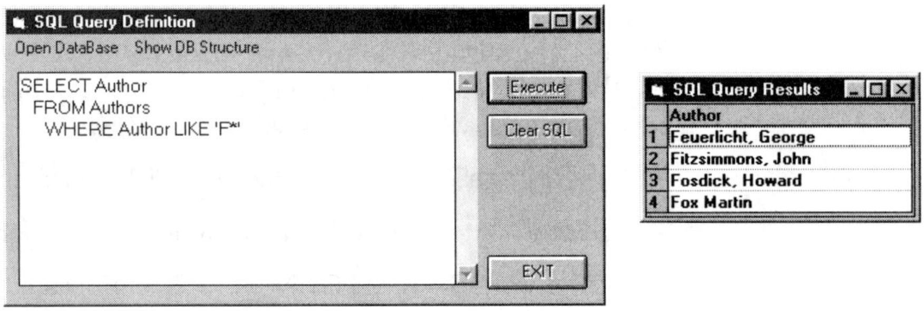


Figure 4-22: Use asterisks as wild card characters in SQL, just as you do to display file names in DOS.

This statement returns all authors whose last name begins with the character F. In string matching, you must use the equals (=) operator only if you know how the full name is stored in the database.

Let's open the VBINC database and recall the Code and Description fields of all products that contain the word *juice* in their description. Open the VBINC database with the Open Database command and then issue the following SQL statement:

```
SELECT Prod_Code, Prod_Description
FROM Products
WHERE Prod_Description LIKE "*juice*"
```

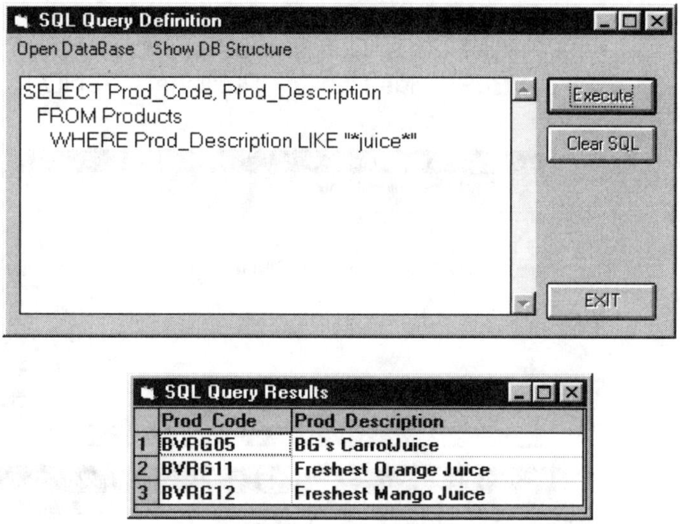


Figure 4-23: SQL string matching is case-insensitive.

This statement retrieves and displays on the Grid the product codes and descriptions of all products that have the string "juice" in their description. Notice that string matching with SQL statements is case-insensitive, as it is with the Find Method.

## Retrieving Data From Multiple Tables

SQL statements are not limited to single Tables. You can just as easily recall data from multiple Tables. In most cases we are interested in combining data from two, or even more, Tables. For example, we can recall all the titles in the BIBLIO database, but what about their publishers? A statement like this would return the titles along with a number, which is the ID of the publisher:

```
SELECT Title, PubID
FROM Titles
```

But the actual name of the publisher resides in a different Table. To make a query from two Tables, we must ask for the Title field in the Titles Table and the Name field in the Publishers Table. To select fields from multiple Tables, the field names must be prefixed by the name of the Tables they belong to. To make sure that each title will be displayed along with its publisher, we must impose the restriction that the publisher ID be the same in both rows:

```
SELECT Titles.Title, Publishers.Company
FROM Titles, Publishers
WHERE Title.PubID = Publishers.PubID
```

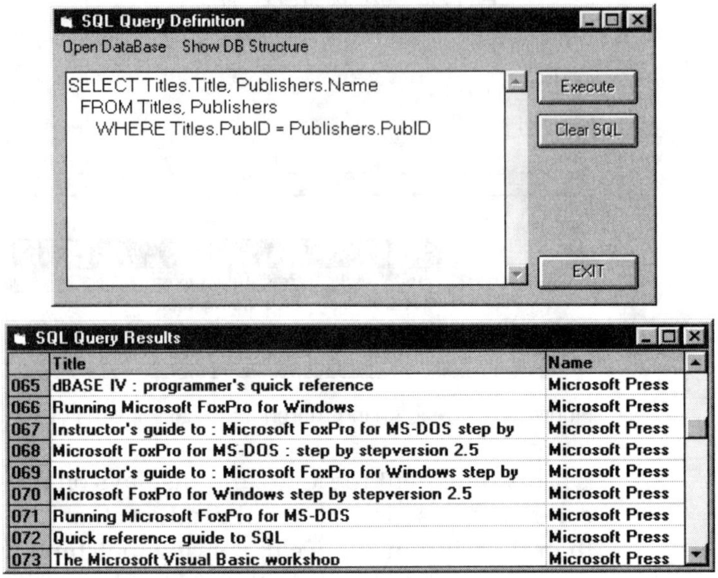


Figure 4-24: Pairing data from two different Tables.

---

If the names of the fields are unique in the specified Tables, they need not be prefixed by the Table's name. In the previous statement, we could have written *Titles.Title* as *Title* and *Publishers.Name* as *Name*. But the PubID field is common to both Tables, and the prefix becomes mandatory—or else Visual Basic wouldn't know which field to use. In the rest of the chapter we will prefix the field names with the corresponding Table names to make the statements easier to read.

---

This statement recalls all the rows of the Titles Table and the Publishers Table whose PubID fields match. The result of the query is a Recordset with two columns and as many rows as there are titles. If some titles were entered without a publisher, these titles will not be displayed.

The previous operation is called an *Inner-Join*. Inner-Joins allow us to combine two Tables on the basis of the value of a field that is common to both Tables. Inner-Joins are so common that SQL provides the keyword INNER JOIN for that purpose:

```
SELECT Titles.Title, Publisher.Name
FROM Titles, Publishers,
Titles INNER JOIN Publishers
ON Titles.PubID = Publishers.PubID
```

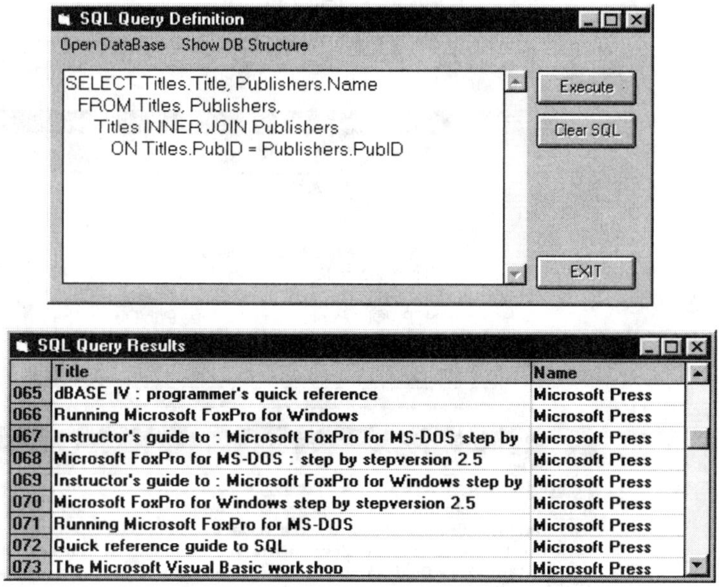

Figure 4-25: The Titles/Publishers collection as an Inner-Join.

When you execute this statement, the Titles and Publishers Tables are joined by the PubID column of both Tables. The INNER JOIN keyword appears between the names of the two Tables to be joined. Following the name of the second Table is the keyword ON, which specifies the fields to be used for joining the Tables and their relationship. The ON clause is identical to the WHERE clause of the last example.

If you omit the INNER JOIN clause in the previous SQL statement, the Recordset will contain all possible combinations of titles and publishers! This is called a Cross-Join, and it's very unlikely that you will ever need a *Cross-Join* in a real-life application. The number of rows in the result is the product of all publishers (67) times the number of all titles (229), which is 25,345 (imagine the size of a Cross-Join in a large database).

The idea of joined Tables can be extended to more than two Tables. The next statement combines all three Tables of the BIBLIO database. This query creates a Recordset that contains all titles, along with the publisher's name and the author's name:

```
SELECT Titles.Title, Authors.Author, Publishers.Name
FROM (([Title Author] INNER JOIN Titles
    ON [Title Author].ISBN = Titles.ISBN)
        INNER JOIN Authors
            ON [Title Author].Au_ID = Authors.Au_ID)
        INNER JOIN Publishers
            ON Titles.PubID = Publishers.PubID
```

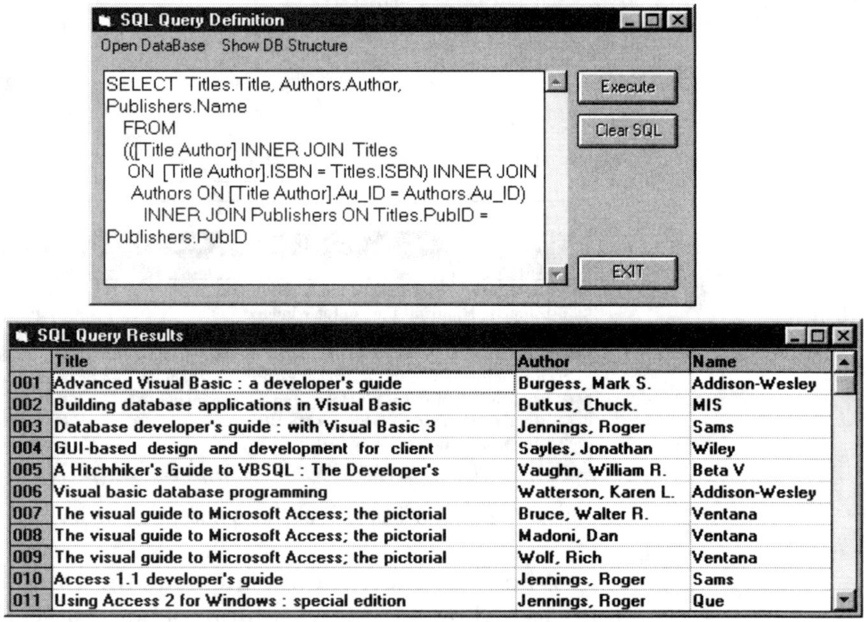


Figure 4-26: Combine data from multiple Tables with successive Inner-Joins.

To understand the previous SQL statement, you must examine the placement of the parentheses. The inner pair of parentheses creates a "ghost" Recordset that contains the records in the [Title Author] and Titles Tables whose ISBN fields match. We called this Recordset "ghost" because its contents will not appear in the final Recordset. We use it to go from the title's ISBN to the author names—the [Title Author] Table contains ISBN numbers and author IDs, neither of which show up on the Grid.

Then we create another Recordset, which contains the matching entries in the Authors Table (the one with the actual author names). The last INNER JOIN simply matches the Titles and Publishers Tables, based on the PubID field.

Here's another way to look at the SQL statement:

```
SELECT Titles.Title, Authors.Author, Publishers.Name
FROM (A Recordset that contains Titles and Authors)
INNER JOIN Publishers
ON Titles.PubID = Publishers.PubID
```

The definition of the first Recordset is more complicated than the Recordsets of the previous examples because we must combine three Tables. Get the title's ISBN, use it to find the corresponding entry in the [Title Author] Table, then get the Au_ID field and use it to find the corresponding entry in the Authors Table. Here is the definition of the first Recordset:

```
([Title Author] INNER JOIN Titles
    ON [Title Author].ISBN = Titles.ISBN)
INNER JOIN Authors
        ON [Title Author].Au_ID = Authors.Au_ID)
```

First we join the [Title Author] and Titles Tables based on the ISBN fields, and then the result with the Authors Table, based on the Au_ID field.

### Left- & Right-Joins

Besides the INNER JOIN, you can create *Left-Joins* and *Right-Joins.* The INNER JOIN operation combines records from two Tables whenever there are matching values in a field common to both Tables. The Right-Join includes all the records from the second (right-hand) Table, even if there are no matching values in the first (left-hand) Table.

If you want a list of all publishers, even if they have no titles in the Titles Table, use the following statement:

```
SELECT Titles.Title, Publishers.Name
FROM Titles, Publishers,
    Titles RIGHT JOIN Publishers
    ON Titles.PubID = Publishers.PubID
```

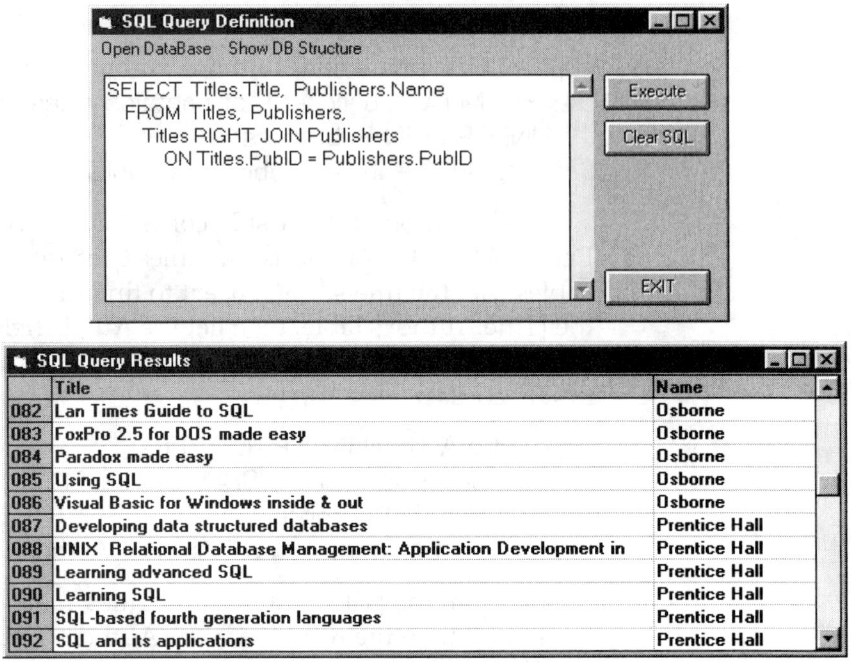


Figure 4-27: Right-Joins include all the records from the right-hand Table but only the matching records of the left-hand Table.

This statement returns all rows of the Publishers Table and the titles they have published from the Titles Table. The INNER JOIN would not have returned the publishers that don't have a matching value in the Titles Table.

The LEFT JOIN includes all the records (rows) from the first of the two Tables (the one appearing on the left), even if there are no matching values for records in the other Table (the one on the right). If you create a Left-Join on the Titles and Publishers Tables of the BIBLIO database, the resulting Recordset will contain some publishers without any titles:

```
SELECT Titles.Title, Publishers.Name
FROM Titles, Publishers,
    Publishers LEFT JOIN Titles
    ON Titles.PubID = Publishers.PubID
```

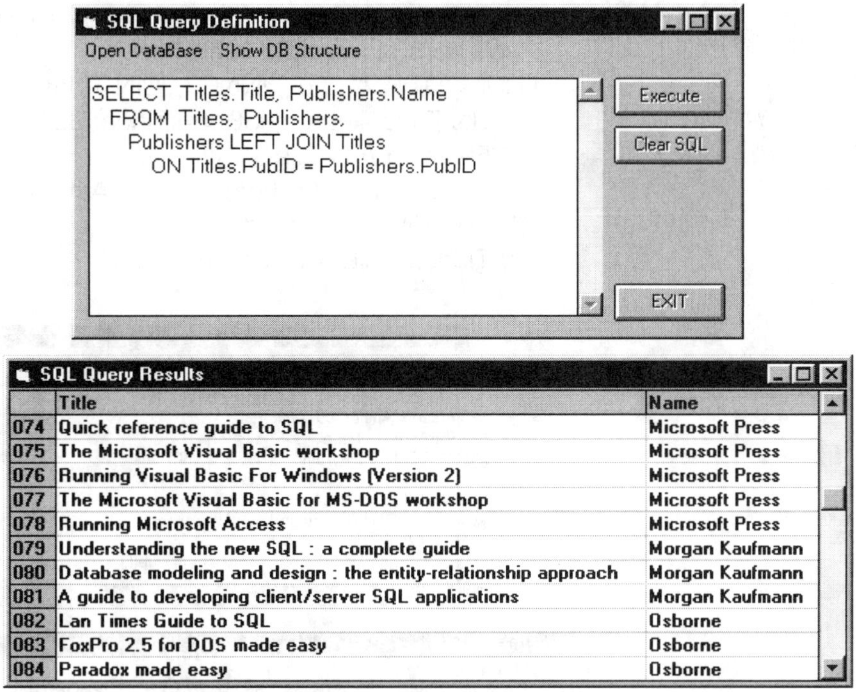


Figure 4-28: Left-Joins return all the records from the left-hand Table, but only the matching records of the right-hand Table.

Both statements returned the same Recordset—notice the similarity between the Left- and Right-Joins. Apart from differing in the LEFT (RIGHT) keyword, the names of the Tables joined are inverted. Execute the same two SQL statements without switching the order of the Tables.

## The AS Option

As you may have noticed, the title of each column of the Recordset returned by an SQL statement is identical to the field name as it appears in the SQL statement. That's why the heading for the author's name is always "Author." (You could have typed **AUTHOR** as well. Field names are not case-sensitive, and this poses no problem to Visual Basic.)

But what if you wanted to use a different heading, like "By" or "Author's Name?" The keyword AS lets you specify the column title for each field in the resulting Recordset. Here is the SQL statement that combines all the Tables in the BIBLIO database with different headings for each column of the Recordset:

A column's title is by default the field's name, but you can change it with the AS keyword.

```
SELECT Titles.Title AS [Book Title], Authors.Author AS [Author],
Publishers.Name AS [Publisher]
FROM ([Title Author] INNER JOIN Titles
    ON [Title Author].ISBN = Titles.ISBN)
INNER JOIN Authors
        ON [Title Author].Au_ID = Authors.Au_ID)
INNER JOIN Publishers
ON Titles.PubID = Publishers.PubID
```

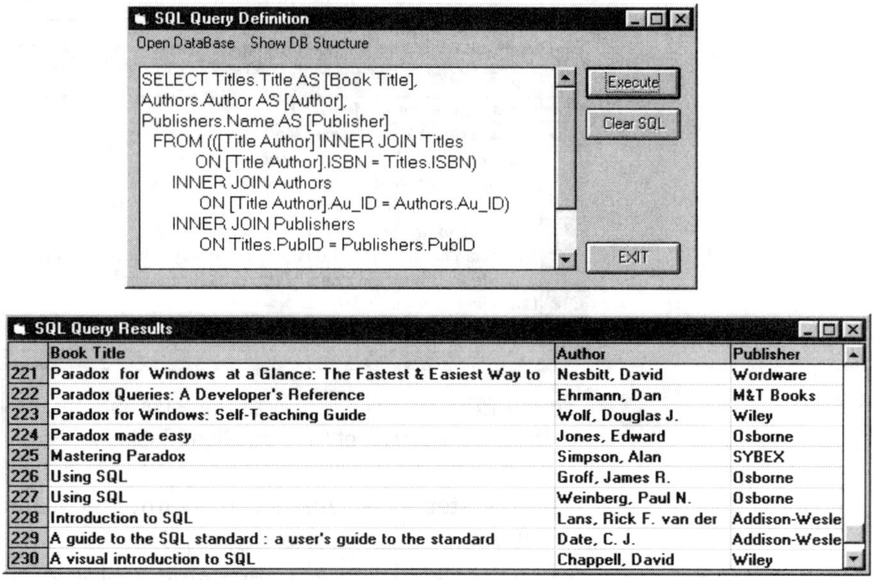


Figure 4-29: Use the AS option to define headings for the Recordset's columns.

## The ORDER BY Option

Another noticeable problem with many of our example queries is the order of the Recordset's rows. The data don't seem to be sorted in any specific way. To rearrange them, use the ORDER BY keywords, followed by the name of the field on whose value you wish to order the Table.

This statement displays all the authors in alphabetical order:

```
SELECT Publishers.Pub_ID, Publishers.[Company Name]
FROM Publishers
    ORDER BY Publishers.[Company Name]
```

The PubID field is displayed so that you can see the records are displayed in a different order than the order they were entered (reflected by the PubID field, which is a counter).

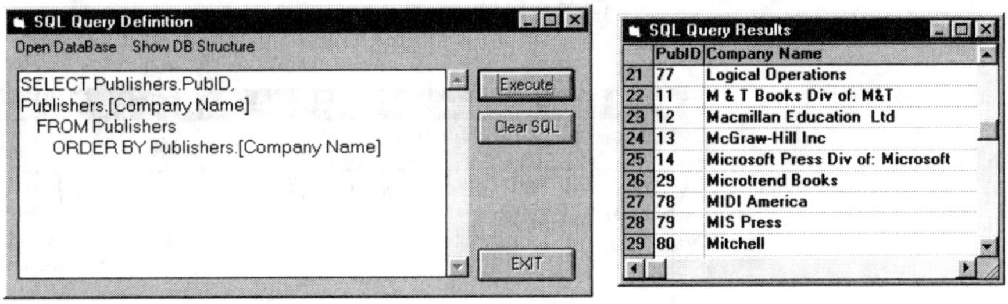


Figure 4-30: To order the rows of the Recordset in a particular sequence, use the ORDER BY option.

## Using Aggregate Functions in SQL Statements

The list of fields following the SELECT keyword can also contain functions. SQL supports five aggregate functions, shown in Table 4-6:

| Function | Description |
|---|---|
| COUNT(field_name) | Returns the number of rows in which field_name is not NULL. A field is NULL if it has not been initialized—an empty field is not NULL. If you specify COUNT(*), the total number of rows will be returned, regardless of whether some of their fields are NULL or not. |
| MAX(field_name) | Returns the largest value of field_name in the Recordset. |
| MIN(field_name) | Returns the smallest value of field_name in the Recordset. |
| SUM(field_name) | Returns the total value of field_name in the Recordset. |
| AVG(field_name) | Returns the average (mean) of the values of field_name in the Recordset. |

Table 4-6: Aggregate functions supported by SQL.

Access SQL supports a few more functions, such as FIRST( ), LAST( ) and STDEV( ), but we will not discuss them here. Let's look at some examples of using aggregate functions with the VBINC database.

The following statement returns a single number, which is the total number of items stored in the Products Table of the VBINC database:

```
SELECT COUNT(Prod_Code) AS [TOTAL]
FROM Products
```

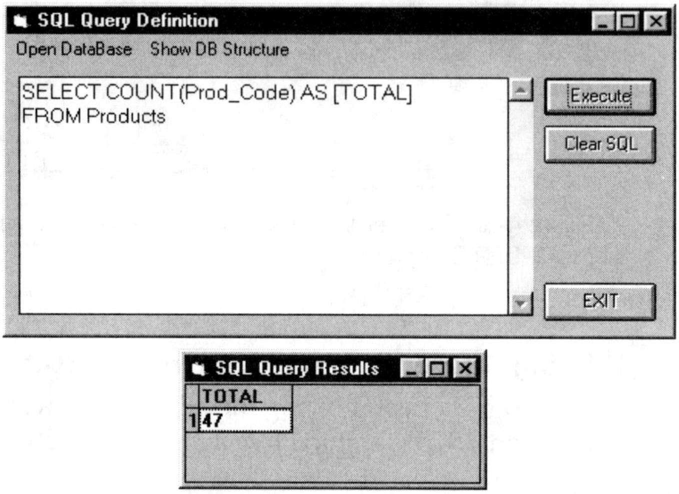


Figure 4-31: It is possible for an SQL statement to return a single number.

## Grouping the Query's Results

It would probably make more sense to break down the total into categories. The following statement returns the number of items in the Products Table for each product category:

```
SELECT Prod_Category AS CATEGORY, COUNT(Prod_Category)
AS Items
FROM Products
    GROUP BY Prod_Category
```

The results of aggregate functions are usually grouped by some field with the GROUP BY option.

When you want to break down the aggregate functions according to some classification scheme, you must specify the GROUP BY option. GROUP BY is a keyword that is used with aggregate functions to specify the classification scheme. In our example, it groups the totals (the numbers returned by the COUNT function) according to their category.

Let's say you want to keep track of the lowest, highest and average price of the products in each category. Here is the SQL statement that does exactly that:

```
SELECT Prod_Category AS CATEGORY,
COUNT(Prod_Category) AS Items,
    MIN(Prod_Price) AS Min,
    MAX(Prod_Price) AS Max,
    AVG(Prod_Price) AS AVRG
FROM Products
GROUP BY Prod_Category
```

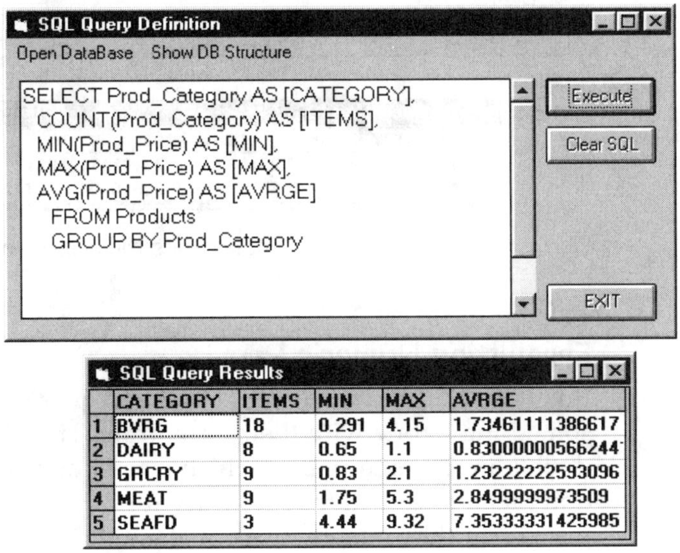


Figure 4-32: The GROUP BY option groups the results of an SQL query according to the value of a field.

If you want to limit the scope of the SQL statement to certain categories, you can't use the WHERE clause. The WHERE clause applies to the entire Table. Instead, you can follow the GROUP BY clause with the HAVING keyword. HAVING is similar to a WHERE clause, but it applies to the results of the query. Here is the same query, only this time applied to products of the DAIRY and BVRG categories:

```
SELECT Prod_Category AS CATEGORY, →
COUNT(Prod_Category) AS Items,
    MIN(Prod_Price) AS Min,
    MAX(Prod_Price) AS Max,
    AVG(Prod_Price) AS AVRG
FROM Products
    GROUP BY Prod_Category
        HAVING Prod_Category IN ("DAIRY", "BVRG")
```

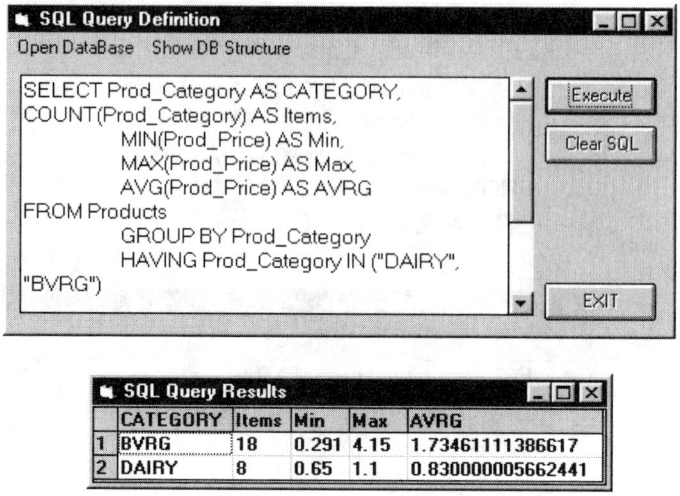


Figure 4-33: The HAVING IN option limits the classes of the GROUP BY option.

### Formatting Numeric Results

If you look at the results of the last two queries, you'll realize there is something wrong with their formatting. The AVG function returns a double-precision number (which is fine for calculations, but you don't really need all that accuracy for printing the average dollar prices), and the integers are not aligned. To fix the appearance of the results on the Grid, we can use the FORMAT command, which is identical to Visual Basic's Format$( ) Function. You can rewrite the previous SQL statement as follows to format and align the numeric columns:

```
SELECT Prod_Category,
    FORMAT(COUNT(Prod_Category), "000") AS Items,
    FORMAT(MIN(Prod_Price), "$0.00") AS [MIN],
    FORMAT(MAX(Prod_Price), "$0.00") AS [MAX],
    FORMAT(AVG(Prod_Price), "$0.00") AS [AVRG]
FROM Products
GROUP BY Prod_Category
```

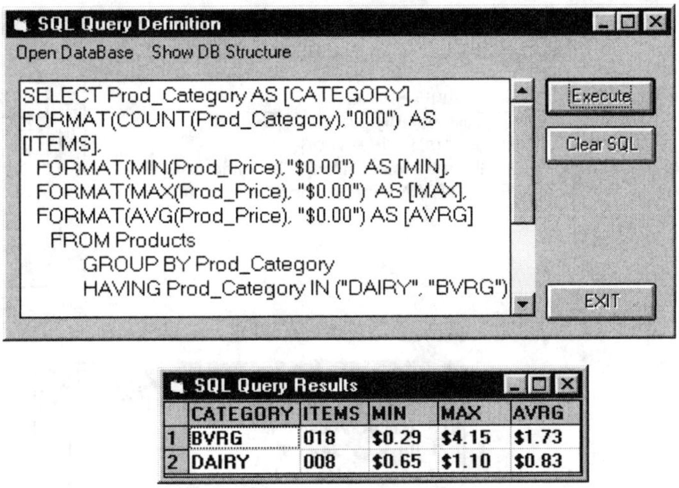


Figure 4-34: SQL's FORMAT function is the same as Visual Basic's Format$( ) Function.

All we did in the previous statement was include the aggregate functions as arguments to the FORMAT function.

### More Examples of Aggregate Functions

Let's look at some examples of the COUNT function involving data from more than one Table. The following examples are based on the BIBLIO database, and if you are using the SQLGRID application to follow the examples, don't forget to open the BIBLIO database.

We'll start by displaying the authors and the number of titles their names appears on. Here is the SQL statement:

```
SELECT Authors.Author, Count([Title Author].ISBN) AS [BOOKS]
FROM Authors, [Title Author]
WHERE Authors.Au_ID = [Title Author].Au_ID
GROUP BY Authors.Author
```

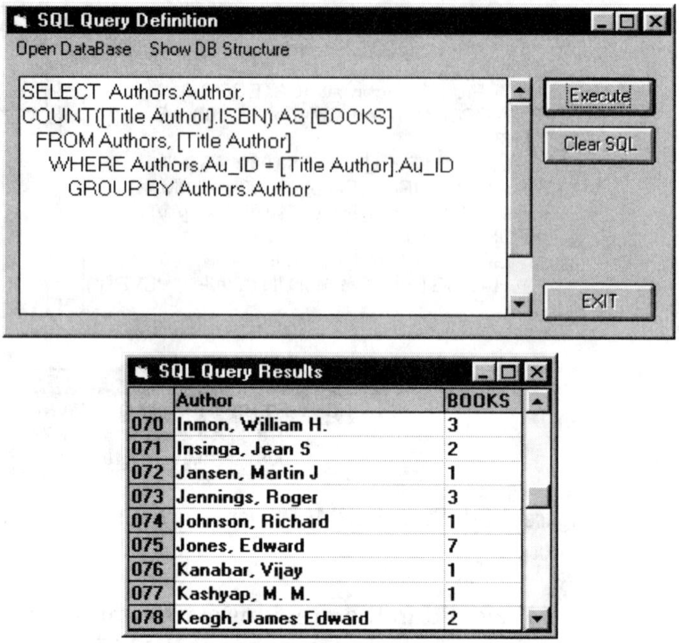


Figure 4-35: The number of titles per author.

This query returns all the authors, along with the number of books per author. The result of the query is a Recordset with 173 records. We know there are 229 titles in the Table, therefore there must be 56 titles written by authors who have written at least one other book. To verify this, we can select only the authors who have written more than one book:

```
SELECT Authors.Author, COUNT([Title Author].ISBN) AS
[BOOKS]
    FROM Authors, [Title Author]
    WHERE Authors.Au_ID = [Title Author].Au_ID
        GROUP BY Authors.Author
            HAVING Count([Title Author].ISBN)>1
```

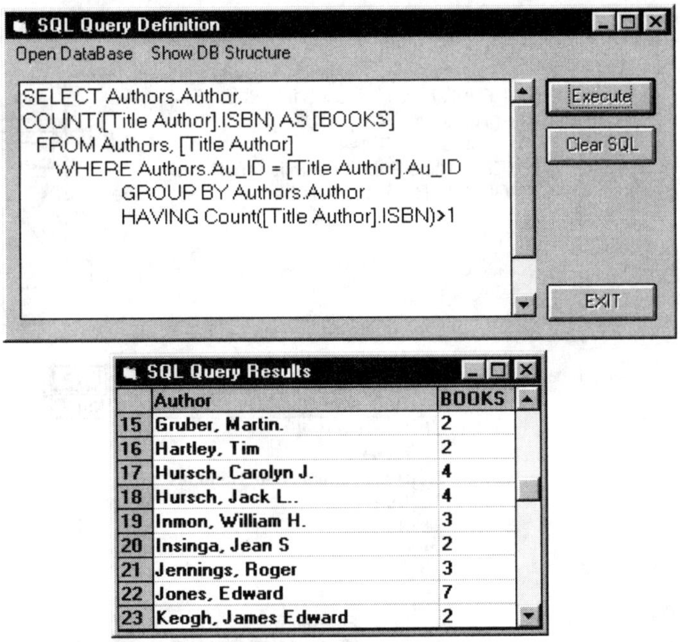


Figure 4-36: The authors with more than one title in the BIBLIO database.

As another example, consider creating a list of all publishers whose names appear in one (possibly more) titles in the Titles Table. This time, we'll count the number of books published by each publisher, and our query will not include the names of publishers without any titles in the Titles Table:

```
SELECT Publishers.Name AS [PUBLISHER],
COUNT (Titles.Title) AS [BOOKS]
FROM Publishers, Titles
    WHERE Titles.PubID = Publishers.PubID
GROUP BY Publishers.Name
```

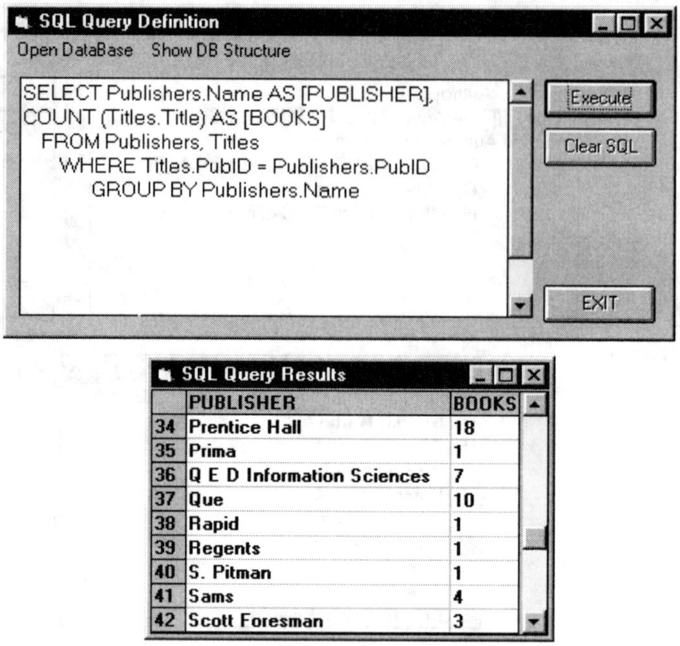


Figure 4-37: This is the list of publishers with one or more titles in the Titles Table.

This query returns 58 records—there are 58 publishers with titles in our database. The total number of titles per publisher varies from 1 to 23 books.

One detail you should notice in this example is the fact that the field on which the grouping is based is different than the field specified in the aggregate function. However, the field following the GROUP BY option must appear in the selection_list.

You could obtain the same result with a RIGHT JOIN too:

```
SELECT Publishers.Name, COUNT (Titles.Title)
FROM Publishers, Titles,
Publishers RIGHT JOIN Titles
    ON Titles.PubID = Publishers.PubID
GROUP BY Publishers.Name
```

As a reminder, the RIGHT JOIN includes all the records from the right-hand Table, but only those records of the left-hand Table that have matching values. Therefore, publishers without one or more titles in the Titles Table will not appear in the query's result.

Now change the RIGHT JOIN to LEFT JOIN:

```
SELECT Publishers.Name, COUNT (Titles.Title)
FROM Publishers, Titles,
Publishers LEFT JOIN Titles
    ON Titles.PubID = Publishers.PubID
GROUP BY Publishers.Name
```

You'll get a complete list of publishers, even the ones that have no titles published.

### The DISTINCT Keyword

The DISTINCT keyword omits records that contain duplicate data in the selected fields. In other words, if a query result contains the same field value in more than one row, the DISTINCT keyword will eliminate all duplicates after the first one. Let's say you want to see the list of all publishers who have at least one title in the database (some publishers appear in the Publishers Table, but no rows in the Titles Table point to them). A statement that involved a single Table (Publishers) wouldn't work. It would return all the publisher names, regardless of whether they have a title in the Titles Table or not.

Use the DISTINCT keyword to eliminate duplicate rows.

The following query would return the names of all publishers:

```
SELECT Name FROM Publishers
```

Let's try to get the list of publishers who have at least one title in the Titles Table. The following query returns a Recordset of all publishers with at least one title.

```
SELECT Publishers.Name
FROM Publishers, Titles
WHERE Publishers.PubID = Titles.PubID
```

The Recordset contains 229 publishers because there are 229 titles. Some of them have the same publisher, whose name is repeated for each one of its titles. To reject all duplicates, use the DISTINCT keyword in the last SQL statement:

```
SELECT DISTINCT Publishers.Name
FROM Publishers, Titles
WHERE Publishers.PubID = Titles.PubID
```

This time the query returns all publishers that appear in one or more entries in the Titles Table. Each publisher's name appears once, regardless of the number of books published.

## Action Queries

Now we will turn our attention from the select queries to the action queries. SQL provides a few options for performing certain actions on the database. The two most common and useful action queries are UPDATE and DELETE.

Action queries do not create (or return) Recordsets. They simply change selected records in one or more Tables and return control to the program. Action queries are especially useful when updating more than one Table en masse. For example, you would use an action query to increase the value of all products in a certain category by some percentage, or to remove all of the invoices issued last year that have been paid for. Performing similar actions on a record-by-record basis is not only time-consuming, it's error-prone too.

Action queries do not return any Recordsets. They act on the data in the database.

CD-ROM

If you are using a database to experiment with action queries, especially if you are going to use the DELETE action query, be sure to first make a copy of the database. If you accidentally destroy data from a database, you can copy the VBINC database from the CD. The BIBLIO database must be copied from Visual Basic's distribution disks.

The SQLGRID application can't be used with action queries. Where select queries can be used to build Recordsets, action queries do not report any results. Where selection queries are usually used as arguments in building Recordsets, action queries must be executed with the Execute Method. The Execute Method applies to the database object, and its syntax is as follows:

```
DB.Execute SQL_statement
```

DB is a properly dimensioned Database variable, and SQL_statement is an action query. The following commands open the BIBLIO database and delete all the titles containing the string "SQL":

```
Dim DB As Database
Set DB = OpenDatabase("BIBLIO.MDB")
DB.Execute = "DELETE FROM Titles WHERE Title LIKE '*SQL*' "
```

Action queries must be executed with the Execute Method.

If you attempt to use an action query in the way you would use a select query (as we have been doing so far), Visual Basic will generate an error message. Do not execute any of the following examples in the SQLGRID application. To execute any of the action query examples below, create a string (text enclosed in quotes) with the SQL statement and use it as argument of the Execute Method of the database.

### Updating Records

The UPDATE verb lets you specify an action query to update a large number of records in a single step. Let's say you want to increase the price of the dairy products in the VBINC database by 3 percent. You can start the VBPRODS application and change each price individually. Or you can issue a single SQL statement that increases the price of all products whose PROD_CATEGORY field equals "DAIRY." The UPDATE verb is even more useful when we want to change data in multiple Tables.

The syntax of the UPDATE verb is very similar to that of SELECT, only this time you must use the keyword SET to specify the changes that will take place. The following statement increases the price of all dairy products by 3 percent:

```
UPDATE Prod_Price
FROM Products
SET Prod_Price = 1.03 * Prod_Price
WHERE Prod_Category = "DAIRY"
```

The UPDATE verb performs an action, and it doesn't return any records. The SET option specifies the action that will take place (sets the new values of the fields).

### Deleting Records

Another action you can specify with SQL is the deletion of certain records. The DELETE verb's syntax is similar to that of UPDATE, without the SET keyword. You can't delete specific fields from a Table, only entire rows (records). The FROM word lets you specify the Table(s) from which data will be deleted, and the WHERE option specifies the criteria. All rows meeting the criteria are deleted.

If your company hires students during the summer, you can delete their names from the employee database when the fall semester begins with a single statement (assuming that the database with the employee data is called Employees and the Title field contains the value "Trainee" for all students):

```
DELETE FROM Employees
WHERE Title = "Trainee"
```

Similarly, if the owner of the VBINC company decides that dairy products don't sell well, he can remove all the items from the Products Table that have the value "DAIRY" in their Prod_Category field:

```
DELETE FROM Products
WHERE Prod_Category = "DAIRY"
```

Because of the referential integrity rules we have specified, the Jet Engine will not allow you to delete any of the products that appear in the invoices. You must first delete the corresponding invoice details from Invoice Details Table and then the products from the Products Table.

Before deleting rows from one or more Tables, create the equivalent Recordset to see the rows you are about to delete.

Let's look at a more complicated deletion process. This time we'll delete from the BIBLIO database all publishers that do not appear in a title—in other words, all publishers that happen to be in the database, but that are not connected to any title. As you may have guessed, we will create an Inner-Join between publishers and titles. To be on the safe side, we will first create a Recordset with the rows that will be removed with a SELECT statement:

```
SELECT Publishers.PubID, Publishers.Name
FROM Publishers
INNER JOIN Titles
    ON Publishers.PubID <> Titles.PubID
```

Or we could use the following SELECT statement, which is even simpler:

```
SELECT Publishers.PubID, Publishers.Name
FROM Publishers
WHERE Publishers.PubID <> Titles.PubID
```

The Recordset returned by this query will contain the names of the publishers without any titles—that is, the publishers we wish to delete. Even if you are not familiar with the database, you will easily spot any mistakes—the wrong Recordset will probably contain too many rows. If the Recordset contains the entries you want to delete, then you can use the WHERE clause with a DELETE statement:

```
DELETE FROM Publishers
WHERE Publishers.PubID <> Titles.PubID
```

The SQL DELETE statement is identical to the SELECT statement, with the exception that you don't have to specify any fields. All fields in the selected rows will be deleted. You can also delete entries in multiple Tables by creating Inner-Joins. The two databases we are using for the examples of this chapter do not lend themselves to this type of operation, so let's return to our hypothetical employee database example. If the trainee names appear also in the company's payroll, when removing their names from the Employees Table, we should also remove them from the Payroll Table. Here is the SQL statement that removes all employees with a title of "Trainee" from both the Employees and the Payroll Tables (where EmployeeID is the common field between the two Tables):

```
DELETE FROM Employees, Payroll
Employees INNER JOIN Payroll
    ON Employees.EmployeeID = Payroll.EmployeeID
WHERE Title = 'Trainee'
```

## Defining Query Objects

In the previous section, we discussed the topic of SQL, and you saw how to retrieve the data you want from the database. The most common use of SQL statements is in creating Recordsets (of the Dynaset and Snapshot types). The SQLGRID application shows how to create Recordsets with SQL statements and how to manipulate their data. In our example, we simply place them on a Grid Control, but you can perform any operations on them or export them to any other program. SQL statements also can be used as values for the RecordSource Property of the Data Control, to limit the scope of the Data Control. In the discussion of the BOOKS example, we used selection queries to limit the scope of the Data Controls. Doing so lets the Data Controls "see" only the part of the database we are interested in.

The queries you use most often can be named and attached to the database itself so that you can call them by name.

Queries are so common when working with databases that they can become part of the database. In other words, you can create queries and store them in the database along with the Tables and their indices. Then you can use them again and again. If you are using the same query with some frequency, you can attach it to the database and have it at your disposal each time you need it. You can even specify parameters so that the scope of the statement can be altered each time the query is executed.

To create a query and attach it to the database, you must first dimension a new variable of type QueryDef:

```
Dim QUERYCust As QueryDef
```

Then create the new variable with the CreateQueryDef Method:

```
Set QUERYCust = DB.CreateQueryDef("CACustomers")
```

"CACustomers" is the name of the query, and DB is a properly initialized Database variable. From now on, you'll be using the name

"CACustomers" to refer to the query in the DB Database. To complete the definition, assign the desired SQL statement to the variable's SQL Property:

```
QUERYCust.SQL = "SELECT * FROM Customers WHERE →
CUST_STATE = 'CA' "
```

This query recalls all the customers from California. To create a Recordset based on the QUERYCust query, use the OpenRecordset Method on the QueryDef object (where DYNACust has been dimensioned as a Dynaset variable):

```
Set DYNACust = QUERYCust.OpenRecordset( )
```

You can also create and define a query in one step, by supplying both the name of the query and its SQL statement as arguments to the CreateQueryDef Method:

```
Set QUERYCust = DB.CreateQueryDef("CACustomers",  →
"SELECT * FROM Customers WHERE CUST_ID = 'CA' ")
```

Similar to the CreateQueryDef Method, which attaches new query definitions to the database, Visual Basic provides the DeleteQueryDef Method for removing existing QueryDef objects from the database. The following line removes the CACustomers query from the database:

```
DB.DeleteQueryDef "CACustomers"
```

*Note:* QUERYCust is only the name of a variable that was used to create the QueryDef object. Once the query has been attached to the database, you can't use the QUERYCust name to refer to it. You must use the QueryDef object's name ("CACustomers").

Before using a query, you must open it, just like any other object stored in the database. Similar to the OpenRecordset Method, use the OpenQueryDef Method to open an existing QueryDef:

```
Dim QUERY As QueryDef
Set QUERY = DB.OpenQueryDef("CACustomers")
```

Then use the QUERY object to create Recordsets. If it's an action query, use the Execute Method of the QueryDef object. Let's define an action query that deletes all the products in the SEAFD category (Table Products of the VBINC database):

```
Dim DELQUERY As QueryDef
Set QUERY = DB.CreateQueryDef("Delete", "DELETE FROM →
Products WHERE PROD_CATEGORY = 'SEAFD' "
```

These lines create the query "Delete" and attach it to the database. To delete the products in the SEAFD category, you must first open the QueryDef object:

```
DIM DELQUERY As QueryDef
Set DELQUERY = DB.OpenQueryDef("Delete")
```

Then you must execute it:

```
DB.Execute DELQUERY
```

## Parameter Queries

Finally, you can define queries with parameters, which are specified when the query is executed. The PARAMETERS option, which determines the parameters, must always appear first in an SQL statement, followed by the parameter names and their types. Here is the syntax of the PARAMETERS option:

Queries attached to a database can contain parameters, which are assigned values when they are executed.

```
PARAMETERS parametertext parametertype;
```

The semicolon at the end is mandatory. The parametertext argument is the name of the parameter. It can be a single word, like "Value" or "Month," or an entire sentence, such as "[Please enter the value]". Note that if the parametertext argument contains spaces, then it must be enclosed in brackets.

The parametertype argument is the data type of the parameter (Text, Date, Currency, etc.). You can also specify more than one parameter, as long as you separate them with commas:

```
PARAMETERS parametertext parametertype, parametertext →
 parametertype;
```

Here is an SQL statement that recalls the invoices with a total that exceeds a user-specified value (parameter) and displays the name of the customer to whom the invoice was issued, along with the invoice's total:

```
PARAMETERS [InvTot] Currency;
SELECT Customers.Cust_Name, Invoices.Inv_Total
FROM Customers, Invoices
WHERE Invoices.Inv_CustID = Customers.Cust_ID
    AND Invoices.Inv_Total > [InvTot]
```

You can't execute this statement with SQLGRID. You must first attach it to a database and then execute it with the Execute Method of the database. Let's follow the steps.

First append this query to the VBINC database. Start a new project and enter the following lines in a Command Button's Click Event:

```
Private Sub Command1_Click ( )
Dim DB As Database
Dim QUERYInv As QueryDef
    Set DB = OpenDatabase("C:\VB\VBINC.MDB")
    Set QUERYInv = DB.CreateQueryDef("InvTotals")
    QSQL = "PARAMETERS [InvTot] Currency; "
    QSQL = QSQL + "SELECT Customers.Cust_Name, →
    Invoices.Inv_Total "
    QSQL = QSQL + "FROM Customers, Invoices "
    QSQL = QSQL + "WHERE Invoices.Inv_CustID = →
    Customers.Cust_ID "
    QSQL = QSQL + " AND Invoices.Inv_Total > [InvTot]"
    QUERYInv.SQL = QSQL
    QUERYInv.Close
    DB.Close
End Sub
```

Note that you may have to change the full name of the database if it is stored in a different location in your computer.

First, we create the QUERYInv object (of type QueryDef) and attach it to the database with the following line:

```
Set QUERYInv = DB.CreateQueryDef("InvTotals")
```

Then we create a string variable (QSQL) that contains the previous SQL statement, and assign it to the QUERYInv object's SQL Property. The "InvTotals" QueryDef object has been attached to the database.

To use this query we must create a QueryDef variable. As soon as this variable is assigned the "InvTotals" query from the VBINC database, the names of the query's parameters can be accessed through the QUERYInv object. Let's examine the following code segment that makes use of the "InvTotals" query:

```
Private Sub Command2_Click ( )
Dim DB As Database
Dim QUERYInv As QueryDef
Dim SNAPInv As Recordset
    Set DB = OpenDatabase("C:\VB\VBINC.MDB")
    Set QUERYInv = DB.OpenQueryDef("InvTotals")
    QUERYInv!InvTot = 50
    Set SNAPInv = QUERYInv.OpenRecordset()
    Print SNAPInv.Fields(0), SNAPInv.Fields(1)
```

```
        SNAPInv.MoveNext
        Print SNAPInv.Fields(0), SNAPInv.Fields(1)
    End Sub
```

First, we open the database and assign the "InvTotals" query to a QueryDef object (which is the QUERYInv variable). Then, we use the QUERYInv!InvTot expression to assign a value to the query's parameter:

```
    QUERYInv!InvTot = 50
```

As you can see, the parameter name we used in the definition of the SQL statement becomes a "property" of a QueryDef object. (Actually it's not a real Property because if you use the period in the place of the exclamation mark, Visual Basic will generate the error message "Property Not Found.")

Then, we can use the query to create a Recordset with the following command:

```
    Set SNAPInv = QUERYInv.OpenRecordset( )
```

Notice that the OpenRecordset Method is applied to the QueryDef object, and not to the database.

Finally, to test the results of the parameter query, we print the first two rows of the resulting Recordset.

This concludes our presentation of the SQL statements. In the next section we will present the actual code of the SQLGRID application. The SQLGRID application will help you understand how select queries are used in programs and how you can access the Recordsets they return.

## Example: The SQLGRID Application

Now we can look at the code of the SQLGRID application. The SQL statement the user types in the Text Box is used to build a Dynaset-type Recordset (DYNA). Then we use the Recordset Methods and Properties to read all the data in the Grid. The core of the SQLGRID application is similar to the DAGRID application we presented earlier in the chapter. Each SQL statement is used to create a Recordset variable (called DYNA). This variable is a table (or array), with DYNA.RecordCount rows and DYNA.Fields.Count columns. These two numbers are used to set up a Grid of the appropriate dimensions. Then, we loop through each row of the DYNA variable (with the MoveNext Method) and transfer all the fields from the variable to the Grid. Here is the code of the Execute Command Button:

```
Private Sub ExecuteButton_Click()
Dim DB As Database
Dim DYNA As Dynaset
Dim SNAP As Snapshot

    SQLline$ = Trim(Text1.Text)
    cr = Chr$(10) + Chr$(13)
    If DataBaseName = "" Then
        MsgBox "You must first open a database"
        Exit Sub
    End If
    Screen.MousePointer = 11
    Form1.Caption = "Building Dynaset..."

On Error GoTo DBError
    Set DB = OpenDatabase(DataBaseName)
On Error GoTo SETError
    Set DYNA = DB.OpenRecordset(SQLline$, dbOpenDynaset) →
    DYNA.MoveLast
On Error GoTo GridError
    Form2.Grid1.Rows = 1
    Form2.Grid1.Cols = 1
    Form2.Grid1.Rows = DYNA.RecordCount + 1
    Form2.Grid1.Cols = DYNA.Fields.Count + 1
    Form2.Grid1.FixedRows = 1
    Form2.Grid1.FixedCols = 1
    NumberGrid (DYNA.RecordCount)
    For i = 0 To DYNA.Fields.Count - 1
        DYNA.MoveFirst
        Form2.Grid1.Col = i + 1
        Form2.Grid1.Row = 0
        Form2.Grid1.Text = DYNA.Fields(i).Name
        For j = 0 To DYNA.RecordCount - 1
            Form2.Grid1.Row = j + 1
            If Not IsNull(DYNA.Fields(i)) Then
                Form2.Grid1.Text = DYNA.Fields(i)
                s$ = DYNA.Fields(i)
                If TextWidth(s$) > Form2.Grid1.ColWidth(i + 1) →
                Then Form2.Grid1.ColWidth(i + 1) = →
                TextWidth(s$ + " ")
            End If
            DYNA.MoveNext
```

```
        Next
    Next

    Form1.Caption = "SQL Query Definition"
    Screen.MousePointer = 0
    Form2.Grid1.Row = 1
    Form2.Grid1.Col = 1
    Form2.Show
    Exit Sub

DBError:
    Form1.Caption = "SQL Query Definition"
    Screen.MousePointer = 0
    Exit Sub

SETError:
    ErrorMsg$ = "Couldn't create Dynaset" + cr + Error
    MsgBox ErrorMsg$
    Form1.Caption = "SQL Query Definition"
    Screen.MousePointer = 0
    Exit Sub

GridError:
    ErrorMsg$ = "Couldn't fill the Grid" + cr + "VB Error →
    Message: " + Error
    ErrorMsg$ = ErrorMsg$ + cr + "Query result probably →
    a cross-join"
    MsgBox ErrorMsg$
    Form1.Caption = "SQL Query Definition"
    Screen.MousePointer = 0
    Exit Sub

End Sub
```

The DataBaseName variable is defined in the application's Module as a global variable so that all Modules can access it. The Show DB Structure command leads to the MAPDB application, which will be explained under "Database Definitions" near the end of this chapter.

One item worth discussing in the previous code is the use of the IsNull Function. If a certain field in a row hasn't been assigned a value, it contains a NULL "value." A NULL value is just that: no value. It is not an empty string (""); neither is it zero (for numeric fields). Visual Basic initializes all fields of a record to NULL values. NULL values, however, can't be assigned to Properties. If you attempt to assign a NULL value to the Grid's Text Property, Visual Basic will generate the error message "Invalid Use of Null."

Notice also the line that adjusts the width of each column according to the contents of the current cell. Of course, if you don't like the appearance of the Grid, you can always adjust the width of its columns individually.

Of course, you'll get the same error message if you assign a NULL value to the Text Property of a Text Box, the Caption Property of a Label, and so on. The NULL value can't be used in operations; neither can it be assigned to variables. That's why it is necessary to always check for NULL values and skip them, or take some other action.

Notice also the number of error-trapping statements. There are many distinct things that can go wrong in this application. The user may attempt to execute an SQL statement before opening a database with the Open Database command. The most common error is an incorrect SQL statement. In that case, we display the error message generated by Visual Basic and exit. An SQL statement that creates a Cross-Join can easily overflow the Grid. If that happens, the program exits again.

## TRANSACTION PROCESSING

We have seen how to handle databases in many ways: How to navigate through a Recordset's rows, how to combine multiple Recordsets, how to recall information in any way we see fit, and how to change and update the information in the database. There is one very practical situation we have been avoiding so far: how to update multiple Recordsets. If you think about it, in most databases we don't add new publishers and titles, or customers and products. The most common operation performed on a database is a *transaction*. A transaction is a series of operations that must be performed at once, as a group. When you use your bank's ATM to transfer funds from your checking account to your savings account, you perform a transaction that involves two steps: removing money from your checking account (decreasing the balance) and adding the same amount to your savings account (increasing the balance). If these two operations aren't performed together, some money will be lost. Either you or the bank will be unhappy about it.

Transactions are very common in everyday business life. Issuing an invoice is a transaction. The customer is debited, the company's accounts are credited, and the inventory is decreased accordingly. Like an ATM transaction, all these actions must be performed at once. If you credit your company's accounts but something goes wrong and the program stops before the invoice has been issued, the transaction can't be considered complete.

If even a single step in a transaction fails, the entire transaction must be aborted.

If the transaction is interrupted for some reason, the computer should be able to undo the changes. In database terminology, this is called *rollback*. If the transaction can't complete, the computer must roll back to the last known "good" state. By good state we mean the last state before the database's integrity was impaired. And this state is the state of the database right before the transaction started.

To handle transactions, Visual Basic keeps track of all changes in a log file. If the transaction completes successfully, it commits the changes to the database. If the transaction fails for some reason, then it rolls back (it "undoes") the changes in the database. This isn't exactly what goes on, but we needn't be concerned with the mechanics of the process.

What can go wrong in a transaction? Everything that can go wrong in a program. A transaction involves several steps, such as checking a customer's current balance, subtracting items sold from inventory, etc. Any of these steps may fail. Even a programming bug can cause a transaction to fail. Even more things can go wrong in a multiuser environment (another user has locked the record you want to update, you lost your connection to a server, and so on). With Visual Basic's transactional capabilities, however, no matter what happens to the program, the database will not become corrupted.

Visual Basic provides three statements for handling transactions, shown in Table 4-6.

| | |
|---|---|
| BeginTrans | Begins the transaction. |
| CommitTrans | Commits a successful transaction (commits all the changes made to the database since the last BeginTrans statement). |
| Rollback | Rolls back all changes made since the last BeginTrans statement. |

Table 4-7: VB's transaction-handling statements.

Here is a sequence of commands that shows how these statements are used:

```
On Error Goto RollBackLabel
BeginTrans
{perform the transaction}
{use the Update Method for the changes to take effect}
CommitTrans
{program continues}
On Error Goto 0
RollBackLabel:
    RollBack
    Exit Sub
```

Let's explain this sequence of commands. First we issue an On Error Goto RollBackLabel command. Should an error happen during the transaction, we simply roll it back and exit. By default, when Visual Basic detects an error, it displays an error message and stops the execution of the program. This certainly isn't what we want to happen. While in another situations you might attempt to remedy the situation that caused the problem, in transaction processing it is imperative that we roll back the transaction to protect the database.

If the Update statement is successful, then the CommitTrans Statement will be executed and the procedure will exit normally. If not, the On Error statement will send the program to the RollBackLabel line, and the changes will be undone with the RollBack statement.

Notice that the On Error Goto RollBackLabel statement appears right in front of the commands that take care of the transaction. The program above should use its own error-trapping routines. Moreover, as soon as the transaction is committed to the database, the On Error statement must change. Any error that may occur after the successful completion of a transaction shouldn't be handled by the RollBack statement. Besides, you can't execute a RollBack after a CommitTrans. The CommitTrans Method commits the changes to the database irreversibly.

Every BeginTrans statement in a procedure must have a matching CommitTrans or Rollback statement.

Notice that you can have nested transactions too—up to five levels. We won't discuss this possibility any further here, but if you nest multiple transactions, make sure they are all committed (or rolled back) in the same Subroutine. Also, if you begin a transaction, you must either complete it or roll it back. If you forget to, then the transactions will accumulate and eventually Visual Basic will generate an error message. An error message will also be generated if you attempt to close the database while any transactions are pending.

### EXAMPLE: PREPARING INVOICES

To demonstrate the concepts presented in this section, we will implement the application shown in Figure 4-38. This is an invoice-issuing application based on a Grid Control. This program may not be suited for your needs, but we decided to demonstrate an alternative (and very interesting) approach. The Grid Control contains all the items in the Products Table, and the user can select the desired item and type the quantity—as opposed to many invoicing applications that require that the user types the item's code as well.

As you know, the Grid Control doesn't accept input. We therefore must program the Control KeyPress Event to fake user input on the Grid. This program accepts only numeric digits and lets you edit an entry with the Backspace key only. If you like the idea of preparing invoices with a Grid Control, your best bet would be to buy a Grid Control that accepts user input, such as FarPoint's Spread/VBX. We decided to use the standard Grid Control in our application so that all readers can follow the example on their computers. It's not as flexible as it should be, but our goal is to demonstrate the transaction processing mechanism of Visual Basic and not to present a complete invoicing application.

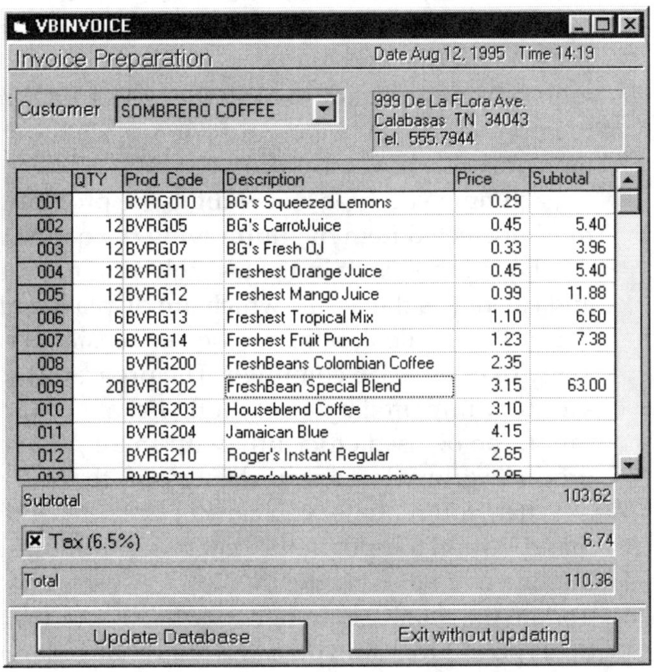


Figure 4-38: The VBINV application uses a Grid Control to prepare invoices.

To use this application, familiarize yourself with the VBINC database. You can open the database with the Data Manager application to see the contents of the Tables, or use the VBCUST and VBPRODS data entry applications to browse through the database's customers and products, and possibly add new entries.

CD-ROM

The VBINV application (located in the 4\APPS\VBINV subdirectory of the CD) is a stand-alone application that lets you prepare one invoice only. Normally, you would call a similar Form from another application's menu. To prepare an invoice, you must select a customer's name from the Combo Box in the upper section of the Form. The customers' names are placed in the Combo Box when the program starts, and you can specify only a valid customer name. The customer's data will be displayed on the Panel next to the name, to help ensure that you have indeed selected the correct name.

With a few lines of code in its KeyPress Event, you can use the Grid Control for simple data entry too.

Then you can click on any line of the Grid and type the quantity for the selected item. The numbers you type always appear in the second column of the Grid. Use the arrow keys or the mouse to move up and down the Grid. To correct an entry, you must press the Backspace key to delete digits from the end of the number and then type new digits. For example, you can't select the entire number and delete it or replace it. This, however, isn't a serious limitation, since most data entry operators use a few keys only, and it is so much faster to hit the Backspace key a few times rather than reach for the mouse. You can either modify the Grid's KeyPress Event's subroutine to improve the keyboard entry, or replace the standard Grid with a more flexible third-party Control.

Each time you type a new digit, the program updates the subtotal for the selected item by multiplying the quantity by the price and displaying the result in the last column. It also scans the entire Grid and calculates the totals, which are displayed at the bottom of the Form. These calculations can be very easily performed between keystrokes on a 386 computer. The program's response time would be seriously impaired by a very long list of products. The VBINV application can be used efficiently with small product lists, but if the list of products grows large, you must resort to a different type of interface.

When you're done, you can click on the Update Database Command Button to update the database, or on the Exit Without Updating Button to discard the invoice. Let's see what happens when you update the database. Either action will end the program. VBINV is the type of program you call from within a larger application, not a stand-alone application.

First, the program must add an entry to the Invoices Table of the VBINC database. The Inv_CustID field of the invoice will be set to the Cust_ID field of the Customers Table so that the invoice will be linked to its customer. The InvDate field will be also set to the current date so that you can later recall invoices on the basis of their dates. Finally, the Inv_Total must be set to the invoice's total amount.

Then, the program must scan the entire Grid, and for each entry that has a nonzero quantity, it must add a new line to the Invoice Details Table. This Table holds the individual lines of the invoices. For each row we add to the Invoice Details Table, we must set its InvDet_ID field equal to the value of the INV_ID field of the invoice, its InvDet_Item to the product's code, and the InvDet_Qty field to the quantity entered in the Grid.

Next we list the code behind the Update Database Command Button. Notice the use of the BeginTrans, CommitTrans and Rollback statements, along with the On Error Goto RollBackLabel statement.

```
Private Sub UpdateButton_Click()

Dim TBLInvoices As Recordset
Dim TBLInvDetail As Recordset
Dim InvNumber As Long
Dim ProdCode As String * 12

   If Combo1.TEXT = "" Then
      MsgBox "Invalid customer name. Please select a →
      customer from dropdown list"
      Exit Sub
   End If

   On Error GoTo RollBackLabel
   Set TBLInvoices = DB.OpenRecordset("INVOICES", →
   dbOpenDynaset)
   BeginTrans
   TBLInvoices.AddNew
   TBLInvoices.Fields("INV_TOTAL") = Val(Panel3D6.Caption)
   TBLInvoices.Fields("INV_CUSTID") = →
   SNAPCust.Fields("CUST_ID")
   TBLInvoices.Fields("INVDATE") = Date
   TBLInvoices.UPDATE
   TBLInvoices.MoveLast
   InvNumber = TBLInvoices.Fields("INV_ID")
```

```
    Set TBLInvDetail = DB.OpenRecordset("INVDETAILS", →
    dbOpenDynaset)
    For i = 1 To Grid1.Rows - 1
        Grid1.Row = i
        Grid1.Col = 1
        If Val(Grid1.TEXT) > 0 Then
            TBLInvDetail.AddNew
            TBLInvDetail.Fields("INVDET_ID") = InvNumber
            Grid1.Col = 2
            TBLProds.Seek "=", Trim(Grid1.TEXT)
            ProdCode = TBLProds.Fields("PROD_CODE")
            TBLInvDetail.Fields("INVDET_ITEM") = ProdCode
            Grid1.Col = 1
            TBLInvDetail.Fields("INVDET_QTY") = Grid1.TEXT
            TBLInvDetail.UPDATE
        End If
    Next
    CommitTrans
    MsgBox "Invoice saved OK"
    End

RollBackLabel:
    MsgBox "Could not write to database. Program ends"
    Rollback
    End

End Sub
```

The following lines add a new record to the Invoices Table and assign the proper values to its fields:

```
TBLInvoices.AddNew
TBLInvoices.Fields("INV_TOTAL") = Val(Panel3D6.Caption)
TBLInvoices.Fields("INV_CUSTID") = SNAPCust.Fields("CUST_ID")
TBLInvoices.Fields("INVDATE") = Date
TBLInvoices.Update
TBLInvoices.MoveLast
InvNumber = TBLInvoices.Fields("INV_ID")
```

The values for the InvTotal and InvDate fields are readily available. The Customer's ID must be looked up in the Customers Recordset (created when we fill the Combo Box with customer names). The last two lines read the invoice's ID so that it can be used later in the

Invoice Details Table. The invoice's ID is not assigned by the program. It's a long number (Counter) assigned to each new invoice automatically by Visual Basic. That's why we must go to the end of the Table (where the new line is added) and read it.

Then, we scan the Grid, and for each row with a nonzero quantity we append another record to the Invoice Details Table.

Run the application and see how it works. Prepare an invoice, and before you update the database, switch to the Data Manager application and delete one of the products you have included in the invoice. Then switch back to the VBINV application and try to update the database. Predictably, the program will fail to add a line for the product you deleted to the Invoice Details Table and will abort the operation. No changes will be made to the database.

The Rollback statement protects your database's integrity, no matter what has gone wrong.

If you do the same with a customer's name, the program will update the database. Why? The customers' names are kept in a Snapshot. Deleting a customer entry from the actual Table has no effect on the Snapshot. That's why the program doesn't fail to update the database (it makes no changes to the Customers Table). In a practical situation, you must either make sure that the customer's ID is valid at the moment the invoice is issued, or (most likely) prevent users from deleting records for no reason at all as long as other users rely on these records.

Before we end this discussion, we'll show the Grid's KeyPress Subroutine:

```
Private Sub Grid1_KeyPress (KeyAscii As Integer)
Dim QTY As Integer, PRICE As Single, SUBTOT As Single
    If KeyAscii >= 48 And KeyAscii <= 57 Then
        Grid1.Col = 1
        Grid1.Text = Grid1.Text + Chr$(KeyAscii) →
        ElseIf KeyAscii = 8 Then
        Grid1.Col = 1
        If Len(Grid1.Text) > 0 Then
            Grid1.Text = Left$(Grid1.Text, Len(Grid1.Text) - 1)
        End If
    End If
    QTY = Val(Grid1.Text)
    Grid1.Col = 4
    PRICE = Val(Grid1.Text)
    SUBTOT = QTY * PRICE
    Grid1.Col = 5
    Grid1.Text = Format$(SUBTOT, "0.00") + " "
```

```
        Call ShowTotals
    End Sub
```

This Subroutine responds only to numeric digits and the Backspace key. Every time a digit is typed, it is appended to current contents of the cell. When the user presses the Backspace key, the last character of the same cell is removed. Then the program calculates the subtotal for the current item and finally calls the ShowTotals Subroutine to update the invoice's totals at the bottom of the Form.

You can load the project in Visual Basic's editor and look at the ShowTotals Subroutine. You can also see the code that is executed when the program starts, which transfers the names of the customers to the Combo Box and the descriptions and prices of the products to the Grid Control. We've seen similar pieces of code earlier in the chapter, and we need not repeat them here.

The VBINC database was intended to be used as an example. If you want to write an invoicing application, you can use it as a starting point, but you must modify its structure and the programs. You may have noticed that we store only the quantities of the invoice lines and not their prices, in accordance to the rule of avoiding data duplication. But what if certain prices change? The old prices are not included in the invoice details, and it seems that even the old invoices were issued with the new prices. In a practical situation, we should save the item prices along with the product codes in the Invoice Details Table. This isn't considered data duplication because the current product price (the one stored in the Products Table) may change, but the one stored in the Invoice Details Table must not change.

## DATABASE DEFINITIONS

To conclude the chapter on databases, we're going to look into the structure of databases and see how the definition of the database itself is stored in the MDB file. You don't need to know how the description of a database is stored in an MDB file in order to use the database, and you can skip this section if you aren't interested in this information. Knowing where and how these descriptions are stored, however, will enable you to write programs that open databases and manipulate them, and even create new databases without the Data Manager tool. The information presented in this chapter will be used shortly to build the MAPDB application, which you have already seen in action in the SQLGRID application. MAPDB reads the description of the database from the MDB file and displays its complete structure in an Outline Control.

A database consists of Tables, each one having its own collection of fields. Each field in turn has a type. Moreover, each Table can be indexed in more than one way (though it may not be indexed at all). Visual Basic must therefore maintain lists of all Tables and indices in a database.

TableDefs describes all the Tables in the database and is a list of TableDef objects, one for each Table.

The description of a database is stored in an object called TableDefs. TableDefs is a list of TableDef objects; there's one TableDefs object for each Table in the database. TableDefs's elements can be accessed with the Name Property or an index value, similar to the ListIndex Property of a List Control. The total number of Tables in the database is returned by the Count Property of the TableDefs object. The following code shows how you can read the names of all Tables in the database and put them in a List (assuming that DB is a Database object, set to an actual database):

```
For i% = 0 To DB.TableDefs.Count - 1
    LstLine$ = DB.TableDefs(i%).Name
    List1.AddItem LstLine$
Next
```

For each Table in the database, there is a TableDefs object, which describes the corresponding Table. Strictly speaking, TableDefs is a collection of objects—specifically, the TableDefs objects for each Table.

TableDefs is also a collection of objects called Fields. Fields in turn have Properties, the most common of which are shown in Table 4-8.

| Property | Description |
|---|---|
| Count | The number of fields in the Table. |
| Name | The field's name. |
| Type | The field's type. |
| Size | The field's maximum size. |

Table 4-8: Some common Properties of Fields.

Here is how you can add the Fields of the first Table of the DB database in a separate List, along with their definitions (data type and size):

```
For i% = 0 To DB.TableDefs(0).Fields.Count - 1
    LstLine$ = DB.TableDefs(0).Fields(i%).Name + "("
    LstLine$ = LstLine$ + DB.TableDefs(0).Fields(i%).Type + ")"
    LstLine$ = LstLine$ + DB.TableDefs(0).Fields(i%).Size
    List2.AddItem LstLine$
Next
```

Besides fields, each Table contains indices, which are stored in Index objects. All the Index objects of a TableDef form another collection, called the Indexes collection. As you may expect, the Index objects contain information describing the Table's indices, and their basic Properties (shown in Table 4-9) are appropriately named:

| Property | Description |
|---|---|
| Count | The number of indexes in the Table |
| Name | The name of the index. |
| Fields | The fields used in the index. |
| Unique | True if the index is unique, false otherwise. |
| Primary | True if it's the primary index, false otherwise. |

Table 4-9: Properties of Index objects.

The previous Properties are straightforward, except for the Fields Property, which is the name of the field(s) used in the index. An index can use multiple fields. Moreover, their order can be different. Some may be in ascending order, others in descending order. The Fields Property is made up of the name(s) of the fields used in the index, with the symbols + and – in front of each name, depending on whether the corresponding field is used in ascending or descending order. Multiple fields are separated with semicolons.

An index that sorts addresses according to state, and within each state according to the city, has the following form:

```
+State;+City
```

When you create this index with the Data Manager application, you don't have to type the previous expression. You select the State and City fields and move them to the Fields In Index Box by clicking on the "Add (Asc)" (ascending) or the "Add (desc)" (descending) Command Button. Data Manager creates the index and stores its description in the database definition.

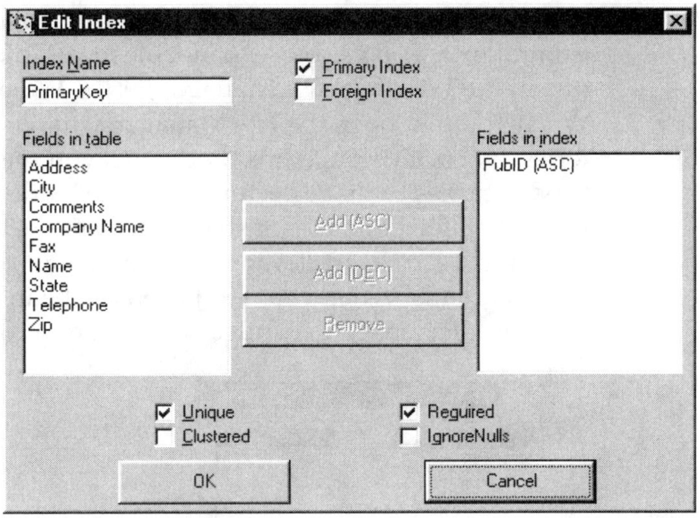


Figure 4-39: Looking at the descriptions of a Table's indices with the Data Manager.

The following lines place all the indexes of the first Table of the DB database in a List:

```
For i% = 0 To DB.TableDef(0).Indexes.Count - 1
    LstLine$ = DB.TableDefs(0).Indexes(i%).Fields
    If DB.TableDefs(0).Indexes(i%).Unique Then
        LstLine$ = LstLine$ + " U"
    End If
    If DB.TableDefs(0).Indexes(i%).Primary Then
        LstLine$ = LstLine$ + " P"
    End If
    List3.AddItem LstLine$
Next
```

Notice the similarity among the last three code segments (the one that reads the database's Table names, the one that reads a Table's field names and the one that reads a database's indices). The last program is somewhat different because it prints the characters U and P only if the corresponding index is unique or primary.

### Example: Mapping a Database

Let's put all of the information we've presented here together to build a useful example. What you see in Figure 4-36 is an Outline Control for displaying the structure of a database. If you don't know how the Outline Control works, it's like a List. We add items with the

AddItem Method. Unlike the List Control, however, the Outline Control provides various expandable levels, like the directory structure of the Windows File Manager (or the Windows 95 Explorer). When you first open the File Manager, you see the root's subdirectories. By clicking on a directory name, you see the names of the subdirectories of that directory. With the Outline Control, the user can view the information he or she is interested in by expanding a given item, and keep the irrelevant information out of sight by collapsing all other items. When you don't need all the information on the Control, click on the expanded item again to collapse it.

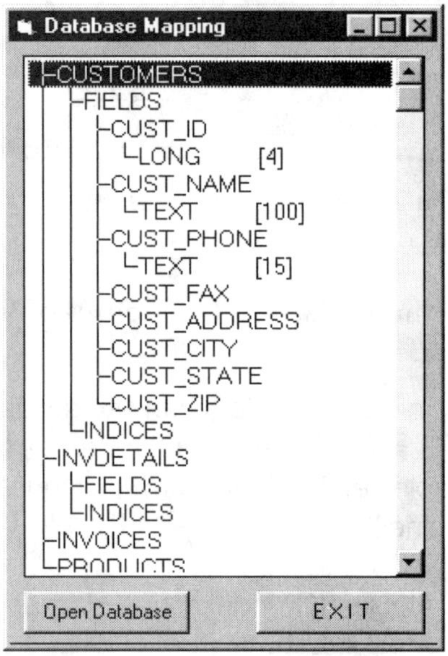


Figure 4-40: The MAPDB application displays the structure of any database.

In the first level you see the names of the Tables in the database. When you click on a Table name, two more items will appear: FIELDS and INDICES. Click on FIELDS to see the list of the fields, or on INDICES to see the list of indices for the specific Table. Once the field names appear, you can click on a field name to see its type. Similarly, you can click on an index name to see the structure of the index. An index is made up of one or more fields, in ascending or descending order, indicated by the + or – sign in front of the field's name. Consecutive fields are separated by a semicolon. If an index is Unique, or Primary, the corresponding indication appears in front of the first field's name.

The code that implements the MAPDB application is entered in the Click Event of the Show DB Structure Command Button.

```
Private Sub OpenDB_Click ( )
    CMDialog1.Filter = "Databases|*.MDB"
    CMDialog1.InitDir = App.Path
    CMDialog1.Action = 1
    If CMDialog1.Filename = "" Then Exit Sub
    Set DB = OpenDatabase(CMDialog1.Filename)
    Outline1.Clear
    Tables% = DB.TableDefs.Count          ' number of tables
    For itables = 0 To Tables% - 1
        If (DB.TableDefs(itables).Attributes And →
        DB_SYSTEMOBJECT) = 0 Then
            Outline1.AddItem DB.TableDefs(itables).Name
            Outline1.Indent(item) = 1
            item = item + 1
            Set FldDef = DB.TableDefs
            Set Fld = FldDef(itables).Fields
            Fields% = Fld.Count      ' Number of fields
            If Fields% > 0 Then
                Outline1.AddItem "FIELDS"' Add literal FIELDS
                Outline1.Indent(item) = 2
                item = item + 1
                For ifield = 0 To Fields% - 1
                ' Add each field to the list
                    FLine = Fld(ifield).Name
                    FldDesc = TypeNames(Fld(ifield).Type) + "[" →
                    + Format$(Fld(ifield).Size, "####") + "]"
                    Outline1.AddItem FLine
                    Outline1.Indent(item) = 3
                    item = item + 1
                    Outline1.AddItem FldDesc
                    Outline1.Indent(item) = 4
                    item = item + 1
                Next
            End If
            Set Idx = FldDef(itables).Indexes
            Indices% = Idx.Count          ' number of indices
            If Indices% > 0 Then
                Outline1.AddItem "INDICES"
                Outline1.Indent(item) = 2
```

```
                item = item + 1
                For iindex = 0 To Indices% - 1 ' Add each index
                    IndxName = Idx(iindex).Name
                    Outline1.AddItem IndxName
                    Outline1.Indent(item) = 3
                    item = item + 1
                    indxStr = ""
                    If Idx(iindex).Unique Then indxStr = "[U]"
                    If Idx(iindex).Primary Then indxStr = →
                    indxStr + "[P]"
                    indxStr = indxStr + Idx(iindex).Fields
                    Outline1.AddItem indxStr
                    Outline1.Indent(item) = 4
                    item = item + 1
                Next
            End If
        End If
    Next
End Sub
```

If you haven't programmed an Outline Control before, you can think of the lines that refer to the Outline1 Control as adding items to a regular List. An Outline Control is very similar to a List, with the exception that it accepts various levels of indentation. Each item is placed on the Outline Control with the proper indentation, and from there on the Control takes over. Expanding and collapsing its contents is done simply by clicking on the line in front of each item.

The databases you create contain a few system tables in addition to the ones you specified.

There is one item worth discussing in this application. When a new database is built, along with the Tables you define, some extra Tables are stored in the same MDB file. These Tables are used by the system, and you never see them with the Data Manager application, but their definitions are present in the TableDefs object. The first If statement in the For...Next loop checks the attributes of each Table and skips it if it's a system Table:

```
If (DB.TableDefs(itables).Attributes And →
DB_SYSTEMOBJECT) = 0 Then
{it's a regular table, process it ... }
```

For other uses of the Attributes Property, see the documentation of the Professional Edition of VB. DB_SYSTEMOBJECT is a constant defined in the DATACON.TXT file.

The variables DB, FldDef, Fld and Idx are Form-wide variables, defined in the Form's declarations section as follows:

```
Dim DB As database
Dim FldDef As TableDefs
Dim Fld As Fields
Dim Idx As Indexes
Dim item As Integer
```

The MAPDB application works with any database and is a handy development tool. If you need quick access to names of Tables and fields in a database (as when writing SQL statements), you can add this Form to your application. The SQLGRID application incorporates the MAPDB application in a separate Form.

## MOVING ON

Graphics are among the most interesting and exciting things modern computer languages can do. Visual Basic is a graphics-rich language, and we are devoting several chapters in this book to its graphics capabilities. In Chapter 5 we will explore the basic graphics capabilities of the language. We'll discuss in depth the Properties and Methods you must master in order to fully exploit the visual aspect of the language. After covering the basics, in Chapter 6 we'll see how to use Visual Basic in image processing and other sophisticated techniques.

# Chapter 5

# Graphics for Business & Science

Visual Basic's drawing facilities are widely overlooked and rarely given sufficient attention in books and magazines. Although there are only a few VB Methods and Properties relating to drawing, they interact. The number of options available with each command offers great flexibility for creating all kinds of graphics. In this chapter, we'll explore all the options of the graphics Methods and explain how to combine graphics Methods and Properties for the most efficient graphics programming.

At the end of this chapter, we'll sum things up by examining a complete application, VBPlot, that makes use of all the topics covered in the chapter and demonstrates how to create a functional business or scientific plotting application.

Let's start with the simplest graphics operation in Visual Basic, loading of a BMP graphic file into a Control. There are a few things you should know, even for this seemingly elementary maneuver.

## LOADING A GRAPHIC ONTO A CONTROL

Visual Basic provides three Controls that accept graphics: Forms, Picture Boxes and Image Boxes. (In the professional version of VB, the three-dimensional Command Buttons also accept graphics, but we'll limit our discussion here to the standard VB Controls.) All three have a Picture Property, which lets you assign a graphic to the Control.

To load a graphic onto a Form, Picture Box or Image Box at design time, type the file name (or browse the disk drive) in the Picture Property field of the Properties window. You cannot directly assign a file name to the Picture Property during run time. For example, the following line won't load a graphic on your Form. Instead, it will produce an error message.

```
Form1.Picture = "C:\IMAGES\MISSION.BMP"
```

To load a graphic on a Control at run time, use the LoadPicture Method, like this:

```
Form1.Picture = LoadPicture(FileName)
```

FileName is the name of the file containing the graphic. This file can have the extension BMP, DIB, WMF or ICO. At present, Visual Basic doesn't support other types of graphic files.

The LoadPicture Method without arguments clears the contents of a Picture Box or Form.

If you use the LoadPicture Method without an argument, the current picture will be unloaded (along with any drawing or printing painted onto the Control or Form via the Circle, Line, PSet or Print commands). Using LoadPicture with no file name specified clears the control. To remove a graphic from a Picture Box, issue the command:

```
Picture1.Picture = LoadPicture( )
```

This technique is similar to the Cls Method, which clears any drawing or printing from a Form or Control.

When you assign the graphic during design time with the Picture Property, the graphic becomes part of your program. This means it is stored along with the other elements of the Form file (increasing its size and the time it takes to load the file from disk into memory).

The alternative is to load the graphic dynamically during run time. Graphics loaded with the LoadPicture Method at run time keep the program's size smaller, but they must be on the disk at run time. So, this is a type of hard coding and can cause problems if the requested graphics are deleted or relocated on the user's disk. If your application lets the user choose between various graphics during run time, you must use the LoadPicture Method.

## Size the Graphic, or the Control?

There is nothing you can do about a graphic's size when it is loaded onto a Form—short of resizing the Form so that it embraces the graphic. If a Form in your application contains a graphic, you must size the Form according to the graphic. To prevent the user from resizing the form, you must also change its BorderStyle Property from the default, Sizeable, to any other setting. If a Form with a graphic is resized, it won't look as you intended it.

"BitBlt( ): Instant Tiled Wallpaper on Forms" (under "General Programming Utilities" in Chapter 8) describes an interesting technique for loading background textures and graphics quickly at run time. This technique dynamically resizes the interior graphic if the Form's size is changed, solving the problem of user-resizing.

Picture Boxes, however, have an AutoSize Property, which automatically resizes the Picture Box to the dimensions of the graphic. The graphic itself doesn't change size; the Picture Box adjusts itself to whatever graphic it contains.

Figure 5-1: Picture Boxes can either crop the image, so that its upper-left corner is always displayed, or resize themselves to fit the image.

Figure 5-2: Image Boxes can either change their own size or resize the graphic they contain. The graphic in an Image Box is never cropped.

Image Boxes have a Stretch Property, which when True expands or contracts the graphic to fit within the Image Box's size. Notice in Figure 5-2 that an Image Box with Stretch set to True resizes the graphic without regard to its original aspect ratio. This means that you must size an Image Box properly, or else the graphic can be distorted. If the Stretch Property of the Image Box is set to False, the Image Box will adjust to accommodate the graphic's size (like a Picture Box with its AutoSize property set to True).

Image Boxes can stretch the image to fit in the available space.

However, an Image Box uses fewer resources than a Picture Box. For one thing, you can't draw with Visual Basic's Line, Circle, PSet or Print commands on an Image Box. But unless you need the extra facilities provided by a Picture Box, use an Image Box instead.

Now let's turn our attention from predrawn graphics loaded into VB from disk files to graphics dynamically drawn during run time. To fully utilize VB's drawing commands (Circle, Line, PSet and Point), we must first understand its highly flexible coordinate features.

## COORDINATE SYSTEMS

Before you can draw anything on a Control, before you can even draw a single line on it, you must know a few things about coordinates. Coordinates describe the position of the individual pixels on the screen, or of the points on a piece of paper in the printer.

## What Is a Coordinate System?

The coordinate system in VB is similar to a city map with columns labeled A, B, C, etc., and rows labeled 1, 2, 3, etc. Each little square on the map has its own unique address: a combination of a column and a row number. In this way, a location on the map is specified with two coordinates. The horizontal coordinate (the column letter on the map example) is called the X coordinate and the vertical coordinate (the row number) is called the Y coordinate. In Figure 5-3 you see a Picture Box, and the coordinates of its four corners.

You could also think of the screen (or part of it) as a two-dimensional array, Screen(X, Y). Each element of the Screen( ) array describes the value (color) of a pixel on the screen. The index X refers to the horizontal position, and Y to the vertical position. With the help of X and Y you can access any point on the screen and read or set its color value, thereby making drawings.

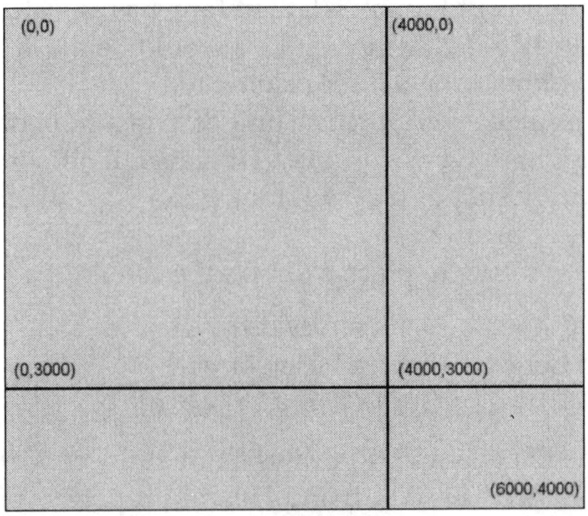


Figure 5-3: The default coordinate system of a Picture Box. Each point is identified with the help of two numbers (its X and Y coordinates).

In Visual Basic, the *origin* of the coordinate system (the point with the smallest X and Y coordinates) is the upper-left corner of the Control or Form. The X coordinates increase to the right and the Y coordinates, downward.

Each coordinate is a number, but what does it represent? Why are there 6,000 horizontal units and 4,000 vertical units in the example of Figure 5-3 (there aren't nearly that many pixels on a computer monitor). Coordinate systems are more or less arbitrary, just like a city map's row and column numbers. There could be more, or fewer, of them, depending on the map's size and contents and the density of the grid being superimposed on the map itself. How dense the grid *is* will be up to the designers of the map; how dense your coordinate system is will be up to you in a VB project.

Visual Basic provides eight different ways to specify coordinates.

You might expect VB coordinates to be expressed in pixels, which are the smallest addressable unit on the screen. However, your application doesn't start and end with the display. A year from now you may have a larger monitor, or some user of your application might use a greater resolution such as 1024 X 768 or 1280 X 1024. Your printer has much greater resolution than your monitor. So, your applications should be designed to perform equally well on a variety of output devices, not just your current video system.

This is why the coordinate systems used by Visual Basic are not limited to the resolution of current monitors. VB's default coordinate system uses a unit called *twip*, and there are 1,440 twips per inch. The Picture Box in Figure 5-3, therefore, has an actual size of approximately 4.15 X 2.75 inches. This would be the size of the Picture Box if you printed it on a laser printer.

A twip is a very precise unit of measurement, probably more precise than we need today. However, it allows us to design screens and draw shapes that will look good even when printed on a 1,200 dpi laser printer.

Here's how to place a dot on the center of a Picture Box:

```
XCoord = Picture1.Width / 2
YCoord = Picture1.Height / 2
Picture1.PSet (XCoord, YCoord)
```

The PSet command draws a dot at the coordinates provided as its arguments. The Width and Height Properties of a Picture Box return its dimensions. This way, you can draw a dot in the center of a Picture Box regardless of the units used to measure its dimensions. This is the very essence of a coordinate system: the units that describe position are *arbitrary* and don't affect the Picture Box size.

However, twips are not convenient in all situations. That's why Visual Basic provides the eight different coordinate systems listed in Table 5-1. To switch to a different coordinate system, assign the proper value to the ScaleMode Property of the Form or Control you're working with.

| Value | Description | Constant Name |
|---|---|---|
| 0 | User-defined coordinate system | USER |
| 1 | Twips (1,440 twips per inch) | TWIPS |
| 2 | Points (72 points per inch) | POINTS |
| 3 | Pixels | PIXELS |
| 4 | Characters (120 twips wide, 240 twips high) | CHARACTERS |
| 5 | Inches | INCHES |
| 6 | Millimeters | MILLIMETERS |
| 7 | Centimeters | CENTIMETERS |

Table 5-1: The values used with the ScaleMode Property, and the corresponding coordinate systems.

The ScaleMode Property determines how you refer to the pixels of your screen or the dots on your printer's page. In other words, it determines how you "address" the points on the output device. Points are the units used by typographers (and DTP software) to accurately measure and position text characters on a page. The Points and Characters coordinate systems are probably the least often used by Visual Basic programmers. The Pixels system allows you to access each individual pixel on the screen, and is therefore the most appropriate for processing images. The three coordinate systems listed last in Table 5-1 are used mostly to design forms that must be printed very accurately. Old BASIC programmers are familiar with Pixels, since it and Character were the only coordinate systems used by most previous BASIC dialects.

The most flexible system of coordinates is the one you define.

But perhaps the most interesting and useful coordinate system of all is the User-defined one.

## User-Defined Coordinate Systems

When you create a drawing representing some actual entity, such as a house or a molecule, the most convenient coordinate system is one that you define. For instance, to make the drawings of your new house, which is 10 yards wide by 12 yards long, you can set a new coordinate system that extends horizontally from 0 to 12 and vertically from 0 to 10. This way, all the distances are described in their natural units, and you won't have to convert them to pixels or twips. Similarly, if you are plotting a mathematical function, as we will do at the end of this chapter, the coordinate system should reflect the values of the function, and not characters or points, which have no physical meaning in most practical applications.

User-defined coordinates differ from any other type in that they must be defined. Setting the ScaleMode Property to 0, the User-defined mode, is not enough. You must then also use the Scale command to tell Visual Basic what units it must use to access the screen. (Note that you need not actually set ScaleMode to 0. As soon as you issue the Scale command, the ScaleMode Property automatically will be set to 0, to reflect the fact that you have switched to a User-defined coordinate system.)

```
Picture1.Scale (0,0) - (12,10)
```

This example sets up a coordinate system whose origin is at coordinates (0, 0) and which extends 12 units horizontally and 10 units vertically. The units can be inches, miles or light-years. Visual Basic doesn't really care. It's up to you, the programmer, to make these numbers meaningful. If you are drawing a map, it makes sense to measure distances in miles. If you're drawing a house, yards or feet would be more meaningful.

Another important distinction between a User-defined coordinate system and the others is that the User-defined system considers only the pixels *within* the Form or Control. All other coordinate systems take into consideration the frame around the Form or Control too. We will return to this important distinction shortly in "Sizing & Positioning Objects."

A User-defined coordinate system need not start at (0, 0). The command

```
Picture1.Scale (25, 28) - (37, 38)
```

By default, the origin of a coordinate system is at the upper-left corner of the Control.

sets up a coordinate system that extends 12 units horizontally and 10 units vertically, as before. But its coordinates go from 25 to 37 and 28 to 38. The origin of this coordinate system is at (25, 28).

If you are more comfortable with a coordinate system that starts at the lower-left corner of the Control or Form, then invert the minimum and maximum Y coordinates in the Scale command. The command

```
Picture1.Scale (10, 100) - (80, 50)
```

defines a coordinate system with its origin at the lower-left corner of the Control. The Control's coordinates extend horizontally from 10 to 80 (left to right) and vertically from 50 to 100 (bottom to top). You can also change coordinate systems during run time, as you'll see in the VBPlot application discussed under "Example: Plotting Functions & Data Sets" later in this chapter.

The four parameters of the Scale Method are actually properties of the Control or Form, with the names ScaleLeft, ScaleTop, ScaleWidth and ScaleHeight. ScaleLeft and ScaleTop are the coordinates of the upper-left corner (origin), and ScaleWidth and ScaleHeight are the width and height of the Control (expressed always in the units of the User-defined coordinate system). The commands

```
Picture1.ScaleLeft = 10
Picture1.ScaleTop = 100
Picture1.ScaleWidth = 80
Picture1.ScaleHeight = 50
```

are equivalent to the following Scale Method:

```
Picture1.Scale (10, 100) - (80, 50)
```

All properties that begin with the prefix Scale use the User-defined coordinate system. Setting any of these properties switches you to a User-defined coordinate system and sets the ScaleMode Property to 0. However, it doesn't reposition or rescale the Control or Form. Similarly, every time you issue a Scale command like Picture1.Scale (10, 100) – (80, 50), these four properties change value according to the Scale command's arguments.

You can, of course, make your grid as fine, as high-resolution, as your purposes demand. A map of a desert, for instance, might require only 16 large squares to locate or position the few features on the map. A map of New York City, on the other hand, might require a high-resolution grid with 100 X 100 tiny squares to be useful.

Here is a way to double the number of horizontal and vertical units (the squares or intersections created when you superimpose a coordinate system) in a Picture Box:

```
Picture1.Scale (Picture1.ScaleLeft, Picture1.ScaleTop) –
(Picture1.ScaleWidth * 2, Picture1.ScaleHeight * 2)
```

Or, more simply:

```
Picture1.ScaleWidth = Picture1.ScaleWidth * 2
Picture1.ScaleHeight = Picture1.ScaleHeight * 2
```

## Sizing & Positioning Objects

Each VB Control or Form has two Properties for setting its size, Width and Height, and two Properties for setting its position, Top and Left. All four are expressed in the coordinate system of the "container," the object that contains the Picture Box or Form. A Form is always positioned with respect to the Screen "Object," and a Picture Box is positioned with respect to the Form or any other object it can belong to (such as a Form, another Picture Box, or a 3-D Panel). In most but not all situations, the Width, Height, Left and Top Properties are expressed in twips.

The Left, Top, Width and Height Properties are used for positioning Controls and *must* be expressed in the Form's or other container's coordinates.

Remember that you cannot use the object's *internal coordinates* to position it on the screen. The coordinate system you set up with the Scale Method has nothing to do with other objects, and therefore cannot be used for positioning or sizing the object relative to the outside objects. In other words, if a Picture Box has a User-defined coordinate system, the Form that contains it still uses the default twips. To reposition or resize the Picture Box, you must use twips. (Of course, you can also change the coordinate system of the container. But the point is this: changing the user-defined system *within* a Picture Box doesn't permit you to use that new system to affect the Picture Box's Height, Width, Left or Right Properties.)

## Experimenting With Coordinate Systems

Many people find the close relationship among graphics Properties and Methods confusing. Even experienced VB programmers must experiment with settings sometimes to get what they want.

CD-ROM

The SCALE application, shown in Figure 5-4, lets you experiment with the various Properties we've discussed so far and with their interdependence. You will find the application in the 5\APPS\SCALE subdirectory on the CD.

### Example: SCALE

The SCALE application consists of two Forms. One (called Image) contains a Picture Box whose position and size can be manipulated using the scroll bars of the other Form (called Properties). All Properties refer to the Picture Box. The scroll bars beneath each Text Box allow you to change the current setting of each Property and see the results.

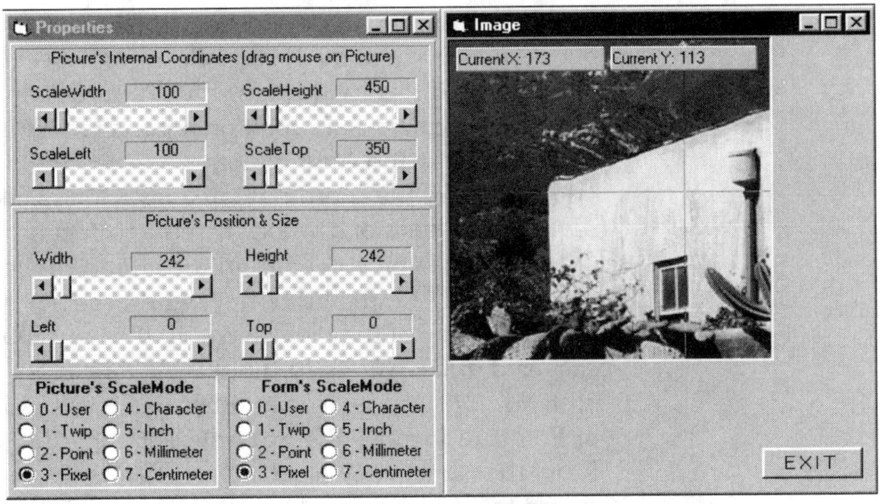


Figure 5-4: The SCALE application lets you experiment with various options for coordinate system settings.

The first group of Controls changes the Picture Box's coordinate system (we call it the "internal" coordinate system to distinguish it from the Form's coordinate system). You can change the Picture Box's coordinate system any way you like. To verify your changes, drag the mouse pointer within the Picture Box. Its current coordinates will be displayed in the two gray frames on top.

For example, change the ScaleLeft setting to 1,000 and then drag the mouse pointer over the Picture Box. The horizontal coordinate (X) will be always larger than 1,000. Then change the ScaleTop Property to 5,000 and watch the coordinate display as you move the mouse pointer over the Picture Box. The vertical coordinate will be larger than 5,000 because this is the new minimum value for the Y axis. Changing any of the four Scale Properties in the upper group of Controls will affect only the way the Picture Box's coordinates are measured. You will have to drag the mouse over the Picture Box and read the coordinates to see the changes.

Changing the ScaleTop, ScaleLeft, ScaleWidth and ScaleHeight Properties does not affect the size of the Control.

Now change settings in the second group of Controls, which determines the Picture Box's position and size. Increase or decrease the dimensions of the Picture Box with the Width and Height Properties, or change its position with the Left and Top Properties. If the Form's coordinate system is twips, it takes a substantial change in the value of any of the properties before something visible happens. There are many twips in a pixel. But set the Form's coordinate system to Pixel, and the Picture Box changes size or moves by 1 pixel with every click on the corresponding scroll bar. Set it to Inch, and with every small change the Picture Box jumps because the program allows only integer values for the Properties. In your applications, of course, you can specify fractional parts too. Some coordinate systems, such as Inches and Centimeters, allow for fractional coordinates, as you can see in the coordinate display. Others, like Twips and Pixels, require that positions be expressed as integers.

Every time you switch from the User-defined system to another one, the ScaleWidth and ScaleHeight Properties change value to reflect the size of the Picture Box in the new coordinates. This is an easy and quick way to find out the relationship between any two systems of coordinates to another one (such as Pixels to Millimeters or Points to Inches). For example, set the Form's Width and Height Properties to 2,880 twips. Click on Points to see how points correspond to 2,880 twips (144). Then click on Pixels to find out that there are 192 pixels in 2,880 twips.

When you switch to the User-defined system from another system, the Scale Properties don't change value. Visual Basic cannot guess your intentions, so it retains the old number of units. If you issue the Scale Method, however, the ScaleLeft, ScaleTop, ScaleWidth and ScaleHeight Properties change value immediately and the ScaleMode Property is set automatically to 0. Change one of the scroll bars in the first group, and the User Option Button is automatically selected.

### Which Coordinate System?

This question will be answered by your application's needs. If you design Forms that must look pretty and accurate when printed, use any of the last three coordinate systems (Inches, Millimeters or Centimeters) or the typographical coordinate system (Points). For image processing applications, where the distance of pixels has no physical meaning, you can choose Pixels. Finally, for drawing shapes with physical analogs in the real world, such as buildings or geographical areas, set up your own coordinate system to relate to the real-world measurements.

Changing the coordinate system does not change the actual size of the Picture Box or Form. Therefore, it is possible to set up a coordinate system, perform some operations and then switch to another coordinate system, as shown here:

```
Picture1.Scale (0, 0) - (1 ,1)
{..graphics commands here..}
Picture1.Scale (0, 0) - (100, 300)
{.. more graphics commands follow..}
```

Think of the coordinate system as the scale of a map. The larger the object, the larger the scale.

The previous Scale commands won't affect the size of the Picture Box. The Width and Height Properties won't change value, but the ScaleWidth and ScaleHeight Properties will. Remember that ScaleWidth and ScaleHeight have nothing to do with the Control's actual size. They are the horizontal and vertical dimensions of the Control in the User-defined system of coordinates. You will use larger coordinates to draw the map of California on a Picture Box than you would to draw the map of Connecticut. Think of the coordinate system as the *scale* of a map. The larger the object you want to describe, the larger the scale will be. But the size of the Picture Box (or the actual paper on which the map is printed) won't be affected.

### Twips, Pixels & Inches

The size of any Control you place on a Form is defined in twips; that's the default coordinate system. However, twips are pretty meaningless when it comes to the size of Picture Boxes. A Control that is 1,440 twips wide extends 1 inch horizontally. But 1 inch is perceived very differently on a notebook screen than on a 21-inch monitor. Visual Basic doesn't know what size monitor you're using, so it defines a "logical" inch, which is close to a physical inch. A logical inch is not always an inch in length if you measure it with a ruler on your screen. When the output is directed to the printer, though, you can expect a logical inch to exactly equal a real, physical inch.

A logical inch equals a physical inch on a 96-dpi monitor.

A more common way to define a Picture Box's dimensions is in pixels. If the container Form or Control is using the default coordinate system, the Width and Height Properties cannot be expressed in pixels. But you can convert pixels to twips using the TwipsPerPixelX and TwipsPerPixelY Properties of the Screen Object. TwipsPerPixelX is the number of twips in each pixel in the horizontal dimension. TwipsPerPixelY is the number of twips in each pixel in the vertical dimension. For a monitor with resolution 640 X 480, both values are 15. If the resolution of the monitor is raised to 600 X 800, the values won't change. Given that there are 1,440 twips in an inch and 15 twips in a pixel, it follows that Windows assumes a monitor resolution of 96 pixels per inch (or dots per inch, dpi), and this is how the logical inch is defined.

Can a logical inch be anything else than 96 dpi? The answer is yes. If you are using a very high resolution, such as 1024 X 768 or more, chances are you are using Large fonts too. Most graphics adapters offer two options when you install a driver with very high resolution: Large fonts and Small fonts. If you select Large fonts, then the monitor's resolution is raised to 120 dpi. And this is a source of headaches for developers. Forms designed to look good at 96 dpi may not look the same at 120 dpi.

Here's a typical example: Let's say you design a Form with a Picture Box on a system with a monitor resolution of 96 dpi. Then you load an image onto the Picture Box. You make sure that the image fills the Picture Box exactly (by adjusting the size of the Picture Box with the image in it). Your Form looks great at various resolutions, and your code works even better.

When designing Forms, never assume that a logical inch is always 96 dpi.

When this application is run on a monitor with 120 dpi, your carefully crafted Form will be thrown out of kilter. For one thing, the image will no longer fill the Picture Box. The Picture Box now contains more pixels! A logical inch is no more 96 dpi, and therefore the TwipsPerPixelX and TwipsPerPixelY Properties are no longer 15 . Since the Picture Box contains more pixels, it can't be filled with the same image. To cope with this situation, you must either position all the elements on the Form with the proper code at run time, or design two Forms, one for 96 dpi and one for 120 dpi. Then, at run time, your program can examine the value of the TwipsPerPixelX Property and decide which Form to load.

Figures 5-5 and 5-6 demonstrate what happens to a Form designed on a system with a specific resolution when it is displayed on a different system, with higher dpi.

Figure 5-5: A Picture Box with an image at 96 dpi. The Picture Box was carefully adjusted to the size of the image at design time.

Figure 5-6: The same Form at 120 dpi. Now, the Picture Box is larger (it contains more pixels), and the image can't fit exactly into the Picture Box.

Most Forms will still look the same, but Forms that contain Picture Boxes with images must be handled carefully. If you want to display an image on a Picture Box, do not resize the Picture Box at design time (snagging the image). When run at a system with higher dpi, the Picture Box will contain more pixels, and the image will fill it partially. Use the ScaleWidth and ScaleHeight Properties from within your code to properly size and position the Picture Boxes (or Image Boxes) along with their contents.

CD-ROM

The programs we offer on the CD were designed to look good with resolutions 640 X 480 and 800 X 600, which are by far the most commonly used. At those resolutions, a logical inch is the same. Although we took care so that our Forms will look good at higher resolutions too, you may run into a Form that doesn't look quite right on a system with a resolution of 120 dpi. You know where the problem lies, and it should be easy to fix.

Suppose you have a Picture Box on a form whose coordinate system is Twips. If you want the Picture Box to be 200 pixels wide and 160 pixels high, you can combine the TwipsPerPixelX and TwipsPerPixelY Properties with the Width and Height Properties, as shown here:

```
Picture1.Width = 200 * Screen.TwipsPerPixelX
Picture1.Height = 160 * Screen.TwipsPerPixelY
```

The new dimensions *include the width of the frame* of the Picture Box. Width and Height Properties include the Control's frame. ScaleWidth and ScaleHeight, on the other hand, are the inside dimensions of the Control, excluding any frame. In other words, they are the number of pixels you could turn on or off within the Control using the drawing commands like PSet. The actual number of pixels you have at your disposal, excluding the single-pixel frame, is given by ScaleWidth and ScaleHeight.

To demonstrate this distinction, set both coordinate systems of the SCALE application to "1 - Twip". Then look at the values of the Picture Box's size Properties. Width and Height are larger than ScaleWidth and ScaleHeight, respectively, by the frame's thickness, measured in twips. On a VGA monitor, this 2-pixel thickness equals 30 twips, but this may vary as we discussed earlier. Switch to different coordinate systems to see the same difference in all types of units.

ScaleWidth and ScaleHeight report the inside dimensions of a Control. Width and Height include the thickness of the frame.

This distinction between internal and external dimensions becomes important with Forms, which have a thick border. The size of a Form must always be expressed in twips (you can't change the screen's coordinate system). To create a Form with a specific number of pixels, you must use the TwipsPerPixelX and TwipsPerPixelY Properties and take into consideration the thickness of the border too. The following code segment resizes a Picture Box so that it has an internal width of 180 pixels and an internal height of 200 pixels, provided that the ScaleMode of both the Form and the Picture Box is 3 (pixels):

```
Picture1.Width = 180 + Picture1.Width - Picture1.ScaleWidth
Picture1.Height = 200 + Picture1.Height -
Picture1.ScaleHeight
```

Notice that the internal size of the Picture Box is 180 X 200, regardless of the width of its frame.

## AND NOW FOR SOME DRAWING

Now let's look at the actual drawing mechanisms of Visual Basic: the Line, Circle, Point and PSet Methods. The Line and Circle Methods accept many arguments that extend Visual Basic's drawing capabilities. With these two Methods you can draw elaborate geometric shapes such as pie charts. The Point and Pset Methods handle images that are made up of pixels rather than shapes and are usually scanned into the computer. We explore all four Methods in the examples below. You can also find many examples of using the Point and PSet Methods in Chapter 6, "Color & Imaging."

## Drawing Lines & Boxes

The Visual Basic command for drawing lines and boxes is appropriately named Line. Like the other graphics Methods, it applies to Forms and Picture Boxes. The complete syntax of the Line Method is

```
Line[[Step] (X1, Y1)] - [Step] (X2, Y2) [,[color], [B][F]]]
```

It is a simple command, in spite of its syntax, but it's also quite flexible. Here's the simplest line:

```
Line (X1, Y1) - (X2, Y2)
```

This command draws a line from point (X1, Y1) to (X2, Y2). The coordinates of the endpoints are expressed in the units of the Control's coordinate system. The thickness of the line is determined by the DrawWidth Property, and its style by the DrawStyle Property, whose settings are shown in Table 5-2. If the width of the line is greater than 1 pixel, then the settings 1 through 4 are identical to setting 0—that is, you cannot draw dashed or dotted lines that are thicker than 1 pixel.

| Value | Description | Constant Name |
|---|---|---|
| 0 | Solid line | G_SOLID |
| 1 | Dashed | G_DASHED |
| 2 | Dotted | G_DOT |
| 3 | Dash-Dot | G_DASHDOT |
| 4 | Dash-Dot-Dot | G_DASHDOTDOT |
| 5 | Invisible | G_INVISIBLE |
| 6 | Inside | G_INSIDE |

Table 5-2: The settings of the DrawStyle Property.

By default, the width of a line is split on both sides of the specified coordinates.

The meaning of each property is obvious, except for the last value, G_INSIDE. When drawing with a line width larger than 1 pixel, Visual Basic splits the width of the line on both sides of the specified coordinates. If you set the DrawStyle Property to 6 (Inside), the shape (line, box or circle) will be drawn entirely within the specified coordinates. In Figure 5-7 you see two identical rectangles, drawn with the Inside setting on the left and the Solid setting on the right. The dashed lines correspond to the Y coordinates of their corners.

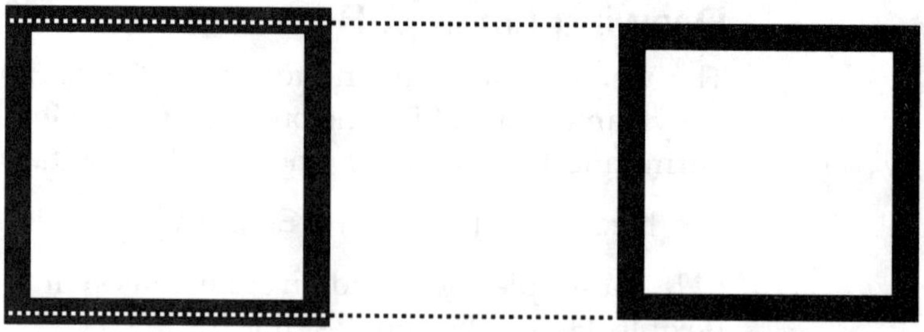


Figure 5-7: When the DrawStyle Property is 6, the rectangle lies entirely inside the coordinates of its corners. Otherwise, the width of the line is split on the inside and outside of the rectangle.

The following short program draws lines of different styles on the Picture Box Picture1:

```
Private Sub Picture1_Click( )

H = Picture1.ScaleHeight
W = Picture1.ScaleWidth
Hstep = H / 6
For i% = 1 to 6
    Picture1.DrawStyle = i% - 1
    Picture1.Line (.1 * W, Hstep * i%) - (.0 *W, Hstep * i%)
Next

End Sub
```

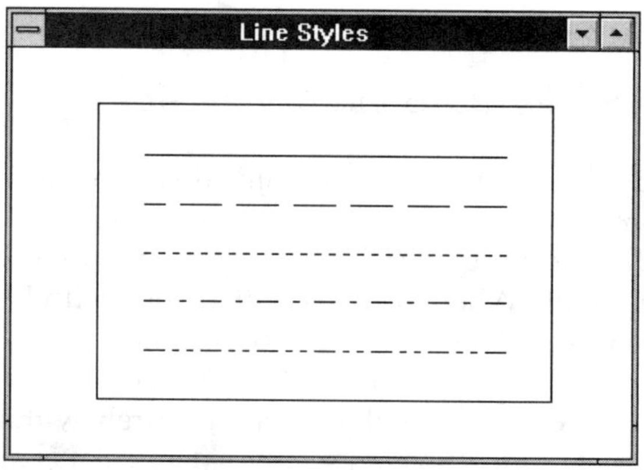


Figure 5-8: To generate different line styles, change the DrawStyle Property.

The ForeColor Property of the Picture Box or Form determines the color of the line. But you can draw lines in different colors by specifying the optional argument, *color*, available with the Line, Circle and PSet commands. The following commands show how the color argument can be used:

```
Line (10, 10) - (100, 100), RGB(0, 0, 255)
Line (10, 10) - (100, 100), &H0000F0
Line (10, 10) - (100, 100), QBColor(4)

BlueColor# = RGB(0, 0, 128)
Line (10, 10) - (100, 100), BlueColor#
```

All three example draw a blue line from (10, 10) to (100, 100), regardless of the current setting of the ForeColor Property. Any valid expression of color, or variable, can be used in the place of the color argument.

If the coordinates of the first endpoint are zero, they can be omitted. The commands Line (0,0) - (100,100) and Line - (100,100) are equivalent, as long as you don't forget the minus sign in front of the second endpoint.

## Using Relative Coordinates

With the Step option you can define the endpoints relative to the current point. In other words, the Step option defines a point not in terms of its coordinates, but in terms of its distance from the current point. (This distance is given by the properties CurrentX and CurrentY, which are updated each time you use a drawing command.)

The coordinates we have used so far are *absolute* because they specify a unique point on the screen as measured from the ScaleLeft and ScaleTop Properties.

The coordinates following the Step option are *relative*. The difference between the two types of coordinates is their origin. Absolute coordinates are always measured from the origin (ScaleLeft, ScaleTop), while relative coordinates are measured from the current position, wherever it might be. When using absolute coordinates, you're always referring to the same point, no matter where the current point is. Placement of a point in relative coordinates depends on the current point.

For example,

```
Line (100, 100) - (300, 300)
```

draws a line that starts at point (100, 100) and extends 200 units down and 200 units to the right from that starting point. The command

```
Line (100, 100) - Step (300, 300)
```

draws a line from the same starting point, but this one extends 300 units down and 300 units to the right. The two numbers following the Step option are not the coordinates of the second endpoint, but its distance from the current point.

To translate relative coordinates to absolute ones, we must add them to the coordinates of the current point. The previous command draws a line from point (100, 100) to the point (100 + 300, 100 + 300) or (400, 400). As you see, we add the relative coordinates of the second endpoint to coordinates of the first one because, as soon as Visual Basic starts drawing the line, the first endpoint becomes the current point. The Step option can also appear in front of the starting coordinates, or both. Here are some examples:

```
Line Step(-10, 20)-(300, 300)
```

This draws a line which starts 10 points to the left and 20 points below the current point and ends at coordinates (300, 300). The command

```
Line (34, 55) - Step (100,100)
```

draws a line that extends 100 units in both directions and starts at the point (34, 55).

Figure 5-9 shows lines drawn with absolute and relative coordinates. The lines were drawn with the commands:

```
Picture1.Line (100, 100) - (500, 500)
Picture1.Line Step (100,150) - (300, 600)
```

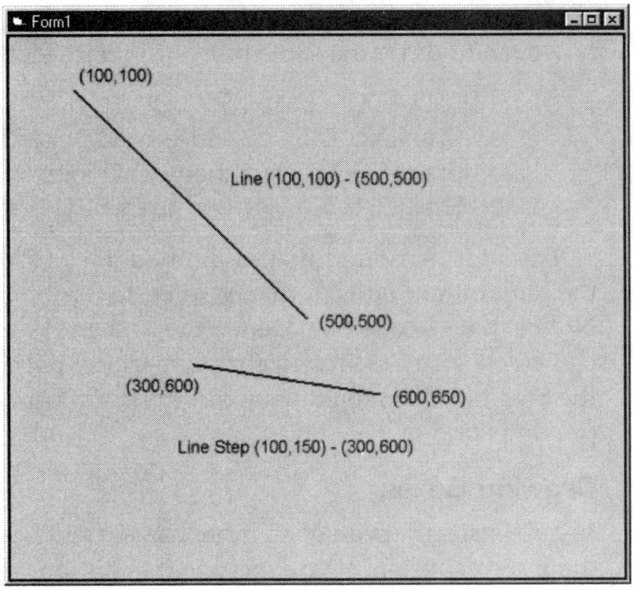


Figure 5-9: Drawing lines with absolute and relative coordinates.

The first line starts at point (100, 100), no matter what the current point was at the time. Before the second command was executed, the current point was moved to (500, 500). The absolute coordinates of the starting point of the second line are (500+100, 500+150) = (600, 650), while the ending point is already expressed in absolute coordinates.

To convert relative to absolute coordinates, add them to the coordinates of the current point.

```
Absolute Coordinates  = Current Point + Relative Coordinates
(Xabs, Yabs)          = (CurrentX, CurrentY) + (Xrel, Yrel)
                      = (CurrentX + Xrel, CurrentY + Yrel)
```

Relative coordinates are used frequently in drawing closed shapes, where it is easier to define an endpoint in terms of its distance from the previous one. Let's say we want to draw a box with dimensions 300 X 500, with its upper-left corner at the point (100,100). This box can be drawn in absolute coordinates, with the following commands:

```
Line (100,100) - (400,100)   ' Move along the X axis
Line (400,100) - (400,600)   ' Move down
Line (400,600) - (100,600)   ' Move back along the X axis
Line (100,600) - (100,100)   ' and back to the starting point
```

For each of the previous commands, we had to calculate the absolute coordinates of each corner of the frame by adding the appropriate dimensions to the previous endpoint. It is much easier, however, to draw the same box with relative coordinates. Here's how:

```
Line (100,100) - Step (300,0)
Line - Step(0,500)      ' Move 500 units down
Line - Step(-300,0)     ' then 300 units to the left
Line - Step(0,-500)     ' and then 500 units up
```

Relative coordinates simplify the drawing of closed shapes.

The starting point must be defined in absolute coordinates, but for the remaining points, it makes sense to use relative coordinates. Notice that we need not define the first endpoint of each side, since it coincides with the second endpoint of the previous side. Following the Step option is the distance of the next corner of the box from the previous one.

### Drawing Boxes

Visual Basic offers an even more convenient way of drawing boxes—the B (Box) option. If you include this option, you can draw a box whose upper-left corner is defined by the first coordinate pair and whose lower-right corner is defined by the second coordinate pair. The last four commands in our previous example could be replaced by the following line:

```
Line (100,100) - (400,600), , B
```

Notice the two consecutive commas. They are necessary to denote the absence of the color argument. If you wanted to include the color argument, you could have typed

```
Line (100,100) - (400,600), QBColor(4), B
```

If you omit the color argument, you must type the two commas, or else Visual Basic will think that B is a variable name specifying the color of the box. If you have declared a variable B in your program, it will be used as a color value. If you have not declared a variable B, Visual Basic will create one and assign it the value 0, and you will end up drawing a black line rather than a box.

As you may have guessed already, there is an even easier way to draw a box on the screen, using relative coordinates. All we wanted was a rectangle with known dimensions and its upper-left corner fixed at point (100, 100). Here's the command that does just that:

```
Line (100,100) - Step (300,500), , B
```

Here we specified the coordinates of the upper-left corner and the dimensions of the box. The advantage of the last command is that we don't have to perform any calculations; we just type the known data.

The BF option of the Line Method draws solid, filled boxes, regardless of the current setting of the FillStyle Property.

The Line method accepts one more option that can be used only along with the B option. If you want to fill the box, use the F (Fill) option immediately after the B option. There is no comma between the B and the F options. It might be easier to think of the two options as being the B (for box) and BF (for filled box) options, since you cannot use the F option alone. The color used for the filling is determined by the property FillColor.

The characters B and F that can follow a Line command are literal and not variables. You don't have to declare any variables of that name and assign values to them. However, you can declare and use variables named B and F in your program. The Line method won't affect them in any way.

This property can take on any of the values of Table 5-3. The default value of this property is 1, which means that the boxes you draw on the screen will be transparent.

| Value | Constant Name | Description |
|---|---|---|
| 0 | FILL_SOLID | Solid Color |
| 1 | FILL_TRANSPARENT | Transparent |
| 2 | FILL-HORIZONTAL | Horizontal Lines |
| 3 | FILL_VERTICAL | Vertical Lines |
| 4 | FILL_UPWARD | Upward Diagonal |
| 5 | FILL_DOWNWARD | Downward Diagonal |
| 6 | FILL_CROSS | Cross |
| 7 | FILL_DIAGONAL | Diagonal Cross |

Table 5-3: The Settings of the FillStyle Property.

## Which Color Goes Where?

We've arrived at a good point to review the properties ForeColor, BackColor, FillStyle and FillColor. BackColor is what fills the Form or Picture Box or other Control. Text and shapes appear on top of the BackColor. ForeColor is the current drawing color (or if you're printing some text, the color that the text characters will be). The FillStyle Property, whose values are shown in Table 5-3, determines how closed shapes (circles or rectangles) will be filled. You needn't specify that a rectangle will be filled with the F option. If the FillStyle Property of the Form is set to any value other than Transparent (1), the rectangle will be filled with the corresponding pattern.

However, the BF option of the Line Method always fills the rectangle with a solid color. It is not affected by the current setting of the FillStyle Property. To fill a rectangle (or a circle, for that matter) with a specific pattern, you must set the value of the FillStyle Property and then draw the rectangle with the B option *only*. Should you specify the F option too, the rectangle will be filled with a solid color.

In spite of its name, the FillColor Property does not affect the filling color. It affects only the color of any lines in the pattern used to fill the shape. In Figure 5-10 you see some boxes and circles filled with all available patterns.

FillColor determines the color of the lines of the filling pattern, and not the color that fills the shape.

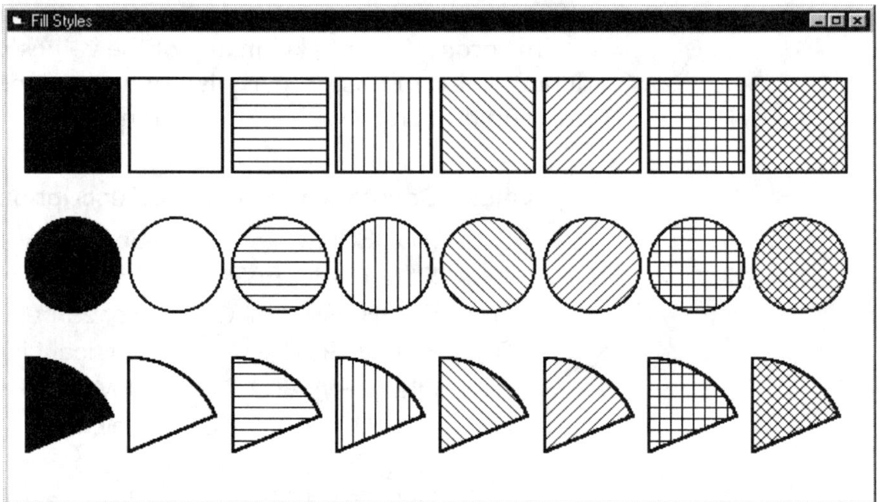


Figure 5-10: Visual Basic's fill patterns applied to boxes, circles and wedges (arcs).

The code that created the filled shapes of Figure 5-10 is quite simple (you may want to look at this routine again after reading the discussion of the Circle Method in the next section):

```
Sub Form_Load ( )
Show

    Form1.DrawWidth = 2
    For i = 0 To 7
        Form1.FillStyle = i
        Form1.Line (i * 1100 + 200, 500)-Step(1000, →
1000), , B
    Next
```

```
    For i = 0 To 7
        Form1.FillStyle = i
        Form1.Circle (i * 1100 + 700, 2500), 500
    Next

    pi# = 4 * Atn(1)
    phi1# = pi# / 8#
    phi2# = pi# / 2
    For i = 0 To 7
        Form1.FillStyle = i
        Form1.Circle (i * 1100 + 200, 4500), 1000, , →
-phi1#, -phi2#
    Next

End Sub
```

CD-ROM

You can find this short program in the 5\APPS\FILLSTLS subdirectory of the CD. The expression 4 * Atn(1) returns the value of pi (3.14159...). phi1# and phi2# are the starting and ending angles of the wedges.

## Drawing Modes

Another property that is of great interest in drawing is the DrawMode Property, which determines how the new pixels (such as the pixels in a line drawn with the Line command) will be combined with the existing ones on the screen (the BackColor). The settings of this property are shown in Table 5-4. Most correspond to logical operators such as AND, OR or NOT. The default Drawmode setting is 13 (Copy Pen), which transfers the new pixels onto the screen, *replacing* whatever pixels used to be there. Setting 4 (Not Copy Pen) works the same way, only it reverses the color of the pixels being drawn. Setting 9 combines the new pixels with the existing ones with the logical AND operator. Setting 5 combines the new pixels with the inverse of the existing ones with the AND operator. As you can see, there are many ways to combine the color of the new pixels with the existing ones. Some are more interesting than others, but most likely you will never use more than a few.

| Value | Name | Meaning |
|---|---|---|
| 1 | BLACKNESS | Draws in black color. Draws pixels as if they were black. |
| 2 | NOT_MERGE_PEN | NOT (drawing color OR background color). The inverse of mode 15. |
| 3 | MASK_NOT_PEN | (Background color) AND (NOT drawing color). Produces colors that are common in the background and the inverse of the drawing color. |
| 4 | NOT_COPY_PEN | The inverse of the drawing color. |
| 5 | MASK_PEN_NOT | (Drawing color) AND (NOT background color). Produces colors that are common to the drawing color and the inverse of the background colors. |
| 6 | INVERT | The inverse of the drawing color. |
| 7 | XOR_PEN | (Drawing color) XOR (background color). |
| 8 | NOT_MASK_PEN | NOT (drawing color AND background color). The inverse of mode 9. |
| 9 | MASK_PEN | (Drawing color) AND (background color). Produces colors that are common in the background and the drawing color. |
| 10 | NOT_XOR_PEN | NOT (background color XOR drawing color). The inverse of mode 7. |
| 11 | NOP | No operation. |

| Value | Name | Meaning |
|---|---|---|
| 12 | MERGE_NOT_PEN | (Background color) OR (NOT drawing color). Combines all colors in the background and the inverse of the drawing color. |
| 13 | COPY_PEN | Uses the drawing color (default mode). |
| 14 | MERGE_PEN_NOT | (Drawing color) OR (NOT background color). Produces colors that exist in the drawing color, but not the background. |
| 15 | MERGE_PEN | (Drawing color) OR (background color). Produces all colors that are present to either the background or the drawing color. |
| 16 | WHITENESS | Draws in white color. Draws pixels as if they were white. |

Table 5-4: The settings of the DrawMode Property.

Neither the names nor the descriptions of the drawing modes are of much use in most programming. In "Painting With PaintPicture" below, you'll find more on the DrawMode settings, as well as a program that lets you experiment with them.

Visual Basic provides more drawing modes than you will ever need.

For now, we'll put the XOR_PEN option to use to draw "rubber" lines. A rubber line is a line with one of its endpoints fixed on the screen and the other one moving around, following the mouse pointer. You have seen this tool in action in just about any drawing application you have used. In the next section you'll see how to include this tool in your applications.

### Rubber Shapes

One of the most interesting and practical settings of the DrawMode property is 7 (XOR_PEN). With this setting, the values of the new pixels are XORed with the existing ones. Technically, the XOR operator combines bits, according to the following table:

| Bit 1 | Bit 2 | Result |
|---|---|---|
| 0 | 0 | 0 |
| 0 | 1 | 1 |
| 1 | 0 | 1 |
| 1 | 1 | 0 |

In other words, the result is 1 only if the bits are different. If they are the same (either both 0 or both 1), the result is 0. Let's see why the XOR drawing mode is so useful.

Assume that the color of a pixel on the screen is (33, 55, 33)—this is its RGB representation—and that we wish to draw another pixel with color value (102, 22, 35) on top of the first one, using the XOR mode. We'll start by writing these values in binary format and then perform a bitwise XOR operation on their bits:

```
(102, 22, 35) (01100110 00010110 00100011)
(33, 55, 33)  (00100001 00110111 00100001)
--------------------------------------------
(102, 22, 35) XOR (33, 55, 33) (01000111 00100001
00000010)
```

This is exactly how Visual Basic will combine each new pixel with the underlying one. (Notice that the bits you see don't correspond to individual pixels in the screen. Each ensemble of three integers represents the color of a single pixel, its RGB representation.) The decimal representation of the result is (71, 33, 2), and this is the color the pixel will be. Let's see what happens if we apply the same color (102, 22, 35) to the pixel we've just drawn on the screen. We will perform the same XOR operation between the current color of the pixel and the color we just applied:

```
(71, 33, 2)   (01000111 00100001 00000010)
(102, 22, 35) (01100110 00010110 00100011)
--------------------------------------------
(71, 33, 2) XOR (33, 55, 33)  (00100001 00110111
00100001)
```

The result is the color of the original pixel. The same would have happened with any color combination. The XOR mode has an interesting property: the first time we draw a shape on the screen, it is displayed on top of everything else—the colors change, but not the shape. If we draw the same shape again, the net result is to remove the shape

Use the XOR drawing mode to temporarily display a shape on top of another shape or image.

without affecting the background (see Figures 5-11 and 5-12). We need not store the original contents of the screen somewhere else in order to recover them later. Next you will see a very practical application of this drawing mode.

Figure 5-11: When you draw a rectangle over an image in XOR mode, some pixels can change color, but the shape won't be affected.

Figure 5-12: Draw another rectangle on top of the previous one in XOR mode, and it will disappear.

## Example: Rubber Lines

The example that follows is useful in any drawing application, or wherever you want to draw or Print something temporarily and nondestructively. Using rubber lines, you can verify the final position of a line before you commit it to the screen. Figure 5-13 shows a Form on which we have drawn a few black lines. The last one, drawn as dashes in gray color, is a rubber line, with one endpoint fixed and the other following the mouse pointer as it moves around the screen.

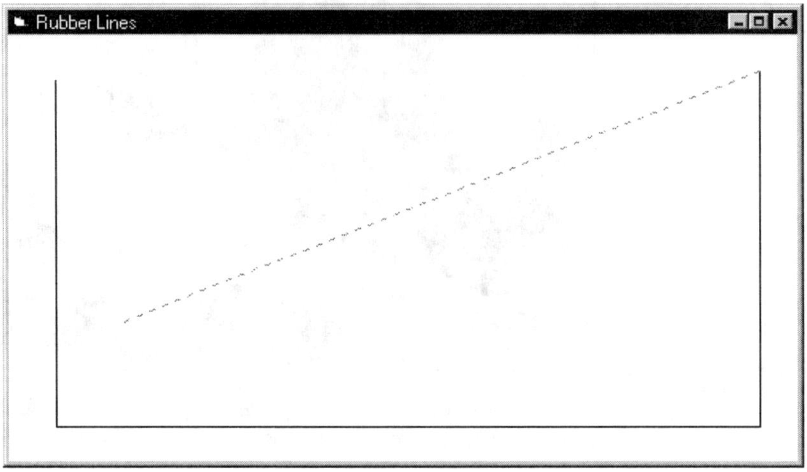


Figure 5-13: The rubber line's first endpoint is fixed. The other one follows the mouse for as long as the user holds down the left button. (The rubber line is dashed. The ones already drawn are solid.)

CD-ROM

This program is called RBBRLINE and can be found in the 5\APPS\RBBRLINE subdirectory of the CD. Run it and press the left mouse button at the starting point of the line. Then you move the mouse around without releasing the button, and the second endpoint of the line follows the movement of the mouse. Every time you move the mouse, a new line is drawn between the starting point and the current position of the pointer. This line is called a rubber line because it can swing, shrink and stretch as needed to follow the mouse, as if you had a rubber band attached to the starting point on one end and to the mouse pointer on the other end. RBBRLINE draws dashed rubber lines. Once you have decided on the exact placement of the line, you can release the mouse button, and the last rubber line will be committed on the screen (it will be a solid line).

Our program will make use of three mouse Events:

1. **MouseDown**—The starting point of a line is determined by pressing the left mouse button. Every time the Form receives a MouseDown Event, it must store the starting coordinates (XStart, YStart).
2. **MouseMove**—From that point on, the MouseMove Event takes over. As long as the user moves the mouse, Visual Basic generates MouseMove Events. The subroutine of this Event must erase the previous line and draw a new one from the starting point to the current point. To be able to erase the old line, we must store the coordinates of the old ending point somewhere. The program uses the variables XOld and YOld for that purpose. We use XOR_PEN mode to draw rubber lines so that erasing them will be as simple as drawing them once again. DrawMode must be set to 7.
3. **MouseUp**—When the mouse button is released, though, we must draw the last line in COPY_PEN mode. Therefore, the MouseUp subroutine changes the drawing mode momentarily to COPY_PEN, draws the line and then restores the mode to XOR_PEN.

Here is the code for the three Events:

```
Private Sub Form_MouseDown(Button As Integer, Shift As
Integer, X As Single, Y As Single)

    If Button <> KEY_LBUTTON Then Exit Sub
    Form1.DrawStyle = 2
    Form1.DrawMode = 7
    Form1.ForeColor = QBColor(8)
    XStart = X
    YStart = Y
    XOld = XStart
    YOld = YStart

End Sub
```

The MouseDown Event changes the line style, so all subsequent rubber lines are drawn with dashes.

```
Private Sub Form_MouseMove(Button As Integer, Shift As
Integer, X As Single, Y As Single)

'   If the mouse has not been moved, do nothing
    If X = XOld And Y = YOld Then Exit Sub
```

```
' React only if left button has been pressed
  If Button And KEY_LBUTTON Then
     Form1.Line (XStart, YStart)-(XOld, YOld)
     XOld = X ' Save X, Y values for the next
     YOld = Y ' MouseMove event
     Form1.Line (XStart, YStart)-(X, Y)
  End If

End Sub

Private Sub Form_MouseUp(Button As Integer, Shift As Integer,
X As Single, Y As Single)

  If Button = KEY_LBUTTON Then
     Form1.DrawStyle = 0
     Form1.ForeColor = QBColor(0)
     Form1.DrawMode = 13
     Form1.Line (XStart, YStart)-(X, Y)
  End If

End Sub
```

The variables XStart, YStart, XOld and YOld are being used in more than one subroutine, so they must be declared Global. Include the following lines in the Form's Declarations section:

```
Dim XStart As Single, YStart As Single
Dim XOld As Single, YOld As Single
Const KEY_LBUTTON = 1
Const KEY_RBUTTON = 2
```

It's easy to modify this application so that it draws rubber rectangles or even rubber circles.

## Erasing With Rubber Lines

The last example of using the Line method involves a new kind of erasing tool found in some drawing applications. Most drawing applications use a tool that resembles an eraser to selectively erase parts of the screen. A variation on that tool is the *screen wiper*. It works like a rubber line, only the line erases everything underneath as the user slides it over the screen. Its first endpoint is fixed, while the second one follows the movement of the mouse. When you see this tool at work, you will think of your car's windshield wiper because it works just like one.

To erase something, all we have to do is change the color of the pixels to the background color (BackColor). We need not check whether a pixel belongs to the background. It's faster to just change all the pixels. This next example program is very similar to the Rubber Line example above. The only difference is that with each MouseMove Event, we draw a new line in the color of the background and we bother to erase the previous line.

### Example: Screen Wiper

Screen Wiper is a unique alternative to the usual eraser tool.

CD-ROM

The example that follows includes the previous code, so you will be able to first draw something on the screen and then erase it. The left mouse button draws rubber lines; the right button erases them. If you wish, you can load a picture onto the Form and erase parts of it. The WIPER example (in the 5\APPS\WIPER subdirectory of the CD) makes use of the three Mouse Events of the Form, just like the RBBRLINE example:

```
Sub Form_MouseDown (Button As Integer, Shift As Integer, X →
As Single, Y As Single)

    Form1.DrawMode = XOR_PEN
    Form1.ForeColor = QBColor(8)
    XStart = X
    YStart = Y
    XOld = XStart
    YOld = YStart
End Sub
```

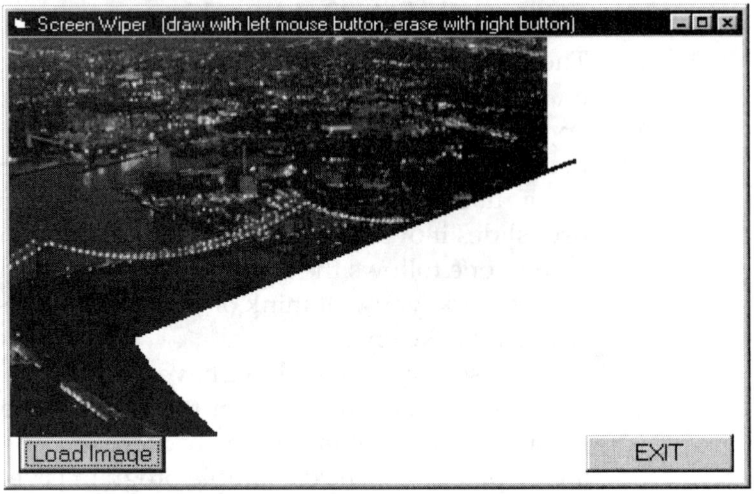


Figure 5-14: The Screen Wiper example. The erasing line is the black one. As it moves, it erases everything it crosses.

In the MouseMove Event we follow the movement of the mouse and either draw a new line (if the left mouse button is pressed) or erase the screen's contents (if the right mouse button is pressed). The global variable TempColor is a long integer, used to temporarily store the Form's foreground color. To erase the screen's contents, we simply draw a line in the background color and, finally, restore the drawing color to its original value:

```
Sub Form_MouseMove (Button As Integer, Shift As Integer, X →
As Single, Y As Single)

    If Button = 0 Then Exit Sub
    If X = XOld And Y = YOld Then Exit Sub
    TempColor = Form1.ForeColor
    If Button = KEY_LBUTTON Then    ' draw rubber line
        Form1.Line (XStart, YStart)-(XOld, YOld)
        XOld = X
        YOld = Y
        Form1.Line (XStart, YStart)-(X, Y)
    ElseIf Button = KEY_RBUTTON Then    ' erase by drawing →
    a solid line
        Form1.DrawMode = COPY_PEN
        Form1.DrawWidth = 2
        Form1.Line (XStart, YStart)-(XOld, YOld)
        XOld = X
```

```
            YOld = Y
            Form1.Line (XStart, YStart)-(X, Y)
            Form1.DrawMode = XOR_PEN
            Form1.Line (XStart, YStart)-(X, Y)
            Form1.ForeColor = TempColor
        End If
    End Sub

    Sub Form_MouseUp (Button As Integer, Shift As Integer, X →
    As Single, Y As Single)

        If Button = KEY_LBUTTON Then
            Form1.DrawMode = COPY_PEN
            Line (XStart, YStart)-(X, Y)
        Else
            Form1.DrawMode = COPY_PEN
            Form1.ForeColor = QBColor(15)
            Form1.Line (XStart, YStart)-(X, Y)
            Form1.ForeColor = TempColor
            Form1.DrawWidth = 1
        End If

    End Sub
```

Run this program and draw some lines. Then hold down the right button and move the mouse until it starts erasing. You will agree that this tool is very precise and really easy to use. The way we implemented it, however, has a small problem. If you move the mouse fast, it does not erase all the underlying pixels. Visual Basic does not generate MouseMove Events for the smallest possible displacement of the mouse pointer, so some pixels are skipped. You can overcome this problem by moving the mouse more slowly. Another quick fix is to change the width of the erasing line to 2, 3 or even 10 pixels. As you can change the size of the eraser of any drawing application, here you change the width of the erasing line. To erase large sections of the screen quickly, use a thicker line. To do some fine work, reduce the width of the line to 1 pixel.

## Drawing Circles, Arcs & Ellipses

Visual Basic's second drawing Method, the Circle command, draws circles, arcs and ellipses. Here is the complete syntax:

```
Circle [Step] (X, Y), radius[, [color] [,[start] [,[end] [,aspect]]]]
```

The only mandatory arguments are the coordinates (X, Y) of the center and the radius R of the circle, which are both expressed in units of the current coordinate system. Therefore, the simplest form of the Circle method is Circle (X,Y), R. The command

```
Circle (1000, 1000), 500
```

draws a circle centered at point (1000, 1000) with radius 500.

As with the Line command, the Step option makes the coordinates of the center relative to the current point. In other words, the center of the circle is X units horizontally and Y units vertically from the current point. Unlike the Line method, the Circle method does not allow you to use the current point as the center of the circle and omit its coordinates. To draw a circle centered at the current point, you must use the command

```
Circle (CurrentX, CurrentY), R
```

or the equivalent

```
Circle Step (0, 0), R
```

where R is the desired radius.

With the Circle Method, you can't omit the coordinates of the circle's center, even if it is the current point.

Suppose you want to draw a circle in the center of Picture Box Picture1. To draw a circle with radius equal to one-third of the horizontal dimension of the box, use the commands:

```
CX = Picture1.Width / 2
CY = Picture1.Height / 2
R = Picture1.Width / 3
Picture1.Circle (CX, CY), R
```

When drawing circles, you must consider the fact that the radius is expressed in the units of the *horizontal axis*. If the current coordinate system of the Picture Box or Form uses the same units in both directions (such as pixels or twips), it doesn't matter how the radius is defined. If the units of the horizontal and vertical axes are different (as in the case of User-defined coordinate systems), the radius is expressed in the units of the horizontal axis. The circle is not distorted in any way, but you must consider this fact when defining the length of the radius.

The last parameter, *aspect*, allows you to draw ellipses. This parameter is the ratio of the vertical to the horizontal radius of the ellipse. It can be an integer or floating-point number, and even less than 1, but it cannot be a negative number. If the aspect is smaller than 1, the ellipse extends horizontally and is squashed in the vertical direction. If it's larger than 1, the ellipse extends vertically. In Figure 5-15 you see a variety of ellipses and the aspect settings used to create them:

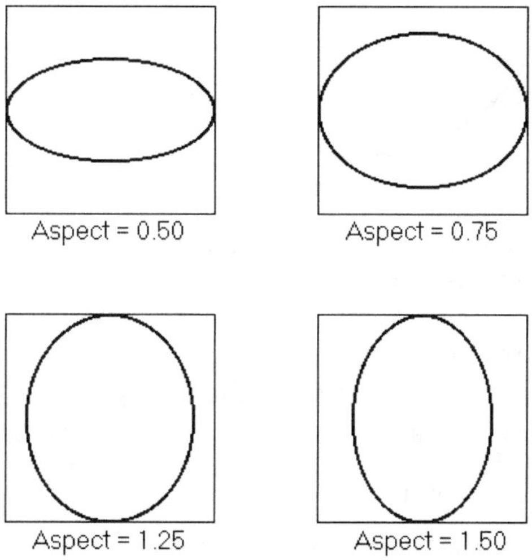


Figure 5-15: Various settings of the aspect parameter yield different ellipses. Notice that the radius (which equals half the width of the squares) is the same for all of the ellipses.

## Drawing Arcs & Wedges

The parameters *start* and *end* are used to draw circular and elliptical arcs. They represent angles and are expressed in radians, the same unit used by the trigonometric functions. If you are more familiar with degrees, remember that a full circle contains 360 degrees, which corresponds to 2*π radians (π=3.14159625...). To convert an angle of phi degrees to radians use the formula 2*π*phi/360, or π*phi/180. For greater precision, you can calculate the value of π as a double value with a statement like this one:

```
Pi# = 4*Atn(1)
```

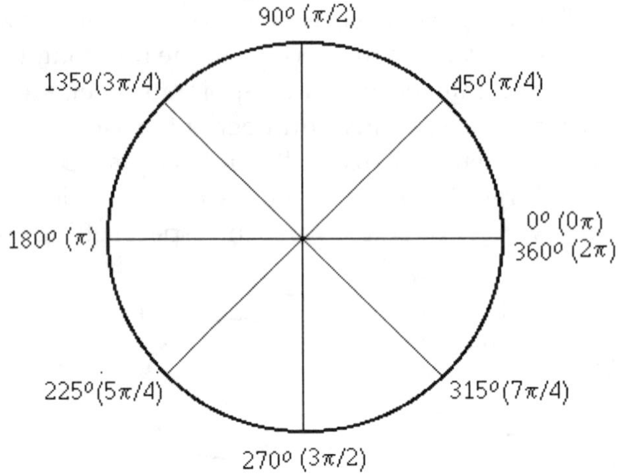


Figure 5-16: Most people measure angles in degrees, but to computers, radians (shown in parentheses) make more sense.

When drawing arcs, keep in mind that angles are measured counterclockwise. If the starting angle is larger than the ending arc, you will still draw an arc counterclockwise. For example, the statement

```
Form1.Circle (CX, CY), R, , Pi/2, Pi
```

draws an arc that covers the second quarter of a full circle, while the statement

```
Form1.Circle (CX, CY), R, , Pi, Pi/2
```

draws an arc that covers the remaining three quarters of the circle.

Negative angles don't reverse the direction of the arc. They simply tell Visual Basic to

- Draw the arc based on their absolute value, and
- Connect the end that corresponds to a negative angle with the center of the circle.

Circles, ellipses and closed arcs will be automatically filled if the FillStyle Property is not set to Transparent.

This technique can be used for drawing pie charts, as we will see.

Because circles, ellipses and connected arcs are closed shapes, you can fill them with a given pattern and color. The filling pattern is determined by the FillStyle Property, while the filling color by the FillColor Property. You can set FillColor to any valid color, and FillStyle Property to any of the values of the Table 5-3.

As with the Line command, you can omit any of the optional arguments when using the Circle command, but not the commas that separate the arguments. If you find the arc drawing options of the Circle Method confusing, take a good look at Figure 5-17, which demonstrates most of the simple forms of the method. The shapes of this figure were created with the following commands:

```
A: Circle (X, Y), R        B: Circle (X, Y), , , , .5
C: Circle (X, Y), , , , 2       D: Circle (X, Y), R, , 0, PI / 2
E: Circle (X, Y), R, , PI / 2, 0 F: Circle (X, Y), R, ,PI / 2, 0, .5
G: Circle (X, Y), R, ,PI / 2, 0, 2
H: Circle (X, Y), R, ,-2 * PI, -PI / 2
I: Circle (X, Y), R, , -PI / 2, -2 * PI
```

Notice that we cannot use the negative zero to connect the end of an arc to the center—to Visual Basic 0 and –0 are the same number. So we have used the equivalent expression 2*π in its place.

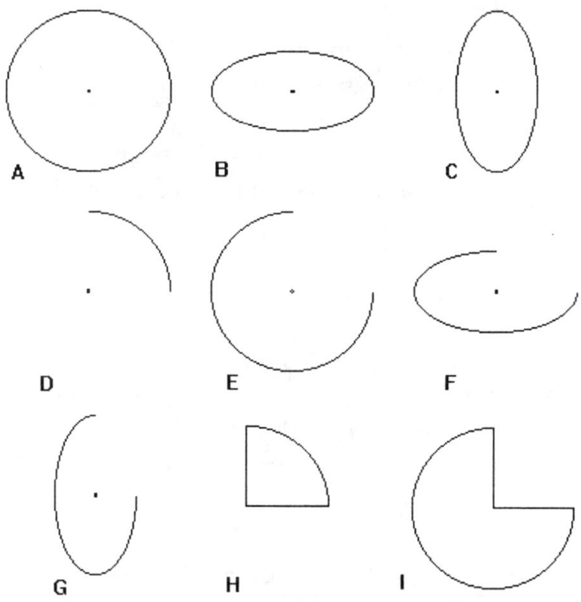


Figure 5-17: The various options of the Circle Method for arc drawing.

### Drawing Pie Charts

You can draw pie charts using the Circle Method—with the help of closed arcs (negative starting and ending angles) and the FillStyle and/or FillColor Properties. Figure 5-18 displays the screen of a short program that generates pie charts based on data stored in an array.

CD-ROM The program is called PIECHART and can be found in the 5\APPS\PIECHART subdirectory on the CD.

#### EXAMPLE: PIECHART

The Form contains two Command Buttons: Plot PieChart and Exit. The second Button simply ends the application. The "Plot PieChart" Command Button draws a pie with 10 slices, based on the data of the DataSet array. Our DataSet array contains random data, but in a practical situation, it would contain such meaningful data as the results of a database query or calculations.

Here is the Click Event's subroutine for the Command Button Plot PieChart:

```
Private Sub Command1_click( )
Dim Legend As String
Dim R As Integer
Dim Cx As Integer, Cy As Integer
Dim Phi As Double, Phi1 As Double, Phi2 As Double

    Form1.Cls
    Form1.DrawWidth = 1
    ' calculate radius
    LSide = Form1.Width
    If LSide > Form1.Height Then LSide = Form1.Height
    Cx = Form1.Width / 2
    Cy = Form1.Height / 2
    R = LSide / 4

    ' Assign random values to data
    For i = 1 To 10
        DataSet(i) = Rnd(Second(Now)) * 3000 + 1000
        Total = Total + DataSet(i)
    Next
```

```
    ' and make pie chart
    For i = 1 To 10
        Phi2 = Phi1 + 360 / Total * DataSet(i)
        Form1.FillStyle = 0
        Form1.FillColor = QBColor(i * 2 Mod 15)
        Form1.ForeColor = Form1.FillColor
        Form1.Circle (Cx, Cy), R, , -Rad(Phi1), -Rad(Phi2)
        Phi = Phi1 + (Phi2 - Phi1) / 2
        Legend = Format$(100 * DataSet(i) / Total, "00.00")
        Form1.CurrentX = 1.25 * R * Cos(Rad(360 - Phi)) + →
        Cx - 0.5 * TextWidth(Legend)
        Form1.CurrentY = 1.25 * R * Sin(Rad(360 - Phi)) + →
        Cy - 0.5 * TextHeight(Legend)
        Form1.ForeColor = QBColor(0)
        Form1.Print Legend
        Phi1 = Phi2
    Next

End Sub
```

The line

```
Phi2 = Phi1 + (360# / Total) * DataSet(i)
```

converts the percentage of each value to the equivalent angle. Each new slice begins where the previous one ends (that's why we add the new angle to the ending angle of the previous slice). The sum of all angles is 360 degrees (a full circle). Notice that most of the code concerns the appearance of the chart, that is, each slice's color and the placement of its percentage. The code for calculating and drawing the arc for each slice is very simple, but the pie wouldn't look as nice without the colors and percentages. The Rad( ) Function converts degrees to radians. We chose to use degrees in our application because most people are more familiar with degrees rather than radians. Here's the Rad( ) Function:

```
Private Function Rad(angle As Double) As Double
Dim Pi As Double

    Pi = 4# * Atn(1#)
    Rad = 2# * Pi * angle / 360#

End Function
```

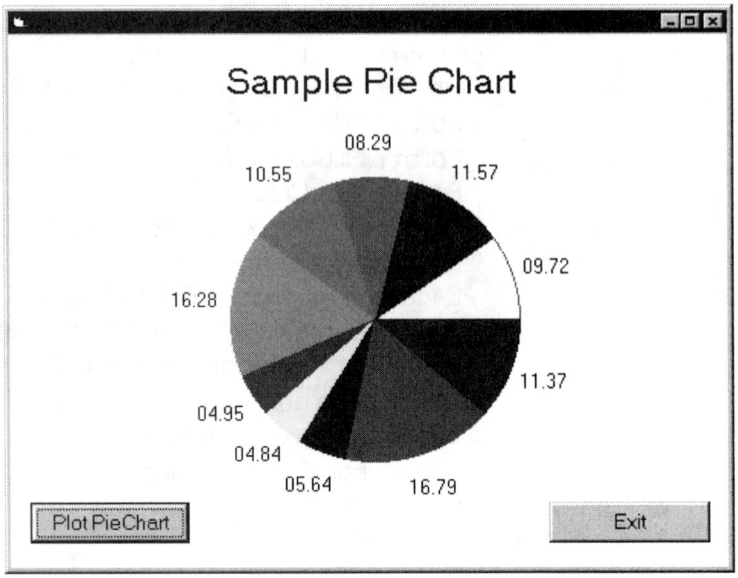


Figure 5-18: Drawing pie charts with the arc drawing options of the Circle Method.

One item worth mentioning here is the placement of the legends. The program locates a point on the radius that crosses the middle of the corresponding arc and lies outside the circle, at a distance 1.25*R from the center of the circle. The TextWidth and TextHeight Properties are also used to center the legend on that point. Figure 5-19 depicts this procedure.

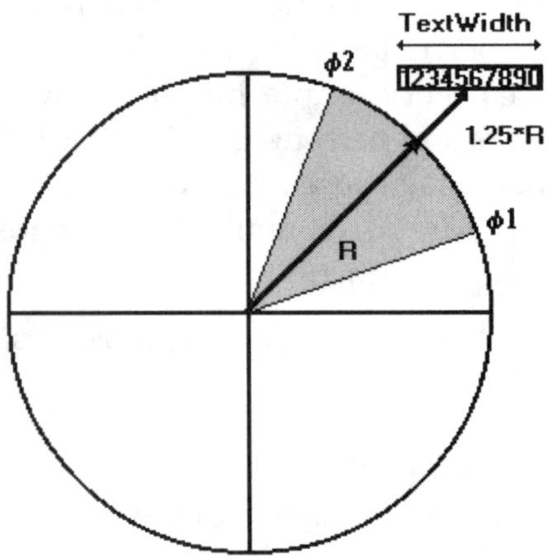


Figure 5-19: Calculating the coordinates of a slice's title. ø1,ø2 are the starting and ending angles of the slice, and TextWidth is the width of the title.

You can modify the previous code to detach any slice. To do this, move the slice's center in the same direction we use to display the legend. You can also replace the line that changes the color of each slice to fill each with a different pattern, according to Table 5-3. Finally, you can easily add small squares with the color or pattern of each slice and a legend next to it, to better describe the chart.

Notice that this short subroutine uses the Form's dimensions to size the pie chart. The circle is centered on the Form, and its radius is one fifth of the Form's width. As a consequence, the graph will be displayed correctly, regardless of the size of the Form. Just resize the Form and click on the Plot PieChart Command Button to see how it behaves. The Resize Event's code is shown next:

```
Sub Form_Resize ( )

    Label1.Left = (Form1.Width - Label1.Width) / 2
    Command1.Left = 200
    Command1.Top = Form1.Height - Command1.Height - 600
    Command2.Left = Form1.Width - Command2.Width - 300
    Command2.Top = Command1.Top
    Call Command1_click

End Sub
```

### Rubber Circles

The techniques we explored earlier for drawing rubber lines can be easily converted to draw rubber circles. The only difference is that instead of keeping track of the second endpoint of the rubber line (XOld, YOld), we must keep track of the radius of the last-drawn circle.

Rather than repeating the rubber lines example, let's look at a way to generate circles based on two opposite endpoints of their diameter. In some cases you want to be able to draw a circle, or an ellipse, based on two points that lie on its diameter, rather than its center and radius, and that's exactly what our next example does.

When the user presses the left mouse button, he or she defines the first endpoint of the diameter of the circle, which will remain fixed. As the user moves the mouse around, our program must draw a circle whose diameter is determined by the first point and the current location of the pointer. The center of this circle is midway between the fixed and the current point, while its radius is half the distance between these two points. The following statements calculate the center and radius of this circle:

```
DX = XEnd - XStart
DY = YEnd - YStart
Radius = .5 * Sqr(DX ^ 2 + DY ^ 2)
X1 = XStart + DX / 2   ' X coordinate of the circle's center
Y1 = YStart + DY / 2   ' Y coordinate of the circle's center
```

XStart, YStart are the coordinates of the starting (fixed) point of the diameter. XEnd, YEnd are the coordinates of the other end of the diameter. We can draw the circle with the method Circle (X1, Y1), Radius.

We place the code in the three mouse Events of the Form of the Picture Box used as the drawing area:

```
Sub Form_MouseDown (button As Integer, Shift As Integer, X →
As Single, Y As Single)

    XStart = X
    YStart = Y
    XOld = X
    YOld = Y
    DrawMain.DrawMode = XOR_PEN

End Sub
```

In the MouseMove Event, we draw rubber circles with a call to the RubberCircle( ) subroutine:

```
Sub Form_MouseMove (button As Integer, Shift As Integer, X →
As Single, Y As Single)

    If Button = KEY_LBUTTON Then
        Call RubberCircle(X, Y)
        Exit Sub
    End If

End Sub
```

All the work is done in the RubberCircle( ) subroutine, which erases the previous circle (by redrawing it in XOR mode) and then draws a new one:

```
Sub RubberCircle (XEnd As Single, YEnd As Single)

    DX = XOld - Xstart
    DY = YOld - YStart
    Radius = .5 * Sqr(DX ^ 2 + DY ^ 2)
    X1 = XStart + DX / 2
```

```
        Y1 = YStart + DY / 2
        Form1.Circle (X1, Y1), Radius' This line erases previous →
        circle
        DX = XEnd - Xstart
        DY = YEnd - YStart
        Radius = .5 * Sqr(DX ^ 2 + DY ^ 2)
        X1 = Xstart + DX / 2
        Y1 = YStart + DY / 2
        Form1.Circle (X1, Y1), Radius' This line draws new circle
        XOld = Xend
        YOld = YEnd

End Sub
```

Finally, in the MouseUp Event we commit the last drawn circle to the screen:

```
Sub Form_MouseUp (button As Integer, Shift As Integer, X →
As Single, Y As Single)

    If Button = KEY_LBUTTON Then
        DX = XEnd - Xstart
        DY = YEnd - YStart
        Radius = .5 * Sqr(DX ^ 2 + DY ^ 2)
        X1 = XStart + DX / 2
        Y1 = YStart + DY / 2
        Form1.Circle (X1, Y1), Radius
    End If

End Sub
```

At each MouseMove we calculate the distance between the current point and the initial point. This distance is the diameter of the circle, and therefore the radius is half this distance. The center of the circle is in the middle of the line connecting the two points, as shown in Figure 5-20.

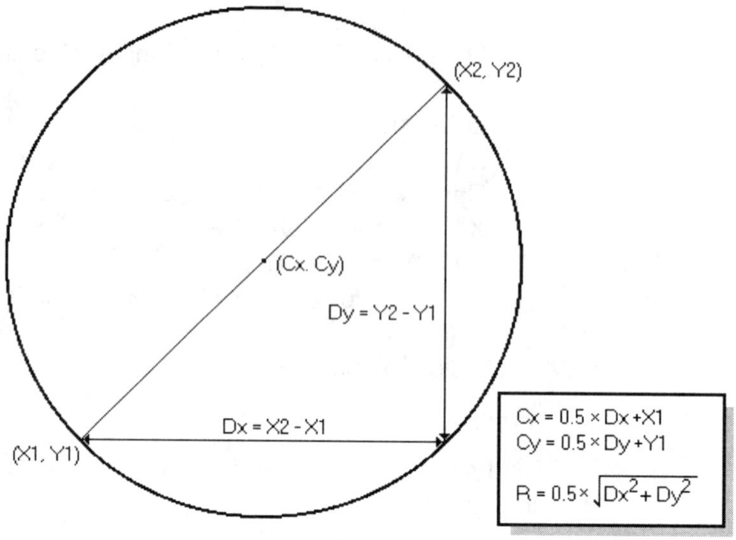


Figure 5-20: Drawing a circle based on the two endpoints of its diameter.

### Turning Pixels On & Off

The PSet command is one of the oldest graphics commands in BASIC, along with Point. Although they are the simplest graphics commands that deal with pixel drawing, they are not as commonly used as the Line and Circle Methods. There are so many pixels that manipulating individual pixels is usually unacceptably slow. If you are interested in image processing, however, these two might well be the only commands you will ever need. Here is the complete syntax of both commands:

```
PSet [Step] (X, Y) [,color]
Point [Step](X, Y)
```

PSet sets the color of the pixel at coordinates (X, Y) to color. Point is a function that reports the color of the pixel at coordinates (X, Y). The Step option allows you to choose between absolute and relative coordinates, as it does in the Line and Circle commands. If you use the Step option, X and Y are the horizontal and vertical distances of the pixel from the current point (see the discussion of the Line command under "Drawing Lines & Boxes" earlier in this chapter).

The PSet command draws "points," or dots on the screen. With the default DrawWidth setting, the size of the dot is 1 pixel. Change the size of the DrawWidth Property to draw dots larger than a single pixel. Whereas the PSet method can set more than 1 pixel at a time, the Point method provides the color of a single pixel only, not a larger dot. As with all other drawing commands, the new pixels are combined with the ones already on the screen according to the current setting of the DrawMode Property (see Table 5-4).

A pixel's color is reported by the Point Method as a Long Integer, even on a 16-color system.

Point is a function that returns a long integer representing the color of the pixel (X, Y). So far we have not mentioned how color is represented in Visual Basic, since this is one of the major topics of the next chapter. A VB description of a color is a long integer (4 bytes). These bytes can represent practically any color imaginable. There are simpler ways to *define* a color, such as the QBColor( ) function, which allows you to specify one of 16 fundamental colors. But when you want to *find out* the color value of a specific point, Visual Basic returns the complete description of the color as a long integer. (In Chapter 6, you will likely find everything you could want to know about colors in the Windows environment.)

The coordinates (X, Y) of the PSet and Point commands can be in any coordinate system (whatever is currently in effect for the Form or Control). You'll usually use pixels because that's what PSet is capable of changing and what Point is capable of reporting on. Both commands are used in image processing applications, where we must be able to handle each pixel individually. For larger shapes, it is best to use the Line and Circle Methods.

### Example: Image Flipping

CD-ROM

In Figure 5-21 you see a simple application that flips an image vertically and horizontally. The application is called FLIPIMG and can be found in the 5/APPS/FLIPIMG subdirectory on the CD.

The image is loaded on the left Picture Box with the help of its Picture Property. The application doesn't know the image's format. It simply reads all the pixel values of the first Picture Box, rearranges them and then transfers them to the Picture Box on the right. For this application to work, you must set the ScaleMode Property of both Picture Boxes to 3 (pixels).

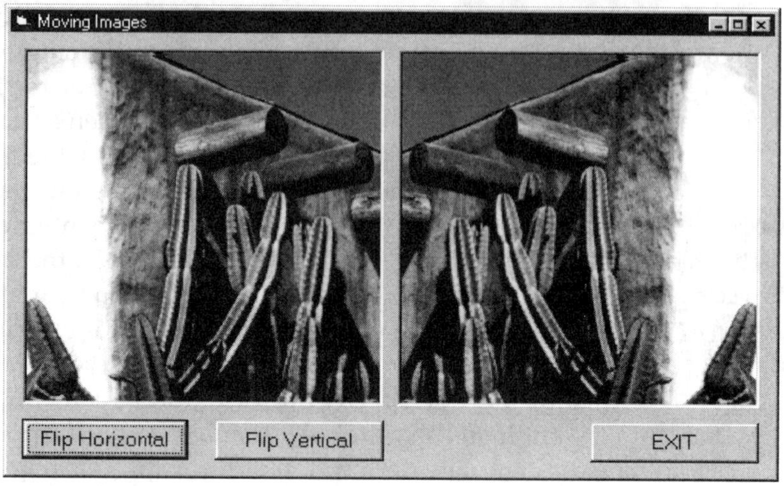


Figure 5-21: An image-flipping application based on the two pixel-handling methods of Visual Basic, PSet and Point.

Here is the code of the Flip Vertical Command Button:

```
Sub Command2_Click ( )
' Flips Vertical

    Picture2.Cls
    For irow = 0 To Picture1.ScaleHeight - 1
        For icol = 0 To Picture1.ScaleWidth - 1
        color# = Picture1.Point(icol, irow)
            Picture2.PSet (icol, Picture2.ScaleHeight - irow →
            - 1), color#
        Next
    Next

End Sub
```

This program reads the pixels of the first Picture Box, one line at a time, and transfers them to the other Picture Box. *irow* is the index to the image's rows and *icol,* the index to the image's columns. While the pixels are read from top to bottom, they are copied to the second Picture Box in the reverse order, from bottom to top. The code of the Flip Horizontal Button is quite similar, except that it reverses the direction of each line of pixels: it reads each line from left to right and copies it from right to left.

## Painting With PaintPicture

The previous example demonstrated the use of the Point and PSet commands for pixel handling. If you need to add a similar feature to your applications, the PaintPicture Method is a much faster way to do it. PaintPicture was introduced with Visual Basic 4.0. If you are using Visual Basic 3.0, you can still achieve the same functionality with the BitBlt( ) and StretchBlt( ) API Functions. These two API Functions were so popular with previous versions of Visual Basic that they were finally incorporated into the latest version of the language in the form of the PaintPicture Method.

The PaintPicture Method allows you copy pixels from one object onto another. It's similar to our FLIPIMG example above, only PaintPicure is much, much faster. PaintPicture can transfer a rectangular portion of a Picture Box onto another Picture Box or a Form in a split second. The rectangular portion can be any part of the Picture Box and can be transferred anywhere on any other Picture Box, Image Box or the Form itself. Moreover, source and destination pixels can be combined in many different ways in addition to simply replacing the destination pixels with the source pixels.

The PaintPicture Method can copy pixels instantly from one Picture Box to another.

If the destination object contains an image already, the new pixels can overwrite the existing ones or be combined with them in many different ways, similar to varied options of the DrawMode Property. Here's the syntax of the PaintPicture Method:

```
PaintPicture picture, DestX, DestY, DestWidth, DestHeight,
SourceX, SourceY, SourceWidth, SourceHeight, RasterOp
```

The first argument is the Picture Property of the Control (Picture Box or Form) from which the pixels will be copied—in other words, it is the source of the transfer. These pixels will be copied onto the Control for which the PaintPicture Method was issued.

The following arguments are all single-precision numbers, with the exception of the last one, which is a long integer. SourceX and SourceY describe the origin (upper-left corner) of the block to be transferred, and SourceWidth and SourceHeight describe the size of the block. Similarly, DestX and DestY describe the origin of the block's destination, and DestWidth and DestHeight, its dimensions. Notice that the arguments relating to the destination appear first.

The last argument, RasterOp, is the drawing mode to be used while copying the image's pixels. RasterOp determines how the copied pixels will be combined with the existing ones (this is quite similar to VB's DrawMode Property). You would expect the RasterOp argument to take on any of the DrawMode Property's values. Actually, the RasterOp argument can take 255 different values. Each value is a Boolean combination of the source pixels with the pixels of the destination image. The possible values of Visual Basic's DrawMode Property are a subset of the possible values of the RasterOp argument. Table 5-5 lists some of the most common values of the RasterOp argument. A complete list is beyond this book's scope, and it is doubtful that you will need it, ever.

| Value | Constant | Description |
|---|---|---|
| &H42 | BLACKNESS | Copies black pixels to destination. |
| &HFF0062 | WHITENESS | Copies white pixels to destination. |
| &H330008 | NOTSRCCOPY | Copies the inverse of the source pixels to destination, overriding existing pixels. |
| &HCC0020 | SRCCOPY | Copies the source pixels to destination, overriding existing pixels. |
| &H550009 | DSTINVERT | Inverts the destination pixels (source pixels are ignored). |
| &H8800C6 | SRCAND | Source pixels are ANDed with destination pixels (Source AND Destination). |
| &HBB0226 | MERGEPAINT | Destination pixels are ORed with the inverse of source pixels ((NOT Source) OR (Destination)). |
| &HEE0086 | SRCPAINT | Source Pixels are ORed with destination pixels (Source OR Destination). |
| &H440328 | SRCERASE | Destination pixels are ANDed with the inverse of source pixels ((NOT Source) AND (Destination)). |

| Value | Constant | Description |
|---|---|---|
| &H1100A6 | NOTSRCERASE | Source pixels are ORed with the inverse of destination pixels (Source OR (NOT Destination)). |
| &H660046 | SRCINVERT | Source pixels are XORed with destination pixels (Source XOR Destination). |
| &H990066 | NOTSRCINVERT | The inverse of SRCINVERT (NOT (Source XOR Destination)). |

Table 5-5: The most commonly used values of the RasterOp argument.

The numeric values are given in hexadecimal notation, and you can type them in your programs as they appear in Table 5-5. We didn't convert them to decimal here because hex is how you will find them in Microsoft's documentation.

To transfer the contents of a Picture Box to another Picture Box, use the command:

```
Picture2.PaintPicture Picture1.hDC, 0, 0,
Picture1.ScaleWidth,
Picture1.ScaleHeight, Picture1.hDC, 0, 0, &HCC0020
```

This command copies the image of Picture1 onto Picture2. The values of the various arguments are expressed in the current ScaleMode. If the ScaleMode of both Picture Boxes is 3 (pixels), the command

```
Picture2.PaintPicture Picture1.hDC, 10, 10,
Picture1.ScaleWidth,
Picture1.ScaleHeight, Picture1.hDC, 0, 0, &HCC0020
```

copies the pixels of Picture2 onto Picture1, starting at 10 pixels to the right and 10 pixels down from the Picture2 origin. Since these values are pixels, they correspond to a small frame near the top and left side of the image.

## The BitBlt & StretchBlt API Functions

If you are using VB3, you can still perform the same pixel copying operations with the help of the BitBlt and StretchBlt API Functions. Here are their declarations:

```
Declare Function BitBlt% Lib "GDI" (ByVal DestDC%,
ByValDestX%, ByVal DestY%, ByVal DestWidth%, ByVal
DestHeight%, ByVal SourceDC%, ByVal SourceX%, ByVal
SourceY%, ByVal RasterOp&)

Declare Function StretchBlt% Lib "GDI" (ByVal DestDC%, ByVal
DestX%, ByVal DestY%, ByVal DestWidth%, ByVal DestY%,
ByVal SourceDC%, ByVal SourceX%, ByVal SourceY%, ByVal
SourceWidth%, ByVal SourceHeight%, ByVal RasterOp&)
```

The BitBlt( ) API Function can copy pixels instantly from any place to any other place on the screen.

DestDC% and SourceDC% are the handles of the destination and source Controls respectively (the value of the hDC Property). As you can see, the two Functions differ in a single point: the BitBlt( ) Function doesn't provide the DestWidth and DestHeight arguments. In other words, it makes a straight copy of the source pixel onto the destination, without resizing the block. Other than that, the two functions are identical, with StretchBlt( ) being a superset of BitBlt( ). If you set the arguments DestWidth% and DestHeight% equal to SourceWidth and SourceHeight, the StretchBlt( ) Function behaves like the BitBlt( ) one. Also notice that the arguments regarding position and size are integers because when you work with BitBlt( ) and StretchBlt( ), the ScaleMode of both source and destination must be 3 (pixels).

### Example: Experimenting with PaintPicture

CD-ROM

Figure 5-22 shows the PAINTPIC application, which lets you experiment with the PaintPicture Method and the various drawing modes. It can be found in the 5\APPS\PAINTPIC subdirectory on the CD.

VB3 users can open the STRCHBLT application in the 5\APPS\STRCHBLT subdirectory on the CD, which is identical to PAINTPIC, only it makes use of the StretchBlt( ) API Function, instead of PaintPicture.

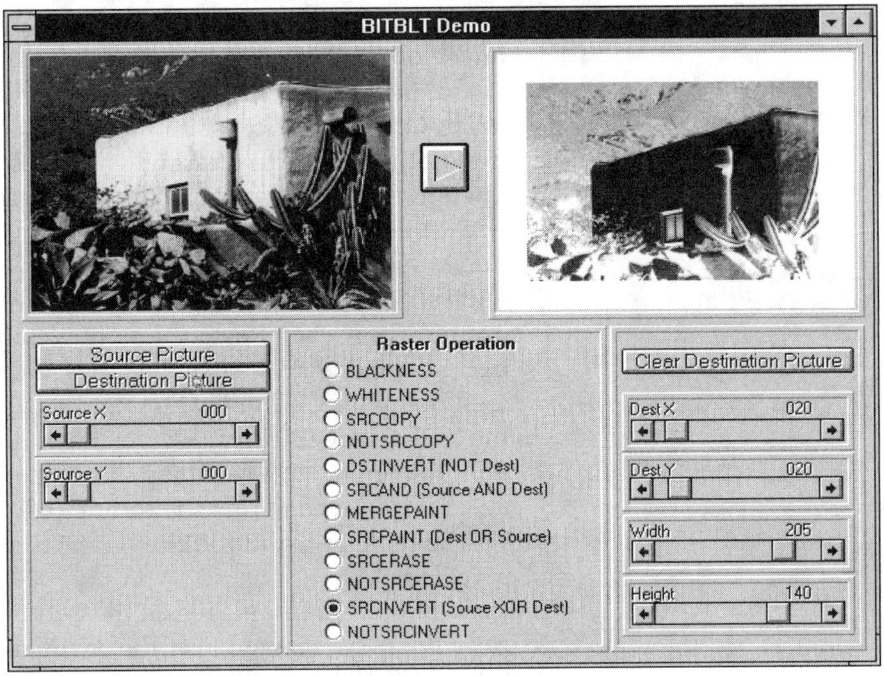


Figure 5-22: The PAINTPIC application lets you experiment with the PaintPicture Method and the various drawing modes. The image on the left Picture Box was copied on the right Picture Box in SRCINVERT (XOR) mode, and the colors were inverted. Moreover, only part of the original image was copied (as indicated by the parameters Width and Height). The origin of the copied image is at coordinates (20, 20) of the Destination Picture Box.

The BitBlt arguments must be expressed in pixels.

The scroll bars on the left control the source arguments of the PaintPicture Method, that is, where the pixels to be copied come from. The scroll bars on the right control the destination: where the pixels will end up. The ScaleMode Property of both Picture Boxes is 3 (pixels), for reasons of simplicity. PaintPicture supports all ScaleMode settings, unlike the BitBlt( ) and StretchBlt( ) Functions, which require that their arguments are expressed in pixels.

Here are some things to try:

- Load an image onto the Source Picture Box and transfer parts of it to the other Picture Box with the help of the scroll bars. You have control over the source, as well as the destination. The program transfers a part of the source image to the destination every time you click on the Command Button. To clear the destination Picture Box, right-click the mouse on it.

- To experiment with the various raster operations, load an image on the Source Picture Box. Transfer sections of the source image to the destination, using various settings of the RasterOp Option Boxes. Between transfers, right-click on the destination image to clear it.
- Then try loading a graphic into the destination Picture Box with the Destination Picture Command Button. The destination image should be a simple one—an image with a few wide stripes of different colors, for example—so that you can examine how each RasterOp setting combines the pixels being copied with the existing ones. One such image is included with the application, and it is called BASIC.BMP. Try the XOR mode (SRCINVERT, as it is called in the Windows API) to copy an image on top of another one. Then copy it again without changing the setting of RasterOp. The image will be removed, and the one on the background will be revealed.
- Load two different images on the two Picture Boxes and then copy the source image over the destination one, using the SRCINVERT mode. The two images will be combined. You will see the inverse of the source image over the destination image. If you copy the source image again, the underlying image will be revealed. (For more information on the properties of the XOR drawing mode, see "Rubber Shapes" under "Drawing Modes" earlier in this chapter.)

Now run the STRCHBLT application and see how BitBlt behaves when we copy a large section of the image, starting at the center of Source Picture Box (see Figure 5-23). This isn't a bug in the program. It's the way BitBlt behaves. If the coordinates of the upper-left corner of the source image are not at the origin, or if the dimensions of the source image are larger than the actual dimensions of the image, then BitBlt( ) and StretchBlt( ) will copy part of the Form itself. BitBlt( ) could, for one thing, be used as a screen capture utility. Assign the hDC Property of a Form to the SourceDC% argument, and BitBlt will copy the contents of the Form onto a Picture Box. The Picture Box can be hidden too, but it will be filled with the image of the active Form, which you can then save in a BMP file or copy to the Clipboard. PaintPicture will not copy parts of the Form that don't belong to the image.

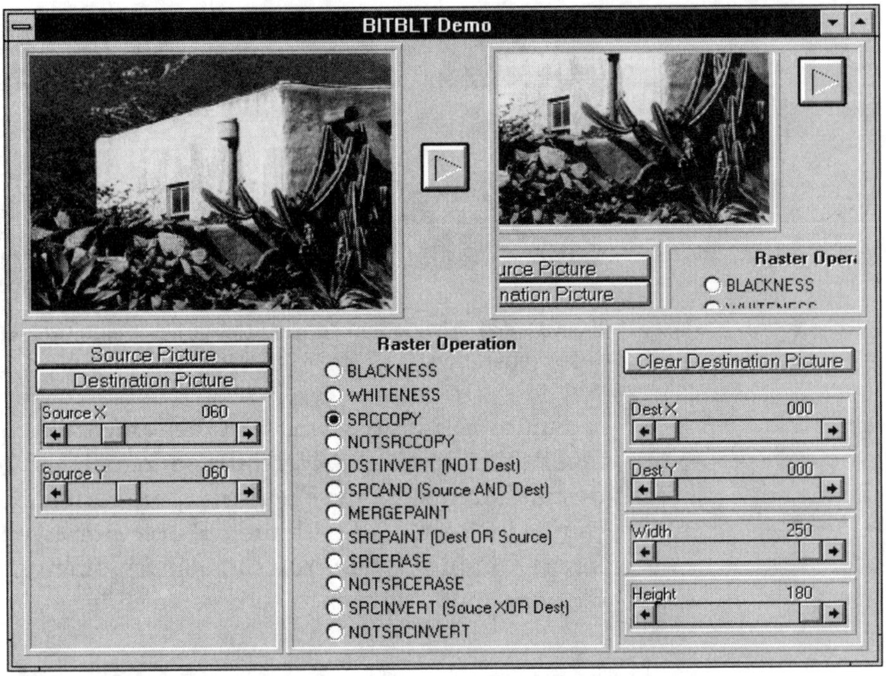


Figure 5-23: BitBlt( ) will fill the destination image, even if it has to copy part of the Form itself.

Combining images with different drawing modes can produce interesting effects.

The various drawing modes can be used to create special effects on images. Although we'll cover many image processing techniques in the next chapter, here are some simple tricks you can achieve with the BITBLT application. Load an image on the Source Picture Box and then copy it with the SRCCOPY operation. To make sure the entire image is copied into the second Picture Box, set the source origin to (0, 0) and its dimensions to the maximum values (the actual width and height of the Picture Box). Then increase the destination's origin by 1 pixel vertically or horizontally and copy it again, only this time with a different drawing mode (SRCPAINT or SRCAND). You can repeat the same process again and again. The result depends on which raster operation you select, as well as on the contents of the original image. The destination image is distorted in a "painterly" manner with each successive copy. Figure 5-24 is an example of this "slide and copy" technique with the SRCAND mode. The dark areas of the image tend to smear in the direction of the slide because bits that become 0 (darker colors) will never be turned on with the AND operator.

Figure 5-24: Sliding and copying the same image over and over with the SRCAND raster operation.

Figure 5-25 is an example of the same technique with the SRCPAINT operation. Here, the source pixels are ORed with the destination pixels, and the image gets lighter. Bits that become 1 cannot be turned off with the OR operator. Eventually, the entire image will turn white. You can also try different settings for the drawing mode with each successive slide.

Figure 5-25: The same technique with the SRCPAINT operation.

Notice that if the source and destination sizes are different, the image is resized as it is copied. The following lines copy the image of Picture1 onto Picture2. The destination image is centered and reduced in size by a factor of 2.

```
SourceX = 0
SourceY = 0
DestX = Picture1.ScaleWidth / 4
DestY = Picture1.ScaleHeight / 4
SourceWidth = Picture1.ScaleWidth
SourceHeight = Picture1.ScaleHeight
DestWidth = SourceWidth / 2
DestHeight = SourceHeight / 2
```

```
RasterOp& = &HCC0020
Picture2.PaintPicture Picture1.picture, DestX, DestY,
DestWidth, DestHeight, SourceX, SourceY, SourceWidth,
SourceHeight, RasterOp&
```

Figure 5-26: Copying and resizing an image with PaintPicture.

The StretchBlt Function was optimized for speed, not palette handling.

If you have a 256-color system, you will notice that the resized images don't look right on your monitor. PaintPicture doesn't optimize the palette of both the source and destination images, so the destination image can look bad. PaintPicture is optimized for speed, not performance. If you have used the Resize operation of any image processing application, you will instantly recognize the trade-off between speed and image quality.

One last feature of the PaintPicture Method is its ability to flip an image while copying it. If the width or height of the source image is negative, the image will be flipped horizontally or vertically. To invert an image vertically, set its width to a negative number. PaintPicture (or BitBlt) will copy as many pixels as the absolute value of the width, but the copied pixels will all be located to the left of the origin. Therefore, the horizontal origin of the source must be set to its maximum value. The commands

```
SourceX = 0
SourceY = 0
DestX = 0
DestY = Picture1.ScaleHeight
SourceWidth = Picture1.ScaleWidth
SourceHeight = Picture1.ScaleHeight
DestWidth = SourceWidth
```

```
    DestHeight = -SourceHeight
    RasterOp& = &HCC0020
    Picture2.PaintPicture Picture1.picture, DestX, DestY,
DestWidth, DestHeight, SourceX, SourceY, SourceWidth,
SourceHeight, RasterOp&
```

copy the contents of Picture1 onto Picture2 and flip it horizontally. Contrast this command with the one that makes a straight copy of the source image onto the destination. They differ in two parameters: the width of the source and the origin. Load the FLIPBMP application (subdirectory 5\APPS\FLIPBMP on the CD) to examine the code for flipping an image in all directions while copying it.

CD-ROM

The operations performed by the PaintPicture Method—and the BitBlt( ) and StretchBlt( ) API Functions—are raster operations; that is, they work on pixels, and they are collectively called "bitblt" (read "bit blit") operations. Even if most pixels on the original image have the same color, neither function will finish any sooner because they must process all pixels. Behind both functions is a powerful mechanism known as Bit Block Transfers (BitBlt). This mechanism consists of highly optimized code for manipulating and moving bits around in memory. Even when copying large sections of memory, BitBlt( ) and StretchBlt( ) are extremely fast.

In Chapter 8, "The Best of API," you will learn how to accomplish some interesting tricks with the BitBlt function. In Chapter 9, you will see how the same function is used to implement video-like wipes with images in Visual Basic. Now we'll move on to a discussion of the way Visual Basic handles graphics and how you can exploit the built-in mechanism to optimize your graphics applications.

## AUTOREDRAW & REFRESH

The setting of the AutoRedraw Property can seriously affect your application's speed of execution.

One of the most important properties affecting VB graphics is the AutoRedraw Property. It has two possible settings, True and False, but the way you use it can seriously affect the speed and behavior of your application. Speed might not be of the essence when you are drawing a few lines or circles on a Form or a Picture Box. However, if you are writing an application that performs many graphics operations such as plotting functions or image processing, speed is important.

When AutoRedraw is set to True, Visual Basic maintains a private copy of the contents of a Picture Box or Form in memory. When you draw a line, Visual Basic draws it first on this hidden copy and then transfers the contents of that zone of memory to the visible Control. You have no direct access to this copy of the image, but Visual Basic uses it to redraw the Control when needed (the Control is moved, the Form is resized, etc.) or to save its contents in a file with the SavePicture Method.

Visual Basic does all the drawing in an area of memory called a *device context*. A device context is a copy of the actual picture of the Picture Box or Form, and Visual Basic uses it to update the image of the actual object from time to time. If the AutoRedraw Property is False, then Visual Basic draws directly on the Control or Form and is not responsible for maintaining the drawing in the Form or Control (moving or resizing during run time will *erase* the drawn image).

The SavePicture command uses the memory copy of the Control's image to create a file. As a result,

- SavePicture won't work if AutoRedraw is set to False. (Actually, it will create a file as large as the object, but it will store nothing in it.)
- If a Picture Box has AutoRedraw set to False, you can't copy an image from it to another Picture Box or Form.
- Even worse, if you switch to another Form or application, when you return, the images of the Picture Boxes or Forms won't be redrawn if their AutoRedraw Property was False.

Without the device context, Visual Basic wouldn't be able to update the contents of the various Picture Boxes and Forms of the applications. Technically, the device context is not a copy of the object's image; the object's image is a copy of the device context.

The safest approach when you create simple graphics is to set AutoRedraw to True. This way, the images you create will not be erased. For more demanding applications, however, this approach won't work because it slows things up too much. There are a few tricks you should remember in order to write an efficient graphics application, and we are going to explain them in this section with simple examples.

The AutoRedraw Property applies only to graphics created with graphics methods (Line, Circle, PSet and Print).

## Balancing Speed & Convenience

CD-ROM

The smooth curve you see in Figure 5-27 was created by the application CURVE (in the subdirectory 5\APPS\CURVE on the CD). CURVE draws a smooth curve with the help of the SIN( ) and COS( ) functions in Visual Basic. Don't worry if you haven't taken any trigonometry courses. All you need to know about this curve is that every point is calculated by a math formula, and it takes a while to complete.

```
Sub Command1_Click ( )

    Picture1.Cls
    DoEvents
    If Check1.Value Then
        Picture1.AutoRedraw = True
    Else
        Picture1.AutoRedraw = False
    End If

    MidY = Picture1.Height / 2
    XOld = 1
    YOld = MidY + 100 * (3 * Cos(x / 200) + 4 * Sin(x / →
    300) + 5 * Cos(x / 400) + 4 * Cos(x / 200) + 3 * →
    Sin(x /100))

    For I = 1 To Picture1.ScaleWidth
        x = I
        y = MidY + 100 * (3 * Cos(x / 200) + 4 * Sin(x / →
        300) + 5 * Cos(x / 400) + 4 * Cos(x / 200) + 3 *  →
        Sin(x /100))
        Picture1.Line (XOld, YOld)-(x, y)
        XOld = x
        YOld = y
        If Check2.Value Then Picture1.Refresh
    Next

End Sub
```

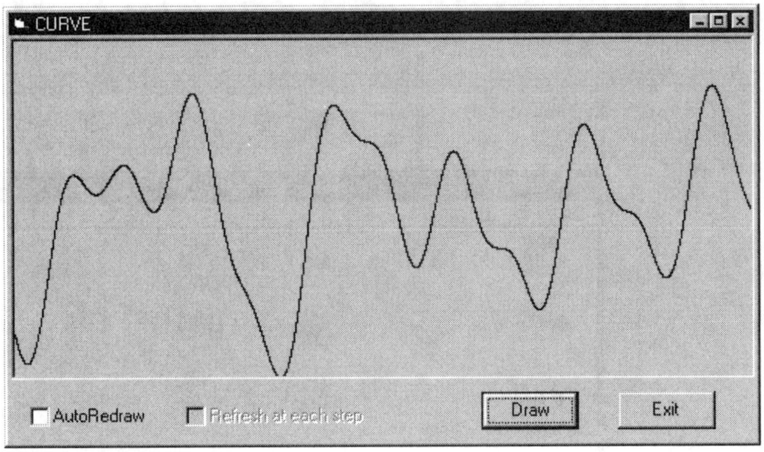


Figure 5-27: The CURVE application draws a smooth curve with various settings of the AutoRedraw Property.

Run the CURVE application without checking any of the Check Boxes at the bottom of the screen. Simply click on the Draw Curve Command Button and watch the curve being drawn. Even on the fastest PC—which at the time of the writing is a Pentium/90MHz—the drawing won't be instant. As each new pixel is calculated and displayed, you can watch the progress of the curve drawing. This is how Visual Basic displays graphics on a Form (or other Control) when its AutoRedraw Property is False.

Once the curve has been drawn, switch to another application by pressing Alt+Tab. Make sure that part of the CURVE Form is covered by another Form. Then return to Visual Basic by pressing Alt+Tab again and look at the Form. Part of the curve is missing. The portion of the Form that had been covered by another window has not been redrawn (see Figures 4-28 and 4-29).

If AutoRedraw is False, it's up to you to Refresh your application's Forms.

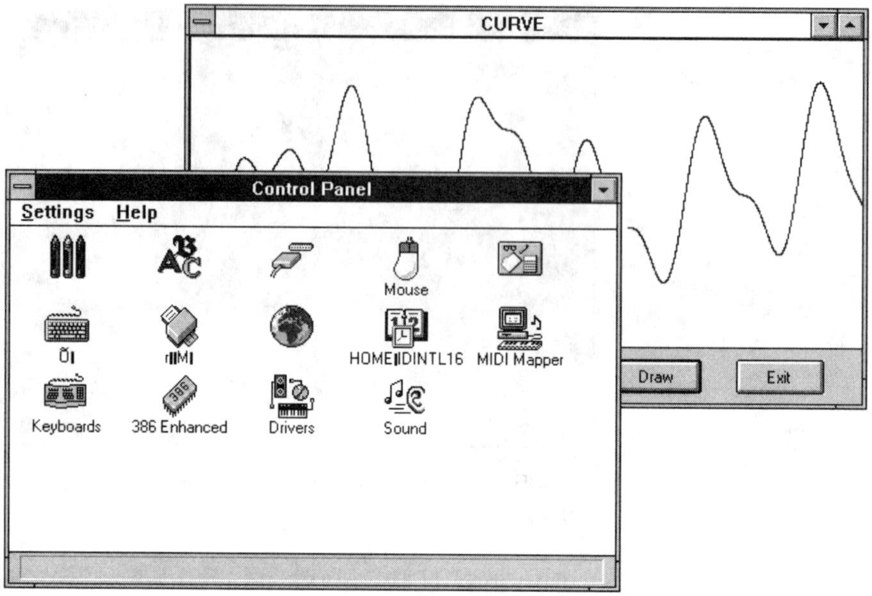


Figure 5-28: Switch to another application to cover part of the CURVE's main Form.

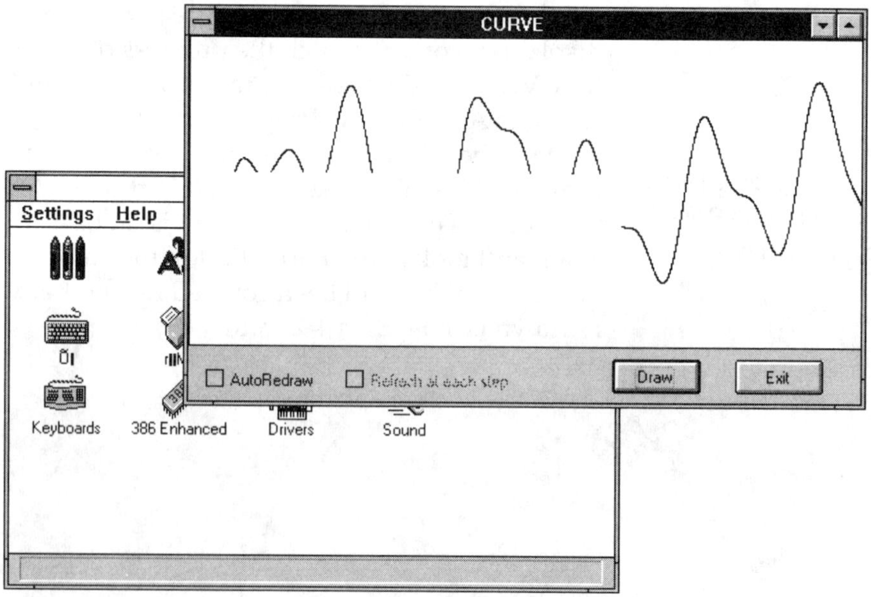


Figure 5-29: When you return to CURVE, the Form is not redrawn automatically for you.

This is where the AutoRedraw Property comes in. Run the application again, but this time click on the AutoRedraw Button to set the AutoRedraw Property to True. The same curve is being redrawn, but this time you can't see anything. If you wait long enough, the entire curve will appear on your screen as soon as it has been completed.

When the AutoRedraw Property is set to True, Visual Basic works with the copy of the image (the device context), and not the image itself. In other words, it updates the hidden copy of the image, and not what you see on the screen. When the drawing is complete, Visual Basic transfers the results all at once to the screen.

But how does Visual Basic know that we are done drawing? It doesn't. VB updates the image every time it gets a chance. That is, every time your program idles, or whenever the DoEvents( ) Function is called. The program that generates the curve is a tight loop. While VB executes it, it doesn't have a chance to redraw the screen. Once it's done drawing, however, it can update the screen contents and display the curve.

To be exact, the redrawing of the screen is actually performed by Windows itself, and not by VB. It is one of the things that happen during a call of the DoEvents( ) Function. If you insert the line

```
DoEvents
```

somewhere in the loop, you will be able to see the progress of the drawing, even with AutoRedraw set to True, but the program will run very slowly. Consider leaving the DoEvents( ) Function out of your programs in similar calculation-intensive situations, because it really does slow things down. DoEvents( ) returns the control of the processor to Windows, which performs certain operations and then returns control to Visual Basic. This "context switching" is very taxing on your application.

## The Refresh Method

The DoEvents( ) Function can be useful in some situations, but other times it does more harm than good. Instead, you can call the Refresh Method. The Refresh Method has the same effect as far your application goes—it refreshes the contents of the Control—but unlike DoEvents( ) it doesn't relinquish control to the Windows operating system. Refresh synchronizes the display with the calculations, by copying the contents of the hidden image onto the Control. Refresh is not as slow as DoEvents( ), but it is not instantaneous either. Calling Refresh after drawing each pixel can degrade the performance of any computer. Run the CURVE application and check both Option Buttons to see how the Refresh Method affects the speed of the application on your computer. Since no calls to DoEvents are employed, the only way to stop the CURVE application is to hit Ctrl+Break.

One way to improve the application's speed is to call Refresh only after a certain number of points have been calculated. This technique makes the display "jumpy." The user won't see the curve being drawn steadily, but will see entire segments displayed as they are calculated.

However, in other types of applications, this technique is useful. For example, in an image processing application, we can call Refresh to display each new row of pixels after they have been calculated (you'll see an example of this technique in the next chapter). Similarly, in a fractal-drawing application, you can refresh the display after calculating an entire line of pixels.

The Refresh Method can slow things down, especially when used with Forms, because the device context where VB does all the drawing is larger than the Form itself. In most cases, the size of the device context is the size of the screen. In other words, you can draw beyond the edges of the Form and then resize the Form to see more of your design. This is a very convenient feature, but it can affect the speed of an application.

Speed is not the only drawback of setting AutoRedraw to True. The device context requires a substantial amount of memory to store the image (as much as is required for storing the actual image of the Control). Memory is becoming less and less of an issue for today's computers, so we won't address this topic here. Conserving memory is not nearly as important in Windows as it used to be with DOS.

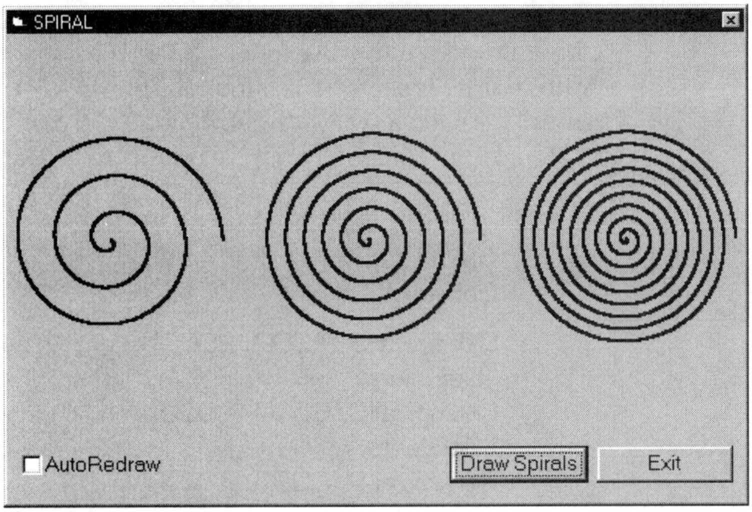


Figure 5-30: A spiral is another mathematically generated curve that requires quite a few calculations.

CD-ROM

Figure 5-30 shows a similar application. The SPIRAL application, in the 5\APPS\SPIRAL subdirectory on the CD, draws three different spirals on the screen. The Subroutine spiral( ), which generates a spiral, accepts three arguments: the number of rotations and the X and Y coordinates of the spiral's center point. A spiral is the trace of a point that moves along the perimeter of a circle, whose radius is increased at each step and thus gets further and further away from the center. Here is the spiral( ) Subroutine:

```
Sub spiral (rotations As Integer, centerX As Integer, centerY →
As Integer)

Dim XOld As Integer, YOld As Integer

    For i = 1 To 360
        r = i * 3
        theta = rotations * (i * 3.14159 / 180)
        x = r * Cos(theta)
        y = r * Sin(theta)
        Line (XOld + centerX, YOld + centerY)-(x + centerX, →
        y + centerY)
        XOld = x
        YOld = y
    Next

End Sub
```

The Form's AutoRedraw Property is controlled by the AutoRedraw Check Box. Set it to False to watch the spirals being drawn. If AutoRedraw is set to True, all three spirals will be displayed simultaneously as soon as they are calculated.

Here is the code of the Draw Spirals Command Button:

```
Sub Command1_Click ( )

    Form1.Cls
    DoEvents

    Call spiral(3, 1000, 2000)
    ' DoEvents
    Call spiral(6, 3500, 2000)
    ' DoEvents
    Call spiral(9, 6000, 2000)

End Sub
```

If you uncomment the two lines of the subroutines, or insert the Form1.Refresh command after each call to the spiral( ) routine, each spiral will be displayed as soon as it's drawn. This is better than having to wait for the completion of all three spirals, but there are moments of inactivity between the appearance of successive shapes, which can be disturbing to the user. If you set the Form's AutoRedraw Property to False, the spirals will be drawn faster. The user will be able to watch the progress of the drawing, but he must not switch to another Form or application.

## Should We AutoRedraw or Refresh?

When AutoRedraw is False, the Refresh Method doesn't refresh at all. It erases everything.

From our simple experiments, it's clear that AutoRedraw must be set to False when you are drawing on the screen for more than a second or two. If you want to be able to save the Control's contents with the SavePicture method, or allow the user to switch to another application and then return, you have no choice but to set this Property to True. This in turn forces you to refresh the screen manually with the Refresh Method. But if you call Refresh too often, it will slow things down.

You can't use the Refresh Method when the AutoRedraw Property is set to False because it will erase everything on the screen (it gives you a fresh start). The Refresh Method works by copying the contents of the device context to the Control. Because shapes or pixels drawn with AutoRedraw = False aren't sent to the device context, the Refresh Method ignores them. Calling Refresh for a Control with

AutoRedraw=False, in effect, erases everything. This behavior sounds quite annoying, but as you'll see, you can exploit it to speed up certain operations.

### Transparency Drawing

The AutoRedraw Property can also be changed during the execution of the program. Everything you draw while the AutoRedraw Property is set to True updates the internal (hidden) copy of the image, and it also appears on the Control. Everything you draw while the AutoRedraw Property is set to False appears on the Control, but it doesn't update the internal copy. This behavior may sound strange, but it isn't. In Figures 5-31 and 5-32 you see a practical example of the things you can do with the two settings of the AutoRedraw Property.

CD-ROM

The Grid application is in the 5\APPS\GRID subdirectory on the CD.

Figure 5-31: An image, with a grid on top of it. The grid was drawn with the AutoRedraw Property set to False.

Figure 5-32: Because the grid was drawn with AutoRedraw = False, we can remove it by simply refreshing the Picture Box.

The grid you see in Figure 5-31 is not part of the image. It is displayed to help the user in certain operations, and it disappears when it's not needed any more. The grid is displayed with a subroutine that draws horizontal and vertical lines. Here is the code of the Show Grid Command Button:

By manipulating the AutoRedraw Property, you can temporarily display graphics on top of other graphics, and then remove them instantly.

```
Sub Command3D1_Click ( )
    GridLines = 20
    Picture1.AutoRedraw = False
    GridSpaceX = Int(Picture1.ScaleWidth / GridLines)
    GridSpaceY = Int(Picture1.ScaleHeight / GridLines)
    For i = 0 To GridLines + 1
        Picture1.Line (GridSpaceX * i, 0)-(GridSpaceX * i, →
        Picture1.Height - 1)
        Picture1.Line (0, GridSpaceY * i)-(Picture1.Width - 1, →
        GridSpaceY * i)
    Next
End Sub
```

To remove the grid, we must either reload the graphic—to overwrite the contents of the Picture Box—or refresh the contents of the Control with the Refresh method. The RemoveGrid subroutine that removes the grid from the Picture Box couldn't be simpler:

```
Picture1.Refresh
```

The trick is in the second line of the ShowGrid( ) subroutine:

```
Picture1.AutoRedraw = False
```

Everything drawn after this command (in other words, everything drawn while the AutoRedraw Property is False) is ignored when Visual Basic updates the contents of the Control because it is not part of the device context. This simple technique allows you to display all kinds of graphics on top of an image and then remove them with a simple Refresh command, as if they were drawn on a transparency over the actual image.

The graphic elements drawn on the Control while AutoRedraw is set to False are ignored in future operations. The elements drawn while AutoRedraw is True, however, are permanent. They will be redisplayed after covering the Form with another Form or changing its size. These elements form the so-called *persistent bitmap*.

Now let's put together what we've discussed so far. We'll create a useful and practical application to plot data and functions. VBPlot is an interesting application on its own, but it also demonstrates many of the graphics Properties and Methods we've presented and their interdependence.

## Example: Plotting Functions & Data Sets

VBPlot is a showcase of the various graphics capabilities of Visual Basic. It also demonstrates the essentials of a business or scientific graphing application. Take a look at Figure 5-33 to see what it does. The line plots were generated by two functions, and the markers represent data points (these would normally correspond to measurements). The VBPlot application can be found in the 5\APPS\VBPLOT subdirectory on the CD.

CD-ROM

VBPlot is a simple plotting application that lets you display data sets and functions.

Every element (or parameter) of the plot can be altered: the color of the tic marks, the background color, the plotting color, and so on. You can plot as many functions and data points as you wish and change the size of the window. With a little extra effort, you can add legends and more titles on the plot. You can use VBPlot as is or incorporate it in your applications. Just define the functions and the data sets to be plotted and connect them to the rest of the application—which can be as simple as loading a new Form.

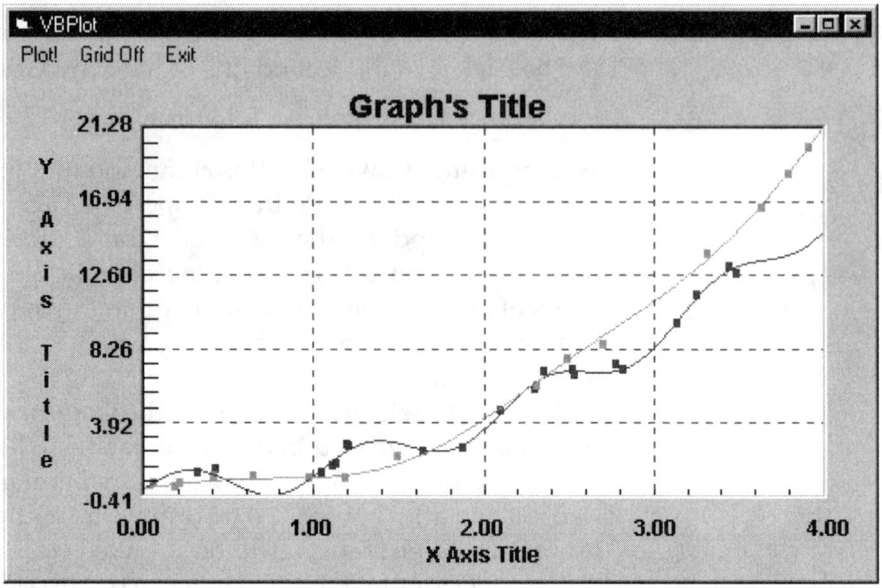


Figure 5-33: Incorporate versatile VBPlot into your applications, or use it as a stand-alone application.

VBPlot demonstrates most of the topics we covered in the previous sections. We'll see how to set up a User-defined coordinate system with the Scale method. We'll see the difference between the Width/Height and ScaleWidth/ScaleHeight Properties. And we'll see how to use the AutoRedraw property (with the Refresh method) to remove the grid from the screen instantly, without affecting the plot.

The VBPlot menu bar contains three commands (none of which leads to a submenu). The Plot command draws the functions and data points you see in Figure 5-33, and the Grid On/Grid Off command displays and removes the grid. Finally, the Exit command terminates the application.

### The Structure of VBPlot

Without any further introduction, let's see how the application works. There are five basic operations, which correspond to the following subroutines:

| | |
|---|---|
| SetUserScale( ) | Scans all functions and data sets to determine the range of the Y axis. The user must set the minimum and maximum values of the X axis. |
| PlotFunction( ) | Plots the functions and/or the data sets. |
| GridOn( ) | Draws the major/minor tic marks. The major tic marks are drawn as a grid and the minor tic marks as small lines. The user determines the number of major divisions on each axis. |
| AxisNumbers( ) | Prints axis numbers on each major tic mark. The numbers are formatted and placed on the form automatically. |
| AxisTitles( ) | Prints the titles for the two axes and the entire graph. The program determines the placement of the titles. |

Table 5-6: Basic operations of VBPlot.

Every time you execute the Plot command from the main menu, these routines (with the exception of the GridOn( ) subroutine) are called in the same order. The main program, which is the subroutine under the Plot menu command, is very simple:

```
Private Sub Plot_Click( )
Dim WidthInDots As Integer

    Picture1.ScaleMode = 3
    WidthInDots = Picture1.ScaleWidth
    Screen.MousePointer = 11
    a% = SetUserScale(XAxisMin, XAxisMax, WidthInDots)
    a% = PlotFunction(XAxisMin, XAxisMax, WidthInDots)
    Call AxisNumbers
    Call AxisTitles
    If GridOnOff.Caption = "Grid Off" Then
        Call GridOn
    End If
    Screen.MousePointer = 1

End Sub
```

First it sets the Picture Box's ScaleMode to 3 (pixels) and determines the number of pixels in the horizontal direction of the Picture Box, where the data will be plotted. Then it plots the function and data sets, numbers the axes and places the graph's titles. (Later in this chapter, we'll examine in detail the routines that perform these operations.)

The SetUserScale( ) routine is identical to PlotFunction( ), except that SetUserScale( ) does not plot anything on the screen. Instead, it keeps track of the minimum and maximum Y values and sets the limits of the plotting area according to these values. If the user has specified values for the Y axis, SetUserScale( ) sets the Scale accordingly and returns, without performing any calculations.

PlotFunction( ) plots the data points and the functions on the Picture Box. This subroutine is the core of the application, and we shall present it in detail shortly.

GridOn( ) places the tic marks on the plot, and it does not require any arguments. It picks up the needed information from the properties of the Picture Box and some global variables, such as the number of tic marks and their color.

The same is true for AxisNumbers( ), which formats and places numbers at the major tic marks. For purposes of this application, the numbers are formatted with two decimal digits. Although straightforward, a subroutine for formatting axis numbers for all cases is rather lengthy and wouldn't demonstrate any graphics methods. Finally, AxisTitles( ) places the X and Y axis titles and the graph title. This subroutine centers the axis titles on the sides of the Picture Box and centers the graph title within the width of the Form.

## Math Functions & Plots

A plot is the visual representation of a numerical relationship.

A function is a mathematical formula that maps an *independent* variable to the *dependent* one. An example of a function is $Y = X^2 + 3*X - 8$. For every value you assign to X, Y gets a new value. If X = 2, then $Y = 2^2+3*2-8 = 2$. The variable X is the independent variable and Y is the dependent one, because Y's value depends on the value of X. A function is the mathematical relationship between two (and possibly more) quantities such as distance traveled and velocity; or your capital in the bank and the interest rate; or even the crime rate and number of guns. The plot of a function is a visual representation of this relationship.

Before we plot a function, we must decide the range of values its independent variable can take on. The previous function can be plotted in the range –0.1 to +0.1, or in the range –10 to +1000. The axis of X values we wish to plot is arbitrary and entirely up to the user. The range of Y values, however, is determined by the function. We must set the limits of the Picture Box, where the function will be plotted, so the entire plot will fit. The question is, at how many points we must calculate this function? The Picture Box has just so many pixels, and the range of X values will not change the number of pixels. Therefore, it makes no sense to calculate the function more times than there are pixels in the horizontal direction, because we cannot display them. We can calculate a function at many thousand values of X, but only a few of the Y values result in new pixels on the screen.

### Setting the Plot's Scale

The range of X values is determined by the user, and the range of Y values depends on the functions being plotted. The range of Y values can be extremely small, or extremely large. Therefore, we must come up with a technique to map the function's coordinates to the screen's pixels. Visual Basic provides this technique, and it is the Scale Method. If we set the ScaleMode Property to 0 (User-defined coordinates), we can specify the size of the Picture Box in whatever units we wish. For example, if we wish to plot the function in the range from –1 to +1, and the minimum and maximum values of the function in this range are –10 and 40 respectively, the command

```
Picture1.Scale (-1, -10) - (1, 40)
```

sets the proper coordinate system of the Picture Box. This coordinate system extends from –1 to 1 horizontally and from –10 to 40 vertically. Again, the Scale Method has no effect on the size of the Picture Box. It simply changes the coordinate system used to access its pixels. The coordinates of the top left pixel are (–1, 40), and the pixel on the center of the Picture Box has coordinates (0, 25).

As you recall, Visual Basic assumes that the origin is always at the upper-left corner of the control. When displaying functions, however, the origin should be at the lower-left corner. Unless you want to view the plots upside-down, you must switch the minimum and maximum values of the Y coordinates. This relocates the origin to the lower-left. The Scale method of the previous example must be used with the following arguments:

```
Picture1.Scale (-1, 40) - (1, -10)
```

The last command specifies a coordinate system whose origin is at the lower-left corner of the Picture Box. This is what the SetUserScale( ) Subroutine does. It accepts the minimum and maximum values of X,

To plot a function, we must calculate its value for every pixel in the horizontal direction of the Picture Box.

then calculates the minimum and maximum values of the function (Y values) in this range and sets a new coordinate system.

To avoid calculating the value of the function at more points than necessary, the program figures out at the very beginning how many pixels are in the Picture Box. It assigns this number to the variable Hsteps, which is passed to both the SetUserScale and PlotFunctions subroutines. HSteps is the minimum (and necessary) number of repetitions of the calculations; it is the value of the Picture Box's ScaleWidth property when its coordinate system (property ScaleMode) is set to 3 (Pixels). The following lines retrieve the number of pixels in the horizontal direction:

```
Picture1.ScaleMode = 3
WidthInDots = Picture1.ScaleWidth
```

Here is the SetUserScale Subroutine:

```
Private Function SetUserScale(XStart As Double, XEnd As
Double, HSteps As Integer)
Dim YMin As Double
Dim YMax As Double
Dim NewPoint As Double

    If Not (YAxisMin = 0 And YAxisMax = 0) Then
        Picture1.Scale (XAxisMin, YAxisMax)-(XAxisMax,
YAxisMin)
        Exit Function
    End If

    XIncrement = (XEnd - XStart) / HSteps
    YMin = F1(XStart)
    YMax = YMin
' calculate min and max value of each function
' and data set.
    If PlotYesNo(1) Then
    For i = 1 To HSteps - 1
        NewPoint = F1(XStart + i * XIncrement)
        If NewPoint > YMax Then YMax = NewPoint
        If NewPoint < YMin Then YMin = NewPoint
    Next
End If
```

```
' Repeat the same calculations for each function & data set

Picture1.Scale (XStart, YMax)-(XEnd, YMin)

End Function
```

XStart and XEnd are the minimum and maximum X coordinates of the plotting area, and they must be specified by the user. The last argument of the Subroutine, HSteps, is the number of pixels in the horizontal direction of the Picture Box. As we have mentioned already, it doesn't make sense to calculate the function at more points than we can display.

The YAxisMin and YAxisMax are global variables. If they are both 0, the user hasn't set the vertical range of the plot, and SetUserScale( ) proceeds with its calculations. On the other hand, if their values have been set, then the subroutine simply sets the coordinate system and returns. Notice that in the code we present here, the range of Y values is calculated according to the first function to be plotted. In your application, consider all other functions or data sets to be plotted in calculating the range of the plot area (you can find the full implementation of the SetUserScale( ) Subroutine on the CD).

The functions to be plotted are called F1, F2, etc. The code for the two functions of this chapter's figures are

```
Function F1 (x As Double) As Double

    F1 = Sin(x * 6) + x ^ 2 * Exp(.002 * x)

End Function
```

and

```
Function F2 (x As Double) As Double

    F2 = Cos(x * 2) * Sin(x * 1.12) + Abs(x) ^ 2.2 * →
Exp(.002 * x)

End Function
```

They implement the functions $F1(X) = \sin(6X) + X2e.002X$ and $F2(X) = \cos(2X)*\sin(1.12X) + \text{abs}(X)^{2.2}e(0.002X)$ correspondingly. Modify these functions' definitions according to your needs. To plot more functions, simply add the definitions of the functions F3, F4 and so on.

### Plotting the Function

Now we can look at the PlotFunction( ) Subroutine, which plots the data. It is similar to the SetUserScale( ) Subroutine, except that after each calculation it plots a line connecting the previous point to the current one.

```
Private Function PlotFunction(XStart As Double, XEnd As
Double, HSteps As Integer)
Dim X1 As Double, Y1 As Double
Dim XPoint As Double, YPoint As Double

' Make sure the AutoRedraw property is True
   Picture1.AutoRedraw = True

' Plot 1st data set
   Picture1.ForeColor = PlotColor(1)
' Each data point will be marked with a small circle
   Picture1.DrawWidth = 4

   For i = 1 To DataPoints(1)
      XPoint = DataSet1(1, i)
      YPoint = DataSet1(2, i)
      Picture1.PSet (XPoint, YPoint)
   Next

' Similar statements for the other data sets

' Now plot 1st function
   If PlotYesNo(1) Then
      Picture1.ForeColor = PlotColor(1)
      X1 = XStart
      Y1 = F1(X1)
      Picture1.CurrentX = X1
      Picture1.CurrentY = Y1

      For i = 1 To HSteps
         XPoint = XStart + i * XIncrement
         YPoint = F1(XStart + i * XIncrement)
         Picture1.Line -(XPoint, YPoint)
      Next
   End If
```

```
' Similar statements for the other functions

End Function
```

Here we have shown how to plot the first data set and the first function. Adding the code for the remaining data sets and functions is straightforward. The data sets are stored in the global arrays, DataSet1, DataSet2, etc. In a practical application, they will be read from a file or entered by the user on a different form. You can find the complete implementation of the PlotFunction subroutine, which plots all functions and data sets of Figure 5-33, in the subdirectory 5\APPS\VBPLOT on the CD.

CD-ROM

## Drawing the Grid

The Grid On/Grid Off option of the menu draws and removes the grid on top of the plot. When you make a new plot, the grid is not drawn automatically. Instead, you must click on the Draw Grid Subroutine to overlay a grid on the plot. Here is the GridOnOff( ) Subroutine:

The grid can be overlaid on the function and removed instantly with the help of the AutoRedraw Property.

```
Private Sub GridOnOff_Click( )

   If GridOnOff.Caption = "Grid Off" Then
      GridOnOff.Caption = "Grid On"
      Picture1.Refresh
      Exit Sub
   Else
      GridOnOff.Caption = "Grid Off"
      Call GridOn
   End If

End Sub
```

The name of the menu option Grid On (and Grid Off) is GridOnOff, and it is a toggle option. When its caption is Grid Off and the user clicks on it, its caption becomes Grid On; the grid is removed by a simple call to the Refresh Method. This is possible because the grid was drawn with the AutoRedraw Property off. The Refresh Method redraws the so-called *persistent* bitmap, which consists of all the elements drawn with the AutoRedraw Property set to True. When the GridOn command is clicked, the grid is redrawn by calling the GridOn( ) subroutine—there is no simple method to bring it back on.

For more information on this technique of overlaying a grid on top of an image, see the "Transparency Drawing" earlier in this chapter.

We could have achieved the same result by setting the DrawMode Property to XOR and redrawing the grid, but this is neither as fast in removing the grid (Refresh requires no calculations) nor as accurate. With the XOR drawing mode, the shapes are retained, but not the colors. In other words, we would get dots of different color at the intersections of the function plots and the grid lines. (See Figures 5-11 and 5-12 for an example of XOR drawing over an image.)

If you would like to see the functions as they are being plotted, set the AutoRedraw Property of the Picture Box to False before calling the PlotFunction( ) Subroutine, or issue the Refresh Method every so often, as discussed earlier in this chapter.

The GridOn( ) Subroutine is lengthy but straightforward. It calculates the location of the horizontal and vertical tic marks and draws them as lines. Notice that AutoRedraw is False while the grid is being drawn, so that we can remove the grid easily with the Refresh Method. The GridOn( ) Subroutine accepts no arguments. Instead, it uses the global variables HTics and VTics, which are the number of horizontal and vertical major tic marks respectively, and calculates their positions on the Picture Box. The number of minor tic marks is fixed (five divisions between two major tic marks).

```
Private Sub GridOn( )

' Set AutoRedraw to False, so that the grid can
' be removed easily with the Refresh method
   Picture1.AutoRedraw = False

' Distance between major tic marcs (Grid)
   GridSpaceX = Picture1.ScaleWidth / (HTics - 1)
   GridSpaceY = Picture1.ScaleHeight / (VTics - 1)
' distance between minor tic marcs
   MinorSpaceX = GridSpaceX / 5
   MinorSpaceY = GridSpaceY / 5
' Length of each horizontal and vertical minor tic amrc
   MinorXTic = Abs(Picture1.ScaleWidth) / 50
   MinorYTic = Abs(Picture1.ScaleHeight) / 50
' Use dashed lines for the grid
   Picture1.DrawStyle = 2
   Picture1.ForeColor = MajorTicColor
```

```
' Draw vertical grid lines
   For ix = 1 To VTics - 1
      XFrom = Picture1.ScaleLeft + ix * GridSpaceX
      XTo = XFrom
      YFrom = Picture1.ScaleTop
      YTo = Picture1.ScaleTop + Picture1.ScaleHeight
      Picture1.Line (XFrom, YFrom)-(XTo, YTo)

   Next
' Draw Horizontal grid lines
   For iy = 1 To HTics - 1
      XFrom = Picture1.ScaleLeft
      XTo = Picture1.ScaleLeft + Picture1.ScaleWidth
      YFrom = Picture1.ScaleTop + iy * GridSpaceY
      YTo = YFrom
      Picture1.Line (XFrom, YFrom)-(XTo, YTo)
   Next

' Minor Tic marks
   Picture1.ForeColor = MinorTicColor
   Picture1.DrawStyle = 0
' X-Axis minor tics
   For jx = 1 To 5 * (HTics - 1)
      XFrom = Picture1.ScaleLeft + jx * MinorSpaceX
      YFrom = Picture1.ScaleTop + Picture1.ScaleHeight
      XTo = XFrom
      YTo = YFrom + MinorYTic
      Picture1.Line (XFrom, YFrom)-(XTo, YTo)
   Next

' Y-Axis minor tics
   For jy = 1 To 5 * (VTics - 1)
      XFrom = Picture1.ScaleLeft
      YFrom = Picture1.ScaleTop + jy * MinorSpaceY
      XTo = XFrom + MinorXTic
      YTo = YFrom
      Picture1.Line (XFrom, YFrom)-(XTo, YTo)
   Next

End Sub
```

One last implication: Let's say we have plotted some functions along with their grid on the Picture Box, and we switch to another application. What will happen when we return to VBPlot? Visual Basic will automatically redraw the Picture Box, but only the parts generated while AutoRedraw was True. The grid, drawn with AutoRedraw = False, will be lost. Moreover, the grid and the menu option will get out of sync (in other words, the menu option will be Grid Off while no grid is displayed).

The simplest solution is to activate the Grid On/Off command from the main menu and redraw the grid. There is a better way to restore the grid, which does it automatically. When a window has to be redrawn, Visual Basic generates its Paint Event. If we called the GridOn( ) subroutine from the Paint Event of our main window, we could update the VBPlot window as if everything on it was drawn with AutoRedraw set to True.

Notice that the grid can be drawn even before any data or functions have been plotted on the screen. The reason is that the GridOn subroutine depends on the size of the plotting area (the Picture Box) and some global variables only.

### Numbering the Axes

The AxisNumbers and AxisTitles subroutines demonstrate the use of the Width and Height Properties. We must print the numbers and titles on the Form, but align them with the major tic marks of the plot's grid. The Form's coordinates are expressed in twips. But the numbers on the tic marks must be expressed in the units of the Picture Box's coordinate system. In our subroutine, we must use the ScaleWidth and ScaleHeight Properties of the Picture Box to calculate

- The X axis number.
- The Y axis number.
- The Width and Height Properties of the Picture Box for the placement of these numbers on the Form.

In the following program we calculate the coordinates of each major tic mark. Then we subtract half of the number's width or height. This centers the numbers around the corresponding major tic marks.

```
Private Sub AxisNumbers( )

    Picture1.ForeColor = NumberColor
    XNumInc = Picture1.ScaleWidth / (HTics - 1)
    YNumInc = Picture1.ScaleHeight / (VTics - 1)
```

```
    XNum1 = Picture1.ScaleLeft
    YNum1 = Picture1.ScaleTop
    GridSpaceX = Picture1.Width / (HTics - 1)
    GridSpaceY = Picture1.Height / (VTics - 1)

    For ix = 0 To HTics - 1
        Number$ = Format$(XNum1 + ix * XNumInc, "0.00")
        X1 = Picture1.Left + ix * GridSpaceX - 0.5 * →
        TextWidth(Number$)
        Y1 = Picture1.Height + Picture1.TOP + 0.5 * →
        TextHeight("0")
        Form1.CurrentX = X1
        Form1.CurrentY = Y1
        Form1.Print Number$
    Next

    For iy = 0 To VTics - 1
        Number$ = Format$(YNum1 + iy * YNumInc, "0.00")
        If TextWidth(Number$) > LongestYNumber Then →
        LongestYNumber = TextWidth(Number$)
        X1 = Picture1.Left - TextWidth(Number$) - TextWidth(".")
        Y1 = Picture1.TOP + iy * GridSpaceY - 0.5 * →
        TextHeight("0")
        Form1.CurrentX = X1
        Form1.CurrentY = Y1
        Form1.Print Number$
    Next

End Sub
```

During the calculations of the Y numbers' coordinates, we keep track of the longest number. We do so because we must consider it when calculating the placement of the Y axis title. The X coordinate of this title must be chosen so that it won't run over the axis numbers. The LongestYNumber is another global variable, used later in the AxisTitles( ) Subroutine.

### Placing the Titles

The AxisTitles( ) Subroutine places the axis and graph titles on the Form. It centers the axis titles on the sides of the Picture Box and the graph title within the width of the Form. Notice that here we make use of the Width and Height Properties of the Picture Box, and not

ScaleWidth and ScaleHeight, because the calculations must be carried out in twips, the units of the Form.

```
Private Sub AxisTitles( )

   Picture1.ForeColor = TitleColor
   YTitleX = (Picture1.Left - 1.5 * LongestYNumber) / 2
   YTitleY = (Form1.Width - TextWidth(YTitle$)) / 2
   XTitleX = Picture1.Left + (Picture1.Width - →
   TextWidth(XTitle$)) / 2
   XTitleY = (Picture1.Height + Picture1.TOP + 1.5 * →
   TextHeight("O"))

' Calculate vertical title's Height
   TitleHeight = 0
   For i = 1 To Len(YTitle$)
      TitleHeight = TitleHeight + TextHeight(Mid$(YTitle$, i, 1))
   Next
' Print Vertical (Y) title, one character at a time
   Form1.CurrentX = YTitleX
   Form1.CurrentY = (Form1.Height - TitleHeight) / 2 - →
   0.1 * Form1.ScaleHeight
   For i = 1 To Len(YTitle$)
      CurChar$ = Mid$(YTitle$, i, 1)
      Form1.CurrentX = YTitleX + TextWidth("X") - →
      TextWidth(Mid$(YTitle$, i, 1)) / 2
      Form1.Print CurChar$
   Next
' Print Horizontal (X) title
   Form1.CurrentX = XTitleX
   Form1.CurrentY = XTitleY
   Form1.Print XTitle$
' Change font size temporarily and print graph title
   TmpSize = Form1.FontSize
   Form1.FontSize = 1.5 * Form1.FontSize
   Form1.CurrentX = (Form1.Width - TextWidth(Title$)) / 2
   Form1.CurrentY = Picture1.TOP / 2 - 0.5 * TextWidth("A")
   Form1.Print Title$
   Form1.FontSize = TmpSize

End Sub
```

XTitleX, XTitleY, YTitleX and YTitleY are the X and Y coordinates of the two axis titles (XTitle$ and YTitle$). We consider the height of each title in calculating the Y coordinate and the width of each title in calculating the X coordinate.

### Finally, the Plot

Now let's look again at the Plot command's code:

```
Private Sub Plot_Click( )
Dim WidthInDots As Integer

    Picture1.ScaleMode = 3
    WidthInDots = Picture1.ScaleWidth
    Screen.MousePointer = 11
    a% = SetUserScale(XAxisMin, XAxisMax, WidthInDots)
    a% = PlotFunction(XAxisMin, XAxisMax, WidthInDots)
    Call AxisNumbers
    Call AxisTitles
    If GridOnOff.Caption = "Grid Off" Then
        Call GridOn
    End If
    Screen.MousePointer = 1

End Sub
```

The Plot command simply calls the four basic subroutines in the proper order. The variable WidthInDots is the number of pixels in the horizontal direction; it corresponds to the HStep variable of the SetUserScale( ) and Plot( ) functions.

### Resizing the Form

We have implemented all the functions so that they are independent of the actual size of the Form. As a consequence, we can easily change the Form's dimensions and call the Plot command again to redraw the Form's contents. Any change in the Form's dimensions is signalled to the program by the Resize Event of the Form. If you add the following lines in the Form's Resize Event, the VBPlot application will keep drawing the functions and the data sets correctly, regardless of the Form's actual size.

```
Private Sub Form_Resize( )

    Picture1.Cls
    Picture1.Left = 0.15 * Form1.ScaleWidth
    Picture1.Width = 0.8 * Form1.ScaleWidth
    Picture1.TOP = 0.1 * Form1.ScaleHeight
    Picture1.Height = 0.75 * Form1.ScaleHeight
    Form1.Cls
    Picture1.Cls
    Form1.FontSize = Form1.Width / 800

End Sub
```

Notice that the size and placement of the Picture Box is specified in terms of the Form's dimensions. You can change the percentages that define the Picture Box's dimensions to make a larger plot or leave more room for the titles. This subroutine also changes the size of the font, to avoid very large titles on a small Form or very small titles on a large Form (but you must use a TrueType font for this technique to work).

### Adding a Cross Hair Cursor

One last feature of the program, which you can see in Figure 5-34, is the cross hair cursor that appears when the mouse pointer is within the Picture Box and the left mouse button is held down. When you move the mouse in the Picture Box and hold down its left button, a cross hair cursor follows the movement of the mouse. At the same time, the coordinates of its hot spot are displayed on the program's title bar. This cursor helps you locate the plot areas you are interested in by providing a numerical feedback. You can also use it to measure the distances between measurements, or the function's value at any X value (or the opposite).

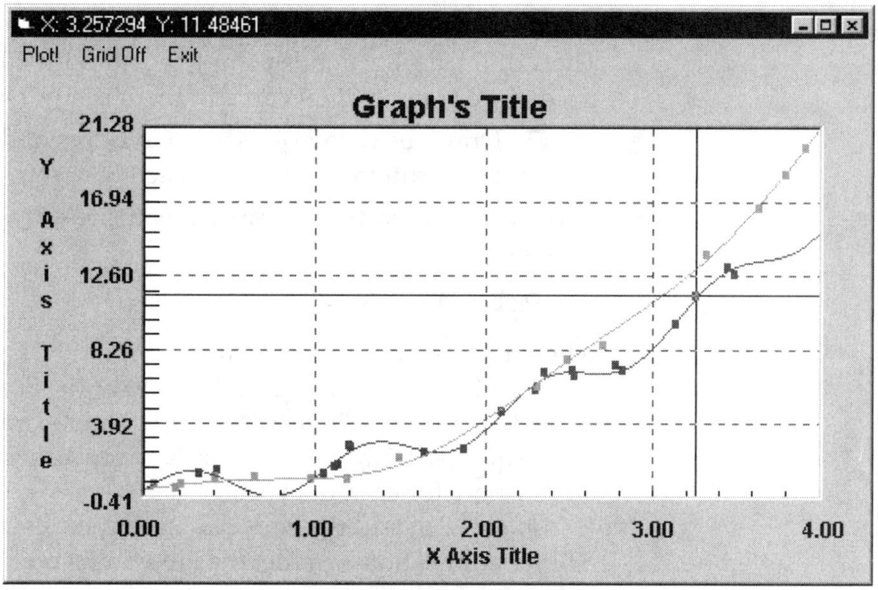


Figure 5-34: The cross hair cursor allows the user to read the (X,Y) coordinates easily and accurately.

We implement this feature within the Mouse Events and base it on the Rubber Lines example earlier in the chapter. In the MouseDown Event we set the DrawMode Property to XOR and draw the cross hair cursor for the first time. In each successive MouseMove Event we erase the old cross hair cursor (by drawing another one on top of it), store its coordinates in the global variables CursorOldX and CursorOldY, and then draw another cross hair cursor at the current location. The variables CursorOldX and CursorOldY become the coordinates of the previous cursor for the next MouseMove Event. This process is repeated for as long as the left mouse button is held down. Finally, in the MouseUp Event we erase the last cross hair cursor and clear the coordinates from the menu bar.

While the mouse moves over the Picture Box with the left button pressed, the title bar displays the coordinates of the current point. When the mouse button is released, the title bar is reset to the string "VBPLOT." The actual programming of the cross hair feature is very similar to the code used to display the Picture Box's coordinates in the SCALE application; we will not repeat it here. You can load the VBPlot application into Visual Basic's editor and look at the code behind the Picture Box's MouseDown, MouseMove and MouseUp Events.

## Further Improvements

The VBPlot application is complete and quite functional, but if you need more features, you can add them easily. Here are some ideas:

- ❒ Draw the data points as solid boxes of different color.
- ❒ Use a different shape for each data set.

For example, you can draw a small circle at each data point with the command

```
Picture1.Circle (XPoint, YPoint), R
```

where R is the radius of the circle.

A good choice for R would be 1/100 of the ScaleWidth or the ScaleHeight of the Picture Box. With a few extra commands you can draw squares, triangles, diamonds or any other shape you find appropriate for each data set.

You can also add the code for storing the current state of the VBPlot application to a file; the next time you run it, it will start where it left off. The state of the application consists of the data sets and the functions to be plotted, the various parameters of the plot and the status of the Grid On command of the main menu.

We specify the application's parameters in the Form's Load Event by setting the appropriate values to a number of global variables. To make VBPlot even more functional, you can add a new Form that lets the user specify all these parameters through a graphical user interface.

This application's major drawback is that it doesn't let the user enter the expression (or formula) to be plotted at run time. The functions to be plotted must be hard-coded into the application itself. As easy as it is to calculate an expression's value in Visual Basic's Debug Window, it is difficult to write a program to evaluate an expression in Visual Basic (or any other language, for that matter). A program that evaluates expressions is called a *parser.* We'll return to this example in Chapter 12, "Recursive Programming." There, we'll expand VBPlot, adding a parser so that it can plot any user input function.

## MOVING ON

We're ready to move on to more advanced and interesting topics, such as image processing. In the next chapter, "Color & Imaging," you'll learn how to use color efficiently with Visual Basic. You'll become familiar with the structure of the Windows BMP files, how images are stored in them and how color is used. These topics will be demonstrated with VBImage, an image processing application.

By chapter's end, you will have learned the basics of image processing and a number of image processing techniques, and you'll be able to develop your own routines for processing images. We also use many of the concepts of Chapter 6 in generating the fractal images of Chapter 14.

# Chapter 6

# Color & Imaging

In this chapter we'll focus on Visual Basic's color handling capabilities. We'll start with the definition and handling of colors in Visual Basic. There are many and various computers out there—some with higher resolutions, and others with more or fewer colors—and your application should work with all of them. To develop applications that can handle color efficiently, you must learn to cope with different situations. We'll see how images are stored in files and then build an image processing application. Figures 6-1 and 6-2 are samples of what you can do with this chapter's major application, VBImage.

Figure 6-1: VBImage can create many special effects on images, such as the Neon effect shown here.

Figure 6-2: This attractive transformation is called Emboss.

Visual Basic supports so many colors that handling them can pose problems.

Visual Basic supports many more colors than you could wish for—up to 16,777,216, to be exact. You can create and display all kinds of images with Visual Basic, but how do we specify colors? Obviously, 16.7 million color names, or color numbers, wouldn't help.

## THE RGB COLOR MODEL

Computers use the RGB model to specify colors. The RGB model is based on three primary colors: Red, Green and Blue. Every color you can imagine can be reconstructed by mixing the appropriate percentages of the primaries. Each color, therefore, is represented by a triplet (Red, Green, Blue), where Red, Green and Blue are three bytes representing the primary color components. The smallest value, 0, indicates the absence of the color. The largest value, 255, indicates full intensity, or saturation. The triplet (0, 0, 0) is black, because all colors are missing, while the triplet (255, 255, 255) is white. Other colors have various combinations: (255, 0, 0) is a pure red, (0, 255, 255) is a pure cyan (what you get when you mix green and blue) and (0, 128, 128) is a mid-cyan, a mix of mid-green and mid-blue tones. The possible combinations of the three primary color components are 256 X 256 X 256, or 16,777,216 colors in all.

The process of generating colors with three basic components is based on the RGB Color Cube, shown in Figure 6-3. The Color Cube has three dimensions, because each color is described in terms of three basic colors. The cube's corners are assigned each of the three primary colors, their complements and the colors black and white.

A color's complementary color is calculated by subtracting its primary components from 255. For example, the color (0, 0, 255) is a pure blue tone. Its complementary color is (255-0, 255-0, 255-255) =

(255, 255, 0), which is a pure yellow tone. Blue and yellow are complementary colors, and they are mapped to opposite corners of the cube. The same is true for red and cyan, green and magenta, and black and white. If you add a color to its complementary, you get white.

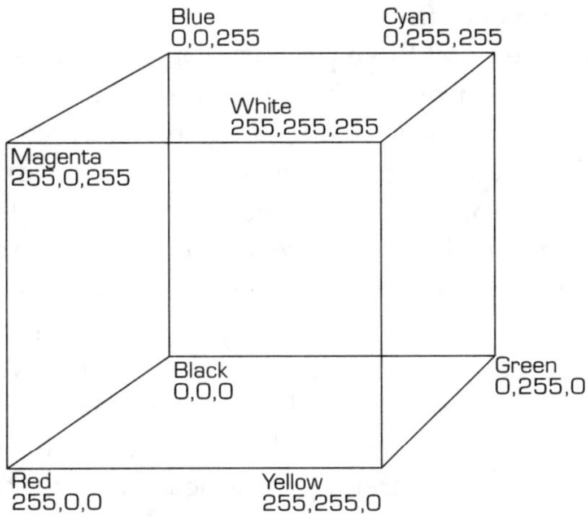


Figure 6-3: Color specification with the RGB Cube.

The RGB Cube is an easy way to visualize all colors available to you and your application.

Notice that the components of the colors at the corners of the cube have either zero or full intensity. As we move from one corner to another along the same edge of the cube, only one of the primaries changes value. For example, as we move from the green to the yellow corner, the red component changes from 0 to 255. The other two components remain the same. As we move between these two corners, we get all the available tones from green to yellow (256 in all). Similarly, as we move from the yellow to the red corner, the only component that changes color is the green one, and we get all the available tones from yellow to red. This range of similar colors is called *gradient*.

## Specifying Gradients

Gradients are sets of colors, with subtle changes in shade between successive colors. When we move to an opposite corner on the same side of the cube (as from red to white, or from green to blue), two of the primary components change value, and we obtain a larger range of colors. For example, there are more ways than one to get from the yellow to the magenta corner. If we move through the red corner, we get all the tones between yellow and red and then all the tones from red to magenta. If we move through the white corner, we obtain a different range of colors. Finally, if we move on the diagonal—which means that the green and blue components change equally at each step—we obtain the smoothest and most natural transition from yellow to magenta.

To specify a gradient, pick up all the colors along an edge (or a diagonal) of the color cube.

A change in all three primary components is required to move between two opposite corners of the cube. And, as you can see, there are even more ways to move from black to white. We can move from the black to the white corner by visiting any other color. As expected, the shortest route, which is the cube's diagonal, yields the simplest transition, which is the range of all available gray tones.

Despite the fact we can specify more than 16 million colors, you can't have more than 256 shades of gray, including black and white. The reason is that a gray tone, including the two extremes (black and white), is made up of equal values of all three primary colors. The value (128, 128, 128) is a mid-gray tone, but the values (127, 128, 128) and (129, 128, 128) aren't gray tones, although they are too close for the human eye to see the difference. That's why it's wasteful to store grayscale pictures using 16-million color True Color file formats. A 256-color file format will store a grayscale just as accurately and more compactly. Once we know an image is grayscale, we needn't store all three bytes per pixel. One value is adequate (the other two components have the same value).

The RGB cube is a very descriptive representation of the color spectrum and can come in very handy when you are choosing or designing colors. For example, when you wish to fill a shape with a gradient, just choose the starting and ending colors and then calculate the tones between them. The more colors you assign, the smoother the gradient will be.

## Channels

Since color is specified by three primary components, each image is made of the three basic images: a red image (an image that contains red shades only), a green image and a blue image. Figure 6-4 shows an image and the three *channels* that make it up.

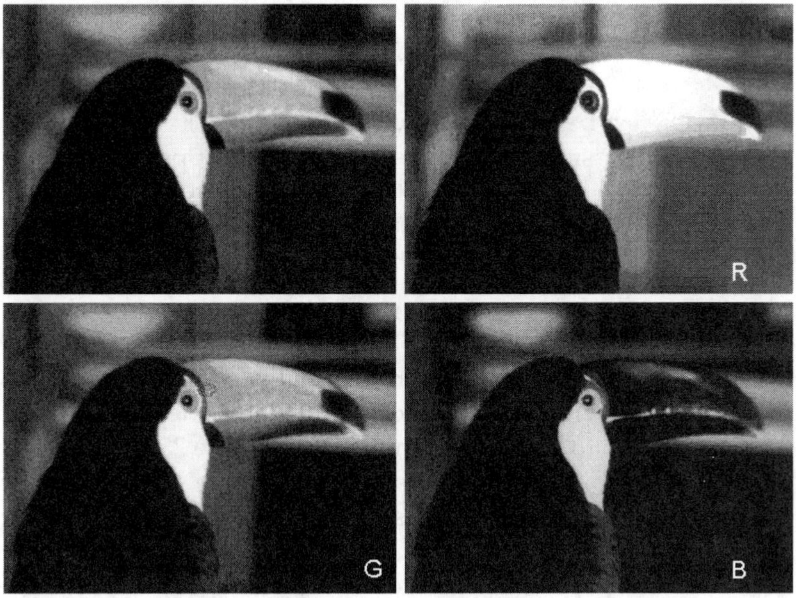


Figure 6-4: The three channels of a color image.

The three channels are monochrome images. The red channel, for example, is a monochrome image, which represents the intensity of the red color over the image. The same is true for the other two channels. The three images are combined electronically by the VGA circuitry to produce a True Color image.

These channels are at the heart of every image processing application. When we process an image, we must process each channel separately. The result will be the combination of the three processed channels.

## Specifying Colors

For defining colors, Visual Basic provides the RGB function, which accepts three arguments: RGB(Red, Green, Blue). VB's RGB( ) Function can define any color imaginable, but there is no guarantee that it will be ever displayed on your screen. What good is it to be able to define 16.7 million colors, if your VGA card can display no more than 16?

Visual Basic provides the means for specifying any color you can display under Windows. However, what you see depends on what you paid for your video system. If you are running Visual Basic on a 16-color system, the RGB function will not help you much. You are better off with VB's QBColor( ) Function, which produces the elementary 16 colors.

On the other hand, if you have a True Color VGA adapter, capable of the full 16,777,216 colors, you can display any color imaginable (well, nearly any, since there are a few colors in nature which cannot be represented on the computer).

Most systems today are equipped with a 256-color VGA and they can display up to 256 different colors. But which 256? The answer is any collection that you wish. The 256 colors are displayed based on the *palette currently in use.*

## 256-Color Palettes

As we have mentioned already, many computers can't display the entire color spectrum. Instead, they allow the application to select up to 256 colors, and use them. The 256 colors form a palette, and your application must use the palette's colors only. If it requests a color that doesn't exist in the palette, Visual Basic approximates it with one of the palette's colors. While it may seem small compared to the full spectrum, 256 colors are plenty for displaying a high-quality image on the monitor.

The average True Color image doesn't really use more than a few thousand colors.

You can't even come close to using 16 million colors. An image with 16 million pixels (one for each color) would have a size of 4,000 by 4,000 pixels.

In the next section we will explore the use of color palettes with simple examples. The examples will work with 256-color systems. If you have a True Color display, your computer doesn't use palettes. However, if you plan to distribute your applications, you must know how Visual Basic handles palettes.

### Where Are the 256 Colors?

Let's see how palettes work with a simple experiment. If you have a 256-color VGA adapter, open a new Form and place a Picture Box on it. Then load an image with the LoadPicture Method, or assign an image's filename to the Picture Property. Visual Basic selects 256 colors (maybe fewer) that best describe this picture, and then displays it. And it does a good job, too. As you can see, 256 colors is adequate for displaying practically any image.

Now add a second Picture Box on the Form, and load another image. If the colors of the two images are drastically different, some pixels in the first Picture Box will change color. Add more images, and these strange effects will become more and more obvious. You may also at times notice a sort of green X-ray effect when loading a new Windows application. This, too, is a result of a palette conflict. Visual Basic has only 256 colors at its disposal and does its best to accommodate all images, but sometimes, 256 colors just isn't enough.

When Visual Basic runs out of colors, it approximates some of them and thereby introduces artifacts.

Here is what happens. Let's say the first image contains one particular palette of 256 colors, and Visual Basic displays them properly. The second image perhaps includes a few colors common to both images, but also new colors. Visual Basic doesn't know what to do with the extra colors, so it replaces a few of the existing colors with the new ones to accommodate the second image. As a result, some pixels change color.

When you load an image on a Visual Basic control, the colors are determined by the image itself. But what if you want to create a new image? You can create palettes with any combination of colors, as long as you do not exceed 256 colors. If you use the RGB( ) Function to draw shapes with random colors on a Picture Box or a Form, you will realize that you can't display more than 20 colors on a 256-color system. These are the 20 basic Windows colors. The rest are not displayed because you have not yet defined a palette. How do we then define the palette?

### Specifying a Palette

You can use the RGB( ) Function to display a palette's colors, but the appropriate color palette must be loaded on a Picture Box or a Form before you can call the RGB( ) Function. The simplest way to do this is to load an image with the palette you want. Every time you load an image on a Control, the image's colors automatically become the palette colors since the palette is included in the file format.

To load a palette on a Visual Basic Control, load an image with the palette you're after. The image itself need be no larger than a pixel.

Visual Basic itself comes with three different palettes, which are stored in DIB (Device-Independent Bitmap) files: RAINBOW.DIB, BRIGHT.DIB and PASTEL.DIB. The first one contains an evenly spread set of colors, the second one contains shades of bright colors, and the third, a spectrum of pale tones. All three files include a single-pixel "stub" image, but they contain a full 256-color palette which is loaded into the Picture Box along with the image. The single-pixel stub image is displayed, but doesn't show on the default white BackColor of the Control. In the \PALETTES subdirectory of the CD are a few more single-pixel images with a full palette; we'll use these in Chapter 13.

CD-ROM

Once the palette is loaded, you can use the RGB( ) Function to specify any of its colors. While there are other ways to load a palette on a Picture Box or Form, this approach is simplest, is recommended by Microsoft, and is the approach we use in this book. For simple applications, you can load a palette with many colors, such as BRIGHT.DIB, and even the approximated colors will look fairly good.

To check out this approach, load one of Visual Basic's DIB palettes on a Picture Box. You will see nothing, since the image is a single pixel only. Enter the following code in the Form's Load Event and run the program:

```
Sub Form_Load ( )

For i = 1 To 100
    centerX = Rnd * Form1.Width
    centerY = Rnd * Form1.Width
    Form1.FillColor = RGB(Rnd * 255, Rnd * 255, Rnd * 255)
    Circle (centerX, centerY), Rnd * Form1.Width / 5
Next

End Sub
```

Circles appear, filled with colors taken from the palette.

### Copying Palettes to the Clipboard

There is another way to load palettes on a Picture Box. How would you load the palette of an image that contains more than just a pixel? Loading the entire image when you only need its palette isn't really a solution (you would actually be loading an image, not just a palette). It is possible to copy palettes to the Clipboard, and then paste them on a Picture Box. Here's how it's done.

Start a new project and place two Picture Boxes on the Form. Then load a 256-color image on the first Picture Box (Picture1). If you want to use the image's colors in the second Picture Box, you can isolate the image's palette and transfer it to the second Picture Box through the Clipboard.

To exchange data between your application and the Clipboard, Visual Basic provides the SetData and GetData Methods. These functions can handle a variety of data structures, including palettes. All we have to do is copy the first Picture Box's palette to the Clipboard, and then paste it on the second Picture Box:

```
Clipboard.SetData Picture1.Image, CF_PALETTE
Picture2.Picture = Clipboard.GetData(CF_PALETTE)
```

The CF_PALETTE constant defines the type of information to be copied to the Clipboard and has the value 9 for palettes. If you look carefully at the second Picture Box, you will see that it contains a single pixel at its upper-left corner. Visual Basic uses the same technique we described earlier to move palettes to and from the Clipboard.

Now we can construct a single-pixel image with a custom palette. Make the size of the second Picture Box equal to 1 pixel, and then save its contents with the SavePicture command. We will use this technique of copying and pasting palettes later in this chapter, in the VBImage application.

How do we know in advance the colors we may need? And even if we do, how do we create a DIB file with them? That's the subject of the next section.

In most cases, you don't know in advance how many colors are required.

So far you have been using images in a variety of ways, either within your Visual Basic application or with other Windows applications. You know how to load images on Forms and other Controls and how to use them to make your interface more visually appealing. Next we'll see how images are stored in files and how you can handle these files in ways that are not possible with a simple method, such as LoadPicture( ) or SavePicture( ). We will start by examining how palettes and images are stored in DIB files. Whether you are using a palette or True Color system, you must be able to read image files in your applications.

## DIB FILE STRUCTURE

The file structure used to store bitmapped images is called DIB, which stands for *Device Independent Bitmap*. A DIB file contains the following:

- Information about the size and other characteristics of the image.
- The definitions of the colors used by the image.
- The values of the pixels that make up the image.

These are the files with extension DIB and BMP (for BitMaP), recognized by all graphics applications under Windows. The image in a DIB file is stored in such a way that it will look the same regardless of the device on which it will be displayed or printed.

Although you can load an image directly to a Picture Box, or save the contents of a Picture Box to a file with a single command, it will come in handy to be able to access DIB files from within your own programs. In a later section we will discuss the implementation of an image processing application that must be able to read DIB files directly from disk. The implementation of the fractal-generating algorithms of Chapter 14 also require reading some data from DIB files.

The structure of a DIB file is straightforward as shown in Table 6-1:

| | |
|---|---|
| BITMAPFILEHEADER | Structure containing information about the file (type, size, etc.). |
| BITMAPINFOHEADER | Structure containing information about the image (resolution, number of colors, etc.). |
| DIB Image Palette | The definitions of the colors used in the image. |
| DIB Image Pixel Values | The actual pixel values. |

Table 6-1: Structure of a DIB file.

## The BITMAPFILEHEADER Structure

The BITMAPFILEHEADER is always 14 bytes long. It identifies the file structure as DIB and contains information about the file itself, rather than the image stored in it:

```
Type BITMAPFILEHEADER
    bfType As Integer
    bfSize As Long
    bfReserved1 As Integer
    bfReserved2 As Integer
    bfOffBits As Long
End Type
```

There's always a "BM" at the start of any BMP or DIB file.

The first integer identifies the file as being a DIB or BMP type. This integer (two bytes) is really the two-character string BM, for BitMap. As a result, the two bytes of the integer field bfType are the ASCII codes of the characters "B" and "M". (The value of this integer is always going to be 19778.) The next field is the length of the file in bytes, followed by two reserved integers that should be set to zero.

The last field is an integer that represents the distance of the first pixel of the image from the beginning of the file. This distance is the total number of bytes in the BITMAPFILEHEADER and BITMAPINFOHEADER structures and the palette.

**Example: The Windows Logo**

Here are the bytes that make up the WINLOGO.BMP image, which should be in your Windows directory. You can open this file with a paint application, such as Paintbrush, to verify the values.

| BITMAPFILEHEADER | | | |
|---|---|---|---|
| 66, 77 | = 19778 | bfType | FileType field ("BM"). |
| 118, 150, 0, 0 | = 38518 | bfSize | The size of the file. |
| 0, 0 | | bfReserved1 | Reserved integer (0). |
| 0, 0 | | bfReserved2 | Reserved integer (0). |
| 118, 0, 0, 0 | = 118 | bfOffBits | Offset of the first pixel. |

Table 6-2: The bytes that make un WINLOGO.BMP.

## The BITMAPINFOHEADER Structure

The next structure, BITMAPINFOHEADER, contains the general characteristics of the image. Its structure is as follows:

```
Type BITMAPINFOHEADER
    biSize As Long
    biWidth As Long
    biHeight As Long
    biPlanes As Integer
    biBitCount As Integer
    biCompression As Long
    biSizeImage As Long
    biXPelsPerMeter As Long
    biYPelsPerMeter As Long
    biClrUsed As Long
    biClrImportant As Long
End Type
```

The second record of a DIB file contains a detailed description of the image. The field biSize is the size of the BITMAPINFOHEADER structure in bytes, and its value is 40. The next two fields are long integers, which hold the dimensions of the image in pixels. The first long integer,

True Color images require 3 bytes to describe each pixel.

biWidth, is the number of pixels per line, and the second, biHeight, is the number of lines in the image. The biPlanes field specifies the number of planes in the target device and should be the integer 1.

The next field, biBitCount, is the number of bits used for representing the color of each pixel. For black-and-white images, biBitCount is 1—we don't need more than 1 bit to describe one of two possible colors. Therefore, we can store 8 consecutive pixels of a black-and-white image in a byte. For a 16-color image, we need 1 byte for two pixels. But the most common images today are those with 256 colors, and for these, the value of biBitCount is 8 ($2^8$=256). In other words, we need 1 byte to describe each pixel of a 256-color image. Finally, for True Color images, this value is 24 (i.e., 1 byte for each of the primary colors, grouped as 3 bytes describing each pixel).

To summarize, the biBitCount field usually takes one of the following values:

| | | |
|---|---|---|
| 1 | For monochrome images | ($2^1$=2) |
| 4 | For 16-color images | ($2^4$=16) |
| 8 | For 256-color images | ($2^8$=256) |
| 24 | For True Color images | ($2^{24}$=16,777,216 colors) |

Table 6-3: Values of the biBitCount field.

The biCompression field specifies whether or not the pixel values are compressed. The value of the biCompression field is zero for uncompressed files. Uncompressed images take up more disk space, but the compression algorithms will increase the complexity of the algorithms. Many applications, including Windows Paintbrush, support only uncompressed DIB images, so we will be concerned with uncompressed DIB files only. (For more information regarding the compression of DIB files, see Microsoft's SDK documentation.)

The next field, biSizeImage, is the size of the image in bytes. biSizeImage is the number of bytes of the last section of a DIB file (the pixel values). The total size of the DIB file is the sum of biSizeImage, the size of the two headers and the size of the palette.

The following two fields, biXPixelsPerMeter and biYPixelsPerMeter, specify the horizontal and vertical resolution in pixels per meter of the target device. These fields allow you to choose from within your application the bitmap resource that best matches the characteristics of the current device. In our examples, we will not make use of these two fields of the BITMAPINFOHEADER structure.

The biClrImportant field specifies the number of colors considered "important" when displaying a particular image.

The last two fields relate to the colors used by the image. A 256-color image may not actually use all 256 colors, but it has a color depth of 8 bits. In other words, every pixel value is represented by a byte (8 bits). An image with 130 different colors has a color depth of 8 bits, but it doesn't use all colors that may be present in the palette. The biClrUsed is the number of colors actually being used by the bitmap.

Applications that open multiple windows with images may need this information, as well as the next field, biClrImportant. The biClrImportant field specifies the number of colors that are considered important for displaying the bitmap. If this value is zero, then all colors are important. We will not use these two fields.

Let's continue our example with the WINLOGO.BMP image. Here are the bytes making up the BITMAPINFOHEADER:

| BITMAPINFOHEADER | | | |
|---|---|---|---|
| 40, 0, 0, 0 | = 40 | biSize | Length of BITMAPINFOHEADER |
| 64, 1, 0, 0 | = 320 | biWidth | Width of the bitmap |
| 240, 0, 0, 0 | = 240 | biHeight | Height of the bitmap |
| 1, 0 | = 1 | biPlanes | Number of planes (=1) |
| 4, 0 | = 4 | biBitCount | Color depth (Colors in image=$2^4$=16) |
| 0, 0, 0, 0 | = 0 | biCompression | Is zero for noncompressed images |
| 0, 0, 0, 0 | = 0 | biSizeImage | Size of image (optional) |
| 0, 0, 0, 0 | = 0 | biXPelsPerMeter | (unused) |
| 0, 0, 0, 0 | = 0 | biYPelsPerMeter | (unused) |
| 0, 0, 0, 0 | = 0 | biClrUsed | All colors used |
| 0, 0, 0, 0 | = 0 | ClrImportant | All colors important |

Table 6-4: The bytes that make up the BITMAPINFOHEADER.

True Color images do not have palettes.

## The Palette Section

The next section of a DIB file is the palette. Here we store the descriptions of the colors that will be used in displaying the image. The size of this section depends on the number of bits per pixel (field biBitCount). A black-and-white image contains only two colors (which need not be black and white). The description of the two colors is stored in the palette section. Similarly, a 16-color image contains 16 color descriptions in the palette section, and a 256-color image contains 256 color descriptions. True Color images do not contain a palette because it wouldn't make sense to store 16.7 million descriptions. Instead, the description of each pixel's specific color is stored in the pixel section of the DIB file—that is, the data of the image itself contains specifications for each pixel's actual color.

In images other than True Color, each pixel's value is not a color value, but a pointer to the palette. To display a 256-color image, for example, Visual Basic reads the value of the pixel, uses it to locate the corresponding entry in the palette and then paints the pixel on the screen with the specific color. (In reality it is the hardware that looks up the palette and paints the pixels, but for this discussion we can pretend that Visual Basic is in control.) The pixels of a monochrome image are stored as 0 or 1, and we can store 8 such values in a byte. If the pixel value is 0, it will be rendered on the screen with the first color of the palette. If it's 1, it will be rendered with the second color. Each pixel of a 256-color image is represented with one byte (0 to 255), which is used as an index to the palette. A pixel whose value is 32 is rendered on the screen with the 33rd color of the palette.

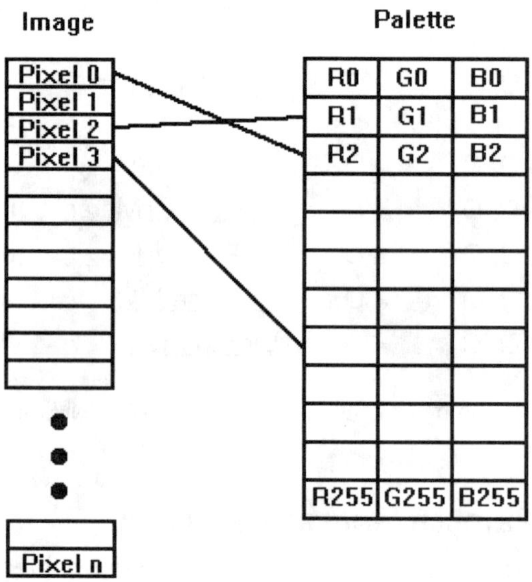


Figure 6-5: The palette is used as a "look-up table" for figuring out how an image will be displayed.

## What's in a DIB Palette?

Now let's take a closer look at the palette section of a DIB file. Each palette entry is described with four bytes. Three of them make up an RGB triplet and the fourth could be used as an *alpha channel.* The alpha channel contains information about the degree of transparency of this palette color. When this byte is 0, the image is opaque, which means that every pixel of the image is displayed as is. When the alpha byte is 255, then the picture is completely transparent and the image has practically no effect on the underlying contents of the screen. Any other alpha value controls the degree of blending between the colors of the image and the colors that exist beneath it on the screen.

The alpha channel is used primarily for special effects. For instance, some image retouching software (such as Micrografx's Picture Publisher) allows you to select the degree of transparency when combining two images. Fade-in and fade-out effects, which you frequently see on TV, can also be produced with the alpha channel. According to Microsoft's documentation, however, the fourth channel is "unused."

The RGB description of each of the 256 colors in the palette is stored as three successive bytes, representing the Red, Green and Blue components of the color. (The components are stored in the file in reverse order: Blue, Green, Red. In our applications, however, we will be storing the components in the order of the RGB( ) Function (Red, Green, Blue) simply to make the code a bit easier to read.) These bytes are followed by a zero byte. Next you see the previous file's palette section as it is stored in the file.

| 16 PALETTE ENTRIES | | | | |
|---|---|---|---|---|
| 0, | 0, | 0, | 0 | Black |
| 0, | 0, | 191, | 0 | Light red tone |
| 0, | 191, | 0, | 0 | Light green tone |
| 0, | 191, | 191, | 0 | Light yellow tone |
| 191, | 0, | 0, | 0 | Light blue tone |
| 191, | 0, | 191, | 0 | Light magenta tone |
| 191, | 191, | 0, | 0 | Light cyan tone |
| 192, | 192, | 192, | 0 | Light gray tone |
| 128, | 128, | 128, | 0 | Mid-gray tone |
| 0, | 0, | 255, | 0 | Pure red |
| 0, | 255, | 0, | 0 | Pure green |
| 0, | 255, | 255, | 0 | Pure yellow |
| 255, | 0, | 0, | 0 | Pure blue |
| 255, | 0, | 255, | 0 | Pure magenta |
| 255, | 255, | 0, | 0 | Pure cyan |
| 255, | 255, | 255, | 0 | White |

Table 6-5: The palette section. The color values are in the order they appear in the DIB file's palette section.

Images are stored in reverse order—the first line in the file will be the lowest line on the screen.

## The Image Pixels

Following the color descriptions, the final section of a DIB file contains the pixel values of the actual image itself. If the image is monochrome (two pixel values, usually black and white) each byte contains eight pixel values, because in this case only one bit is needed to represent each pixel. For a 16 color image (VGA colors) we can store 2 pixel values in a byte, because each pixel is represented by 4 bits ($2^4$=16). For 256-color images, we need 1 byte per pixel ($2^8$=256) and the size of the DIB file is larger in bytes than the number of pixels in the image. Finally, for True Color images we need 3 bytes to represent each pixel.

One crucial detail: an image's pixels are stored as successive "lines" of the image, but they're stored in reverse. The first line in the file is the last line in the displayed image (in other words, the last line of pixels in the Picture Box, where it's displayed). You would expect that the lines are stored in the file from top to bottom, but this isn't the case. If you display each line as you read it, the image will be displayed upside-down. We'll demonstrate how the pixels are read and displayed in "An Image Processing Application" later in this chapter.

Another peculiarity of BMP files is the fact that they may contain extra bytes at the end of each line. Each line of pixels must end at a double word boundary: the number of pixels per line must be a multiple of four. This means that there may be up to 3 empty bytes at the end of each line of pixels. When you create DIB files you may have to waste a few bytes at the end of each line, and ignore them when reading.

### **Example:** Looking at an Actual BMP File

Let's put together the parts we have presented so far by looking at the WINLOGO.BMP file, displayed in Figure 6-6. The left column lists the bytes as they are stored in the file and the values of the integers or long numbers the bytes form (the bytes are stored sequentially in the file, but we have grouped them by two or four depending on whether they form an integer or a long number). At right are the names of the corresponding fields and some comments.

| | | | |
|---|---|---|---|
| BITMAPFILEHEADER | | | |
| 66, 77 | = 19778 | bfType | FileType field ("BM") |
| 118, 150, 0, 0 | = 38518 | bfSize | The size of the file |
| 0, 0 | = 0 | bfReserved1 | Reserved integer (0) |
| 0, 0 | | bfReserved2 | Reserved integer (0) |
| 118, 0, 0, 0 | = 118 | bfOffBits | Offset of the first pixel |
| BITMAPINFOHEADER | | | |
| 40, 0, 0, 0 | = 40 | biSize | Length of BITMAPINFOHEADER |
| 64, 1, 0, 0 | = 320 | biWidth | Width of the bitmap |
| 240, 0, 0, 0 | = 240 | biHeight | Height of the bitmap |
| 1, 0 | = 1 | biPlanes | Number of bitplanes (=1) |
| 4, 0 | = 4 | biBitCount | Color depth |
| Colors in image = $2^4$ = 16 | | | |
| 0, 0, 0, 0 | = 0 | biCompression | Noncompressed image |
| 0, 0, 0, 0 | = 0 | biSizeImage | Size of image (optional) |
| 0, 0, 0, 0 | = 0 | biXPelsPerMeter | (unused) |
| 0, 0, 0, 0 | = 0 | biYPelsPerMeter | (unused) |
| 0, 0, 0, 0 | = 0 | biClrUsed | All colors used |
| 0, 0, 0, 0 | = 0 | ClrImportant | All colors important |

16 PALETTE ENTRIES

| | | | | |
|---|---|---|---|---|
| 0, | 0, | 0, | 0 | Black |
| 0, | 0, | 191, | 0 | Light red tone |
| 0, | 191, | 0, | 0 | Light green tone |
| 0, | 191, | 191, | 0 | Light yellow tone |
| 191, | 0, | 0, | 0 | Light blue tone |
| 191, | 0, | 191, | 0 | Light magenta tone |
| 191, | 191, | 0, | 0 | Light cyan tone |
| 192, | 192, | 192, | 0 | Light gray tone |
| 128, | 128, | 128, | 0 | Mid-gray tone |
| 0, | 0, | 255, | 0 | Pure red |
| 0, | 255, | 0, | 0 | Pure green |
| 0, | 255, | 255, | 0 | Pure yellow |
| 255, | 0, | 0, | 0 | Pure blue |
| 255, | 0, | 255, | 0 | Pure magenta |
| 255, | 255, | 0, | 0 | Pure cyan |
| 255, | 255, | 255, | 0 | White |

Table 6-6: At left are the Bytes of the WINLOGO.BMP file and their values. At right are the corresponding field names and some comments.

Figure 6-6: The bytes described in Table 6-6 correspond to the headers and palette sections of the WINLOGO.BMP image.

The value of the bfOffBits is 118 because the two headers have a total length of 54 (40 + 14) bytes, and the palette size in bytes is 16 * 4 = 64. You may wonder why some palette entries have a value of 191 and others, the value 192, in their color definitions. The difference is probably due to the algorithmic way they were generated, but for all practical purposes you may consider them identical.

Sixteen-color images store two pixel values in a byte.

Following the palette entries are the values of each pixel in the image. Since the image contains only 16 colors, each pixel value is described with four bits, and therefore each following byte contains two pixel values, each in the range (0, 15). The four most significant bits of the byte correspond to the first pixel; the four least significant bits correspond to the pixel immediately following. The first byte after the palette entries in the WINLOGO.BMP file is 135, which in binary form is written as 10000111. The values of the first two pixels of the image are 1000 (=8 decimal) and 0111 (=7 decimal). From the palette entries, we know that their colors are two gray tones: (128, 128, 128) for the first pixel and (192, 192, 192) for the second.

Fortunately, we don't have to read a BMP file and paint each pixel of a Picture Box or a Form with the PSet method. Visual Basic's LoadPicture Method does the same thing, only much faster. However, there are occasions when we might need to read specific fields of a BMP file (its resolution or number of colors, for example) or its palette (if we plan to use it with another image). We'll look at some practical examples of reading BMP files shortly. For now, let's see how to read BMP files' headers and palettes.

### Example: Looking at Images

CD-ROM

Our first example is a simple application that allows the user to locate any DIB (or BMP) file on the disk, see its size and the color depth, and display its bitmap on the screen. It is called IMGSHOW, and you can find it in the 6\APPS\IMGSHOW subdirectory of the CD. The application consists of a single Form, shown in Figure 6-7, and resembles a File Open dialog box. This application understands only DIB and BMP files, so the File List's Pattern Property is set to "*.BMP;*.DIB".

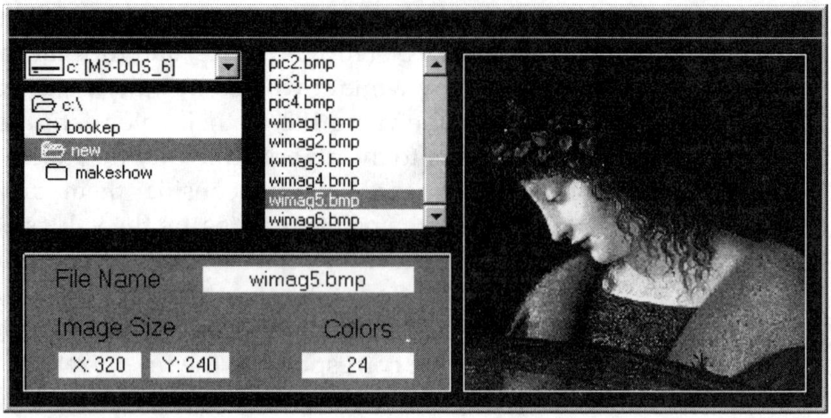


Figure 6-7: The IMGSHOW application.

The Drive, Directory and File Lists help the user locate the image files, and the image's data are displayed in Labels at the bottom of the Form.

The basic data types of a DIB file (BITMAPFILEHEADER and BITMAPINFOHEADER) must be defined in a global Module so that they are available to all other applications as well. Here are their definitions:

```
Type BITMAPFILEHEADER
    bfType As Integer
    bfSize As Long
    bfReserved1 As Integer
    bfReserved2 As Integer
    bfOffBits As Long
End Type

Type BITMAPINFOHEADER
    biSize As Long
    biWidth As Long
    biHeight As Long
    biPlanes As Integer
    biBitCount As Integer
    biCompression As Long
    biSizeImage As Long
    biXPelsPerMeter As Long
    biYPelsPerMeter As Long
    biClrUsed As Long
    biClrImportant As Long
End Type
```

```
Global h1 As BITMAPFILEHEADER
Global h2 As BITMAPINFOHEADER
```

The global variables h1 and h2 are used for storing the two headers of the BMP file.

The Drive1_Click( ) and Dir1_Click( ) Subroutines of the Drive and Directory Lists are very simple. Here's one:

```
Sub Drive1_Change ( )
On Error Resume Next

    Dir1.Path = Drive1.Drive

End Sub
```

And here's the other:

```
Sub Dir1_Change ( )
On Error Resume Next

    File1.Path = Dir1.Path

End Sub
```

The Subroutine File1_Click( ) does all the work. When the user clicks on a file name, the program reads the file's headers, displays the basic image data on the Form and finally loads the image into the Image Box. Here's the code:

Make sure the file being read is indeed a bitmap file.

```
Sub File1_Click()

   If Right$(Dir1.Path, 1) = "\" Then
      FileName = Dir1.Path + File1.FileName
   Else
      FileName = Dir1.Path + "\" + File1.FileName
   End If
' Open the file
   Open FileName For Binary As #1
' Read the headers
   Get #1, , h1
   Get #1, , h2
   Close #1
' Is it a BMP file ?
   If h1.bfType <> 19778 Then
      ImageName.Caption = "Not a DIB File"
      ImageSizeX.Caption = ""
      ImageSizeY.Caption = ""
```

```
        ImageColors.Caption = ""
        Exit Sub
      End If
   ' Display file name, dimensions and number of colors
      ImageName.Caption = File1.FileName
      ImageSizeX.Caption = "X: " + Format$(h2.biWidth, "####")
      ImageSizeY.Caption = "Y: " + Format$(h2.biHeight, "####")
      ImageColors.Caption = Format$(h2.biBitCount, "##")  →
      If h2.biBitCount < 24 Then
         PaletteSize = 2 ^ h2.biBitCount
         ImageColors.Caption = ImageColors.Caption + " (" + →
         Format$(PaletteSize, "###") + ")"
      Else
         ImageColors.Caption = ImageColors.Caption + " (16M)"
      End If
   ' And show picture
      Call DisplayImage

   End Sub
```

ImageName, ImageSizeX, ImageSizeY and ImageColors are the names of the Labels we use to display the data of the image. The DisplayImage Subroutine loads the image to the Image Box with the PictureLoad command, but our implementation does some error checking as well:

```
   Sub DisplayImage ( )

   ' Change mouse pointer to hourglass while reading file
       Form1.MousePointer = 11      ' HOURGLASS cursor shape
       On Error GoTo NotValidDIB
   ' Display file
       Image1.Picture = LoadPicture(FileName)
   ' Restore mouse pointer
       Form1.MousePointer = 0          ' DEFAULT cursor shape
       Exit Sub

   ' Handle any error while loading picture
   NotValidDIB:
       msg$ = "Can't Display this File" + Chr$(13) + "Click on OK →
       and Select another DIB File"
       P = MsgBox(msg$, OKbutton + QMarkicon, "Unknown →
       Error")
```

```
        Image1.Picture = LoadPicture( )
        Resume Next

    End Sub
```

The second half of the subroutine simply handles any error that may occur during the loading of the file. Our program checks only the bfFileType field; every other error will be handled with On Error statement.

Notice that we are reading only a small section of the file, the one that contains the two headers we are interested in. The rest of the image (palette and pixel values) are of no interest to us, since the image is loaded with the LoadPicture method. Moreover, the Stretch Property of the Image Box is set to True, so that the entire image can be displayed, even if it is distorted.

With some extra effort, you can create a scrollable Picture Box.

It would be nice if we could attach two scroll bars on a *Picture Box* to allow the user to move its contents around and bring any part of the image in view. (If you set its AutoSize Property to False, a Picture Box will display only a portion of a large image. However, you can add scroll bars and allow the user to move the "window" into the image. To see how, look at "Scrolling Windows" in Chapter 8.)

## Looking at a Palette's Colors

Remember that every time a DIB file is loaded on a Picture Box, its palette is loaded as well. This means that the Picture Box contains all the colors. But we don't know which colors, so how can we use them? To make optimal use of the palette, we must be able to read the palette from a file.

Reading a palette from a DIB file isn't complicated. We read the two headers (BITMAPFILEHEADER and BITMAPINFOHEADER), find out how many colors the file contains and then read that many color descriptions from the file and store them to an array of integers. Once you know the structure of a DIB file, you can handle it just like any other file. Here's a code segment that extracts a palette from the DIB file and stores it in an array:

```
Function GetPalette ( ) As Integer
Dim R As String * 1
Dim G As String * 1
Dim B As String * 1
Dim A As String * 1
Dim NColors As Integer
```

```
Open #FNUM As
Get #FNUM, , h1
Get #FNUM, , h2
NColors = 2 ^ h2.biBitCount
For i = 1 To NColors
        Get #1, , B: Get #1, , G: Get #1, , R: Get #1, , A
        Palette(i, 0) = Asc(R)
        Palette(i, 1) = Asc(G)
        Palette(i, 2) = Asc(B)
Next

End Function
```

The Palette( ) array must be defined as a global variable:

```
Global Palette(256, 2) As Integer
```

(assuming that the array indexing starts at 0—use the Option Base 0 statement to be sure). The variables h1 and h2 must be defined as in the previous example. Notice the order in which the color bytes are read. Having read a file's palette, we can use it for our own purposes. As Microsoft suggests, we can load a DIB file with colors similar to the ones we need on a Picture Box. Then, every color we define with the RGB function is mapped to the closest solid color of the palette. This approach works in most situations, but we don't know whether we are using the exact color or an approximation. However, being able to build and read the palette of a DIB file allows us more flexibility and control over the images we generate. Soon you will see this technique in action.

## Reading an Image's Pixels

The last step in reading a BMP file is reading the samples of the image. Why read the pixels, when Visual Basic can load a BMP or a DIB file on a Picture Control with a simple command? Granted, you will never have to read an image's pixels and then draw each one. But what if you wish to process the pixels of an image, or you simply want to convert a 256-color image to a monochrome one? Our presentation of DIB files had more than just theoretical interest. In the VBImage application, where we present some image processing techniques, you will see some real examples of reading BMP files. For now, we will only look at code segments for reading the pixels of a DIB file.

To process an image, you must use an RGB description of its colors, even if the image contains a palette.

When processing images, we must store them in memory so we can access them faster. In processing an image, we may use the same pixel's value many times, and therefore it makes sense to trade off some memory for speed. The pixel values are stored in memory in their original RGB representation (that is, as three integer values, one for each of the three primary colors). Therefore, if the image's dimensions are XRes and YRes respectively, the array must be defined as

```
Dim pic(XRes, Yres, 2)
```

To make the coding simpler, we assume that indexing of the arrays begins at zero. The element pic(XRes, Yres, 0) holds the red component of the pixel's color, the element pic(XRes, YRes, 1) holds the green component, and pic(XRes, YRes, 2) holds the blue component. The pic( ) array holds the image's pixels, regardless of whether they were read from a 256-color DIB file or a True Color one. The color value of a pixel in a 256-color image is only an index to its palette, and has nothing to do with the actual color of the pixel.

### Reading True Color Images

The simplest images to read are the True Color images, because they contain the values needed for our pic( ) array. Every three bytes form a pixel's definition and they are assigned to the elements of the pic( ) array. Here's how to read True Color images in an array:

```
Dim pix As String * 1
Dim RGBentry As String * 3

Open "C:\IMAGES\CITY.BMP" For Binary As #1
Get #1, , h1
Get #1, , h2

XRes = h2.biWidth
YRes = h2.biHeight

For i = 0 To YRes - 1
   For j = 0 To XRes - 1
      Get #1, , RGBentry
      pic(j, i, 0) = Asc(Mid$(RGBentry, 3, 1))
      pic(j, i, 1) = Asc(Mid$(RGBentry, 2, 1))
      pic(j, i, 2) = Asc(Mid$(RGBentry, 1, 1))
   Next
```

```
        If Int((XRes * 3) / 4) <> (XRes * 3) / 4 Then
            For kk = 1 To 4 - ((XRes * 3) Mod 4)
                Get #1, , pix
            Next
        End If
    Next
    Close #1
```

Notice the If structure that reads (and ignores) the extra bytes that pad each line of pixels. Notice also that the three color components are stored as Blue, Green, Red, and not in the order they appear in the RGB( ) Function.

### Reading 256-Color Images

To read an image with a palette, we must first extract the palette definitions and then assign them to the pic( ) array's elements. Each time we read a pixel's value, which is a number between 0 and 255, we use it as an index to the palette. We assign the three palette colors at the row specified by the pixel's value to the three elements of the corresponding element of the array pic( ). For example, if the third palette color is (128,64,255), and the pixel at location (i, j) has the value 2, the element pic(i, j, 0) gets the value 128, the element pic(i, j, 1) gets the value 64 and the element pic(i, j, 2) gets the value 255.

Monochrome images pack 8 pixels into a single byte.

```
Dim PALentry As String*4
Open ImageName$ For Binary As #1
Get #1, , h1
Get #1, , h2

XRes = h2.biWidth
YRes = h2.biHeight
PaletteSize = 2 ^ h2.biBitCount

' This loop reads the palette's color definitions
For i = 0 To PaletteSize - 1
    Get #1, , PALentry
    RGBPalette(i, 0) = Asc(Mid$(PALentry, 1, 1))
    RGBPalette(i, 1) = Asc(Mid$(PALentry, 2, 1))
    RGBPalette(i, 2) = Asc(Mid$(PALentry, 3, 1))
Next
' and the next two loops read the image's pixels and assign
' the proper values to the pic( ) array
For i = 0 To YRes - 1
```

```
        For j = 0 To XRes - 1
            Get #1, , pix
            pic(j, i, 0) = RGBPalette(Asc(pix), 0)
            pic(j, i, 1) = RGBPalette(Asc(pix), 1)
            pic(j, i, 2) = RGBPalette(Asc(pix), 2)
        Next
        If Int(XRes / 4) <> XRes / 4 Then
            For kk = 1 To 4 - XRes Mod 4
                Get #1, , pix
            Next
        End If
    Next
```

Again, the padding pixel values at the end of each line are ignored.

To save memory, the array pic( ) may be defined as an array of characters. However, if the pixel values are going to be used in mathematical operations, they will have to be converted to arithmetic values before they can be used. In our examples, we prefer to trade off some memory for speed and store the pixel values as integers. This way, the coding is simplified and the programs run much faster. A (256 X 256) image is made up of 64k pixels. If we stored the pixel values in characters and we wanted to process it, we would have to call the Asc( ) Function at least 64k times just for a small picture.

By the way, we could have used the Byte data type with VB4, but this wouldn't make our code faster. Moreover, if the result of some arithmetic operation exceeds the Byte range (0 to 255) an overflow error will occur. In the section "VBImage's Internal Mechanisms," we are going to use Bytes to store the palette entries.

With a similar loop you can read black-and-white DIB files too, only here you must extract 8 pixel values from each byte. It's best to store the values in a character array because allocating an integer for a single bit is a real waste of memory.

In the section "An Image Processing Application" you will see a subroutine that reads both 256-color and True Color images. Since there is little image processing that can be done with 16-color or black-and-white images, we address only 256-color and True Color images through the rest of this chapter.

## Handling Color Palettes

If your computer supports 16 colors only, the VB QBColor( ) command is all you need. If it supports True Color, the VB RGB( ) command is all you need again. You can display any color you wish on your monitor. As always, between the two extremes there is a happy medium, which in this case is 256 colors. In the case of color palettes, the "happy medium" isn't as simple to cope with. We have seen the problems that 256-color systems introduce. However, until True Color displays become commonplace, we must be able to deal with palettes.

We will end our discussion of palettes with an application that reads and displays an image's palette.

### Example: Looking at a Palette's Colors

CD-ROM

Figure 6-8 shows a simple application that displays the entries of a 256-color palette. The application is called PALET256, and you can find it in the directory 6\APPS\PALET256 on the CD, along with a few palettes you can look at. The palette is loaded onto the Picture Box using the method we mentioned previously, through the Clipboard. Then we draw 256 small squares on the Picture Box and display in each one a different color from the palette. The Text Boxes to the left display the values of the three primary components of the selected color. To select a color, the user must click on it with the mouse. Use the New File Command Button to select another file and look at its palette.

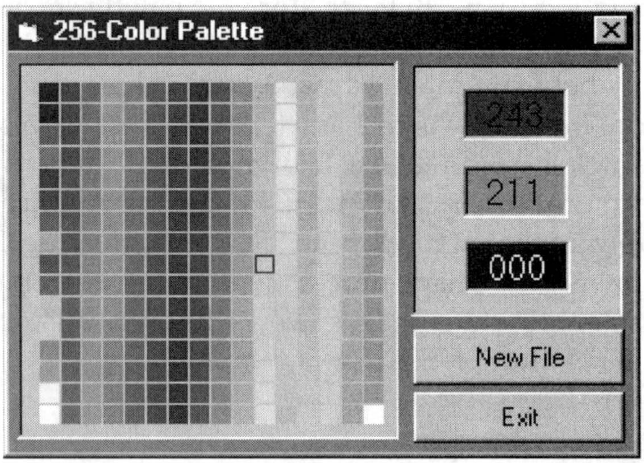


Figure 6-8: The PALET256 application.

Here is the code that loads the palette, reads its colors and draws the 256 small Picture Boxes in which the palette's entries are displayed. It is executed every time we load a new palette with the New File Button:

```
Sub Command1_Click ( )
Dim PALETTEFILE As String

Dim h1 As BITMAPFILEHEADER
Dim h2 As BITMAPINFOHEADER
Dim chcolor As String * 1
CurrentColor = -1
CF_PALETTE = 9

    On Error GoTo endApp
    CMDialog1.Action = 1
    PALETTEFILE = CMDialog1.Filename
    If PALETTEFILE = "" Then Exit Sub
    PaletteBox.Cls
    SampleColorBox.Cls
    Clipboard.Clear
    PaletteBox.Picture = LoadPicture(PALETTEFILE)
    Clipboard.SetData PaletteBox.Image, CF_PALETTE
    PaletteBox.Picture = Clipboard.GetData(CF_PALETTE)
    SampleColorBox.Picture = Clipboard.GetData(CF_PALETTE)

    Open PALETTEFILE For Binary As #1
    Get #1, , h1
    Get #1, , h2

    If h2.biBitCount <> 8 Then
        MsgBox "This image doesn't contain a palette!"
        Close #1
        Exit Sub
    End If

    For i = 1 To 256
        For j = 1 To 3
            Get #1, , chcolor
            Palette(i, j) = Asc(chcolor)
        Next
        Get #1, , chcolor
    Next
    Close #1
```

```
        On Error Resume Next
        BWidth = 8
        BHeight = 8
        BSpace = 2

        PaletteBox.ScaleMode = 3
        PaletteBox.Width = 16 * (BWidth + BSpace) + 2 * BWidth
        PaletteBox.Height = 16 * (BHeight + BSpace) + 2 * →
        BHeight

        For ih = 0 To 15
        For iv = 0 To 15
            CIndex = ih * 16 + iv + 1
            bxstart = BWidth + ih * (BWidth + BSpace)
            bystart = BHeight + iv * (BHeight + BSpace)
            Palet256.PaletteBox.Line (bxstart, bystart)- →
            Step(BWidth, BHeight), RGB(Palette(CIndex, 1), →
            Palette(CIndex, 2), Palette(CIndex, 3)), BF
        Next
        Next
        Exit Sub

    endApp:
        MsgBox "Error in opening file!"
        Exit Sub
    End Sub
```

The BITMAPINFOHEADER and BITMAPFILEHEADER structures are defined as global variables, as in the previous example. This subroutine draws 256 small squares with dimensions BWidth and BHeight (spaced apart by BSpace) and assigns one of the palette's colors to each. The ScaleMode Property of the Picture Box must be set to pixel (3).

Each time the user clicks on a square, the application determines the color of the selected square, draws a frame around it and displays the three primary values on the three Text Boxes. At the same time, it assigns the current color to the BackColor property of the Frame. These actions take place in the Picture Box's MouseUp Event, because we need the coordinates of the mouse at the click. Here is the code:

The main job of this subroutine is to simply identify which box was clicked on.

```
Sub PaletteBox_MouseUp(Button As Integer, Shift As Integer, X
As Single, Y As Single)

' If X, Y lie outside the color box, beep and return
    If X < BWidth Or X > 16 * (BWidth + BSpace) + BWidth Or
Y < BHeight Or Y > 16 * (BHeight + BSpace) + BHeight Then
        Beep
        Exit Sub
    End If
' First, remove border from previously selected color - if any
    If CurrentColor > -1 Then
        cy = (CurrentColor - 1) Mod 16
        cx = Int((CurrentColor - 1) / 16)
        bxstart = BWidth + cx * (BWidth + BSpace)
        bystart = BHeight + cy * (BHeight + BSpace)
        PaletteBox.Line (bxstart, bystart)-Step(BWidth, →
        BHeight), RGB(Palette(CurrentColor, 1), Palette
        (CurrentColor, 2), Palette(CurrentColor, 3)), B
    End If
' Now draw border around new square
    cx = Int((X - BWidth) / (BSpace + BWidth))
    cy = Int((Y - BHeight) / (BSpace + BHeight))
    CurrentColor = cx * 16 + cy + 1
    bxstart = BWidth + cx * (BWidth + BSpace)
    bystart = BHeight + cy * (BHeight + BSpace)
    PaletteBox.Line (bxstart, bystart)-Step(BWidth, BHeight), →
    RGB(255 - Palette(CurrentColor, 1), 255 - Palette
    (CurrentColor, 2), 255 - Palette(CurrentColor, 3)), B
' and display values of primaries
    Label1.Caption = Format$(Palette(CurrentColor, 1), "000")
    Label2.Caption = Format$(Palette(CurrentColor, 2), "000")
    Label3.Caption = Format$(Palette(CurrentColor, 3), "000")
    SampleColorBox.BackColor = RGB(Palette(CurrentColor, 1),
Palette(CurrentColor, 2), Palette(CurrentColor, 3))
End Sub
```

This program figures out which square was clicked and displays its three color components on the corresponding Text Boxes. The program is rather lengthy, but most lines deal with drawing the small boxes and not with direct palette manipulation.

CD-ROM

The PALET256 application will work on systems with 256 (or more) colors only. If you run this application on a 16-color system, most colors will be approximated with a technique called dithering. The dithered colors have a textured appearance, and they are Visual Basic's best approximation to the real colors. Try it out with the DIB palette files that come with Visual Basic, or the ones in the \PALETTES subdirectory of the CD that comes with this book.

PALET256 will *display* an image's colors, but changing their values is significantly more complicated.

The PALET256 application doesn't allow you to set the colors, but only to view them. Visual Basic provides no simple mechanism for manipulating the current palette's entries. The only way to set new colors is by using API calls, but this approach isn't very simple.

So far we have covered the basic topics necessary to explore a real image processing application. In VBImage, we will combine all the information of this chapter to create an impressive yet surprisingly easy-to-write application for handling color images. The same basic concepts will be used in a later chapter for creating fractal images.

## AN IMAGE PROCESSING APPLICATION

Our next example, VBImage, reads an image from a BMP file, processes it and then displays the processed image next to the original one, as shown in Figure 6-9. The same example will also vividly demonstrate how Visual Basic handles palettes, as well as the structure of BMP files. Apart from its educational value, however, this application is interesting and may inspire you to experiment.

An image is a two-dimensional arrangement of pixels. The pixels are arranged in lines, and each line contains the same number of pixels. Each pixel represents the color of the image in the tiny area it occupies on the screen. When we place a large number of pixels next to one another, we create the impression of a solid image. The human eye can't distinguish the successive pixels from a normal viewing distance—provided you have a high-resolution monitor that can display many colors.

Smooth as images often appear on a computer display, they are still made up of pixels.

You can think of an image as a two-dimensional array whose elements represent the image's colors on a grid. In a black-and-white image each pixel is represented by one bit. The most common types of images are those with 256 colors (1 byte per pixel). For the best possible image quality, we need 3 bytes per pixel (True Color images).

## What Is Image Processing?

Image processing is the science of extracting or manipulating information from pictorial data (images). This information is at least indirectly present in the original image, but is sometimes not obvious to the human eye. Originally, the role of image processing was to make useful information stand out, and at the same time remove unwanted effects, such as noise and over- and underexposure. For example, enhancing the edges of an image makes the objects stand out. However, the basic image processing techniques now are widely used in fields such as desktop publishing (DTP), graphic arts, and so on. The emphasis in these applications is on the artistic transformation of the image, rather than the extraction of hidden information. Today, there are hardly any systems without some image processing software, even a very basic image processing application.

### Example: Processing Images

Our image processing application is called VBImage, and its main Form is shown in Figure 6-9. You can find it in the subdirectory 6\APPS\VBIMAGE of the CD. It's not a professional tool, such as Picture Publisher or PhotoStyler, but it can be easily implemented in Visual Basic and will give you the opportunity to explore image processing techniques on your own. The techniques we will cover in this chapter are simple and basic ones, but so are most image processing techniques.

Figure 6-9: The main Form of the VBImage application.The image on the left has been processed with the Emboss algorithm, and the result is shown on the right.

To use VBImage you should, ideally, have a True Color display. Any image will be displayed accurately on a True Color display, and you need not worry about palette problems. You can still use it with a 256-color display, although you should expect some artifacts. If you have a 256-color display, we suggest that you process grayscale images. Grayscale images, like the ones printed in this book, contain at most 256 shades of gray, and they can be displayed properly on a 256-color display. Color images may contain many more tones than your display can support, and Visual Basic may not approximate them all correctly. However, since many image processing algorithms produce colors similar to the ones in the original image, VBImage will work well with 256-color systems.

To best exploit the VBImage application on a 256-color system, use grayscale images.

To experiment with the VBImage application, you will need a few sample pictures. If you don't own a scanner, use the sample images on this book's CD, or connect to a bulletin board service such as CompuServe and download images.

The images of our examples, along with a few dozen more, can be found in the subdirectory with the application (6\APPS\VBIMAGE) as well as in the IMAGES subdirectory of the CD. We have included grayscale, 256-color and True Color images.

## The Application

Let's start with a short description of the VBImage application. The main Form contains two Picture Boxes called *Source* and *Target*. The Source Picture Box is used for loading the original image (a DIB or BMP file), and the Target Picture Box is used for displaying the processed image. The dimensions and the palette of the Source Picture Box are determined by the image loaded onto it. The Target Picture Box must have the same dimensions as the Source. The Source Picture Box's AutoSize property must be set to True, so that it will be resized to the image loaded onto it. The VBImage application on the CD accepts images with dimensions up to (400 X 400).

The two Picture Boxes are placed next to each other. The program will try to place the two Picture Boxes side to side. If it can't, it will place the Target Picture Box under the Source Picture Box. With large images, the target image may end completely outside the screen (its contents, however, will be saved with the File/Save command).

The operation of the application is straightforward. It loads a user-selected image onto the Source Picture Box, then copies the original image's palette to the Target Picture Box through the Clipboard and finally processes the source image with the algorithm the user selects from the Process menu. It then displays the result on the Target Picture Box. Every time the user selects a new algorithm from the Process menu, the original image is processed and the result overwrites the contents of the Target image. In other words, the effects of various processes do not accumulate. Finally, the Save command of the File menu stores the contents of the Target Picture Box to a BMP file.

### VBImage's Internal Mechanisms

Before we present the actual code of VBImage we must say a few words about the structure of the application. The application uses an integer array for storing the source image. This array is called pic( ) and is redimensioned every time a new image is loaded, according to the dimensions of the image. All images are stored in the pic( ) array in their True Color representation (RGB), as we discussed earlier in "Reading an Image's Pixels." This way, the result of the processing is not dependent on the original image's palette. In other words, the processing of an image will most likely introduce colors that are not present in the palette. (This will not happen with monochrome images, since you can't have more than 256 gray tones.)

Even 256-color images must be processed as True Color images.

RGB values go from 0 to 255 (1 byte), while integers take up 2 bytes, resulting in a waste of half the memory allocated to the array. Unfortunately, VB3 does not provide an integer data type that is 1 byte long. We could have used an array of characters, but then we would have to convert the characters to integers before using them. This approach would have introduced significant delays, so we have decided to trade off some memory for execution speed. Visual Basic 4.0 provides this single-byte data type, which is called *Byte*. Unfortunately, Byte variables are not processed any faster than Integers, so there will be no speed benefit in using a Byte array to store the image's pixels. Moreover, the Byte data type can only store integer values in the range 0 to 255. Our image processing algorithms will eventually produce negative values, or values larger than 255. Because these cases must be handled specially, we decided to store the pixel values to an array of integers.

However, the Byte data variable is ideal for storing palette values because we can read the color components of the palette's entries directly from the DIB file. Here is the Visual Basic 4.0 implementation of the routine that reads a 256-color palette from a DIB file:

```
For i = 0 To PaletteSize - 1
    Get #1, , PALentry
    RGBpalette(i, 0) = Asc(Mid$(PALentry, 3, 1))
    RGBpalette(i, 1) = Asc(Mid$(PALentry, 2, 1))
    RGBpalette(i, 2) = Asc(Mid$(PALentry, 1, 1))
Next
For i = 0 To YRes - 1
    For j = 0 To XRes - 1
        Get #1, , pix
        pic(j, i, 0) = RGBpalette(pix, 0)
        pic(j, i, 1) = RGBpalette(pix, 1)
        pic(j, i, 2) = RGBpalette(pix, 2)
    Next
    If Int(XRes / 4) <> XRes / 4 Then
        For kk = 1 To 4 - XRes Mod 4
            Get #1, , pix
        Next
    End If
Next
```

The menu structure of the application is the following:

| | |
|---|---|
| File | |
| Open | Loads a Source image from a disk file. |
| Save | Saves the Target image in a file. |
| Exit | Terminates the application. |
| Process | |
| Smooth | Smoothes (blurs) the image. |
| Sharpen | Sharpens the image. |
| Emboss | Gives the image a raised 3D look. |
| Engrave | Gives the image an inset (carved) 3D look. |
| Mosaic | Gives the image a block-like effect. |
| Diffuse | Scrambles pixels to give image a painterly look. |
| Neon | Another sharpening effect with neon highlights. |
| Invert | Inverts the colors of the pixels. |
| Color to Mono | Converts color images to monochrome ones. |

Table 6-7: The menu structure of VBImage.

The Open command displays the Open File Dialog Box, which allows the user to select a BMP or DIB file and then load it in the Source Picture Box with a double-click. Once the image is loaded, the user can apply a special effect to the Source image by making a selection from the Process menu. The result is another image, which appears on the Target Picture Box. The Save command stores the contents of the Target Picture Box in a BMP file, whose name is specified by the user with the help of the Save File Dialog Box.

When loading True Color images with certain high-color graphics adapters, you may experience long delays. This problem originates in the adapter's driver and can't be fixed from within Visual Basic. The problem does not come up when VBImage is used with 256 colors or True Color systems—or most high-color systems. For more information, read the section "High Color Systems" later in this chapter.

### Implementing VBImage

The File/Open command reads the image into the Source Picture Box with the LoadPicture command and positions the two pictures on the Form. It also extracts the dimensions of the image from the BITMAPINFOHEADER and stores them in the global variables XRes and YRes, which are available to all other modules. Finally, it reads the pixels of the image and stores them to the pic( ) array. You could also read the image's pixels directly from the Source Picture Box with the Point method, but it is faster to read them from the file.

When reading an image's pixel values, your program must make a distinction between 256-color and True Color images. No matter what the type of the image, its pixels are stored in the pic( ) array. The pic( ) array is a three-dimensional array, defined as pic(m, n, 2), where m, n are the dimensions of the image. The element pic(i, j, 0) holds the red color component of the pixel at position (i, j), pic(i, j, 1) holds the green component at the same position, and pic(i, j, 2) holds the blue component at the same location.

VBImage stores all the pixels of an image in an array in memory so it can access them as fast as possible.

When reading True Color images, we can read each byte directly into its corresponding array element. But 256-color images must be read differently. First, we must read the palette and store it in the array RGBPalette( ), which is two-dimensional, and is defined as RGBPalette(256, 2). The element RGBPalette(i, 0) holds the red color component of the *i*th color in the palette, the element RGBPalette(i, 1) holds the green component, and RGBPalette(i, 2) holds the blue component.

Then we start reading the image's pixel values. Each pixel value we read is used as an index to the RGBPalette( ) array, so that we can assign the pixel's primary colors to the corresponding element of the pic( ) array with the lines

```
Get #1, ,pix
    pic(j, i, 0) = RGBPalette(Asc(pix), 0)
    pic(j, i, 1) = RGBPalette(Asc(pix), 1)
    pic(j, i, 2) = RGBPalette(Asc(pix), 2)
```

where pix is a 1-byte variable (String * 1).

The complete code for the Open command is given next:

If the image contains a palette, we must read it before reading the pixels.

```
Private Sub File1_DblClick()
CF_PALETTE = 9

Dim pix As Byte
Dim PalEntry As String * 4
Dim RGBEntry As String * 3

ImageFind.Hide
' Load image & palette
Clipboard.Clear
ImageForm.Source.picture = LoadPicture()
ImageForm.Target.picture = LoadPicture()
ImageForm.Source.picture = LoadPicture(imagename$)
Clipboard.SetData ImageForm.Source.IMAGE, CF_PALETTE
ImageForm.Target.picture = Clipboard.GetData(CF_PALETTE)

ImageForm.Target.Width = ImageForm.Source.Width
ImageForm.Target.Height = ImageForm.Source.Height

' Arrange images on Form
Call ArrangePics
ImageForm.Source.picture = LoadPicture(imagename$)

ImageForm.Source.ScaleMode = 3
ImageForm.Target.ScaleMode = 3
ImageForm.Target.Cls

' Open Image and read palette and pixels
Open imagename$ For Binary As #1
Get #1, , h1
Get #1, , h2
```

```
XRes = h2.biWidth
YRes = h2.biHeight

If XRes > 400 Or YRes > 400 Then
    MsgBox "Image too large", 32, "VBImage Error"
    XRes = 0
    YRes = 0
    Close #1
    Exit Sub
End If

If h2.biBitCount <> 8 And h2.biBitCount <> 24 Then
    MsgBox "Not a Color Image", 32, "VBImage Error"
    Close #1
    Exit Sub
End If


PaletteSize = 2 ^ h2.biBitCount

PlsWaitForm.Show
DoEvents
If h2.biBitCount = 8 Then
    For i = 0 To PaletteSize - 1
        Get #1, , PalEntry
        RGBpalette(i, 0) = Asc(Mid$(PalEntry, 3, 1))
        RGBpalette(i, 1) = Asc(Mid$(PalEntry, 2, 1))
        RGBpalette(i, 2) = Asc(Mid$(PalEntry, 1, 1))
    Next
    For i = 0 To YRes - 1
    For j = 0 To XRes - 1
        Get #1, , pix
        pic(j, i, 0) = RGBpalette(pix, 0)
        pic(j, i, 1) = RGBpalette(pix, 1)
        pic(j, i, 2) = RGBpalette(pix, 2)
    Next
    If Int(XRes / 4) <> XRes / 4 Then
        For kk = 1 To 4 - XRes Mod 4
            Get #1, , pix
        Next
    End If
```

```
        Next
    Else
        For i = 0 To YRes - 1
            For j = 0 To XRes - 1
                Get #1, , RGBEntry
                pic(j, i, 0) = Asc(Mid$(RGBEntry, 1, 1))
                pic(j, i, 1) = Asc(Mid$(RGBEntry, 2, 1))
                pic(j, i, 2) = Asc(Mid$(RGBEntry, 3, 1))
            Next
            If Int((XRes * 3) / 4) <> (XRes * 3) / 4 Then
                For kk = 1 To 4 - ((XRes * 3) Mod 4)
                    Get #1, , pix
                Next
            End If
        Next
    End If
    PlsWaitForm.Hide

    Close #1

    End Sub
```

This Subroutine is a combination of the two pixel subroutines we presented earlier, in "Reading an Image's Pixels." First it loads the image on the Source Picture Box. Then, it copies its palette to the Target Picture Box through the Clipboard, so that the image's colors will be available to the application in the Target Picture Box too. Next, it reads the image's pixels and stores them in the array pic( ), as RGB values. The routines for reading 256-color and True Color images were covered earlier in "Reading an Image's Pixels." Once the image has been loaded onto the Picture Box and its pixels read into the pic( ) array, we are ready to process the image. As soon as the user selects an option from the Process menu, the processing starts. The results are displayed on the Target Box as soon as they become available.

In the following sections we'll explore each of the program's effects.

## Smoothing

The Smoothing algorithm blurs the image, as you can see in Figure 6-10. The smoothed image contains less abrupt changes than the original, and here is where its value lies. Abrupt changes may be part of the image, but sometimes these changes are noise—pixels that differ significantly from their neighboring ones. The noise pixels are usually caused by spurious effects, and removing them is an important step in image processing.

Figure 6-10: An original image and its smoothed version.

How do we blur an image? The idea is to smooth out the edges of the image. As you can see, the blur effect is most obvious on the edges. Flat areas of the image can't be blurred much, anyway. If you look at an image with edges, you will see that the edge pixels are those that differ significantly from their adjacent ones. Therefore, the average, or the median, of the surrounding pixels would be a good choice to replace them. Indeed, this is how smoothing is achieved. Every pixel of the original image is replaced by the average of its adjacent pixels. We can use a 3 X 3 neighborhood, where a pixel is replaced by the average of its 8 neighboring pixels and itself, or an even larger neighborhood. The more pixels we use, the smoother the image will be. Of course, if you use a very large neighborhood, the result will be not only the removal of noise, but the loss of information too. Too much smoothing may essentially obliterate some details.

Smoothing an image is very similar to low-pass filtering a sound.

The smoothing operation is equivalent to low-pass filtering in audio. Just as you can cut off a hissy tape's high frequencies in your stereo with the help of an equalizer, you can cut off the high frequencies of an image. If you are wondering what high frequencies of an image are, think of them as areas with abrupt changes in intensity. These are the areas that are mainly affected by a low-pass filter. Where in sound we talk about frequency, in image processing we talk about *spatial frequency*, which is defined as the number of changes per length unit in intensity across the picture. Reducing the number of these changes reduces the spatial frequency of the image as well. Many times a smoothing filter yields interesting results in images that contain no noise at all. This filter is also known as *low-pass* filter, because it cuts off high frequencies and allows the lower ones to show.

The square over which the pixels are averaged is selected so that the pixel being processed is located at its center (in other words, its dimensions must be odd numbers). In Figure 6-11 you can see a very small section of an image. The numbers represent pixel values of a grayscale image. The pixel values of a (3 X 3) area are averaged, and the result is placed in the square's center pixel in the processed image.

To smooth an image, we must visit each pixel of the original image and calculate the average of this pixel and its neighboring ones. The new value should replace the value of the current pixel, but in another array. If we replaced the same pixel, we would have lost the original pixel, which is needed for the following calculations.

| | | | | | | | | | | |
|---|---|---|---|---|---|---|---|---|---|---|
| 4 | 17 | 11 | 13 | 3 | >> | ? | ? | ? | ? | ? |
| *13* | *12* | *7* | 17 | *9* | >> | ? | 10 | 12 | 10 | ? |
| *9* | *6* | *10* | 12 | 10 | >> | ? | 9 | *11* | 12 | ? |
| *3* | *9* | *11* | 15 | 12 | >> | ? | ? | ? | ? | ? |

(13+12+7+9+6+10+3+9+11) / 9 = 9

Figure 6-11: The Smoothing algorithm in action. The question marks indicate that the corresponding pixels can't be computed (we don't know the values of all the pixels required for the calculation).

Of course we must calculate three averages: one for the red, one for the green and one for the blue component. The three values are later combined with the RGB( ) Function to yield the color of the processed pixel.

Assuming that the image's pixels have been read into the pic( ) array and that the size of the block is BlockSize, here is the smoothing subroutine:

```
Sub SmoothProc_Click()
' Smooth (LPF)
BlockSize = 3
IMPARAM3.Show 1          ' Prompt use to enter Blocksize
If BlockSize < 0 Then Exit Sub
Target.Cls
' for each pixel in the image
For i = Int(BlockSize / 2) To YRes - Int(BlockSize / 2)
    For j = Int(BlockSize / 2) To XRes - Int(BlockSize / 2)
      ' for each element in filter
```

```
            For k1 = -Int(BlockSize / 2) To Int(BlockSize / 2)
                For k2 = -Int(BlockSize / 2) To Int(BlockSize / 2)
                    ' and for each color component
                    For k = 0 To 2
                        vpic(k) = vpic(k) + pic(j + k1, i + k2, k)
                    Next
                Next
            Next
            For k = 0 To 2
                vpic(k) = vpic(k) / BlockSize ^ 2
            Next
            Target.PSet (j, YRes - i - 1), RGB(vpic(0), vpic(1), vpic(2))
        Next
        Target.Refresh
    Next

    End Sub
```

To avoid shifting the image, we must be sure that we are using a pixel at the center of each block.

BlockSize is the size of the block in which the average is calculated. The user enters the block size in a dialog box that appears when the Smooth filter is selected (in the Form IPARAM3). The two outer loops (i, j) scan each pixel of the image. At each pixel, the two inner loops (k1, k2) scan all the pixels of the block centered on the current pixel (i, j). The last loop (k) repeats the operation three times, once for each color component. vpic(0) is the red component of the new pixel, vpic(1) is the green component and vpic(2) is the blue component. These values are used by the RGB command to set the color of the processed pixel.

Notice that the current pixel is located at the center of the block with size BlockSize. This means that we cannot smooth the pixels along the edges of the image, because some of the values needed in the calculations are not defined. In other words, we can't process the top left pixel, because there are no pixels on top or to the left of that value. We will see what can be done about such boundary pixels toward the end of the chapter.

## Sharpening

The opposite operation of smoothing is sharpening. As you can see in the right image of Figure 6-12, sharpening brings out the edges of the objects in the image; it enhances by highlighting areas that are not obvious enough in the original image. What the eye perceives as edges are the sharp changes in color between adjacent pixels. The changes in the original image may not be sharp enough for the eye to isolate them, or we may just wish to enhance them. A sharpening operation can improve the edges and reveal new ones.

Figure 6-12: An original image and its sharpened version.

Obviously, the image-sharpening algorithm is the opposite of the Smoothing algorithm. Whereas addition was used in the Smoothing algorithm, subtraction is used in the Sharpening algorithm. Consider for a moment that you have two slides of the same image: the positive and the negative. If you align them perfectly, you won't see anything. Where one slide is white, the other is black. If you shift them slightly, some light will come through. The areas where the light goes through are the areas where the adjacent pixels are different, that is, the edges of the image. If you shift the two slides horizontally, you see the vertical edges; if you shift them vertically, you see the horizontal edges. If you shift them in both directions, you see both the vertical and horizontal edges, as shown in Figure 6-13. This operation enhances the edges, indeed, but it totally blackens the smooth areas.

Figure 6-13: Isolating the image's edges by calculating the absolute value of the differences between adjacent pixels.

Pixel values change drastically at the edges of an image.

The operation just described corresponds to the subtraction of adjacent pixels. Figure 6-14 shows an example of this sharpening algorithm. The image section you see has a constant gray level, except for a diagonal line 2 pixels wide. This line represents two edges: from a light gray tone to a darker one, and from the dark gray tone back to the light one. (One object, but two edges!) In the processed image section you see that all areas with the constant gray tone turn black. There are no edges in this area and therefore nothing to be sharpened. Nonblack areas indicate transitions between different pixel values. The differences are calculated in the horizontal direction.

| | | | | | | | | | | | | |
|---|---|---|---|---|---|---|---|---|---|---|---|---|
| 2 | 2 | 2 | 18 | 18 | 2 | >>> | 0 | 0 | 16 | 0 | 16 | 0 |
| 2 | *2* | *18* | 18 | 2 | 2 | >>> | 0 | *16* | 0 | 16 | 0 | 0 |
| 2 | *18* | *18* | 2 | 2 | 2 | >>> | 16 | 0 | 16 | 0 | 0 | 0 |
| 18 | 18 | 2 | 2 | 2 | 2 | >>> | 0 | 16 | 0 | 0 | 0 | 0 |
| 18 | 2 | 2 | 2 | 2 | 2 | >>> | 16 | 0 | 0 | 0 | 0 | 0 |

Figure 6-14: Detecting an image's edges by subtracting adjacent pixels. All differences are considered positive (absolute values), because an image's pixels can't have negative values.

This technique extracts edges, but it completely flattens out the smooth areas of the image. This isn't what we really want from a Sharpen operation, so we must modify it by adding the result of the subtraction to the original pixels. The result is what you saw in

Figure 6-12. The original image is still there, but the edges are now more pronounced. This operation can be expressed mathematically as

```
picture(i, j) = picture(i, j) + 0.5 * (picture(i, j) - picture(i - 1, j - 1) )
```

This formula says that each pixel of the new image is the original pixel plus a percentage of the difference between this pixel and another, adjacent one. We chose a value of 0.5 (50%) for the percentage, but it can be adjusted.

Let's examine what this algorithm does. In flat areas of the image, the difference between adjacent pixels is zero, and the value for the new pixel is the same as the original value. If there's an edge, though, the difference becomes significant and introduces a disturbance when added to the original value of the pixel.

In the following Subroutine we are using the adjacent pixel on the previous line and previous column. If you want, you can use the adjacent one in the previous line, or previous column only. You can even use distances larger than 1 pixel, but the effect will be more noticeable than we want. This effect is meant to be subtle, to improve the quality of an image without distorting it, as most of the other effects do.

"Sharpening," or "edge enhancement," emphasizes detail; it's the same as turning up the treble control on a stereo receiver.

As the smoothing effect can be controlled by the size of the block over which the average is calculated (variable BlockSize), the sharpening effect can be controlled by the percentage of the difference (edge) we add to the original pixel. If we call this parameter SharpenPercent, here is the implementation of the Sharpen algorithm in VB:

```
Sub SharpenProc_Click()
' Sharpen
Target.Cls
SharpenPercent = 0.25
IMPARAM2.Show 1
If SharpenPercent < 0 Then Exit Sub
' Get degree of sharpness
SharpenX = 1
SharpenY = 1

' for each pixel in the image
For i = SharpenY To YRes - SharpenY
    For j = SharpenX To XRes - SharpenX
        ' for each color component
        For k = 0 To 2
            vpic(k) = pic(j, i, k) + SharpenPercent *    →
```

```
            (pic(j, i, k) - pic(j - SharpenX, i - SharpenY, k)) →
            'Abs(pic(j, i, k) - pic(j - BRelX, i - BRelY, k))
            If vpic(k) < 0 Then vpic(k) = 0
            If vpic(k) > 255 Then vpic(k) = 255
        Next
        Target.PSet (j, YRes - i - 1), RGB(vpic(0), vpic(1), vpic(2))
    Next
Target.Refresh
Next

End Sub
```

The variables SharpenX and SharpenY are used in the Subroutine so that you can modify the algorithm by taking into consideration just the vertical or just the horizontal distances between adjacent pixels (or even distances larger than 1 pixel).

To achieve the result of figure 6-13, change the line that calculates vpic( ) to:

```
vpic(k) = abs(pic(j, i, k) - pic(j - SharpenX, i - SharpenY, k) )
```

### Emboss & Engrave

This time we will use the edge detection method we presented earlier. If we take the differences between pixels and add a constant value to them (say 128), the smooth areas of the image will be colored with a mid-gray tone, while transitions from light to dark pixels will produce lighter lines and transitions from dark to light pixels will produce darker lines. The result is an image with a gray background, with white and black lines along the objects' edges. These lines creatie the illusion of depth by adding white highlights and black shadows.

This method often yields more interesting results than simple edge extraction, as you can see in Figure 6-15. These images have a three-dimensional look. If you examine them carefully, you will see that the white and black lines appear to have a pattern. Don't they form objects that seem to be illuminated from one side? This effect is called *emboss.*

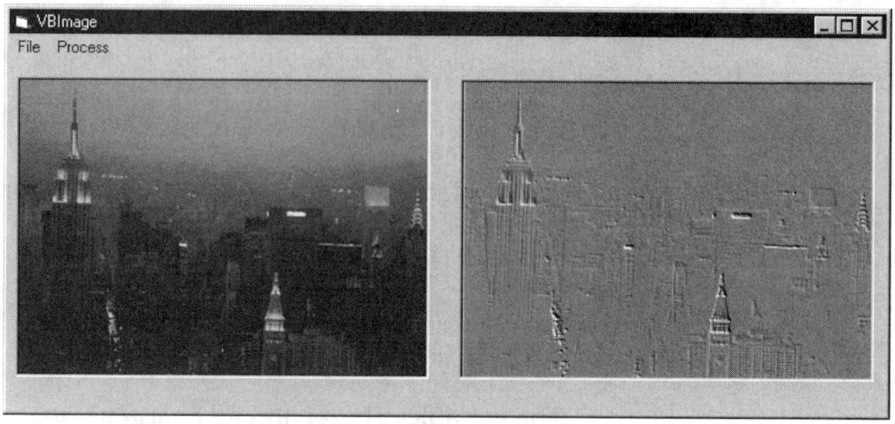

Figure 6-15: An original image and its embossed version.

Emboss and Engrave add a three-dimensional look.

The emboss effect can be controlled by the number of pixels the two images are shifted—in other words, the distance of the pixels being subtracted. Moreover, you can calculate the differences vertically, horizontally or in both directions to get the desired result. Photographers use a darkroom technique called *bas-relief* to achieve similar results.

Here is the Subroutine that embosses an image:

```
Sub EmbossProc_Click()
' Emboss
Dim vpic(2) As Integer
BRelX = 1
BRelY = 1
IMPARAM1.Show 1
If BRelX < 0 Then Exit Sub
Target.Cls
For i = BRelY To YRes - BRelY
    For j = BRelX To XRes - BRelX
        For k = 0 To 2
            vpic(k) = pic(j, i, k) - pic(j - BRelX, i - BRelY, k) + 128
            If vpic(k) < 0 Then vpic(k) = 0
            If vpic(k) > 255 Then vpic(k) = 255
        Next
        Target.PSet (j, YRes - i - 1), RGB(vpic(0), vpic(1), vpic(2))
    Next
    Target.Refresh
Next

End Sub
```

BRelX and BRelY are the horizontal and vertical distances of the pixels being subtracted, and the user enters them with the help of a Dialog Box (IPARAM1 in the listing).

In Figure 6-15 you see a similar effect, only now the light is coming from a different direction. Instead of the upper right corner, it seems to come from the lower left. This is done by simply inverting the order of the subtraction. It's the opposite effect of embossing, and it's called engraving. Instead of subtracting the previous pixel on the same row (or column) from the current pixel, we subtract the next pixel.

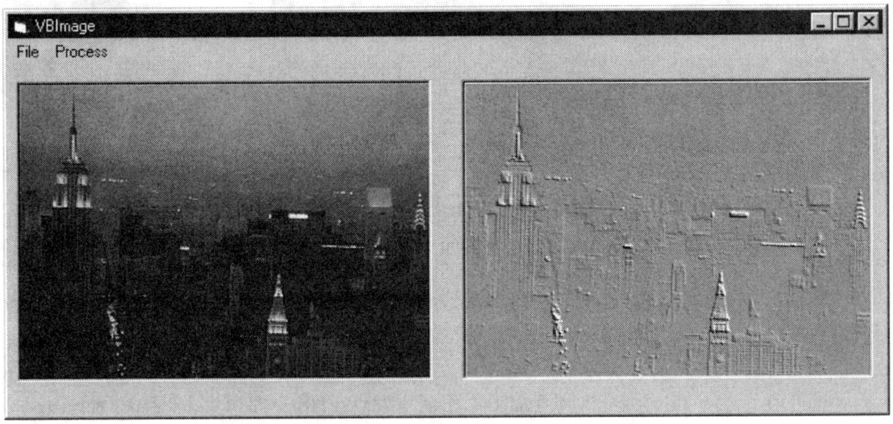


Figure 6-16: An original image and its engraved version.

The algorithm differs in a single line only:

```
vpic(k) = pic(j, i, k) - pic(j + BRelX, i + BRelY, k) + 128
```

The Emboss and Engrave algorithms not only detect edges, but they distinguish between positive and negative edges. Positive edges are colored with lighter gray tones (128 plus a small value) and negative edges are colored with darker gray tones (128 minus a small value).

## Neon

The Neon effect is yet another sharpening algorithm, as you can see in Figure 6-17. This algorithm is also based on the differences between adjacent pixels, but it is a bit more complicated. Instead of calculating the absolute value, or adding a constant, we calculate a quantity that is called *gradient*. The gradient is the square root of the sum of the squares of the differences. That's easier coded than said.

Let's say that the current pixel's value is 78 and the adjacent one in the same row has the value 82, while the value of the adjacent pixel on the same column is 73. The differences are (82 - 78) = 4 and (78 -73) = 5. Then we calculate their squares: 4 * 4 = 16 and 5 * 5 = 25. The sum of the squares is 25 + 16 = 41. Finally we take the square root of 41, which is approximately 6. This number is a measure of the distance of the current pixel from two adjacent pixels. The same calculations must be performed for each of the three components.

Figure 6-17: An original image and its Neon-enhanced version.

First, we calculate the squares of the differences. The squares are bound to be positive, regardless of the actual values of the differences. Then we add the two squares—in other words we get the "total" difference. This is a large number, and we take its square root to reduce its size. The gradient is a measure of the difference in both directions simultaneously, which exaggerates the differences. It is subtle for small differences and more dramatic for larger differences. It also does not depend on the orientation of the edges.

The gradient is a measure of the "abruptness of change" between pixels.

A gradient indeed brings out the edges of an image, much more than the previous algorithms, but in a more impressive manner too. Here is the Subroutine that implements the Neon effect:

```
Sub NeonProc_Click()
' Neon effect (image gradient)
Target.Cls
For i = 0 To YRes - 1
   For j = 0 To XRes - 1
      For k = 0 To 2
         g1 = (pic(j, i, k) - pic(j + 1, i, k)) ^ 2
         g2 = (pic(j, i, k) - pic(j, i + 1, k)) ^ 2
         vpic(k) = 2 * (g1 + g2) ^ 0.5
         If vpic(k) > 255 Then vpic(k) = 255
```

```
            Next
            Target.PSet (j, YRes - i - 1), RGB(vpic(0), vpic(1), vpic(2))
        Next
        Target.Refresh
    Next

    End Sub
```

This algorithm is also known as the *Gradient* method. g1 and g2 are the squares of the differences between adjacent pixels in the horizontal and vertical direction. Then we take the square root of their sum and multiply it by 2, to enhance the edges even more. There are no parameters here to control the effect, but if you want you can calculate the horizontal or vertical differences only. The Gradient method extracts the edges of an image, just like the absolute value of the differences, but we prefer it over the absolute values, because the gradient is proportional to the square of the difference and yields more dramatic results for larger differences between pixel values.

## Mosaic

Another very simple and interesting algorithm is called Mosaic. Here, we replace a block of pixels with their average, to give the image a block-like look. This process is depicted with a small image section in Figure 6-18.

| | | | | | | | | | | |
|---|---|---|---|---|---|---|---|---|---|---|
| 4 | 17 | 11 | 13 | 3 | >> | 10 | 10 | 10 | ? | ? |
| 13 | 12 | 7 | 17 | 9 | >> | 10 | 10 | 10 | ? | ? |
| 9 | 6 | 10 | 12 | 10 | >> | 10 | 10 | 10 | ? | ? |
| 3 | 9 | 11 | 15 | 12 | >> | ? | ? | ? | ? | ? |

(4+17+11+13+12+7+9+6+10)/9 = 10

Figure 6-18: The operation of the Mosaic algorithm for a blocksize 3. The question marks correspond to pixels that cannot be determined without knowledge of values not shown in the picture.

Here is the Subroutine that implements the Mosaic algorithm:

```
Sub MosaicProc_Click()
' Mosaic
Dim mosaic As Integer, vpic As Integer
BRelX = 5
BRelY = 5
```

```
IMPARAM1.Show 1
If BRelX < 0 Then Exit Sub
Target.Cls
BlockSize = BRelX * BRelY
For i = 0 To YRes - BRelY Step BRelY
    For j = 0 To XRes - BRelX Step BRelX
        mr = 0: mg = 0: mb = 0
        For k1 = 0 To BRelY
            For k2 = 0 To BRelX
                mr = mr + pic(j + k1, i + k2, 0)   ' red tones
                mg = mg + pic(j + k1, i + k2, 1)   ' green tones
                mb = mb + pic(j + k1, i + k2, 2)   ' blue tones
            Next
        Next
        mr = mr / BlockSize   ' red average
        mg = mg / BlockSize   ' green average
        mb = mb / BlockSize   ' blue average
        For k1 = 0 To BRelY
            For k2 = 0 To BRelX
                Target.PSet (j + k2, YRes - i - 1 + k1), RGB(mr, →
                mg, mb)
            Next
        Next
        mosaic = 0
    Next
    Target.Refresh
Next

End Sub
```

The Mosaic algorithm "blurs" an image, but by degrading it into square shapes.

Notice the similarities between the Mosaic algorithm and the Blur algorithm. They both calculate the average of a block of pixels, but the Mosaic algorithm assigns the result to all the pixels of the block, while the Blur algorithm replaces only the pixel at the center of the block.

Figure 6-19: Example of the Mosaic algorithm (BlockSize = 4).

The Mosaic algorithm is frequently used in TV to censor a certain part of an image. The larger the size of the block, the more the image will be blurred. For an interesting animation, you can create a sequence of pictures starting with a block that is the size of the image, then two blocks half the size of the original image. Keep halving the image until the size of the block becomes 1 pixel. If you play all those images back in rapid succession, you can bring a picture on the screen, which starts with little information and at each successive frame reveals more and more detail.

## Diffuse

This effect differs from the previous ones in that it uses random numbers, and gives the image a "painterly" effect. Figure 6-20 demonstrates what the Diffuse effect does to an image. The splatter of the paint depends on a user-input parameter, which helps you control the depth of the effect.

Figure 6-20: The Diffuse effect gives an image a clearly painterly effect.

This technique is based on the displacement of the image's pixels. Each pixel is swapped with another one in its neighborhood. Which pixels are swapped at each step is determined with two random numbers. Of course, the pixels being swapped must be very close, or else the image will be scrambled to a point that it will become unrecognizable. The distance of the two pixels being swapped is determined with two random numbers, one for the horizontal and one for the vertical direction. The maximum values of the random numbers are BRelX and BRelY respectively. Here is the implementation of the Diffuse algorithm:

```
Sub DiffuseProc_Click()
' Diffuse
Dim rdx As Integer, rdy As Integer

BRelX = 5
BRelY = 5
  IMPARAM1.Show 1
If BRelX < 0 Then Exit Sub
Target.Cls
' get max. random displacement in x and y
For i = BRelY To YRes - BRelY
    For j = BRelX To XRes - BRelX
        rdx = Rnd * BRelX   ' random x displacement
        rdy = Rnd * BRelY   ' random y displacement
        dr = pic(j + rdx, i + rdy, 0)
        dg = pic(j + rdx, i + rdy, 1)
        db = pic(j + rdx, i + rdy, 2)
        Target.PSet (j, YRes - i - 1), RGB(dr, dg, db)
    Next
```

```
    Target.Refresh
Next

End Sub
```

## Invert

This very simple algorithm inverts the pixels' colors, as shown in Figure 6-21.

Figure 6-21: The negative of an image.

As mentioned before, to invert color (what in photography is called the negative) we must subtract each color component from 255 (which produces the complementary color). Here is the implementation of the Invert algorithm in Visual Basic:

```
Sub InvertProc_Click ( )
Target.Cls
' Invert Colors
    For i = 0 To YRes - 1
    For j = 0 To XRes - 1
        For k = 0 To 2
            vpic(k) = 255 - pic(j, i, k)
        Next
        Target.PSet (j, YRes - i - 1), RGB(vpic(0), vpic(1), →
        vpic(2))
    Next
    Target.Refresh
    Next

End Sub
```

## Color to Monochrome

One of the most useful algorithms in image processing is the one that converts color to monochrome. This algorithm is especially useful for users with 256-color displays. A color value is defined with the help of its three primary components (R, G ,B). The equivalent gray value is another triplet, in which all three components are identical. The following relationship maps the color value (R, G, B) to a gray value (GrVal, GrVal, GrVal):

```
GrVal = 0.30*R + 0.59*G + 0.11*B
```

The coefficients of the primary colors are based on the physiology of the human eye and the way it perceives color. This choice of coefficients yields good results, but you can try different combinations, especially for images that were not exposed or scanned properly. Just remember that the sum of the coefficients must be exactly 1. This is the color-to-grayscale technique:

```
Sub Color2MonoProc_Click ( )
Target.Cls
' Color 2 Mono
For i = 0 To YRes - 1
    For j = 0 To XRes - 1
            GrVal = .3 * pic(j, i, 0) + .59 * pic(j, i, 1) + .11 →
            * pic(j, i, 2)
            Target.PSet (j, YRes - i), RGB(GrVal, GrVal, GrVal)
        Target.Refrsh
    Next
Next

End Sub
```

Grays are produced when you mix equal amounts of red, green and blue.

GrVal is the gray value of the new pixel, and it is the same for all three components of the RGB( ) Function.

## Handling Edge Pixels

You may have noticed that the target image is slightly smaller than the source image in our VBImage application. This happens because the pixels along the edges of the source image cannot always be processed. When we calculate the filtered value of the first pixel in a row of the original image, there is no previous pixel on the same row. The same is true for all the pixels along the edges of the image. The code we presented earlier simply ignores those pixels, because they cannot be calculated. To make the two images equal in size, you could repeat the values of the original pixels. Alternatively, you could assume that the nonexistent pixels have the same value as the pixel being processed, or a constant value (0 or 128, for example), so that the algorithm can process them. You can also add a constant color frame around the processed image to make up for the "lost" pixels.

Of course, you can devise additional techniques for handling edge pixels, depending on the algorithm. To smooth the top left pixel, for example, you can use its neighbors to the right and below—in other words, violate the rule about centering the pixel being processed in the filter for the few edge pixels.

## High-Color Systems

VBImage saves the processed image to a file by calling VB's SavePicture Method. After prompting the user for a file name by displaying the File Open Dialog Box, VBImage saves the contents of the Target Picture Box to a file with the line:

```
SavePicture Target.Image, CMDialog1.Filename
```

On 256-color or True Color systems, the images saved by VBImage can be used by any other Windows application, including VBImage. You can load a processed image in VBImage and process it again. If you are using VBImage with a High-Color system, however, you will not be able to open an image previously processed by VBImage. The reason is a High-Color system is one that uses 15 or 16 bits to represent each color value. A 16-bit High-Color system allocates 5 bits to each primary color. Therefore, you have 32 instead of 256 levels for each primary color and a total of 32 * 32 * 32 = 32k colors. When images are saved with the SavePicture Method, Visual Basic doesn't translate them to 24 bits. It saves them as 15- (or 16-) bit images. VBImage doesn't understand High-Color images. Many image processing applications can't read these images either. Under Windows 95, High-Color images are saved in True Color format, so this isn't going to be a problem.

To overcome this problem, you could write a subroutine to save the contents of the Target Picture Box to a file. This subroutine must read each pixel with the Point function, extract the three bytes of the RGB representation and then store them to the BMP file. The code will be very similar to the code we presented for reading True Color images. Instead of reading the pixels, it will send them to the file. The two headers of the file will be the same as in the original file. We do not use this technique here because it is much slower than the SavePicture Method, which works fine with both 256-color and True Color images (16.7 million colors vs. High-Color's 32k colors).

## Further Improvements

The algorithms in the previous paragraphs were chosen to demonstrate how much simpler image processing really is. It's interesting to experiment with other algorithms too. For example, to obtain the negative of an image, subtract its pixel values from 255 (see "Invert" earlier in this chapter). You can obtain even more impressive results if you don't invert *all* the pixels, but only those with a color component smaller or larger than a threshold. Or invert a single channel. The effect of inverting selected pixels in an image is called *Solarizing*.

Pixels can be processed with logical operators like XOR, too.

You could try to combine the pixels of two images with the logical operators AND, OR or XOR. Load two different monochrome images on the two Picture Boxes, and replace each pixel of the second one with an expression such as

```
vpic(k) = pic1(i, j, k) AND pic2(i, j, k)
```

for all three values of the variable k (0, 1 and 2).

You can also try various combinations of the three channels of a single image, such as

```
vpic(k) = pic(i, j, 1) AND pic(i, j, 2)
```

which ANDs the pixels of the blue and green channels. The results depend a lot on the original image, but experimentation may lead you to unpredictable and unexpected results.

Try the Min and Max operations to replace each pixel of the new image with the smallest or largest corresponding pixel value of the two images. Actually, you can use these operators with one image only. Modify the Mosaic algorithm so that instead of the average, it calculates the minimum or maximum values of the pixels in the corresponding square.

## Masking

Another interesting way of combining images is to let the second image show through certain colors of the first one. Select a color, or a range of colors, and when you locate a pixel with this specific color in the first image, display the corresponding pixel of the second image. The color which lets the underlying image show through is called *mask*. If the pixels of the images are stored in the arrays pic1( ) and pic2( ), the basic algorithm can be implemented with a line such as

```
If pic1(i, j, k) = MaskColor then v = pic1(i, j, k) Else v = pic2(i, j, k)
```

for all three values of k. To make a mask with a range of colors, use one or more components:

```
If Palette( pic1(i, j, 2 ) > 32 then
    v = pic1(i, j, 2)
Else
    v = pic2(i, j, 2)
End If
```

The new image's pixel at location (i, j) is

```
RGB(pic1(i, j, 0), pic1(i, j, 1), v)
```

The previous line uses all colors with a blue component larger than 32 as the mask. The result is an image shown through the blue components of another image. By selecting carefully the two images and the color of the mask, you can create very interesting results.

You can also implement some even more basic operations, such as trimming an image, exchanging rows and columns and so on. These are trivial operations, but extremely useful in handling images. Remember, Visual Basic is not the most appropriate tool for writing this type of application. It is rather slow when it comes to number processing, at least when you compare it with compiled languages like C++ or Pascal. However, you can experiment with image processing techniques and discover a new world of exciting capabilities, even with a not-so-fast tool.

## MOVING ON

In Chapter 7, we'll find out how to make VB applications look good. We'll go through the rules of effective, ergonomic user-interface design. Currently Visual Basic is used largely by independent solution providers and in-house corporate developers. In most cases, this means a single person designs and programs any given application. Even when there is a team, it's rare that one of its members is a graphics designer, someone to polish the surface and ensure that the Forms are clean, balanced and professional-looking. Fortunately, there are principles of design for Windows applications that anyone can learn. This set of visual guidelines is our next topic.

# Chapter 7

# Designing Windows

If you're like many programmers, you ask your spouse or a friend if this tie goes with that suit. You leave it up to someone else to arrange furniture, to select colors, patterns and designs. In other words, you don't have much experience thinking visually.

Fear not. In this chapter you'll find the rules of good Windows design. There *are* guidelines. Talented artists at various software companies have spent lots of time developing these rules. You can see the results by comparing the homely flat black-on-white look of older Windows applications with the sleek, sculpted look that has become the standard in Windows 95.

## MAKE APPLICATIONS *LOOK* RELIABLE

How your application looks contributes to the user's impression of how it works.

We'll explore a variety of techniques you can use to make your VB programs look better. At first we'll work with tools that VB provides—the Picture Property of Forms and of a few Controls; Sheridan's Custom Control set (in particular, the SSPanel for framing and the SSCommand for engraved text effects); and the famous gray-steel look. Then we'll go beyond what VB provides, demonstrating how to do pretty much anything visual that you want to do. You've seen commercial software with slick lighting effects, embossed and shadowed text and all the rest. We'll see how to accomplish those tricks, how to create flashing lights and other effects. But before anything else, we've got to deal with a fundamental question: Why bother?

A pretty Form is more than merely a desirable luxury. If your work looks coordinated, polished and professional on its surface, people will think it is equally solid on the inside. They will trust it. Study after study has demonstrated that a handsome man or a beautiful woman is far more likely to be believed than the alternative. That's why so many companies pay huge sums to improve their logo and millions to get movie stars to recommend their products.

You know the effect. Which stranger do you trust: the woman in sweatpants with greasy hair, heavy makeup, vacant dancing eyes, chewing gum and laughing loudly? Or the calm, intelligent woman in a well-cut beige silk dress, wearing a single strand of pearls around her clean, strong neck?

Beyond the value of first impressions, users unconsciously make good use of visual conventions, the rules of the road. For example, notice the difference between the Forms in Figures 7-1 and 7-2:

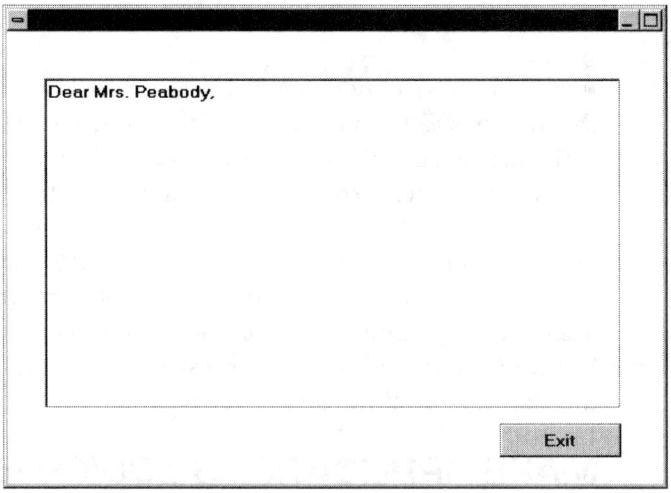


Figure 7-1: BEFORE. Avoid flat, dull Forms.

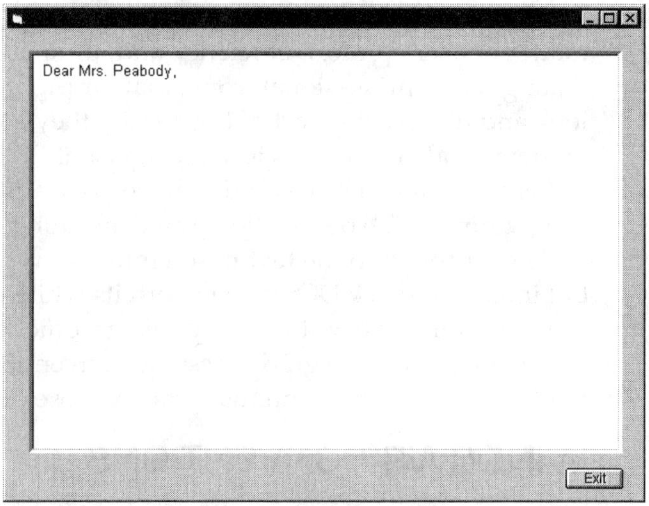


Figure 7-2: AFTER. Much improved by adding backcolor, a 3D frame, turning off boldface text, and shading the button caption.

In the best-designed applications, these visual conventions include placement of the Exit Button in the lower right, a gray (or at least not white) background, related Controls grouped into zones separated by frames and so on. If one of your Visual Basic Forms has its BackColor set to white, is unzoned, and locates the Exit Button on the left, your application will slow users down. It will confuse them because it's both homely and, in the wrong way, unique. They're just not used to these odd design elements.

They might not know why, but they will be uncomfortable using your program. Your project will resemble an early Windows 3 application or, worse, DOS, instead of the sleek surfaces of contemporary applications.

## Focus Groups Produce Visual Guidelines

Microsoft and others have tested thousands of people in focus groups and found that certain design elements result in the most efficient and most visually appealing "looks." One finding that might surprise you: you should use very little color in an icon.

If you've never studied, or even thought about, pictorial design, here's your chance. VB, and Windows, offer rich graphic possibilities. Computing is becoming increasingly, even relentlessly, visual. (This trend will not stop until computer programs are photo-realistic, until a telephone icon looks like a 3D hologram of a telephone. So prepare yourself.)

Design is not just a matter of making things look better—it's also a matter of user-comfort, efficiency and, ultimately, a quality that distinguishes professional from amateur programming. How things look and feel is a big part of how easily they are used. Ergonomics matters. And ergonomics is, in part, visual.

Programming now requires graphic design as well as interface design.

Visual design and decoration have not traditionally been part of a programmer's job description. But computing is graphical now and will never revert to the text-based interface typified by the beloved but infamous black DOS screen with its white words. These days you must communicate with the user via graphics as well as with text. Fortunately there are guidelines and conventions you can learn. Explaining these conventions is the purpose of this chapter.

## WINDOWS CONVENTIONS

There are several graphic conventions to which virtually all Windows programs now submit.

### The Metallic Look

First, Windows programs aspire to look "metallic." You can achieve this look by building highlights and shadows into such Controls as Command Buttons, and by using a "metallic gray" background. So when designing a program, a good first move is to make sure the Form's backcolor to light gray. If you leave the new VB4 Appearance Property of Forms and Controls set to the default (3D), light gray automatically will be your BackColor.

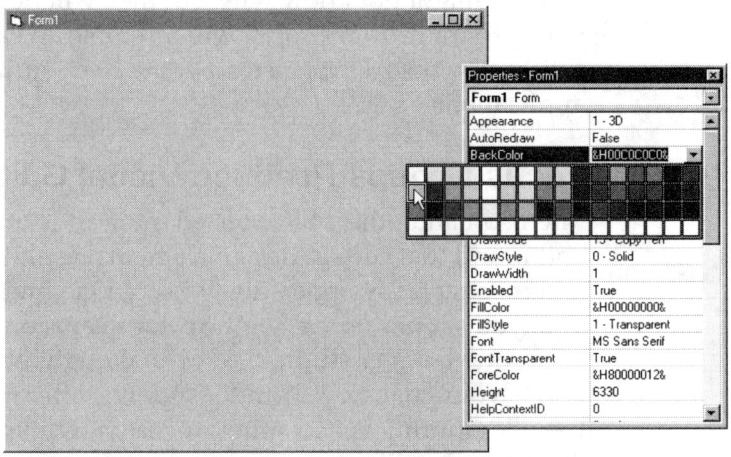


Figure 7-3: In VB4, leave the Appearance Property set to its default, 3D, for a backcolor of light gray (for a gray backcolor in VB3, change the Form's Backcolor Property from the default white).

Textures like marble or stucco are becoming an increasingly popular alternative to the common gunmetal gray background. This welcome trend is explored later in this chapter.

## FontBold Off

Second, FontBold should be False (normal text weight is used, not boldface) in the button captions, menu titles and other text in most applications, including those from Microsoft. Unfortunately, Visual Basic 3.0 defaults to FontBold True. You should therefore routinely change the FontBold Property of all your Forms and Controls (including Text Boxes) to False. However, in VB4 it fortunately defaults to bold off.

Normal text looks neater and cleaner than boldface text. Reserve boldface for highlighting something—to indicate, for instance, that a particular Command Button has the focus (will activate if you press Enter). Interestingly, Windows (and VB) do change normal caption text to boldface automatically when you click on a Command Button (thus giving it the focus). However, if you use bold in the captions in your Controls, this worthwhile visual clue is lost. Beyond that, more than an occasional touch of boldface is crude and unsightly.

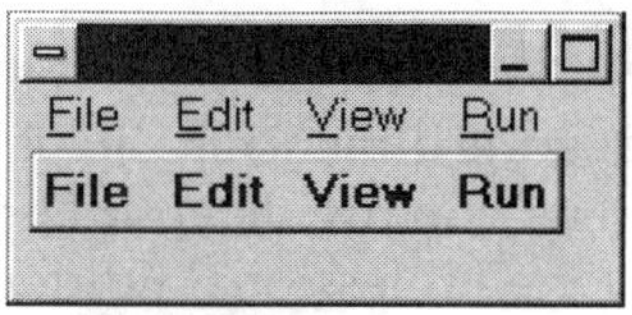


Figure 7-4: Boldface, shown on the panel here, is too strong and coarse for most text.

## Use a Sans-serif Typeface

Avoid Serif typefaces like Times Roman.

Luckily, VB's default Font Property is MS Sans Serif, which is also the Windows default typeface. Of the fonts that ship with Windows, Arial is the best choice for most text. Arial differs from MS Sans Serif primarily in that the midpoint of its uppercase letters is lower than the midpoint of MS Sans Serif's capitals. Arial also spaces its letters somewhat more widely apart. Both effects are usually undesirable (both make text less readable on a video monitor).

But Arial does have two major advantages over MS Sans Serif. MS Sans Serif turns bold if you increase its FontSize from 9.75 to 12; Arial does not. In addition, MS Sans Serif becomes so grainy at large type sizes that it is unusable. On the other hand, since MS Sans Serif is not a TrueType font, slower machines can draw it more quickly than Arial.

### Choosing a Type Size

For most purposes, the default FontSize (9.75) is right. FontSizes are not a continuum; you can only move in steps (9.75, 12, 15, 17.25, 22.5 and so on). VB automatically selects the nearest possible value, no matter what you type in as the FontSize. If you need a larger FontSize than 9.75, switch to Arial and you can go up to 12 and still retain the desirable qualities of normal, nonbold lettering. (Note that the preceding numbers apply if your Windows screen resolution is set to Large Fonts. If you're using Small Fonts, the size defaults at 8.25, and both MS Sans Serif and Arial remain nonbold up to 12.)

Arial
MS Sans

Figure 7-5: VB's default MS Sans Serif comes apart in the larger sizes. For headlines, use Arial.

## LAYERING & FRAMING

Another technique that adds dimensionality is layering, a kind of rice-paddy effect whereby you divide your Form into logical zones. Visual Basic, especially the Professional Edition, comes with many Controls. To the visual designer, no other feature of VB is more important than the Sheridan 3D Controls (THREED.VBX in VB3), the primary set of add-on Controls with which you add depth to Forms.

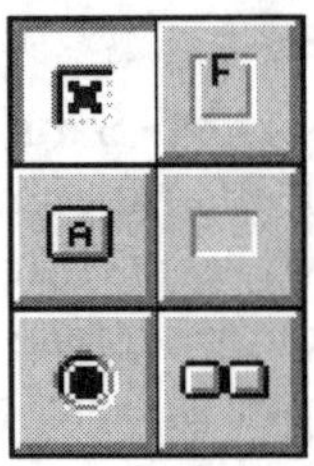

Figure 7-6: The Custom Controls available in the Sheridan 3D Controls.

The Sheridan Controls add a new, more flexible Option Button, Check Box and Command Button. It also adds a Group Push Button, a 3D Frame Control, and perhaps the best of all, the SSPanel Control.

To make their Toolbar more manageable, many VB programmers remove infrequently used custom Controls from the default Toolbar (this is done by adjusting the AUTO16ID.VBP or AUTO32ID.VBP files in VB4, and AUTOLOAD.MAK in VB3). But they leave Sheridan (or THREED.VBX, in VB3) in the default startup file—they would never think of designing a Form without it.

## Adding Depth

The first and most important graphics technique when designing visually pleasing windows is to add depth, to make them look three-dimensional. Flat, monochromatic screens, so typical of DOS programs, should never be used in Windows. No design error makes your application look more amateurish than a lifeless, boring, flat surface.

Not only does a sculpted, 3D window look more attractive, it also more efficiently conveys information to the user. One reason is that we are not Cyclopes—we have two eyes, so depth, the Z-axis, provides us with additional useful information.

Also, the user is supposed to interact with some Controls, and these Controls should have highlights and shadows to make them look physical, to make them look as if clicking on them will do something.

Dimensional Controls cue users that they can interact with the object.

A Control Button looks as if it could be depressed; it seems to protrude from the window (unlike Labels, which seem merely printed on the flat surface of the window). The Windows user understands that a captioned three-dimensional rectangle is a button—just like buttons on appliances in the real world. Likewise, the user understands that the flat printing on Labels is merely informational—it describes the purpose or contents of something. A Label is generally not something the user should physically interact with. Thus, Command Buttons (and other sculpted Controls like Option Buttons) are interactive. Almost everyone presses the button labeled POWER on their stereo—few try to press the label itself.

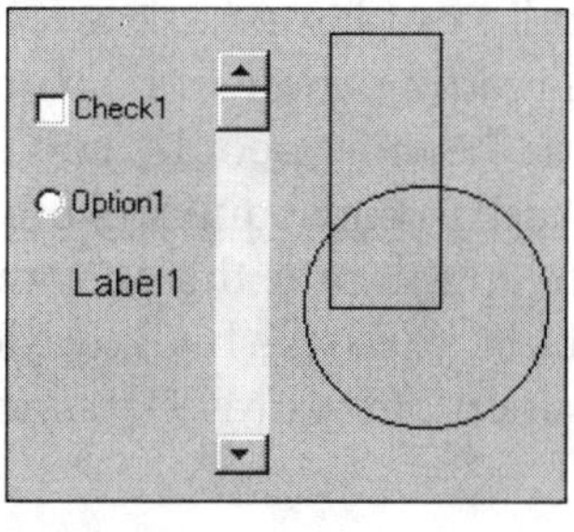


Figure 7-7: Interactive Controls (Check Boxes, Option Boxes and Scroll Bars) are in 3D; informational Controls (Shapes and Labels) are flat.

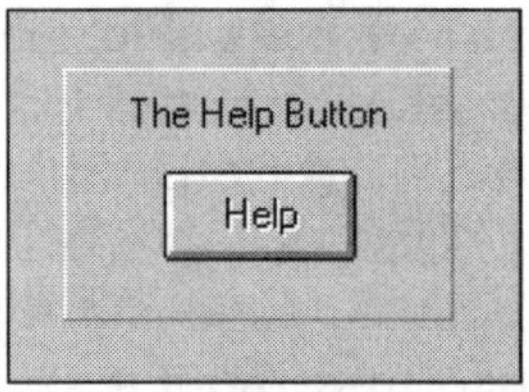


Figure 7-8: Important visual clues distinguish 3D Buttons from 2D Labels.

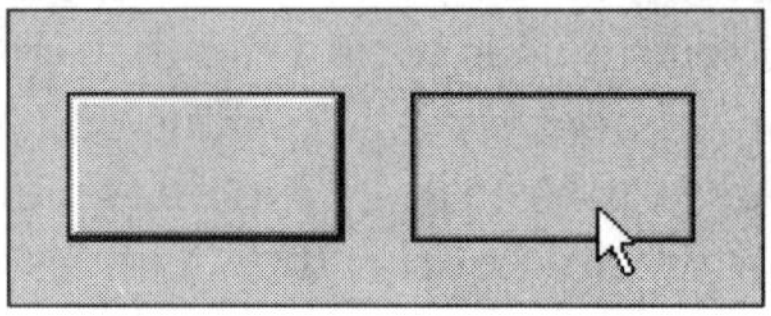

Figure 7-9: When you click on a Button, it seems to sink into the Form, to be physically depressed.

## Light From the Upper Left

In Figures 7-10 and 7-11, notice the way that Windows draws a Button before and after the Button is clicked. In Windows, the light is always assumed to be coming from the upper left corner of the screen. Therefore, a protruding object (Figure 7-10) picks up highlights along its top and left sides. Shadows fall along the right and bottom of the object. However, if the object is supposed to be sinking into the background, the process is reversed (Figure 7-11). To indicate a depressed Control, the black shadow line is drawn along the top and left of the object, the highlight line along the bottom and right. We'll have more to say about this technique below, in the section "Light & Shadow."

Interestingly, most light sources in the real world usually follow this same pattern. People reading outdoors maneuver their bodies until the sun shines from their left side (and, of course, above) onto the book. People generally put lamps to the left of their desk and above it, to the left of a reading chair, and so on. Look at your computer monitor. If you're like most people, you'll have your lamp above and to the left. And, in consequence, the top and left of your monitor will pick up the highlights, the bottom and right will be in shadow. As an experiment, turn this book upside down and see what happens to your perception of Figures 7-10 and 7-11.

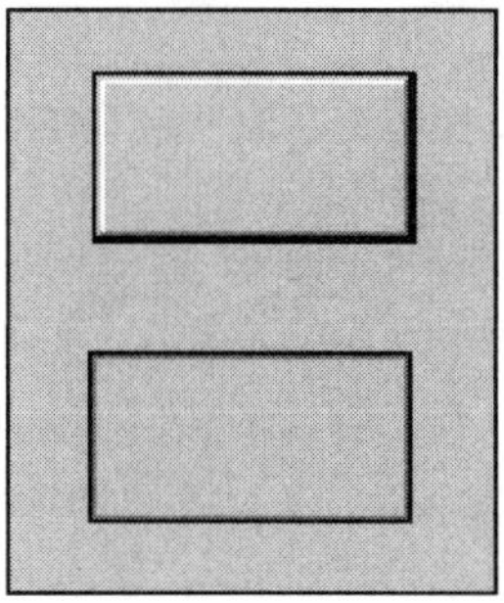

Figure 7-10: Light comes from the upper left in Windows.

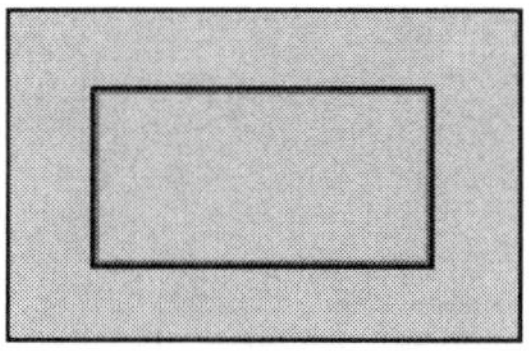

Figure 7-11: To indicate engraving or a depression, simply remove the normal highlight and shadow.

## CREATING ZONES

When you start designing a Form (after you've first set its Backcolor to light gray or filled it with a texture), you'll decide which Controls you're going to put on the Form. But don't put them on yet. First determine which Controls will be merely decorative, which informational and which interactive. Then add some zones to visually separate these Control categories.

### Informational vs. Interactive Zones

Let's design a Form that accepts text input from the user. There will be no Picture or Image Boxes—no decorative sections. The informational zone will include a word-count and the current time. The interactive zone will include a Text Box and a set of Command Buttons.

But, before adding these Controls, we'll add several 3DPanels, found in THREED16.OCX or THREED32.OCX, depending on your version of VB4 (in VB3, they're in THREED.VBX). These will add variety and depth to the Form, and they serve to group the various objects into their logical sections as well.

Figure 7-12: The indispensable 3DPanel Control.

First, as background for our Text Box, we'll put a large Panel on the Form:

Figure 7-13: A large, understated Panel improves the appearance of the Text Box.

When you place a Panel Control on a Form, the subtlest effect results if you set the following Properties of the Panel Control: Outline = False; BevelInner = 1-Inset; BevelOuter = 0-None; BevelWidth = 1; BorderWidth = 0. These are the settings used in Figure 7-13.

We didn't change the RoundedCorners Property because that property affects the corners of an outline, and we have set the Outline Property for this Panel to False (invisible).

The RoundedCorners Property is subtle, like most visual design.

An outline is a black line surrounding a Panel or other Control. If you are using a conspicuous, high-relief Panel (BevelWidth 2, 3 or greater), set the Outline to True. The RoundedCorners Property then defaults to True. A single pixel of black will be removed from each corner of the outline (see Figure 7-14), resulting in a smoother, more sophisticated look. (However, if you are putting the Panel or other Control onto a dark or black background, turn RoundedCorners to False—otherwise there will be strange and annoying light dots at each corner.)

## The All-Important 3D

The Sheridan 3D Controls include 3DCommand Button and 3DGroup PushButton Controls, which also feature rounded corners. (You'll notice that the buttons and toolbar icons in most Microsoft Applications, indeed in Windows itself, remove those four corner pixels to achieve this look. Unfortunately, VB's Command Buttons and other Controls do not. Curiously, the VB ToolBar has rounded corners, but the VB ToolBox does not. Eventually, all Windows applications and objects will likely use the superior rounded-corner look.)

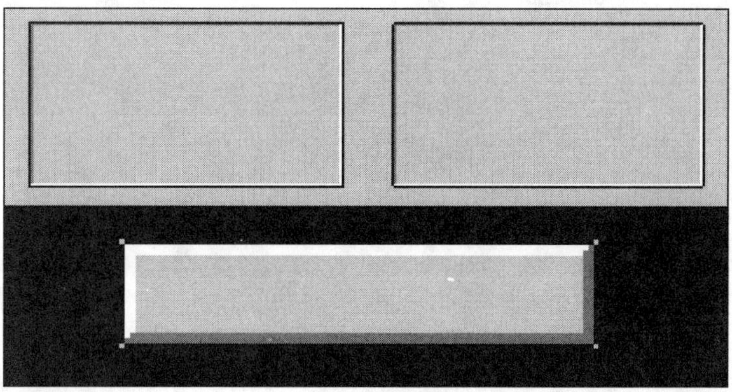

Figure 7-14: The RoundedCorners Property is set to True in the Panel on the right. But with a dark background, turn RoundedCorners off or you'll get the white dots shown around the Button at bottom.

After placing a Text Box on the Panel, we turn off the Text Box's BorderStyle Property (removing the black frame along the left and top). We draw the Text Box within the borders of the Panel, sizing the Box to be a pixel or two smaller than the four sides of the Panel. The result is shown in Figure 7-16. A Text Box with its own border and no underlying Panel is shown in Figure 7-15.

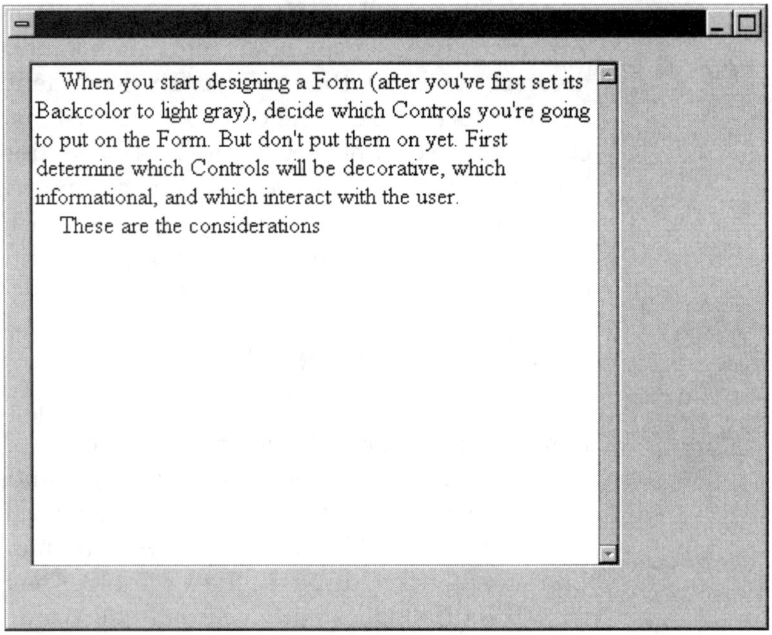

When you start designing a Form (after you've first set its Backcolor to light gray), decide which Controls you're going to put on the Form. But don't put them on yet. First determine which Controls will be decorative, which informational, and which interact with the user.
These are the considerations


Figure 7-15: BEFORE. An unmodified Text Box includes a black line along the left and top.

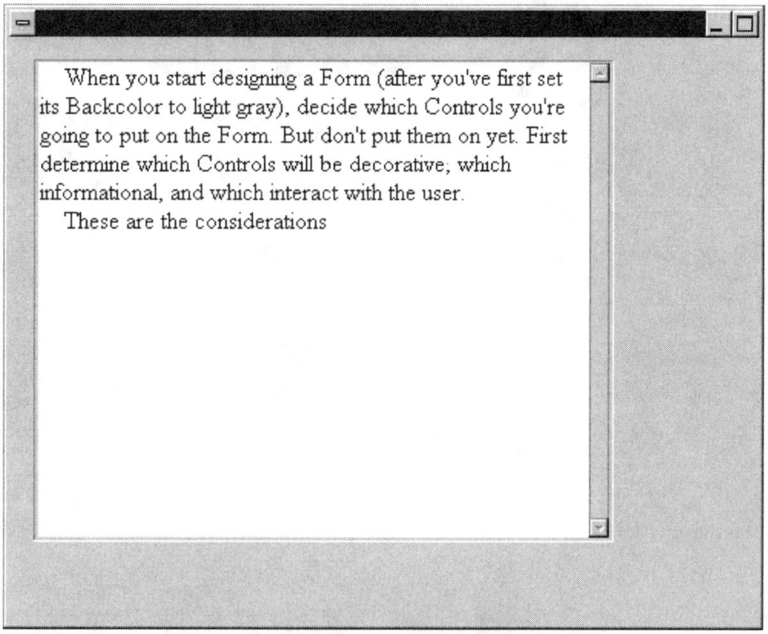
When you start designing a Form (after you've first set its Backcolor to light gray), decide which Controls you're going to put on the Form. But don't put them on yet. First determine which Controls will be decorative, which informational, and which interact with the user.
These are the considerations

Figure 7-16: AFTER. A borderless Text Box surrounded by a Panel looks more polished.

## Minor Improvements Are Cumulative

The primary difference between the Text Boxes in Figures 7-15 and 7-16 is the black line along the left and top in Figure 7-15. This line is replaced by a dark gray line in Figure 7-16. A small difference, but it makes for a more handsome Form. Collectively, these small graphic adjustments can make the difference between a sleek or a relatively crude-looking window. Consider that to achieve rounded corners, only four pixels are changed.

## THE STATUS BAR

As a convenience for users, you'll often find status bars along the bottom of spreadsheets, word processors and other applications. Let's add one that displays the approximate word count, and the day, date and time. First place a long, thin Panel Control at the bottom of the Form. Set the Panel's BevelInner Property to 2-Raised (otherwise leave the Panel Properties as before: Outline = False; BevelOuter = 0-None; BevelWidth = 1; BorderWidth = 0).

Figure 7-17: Shift-click to align multiple Controls.

Now add additional Panels to the long indented one—stretch a new Panel for each field you want to add within the status bar. For each interior Panel, set  the BevelInner Property to 1-Inset. Then hold down the Shift key and click on each interior Panel until they are ganged as a unit, as shown in Figure 7-17. Now use the Properties Window to set their collective Top and Height Properties so that they line up perfectly.

People are affected by even mild asymmetry.

The eye is extremely sensitive to small variations in symmetry and alignment. When you've finished a Form, shift-click to group Controls and adjust their various Width, Height, Top and Left Properties to make sure they line up like Rockettes, equivalent in shape and linear in position.

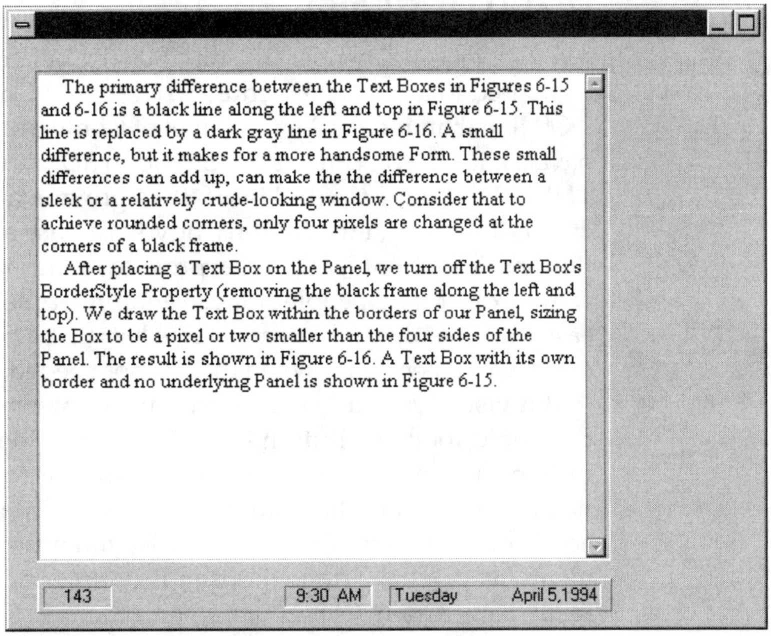

The primary difference between the Text Boxes in Figures 6-15 and 6-16 is a black line along the left and top in Figure 6-15. This line is replaced by a dark gray line in Figure 6-16. A small difference, but it makes for a more handsome Form. These small differences can add up, can make the the difference between a sleek or a relatively crude-looking window. Consider that to achieve rounded corners, only four pixels are changed at the corners of a black frame.
After placing a Text Box on the Panel, we turn off the Text Box's BorderStyle Property (removing the black frame along the left and top). We draw the Text Box within the borders of our Panel, sizing the Box to be a pixel or two smaller than the four sides of the Panel. The result is shown in Figure 6-16. A Text Box with its own border and no underlying Panel is shown in Figure 6-15.
143
9:30 AM
Tuesday
April 5,1994


Figure 7-18: Our Status Bar Fields in action.

To get the results displayed in Figure 7-18, put the day-date generator in the Form Load Event:

```
Sub Form_Load ()
    Show
    Panel3d4.Caption = Format(Now, "dddd        mmmm d,yyyy")
End Sub
```

To display the time, place that code within a Timer and set its interval to 1 minute:

```
Sub Timer1_Timer ()
    Panel3d5.Caption = Format(Now, "h:mm AM/PM")
End Sub
```

And to show the approximate word count, divide the total number of characters in the Text Box by six, the average characters-per-word in English:

```
Sub Text1_Change ()
    Panel3d3.Caption = Int(Len(text1.Text) / 6)
End Sub
```

## BUTTON PANEL

Avoid overusing menus. One nice Star Trek effect—particularly when compared to traditional menus (what could be more uninterestingly DOS-like than menus?)—is a panel of Command Buttons. Here you have a choice: you can use the Sheridan 3D Controls in VB4 (or THREED's Frame Control in VB3) to provide what looks like an etched line around the Buttons, or you can use a Panel underneath the Buttons. You should, of course, provide menus in applications of any complexity. Many people still use and prefer menus because you can easily browse through menus while learning a program. And menus don't use screen space when they're not needed.

Icons are superior to menus.

But visually, simple text-based, drop-down menus are anachronistic. Iconic Toolbars, Button Bars, detachable ToolBoxes and Command Buttons in series are now preferred. The reason is that a list of words, no matter how familiar, must be read each time the user wants to accomplish something. To save a file, you must first click on the File menu (as you have done thousands of times before), then you must read "New, Open, Close...Save," and then click on Save. However, if a Toolbar is visible, you merely click on an icon of a small disk immediately. The icon's position and appearance are both more memorable than the plain word *Save*, buried within a list of words.

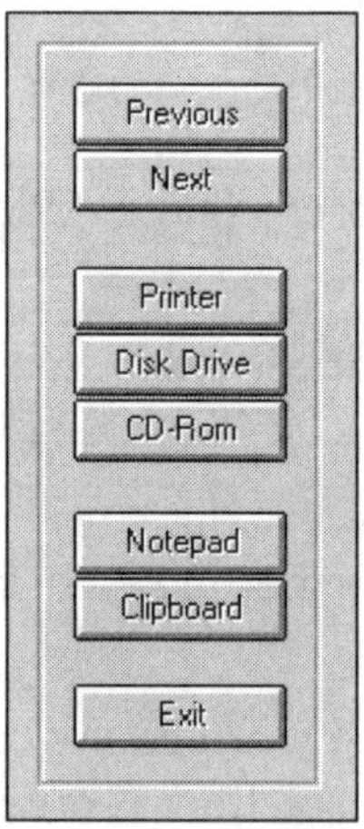


Figure 7-19: Use clustered Command Buttons to avoid menus.

The Panel Control on the left in Figure 7-20 creates an embossed, protruding frame (set the Panel's Properties: BevelInner to 1-Inset, BevelOuter to 2-Raised). The 3DFrame Control on the right in Figure 7-20 (when you set its Caption Property to empty) creates an etched, "carved" frame.

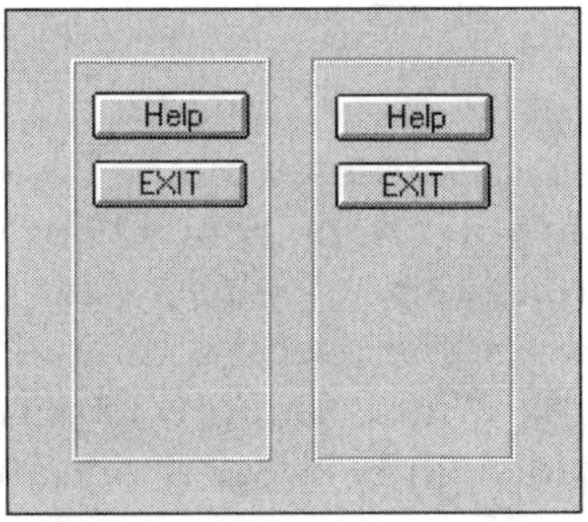


Figure 7-20: You can cordon off a set of Buttons within an embossed (left) or etched (right) frame.

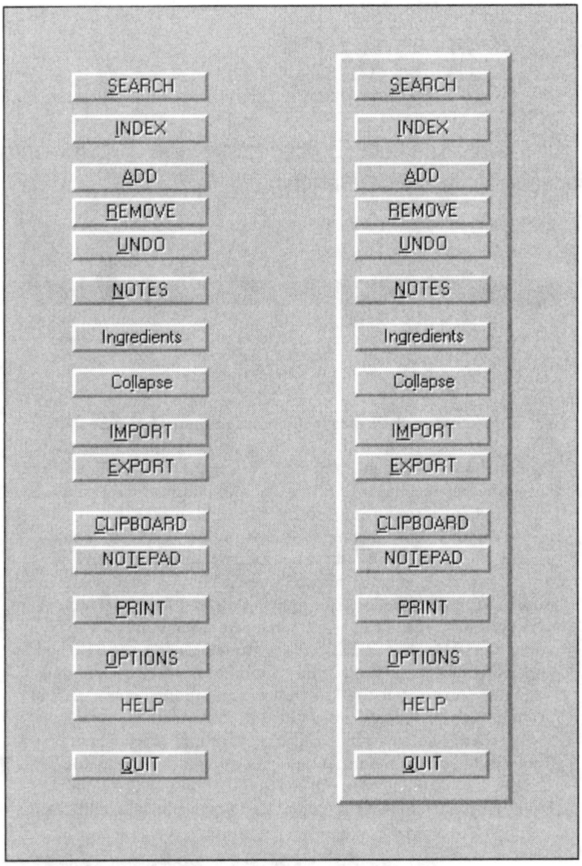


Figure 7-21: Both styles look good: Buttons clustered on a plain background or grouped onto a flat, raised Panel.

## Grouped Buttons

As you can see in Figure 7-21, grouped Buttons look attractive either on top of a Panel or simply arrayed on the Form itself. Note also the handsome effect when you set the Font3D Property of the Command3D (Button) Control to 3-Inset with Light Shading. Finally, Figure 7-21 illustrates another useful zoning technique: related Buttons—Add/Remove/Undo; Import/Export; and Clipboard/Notepad—are grouped slightly closer to one another.

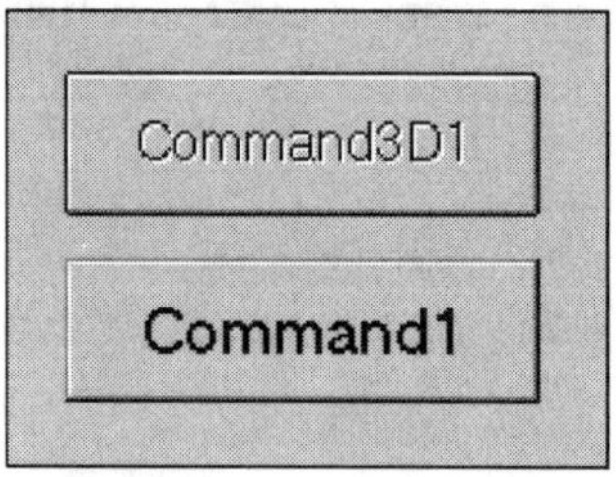


Figure 7-22: The Font3D Property (of the 3Dcommand button) is nearly always superior to flat black captioning.

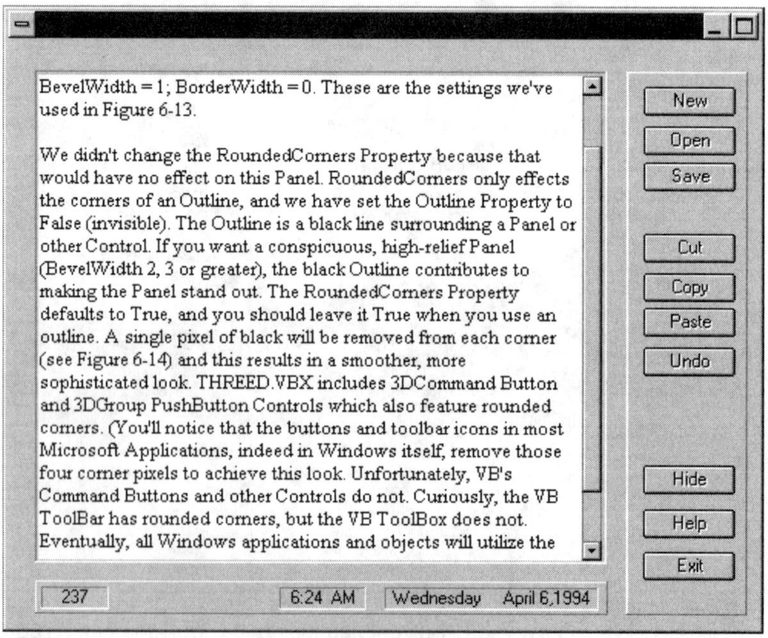


Figure 7-23: The finished Form, grouping Buttons on a Panel.

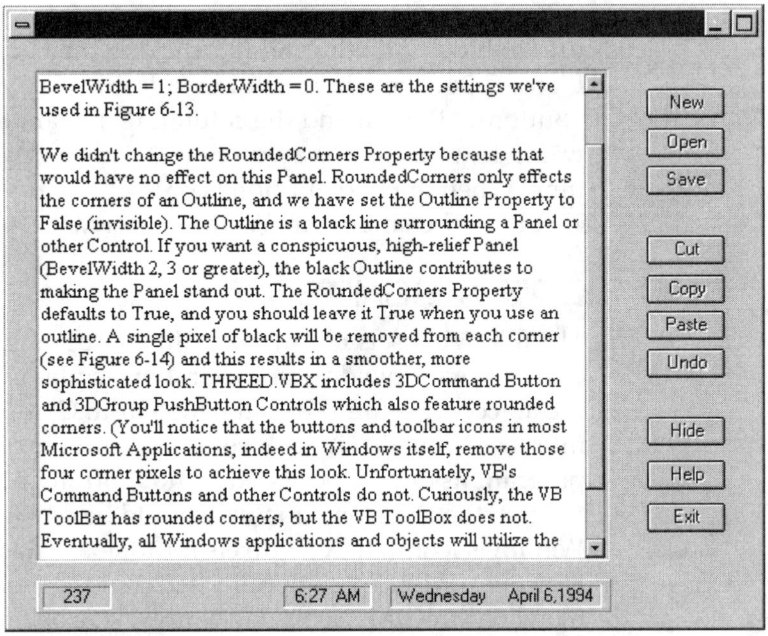


Figure 7-24: The same Form, with Buttons placed directly on the background.

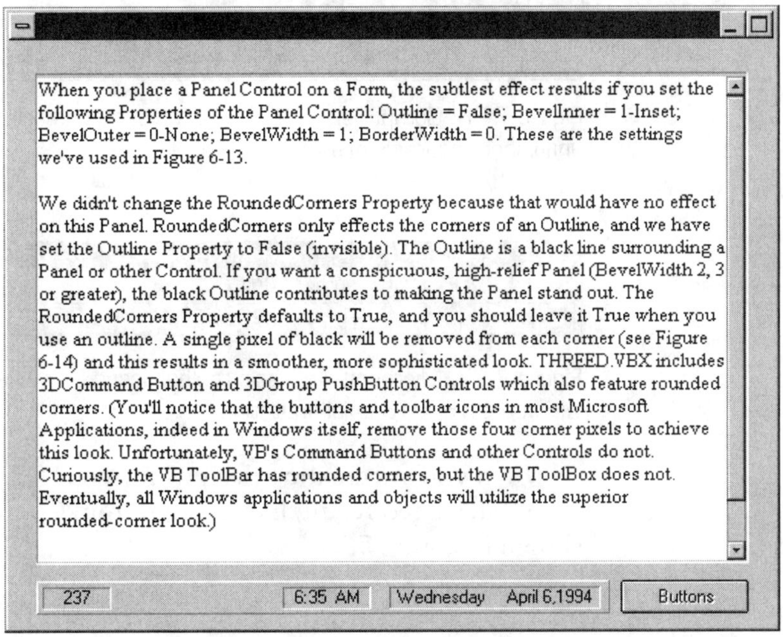


Figure 7-25: It's also nice to let the user hide a row of Buttons. Pressing the Hide Button collapses them and widens the Text Box.

In a panel of buttons, include one that hides all the rest.

Figure 7-25 demonstrates another useful technique—allowing the user to hide all the buttons by clicking the Hide Button shown in Figure 7-24. The whole column falls into a single Button labeled "Buttons." Press it and the column reappears. This gives the user a wider Text Box; this way, more text can be viewed on screen at one time. When the Hide Button is pressed, your VB program widens the Text Box by changing its Width Property.

## DO'S & DON'TS

The following sets of examples illustrate some additional do's and don'ts of window design. Several principles can be learned by looking at icons. Figure 7-26 is the toolbar in CompuServe's Windows interface WinCIM. It has a couple of graphic problems, although the program itself runs well and is thoughtfully organized.

First, the icons on a toolbar should be one-fourth the size of normal Windows icons (16 X 16 pixels for toolbars, 32 X 32 for regular icons). However, WinCIM's are full-sized. But the worst problem is that many of WinCIM's icons are simply, let's be honest, amateurish.

Figure 7-26: CompuServe WinCIM's toolbar icons are too large and some look unfinished, coarsely drawn.

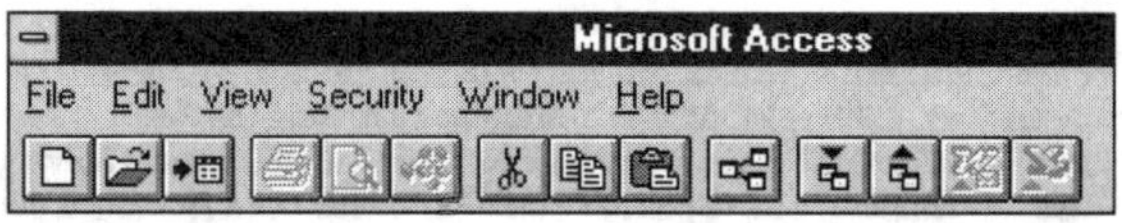


Figure 7-27: Microsoft Access's toolbar icons convey a clean dimensionality, even within the 16 X 16-pixel limitation.

When you are creating designs for your forms or icons, don't settle for a flat, jagged result, like the two from CompuServe's interface shown in Figure 7-28:

Figure 7-28: Two icons that look unfinished.

Figure 7-29: Simple and clean, these icons are excellent.

In the limited space permitted an icon, try to avoid using diagonal lines (which will stairstep); circles (even more ragged); and text (which cannot reproduce well in this confined an area). Notice that the icons in Figure 7-28—even though they use a large icon's 1,024 pixels—look rough because they attempt text and circular lines. Compare that to the neat rectangular designs—using only 256 pixels—in Figure 7-29.

## LIGHT & SHADOW

The play of highlights and shadows across a window creates both solidity and depth. One convention that you should observe is the use of highlight/shadow line drawings to indicate that an icon or other element is unavailable to the user. "Grayed out" elements are used, for example, to show that the printer icon is currently inoperative because there is no active document that could be printed. When the user creates or loads a document, the icon reverts to its normal, more vibrant appearance. Again, to see how to gray-out a graphic, let's compare the WinCIM to the Access designs:

Figure 7-30: Simply fading the original icon indicates inactivity, but this is hard to recognize—it looks like noisy TV.

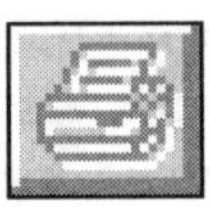

Figure 7-31: A highlight/shadow line drawing is tidy and more legible.

## Superimposition

All this should not be taken to mean that you can't create complex, interesting icons. The two icons in Figure 7-32 show the well-drawn but static Windows 3.0 File Manager icon compared to the more dramatic Windows 95 settings icon.

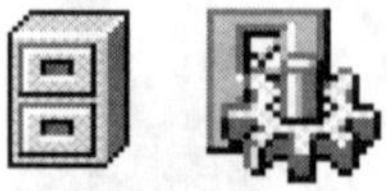

Figure 7-32: The Windows 95 icon at right is more detailed and more unique.

Another tip: In the real world, things overlap—one thing will be in front of another. Only on two-dimensional flat surfaces like paper, or in cartoons, do things separate and space themselves apart so that nothing covers anything else.

Note that the icon on the right in Figure 7-32 superimposes the gear. Note also the shadow behind the gear. Both superimposition and shadowing contribute to the 3D, real-world effect. And the greater detail contributes to the uniqueness and the greater recognizability of the revised icon. Put simply, the user can locate this icon more quickly on the screen. It looks less like other icons.

If you prefer not to design your own icons and toolbar buttons, you can use those in the excellent set of professionally designed icons bundled with VB.

## Large-Scale Balance

Another trend in Windows design is to spread gray across most of a window or Form. This helps unify the elements within the window—it ties the individual Controls together. In earlier Windows applications, white was the prevalent background in Microsoft's and everyone else's designs. New Windows applications from Microsoft and others are using white only to indicate places on a Form (Window) where the user can enter information, places that can be "filled in." All else is gray. (Controls the user can click on, like List Boxes, File access and Drop Down selection Controls, are also left white.) However, unless the user can directly type something into a Control, or select from a list inside it, set the Control's BackColor Property to light gray (H00C0C0C0& in RGB). Containers for information provided by the application (like Labels) remain gray; information provided by the user (like Text Boxes) remains white. (See "New in VB4" at the end of this chapter.)

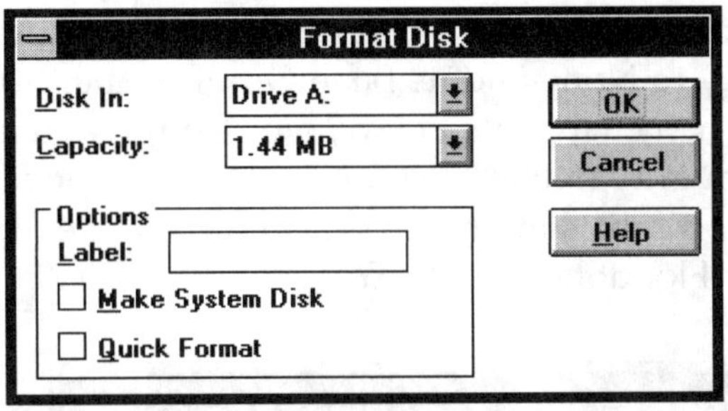


Figure 7-33: BEFORE. The Format Disk input box in Windows 3.1 is largely white, largely two-dimensional and, let's face it, largely dull.

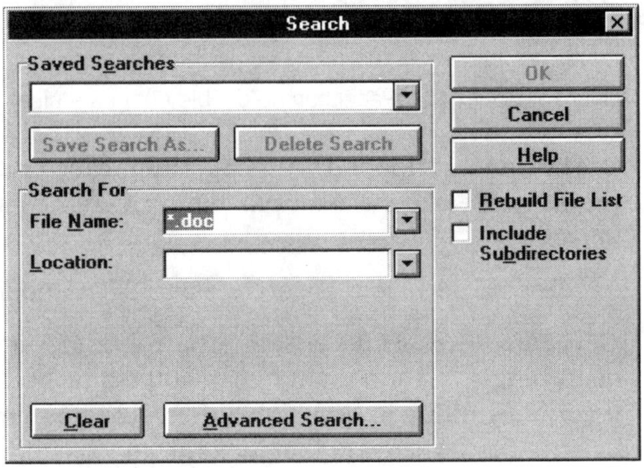


Figure 7-34: AFTER. Word 6.0 displays disk-access information far more attractively and ergonomically.

## Emphasizing the Third Dimension

Most applications now use gray to unify a window.

Notice the parallels in Figure 7-34 between this window's set of Controls and those that come with VB. Options Buttons and Check Boxes in VB are two-dimensional. But VB also supplies Option3D and Check3D Controls, and you should always use them. (The VB 3D Option Buttons are circular; their Windows counterparts are diamond-shaped. The backcolor of the Windows List Box is white, but you should set the BackColor Properties of VB List Boxes to light gray. These discontinuities will doubtless eventually be resolved in favor of the VB versions.) Figure 7-34 also illustrates how to organize a window using the VB Frame3D Control to zone related options.

Currently, a Panel is the most elegant way to show the passage of time in Visual Basic. To use such a progress indicator in your own programs, draw a long rectangular Panel. Set the Panel's BevelInner Property to None and its BevelOuter Property to Inset (see Figure 7-35). Then change its FloodColor from the default deep blue to medium gray (H00909090&), and change the FloodType Property to 1-Left to Right. Finally, if you want a text description of the percentage, set FloodShowPct to True.

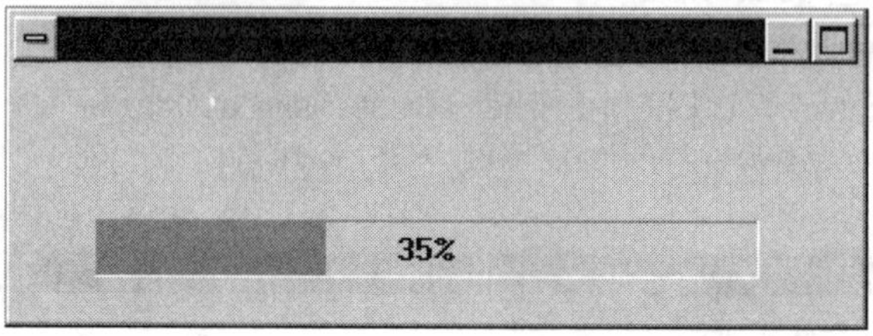


Figure 7-35: The 3DPanel can do double duty as a sleek progress indicator.

The Panel is flooded with color by means of its FloodPercent Property. Here's one example, which increments the indicator by five percent:

```
Panel3D1.FloodPercent = Panel3D1.FloodPercent + 5
```

There's also a gauge custom Control from Microhelp, but it is disturbingly flat and unattractive at the time of this writing. However, if you're working in VB4 32-bit, there's an excellent new ProgressBar Control from Microsoft that looks as good as the 3D Panel.

## NEW CONTROLS

A relatively new Windows Control is the Button Bar (a.k.a. "Toolbar"). In VB it isn't a Control in the strict sense—you cannot drag it from the toolbox to a Form. However, it's easy to construct a Button Bar. Put a Picture Box on a Form and set its Align Property to 1. On this Picture Box draw a set of Image Controls, filling each with a button icon (from VB's set of icons). This approach, though, isn't as attractive as the standard Windows button bar. The buttons are not 3D and you cannot put a Panel behind the Picture Box itself to give it a three-dimensional look.

The tabbed Controls shown in Figures 7-36 and 7-37 are now available in VB4 (Sheridan Tabbed Dialog).

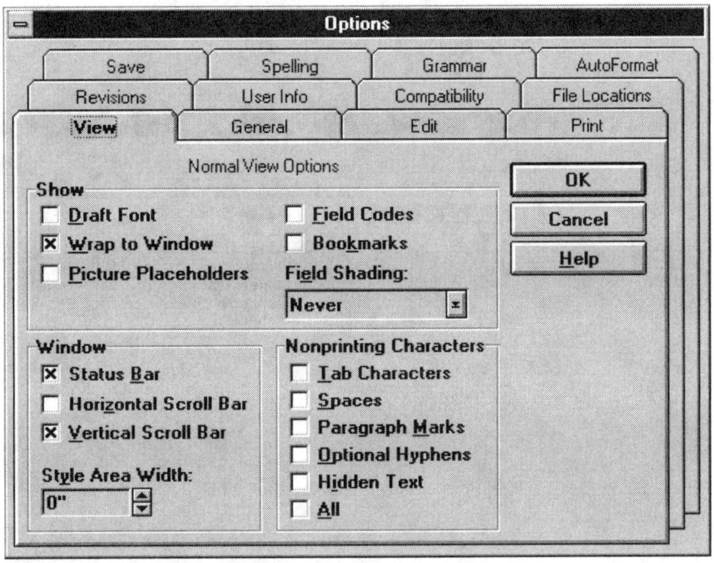


Figure 7-36: This Cardfile metaphor, from Word 6.0, is an effective way to present the user with a group of related windows.

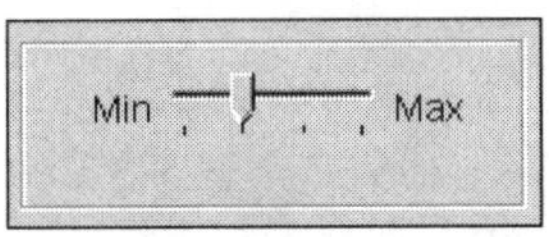


Figure 7-37: A slider is a visually superior alternative to a group of Option Buttons, or a Scroll Bar, when choosing a point within a range. There is also a vertical version.

## ALTERNATIVE BACKGROUNDS

The light gray background is a good, safe choice for any Form. But if you're feeling adventurous, you could use a texture. As time goes on, we'll see more and more subtle textures in Windows design. The key word here is subtle. Using a bright floral pattern as a background would be the same kind of error (causing confusion and mistrust) as would occur if a banker wore a suit printed with roses. Designers call this kind of thing a honker (flaw).

Avoid honkers.

Often it's generally best to avoid color altogether—translate your texture into shades of gray. All photo-retouching programs (Corel's PHOTO-PAINT!, Adobe's Photoshop and so on) include a "Convert to grayscale" option that takes color down to monochrome. For a "Materials Inventory" window within a program for a construction company, the background in some of the following figures might be just the ticket.

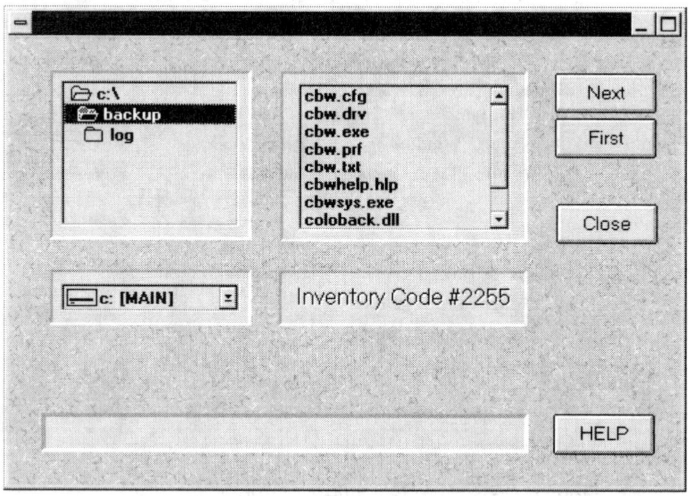


Figure 7-38: PAPER. Your Forms need not be grounded upon a simple, gray backcolor.

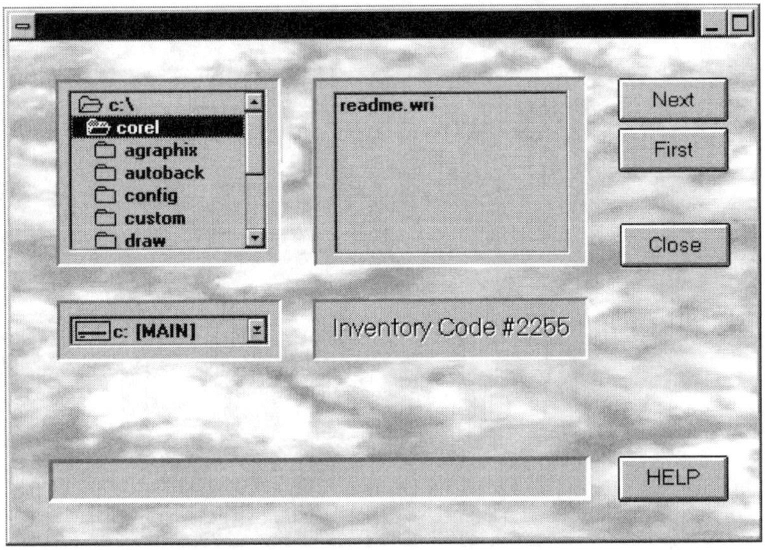


Figure 7-39: SKY.

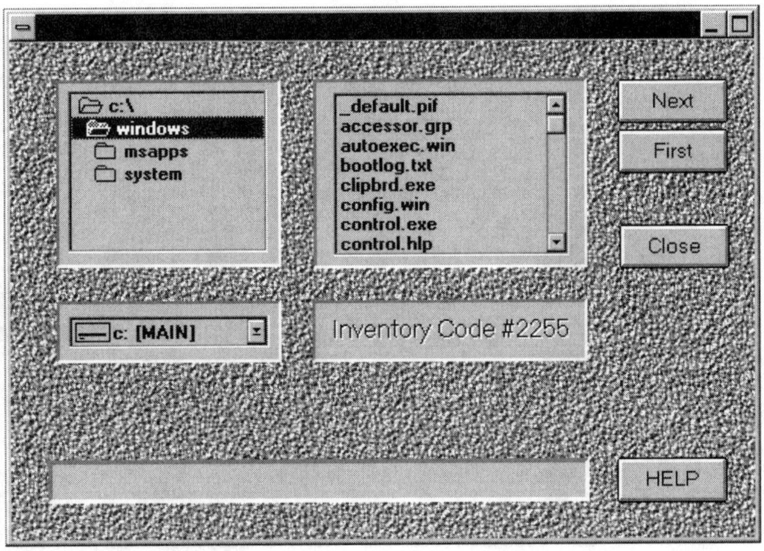


Figure 7-40: STUCCO.

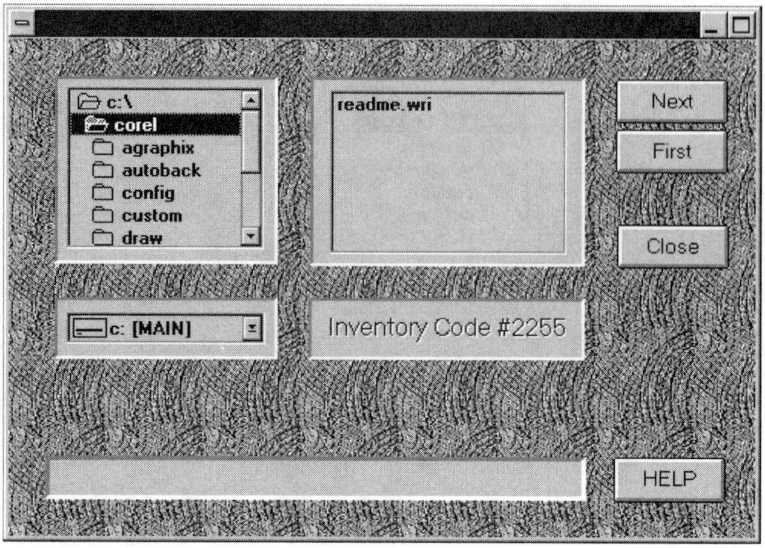


Figure 7-41: CEMENT.

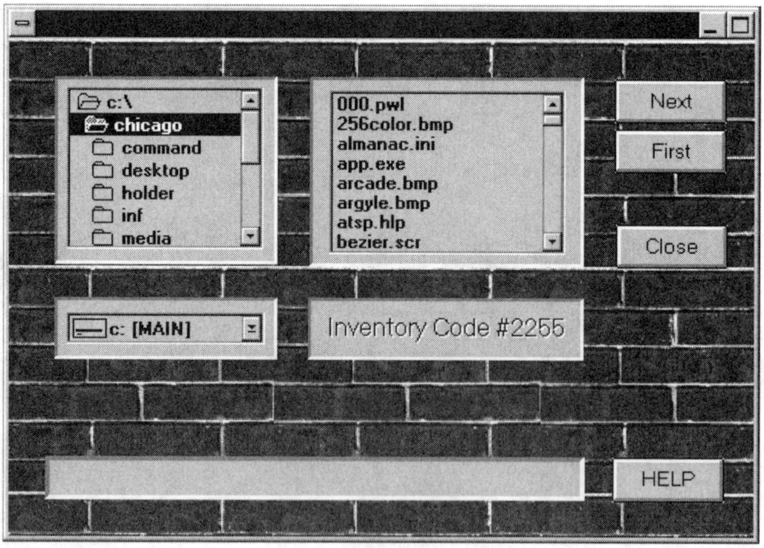


Figure 7-42: BRICK, Large.

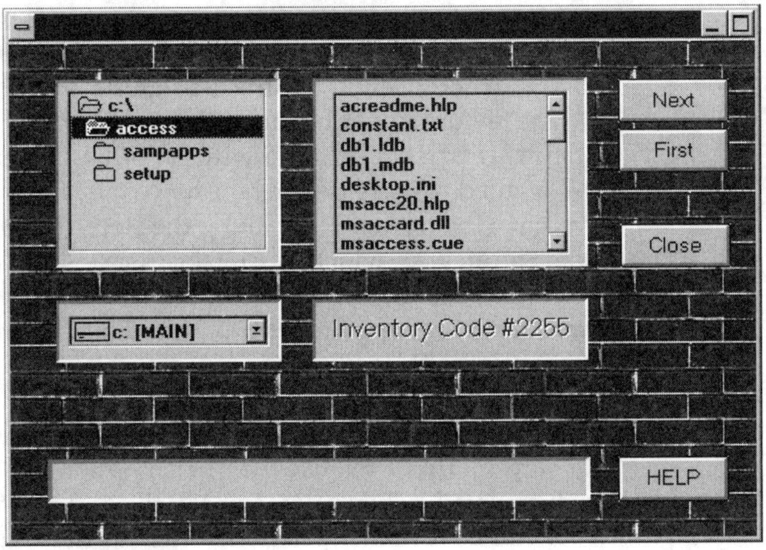


Figure 7-43: BRICK, Small.

## Creating Textures

Creating background textures is easy if you have a graphics program like Corel PHOTO-PAINT!, Micrografx's Picture Publisher, or some other "retouching" application. All the sample backgrounds in Figures 7-38 through 7-43 were built in Corel PHOTO-PAINT! except Cement and Brick, which are from Picture Publisher. *Note:* We've included a set of 114 textures on this books CD.

CD-ROM

Here are the steps to creating a background BMP file:

1. Start a new picture (from the File menu, select New). Specify that it be roughly the same size as the Form you'll be using it in—perhaps 2 X 2 inches. Select Grayscale (we don't want color to wash out the icons or other color we're using elsewhere on the Form).
2. Click on the Fill tool in the toolbar (usually a tipping paint bucket). Choose "Texture Fill." Then select one of the textures from the texture drop-down window (Corel) or the drop-down List (Micrografx).
3. Fill the picture.
4. Save it as a .BMP file to disk.
5. Change the Form's Picture Property to the name of your .BMP file.

Make sure it's a fairly light gray (some will be too dark). If it's obtrusively dark, go back to the originating graphics application, load it in and use the Contrast/Brightness control to make it brighter.

The texture might be too grainy, or the details too large (for instance, a brick background with six bricks, when you wanted 100). We wanted to increase the density of the bricks in Figure 7-42 (which has 65 bricks). After completing the steps described below, the result was Figure 7-43, which has 180 bricks.

To increase the density and detail of the background, start another new image in the graphics program. This time, make it 4 X 4 or 8 X 8 inches large. Then fill it.

Now from the Image menu, select Size (Picture Publisher) or Resample (Corel). Reduce the size of the picture by 50 percent or even 25 percent. (In Corel, use the Stretch option; the other options will reduce detail.) Then save the BMP file and try it in the Form.

If you use another program—such as the excellent shareware PaintShop Pro—to resize a BMP file, try to resize by 50%, 25%, 200% or 400%. Using fractions or multiples like these (halving, quartering, doubling the size, for example, for your percent resize) will prevent dithering and other unfortunate side effects. (For more on dithering, see Chapter 6.)

### Rapid Tiled Wallpaper

Tiling a texture is one of the most useful graphic techniques.

Textured backgrounds do have a serious shortcoming: they can take too much time to display on screen (particularly on older, slower machines like 386s). And they can make your finished VB EXE files immense. The solution is to rapidly "tile" a small bitmap, making it fill a large area without adding significantly to the file size. For a complete description of this simple but powerful technique, see "BitBlt( ): Instant Tiled Wallpaper on Forms" in Chapter 8.

## PRINTING, RAISED & EMBEDDED

The fastest special effects of all (and the least costly in memory or resources) are those created with the Print command or the Line command. You can do a variety of things with these techniques. For example, if you want to display a modal form (like a MsgBox) that alerts the user to something or gets necessary information (like an InputBox), don't use the unsightly MsgBox or InputBox built into VB. Consider the trend—the obvious ramp up in graphic quality—from DOS through Windows 3 to the latest applications, shown in Figure 7-44.

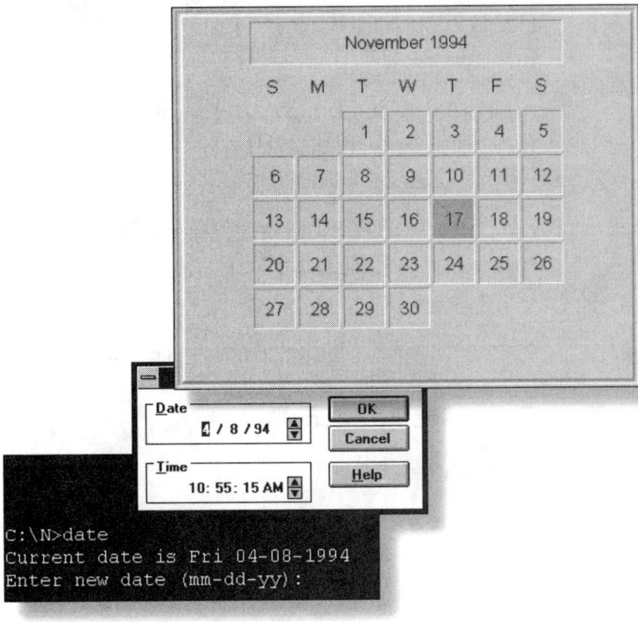


CD-ROM

Figure 7-44:The evolution of user input: increasingly detailed, increasingly subtle. The calendar is a custom control from Crescent (see the demo on this book's CD).

## Drop Shadowing

The built-in VB MsgBox and InputBox are typical Windows 3-style modal Forms. Your programs will look far nicer if you create your own "alert" boxes in the spirit of the ongoing Windows design advances described in this chapter. Try, for instance, drop-shadow effects as illustrated in Figure 7-45:

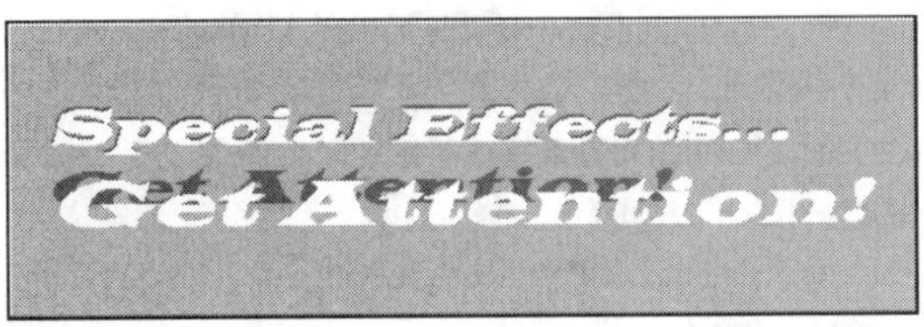


Figure 7-45: Overprinting can grab the reader's attention through drop-shadowing.

Here's the programming that produces Figure 7-45:

```
Sub Form_Load ()
Show
```

```
Backcolor = QBColor(7)
Fontsize = 24

currentx = 300: currenty = 600
forecolor = QBColor(8)
Print "Special Effects..."

currentx = 320: currenty = 630
forecolor = QBColor(15)
Print "Special Effects..."

currentx = 300: currenty = 1200
forecolor = QBColor(8)
Print "Get Attention!"

Fontsize = 32

currentx = 340: currenty = 1260
forecolor = QBColor(15)
Print "Get Attention!"

End Sub
```

## Embossing & Engraving

A similar offsetting technique, also using Print and CurrentX/Y, results in embossed (raised) or engraved (sunken) lettering effects. Here are general purpose Functions to etch or emboss text. Just put them into a Module and call them:

```
Function Etch (fname As Form, a$, x, Y)

fname.CurrentX = x
fname.CurrentY = Y
fname.ForeColor = QBColor(15)
fname.Print a$
fname.CurrentX = x - 28
fname.CurrentY = Y - 20
fname.ForeColor = QBColor(0)
fname.Print a$

End Function

Function Emboss (fname As Form, a$, x, Y)
```

```
fname.CurrentX = x
fname.CurrentY = Y
fname.ForeColor = QBColor(15)
fname.Print a$
fname.CurrentX = x + 6
fname.CurrentY = Y + 8
fname.ForeColor = QBColor(0)
fname.Print a$

End Function
```

You provide four variables when you call these functions: the Form's identity (Me), the text you want printed, and the currentx and currenty position on the Form where you want the text printed.

Figure 7-46: Embossing and etching effects are easy in VB.

To get the results shown in Figure 7-46, use this programming:

```
Sub Form_Load ()
Show
AutoRedraw = True
fontname = "Times New Roman"
fontsize = 56
x = etch(Me, "This is Etched", 500, 500)

x = emboss(Me, "This is Embossed...", 500, 1800)

End Sub
```

To get different effects, try changing the amount of offset in the lines

```
fname.CurrentX = x - 28
fname.CurrentY = Y - 20
```

to, perhaps

```
fname.CurrentX = x - 38
fname.CurrentY = Y - 30
```

Also try changing one of the colors from black to dark gray:

```
fname.ForeColor = QBColor(8)
```

## FRAMING

The Line command creates efficient, attractive layering, zoning and highlighting effects.

Just as printing is the fastest and most memory-efficient approach to special effects with text, the Line command is the most rapid, efficient way to add frames around Controls. You can use multiple Sheridan Panel Controls to achieve these effects, but at a cost in repaint speed. (You could also use superimposed Shape Controls, but the effect is not attractive—the corners don't come out right.)

CD-ROM

We've created a multipurpose framing subroutine called DrawFrameOn that can create all possible kinds of frames quickly and easily. It's a bit of typing, so you might want to copy this one off the CD:

```
'TopLeftControl, and LowestRightControl should be the
' names of the upper-left and lower-right Controls
' which you want to have framed. (To frame a single
' Control, name it twice.)
'
' "Style" should be "inward" or "outward"
'
' "FrameWidth" is the size you want the frame to be, in Twips.
'
Sub drawframeon (TopLeftControl As Control,
LowestRightControl As Control, Style As String, Framewidth)

dw = drawwidth
fs = fillstyle
sm = scalemode
drawwidth = 1
fillstyle = 1
scalemode = 1
st$ = LCase$(Left$(Style$, 1))
Lft = TopLeftControl.Left
Toplft = TopLeftControl.Top
Hite = TopLeftControl.Height
```

```
Rite = LowestRightControl.Left + LowestRightControl.Width →
Ritebotm = LowestRightControl.Top + →
LowestRightControl.Height
'Use tallest Control as Y
If Ritebotm > Hite Then Hite = Ritebotm
'Draw a Thick Box
Line (Lft - Framewidth, Toplft - Framewidth)-(Rite + →
Framewidth, Ritebotm + Framewidth), QBColor(7), BF
'Draw Highlight and Shadow lines
lt = 15: rb = 8
If st$ = "i" Then lt = 8: rb = 15
Line (Lft - Framewidth, Toplft - Framewidth)-(Rite + →
Framewidth, Toplft - Framewidth), QBColor(lt)
Line (Lft - Framewidth, Toplft - Framewidth)-(Lft - →
Framewidth, Hite + Framewidth), QBColor(lt)
Line (Rite + Framewidth, Toplft - Framewidth)-(Rite + →
Framewidth, Ritebotm + Framewidth), QBColor(rb)
Line (Rite + Framewidth, Ritebotm + Framewidth)-(Lft - →
Framewidth, Hite + Framewidth), QBColor(rb)
If st$ <> "i" Then 'comment this next line out to remove thin →
black line.
Line (Lft - Framewidth - 17, Toplft - Framewidth - 16)-(Rite + →
Framewidth + 10, Ritebotm + Framewidth + 10), QBColor(0), B
End If
drawwidth = dw
fillstyle = fs
scalemode = sm

End Sub
```

Figure 7-47: The molded framing around Bossy is easy with the DrawFrameOn routine.

## Layered Frames

The multiple-frame effect in Figure 7-47 was created by repeatedly calling the DrawFrameOn routine. Notice that you start by describing the outermost frame (500) and working down closer to the image. This way, the larger frames don't overprint (and destroy) the smaller inner frames:

```
Sub Form_Load ()
Show
    DrawFrameOn image1, image1, "outward", 500
    DrawFrameOn image1, image1, "inward", 360
    DrawFrameOn image1, image1, "outward", 280
    DrawFrameOn image1, image1, "outward", 200
End Sub
```

For a quieter, less dramatic effect (see Figure 7-48), remove the black line around the frames by commenting out the following line in the DrawFrameOn routine:

```
'Line (Lft - Framewidth - 17, Toplft - Framewidth - 16)-(Rite + →
Framewidth + 10, Ritebotm + Framewidth + 10), QBColor(0), B
```

Figure 7-48: The DrawFrameOn routine can also produce these gentler, less muscular frames. This one looks like a matted print.

Figure 7-48 was created with these lines:

```
Sub Form_Load ()
Show
    drawframeon image1, image1, "outward", 400
    drawframeon image1, image1, "inward", 180
    drawframeon image1, image1, "outward", 100
End Sub
```

## COMPLETE COORDINATION

Before leaving the topic of good-looking applications, let's look at some additional techniques that produce highly sophisticated visual effects. You can complement a textured background by using the same texture in the Picture Property of a 3DCommand Button. Coordinated textures can create a visual unity on a window in the same way that coordinated backcolors do.

Here are the Property settings for the 3DCommand Button, which create the carved marble effect shown in Figure 7-49:

```
Begin SSCommand Command3D1
    BevelWidth=   3
    Caption=   "E X I T"
```

```
    Font3D=   4  'Inset w/heavy shading
    FontBold   =   0   'False
    FontItalic   =   0   'False
    FontName =   "Gravure"
    FontSize   =   18
    FontStrikethru =   0   'False
    FontUnderline =   0   'False
    ForeColor   =   &H00808080&
    Height =   660
    Left=   3075
    Outline =   0   'False
    Picture =   FORM1.FRX:2A9F0
    TabIndex   =   0
    Top=   4980
    Width   =   1635
End
```

Try using identical textures on the background and a Control.

Figure 7-49: Visual unity can be achieved by repeating a texture. Here we put the background marble on the Command Button as well as the Form.

## Metallic Shading

One of the best ways to avoid dull-looking Forms is to use gradient metallic shading. It's subtle and conservative enough for any business application, yet considerably more attractive than plain gray.

CD-ROM

We've included on the CD several gradients to put into the Picture Property of 3D Button Controls and Forms (see subdirectory 7), but you can make your own with Corel PHOTO-PAINT!, Picture Publisher or most any photo-retouching program. Here's how to do it.

The best metallic gradient is a gradual shift between two shades: white and the typical Windows gray (the light gray often used as backcolor; the same gray that's used on the VB Command Button and many other Controls). So put a Command Button on a Form, and then press Alt+PrintScreen to capture the Form to the Clipboard. Then open a photo-retouching program like Photoshop. From the Edit menu, select Paste to bring in the Form.

All retouching programs have a "color picker" tool. It sometimes looks like an eyedropper. Use it to select the color of the Command Button's shadow, thereby placing it into the main color selection. Change the alternate color (sometimes called "backcolor" or "secondary color") to white. (If you don't want to use the picker, adjust the main color directly to shadow gray by setting RGB to 75% each, or to white, by setting RGB to 100% each. If you're specifying colors in CYMK rather than RGB, the percentages for gray are 25% for the first three and 0% for K.) For a more dramatic effect, use 50% gray.

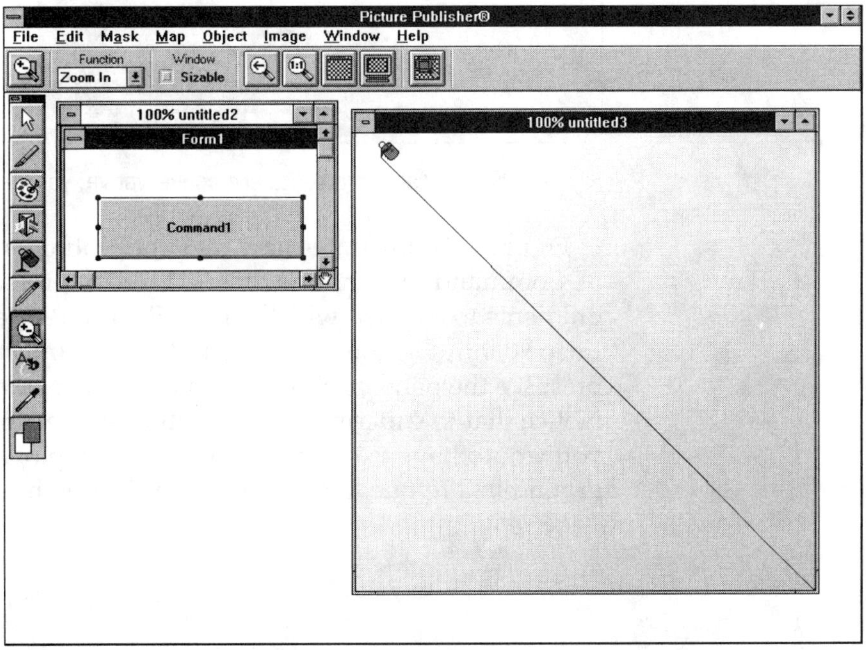


Figure 7-50: Creating a metallic gradient for a Form's background.

Now create a new graphic (File/New) and drag your gradient so that the gray shadow is strongest in the lower right corner and white is strongest in the upper-right corner. Use the linear gradient option. Save the results to disk for later use. Also make several small gradients to load into the Picture Property of 3DCommand Buttons.

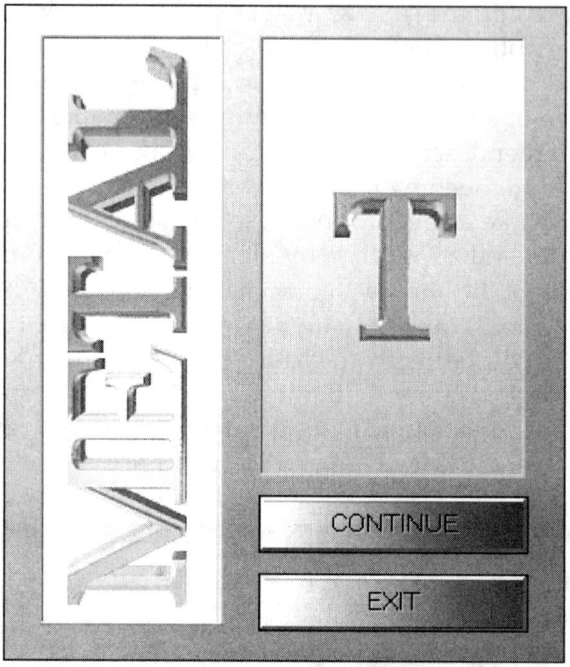


Figure 7-51: Metallic gradients are conservative, yet sophisticated.

Figure 7-51 illustrates how metallic gradients look on a Form, on 3DCommand Buttons and inserted into depressed 3DPanels. To add gradients to a panel (which has no Picture Property), just put an Image control inside the panel and size it almost to the edges to preserve the panel framing. Then load your gradient into the Image. Notice that to superimpose a graphic, like the metallic lettering here, you would have to create the graphic on top of a gradient background in a retouching graphics application like Picture Publisher.

## FLASHING LIGHTS, DEEP COLOR

With the techniques described below, you can make your VB applications as decorative and photo-realistic as any commercial software. Essentially the trick is this: *design your forms in Photoshop or Picture Publisher*. Go beyond the techniques described on the previous pages. Do more than create an attractive gradient or textured background. When you're working in a graphics program, you can add shadowing, neon, 3D, animation, sculpted labels and other effects to VB *Controls*. We recommend Picture Publisher because it's attractively priced, does pretty much everything, includes a simple macro language, and is easy to use. However, Photoshop is the de facto standard graphics editor and, though more complex, produces excellent results too.

*Warning:* This technique requires that any user of your application have his or her settings for Large Fonts or Small Fonts (in Windows) the same as you had it when you designed the Form. If the user changes resolution from, say, 1024 X 768 to 800 X 600, all will be well. But if the user has chosen Large Fonts and you designed for Small Fonts, the visual effects will be misaligned. *Solution:* Provide two applications and tell the user to run the alternative application if the font size is wrong. You can use the GetDeviceCaps API call to detect resolution and font size. Here's how, for the VB4 32-bit version:

```
Public Declare Function GetDeviceCaps Lib "GDI32" (ByVal  →
hDC As Long, ByVal nIndex As Long) As Long

Public Function fixres() As Single
Dim xDPI As Long
Dim horresol As Long
Dim vertresol As Long

    '—Get display's horizontal dots per logical inch
xDPI = GetDeviceCaps(Form1.hDC, LOGPIXELSX)

    '—Figure fonts ratio
px = 1440 / xDPI

    '—Get resolution
horresol = GetDeviceCaps(Form1.hDC, HORZRES)
vertresol = GetDeviceCaps(Form1.hDC, VERTRES)
```

```
If px = 12 Then 'they're using large fonts

MsgBox ("Your video display is set to LARGE FONTS. This →
application requires a setting of Small Fonts. Right click on →
your desktop, select PROPERTIES, then SETTINGS. Change →
Fonts from Large to Small. Or, run our other application →
named LARGEAPP.EXE")

End If
End Function
```

If you just want to try your hand at design, you can use Corel PHOTO-PAINT! or the excellent shareware product, Paint Shop Pro. You could even create backgrounds with Windows's Paint applet, but why torment yourself?

CD-ROM

Alas, we can't show you here in print the color, texture and animated lighting effects we've added to the applet illustrated in Figures 7-52 and 7-53. However, this sample applet is on the book's CD, so you can load it in and take a look. It features high-resolution detail (75 pixels per inch) and considerable color depth (24-bit color), so it looks best on a 1024 X 756 True Color display.

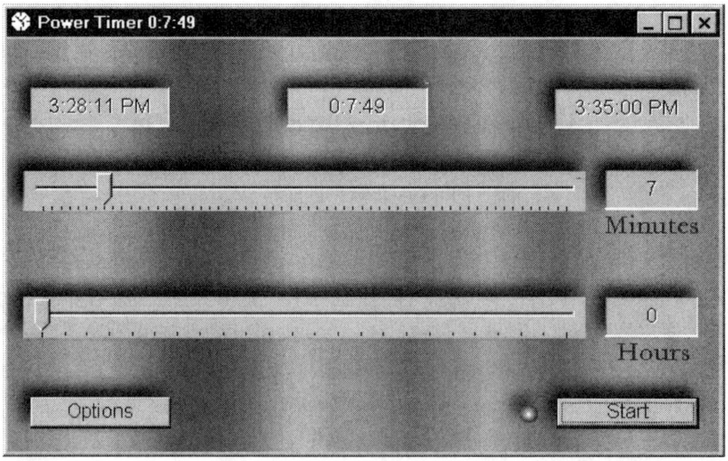


Figure 7-52: Shadowing, custom labels and a subtle glimmering light animation have been added to this Form.

Figure 7-53: The sculpted gold lettering was created in Picture Publisher; the high-res alarm clock graphic is from Fractal Design's Painter.

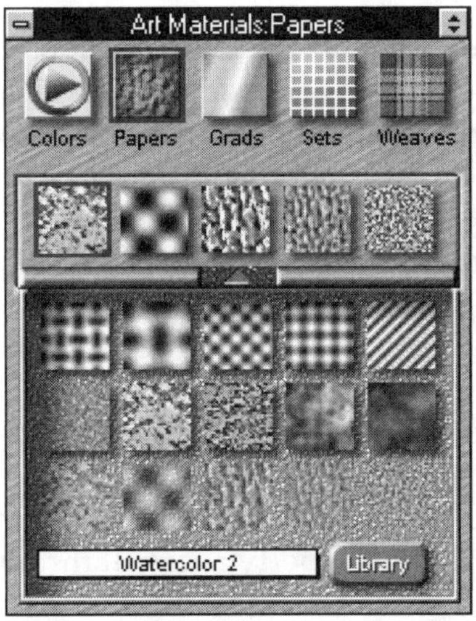


Figure 7-54: Fractal Design's Painter includes extensive and excellent features for creating textures and gradient backgrounds.

Here's how we shadowed the Controls, added special effects to labels and created the animation illustrated in Figures 7-52 and 7-53. First, put all the Controls you'll want onto a Form, as shown in Figure 7-55.

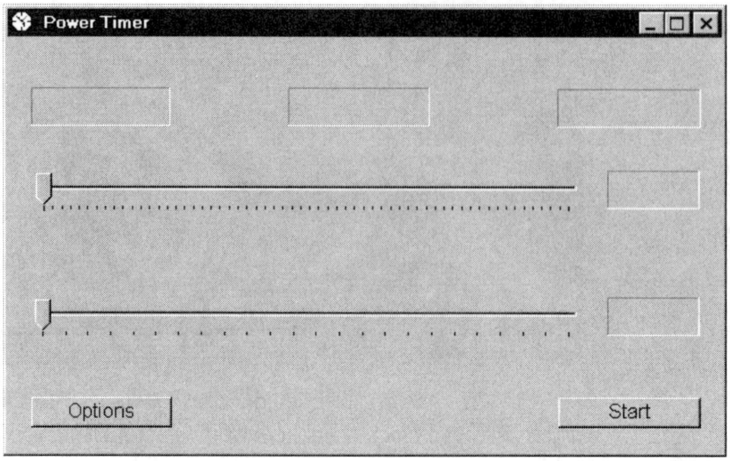


Figure 7-55: Start by arranging the Controls on a Form within VB.

Make sure the Form has the focus (click on its title bar). Then take a snapshot of the Form by pressing the Alt+PrintScrn key to send the image of the Form to the Clipboard. Now run your graphics program and, from its Edit menu, choose Paste (or Paste as New Image). Depending on the graphics application, you may have to first create a new blank picture into which the Form can be pasted (see the File menu).

Now you can freely *paint* and otherwise manipulate the visuals of your Form. You can even paint on top of the Controls if you wish—the real Controls will reappear when you load this image as the Picture Property of the real Form.

However, you should use the *crop* tool to remove the title bar—it's not part of the Picture Property and will throw things off unless you remove it. Next you want to "select" or "mask" the Controls—so they will remain visible (that's because we're going to shadow them later). Use the magic wand masking feature that selects and zones the graphic based on similarity of color, as shown in Figure 7-56.

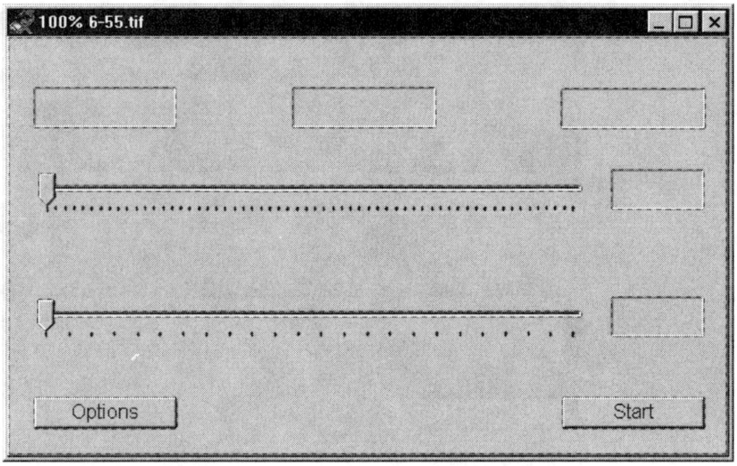


Figure 7-56: We've removed the VB title bar and used the magic wand to select only the non-Controls' background.

Now add whatever background texture you want. After adding a golden gradient from Painter (created as a separate .BMP file, then cut and pasted into the masked graphic shown in Figure 7-56), we used the Alien Skin drop shadow plug-in (set to "very soft" and –1 x/y offset).

The throbbing light animation effect is also simple to create. First drag a circular selection using the "elliptical" selection tool, while holding down the Ctrl key to constrain it to a circle. Create a gradient by choosing foreground and background colors that you want to represent the extremities of the effect (we used a medium and dark purple). Then use the gradient fill tool (set to "circular") to create the ball of light illustrated in Figure 7-52. This is your light in the "off," or dark, position. It's embedded right there as a permanent part of the background Picture Property. Save this file so you can load it into your form.

To create the animation (the light throbbing on and off), we'll want to put an identical ball light into an Image Control. So crop the light so you have a small square image, then select (mask) the light so you won't affect the background when you repeat the steps above to give it a circular gradient. We used medium to light purple to indicate that the light is "on." Save this as a separate .BMP file and load it into an Image Control, as shown in Figure 7-57:

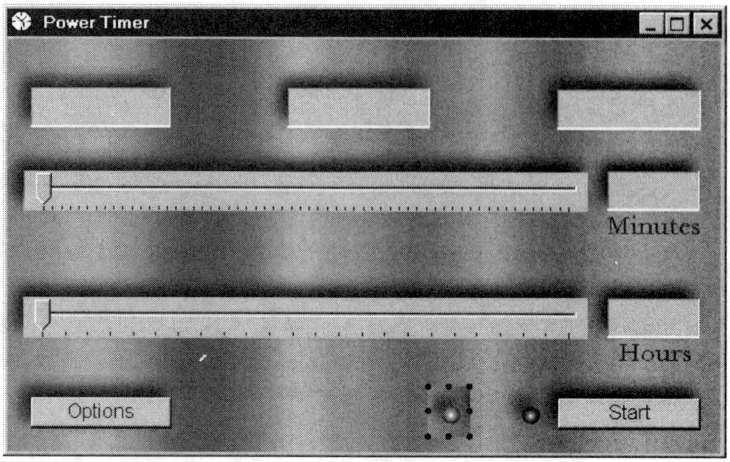


Figure 7-57: Position the "on" light in the Image Control directly on top of the "off" light embedded in the background on the Form.

Now all you have to do is click on the Image Control, then hold down Ctrl while you use the arrow keys to position the Image's light ball directly over the one on the background. You might have to run the program and trigger the animation a few times until you get it just right—you don't want the ball jumping around, just throbbing. Here's the code that, within a Timer with its Interval set to 1,000, will turn the light on and off every second:

```
Private Sub Timer1_Timer()
Static toggle As Boolean
If toggle = True Then
    Image1.Visible = False
    toggle = False
Else
    toggle = True
    Image1.Visible = True
End If
End Sub
```

## Special Lettering

The Print command and Label Control in VB rather limit your creativity with lettering. Go ahead and *draw* labels onto the background .BMP that you'll import into the Picture Property of a Form.

Figure 7-58: This gold-toned lettering was fabricated in Picture Publisher.

To get the lettering effect shown in Figure 7-58, we first used the Picture Publisher text tool, with a forecolor of dark brown. When you finish typing in the label, click on the pointer tool. This leaves the text selected (masked), and you can also now drag it into position. Start a new image (File/New), then press Ctrl+C to copy the selected text. Paste it into the new image. Then in the new image, fill the selected text with a white-to-golden gradient. Copy it, then paste back into the original image and position it just one pixel to the right and one pixel down from the position of the original dark brown text.

## NEW IN VB4

Several attractive new Controls have been added to VB4, Controls that conform to the Windows 95 standards. These Controls work only under 32-bit operating systems such as Windows 95 and Windows NT version 3.51 or higher.

The new Controls are all clustered in a file named COMCTL32.OCX. If you don't see the Controls on your VB Toolbar, click on the Tools menu, then select Custom Controls. Choose "Microsoft Windows Common Controls," and they will appear on your Toolbar. Also remember that when you give somebody else a VB application you've written that uses some of these Controls, you must ensure that the COMCTL32.OCX file is in his or her Windows SYSTEM directory.

## MOVING ON

Perhaps no one topic contributes as much to a VB programmer's bag of tricks as learning to use the Application Programmer's Interface (API). The API is a collection of over 1,000 Functions (and a few Subroutines) built into the Windows operating system itself. Tapping into this huge toolbox allows you do accomplish many things more quickly or more easily than you can with VB alone. Beyond that, the API does lots of things that are impossible to do in VB.

Although many books touch on the API, and a couple cover it in depth, we've yet to see one that provides complete, runnable examples written in Visual Basic. Most books provide only a few examples in VB, some provide examples in C, and some provide many API listings, but none provides lots of useful examples.

Chapter 8 is a collection of what we consider to be all the most important API Functions—the Functions every VB programmer should know about in order to improve his or her VB applications. Most entries include figures to show the results you can expect. Above all, each entry includes a full, executable example written in Visual Basic.

Chapter 8

# The Best of the API

Here, in one place, are what we believe to be all the most useful Functions that a VB programmer can add to VB's built-in commands. The API is the Application Programming Interface, a collection of routines used by the Windows operating system itself.

The tips, tricks and techniques in this chapter are for those who prefer tested, explicit examples. Unfortunately, most books that explain how to contact the API from VB assume that, since the *topic* is relatively advanced, the reader already knows a lot about C, locates bugs instantly and has memorized the SDK.

We're taking a different approach. There is nothing inherently difficult or bewildering about using the API from VB. In this chapter, you don't have to translate from C into VB, or figure out how to provide parameters, or decide what Controls to use. It's all here *in Visual Basic*—and each API routine is illustrated by a complete example you can type in or cut and paste from the CD and explore.

CD-ROM

Section 1 provides background on the API. Section 2 lists API Functions by name and purpose, in the following categories: Bitmapped Graphics, Drawing & Geometric Graphics, Manipulating Windows, General Programming Utilities, Managing INI Files, Video & Animation and Music & Sound.

## SECTION 1: BACKGROUND

The API is Windows's own toolbox. Windows applications can utilize most of the over 600 prewritten Functions contained within several related Windows libraries. Your VB programs can utilize the API as well. And if you are interested in VB, you should become familiar with the API. It is a substantial resource, and one that supplements Visual Basic in important ways, as you will see.

Some API Functions merely duplicate existing VB commands; others are awkward or impossible to use with VB. We won't describe those in this chapter.

There are more than 1,000 procedures in the API at your disposal.

Yet, there are actually more than 1,000 procedures in the API, when you consider that some Functions can perform dozens of separate tasks (see "SendMessage( ): Many Functions in One" in Section 2). API commands can also be faster than their VB equivalents because they are less generic.

For other API commands, there *is* no VB equivalent at all. In this chapter, we will demonstrate precisely how to use what we think are the best, most important API commands for the Visual Basic programmer. They are *best* in the sense that they can make your VB program run faster, or can do things that are impossible to do with VB commands alone, or both.

Using an API Function is hardly more difficult than using a Function you write yourself. You first declare the API Function (providing its name, library, data type and any parameters). Thereafter, you are free to use the Function within your VB program, simply by calling it as if it were a normal Function and furnishing the already-declared parameters (arguments).

### Calling Conventions

API routines are usually Functions, but a few are Subroutines. You treat them essentially the same as if they were a normal VB Function or Sub. Functions require a return argument and the parameters listed in parentheses: x% = FunctName (param1, param2). Subs don't: SubName param1, param2.

Each Function has a variable type.

When declaring an API Function (so you can call it later), remember that the entire Function has a *variable type*. This means that you can either append a variable type symbol (like % or &) to the Function name:

```
Declare Function GetCaretBlinkTime% Lib "User" ( )
```

Or you can add the type at the end, as descriptive words:

```
Declare Function GetCaretBlinkTime Lib "User" ( ) As Integer
```

Though there are few of them in the API, remember that, unlike Functions, *subroutines are not typed.* (Subs don't return a value, so they don't need to be "of a particular variable type.") There is no % or As Integer:

```
Declare Sub SetCaretBlinkTime Lib "User" (ByVal Timing%)
```

### All Function Calls Require a Return Variable

Remember that when you call a Function you must provide the return variable (even if you don't use it), like the x% here:

```
x% = GetCaretBlinkTime( )
```

Alternatively, you can implicitly provide a place for the returned value, by including the Function in an expression:

```
If GetCaretBlinkTime( ) > 300 Then End
```

Even if there are no parameters being passed to a Function, you must still include the ( ).

By contrast, a Sub is called without the x% = or the ( ). Any parameters are simply listed, separated by commas if necessary:

```
SetCaretBlinkTime 500
```

What about parameter *names*? They don't matter at all—you can use any names you want. All that matters is that you get the variable *types* exactly the way the API wants them (and the *name* of the API Function must be accurate, too).

### Microsoft's Variable-Naming Convention

Microsoft has developed an elaborate formal set of rules about how variables (and constants) should be named. For instance, wMsg means a "message" parameter that is a "word" type (integer). Or lParam means a generic parameter of the "long integer" type. You are free to ignore this naming convention if you wish. Just keep the variable types straight.

It's OK to use the same names in the Declare and the call to an API Function.

RIGHT:

```
Declare Function ExitWindows% lib "User" (ByVal L as Long, →
ByVal I as Integer)
```

```
x% = ExitWindows (L&, I%)
```

It's also OK to use different parameter names.

RIGHT:

```
Declare Function ExitWindows% lib "User" (ByVal L as Long, →
ByVal I as Integer)
```

```
x% = ExitWindows (FirstParam&, SecondParam%)
```

But you cannot change the variable types. If you do, you'll likely get a "Bad DLL Calling Convention" error message.

WRONG:

```
Declare Function ExitWindows% lib "User" (ByVal L as Long, →
ByVal I as Integer)
```

```
x$ = ExitWindows (L%, I$)
```

### ByVal & ByRef

You must get the API Declare variable types correct.

The most important part of an API declaration is the list of arguments. It's no different from the list of arguments of any built-in VB Function (like MsgBox), or any Function you create. However, you do want to make sure when declaring the API functions that you get the *variable types* of the parameters correct. tParam% is quite different from tParam$. Or, to use the other, equivalent type notation: tParam As Integer is quite different from tParam As String.

There is also a fundamental difference between Visual Basic and most other languages. Visual Basic provides two ways to pass arguments (parameters): *by reference* (the default), which passes to the Function the actual *address* (location) of the variable, and *by value*, which passes to the Function only a *copy* of the variable.

When passing arguments by reference, any changes the Function makes to the variable are permanent. In other words, the Function can manipulate the same variable as the rest of the VB program. But, when passing arguments by value, VB just makes a copy of the variable and gives it to the Function. This is for the Function's information, but if the Function makes any changes to the variable, the changes will have no effect on the original variable. When the Function is finished, and control returns to the VB program, the variable retains its original value.

Most programming languages pass arguments by value (just a copy is passed). Visual Basic passes them by reference (the actual address of the variable is provided, so the variable can be permanently changed). If you are accessing an outside language (or an API Function), you often must pass parameters by value, which is not the VB default. To specify passing by value, you use VB's ByVal command.

Arrays and text (string) variables are always passed by reference, the VB default. So you can simply pass them, as in

```
Declare Function APIFunction% Lib "GDI" (MyVarNam$)
```

or

```
Declare Function APIFunction% Lib "GDI" (MyVarNam As String)
```

But you must use ByVal to pass an integer:

```
Declare Function APIFunction% Lib "GDI" (ByVal MyVarNam →
As Integer)
```

### You Must Conform

Note also that each API Function expects parameters to be passed either by value or by reference. This isn't something you can change just by the way you list the parameters when calling the API Function. You must conform to the API's expectations.

You cannot pass an argument by reference when the DLL expects it by value, and vice versa. Of course, any given API Function might want both kinds of passing:

```
Declare Function PixelRGB% Lib "\MYDLLS\GRAPHDLL.DLL" →
(ByVal X As Integer, ByVal Y As Integer, R As Integer, G As →
Integer, B As Integer)
```

Notice that we can omit ByRef (with R As Integer, etc.) since *by reference* is the VB default.

This above all: copy Declares accurately.

Most important, type in the Declare statements accurately—get the variable types correct, and insert the ByVal command wherever it appears in the book, magazine or other reference from which you are copying the Declare.

## If You Have Trouble

If you have problems in the examples in this chapter, be sure you've included the % or & (or As Integer or As Long) in Function Declarations. Make sure you have the ByVal command if it appears in the example code in this book. Also be sure that the entire Declaration *is on a single line.*

API Function Declarations can be placed into a Module (making them default to program-wide in scope) or placed into a Form (making them only usable in that Form). In both Forms and Modules, put the Declare in the General Declarations section.

If you're still not getting the expected results from the API, check the following:

1. Proof your code: have you typed something incorrectly in the Declare statement? Have you remembered to include the ByVal command within the parameter list where necessary?
2. Is your Picture Box's AutoRedraw Property set to True? (It must be False for some of these examples to work.)
3. Are the variables you are using to call the API Function of the correct type (that is, do they match the variable types in the Declare statement)?

If the Declare says:

```
Declare FunctName% Lib "User" (n%, r&)
```

you are responsible for providing an Integer (%) for the return value, followed by parameters which are integer, then long (&), as in

```
x% = FunctName (y%, z&)
```

or

```
Dim x As Integer, y As Integer, Z As Long
x = FunctName (y, z)
```

## For Further Information

The most immediate source of help is, not surprisingly, pressing F1 to get help. There is no direct API help from VB, but it's easy enough to locate. The Professional Edition of VB comes with two API help files. From within VB, press F1 to get to the Help window. Then click on the File menu, then the Open option (or press Alt+F, O). Now you can browse your VB directory looking for HLP files to load.

Here are a few other resources:

- *Microsoft Windows Programmer's Reference* (Microsoft Press). This giant book is the most exhaustive reference book to the API. It contains all the API routines listed alphabetically. It also provides a complete list of Constants for use with the API, and data structures. (The descriptions of how to use each API routine are a bit cryptic to the Basic programmer. They are written for programmers wrestling with the C language.)
- *Visual Basic Programmer's Guide to the API* (Ziff-Davis Press). This is an excellent reference book on the API specifically written for the VB programmer. The primary value of the book is that it presents the API Functions and Subs in VB syntax. The author also describes the utility of the API Functions to the VB programmer. It includes a disk with complete Declare statements as well as Constants and structures. The book has few examples, and for most of the API calls you are left on your own to work out precisely how to incorporate a particular procedure. Nonetheless, this book is essential for a VB programmer interested in utilizing the API.

## NEW IN VB4

There are a few things to be aware of when translating API calls from their 16-bit versions that work with VB3 under Windows 3.x and their 32-bit versions that work with VB4 32-bit under Windows 95. For the correct syntax for 32-bit API calls, you can cut and paste them from the file WIN32API.TXT supplied with VB4. However, here is a list of the four main adjustments to make when turning a 16-bit Windows 3.x API Declare into a 32-bit Windows 95 Declare:

- The primary change is that a library name gets "32" appended to it. Often, this is all you have to do to make a Windows 3.x API call work for Windows 95:

  ```
  Declare Sub BringWindowToTop Lib "User" (ByVal hwnd%)
  ```

  becomes:

  ```
  Declare Sub BringWindowToTop Lib "User32" (ByVal hwnd%)
  ```

- Also, if an API Function is an Integer type, it generally becomes a Long type under Windows 95:

  ```
  Declare Function GetCaretBlinkTime Lib "User" ( ) As Integer
  ```

becomes

```
Declare Function GetCaretBlinkTime Lib "User32" ( ) As Long
```

or the alternative syntax:

```
Declare Function GetCaretBlinkTime& Lib "User32" ( )
```

(The type symbol is appended to the Function name.)

- If arguments also change from Integer to Long, you must make that change as well. For example,

```
Declare Function arc% Lib "GDI" (ByVal hDC%, ByVal →
xa%, ByVal ya%, ByVal xb%, ByVal yb%, ByVal xc%, →
ByVal yc%, ByVal xd%, ByVal yd%)
```

changes to

```
Declare Function Arc Lib "gdi32" (ByVal hDC As Long, →
ByVal X1 As Long, ByVal Y1 As Long, ByVal X2 As →
Long, ByVal Y2 As Long, ByVal X3 As Long, ByVal Y3 →
As Long, ByVal X4 As Long, ByVal Y4 As Long) As Long
```

However, it doesn't matter if you permit the return variable to be an Integer, when you *call* a Long Function. For example,

```
x% = GetCaretBlinkTime( )
```

will work as well as

```
x&= GetCaretBlinkTime( )
```

- The final adjustment is required when you are working with 32-bit API calls involving text ("string") variables. You append an "A" to the name of the API procedure to indicate that this is an ASCII code text. Windows 95 works with the new 2-byte character code called UniCode, whereas ASCII holds each character code in a single byte.

```
Declare Function SystemParametersInfo% Lib "User" →
(ByVal Action As Integer, ByVal Param As Integer, →
Returned As Any, ByVal ChangeIni As Integer)
```

changes to

```
Declare Function SystemParametersInfo Lib "user32"  →
Alias "SystemParametersInfoA" (ByVal uAction As Long,  →
ByVal uParam As Long, lpvParam As Any, ByVal fuWinIni  →
As Long) As Long
```

### Where To Put Them

Another difference: whereas in VB3 you could put Declares into a Form's General Declarations section, in VB4 32-bit, put them in a Module. Otherwise, you'll get a mystery error message: "Constants, Fixed-length strings and arrays not allowed as public members of a Class Module." Since you're not using any Constants or strings or arrays here, nor are you in a Class Module, you might well pause when you see this message. (Perhaps it has been fixed, but at the time of this writing you'll get that message.) If you do want to put your Declare into the General Declarations section of a Form, add the word Private to the start of the Declare, as in the line

```
Private Declare Function GetCaretBlinkTime Lib "User32" ( )  →
As Long
```

and all will be well.

# SECTION 2: API FUNCTIONS

The rest of this chapter lists API Functions by name and purpose or technique. The Functions appear in these categories:

- Bitmapped Graphics
- Drawing & Geometric Graphics
- Manipulating Windows
- General Programming Utilities
- Managing INI Files
- Video & Animation
- Music & Sound

## Bitmapped Graphics

Before getting into API graphics, we'll briefly digress to explain *hDC* and *hWnd*, two variables that often appear in API calls that manipulate images. The hDC is the "handle"—a unique ID number assigned to the screen, printer or other "surface" on which the computer can create visual effects. Windows itself assigns these ID numbers, and Forms and Controls can be identified as part of an hDC.

Handles are used when you access the API to create graphics effects. Technically speaking, the hDC is not a handle assigned to a particular Form or Control per se. Rather, the hDC is a handle to what in Windows is called the "device context." A device context describes a drawing surface and its capabilities (in the case of VB, this surface is the entire video screen).

The hWnd, by contrast, is the actual handle to a particular Form or Control (in other words, hWnd is a locale within the larger space of the hDC). Although they are called Properties, hDC and hWnd are actually Windows Variables. You cannot change them; you can only "pass" them when you are calling an API Subroutine. Also, the hDC is assumed to be dynamic (it can change at any time while Windows is active), so you should not put the value of hDC into a Variable and then try to use that Variable later when calling the API. Always use the hDC itself in your API call, in case the hDC has changed.

Now, on to the API graphics calls.

### StretchBlt( ): Distorting Images

The first step when using an API function is to declare it. *A declare statement must be on a single line—do not press the Enter key until you have typed in all the parameters inside the parentheses.* We're going to manipulate some BMP files. The best API function for this task is called StretchBlt—it can transform a Picture Box or Form Pictures in hundreds of ways.

So, in the General Declarations section of the Form where you want to use the Function (or in the General Declarations section of a Module, to be able to use it anywhere in the program), type in the following declaration. Remember, always type a Declare on a single line:

```
Declare Function StretchBlt% Lib "GDI" (ByVal hDC%, ByVal →
x%, ByVal Y%, ByVal nWidth%, ByVal nHeight%, ByVal →
hsourceDC%, ByVal Xsource%, ByVal Ysource%, ByVal →
nsourceWidth%, ByVal nsourceHeight%, ByVal dwRop&)
```

(For VB4 32-bit, use **"GDI32"** instead of **"GDI"**.)

Set a Form's Picture Property to the name of a BMP file that you have on your hard drive somewhere. Now, put a Picture Box on the Form. In Figure 8-1, we made the Picture Box about half the size of the Form, and placed it on the right side. You can do what you want; we're going to illustrate how to manipulate the various parameters of the StretchBlt Function to get the desired result. Notice, also, that the original picture—the BMP file that we loaded as the Form's Picture Property—appears on the left side and only takes up about 1/3 of the Form. If you wish, set the Form's BackColor Property to black, or whatever color matches the background of your BMP picture. In our example, it's black.

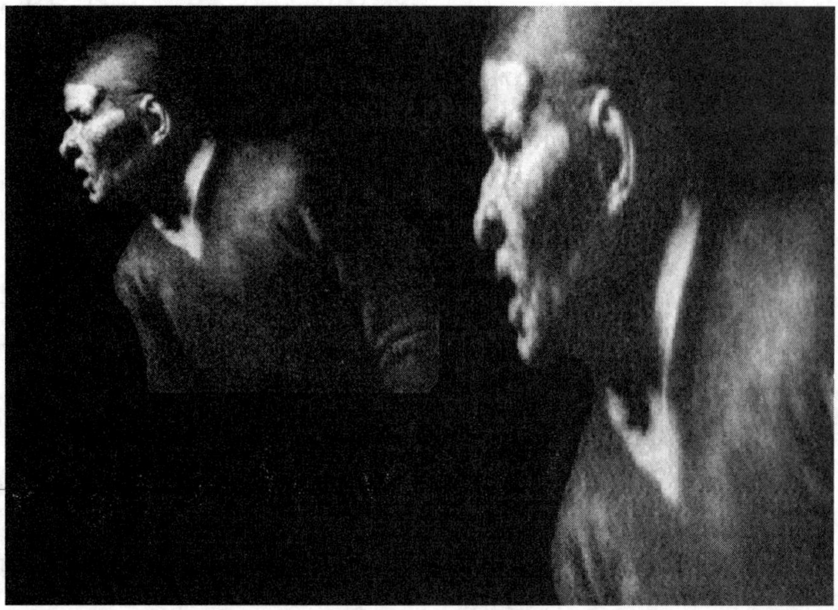

Figure 8-1: The picture on the left is simultaneously enlarged and elongated into the Picture Box on the right.

To get an effect similar to Figure 8-1, type the following into your Form's Click Event. Again, be sure that the entire function description (the line that starts with x% = StretchBlt) is *on a single line*:

```
Sub Form_Click ( )
form1.ScaleMode = 3
picture1.ScaleMode = 3

copymode& = &HCC0020
srcwid% = form1.ScaleWidth / 3
srchgt% = form1.ScaleHeight / 1.5 - 150
destwid% = picture1.ScaleWidth
desthgt% = picture1.ScaleHeight

x% = StretchBlt(picture1.hDC, 0, 0, destwid%, desthgt%, →
form1.hDC, 30, 50, srcwid%, srchgt%, copymode&)

End Sub
```

### Change VB's Default Twips to Pixels

The first thing required by StretchBlt is that the ScaleMode of the source picture (the Form) and the destination picture (the Picture Box) be set to Pixels. Then, we describe the "copymode," one of the parameters expected when we call this Function. CopyMode tells the API just *how* we want the image copied (x-ray, black, OR, white, XOR and 10 other options). You can find the various CopyModes listed with all the other API constants in a file included with VB called WINAPI.TXT (or WIN32API.TXT). Also look in the Help file called WIN31WH.HLP included with the Professional Edition of VB4.

Table 8-1 lists the possible CopyModes:

```
Global Const SRCCOPY = &HCC0020 ' (DWORD) dest = source
Global Const SRCPAINT = &HEE0086 ' (DWORD) dest = source →
OR dest
Global Const SRCAND = &H8800C6 ' (DWORD) dest = source →
AND dest
Global Const SRCINVERT = &H660046 ' (DWORD) dest = source →
XOR dest
Global Const SRCERASE = &H440328 ' (DWORD) dest = source →
AND (NOT dest )
Global Const NOTSRCCOPY = &H330008 ' (DWORD) dest = (NOT →
source)
```

```
Global Const NOTSRCERASE = &H1100A6 ' (DWORD) dest = (NOT →
src) AND (NOT dest)
Global Const MERGECOPY = &HC000CA ' (DWORD) dest = →
(source AND pattern)
Global Const MERGEPAINT = &HBB0226 ' (DWORD) dest = →
(NOT source) OR dest
Global Const PATCOPY = &HF00021 ' (DWORD) dest = pattern
Global Const PATPAINT = &HFB0A09 ' (DWORD) dest = DPSnoo
Global Const PATINVERT = &H5A0049 ' (DWORD) dest = →
pattern XOR dest
Global Const DSTINVERT = &H550009 ' (DWORD) dest = →
(NOT dest)
Global Const BLACKNESS = &H42& ' (DWORD) dest = BLACK
Global Const WHITENESS = &HFF0062 ' (DWORD) dest = WHITE
```

Table 8-1: Possible CopyModes.

If you load the WINAPI.TXT file into your Visual Basic program, you can use the words like SRCCOPY instead of the actual values:

```
copymode& = SRCCOPY
```

Some say that CONSTANT.TXT is more trouble than it's worth.

However, many programmers find all this loading of Constant definitions more trouble than it's worth (VB has its own set of constants in a file called CONSTANT.TXT, which contains descriptive translations for such things as the QBCOLORs and so on.) Likewise, you can press F2 in VB4 and look under "Constants" in the VB or VBA Libraries. These Constant definitions are built into VB4. However, you can just look up the CopyMode you are interested in (in the WINAPI.TXT file) and assign the actual numeric code, as we did above:

```
copymode& = &HCC0020
```

The following four lines in our program tell StretchBlt the piece of the original (source) picture we want copied

```
srcwid% = form1.ScaleWidth / 3
srchgt% = form1.ScaleHeight / 1.5 - 150
```

and the part of the destination picture into which we want that image placed:

```
destwid% = picture1.ScaleWidth
desthgt% = picture1.ScaleHeight
```

### Sizing the Image

Because, in this example, our Form happens to be larger than the picture we put into its Picture Property—we set the source width and height to a fraction of the Form's actual size. This way, StretchBlt will only copy the region within the Form where the picture actually exists. We won't copy extraneous background from the Form. The picture is about one-third as wide as the Form, so we describe the source-width (srcwid%) as the ScaleWidth (the Form, minus its frame), divided by 3. The height of the picture within the Form is similarly shaved off the total ScaleHeight. You can just repeatedly type in different subtractions or divisions, then run the program by pressing F5—until you get the right size, the amount of the Form you want copied.

We want the entire Picture Box filled with the image, so we set the destination width and height (destwid%, desthgt%) to the actual full ScaleWidth and ScaleHeight of the Picture Box. Setting it higher or lower than the dimensions of the Picture Box would result in the following:

Figure 8-2: With the destination width higher than the container, we simply blow up the picture, without distortion (destwid% = picture1.ScaleWidth + 300).

Figure 8-3: With the destination height higher than the container, we distort the picture (desthgt% = picture1.ScaleHeight + 500).

Gain unlimited flexibility.

The effects in figures 7-2 and 7-3 are *relative*. The amount and direction of any stretching is a factor of the ratio between the height and width of the source and destination container. Therefore, unless you're Isaac Newton and can do complicated math in your head—just try different adjustments until you get the result you want.

Finally, after all the parameters have been defined, we call the API Function itself and, bam! The man in the Form is copied to the Picture Box. How fast is it, compared to the VB approach, if we are just copying?

In VB, you can make a direct one-for-one copy of the graphic faster:

```
Picture1.Picture = Form1.Picture
```

This VB approach takes .077 seconds; the API call takes .511 seconds. So it's not speed that we gain, this time, by calling on the API. Instead, it's unlimited flexibility in transforming, distorting and resizing the image.

## NEW IN VB4

With VB4, the capabilities of StretchBlt and BitBlt are provided by a new VB command: PaintPicture. With PaintPicture, you can avoid the necessity to Declare the API Function, and you can leave out setting the ScaleModes of the source and target objects. The same arguments are used, but in a somewhat different order. The target is the first item you mention, as an "object" prepended to the word PaintPicture and separated by a dot: Picture1.PaintPicture, for example. Also, the *source* of the copied graphic is the first argument (Form1.Picture, for example). The rest is the same.

Here's how to reproduce the results shown in Figure 8-1, but using PaintPicture instead of StretchBlt:

You must fiddle some with the source width and height because the measurement is in the default ScaleMode, Twips. (We don't have to change it to Pixels as we did for StretchBlt):

```
srcwid% = Form1.ScaleWidth / 2
srchgt% = Form1.ScaleHeight / 2

Picture1.PaintPicture Form1.Picture, 0, 0, destwid%, →
desthgt%, 30, 50, srcwid%, srchgt%, copymode&
```

Interestingly, PaintPicture is about five times as fast as StretchBlt when accomplishing Figure 8-1. However, they're both faster than the eye, so the extra speed doesn't, for most applications, matter. We measured them by having each technique transfer the picture 10,000 times. StretchBlt took 361 seconds, PaintPicture 65 seconds.

### GetDeskTopWindow & ArrangeIconicWindows: Arranging Icons

These two routines cause all icons on the Windows desktop to line up along the bottom. If any have been moved around on the desktop, they will be moved and arranged along the bottom.

In General Declarations:

```
Declare Function ArrangeIconicWindows Lib "User" (ByVal →
hWnd%) As Integer
Declare Function GetDeskTopWindow Lib "User" ( ) As Integer
```

In an Event:

```
Sub Command1_Click ( )
    n% = GetDeskTopWindow( )
    x% = ArrangeIconicWindows(n%)
End Sub
```

(For VB4 32-bit: Windows 95 doesn't utilize this routine.)

### BringWindowToTop( ): Bring a Window to Top

If you want a particular Form or Window to be on top of anything else on screen, use this technique. Create two Forms, then in Form1, type this:

In General Declarations:

```
Declare Sub BringWindowToTop Lib "User" (ByVal hwnd%)
```

(For VB4 32-bit: change **"User"** to **"User32"**.)

In an Event (in Form1):

```
Sub Form_Load
    Form2.Show
End Sub

Sub Form_Click ( )
    BringWindowToTop Form2.hWnd
End Sub
```

### RoundRect( ): Rounded Rectangles

You can round off the corners of any rectangle to any amount.

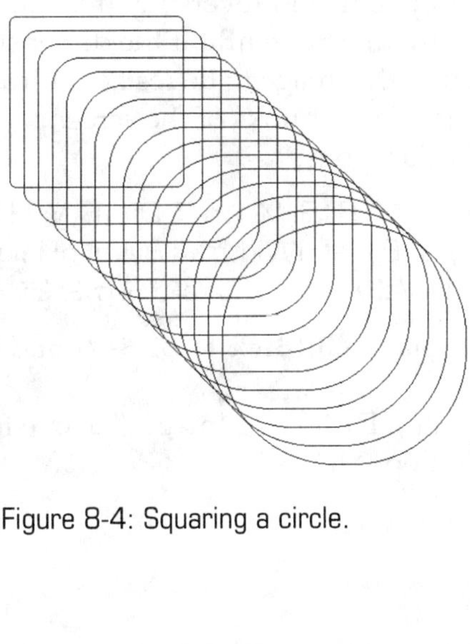

Figure 8-4: Squaring a circle.

In General Declarations (all on a single line, remember):

```
Declare Function RoundRect Lib "GDI" (ByVal hdc As Integer, →
ByVal X1 As Integer, ByVal Y1 As Integer, ByVal X2 As →
Integer, ByVal Y2 As Integer, ByVal X3 As Integer, ByVal →
Y3 As Integer) As Integer
```

(For VB4 32-bit, change **"GDI"** to **"GDI32"** and change the final **As Integer** to **As Long**.)

In an Event:

```
Sub Form_Click ( )

For i = 200 To 500 Step 20
    j = j + 15
    x% = RoundRect(hdc, i, i, j, j, j, j)
Next i

End Sub
```

(For VB4 32-bit, change **x%** to **x&**.)

The parameters here are the hdc of the Form (or Picture Box) on which you want to draw. Then follow three paired sets: the x,y location (using Pixels as the ScaleMode—all API calls do) of the upper left corner of the rectangle; the x,y location of the lower right corner of the rectangle; the width, height of the rounded corner (this describes the amount of curvature).

### BitBlt( ): High-Speed Copying

BitBlt is a fast way to move graphics.

The BitBlt API Function can copy any section of the screen to anywhere else on the screen. It can also transform images in a variety of ways, such as stretching and reversing. It is quite similar to StretchBlt and, in fact, will invoke StretchBlt if the dimensions you supply as parameters require the image to be resized. BitBlt, though, is usually the fastest way to move chunks of the screen.

In General Declarations:

```
Declare Function BitBlt% Lib "GDI" (ByVal hDestDC%, ByVal →
x%, ByVal y%, ByVal nWidth%, ByVal nHeight%, ByVal →
hSrcDC%, ByVal XSrc%, ByVal YSrc%, ByVal CopyMode&)
```

(For VB4 32-bit, change **BitBlt%** to **BitBlt&** and change **"GDI"** to **"GDI32"**.)

(See "StretchBlt( ): Distorting Images" above for a table of the various possible CopyModes.)

We've put two Picture Boxes on a Form. You could use an Image Box or some other Control, but you'd have to use the Form's hDC and describe the location of the Control (rather than using the Control's hDC Property). An Image Box, for instance, has no hDC Property).

The simplest copying is a direct one-for-one copy:

```
Sub Form_Click ( )

CopyMode& = &HCC0020

x% = BitBlt(picture2.hDC, 0, 0, picture2.Width, →
picture2.Height, picture1.hDC, 0, 0, CopyMode&)

End Sub
```

(For VB4 32-bit, change **x%** to **x&**.)

### Parameter Order Is Often Counterintuitive

Notice that some API Functions require parameters listed in counter-intuitive order (wouldn't you know!). Humans normally think of source and destination.

However, in the parameter list you first provide the *destination* hDC, then the offset in the *destination* from the upper left corner of the destination object. In this case, our destination is Picture2 and we want the copy to reside right up at the top and right against the left of Picture 2 (we're just making a direct copy, so we don't want any offset).

Then you provide the dimensions of the item to be copied. In this case, we have equal-sized Picture Boxes, so we can use the Width and Height of Picture2. Finally, identify the *source* hDC, and any desired offset in the *source* from the upper left corner of the source object. Then, you name the copy-mode, in this case a simple source = destination style of copying.

Figure 8-5: Direct copy so fast you cannot measure the elapsed time.

### Time Trials

Interestingly, using the API BitBlt to copy one Picture Box to another is much faster than using the VB equivalent:

```
picture2.Picture = picture1.Image
```

The first time you try the VB approach in this example on our test machine, it takes 1.76 seconds. Thereafter it goes down to .178 seconds. However, the first time you use the API approach, it takes .055, and thereafter 0 seconds—it's immeasurably fast.

The API isn't just faster than VB in this operation—it can also do hundreds of things that VB simply cannot do. (However, see "StretchBlt( ): Distorting Images" at the start of this section for a discussion of VB4's new ultra-swift PaintPicture method.)

Figure 8-6: BEFORE. We'll BitBlt into this texture.

Figure 8-7: AFTER. The two images are combined, superimposed with translucence.

If you put a texture into the target Picture Box and set the CopyMode parameter to CopyMode& = &HEE0086 (dest = source OR dest), you'll get a blended effect, as in Figure 8-7. This is a way to "texturize" images. (See Chapter 7 for more on textures.)

Figure 8-8: BEFORE. We'll XOR these two images.

Figure 8-9: AFTER. This eerie, negative superimposition transforms the birds into *bats*.

The effect in Figure 8-9 is achieved by changing the CopyMode& parameter to the API Constant "SRCINVERT": CopyMode& = &H660046.

Figure 8-10: You can also copy and manipulate an area *outside* a VB Form.

Copy anything you can see onscreen via BitBlt.

In Figure 8-10, we've copied part of the Windows *desktop* itself; the VB button bar shows up, in addition to our man. BitBlt isn't limited to VB and the Forms it creates. You can copy Controls, the Windows desktop—anything that's onscreen. Clearly, this is how you would write a "snapshot" feature that would take a screen shot, then allow the user to save it. Your program can specify which Forms, Controls, or any other rectangle on the currently visible screen will be captured.

### Using Negative Coordinates

To achieve the beyond-the-Form capture in Figure 8-10, you can merely make the source rectangle coordinates negative:

```
x% = BitBlt(picture2.hDC, 0, 0, picture2.Width, →
picture2.Height, picture1.hDC, -100, -100, CopyMode&)
```

## Drawing & Geometric Graphics

### Arc( ), Chord( ), Pie( ), Ellipse( ): Drawing Arcs, Chords & Pies

The changes indicated below for Arc using VB4 32-bit apply as well to all the following geometric API calls.

An ellipse is a round shape, but it need not be a perfect circle. An arc is a segment of an ellipse; the lines don't connect. A chord is an enclosed arc and a pie shape is an enclosed arc that has a wedge taken out of it.

To draw an arc:
In General Declarations:

```
Declare Function arc% Lib "GDI" (ByVal hDC%, ByVal xa%, →
ByVal ya%, ByVal xb%, ByVal yb%, ByVal xc%, ByVal yc%, →
ByVal xd%, ByVal yd%)
```

(For VB4 32-bit, change **"GDI"** to **"GDI32"** and change all % symbols to **&**.)

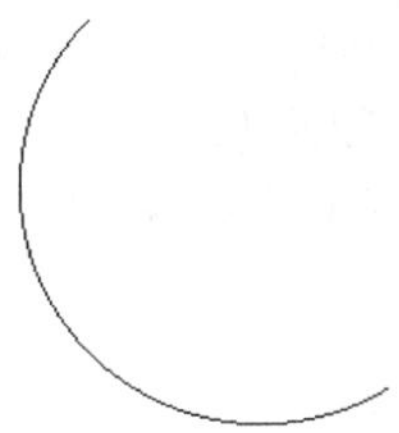

Figure 8-11: Drawing an Arc.

In an Event:

```
Sub Form_Load ( )

Show

z% = arc(form1.hDC, 50, 50, 260, 260, 114, 115, 164, →
170)

End Sub
```

To draw a Chord:
In General Declarations:

```
Declare Function chord% Lib "GDI" (ByVal hDC%, ByVal xa%, →
ByVal ya%, ByVal xb%, ByVal yb%, ByVal xc%, ByVal yc%, →
ByVal xd%, ByVal yd%)
```

In an Event:

```
Sub Form_Load ( )
Show

z% = chord(form1.hDC, 50, 50, 260, 260, 114, 115, →
164, 170)

End Sub
```

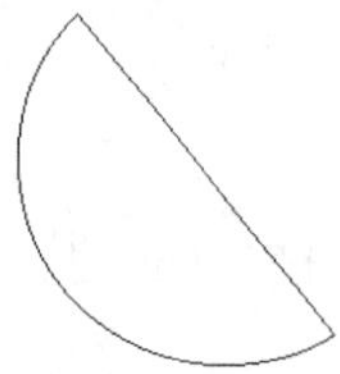

Figure 8-12: Drawing a chord.

To draw a Pie:
In General Declarations:

```
Declare Function Pie% Lib "GDI" (ByVal hDC%, ByVal xa%, →
ByVal ya%, ByVal xb%, ByVal yb%, ByVal xc%, ByVal yc%, →
ByVal xd%, ByVal yd%)
```

In an Event:

```
Sub Form_Load ( )
Show

z% = pie(form1.hDC, 50, 50, 260, 260, 114, 115, 164, →
170)

End Sub
```

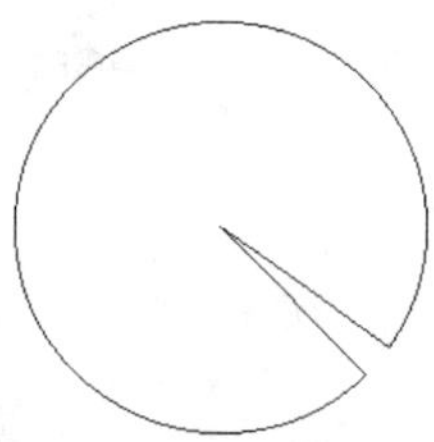

Figure 8-13: Drawing a pie shape.

To draw an Ellipse:
In General Declarations:

```
Declare Function Ellipse% Lib "GDI" (ByVal hDC%, ByVal xa%, →
ByVal ya%, ByVal xb%, ByVal yb%)
```

In an Event:

```
Sub Form_Load ( )
Show
z% = Ellipse(form1.hDC, 50, 50, 100, 260)

End Sub
```

Figure 8-14: Drawing an ellipse.

Note that arc, chord and pie shapes are based on the ellipse shape. The parameters for an ellipse are essentially the same as those you provide to describe a rectangle—the four corners: x (horizontal), y (vertical) for the upper-left location, followed by another x (horizontal), y (vertical) for the lower-right location. These four parameters construct an imaginary rectangle, and the ellipse is fitted within that rectangle—it "bumps" the four sides of the imaginary rectangle.

So an ellipse has four parameters. The arc, chord and pie shapes must have an additional four parameters specifying the coordinates of the start and end of their deformation of the basic ellipse. An arc's final four parameters specify where to start and end the piece of the ellipse that will be cut out of the ellipse. A chord is merely an arc with a line drawn between the breaks in the ellipse's line. A pie shape is a chord with the line drawn between the breaks and the center of the ellipse.

## DrawFocusRect( ): Draw a "Focus Band"

Figure 8-15: The Image on the left has the "focus." This is a good way to highlight Controls that don't have a TabIndex Property.

Adding a focus band is yet another way to cue the user.

It is a convention in Windows that when something has the "focus" (is the window or Control that will react if the user types something on the keyboard)—this focus is usually illustrated to the user by a surrounding, dotted line. (Other Controls show focus by turning their captions boldface, etc.) Many Controls, though, like the Images in Figure 8-19, don't get the focus (cannot be typed into). However, if you were building a database for BMP graphic files, for example, adding this focus band would be a good way of indicating to the user which file was most recently loaded or otherwise manipulated by your application.

If you want to create a "focus rectangle," do this:

In a Module:

```
Type rect
    x1 As Integer
    y1 As Integer
    x2 As Integer
    y2 As Integer
End Type

Declare Sub DrawFocusRect Lib "User" (ByVal hdc As Integer, →
rectang As rect)
```

(For VB4 32-bit, change all five occurrences of **As Integer** to **As Long** and change **"User"** to **"User32"**.)

In a Form's General Declarations:

```
Dim lprect As rect
```

In an Event:

```
Sub Form_Click ( )
scalemode = 3
'defines the rectangle
lprect.x1 = image1.Left - 10
lprect.y1 = image1.Top - 10
lprect.x2 = lprect.x1 + image1.Width + 20
lprect.y2 = lprect.y1 + image1.Height + 20

DrawFocusRect form1.hDC, lprect

End Sub
```

Note that since we are calculating the position of the rectangle based on a Control, we want our Form's ScaleMode to match the scalemode used by the API (3-Pixels rather than the VB Default, 1-Twips).

## LineTo( ): Draw a Line

For drawing applications, to underline things—whenever you want to draw a line on a VB Form (or any Control that has an hDC Property)—use the LineTo Function.

In General Declarations:

```
Declare Function LineTo% Lib "GDI" (ByVal hDC%, ByVal x%, →
ByVal y%)
```

(For VB4 32-bit, change all four % symbols to **&** and change **"GDI"** to **"GDI32"**.)

In an Event:

```
Sub Form_Load ( )
Show

For i% = 1 To 500 Step 100
    For j% = 1 To 200 Step 5
        z% = LineTo(form1.hDC, i%, j%)
Next j%, i%

End Sub
```

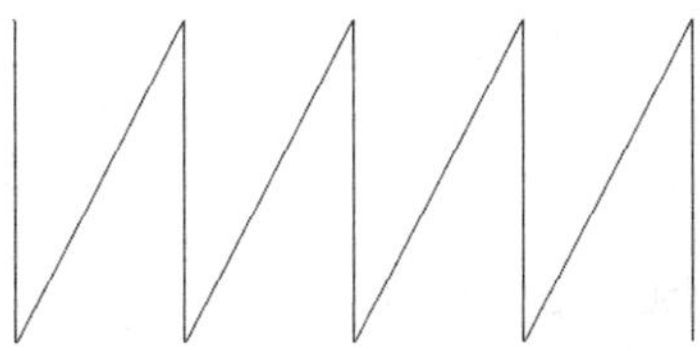

Figure 8-16: Draw lines anywhere with the LineTo Function.

## Rectangle( ): Regular Rectangles

You can draw any rectangle (see "RoundRect( ): Rounded Rectangles" above for another technique).

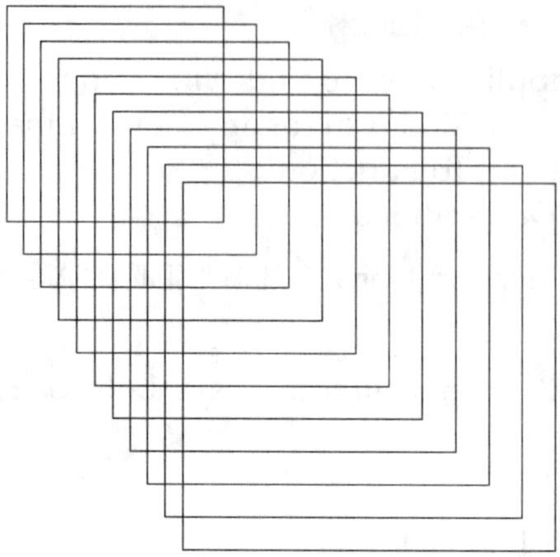

Figure 8-17: Rectangles of any size, in any position, via the Rectangle Function.

In General Declarations:

```
Declare Function Rectangle Lib "GDI" (ByVal hdc As Integer, →
ByVal X1 As Integer, ByVal Y1 As Integer, ByVal X2 As →
Integer, ByVal Y2 As Integer) As Integer
```

(For VB4 32-bit, change all six occurrences of **As Integer** to **As Long** and change **"GDI"** to **"GDI32"**.)

In an Event:

```
Sub Form_Click ( )

For i = 200 To 500 Step 28
    j = j + 15
    x% = Rectangle(hdc, i, i, j, j)
Next i

End Sub
```

The parameters here are the hDC of the Form (or Picture Box) on which you want to draw; the x,y location of the upper left corner of the rectangle; and the x,y location of the lower right corner of the rectangle.

## Manipulating Windows

### ExitWindows( ): Going to DOS

Windows expects you to exit through a series of queries: "This will shut down Windows" and so on. You can obviate this by calling ExitWindows from the API.

Also, if you are permitting the user to reset his video resolution or other Windows defaults, from within your VB program, set the "code&" parameter to 66 (decimal) and Windows will go to DOS, then restart. (There isn't any danger here that you can shut down Windows without giving running applications a chance to properly close, prompting the user to save any modified files within them. This API call permits applications to close gracefully.)

In General Declarations:

```
Declare Function ExitWindows% Lib "User" (ByVal code&, →
ByVal nonsense%)
```

(*Note:* This API call has been removed in Windows 95.)

In an Event:

```
Sub Form_Load ( )

'67 causes a warm reboot.
'66 causes a trip down into DOS, then back to Windows.
'the second parameter, 0, does nothing.

x% = ExitWindows(66, 0)

End Sub
```

### GetCaretBlinkTime( ) & GetDoubleClickTime( ): Caret & Double-click Timing

Get some user settings in milliseconds.

To find out the user's current settings for the blinking caret (the vertical line that shows the insertion point in text documents) and the double-click speed (as set by the user in Windows Control Panel), these API calls return the time in milliseconds):

In General Declarations:

```
Declare Function GetCaretBlinkTime Lib "User" ( ) As Integer

Declare Function GetDoubleClickTime Lib "User" ( ) As Integer
```

(For VB4 32-bit, change **As Integer** to **As Long** and change **"User"** to **"User32"**.)

In an Event:

```
Sub Form_Load ( )
    x% = GetCaretBlinkTime( )
    y% = GetDoubleClickTime( )
MsgBox "CaretBlink = " & x% & " DoubleClick = " & y%
End Sub
```

To change these settings:
In General Declarations:

```
Declare Sub SetCaretBlinkTime Lib "User" (ByVal Timing%)
Declare Sub SetDoubleClickTime Lib "User" (ByVal Timing%)
```

(For VB4 32-bit, change % to **&** and change **"User"** to **"User32"**.)
In an Event:

```
Sub Form_Load ( )

    SetCaretBlinkTime 500
    SetDoubleClickTime 500

End Sub
```

## SystemParametersInfo( ): Read/Change Windows Options

The Windows Control Panel allows the user to read or adjust various aspects of Windows behavior—should icon titles wrap or be truncated? How many minutes should elapse before the screen saver clicks in? Here is a list of these settings and the codes you use to GET or SET them.

### Action: Setting & Getting

The Action parameter (the name we've given the first parameter in the SystemParametersInfo% API Function used in the following two examples) can have any of the following values. "SET" means change a WIN.INI definition; "GET" means find out how it's currently set. So, to find out, to "GET," the current keyboard speed settings for example, you would use 10 for the Action parameter:

```
GETBEEP=1
SETBEEP=2
GETMOUSE=3
```

```
SETMOUSE=4
GETBORDER=5
SETBORDER=6
GETKEYBOARDSPEED=10
SETKEYBOARDSPEED=11
LANGDRIVER=12
ICONHORIZONTALSPACING=13
GETSCREENSAVETIMEOUT=14
SETSCREENSAVETIMEOUT=15
GETSCREENSAVEACTIVE=16
SETSCREENSAVEACTIVE=17
GETGRIDGRANULARITY=18
SETGRIDGRANULARITY=19
SETDESKWALLPAPER=20
SETDESKPATTERN=21
GETKEYBOARDDELAY=22
SETKEYBOARDDELAY=23
ICONVERTICALSPACING=24
GETICONTITLEWRAP=25
SETICONTITLEWRAP=26
GETMENUDROPALIGNMENT=27
SETMENUDROPALIGNMENT=28
SETDOUBLECLKWIDTH=29
SETDOUBLECLKHEIGHT=30
GETICONTITLELOGFONT=31
SETDOUBLECLICKTIME=32
SETMOUSEBUTTONSWAP=33
SETICONTITLELOGFONT=34
GETFASTTASKSWITCH=35
SETFASTTASKSWITCH=36
```

Table 8-2: Values of the Action parameter.

Our first example will find out ("GET") how many seconds of screen activity will elapse before the screen saver kicks in:

In General Declarations:

```
Declare Function SystemParametersInfo% Lib "User" (ByVal →
Action As Integer, ByVal param As Integer, Returned As Any, →
ByVal ChangeIni As Integer)
```

## NEW IN VB4 32-BIT

Although WIN.INI and SYSTEM.INI are present in Windows 95, they are only tolerated—so that 16-bit Windows 3.x programs won't crash when looking for information in these files. Windows 95 programs are expected to store their initialization details (user customization, location of special files on the hard drive, etc.) within the immense Registry. This behemoth starts out as about 75% of a megabyte and grows and grows.

In any case, the SystemParameterInfo API call has been adjusted to work with the Registry, so you don't have to concern yourself with the new target for application and system data. All you have to do to use SystemParameterInfo is to change the Declare to:

```
Declare Function SystemParametersInfo Lib "user32" Alias →
"SystemParametersInfoA" (ByVal uAction As Long, ByVal →
uParam As Long, lpvParam As Any, ByVal fuWinIni As Long) →
As Long
```

Now let's look at some of the things you can do with SystemParameterInfo in either a 16-bit or 32-bit context.

The Action parameter should be set to one of the codes listed above. When you are getting information, the second parameter, *param*, should be 0. When you are setting (changing) one of the settings, *param* should be the new value that you want (for instance, if you want the SCREENSAVETIMEOUT to wait for 9 minutes of inactivity before activating the screen saver, you would enter 540 as the param—60 seconds * 9). If you are *getting* information, not changing it, make *param* a zero.

The *Returned* parameter is quite strange. Most functions return their information in the x% in the following way:

```
x% = FunctName (param1, param2)
```

So to see the results of calling a normal Function, you would:

```
Print x%
```

However, this SystemParametersInfo Function returns information *in a parameter variable,* the parameter we've named *Returned.* So, even

You must remember to Dim the returned value.

if you use literals like 14, 0, or 0& for the other parameters, use a variable name for *Returned* and also, be sure to Dim *Returned*, or you can cause a GPF crash. Also, remember to use or display the value in *Returned* rather than the usual x%.

Here's how to find out how many minutes of inactivity are to elapse before the user's screen saver activates:

In an Event:

```
Sub Form_Load ( )

Show
Dim Returned As Long

x% = SystemParametersInfo(14, 0, Returned, 0)
Print Returned

End Sub
```

This results in 600 (if the user's screen timeout is set to 10 minutes).

### Changing a Setting

You can use SystemParametersInfo to change the settings as well as to read them. You first set the appropriate Action parameter (see Table 8-2 and find the code for SETKEYBOARDSPEED, which is 11). Then, you provide the actual value of the change. If we wanted to make the keyboard repeat rate as fast as possible, we would make Param 30, because the keyboard rate can range from 0 to 30. In this case, the *Returned* parameter does nothing. However, when *changing* a setting with the SystemParametersInfo Function, the final parameter, which we've called *ChangeIni*, does matter.

The final parameter makes a permanent change to the user's WIN.INI file if you use 1, notifies all applications of the change if you use 2, and makes no change to WIN.INI if you use 0. The change will remain temporary (effective during the current Windows session only) unless you set 2. If you do make the change, it's a good idea to have the API notify all applications of the change. So, you can combine setting 1 and 2—change WIN.INI and notify everyone—by using, as we do below, 3.

You can make INI changes permanent for "this session only."

### Adjusting the Repeat Rate

Here's a little applet that allows the user to adjust the keyboard repeat rate. Put a Label on a Form. This Label will always show the current setting of the keyboard rate. Put a Scroll Bar below the Label, then add a Text Box within which the user can depress a key and test the effect of any changes. Finally, put a Command Button at the bottom of the Form to permit the user to make the change permanent (by forcing it to be written to WIN.INI).

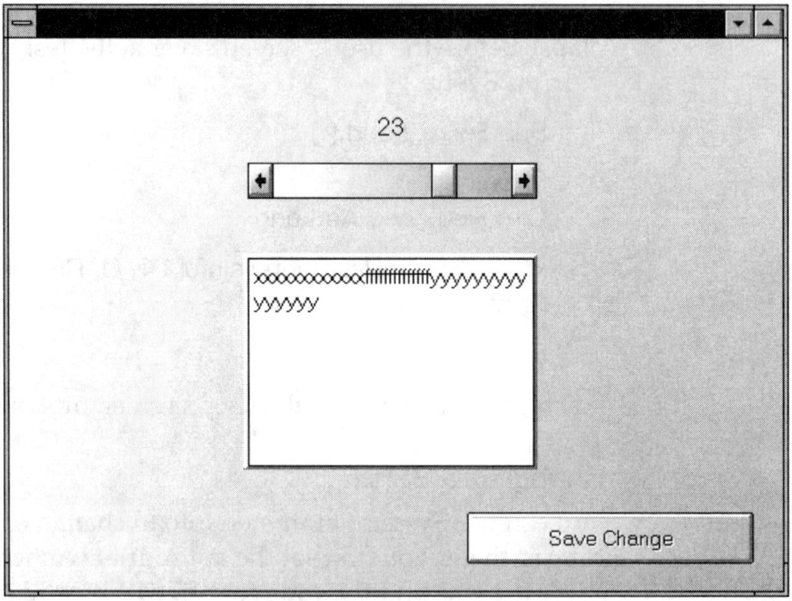


Figure 8-18: Allowing the user to change the keyboard repeat rate.

In General Declarations:

```
Declare Function SystemParametersInfo% Lib "User" (ByVal →
Action As Integer, ByVal Param As Integer, Returned As Any, →
ByVal ChangeIni As Integer)
```

In the Form_Load Event:

```
Sub Form_Load ( )
Show

HScroll1.Max = 31
Command3D1.Caption = "Save Change"

Dim Returned As Long, Param As Integer

x% = SystemParametersInfo(10, 0, Returned, 0)

Label1.Caption = Int(Returned)
HScroll1.Value = Int(Returned)

End Sub
```

Here in Form_Load, we leave the ScrollBar's minimum to the default zero, but permit its maximum to reach only 31, the upper limit of the keyboard repeat rate. Then, we find out the current WIN.INI setting, print it into the Label and set the Scroll Bar Tab to the appropriate location within the Bar.

Now, when the user changes the ScrollBar, we want the change to be made temporary (so we make the final parameter, the one called ChangeIni, zero and, therefore, no change will be written to WIN.INI):

```
Sub HScroll1_Change ( )

Dim Returned As Long, Param As Integer
Label1.Caption = HScroll1.Value

Param = HScroll1.Value

x% = SystemParametersInfo(11, Param, Returned, 0)

End Sub
```

Finally, if the user clicks on the Command Button, requesting a permanent change be written to WIN.INI, we replace the final zero with three:

```
Sub Command3D1_Click ( )

Dim Returned As Long, Param As Integer
Param = HScroll1.Value

x% = SystemParametersInfo(11, Param, Returned, 3)

End Sub
```

In the WIN.INI file, the changes you make in this fashion are then written, like this:

```
[windows]
ScreenSaveTimeOut=540
ScreenSaveActive=1
TransmissionRetryTimeout=45
device=HP LaserJet III,winspl16,LPT1:
MouseThreshold1=2
MouseThreshold2=0
MouseSpeed=1
KeyboardSpeed=30
KeyboardDelay=0
```

## GetFreeSpace( ) & GetFreeSystemResources( ): Memory & System Resources

GetFreeSystem-Resources responds three ways.

To find out how much free memory and free system resources the user currently enjoys, you can use the following two Functions. Note that GetFreeSystemResources can provide three different responses, based on the parameter described below in the comments just above the API call.

In General Declarations:

```
Declare Function GetFreeSpace& Lib "Kernel" (ByVal flag%)
Declare Function GetFreeSystemResources& Lib "User" →
(ByVal flags%)
```

(For VB4 32-bit, see "New in VB4 32-Bit" below.)

In an Event:

```
Sub Form_Load ( )
x& = GetFreeSpace(0)

' For Resources, 0 provides percentage of resources
' 1 provides GDI resources
' 2 provides User resources
y& = GetFreeSystemResources(0)

MsgBox "Free Memory = " & x& & " Free Resources = " & →
y& & "%"

End Sub
```

## NEW IN VB4 32-BIT

The GetFreeSpace and GetFreeSystemResources Windows 3.x API calls have been dropped from the Windows 95 32-bit API. Just as ExitWindows is too simple a way to shut things down in the new Windows 95 network-sensitive, multilevel, OLE- and object-capable OS, so too are such things as GetFreeSpace too simple for the complexities of Windows 95 memory management. Instead, you can get the same information (and more) by using the GlobalMemoryStatus API call in Windows 95.

In a Module, type this:

```
Type MEMORYSTATUS
   dwLength As Long
   dwMemoryLoad As Long
   dwTotalPhys As Long
   dwAvailPhys As Long
```

```
    dwTotalPageFile As Long
    dwAvailPageFile As Long
    dwTotalVirtual As Long
    dwAvailVirtual As Long
End Type

Declare Sub GlobalMemoryStatus Lib "KERNEL32" →
(lpmstMemStat As MEMORYSTATUS)
```

Then, in a Form, type this:

```
Private Sub Form_Click()
    Dim MemStat As MEMORYSTATUS
    MemStat.dwLength = Len(MemStat)
    GlobalMemoryStatus MemStat
    Print MemStat.dwMemoryLoad
    Print MemStat.dwTotalPhys
    Print MemStat.dwAvailPhys
    Print MemStat.dwTotalPageFile
    Print MemStat.dwAvailPageFile
    Print MemStat.dwTotalVirtual
    Print MemStat.dwAvailVirtual
End Sub
```

TotalPhys and AvailPhys will probably be the ones of interest. We haven't been able to locate an equivalent for GetFreeSystemResources.

### WinHelp( ): Bring Up Help Search

Many people find themselves wanting to use a HLP file's search feature, but are annoyed at having to go through the process of clicking on Search, etc. Here's how to directly bring up a Help File's search feature.

In General Declarations:

```
Declare Function WinHelp% Lib "User" (ByVal hWnd As →
Integer, ByVal HelpFileName As String, ByVal MainParam As →
Integer, ByVal param As Any)
```

In an Event:

```
Sub Form_Click ( )

Buffer$ = ""

x% = WinHelp(Form1.hWnd, "c:\vbapi\winapi\win31wh.hlp", →
261, Buffer$)

End Sub
```

The second parameter, HelpFileName, should be set to the full path of the desired Help file. The third parameter MainParam, describes how the Help file will be accessed. The code 261 goes directly to the Search feature. Here are some useful codes for MainParam:

| | |
|---|---|
| HELP_QUIT = 2 | Quit Help. Use this before shutting down your application. |
| HELP_INDEX = 3 | Show index. |
| HELP_PARTIALKEY = 261 | Go directly to Search feature. |
| HELP_HELPONHELP 4 | Show "How to Use Help." |

Table 8-3: Useful codes for MainParam.

If you want to go directly to a particular Search entry, fill Buffer$ with the target:

```
Buffer$ = "Constant"
```

## General Programming Utilities

### BitBlt( ): Instant Tiled Wallpaper on Forms

This technique using BitBlt is one of our favorites, so we've put it in the general utilities section rather than with graphics above. It's the solution to a problem that has plagued VB programmers from day one (1991) if they were trying to make their Forms more visually attractive.

#### The Problem

Forms often look nicer with a bitmapped background. A sophisticated texture is more pleasing to the eye and more professional-looking than a simple, plain background. Obviously, you want your Forms to be visually attractive as well as functional. Your competitors also are beginning to realize the value of attractive screens.

Figure 8-19: BEFORE. A plain background is boring, homely, unprofessional.

Figure 8-20: AFTER. Adding a texture often brings a window to life, but this concrete and granite adds over a million bytes to the EXE file.

A bitmapped background makes your Form much better looking, and also adds about a million bytes to the EXE file.

Until recently, most graphic design activity was focused on the title screen—the window the user sees while the program is loading itself into the computer from disk. However, more and more effort is now going into the look of all the other workhorse windows in an application.

The problem is that bitmapped graphics, although they do provide the best-looking backgrounds, take up lots of computer memory. Adding a *single* BMP graphic to a Form can inflate the final EXE file's size enormously. (Adding the color BMP to Figure 8-19, for example, increased the program's EXE file size from less than 5,000 bytes in Figure 8-19 to over a million bytes in Figure 8-20.)

And if you want a textured background on several, or all, your Forms—things can quickly get out way of hand. Nobody wants gigantically plump files. Shareware authors want to keep their EXE files a reasonable size so people will download them and try them out. In-house developers want programs to load and display quickly—particularly on those older, slower machines that most companies always seem burdened with. And everyone wants their programs to be as lean as possible so they will use up less disk space.

### The Solution

Have it both ways by tiling textures across a Form.

Windows solves this problem by permitting you to *tile* wallpaper. This technique takes a single, small, seed BMP—it can be little more than the size of an icon—then rapidly repeats it to fill the entire screen. The key word here is *rapidly*. Windows has optimized facilities for copying regions of the screen extremely quickly—so fast that you won't notice it: the screen will simply appear filled with your texture (even on older, slower 386 machines). It's the same effect that is used in movies: the individual frames move by so rapidly they appear to be fluid and instantaneous. You just don't see the separate tiles or frames. What's more, wallpaper or texture, by its very nature, repeats a graphic to fill the allotted space.

### Anything Windows Can Do

With API calls, we can theoretically do anything with our VB program that Windows can do. We can certainly tile a graphic. Here's a quick, effortless way to do it. It works in all screen resolutions, instantly filling a Form—the user never sees the effect. They won't be able to tell the difference between this technique and a full, million-byte BMP. It also works when a Form is clipped (covered by another Form or window), stretched, minimized—whatever. And, best of all, it's easy to put into your VB programs.

Because this technique is so valuable, we're going to spend several pages describing it in detail. It's quite simple, but many programmers are unfamiliar with computer graphic techniques, so we'll go through the process from start to finish, step by step.

First, where do you get a texture that will make a good wallpaper? Windows makes it easy to capture *anything* visual—anything that appears on screen can be utilized.

Choose any texture you like—fractals, captured marble—or draw your own.

1. Start any photo-retouching or image capture application (HiJaak, Paint Shop Pro, Corel PHOTO-PAINT!, Adobe's Photoshop, Micrografx's Picture Publisher, etc.).
2. Put a nice texture on screen. (Start an application that has a background you like; use one of Windows's supplied wallpapers; generate a fractal texture in Corel's Photo-Paint.) Just so about an inch or so of some texture is showing on screen. Display a texture that regularly repeats (like bathroom tiles), or is inherently fairly even (like sandpaper rather than, say, a picture of a tree—because the section you tile from a tree will end up looking like a puzzle rather than wallpaper).

Figure 8-21: You can capture a piece of "seed" tile from any texture. Here we'll use part of this starfield background.

3. Press the PrintScreen key which puts the entire screen into the clipboard.
4. Now switch to the photo-retouching program you're using. From the Edit menu, select Paste to import your screen capture.

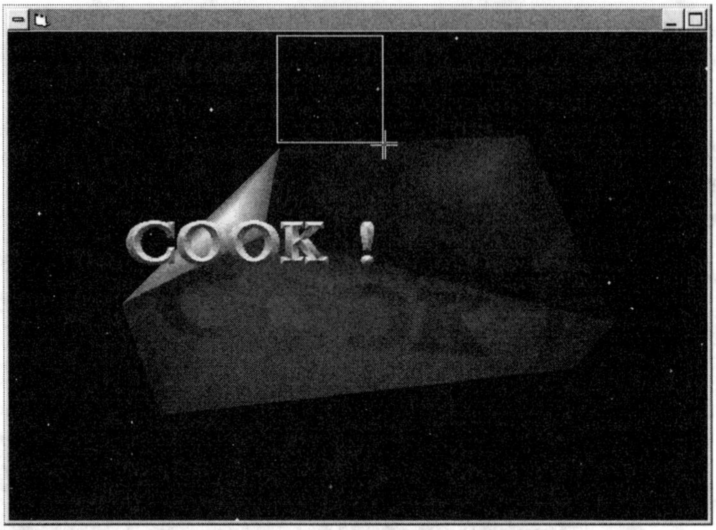


Figure 8-22: Select about an inch of the texture you want to use as your "seed."

5. Use the selector tool of the retouch program to choose a section for your "seed" tile (see Figure 8-22).
6. Select "Crop" from the Edit menu. (*Crop* means "remove everything but the selected area." Some programs, such as PHOTO-PAINT!, require that you select an area, choose Copy from the Edit menu, then choose Paste As New Image from the Edit menu.)
7. At this point you can save even more space if your tile has no color (like our black-and-white starfield tile in this example). Convert the image type to Grayscale using the Color or Image menu. In any case, Save this tile as a BMP file. We'll call it STAR.BMP.
8. Start VB and into a blank Form's Picture Property, load STAR.BMP or whatever you called your seed tile.

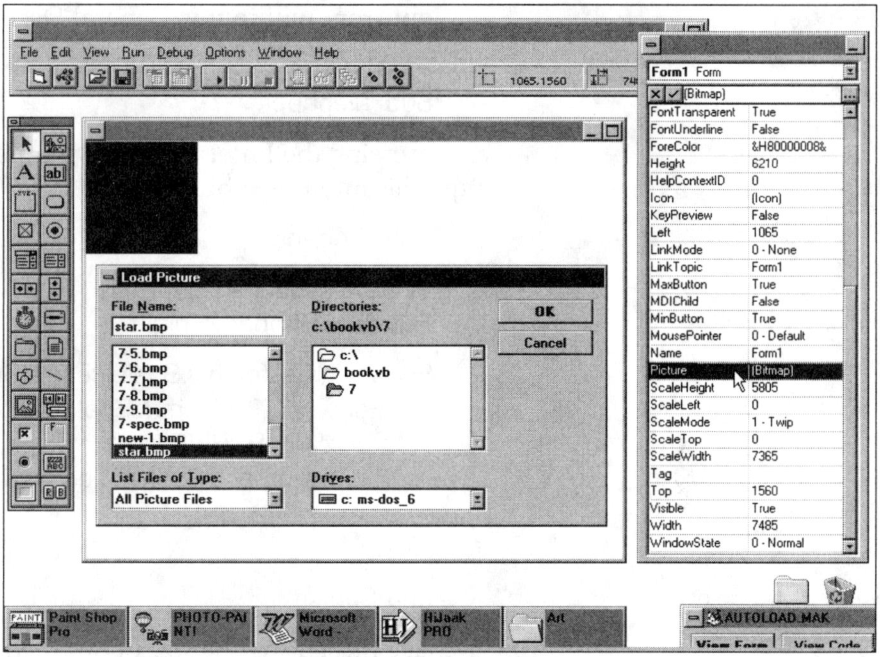


Figure 8-23: Simply load in your piece of texture using the Picture Property of the Form. The seed can be any size and need not be perfectly square.

9. Now type in the programming that will blast your tiles across the Form faster than the eye can see. Into your Form's General Declarations section (or the General Declarations section of a Module, if you want to use this technique in several Forms), type this *on a single line*:

```
Declare Function BitBlt% Lib "GDI" (ByVal hdestDC As →
Integer, ByVal x As Integer, ByVal y As Integer, ByVal →
nWidth As Integer, ByVal nHeight As Integer, ByVal →
hsrcDC As Integer, ByVal xsrc As Integer, ByVal ysrc As →
Integer, ByVal dwRop As Long)
```

(For VB4 32-bit, change **"GDI"** to **"GDI32"**, % to **&**, and all eight occurrences of **As Integer** to **As Long**.)

Then, below this Declare, type in the code identifying the particular *kind of copying* that we want BitBlt to do (there are several). In this case, just straight one-for-one copying:

```
Const copyit& = &HCC0020
```

Now, from within this General Declarations section, create a Sub by typing

```
Sub Tilepaper
```

and pressing the Enter key. VB will make a new Sub for you. Type this into the Sub:

```
Sub Tilepaper ( )

Wide% = Shape1.Width
High% = Shape1.Height

For y = 0 To form1.ScaleHeight Step High%
    For x = 0 To form1.ScaleWidth Step Wide%
        z% = BitBlt(Form1.hDC, x, y, Wide%, High%, →
        Form1.hDC, 0, 0, copyit&)
    Next x
Next y

End Sub
```

Using an invisible Image or Shape Control makes measuring the size of your tile a snap.

10. To make measuring the size of our seed tile easy, add an Image Control to the Form and stretch it to the size of the seed tile. Set the Image's Visible Property to False. (You can just as easily use a Shape Control with its Visible Property set to False or its BorderStyle set to transparent.) We're just using it as a quick way of letting VB know the dimensions of the tile it will be copying. Again, you don't have to be precise—you can stretch the Image inside the BMP a little. Whatever shape and size you make the Image—that's what BitBlt will reproduce.
11. Type this into the Form's Form_Load Event, to set the proper ScaleMode for an API call:

```
Sub Form_Load ( )
    ScaleMode = 3
End Sub
```

12. Type this into the Form's Resize *and* Paint Events, to trigger the repainting every time it's needed (during Form Load; when the Form is restored from an icon; when the Form is covered, then uncovered, by another window; when the Form is resized by user dragging or other activity):

```
Sub Form_ReSize ( )
    Tilepaper
End Sub

Sub Form_Paint ( )
    Tilepaper
End Sub
```

13. A few housekeeping details:
    - ❒ Make sure the Form's AutoRedraw Property is set to False (the VB default).
    - ❒ Make sure the Form's ClipControls property is set to True (the VB default).
    - ❒ Set the Image Control's BorderStyle to None.

Now press F5 to run your program, and you should get results like those in Figure 8-24.

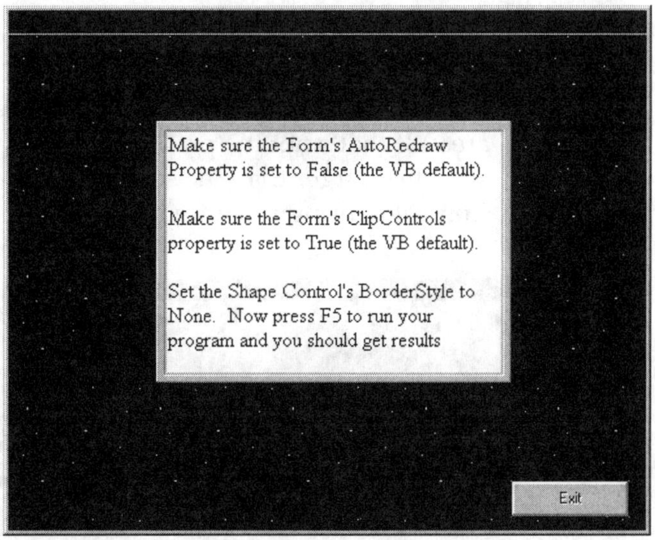


Figure 8-24: When we run this program, our wallpaper is splashed across the Form.

### Bordering & Problems

1. *Borders:* If you get borders between the tiles, the original picture BMP might contain a line of white or some other color that's not part of your texture. This means that you didn't

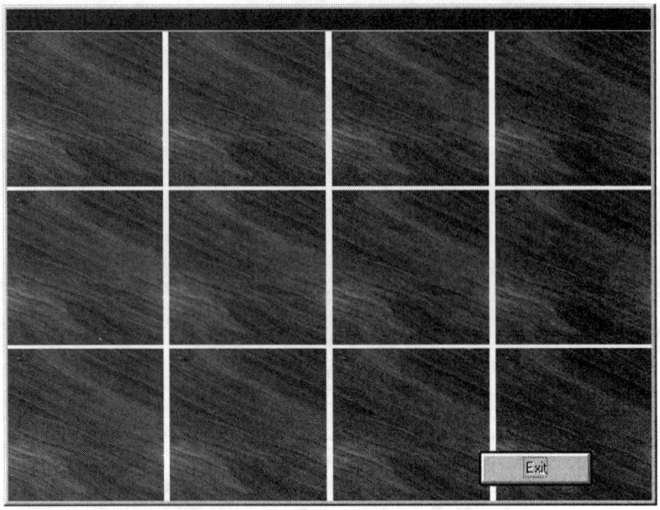


Figure 8-25: Separate tiles will result if your Shape Control is larger than the seed tile.

completely crop the image. (*Solution:* Crop the picture again in your photo-retouching program to remove the nontextured area.) If that's not the problem, your Image Control is stretched larger than the seed tile. (*Solution:* Drag the Image Control to bring it within the borders of the tile.)

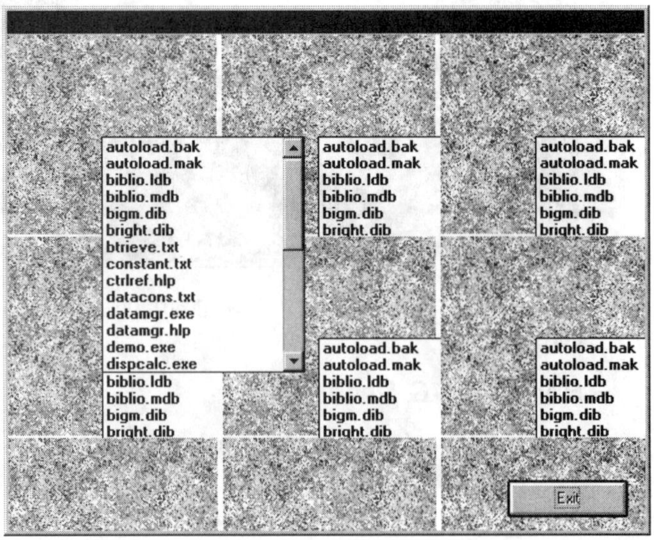


Figure 8-26: Artifacts from your Form's Controls will also be reproduced by BitBlt.

2. *Artifacts:* Anything that lies within the Shape Control's boundaries will be copied across the Form via BitBlt. In Figure 8-26, the List Box is invading the space of our seed tile, so that portion of the Box is reproduced. (*Solution:* Move the Control or reduce the size of the Shape Control.)
3. *It just doesn't work:* Check again the settings of the Properties for the Form. Check that you've correctly typed in the Declare and the call to BitBlt. Look once again: is the Form's AutoRedraw Property set to False? (And if you're using a Picture Box to hold the tile, is its AutoRedraw Property set to True?) If all else fails, just copy the programming from the CD example program, then strip it down to a bare Form and add your own Controls and programming for those Controls.
4. Try putting Show in the Form_Load Event.

Be sure the Form's AutoRedraw is False.

### The Easy Way

If you want to avoid all these problems (at a little expense of system resources and a larger EXE file size), use a Picture Box instead of placing the tile onto the Form itself. Just make these changes to the Sub (assuming that your Picture Box is named "Picture1"):

```
Sub Tilepaper ( )

Wide% = Picture1.Width
High% = Picture1.Height

For y = 0 To form1.ScaleHeight Step High%
    For x = 0 To form1.ScaleWidth Step Wide%
        z% = BitBlt(Form1.hDC, x, y, Wide%, High%, →
        Picture1.hDC, 0, 0, copyit&)
    Next x
Next y

End Sub
```

Then, put the Picture Box in the upper left corner of the Form and set the Picture Box's AutoRedraw, AutoSize and ClipControls Properties to True, and its BorderStyle to "None."

### GetWinFlags( ): User System Info

The GetWinFlags Function can tell you some details about the user's computer.

In General Declarations:

```
Declare Function GetWinFlags Lib "kernel" ( ) As Long
```

(This function is not available in Windows 95.)

In an Event:

```
Sub Form_Load ( )
Show

    Dim Flags As Long
    Flags& = GetWinFlags( )

    ' You get back a long integer which contains "flags"
    ' Particular bits within this long integer indicate
    ' particular information. You can test flags by using
    ' the AND command, as follows:

'Some of the flags are:
' 2 = 286, 4 = 386, 8 = 486, 1024 = coprocessor, 32 = →
' enhanced mode

    If Flags And 8 Then Print "486 CPU"
    If Flags And 4 Then Print "386 CPU"
    If Flags And 2 Then Print "286 CPU"

    If Flags And 1024 Then Print "Coprocessor"

    If Flags& And 32 Then
    Print "Enhanced Mode "
    Else
    Print "Standard Mode "

    End If

End Sub
```

### GetVersion( ): Windows & DOS Versions

Which DOS and Windows versions does the user have?

If you need to determine the user's DOS and Windows versions, here's how. As with the GetWinFlags Function above, you get back a long integer that contains "flags." (Particular bits within this long integer indicate particular information.) You can test flags by using the AND command, as follows:

In General Declarations:

```
Declare Function GetVersion Lib "Kernel" ( ) As Long
```

(For VB4 32-bit, change **"Kernel"** to **"Kernel32"**.)

In an Event:

```
Sub Form_Load ( )
Show

Ans& = GetVersion( )

    Dos& = Ans& \ 65536
    Main = Dos& \ 256: Sec = Dos& Mod 256
    Print "DOS " & Main & "." & Sec

    Win& = Ans& And 65535
    Main = Win& Mod 256: Sec = Win& \ 256
    Print "Windows " & Main & "." & Sec

End Sub
```

## GetWindowsDirectory( ) & GetSystemDirectory( ): Windows Pathfinding

Sometimes you need to find out the path to the user's Windows directory or to the WINDOWS\SYSTEM directory. (But avoid storing your application's data in the WINDOWS\SYSTEM directory. It, like WIN.INI, has been too widely used by too many Windows applications. Particularly if you have many font files, the WINDOWS\SYSTEM directory can become huge and unwieldy.)

In General Declarations:

```
Declare Function GetWindowsDirectory% Lib "Kernel" (ByVal →
buffer$, ByVal buffersize%)
Declare Function GetSystemDirectory% Lib "Kernel" (ByVal →
buffer$, ByVal buffersize%)
```

(For VB4 32-bit, change **Lib "Kernel"** to **Lib "Kernel" Alias "GetWindowsDirectoryA"** and change all % symbols to **&**.)

In an Event:

```
Sub Form_Load ( )
Show
buffer$ = Space(200)
buffersize% = 200
n% = GetWindowsDirectory(buffer$, buffersize%)
```

```
buffer$ = Left$(buffer$, n%)
Print buffer$

buffer$ = Space(200)
buffersize% = 200
n% = GetSystemDirectory(buffer$, buffersize%)
buffer$ = Left$(buffer$, n%)
Print buffer$

End Sub
```

### GetModuleHandle( ): Is an Application Running?

If you are doing some OLE Automation (see Chapter 10), it's sometimes useful to know if the user is currently running a particular application in Windows. For one thing, Automation is faster and sometimes behaves differently with an executing application vs. one that must first be loaded in from disk.

The GetModuleHandle routine tells you which applications are currently running in Windows. In this example, all we want to know is whether or not Microsoft's Word for Windows is running.

In General Declarations:

```
Declare Function GetModuleHandle Lib "KERNEL" (ByVal App →
As String) As Integer
```

(At the time of this writing, this doesn't work correctly under Windows 95.)

In an Event:

```
Sub Form_Load( )
    handle = GetModuleHandle("WINWORDEXE")
    If handle = 0 Then
        MsgBox "Word isn't running."
    Else
        MsgBox "Word is running."
    End If
End Sub
```

### GetCurrentTime( ): High-Precision Timing

The API GetCurrentTime Function provides the number of milliseconds that have elapsed during the current Windows session. With GetCurrentTime, you can measure how long things take to accomplish in VB (or Windows), as well as set highly specific delays, etc.

GetCurrentTime measures to a precision of 55 milliseconds. That is, even if you call it 12 times within a given 55-millisecond span, you'll get the same results.

Figure 8-27: The Elapse( ) Function measures how long it takes to float an apple down a mountain.

To try it out, type this into the General Declarations section of a Form or Module:

```
Declare Function GetCurrentTime& Lib "User" ( )
```

(This function is not working in Windows 95 at the time of this writing.)

Then type in the Elapse Function:

```
Function Elapse ( )       ' Returns the elapsed time.

Static c As Integer, Start As Long, Done As Long

c = c + 1

If c = 1 Then
    Start = GetCurrentTime( )
```

```
Else
    Done = GetCurrentTime( ) - Start
    MsgBox "Time Elapsed: " & Done / 1000 & " seconds."
c = 0
End If

End Function
```

What's faster: changing the .Left Property or using the Move command? We'll scoot an Image Box across a Form and use Elapse( ) to tell us which approach is quicker. Put in the Click Event of the Form:

```
Sub Form_Click ( )
z = Elapse( )

x = image1.Left: x1 = image1.Left + 2000
y = image1.Top
For i = x To x1 Step 10
    y = y + 10
    image1.Top = y
    image1.Left = i
Next i

z = Elapse( )

End Sub
```

Now try it again, but this time with the Move command (which, in addition to being faster, is also smoother):

```
Sub Form_Click ( )
z = Elapse( )

x = image1.Left: x1 = image1.Left + 2000
y = image1.Top
For i = x To x1 Step 10
    y = y + 10
    image1.Move i, y
Next i

z = Elapse( )

End Sub
```

The results:

- Move = 9.353 seconds
- Top/Left = 12.41 seconds

## GetKeyboardStateBystring( ): Keyboard Snapshot

CONSTANT.TXT is a good place to look up nonstandard key codes.

You can get an instant picture of the current state *of the entire keyboard*. If you need to test the status of more than one key, this is a way to do it. The alphabetic keys on the keyboard are mapped according to the normal ANSI code (a = 66, b = 67 and so on). See ANSI in VB's Help feature. The nonalphabetic keys, like function keys, are also mapped. Their codes can be found by loading in the text file (in VB, press Alt+F, L) called CONSTANT.TXT that comes with VB. Here is a partial listing from the key codes section of CONSTANT.TXT:

```
' Key Codes
Global Const KEY_LBUTTON = &H1
Global Const KEY_RBUTTON = &H2
Global Const KEY_CANCEL = &H3
Global Const KEY_MBUTTON = &H4 ' NOT contiguous →
with L & RBUTTON
Global Const KEY_BACK = &H8
Global Const KEY_TAB = &H9
Global Const KEY_CLEAR = &HC
Global Const KEY_RETURN = &HD
Global Const KEY_SHIFT = &H10
Global Const KEY_CONTROL = &H11
Global Const KEY_MENU = &H12
Global Const KEY_PAUSE = &H13
Global Const KEY_CAPITAL = &H14
Global Const KEY_ESCAPE = &H1B
```

(In VB4, look in the Object Browser by pressing F2, then see "Constants" in the VB Library.)

### Interpreting the Results

To get a keyboard snapshot, put a Text Box on a Form, then type in the following:

In General Declarations:

```
Declare Sub GetKeyboardStateBystring Lib "User" Alias →
"GetKeyboardState" (ByVal keystate$)

Dim a$
```

(This function is unavailable in Windows 95.)

We're going to use the variable a$ to hold the results. We'll display it in the Text Box, so set the Text Box's MultiLine Property to True.

In the Form_Load Event, make *a$* 256 spaces large. This, by no coincidence, is the number of key-codes and the number of "characters" that the GetKeyboardStateBystring Function returns:

```
Sub Form_Load ( )
    a$ = Space(256)
End Sub
```

Finally, in the Text Box's KeyPress Event, type this:

```
Sub Text1_KeyPress (KeyAscii As Integer)

GetKeyboardStateBystring a$

For i = 1 To 256
    p$ = Mid$(a$, i, 1)
    z$ = z$ & i & ":" & Asc(p$) & " "
Next i

Text1.Text = z$

End Sub
```

When you run this program, try pressing the *a* key on your keyboard. You should see something like Figure 8-28. You can use the Mid$ Function to pick off a particular key: Print Mid$(a$, 66, 1) would show the status of the 66th key in the code (the lowercase *a*). If the value is 128, the *a* key is pressed. If the value is 129 (zeroth and seventh bits set), that means the *a* key is pressed and one of the toggled keys (like Caps Lock) is also on. If you press Shift+A, the 66th key will be a 128 and the 17th key (the Shift key code) will also be a 128 (or 129).

(*Note:* The potential VB4 32-bit alternative GetKeyboardState Function is inoperable at the time of this writing.)

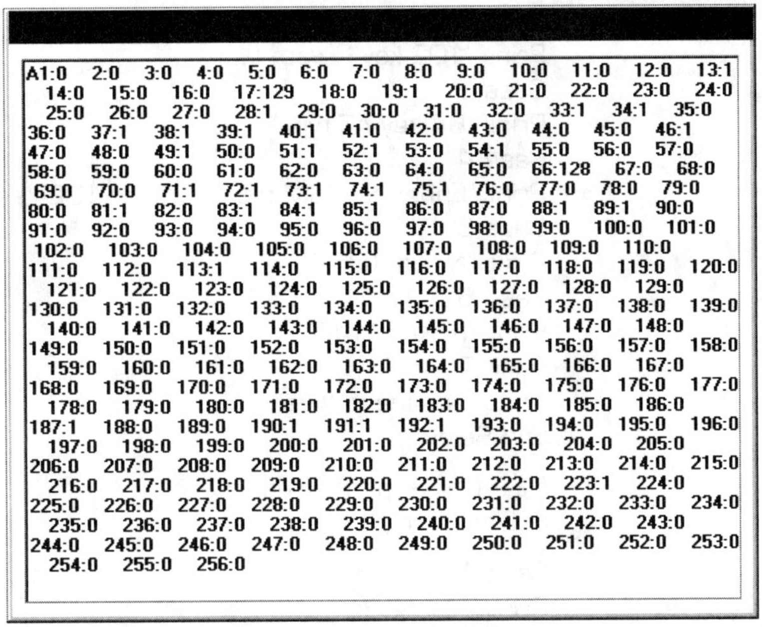


Figure 8-28: A snapshot of the keyboard. Shift (17) and the letter *a* (66) were both depressed when this picture was taken.

## GetKeyBoardType( ): What Kind of Keyboard?

If your program needs to determine what kind of keyboard the user has (how many keys, how many function keys), use this:

In General Declarations:

```
Declare Function GetKeyboardType% Lib "Keyboard" (ByVal →
flag%)
```

(This Function is not currently operative in Windows 95.)

In an Event:

```
Sub Form_Load ( )
Show
'0 provides the keyboard type
'1 provides a manufacturers code
'2 provides the number of function keys
f% = GetKeyboardType(0)
Select Case f%

Case 1
Print "83-key"
```

```
Case 2
Print "102-key Olivetti type"
Case 3
Print "84-key AT type"
Case 4
Print "Enhanced IBM type 101- or 102-key"
Case 5
Print "Nokia 1050"
Case 6
Print "Nokia 9140"
Case 7
Print "Japanese type"
End Select

f% = GetKeyboardType(2)
Select Case f%

Case 1
Print "10";
Case 2
Print "12 or 18";
Case 3
Print "10";
Case 4
Print "12";
Case 5
Print "10";
Case 6
Print "24";
Case Else
Print "Unknown";
End Select

Print " Function Keys"

End Sub
```

### SwapMouseButton( ): Swap Mouse Buttons

You can switch the actions normally associated with the left mouse button to the right button. And vice versa.

In General Declarations:

```
Declare Function SwapMouseButton% Lib "User" (ByVal →
toggle%)
```

(For VB4 32-bit, change % symbols to **&**, and change **"User"** to **"User32"**.)

In an Event:

```
Sub Form_Load ( )
'1 swaps them (making right-button act like left, & vice versa)
'0 restores to normal.
'the return value (n% here) is true if they were reversed →
' before this call.
' n% = false if they were normal.
n% = SwapMouseButton(0)
End Sub
```

## GetDriveType( ): What Kind of Disk Drive?

If you need to know the number and type of disk drives the user has available to the computer, this Function will tell you. In this example, we use the GetDriveType Function to query all possible drive names (A: through Z:). The Function returns a zero if there is no drive; a 2 if it's a floppy (or other removable type); a 3 if a hard drive; and a 4 if a "remote" drive like a CD-ROM, network server, etc.

In General Declarations:

```
Declare Function GetDriveType Lib "Kernel" (ByVal thetype%) →
As Integer
```

(For VB4 32-bit, change **"Kernel"** to **"Kernel32" Alias "GetWindowsDriveTypeA"**, and change % to **&**, and **As Integer** to **As Long**.)

In an Event:

```
Sub Form_Load ( )
Show
For i% = 0 To 25
    x% = GetDriveType(i%)
    If x% <> 0 Then c = c + 1
Select Case x%
    Case 2
    Print "Drive " & Chr$(i% + 65) & ": is a floppy."
    Case 3
    Print "Drive " & Chr$(i% + 65) & ": is a hard drive."
    Case 4
    Print "Drive " & Chr$(i% + 65) & ": is a CD-ROM, a →
    network server, or other remote drive."
```

```
        Case Else
    End Select

    Next i%

    Print "There are " & c & " drives accessible by this computer."

    End Sub
```

Results will, of course, differ depending on what computer you run it on. But here's a typical printout:

```
Drive A: is a floppy.
Drive B: is a floppy.
Drive C: is a hard drive.
Drive D: is a CD-ROM, a network server, or other remote drive.
Drive H: is a hard drive.
There are 5 drives accessible by this computer.
```

## SendMessage( ): Many Functions in One

SendMessage is really many dozens of "functions" in one. Depending on the parameters (the "message" and two subarguments that follow it) SendMessage can do sundry jobs for you.

SendMessage is a particularly versatile API Function; it performs many dozens of services.

The SendMessage essentially sends messages to windows. Messages can be a notification that something is happening (a Control has been clicked, a window is shutting down, etc.) or that something should happen (selected text should be sent to the clipboard, scrolling is requested, etc.). Thus, SendMessage has the potential for variety and impact typical of something powerful and pervasive, like the telephone exchange in a small town.

### Using WIN31WH.HLP

Obviously, a complete description of everything you can do with SendMessage is beyond the scope of this (or, to date, any other) book. However, here is a brief taste, should you want to explore this little powerhouse further. The only book containing a complete list and brief description of all possible messages is *Microsoft Windows Programmer's Reference* (Microsoft Press).

However, the WIN31WH.HLP file that comes with VB Professional, contains a complete list of all messages, along with descriptions of their purpose(s) and parameters. Here's an example of the entry in WIN31WH.HLP describing the WM_UNDO message:

```
WM_UNDO
```

An application sends the WM_UNDO message to an edit control to undo the last operation. When this message is sent to an edit control, the previously deleted text is restored or the previously added text is deleted. This message has no parameters. The return value is nonzero if the operation is successful, or zero if an error occurs. (See also WM_CLEAR, WM_COPY, WM_CUT and WM_PASTE.)

The other API .HLP file (WIN31API.HLP) supplied with VB also contains a list of the messages *and their codes.* We'll utilize this HLP file in a moment. Now let's try WM_UNDO.

## Undoing a Change in a Text Box

It all depends on the codes.

What kind of message SendMessage sends, what happens, and what is returned all depend on the codes you use for SendMessage's three parameters: wMsg, wParam and lParam. wMsg is the main one (the actual message); wParam and lParam are subsidiary, refining the meaning of the actual message. With WM_UNDO, wParam and lParam are unused, so we'll use zeros for them.

Put a Text Box and a Command Button on a Form, then type this into the Form's General Declarations:

```
Declare Function SendMessage% Lib "user" (ByVal hWd%, →
ByVal wMsg%, ByVal wParam%, ByVal lParam As Any)
```

(For VB4 32-bit, change all % symbols to & and change **"User"** to **"User32" Alias "SendMessageA"**.)

Now we need to find out what to put in for the wMsg% parameter. It will be an integer, a code, identifying the particular message we want to send—in this case, the one called WM_UNDO (Windows Message_UNDO). So press F1 in VB and then press Alt+F, O and browse around your disk until you find the API Help file that comes with VB, called WIN31API.HLP. (Look in the subdirectory called WINAPI.) Click on "Global Constants" and locate WM_UNDO. You'll see this:

```
WM_UNDO

Public Const WM_UNDO = &H304
```

(Or use **Private**, if you're using VB4 and are placing this in a Form.)

This tells us what we need to know: the code is &H304. Unfortunately, codes are still supplied as hex numbers for most computer languages. Probably VB, which is after all the highest level serious programming language in the world today, will lead the way in abandoning hex. In this book, we have provided all codes in decimal, the number system humans use in daily life. If you wish, you can just use the hex version—simply leave the &H in front of the number so the computer will know you are conforming to its preferred number base. If, however, you want to use decimal, simply remove the &H and use the decimal equivalent of &H304, which is 772. In a Command Button's Click Event, type the API SendMessage call:

```
Sub Command1_Click ( )
    x% = SendMessage(Text1.hWnd, 772, 0, 0&)
End Sub
```

Now type some text into the Text Box, select a few words—highlight them by dragging the mouse over them with the left button held down. Then press the Del key to remove those selected words. Now, click on the Command Button to see the undo. Click again and note that you can toggle between cutting and pasting.

Note that 0& in the parameter list. If the API wants a Long Integer, that's all it will accept—so we had to add the & onto the 0. Even though those last two parameters are unused, the API still expects you to follow the rules of variable typing. A Variant just isn't good enough here.

Let's try a few more SendMessages.

### How Many Lines in a Text Box?

There is no predictable way in VB to calculate how many actual lines of text will be in a Text Box, or to extract a particular line. The number of lines depends on the width and height of the Box, the font and font size, the number of carriage returns and so on. A Text Box automatically wraps lines as necessary, dynamically (assuming its MultiLine property is set to True).

Sometimes, though, it's useful to isolate individual lines within a Text Box. This can assist, for instance, if you want to control how the text is printed, rather than just simply dumping the Text Property to the printer. Here we'll use the EM_GETLINECOUNT Message, requesting a count of the lines. (EM stands for Edit Message, the API refers to all Controls like Text Boxes and Combo Boxes as "Edit Controls.") In any case, we'll again look up EM_GETLINECOUNT in the API HLP files.

WIN31API.HLP describes EM_GETLINECOUNT like this:

```
EM_GETLINECOUNT

Global Const EM_GETLINECOUNT = WM_USER+10
```

When using SendMessage with a Text Box—when trying as we are to get a count of the number of lines—the final two codes are just zero (unused), but the wMsg parameter is the Global Const EM_GETLINECOUNT = WM_USER + 10. The WM_USER Constant is 1024, so to use the GETLINECOUNT code, we add 10, resulting in 1034.

Put a Text Box on a Form, set the Text Box's MultiLine Property to True. Also, put a Command Button on the Form.

In General Declarations:

```
Declare Function SendMessage% Lib "user" (ByVal hWd%, →
ByVal wMsg%, ByVal wParam%, ByVal lParam As Any)
```

In the Command Button's Click Event:

```
Sub Command3D1_Click ( )

cnt& = SendMessage(Text1.hWnd, 1034, 0, 0&)
MsgBox "There are " & cnt&

End Sub
```

Now type in some words until you have a few lines in the Text Box, then click on the Command Button to get the report of the number of lines.

| **Other EM_ Messages** | |
|---|---|
| EM_EMPTYUNDOBUFFER | Clear the undo flag. |
| EM_FMTLINES | Turns soft line-break characters (CR+CR+LF) on or off. |
| EM_GETFIRSTVISIBLELINE | Locates the highest nonblank line. |
| EM_GETLINE | Gets an individual line of text. |
| EM_GETMODIFY | Tells you if the text is "dirty" (has changed). |
| EM_LIMITTEXT | Specifies how many bytes the user can type into a Text Box. |
| EM_LINELENGTH | Tells you the length of a particular line. |

Table 8-4: Here are some other messages you can send relating to Text Boxes.

## Get a Particular Line in a Text Box

How about retrieving a particular line from within a Text Box? We use the same GetMessage Function as above, but change the wMsg% parameter to 1,044; use the wParam% parameter to signal which line we want (starting from line 0), and use a padded string for the final parameter, lParam.

Put a Text Box on a Form and set the Text Box's Multiline Property to True. Put a Command Button on the Form.

In General Declarations:

```
Declare Function SendMessage% Lib "user" (ByVal hWd%, →
ByVal wMsg%, ByVal wParam%, ByVal lParam As Any)
```

In the Command Button's Click Event:

```
Sub Command3D1_Click ( )

buffer$ = Space(100)
cnt& = SendMessage(text1.hWnd, 1044, 1&, buffer$)
buffer$ = Left$(buffer$, cnt&)
Print buffer$
MsgBox "There are " & cnt& & " characters."

End Sub
```

You'll want to strip off the extra spaces the API sends back.

Then, press F5 to run this, type in a few lines of text and click on the Command Button. The line you've requested will be printed on the Form. Notice that the API Function doesn't insert a delimiter (such as a 0, NULL character at the end of the line of text in Buffer$). Instead, the Function returns the number of characters in the line into our variable cnt&. We can then use that to adjust buffer$ to the correct length (stripping off the extra space characters we originally padded into it with the Space command). You could also use the RTrim$ command if you wished.

## Limiting Text Box Input

There are, as you can see from the list of Text Box-related messages above, many things you can do with SendMessage. Here's one final example that limits the number of characters the user can enter into our Text Box to 10:

```
Sub Form_Load( )
cnt& = SendMessage(text1.hWnd, 1045, 10&, 0&)
End Sub
```

### Automatic Box Dropping

Some programmers and users really dread the Combo Box Control when it's set to the default style (its Style Property set to 0-DropDown Combo or to 2-DropDown List). Sure, it saves screen space because only the first item in the list is visible. But that's also its drawback—the user cannot see the other items on the list without going to the trouble of locating and clicking on the little arrow.

Here's a way to permit the user to drop it by clicking anywhere in the Box, not just on that arrow. Also, it will drop when Tabbed to via the keyboard. In other words, when it gets the focus, this Box will respond by gaping wide open. There is no VB command to drop a Box, but we can do it via the API.

Put a Command Button on a Form. Then put on a Combo Box (put this on second, so the Command Button will have a TabIndex of 0). Then, in the General Declarations:

```
Declare Function SendMessage% Lib "user" (ByVal hWd%, →
ByVal wMsg%, ByVal wParam%, ByVal lParam As Any)
```

In the Combo Box's GotFocus Event:

```
Sub Combo1_GotFocus ( )
    x& = SendMessage(Combo1.hWnd, 1039, 1, ByVal 0&)
End Sub
```

Now try clicking on the Form, the Command Button, or *anywhere* within the Combo Box. Also try pressing Tab to move the focus between the Controls.

### Scrolling a Text Box

Here's a way to imitate the scrolling credits in a movie.

Your program can scroll the text in a Text Box. This would be a nice way to display messages to the user, such as copyright information at start-up. Put the scrolling within a loop, add some delays (via a Timer) and you can list credits the way a movie does. Add a Text Box and a Timer to a Form.

In General Declarations:

```
Declare Function SendMessage% Lib "user" (ByVal hWd%, →
ByVal wMsg%, ByVal wParam%, ByVal lParam As Any)
```

In the Form_Load Event:

```
Sub Form_Load ( )
Show
'build the text
```

```
bl$ = Chr$(13) & Chr$(10)
a$ = "Special Effects by VBFX..."
b$ = "Program Design by BIBI of Montreal..."
c$ = "Credit Scroll by Saunders Gas & Design... "

'insert blank lines between text lines:
t$ = bl$ & bl$ & a$ & bl$ & bl$ & b$ & bl$ & bl$ & c$
t$ = t$ & bl$ & bl$ & bl$ & bl$ & bl$ & bl$

Text1.Text = t$

timer1.Interval = 200 ' turn the Timer on

End Sub
```

In the Timer Event:

```
Sub Timer1_Timer ( )

Static c
c = c + 1

howmanylines& = 1 'the number of lines to scroll down
x& = SendMessage(Text1.hWnd, 1030, 0, ByVal →
howmanylines&)

If c = 10 Then timer1.Interval = 0 'turn off timer when done

End Sub
```

(You can get a smoother scroll with the ScrollWindow command. See "ScrollWindow" in the "Video & Animation" section below.)

## SetParent( ): Control Erector Set

Here's a way to move a Control from one Form (or "container" Control such as a Picture Box or Frame) to another, *while your program is running*. This is a way to permit the user to design how your program looks, as if it were an erector set whose pieces could be maneuvered by the user.

### Moving Between Containers

Of course, you can use VB's Visible Property or Move Method to manipulate the appearance or location of a Control during run time. But the SetParent API Function is a way to move a Control *between* containers, like Forms, Frames or Picture Boxes, while a program is running.

Figure 8-29: This Button dances back and forth between the Picture Boxes (clip art courtesy CorelDRAW!).

Here we'll make a Command Button flip back and forth between two Picture Boxes (in VB4, the control named **Command3D** has been changed to **SSCommand**):

In General Declarations:

```
Declare Function SetParent% Lib "User" (ByVal hwndCtrl%, →
ByVal hwndContainter%)
```

(For VB4 32-bit, change all % symbols to **&** and change **"User"** to **"User32"**.)

In an Event:

```
Sub Command3D1_Click ( )

Static Toggle As Integer
Toggle = Not Toggle

If Toggle Then
     z% = SetParent(Command3D1.hWnd, ByVal
Picture2.hWnd)
Else
     z% = SetParent(Command3D1.hWnd, ByVal
Picture1.hWnd)
End If

End Sub
```

### ClipCursor( ): Imprison the Mouse

You can use the API to punish the user.

As you probably know, modal windows (like MsgBoxes and InputBoxes) can really annoy users. The whole program comes skidding to a halt and users *must* respond to your little window before they can regain control of their computer. It's so DOS-like, so un-Windows. You, the programmer, suddenly co-opt the system and force users to react.

You can annoy users in a similar fashion with this API call—it creates a prison on the screen from which their mouse cannot escape. If there is no provision for releasing their mouse, they'll have to reboot. If you want it, here it is.

In a Module:

```
Type rect
    x1 As Integer
    y1 As Integer
    x2 As Integer
    y2 As Integer
End Type
```

In General Declarations:

```
Dim Prison As Rect
Declare Sub ClipCursor Lib "User" (Rect As Any)
```

(For VB4 32-bit, change **As Integer** to **As Long** and change **"User"** to **"User32"**.)

In an Event:

```
Sub Form_Click ( )

'defines the rectangle in screen pixels
Prison.x1 = 0
Prison.y1 = 0
Prison.x2 = 200
Prison.y2 = 200

ClipCursor Prison

End Sub
```

### EnableHardwareInput( ): Freeze the Mouse

If imprisoning the user's mouse isn't enough (via the ClipCursor API Function), here's how to simply freeze the mouse and keyboard entirely. Perhaps you might employ this lockout if a user incorrectly enters a password.

In General Declarations:

```
Declare Function EnableHardwareInput% Lib "User" (ByVal →
toggle%)
```

(For VB4 32-bit, change **"User"** to **"User32"** and change % to **&**.)

In an Event:

```
Sub Form_Load ( )
    MsgBox "Password invalid!! Suspended for 10 seconds"
    Timer1.Interval = 10000
    x% = EnableHardwareInput(False)
End Sub
```

In the Timer Control:

```
Sub Timer1_Timer ( )
    x% = EnableHardwareInput(True)
    MsgBox "Control restored... NOW TURN YOURSELF IN →
IMMEDIATELY!"
End Sub
```

## Managing INI Files

### GetPrivateProfileString( ) & WritePrivateProfileString( ): Managing INIs

Applications of any significant size generally need to remember such things as user preferences (as selected in an Options menu). These settings and other initialization information are normally kept in a file with the extension INI.

Avoid adding to already gargantuan WIN.INIs. Use your own INI for each application.

Windows itself stores initialization information in such files as WIN.INI and SYSTEM.INI. Until recently, many applications stored their initialization data within WIN.INI, but this is proving impractical—the WIN.INI file can become bloated, particularly since there is no standard for *uninstalling* information in WIN.INI if the related application is deleted from the user's system. Also, Windows won't load if WIN.INI becomes larger than 64k.

Most applications now provide their own INI file. And if you write a VB program that needs an INI file, you should too. The API includes two Functions that assist in this task: WritePrivateProfileString( ) inserts some data into your INI file (when the user, for example, changes an option). GetPrivateProfileString( ) retrieves data so your program can examine it when initializing.

### INI Management

To se how to handle a typical INI file, let's create an example application called TRACER.EXE; our INI file will be TRACER.INI. A VB application's first job is to create an INI file if one doesn't exist (either because the application is being executed for the first time, or because the INI file has been deleted). The WritePrivateProfileString API Function will create an INI for you automatically, if one doesn't exist. Here's a typical Form_Load Event:

In General Declarations:

```
Declare Function WritePrivateProfileString% Lib "Kernel" →
(ByVal section$, ByVal itemname As Any, ByVal itemvalue →
As Any, ByVal inifilename As String)
Declare Function GetPrivateProfileString% Lib "Kernel" (ByVal →
section$, ByVal itemname As Any, ByVal Default$, ByVal →
Buffer$, ByVal Buffersize%, ByVal inifilename As String)
```

(For VB4 32-bit, change **"Kernel"** to **"Kernel32" Alias "GetPrivateProfileStringA" and Alias "WritePrivateProfileStringA"** and change all % symbols to **&**. Note that VB4 32-bit sends information from the API calls into the Windows 95 Registry. For more on this, search for Registry Functions in VB's online Help.)

In an Event:

```
Sub Form_Load ( )
Show
On Error Resume Next

directoryname$ = app.Path
If Right$(directoryname$, 1) <> "\" Then directoryname$ = →
directoryname$ + "\"

fname = directoryname$ & "TRACER.INI"
fnum = FreeFile

Open fname For Input As fnum 'see if .INI exists
Close

If Err = False Then GoTo FoundIni 'INI file exists
```

```
If Err = 53 Then 'INI file doesn't exist, so build one.
'set default startup conditions & create INI file

section$ = "Fonts"
itemname$ = "Favorite"
itemvalue$ = "Arial"
x% = WritePrivateProfileString%(section$, itemname$, →
itemvalue$, fname)

section$ = "Colors"
itemname$ = "Highlight"
itemvalue$ = "Blue"
x% = WritePrivateProfileString%(section$, itemname$, →
itemvalue$, fname)

section$ = "Colors"
itemname$ = "Inactive"
itemvalue$ = "Gray"
x% = WritePrivateProfileString%(section$, itemname$, →
itemvalue$, fname)

End If

'Put normal initialization here:
FoundIni:

End Sub
```

The code above results in a new INI file in the same directory in which your VB application's EXE file resides. This new INI file contains the following items in the following format:

```
[Fonts]
Favorite=Arial

[Colors]
Highlight=Blue
Inactive=Gray
```

The API punctuates these entries for you.

Note that the API *provides the punctuation* (the carriage returns, the [] and the = symbols). You merely provide the section name, item name and value to be assigned to that item. By using WritePrivateProfileString( ), the API automatically builds a typical INI file—structured just like WIN.INI or any other INI file.

Now, let's see how to use GetPrivateProfileString( ) to read from our INI file.

### Reading an INI

Using the same example above in which we created a new INI, let's assume that this time we run our VB application, the file TRACER.INI already exists. So, during the start-up of our application we'll just want to *read* this INI file—not make a new one.

Since the INI file exists, this line sends us down to the label *FoundIni:*

```
If Err = False Then GoTo FoundIni 'INI file exists
```

There we'll do normal INI processing, between the FoundIni label and the End Sub:

```
'Put normal initialization here:
FoundIni:

section$ = "Colors"
itemname$ = "Inactive"
default$ = "NONE" 'what you get back if nothing matching →
section/itemname is found
Buffer$ = Space(50) 'a place to put the returned data. Pad it →
as large as necessary.
Buffersize% = 50 'describes size in characters of Buffer$

x% = GetPrivateProfileString(section$, itemname$, default$, →
Buffer$, Buffersize%, fname)

MsgBox "The Inactive Color is listed as " & Buffer$

End Sub
```

The above results in a Message Box, saying "The Inactive Color is listed as Gray."

In this way, you are given a piece of data (stripped of the Section and Itemname and = symbol) for whatever items in your INI file that your program needs.

### Getting All ItemNames in a Section

Your application can also use GetPrivateProfileString( ) to find out all the Items within any given section. In our example, we've created a section called [Colors] that contains two items, Highlight and Inactive:

```
[Colors]
Highlight=Blue
Inactive=Gray
```

Let's say that we want to find out, during our initialization, which of perhaps dozens of potential color items the user could have customized, really exist in the INI file. To get this list, you set the itemname$ to zero. Notice that when we Declared the GetPrivateProfileString( ) function, we described the Itemname parameter as "any."

```
ByVal itemname As Any
```

You can't always do this, but in some API calls, it permits the parameter to behave in different ways—depending on the variable type used (somewhat like a Variant Variable). In any case, we're going to change ItemName this time to a long integer. (We'll also adjust the word *ItemName* somewhat to avoid conflict with its previous use in this Form_Load Event):

```
section$ = "Colors"
itemn& = 0
default$ = "NONE" 'what you get back if nothing matching →
section/itemname is found
Buffer$ = Space(50) 'a place to put the returned data. Pad it →
as large as necessary.
Buffersize% = 50 'describes size in characters of Buffer$

x% = GetPrivateProfileString(section$, itemn&, default$,  →
Buffer$, Buffersize%, fname)
```

Use Mid$ to parse the results.

Notice that we've made only two changes here: *itemn& = 0* and a matching *itemn&*, in the API call. You can't use a MsgBox to report the results here, because after the API call, Buffer$ will now return all the ItemNames (within the Colors section), separated by zeros (null). This way, your program will be able to use the Mid$ command to parse (search through the Buffer$) for zeros, picking off each ItemName. The end of this list of ItemNames within Buffer$ is indicated by two zeros. Buffer$ looks like this, in our example:

```
Highlight0Inactive00
```

## Editing INIs

So far so good. But a truly useful little database must also permit us to *edit* the data—to add, delete and change items.

- To add a new item, just use WritePrivateProfileString( ) again:

  ```
  section$ = "Colors"
  itemname$ = "Frames"
  itemvalue$ = "Black"
  x% = WritePrivateProfileString%(section$, →
  itmname$, itemvalue$, fname)
  ```

  This results in:

  ```
  [Fonts]
  Favorite=Arial
  [Colors]
  Highlight=Blue
  Inactive=Gray
  Frames=Black
  ```

- To delete an Item, set ItemValue$ to zero. Again, this means changing its type from $ to &. Also, we'll change the parameter's name, since we get conflicts using two different variable types with the same name within the same procedure. You might find it more convenient, therefore, to create separate Functions—one to delete an INI item, one to read the INI file, one to create a new INI file and so on. In any case, the following will delete the Inactive item:

  ```
  section$ = "Colors"
  itemname$ = "Inactive"
  itemvalu& = 0
  x% = WritePrivateProfileString%(section$, itemname$, →
  itemvalu&, fname)
  ```

  This results in:

  ```
  [Fonts]
  Favorite=Arial

  [Colors]
  Highlight=Blue
  Frames=Black
  ```

- To change an item, simply call the API again, substituting the new value. Here we'll change Highlight=Blue to Highlight=Azure:

```
section$ = "Colors"
itemname$ = "Highlight"
itemvalue$ = "Azure"
x% = WritePrivateProfileString%(section$, itemname$, →
itemvalue$, fname)
```

  This results in:

```
[Fonts]
Favorite=Arial

[Colors]
Highlight=Azure
Frames=Blac
```

- To delete all Items in an entire section, set ItemNam& to zero. Once again, this means changing *ItemName* to *Itemnam* and changing its type from $ to &. The following will delete the entire Colors Section:

```
section$ = "Colors"
itemnam& = 0
itemvalue$ = ""
x% = WritePrivateProfileString%(section$, itemnam&, →
itemvalue$, fname)
```

  This results in:

```
[Fonts]
Favorite=Arial
```

### Other INI Functions

There are several additional API Functions that manipulate INI files. They behave essentially as described above for WritePrivateProfileString( ) and GetPrivateProfileString( ), except for the differences described below:

- *WritePrivateProfileStringByNum( ).* This one is identical to WritePrivateProfileString( ), except it utilizes long integers instead of "Any" for the ItemName and ItemValue parameters:

```
Declare Function WritePrivateProfileString% Lib "Kernel" →
(ByVal section$, ByVal itemname&, ByVal itemvalue& →
,ByVal inifilename As String)
```

You can use this Function, if you wish, to delete sections or items. Or use it if you want to store numeric (rather than text) data as the itemvalue.

You can use WIN.INI, but it's best left alone.

- *Manipulating WIN.INI.* There is a parallel set of Functions that deal exclusively with WIN.INI—in this way, you avoid having to specify the path name for your own "private" INI. However, for reasons of WIN.INI bloat, it is recommended that you store your own application's data in private INI files. If, though, you need to read some general Windows parameters from WIN.INI, you could use the GetProfileString( ) Function. Note that the fname (filename and path to look for) is missing here; Windows knows where WIN.INI is:

```
Declare Function GetProfileString% Lib "Kernel" (ByVal →
section$, ByVal itemname As Any, ByVal Default$, ByVal →
Buffer$, ByVal Buffersize%)
```

(There's also an alternative, parallel Function—GetProfileInt( )—which pulls in an Integer from a particular WIN.INI entry.) To write to WIN.INI:

```
Declare Function WriteProfileString% Lib "Kernel" (ByVal →
section$, ByVal itemname As Any, ByVal itemvalue As Any)
```

Again, no file name or path is necessary here. The alternative, parallel Function, which writes to WIN.INI using Long Integers, is WriteProfileStringBynum( ).

## Video & Animation

### FlashWindow( ): Flash a Title Bar

If you want to, you can make a Form's Title Bar seem to blink on and off. For most users, this is probably overkill as a way of attracting attention, but it is used in applications for the deaf.

In General Declarations:

```
Declare Function FlashWindow% Lib "User" (ByVal hWnd%, →
ByVal Toggle%)
```

(For VB4 32-bit, change all % symbols to & and change **"User"** to **"User32"**.)

The Toggle% parameter, when set to anything nonzero, causes the Title Bar to be turned on, then off, with each successive call to the FlashWindow Function. When set to zero, the Title Bar is restored to its original condition. The changes are the equivalent of what happens to a Title Bar when you click on that window, making it "active" and when you click on another window, making the first one "inactive." The colors used for the text and background depend on the settings in your Windows Controls for Colors.

Here we'll flash the Title Bar of Form2 10 times. In Form1's Load Event, make Form2 visible, we then make it blink:

```
Sub Form_Load ( )

Form2.Show
For i = 1 To 10
For j = 1 To 30000
Next j
x% = FlashWindow(Form2.hWnd, 1)
Next i

End Sub
```

### ScrollWindow( ): Scrolling Windows

Create smooth wipes and other special effects with ScrollWindow.

You can create various special effects, including the following smooth horizontal wipe. We'll clean out a Text Box, by moving a sliding shade across it from left to right. When finished, the Text Box will be empty. This effect could be attractive when the user clicked on a button labeled CLEAR.

In a Module's General Declarations section, enter the following User Defined variable type and the API Declare statements. Note that you can put the API declarations in either a Module or a Form, though in VB4 you must put Private in front of the Declare if it's in a Form. However, you must put a user-defined variable declaration in a Module, and you must put the Dim statements associated with it in a Form:

```
Type rect
    x1 As Integer
    y1 As Integer
    x2 As Integer
    y2 As Integer
End Type
```

```
Declare Sub ScrollWindow Lib "User" (ByVal hWnd As →
Integer, ByVal XAmount As Integer, ByVal YAmount As →
Integer, lprect As rect, lpcliprect As rect)
```

(For VB4 32-bit, change all occurrences of **As Integer**, including those in the rect definition, to **As Long**, and change **"User"** to **"User32"**.)

In your Form's General Declarations:

```
Dim lprect As rect
Dim lpcliprect As rect
```

In an Event:

```
Sub Form_Click ( )

Form1.ScaleMode = 3

Dim i As Integer

a% = text1.Left: b% = text1.Top
c% = a% + text1.Width
d% = b% + text1.Height

'defines the rectangle to move
lprect.x1 = a%
lprect.y1 = b%
lprect.x2 = c%
lprect.y2 = d%

'defines the window that will clip the rectangle.
lpcliprect.x1 = a%
lpcliprect.y1 = b%
lpcliprect.x2 = c%
lpcliprect.y2 = d%

For i = 1 To 30
    scrollwindow Form1.hWnd, i, 0, lprect, lpcliprect
Next i

text1.Text = ""
End Sub
```

To slow down the wipe, insert a delay function, or use a VB Timer, within the For...Next loop.

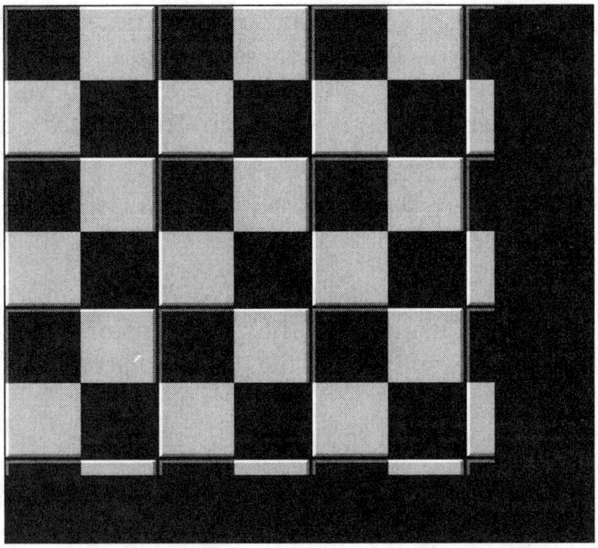

Figure 8-30: BEFORE. The checkerboard, in its unsullied state.

Figure 8-31: AFTER. ScrollWindow smears the graphic, creating a new background.

You can, of course, specify horizontal movements and also move such things as BMP pictures. In Figure 8-31, we've used the For...Next loop counter variable *I* to move down *both* vertically and horizontally by the same amount each time. This creates a diagonal move:

```
For i = 1 To 30
    scrollwindow Form1.hWnd, i, i, lprect, lpcliprect
Next I
```

Also, we specified the precise dimensions of the two rectangles (instead of using a Text Box's dimensions). Set the Form's Picture Property to some BMP file, then replace the following lines in the Click Event:

```
'defines the rectangle to move
lprect.x1 = 20
lprect.y1 = 20
lprect.x2 = 1350
lprect.y2 = 1400

'defines the window that will clip the rectangle.
lpcliprect.x1 = 0
lpcliprect.y1 = 0
lpcliprect.x2 = 1050
lpcliprect.y2 = 1000
```

### mciSendString( ): Show a Video Full Screen

For many more multimedia tricks, see Chapter 9.

This uses up memory—a few seconds costs megabytes—but it will knock their socks off when users see their monitors turn into full-motion television. (This won't work on most slow video cards.)

In General Declarations:

```
Declare Function mciSendString& Lib "mmsystem" (ByVal →
lpstrCommand$, ByVal lpstrReturnStr As Any, ByVal →
wReturnLen%, ByVal hCallBack%)
```

(For VB4 32-bit, change **"mmsystem"** to **"winmm" Alias "mciSendStringA"** and change % to **&**.)

In an Event:

```
Sub Form_Load ( )
Show

'provide here the full path of an .AVI file on your hard drive:
```

```
s$ = "play c:\winvideo\wndsurf1.avi fullscreen"
x& = mciSendString(s$, 0&, 0, 0)

End Sub
```

### mciSendString( ): Play a Video Anywhere

Here we'll play an AVI video (and sound) file—locating a child window *anywhere* on our Form that we wish, and making the video whatever size we want it to be.

Figure 8-32: Display a Video clip at any size, in any location on your Form.

Put a 3DPanel on a Form and add a Command Button.
In General Declarations:

```
Declare Function mciSendString& Lib "mmsystem" (ByVal →
WhatToDo$, ByVal Buffer As Any, ByVal BufferLen%, ByVal →
param%)
```

(For VB4 32-bit, change **"mmsystem"** to **"winmm" Alias "mciSendStringA"** and change % to **&**.)

In an Event:

```
Sub Command1_Click ( )

Last$ = form1.hWnd & " style " & &H40000000
ToDo$ = ("open c:\morph\twoguys.avi type AVIVideo alias →
Animation parent " & Last$)
```

```
x% = mciSendString(ToDo$, 0&, 0, 0)
x% = mciSendString("put Animation window at 40 40 210 →
210", 0&, 0, 0)
x% = mciSendString("play Animation wait", 0&, 0, 0)
x% = mciSendString("close Animation", 0&, 0, 0)

End Sub
```

The wait command forces the video to finish; it can't be interrupted.

Figure 8-33: You can create a video "child window" of any size.

The following will calculate the size and position of your video window for you—based, in this case, on the dimensions of the surrounding 3DPanel Control:

```
' Calculate relative video size:
scalemode = 3
x1 = panel3d1.Left + 5: y1 = panel3d1.Top + 5
x2 = x1 + panel3d1.Width - 25: y2 = y1 + panel3d1.Height - →
22
frame$ = " " & x1 & " " & y1 & " " & x2 & " " & y2 & " "
frame$ = "put Animation window at" & frame$

x% = mciSendString(ToDo$, 0&, 0, 0)
x% = mciSendString(frame$, 0&, 0, 0)
```

# Music & Sound

## sndPlaySound( ): Play a WAV file

To play a sound file (a file with a WAV extension), do this:
In General Declarations:

```
Declare Sub sndPlaySound Lib "MMSYSTEM" (ByVal WavFile as
String, ByVal wFlags As Integer)
```

In an Event:

```
Sub Form_Load( )
    sndPlaySound "chord.wav", 1
End Sub
```

(For VB4 32-bit, change **"mmsystem"** to **"WINMM.DLL" Alias "SndPlaySoundA"** and change **As Integer** to **As Long**.)

The last parameter (wFlags, which is 1 in this example) has four possible values:

| | |
|---|---|
| 0 | Synchronous (sound will take over the computer until finished, like a VB modal window—such as a MsgBox). |
| 1 | Asynchronous (other things can happen; multitasking permitted as in VB's DoEvents Function). |
| 2 | No Default Beep (avoids the warning sound the computer makes when something fails to work). |
| 4 | Default Beep (makes the warning sound that the user has chosen in sound settings for Windows). |

Table 8-4: Possible values for wFlags.

## mciSendString( ): Play a MIDI File

MIDI is a full language—the computer language for music.

The MIDI standard is the computer's musical language. Adopted by agreement among synthesizer manufacturers in the mid-'80s, MIDI can specify tone, timbre, duration, vibrato and dozens of other aspects of sound and music.

The Professional Edition of VB includes an MCI Control (Media Control Interface) that you can use to play MIDI music files (along with CD players, video, etc.). However, if you prefer to control a MID file directly from within your VB application, the API offers a Function called mciSendString.

Put two Command Buttons on a Form. Find out the name of a MIDI file somewhere on your hard drive (most people have one called CANYON.MID in their Windows directory, but any MID file will do).

In General Declarations:

```
Declare Function mciSendString& Lib "mmsystem" (ByVal →
lpstrCommand$, ByVal lpstrReturnStr As Any, ByVal →
wReturnLen%, ByVal hCallBack%)
```

(For VB4 32-bit, change **"mmsystem"** to **"Winmm" Alias "mciSendStringA"** and change % to &.)

In the Click Event of the Command Button:

```
Sub Command3D1_Click ( )

x% = mciSendString("open C:\WINDOWS\CANYON.MID type →
sequencer alias canyon", 0&, 0, 0)

x% = mciSendString("play canyon", 0&, 0, 0)

x% = mciSendString("close Animation", 0&, 0, 0)

End Sub
```

In a second Command Button (to stop the song):

```
Sub Command1_Click ( )

x% = mciSendString("open C:\WINDOWS\CANYON.MID type →
sequencer alias canyon", 0&, 0, 0)

x% = mciSendString("stop canyon", 0&, 0, 0)

x% = mciSendString("close Animation", 0&, 0, 0)

End Sub
```

For more on the MCI command set (it's really a complete multimedia control language), see "The Multimedia Control Interface" in Chapter 9).

Additional information on how to manipulate multimedia devices via the mciSendString Function can be found in Microsoft's Windows SDK (Software Development Kit) in the "Multimedia Programmer's Reference" section.

## MOVING ON

The next chapter is almost like school recess—we'll take a break from staid, traditional computer programming and try out some great tricks. Multimedia is the cutting edge of computing these days, and adding nifty sound and video effects to your VB programs can really bring them to life. Among many other effects, we'll even see how easy it is to incorporate TV-like "wipes" as transitions between sections of an application.

Chapter 9

# Multimedia: The New Technology

This chapter is fun. You'll find out how easy it is to create special effects with your voice; to wipe images or text for dynamic special visual transitions; to create animation; to make spreadsheets talk; and to control a variety of multimedia devices with Visual Basic.

Multimedia is the core of tomorrow's computing. Until recently they were considered a luxury expansion of a personal computer. Not any more. Today, multimedia are one of the fastest-growing sections of the personal computing market and they are slowly forming the foundation of tomorrow's user interface. In this chapter we are going to look at various multimedia components in the Windows environment, from both a user's and a programmer's point of view.

Multimedia is not a new idea; it's just relatively new to computing. Combining media is commonplace in art. For example, drama is mixed with music in movies. However, the computer adds a new dimension to mixed media—interactivity. With a personal computer, the user can manipulate sound and video, controlling the composition.

We must at the start dispense with two myths. First, multimedia applications don't require expensive computers. With VB you can even add multimedia capabilities to plain vanilla PCs. Second, multimedia isn't hard to program in VB (though, like any Windows programming, it would be hard indeed *without* Visual Basic; an alternative, "authoring" tools like ToolBook, can't match VB for robustness or depth).

Visual Basic provides a specialized Control, called MCI (Multimedia Control Interface), which lets you program the various multimedia components of your PC. The MCI Control uses VCR-style buttons and, with the appropriate property settings, you can both record and play back sounds and animation. However, we're going to go beyond this Custom Control in this chapter, showing you how to really take charge of the powerhouse multimedia engines built into Windows.

As you know, Visual Basic is your gateway to various "languages" hidden within Windows. Broadly defined, we can consider any collection of related commands or functions a "language," and VB's inherent power can be expanded and deepened in several directions via such languages. You can create a variety of interesting effects by utilizing the API (Application Programmer's Interface), which provides what is virtually a "language of Windows" hidden inside the operating system (see Chapter 8). Likewise, VB now contains a full-featured, database-manipulation language, called the Data Definition Language, or DDL.

MCI is another specialized language of the Windows operating system.

There are also the database query language, SQL (see Chapter 3, if you're using VB3, or Chapter 4, if you're using VB4)); the MAPI, for sending messages between applications and users (see Chapter 14); OLE, for various kinds of data exchange and interprogram control (see Chapter 10); and so on. In this chapter, we focus on the MCI (a language devoted to the "Multimedia Control Interface"); the BitBlt and SndPlaySound API calls; the structure of sound files and techniques for processing them; several animation techniques; and a set of routines with which you can add dynamic "wipes"—exciting television-style transitions between sections of your programs.

## MULTIMEDIA COMPONENTS

To best exploit the multimedia capabilities of Windows you should have a sound card and a video capture board (or at least a graphics accelerator) installed on your computer. Don't give up if you don't, though. We will also give you a collection of tools to make use of sound and animation even on a "plain" PC.

(There are a few things you can't do without the specialized hardware. You must have a sound card if you want to be able to play back MIDI files or record WAVE files. You must have a video capture card if you want to be able to record live video from your VCR or cable. Also, we won't be covering esoteric devices, such as videodisc players.)

The basic multimedia components under Windows 3.1 and Windows 95 are images, sound and animation (moving images). Images have been covered extensively in Chapter 6. In this chapter we will explore the last two components of multimedia, as well as techniques for manipulating them and ways to combine them to build multimedia applications.

## SOUND

In the Windows multimedia environment, sounds fall into two major categories: waveforms and MIDI. Waveforms are recorded sounds, like those recorded on a cassette player; but instead of tape, they are stored in a disk file. MIDI files, on the other hand, are like sheet music, containing a coded description of music—the pitch, instrument and duration of each note, along with additional codes for such things as vibrato. (Think of WAV files as similar to BMP files; there is an entire copy of the original. Think of MIDI files as similar to WMF files; there is a mathematical description of the original.) We will start with the first category, the waveform files, which are simpler and familiar to everyone.

### How to Play a WAVE File

If you don't have a sound card, you can install a freeware program by Microsoft, SPEAKER.DRV, which lets you play WAVE files through your computer's built-in speaker. Why isn't the Speaker Driver built into Windows? Microsoft's testing found that it is incompatible with a few particular makes of PCs, so they decided to make it available separately to cut down on potential problems. The quality of the sound it produces through that tiny speaker is not, of course, as good as what you would get with a sound card. SPEAKER.DRV can be downloaded from Microsoft Library Forum on CompuServe (GO MSL, then select the Software Library and download the SPEAK.EXE file).

There are two ways to play back a sound file. The first one is to use the MCI commands explained later in this chapter. Unfortunately, MCI doesn't support SPEAKER.DRV.

SPEAKER.DRV will allow you to play WAVE files through your PC's speaker.

There is, however, an API function that can be used with both a sound card and the SPEAKER driver. It is the sndPlaySound( ) Function. To play the TADA.WAV file (a recorded sound that comes with Windows) put the following in the General Declarations section of a Form:

```
Declare Function sndPlaySound Lib "WINMM" Alias
sndPlaySoundA (ByVal waveFile As String, ByVal wFlags As
Long) As Long
```

If you are working with Visual Basic 3.0 under Windows 3.1 (or the 16-bit version of VB4), you must declare this Function as follows:

```
Declare Function sndPlaySound Lib "MMSYSTEM" (ByVal
waveFile As String, ByVal wFlags As Integer) As Integer
```

Then, put this line in your Form_Load or some other Event:

```
sndPlaySound "c:\windows\tada.wav",0
```

WavFile is the name of the sound file to be played (one with extension WAV) and wFlags is a flag that tells the computer how to play it. Here are the valid values of the wFlags parameter:

| Value | Constant Name | Description |
|---|---|---|
| 0 | SND_SYNC | Synchronous (sound will take over the computer until finished). |
| 1 | SND_ASYNC | Asynchronous (other things can happen; multitasking permitted like using VB's DoEvents Function). |
| 2 | SND_NODEFAULT | No Default sound (avoids the warning sound the computer makes when there is a problem playing the sound). |
| 4 | SND_MEMORY | The first parameter is not a file name, but a pointer to an area in memory where the sound is stored (it is an "image" of a WAVE file in the memory). |
| 8 | SND_LOOP | Plays the sound repeatedly, until a subsequent call to sndPlaySound( ). |

Table 9-1: The values of the sndPlaySound wFlags parameter.

There is a major limitation with sndPlaySound( )—the entire sound must fit in the computer's available RAM memory. So sndPlaySound( ) must be used only with small files—Microsoft suggests files up to 100k. For long sounds, you must use the MCI commands (described below). Also, note that sndPlaySound( ) can only be used with WAV files, not MIDI files.

## What Is Sound?

Sound is vibrations in the air. A "waveform" is the plot (or shape, over time) of these vibrations that have been detected by a microphone. Waves have two primary qualities. First, they can vary in frequency—the rapidity with which the waves of air are hitting a mike or your ear. This frequency of vibration is what our brain translates into what we call the "pitch" of a sound, how low or high it is, a bass drum being low and a flute being high. Second, the waves can vary in amplitude—the amount of air being displaced, what we hear as the "loudness" or "volume" of the sound.

The basic characteristics of sound are amplitude and frequency.

This same distinction can be seen in any waves. For example, on the ocean, waves of high frequency crash quite frequently against the sand; waves of high amplitude are tall, they rise high above the surface and are good for surfing.

A waveform can be made visual (via a plot) or digitally stored (in a computer, on a CD, etc.). A waveform is a representation of the combined frequency and amplitude information of a particular sound or series of sounds. When you open a WAV file with the Sound Recorder application in Windows, a waveform, a pictorial representation of the sound, is displayed.

Figure 9-1: The "picture" of a sound, or waveform, shows the variations of the sound's amplitude and frequency.

When you look at a waveform, the vertical size of the waves is the amplitude and the number of times the waves cross the center (X-axis) line shows the frequency. Sounds have both positive and negative values, just as ocean waves can rise over the surface of the ocean or sink below it.

## Digitizing Sound

Natural sound, the kind your ears hear, is continuous. If you could see it, it would look like an ocean wave. Digitized sound is not continuous, and looks more like a set of stairways going up and down along an apartment complex.

For CDs, computers and, soon, television, sound and video are translated from their natural, original analog status into digital format. There are several advantages to storing information digitally, not the least of which is that complex manipulations by computer are possible (extraordinary audio effects via synthesizer, realtime video image stabilization, morphing, etc.). Also, digital information is virtually impervious to noise (static, hiss, ghosting, etc.), since the digital signal can contain error correction information and be mathematically "cleaned up" to correct distortion.

To store sounds in your computer, you must first digitize them: convert them to sequences of numbers your computer can understand.

Sound digitization—that is, sound's translation into digital format—results in a series of numbers, rather than a copy of the original waveform (a cassette recorder or videorecorder maintains analog copies of waveforms on tape). If you could make yourself very small and walk along a cassette tape, you would see wavy patterns in the iron filings on the tape. It would look like those bands of rock you see along a highway cutting through a mountain. If you walked along a CD, you would see an orderly sequence of tiny pits that stand for 0s and 1s, which make up the numbers representing the samples.

The goal is to transform the smooth original sound waves into *enough* numbers to permit them to eventually be translated back again into reasonably smooth waves—so we can play them back.

## Sound Samples

When digitized, the original continuous analog wave is "sampled" so that you get a position on the wave only every so often. If it is sampled with sufficient frequency, it can be restored later—for all practical purposes—as a copy of the original continuous waveform. The conversion from analog to digital is done by polling the sound at a regular interval, as if you were reducing a cartoon to a connect-the-dots representation of the original drawing. What you are left with is a series of positions, each position simply a number, *a sample*. The success of the eventual reconstruction (from digital back to analog) depends on how often you take a sample. This process is depicted in Figures 9-2 through 9-4.

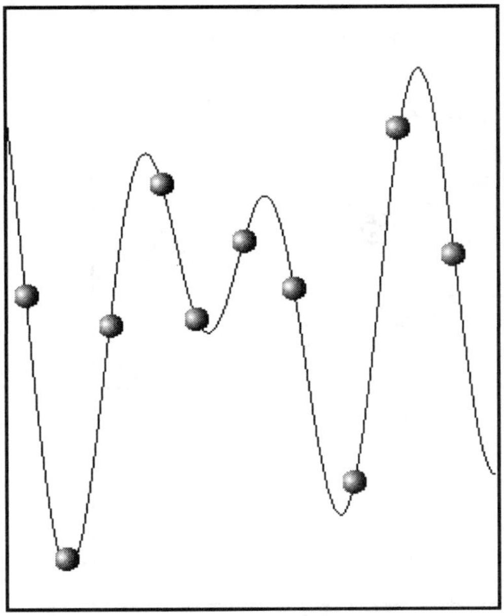

Figure 9-2: Sampling an analog waveform. To convert a sound to digital form, we select certain samples and throw away the rest. After this conversion, only the spheres (individual samples) will remain.

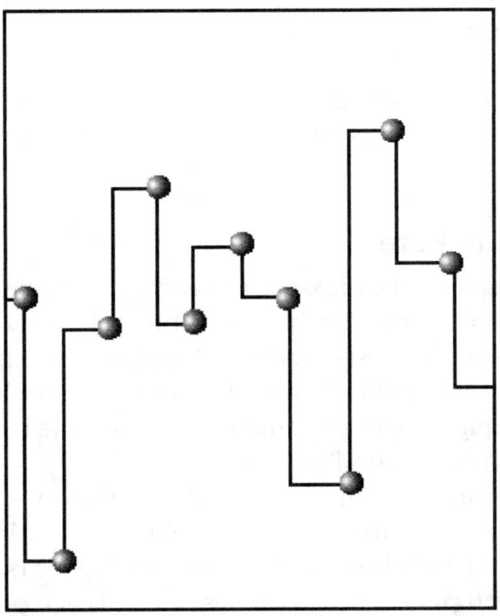

Figure 9-3: When the waveform is described only by the spheres, digital pulses describe discrete locations (samples) representing the position of each sphere.

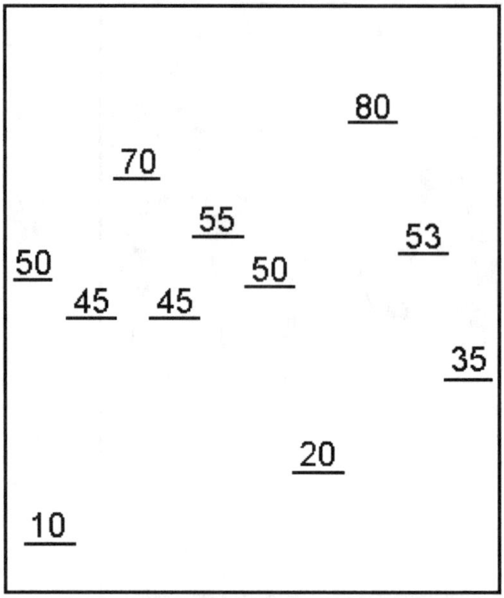


Figure 9-4: Boom. The lines go away. Removing these connecting lines, we are left with the actual samples: the numbers that describe the implied (but now invisible) wave. These samples are simply a series of numbers. And numbers have an advantage over waves: they cannot be distorted. The number 12 is always 12. A wave can lose its shape during storage, like a candle in the summer heat. A number will always be exactly what it is.

Notice that between Figures 9-2 and 9-4 we have moved from an analog wave to a group of digits. This, in essence, is analog-to-digital conversion.

### Sampling Rate

Samples should be taken close enough together for the computer to be able to reconstruct the signal, but not any closer than necessary (storage media costs money). One of the specifications of any computer sound card is its sampling rate, or samples per second. All else being equal, the more samples you take, the better the quality of the reconstructed sound will be.

A picture of a sampled sound (like the one displayed by Sound Recorder in Figure 9-1) might fool you into thinking that you're looking at a continuous analog pattern. This is just an illusion created when you put enough samples close to each other (much the way things appear to move fluidly in a film when still pictures are displayed at 30 samples, or "frames," per second).

"Samples per second" in sounds are equivalent to "dots per inch" in images.

Some sound processing applications let you zoom into their waveform display, and then as you get further "down" you can see the "grain" or the discontinuities that are characteristic of sampled, digitized sounds or images. This same granularity is easily seen when you zoom into a BMP file, as you can see in Figures 9-5 through 9-9.

Figure 9-5: A digitized sound or image will reveal its true, sampled texture. Like this BMP file, sampled data gets progressively more blocky and discontinuous as you zoom down into it.

Figure 9-6: Zooming down further . . .

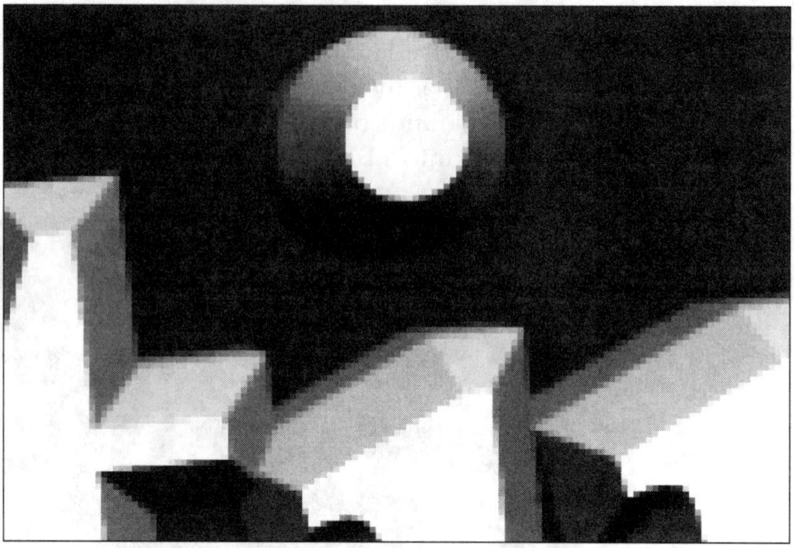

Figure 9-7: Closer still . . .

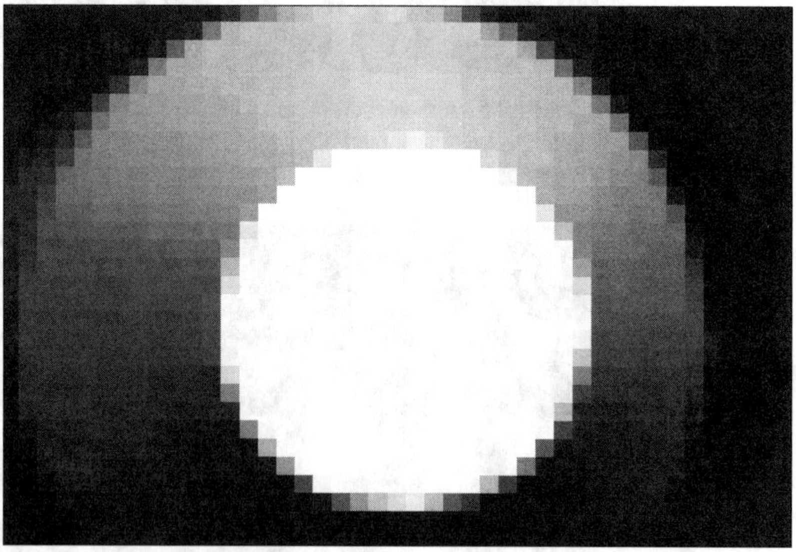

Figure 9-8: Now we can see the individual discrete samples.

Figure 9-9: Now it really gets chunky.

When you are only mildly concerned about accuracy, you might only ask a couple of friends how they feel about the next election. But if accuracy is your business, if you are Mr. Gallup, you must ask thousands of people. So, when taking a poll, the quantity of your sample is directly related to the quality of the result.

Your goal is to set a sampling rate that won't seriously degrade the source, yet won't use too much memory or require too much computer processing either. In Figure 9-10, when sampled at 50 dpi (dots per inch), the rocks are essentially unrecognizable. When sampled at 200 dpi (on the right), the image becomes clear.

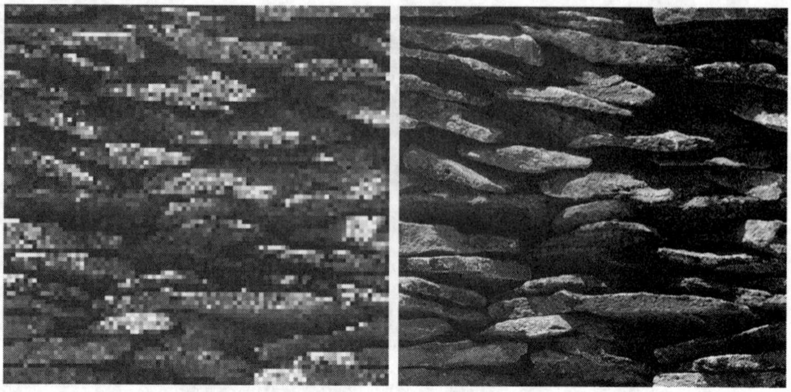

Figure 9-10: When scanned at too low a sampling rate (resolution), the picture of rocks on the left is almost too crude to be recognized.

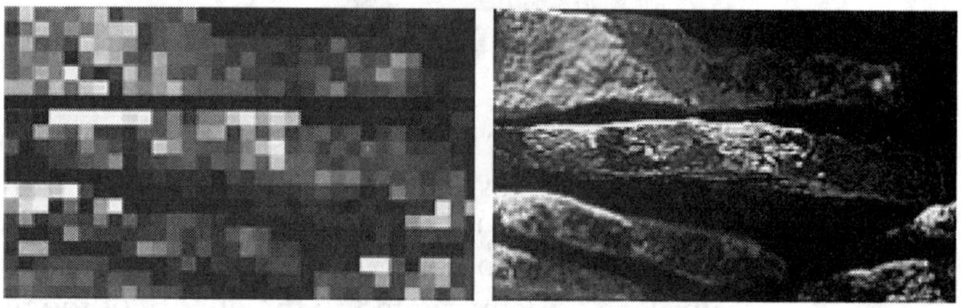

Figure 9-11: A close-up of Figure 9-10. Notice how the irregular shadow between the upper rocks is rendered as a simple, straight black line because our sampling rate is so low on the left.

When sampling a sound, the sampling rate should be determined by the frequencies present in the sound (the complexities of the sound). Voice is simpler than singing (the pitch varies less). Solo singing is simpler than opera (there are fewer instruments, and thus a narrower range of frequencies.) You might think of "frequency" as how many abrupt irregular changes happen in this thing you are trying to turn into a code of numbers.

Sounds with high frequency content call for higher sampling rates (more samples per second). A fundamental theorem in digital signal processing states that an analog signal should be sampled at a rate which is twice as high (or higher) than the highest frequency present in the signal. To properly sample a signal, therefore, we must have an idea of the frequencies it carries. A scream, for example, carries much higher frequencies than a newscaster describing that scream.

The higher the frequencies present in a sound, the higher the sampling rate should be.

Fortunately, we don't usually have to specify a sampling rate. It's built into things we use like the telephone (where, because of its relatively restricted frequency range, a scream sounds like a squawk) or our computer's sound card. (Modern telephones use digital sound. Your voice is converted to a digital signal behind the scenes, transmitted, and then converted back to analog form on the other end.)

### Sampling Rates vs. Frequency

Let's look at some common digital sounds to get an idea of typical sampling rates.

When you talk over the phone, your voice is sampled at approximately 11,000 times per second. In other words, the sampling rate for telephone quality sound is 11 KHz. Therefore, because the rate is twice the highest frequency (the maximum frequency carried over the telephone lines is around 5 KHz), the quality of the reconstructed voice—what you hear on the other end of the line—is fairly clear. The sounds made by a talking human are generally restricted within 5 KHz. If you attempt to sing a song, though, the quality will be less than perfect, because telephones were designed to transmit conversations.

The songs on a CD are sampled at 44.1 KHz and represent the best quality digital sound widely available today. This is referred to as *CD Quality*. Moreover, CDs are recorded in stereo, which means they contain close to 90,000 samples per second. If you attempt to store sound of this quality on your computer, you will run out of disk space very quickly. However, most sound cards are capable of digitizing sounds at CD quality.

Between these two values, there is another sampling quality, called Radio Quality. This quality is equivalent to the quality of a radio broadcast and corresponds to a sampling rate of approximately 22 KHz.

The most common default sampling rate used by sound cards today is 11.025 KHz, which means that, like the telephone, they can reconstruct all frequencies up to approximately 5 KHz. This value is very reasonable for voice and most sounds, but it will fall short if you attempt to record a soprano. When recording music, you might want to raise the sampling rate to 22.050 KHz. Any higher sampling rates will hardly justify the additional disk space. If you want to accurately record the sound of a breaking glass or a gunshot, you will have to raise the sampling rate to 44.1 KHz. Doing so, you will record frequencies most of us cannot even hear. The most sensitive human ear can detect frequencies up to 20 KHz, but no more.

Voice is usually sampled at 11 KHz (11,025 times per second).

CD-ROM

So when you are recording a sound into your computer, simply select a sampling rate that seems adequate for the purpose. All of the sound samples you will find in the \SOUNDS subdirectory of the CD were sampled at 11.025 KHz, and they are monophonic. In rare occasions you may need to raise your sampling frequency, but remember that the resulting files will take up a lot of space on your disk.

### Quantization Levels

Another term you have seen in the specs of a sound card is *bits per sample*, or *quantization levels*. This determines the "quality" of the number that is used to store each sample—in other words, the variable type. Clearly, double-precision floating point would be the most precise way of describing samples. But each double requires 8 bytes per sample. This would result in a waste of disk space—speakers are not nearly this sensitive.

The variable type used to hold each sample determines the number of quantization levels—the granularity of the digital sound. Samples with very similar amplitudes are approximated by the same number. A quantization level is the smallest difference in amplitude that will cause a different classification of the sample. For most sounds, we can use 1 byte per sample. Some sounds can be digitized with less than 1 byte per sample. You can go as low as 4 bits per sample (a half-byte) and still produce intelligible sounds.

The more bits you allocate for each sample, the better you will be able to reconstruct a sound.

Nonetheless, 8 bits per sample is typical. Using this approach, each sample can have one of 256 different values, 0 being the smallest and 255 the largest. Note that these values do not represent physical quantities. Silence corresponds to the value 128. (Waves can have both positive and negative values.) In order to plot the amplitude of a sound, or process its samples, we subtract 128 from each sample. After the processing, we add back the value 128 before we write the sample to a WAVE file.

For higher-quality sound, use 2 bytes (giving you 16 bits per sample). In VB, this would be an integer variable, which can express numbers from –32,768 to 32,767. Again, these values are arbitrary and represent the relative loudness (or amplitude) of each sample. Because integers can range from –32,768 to 32,767, the silence level of sounds

CD-ROM

sampled at 16 bits is at zero. The sound files included in this book's CD (subdirectory \SOUNDS) were digitized at both 8 and 16 bits per sample (in separate subdirectories, of course). The settings of 11.025 KHz for the sampling rate and 8 bits per sample work very well for most everyday sounds. For the very best (to record an orchestra at high fidelity), you will probably have to raise both the sampling rate and the quantization level. But keep in mind that without the proper hardware, you will not be able to hear the difference.

Figure 9-12: Changing the bits per sample has a somewhat different and less drastic effect than changing the sampling rate (see Figure 9-10). When we have few bits per sample (two, in this figure), the geometric shapes are preserved (circles don't degrade into ragged tiles), but interior texture, shading within the main shapes, is lost. It's clear that there are four bands of color in this image.

Figure 9-13: Here, at 4 bits per sample (16 gray levels), grayscale transitions begin to improve.

Figure 9-14: Now, increasing to 5 bits per sample (32 gray levels), the true texture of the shape becomes evident.

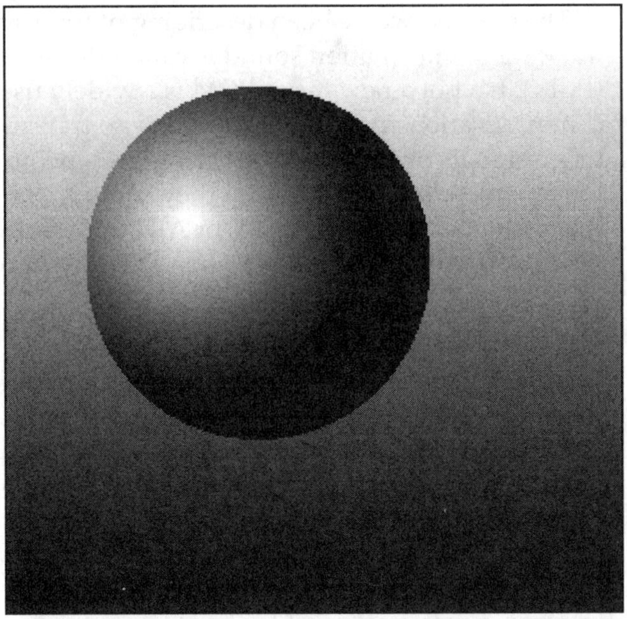

Figure 9-15: At 8 bits per sample (or 256 gray levels), we reach a level of resolution that, at least for gray scale images, approaches the best the human eye can discern.

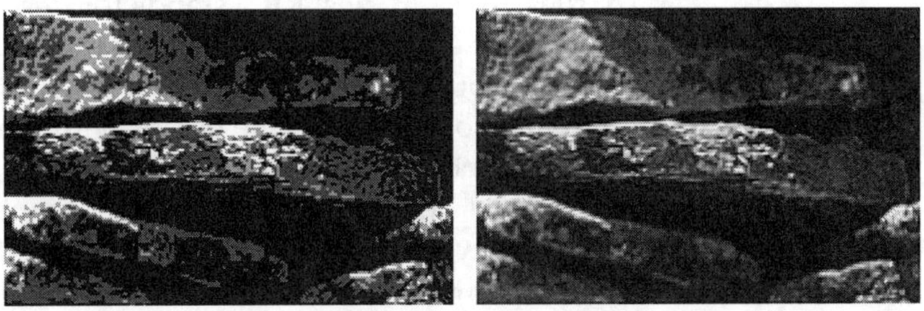

Figure 9-16: Here we reduce 256 gray levels down to 16, or 4 bits per sample. Compare this effect to Figure 9-11, where we reduced the rate at which we are sampling. The image on the left in Figure 9-11 was scanned at 50 dots per inch; the one on the right at 200 dpi.)

The effect on an image when you reduce bits per sample can be seen in Figures 9-12 through 9-16—you can still see the essential shapes, but you lose texture. The effect of reducing the sampling rate (samples per sample) on sound is similar: you might still be able to recognize the words, but be unable to tell which person is speaking. In music, you might still hear the rhythm, but not be able to tell what instruments are playing or even at what pitches.

The method we've been describing of translating an analog sound into digital information sound is called Pulse Code Modulation (PCM). It's not a new term. PCM is a widely used standard in telecommunications that opened the way to transmission of audio and video signals over digital (i.e., error-free) media. Other formats exist that are more efficient because they compress the sound as they store them (such as Adaptive PCM, or ADPCM). However, we will not be concerned with formats other than PCM in this chapter.

## Storing Sounds in Files

WAV files are quite similar to BMP files.

Now let's take a look at the structure of a WAV file, the format in which Windows stores digitized sound. Just like DIB (BMP) files (Device Independent Bitmap graphics files), WAV files contain a "header" (introduction) with information about the sound, followed by the actual sound samples. WAV files are in many ways similar to DIB files. DIB files contain pixel values, which when displayed very close to one another produce the illusion of a continuous-tone image. In other words, you must try hard to see the individual dots on your screen. The same thing happens with WAV files. When the samples are played back in rapid succession, we hear a continuous sound as if it were analog audio.

WAV files are RIFF files. RIFF stands for Resource Interchange File Format and is used by Microsoft to store many different types of multimedia resource files such as movie files, sound files, palettes, MIDI files and so on. A RIFF file begins with the text "RIFF," which identifies the type of the file, followed by a long integer representing its size. The next item in the RIFF file is a four-character piece of text identifying the type of the RIFF file. For sound files, this word is "WAVE." The RIFF file structure is a bit more complicated than the DIB structure, because it is flexible enough to accommodate any new types of multimedia that will appear in the future.

WAV files contain two chunks, the header that describes the structure (sampling rate, bits per samples, etc.) of the waveform, and the body of the file—the actual data in which the waveform is stored.

## The Structure of WAVE Files

Now let's look at the structure of a WAV file. The highest-level description of a WAV file consists of two headers:

```
Type WAVEFORMHEADER
    RiffChunk As RFORMAT
    fmtchunk As WFORMAT
End Type

Type DATAHEADER
    DataString As String * 4
    DataLength As Long
End Type
```

The WAVEFORMATHEADER structure contains information about the type of the sound (sampling rate, bits per sample, etc.). The DATAHEADER structure describes the sound samples that follow.

A full breakdown of the first structure (WAVEFORMHEADER) looks like this:

```
Type RFORMAT
    Name As String * 4
    FileSize As Long
End Type

Type WFORMAT
    fmtName As String * 4
    fmtType As String * 4
    fmtSize As Long
    fmt As WAVEFORMAT
    pcm As PCMSPECIFIC
End Type
```

The RFORMAT structure identifies the file as a RIFF file. The first field is always the four-character string "RIFF." Then there is a long integer, which tells the size of the file. (In reality, the FileSize field is the number of bytes following the RFORMAT section, so FileSize is always 8 bytes less than the actual file's size.

A WAVE file always begins with the word "WAVE."

The WFORMAT structure identifies the type of the RIFF file. In the case of sound files, it begins with the text string "WAVE," followed by the string "fmt," which says that the following bytes determine the format of a WAV file. (Notice that the string "WAVE" must be in uppercase, while the "fmt" string is always in lowercase, padded with a space.)

fmtSize is the size of the two pieces of information that follow fmtSize—that is, the size of the structures WAVEFORMAT and PCMSPECIFIC. These last two structures describe the actual waveform (sampling rate, bits per sample, etc.).

Finally, here is the information contained in the WAVEFORMAT and PCMSPECIFIC structures:

```
Type WAVEFORMAT
    FormatTag As Integer
    nchannels As Integer
    nSamplesPerSec As Long
    nAvgBytesPerSec As Long
    nBlockAling As Integer
End Type

Type PCMSPECIFIC
    nBitsPerSample As Integer
End Type
```

- FormatTag is an integer that identifies the method of coding the waveform. Currently, this field always has the value 1, which means PCM. In the future, there will be more values for the FormatTag. (See the discussion of the PCMSPECIFIC data structure below.)
- nChannels is the number of channels used in the recording process. It has the value 1 for mono sounds and 2 for stereo sounds. Stereo WAV files contain two channels, numbered 0 and 1. Channel 0 represents the left channel and channel 1 the right channel. In the future, we will probably see more values for nChannels, but the speaker position-mapping for more than two channels is not defined yet.

  Ordinary monophonic (single channel) sound is stored in a simple sequence (each sample usually takes up 1 byte):

  sample 1
  sample 2
  sample 3 , and so on.

  Stereo has two channels, and each sample usually requires 2 bytes:

  | | |
  |---|---|
  | sample 1 (left channel) | sample 1 (right channel) |
  | sample 2 (left channel) | sample 2 (right channel) |
  | sample 3 (left channel) | sample 3 (right channel) |

  and so on.

For stereo sounds we first store the sample(s) of the left channel and then the sample(s) of the right channel. When you read a sound file, you must first determine the number of channels and the size of the samples. You really need to use different subroutines for mono and stereo, and different ones for single-byte (mono) and 2-byte samples (stereo).

In this chapter, our examples will be limited to monophonic sounds, sampled at 1 byte per sample. This will not only make our programming simpler, it will also help run the applications efficiently on systems with small amounts of memory. However, the examples can be expanded relatively easily to handle stereo.

- nSamplesPerSecond is the sampling rate (in samples per second) at which each channel was sampled, and should therefore be used to play the sound back.
- nAvgBytesPerSec is the average number of bytes per second at which the data should be transferred. This number is used by the playback software to determine the size of a buffer. (Playback software can't slow things down by pulling the bytes off from the hard drive one at a time, so the whole sound or large pieces of it are stored in a temporary buffer in the user's RAM memory where it can be rapidly accessed.)
- nBlockAlign is the block alignment (in bytes) of the samples and should be nChannels*nBitsPerSample, divided by 8. This number is needed by the playback software to align the data in a buffer, and you can ignore it.
- Finally, there is the PCMSPECIFIC data structure, which contains the number of bits per sample. Currently all WAV files are in the PCM format, but another format has appeared recently. It is called ADPCM (ADaptive PCM) and is a form of compressed PCM. ADPCM requires more powerful hardware to uncompress the waveform in realtime, and is not used widely yet. You should expect, however, that newer sound cards will support this new compression technique.

RIFF files weren't designed for storing WAVE files only.

You may be wondering why the header information isn't simpler. You can make it simpler by combining fields, but the structure of waveform files isn't finalized yet. It is very likely that there will be other methods for digitizing sounds in the future, and the PCMSPECIFIC data structure will be augmented. Also, recall that RIFF files are a standard for storing many types of multimedia files. (You could even come up with your own file structure for storing some new type of information. Your file type might be some custom animation technique or something, instead of a sound WAVE, and so it will contain a completely different format chunk.)

If it helps you, you can simplify the WAVE data structure for reading WAV files, but in our examples we will follow Microsoft's standard. And, once these data structures have been typed into VB, all their fields can be extracted very easily.

Here is a very familiar example. In the Windows subdirectory you will find four WAV files, one of them named TADA.WAV. Even if you don't have a sound card, you can play it with Microsoft's Speaker Driver, which lets you play WAVE files through your computer's built-in speaker. Here are the values of the bytes stored in this file and their meanings:

| Byte (Hex) | Value | Meaning |
|---|---|---|
| 52 49 46 46 | 'RIFF' | The type of the file. |
| 94 6C 00 00 | 27,796 | Length of file (minus 8 bytes). |
| 57 41 56 45 | 'WAVE' | The type of RIFF file. |
| 66 6D 74 20 | 'fmt ' | The type of the following header. |
| 10 00 00 00 | 16 | The length of the following header. |
| 01 00 | 1 | It's a PCM sound. |
| 01 00 | 1 | Number of channels. |
| 22 56 00 00 | 22,050 | Sampling rate. |
| 22 56 00 00 | 22,050 | Average number of bytes/second. |
| 01 00 | 1 | Block alignment (no padding bytes). |
| 08 00 | 8 | Bits per sample (byte). |
| 64 61 74 61 | 'data' | Start of data header. |
| 70 6C 00 00 | 27,760 | Number of samples (one-per-byte in this case). |

Table 9-2: The bytes making up a well-known WAV file (Windows's TADA.WAV in the Windows directory) and their meanings. The values in the first column are hexadecimal numbers, as you would see them with any file viewer program. The quotation marks are a convention for signifying strings and are not part of the file.

Notice the spelling of the keywords "RIFF," "WAVE," "fmt " and "data" as well as the space padding the "fmt " string. The sampling rate is 22.050 KHz, and because there are 8 bits (1 byte) per sample, the average number of bytes per second is 22,050 also.

The size of the file as reported by the FileSize field is 8 bytes shorter than the actual size. The total size of the file is the 36 bytes needed to store the headers plus 27,760 bytes of samples. In other words, the FileSize field doesn't take into consideration the first two fields of the WAVE file.

If you look at the first few actual samples in this WAV file, you will see that their value is 80 (or 128 decimal), which corresponds to silence. If you want to experiment with the structure of other WAVE files and find out how they store information, you can use the FullView application included on the CD.

The values of a WAV file are determined when the sound is recorded. Unlike images, sound files are not created with simple user-interactive applications (i.e., you cannot draw, or paint, sound files). The only way to create sound files is to use your sound card's software. However, we will demonstrate some ways to manipulate sound files to produce interesting special effects.

In Figure 9-17 you see the structure of a WAVE file, with the field names in lowercase and the structures they form in uppercase. You can use this single structure to access WAVE files if you find it simpler. In our example applications, however, we use the full RIFF structure.

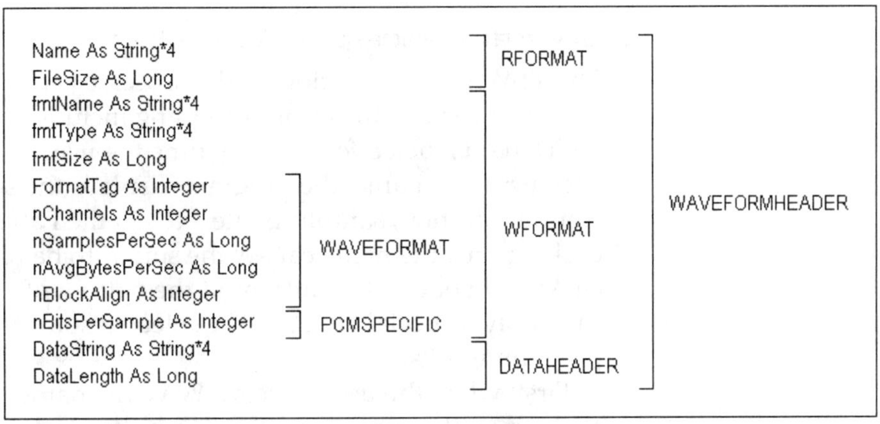


Figure 9-17: A different, simplified look at the structure of a WAVE file. All field definitions of the file's header are shown in their proper order on the left side of the figure in lowercase, and the RIFF structures they form are shown on the right, in uppercase.

## MANIPULATING SOUND

This example, VBWAVE, is analogous to the IMGSHOW example we explored in Chapter 6. Its main Form, shown in Figure 9-18, allows you to locate any WAV file on your hard disk, see its characteristics and play it back. To see the characteristics of a sound file, click on its name; to play it back, double-click on its name. VBWAVE is stored in the 9\APPS\VBWAVE subdirectory of the CD.

CD-ROM

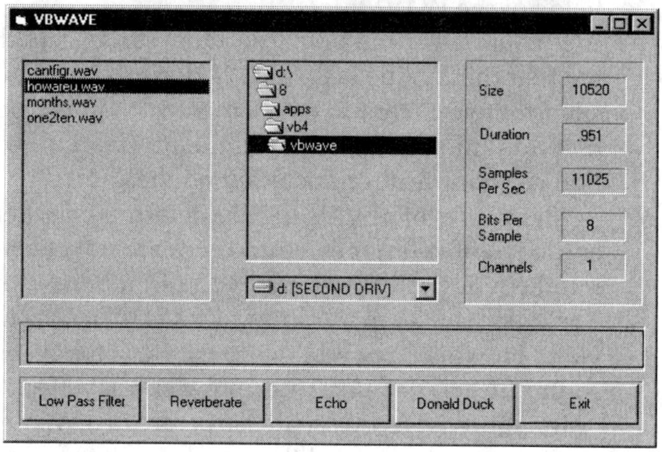


Figure 9-18: This application displays information about sound files, and also filters them in various ways.

### EXAMPLE: PROCESSING WAVE FILES

The VBWAVE application reads, processes and plays back WAVE files. The various forms of processing include echo, reverberation and the Donald Duck effects. Every time the user selects a sound file by clicking on its name, the program displays the sound's characteristics (sound duration, sampling rate, etc.) in the Labels on the left. Double-clicking on a file name causes the sound to be played back. Finally, by clicking on one of the Buttons at the bottom of the screen, the user can apply a special effect on the selected sound. Let's see how the program works.

First, when the user selects a WAV file name in the File List by clicking on its name, the following happens:

```
Private Sub File1_Click( )
Dim SFileName As String
Dim NextByte As String * 1
```

```
Dim w As WAVEFORMHEADER
Dim d As DATAHEADER

   If Right$(dir1.Path, 1) = "\" Then
      SFileName = dir1.Path + File1.FileName
   Else
      SFileName = dir1.Path + "\" + File1.FileName
   End If

   On Error GoTo OpenError
   Open SFileName For Binary As #1
   On Error Resume Next
   Get #1, , w          ' Read waveform header
   Get #1, , d          ' Read data header

   If w.RiffChunk.Name <> "RIFF" Or w.fmtchunk.FmtName   →
   <> "WAVE" Then
      MsgBox "Not a Valid WAV File"
      FSize.Caption = ""
      SPerSec.Caption = ""
      BPerSample.Caption = ""
      channels.Caption = ""
      SDuration.Caption = ""
      Exit Sub
   End If
   FSize.Caption = Format$(w.RiffChunk.FileSize, "######")
   SPerSec.Caption =    →
   Format$(w.fmtchunk.fmt.SamplesPerSec, "#####")
   BPerSample.Caption =    →
   Format$(w.fmtchunk.pcm.BitsPerSample, "##")
   channels.Caption = Format$(w.fmtchunk.fmt.channels, "#")
   SDuration.Caption = Format$(d.DataLength /    →
   w.fmtchunk.fmt.SamplesPerSec, "###.###")

   Close #1
   Exit Sub

OpenError:
   MsgBox "Can't Open " + FileName
   Close
   Exit Sub
End Sub
```

The program opens the selected file, reads the headers and displays the appropriate fields in the Labels on the right side of the Form. These Labels are named Fsize, SPerSec, BPerSample, Channels and SDuration. We define the structures WAVEFORMHEADER and DATAHEADER in a separate Module (SOUND.BAS), along with the declaration of the sndPlaySound( ) Function (discussed above). Here are the contents of the SOUND.BAS Module:

```
Declare Function sndPlaySound Lib "winmm" Alias  →
"sndPlaySoundA" (ByVal WavFile As String, ByVal wFlags As  →
Long) As Long

Type RFORMAT
    Name As String * 4
    FileSize As Long
End Type

Type WAVEFORMAT
    FormatTag As Integer
    channels As Integer
    SamplesPerSec As Long
    AvgBytesPerSec As Long
    BlockAling As Integer
End Type

Type PCMSPECIFIC
    BitsPerSample As Integer
End Type

Type WFORMAT
    FmtName As String * 4
    FmtType As String * 4
    FmtSize As Long
    fmt As WAVEFORMAT
    pcm As PCMSPECIFIC
End Type

Type DATAHEADER
    DataString As String * 4
    DataLength As Long
End Type
```

```
Type WAVEFORMHEADER
    RiffChunk As RFORMAT
    fmtchunk As WFORMAT
End Type

Global voice(5000) As Integer
```

The global array voice( ) is used by the various special effect generating algorithms we are going to present in the next few paragraphs. We use it as a temporary storage place for previous samples. Depending on the version of the application you are using, the declaration of the sndPlaySound( ) Function may differ from the one in the previous listing.

The sndPlaySound( ) Function is the simplest way to play a sound file from within a VB application.

To play back the sound, we use the sndPlaySound( ) API Function. Here is the code executed when the user double-clicks on a file name:

```
Sub File1_DblClick( )
Dim SFileName As String

    If Right$(dir1.Path, 1) = "\" Then
        SFileName = dir1.Path + File1.FileName
    Else
        SFileName = dir1.Path + "\" + File1.FileName
    End If
    wFlags% = &h2
    x% = sndPlaySound(SFileName, wFlags%)

End Sub
```

## Voice Processing

Just as you can filter, process and variously distort a picture (smoothing, embossing, etc.), so too can you process a sound in many ways. VBWAVE works with mono sounds only, at 8 bits per sample. It is straightforward to convert the application so that it supports stereo sounds and 16 bits per sample, but we want to present the basics of sound processing and keep the complexity of the programs to a minimum. Here are a few manipulations of WAV files you might want to experiment with.

The examples of sound processing in this section correspond to the Command Buttons at the bottom of our VBWAVE application. Each time the user clicks on one of these Buttons, the selected .WAV file is read, processed and played for the user to hear. The processed file is stored always under the same file name, which is VBFX.WAV in the current directory. If you want to keep any of the resulting special effects, adjust the source code to remove the command

```
Kill OutFile
```

Under Windows 3.1 you sometimes may not hear the latest file (modified to include special effects). This isn't a bug in the application, but a problem with the sndPlaySound( ) Function, which doesn't load a file from disk if it already exists in memory. If you call the sndPlaySound( ) Function twice with the same file name, the second time around it will play the file already in memory (even if the file on disk has been modified). Moreover, there is no argument that will force sndSoundPlay( ) to reload the file from disk. If you play the VBFX.WAV file and you don't hear the sound you expected, just play a different sound file and then try again.

## Echo

One of the most common audio special effects is echo. Here we'll see how you can control echo with your own Visual Basic routine. Echo will also offer additional insight into the nature of digital sound.

Echo is the what you hear when a sound is reflected coherently; it's a repeat of the original, but somewhat less sharp and loud. This description can be translated to the following relation between samples:

```
s(i) = s(i) + 0.5 * s(i-N)
```

This line says that the sample s(i) is heard at the same time as a previous (now echoing) sample s(i-N). And this echoing sample was heard N samples ago. Here we are using a factor of 50 percent (0.5) to reduce the loudness of the echo (an "attenuation factor"). This choice of 50 percent is rather arbitrary and determines the percentage of the signal that was "reflected." You can change this value to control the echo's relative loudness, and change N to control the echo's delay.

To control the Echo effect, change the distance (N) and the attenuation factor.

A very small value for N has practically no effect. To find a reasonable value for N, let's say we want to add the echo of an obstacle that's 20 meters away. The sound travels at the speed of 340 m/sec. The distance it must cover to return to our ears is 40 meters (20 meters to reach the obstacle and 20 more meters back). This distance is traveled in 40/340, or approximately .117 of a second. To express this time in samples, we must take into consideration the sampling rate. If the sound was sampled at 11,025 samples per second, .117 seconds correspond to 11,025 * 0.117, or 1300 samples approximately. Therefore, if you set N to 1300 you will create the echo effect that you would get from an obstacle 20 meters away. In our sample code we use a value of 3,000 to make the echo effect very clear.

Under the Echo Button on our the Form, this is the programming:

```
Private Sub ECHOButton_Click( )
Dim NextByte As Byte
Dim SFileName As String
Dim w As WAVEFORMHEADER
Dim d As DATAHEADER

    If File1.FileName = "VBFX.WAV" Then
        MsgBox "Can't use this file name!"
        Exit Sub
    End If

    If Right$(dir1.Path, 1) = "\" Then
        SFileName = dir1.Path + File1.FileName
        OutFileName = dir1.Path + "VBFX.WAV"
    Else
        SFileName = dir1.Path + "\" + File1.FileName
        OutFileName = dir1.Path + "\" + "VBFX.WAV"
    End If

    On Error GoTo OpenError2
    Open SFileName For Binary As #1
    On Error Resume Next
    Kill OutFile
    File1.Refresh
    On Error GoTo OpenError2a
    Open OutFileName For Binary As #2

    Get #1, , w
    Get #1, , d
    If w.fmtchunk.pcm.BitsPerSample <> 8 Then
        MsgBox "VBWAVE can process only sounds sampled  →
        at 8 bits/sample"
        Exit Sub
    End If
```

```
    Put #2, , w
    Put #2, , d

    NSamples = 3000
    For i = 1 To NSamples
        Get #1, , NextByte
        voice(i) = NextByte - 128
        Put #2, , NextByte
    Next

    FLen = LOF(1)
    While Not EOF(1)
        i = i + 1
        Get #1, , NextByte
        vecho = 0.8 * (NextByte - 128) + 0.4 * voice(i Mod  →
        NSamples)
        voice(i Mod NSamples) = NextByte - 128
        vecho = vecho + 128
        If vecho > 255 Then vecho = 255
        If vecho < 0 Then vecho = 0
        NextByte = vecho
        Put #2, , NextByte
        If i Mod 100 = 0 Then
            Gauge1.Value = 100 * (i / FLen)
            Gauge1.Refresh
        End If
    Wend
    Close #1
    Close #2
    File1.Refresh
    Gauge1.Value = 0

    wFlags& = &H2
    xx = sndPlaySound(OutFileName, wFlags&)
    Kill OutFileName
    File1.Refresh
    Exit Sub

OpenError2:
    MsgBox "Can't Open  " + SFileName
    Close
    Exit Sub
```

```
OpenError2a:
    MsgBox "Can't Open  " + OutFile
    Close
    Exit Sub

End Sub
```

The programming that creates the echo effect is only a few lines of the above. (The rest of it takes care of the Gauge Control that displays the progress of the operation and possible file error conditions.)

These are the lines that actually produce the echo effect:

```
While Not EOF(1)
        i = i + 1
        Get #1, , NextByte
        vecho = 0.8 * (NextByte - 128) + 0.4 * voice(i Mod  →
        NSamples)
        voice(i Mod NSamples) = NextByte - 128
        vecho = vecho + 128
        If vecho > 255 Then vecho = 255
        If vecho < 0 Then vecho = 0
        NextByte = vecho
        Put #2, , NextByte
        If i Mod 100 = 0 Then
            Gauge1.Value = 100 * (i / FLen)
            Gauge1.Refresh
        End If
Wend
```

The array voice( ) holds enough samples to create the echo effect—to be exact, the last NSamples samples. This is all the past samples we need to create the echo effect. (Because an echo effect repeats a sound only once, we don't need the already-heard echo again, so we can forget about it. If we stored all the data in an array, they would be always available, but this approach would needlessly use up memory. So we slide a "window" (the array voice) over the sound samples, dropping the trailing, unnecessary data as we move forward through the sound. Note that the Mod command assists in this process by ensuring that we always remain within the "sliding window" as we go forward through the array.)

Each sample of an 8-bit sound file has a value between 0 and 255, and the value 128 corresponds to silence. That's why we have to subtract 128 from each sample in order to process it, and then we add 128 to the result before saving it to disk.

## Reverberation

For a more dramatic trick, a sound can bounce around between several obstacles at various distances. This results in various attenuations (reductions in loudness). In effect, the difference between reverb and echo is the difference between sound indoors versus outdoors, between sound bouncing around within a room versus flying back from a canyon wall.

Reverberation adds a kind of depth or "presence" to a sound. Most music, for example, contains reverb since it is usually played indoors. Here is a formula for reverb that's based on three different reflections:

$$s(i) = 0.7 * s(i) + 0.25 * s(i\text{-}1000) + 0.20 * s(i\text{-}2000) + 0.15 * s(i\text{-}3000)$$

Notice that this time we have added four amplitude factors (.7 for the original sample, then .25, .20 and .15 for the reflected one). Since so much is being added here, we want to guard against "clipping" the sound by exceeding the maximum value allowed for a sample (255, in the case of these byte-sized samples we're using here).

Reverberation is the combination of multiple echo effects, from different distances and with different attenuation factors.

Also notice that the sum of these amplitude factors exceeds 1. This means that sound+reverb is louder than the volume of the original sound, which is what happens when you are talking in a reverberant room. However, the sum of the factors (technically "coefficients") shouldn't exceed 1 by much, or else the dynamic range of the output will be exceeded. (Dynamic range is the amount of the difference between silence and the loudest sound.)

Here's the programming to add reverberation to a sound. (We show only the lines that implement the reverberation effect. The rest of the lines behind the Button's subroutine open the file and handle errors, and these are identical to the previous Subroutine.)

```
NSamples = 3000
While Not EOF(1)
     i = i + 1
     Get #1, , NextByte
     Sample = NextByte - 128
     vecho = 0.7 * Sample + 0.25 * voice((i - 1000) Mod  →
     NSamples) + 0.2 * voice((i - 2000) Mod NSamples) +  →
     0.15 * voice((i - NSamples) Mod NSamples)
```

```
            voice(i Mod NSamples) = Sample
            vecho = vecho + 128
            If vecho > 255 Then vecho = 255
            If vecho < 0 Then vecho = 0
            NextByte = vecho
            Put #2, , NextByte
            If i Mod 100 = 0 Then
                Gauge1.Value = 100 * (i / FLen)
                Gauge1.Refresh
            End If
    Wend
```

Notice that the reverberation effect is performed by a single line of code—a fairly lengthy one:

```
    vecho = .7 * Sample + .25 * voice((i - 1000) Mod NSamples) →
    + .2 * voice((i - 2000) Mod NSamples) + .15 * voice((i - →
    NSamples) Mod NSamples)
```

The array voice( ) is used again for storing the previous samples we are going to need in future computations, and no more.

## Low-Pass Filtering

One of the most useful kinds of sound processing is the filtering of the high frequencies. Low frequencies are what make the voice of a baritone so distinct, while high frequencies are dominant in a soprano's voice. Before we look at the next example, let's see what low and high frequencies look like.

In Figures 9-19 and 9-20 you see two waveforms, which could be parts of a sound signal. Which one do you think contains higher frequencies? High frequencies are easy to distinguish by the ear, but not quite so obvious in a waveform. In general, the more rapidly a signal changes, the higher its frequencies.

In Figure 9-20 you see the same waveform as in 9-19, but after the removal of its highest frequencies. The filtered signals maintain their basic structure, but the most abrupt changes have been removed. Notice also that there's a decrease in amplitude.

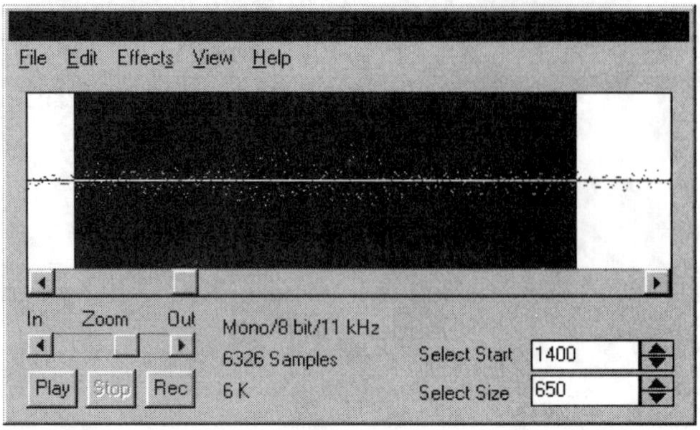


Figure 9-19: The original waveform.

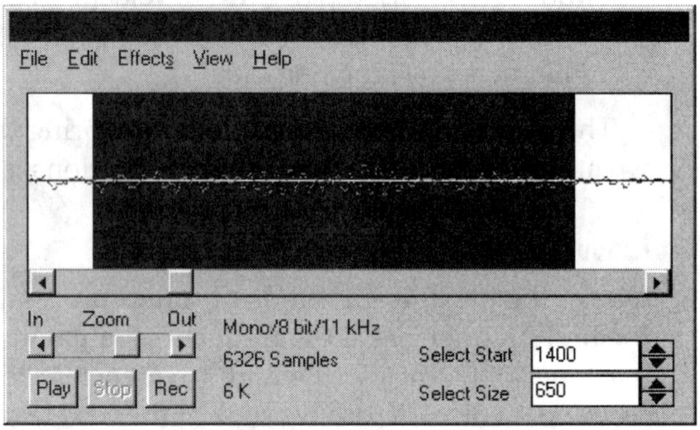


Figure 9-20: The same waveform after removing its high frequencies.

Removing high frequencies from sound is accomplished the same way as blurring a picture, and has an analogous effect. (See the Smooth image processing algorithm in Chapter 6.) To our ears, high frequency sounds seem squeaky, strident, sibilant and so on—a struck cymbal versus a bass drum.

If you listen to a sound after removing its high frequencies, you will hear a diffuse, "flatter," less precise sound. It's as if you were listening to a band playing in another room on the other side of a wall.

Low-pass filtering a sound is similar to "blurring" an image.

How do we remove high frequencies from a sound file? The technique is no different than the one we used to remove high frequencies from images: each sample is replaced by the average of its neighboring ones. The result is that samples considerably "higher" or "lower" than their neighbors (in other words samples that cause abrupt changes in the signal and therefore contribute to higher frequencies) are pulled toward the rest of the samples.

Taking the average of a number of samples smoothes out the signal. This operation is called low-pass filtering, because it lets the low frequencies go through unhampered, but cuts off the high frequencies. In many cases high frequencies represent an unwanted portion of the signal—noise (the scratches on an old LP, for example, or hiss in tape). Low-pass filtering is the equivalent of turning down the "tone" control on a stereo system.

### The Filter's Length

The main parameter that we can fiddle with when averaging is how many neighbors should be considered. If you only average three samples at a time (the one before and the one after the current sample), the effect will be hardly noticeable. If you stretch your "filter" too much (averaging say 50 samples at a time), the sound will flatten so much as to become unintelligible. A good choice for the filter's length is between 3 and 10 samples.

Here is the programming to add a low-pass filter. (This and the other sound manipulation functions use the same gauge and file programming, so we are only reprinting the section that does the actual filtering. To see the complete listing, look for VBWAVE.MAK on the CD's 9\APPS\VBWAVE subdirectory):

CD-ROM

```
FilterLength = 8
While Not EOF(1)
    Get #1, , NByte
    v = Asc(NByte) - 128
    voice((i Mod FilterLength) + 1) = v
    v = 0
    For j = 1 To FilterLength
        v = v + voice(j)
    Next
    v = 1.6 * v / FilterLength
    v = v + 128
    If v > 255 Then v = 255
    NByte = Chr$(v)
    Put #2, , NByte
    i = i + 1
Wend
```

The length of the filter we are using here is 8 samples, and it produces an obvious effect on the sound.

Notice that we are also multiplying each filtered sample by 1.3, because low-pass filtering generally reduces the amplitude (loudness) of the original signal. The factor 1.3 restores to some extent this loss of amplitude—a rather crude approach, but it works without introducing any math complexity to our application. Try low-pass filtering some of the female voice samples included on the CD with a filter length of 3 to 5 samples to see how the filter operates.

CD-ROM

Low-pass filtering smoothes out high frequencies, but it decreases overall amplitude as well.

The opposite operation, removal of low frequencies, is also possible, but hardly useful. (Most information in voice or music is carried on relatively low frequencies. Removing them would leave you with the mountain peaks but no mountains. It would sound like interrupted static. There used to be "rumble filters" on stereo receivers, which removed subsonic artifacts induced by old-style needle-in-groove record players. However, with the advent of the CD, this is no longer necessary.)

Notice that the speed of the program can be improved by adjusting the calculation of the variable v. Instead of adding all the adjacent samples for each sample we process, we could subtract the oldest sample, and add the most recent one (so that v will always be the sum of the 8 most recent samples). Again, we sacrificed some efficiency for clarity.

### Sound vs. Image Processing

Many operations can be carried out on visual images as well as sounds. But there is a basic difference: images can be processed to the extent that they become unrecognizable. As long as the result is aesthetically pleasing, nobody will object. Sounds should not lose their basic content, or else they will become noise and certainly not pleasing to the ear at all.

A primary reason for this distinction is that an image, a painting for instance, is seen holistically—all at once. A sound, however, moves through time in a linear fashion. So, a sound generally contains less information at any given point in time, and the effect of a sound is cumulative. You can visualize this distinction by considering dance. If seen in a painting, there is almost no position that would make a dancer seem awkward. However, move the dancer through time in a movie and then clumsy movements, if any, are clearly revealed.

Also, the human brain devotes considerably more processing power to visual events than it does to auditory events. As you might expect, the brain can supply meaning to and enjoy nearly featureless pictures (otherwise there would be less appreciation of "modern" art). However, randomized, homogeneous sound (noise) or extremely low amplitude (silence) are seen as the absence of information or an unpleasant distortion of it. We call degraded sound "noise," but there is no word for a degraded picture, except, perhaps, "texture."

## Donald Duck Effect

Our last example is a surprisingly simple effect that changes the waveform by pinching it together like a squeezed accordion. This results in a helium-balloon, "Donald Duck" effect.

What are the characteristics of Donald Duck's voice? It is fast and contains relatively high frequencies. We can achieve both by simply changing our sampling rate (during playback only). If your voice has been recorded at a given sampling rate, it will sound normal only if played back at that same rate. If you change the sampling rate for the playback, the computer will play it back slower (and lower), or faster (and higher). Try both effects.

It's interesting to see what happens when we increase the sampling rate. The computer thinks the sound was sampled at a higher rate and tries to play it back faster. The variations in the signal will not change (you can still understand the words), but they must take place in a shorter period of time. This in turn means that the changes in the signal will become more abrupt, therefore producing higher frequencies. The opposite is true when we play back the sound at a lower sampling rate. The same samples are spaced further apart and the changes in the sound become less abrupt.

There is a peculiar relationship between time and frequency. When a signal is compressed in time, its frequencies expand. Likewise, when the signal expands in time, its frequencies shrink. You can observe (actually hear) this relationship by changing the sampling rate of a sound file and then playing it back.

Here is the programming for this effect:

```
Private Sub DONALDButton_Click( )
Dim w As WAVEFORMHEADER
Dim d As DATAHEADER
```

```
    ScaleBy = 1.5

    If File1.FileName = "VBFX.WAV" Then
        MsgBox "Can't use this file name!"
        Exit Sub
    End If

    If Right$(dir1.Path, 1) = "\" Then
        SFileName = dir1.Path + File1.FileName
        OutFileName = dir1.Path + "VBFX.WAV"
    Else
        SFileName = dir1.Path + "\" + File1.FileName
        OutFileName = dir1.Path + "\" + "VBFX.WAV"
    End If

    On Error Resume Next
    Kill OutFileName
    On Error GoTo OpenError5
    FileCopy SFileName, OutFileName
    a% = DoEvents( )
    Open OutFileName For Binary As #1
    Get #1, 1, w
    w.fmtchunk.fmt.SamplesPerSec = ScaleBy *   →
    w.fmtchunk.fmt.SamplesPerSec
    w.fmtchunk.fmt.AvgBytesPerSec = ScaleBy *   →
    w.fmtchunk.fmt.AvgBytesPerSec
    Put #1, 1, w
    Close #1

    wFlags& = &H2
    xx = sndPlaySound(OutFileName, wFlags&)
    Kill OutFileName
    File1.Refresh

    Exit Sub

OpenError5:
    MsgBox "Can't Open  " + SFileName
    Close
    Exit Sub

End Sub
```

This Subroutine is shorter and transforms the WAV file much faster than the other special-effects Subroutines because it doesn't have to process each sample. It copies the entire file and then it changes the sampling rate by multiplying the SamplesPerSec field with a constant. (We also change the AvgBytesPerSec field, which is used by Windows's or other playback software, to make sure that the sound file will be played back properly.)

You can scale the sampling rate up and down to hear what it does to the waveform: just change the ScaleBy factor above. You could also add a scroll bar to calibrate the scaling of the playback rate.

Playing a WAVE file faster or slower is similar to playing an LP at the wrong speed.

Like pictures, sounds are made up of samples, and their processing can be a simple matter of arithmetic operations on these numbers.

One last remark before leaving WAVE files. As you may have noticed, in the algorithms presented here the processed sound files have the same length as the original ones. This isn't quite right because we are, for instance, ignoring the echo or reverberation aftereffects on the last few samples in the sound. In theory, we should extend the length of a sound file to accommodate this. However, we assume that the last few moments of each WAVE file are silent (generally the case), so that the echo or reverberation of the last audible samples will fit in the space of the trailing silent samples. We chose this approach because it works well and also simplifies the programming. If you want to change the length of the processed file by appending more samples at the end, don't forget to change the values of the DataLength and FileSize fields.

### Processing 16-Bit Sounds

The VBWAVE application can process mono sounds, sampled at 8 bits per sample. You can easily adjust it to handle other types of sounds. If you want to process 16-bit sounds, all you have to do is read the sample directly into an integer variable (just skip the step of converting the character to a number). For stereo sounds, you have to perform the processing twice, once for the right and once for the left channel, and put both samples back on the file in the same order. The two channels of a stereo sound are always processed separately.

### Further Improvements

As we have demonstrated, processing sounds is straightforward, not unlike image processing. Both images and sounds are made up of numeric values, which represent color intensity or volume respectively. Manipulating sounds and images is a matter of combining integer values with the basic arithmetic operators. VBWave can serve as your starting point to create additional sound effects.

For example, you can add fade-ins and fade-outs by combining the samples of two different sound files. Let's say the two sounds are stored in the files SOUND1.WAV and SOUND2.WAV, and you want to mix them by fading out SOUND1.WAV and fading in SOUND2. The resulting waveform will be stored in a new file, SOUND.WAV. Copy a few seconds worth of samples from SOUND1 to SOUND. Then start adding the samples of the two files, as follows: Multiply the sample of SOUND1 by 0.99 and the corresponding sample in SOUND2 by 0.01 and then add them. This sample has 99% of the intensity of the first sound and only 1% of the intensity of the second sound. Then multiply the next samples with 0.98 and 0.02 respectively. Continue decreasing the percentage of the first sound and increasing the percentage of the second sound until you reach 100% of the second sound.

If you play back the file SOUND, you'll hear the sound SOUND1 for a while, and then SOUND1 will fade out (you'll be hearing less and less of it) while SOUND2 fades in (you'll be hearing more and more of it).

CD-ROM

In the \COOL subdirectory of the CD you will find a great sound processing application. It is called Cool Editor (COOL.EXE) and provides numerous sound effects, such as talking underwater or talking like an alien. It also provides the tools to create your own special sound effects. The algorithms of the application are more complicated than the ones we presented in this chapter, but once you've become familiar with sound processing techniques, you should be able to understand how Cool Editor implements the sound effects.

Cool Editor is a shareware application and offers a variety of registration methods. Please read the registration information to find out about the program and its author.

## MIDI FILES

The second category of sounds in the Windows environment are MIDI sounds. MIDI is now the accepted standard computer language for music. Adopted by agreement among synthesizer manufacturers in the mid-'80s, MIDI can specify tone, timbre, duration, vibrato and dozens of other aspects of sound and music.

As you have doubtless realized, information has two possible forms: symbolic (coded) and imitative (sampled). The English language, for example, is a code—it uses a subset of 26 symbols to represent a fish, like this: FISH. The Egyptian and Oriental languages, by contrast, use pictures to *imitate* what the pictures portray. A fish, in an Egyptian tomb or in Japanese, can look like this:

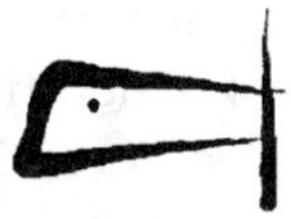

Imitative information always endeavors to duplicate an object (the success of this endeavor is determined by the amount of "resolution," by the sampling rate).

Descriptive information, by contrast, endeavors to symbolize the object it describes. This is why a photo of President Clinton actually looks like him, whereas a clip-art rendering of Mr. Clinton can only remind you of him by exaggerating any unusual features in his appearance, the way cartoonists must. In other words, photos are representative of an original, cartoons are symbolic of the original.

MIDI files are descriptive. WAVE and BMP files are imitative.

Like any other information, data that's stored, manipulated or played back by a computer must be either coded or imitative. A WMF graphic file is symbolic; a BMP is imitative.

A WMF graphic contains a set of equations describing positions and sizes of geometric objects, along with codes for the colors and textures that fill those objects. It's a set of coordinates and a list of colors to fill those coordinates with. When a WMF is displayed, the computer calculates these rectangles, ellipses, colors and so on. Then it can reproduce them on the printer or the screen. However, this reproduction—based as it is on maplike coordinates—will always look like a drawing, no matter how detailed. You can see one layer upon another—like rice paddies viewed from above.

A BMP graphic, by contrast, is like a Xerox copy of the original: it contains a bit-by-bit imitation of the original. So there is little calculation required to display it. The computer merely feeds to the screen or printer, line by line, the spots (pixels) in whatever degree of gray or color that they were stored when the image was copied. A circle in a BMP file doesn't have to be mathematically calculated, it merely appears on screen as the by-product of sending the stream of bits within the BMP, the "bitmap." A high-resolution bitmap (the original was sampled often so the visual information is quite dense) looks like a photograph, not a drawing.

WAV files are imitative. They contain the actual sounds, because we cannot yet describe many sounds in rigorous, unambiguous form.

If there were a way to describe sounds with notes, then the sound files could be stored much more efficiently. Attempts have been made to that end, but the results are far from satisfactory. If you have heard computer-generated speech, you will agree that it doesn't come close to sampled voice. The symbols used to code sounds are called phonemes, and there are 64 of them. The phonemes are used in text to voice conversion, but they fall short of generating natural sounds. The day computers will be able to listen and talk is coming, but it's not near yet. Until then, voice and other simple sounds will be recorded and played back.

Music, however, has its own rich coded language, where the symbols are the notes and rests and accents and so on. Therefore, music can be stored as a mathematical description of the components of each sound (duration, timbre, etc.). So with music, as with images, we have the same option of either coding or sampling the original sound. Sheet music contains coded music; a CD or cassette tape contains a stream of waveforms sampled from an actual performance of the music.

The MIDI Language grew out of existing music notation, and added new descriptions such as depth of vibrato.

The MIDI language, and a MID music disk file, is a coded description in mathematical terms of each moment of music. A WAV file is the opposite: it contains a copy of the original waveforms making up the sound—sampled via microphone.

Descriptive data like MIDI music is far less bulky—it takes up much less room on disk than imitative, sampled data. Another advantage of descriptive data is that it is inherently scalable—you can blow it up or reduce it without changing the resolution, without getting jaggies, stairsteps or a mosaic effect. The resolution of descriptive data depends only on the capabilities of the reproducing medium (how good your monitor or synthesizer is). The resolution of imitative data depends on the original sampling rate, and the degree to which you are magnifying or amplifying the information.

To play a MIDI file you will need a sound card because it takes specialized hardware to convert the music codes to waveforms. That means you cannot use the SPEAKR.DRV driver to play back MIDI files. It is not unthinkable that someone could develop a utility for converting MIDI notation to a WAV file, but its usefulness would be very limited.

Every sound card we have run across comes with its own MIDI applications, but we will not present one here. The MIDI language is so full and complex that describing it is beyond the scope of this book. There are, for those interested, books on MIDI available.

## ANIMATION

Now let's look at another multimedia component, moving pictures. Video information requires even more storage space on the computer's hard drive than does audio information, and its processing is much more complicated than sound or image processing.

Moving pictures fall into two major categories: computer-generated animation (coded) and "digital" (sampled) video. Animation is created with special and, so far, usually expensive software. Programs such as Autodesk's 3D Studio and Animator Pro, Caligari's trueSpace and PIXAR's Typestry are typical examples of animation programs. 3D Studio and trueSpace are photorealistic animation applications that let you define a scene, the objects that will appear in it, their movement, the light sources and the movement of the camera. Having defined all of these elements, they produce an animation of what you would see through the camera.

Typestry is a less ambitious application that allows you to animate text characters only. Nevertheless, its output is extremely realistic.

These programs produce files with the extension FLI, FLC or AVI, which can be played back with the appropriate software. Fortunately, the playback software is not nearly as expensive as that used to create the animation.

CD-ROM

One of the tools for playing back animation files is called AAWIN and can be downloaded from CompuServe (GO ADESK and then Join the Autodesk Multimedia Forum; the file you need is called AAPLAY.EXE). To install it, follow the instructions of the README.DOC file. With AAWIN you can play back FLI and FLC files, as well as sequences of BMP files in rapid succession. You can try out the AAWIN application with some of the FLI files we've included on the CD (subdirectory ANIMATIO). Later you'll see how you can create animation as a sequence of BMP files.

The second category of moving pictures in computers is digital video. With the appropriate hardware you can capture (digitize) video from your VCR or TV, store it in a file on your hard disk and play it back later, just as you can capture sounds with the sound card. This is called digital video, since the video image is stored in your computer in digital form.

Video cards are not needed for playback. With Microsoft's Video for Windows applet you can play back a digital video file (one that has extension AVI). You will find several AVI files on the CD, under the subdirectory ANIMATIO.

Just as you can create animation files, it is possible to process digital video and create special effects with video, text and graphics. A new generation of software has made possible the combination of digital video sequences with more traditional media, such as graphics and animation. Perhaps the most important tool in this category is Adobe's Premier, which lets you create numerous special effects with video, graphics and animation files.

Now let's see how to create and use AVI and FLI files with the simple tools. Later on, we will demonstrate a few simple ways to create surprisingly sophisticated animation on your computer, without expensive hardware or software.

## Capturing & Playing Back Video

The simplest form of moving pictures you can display on your computer's monitor is digital video. If you have a video capture card installed on your computer you can display live video from your VCR or cable in a window. To store a video sequence on your hard disk, you can use the VidCap application which comes with Microsoft's Video for Windows (often included with a video capture card). VidCap digitizes video and stores it in a file. The files created by VidCap are called AVI (Audio Video Interleave), which is a standard proposed by Microsoft for storing synchronized video and audio information in the same file.

Digital video is still in its infancy. The movement is jerky on all but the fastest systems and it must be captured in a low resolution and displayed in a small window to look good. To appreciate the difficulties of working with video in the digital domain, consider what's involved in digitizing a video sequence. At first, we must decide upon the resolution of the image. A *single* 240 X 320 image (a "frame" as it's called) at 256 colors contains 76,800 bytes. This picture is only one frame of the video sequence. Multiply this by the number of frames in the video signal (12 or more for reasonable quality animation, 30 for TV or movie quality) and you end up with nearly a megabyte of storage required for a single second of digital video.

A greater concern than your hard disk's capacity is how fast your machine can get the video data off of the disk and onto the screen. Can your hard disk maintain a transfer rate of 1mb per second?

Of course, digital video files can be compressed, but the decompression itself takes time and you cannot achieve any reasonable compression without the proper hardware. These operations are computationally intensive even for the fastest Pentium processor—

that's why less swift computers have to resort to this specialized MPEG hardware. Compression/decompression cards are expensive and you can assume that most users of your applications don't have one installed in their systems. However, techniques for compression/decompression of video signals are under continual study and development—major advances in this field have been expected for several years.

Another category of animated images involves images you create on the computer. We will explore how to make animation without special programs. One advantage of this approach is that you have control over the colors and frame rate, and you can fine-tune the animation. When you capture video with a video card, you can't easily change the content of the images.

### MPEG Hardware

To record and play back video in a relatively high resolution, you need an MPEG card. MPEG is a video compression standard (designed by the Motion Picture Experts Group), which can deliver near-VHS-quality video to your desktop computer. To be more specific, MPEG is a highly efficient compression/decompression technique that is currently implemented in hardware. In order to record or play back video in MPEG format, you need dedicated hardware.

Currently, the MPEG standard defines a resolution of 352 X 240, at 30 frames per second, with a bandwidth of 150 KB per second. This is a pretty good window size for video playback, at the highest rate. The best part of MPEG is the required bandwidth. Even with a first-generation CD-ROM, you can maintain a rate of 30 frames per second. Since triple speed (3X) and quad speed (4X) CD-ROMs have appeared in the market, manufacturers of MPEG cards can provide even higher resolutions. You can buy an MPEG card capable of playing back digitized video at a resolution of 640 X 480, at 30 frames per second.

MPEG playback cards are within reach for most power users (they start at $300). The less expensive MPEG cards can only decompress (playback) video. To compress digitized video with the MPEG algorithm, you need a much more expensive card—a rather strange situation, since compression and decompression algorithms are usually very similar. Not so with MPEG. The design of the MPEG standard was based on the assumption that playback should be real-time and cost as little as possible. Compression, on the other hand, is a complicated process that need not even be performed in real-time. A video clip will be compressed once but played back by a million users. The compression algorithms are more complicated so that the decompression algorithms will be significantly simpler.

A real-time MPEG compression card today can cost anywhere from $5,000 to $20,000. There are hardly any systems out there with MPEG compression capabilities, and we will not deal with these techniques in this chapter. We will concern ourselves only with animation techniques that can be used on any PC, even if the final result is a little crude (or "video in a stamp," as its critics call it). All the techniques we will discuss in this chapter, however, can be used with MPEG compression/decompression hardware to produce much more impressive results.

Computer digital video has not yet reached its full potential.

As CPUs become more and more powerful, though, we are going to see software MPEG solutions—that is, programs, that, with the help of powerful CPUs, can perform MPEG decompression without any assistance from specialized hardware.

## Fractal Animation

If you have read Chapter 14 on fractals, you may recall that certain fractal images (Julia Sets) are based on a few simple algorithms, and the end result depends upon the value of a single parameter. The Julia Set, for example, begets many different shapes based on the values of the cx and cy parameters. By slowly varying the value of these parameters, we can create sequences of animated fractals. To see this often lovely effect, run the AVI files in the \ANIMATIO\AVI subdirectory of the CD with the Media Player that comes with Windows. You must also have the two Microsoft run-time files AVIPLAY.DLL and VIDEO.DLL in your Windows\System directory. If you don't, you can download them from Microsoft's Software Library on CompuServe (GO MSL and download the file VFW11D.EXE, which contains all the files you need). The files under the ANIMATIO\AVI subdirectory are animated fractals, generated with the applications you will find in this chapter.

CD-ROM

There are many ways to create animated fractals. The simplest one is to zoom slowly into a small area of the Mandelbrot or Julia Set you are interested in. As you zoom in, new patterns and colors are revealed slowly. Julia Sets depend on the value of the complex constant *c* and they offer another possibility for animation: if you change the value of the constant slowly, the shape of the Julia Set changes progressively into new, often magnificent images. We can take advantage of the dependence of certain fractal images on a specific constant to create sequences of BMP files, which when played back in quick succession produce some stunning animations.

Figure 9-21: A new type of fractal image. It is a Julia Set, but very different from the ones in Chapter 14.

Figure 9-22: These cosine-driven images lend themselves particularly to animation.

## A New Type of Fractal

We will not explore the type of fractals shown in Figures 9-21 and 9-22 in Chapter 14 because we want to look at them here—this type produces pictures that are well suited for animation. (We also avoid this type of fractal in Chapter 14 because the calculation of the cosine of a complex number involves more trigonometry than we can present in this book.)

Although it is a member of the Julia Set, this fractal paradigm differs from the other Julia Sets because it uses a different transformation. The Julia fractals in Chapter 14 are based on the function $z=z^2+c$, where z is a point on the complex plane and c, a complex constant. This time the transformation is defined as

```
z = λ*cos(z)
```

Here, λ (pronounced "lambda") is a real constant that controls the shape of the fractal, similar to the c constant of the Julia Set. z takes on all the values of the complex plane as before. The function for calculating the new fractal is included in Visual Basic code in the COSJULIA application—function cosFractal( ).

You can use cosFractal instead of the VBMandel( ) or VBJulia( ) Functions (see Chapter 14) without having to know how it works. It simply performs its transformation on whatever point of the complex plane you pass to it as arguments. cosFractal( ) accepts four arguments: the two coordinates of a point on the complex plane, the value of the parameter λ and the maximum number of iterations.

The cosFractal( ) Function returns the number of iterations it took for the specified point to escape to infinity. If this number is equal to MaxIter, then the point is bounded. If not, the point is an escapee and is colored according to the number of iterations. (See Chapter 14 for a more detailed explanation of fractal generation.)

To implement a new application based on this fractal type, you can copy the files of the VBFract application to a new subdirectory and replace the line that calls the VBMandel( ) Function, shown here,

```
Color = VBMandel(x, y, maxIter)
```

with the following line

```
Color = cosFractal(x, y, maxIter, ParameterValue)
```

where ParameterValue is the value of the parameter λ in the previous math expression. The rest of the program remains the same.

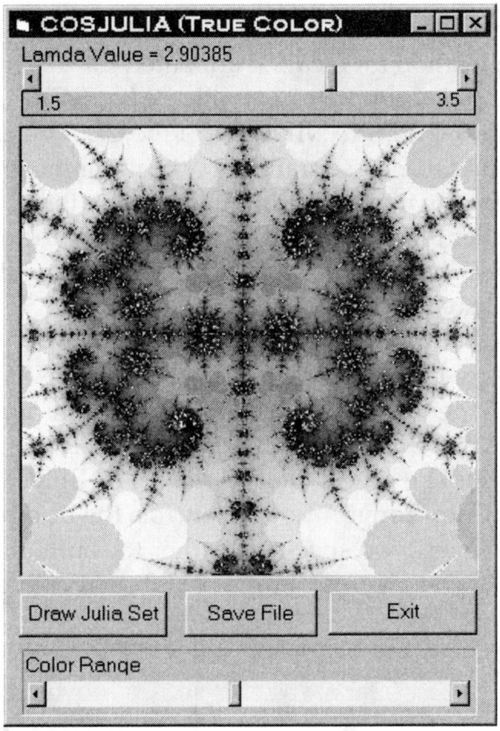


Figure 9-23: The fractal image changes when you move the scroll bar. You can also drag the mouse over the image to select the area you want to zoom into.

CD-ROM

COSJULIA is a variation on the basic Julia Set suited for animation.

Figure 9-23 shows a new application, COSJULIA, that allows you to change the value of the parameter as the program runs and see the effect it has on the image. This application can be found in the directory 9\APPS\COSJULIA on the CD.

The programming involved is identical to the fractal applications discussed in depth in Chapter 14. The only difference is that this time we call the cosFractal( ) Function instead of the VBMandel( ) or VBJulia( ) Function.

## Animating Fractals

Where is the animation? If you draw a number of fractal images by slowly varying the value of $\lambda$, you will get a sequence of images like the ones shown in Figure 9-24. These images are saved as BMP files, which you can later play back with AAWIN (from AutoDesk) or convert to an AVI file with Video for Windows and play it with the Windows Media Player applet.

## EXAMPLE: ANIFRCTL

CD-ROM

The application for creating animated fractals of the type shown in Figures 9-21 through 9-24 is called ANIFRCTL and is located in the directory 9\APPS\ANIFRCTL of the CD. You can use the COSJULIA application to choose starting and ending images you like and then decide on the number of frames between them. The more images, or the smaller the difference between the starting and ending images, the smoother the animation will be. The corresponding values of the parameter can be set in the "From" and "To" Text Boxes in the ANIFRCTL application, shown in Figure 9-25. We are including two versions of the ANIFRCTL application—one for 256-color systems and one for True Color systems. The applications are stored in the subdirectories 9\APPS\ANIFRCTL\256 and 9\APPS\ANIFRCTL\TRUECLR of the CD. The True Color version of ANIFRCTL provides a scroll bar called "Color range," which controls the number of colors in the images (it lets you specify whether the animation will contain more shades of a few colors, or many different colors).

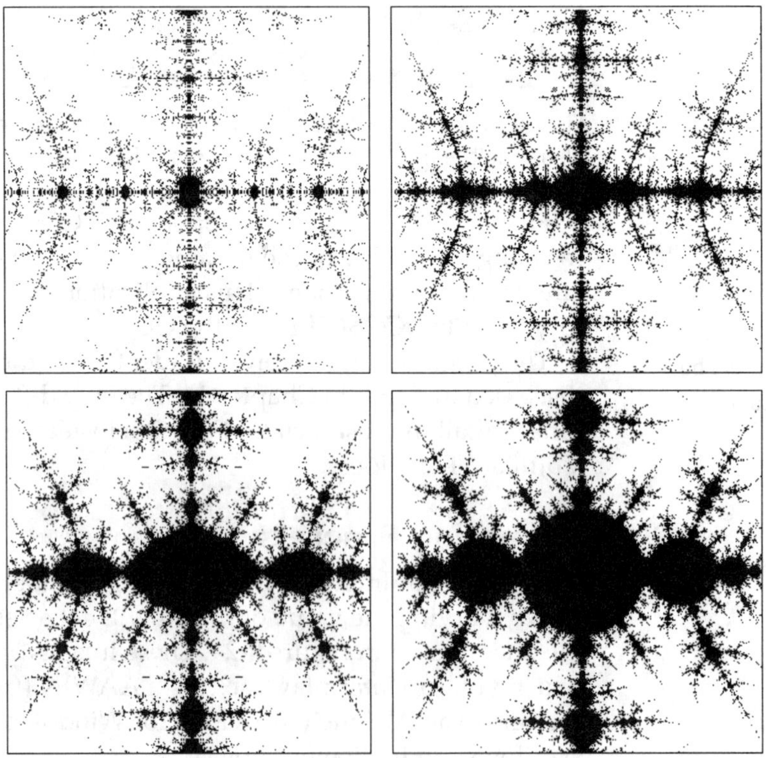

Figure 9-24: Excerpts from an animated fractal sequence.

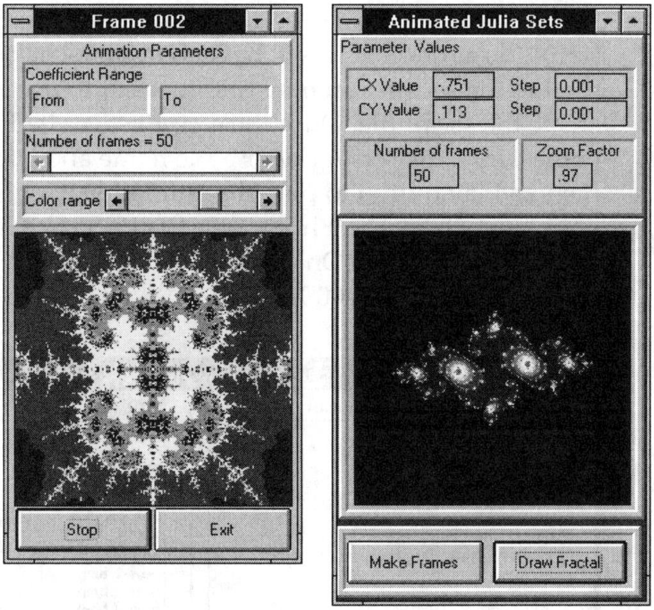


Figure 9-25: The ANIFRCTL (left) and ANIJULIA (right) applications let you generate animated fractals by controlling the various animation parameters.

The program will loop from the starting to the ending image by the step you have specified and will create a new BMP file during each loop. The names of the resulting files will be FRCTL000.BMP, FRCLT001.BMP and so on.

## Animating BMP Files

Once the BMP files have been created, you have two options: either play them back with AAWIN, or convert them to an AVI file with Video for Windows. We'll describe both methods. You may have other applications that translate BMP to playable video, and it is very likely that new utilities will soon be available that do the same thing even better.

### Animating With AAWIN

Let's start with AAWIN. To play back a sequence of BMP files with AAWIN you must create a script—a list of the images that will be played back.

Start the AAWIN application, select File/New Script, and you'll see Figure 9-26. Select each one of the BMP files in the file list and add them to the script with the Add to Script Button. Unfortunately,

AAWIN doesn't let you select multiple files and transfer them to the script file at once. You will have to double-click on each file to transfer it to the script. You may find it easier to use a word processor to create the script file. Once the script list is filled with the BMP file names, save the script under a file name and click on the main menu's Play button to play the animation. Depending on how fast your hard disk is, and how large the BMP files are, the animation may be a little jerky. On our 486/66 system we got smooth animation with images up to (200 X 200).

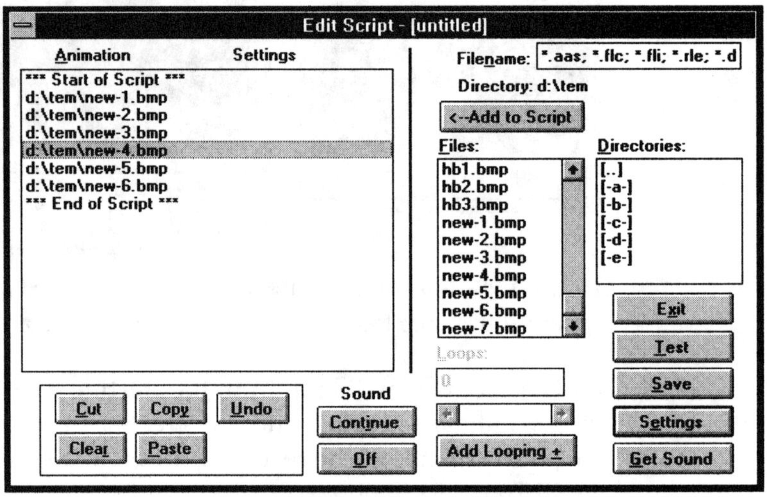


Figure 9-26: AAWIN produces surprisingly effective animations by playing back sequences of BMP files. Here you see the Form that allows the user to create a script (a list of the image files to be played back).

The drawback of AAWIN is that it doesn't convert the images to a single file. Instead, it requires that all files listed in your script be present on your hard disk. By storing the entire animation in a single file we would not only save disk space (even with the crudest form of compression), the program would also be able to get the information from the disk faster. Video for Windows does just that.

### Animating With Video for Windows

Video for Windows will play a sequence of BMP files directly from disk, but it will also convert them to an AVI file. If you have a compression/decompression card installed on your computer, Video for Windows will take advantage of it.

To use Video for Windows, first start the VidEdit application and read the BMP files with the File/Open command. In the File List select the name of the first file in the animation sequence (FRCTL001.BMP). Video for Windows will figure out which files belong to the sequence and will open them in the proper order. Next, create an AVI file with the File/Save As command. Video for Windows will convert the BMP sequence to AVI format and then you can play back (or distribute) this file.

### Other Products

Both AAWIN and Video for Windows can create animation from a sequence of bitmap files.

There are other products that can help you animate BMP sequences. We have used an application called VFD (Video for DOS) that reads a sequence of BMP files and produces an FLI file. VFD is a shareware application that you will find useful if you want to convert BMP sequences to FLI files. FLI files seem to be smoother than AVI files, but the ones produced by VFD can't contain more than 256 colors.

## EXAMPLE: ANIJULIA

CD-ROM

In the 9\APPS\ANIJULIA subdirectory of the CD, you will find another application for generating animated fractals. It is called ANIJULIA and is based on the classic Julia Set. Like ANIFRCTL, there are two versions of the ANIJULIA applications, one for 256-color systems and one for True Color systems. This application lets you animate the Cx and Cy parameters of the Julia Set. By slowly changing the values of two parameters, the Julia Set is constantly transformed into new shapes, creating interesting animations. Along with the range of the parameters Cx and Cy, the ANIJULIA application lets you specify a zooming factor. If the zooming factor is different than 1, each successive frame is a fraction of the previous one. To zoom by 3 percent at each step, specify a zooming factor of .97. If you make the zooming factor larger than 1, successive frames will zoom out.

The ANIJULIA application, shown in Figure 9-25, has two Command Buttons named "Draw Fractal" and "Make Frames." The first Command Button lets you draw a single frame. Then, you can use the mouse to zoom into it. Drag the mouse over the area you wish to zoom into and then click again on the Draw Fractal Command Button. The program will loop through the frames, varying the Cx and Cy variables by the specified step, each time zooming in or out by the specified zooming factor. The frames of the animation are stored as BMP files on the current directory, and they are named JULIA001.BMP, JULIA002.BMP, etc. The step values depend strongly on the current zoom level. If you have zoomed deeply into a Julia Set, a small change in the step will go a long way. Successive frames may not even resemble one another.

So far, we have explored the Windows multimedia aspect without any requirements on the hardware. We looked at how to play back sound and animation files, as well as how to create animation. In the next section we are going to look at the MCI commands. These offer much more flexibility, but they also require specialized hardware, such as a sound card.

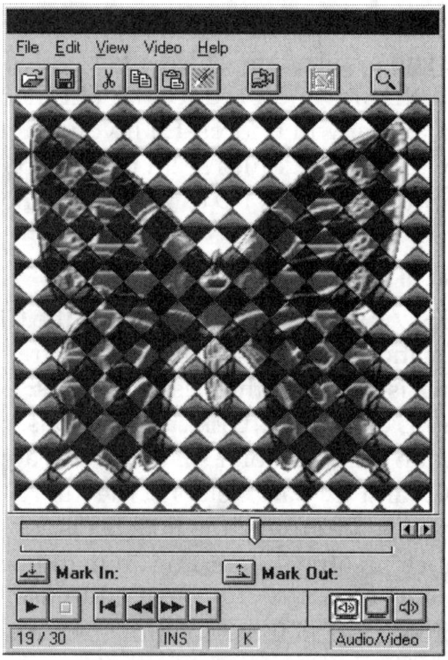


Figure 9-27: The Video for Windows editor in action.

## THE MULTIMEDIA CONTROL INTERFACE

All multimedia activities on your computer are controlled by a set of MCI device drivers (they're listed in your SYSTEM.INI file under [mci]). MCI stands for Multimedia Control Interface, and it is the Windows mechanism that provides high-level applications with multimedia capabilities.

MCI used to be an extension of the operating system (remember the Windows Multimedia Extensions, MME, of Windows 3.0?), but with the new version of Windows, it—like faxing and many other features—has become part of the operating system itself. This same integration is happening with other operating systems, such as the Macintosh and the operating systems on more expensive workstations. Multimedia services are no longer extensions of the operating system but an integral part of it.

## Device Drivers

A device driver is an executable file that controls the hardware. In other words, it accepts high-level commands from an application and translates them to low-level commands, which, in the case of MCI, control the various multimedia devices—a CD player, for example, or a MIDI synthesizer. One value of a device driver is that it hides the peculiarities of a specific device from the programmer. Outboard function libraries like these also make it easier for manufacturers to tweak performance—they can just supply new device drivers when there is an improvement rather than having to ship a whole new release of the application proper.

A multimedia device driver is like a printer driver. You don't have to know how it works in order to use it.

Each sound card has different hardware and a different set of commands, but your VB application doesn't see these details. The *play* command, for example, plays a multimedia file on all sound cards. Similarly, the *pause* command interrupts the playback of the file. You, the programmer, don't need to know anything about the low-level commands of the specific sound card, just as you don't have to know PostScript to print to a PostScript-capable printer. The operating system takes care of the details, with the help of a device driver.

The device driver is usually supplied by the manufacturer of the device. When you buy a new printer, a printer device driver is installed in your system. Similarly, when you buy a sound card, or any other multimedia device, the corresponding device drivers must be installed in your system.

## What Is MCI?

From a VB programmer's point of view, MCI is essentially a language that sits between your VB application and the multimedia device drivers. You tell the computer what you want it to do (play a sound file, or record video from the TV, for example) and MCI translates your requests to low-level commands that tell the device driver how to do it. Every device works differently, but to you, the VB programmer, they all look the same. They obey the same set of commands and the application you developed and tested with a specific sound card will work on any Windows system, equipped with another sound card, which may not even have been available at the time you developed the application.

MCI is as close to English as you can expect from a computer today. The MCI language is very simple and is probably one of the best implemented features of the Windows operating system. Its commands are so straightforward that you may find the MCI language easier to master and use than Visual Basic's MCI Control. In effect, they both do the same thing, but MCI commands are so simple and give you such complete control over the MCI mechanism that you may never want to use the MCI Control. (A similar situation exists with the Data Control—though in this case you gain considerable power and flexibility by using SQL or the database language rather than the VB Data Control. For more on this, see Chapter 3, if you're using VB3, and Chapter 4, if you're using VB4.)

Visual Basic's MCI Control lets you specify MCI commands too.

By the way, one of the MCI Control's Properties is called Command. It lets you specify an MCI command to be executed. It's possible that as you become more comfortable with programming multimedia events, you may eventually make use of the MCI Control's Command property. The MCI commands we describe in this section can all be used with the MCI Control's Command property. However, just as the scroll bar provided with the Data Control is rather restrictive, you might find that the "tape recorder" metaphor used by the MCI Control offers less to the user than you want to provide (both aesthetically and functionally).

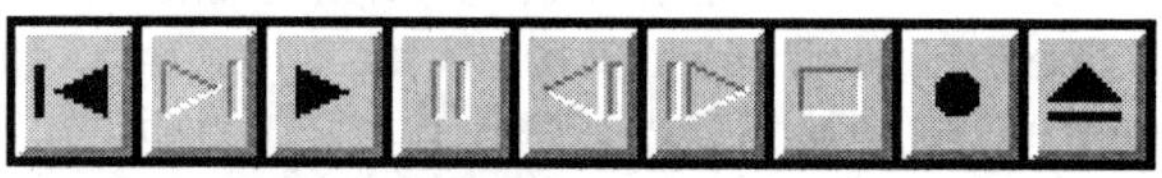

Figure 9-28: The MCI Control's buttons are designed to work with various multimedia devices. All devices are treated uniformly, through a VCR-style panel.

### Some Simple MCI Commands

Before we look at the MCI commands in general, let's look at a few specific examples, to get a feel for the language. Of course, to use these commands within VB, you must first Declare the mciSendString ( ) Function (as described below), and also assign each MCI command that you are going to send to a text variable, like this:

```
cmd$ = "open c:\sounds\mymusic.mid type sequencer alias →
music"
x& = mciSendString(cmd$, 0&, 0, 0)
```

mciSendString( ) is the function that submits commands to the MCI mechanism for execution. For the moment, we'll just consider a few MCI commands in their raw state, and we will say more about this function shortly. Here are the MCI commands for playing back a MIDI file through any sound card:

```
open c:\sounds\mymusic.mid type sequencer alias music
play music
close music
```

There are three basic steps in playing back multimedia files:

1. Open the device.
2. Play a file.
3. Close the device.

The first command (open) tells the computer to open a MIDI file (c:\sounds\mymusic.mid) and make an "alias" for it. By creating this alias, we need no longer specify in subsequent commands the entire file name, just the alias, "music." (This is like using a constant name.) The *type* keyword tells the computer which multimedia driver it must use. In this example, it's the sequencer driver, which is the driver for the MIDI synthesizer.

The second command (play) plays the file. The play command loads the file in memory and streams the data to the appropriate driver, then it returns control to your VB application. The MIDI file may keep playing for several minutes, but this will not prevent the computer from doing other things in the meantime.

The last command (close) closes the device. The command is executed immediately after the play command; so if you want to hear the sound, you must wait before issuing the close command.

Therefore, our example above won't, in fact, play anything. The close command must be somehow separated from the play command. (Shortly, we will look at the various ways to play sounds, wait for them to finish, and close them when done.)

Here are the similar commands for playing back a WAV file:

```
open c:\sounds\myvoice.wav type waveaudio alias voice
play voice
close voice
```

Normally, every new MCI command you issue to a given device will interrupt any still-active MCI command sent to it.

The only difference here is the type of the device (waveaudio instead of sequencer). Other than that, playing a sound file is no different from playing a MIDI file. The two types of files are very different and they have different playback requirements; but to you, the programmer, they are just like two different segments on a cassette, and the basic mechanism for playing them back doesn't differ in the programming. These two examples, although elemetary, reveal the English-like structure of the MCI commands. You can probably understand what any MCI command sequence does without even reading the rest of the chapter, but you need to know the names of the commands.

## Device Types & Device Drivers

Windows supports many types of multimedia devices, but a given computer may not have device drivers for all of them. Here is a complete list of multimedia device types supported by Windows:

| Device Type | Description |
|---|---|
| animation | Animation device |
| cdaudio | Audio CD player |
| dat | Digital audio tape player |
| avivideo | Digital video |
| overlay | Overlay device (analog video in a window) |
| scanner | Image scanner |
| sequencer | MIDI sequencer |
| vcr | Videotape recorder |
| videodisc | Videodisc player |
| waveaudio | Audio device for digital waveforms |
| other | Undefined MCI device type |

Table 9-3: The list of multimedia device types supported by Windows.

This list will no doubt keep expanding, as new multimedia capabilities are added to personal computers. When you open a multimedia device, you must specify its type with the open command (as we did in the previous examples).

The device type determines which MCI commands can be issued, but the actual execution of the commands is carried out by a device driver. This driver connects the MCI commands with the actual device.

Each device type may be served by multiple MCI drivers that operate on different file formats. For example, you may have two device drivers for animation—one for Audio Video Interleave (AVI ) files and another one for MultiMedia Movie (MMM) files.

To uniquely identify an MCI driver, use device names. All device names are identified in the [mci] section of the SYSTEM.INI file. Here is a typical one:

```
[mci]
waveaudio = mciwave.drv
sequencer = mciseq.drv
MMMovie = mcimmp.drv
cdaudio = mcicda.drv
```

The name on the left side of the equals sign is the "device name." The name on the right side is the actual file name of the driver—the program Windows looks for when asked to play a specific multimedia file. The device name can be the same as the device type, as in the case of waveaudio, but this isn't always the case. The device name MMMovie, is a device of type animation (it plays MMM movies). As you will see, there can be more device names for animation (avivideo, for example, which plays digital video).

A device name is an alias for the actual device driver. This simplifies the syntax of the MCI commands.

The device name is nothing but an alias for the actual device driver. The device name is always the same, whereas the device driver name may differ from one computer to another, depending on the multimedia devices installed. Remember that not all multimedia device drivers are supplied by Microsoft. Autodesk's MCIAAP.DRV driver is an animation driver with type animation1. Once you install this driver on your system, you needn't remember the name MCIAAP.DRV. The alias "animation1" is not only easier to remember, but it also makes more sense than an eight-character file name.

If you are using Windows 95, you can also find the same information in the Registry. Run the RegEdit application and search for "waveaudio" with the Find command. You will find the entries for all mci drivers on your computer if you follow the path HKEY_LOCAL_MACHINE -> SYSTEM -> CURRENTCONTROLSET -> CONTROL -> MEDIARESOURCES -> MCI, as shown in Figure 9-29. The Registry entries are placed there by the corresponding installation program every time you install a new multimedia device, such as a sound card or a CD-ROM.

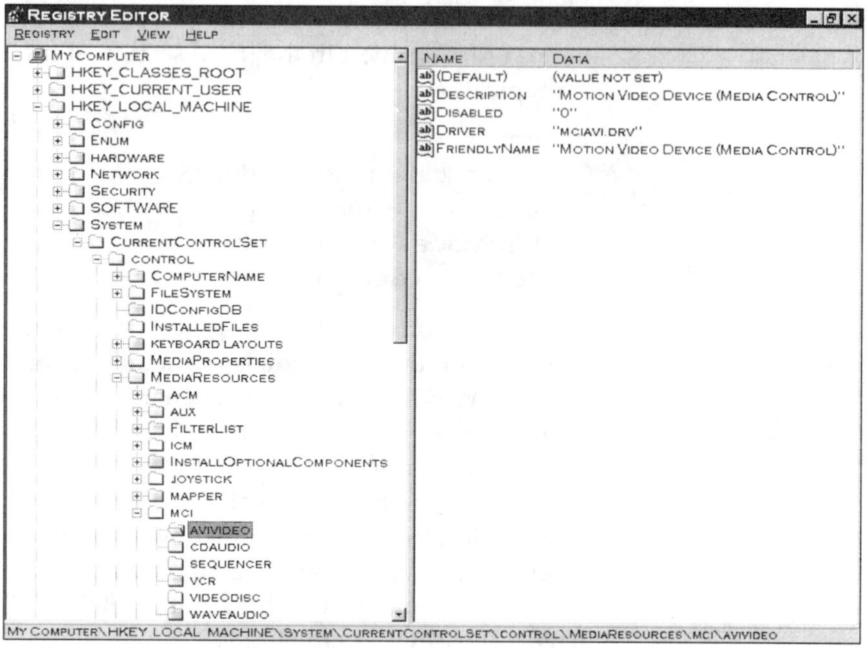


Figure 9-29: Locating the mci drivers in the Windows 95 Registry. Notice that the names of the drives are the same as in the SYSTEM.INI file.

You don't have to know the names of device drivers. Once installed, you can forget about them.

Fortunately, you never have to install the [mci] entries in your SYSTEM.INI file. Every time you install a new program that makes use of a device driver, the installation program registers it in SYSTEM.INI for you. If you buy a video capture and playback card, the installation program will place the appropriate line for the overlay device type in your SYSTEM.INI file. You can also install multiple device drivers for the same device type. For example, you can install two sound cards and have two distinct device names: waveaudio1 and waveaudio2. Both sound cards will likely support MIDI files, too (most all of them do), so you will see two more lines in your [mci] section: sequencer1 and sequencer2.

Windows itself comes with two MCI drivers: sequencer for MIDI files and waveaudio for WAV files. If you have installed the Video for Windows runtime module, you also have a third device called avivideo, for playing back digital video files (AVI files). Once you install Video for Windows, the entry avivideo=mciavi.drv will be added to the [mci] section of your SYSTEM.INI file.

If you have a sound card, which is the most common multimedia expansion card (and most readers have one), you should be able to play MIDI and WAV files.

## Executing MCI Commands

As you may have guessed, the MCI commands can't be executed directly from within Visual Basic (unless they are assigned to the MCI Control's Command Property). They must be passed to MCI, which will execute them for you. This is a simple process, however. To execute an MCI command from within your Visual Basic application, all you need is a function called mciSendString( ), which sends the MCI commands to the MCI drivers. To use it, declare it in the General Declarations section of a Form or Module, typed entirely on a single line:

```
Declare Function mciSendString Lib "winmm" Alias →
"mciSendStringA" (ByVal Command$, ByVal ReturnStr As →
String, ByVal wReturnLen As Long, ByVal hCallBack As Long) →
As Long
```

If you are using VB3, the previous declaration is different:

```
Declare Function mciSendString& Lib "mmsystem" (ByVal→
Command$, ByVal ReturnStr As Any, ByVal ReturnLen%,→
ByVal hCallBack%)
```

Command$ is a text (string) variable that contains the actual MCI command that will be sent; ReturnStr is another string which, when the job is done, contains a message from the MCI driver. This argument is used to request information about the status of the device, or the current operation. ReturnLen is the length of the ReturnStr message in characters (up to 255 characters). The last argument, hCallBack%, is used in C programming and you can ignore it.

The Long Integer returned by the mciSendString( ) Function determines whether the operation was completed successfully, or an error occurred. If the MCI command was completed successfully, the value zero is returned. If the number returned by mciSendString( ) was non-zero, then an error was encountered and the return value represents the error. Fortunately, you don't have to look up all possible error messages. The mciGetErrorString( ) Function can be used to extract a complete text description of the error (and the MCI error messages are very descriptive). We will see examples of this shortly.

Here's how to play a MIDI file with the MCI commands we've explored so far. Put a Command Button on a Form, then type this into the General Declarations section of a Form:

```
Declare Function mciSendString Lib "winmm" Alias →
"mciSendStringA" (ByVal Command$, ByVal ReturnStr As →
String, ByVal wReturnLen As Long, ByVal hCallBack As Long) →
As Long
```

And for VB3, use the following declaration:

```
Declare Function mciSendString& Lib "mmsystem" (ByVal→
Command$, ByVal ReturnStr As Any, ByVal ReturnLen%,→
ByVal hCallBack%)
```

Into the Command Button's Click Event, type this (replacing "c:\sounds\mymusic.mid" with the path to a valid .MID file on your hard drive):

```
Sub Command1_Click ( )

cmd$ = "Open c:\sounds\mymusic.mid type sequencer alias→
music"
x& = mciSendString(cmd$, 0&, 0, 0)

cmd$ = "play music from 0 wait"
x& = mciSendString(cmd$, 0&, 0, 0)

End Sub
```

(The important *wait* parameter causes the computer to play the entire selection before it returns control to your VB application. The parameter *from 0* starts it at the beginning each time you execute this Sub.)

If you have problems getting this to work, read on. MCI provides very generous, and most helpful, error messages.

### Interpreting MCI Messages & Error Codes

MCI responds to each command it executes with a return code, and a text message. The return code is a long integer that is zero if the command was executed successfully, or an error code if it failed. Moreover, it sets the ReturnString string to a text description, relevant to the specific command. When you request information about a specific device, MCI returns the information in this string, which can be up to 255 characters long. Here is how you call the mciSendString( ) Function and retrieve a message:

```
Dim ReturnStr As String

cmd$ = "pause music"
x& = mciSendString(cmd$, ReturnString, 255, 0)
Print ReturnString
```

This results in

```
Paused
```

The mciGetErrorString( ) Function translates MCI's error codes into meaningful text strings.

The ReturnString message contains the result of the operation. Most likely, ReturnString contains the word "paused" after the above example is tested.

The error code (x&) is equivalent to Visual Basic's Err( ) Function. It is a number and can be examined from within your program. Just as Visual Basic provides the Error$( ) Function to convert an error number to a meaningful string, MCI provides the mciGetErrorString( ) Function to convert an MCI error code into a descriptive message. The most common message returned by the mciGetErrorString( ) is "The specified command was carried out," which corresponds to error code zero.

Here is how the mciGetErrorString( ) Function is declared:

```
Declare Function mciGetErrorString Lib "winmm" Alias →
"mciGetErrorStringA" (ByVal ErrorNum As Long, ByVal →
ErrorString As String, ByVal ErrorSize As Long) As Long
```

Again, here is the equivalent declaration of the mciGetErrorString( ) Function for VB3:

```
Declare Function mciGetErrorString Lib "mmsystem" (ByVal →
ErrorNum As Long, ByVal ErrorString As String, ByVal →
ErrorSize As Integer) As Integer
```

ErrorNum is the error number, returned by mciSendString( ) Function, and ErrorString is the corresponding error message. ErrorSize is an integer, holding the maximum allowed size of the error message, just like the ReturnLen argument of the mciSendString( ) Function.

*Before you can use mciGetErrorString,* you must first dimension a string variable to hold the response. So first put this line into any sub or function in which you will be using mciGetErrorString( ):

```
Dim errorstr As String * 255
```

Usually, the mciGetErrorString( ) Function is called immediately after each mciSendString( ) command:

```
x& = mciSendString(cmd$, ReturnString, 255, 0)
if x&>0 Then
    r% = mciGetErrorString(x&, ErrorStr, 255)
    msgbox ErrorStr
End If
```

Here, the cmd$ string contains an MCI command. ReturnString doesn't contain an error description. The error code is the value of the mciSendString( ) Function. ReturnString usually contains information you request from the system, such as the status of a device, the length of a sound file and so on.

## The MCI Language

The MCI language is general enough to accommodate all types of multimedia files. It contains a small number of commands, which accept a large number of parameters and of course not all device types support all of the parameters. In the following section we'll cover the basic MCI commands and their most commonly used parameters. For up-to-date list of MCI commands, contact Microsoft's Multimedia Division.

The MCI language is made up of English-like commands and syntax.

The MCI's relatively few commands provide a general framework for controlling various types of multimedia devices. The main MCI commands are listed alphabetically in Table 9-4.

| Command | Description |
|---|---|
| capability | Requests information about the capabilities of a specific device. |
| close | Closes a device when it's not needed any more. |
| info | Requests information about a specific device (the name of the driver, for example). |
| open | Opens and initializes a device. |
| pause | Pauses playback or recording. |
| play | Begins playback on a device. |
| put | Sets the position and size of the animation playback rectangle. |
| record | Begins recording on a device. |
| resume | Resumes playback or recording on a paused device. |
| save | Saves the data recorded with the record command. |
| seek | Changes the current position in the media. |
| set | Changes control settings for a specific device. |
| status | Requests information about the status of a device. |
| stop | Stops playback or recording on a device. |

Table 9-4: The basic MCI commands.

## Experimenting With MCI Commands

To follow the examples in the next paragraphs, use the MCIDEMO application, shown in Figure 9-32. This application lets you issue MCI commands by typing them in the Text Box next to the Execute Command Button. Once the command is passed to the mciSendString( ) Function for execution, the program reports the error message returned by the function, as well as the system's response, under the heading "MCI Response." The MCIDEMO application will be explained in detail shortly, but first we will take a closer look at the most common MCI commands.

The MCI commands are case-insensitive, so we usually type them all in lowercase. Notice also that whenever we specify file names, we don't have to include them in quotes. MCI is not only structured like English sentences, its syntax is flexible too.

### open

The *open* command initializes the device. After the command name you must specify the device type and a number of optional parameters. The syntax of the open command is

open *file_name* type *device* alias *alias_name*

where *file_name* is the name of the file to be played, *device* is the type of the multimedia device (this must be a name from the first column of Table 9-3) and *alias_name* is the alias with which you refer to the device in subsequent commands. If you specify an alias when opening the device, in subsequent commands you must specify the alias and not the device.

Videodisc players are called "simple" devices; a sound card is a "compound" device.

The devices described so far in the above examples are called "compound," because they require a file name to be supplied. There is another class of multimedia devices, which are called "simple." A Videodisc or CD player is a simple device, because you don't specify a file name when you open it (the user has presumably put a disc in the device). A sound card, on the other hand, is a compound device, because it must be told which MIDI or WAV file to play and it relies on the operating system to supply the stream of data it needs. The file you specify when opening a compound device is called the *media element*. With simple devices, we don't specify file names.

To open the audio CD device, use the command:

```
open cdaudio alias cd
```

To open a waveform file or an animation file, you must supply the name of the file to be played as well, as in

```
open c:\sounds\myvoice.wav type waveaudio alias voice
```

or

```
open c:\morph\vb.avi type avivideo alias video
```

(Notice that you don't have to use quotes around the file name). In the last command, *c:\morph\vb.avi*, is the media element and *video* is the alias for the device. Until you close it, all commands must refer to this device with its alias video.

If you are opening an animation device, you can determine the type of the window in which the animation will be played with the *style* parameter. The style parameter of the open command may be followed by one of the keywords of the following table:

| Keyword | Description |
|---|---|
| child | Opens a window with a child window style |
| overlapped | Opens a window with an overlapped window style |
| popup | Opens a window with a popup window style |
| fullscreen | Shows the movie as if a borderless window were maximized |

Table 9-5: The values of the style parameter.

Here's an example of how to use the style parameter to play an AVI file in a pop-up window (provide here the full path of an AVI file on your hard drive):

```
play c:\winvideo\wndsurf1.avi style popup
```

Note that not all of these options (popup, fullscreen, etc.) may not work on your system. Different drivers will produce different results (see "capability" below).

There's one more parameter you can use with the open command, which lets you specify the Control on which the animation or video will be displayed. It is the *parent* parameter, which is followed by the handle of the desired Control. Let's say you wish to play back an AVI file on the Picture1 Picture Box. First, find the Control's handle:

```
controlID = Picture1.hWnd
```

and then issue the following MCI command:

```
cmd$ = "open \fractals\anijulia.avi type avivideo alias video
parent " & controlID & " style child"
x& = mciSendString(cmd$, ReturnString, 255, 0)
```

This lengthy command tells the MCI mechanism to open an AVI file and prepare to play it back on the Control with the specific handle (which, in our example, is a Picture Box). Notice that you can't pass the controlID variable directly to mci by embedding it into the open command; you must embed its actual value in the open command.

To use the parent parameter with the MCIDemo application, you will have to stop the program and use the Debug Window to determine the handle of the Form or Control on which the video will be played back. Enter the following in the Debug Window,

```
Print Form1.hWnd
```

and use the value returned by the Print command with the parent keyword of the open command. You can also use the window command to specify where an AVI file will be played back, or use the put command to specify the size of the playback window (the window and put commands are explained later in this section).

**play**

The *play* command starts a device playing its file. If the device is an animation device, it will play back an animation file and if the device is a CD player, it will play the first track of the record. The simplest form of the play command is

```
play device
```

where *device* is the device name you used in the corresponding open command (or the device's alias). Assuming you have opened a sound file with the command

```
open c:\sounds\myvoice.wav type waveaudio alias wave1
```

you can play back the file with the command

```
play wave1
```

The playback starts at the current position in the media. If you issue the commands

```
play wave1
play wave1
```

the sound file wave1 will nonetheless be heard only once. (After the first playback, the current position of the "pointer" within the WAV file is at the end of the file, and there is nothing to play the second time. You might say that the tape needs to be rewound.

The *from* and *to* parameters of the play command allow you to play back a section of a file.

To play a file from its beginning, use the *from* parameter. You can also use the *to* parameter to specify an early end of playback, if you don't want to play the entire file. To ensure that each time you start a WAVE file from its beginning, use the *from 0* parameter:

```
play wave1 from 0
```

To play a portion of the file (a specific word, or sentence within the sound file), use a command like

```
play wave1 from 1050 to 1200
```

(See "Example: The Talking Grid" later in this chapter for an example of how to use the *from* and *to* parameters.)

The most common parameter for the play command is *wait*, which tells MCI not to accept any other MCI commands until the song ends.

Avoid the *wait* parameter with very long files because you won't be able to interrupt their execution.

The *wait* parameter is useful when you want to be sure that one MCI command is completed before you issue the next MCI command. This is fine for a succession of short sounds, but for larger files, you will probably not opt to freeze your machine while a MIDI file plays itself out. (You can find out whether playback has completed with the *status* command discussed later in this chapter. This is a more elegant solution to the problem.)

**capability**

The *capability* command must be used with a "capability name," and it responds with a text variable (in ReturnString) saying True if the device supports the specified capability, or False if not. To try this, issue the following MCI commands (and use an AVI file path that exists on your computer instead of c:\winvideo\wndsurf1.avi):

```
open c:\winvideo\wndsurf1.avi type avivideo alias ani1
capability ani1 has audio
```

This example will report if the animation file opened as ani1 has a soundtrack. The *reverse* keyword tells you if the device can play a file backwards. Use it before you play a file backwards, to find out if the device supports this capability.

Here is a list of the capabilities supported by most devices:

| | | | |
|---|---|---|---|
| can eject | can play | can record | can reverse |
| can save | can stretch | uses palettes | compound device |
| has audio | has video | uses files | |

Table 9-6: Capabilities supported by most devices.

You can temporarily interrupt the playback of a device with the pause command.

**pause**
The *pause* command pauses the playback of a file, leaving the current position unchanged. When playback resumes, it will start at the position where it was paused, unless of course you use the *from* parameter.

Issue the following commands to start a playback

```
open c:\winvideo\wndsurf1.avi type avivideo alias ani1
play ani1 from 0
```

and then pause the playback with the command:

```
pause ani1
```

To resume the playback, you can use the *resume* command, explained next.

**resume**
The *resume* command resumes the playback of a device interrupted with the pause command. The playback resumes at the position where it was interrupted. After pausing the playback of ani1, resume it with the command:

```
resume ani1
```

The pause and resume commands do not accept parameters.

**set**
The *set* command establishes various control settings for the driver. For example, you can set on or off individual speakers, turn off the soundtrack of an AVI file, and so on. Here is a list of parameters of the *set* command that are common to all sound and animation devices:

| | |
|---|---|
| audio all off | audio all on |
| audio left off | audio left on |
| audio right off | audio right on |
| video off | video on |

Table 9-7: Parameters of the *set* command.

To turn off the soundtrack of an AVI file, use the commands:

```
open c:\winvideo\wndsurf1.avi type avivideo alias ani1
set ani1 audio all off
play ani1 from 0 wait
close all
```

Another parameter, which lets you set the units for measuring the length of the file (or the current song, if it's a CD device), is called *time format* and can take different values for different types of devices. For waveaudio devices, time format can be *milliseconds* (abbreviated *ms*), *bytes*, or *samples*. For animation devices, the time format parameter can take the values *milliseconds* or *frames*. The command

```
set wave time format samples
```

sets the time format for the device opened with the alias wave to samples. When you request the length or the current position in this file, its value will be returned in samples (see *status* command). Other devices use more complicated time formats. A CD, for example, uses the *tms* format, which stands for "track, minutes, seconds." When you ask for the current position on a CD, the reply in this format will be something like "1:02:03" (first track, 2 minutes and 3 seconds).

**status**

The *status* command returns status information about a device. Because of the variety of multimedia devices, the status command accepts many parameters. The syntax of the command is:

status *device parameter*

Table 9-8 is a list of the status parameters commonly used with sound and animation devices.

| Parameter | Description. |
|---|---|
| length | Returns the total number of frames in animation, or samples in a sound file. |
| mode | Returns one of the strings "not ready," "paused," "playing," "seeking" or "stopped." |
| position | Returns the current position in the file. |
| ready | Returns true if the device is ready. |
| window handle | Returns the handle of the window used for animation playback. |

Table 9-8: The status command's parameters and their meanings.

For example, if you open a MIDI device as music, you can issue the status command and inquire information about the mode of the device:

```
open c:\sounds\enya.mid type sequencer alias music
status music mode
close all
```

At this point you should receive the string "stopped" from MCI. If you start playback, and then issue the status command again, this time MCI will return the string "playing."

Recall that your VB application must wait for a sound to finish playing back before VB issues another command for playback, or attempts closing the device. The *wait* parameter of the play command is one way to make sure that playback will complete before the next command is issued. This approach, however, freezes your VB program. You can't issue any other MCI command during a *waiting* playback.

The status command allows you to monitor the progress of the playback.

The *mode* parameter of the status command allows you to check the progress of playback, while using the computer for other purposes. In other words, you can execute other calculations and—prior to issuing another MCI command, such as play or close—use the *status mode* command to find out whether the playback has finished or not. If it's playing, the application must wait for a while (or do more calculations) and check again. This approach is best with longer MCI activities which do not require much of your computer's resources, such as playing MIDI files. For shorter sounds, such as WAVE files, the *wait* command works just as well, and it's simpler too.

Here's how to use the *mode* parameter to start the playing a MIDI file, then perform a few calculations and finally close the device when the music completes:

```
cmd$ = "open c:\sounds\mymusic.mid type sequencer alias→
music"
x& = mciSendString(cmd$, 0&, 0, 0)
cmd$ = "play music from 0"
x& = mciSendString(cmd$, 0&, 0, 0)

'Busy ourselves
For i = Form1.Width to Form1.Width - 500, Step -1
    Form1.Width = i
    Form1.Height = i
Next i

cmd$ = "status music mode"
x& = mciSendString(cmd$, 0&, 0, 0)
While not ReturnStr ="playing"
    x& = mciSendString(cmd$, ReturnStr, 0, 0)
Wend

cmd$ = "close music"
x& = mciSendString(cmd$, 0&, 0, 0)
```

Another application of the status command is to find the length of the playback file or your current position in it. Assuming that you have set the wave device's time format to samples, you can find the WAVE file's length with the command:

```
status wave length
```

Then start playing the sound with the command:

```
play wave
```

And before the playback completes, interrupt it with the command:

```
pause wave
```

At this point issue the command

```
status wave position
```

to find out the current position in the file in samples or any other unit you have specified with the *set time format* command.

**seek**
The *seek* command repositions the pointer in a device. The syntax of the seek command is

```
seek to position
```

where position is a number, expressed in the current time format. The seek command repositions the current pointer in the device and stops the playback. The command

```
seek to 0
```

repositions the pointer in the device to the beginning.

**window**
The *window* command is very useful when playing back animation. It lets you control the window in which the animation is displayed. In Windows, it's quite easy to cover the active window by switching to another application, especially if the active window is a small one, which is presently the case with digital video. To show the animation display window opened with the alias video, use the command

```
window video state show
```

If the display window is totally, or partially, covered by other windows, use the command

```
window video state action
```

to display the animation window on top of every other active window, without changing the focus of the active window. In other words, the previous command brings the animation window on top of all other windows, without making it the active one.

To hide the animation window use the command:

It is possible to keep the window displaying animation on top of all others, without making it active.

```
window video state hide
```

The parameter text of the window command lets you change the title of the animation window. The command

```
window video text "Uncle Bob's party"
```

displays the string in quotes on the title bar of the playback window.

Another useful parameter of the window command is the *handle* parameter, which is followed by the handle of the Control (or Form) where digital video, or an animation file, will be played back. To play back an AVI file on the Picture1 Control, open it as usual and then define the playback window as Picture1. First get the handle of the Picture Box:

```
Debug.Print Picture1.hWnd
```

Then use the number you see on the Debug Window in the window command:

```
open venice.avi type avivideo alias video
window video handle <handle>
```

where <handle> is the actual handle number. When the play command is issued, the AVI file will be played back on Picture1.

Notice that you can't include any VB statements or variables within an MCI command. To pass the handle of the Picture Box Control to MCI, you must first generate a VB string, which will be used as the first argument in the mciSendString( ) Function:

```
cmd$ = "window video handle "&Picture1.hWnd
x& = mciSendString(cmd$, ReturnStr$, 0, 0)
```

**put**

The *put* command lets you specify the exact placement of the playback area in the playback window. The playback window can be the default one, or a Picture Box or Form, you've specified with the window command. Playback will take place in this window, but you may wish to change the size of the playback area or its origin.

For example, you may wish to play back an AVI file, so that it fills the entire playback window. Let's say the Picture Box on which the playback will take place has dimensions 250 X 250 pixels. The commands:

```
window video handle <handle>
put video destination at 0 0 250 250
```

will cause the AVI file to cover the entire Picture Box. Again, <handle> is the value of the hWnd Property of the Picture Box and must be entered as a number. The arguments of the *desination at* parameter are the x and y coordinates of the origin, and the width and height of the playback area. To leave a 10-pixel frame around the playback area, use the command:

```
put video destination at 10 10 230 230
```

### configure

The *configure* command lets you specify various playback parameters, such as frame rate, zoom factor, etc. When you execute this command with the avivideo device, you will see a window like the one in Figure 9-30. This window allows the user to set certain parameters of the animation. Your application is not aware of the changes the user makes on this window, but it doesn't really need them. The next time you play back an animation file, it will be played back with the new parameters. In other words, your application need not extract the information from the configuration window and use it in subsequent commands.

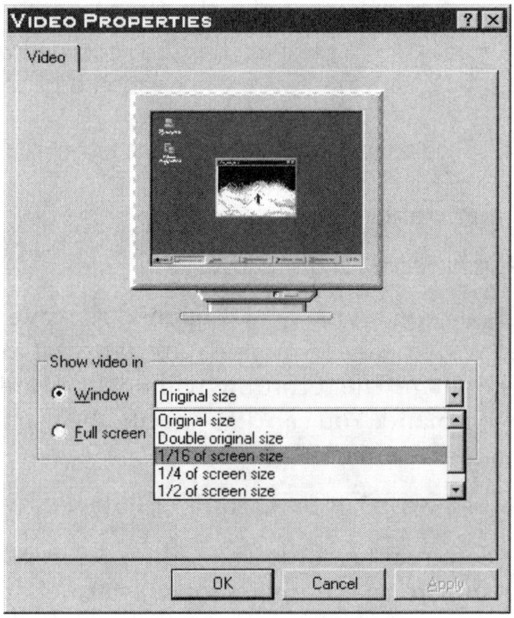


Figure 9-30: Video for Windows configuration window.

### record

The *record* command starts recording sounds or digital video. The data are stored in a temporary buffer and will be discarded unless you save them with the save command (explained next). The syntax of the record command is

record *device parameters*

where *parameters* can have one or more of the text strings of Table 9-9:

| Parameter | Description |
|---|---|
| from | Specifies the starting position for the recording. This position must be expressed in the current time format (ms, bytes, or samples). If you omit the *from* parameter, the recording starts at the current location in the file. |
| to | Specifies where the recording will end. If you omit this parameter, the recording will go on until you issue a pause, or a stop command. |
| insert | Specifies that the recorded data will be inserted in the file, after the current position. |
| overwrite | Specifies that the recorded data will overwrite the existing data in the file. |

Table 9-9: The parameters of the record command.

The command

```
record wave1 from 0 overwrite
```

starts recording on the device opened as wave1, starting at the beginning of the file. Any previous data that existed in the buffer will be overwritten. The recording will not end, unless you issue a stop or pause command. You can also specify the start and end of a recording in the same command:

```
record wave1 from 0 to 3000 overwrite
```

This command records a sound for 3 seconds (assuming that the current time format is milliseconds) starting at the beginning of the buffer.

**save**

The *save* command saves the data recorded on a device. The record command must be followed by a save command, or the data will be lost. To save the recording of the previous example to the file C:\SOUNDS\NEWSOUND.WAV, use the command:

```
save wave1 c:\sounds\newsound.wav
```

### info

The *info* command requests information from the device driver. The only type of information you can retrieve with *information* is the product's name and model. Here's how the info command is used:

```
info wave1 product
```

## Example: Monitoring MCI Devices

Figure 9-31 shows an example program called MCISTAT (in the subdirectory 9\APPS\MCISTAT). It controls three basic multimedia devices: waveaudio, sequencer and avivideo. (If your computer isn't equipped with a sound card, then you can only use the avivideo device—or other devices for which you must provide the programming, using MCISTAT as a template.)

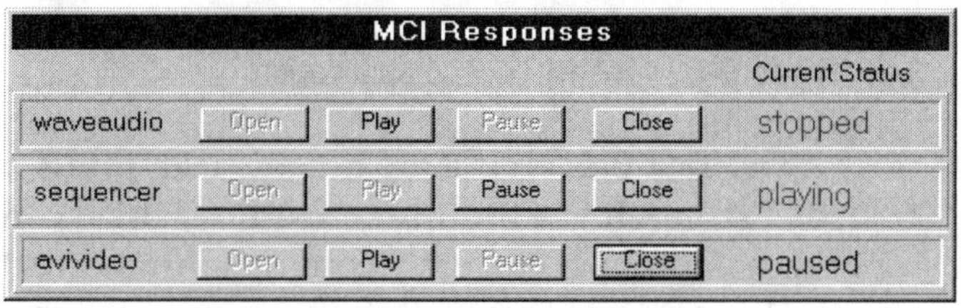


Figure 9-31: Our MCISTAT application reports that the waveaudio device is stopped, the sequencer device is playing and the avivideo device is paused.

The programming in this application is spread among the Command Buttons' Click Events. This application makes extensive use of the mciSendString( ) Function to invoke actions (open files, play, stop and close them) and then displays the results of each action in the three Label Controls at the right side of the Form. Please load MCISTAT.MAK from this book's CD (subdirectory 9\APPS\MCISTAT) to experiment with the various commands. You will have to change the names of the multimedia files.

CD-ROM

## Example: MCIDemo

Our second example program, MCIDemo (see Figure 9-32), lets you try out the various multimedia devices connected to your computer and see how to govern them with MCI commands. MCIDemo can also be used to generate program lines that you can insert into your own VB applications to control multimedia devices.

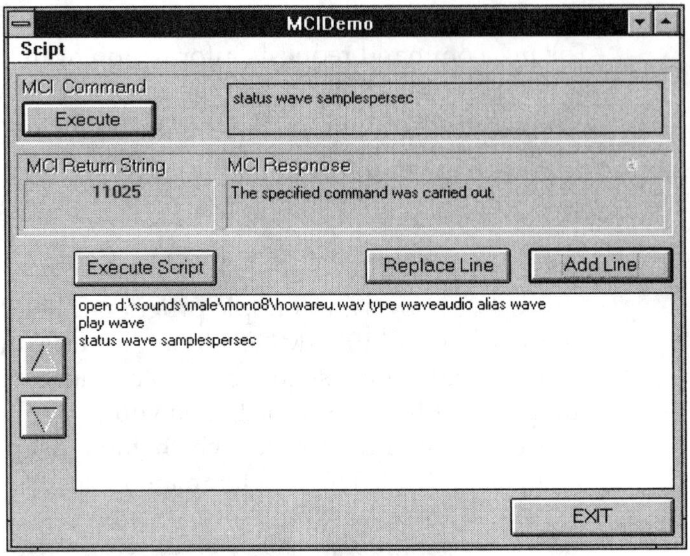


Figure 9-32: The MCIDemo application.

MCIDemo allows you to test MCI commands before you incorporate them into your programs.

The Text Box on the top accepts user input, which must be a valid MCI string. It is a multiline Text Box which can accept up to 255 characters. To execute the command in the Text Box, you can click on the Execute Command Button, or press Enter (this is the default Command Button of the Form).

The Execute Button will pass the Text Box's contents to the mciSendString( ) Function, and the results of the operation will appear in the Text Box below. The second Text Box displays the interpretation of the code returned by mciSendString( ) Function. Under the heading "MCI Response," you will see the message returned by the command itself.

The most common message displayed in this Text Box is "The specified command was carried out," unless an error was encountered. If there is a problem, you'll see a descriptive message such as "The specified device is not open, or is not recognized by MCI," or "Cannot find the specified file" or something similar. This message is extracted from the mciSendString( ) Function's result with the help of the mciGetErrorString( ) Function. The message returned by mciSendString( ) Function can provide either a number or a text string. For example, you may require a numeric response: the length of a sound file in samples, or seconds. Or you might want the name of the animation file being played, in which case the message is a string.

As usual, the first thing is the declaration of the two MCI Functions, in the General Declarations section of a Form or Module:

```
Declare Function mciSendString Lib "winmm" Alias →
"mciSendStringA" (ByVal Command As String, ByVal →
ReturnStr As String, ByVal wReturnLen As Long, ByVal →
hCallBack As Long) As Long

Declare Function mciGetErrorString Lib "winmm" Alias →
"mciGetErrorStringA" (ByVal ErrorNum As Long, ByVal →
ErrorString As String, ByVal ErrorSize As Long) As Long
```

The core of the application is found in the Click Event of the Execute Command Button (again, the declaration of the API Functions is different in the VB3 version of the application):

```
Private Sub ExecuteButton_Click( )
Dim ReturnString As String * 255
Dim ErrorStr As String * 255
Dim strLen As Integer

    ExecuteButton.Enabled = False
    strLen = 255
    ' Execute command and intercept return string
    X& = mciSendString(Trim(ScriptText.Text), ReturnString, →
    strLen, 0)
    Label3.Caption = ReturnString
    ' Obtain error message from error number
    r& = mciGetErrorString(X&, ErrorStr, strLen)
    label1.Caption = ErrorStr
    ExecuteButton.Enabled = True

End Sub
```

First, the Command Button is disabled for as long as the command executes, so that the user knows when not to click on it. The string returned by mciSendString( ) Function is displayed in a Label, and the return code is interpreted with the mciGetErrorString( ) Function and displayed in a second Label.

The rest of the application is a collection of simple tools that allow the user to create a multimedia script by adding the current command to the List Box and loading or saving scripts. You can use the

MCIDemo application to create a working script, by checking each command separately. When you have tested the entire script, save it under a file name with extension SCR. The script file is a text file which can be later imported into any Visual Basic application for governing multimedia activities. You may find the Copy to Clipboard menu option even more useful. It copies the contents of the Script List into the Clipboard. From there, you can paste the commands into your VB project.

Here are a few examples of MCI commands and their responses on our system. You may get different responses on your system, depending on your sound card, but most of them should be identical.

```
Command: open c:\morph\twoguys.avi type avivideo alias video
Response: 1

Command: info video file
Response: C:\MORH\TWOGUYS.AVI

Command: status video length
Response: 30
```

To add an MCI command from the Text Box to the List, click on the Command Button Add Line. The Replace Line Button replaces the selected line in the List Box with the current command. You can copy any of the List Box's lines to the command Text Box by double-clicking on it, and delete a line from the List Box by selecting it first and then right-clicking on it. The two Buttons with the arrows allow you to reposition the selected line in the List Box, by moving it up and down. Finally, the Execute Script Command Button executes each line in the script:

```
Sub ScriptExecute_Click ( )

' Execute all lines in list. No error checking here
    For i = 0 To ScriptList.ListCount - 1
        ScriptList.ListIndex = i
        X& = mciSendString(ScriptList.List(i), 0&, 0, 0)
    Next

End Sub
```

Notice that this Subroutine doesn't check for errors—the MCI commands will have already been tested with the "Execute" Command Button. There are, however, a few situations where the script may not execute as expected. For example, if you typed in the commands to play three sound files, hitting the Execute String Command

Button each time, the songs will play as you would expect. However, if you add each of those three commands to a script, when you execute the script, you will hear only the third sound file (unless you have specified the *wait* option described above). Remember that MCI commands are not queued. Each new command will interrupt the previous one and take over. To prevent this behavior, you must specify the wait option with each play command:

```
play wave wait
```

or

```
play ani1 wait
```

The MCI commands may behave differently when executed sequentially as a script.

Another situation where an entire script's execution may differ from simple single command execution is when you play a file without the *from* option. When a file is played for the first time, playback starts from the beginning of the file and stops at the end. If you attempt to play the same file again, nothing will happen, because the current position in the file is at the end of the file. To replay the file, you must rewind it, or play it with the *from 0* option. We repeat these small details because they can be a source of frustration when you are first getting used to the MCI language—especially if your multimedia application allows the user to interact with it.

### Example: The Talking Grid

CD-ROM

Before we leave the MCI, we offer one final and, we hope, useful, example. VBReader is a nice tool for proofing spreadsheets. The application is stored in the 9\APPS\VBREADER subdirectory of the CD, along with all the support files, as will be explained shortly. If you've ever had to proofread an entire spreadsheet with dozens, or hundreds of numbers, you will appreciate this application. Switching your attention back and forth between a printed or handwritten document and the computer screen rapidly induces both fatigue and errors.

Most people would ask a co-worker to read the number, while they keep their attention and their finger on the numbers on the screen. But what if you are working alone? And, even if you work with other people, why not let the computer do the talking for you? You listen and check the paper copy.

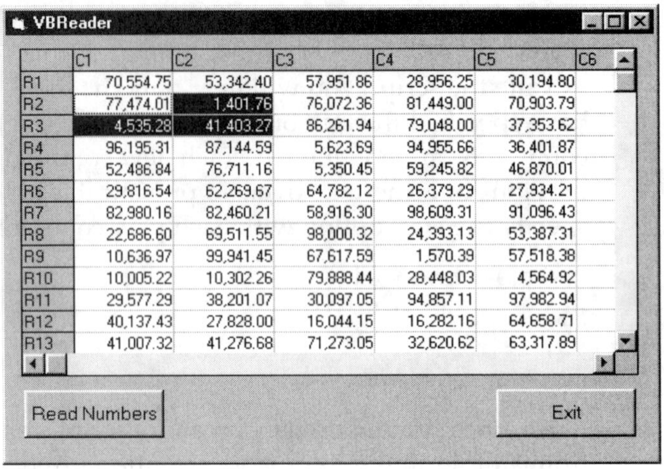


Figure 9-33: This spreadsheet talks.

The numbers in the Grid's cells were generated randomly, but it is not really difficult to connect this application to Excel, for example, and bring in your data from a spreadsheet. To focus our attention on demonstrating the multimedia aspect of the application, however, we'll just use random numbers.

When the application starts, it fills an area of the Grid with random numbers. As soon as the user clicks on the Command Button "Read Numbers," it starts reading the number of each selected cell, in columns. In other words, drag the mouse to select a range of cells you want read, then click the Button.

The application will read all the numbers in the first column, then the numbers in the second column, and so on. To help the user follow its progress, it highlights the number it is currently reading and it also tells you (vocally) the coordinates of the first element of each column. The numbers selected in Figure 9-31 will be read by the computer as follows:

"Column 1"

"Row 2"

"Seven Seven Four Seven Four Zero Point One"

"Four Five Three Five Two Point Seven Six"

"Column 2"

"Row 3"

"One Four Zero One Seven Point Six Four"

"Four One Four Zero Three Two Point Seven"

Reading the coordinates of each cell would be rather tedious and would annoy rather than help the user. Reading the coordinates of the first element each time the program moves to the next column, however, is a helpful feature. Of course, you can eliminate the reading of the coordinates altogether, or substitute the column and row number with a different message.

The program speaks the digits making up each number. The value 345.1 is read as "Three Four Five Point One" and not as "Three hundred forty-five point one." To run the VBReader application, you must use the GRIDNUMS.WAV file included in the same sub-directory on this book's CD. The GRIDNUMS.WAV file contains the sounds for the numbers zero to nine and the words "minus," "point," "comma," "row," "column," "oops" and "invalid entry" (just in case it tries to read a blank cell). The application extracts each digit from a number and reads it by playing the waveform using the MCI's *from* and *to* parameters. It must, therefore, be told where within the sound file each digit and punctuation word begins and ends.

CD-ROM

The WAVE file used by VBReader shouldn't contain any zone of silence.

Isolating the digit sounds was accomplished outside the VBReader application, with a utility (included with virtually all sound cards) that allows you to select a portion of a waveform and play it back. In Figure 9-34 you can see what the GRIDNUMS.WAV waveform looks like. Notice that the utility provides you with the data you need for the *from* and *to* arguments down in the lower-right corner.

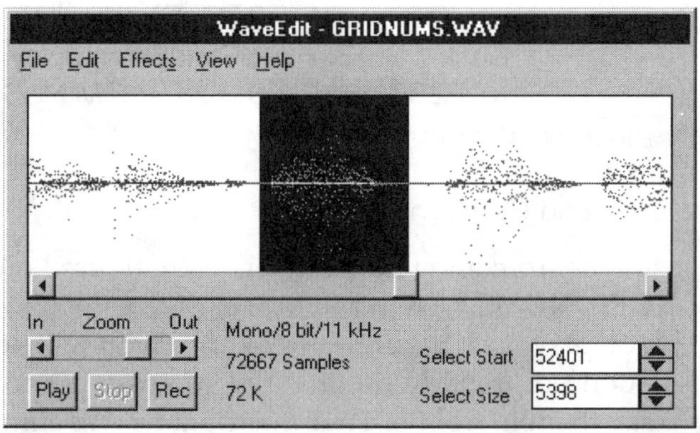


Figure 9-34: The file GRIDNUMS.WAV containing the numbers for the Talking Grid application. You can guess where each word begins and ends. Play the selection and note the positional information.

Once the positions of each word in the waveform were isolated, we can implement the Function that reads them:

```
Function ReadDigit(digit As Integer) As Integer

   Select Case digit
      Case 0: x& = mciSendString("play voice from 4400 →
      to 4900 wait", 0&, 0, 0)
      Case 1: x& = mciSendString("play voice from 0 to →
      432 wait", 0&, 0, 0)
      Case 2: x& = mciSendString("play voice from 485 →
      to 880 wait", 0&, 0, 0)
      Case 3: x& = mciSendString("play voice from 890 to →
      1350 wait", 0&, 0, 0)
      Case 4: x& = mciSendString("play voice from 1375 →
      to 1900 wait", 0&, 0, 0)
      Case 5: x& = mciSendString("play voice from 1910 →
      to 2400 wait", 0&, 0, 0)
      Case 6: x& = mciSendString("play voice from 2450 →
      to 2830 wait", 0&, 0, 0)
      Case 7: x& = mciSendString("play voice from 2850 →
      to 3400 wait", 0&, 0, 0)
      Case 8: x& = mciSendString("play voice from 3410 →
      to 3810 wait", 0&, 0, 0)
      Case 9: x& = mciSendString("play voice from 3825 →
      to 4400 wait", 0&, 0, 0)
      Case 11: x& = mciSendString("play voice from 6710 →
      to 7200 wait", 0&, 0, 0)  ' "POINT"
      Case 12: x& = mciSendString("play voice from 8500 →
      to 9250 wait", 0&, 0, 0)  ' "MINUS"
   End Select

End Function
```

The from and to parameters were figured out for the GRIDNUMS.WAV waveform earlier, using the WaveEdit utility. If you play back the entire waveform, you will hear all words pronounced properly, but in rapid succession—not the way you would say them in front of your microphone. We eliminated the silence and pauses by cutting and pasting the words to minimize memory usage. We wanted the file to be small enough so that it would easily fit in memory and to avoid delays when the computer speaks the numbers. If you want to use a waveform different from the one we supplied on the CD, possibly a WAVE file with your own voice, you should adjust the values of the *from* and *to* parameters in the readDigit( ) Function.

The readDigit( ) Function must be told where each word starts and ends in a WAVE file.

The Function readDigit( ) accepts a number as argument and reads the corresponding word from the GRIDNUMS.WAV file. Notice that the words "point" and "minus" are just treated as if they are digits. However, the words "column," "row" and "oops," which are not part of the numbers, are handled by three different functions, which are called sayCOLUMN( ), sayROW( ) and sayOOPS( ). Here is the code of the sayCOLUMN( ) Function:

```
Function sayCOLUMN(colNum As Integer) As Integer
Dim digit As Integer

    If colNum < 0 Or colNum > 99 Then
        success% = sayOOPS( )
        Exit Function
    End If
    x& = mciSendString("play voice from 5520 to 6040  →
    wait", 0&, 0, 0)
    Number$ = Format$(colNum, "#")
    For i = 1 To Len(Number$)
        digit = Val(Mid$(Number$, i, 1))
        success% = ReadDigit(digit)
    Next
    delay (500)

End Function
```

The sayCOLUMN( ) Function reads the word "column" and then the number specified in the parentheses, which must be a column number. Notice also that the individual words are played back with the *wait* option, to make sure that they are all read properly before the next word.

Having implemented the readDigit( ) Function, reading the numbers in each cell is as easy as printing them one character at a time. Instead of the Print command, we call the readDigit( ) Function to "print" them to the speaker. Most of the lines in the programming here scan the grid and select and highlight the current cell, so that the user can locate the number being read at a quick glance. Here is the listing of the "Read Numbers" Command Button's Click( ) event:

```
Private Sub ReadButton_Click( )
Dim digit As Integer
Dim icol As Integer, irow As Integer
Dim StartRow As Integer
```

```
Dim ErrorString As String * 255
Dim StrLen As Long

ReadButton.Visible = False
StopButton.Visible = True
ExitButton.Visible = False
StopNow = False
DoEvents
' Load WAVE file in memory
voicefile = App.Path + "\gridnums.wav"
On Error GoTo NoFile
Open voicefile For Binary As #1
Close #1
On Error Resume Next
cmdStr$ = "open " + voicefile + " type waveaudio alias voice"
x& = mciSendString(cmdStr$, 0&, 0, 0)
cmdStr$ = "play voice from 0 to 100 wait"
x& = mciSendString(cmdStr$, 0&, 0, 0)
If x& <> 0 Then
   StrLen = 255
   r& = mciGetErrorString(x&, ErrorString, StrLen)
   MsgBox ErrorString
   End
End If

cmdStr$ = "set voice time format samples"
x& = mciSendString(cmdStr$, 0&, 0, 0)

StartCol = Grid1.SelStartCol
StartRow = Grid1.SelStartRow
EndCol = Grid1.SelEndCol
EndRow = Grid1.SelEndRow
DoEvents
' A chance to display selected cell
' The two FOR..NEXT loops scan the selected area,
' column first
For icol = StartCol To EndCol
   DoEvents
   Grid1.SelStartCol = icol
   Grid1.SelEndCol = icol
   success% = sayCOLUMN(icol)
   success% = sayROW(StartRow)
```

```
    For irow = StartRow To EndRow
        Grid1.SelStartRow = irow
        Grid1.SelEndRow = irow
        Grid1.Row = irow
        Grid1.Col = icol
        DoEvents
        num$ = Grid1.Text
        varNum = num$
        If Not IsNumeric(varNum) Then
            success% = sayOOPS( )
        Else
            For i = 1 To Len(num$)
                If StopNow Then          ' User clicked on Stop Button
                    x& = mciSendString("stop voice", 0&, 0, 0)
                    x& = mciSendString("close voice", 0&, 0, 0)
                    Exit Sub
                End If

                symbol$ = Mid$(num$, i, 1)
                If symbol$ = "." Then
                    digit = 11
                ElseIf symbol$ = "-" Then
                    digit = 12
                Else
                    digit = Val(Mid$(num$, i, 1))
                End If
                res% = readDigit(digit)
            Next
            delay (1000)         ' Wait for 1 second
        End If
        Next
    Next

    x& = mciSendString("close voice", 0&, 0, 0)
    ReadButton.Visible = True
    ExitButton.Visible = True
    StopButton.Visible = False
    Exit Sub

NoFile:
    MsgBox "Voice file not found. Make sure the GRIDNUMS.WAV →
    file is in the same directory as the application."
```

```
        ReadButton.Visible = True
        ExitButton.Visible = True
        StopButton.Visible = False

    End Sub
```

(Again, if you experience a problem, first check to see that the open command is pointing to the correct path for what is being opened.)

The StopNow variable is a Global variable set by the Stop Command Button when the user clicks on it to end the operation. As soon as the process of reading starts, we make the Read Numbers Command Button invisible, and in its place we display the Stop Button. Click on this Button to end the process of reading out the numbers. Once the reading process is interrupted, the Stop Button becomes invisible and the Read Numbers Button becomes visible again.

Before the program starts reading out the numbers, it makes sure the proper hardware is available by executing the following lines:

```
cmdStr$ = "open " + voicefile + " type waveaudio alias voice"
x& = mciSendString(cmdStr$, 0&, 0, 0)
cmdStr$ = "play voice from 0 to 10 wait"
x& = mciSendString(cmdStr$, 0&, 0, 0)
If x& <> 0 Then
    StrLen = 255
    r& = mciGetErrorString(x&, ErrorString, StrLen)
    MsgBox ErrorString
    End
End If
```

It just plays back the 10 first samples of the WAVE file and checks the result of the operation. If the computer isn't equipped with a sound card, the program displays the error message and ends.

## SIMPLE ANIMATION TECHNIQUES

So far we've explored multimedia tools. Now let's turn our attention to some useful techniques for manipulating images in very different ways. You will see a few surprisingly simple animation techniques which can be implemented in Visual Basic (no sound drivers, no animation players required). With the following techniques, you can add visual excitement to your applications simply by employing new ways of programming.

## Sprites, Animation & Superimposition

One relatively straightforward animation technique combines a static background image with a moveable foreground image. It's easy to merge two images in Visual Basic. Say that we want to paste the goose in Figure 9-35 into the seascape in Figure 9-36. The essence of this process is called *masking*, and, lucky for us, it's built into the BitBlt( ) API Function as a copy mode (using the XOR technique). VB can, of course, utilize API functions (see Chapter 8).

Figure 9-35: We're going to add this goose to the following figure.

Figure 9-36: This background image is the target of our superimposition.

Figure 9-37: The result: One picture combined with another.

Here's how to make parts of an image transparent, allowing a separate background image to show through.

We'll demonstrate how to display a foreground image with an underlying background image showing through. This technique is clearly more realistic than merely putting an Image or Picture Box on top of an image. Of course, the simplest animation is to use the Move command with (or change the Left or Top Properties of) a Picture Box or Image Control. You can use a Timer to repeatedly slide the Picture or Image across a background. But you end up with a rectangle (the background of the superimposed image) covering up the true background, as you can see in Figure 9-38.

Figure 9-38: The problem: A superimposed Image covers up part of the desired background.

Figure 9-39: The solution: Using BitBlt( ), the desired background “shows through” and the composite image looks more realistic.

One solution would be to make the background (on the Form) pure black or white—or some other untextured, uninteresting color—then fill in the background of the superimposed image with the same color. This approach, though, results in cruder and less dynamic animations.

Let's write a program which merges the image of a goose, then moves it across the sky.

First, load a background BMP file into the Picture Property of a Form. Add a Timer. Then, drag three Picture Boxes onto the Form (it doesn't matter where). Change their Names to Original, Mask and Background. Set to True their AutoRedraw, AutoSize and ClipControls Properties. Now we must make the Original and the Mask.

Figure 9-40: The Original, Mask and Background Picture Boxes, ready to be merged with the clouds in the background.

You want the Original to have a pure white background and the Mask to have a pure black background. (When XOR does its magic, it expects to find these colors.) It's easy to remove a background from an image, then pour in ("fill") the empty background with black or white—if you use a photo-retouching program like Photoshop, Corel's PHOTO-PAINT!, Micrografx's Picture Publisher, etc. (If all you have is Windows's Paintbrush, you'll have to do it the hard way—try to paint in white and then black around whatever graphic you want to animate.)

Use a "magic wand" to isolate, then manipulate, graphic objects.

However, in a retouching program, all you have to do is use the "magic wand" to create a mask (possibly "invert" the mask), copy the mask, then paste it into a "New Image." This will leave it with a white background, so you can save it as "Original." Then, just fill the white background with black, and save it as "Mask." (See Figure 9-41.)

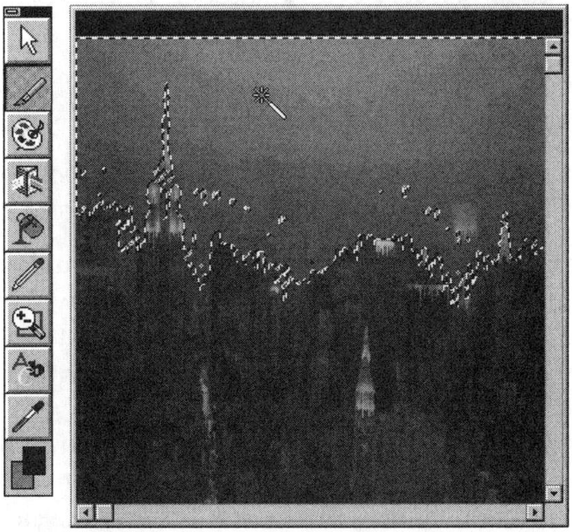

Figure 9-41: Use the Mask tool to isolate the image you want to animate from its original background.

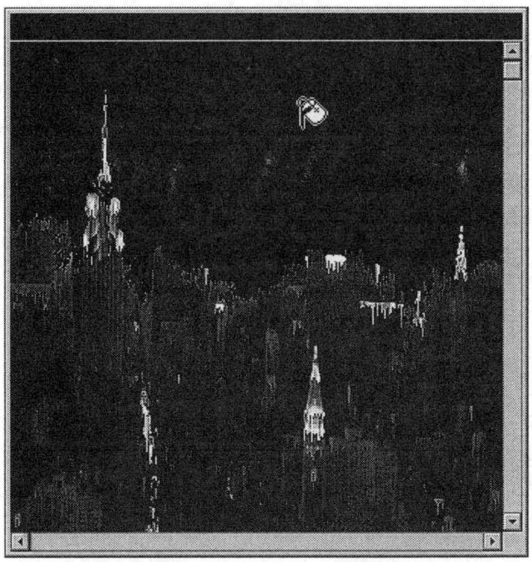

Figure 9-42: Then, pour pure black (or white) into the sky. We're using Picture Publisher here.

Now for the programming: In the General Declarations section of a Form (all on one line) type the BitBlt declare:

```
Public Declare Function BitBlt Lib "GDI" (ByVal hDestDC As→
Integer, ByVal X As Integer, ByVal Y As Integer, ByVal nWidth→
As Integer, ByVal nHeight As Integer, ByVal hSrcDC As→
Integer, ByVal XSrc As Integer, ByVal YSrc As Integer, ByVal→
dwRop As Long) As Integer
```

And right below that, create two pairs of variables to allow the program to remember the position, and size, of our sprites.

```
Dim X As Integer, Y As Integer 'The location of the sprite.
Dim wi As Integer, hi As Integer 'The size of the sprite.
```

Then, in the Form_Load, we'll do the usual housekeeping in preparation for the program proper. First, we establish the starting point for our bird's flight, by storing 12 and 300 into our position variables (slightly over from the left side of the Form, and about halfway down).

Then we put the size of the Original Picture Box into our "size" variables, wi and hi, and make sure that the "Background" Picture Box (into which we will repeatedly copy the clouds and sky as the bird flies across the background) is the same size as our Original and Mask bird images. Then we set the Timer to move the bird every 150 milliseconds. You want to fiddle with this Interval value, to get the smoothest animation based on the size of the sprite you are working with.

Finally, we make all Picture Boxes invisible, then copy the clouds at the starting location into the Background Picture Box so we can restore the background once the bird has flown on up past this area.

```
Private Sub Form_Load( )
Form1.Show

X = 12
Y = 300

wi = Original.Width
hi = Original.Height
Background.Width = wi
Background.Height = hi
timer1.Interval = 150

'Make all picture boxes invisible
Original.Visible = False
```

```
Mask.Visible = False
Background.Visible = False

'remember starting background rectangle

z% = BitBlt(Background.hDC, 0, 0, wi, hi, Form1.hDC, X, Y,→
&hcc0020)

End Sub
```

It's a small matter of adding a loop to create animation effects, to make one picture seem to move across another. (This kind of thing used to be called sprites, and facilities for sprite animation were built into early personal computers like the Atari.)

So, here's the meat of our program. Within the Timer's Timer Event, type this:

```
Private Sub Timer1_Timer( )

    'Copy background sample over bird
    z% = BitBlt(Form1.hDC, X, Y, wi, hi, Background.hDC, 0,→
    0, &hcc0020) 'SRCCOPY

    'Move up & to the right
    X = X + 4
    Y = Y - 2

    'Move back down and restart if going off the Form
    If Y < 50 Then Y = 300: X = 12

    'Copy and save new background rectangle
    z% = BitBlt(Background.hDC, 0, 0, wi, hi, Form1.hDC, X,→
Y, &hcc0020) 'SRCCOPY

    'Display the original (white background).
    z% = BitBlt(Form1.hDC, X, Y, wi, hi, Original.hDC, 0, 0,→
&h8800c6) 'SRCAND

    'Display the mask (black background)
    z% = BitBlt(Form1.hDC, X, Y, wi, hi, Mask.hDC, 0, 0,→
&hee0086) 'SRCOR

End Sub
```

Now to make the goose flap its wings.

Looks pretty good. Of course, true animation involves more than sliding a foreground image across a background. There should also be motion within the sprite. Let's make our goose flap its wings.

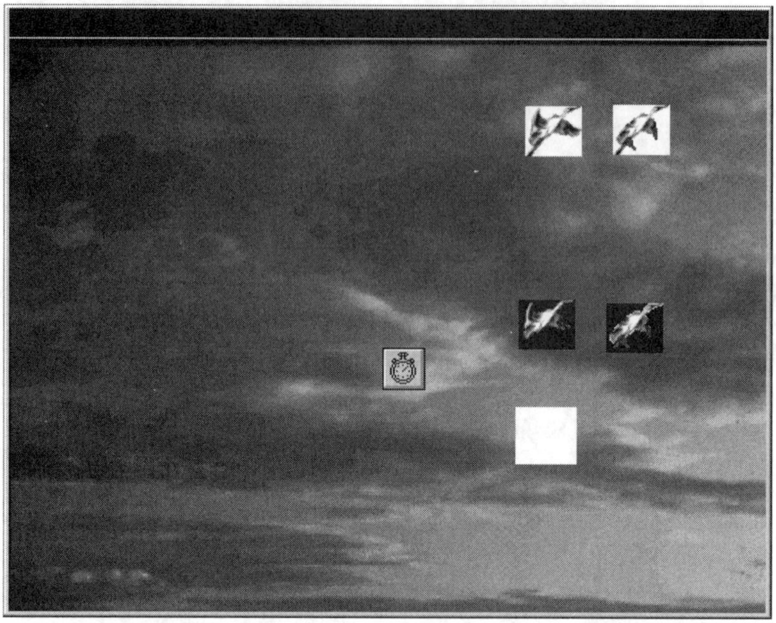

Figure 9-43: To add additional animation, we'll create a second set of geese—this time flapping their wings.

Put two more Picture Boxes on the Form, containing the black-and-white masked goose, but this time with its wings down. We'll call these new images O1 and M1. Add this to the Form_Load Event:

```
O1.Visible = False
M1.Visible = False
```

Then change the Timer routine to show the wings up, then down, alternating the flapping across the sky:

```
Private Sub Timer1_Timer( )
Static toggle As Integer
toggle = Not toggle

    'Copy background sample over bird
    z% = BitBlt(Form1.hDC, X, Y, wi, hi, Background.hDC, 0, →
    0, &hcc0020) 'SRCCOPY

    'Move up & to the right
    X = X + 4
    Y = Y - 2

    'Move back down and restart if going off the Form
    If Y < 50 Then Y = 300: X = 12
```

```
        'Copy and save new background rectangle
        z% = BitBlt(Background.hDC, 0, 0, wi, hi, Form1.hDC, X,→
        Y, &hcc0020) 'SRCCOPY

    If toggle Then

        'Display the original (white background).
        z% = BitBlt(Form1.hDC, X, Y, wi, hi, Original.hDC, 0, 0,→
        &h8800c6) 'SRCAND

        'Display the mask (black background)
        z% = BitBlt(Form1.hDC, X, Y, wi, hi, Mask.hDC, 0, 0,→
        &hee0086) 'SRCOR

    Else

        'Display the second original (white background).
        z% = BitBlt(Form1.hDC, X, Y, wi, hi, O1.hDC, 0, 0,→
        &h8800c6) 'SRCAND

        'Display the second mask (black background)
        z% = BitBlt(Form1.hDC, X, Y, wi, hi, M1.hDC, 0, 0,→
        &hee0086) 'SRCOR

    End If

    End Sub
```

Sprites, of course, can also be used to animate text—they can make a nice show for the user while your program loads and sets itself up.

## Wipes: TV Transitions

Our next topic is the creation of transitions (or wipes) between images, which can be used in a variety of ways. You can set up slick slide shows for presentations.

Why bother with visual transitions? For the same reason that transitions are used in writing, in music or anywhere else, even in conversations. Abrupt changes annoy people. If you suddenly change the subject, people notice. If one paragraph bears no relation to the previous one, people think you're illogical, clumsy or perhaps just a bad writer. However, until now, visual transitions were not possible in computers—there wasn't enough processing power to imitate the way movies and TV move from one visual subject to another (they are called "dissolves" or "wipes").

Wipes make transitions between images more natural.

The alternative—"jump cuts"—is avoided in television or movies during major shifts in time or space. The noticeable exception is MTV videos where jarring is the operative goal. Also, music videos often make their jumps on the drumbeat because it would be too strange to create a different visual rhythm.

But when a movie switches scenes from the inside of a house to the street, the camera usually follows the actors outside or sometimes fades the new outdoor image into the previous, inside scene. A jump cut would simply abruptly replace the couch and chairs with cars and telephone poles.

And now that computers can wipe between windows, we'll likely see this effect used more and more to smoothly move the user between the "scenes" of a program. With the techniques demonstrated and explained below, you can add these special effects to your VB programs right now. It's fast, effective, fully professional.

In previous chapters we've explored how to design attractive and functional Forms, how to use graphics to enhance even the simplest Forms, and numerous ways to manipulate bitmaps. Here we'll add a new and quite valuable technique to your bag of tricks—a slew of sleek transitions.

One little-discussed phenomenon: computers aren't merely converging with television in the hardware. Computer software is gradually approaching the skill and élan with which TV and cinema convey visual information.

A wipe is a technique for gradually replacing one image with another. There are dozens of wipes. An image may slide from bottom to top, or be drawn in stripes from left to right. One might move in like a worm from the edges to the center, or shift like venetian blinds. They can make a compelling presentation with a minimum of effort.

### Example: Slide Show Demo

Our example program, WIPEDEMO, shown in Figure 9-44, is a slide show application. First select an image by clicking on its icon on the lower-left corner, and then display it on the Picture Box with any of the special effect Command Buttons on the right half of the Form. You can also use the scroll bar to adjust the duration of each wipe. To speed up the operation, you can let the program select an image at random for you, by checking the Select Image Randomly Check Box.

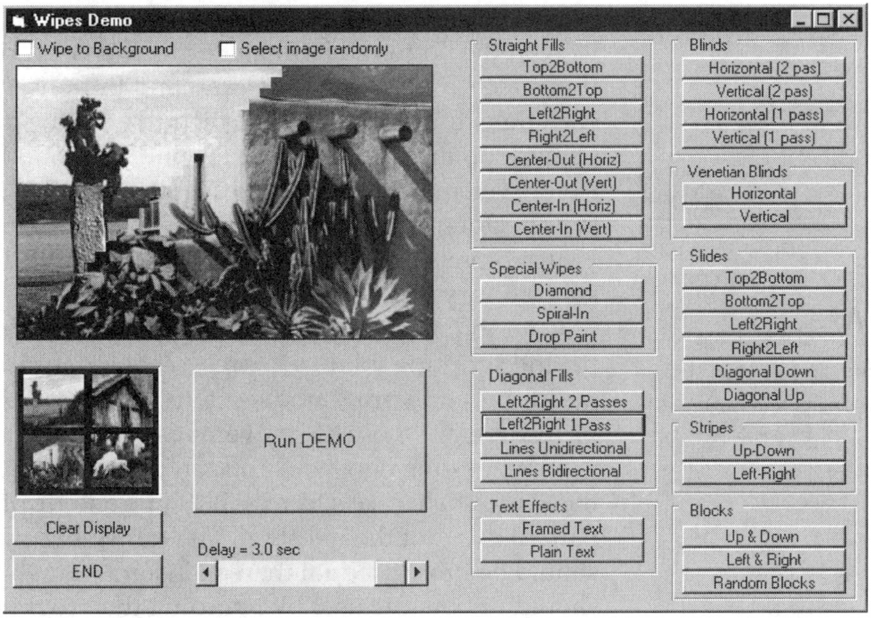


Figure 9-44: Here you see an image being wiped diagonally over another one.

Figure 9-45: WIPEDEMO shows you how to do dozens of special-effect wipes. Here you see the Diamond wipe in progress.

Try it out. Run WIPEDEMO and select an image by clicking on its icon on the bottom left of the Form. Then experiment with the transition effects by clicking the Command Buttons. (Click on a new icon each time, to wipe the visible picture with the picture behind the icon. Or click on the "Wipe to Background" option.) If you have a True Color system, run WIPEDEMO in the 9\WIPEDEMO\TRUECLR subdirectory of the CD. With a 256-color system, you should use the 256-color version of WIPEDEMO in the 9\WIPEDEMO\256COLOR subdirectory. (See "Palette Problems" below.)

CD-ROM

WIPEDEMO is a demonstration of the flexibility and speed of the BitBlt( ) API Function.

Later in this chapter you will find another application for setting up and scripting your own presentations. And, of course, you can insert this wipe programming into any of your own applications.

To wipe, we'll use the powerhouse BitlBlt( ) Function (see Chapter 8) in an interesting new way. You can probably guess that merely reading the appropriate pixels from a .BMP file and displaying them in some pattern is out of the question. The transitions must be swift. A wipe should be more gradual than an instant jump—but the transition shouldn't bore the user by retarding the program. Usually, you'll want to adjust the timing so that a wipe is only a half-second or a second long.

Also, we certainly cannot tolerate the delays induced when reading an image's pixel by pixel from disk. Instead, we must load the image on a hidden Image Box (its Visible Property set to False), and then use the BitBlt( ) Function to move chunks of pixels to the visible Image Box. This approach works very well and Visual Basic (reading from a disk file, or using the PSet Command) cannot even come close to the speed of BitBlt, once the image is in the computer's memory.

The BitBlt( ) Function copies pixels from one rectangular area of the screen to another one. You can, for instance, copy the upper left portion of an Image Box onto the lower right of another one. The API function is first declared in the General Declarations section of a Form (or Module), and typed in all on a single line:

```
Declare Function BitBlt Lib "GDI" (ByVal hDestDC As Integer, →
ByVal X As Integer, ByVal Y As Integer, ByVal nWidth As →
Integer, ByVal nHeight As Integer, ByVal hSrcDC As Integer, →
ByVal XSrc As Integer, ByVal YSrc As Integer, ByVal dwRop →
As Long) As Integer
```

## Looking at Some Wipes

Before we proceed with the actual programming, let's see a few examples of transitions and explain how they are achieved. In Figures 9-46, 9-47 and 9-48, you see some stages of three different transition effects: Top2Bottom (the image is drawn slowly from top to bottom), VerticalBlinds (the image is drawn in vertical stripes from left to right and then vice versa) and Diamond (the image starts as a small diamond in the middle and grows larger and larger until it covers the entire Picture Box).

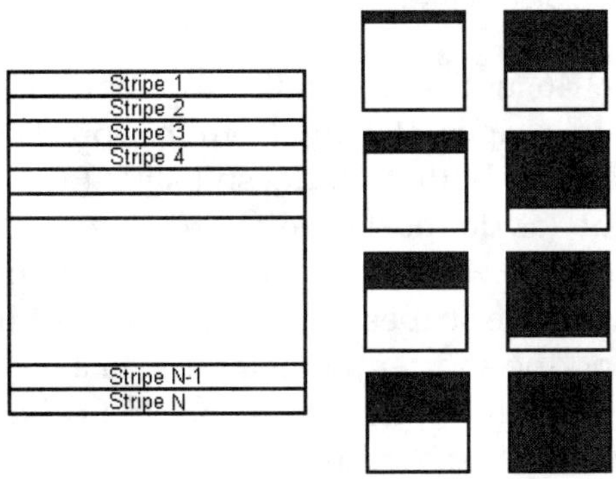


Figure 9-46: The stages of the Top2Bottom wipe.

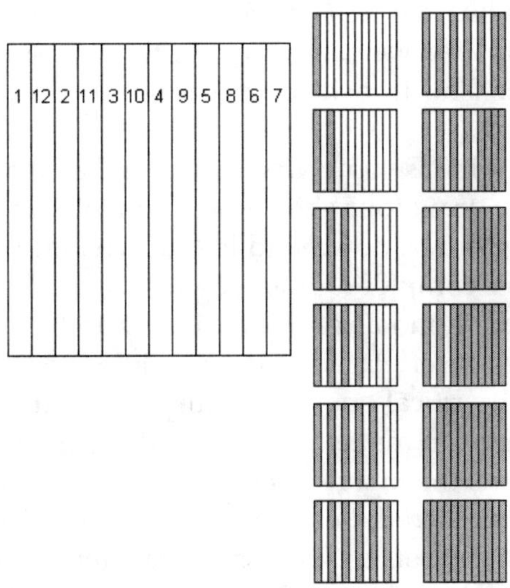


Figure 9-47: The stages of a wipe with vertical blinds (BlindVert2Pass).

Figure 9-48: The diamond wipe.

Wipes are block transfers of pixels, based on various geometric shapes.

In Figure 9-46, notice that in the Top2Bottom transition we draw thin horizontal stripes, starting from the top. The image is actually drawn from top to bottom. It doesn't slide (a slide is a different wipe). This transition (as do most others) offers two parameters for controlling the effect. The width (thickness) of the stripe and the delay in drawing successive stripes. The smaller the width, the smoother the transition, and the shorter the delay, the faster the image is drawn. These parameters interact, so you should fiddle with them to get the best combination of smoothness and speed for whatever size of Image Box you are working with.

The BlindVert2Pass effect works similarly. Here the stripes are not displayed in their natural order. In going from left to right we draw the odd-numbered ones (1, 3, 5, ...) and after we reach the right side of the display area we start drawing the even-numbered stripes in reverse order. This transition covers the entire display area in two passes.

The third wipe is somewhat different. To create an expanding diamond, we draw four short lines of pixels (or groups of pixels) in the following order: down and left, down and right, up and right, up and left. After completing four segments, we display the next four around the diamond already on display. In this transition one can notice a staircase effect, since diagonal lines are never as smooth as horizontal or vertical ones when displayed on a computer.

Our application makes use of two Picture Boxes—a hidden one, which contains the image to be wiped, and the visible one, on which the image is rendered. Let's call them "source" and "target." A wipe, or transition, consists of successive transfers of pixel blocks from the source to the target Picture Box. Depending on the shape and size of the pixel blocks, and the order in which they are transferred, you can create numerous wipes.

Now let's look at the actual code that produces the three effects we just mentioned. The simplest transition is the Top2Bottom one, which reads stripes of the hidden Picture Box (Picture1) and transfers them to the same place on the visible Picture Box (Picture2), with a simple loop. Here is the code for the Top2Bottom transition:

```
Sub Top2Bottom(StripeHeight As Integer, msecdelay As →
Integer)
' STRAIGHT FILL: TOP TO BOTTOM
Dim Stripes As Integer
Dim P1 As Integer, P2 As Integer
Dim mdelay As Integer

    Stripes = Form1.Picture1.ScaleHeight / StripeHeight
    mdelay = msecdelay / Stripes
    P2 = 0
    P1 = Form1.Picture1.ScaleWidth
    While P2 <= Form1.Picture2.ScaleHeight
        Call StartDelay
        r% = BitBlt(Form1.Picture2.hDC, 0, P2, P1, →
        StripeHeight, Form1.Picture1.hDC, 0, P2, &HCC0020)
        P2 = P2 + StripeHeight
        Call EndDelay(mdelay)
    Wend

End Sub
```

P1 is the height of the picture section which is being transferred (it keeps growing larger until the entire picture has been moved). stripeheight is the parameter that the user can set to define how thick the stripes should be.

The BlindVert2Pass transition is slightly more complicated, since now we must use two loops. The first one scans the image from left to right and the second one backwards. Moreover, each loop skips every other stripe (by looping with a Step of 2):

```
Sub BlindVert2Pass(StripeWidth As Integer, msecdelay As →
Integer)
' BLINDES VERTICAL (2 passes)
Dim Stripes As Integer, mdelay As Integer

    Stripes = Form1.Picture1.ScaleWidth / StripeWidth
    mdelay = msecdelay / Stripes
```

```
    P2 = Form1.Picture1.ScaleHeight
' Draw even stripes in upper half ...
    For i = 0 To Stripes - 1 Step 2
        Call StartDelay
        P1 = StripeWidth * i
        r% = BitBlt(Form1.Picture2.hDC, P1, 0, StripeWidth,  →
        P2, Form1.Picture1.hDC, P1, 0, &HCC0020)
        Call EndDelay(mdelay)
    Next
' ... and odd stripes in lower half
    For i = Stripes - 1 To 0 Step -2
        Call StartDelay
        P1 = StripeWidth * i
        r% = BitBlt(Form1.Picture2.hDC, P1, 0, StripeWidth,  →
        P2, Form1.Picture1.hDC, P1, 0, &HCC0020)
        Call EndDelay(mdelay)
    Next

End Sub
```

Table 9-10 lists transition effects in the WIPEDEMO application, the names of the functions that implement them, and short descriptions of the wipe effects.

| | |
|---|---|
| **Slides** | **Image slides into the destination Picture Box from various directions.** |
| Bottom to Top | SlideFromBottom |
| Top to Bottom | SlideFromTop |
| Right to Left | SlideFromRight |
| Left to Right | SlideFromLeft |
| Diagonal Down | SlideDiagonalDown |
| Diagonal Up | SlideDiagonalUp |
| **Straight Fills** | **Image fills the destination Picture Box in stripes from all vertical and horizontal directions.** |
| Bottom to Top | Bottom2Top |
| Top to Bottom | Top2Bottom |
| Right to Left | Right2Left |

| | |
|---|---|
| Left to Right | Left2Right |
| Center-In Horizontal | CenterInHoriz |
| Center-In Vertical | CenterInVert |
| Center-Out Horizontal | CenterOutHoriz |
| Center-Out Vertical | CenterOutVert |
| **Diagonal Fills** | **Image fills the destination Picture Box diagonally.** |
| Left to Right 1 Pass | DiagonalL2R1Pass |
| Left to Right 2 Passes | DiagonalL2R2Pass |
| Lines Unidirectional | LinesUniDir |
| Lines Bidirectional | LinesBiDir |
| **Blocks** | **Image fills the destination Picture Box by drawing small boxes.** |
| Up and Down | BlocksUpAndDown |
| Left and Right | BlocksLeftAndRight |
| Random | BlocksRandom |
| **Blinds** | **Image is displayed gradually in vertical and horizontal stripes.** |
| Horizontal 1 Pass | BlindHoriz1Pass |
| Horizontal 2 Pass | BlindHoriz2Pass |
| Vertical 1 Pass | BlindVert1Pass |
| Vertical 2 Pass | BlindVert2Pass |
| **Venetian Blinds** | **Image is displayed in gradually increasing blinds (like a venetian blind).** |
| Venetian Vertical | VenetianBlindVert |
| Venetian Horizontal | VenetianBlindHoriz |
| **Special** | **Image fills the destination Picture Box from various directions and shapes.** |
| Spiral-In | Spiral Inward |
| Diamond | Diamond |
| Drop Paint | DropPaint |

Table 9-10: The transitions of the WIPEDEMO and MAKESHOW applications.

### Timing the Wipes

Timing the wipes is fairly straightforward for most of them, and here is how it's implemented: What we know is the total duration of the wipe. This interval has to be spread throughout the wipe's steps. Each time a new block of pixels is transferred from the Source to the Target Picture Box, a small delay must be inserted. This delay is the total duration of the wipe divided by the number of blocks to be transferred.

Let's say that we want to fill the Target Picture Box with a blind effect in 2 seconds (or 2,000 milliseconds), and there are 50 blinds in the effect. This means each transfer must take 2,000/50 = 40 milliseconds. Notice that this isn't just a delay. We must take into consideration the time it takes the computer to transfer the designated block. If it takes the computer 13 milliseconds to copy a block of pixels, we must add a delay of 27 milliseconds, so the total duration of a single block transfer is 40 milliseconds.

Visual Basic's Timer Function can't be used for this purpose because its resolution is 55 milliseconds. The Timer Function will return the same value if called many times within the same 55-millisecond interval. Obviously, it wouldn't work in our case, where we need a resolution of 40 milliseconds.

The Function we need here is called timeGetTime( ), and we'll borrow it from the WINMM.DLL (or MMSYSTEM.DLL under Windows 3.1). This Function returns a long integer, which is the system time in milliseconds. Here's its declaration:

```
Declare Function timeGetTime Lib "winmm" ( ) As Long
```

In each wipe, we calculate the duration of each transfer by dividing the total duration by the number of block transfers (which is the number of times the BitBlt( ) Function is called). Then the wipe starts. Before each new block is transferred, we call startDelay( ) to retrieve the current system time and store it in the StartTime global variable:

```
Sub StartDelay ( )
    StartTime = timeGetTime( )
End Sub
```

After each block transfer, we call the EndDelay( ) Subroutine with the number of milliseconds each transfer is supposed to last. The EndDelay( ) routine compares the difference between the current time and StartTime. If their difference is less than the required number of milliseconds, the endDelay( ) Subroutine stalls until this difference becomes equal to (or exceeds) the required delay. Here is the code of the endDelay( ) Subroutine:

```
Sub EndDelay (N As Integer)
    While timeGetTime( ) - StartTime < N
    Wend
End Sub
```

The argument N is the number of milliseconds each block transfer should last. Notice that each individual delay takes into consideration the time it takes the computer to transfer a block of pixels too.

The delay for each wipe is built into the corresponding function and, in most cases, is straightforward. Some wipes, however, are rather complicated. The Random Blocks effect is one of them because we don't always know in advance the number of block transfers it will take to fill the Picture Box. Also, some wipes are too slow to time properly. The Drop Pixels wipe is too slow on a 386 system. In fact, we chose not to time the duration of the Drop Pixels wipe because the calls to the StartDelay and EndDelay Subroutines would introduce additional delays. Instead, you can drop multiple lines of pixels to speed up this wipe.

### Example: Creating a Slide Show

Where the WIPEDEMO application can help familiarize you with the various wipes and their visual effect, this next application, MAKESHOW, helps you build a real slide show. If you are creating a presentation, use MAKESHOW to create a script via simple point-and-click operations.

You can see the main Form of MAKESHOW in Figure 9-49. Use the File Controls to select an image; double-click on its name to add it to the List Control. The file name is inserted at the selected item's place, or at the end of the List if no item is selected. After clicking on a file name, you'll see the image (properly resized) in the Picture Box.

Each image, along with its associated transition effect, is displayed in the List control. To specify a wipe, select a line from the List and then a transition from the Transitions menu. If you don't specify a transition, the default, a simple jump cut, will be inserted. The entire image will be transferred at once onto the Picture Box. The three icons above the List Control allow you to move a selected item up or down the List, or delete it entirely. Finally, to view the script, click on the Play Script Menu command.

Notice that WIPEDEMO will cope with images of any size and will attempt to center them on the Form. In a practical situation, however, all images must have the same size.

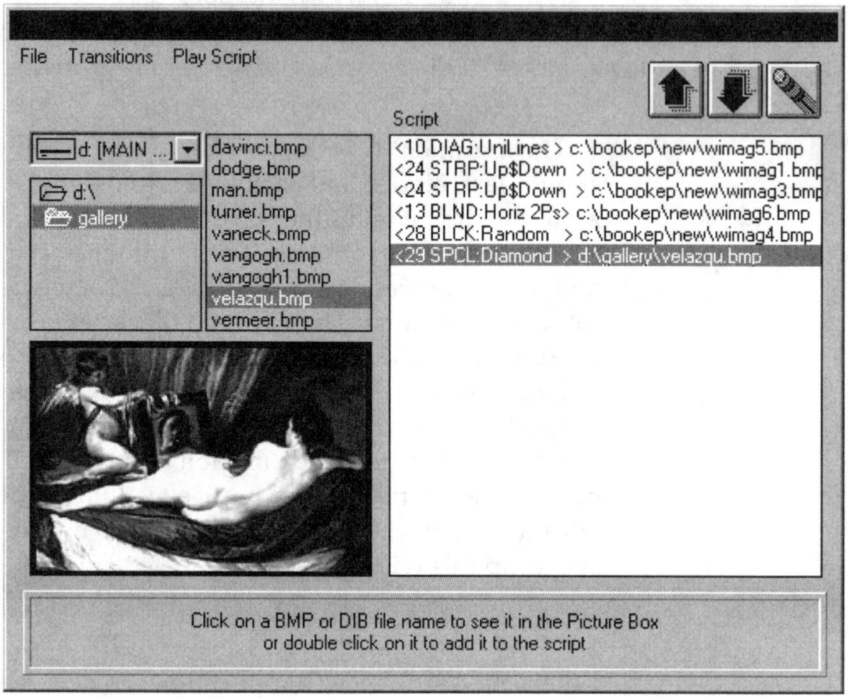


Figure 9-49: With the MAKESHOW application, you can script a series of wipes for inclusion in your VB programs.

The file names of the images in the List are preceded by a string in brackets, like

<10 DIAG: UniLines>

or

<13 BLND:Horiz 2Ps>

These strings describe the transition effect for the specified image. The names are descriptive and short: DIAG: UniLines means that the effect to be used is a diagonal fill, with unidirectional lines. Likewise, the next effect is a blind, in which the stripes cover the entire image horizontally, in two passes. The number in front of them, is used to speed up the logic of the program that runs the script. If you look at the code of the application, you will see that it uses a long Case command based on the number for each special effect, rather than its name. The names of the wipes, along with their numbers, are stored in an array, which is initialized in the Form's Load Event.

## Hints & Tips

Most of the wiping functions accept two arguments: the size of each individual block and the duration of the wipe. For example, the Left2Right( ) Function declaration is:

```
Function Left2Right(StripeWidth As Integer, msecs As →
Integer) As Integer
```

StripeWidth is the width of the stripe, by which the image is advanced at each step, and msecs is the total duration of the wipe in milliseconds.

If the width of the image to be wiped is 200 pixels and you are using a StripeWidth of 10 or 20 pixels, the wipe will work fine. If the StripeWidth is 13, some pixels will not be transferred. This implementation of WIPEDEMO (and MAKESHOW) requires that the Width or Height of the image be an integer multiple of the StripeWidth, or StripeHeight respectively. This restriction makes sense because we want the wipe to take place with equally sized blocks. Since all images must have the same size, you should first clip them so that they all have the same size. Don't use pictures with odd dimensions, like 203 X 311. Crop them to 200 X 300, for example, and use an even value for StripeWidth and StripeHeight (like 2, or 4, or 10, etc). Of course, the code can be adjusted to accommodate any image size, but we chose to omit this optimization step here, to minimize the complexity of the code.

## Palette Problems

Both WIPEDEMO and MAKESHOW work fine on systems capable of displaying True Color images. If your system is limited to 16 colors, you will not be able to display the best possible images. You can, however, use both applications on a 16-color system to display simple drawings or text created with paint programs, or dithered images—as long as you limit your ambitions accordingly.

The situation is a bit more complicated with 256-color systems. When you display an image on top of another one, with different colors, Visual Basic will have to approximate some of the colors, since it is impossible on such computers to display more than 256 colors correctly. Although most of the time you see only one image on the screen, during a wipe you are actually displaying two images for a few seconds.

For a discussion on handling 256-color palettes, see Chapter 6.

To be able to display two images with correct colors, you must make sure that they both utilize the same palette, so that Visual Basic will not be tempted to approximate any of the colors. There are many ways to force two pictures to use the same palette and we will discuss them shortly. However, there is also a surprisingly simple way to overcome the multiple palette problem. You can wipe each image to a simple one, such as a single color or a simple texture, and then wipe the simple picture to the next image. You can use any simple image between images—your company's logo, for example. Just make sure that this image doesn't contain more than a few basic colors. This process insures that all images are displayed with their own palette.

Another way to ensure that all images display properly is to force them to share a single palette. The images of the WIPEDEMO application were created with a common palette. They were scanned all together at 256 colors, and then using Picture Publisher, each was cut (cropped) and saved into a separate BMP file. This gives them the same palette.

If you are using a paint application to create the images, such as CorelDRAW! or PhotoStyler, load the same 256-color palette (see the respective programs' help files). As a result, all the images you will create will share the same palette and can be used without a hinch by the MAKESHOW application.

The images included in the subdirectories with the WIPEDEMO application are 256-color images, with a common palette to ensure that they will work with both 256-color and True Color systems.

## Further Improvements

In setting up a slide show, you might want to display more than just simple images. You could use the mciSendString( ) API function we explained earlier in this chapter to play back animation files on the Picture Box. Or use the sndPlaySound( ) Function to start a WAV file before you begin each wipe. If you prefer MIDI music—which takes less space on the disk, too—you can use the mciSendString( ) Function.

Of course, there are also effective displays you can create with text alone. The point of a slide show is to get your message across, and although images can be the most powerful means of communicating, a few lines of text can be useful as well. There are several ways to superimpose text on top of an image. Here are a few techniques used by commercial applications.

The simplest way to add text to a Picture Box is to use the Print method. To get the viewer's attention, you can print one letter at a time with this Subroutine:

```
Sub DisplayChars (text$)

    For i = 1 To Len(text$)
        Picture1.Print Mid$(text$, i, 1);
        ' Insert some delay here
    Next

End Sub
```

Another interesting way to display text is to first create a small frame and then print the text inside. To see how these effects are accomplished, load in the WIPEDEMO program, and click on Plain Text or Framed Text Command Buttons.

Clearly, VB can accomplish all sorts of multimedia manipulations—you don't need a separate authoring tool to create multimedia applications. Visual Basic offers a wealth of capabilities, without imposing a "do-it-graphically-or-don't-do-it-at-all" approach. Some people misunderstand the acronym BASIC; they assume it must be a simple, elementary language. BASIC stands for Beginner's All Purpose Set of Instructions for Computers. For many years, the key word was "Beginner's." Now, clearly, the emphasis has shifted to "All Purpose." BASIC has evolved so far beyond its humble beginnings that Visual Basic, its ultimate implementation today, can perform quite effectively as one's primary programming language (both during design as well as in the specs of the resulting runtime) in virtually any aspect of computing—including multimedia.

## MOVING ON

In the next chapter, we'll examine another cutting-edge topic—OLE Automation. Introduced in 1994, this technique permits one application to control another, to use its macro language, to transfer data and to dynamically and programmatically gang two or more applications together into a virtual super-application. All this goes considerably beyond the earlier, simpler technologies of dynamic data exchange and such relatively cumbersome techniques as SendKeys and AppActivate.

In Chapter 10, we'll see how to analyze the contents of a VB Text Box, using two facilities (objects) of Word for Windows—Word's spell checker and character counter. We'll also construct examples of OLE Automation involving Microsoft Project and Microsoft Excel and see how macros can be used to create templates for automation. When you've read Chapter 10, you should feel comfortable programming in this intriguing and powerful new way.

# Chapter 10

# OLE Automation

OLE Automation is among the latest in a series of efforts to break applications into their component parts, their objects. Automation also breaks down the barriers between individual applications.

Since computing began, it has usually been awkward to move information from one application to another. Say you were writing a quarterly report. If you kept your company's inventory in a database, you had to retype the data into a word processor to incorporate it into your report.

Custom filters were the first improvement in integrating applications. Each application came with a set of protocols that allowed you to load various types of file structures and thereby import data from an outside application. Likewise, export filters permitted you to "Save As," saving data out to disk more or less successfully in an alien format.

Data transfer became more streamlined with DDE and OLE 1.0.

Then came cutting, copying and pasting—the Clipboard—a way to manually move text, and later graphics, between applications. With dynamic data exchange (DDE) and object linking and embedding (OLE 1.0), data transfers became relatively automatic and invisible to the user. But the user still had to manually activate and specify the links.

## MORE THAN SIMPLE DATA TRANSFER

Now, OLE Automation goes beyond simple data transfer: you can control one application from another. OLE Automation permits virtually unlimited manipulation of outside "objects" (like an equation editor, a word counter and so on). It doesn't matter that these objects are part of a separate, outside application. With OLE Automation, you get essentially unrestricted access to the innards of any application that permits its objects to be used. In the colorful phrase that Microsoft uses for this permission, an application is said to "expose its objects."

With DDE and OLE, the user had to manually activate and specify the links. With Automation, you, the programmer, set up the entire process of sharing data or features ("objects," as they are called). Then, the user merely clicks on an icon in your Visual Basic Form to have the spelling of a Text Box checked, the words counted—whatever services and functionality that Word for Windows provides for its own documents can be "borrowed" by your VB program. The user doesn't have to care how the functionality is implemented, doesn't have to specify the outside document or feature. You, the programmer can automate this process.

In sum, with OLE Automation you can do two new and very valuable things. First, you can directly employ any of the tools in an OLE-capable application (heightening contrast in a photo, sending email, or whatever tasks that application performs). You can employ those tools from the outside, from within a separate application. Second, you can have these services performed automatically between applications. This combination of inter-app communication (OLE) and automation is what OLE Automation means.

### EXAMPLE: BORROWING WORD'S SPELL-CHECKER

Much OLE Automation is surprisingly easy (macros are a shortcut).

It can be surprisingly easy to construct an OLE Automation. Let's try one. We'll have Word for Windows do a spell-check of the text in a VB Text Box. VB cannot check spelling, so we'll borrow the services of Word for Windows 6.0.

How do you contact Word? Create an object. Objects can be virtually anything, but in this example, the object will be Word's macro language, WordBasic. Here's how to create the WordBasic object:

```
Dim Wordobj As Object
Set Wordobj = CreateObject("word.basic")
```

Once the object is created, we can use all the commands and facilities of WordBasic from within VB. But which WordBasic commands should we use to manipulate our text? That's easy, too: record a macro in WordBasic, then copy the result to the Clipboard. WordBasic will do the main work itself, providing the necessary commands and their parameters. We'll just do a little translation to help VB understand what's wanted.

You can feed WordBasic commands to Word from within a VB application.

OLE Automation from VB to Word involves "calling up" WordBasic and then feeding WordBasic commands that it understands (commands written in WordBasic). The easiest way to get the correct commands to accomplish things in Word is to record a macro using WordBasic from within Word. Then copy and paste those commands into the Sub or Function in VB where we want to trigger the OLE Automation.

## Recording the Macro

Let's create our spell-check automation, step by step:

1. Start Word, and then type in a few lines of text. Highlight (select) these words by dragging the mouse across them.
2. Copy the highlighted words to the Clipboard by pressing Ctrl+Ins. (We'll send our VB Text Box's contents to Word via the Clipboard, so we want something that can substitute for the actual text while we're recording this macro.)

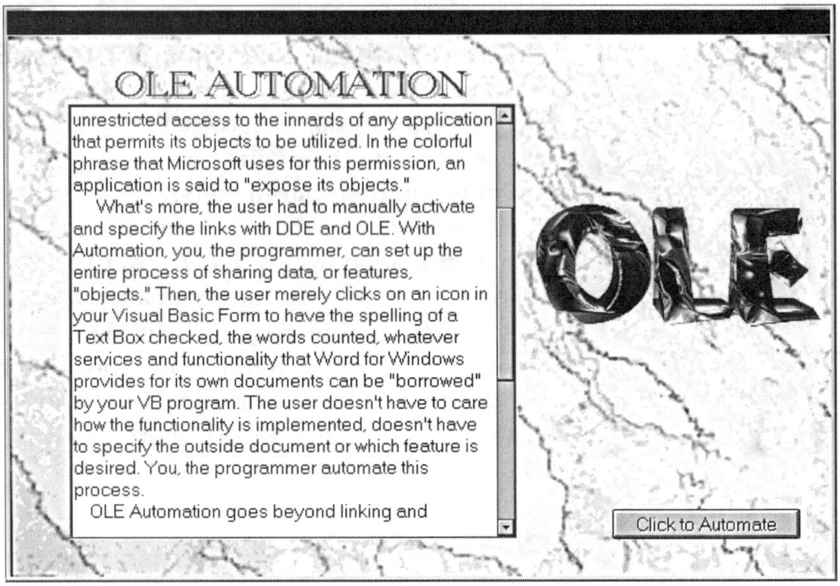


Figure 10-1: We'll borrow Word's spell-checker from within VB.

3. Turn on Word's macro recorder by pressing Alt+T, M.
4. Type in the macro name *ForVB* (or whatever name you want to give the macro).
5. Press Alt+O, Enter to start recording the macro.
6. Now, with WordBasic recording your every move, do this:
   - Press Alt+F, N to create a new document.
   - Press Shift+Ins to paste the clipboard text into the Word document.
   - Invoke the SpellCheck by pressing Alt+T, S, Enter.
   - To select the entire document, press Alt+E, L. Then press Alt+E, C to copy the spell-checked text back into the clipboard.
   - Finally, close the document by pressing Alt+F, C, and stop the macro from recording by pressing Alt+T, M, Alt+O.

At this point, we want to see the results, so press Alt+E to Edit the ForVB macro. You should see this:

```
Sub MAIN
FileNew .Template = "Normal", .NewTemplate = 0
EditPaste
ToolsSpelling
```

```
EditSelectAll
EditCopy
FileClose
End Sub
```

In our VB Sub, we can use this entire piece of programming as is, except for the first line. VB doesn't understand named parameters like .Template = "Normal", so our next task will be to translate the FileNew command so that VB will know what to do with it.

## How VB Handles Parameters

A *parameter* (sometimes called an *argument*) is a modification or list of specifications for a command. For example, the VB Move command has four parameters: left, top, width and height.

```
Move left[, top[, width[, height] ] ]
```

The actual names of the parameters (left, top, width and height) never appear in your programming. You merely list the values of any parameters you use:

```
Move 400, 200
```

Moreover, you have to get the order of the parameters right, or there will be problems. And if you want to change the last parameter in the list, you have to include commas as spacers for any parameters you omit.

## Named Parameters

To make Basic more programmer-friendly, products like Excel, Microsoft Project and Word 6.0 now feature *named parameters.* Named parameters describe each parameter in English. Therefore, your intentions can still be understood by VB even if you list them "out of order" or omit some of them. The parameter names are listed along with the parameter values, separated by an equals sign (The parameter name is preceded by a period.) It looks like

```
Object .Parametername = value, .Parametername = value,→
.Parametername = value
```

rather than the traditional:

```
Object value, value, value
```

Basic is not only the highest-level computer language today, but it is also receiving the most attention, creativity and care. Basic is evolving faster than any other language. The latest versions of Basic in Word, Excel and Microsoft Project have moved ahead of VB. Not only do Excel and Project offer named parameters, but they also boast the latest, slickest version of Basic, Visual Basic for Applications, described in Chapter 11.

In VB4, named parameters are rarely used. You still must write almost all parameter lists like this:

```
ToolsWordCount = 0, "1","3","9","1","1"
```

If you don't care about any of these parameters except the fourth one, you still must preserve the order by using spacer commas:

```
ToolsWordCount 0, , ,"9"
```

The new style (not yet in VB, alas) avoids all this by giving names to each parameter; the line

```
ToolsWordCount .Characters = "9", .Lines = "1"
```

works the same as this:

```
ToolsWordCount .Lines = "1", .Characters = "9"
```

(Notice, too, that there is no = sign between the command and the parameters, but there is an = between each parameter name and its value.)

VB requires that you surround with brackets any WordBasic commands which return a text (string) variable. There aren't all that many of them, nor are most of them useful in OLE Automation, but you should be aware of this anomaly. The little routine that follows uses WordBasic's Time$() function to return a text (string) variable to VB that is then printed in a Message Box. Note that the command [Time$] must be bracketed.

```
Sub Command3D1_Click ()

Dim WordObj As Object
Set WordObj = CreateObject("Word.Basic")
MsgBox WordObj.[Time$]()
Set WordObj = Nothing

End Sub
```

## Translating WordBasic Into VB

Now back to our spell-check automation. How do we translate WordBasic into something that VB can understand? Because, with very few exceptions, VB4 doesn't use parameter names, we must strip those off. VB does not recognize this new VBA-style of parameter listing:

```
FileNew .Template = "Normal", .NewTemplate = 0
```

But it does accept the traditional:

```
FileNew
```

("Normal" and 0 are the default parameters for FileNew, so we can leave them off.)

Just paste a WordBasic macro directly into your VB program.

So let's copy the WordBasic macro. Select the text in Word's Macro Edit screen and press Ctrl+Ins (don't copy the Sub Main or End Sub). Now switch over to VB and double-click on the Command Button to bring up its Click Event. Then paste the WordBasic right into VB:

```
Sub Command3D1_Click ()
Dim Wordobj As Object
Set Wordobj = CreateObject("word.basic")
FileNew .Template = "Normal", .NewTemplate = 0
EditPaste
ToolsSpelling
```

```
EditSelectAll
EditCopy
FileClose

End Sub
```

Now we go through and translate the WordBasic into VB-compatible programming. First, strip off the unneeded default parameter list (.Template = “Normal”, .NewTemplate = 0). Then, to let VB know that each command should be sent to the WordBasic object, add *Wordobj.* to the start of each command:

```
Sub Command3D1_Click ()

Dim Wordobj As Object
Set Wordobj = CreateObject("word.basic")

Wordobj.FileNew
Wordobj.EditPaste
Wordobj.ToolsSpelling
Wordobj.EditSelectAll
Wordobj.EditCopy
Wordobj.FileClose 2

Set Wordobj = Nothing

End Sub
```

One final thing: to release Windows system resources, destroy an object when you’re finished using it. The final line sets our object to Nothing, which makes the object evaporate. More on this below. (Then we add a *2* to the FileClose command; adding that 2 eliminates certain problems that can occur if you use FileClose alone. You just have to remember this kink.)

Now all that remains is to insert the VB commands that will copy the Text Box’s contents to the Clipboard and, at the end, paste the spell-checked result back into the Text Box. Here’s the finished Automation routine:

```
Sub Command3D1_Click ()

On Error Resume Next

Dim wordobj As object
Set wordobj = CreateObject("Word.Basic")
```

```
clipboard.Clear
clipboard.SetText text1.Text, 1

wordobj.FileNew
wordobj.EditPaste
wordobj.ToolsSpelling
wordobj.EditSelectAll
wordobj.EditCopy
wordobj.FileClose 2

Set wordobj = Nothing

text1.Text = clipboard.GetText()

End Sub
```

## Why Not Just Exit?

Setting the object to Nothing (Set wordobj = Nothing) when an automation is done accomplishes two things: (1) it releases any Windows system resources that were used by the object, and (2) it shuts down Word (or whatever application you've automated) if that application wasn't running when the OLE Automation started. You cannot exit an OLE Automated application by using the Exit command on the File menu. This will not work:

```
Wordobj.FileExit
```

The reason it won't work is that OLE Automation very sensibly assumes that if an instance of Word was running prior to the automation activity, it should be the user's responsibility to shut down that instance of Word. After all, the user started that application, and perhaps the user wants to continue using it. However, if the automation started Word (because Word was not already running), then the Set Wordobj = Nothing will, as it should, shut Word down.

Use FileNew if you don't want to make changes to an existing document.

Also note that when you use the CreateObject command, VBA looks to see if Word is already running. If Word is running, OLE Automation uses that copy of Word rather than starting a new "instance." This is why you'll usually want to use the Wordobj.FileNew command to display a new, blank document in Word. You generally won't want your automation to interfere with an existing document that the user is working on, independent of your automation activities.

Under Windows, you can start more than one copy, or instance, of Word and some other applications, such as Notepad, at the same time. Some applications permit multiple instances of themselves; others don't. OLE Automation, though, is not designed for multiple-instance automation and never starts a new instance if an application is already running.

The Clipboard is a temporary compromise.

It is, of course, regrettable that we must use the Clipboard as a postal service for our Automation activities. Rather a throwback, all things considered. For now, we must send the contents of a Text Box to the Clipboard so Word can later be told to import it (EditPaste). Then, after Word has done its job, we must export the text back to the Clipboard (with Word's EditCopy command), and import it to the Text Box.

You can avoid the sending, by directly importing the Text Box contents with WordBasic's Insert command:

```
Wordobj.Insert Text1.Text
```

However, there is no comparable way to export data from Word to VB; the Clipboard is required. Using the Clipboard as a way station isn't exactly as automatic as we'd like things to be. In the future we can look forward to directly describing the location of the text or other data that we want manipulated or imported. After all, the data does reside inside the computer, so we can point to its location rather than making a copy of it. But not yet. OLE Automation, remember, is just in its infancy.

### When You Can't Use a Macro . . .

You can generally find the WordBasic parameters you need, and their correct order, by simply recording a macro. However, some things cannot be recorded because they either aren't on Word's menus or aren't otherwise accessible to the user except as pure WordBasic commands. Often you'll find a complete parameter list by looking at Word's WordBasic Help file. There is a problem with these parameter lists when you want to use them with Visual Basic: the parameters are sometimes listed in the "wrong" order. Position isn't important when you're using named parameters; the order is simply irrelevant to VBA. However, for VB, the order does matter. The order is the only way that VB can know which parameter is which.

Fortunately, Microsoft provides a self-extracting file called POSITION.EXE that contains the information (positional information) in this format:

```
EditReplace
    [.Find = text]
    [.Replace = text]
    [.Direction = number]
    [.MatchCase = number]
    [.WholeWord = number]
    [.PatternMatch = number]
    [.SoundsLike = number]
    [.FindNext]
    [.ReplaceOne]
    [.ReplaceAll]
    [.Format = number]
    [.Wrap = number]
```

You can obtain POSITION.EXE from the Microsoft Software Library on CompuServe (GO MSL), from the Microsoft Software Library on Internet (ftp.microsoft.com cd softlib) or directly from the Microsoft Download Service at (206) 936-MSDL.

## FORMAT TRANSLATION

Let's try another example. You can also use Word's facilities if you need to translate VB text into other file formats. The VB Text Box, for all its utility, is rather limited as a word processor. Word for Windows, by contrast, is full of features.

### Example: Saving a Text Box in RTF

Say that you want to save the contents of a Text Box in RTF (Rich Text Format). If saved directly from VB, the text would be plain vanilla ASCII—no italics, no boldface. But you can send the text into Word and save it in any format you want: WordPerfect, Word, Excel WorkSheet, Word for Macintosh, RTF and so on.

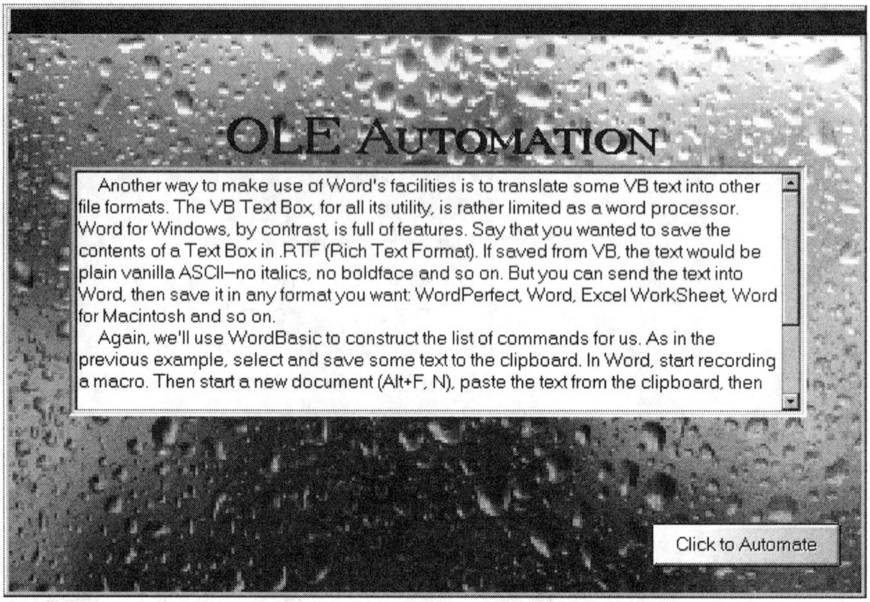


Figure 10-2: No human hands: this text will be automatically saved in RTF format.

Again, we'll use WordBasic to construct the list of commands:

1. Select and save some text to the Clipboard.
2. In Word, start recording a macro.
3. Start a new document (Alt+F, N), and paste the text from the Clipboard.
4. Press Alt+F, A to "File Save As..."
5. At this point, select Rich Text Format from the Save File as Type window.
6. Name the file TEST2.RTF and save it.
7. Now stop the macro recording and open your macro for editing (Alt+T,M). You should see something like this:

```
Sub MAIN
FileNew .Template = "Normal", .NewTemplate = 0
EditPaste
FileSaveAs .Name = "TEST2.RTF", .Format = 6,
   .LockAnnot = 0, .Password = "", .AddToMru = 1,
   .WritePassword = "", .RecommendReadOnly = 0,
   .EmbedFonts = 0, .NativePictureFormat = 0,
   .FormsData = 0
FileClose
End Sub
```

Remove unnecessary default parameters, or leave them in—whatever you prefer.

8. Now start a new VB project, and add a Text Box and a Command Button to the Form.
9. Copy the WordBasic macro, then paste it into the Command Button's Click Event.
10. To translate the macro into VB, first remove the unnecessary default parameters from FileNew. Then remove the entire *Insert "This is some text"* line. Now for the fun part. No one can accuse named parameters of being too concise. Some parameter lists are, like the list for the FileSaveAs command, simply huge. But all we really need is the name of the file and the format, so we can translate it into VB by lopping off everything else, and changing the syntax:

```
FileSaveAs "TEST2.RTF", 6
```

Also, remember to add a 2 to FileClose. Here's the finished result:

```
Sub Command3D1_Click ()

On Error Resume Next

Dim Wordobj As object
Set Wordobj = CreateObject("Word.Basic")

clipboard.Clear
clipboard.SetText text1.Text, 1

Wordobj.FileNew
Wordobj.EditPaste
Wordobj.FileSaveAs "TEST2.RTF", 6
Wordobj.FileClose 2

Set Wordobj = Nothing

msgbox "Your document has been saved as an RTF file."

End Sub
```

## GOING BOTH WAYS

In the preceding two examples we used VB as the *controller* and Word as the target, or *server*, of the Automation. Can Word control VB? Not yet. (Word could certainly use its Shell command, Shell "VBAPP.EXE", to launch an existing VB application. However, the spirit and purpose of automation is to take control of the innards, the individual features, and much if not all of the particular behaviors and properties of another application, not simply load its product—its data or compiled file.)

Currently, most applications expose only two objects: "Application" and "Document"(or whatever is a typical document for the application; for example, the Project document is called a "Project," naturally enough). How, you might ask, can we use Project's macro language if we cannot declare it as our target object (server)? Word exposes its macro language, WordBasic, as an object. That pretty much gives you control over everything Word can do. The answer is that you can declare the "Application" as your server, then proceed to use the macro language anyway.

### Example: Automating Microsoft Project

Suppose you want to automate the formatting of a Project calendar view. The process is quite the same as automating Word. As usual, first fire up Project and use its macro language to get the correct commands.

You create a macro in Project almost the same way you create one in Word, Excel and other applications. To create a macro in either Word or Excel, you can press Alt+T, M. Project is more advanced—the Record Macro option in its Tools menu saves a step.

Since VBA, OLE and the rest are young technologies, you'll find that when you move to a new application, things are nearly the same, but not quite identical. This slight discontinuity is just one of those things that make life a little exasperating. (We can expect conformity across applications as time goes on.)

1. In Project, press Alt+T, R, Enter.
2. Now record some formatting adjustments:
   - ❒ Press Alt+V, C to switch to calendar view.
   - ❒ Press Alt+O, T. Change the size of the text to 12, choose a color, and click OK to close this dialog.
   - ❒ Finally, press Alt+O, I and change the date shading and color.
3. Stop recording with Alt+T, R.

Edit the macro as follows:

1. Press Alt+T, M, select the name of your macro, and then press Alt+E.
2. Drag your mouse across the macro text to select it, and press Ctrl+Ins to copy it to the Clipboard.

3. Then paste the text into a VB Sub.

It should look something like this:

```
ViewApply Name:="Calendar"
TextStyles Item:=0, Size:="12", Color:=5
CalendarDateShadingEdit Item:=0, Pattern:=4, Color:=3
```

Again, the translation process from named parameters to VB is straightforward enough:

```
ViewApply "Calendar"
TextStyles 0, "12", 5
CalendarDateShadingEdit 0, 4, 3
```

## IF YOU HAVE PROBLEMS

When resources run low, Windows gets woozy.

Your OLE Automation might fail or behave strangely if too many other applications are running at the same time, using up memory and system resources. When memory is low, strange behavior occurs in any kind of Windows activity, not just OLE Automation. You may, for example, notice odd screen redraws or sluggish behavior (it takes 30 seconds for something to happen while the madly paging disk drive whirrs). If this or other unusual activity occurs, see if you have too much going on at once. Shut down some of the applications (or better yet, restart the computer). Then try Automation again.

You can check the status of low memory (or resources) by clicking on an application's Help menu and then selecting "About." This will display a percentage of free resources. If you're below 15%, you're in the danger zone: too many applications are using up too many of Windows's resources.

An application's customized startup behavior can also cause problems. You might have defined your Word NORMAL.DOT file so that certain things happen when Word is first fired up. Or you might use an Autoexec macro (this particular macro automatically runs when Word first starts). For example, some people are annoyed that Word doesn't always start full-screen, maximized and ready for them to type something in. To ensure that Word is always maximized on startup, you could create this WordBasic macro and name it Autoexec:

```
Sub MAIN
x = AppMaximize()
If x = 0 Then
    AppMaximize
EndIf
End Sub
```

This tests the window size status of Word. After "reading" the AppMaximize( ) Function, the variable x contains a zero if Windows isn't filling the screen. In that case, the AppMaximize command is used to make Windows full-screen.

When you Automate, check for an application's startup behaviors.

Any other instructions that you've programmed into this macro with the special name "Autoexec" will also be carried out when Word first runs. Recall that OLE Automation directed to Word will start Word if it's not already running. This, of course, will trigger any behaviors specified within an Autoexec macro.

So if things seem strange when you try OLE Automation, see if some startup conditions are being carried out by the target (server) application. To test this, just start the application manually before trying the OLE Automation. (Start Word by clicking on its icon in Program Manager, rather than having OLE Automation start it.) If the automation problem you were having goes away, that points to startup behaviors as the source of the difficulty. Or look in Word's Tools/Macros menu for a macro named Autoexec, then click on the Edit button to read it and see what it does.

## WHICH APPS CAN AUTOMATE?

There are two ways an application can use (or be used by) OLE Automation, just as there are two distinct roles in an employer-employee relationship. The application that initiates communication to a second application is called the *controller*. Microsoft calls the second, target application the OLE Automation Object or, in popular usage, the *server*.

There are two entities during Automation—the controller and the server (the caller and the called upon).

Regardless of what you call them, these two applications are clearly distinguished during their OLE Automation relationship. One application contains the procedure (Sub, Function, macro or Module that starts and controls the action). This is the active, "caller," application. The other application is passive ("called"), and it provides services, like its spell-checker, to the controller application. The passive application exposes its objects to outside access from an OLE Automation controller application.

In other words, the OLE Automation "Object application" includes the technology that permits its various features to be manipulated from the outside. It is possible to see this behavior in nature, too, in almost any field or forest in the spring.

But how do you know which applications can be controllers, which expose their objects, and which do both? Presumably most applications will be able to do both in the next couple of years. However, OLE Automation, and objectification in general, are emerging technologies. At this point, only some applications "expose their objects" and can thus be used as the target, or server, during automation. Others, like VB, can take advantage of exposed objects, but don't yet expose their own.

However, more applications are becoming OLE-automation capable all the time. In fact, eventually Windows itself will expose its objects—its menus, dialog boxes, and all the rest of the things that the Windows shell can do. This will permit extensive manipulation and control of the operating system itself. This is yet one more reason to learn to program in Visual Basic—you'll not only be able to customize and control your applications to your heart's content, you'll also be able to exploit the foundations of the operating system.

But how do you determine which apps can Automate? And, beyond that, how do you know what objects they expose and what you can do with those objects once they are open for use?

Applications are registered, like socialites at a ball.

Windows now requires that applications register themselves during their setup process. They are asked to declare their structure, capabilities, and their contents—like socialites being described and announced by the butler as they arrive at a formal ball.

This registered information goes beyond the data typically listed within the WIN.INI file or other INI files. Descriptions of objects are available by looking in the new Object Browser tool that comes with the latest versions of Excel and Project. Object browsers will be in most applications in the future. However, at this point, you must take a slightly less direct approach to viewing the inner workings of your applications.

### Example: A Peek Into Regedit

Try this. With the Windows Run command, type this:

REGEDIT /V

You should see something like the list shown in Figure 10-3.

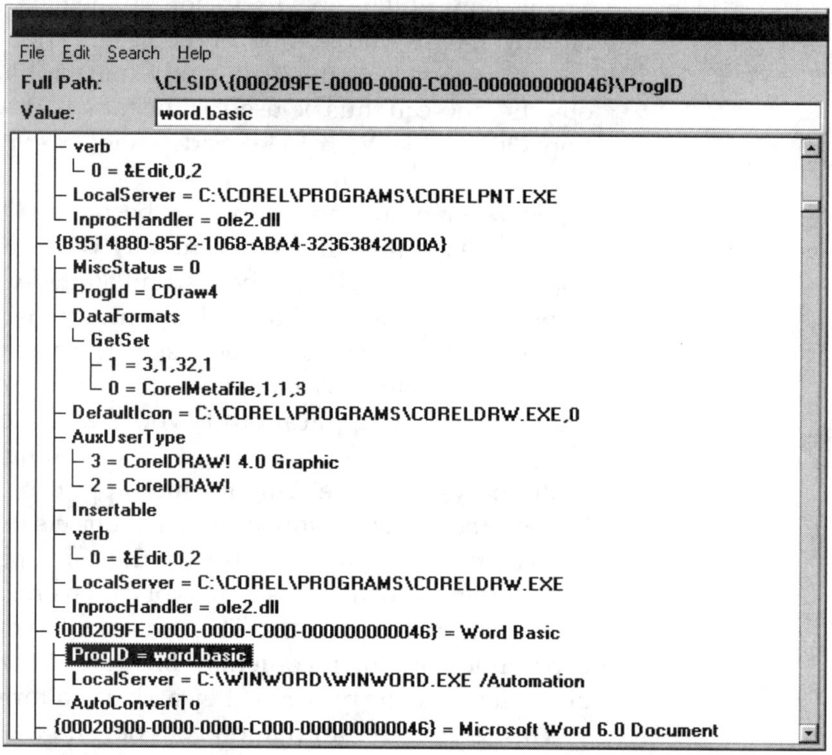


Figure 10-3: Regedit shows you who can do what via Automation.

Then use Regedit's Search menu to locate any definitions of ProgId. Doing so gives you both an object that you can access (one that's exposed) as well as the correct calling syntax to use with the Set = CreateObject line in your program.

Use REGEDIT /V to get a complete list of OLE-Capable applications, and the syntax to call them.

On my computer, the following objects are registered: word.basic, word.document.6, word.picture.6, mplayer, mplayer3, excel.sheet.5, excel.application.5, excel.chart.5, msgraph.chart, msgraph.application, msproject.project, msproject.application and cpaint4. In each case, the first id is the application itself, and the second is an "object" within the application that you can contact and, usually, manipulate.

Of these various objects, being able to contact the application's language, like WordBasic, clearly gives you the most extensive control over that application. The second most powerful contact is to the outermost object, the "Application" object, which contains all other objects in the application. Sometimes this is also a way into the application's embedded macro language. (See "Example: Automating Microsoft Project" above.)

### What to Give the User

If you create an application that OLE Automates, you must provide the user with a series of DLL files. (These DLL files go into the WINDOWS\SYSTEM directory: COMPOBJ.DLL, OLE2.REG, OLE2.DLL, OLE2CONV.DLL, OLE2DISP.DLL, OLE2NLS.DLL, OLE2PROX.DLL, STORAGE.DLL and VBOA300.DLL.) You must also ensure that the user is utilizing the SHARE.EXE from his or her AUTOEXEC.BAT file. If the user is running Windows for Workgroups, SHARE is not necessary. And we can assume, or hope, that OCX files will become part of the Windows operating system itself, relieving VB programmers of the burden of maintaining and distributing current versions of dozens of support files.

## TRIGGERING MACROS

So far we've recorded macros to generate the commands necessary to automate. But we can also just use an application's existing macros, activating them by Automation like any other feature of a server application.

#### Example: Triggering an Alien Macro

You can also trigger an application's macros via OLE Automation.

One useful macro in Word for Windows prepares a document for publication by removing extra spaces. While you're writing, you might insert extra spaces accidentally (not tabs, but unwanted spaces). Some people always press the spacebar twice between sentences. Magazine and book publishers don't want these extra spaces because they look strange when printed in a professional typeface. It's easy, though, for a macro to go through an entire document and replace all instances of two spaces with one. Likewise, publishers prefer the em dash (—) rather than two hyphens (--). So we have a WordBasic macro, named Publish, which replaces spaces as well as hyphens (as shown in Figures 10-4 and 10-5). Here's what it looks like:

```
Sub MAIN
StartOfDocument
EditReplace .Find = "  ", .Replace = " ", .Direction = 0,
.MatchCase = 0, .WholeWord = 0, .PatternMatch = 0,
.SoundsLike = 0, .ReplaceAll, .Format = 0, .Wrap = 1
EditReplace .Find = "--", .Replace = "^+", .Direction = 0,
.MatchCase = 0, .WholeWord = 0, .PatternMatch = 0,
.SoundsLike = 0, .ReplaceAll, .Format = 0, .Wrap = 1
End Sub
```

The macro first goes to the top of the document. It then searches for "  " to replace it with " ", and searches for "--" to replace it with "^+" (Word's code for the em dash). We'll want to transfer the contents of a Text Box to Word, and then trigger this macro. Finally, we'll save the results in a disk file that can be sent to the publisher.

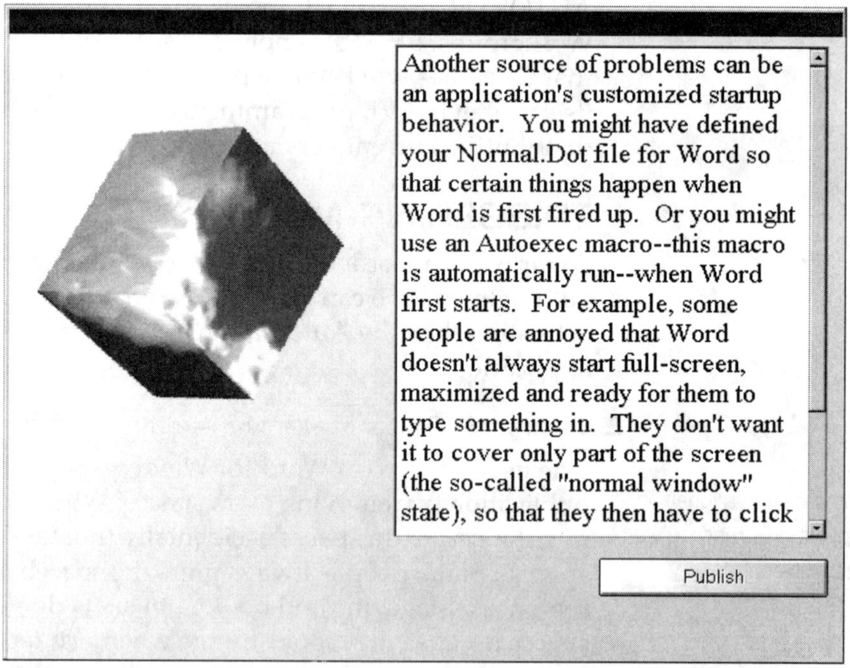
Another source of problems can be an application's customized startup behavior.  You might have defined your Normal.Dot file for Word so that certain things happen when Word is first fired up.  Or you might use an Autoexec macro--this macro is automatically run--when Word first starts.  For example, some people are annoyed that Word doesn't always start full-screen, maximized and ready for them to type something in.  They don't want it to cover only part of the screen (the so-called "normal window" state), so that they then have to click
Publish

Figure 10-4: BEFORE. This cannot be published—it has double hyphens and double spaces.

> Another source of problems can be an application's customized startup behavior. You might have defined your Normal.Dot file for Word so that certain things happen when Word is first fired up. Or you might use an Autoexec macro—this macro is automatically run—when Word first starts. For example, some people are annoyed that Word doesn't always start full-screen, maximized and ready for them to type something in. They don't want it to cover only part of the screen (the so-called "normal window" state), so that they then have to click on the

Figure 10-5: AFTER. Automation has sent the text through a Word macro, cleaning it up.

First, type in the above macro in Word, and save the macro as "Publish." You actually only need the first two parameters, since the rest are defaults:

```
StartOfDocument
EditReplace .Find = "  ", .Replace = " "
EditReplace .Find = "--", .Replace = "^+"
```

Now that we've got a macro, close down Word (you can leave it open, but it's more spectacular, though slower, to have Visual Basic actually start Word running).

In VB, create a Form and put a Text Box and a Command Button on the Form. Double-click on the Command Button, and in its Click Event, type this:

```
Sub Command3D1_Click ()
    Dim WordMacro As Object
    Set WordMacro = CreateObject("Word.Basic")

    clipboard.Clear
    clipboard.SetText text1.Text, 1

    WordMacro.FileNew
    WordMacro.EditPaste
```

```
        WordMacro.ToolsMacro "Publish", True
        WordMacro.FileSaveAs "PUB.DOC"
        WordMacro.FileClose 2

        Set WordMacro = Nothing
    End Sub
```

That's it. Now, to trigger the macro in Word, we just use the ToolsMacro command, followed by the name of the macro and the word True.

The name you give an object variable (or any other variable) is up to you.

As always, we first create an object variable, naming it, just for whimsy, WordMacro. Then we create the WordBasic object and assign it to the WordMacro variable. In the next line, the real action happens. We tell the ToolsMacro feature in Word to run our macro, named Publish. Note that many of the objects in WordBasic are named after the *menu/menu item*—in this case the Tools menu and the Macro item within that menu, hence *ToolsMacro*. Also notice the syntax of this line. In WordBasic, it would be

```
ToolsMacro .Name = "WordMacro", .Run
```

To edit rather than run the macro, the syntax would be:

```
ToolsMacro .Name = "WordMacro", .Edit
```

Since VB doesn't yet support named parameters, you must put the parameters in the correct position, separated by commas. (*True* is VB's substitute for .Run, .Edit or whatever other yes/no options appear in a parameter list):

```
WordMac.ToolsMacro "WordMacro", True
```

But to edit the macro, which is the third parameter, you must insert an extra comma to preserve the .Edit parameter's position in the parameter list:

```
WordMac.ToolsMacro "WordMacro", ,True
```

## EXAMPLE: BORROWING WORD'S WORD-COUNT FEATURE

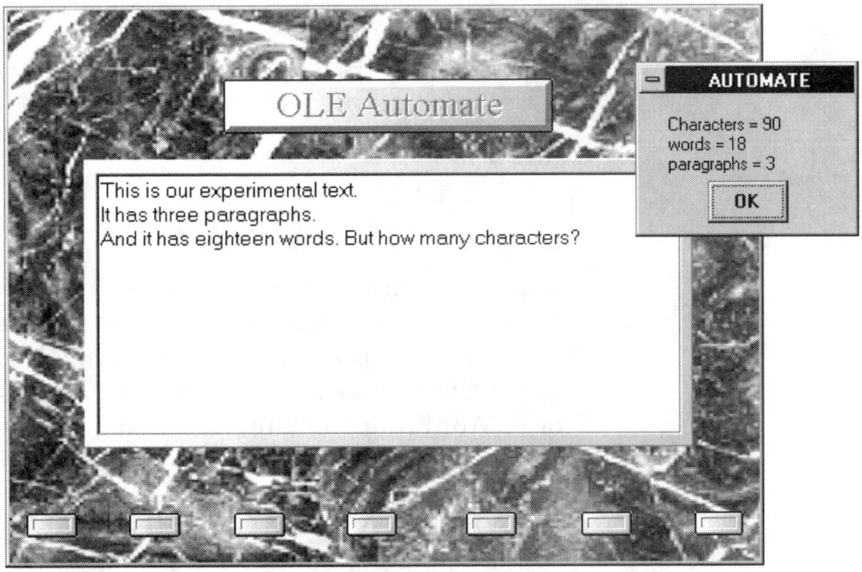


Figure 10-6: Getting information from dialog boxes.

Here's how to get statistics about the text in a VB Text Box. On a new Form, place a Text Box (with its MultiLine Property set to True) and a Command Button. In the Button's Click Event, type this:

```
Sub Command3D1_Click ()

On Error Resume Next
Dim wordcontact As object, dlg As object
Set wordcontact = CreateObject("Word.Basic")

clipboard.Clear
clipboard.SetText text1.Text, 1

wordcontact.FileNewDefault
wordcontact.EditPaste

wordcontact.ToolsWordCount
Set dlg = wordcontact.curvalues.ToolsWordCount

c = dlg.characters
w = dlg.words
p = dlg.paragraphs

cr$ = Chr$(13)
n$ = "Characters = " & c & cr$
```

```
n$ = n$ & "words = " & w & cr$
n$ = n$ & "paragraphs = " & p

msgbox n$
wordcontact.FileClose 2
Set wordcontact = Nothing

End Sub
```

### The Curvalues Powerhouse

The valuable trick in the word-counting example is an unassuming little powerhouse named *curvalues*. You can use it to "read" (find out) the values or information contained in any Word dialog box. We requested the number of characters, words and paragraphs from Word's WordCount feature. We could have asked for lines and pages, too, since the WordCount dialog box also provides those statistics.

## CREATING A CHART WITH EXCEL

At this writing, Excel contains the most robust, most advanced version of Visual Basic—VBA, Visual Basic for Applications (or Visual Basic, Applications Edition, as it's formally known). Among other things, this means that Excel 5.0 exposes more objects than any other current application. In practical terms, you can use Excel's specialized facilities to deal with numbers, graphs or any other spreadsheet feature. In this way, Excel can become a superpowerful "custom Control" for VB. (For more on VBA, see Chapter 11.)

The techniques that permit borrowing functionality from Excel are similar to those needed to use WordBasic from within VB.

We'll use the Chart Wizard.

1. First, start recording a macro within Excel (Alt+T, R, R) to get the syntax of Excel commands.
2. Create a new WorkSheet (Alt+I, W) so we won't disturb any possible existing data on a WorkSheet if Excel is up and running.
3. Type some dummy data into the first few cells, and drag the mouse to select this range of cells.
4. Next create a graph of the selected range of cells by pressing Alt+I, C, O. Excel 5.0 pops up the Chart Wizard, which asks us a few questions about the type and style of the graph we're after.
5. Finally, resize the resulting graph to make it larger, and send the Chart to the Clipboard for importation into VB.

6. Stop recording (Alt+T, R, S) and locate Module1 or wherever Excel stored your new macro.

It should look something like this:

```
'
' Macro1 Macro
' Macro recorded 10/26/94 by Richard Mansfield
'
'
Sub Macro1()
    Sheets.Add
    ActiveCell.FormulaR1C1 = "12"
    Range("A2").Select
    ActiveCell.FormulaR1C1 = "18"
    Range("A3").Select
    ActiveCell.FormulaR1C1 = "22"
    Range("A4").Select
    ActiveCell.FormulaR1C1 = "24"
    Range("A5").Select
    ActiveCell.FormulaR1C1 = "28"
    Range("A6").Select
    ActiveCell.FormulaR1C1 = "34"
    Range("A1:A6").Select
    ActiveSheet.ChartObjects.Add(107.25, 79.5, 223.5, →
    93.75).Select
    Application.CutCopyMode = False
    ActiveChart.ChartWizard Source:=Range("A1:A6"), →
    Gallery:=xl3DColumn, _
        Format:=6, PlotBy:=xlColumns, CategoryLabels:=0, →
        SeriesLabels _
        :=0, HasLegend:=2, Title:="Visual Basic ListBox →
        Data", _CategoryTitle:="", ValueTitle:="", ExtraTitle:=""
    Selection.Width = 440.25
    Selection.Height = 204.75
    Selection.Left = 75.75
    Selection.Top = 25.5
    Selection.Width = 471.75
    Selection.Height = 258.75
    Selection.Copy
End Sub
```

How about expanded "curvalues" and standardized diction, syntax and punctuation?

You've probably thought to yourself: "Some of the things we've had to do in the previous OLE Automation examples were tricks." You're right. FileClose 2 shouldn't need that 2. Curvalues should be available for all objects. You should be able to get or change the status of any object at any time, including the condition of all its qualities (its "Properties") and the state of its behaviors (its "Methods"). All applications should be capable of both exposing their objects and controlling other applications' objects. The syntax, punctuation and diction used to communicate between applications and objects should be standardized, should not require even minor translation. All data should be transferable directly via pointers (a description of the current location in RAM of the data) rather than by temporary storage in the Clipboard. And a list of each application's objects should be easily available.

All these things will happen. Each application (and Windows itself) will join the OLE/Visual Basic bandwagon in the coming months and years. For now, though, the process of OLE Automation requires some special work-arounds, some inconvenience and some indirection. However, if you find yourself unable to accomplish some goal, try different punctuation. That often does the trick.

## MOVING ON

Coming up next: The future of Basic.

In the next chapter, we'll see new directions in Basic. Visual Basic for Applications is now part of Microsoft Excel, Access, Project and VB4. This highly advanced version of Basic is intended to replace over time the disparate macro languages in all Microsoft applications. When it does, the applications will use the same punctuation, employ the same commands and syntax and finally behave the same way. No longer will each application have its unique and peculiar version of Basic. All applications, and Windows itself, will be able to sing in tune, with interchangeable parts and free communication between them.

VBA features many new commands. It also embraces object-oriented programming, with such new structures as For...Each (instead of For...Next) and collections (which can replace traditional arrays). Because of the importance of VBA to Visual Basic programmers, we're devoting more space to the next chapter than to any other topic in this book. Mostly we'll look at Excel, where VBA is now most fully implemented. We'll cover all the new commands, structures and features that are common to VBA/Excel and VB4.

# Chapter 11

# New Directions

## SECTION 1: OVERVIEW

Visual Basic has produced a descendant—Visual Basic for Applications (VBA). In this new guise, VB can manipulate objects more fully, and it offers some valuable new commands as well. In this chapter, we'll examine the philosophy and features of VBA and thereby discover what to expect in future versions of Visual Basic.

Visual Basic 4.0 includes a subset of the VBA commands discussed in this chapter. For example, VB now features the Collection object, but not the GroupObject object (these ideas are discussed later in this chapter). This chapter covers the elements of VBA that have been absorbed into VB4 so you can look for them and use them. It also covers commands and features of VBA that didn't become part of VB4 so we can perhaps anticipate their inclusion in VB5. Some of these elements of VBA may never be absorbed into VB, but our guess is that most, eventually, will.

Currently, VBA is most fully developed within Excel, as Excel's macro language. And new versions of the programs within the Microsoft Office for Windows 95, such as Access, also now include VBA (with the notable exception of Word).

However, VBA isn't merely a good, strong new macro language. It's the latest, fullest implementation of the venerable Basic language itself. VBA is of more than passing interest to the VB programmer—in some ways it represents the destiny of Visual Basic.

## Whither VBA?

Visual Basic is evolving rapidly. New VBA-capable applications should be introduced with increasing frequency during 1996. And we can expect Windows itself to expose its objects to VB. We expect (well, *hope*) that when Windows itself objectifies, some version of Visual Basic will be included with each copy of Windows (Windows 96?). At that point, the user could write scripts controlling how his or her applications and operating system will behave and interact.

But Visual Basic is orders of magnitude more powerful than DOS's batch files. If VB can govern Windows, we'll be able to construct much more than simple scripts or short macros. We'll be able to use all the facilities of each application. And we'll be able to coordinate their collective behavior by conducting the activities and properties of Windows itself.

Our control over the computer will have reached an unprecedented level of flexibility and sophistication. And if you've used Visual Basic, you know that increased power does not mean increased complexity. No previous computer language comes close to VB's efficiency and simplicity while permitting the construction of truly astonishing programs.

Visual Basic and VBA are cross-fertilizing. When a new edition of VBA comes out, it will include features that are not in the current version of Visual Basic. Likewise, each new version of Visual Basic will have capabilities not yet in existing implementations of VBA.

VB is the world's most rapidly evolving language. Leapfrogging like this, VB and VBA should incorporate one another's facilities while adding new commands to the language they share. In our view, they must ultimately converge into a single language.

## VBA: The Guest Language

While much of VBA will be familiar to the VB programmer, much is also novel. Of necessity, many of VBA's commands are currently application-specific. In Excel, for instance, you can look under Help's "Programming with Visual Basic" and find a list of Objects. Most are useful only within Excel (Axis, WorkBook, etc.). Other VBA/Excel Objects are familiar to any VB programmer (TextBox, Option Button, etc.). In this chapter, we will look at what's generic in VBA—those new features and commands that expand the Basic language. These generic features and commands, or some variant of them, will almost certainly become part of Visual Basic itself.

With the introduction of VB4, you'll notice that some of VB's commands have been classified as VBA commands. There are, in fact, two separate "libraries" of commands within VB4. Since VB and VBA are still, to a degree, segregated, we could think of VB as the host language and VBA as the guest. Nonetheless, VBA is here to stay and, over time, the distinction between these two "flavors" of Basic is likely to blur.

In general, the commands that have been moved from the VB to the VBA library are clerical—file manipulation (ChDir, for example); Date and Time manipulation (TimeValue); the set of financial functions; math (Sqr); text string manipulation (Mid); and the set of user-interface commands (Beep, MsgBox, etc.). Other categories of commands remain within the VB library—the various Methods and Properties relating to VB Controls (List Box, for example) and VB behaviors such as Circle, Timer and database manipulation.

What does this bifurcation mean to the eager Visual Basic programmer? Not much at this point. You can still use all the commands by just typing them in. It hardly matters whether a given command is classified as belonging to VB or VBA. Press F2 to look at the new Object Browser. In the Libraries list, you'll see the VB and VBA libraries, along with any Controls associated with your project. Clicking in the Classes/Modules list reveals the Methods and Properties associated with a particular Class or Module (a Class/Module here is generally a logical collection of commands—for instance, all commands that manipulate the date or time). If you click on one of the Methods or Properties, you'll see its syntax. However, pressing F1 for Help is far more useful if you're looking for an example, a real-world example, of a command in action. Click on "Example" in help and then cut and paste the code right into your project.

VBA doesn't kill off an application's macro language when it becomes part of an application. For example, Excel's familiar built-in macro language coexists with the new VBA in Excel. VBA offers an alternative way to program macros for Excel. But this alternative is so clearly superior that we can predict that, over time, all the application-specific (and wildly incompatible) macro languages, like WordBasic and Access Basic, will atrophy.

VBA will soon be inserted into all Microsoft applications and will likely be built into Windows eventually. Like DOS, with its batch language, we can expect Windows to incorporate a script language, but to go far beyond batch programming. The most obvious candidate is VB/VBA. A version of Visual Basic will probably become an essential part of the operating system itself.

When you compare VBA to VB, you'll notice some differences on the surface, but there's a sea change underneath. Below the surface VBA is clearly a participant in the rush to 32-bit and object-oriented programming (OOP). These changes down below bubble up and sometimes compel you to modify the way you use even old familiar commands and techniques. The changes help you think and program in new ways.

For one thing, Controls are now sometimes called *Classes*, meaning that they are paradigmatic—they can be used as templates to create an actual particular object (such as an actual Text Box on a Form). This feature isn't new to VB, but the use of the OOP term *classes* to describe it is.

First, in Section 1 of this chapter, we'll look at some elements of VBA that are general and predictive of the future of Visual Basic. The bulk of this chapter, Section 2, is essentially a dictionary of new commands—VBA Methods, Objects, Functions and Properties that we can expect to see incorporated into Visual Basic (or any other implementation of Basic) as time goes on.

Some new commands are so useful and novel that we'll explore them in detail—for example, we'll look closely at For...Each and Collection and the rather surprising new Property Procedure (Subs and Functions aren't the only Procedures anymore). Other new VBA commands—like PasteFace—have limited functionality, but they *are* new, and they likely will be in future versions of Basic. So they too are discussed, if briefly.

## General Changes

Here's a quick look at some significant changes that are taking place in the Basic language.

### Text Variables Disappearing

Some changes that have occurred since VB 3.0 are subtle. For example, the distinction between the Text ("String") Variable and Numeric Variable is giving way to the new polymorphous Variant variable. The major impact of this on VBA's diction is that the ancient string-manipulating commands like Left$ are dropping the string symbol, $, to become Left, Chr, Right, LCase, UCase, Ltrim, Rtrim, Space, String and Trim. (Some of the commands in this group made this change in VB3.).

For example, it used to be that the lines

```
N$ = " Well, OK"
Print N$
Print Trim$(N$)
```

resulted in

```
 Well, OK
Well, OK
```

Now we get the same result with

```
N = " Well, OK"
Print N
Print Trim(N)
```

### Box Help

MsgBoxes and InputBoxes now have two additional, optional parameters: HelpFile and Context. HelpFile identifies the Help file that should be available when the dialog box is visible. If you use the Helpfile parameter, you must also provide the Context parameter (the "Help context number" pointing to the correct topic in the Help file).

### A Boolean Data Type

There's a new Boolean data type (which, odd as it might seem, uses two bytes in memory to store what could be stored in a single bit). However, it returns the words True or False when you print it. For example

```
Dim n As Boolean
Print n
```

results in

```
False
```

You can assign the older true/false values (–1 and 0, respectively) to a Boolean variable. It will accept them, but will always report with the words *True* or *False*. However, if you convert a Boolean into another data type, *True* does change to -1 and *False* to zero. For example

```
Dim n As Boolean
Dim r As Integer
n = -1
Print n
Print TypeName(n)
r = n
Print r
```

results in

```
True
Boolean
-1
```

And should you ever need to force another data type to compute as if it were Boolean, there's the new command, CBool.

In VBA, there's now a single-byte data type: the Byte type. If you want to pull in bytes one by one from a disk file, you can now use a Byte-type variable rather than resorting to a predefined single-byte text variable: (DIM C As String*1).

## The "Is" Queries

As we move toward object-oriented programming, there will be times, believe it or not, when the *programmer* will not know the data type of a variable. A Variant, like a shape-shifter, can morph into several different variable types dynamically during run time. This can happen without the programmer's knowledge or consent.

In the brave new world of objects, even an application's user can be permitted to create new objects in some situations. One side effect of all this freedom (and the resulting mutations of your original program design) is that you, as a programmer, might sometimes have to ask your running program to tell you the type of a variable.

VB3 provided four IsX variable-query commands: IsDate, IsEmpty, IsNull and IsNumeric.

To these VBA and VB4 now add four more: IsArray, IsError, IsMissing and IsObject. And VB4 also includes the new IsDirty and IsItemVisible commands. (IsDirty means "has the user made any changes to it?") These two Is commands are essentially unrelated to the others in the group. Most Is commands let you get information about variables; these last two report on the user interface.

IsMissing tells a procedure whether or not an Optional parameter has been passed. The following example either prints a string twice or, if the optional second string has been passed, concatenates both strings:

```
Function multiple(A, Optional B)
If IsMissing(B) Then
    multiple = A & A
Else
    multiple = A & B
End If

End Function

Sub Form_Load( )
    A = "Once"
    Print multiple(A)
End Sub
```

The following example uses IsDate to check the user's input. The user's response is put into a Variant variable, *x*, which will adapt itself to *whatever* variable type is appropriate based on what the user might type in. (Any variable you don't formally declare defaults to the Variant type.) However, our program can avoid an error here if it can determine just what the Variant turned into. So we use the IsDate Function to let us know how to proceed:

```
    x = InputBox("Please type in the date of your birthday...")
If IsDate(x) Then
    z = (Now - DateValue(x)) / 365
    Print "You are " & Int(z) & " years old."
Else
    MsgBox "We can't understand your entry: " & x & "...as _
a  date..."
End If
```

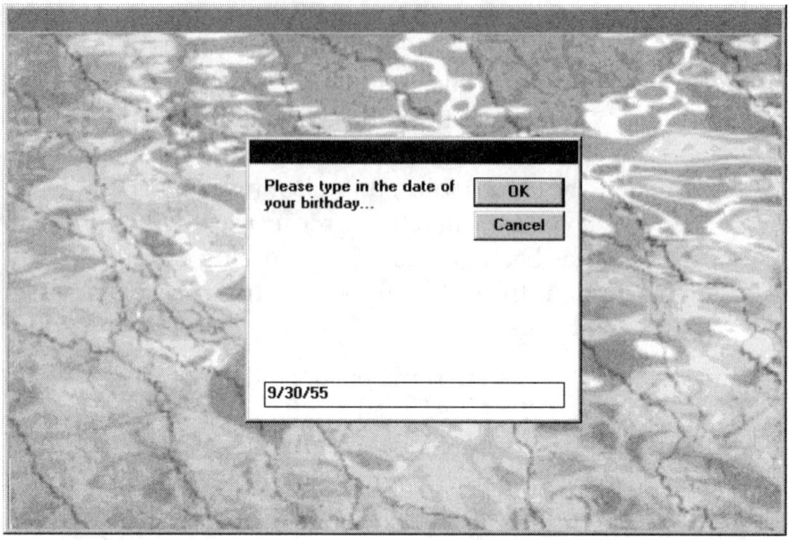


Figure 11-1: The IsDate Function will trap any user-entry errors here.

### Named Properties

Now you can group Properties, using the new With...End With structure. This streamlines your programming and also makes reading the source code easier. Here's the old style:

```
Text1.Text = ""
Text1.Left = 12
Text1.Top = 100
Text1.FontBold = False
Text1.FontSize = 12
Text1.Width = Text2.Width
```

Now you can eliminate all those references to Text1:

```
With Text1
    Text = ""
    Left = 12
    Top = 100
    FontBold = False
    FontSize = 12
    Width = Text2.Width
End With
```

## New Procedure Styles

The old distinction between Subs and Functions is becoming a bit less strict. When you call a Function in all other versions of Basic, you must include a Variable to hold the returned value, even if you don't care what the returned value is. You're also required to "send" any variable (or variables) enclosed within parentheses:

```
X$ = NameofFunct (N$)
```

VBA does not require a return-value variable (though you can use one if you wish). Nor does VBA require parentheses around the "sent" value. You can strip those two things off and write it like this: NameofFunct N$. So, how does this syntax differ from the syntax when calling a Sub? It doesn't. *In VBA, there is no longer any practical distinction between the calling syntax used with a Sub or a Function.* If you like, we can just call them all *procedures*, some of which return a value and some of which don't. The VBA programmer can call Functions and Subs with identical punctuation.

The following example demonstrates the new syntax. It calls a Function named *DoubleIt* by merely naming it and then providing a parentheses-free variable, F$:

```
Sub SendString( )
F$ = "Bingo"
DoubleIt F$
MsgBox F$
End Sub

Function DoubleIt(N As String)
    N = N & N
End Function
```

This results in

```
BingoBingo
```

Notice that correct programming practice would not change the argument that's sent to a function. Instead, you would change the function name itself, passing *that* back to the caller (to preserve variable typing). Properly written, the above should be

```
Function DoubleIt(N As String)
    DoubleIt = N & N
End Function
```

To show how in VBA there is no longer a distinction when calling Functions and Subs, here's the same example, but written using a Sub rather than a Function:

```
Sub SendString( )
    F$ = "Bingo"
    DoubleIt F$
    MsgBox F$
End Sub

Sub DoubleIt(N As String)
    N = N & N
End Sub
```

The only difference between this Sub and the previous Function is that we changed the word *Function* to *Sub,* and the *End Function* to *End Sub.* Therefore, the only remaining distinctions between Subs and Functions in VBA are that Function calls

- Can have a variable on the left of an equal sign (can receive a result).
- Can enclose any arguments sent to the Function within parentheses.

But these punctuational distinctions are preserved only so that VBA can understand programs written for previous versions of Basic. The bottom line is that there are now only procedure calls. It's not possible to predict whether this relaxation of punctuation will remain part of Basic in the future. But for now, these things are fairly loose.

## SECTION 2: SELECTED COMMANDS

For the remainder of this chapter, we'll look at selected commands and features that are not in Visual Basic 3.0, some of which are now in VB4, but are all in Excel's implementation of VBA. We can expect to see more of these VBA commands (or variations of them) in Visual Basic 5.0.

# ACTIVATE

**method**

**Description**

Causes the specified Object—for example, a window in the same application—to be activated (to "get the focus," to be the one on top that the user can type text into if the window or other Object accepts keystrokes). The VB equivalent of this command is SetFocus.

**Used With**

A window, range, item in a list, member of a table, Chart, dialog bar, MenuBar, Module, OLE Object, pane, WorkBook, worksheet or elements within other Objects that can get the focus. (See more about range under "Cautions.")

**Cautions**

The Activate Method is almost indistinguishable from the Select Method. Both cause something to get the focus and become the place where typed characters show onscreen (assuming that Object can display characters).

However, in Excel the Activate Method is supposed to be used to give focus to a single cell in a worksheet; the Select Method is to be used to give focus to more than one cell (a "range," properly so-called). Nonetheless, you can use the Select Method to focus a single cell if you wish; Range("B5").Select works as well as Range("B5").Activate.

Note that if you want to activate a particular cell in a *selected range*, you have to use the Activate method:

```
Sub ZeroIn( )
    Sheets("sheet1").Range("a1:a5").Select
    Sheets("Sheet1").Range("a3").Activate
End Sub
```

If you try to use the Select method in the second line above, you end up with one selected cell. This could be useful if you wanted to use the FillUp or FillDown Methods with the active selection. Those Methods use the value in the "active" cell.

**Example**

```
Sub doit( )
    Sheets("Sheet1").Select
    Range("A5").Activate
End Sub
```

# ActivateMicrosoftApp method

**Description**

Like the AppActivate command, ActivateMicrosoftApp makes another program the active window (starts another program running). However, AppActivate can start up any Windows program, while ActivateMicrosoftApp currently starts only Word, PowerPoint, Access, FoxPro, Mail, Project or Schedule+. Furthermore, the format is strange.

With AppActivate, use the application's name (as listed in its title bar) as the argument. For example, this starts NotePad:

```
AppActivate NotePad
```

However, the ActivateMicrosoftApp is closer in behavior to the Shell command:

```
x = Shell("C:\WINDOWS\NOTEPAD.EXE", 1)
```

AppActivate is useful only for moving between applications. For example, you could design a macro that allows a user to choose applications from a menu or set of buttons—something like Task Manager or Program Manager but much more customizable. However, AppActivate requires that any programs it activates already be running. The Shell command and its more limited cousin, ActivateMicrosoftApp, don't have this requirement and are probably more useful.

**Cautions**

ActivateMicrosoftApp will make the named program active (that is, bring the window to the top, ready to accept keystrokes); if the program isn't running, it will be started first. By contrast, the AppActivate statement merely changes the focus. It makes the named application the active window but will not start an application running.

### Built-in Constants

The format for ActivateMicrosoftApp is somewhat peculiar. You must prepend the built-in Constant *xlMicrosoft* to the name of the application. (To use predefined Constants in VB, you must load the file CONSTANT.TXT; the definitions aren't built into the language itself.) There are many built-in Constants in VBA/Excel, and they all begin with *xl*. For descriptions, look in the Help for the Method or Property with which the Constant works. You can also find a list of xlConstants in Excel's Object Browser. Here's how to activate Access:

```
Application.ActivateMicrosoftApp xlMicrosoftAccess
```

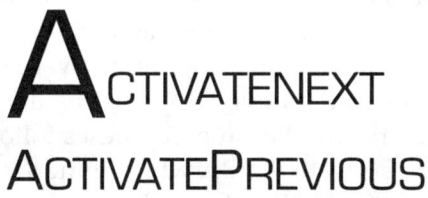

Figure 11-2: ActivateMicrosoftApp is the equivalent of clicking on a button in the "Microsoft Toolbar" that now appears in various Microsoft applications.

**Example**

```
Application.ActivateMicrosoftApp xlMicrosoftWord
```

**See Also** Load, SendKeys, SetFocus, Shell, Show

## ACTIVATENEXT ACTIVATEPREVIOUS

**method**

**Description** These commands rearrange the position of the "child windows" within an application's main window. If you have three workbooks open in Excel, one of them likely is completely or partially covering the other two. The order in which they are visually stacked onscreen is called the *ZOrder*. ZOrder also determines which window is activated, has the "focus" (can accept keystrokes if the user types something). You use ActivateNext, ActivatePrevious to adjust the ZOrder, to change which window is on top, and so on. In other words, ZOrder determines both the visual position of the windows onscreen and which one is activated.

Some people find it useful to think of the x, y and z axes, used in describing geometric forms. The x axis describes a horizontal position, and the y axis describes a vertical position. A z axis moves us into 3D and describes *depth*.

In Word for Windows, each separate document is a child window in this "multiple-document interface," as it's called. In Excel, each workbook is a child window. If only one workbook is open, you can't activate the "next" window—there's only one window. Before trying to ActivateNext or ActivatePrevious, you can use the Count Property of the Windows collection to determine if it's possible to adjust the ZOrder (see the example below). Or just trap the error in the usual ways (with On Error Resume Next).

### How Do They Work?

The ActivateNext and ActivatePrevious commands permit the user (or your program) to make a child window appear on the top or bottom of a pile of overlapping windows. These commands thus give you an alternative to the Visible or Enabled Properties as a way of indicating the active window while a program is running. They also offer an alternative to traditional menus or tiled windowing as a way for the user to select among program options or features.

There are only two ways to affect the ZOrder of a window: ActivateNext and ActivatePrevious. So these commands are not like an Index number or the Tab Property or other indices to groups of objects. You cannot directly specify that a window should assume the second position in a pile by using the ActivateNext and ActivatePrevious commands. To adjust positions, you have to fiddle.

For instance, the number in parentheses following the word Windows—Windows(4)—tells VBA which window to send to the bottom of the pile. "Next" and "Previous" describe which window you want on the top of the pile, relative to the window currently on top. There *is* a ZOrder Property, but it doesn't apply to windows—only to other Objects such as buttons, labels and text boxes. Furthermore, the ZOrder Property (unlike the ActivateNext/Previous Methods) is "read-only"—that is, you can find out an object's position with ZOrder, but you cannot change it. (To change an object's position, you use the BringToFront or SendToBack Methods. They permit you to actually change the relative positions of Objects—by a little fiddling—the way you could adjust the position of cards in a deck, one at a time. However, BringToFront and SendToBack do not work with windows, but only with such Objects as buttons, labels, etc.)

**Used With** A window Object or a windows( ) Object collection.

**Example** Using the Add method, we add two new workbook windows to the default single workbook (or however many workbooks you might currently have). Our main goal here is to make sure that more than one child window is active in Excel. Then we ActivatePrevious the next window (twice) in the ZOrder of this collection of child windows. The number in parentheses, (3) or (2), describes which window to place at the back. Note that we are dealing with a "collection" of window Objects, which is like an Array. After adding two new workbooks, or windows, to Excel, we have Windows(1), Windows(2) and Windows(3) as the objects to manipulate.

In this way, you can organize the cascade of the windows.

```
Sub DoActive( )
    Debug.Print Windows.Count
    Workbooks.Add
    Workbooks.Add
    Windows(3).ActivatePrevious
    Windows(2).ActivatePrevious
End Sub
```

**See Also** ZOrder, BringToFront, Arrange

# ADD method

**Description** You can Add Objects or Controls—almost anything—to a Collection. Many Objects, like toolbars, are generic to the Windows operating system. Many others, like an Excel worksheet, are specific to an individual application.

**Used With** Almost any kind of Object. This includes windows; most Controls, like edit boxes, spinners and scroll bars; buttons; toolbars; menus; OLEObjects; and many application-specific Objects (for example, workbooks, worksheets, Modules, Charts and scenarios in Excel). In VB4, the Add Method works with Buttons, ColumnHeaders, ListItems and Tabs (each of which is a "collection"). You can also use Add with any other collection.

**Cautions**

The parameters you can give to the Add Method vary according to what you are adding. Look at online Help for a complete list. For instance, if you Add a Rectangle Object, you must describe its location and size by specifying Left, Top, Width and Height, the traditional parameters for a graphic Object. But if you add a new toolbar, there is only one parameter, the name of the toolbar, and even that is optional. If you leave the name out, VBA will name it ToolBar1 or Toolbar2, etc., as appropriate.

**Example**

```
Sub Macro4()
    Sheets("Sheet1").Select

ActiveSheet.Buttons.Add(400, 270, 145, 32).Select
Selection.Caption = "See Additional Paintings"
```

Or use this alternative technique:

```
Sub Macro4( )
    Dim Button as Object
    Sheets("Sheet1").Select
    Set Button = ActiveSheet.Buttons.Add(400, 270, 145, 32)
    Button.Caption = "See Additional Paintings"
End Sub
```

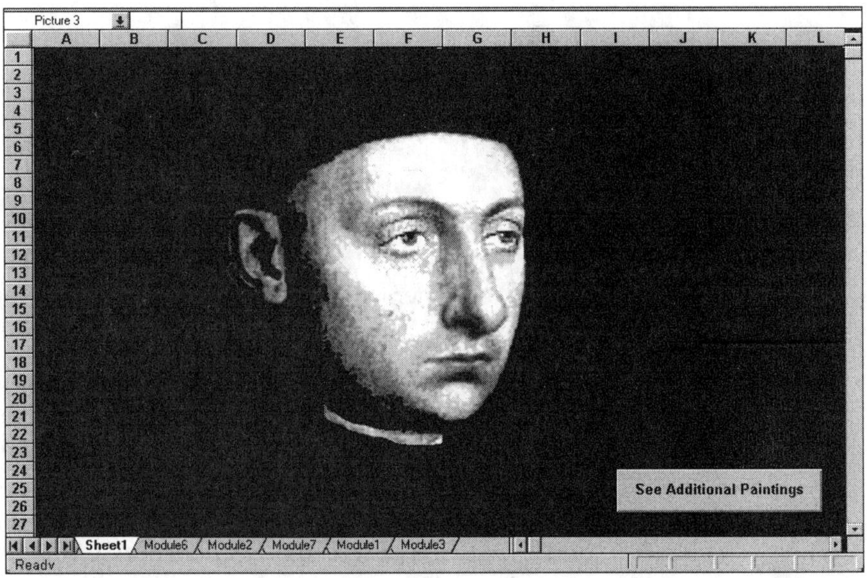


Figure 11-3: VBA uses the Add Method to create new Controls, like the See Additional Paintings Command Button.

Here we add a new button to an Excel worksheet. The four numbers describe the X,Y (400, 270) position of the upper-left corner and the X,Y (145, 32) position of the lower-right corner. In this way, both the position and the size of the new text box are specified. Some objects that you add, such as a new workbook, require no additional specifications (parameters). Others, like a new button on a toolbar, can require descriptive arguments to indicate, for example, which button to use ("Button"), in what position ("Before") and with which macro (OnAction).

**Used With** Copy

# ARRANGE method

**Description** Used to tile or otherwise position an application's windows onscreen. This is the equivalent of selecting the Arrange option from the Window menu found in most applications. You can tile, cascade or arrange the windows horizontally or vertically (nonoverlapping). This command is available in VB4.

This technique does not work with buttons, labels or any other Object except child windows (interior windows within an application). In Word, each separate document is a child window. In Excel, each workbook is a child window.

**Used With** Windows.

**Variables**

```
Arrange (Style, activeworkbook, syncHorizontal, syncVertical)
```

The Style parameter is one of five possible parameters: xlCascade, xlTiled, xlHorizontal, xlVertical or xlIcons. Horizontal and Vertical here determine whether the windows are arranged up and down the screen or side-by-side. The Icons option arranges the icons.

If the activeworkbook parameter is set to True, only the windows in the currently active workbook are arranged. If it is False (the default), all Excel's windows are arranged. The two sync parameters, when True, cause all windows to scroll in sync in the named direction (the default here is False).

**Example** Here we'll add two new workbooks (to be sure we have windows to tile). Then we'll use the Arrange Method with the xlTiled option to display the windows (see Figure 11-4):

```
Sub doit( )
    Workbooks.Add
    Workbooks.Add
    Sheets("Sheet1").Select
    Application.Windows.Arrange (xlTiled)
End Sub
```

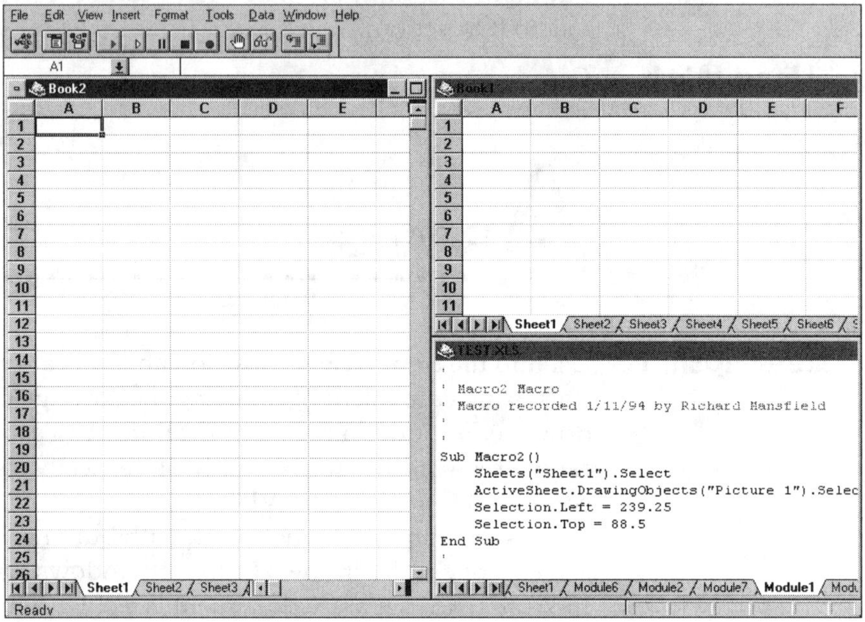


Figure 11-4: Use Arrange to cascade or, as here, tile documents in your applications.

**See Also** ActivateNext

# ARRAY function

**Description** The Array command creates a strange kind of Variable, a Variant that contains a "list" of separate, indexed, interior items of data. This new function replaces the DATA...READ command in previous versions of Basic. It can be used to establish an initial set of data items within a classic array. Don't confuse this new function with the traditional array. Available in VB4.

The Array function is similar to this traditional array:

```
Dim ThisArray (1 to 5) As Variant
    ThisArray(3) = "Susan"
Debug.Print ThisArray(3)
```

**Results in** Susan

However, when you use the Array command, you can *change* the elements in the array, like this:

```
Sub DoChange( )
    Dim vArray As Variant
    vArray = Array(5, 10, 15, 20, 25, 30)
    MsgBox vArray(0)
    vArray(0) = 6
    MsgBox vArray(0)
End Sub
```

The following alternative approach, using the For Each...Next structure, can make traversing arrays (especially dynamic arrays) easier. For Each is also faster than the traditional For Next loop when you're working with objects or Variant variables.

```
Sub DoChange()
    Dim vArray As Variant, element as Variant
    vArray = Array(5, 10, 15, 20, 25, 30)
    For each element in vArray
        debug.print vArray
    next
End Sub
```

And you can access the individual items, or "read them"—for display, for information your program needs or for other purposes.

The now-abandoned DATA...READ commands served the same purpose in early (pre-VB) versions of Basic as does the new VBA Array Function. In earlier versions of Basic, you could insert a (usually brief) list of information into your program this way:

```
DIM NUMBERS(5)
DATA ones, tens, hundreds, thousands, millions
FOR I = 1 to 5
    READ NUMBERS(I)
NEXT I
DEBUG.PRINT NUMBERS(3)
```

**Results in** hundreds

You inserted some pieces of data into your program following the DATA command. Then you used the READ command to fill an array with that data. This was useful for such things as the days of the week, the months of the year and other small lists of data.

When DATA and READ were jerked out of Basic with the development in 1991 of Visual Basic 1.0, some people complained. The response of VB designers was that you should individually assign Variables (the program would run marginally faster, it was said):

```
Numbers(0) = "ones"
Numbers(1) = "tens"
Numbers(2) = "hundreds"
Numbers(3) = "thousands"
Numbers(4) = "millions"
```

As you can see, DATA...READ was easier on the programmer—there was less typing.

Now with VBA, DATA...READ is back, in an improved, high-efficiency format. This technique is now called the Array Function:

```
Numbers = Array("ones", "tens", "hundreds",  →
"thousands", "millions")

Debug.Print Numbers(3)
```

Remember, though, that arrays default to a zeroth item. This means that "ones" is Numbers(0) and "tens" is Numbers(1), and so on. So if you test the above example, you'll find that printing Numbers(3) results in "thousands." To avoid this absurd arrangement in your programs, you can force all arrays to start with element #1 by inserting this command in your Module (outside of any Sub...End Sub):

```
Option Base 1

Sub Testit( )
Numbers = Array("ones", "tens", "hundreds", "thousands",
"millions")
Debug.Print Numbers(3)
End Sub
```

**Results in** hundreds

# BringToFront, SendToBack

**method**

**Description** Puts the designated object at the top of the ZOrder (you see it on top of everything else onscreen). For more on ZOrder, see "ActivateNext."

BringToFront and SendToBack are the equivalent of the same options available on the VB 4 Edit menu. See the ZOrder Method in Visual Basic.

**Used With** All kinds of Objects and Controls. Not used with child windows within an application, such as a Document window in Word.

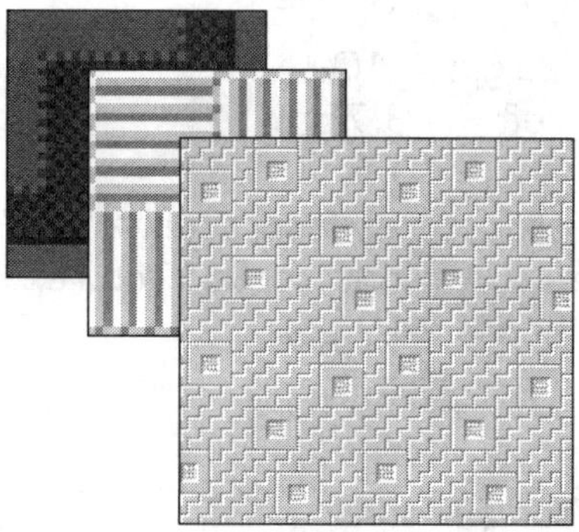

Figure 11-5: Three Picture Objects in their original order.

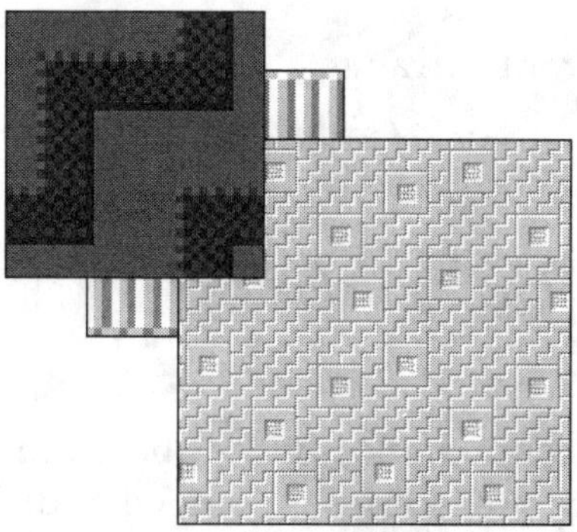

Figure 11-6: After Picture 1 BringToFront, the bottom one moves on top.

**Example** Here we insert three pictures (from Windows's wallpaper BMPs). The first one inserted becomes Picture 1, and so on. Together they form a collection of Picture Objects, called *Pictures*. As each one is inserted in the Excel worksheet, we position and size it. That is the job of Macro1. The second macro, MoveToFront, does the actual arranging. It brings Picture 1 to the front,as you can see in Figure 11-6.

```
Sub Macro1( )
    Sheets("Sheet1").Select
    ChDir "C:\WINDOWS"
    ActiveSheet.Pictures.Insert("zigzag.bmp").Select
    ActiveSheet.DrawingObjects("Picture 1").Select
    Selection.Width = 97.5
    Selection.Height = 102
    ActiveSheet.Pictures.Insert("thatch.bmp").Select
    ActiveSheet.DrawingObjects("Picture 2").Select
    Selection.Width = 96.75
    Selection.Height = 102
    Selection.Left = 78.75
    Selection.Top = 73.5
    ActiveSheet.Pictures.Insert("chitz.bmp").Select
    ActiveSheet.DrawingObjects("Picture 3").Select
    Selection.Left = 113.25
    Selection.Top = 99.75
End Sub

Sub MoveToFront( )
    Sheets("Sheet1").Select
    ActiveSheet.Pictures("Picture 1").BringToFront
End Sub
```

**See Also** ZOrder, BringToFront, Arrange

## BYREF & BYVAL keywords

**Description** These aren't new commands, but they behave in a new way because programming with procedures is somewhat different in VBA. ByRef permits procedures (Subs or Functions) to change Variables that would normally be changeable only within their local Procedure. The companion command, ByVal, denies this permission.

**Used With** Subs, Functions, Declare, Call, Property Get/Let/or Set.

**Cautions** Any Variables passed to a Procedure (a Function or a Subroutine) can be changed by the receiving Procedure. These variables do not have to be given a wide scope (that is, Dimmed or declared Public).

You can define a variable as Private, or local to a particular Module, like this:

```
Private X As Integer
```

But if you then use a procedure within the Module to pass X to another procedure, located in a separate Module, *X will still be changed by the actions of the outside procedure.*

To prevent this, you can either use the ByVal keyword to protect a Variable or use parentheses. If you pass the arguments (variables) within parentheses, VBA understands you are passing them ByVal:

```
Mysub arg1,(arg2), arg3 'the variable arg2 here is passed _ by
Value, and cannot be changed
```

A protected Variable passed to a procedure can be used for information and even changed temporarily while within the receiving Procedure. But when you return to the place that called the Procedure, a Variable passed ByVal will not have been changed. In the following example, X will not be changed, no matter what happens to it inside the Function "Newcost." However, Y can be permanently changed by the Function since it is not described as "ByVal":

```
Function Newcost (ByVal X, Y)
```

Neither ByRef nor ByVal can be used with user-defined types.

You must use ByVal when passing Properties, like the Text Property of an edit box. Here's an example from Visual Basic:

```
Sub updatelabel (ByVal a As String, ByVal b As String)
x = StrComp(a, b)
Select Case x
    Case -1
        Form1.Label1.Caption = a + " is less than " + b
    Case 0
        Form1.Label1.Caption = a + " is equal to " + b
    Case 1
        Form1.Label1.Caption = a + " is greater than " + b
End Select
End Sub
```

We can pass the Text Property of two text boxes to this updatelabel Sub, and it will make its report on how they compare by setting the label's caption. When you pass Properties, you must use the ByVal command. When passing ordinary text Variables, you would just use (a As String, b As String) and forget the ByVal command.

The following would be typed into the KeyPress Events of both Text1 and Text2 when you pass Properties:

```
Sub Text1_KeyPress (KeyAscii As Integer)
    If KeyAscii = 13 Then
            updatelabel text1.Text, text2.Text
    End If
End Sub
```

In each case, we pass the text within both text boxes to our updatelabel Subroutine for processing. The Subroutine, which is designed to accept Properties as arguments, must use the ByVal technique for accepting data.

**Example**

Normally a variable can be changed only within the Sub or Function in which it resides. That is, a variable's "scope" (of influence) doesn't extend past the procedure's End Sub.

In the following example, we place the value 12 into the Variable TheVar. Then we call a separate Subroutine that endeavors to change this value by adding 1. But the result will still be 12 when we print it because TheVar is local to each procedure. In effect, the two "TheVars" are different variables:

```
Sub Showit ( )
TheVar = 12
TryToChangeIt
Debug.Print TheVar
End Sub

Sub TryToChangeIt( )
TheVar = TheVar + 1
End Sub
```

**Results in**

12

However, you can extend a Variable's scope by explicitly defining it as Module-wide. You do this by Dimming it at the top of a Module, outside of any Procedure:

```
Dim TheVar As Integer

Sub Showit ( )
TheVar = 12
TryToChangeIt
Debug.Print TheVar
End Sub

Sub TryToChangeIt( )
TheVar = TheVar + 1
End Sub
```

**Results in** 13

Courtesy of the Dim command, we've created a Variable that can be read or changed anywhere within this Module. Likewise, you can make a Variable available program-wide by using the Public command (Public TheVar) or the older global command (Global TheVar).

But the examples above are artificial. You'd never try to change a variable by assuming that it has enough scope to be changed by an outside procedure. Instead, you'd simply "pass" the variable (send it), and then the scoping rules wouldn't matter at all. This is the purpose of the ByRef command. However, since ByRef is the default method of passing variables, you never see it used in programming.

A local Variable (one not declared to be Module-wide or program-wide) can easily be manipulated by an outside procedure. Just use the ByRef command and pass the Variable to the outside Procedure. Recall that in practice, you need not explicitly insert the ByRef command, since passed variables default to ByRef:

```
Sub Showit ( )
TheVar = 12
TryToChangeIt TheVar
Debug.Print TheVar
End Sub

Sub TryToChangeIt(ByRef TheVar)
TheVar = TheVar + 1
End Sub
```

**Results in** 13

By contrast, if a Variable has been declared Module-wide (or Public and thereby available to all Modules), you could still, for perverse reasons of your own, refuse permission to a procedure to change its value. Just use the ByVal command:

```
Dim TheVar As Integer

Sub Showit ( )
TheVar = 12
TryToChangeIt TheVar
Debug.Print TheVar
End Sub

Sub TryToChangeIt(ByVal TheVar)
TheVar = TheVar + 1
End Sub
```

But if safety is your top priority, use ByVal whenever possible. When speed is the priority, use ByRef.

**Results in** 12

# CHARACTERS method

**Description** The Characters Method allows you to change the font, underlining or any other Properties of a specified group of characters within a larger piece of text. This is similar to the searching permitted by the Instr command. In VB4, look in VB's Help engine for information on the new Font object.

If you are technically inclined, you might ask, "How does the Characters *Method* differ from the Characters *Object*?" Simply put, the Method "returns" (provides) the Object. The Characters Method+Object pair is like the Range Method+Object pair and the many other instances of this "team" approach in Excel's object model.

Strictly speaking, the Characters Method is not, itself, an Object. Like all Methods, it does not have its own Properties or Methods. By contrast, the Characters *Object* does have Properties and Methods. Of course, the Characters Method immediately returns a Characters Object. Because you instantly get this Object, you can access its Properties and execute its supported Methods. In other words, the Characters Method immediately provides you with a Characters Object, so the distinction between Method and Object is purely theoretical. Get it?

When you begin to string Objects, Properties and Methods together, you enter a house of mirrors. Each new Object can add additional Objects, Properties and Methods to those already available to the original Object. For example, here we have Object, Collection Object, Object, Property = Parameter:

```
ActiveCell.Characters(4, 6).Font.Subscript = True
```

Technically, the Characters Method "returns" (provides you with) a "Characters Object." This is a set of characters on which you can perform additional Methods (namely, Insert and Delete). You can also find out or change the Properties of a Characters Object (Application, Caption, Count, Creator, Font, Parent, Text). Of these Properties of a Characters Object, the Font Object is particularly fertile. The Font Object includes a slew of Properties of its own—10, to be exact. You can see all the Properties of a Font object by recording a macro and making a change to some text. When you look at the macro, you see a list of all the Font Properties:

```
Sub Macro3( )
    Sheets("Sheet1").Select
    Range("D11").Select
    With Selection.Font
        .Name = "Arial"
        .FontStyle = "Bold"
        .Size = 32
        .Strikethrough = False
        .Superscript = False
        .Subscript = False
        .OutlineFont = False
        .Shadow = False
        .Underline = xlNone
        .ColorIndex = xlAutomatic
    End With
End Sub
```

**Variables**

```
Object.Characters (start, length)
```

The object can be the ActiveCell (as in the example below) or it can be any of the following: AxisTitle, Button, Buttons, ChartTitle, CheckBox, CheckBoxes, DataLabel, DialogFrame, DrawingObjects, DropDown, DropDowns, EditBox, EditBoxes, GroupBox, GroupBoxes, Label, Labels, OptionButton, OptionButtons, Range, TextBox, TextBoxes.

*Start* refers to the character position where you want the changes to begin. The first character is "1" and counts up from there. Both *Start* and *Length* are optional. Leave them out, and the entire piece of text will change. *Length* refers to the number of characters to change.

**Examples** You can use the Font Property of a selected range of text or cells to change the qualities of text. Here we change the text size:

```
Sub MacroFormat( )
    Sheets("Sheet1").Select
    ActiveWindow.DisplayGridlines = False
    Range("B11").Select
    ActiveCell.FormulaR1C1 = "We want to reformat this →
    message!"
    Range("B11:E11").Select
    With Selection.Font
        .Size = 32
    End With
End Sub
```

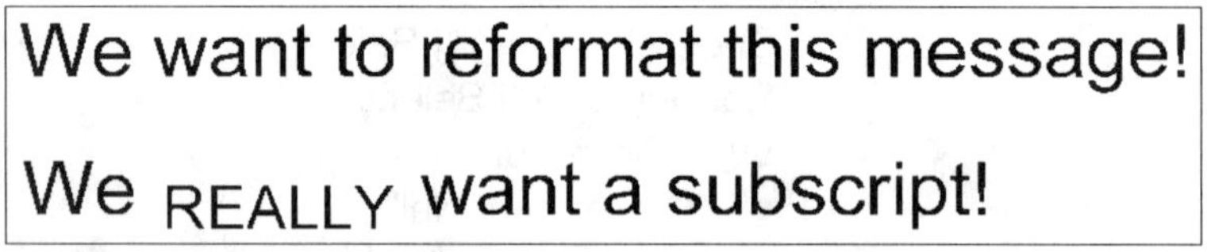
We want to reformat this message!
We REALLY want a subscript!

Figure 11-7: Use the Characters command to make fine adjustments to the properties *within* a text string.

However, we can make fine adjustments to particular sets of characters within a large piece of text. Here we make the word *REALLY* a subscripted text:

```
Sub DoChars( )
    Sheets("Sheet1").Select
    Range("B14").Select
    ActiveCell.FormulaR1C1 = _
        "We REALLY want a SubScript!"
    With Selection.Font
        .Size = 32
    End With
    ActiveCell.Characters(4, 6).Font.Subscript = True
End Sub
```

# CHECKSPELLING method

## Description

Activates the spell-checker utility within the parent application. At this time, Word has its own spell-checker, Excel has a different one, and so on. Soon, though, we can expect them all to activate the same Windows-wide spelling-checker utility. There is no such command in VB4, but see "Example: Borrowing Word's Spell-checker" under "More Than Data Transfer" in Chapter 10.

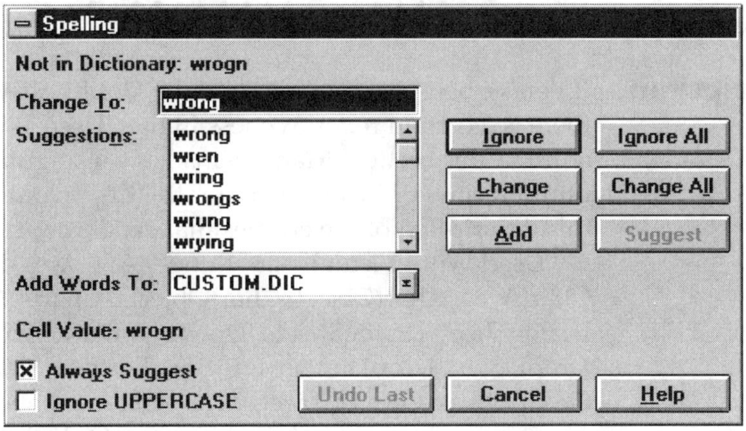


Figure 11-8: The CheckSpelling command brings up this utility.

## Used With

Almost anything that contains text, including an Application, Button, Buttons, Chart, CheckBox, CheckBoxes, DialogFrame, DialogSheet, DrawingObjects, GroupBox, GroupBoxes, GroupObject, GroupObjects, Label, Labels, OptionButton, OptionButtons, Range, TextBox, TextBoxes or worksheet.

## Example

After we deliberately insert a misspelled word into an Excel worksheet, the CheckSpelling feature traps it and displays the problem shown in Figure 11-8.

```
Sub Macro1( )
    Sheets("Sheet1").Select
    ActiveCell.FormulaR1C1 = "This"
    Range("B1").Select
    ActiveCell.FormulaR1C1 = "word"
```

```
        Range("C1").Select
        ActiveCell.FormulaR1C1 = "is"
        Range("D1").Select
        ActiveCell.FormulaR1C1 = "wrogn"
        ActiveSheet.CheckSpelling
    End Sub
```

## COLLECTION object

**Description** If you've been reading sequentially, doubtless you've noticed that there is a certain repetitiveness in the "Used With" listings for each entry in this section. Many items have a singular form, followed by a plural form. For instance, under the Copy command entry, you'll find this description of the entities that can be copied:

"Used With: Virtually anything—Arc, Arcs, Button, Buttons, Chart, ChartArea, ChartObject, ChartObjects, Charts, CheckBox, DialogSheet, DialogSheets, Drawing, DrawingObjects, Drawings, DropDown, DropDowns, EditBox, EditBoxes, GroupBox, GroupBoxes, GroupObject, GroupObjects, Label, Labels, Line, Lines, ListBox, ListBoxes, Module, Modules, OLEObject, OLEObjects, OptionButton, OptionButtons, Oval, Ovals, Picture, Pictures, Point, Range, Rectangle, Rectangles, ScrollBar, ScrollBars, Series, Sheets, Spinner, Spinners, TextBox, TextBoxes, ToolBarButton, worksheet."

Most of the items here seem to be repeated: singular, plural. For example, there isn't just an Oval item, there is also an Ovals item paired with it. That is because the entities that can be used with the Copy command are *Objects*. And most Objects can be part of a collection. Said another way, the Oval Object is a *particular* Oval. The Ovals Object is a *collection* of individual Ovals; in other words, Ovals is a collection of Oval Objects.

("Ovals" here is essentially an array; it is *not* to be confused with the "Class" Oval—or as VB would put it, if it had such a control, the "Custom Control Oval." *Classes* and *Custom Controls* are templates describing the most general, vanilla set of Properties, Methods and Events for an Object. From this generic template, "real" concrete Objects and collections of Objects are created. You can transform a Class Control, like a Text Box, into an actual Object by dragging it from VB's ToolBox onto a Form. Now that you have this Object actualized, it can be used by your programming. Or you can use the CreateObject command, for more about which see "More Than Simple Data Transfer" in Chapter 10.)

A collection is a meta-Object, or cluster (an Array of related Objects). You can use collections to manipulate an individual Object (element) within the collection. Or since a collection is itself an Object, you can manipulate Properties of the entire collection at once. In other words, Collections have their own Properties (such as count) and Methods (such as Add), so Collections are, in all respects, true Objects. They merely have the special capability to manipulate a set of objects simultaneously.

A collection behaves like an Array, and you can often simply use a collection rather than the traditional classic array. You can isolate an individual entity (a single Object) within the Array by specifying its index number. Then you can change that single element's Properties. To remove the fifth worksheet in a worksheets collection, for example, you can say worksheets(5).Delete.

But to change all the items in an Array, you have to loop through the elements, like this:

```
Sub ShowArray
Dim Z (1 to 6)

For I = 1 To 6
    Z(I) = 1
Next I
For I = 1 To 6
    Debug.Print Z(I),
Next I
End Sub
```

**Results in** 1 1 1 1 1 1

Fortunately, a collection is more efficient; you can change an entire collection's Property with a single line of programming. No need to loop. Here's an example:

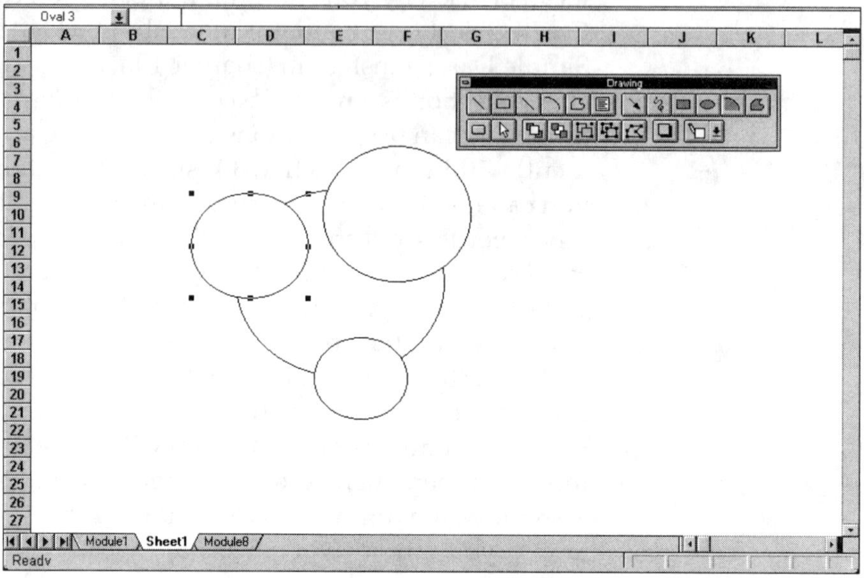

Figure 11-9: A collection of Oval Objects.

In Figure 11-9, we used the Drawing toolbar to put four Ovals on Sheet1. We can refer to them separately or collectively when we want to change their appearance or otherwise manipulate them. In Figure 11-9, Oval 3 is the currently selected Oval, the one with the little black "handles" around it. To make this Oval float, we can refer to it by its own name:

```
Sub Float3( )
    Sheets("Sheet1").Select
    ActiveSheet.DrawingObjects("Oval 3").Select
    Selection.Top = Selection.Top - 100
End Sub
```

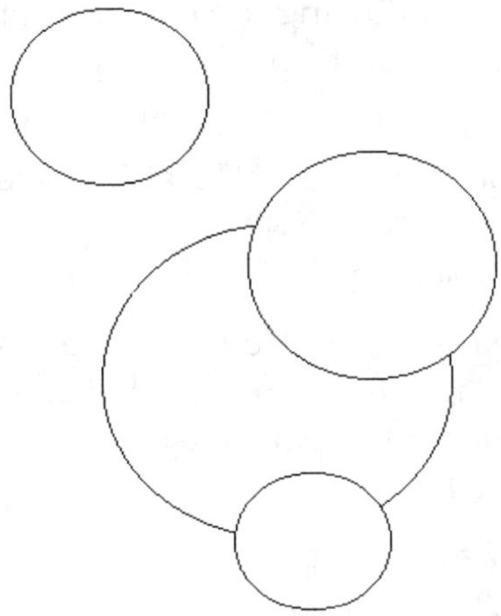

Figure 11-10: We've moved Oval 3 up, away from the others.

Notice that we are using a Sheets collection to move to (Select) a particular worksheet from within this collection: Sheet1. Then we use a DrawingObjects collection to select a particular Oval. Now that we've specified Oval 3 (selected it), we can move it up the screen by 100 twips.

There are several collections that are predefined, which come built into an application. Excel has Sheets, workbooks, DrawingObjects, worksheets, Buttons, Toolbars and many other built-in collections. To see a list of them, look in Excel's VBA Help feature, and then look under "Objects." Anything that is *plural* (such as *EditBoxes*) is a collection.

You can also define your own collections, using the Group command (see "Group" later in this section).

But back to our example. We could also move Oval 3 up the screen by using a different format. Here, instead of the DrawingObjects collection, we use the Ovals collection:

```
ActiveSheet.Ovals("Oval 3").Select
```

However, we are still referring to Oval 3 by name. Since it is an element in what is, for all practical purposes, an Array, we can optionally refer to Oval 3 by its *index*. The first oval we drew onscreen became Ovals(1), the second became Ovals(2) and so on. To move Oval 3 up, we can use this syntax as well:

```
ActiveSheet.Ovals(3).Select
```

Therefore, any of the following three lines of programming will have the same effect, will select the oval in preparation for moving it upscreen:

```
ActiveSheet.DrawingObjects("Oval 3").Select
ActiveSheet.Ovals("Oval 3").Select
ActiveSheet.Ovals(3).Select
```

(However, you are not guaranteed that Ovals(3) is going to be ("Oval 3") all of the time. An item can be inserted at any location within a collection.) Now for the fun part. We can select the entire Ovals collection with a single line:

```
ActiveSheet.Ovals.Select
```

We've now got hold of all four Ovals. So we can move them, color them, border them, whatever—all at once:

```
Sub FloatEmAll( )
    Sheets("Sheet1").Select
    ActiveSheet.Ovals.Select
    Selection.Top = 150
    With Selection.Border
        .LineStyle = xlContinuous
        .ColorIndex = 1
        .Weight = xlMedium
    End With
    Selection.Shadow = True
    With Selection.Interior
        .Pattern = xlSolid
        .ColorIndex = 15
    End With
End Sub
```

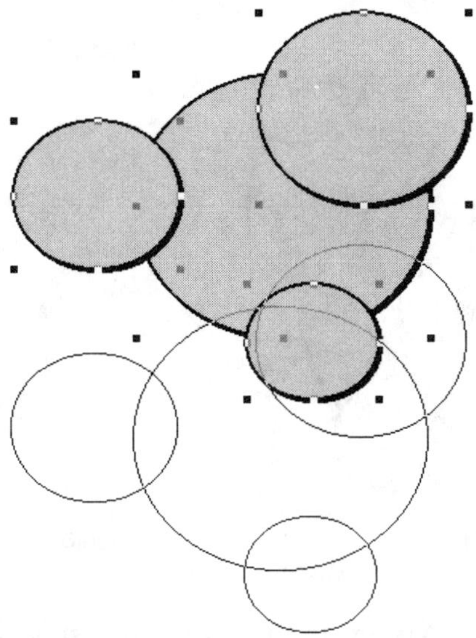

Figure 11-11: Our Ovals during a transformation: we're moving, shading, shadowing and, let's face it, tormenting them—as a group.

If you were going to do a lot of things to Oval 3, you might want to define it as an Object in its own right, with its own unique *Object Variable name*. Then there would be no need to actually move to (select) Sheet1, or use the ActiveSheet identifier. When something has been objectified, it has its own, independent identity and you can refer to it casually and directly from anywhere:

```
Sub Float3( )
    Set AnObj = Sheets("Sheet1").Ovals(3)
    AnObj.Top = AnObj.Top - 100
End Sub
```

This also improves performance dramatically.

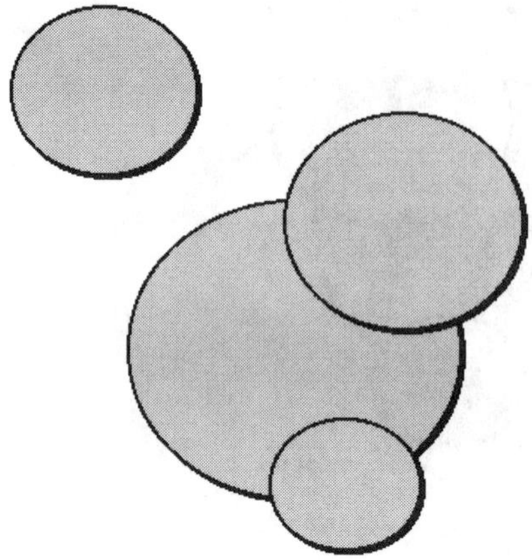

Figure 11-12: Moving Oval 3 after giving it a special Object Variable name.

**Variables**

The Properties or Methods that you can use with a collection depend on the nature of its objects. A TextBoxes collection of text characters has a Font Property, which in turn has a cluster of Properties such as underline, italic and bold. A TextBoxes collection can use the CheckSpelling Method. A Rectangles collection cannot use the CheckSpelling Method, nor can it have italics or boldface Properties. But it *can* use its Border, Width and ZOrder Properties, and can invoke its BringToFront or CopyPicture Method.

To find out which Properties and Methods are used with a given collection of Objects in a Module, type in the name of the collection (for instance, MenuItems). Then with your cursor on that word, press F1. The Help feature will appear, and you can click on either Properties or Methods to see what jobs your collection can do.

**Example**

For generic approaches to manipulating collections of Objects, see the examples above under "Description."

One more trick: what if you wanted to expand Oval 2 and Oval 4, but leave 3 and 1 alone? That's easy. Use the Group command to define *yet another* Object. This new Object is a subset of our Ovals, like this:

```
Sub DragTwo( )
Set TwoOvals = Sheets("Sheet1").Ovals(Array(2, 4)).Group
TwoOvals.Width = 200
TwoOvals.Ungroup
Set TwoOvals = Nothing
End Sub
```

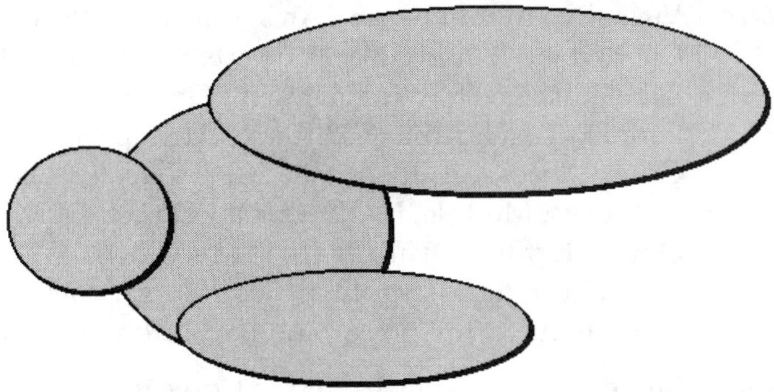

Figure 11-13: Expanding "TwoOvals," our new object made up of Oval 2 and Oval 4.

When you group objects, it's important to remember to later *Ungroup* them. Otherwise, they remain permanently glued together. Grouping Oval 2 and Oval 4 results in three Oval Objects on Sheet1: Oval 1, Oval 2, and Group 5.

"Group 5?" This absurdity is the result of Excel's naming convention. Excel adds numbers to Objects in the order they are created rather than by category. Hence, we created Oval 1, Oval 2, Oval 3 and then Oval 4. So by Excel's logic, this new group should be called Group 5. If we added an edit box to this worksheet, it would be named EditBox6. We can expect this naming convention to be abandoned as VBA moves into other applications. Visual Basic, for example, adds numbers according to the category of Object. (In Visual Basic, we would have Oval 1-4, then Group 1.)

Also remember to always evaporate an object when it is no longer needed: Set TwoOvals = Nothing.

**See Also** GroupObjects, Object, Item

# COPY

**method**

**Description** This method can copy something to the Clipboard or create a new "instance" of some Object. For example, you can make Excel copy worksheet5 and put the new copy between worksheet12 and worksheet13. You can copy a range and relocate the contents to a different range. You can insert a new button on a toolbar. In VB4, see the Clipboard object and the SetData or SetText commands.

**Used With**

Virtually anything—Arc, Arcs, Button, Buttons, Chart, ChartArea, ChartObject, ChartObjects, Charts, CheckBox, DialogSheet, DialogSheets, Drawing, DrawingObjects, Drawings, DropDown, DropDowns, EditBox, EditBoxes, GroupBox, GroupBoxes, GroupObject, GroupObjects, Label, Labels, Line, Lines, ListBox, ListBoxes, Module, Modules, OLEObject, OLEObjects, OptionButton, OptionButtons, Oval, Ovals, Picture, Pictures, Point, Range, Rectangle, Rectangles, ScrollBar, ScrollBars, Series, Sheets, Spinner, Spinners, TextBox, TextBoxes, ToolBarButton, worksheet.

**Variables**

There are four syntaxes for the Copy Method:

- Object.Copy—Sends the object to the Clipboard, like a normal "Copy" from an Edit Menu.
- Object.Copy (destination)—The optional destination can be a new range to copy a Range Object to.
- Object.Copy (before, after)—*Before* or *after* describes the *position* in a collection of worksheets to which this worksheet should be copied. For instance, this will position Sheet4 just before Sheet7:

  Sheets("Sheet4").Copy before := Sheets("Sheet7").

  You can use *before* or *after*, but not both.
- Object.Copy (toolbar, before)—Copies a button to the specified toolbar. The *before* parameter specifies the position for this new button within the existing set, starting from 1.

  **Tip:** To copy a workbook, see the "NewWindow" command.

**Example**

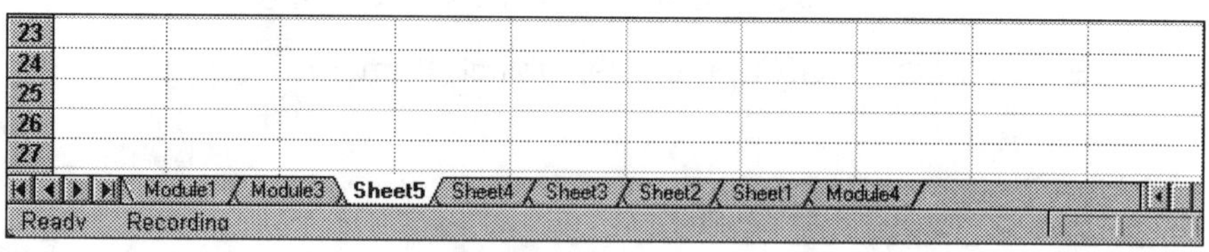


Figure 11-14: Before copying (and relocating) Sheet1.

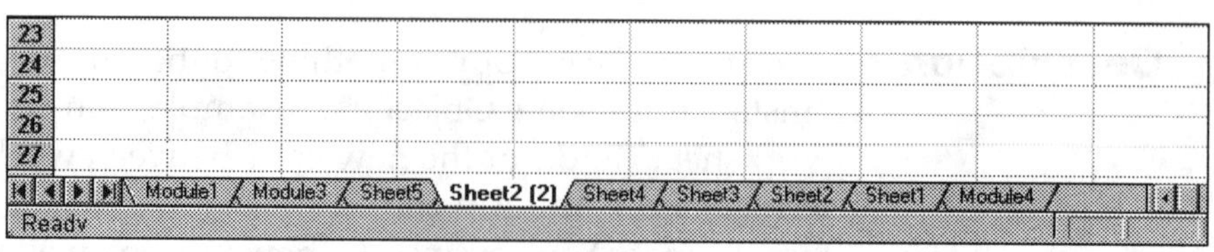


Figure 11-15: Now a clone of Sheet2 has been placed "after" Sheet5.

```
Sub CloneOne( )
    Sheets("Sheet1").Select
    Sheets.Add
    Sheets.Add
    Sheets.Add
    Sheets.Add
    Sheets("Sheet2").Copy after:=Sheets("Sheet5")
End Sub
```

**See Also** Duplicate, Cut, Paste, Move

# COPYFACE method

**Description** You can copy the image (the icon graphic) from one button to another. In VB4, see Help about the ImageList Control.

**Used With** ToolbarButtons only.

**Example** First we make sure that the Excel Drawing toolbar is displayed (by setting its Visible Property to True). Then we copy the first button's image to the Clipboard and paste it onto the third button. Notice that Object collections (like the ToolBars collection and the ToolbarButtons collection) start with item 1, unlike arrays and other computer lists that all too often start with the zeroth item.

To undo this change, choose the original icon that was on Button 3 from the Tools/Customize menu.

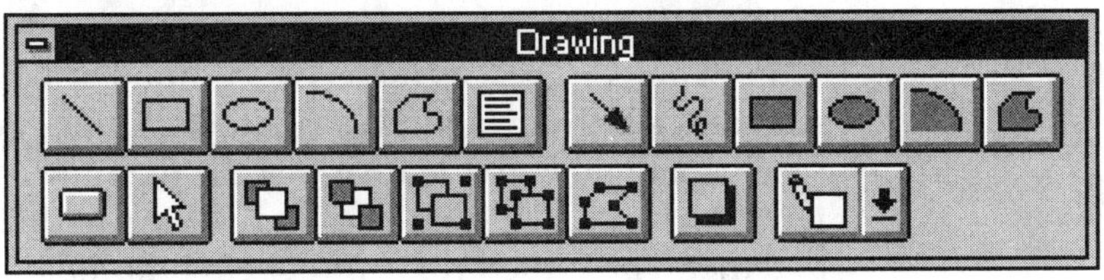


Figure 11-16: The Drawing Toolbar in its virgin state.

Figure 11-17: Now, the first button has been cloned to the third button.

```
Sub SwitchOne( )
    Toolbars(5).Visible = True
    Toolbars(5).ToolbarButtons(1).CopyFace
    Toolbars(5).ToolbarButtons(3).PasteFace
End Sub
```

**See Also** PasteFace

# CopyPicture

**Description** Copies an image of something to the Clipboard. In VB4, see the SetData command. This is different from copying text. Computers hold information in two ways: as descriptions and as true copies. A description is usually mathematical or part of a code. The letter *a* in a Word document is part of a code called the ANSI code. The computer stores *a* as the number 65, and *b* as 66. When displaying, spell-checking or printing a Word document, the number 66 is the same thing as a *b*.

However, if you open Paintbrush and hand-draw a *b*, that will be a "copy," an "image," as far as the computer is concerned. It will be stored as a bitmap (a kind of photocopy, one-for-one, of the dots or pixels that make up the image of the *b*). A bitmap is just a visual pattern and cannot be spell-checked. A bitmap of 2+4 cannot be added together. These pictures cannot be manipulated by logical or mathematical techniques. The only manipulations you can make are *graphic*: you can lighten or change the color of 2+2.

It's like the difference between receiving a fax and downloading the same text file via a modem. You type new words into a fax; it's a picture, not a document. A text file, however, is a set of computer codes and is fully editable.

**Used With** Virtually anything except a window: Arc, Arcs, Button, Buttons, Chart, ChartObject, ChartObjects, CheckBox, CheckBoxes, DialogFrame, Drawing, DrawingObjects, Drawings, DropDown, DropDowns, EditBox, EditBoxes, GroupBox, GroupBoxes, GroupObject, GroupObjects, Label, Labels, Line, Lines, ListBox, ListBoxes, OLEObject, OLEObjects, OptionButton, OptionButtons, Oval, Ovals, Picture, Pictures, Range, Rectangle, Rectangles, ScrollBar, ScrollBars, Spinner, Spinners, TextBox, TextBoxes.

**Example**

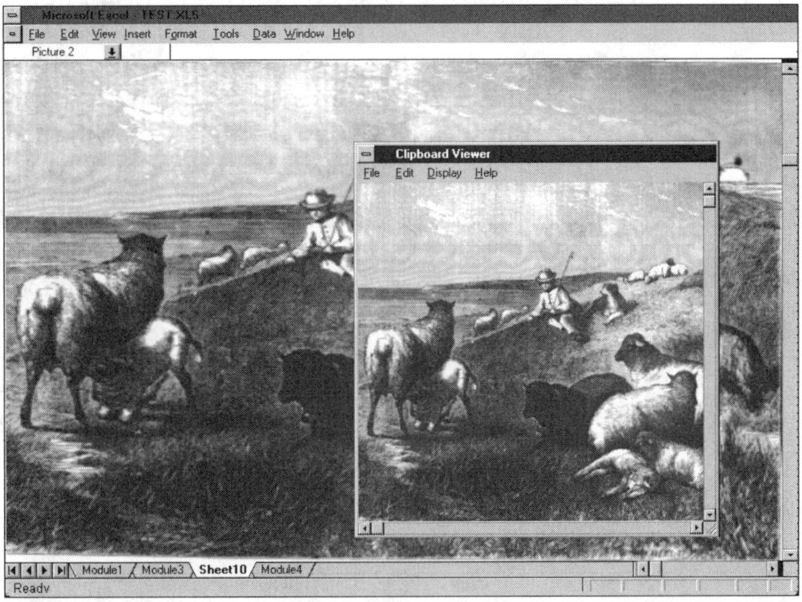


Figure 11-18: The shepherd cloned to the Clipboard using the CopyPicture command.

```
Sub ClonePic( )
    Sheets("Sheet10").Select
    Range("B3").Select
    ActiveSheet.Pictures.Insert("C:\BOOK\SOLDIER.BMP").Select
    Selection.CopyPicture xlScreen, xlBitmap
End Sub
```

This macro puts a graphic image onscreen and then clones it to the Windows Clipboard. From there, it can be further cloned using the Paste command (described later). Run this, and then look in your Clipboard to see your picture. It has been copied.

# CUT

**method**

**Description**

Works the same way as the Cut command on applications' Edit menus. It deletes the Object, but saves a copy in the Clipboard (which can then be used to "move" the Object by pasting it elsewhere).

Note, however, that the Cut command doesn't work in Excel the way it works in most other Windows applications. The Excel Cut is actually a Move command. As soon as you Cut a cell, Excel wants you to select a target location where it can Paste the selection. To accomplish a true Cut in Excel, you have to use the Clear command. See the example below. (Excel will likely abandon this eccentric version of Cut to conform to the Windows standard.)

**Used With**

Virtually any object (including Controls like Text Boxes) except a window. Arc, Arcs, Button, Buttons, ChartObject, ChartObjects, CheckBox, CheckBoxes, Drawing, DrawingObjects, Drawings, DropDown, DropDowns, EditBox, EditBoxes, GroupBox, GroupBoxes, GroupObject, GroupObjects, Label, Labels, Line, Lines, ListBox, ListBoxes, OLEObject, OLEObjects, OptionButton, OptionButtons, Oval, Ovals, Picture, Pictures, Range, Rectangle, Rectangles, ScrollBar, ScrollBars, Spinner, Spinners, TextBox, TextBoxes.

**Example**

```
Sub Macro5( )
    Sheets("Sheet1").Select
    Range("B7").Select
    ActiveCell.FormulaR1C1 = "We'll"
    Range("C7").Select
    ActiveCell.FormulaR1C1 = "remove"
    Range("D7").Select
    ActiveCell.FormulaR1C1 = "this"
    Range("E7").Select
    ActiveCell.FormulaR1C1 = "word"
    Range("D7").Select
    Selection.Cut
End Sub
```

After you run this sample macro, Excel pauses and asks you to "Select destination and press Enter, or choose Paste" in the status bar at the bottom of the Excel window. If you want to program it so the Object is actually cut instead of moved (as discussed in "Description" above), use this:

```
Selection.ClearContents
```

**See Also** ClearContents, Copy, Paste

# DELETE

**method**

**Description** You might think that with Cut and ClearContents commands already available in VBA, a Delete command would be superfluous. You would be right. You might also think that four types, or flavors, of Delete is just too much of a good thing. You would be right again. Among other choices, when you select Delete from the Edit menu in Excel, you are then required to pick between Delete-Contents and Delete-All. Can you guess the difference? If the bank gave you the choice of doubling the *contents* of your checking account, or doubling *all* of your checking account, what would you choose?

Thankfully, Windows is moving toward uniform menus, toolbars and options and toward uniform ways of doing the same things. It shouldn't matter what application you're in: Cut should mean cut, Move should mean move, and Delete should be a cut (with no copy of the cut thing sent to the Clipboard). It's not that simple in Excel, but we can expect Excel to simplify itself in future releases, eliminating its whimsical meaning for Cut, and meaning just one thing when it says "Delete" (instead of the current four meanings).

Now, you might say, synonyms are useful in languages; the Eskimos have 34 words for snow. Well, yes, it's important, it can even be vital, that an Eskimo distinguish between solid and slippery snow. But in computer operating systems (and computer languages), synonyms often cause confusion. It can be reliably predicted that these troublesome synonyms will disappear from VBA. They currently exist in VBA only because VBA has to include all the Menu items and other options offered by Excel. Because Excel is the first of Microsoft's applications to embrace VBA, so VBA perforce inherits some damaged genetic material (another example of this is the existence of text box and edit box objects, which are identical except for the contexts in which they are used).

**Used With**

Virtually any object (including Controls like text boxes) except a window, including Arc, Arcs, Axis, Axis Title, Button, Buttons, Characters, Chart, ChartObject, ChartObjects, Charts, ChartTitle, CheckBox, CheckBoxes, DataLabel, DataLabels, DialogSheet, DialogSheets, DownBars, Drawing, DrawingObjects, Drawings, DropDown, DropDowns, DropLines, EditBox, EditBoxes, ErrorBars, GridLines, GroupBox, GroupBoxes, GroupObject, GroupObjects, HiLoLines, Label, Labels, Legend, LegendEntry, LegendKey, Line, Lines, ListBox, ListBoxes, Menu, MenuBar, MenuItem, Module, Modules, Name, OLEObject, OLEObjects, OptionButton, OptionButtons, Oval, Ovals, Picture, Pictures, Point, Range, Rectangle, Rectangles, Scenario, ScrollBar, ScrollBars, Series, SeriesLines, Sheets, SoundNote, Spinner, Spinners, Style, TextBox, TextBoxes, TickLabels, Toolbar, ToolbarButton, Trendline, UpBars, worksheet, worksheets.

**Example**

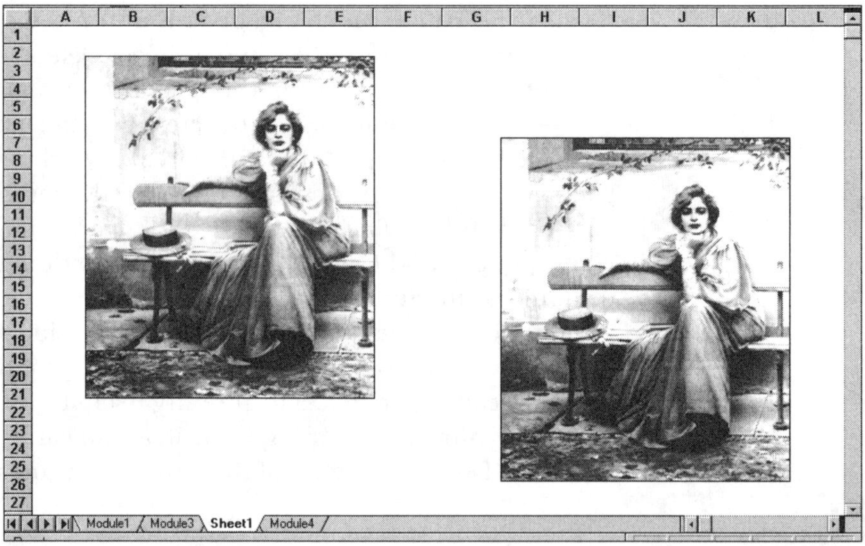


Figure 11-19: Now you see it.

Figure 11-20: After the Delete . . . now you don't.

We'll import a picture, clone it with the Copy command, then Paste it slightly lower and to the right. After that, we can select the original ("Picture1") and use the Delete command to remove it.

```
Sub DelPic( )
    Sheets("Sheet1").Select
    Range("a2").Select

ActiveSheet.Pictures.Insert("C:\GRAPHICS\LADY.BMP").Select
    Selection.Copy
    Range("f4").Select
    ActiveSheet.Pictures.Paste
    ActiveSheet.DrawingObjects("Picture 1").Select
    Selection.Delete
End Sub
```

**See Also** Cut

# DIALOGS

**method**

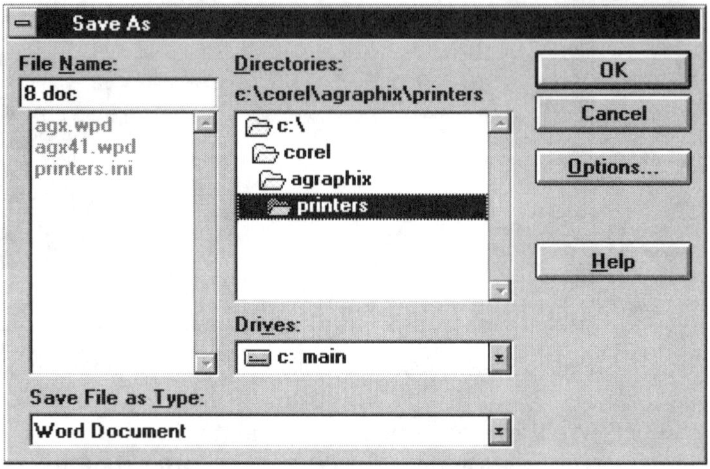


Figure 11-21: You can use any of the hundreds of dialog boxes built into an application.

**Description** The Dialogs Method lets you display any of an application's user-input windows, such as the Print Setup and Search & Replace windows. How do you specify which of the more than 200 dialog boxes to show? Each has its own name, a built-in, predefined constant. In Excel, the names start with the prefix *xlDialog*. To see all available dialog boxes for an application, use the Object Browser.

Before you can look at Excel's Object Browser, you must switch to a Module. If there is no Module in your current workbook, add one by pressing Alt+I,M,M. Then press F2 or Alt+V,O. Under Libraries\workbooks, select Excel; under Objects\Modules, select Constants. Now scroll down the list until you see the group of dialog boxes (they all start with xlDialog).

**Used With** Dialog boxes (such as the one that pops up when you ask a Microsoft application to Save As from the File menu, shown in Figure 11-21).

**Cautions**

You cannot display a dialog box in a context inappropriate to its purpose. That's why we must first switch to a worksheet view in the example below before we can display the Color Selector dialog box.

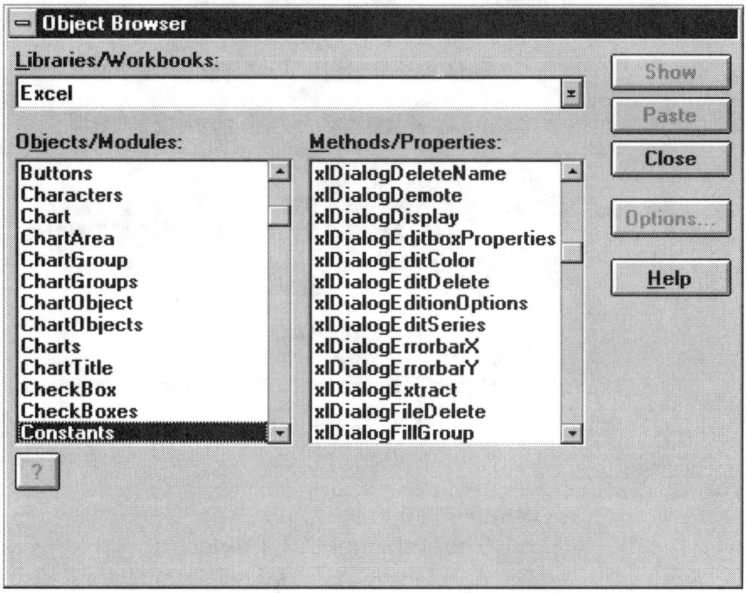


Figure 11-22: The names of Excel's dialog boxes all start with *xl*.

**Example**

You can easily display Excel's color selector window, xlDialogColorPalette, in one of your programs. As you can see, we apply the Show Method to both the Application Object and the Dialogs Object. Therefore, it's possible to have two Objects followed by a Method as we do here, with *Object, Object, Method*:

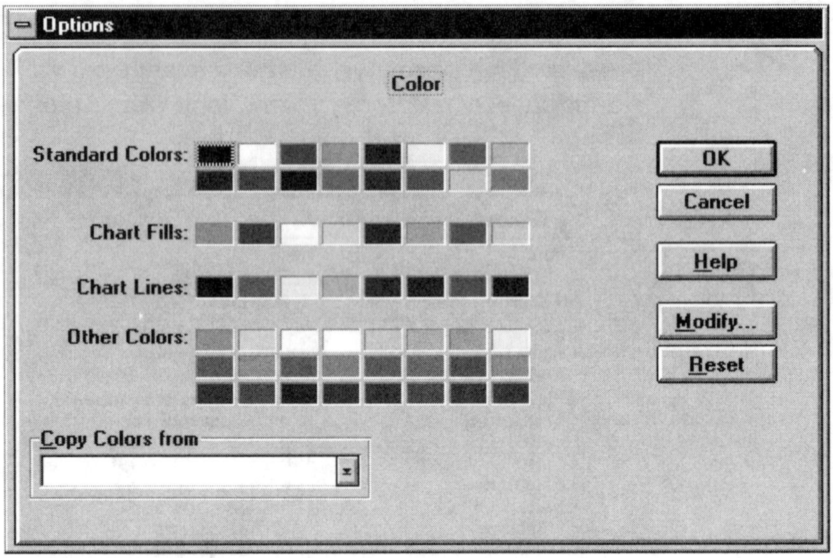


Figure 11-23: The macro below displays this Color Options dialog box.

```
Sub Macro1( )
    Sheets("Sheet1").Select
    Application.Dialogs(xlDialogColorPalette).Show
End Sub
```

One can easily get lost in some of the categories involving Objects. The second line of the example above may appear to have the sequence *Object, Method, Method*. Or is this two Objects, followed by one Method? The answer is that you cannot apply a Method to another Method, but only to an Object. Thus, you are actually applying the Show Method to one Object (Dialogs), which is accessible through another Object (Application). It's analogous to picking an orange. You can't just pick a orange from anywhere; you must first find an orange tree, and next find a branch with a ripe orange on it. So the orange (Object) might have a "Pick" Method, but you access this orange Object via the Tree Object. Thus, picking an orange would be programmed be something like:

```
OrangeTree.Branches("NearBase").Oranges("Ripest").Pick
```

# DOUBLECLICK

**object**

**Description** Imitates a user double-clicking the mouse. Whatever item is currently selected (a document, a spreadsheet cell, a range of text, an embedded object, whatever) receives the double-click and responds in its usual manner. In VB4, see the DblClick Event.

**Used With** The Application (object).

**Example** This example should bring up the Format Object dialog box, just as if you had double-clicked on the Picture Object that we inserted.

```
Sub Macro2( )
    Sheets("Sheet1").Select
    ChDir "C:\WINDOWS" ActiveSheet.Pictures.Insert →
    ("C:\WINDOWS\CARS.BMP").SelectApplication.DoubleClick
End Sub
```

Here's a workaround that will do the job, though it doesn't rely on the currently dead DoubleClick command:

```
Sub bar( )
    Worksheets(1).ActivateWorksheets(1).Pictures.Insert →
    ("C:\WINDOWS\CASTLE.BMP").SelectApplication. →
    Dialogs(xlDialogPatterns).Show
End Sub
```

# DUPLICATE

**method**

**Description** Creates a duplicate of an existing object. The new object is now an entirely separate entity, though its qualities (Properties) are entirely cloned from the original. This is equivalent to creating a "new instance" of an object in Visual Basic using the Set...New command.

**Used With** Arc, Arcs, Button, Buttons, ChartObject, ChartObjects, CheckBox, CheckBoxes, Drawing, DrawingObjects, Drawings, DropDown, DropDowns, EditBox, EditBoxes, GroupBox, GroupBoxes, GroupObject, GroupObjects, Label, Labels, Line, Lines, ListBox, ListBoxes, OLEObject, OLEObjects, OptionButton, OptionButtons, Oval, Ovals, Picture, Pictures, Rectangle, Rectangles, ScrollBar, ScrollBars, Spinner, Spinners, TextBox, TextBoxes.

**Example**

Figure 11-24: A smaller painting is duplicated, then repositioned and blown up relative to the original.

Here we take a graphic BMP picture, insert it into an Excel worksheet and then clone it with the Duplicate command. A clone (a duplicated Object like this picture) inherits all Properties of the original picture, including its position and size. Therefore, the only way to really know that we've now got a clone is to move it away from the original. Note also that the Set command (which must be used with the Duplicate command) permits us to now refer to the clone as "NewPic," the name we gave it during the Duplication. Then we use the Top, Left, Width and Height Properties of the original picture to move and resize the clone. You'll be surprised at how quickly all this happens.

```
Sub NewInstance( )
    Sheets("Sheet1").SelectActiveSheet.Pictures.Insert →
    ("C:\GRAPHICS\CLOUD.BMP").Select
    Set NewPic = ActiveSheet.Pictures(1).Duplicate
    NewPic.Select
    NewPic.Left = ActiveSheet.Pictures(1).Left + 80
    NewPic.Top = ActiveSheet.Pictures(1).Top + 80
    xfactor = ActiveSheet.Pictures(1).Width * 1.5
    yfactor = ActiveSheet.Pictures(1).Height * 1.5
    NewPic.Width = xfactor
    NewPic.Height = yfactor
End Sub
```

**See Also** Copy

# EDIT method

**Description** This command brings up the standard Button Editor window, allowing the user to make changes to the button on the specified toolbar. In VB4, see the Customize Method of the Toolbar Control.

**Used With** ToolBar Buttons only.

**Cautions** Recall that, unlike Arrays, toolbars and the buttons on them start with item #1 and work on up. (Arrays start with a zeroth item.)

**Example** We'll display the edit window for the Open Button:

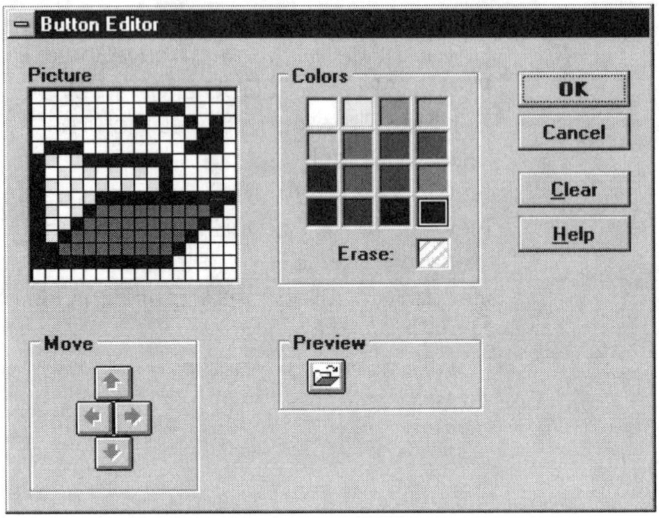


Figure 11-25: You can bring up this Button (icon) Editor with the Edit Method.

```
Sub Macro4( )
    Application.Toolbars(1).ToolbarButtons(2).Edit
End Sub
```

Assuming that you haven't changed the default order of the standard Excel toolbar, you'll see the Open File icon ready to be edited in the Button Editor window.

## EVALUATE method

**Description**

The word *evaluate* in computer programming means "find out the meaning of an expression." For example, evaluating the expression 5 * 6 results in 30. The Evaluate Method is similar; however, it allows you to use a Text ("string") Variable in ways that normally wouldn't work.

For instance, if you want to multiply 25 by whatever value is currently inside cell A3, you can retrieve the contents of A3 by enclosing it in brackets and requesting the value. You use the Value Property. If cell A3 contains the number 3, the following results in (evaluates to) 75:

```
Sub Eval ( )
    Sheets("Sheet1").Select
    Debug.Print [A3].Value * 25
End Sub
```

That's fine if you know when you're programming that you want to use cell A3. (Evaluate was created back when Excel didn't have variables per se. You would have to store expressions in a macro cell and then evaluate it. This is still handy for similar applications in which you might hide a data sheet from the user but could easily modify it without having to touch the code.) Knowing the location of the item you want to manipulate and then specifying that location in your program is called *hard coding*. Hard coding limits a program. For instance, hard coding the location of a graphics file—for example, Pictures.Insert("C:\WINDOWS\ EGYPT.BMP").Select—assumes that your program's user will have Windows in drive C: and, further, that the directory is in fact named *Windows*. If either of these two conditions is untrue, your program will generate an error and fail to accomplish one of its goals. Hard coding is to be avoided whenever possible.

One way to avoid hard code is to ask the user to supply the location of something your program needs. In the following example, we ask the user to type in a cell number. Of necessity, the user will supply a Text ("string") Variable. This will generate an "object required" error because the computer cannot understand [X$]. Inside brackets you must have a *Literal* description (A3), not a Variable like X$.

```
Sub Eval ( )
    Sheets("Sheet1").Select
    X$ = InputBox ("Please type in the name of the cell...")
    Debug.Print [X$].Value * 25
End Sub
```

**Results in** "Object Required" Error

To transform the user's input (the Variable X$) into a usable Object that says to VBA, "We are referring to cell A3," you use the Evaluate Method:

```
Sub Eval ( )
    Sheets("Sheet1").Select
    X$ =   InputBox ("Please type in the name of the cell...")
    Debug.Print Evaluate(X$).Value * 25
End Sub
```

**Results in** 75

**Used With** Application, Chart, DialogSheet, worksheet

**Variables**

```
Object.Evaluate(text)
```

The text name of the thing you want evaluated can be a single cell in Excel (as illustrated in the example above). It can be the text name of a graphic Object, such as a particular rectangle drawing Object. Or it can be a range or a "defined name" in the macro language of the application, a reference to an external item.

---

In Excel, you can reference a cell in another workbook like this: Evaluate("[TESTBOOK.XLS]Sheet4!A3"). Translated, this means, "Get the contents of cell A3 on the worksheet named Sheet4 in the workbook named TESTBOOK."

---

Technically, a *defined name* in Excel is created when you give a range of cells a name, such as AprilSales. This can be done programmatically through the Names collection. Or you can select a range of cells on a Worksheet and enter a name on the formula bar in the leftmost combo box. This can be quite useful when programming. You don't have to specify, or "hard code," a specific range of cells in your program (which might differ from the range the user wants when your program is run). Instead, you refer to the defined name in your program.

**Uses**

- To change a text Variable (like the result of user input from an InputBox question asked by your program) into an Object that VBA can query (*query* means to read or use the contents).
- To "objectify" incoming data. For example, in programming with Objects, the identity of an Object is usually expressed as a text Variable. What's more, with interapplication communications (such as OLE), an external Object is often presented to VBA by its text name—"Microsoft Graph 5.0 Chart" is an external Object. You can't change the width or color or use an Object's Methods while it is merely a name, a piece of text. You must first objectify it, or make it into an Object that VBA can manipulate. Using the Evaluate command, you can transform the text name into a usable object.

**Example** Evaluate can be used in expressions that change the Properties of an object. In other words, when used with Evaluate, a text name (such as Rectangle 4) can be treated as an Object. In this example, we display three rectangles and ask the user to pick one to widen. The user's response will be a Text Variable in our VBA program. To use it as if it were an Object, we put it in parentheses after the Evaluate command. Now we can get at the rectangle's Properties, such as the Width Property.

```
Sub Evalu( )
    Sheets("Sheet1").Select
    Selection.ClearContents
    ActiveWindow.DisplayGridlines = False
    ActiveSheet.Rectangles.Add(60, 100, 140, 85).Select
    Selection.Interior.ColorIndex = 4
    ActiveSheet.Rectangles.Add(160, 60, 273, 135).Select
    Selection.Interior.ColorIndex = 3
    ActiveSheet.Rectangles.Add(126, 175, 206, 117).Select
    Selection.Interior.ColorIndex = 2
    x$ = InputBox("Which box do you want to make wider?")
    Evaluate(x$).Width = Evaluate(x$).Width + 130
End Sub
```

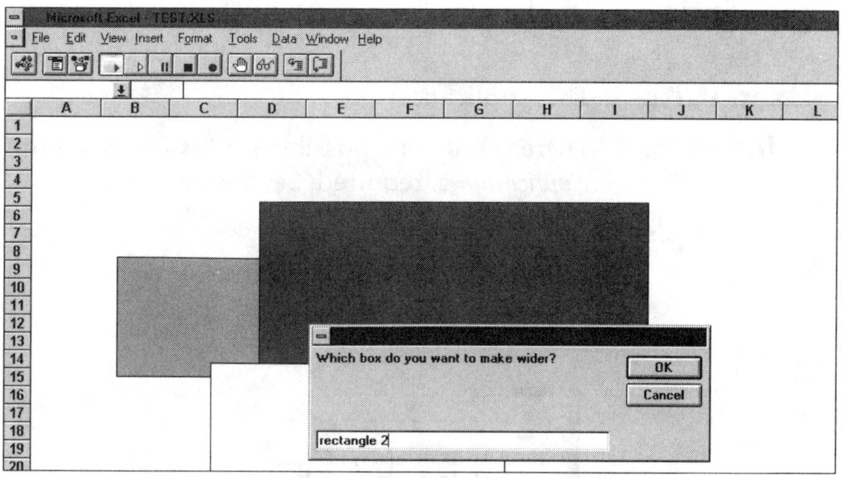


Figure 11-26: Our rectangles, before the user describes which one to widen.

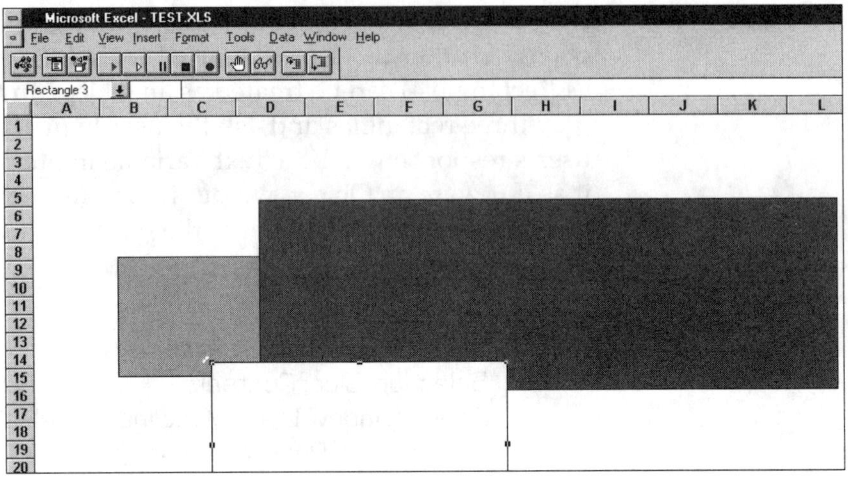


Figure 11-27: One rectangle expands, based on a Text Variable.

## FindFile method

**Description** Displays the file-find utility. This dialog box permits the user to locate a file on disk. This handy option isn't available in VB4.

**Used With** The Application Object.

**Variables** There is only one possible syntax for this command, and the word *Application* is required. See the example.

**Example**

```
Sub check( )
    Application.FindFile
End Sub
```

## For...Each statement

**Description** This useful command is similar to the familiar For...Next command, and is available in VB4. Both allow you to repeatedly carry out some task until completing a specific number of iterations. With For...Each, VBA does something to each item in an Array or each item in a collection of Objects. *But VBA keeps track of the total number of items that must be manipulated.* This saves you the trouble of finding out how many items or Objects are in the group (the Array or collection). VBA just steps through the group and does something for each item, then automatically stops looping when the end of the collection is reached. VBA thereupon moves on to the next command in your program.

**Used With** An Array or a collection of objects.

**Cautions** The Variable you use to access an array must be a Variant type. With an Object collection, the Variable must be either a Variant or Object type. That is, you cannot use For...Each with a Variable that you have specifically declared (with the Dim, Private, Public or Global command) to be a Text Variable, an Integer Variable or some other specific kind of Variable. For instance, this wouldn't work:

```
Dim fetchit as integer
For Each fetchit in MyArray
```

The Array that you manipulate with the For...Each command can be of any variable type. But the *Variable* you use with the For...Each command must be a Variant. If you don't explicitly declare a Variable's type (if you don't use the Dim command in the above example and you just ignore the issue of explicitly describing your variable), the Variable will be, by default, a Variant type.

For...Each cannot be used to affect or change (write to) the items in an Array, like this:

```
For Each whateveritis In ourarray
    whateveritis = whateveritis + 1
Next whateveritis
```

That would be changing the data in the Array (you can do this with the For...Next command). In other words, you can only get the items in the Array (read them); you cannot change them (write to them).

You cannot use For...Each with user-defined variable types. The Variant Variable type cannot handle a user-defined type.

**Example** We'll create an Array in Excel (but we won't specify its Variable type, so it will be the default Variant type). Then we'll fill each element in the Array with a piece of text. Finally, we'll use For...Each to go through the Array and display each item.

```
Dim ourarray(1 To 3)
Sub testit( )
ourarray(1) = "Going "
ourarray(2) = "around "
ourarray(3) = "the bend."
For Each whateveritis In ourarray
    Debug.Print whateveritis
Next whateveritis
End Sub
```

Note that we're using a Variant Variable, whateveritis. It's a Variant because we didn't specifically declare a type (Dim whateveritis as Integer, for example). Notice also that the For...Each command doesn't require that you specify when the loop should stop. VBA does this job for you—that's the benefit of the For...Each structure. To do this same thing with For...Next, you would have to specify the limit of the loop—in this case, three:

```
For whateveritis = 1 to 3
    Debug.Print ourarray(whateveritis)
Next whateveritis
```

You can use the Exit For command to prematurely get out of the For...Each loop:

```
For Each whateveritis In ourarray
    If whateveritis = "around" then Exit For
    Debug.Print whateveritis
Next whateveritis
```

## GETOBJECT function

**Description** This one is not new in VBA; it appears in VB3. But it's new enough to the Basic language as a whole to warrant a brief description here.

GetObject creates a new object, for purposes of OLE. It is similar to the OLE option from an application's Insert/Object menu. When you activate that option, you are given the choice of creating an Object that is "New" or "From File."

Note that you specify a file name and, optionally, the Object's class when you use the GetObject command. By contrast, when you use the CreateObject command, you give only the class name.

**Uses** To create an object *programmatically* (by writing a macro or program rather than selecting Object from the Insert menu), you can use either the CreateObject or the GetObject command. CreateObject is preferable because it's more under your control; it doesn't depend on the possibility that a disk file is missing or has been relocated. CreateObject is the equivalent of Create New from the Insert/Object menu of many applications.

**Example**

```
Sub MakeObj ( )
    Dim wordobj As object
    Set wordobj = GetObject("C:\WINWORD\INVOICE.DOC")
End Sub
```

(*Note:* At this time, GetObject and CreateObject both behave the same was in Word.)

# GETOPENFILENAME method

**Description** Displays the typical Windows File Open dialog (as if the user had pressed Alt+F,O). However, the user's selection is simply returned to your program for further processing. The user-selected file is not opened. A full path is provided (C:\WINWORD\MYFILE.DOC). If the user clicks on the Cancel button or otherwise aborts the dialog box, a False is returned. Not available in VB4, except in the Common Dialog Control.

**Used With** The Application Object.

**Variables**

```
X = GetOpenFileName (FileFilter, FilterIndex, Title)
```

Like a Function, this Method returns a value. So you need the X = or some other Variable on the left side to receive the results. The FileFilter is the text and filter displayed in the list box at the bottom of the File Open dialog. It's the "Any Old Files (*.*)" in Figure 11-28.

The FilterIndex is the file specification you provide, and it determines which files are displayed in the file list box. We used *.* to display all files. The Title is the dialog box's title bar text—a replacement, if you wish, for the "Open" normally displayed there.

If you want to offer the user more than one filter, just add them to your FilterIndex, separated by semicolons: *.txt; *.doc. They are the Filter, Index and Title Properties of the CMDialog Control.

**Uses**

You might use this to prevent a particular file from being opened.

No file is actually opened until you decide to open it within your program (using the Open command). You could thus verify the appropriateness of the user's choice or provide additional information to the user about a file before loading it.

One feature that's built into many Windows applications (such as Word and Notepad) is the default filespec. When you use the application's File, Open dialog box, a default filespec is given, such as *.DOC or *.TXT. If you want to see *all* the files, you have to reset this default to *.*. Many users find this annoying and would prefer to have *.* be the default. In Excel, *.xl* is the default. You could use the GetOpenFilename to create a macro that replaces the *.xl* with *.*.

**Example**

The syntax for displaying all file names is

```
Sub Showall ( )
choice = Application.GetOpenFilename("Any Old Files (*.*),  →
*.*",_
    "Show Them All", "PRESS HERE")
    Debug.Print choice
End Sub
```

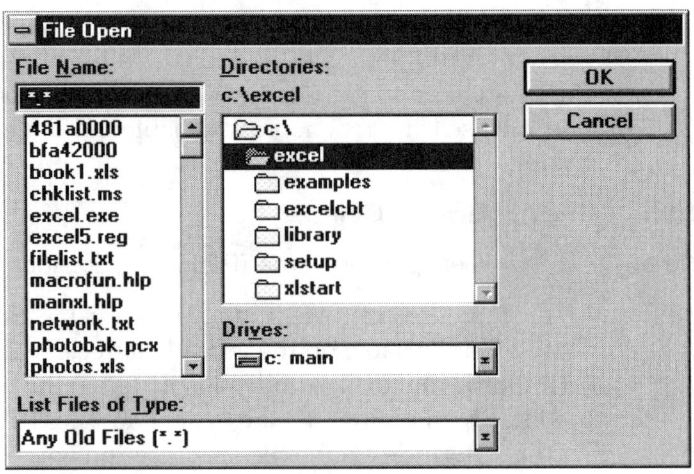


Figure 11-28: A typical File Open dialog box triggered by the GetOpenFilename command.

**See Also** GetSaveAsFileName

# GetSaveAsFileName method

**Description** The twin sister of the GetOpenFileName command. Displays the typical Windows File SaveAs dialog (as if the user had pressed Alt+F,A). However, the user's described file name (and path) is simply returned to your program for further processing. The user-selected filespec is not actually saved to disk. A full path is provided (C:\WINWORD\MYFILE.DOC). If the user clicks on the Cancel button or otherwise aborts the dialog box, a False is returned. Not available in VB4, except in the Common Dialog Control.

**Used With** The Application object.

**Variables**

```
X = GetSaveAsFileName (initialFileName, FileFilter, →
FilterIndex, Title)
```

Like a Function, this Method returns a value. So you need the X = or some other Variable on the left side to receive the results. The initialFileName is optional. If you omit it, VBA inserts the name of the current document (for example, the current worksheet in Excel).

The FileFilter is the text and filter displayed in the list box at the bottom of the File Open Dialog. The FilterIndex is the actual file specification you provide, and it determines which files are displayed in the file list box. We used *.* to display all files.

If you want to offer the user more than one filter, just add them to your FilterIndex, separated by semicolons: *.txt; *.doc.

**Uses**

- You might want to refuse to save a particular file.
- Nothing is actually saved to disk until you decide to save it within your program (using the Save command). You could thus verify the appropriateness of the user's choice or provide additional information to the user about a file before saving it.

**Example** We first use the GetSaveAsFilename command to find out what the user wants to call this file. By omitting the first argument (the empty comma), Excel suggests saving the file using the name it had when loaded. The user's response is then sent to the PathParts function, which extracts the file name from the path (the TEST.XLS from C:\EXCEL\TEXT.XLS). Then we see if it ends in XLS. If not, we put up a message box and request another try (sending the program back up to the label "recycle" and incrementing our counter *c* each time). If the user fails after two tries, we quit with Exit Sub.

Note that we could test the final three letters of the path+filename more easily using the Right$ command, but sometimes you'll want to extract Drive, Directory, Filename from the full path provided by the GetSaveAsFilename (or GetOpenFilename) command. We've included the PathParts Function here to demonstrate a way to do that. For instance, you might want to test the drive name or suggest a different directory if the user is saving a backup copy.

```
Sub filesee( )
recycle:
choice = Application.GetSaveAsFilename(, "(*.*), *.*")
fname$ = PathParts(choice)
If Right$(fname$, 3) <> "XLS" Then
    c = c + 1
    If c > 2 Then Exit Sub
    MsgBox "You entered " & fname$ & ". This file must →
    have an XLS ending. Please try again."
    GoTo recycle
End If
End Sub

Function PathParts(pathname As Variant) As String
    lngth% = Len(pathname)
    x% = InStr(pathname, "\")
    drivename$ = Left$(pathname, x%)
    whatsleft$ = Right$(pathname, lngth% - x%)
    z% = InStr(whatsleft$, "\")
    If z% Then
        lngth% = Len(whatsleft$)
        PathParts = Right$(whatsleft$, lngth% - z%)
    Else
        PathParts = whatsleft$
    End If
End Function
```

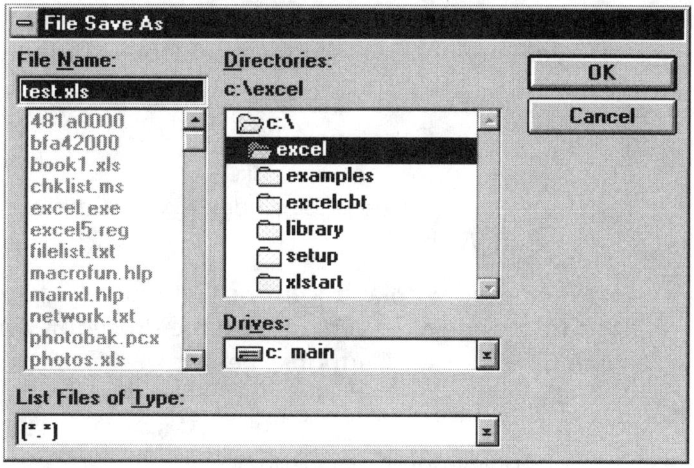


Figure 11-29: A typical File SaveAs Dialog Box triggered by the GetSaveAsFileName command.

**See Also** GetOpenFileName, Open

# GOTO

**method**

## Description

Goto activates an Excel range of cells or a VBA Procedure in any workbook (not necessarily the currently loaded document).

Goto is very similar to the Select Method (described later in this section), but Goto has some unusual distinguishing features. If you Select a range of cells in Excel, you can then manipulate their appearance, their qualities or their contents. However, that range, if hidden (on a different worksheet, for instance), doesn't pop into view onscreen. The Goto command does activate the hidden sheet.

Goto has a Scroll feature that is missing in Select. Goto can use the PreviousSelections Property (which see); Select cannot. Select can use a Replace parameter; Goto cannot.

When used with a range, that range is automatically selected by Goto. Therefore, you can manipulate its Properties, as shown here:

```
With Selection.Interior
        .ColorIndex = 22
        .Pattern = xlSolid
        .PatternColorIndex = xlAutomatic
End With
```

When used with a Procedure, Goto merely displays the target Procedure onscreen. To actually run the Procedure, you must use the Run command. See "Cautions" below.

**Used With** A Range or a Procedure.

**Variables**

```
Application.Goto (Target, Scroll)
```

The Target can be an Excel range or a String (Text) Variable specifying one of your VBA Subs or Functions. (The Target need not be in a currently loaded workbook.)

**Cautions** You can always use one of your VBA Subs or Functions in a different Module, as long as it's in the same workbook. However, to use a Procedure in a different workbook (even though it may be loaded into Excel), you need to activate it with the Run Method, and you need to fully describe the target:

```
Sub Tryit( )
    Application.Run Macro:="TEST.XLS!ScrollWatch"
End Sub
```

However, if you merely want to *display* a Procedure in an outside (or even a local) Module, use the Goto command, like this:

```
Sub Tryit ( )
    Application.Goto reference:="TEST.XLS!ScrollWatch"
End Sub
```

## Example

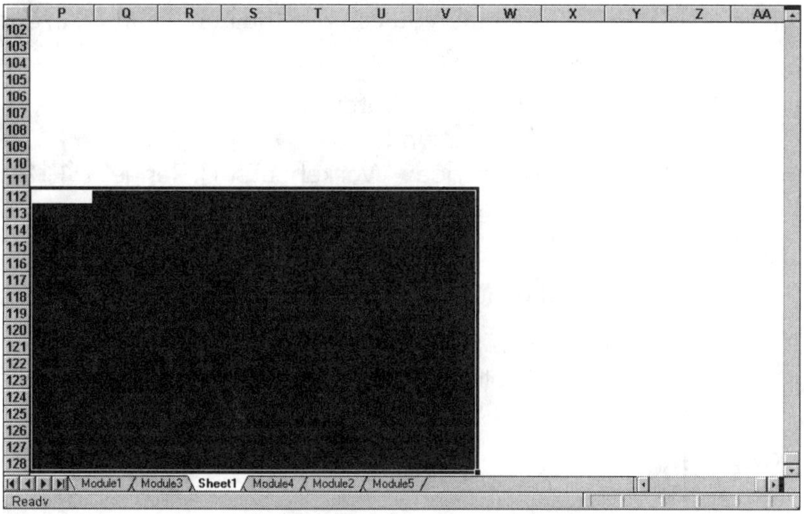


Figure 11-30: With the Scroll feature off (False), the range appears at the bottom.

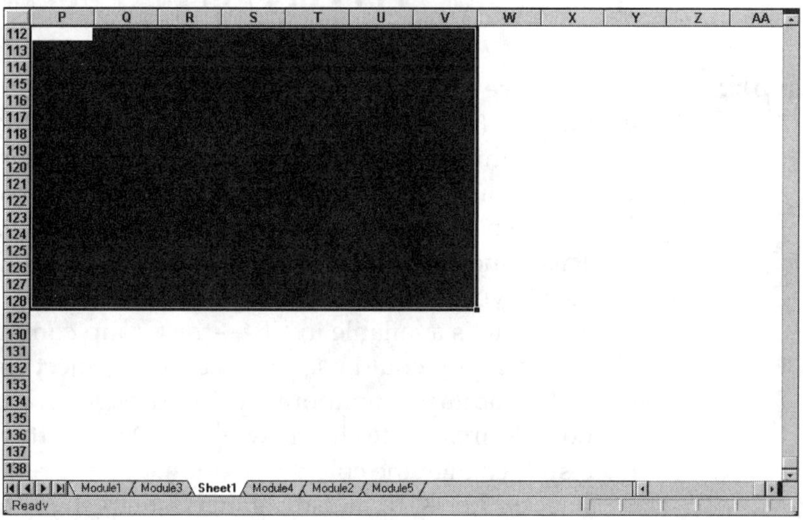


Figure 11-31: With Scroll set to True, VBA automatically positions the target at the top left of the window.

We'll make VBA go to a range of Excel cells. In the first example, with the Scroll option True, the window will be scrolled until the top left of the range appears in the top left of the window.

As usual, you can use the new "named argument" format, shown here:

```
Sub ScrollWatch( )
Application.Goto
reference:=Worksheets(1).Range("P112:V128"),  →
    scroll:=True
End Sub
```

Or the older, position-in-list approach:

```
Sub ScrollWatch( )
Application.Goto Worksheets(1).Range("P112:V128"), False
End Sub
```

**See Also** Select

# GROUP, UNGROUP method

**Description**

If you've programmed in Visual Basic, you know you can have five pictures (or any other visible Object) in a window and you can *group* them (Shift+click). You can even group only certain ones of the five. When thus linked, your group can be moved to a different location onscreen as if they were attached to one another by restraining wires. This same technique can be used in Excel as well, however it's available to you during run time programmatically. The design-time grouping is available in VB4—the Group command is not available in VB4, but you could use a Collection of objects in a similar fashion.

This ability to temporarily "weld" selected (or all) items in a collection has many uses in the world of Objects. It would be a way to resize, change the color, reposition, delete or otherwise maneuver the selected items. In fact, the ganged items themselves become a new Object.

The Ungroup command releases the grouping. For more on this, see the entry titled "Collection."

**Variables**

```
Object.Group
```

**Example**

There are two Subroutines here. The first merely displays and arranges three pictures onscreen (and also removes grid lines and other distractions). The second Sub groups two of the pictures into a single

Object called TwoPictures, then resizes and repositions the grouped images, leaving the other picture unaffected.

Notice that the Group command is used with the command that creates Objects. Also notice the Array command used to define which items within the DrawingObjects collection are to be grouped. The Array command, used within any Object collection, defines a subset of that collection.

Figure 11-32: Before we ganged Picture #1 with Picture #3.

Figure 11-33: We can simultaneously adjust the size and the position of the two Pictures when they are grouped.

```
Sub CreatePictures( )
    Sheets("Sheet1").Select
    With Application ‘ Remove distractions
        .DisplayFormulaBar = False
        .DisplayStatusBar = False
```

```
        .DisplayNoteIndicator = False
    End With
    ActiveWindow.DisplayGridlines = False

    ChDir "C:\GRAPHICS"
    ActiveSheet.Pictures.Insert("VG.BMP").Select 'insert a →
    picture

    Selection.Copy 'make two copies and separate them
    ActiveSheet.Paste
    ActiveSheet.DrawingObjects("Picture 2").Select
    Selection.Left = 184.5
    Selection.Top = 112.5

    ActiveSheet.Paste 'Make second copy
    ActiveSheet.DrawingObjects("Picture 3").Select
    Selection.Left = 348
    Selection.Top = 73.5

End Sub

Sub NowChangeGroup( )
Sheets("Sheet1").Select
Set TwoPictures = ActiveSheet.DrawingObjects(Array(1, →
3)).Group
TwoPictures.Select
    Selection.Width = 417
    Selection.Height = 156.75
    Selection.Left = 36.75
    Selection.Top = 142.5
Set TwoPictures = Nothing
End Sub
```

An alternate way to accomplish this grouping of Objects is to describe an Array in Literal terms. This doesn't use the Group command and therefore doesn't create a group Object. The Objects involved must be affected by the Select command, so this technique is less flexible than using Group (which can gang together any Objects).

The approach

```
ActiveSheet.DrawingObjects(Array("Picture 1", "Picture 3")). →
Select
```

is the same as using Group in this approach:

```
Set TwoPictures = ActiveSheet.DrawingObjects(Array(1,3)).Group
TwoPictures.Select
```

**If You Have Trouble**

If you get errors trying this or other examples in this book, look at the *Literals*—items within quotation marks. If you have no C:\GRAPHICS directory, or no ROMAN.BMP picture file within that directory, the example will not work.

```
ChDir "C:\GRAPHICS" 'insert a picture
ActiveSheet.Pictures.Insert("ROMAN.BMP").Select
```

You must replace these references with locations and files that do exist on your disk drive. Likewise, if your Excel workbook has no Sheet1, you'll need to insert a new sheet with that name or double-click on an existing sheet and rename it Sheet1.

**See Also**

Collection

# GROUPOBJECTS — object

**Description**

When you gang Objects together (using the Group command, described above), they become a new Object. In fact, you could gang one set of Objects, then a second set, then a third and so on. Each of these collections of Objects becomes part of a huge, hovering super Object. When you group some rectangles, they become part of a new GroupObjects collection, GroupObjects(1). If you group a second set of rectangles, they, in turn, can be referred to as GroupObjects(2), and so on.

**Example**

GroupObjects are an Array (of Object collections). Therefore, you refer to each GroupObjects entity with an index number: GroupObjects(3), for instance. Then you can change Properties in this fashion:

```
GroupObjects(2).Left = 340
```

**Example**

Figure 11-34: We'll group the bird and the tree, then move them down.

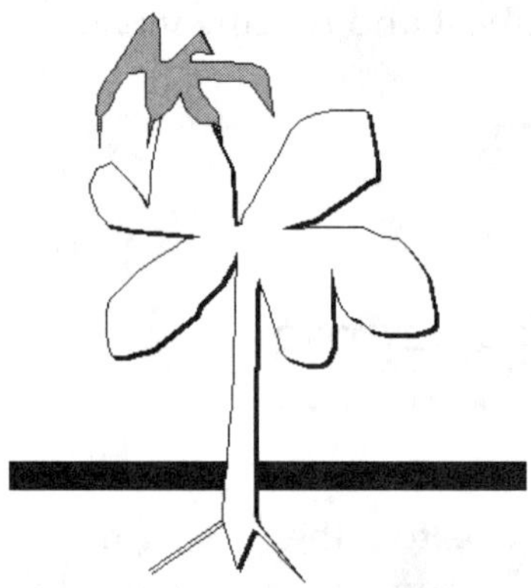

Figure 11-35: Now it looks more natural, with the horizon line higher.

Here we drew a freehand bird and tree, then added a horizon line with a filled rectangle (all from the Drawing toolbar in Excel). For convenience, in a kind of shorthand, we created a new Object Variable out of Sheet1. Now we can just use the Variable name OurSheet–it's simpler than typing **Sheets("Sheet1) or WorkSheets(1)** each time.

Then we grouped the bird and the tree into a collection that we named BirdInTree. This group automatically becomes GroupObjects(1) since it is the first group created on this worksheet. We can now freely use the Object called GroupObjects(1) to find out the common top of the group, and then move the group down onscreen. As always, use the UnGroup command to free them up (return them to their individual identities) after you are finished adjusting their collective behavior. Also release the two Object Variables by setting them to Nothing.

```
Sub Macro3( )
    Set OurSheet = Sheets("Sheet1")
    Set BirdInTree = OurSheet.Drawings(Array(1, 2)).Group
    t = OurSheet.GroupObjects(1).Top
    OurSheet.GroupObjects(1).Top = t + 75
    OurSheet.GroupObjects(1).Ungroup
    Set OurSheet = Nothing
    Set BirdInTree = Nothing
End Sub
```

An alternative would be to use the built-in DrawingObjects collection:

```
t = OurSheet.DrawingObjects(2).Top
OurSheet.DrawingObjects(2).Top = t - 75
```

**See Also** Collection, Group

# HELP

**method**

**Description** Brings up the typical Windows Help window, filled with the .HLP file you've specified.

**Variables**

```
Application.Help "NameOfHlpFile, ID%"
```

The NameOfHlpFile can be a single file name, WRDBASIC.HLP, or a complete path: C:\WINWORD\WRDBASIC.HLP.

If you leave out the NameOfHlpFile, the current application's Help window will appear:

```
Application.Help.
```

The optional ID% is a number that refers to a particular location (a specific topic) within the Help file.

**Example**

```
Sub FindHelp( )
    Application.Help "WRITE.HLP"
End Sub
```

# INCHESTOPOINTS method

**Description** Allows you to specify in inches the size, position, margins or other measurements for Objects. Like publishers and printers, VBA uses a unit of measurement much finer than the inch. A *point* is 1/72 of an inch. So if you see something like Oval.Width = 144, that would translate into 2 inches. We, however, often prefer to express things in inches, so VBA provides the translator feature InchesToPoints. (Actually, a point is 72.27 per inch, but so what?)

But wait. If you try to make something 2" X 2" square onscreen, then measure it, you'll find that it is larger than 2" X 2" and that it is, in fact, a rectangle, higher than it is wide. Computer screens are not intended to represent real dimensions. Instead, a computer screen compensates in various ways. The *true* measurement that is created by InchesToPoints is the measurement *on paper* when the Object is printed.

**Variables** Use it like a built-in Function that translates the measurement you give it (in the familiar inches) into the points the computer uses. Essentially, it multiplies the inches by 72. So

```
MyRectangle.Width = Application.InchesToPoints(4)
```

is the same as

```
MyRectangle.Width = 4 * 72
```

**Cautions** Computer screen measurements are not the same as the true (printed) measurements. Notice that Figure 11-37 is supposed to be 4" x 4" square, yet it appears in this screen capture to be longer than it is wide. In fact, measured onscreen, it is 5.25" x 5.75". However, when printed on paper (which is what InchestoPoints defines), it is a true 4" x 4" square.

**Example**

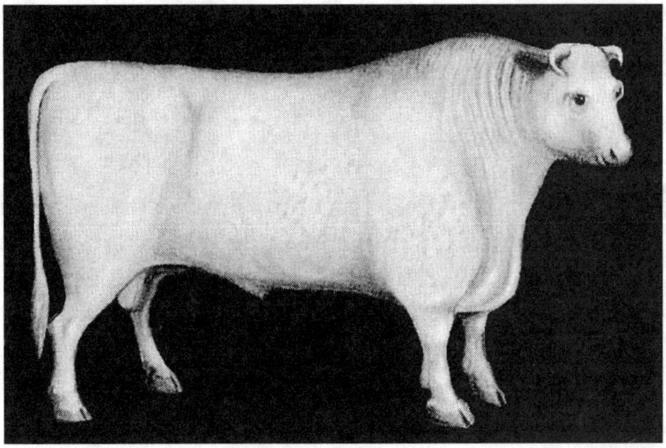

Figure 11-36: Bossy, before we translated inches to points.

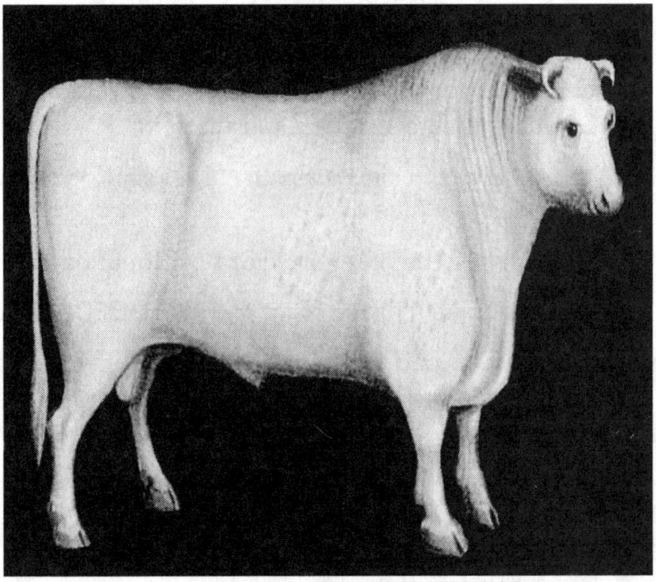

Figure 11-37: Bossy afterward, grown taller.

```
Sub Blowup( )
Worksheets(1).Select
    ActiveSheet.DrawingObjects("Picture 1").Width = _
Application.InchesToPoints(4)
    ActiveSheet.DrawingObjects("Picture 1").Height = _
Application.InchesToPoints(4)
End Sub
```

# INSERTFILE

**method**

**Description**

Similar to Include features found in other languages, VBA's InsertFile loads a text file into a Module while a macro is running. This allows you to add features to your macro on the fly, perhaps depending on a choice the user makes. Alternatively, you could load in a set of standardized Declares or Procedures that you've written before and like to use in most of your programs. However, at the time of this writing, this technique is buggy and we suggest you avoid it.

**Variables**

```
InsertFile Filename, Merge
```

The Merge feature puts the Declarations up at the top of the Module where they belong and keeps Sub...End Sub structures intact (rather than sticking the whole text file right into the middle of wherever the cursor happened to be last). Always use the merge feature, or you can end up with problems like those illustrated in Figure 11-39.

Using the new named parameters:

```
Modules(1).InsertFile fileName:="C:\EXCEL\DECLARES.TXT", →
Merge:=True
```

Or, using the older style of positional parameters:

```
Modules(1).InsertFile "C:\EXCEL\DECLARES.TXT", True
```

**Cautions**

You cannot load a file into the Module where you are currently running a macro. Therefore, if you are using the InsertFile command in Module2, specify that the file should be loaded into Module1 or some other Module.;

**Example**

```
Sub Only()
    Debug.Print "ME ALONE"
End Sub
```

Figure 11-38: This is Module1 prior to inserting the DECLARES.TXT file.

First you must save a text file (such as from Notepad) containing the Declares, Functions or Subroutines that you want included. Since we are going to insert this file into Modules(1) we have to run the following from Module2 or anywhere except Module1:

```
Sub InsertOne ( )
    Modules(1).InsertFile "C:\EXCEL\DECLARES.TXT"
End Sub
```

After we run this, there is a problem. Our little Subroutine in Figure 11-38 has been interrupted by the insertion:

```
  Sub Only()
      Debug.Print "ME ALONE"
Public UserName As String
Public Const Writername = "ME"


Function Square(num As Long) As Long
    Square = num * num
End Function


  End Sub
```

Figure 11-39: Bad news. Always leave the Merge option on if you don't want mangled Procedures like this.

Change the example to the following and run it again:

```
Modules(1).InsertFile "C:\EXCEL\DECLARES.TXT", True
```

```
Public UserName As String
Public Const Writername = "ME"


Function Square(num As Long) As Long
    Square = num * num
End Function


Sub Only()
  Debug.Print "ME ALONE"
End Sub
```

Figure 11-40: This is more like it; the Declares are at the top and our Procedures are intact.

## ITEM **method**

**Description** Not needed unless you want to use a separate Subroutine to adjust the Properties or invoke the Methods of an Object within an Object collection (see "Collection"). Available in VB4.

Normally, you can change the width of Picture #2 like this:

```
Sheets("Sheet1").Select
ActiveSheet.DrawingObjects(2).Width = 200
```

You just use the DrawingObjects collection (Array) and specify which element within that Array you are targeting—in this case, (2).

However, *if you want to pass an Object collection to a separate Function or Subroutine for manipulation, you must use the Item Method.* See the example below.

**Variables**

```
Object.Item(index number)
```

**Example**

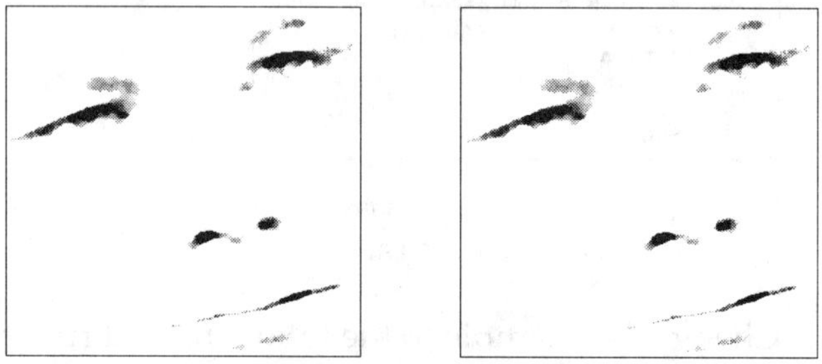

Figure 11-41: Two DrawingObjects at their normal width.

The only use for Item is when you want to pass an Object collection to a Subroutine or Function. In the remote procedure, you must specify the element of the collection—the index, such as (2)—by referring to the Item:

```
Sub DoItRemotely( )
    Sheets("Sheet1").Select
    Widen ActiveSheet.DrawingObjects
End Sub

Sub Widen(WhichOne As DrawingObjects)
    WhichOne.Item(2).Width = 300
End Sub
```

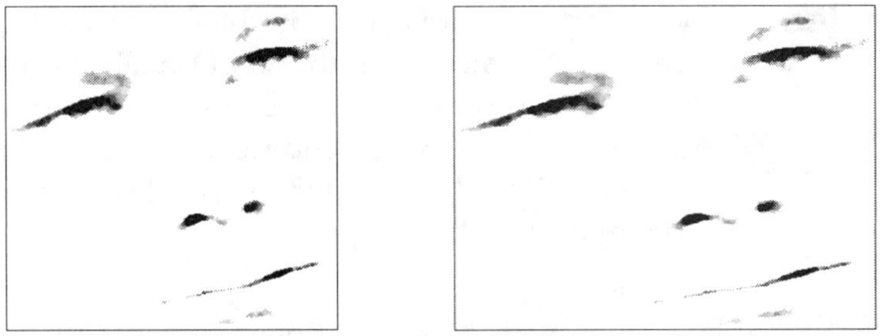

Figure 11-42: In this example, we changed the Width of Item(2).

**See Also** Collection

# LargeScroll, SmallScroll

**method**

**Description**

LargeScroll lets your program imitate the act of the user clicking *within* a scroll bar. In other words, the active window or pane scrolls by its largest amount. The result depends on the window in question. In a word processor, you move to the next visible page; in Excel, you move to the next window full of cells.

SmallScroll imitates the action when the user clicks on an arrow at either end of a scroll bar. In other words, a text document would move one line, and a spreadsheet would move by one row or column of cells.

These are not to be confused with VB's LargeChange and SmallChange Properties, which don't result in visible actions. LargeChange and SmallChange merely describe how much the "Thumb" button within a ScrollBar should move when the user clicks on the ends, or within, a ScrollBar. To imitate this behavior, change the Value Property of a ScrollBar in any version of VB.

**Variables**

```
Object.LargeScroll (down, up, toright, toleft)
```

Use the parameters as *named* parameters (down:=3).

The arguments can be negative, and you can move up, down, right or left.

**Examples** If you start out with cell A1 in the upper left-hand corner of Sheet1 in Excel, this can move you to cell BD55. (The actual cell depends on your screen resolution and the number of active toolbars. In standard VGA resolution, you can end up at cell AT33, for example.) It's just as if you had clicked twice in the vertical scroll bar and five times in the horizontal scroll bar.

```
Sub nanc( )
    Sheets("Sheet1").Select
    ActiveWindow.LargeScroll down:=2, toright:=5
End Sub
```

# MENUBARS method

**Description** MenuBars allows you to retrieve a menu bar, then add to it or find out how many menus are on it. Like most applications, Excel has several MenuBars, including xlWorkSheet, xlChart and xlModule. This permits your programs to manipulate the menu structures, just as if you had selected the Menu Editor from the Tools menu (by pressing Alt+T, D). Not available in VB4.

A MenuBar is the zone onscreen where the titles of menus such as File, Edit and Insert are listed horizontally. A Menu is the entire thing that drops down when you click on one of those titles. If you click on the title File, you'll see the file Menu, which lists the following *MenuItems*: New, Open, Close, Save, Save As and so on.

**Variables** You can manipulate two Objects with the MenuBars Method: a particular MenuBar Object (such as the macro menu that appears when you are viewing a Module) or the application's whole collection of MenuBar Objects.

To work with a single menu bar, use this:

```
Application.MenuBars(index)
```

The index can be an index number, or the name of the MenuBar you are after. (See the example below.)

Or to work with the whole MenuBars collection, use this:

```
Application.MenuBars
```

As the next example shows, you can use one of the application's built-in Constants to specify which menu bar you are after.

## Example

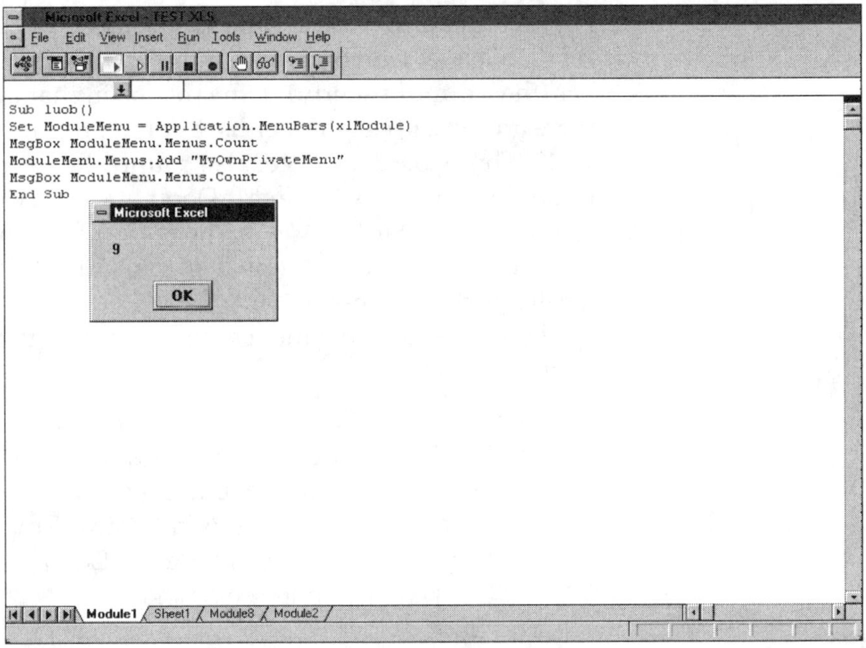


Figure 11-43: Module1's normal menus.

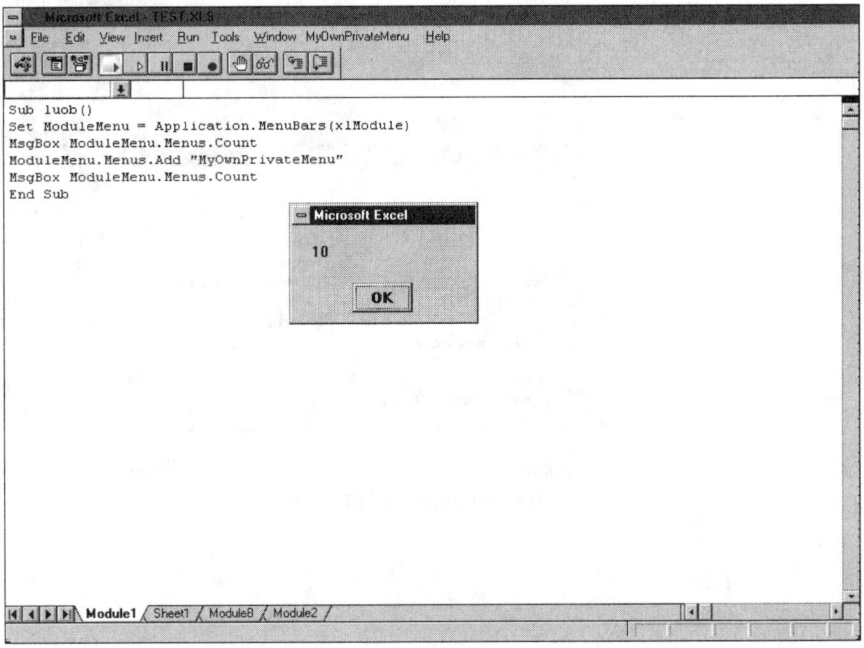


Figure 11-44: We've added a new one.

First we create an Object called *ModuleMenu*. This is the menu bar Excel displays when you are working in a Module. We display the number (the Count Property) of the menus in that menu bar. Note that there are actually eight menus, but the program reports nine in Figure 11-43. This is because Excel also counts the Command Button at the upper-left corner as Menu #1. Don't ask why. (It is more correct to call this button the *System Menu*. The reason Excel does this is directly related to how Windows implements menus: the System Menu is technically part of the menu bar.)

Then we add a new menu, as shown in Figure 11-44, and again display the Count.

```
Sub luob( )
    Set ModuleMenu = Application.MenuBars(xlModule)
    MsgBox ModuleMenu.Menus.Count
    ModuleMenu.Menus.Add "MyOwnPrivateMenu"
    MsgBox ModuleMenu.Menus.Count
    Set ModuleMenu = Nothing
End Sub
```

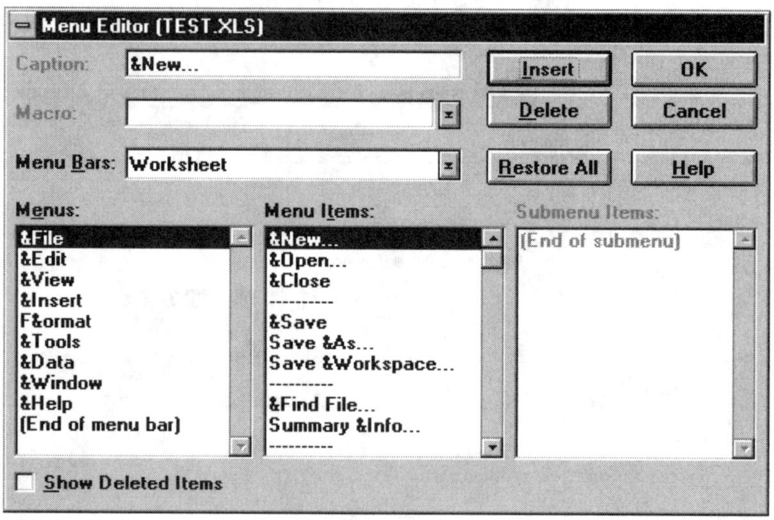


Figure 11-45: The MenuBars Method allows your program to do the things a user can do in this Menu Editor.

# MENUITEMS

**method**

**Description** Allows you to add new items to a menu or to get the Count (the number of items on a given menu).

**Example**

```
Sub SeeMenu( )
    Z = ActiveMenuBar.Menus("Run").MenuItems.Count
    MsgBox "There are " & Z & " menu items listed under Run"
End Sub
```

**See Also** MenuBars

# MENUS

**method**

**Description** Allows you to add new menus to a menu bar or to get the Count (the number of menus on a given menu bar).

**See Also** MenuBars

# MODULES

**method/object**

**Description** Allows you to manipulate the Modules in an Excel workbook. In Excel, a Module is where you write VBA programs (macros). A Module is a plain, blank sheet (as opposed to the typical worksheet, which, being a spreadsheet, is divided into a honeycomb of cells).

The Modules Method is one of a large number of paired entities (paired into a Method and an Object) that share the same name. Other examples are menus, worksheets, toolbars and dozens of others that are building blocks of Excel. When VBA is included in Word, Access and other applications, the elements of each application will be provided to you, the programmer, in this same way: as a Method or as an Object.

When you use one of these Method/Objects, the distinction between *Method* and *Object* becomes somewhat blurry. Everything can happen on a single line in your program. The Method provides you with an Object that you then use in the same line *as an Object* to change one of the Object's Properties or something else. In effect, it is simultaneously a Method and an Object.

As a Method, the Modules command simply provides you with a particular Module (or the whole Modules collection). Then you use this Object or Object collection (it can be done in the same programming line) by changing or querying its Properties or by invoking one of its Methods. For example, to get the Modules Object collection (Modules used as a Method), then immediately utilize that new Object (Modules used as an Object), do this:

```
Sub NewOne( )
    Application.Modules.Add
End Sub
```

In the example above, *Modules* is first being used as a Method. The same command is immediately reused as an Object to invoke the Add command.

The Modules Object has the following Properties: Application, Count, Parent and Visible. The Modules Object has the following Methods: Add, Copy, Delete, Item, Move, PrintOut and Select.

**Variables**

There are two objects you can access with the Modules Method: a particular Module Object (such as Module2) or the application's whole collection of Module Objects.

To work with a single Module, use this:

```
    Application.Modules(index)
```

The index can be an index number or the name of the Module you are after. For example, to make the second Module invisible, use this:

```
Application.Modules(2).Visible = False
```

Or you can use the alternative syntax, providing the name of the particular Module rather than its index number in the collection:

```
Application.Modules("Module3").Visible = False
```

Or you can access the entire collection of Modules, like this:

```
ActiveWorkbook.Modules.Visible = False
```

**Example** First we find out how many Modules exist in the current Excel workbook, then we find out the name of their "Parent." (In Excel, this would be the name of the workbook the Modules are a part of. In Word, it would be the name of the document.)

```
Sub DoMods( )
    Z = ActiveWorkbook.Modules.Count
    N = ActiveWorkbook.Modules.Parent.Name
    MsgBox "In the Workbook named " & N & " there are " _
        & Z & " Modules."
    ActiveWorkbook.Modules(2).Visible = False
End Sub
```

# MOVE method

**Description** In Excel, Move works only with Charts, dialog sheets, toolbar buttons and worksheets. It repositions the Object (as opposed to the Copy Method, which leaves the original in place, and creates a clone in another location). See the VB Move command.

**Variables** For every Object except a toolbar button, you specify the target position for the move with "before" or "after," referring to another Object of the same kind:

```
Application.Modules(2).Move before:=Modules("Module1")
```

Alternatively, you can specify a different *workbook* thus:

```
Application.Modules(2).Move before:= _
Workbooks("Book3").Modules("Module1")
```

Or when moving a toolbar button, you first give the toolbar name (it can be the same one), followed by which button to place it "before" (the button's *number*, with the first button as 1). See the example below.

**Cautions** When figuring out button numbers by their order on the toolbar, be sure to count spacers as well.

**Example**

Figure 11-46: The Forms toolbar in its native state (watch the X).

Figure 11-47: The Forms toolbar, after moving the X (the Check box button).

```
Sub ReOrder( )
    Toolbars(7).Visible = True
    Toolbars(7).ToolbarButtons(7).Move Toolbars(7), 18
End Sub
```

**Tip** To restore a toolbar to its original state, try this:

```
    Toolbars(7).Reset
```

**See Also** Copy, CopyFace

# NAMED ARGUMENTS parameters

**Description** The versions of Basic built into Word, Excel and Project now *name* their parameters, so you can list the parameters in any order. Although VBA in Excel (and even WordBasic) makes extensive, nearly universal use of named parameters, the only place you'll find this useful new syntax in VB4 is the Add and OpenDatabase Methods:

```
MyNames.Add Item := A$(I), Key := "Key#" & I In VB4,
```

However, as time goes on, we can expect VB to join this move toward named arguments. It would be particularly useful (for clarity as well as simplicity) with commands like Circle that have a slew of arguments.

Here's how it works. To define the typeface as 9 points large, not underlined, and turn strikethrough on, do this:

```
FormatFont .Points = "9", .Underline = 0, .Color = 0,  →
.Strikethrough = 1
```

Notice that each parameter (argument) has a label, a name. For example, the label Underline = 0 means that underlining is not turned on. Aside from being easy to read and understand, this labeling has a second advantage—it doesn't matter what *order* the items are in, nor does it matter whether you include them all.

Below, we'll use examples taken from Word. Recall that the punctuation of named parameters currently used by Word differs from the way VBA punctuates parameters. In Word you pass a named argument with a simple equal sign:

```
param = value
```

In VBA you use := (a colon + equals sign):

```
param:=value
```

For example, if you are interested in setting only the point size and strikethrough in Word, you could simply write this:

```
FormatFont .Points = "9" .Strikethrough = 1
```

You know that the default for underlining (or the current state of underlining) is fine as it is.

The order of these parameters is also irrelevant when they are labeled. This line

```
FormatFont .Points = "9" .Strikethrough = 1
```

does the same thing as

```
FormatFont .Strikethrough = 1 .Points = "9"
```

By contrast, in Visual Basic and previous Basics, there are (nearly universally) no such labels. When you want to describe a series of parameters, you have to include them all and in the correct order:

```
FormatFont "9", 0, 0, .Strikethrough = 1
```

Or you could leave out the defaults, but you still have to include spacers, or commas, to create the correct *position* for each item:

```
FormatFont "9", , , .Strikethrough = 1
```

For example, if you were not concerned about strikethrough, you could leave out the extra spacer commas, but if you did want to effect strikethrough, those commas were essential. The full list of parameters for Word's FormatFont command includes 17 items:

```
FormatFont .Points = "9", .Underline = 0, .Color = 0,
.Strikethrough = 0, .Superscript = 0, .Subscript = 0,
.Hidden = 0, .SmallCaps = 0, .AllCaps = 0, .Spacing = "0
pt", .Position = "0 pt", .Kerning = 0, .KerningMin = "", .Tab
= "0", .Font = "Modern", .Bold = 1, .Italic = 0
```

Obviously, turning on italics, the final item in the list, is cumbersome in the old style, where position matters:

```
FormatFont "9", , , , , , , , , , , , , , , 1
```

Yet it is very simple in the new style:

```
FormatFont .Italic = 0
```

As a plus, programs are more readable when you are allowed to mix and match parameters. We can all look forward to the time when Visual Basic and all other versions of Basic join VBA Excel, VBA Project and WordBasic in this more efficient and more natural approach to describing things. This should happen soon.

## NewWindow — method

**Description** Creates a new window in the application. A new window in Word would be a new "instance" of the document; in Excel, it's a new window, with a copy of the contents of the original window. In VB, see "MDI Form."

**Variables**

```
workbooks("TEXT.XLS").NewWindow
```

**Example**

Figure 11-48: A single window (in Excel, it's a workbook).

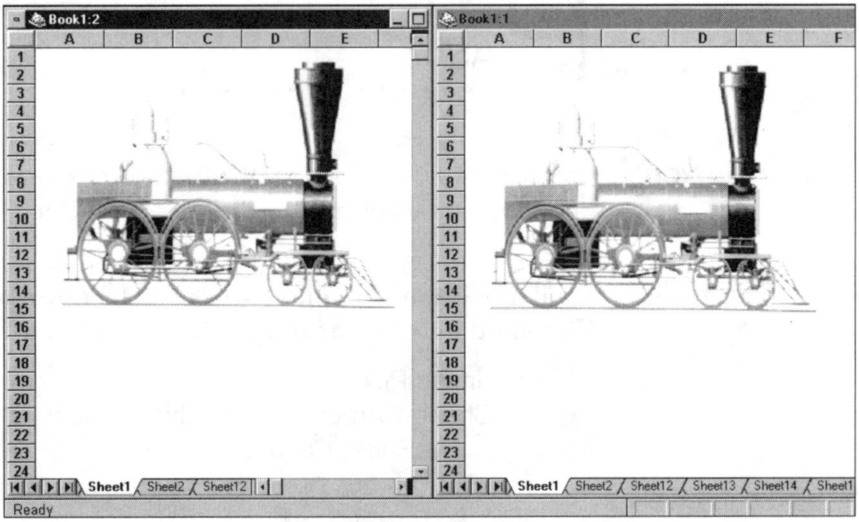

Figure 11-49: After NewWindow, we have a clone.

```
Sub DoName( )
    Workbooks(1).NewWindow
End Sub
```

**See Also** Copy

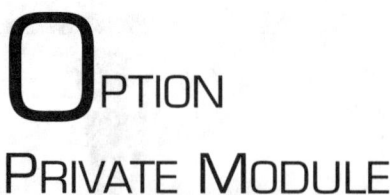

# OPTION PRIVATE MODULE

**statement**

This command, placed at the top of a Module, makes the Module's Procedures unavailable to any other Modules in the program. However, its public (see Public) Variables, Objects or user-defined Type Variables are still available outside the Module. See Private and Public in VB.

**Uses** To limit the range of influence of a Variable, Constant or Procedure to the Module in which it is located.

# PASTE

**method**

**Description** Can paste something from the Clipboard to a worksheet, dialog sheet or Chart. For additional techniques, see "Copy." In VB, see GetData or GetText.

**Example** We'll move a picture into a worksheet. Paste stuffs *whatever* is in the Clipboard into the currently active document.

```
Sub InsertPic( )
    Sheets("Amortization Table").Select
    ActiveSheet.Paste
End Sub
```

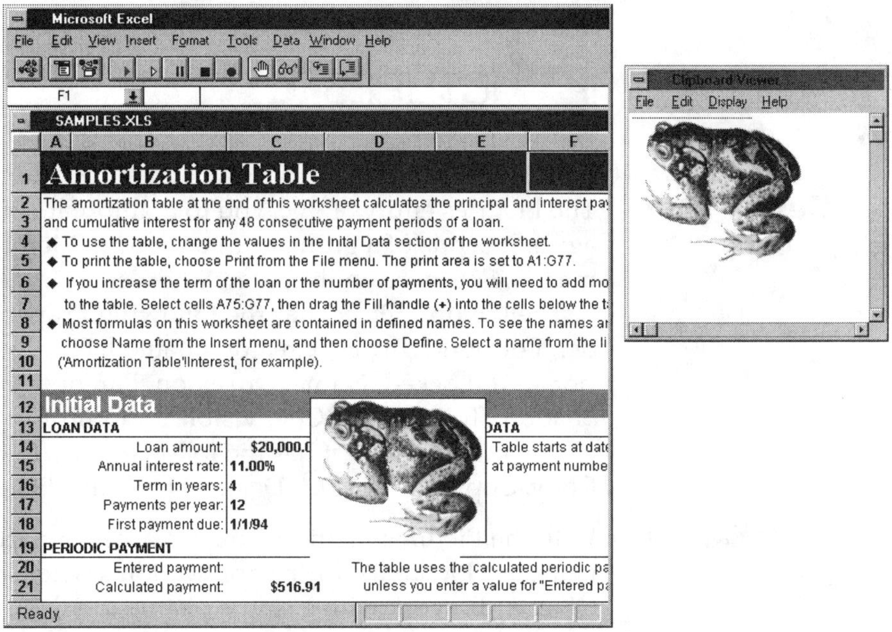


Figure 11-50: Paste moves the contents of the Windows Clipboard into the currently active document.

**See Also** Duplicate, Cut, Copy, Move

# PASTEFACE *method*

**Used With** Toolbar buttons only.

**Description** You can copy the image (the icon graphic) from one button to another. Use the CopyFace command, followed by the PasteFace command. In VB4, see the ImageList Control.

**Example** See CopyFace.

# PICTURES

**method/object**

**Description**

The Pictures entity allows you to manipulate pictures (graphic images). It is one of a group of dual-nature (Method/Object) commands. For more on this, see "Modules."

The Pictures Object has the following Properties: Application, Border, BottomRightCell, Creator, Enabled, Formula, Height, Index, Interior, Left, Locked, Name, OnAction, Parent, Placement, PrintObject, Shadow, Top, TopLeftCell, Visible and Width.

The Pictures Object has the following Methods: BringToFront, Copy, CopyPicture, Cut, Delete, Duplicate, Select and SendToBack.

**Variables**

With the Pictures Method, you can access a particular Picture Object (such as "Picture2") or the application's whole collection of Picture Objects. To work with a single picture, do this:

```
Application.Pictures(index)
```

The index can be an index number or the name of the picture you are after. You can make the second picture invisible like this:

```
Application.Pictures(2).Visible = False
```

Or you can use the alternative syntax, providing the name of the particular picture rather than its index number in the collection:

```
Application.Pictures("Module3").Visible = False
```

Or you can access the entire collection of pictures in the currently active workbook:

```
ActiveWorkbook.Pictures.Visible = False
```

Or do this, to work with the whole Pictures collection:

```
Application.Pictures
```

**Example**

Insert a picture (Alt+I, P) into a document or spreadsheet. Then copy it using the Duplicate command. The copy inherits all the qualities (Properties) of the original picture, including *position*. So to see it, you have to adjust its position after you've made the copy.

```
Sub MM( )
    Sheets("Sheet1").Select
    Set Marilyn = ActiveSheet.Pictures("Picture 1").Duplicate
    Marilyn.Select
    Marilyn.Left = 300
    Set Marilyn = Nothing
End Sub
```

**Note** You can also use the syntax:

```
Set Marilyn = ActiveSheet.Pictures(1).Duplicate
```

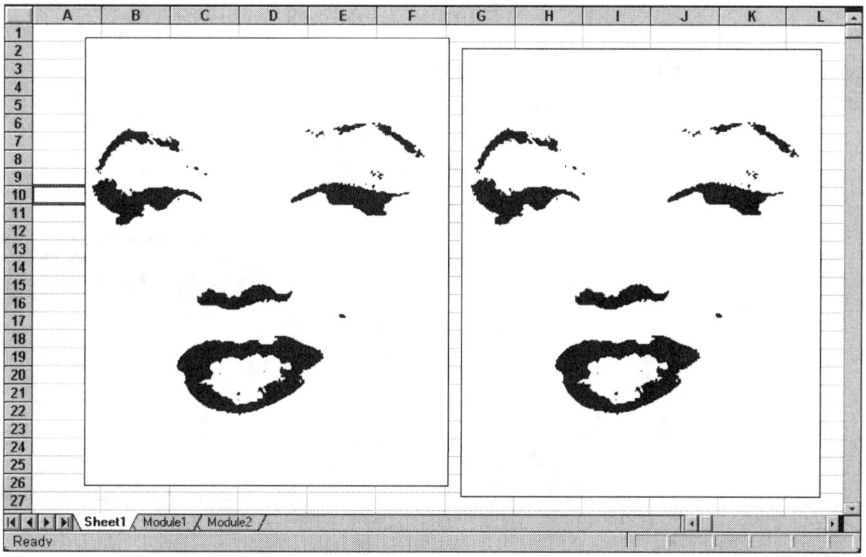


Figure 11-51: Copying pictures of Marilyn.

# PRINT method

**Description** The Print command can be used only with the Debug Object, for purposes of debugging your programs. If you want to print something to your printer, use the PrintOut command (described later).

Debug.Print and MsgBox are currently the best ways to watch how your program is behaving. In Excel, you cannot print Intermediate results directly to a document (as in Word) or to a Form (as in Visual Basic). Often, when you want to see what's happening to your Variables or expressions, you'll step through a program and use Debug.Print. Whatever is printed is sent to the Immediate pane of the Debug window, as shown in Figure 11-52.

**Variables**

Debug.Print *expression*.

The thing you print, the expression, can be any Text or Numeric Variable or combination of the two (an expression is a Compound Variable). You can also include Constants or *Literals* (the actual number 13, for instance, in our example below).

**Example**

```
Sub ToImmediate( )
    Z = 12
    Debug.Print Z * 13
End Sub
```

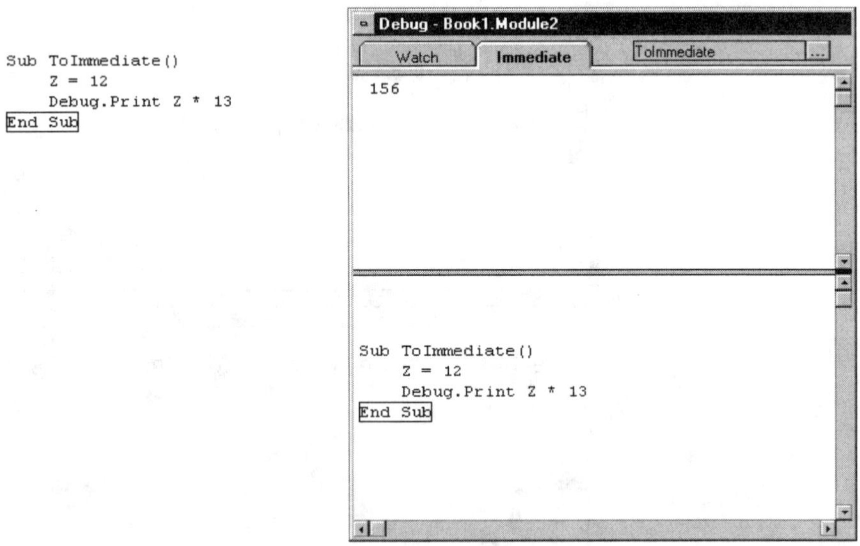


Figure 11-52: The Module on the left sends its results to the Immediate window, via Debug.Print.

**See Also** PrintOut, PrintPreview

# PRINTOUT, PRINTPREVIEW method

**Description**

PrintOut prints something to your printer. Which Objects (windows, documents, etc.) can actually be sent to the printer differs from application to application. Excel can PrintOut Charts, dialog sheets, Modules, ranges, worksheets or the singular equivalent of each. In other words, you can PrintOut all Modules or a specified Module.

In addition, you can PrintOut a window or any entire workbook. Using the From and To parameters, you can specify a range within these Objects. You can also specify the number of copies and request a print preview onscreen.

The Print Preview feature can be incorporated into the PrintOut command (as the final parameter). Alternatively, you can use PrintPreview alone, in this fashion:

```
ActiveSheet.PrintPreview
```

PrintPreview shows onscreen exactly how the document will look when printed by the printer.

**Variables**

```
Object.PrintOut From, To, Copies, Preview
```

From and To describe which range of *pages* (or other subdivision appropriate to the Object being printed) to send to the printer. Note that in Excel, these numbers do not refer to the worksheets' Array numbers: worksheets(1) might well print as page 3. Nor do the numbers refer to the default names Excel provides when you create a new worksheet: WorkSheets("Sheet2") might print as the first page. *The pages are printed in order of the tabs on the scroll bar at the bottom of an Excel window.*

Copies describes the number of separate copies you want printed. Preview is False (off) by default. If you request it, you will be shown the Print Preview screen, where you can view a WYSIWYG display of the pages. The following will print a single copy from pages 1 to 3, with no print preview:

```
WorkSheets.Printout 1, 3, 1
```

**Example** This example uses the *named* parameters rather than the *positional* parameters illustrated under Variables above. Here we print page 2 only, a single copy, and provide a print preview (in which the user can cancel the print job).

```
WorkSheets.Printout From:=2, To:=2, Copies:=1, →
Preview:=True
```

# PRIVATE

**statement**

**Description** If you want to limit the scope of a Variable, Procedure, Constant, Array or all the Procedures inside a particular Module, describe these things with the Private command. Thereafter, nothing outside the current Module can change or find out the contents of (read or write to) that entity.

```
Private MyVariable As Integer
    Private MyVar%
    Private MyArray(1 To 5) As String
    Private MyVar, OtherVar, SomeText$, NewText as String
    Private MySub ( )
```

The Private Statement is, you must have guessed, the inverted counterpart to the Public Statement.

**Cautions** Note that the Private Statement is quite similar to the Dim Statement. Dim differs from Private only in that Dim can also be used within a Procedure (a Sub or Function); Private cannot.

Private can also be used to restrict the scope (the effective range of influence or access) of a Procedure. One way is to define the Procedure by including the Private Statement:

```
Private Function MyFunction ( )
```

Private can also be an "adjective" describing the scope of the following:

- Subroutines:

```
Private MySub ( )
```

- Constants:

```
Private WhiteHouse = "Big Government"
```

- Property Procedures:

```
Private Property Get MyProp
```

- Type Variables (which see):

```
Private Type OurCompany
    Num As Integer
    FirstName As String * 30
    LastName As String * 50
    Address As String * 100
    PhoneNum As Long
    HireDate As Date
End Type
```

# Property Get, Property Let, Property Set (see "Property Procedure")

# Property Procedure procedure

**Description**

A *Property* is a quality of an object. For example, an application's title bar has a "caption," some text that describes the application. By default, the application's Caption Property will be the name Microsoft gave the application, such as "Microsoft Excel" or "Microsoft Word." However, you can change this default caption. The normal way to change a Property is to simply assign a new value to it:

```
Application.Caption = "Not Excel Anymore"
```

However, VBA lets you create a special kind of Procedure that also changes a Property. Most people have learned that a *Procedure* is a Subroutine or a Function. However, VBA now adds a somewhat peculiar kind of Procedure to the Basic language.

You can think of a Property Procedure as a kind of Global Variable that can *react* to values assigned to it or returned by it. The created Property is *a Property of the Module*, though, unlike an ordinary Property of an Object (such as the Color Property of a text box). In VB4, see the Property Let, Property Set and Property Get statements.

### The Purpose of Property Procedures

What's the point of creating this new category of Procedure? Objects are supposed to be sealed off from the outside world, except for a select few doors through which the outside world can influence their Properties (like their color) or trigger their behaviors (their Methods). People aren't supposed to get into the Object's innards and start making changes. But you want some way that something outside an Object can change its Properties. The Property Procedure is the way an object exposes its qualities, giving permission for an outside agent to make changes in this limited way.

A case in point: Let's say that you want to create an Object that shuts down Excel. You've decided that this Object will be a blue button that sits on the Excel toolbar. All Objects have two essential parts: what they do and how they look. What this one does is kill the running Excel (that's its Method, its activity). How this Object looks is blue, by default. We want the user to be able to access the Method, so we program a Function or Subroutine to shut down Excel. And we give the user permission to access this Function or Procedure to trigger the collapse of Excel. But we also want to let the user optionally change the color of the object from blue to something that pleases him or her more. To do this, we also expose (give permission to access) this new kind of Procedure, the Property Procedure, which accepts the user's choice of color and modifies the Object accordingly.

There are three flavors of Property Procedures: Property Let "sets" a value (like changing the contents of a Variable); Property Get "reads" or "returns" a value (like finding out the contents of a Variable); and Property Set creates a reference to an Object (like using the Set command to create a new Object Variable; see Chapter 4).

❒ Use Property Let when you assign a value to the Property.

❒ Use Property Set when you assign an object reference to the variable with the Set statement.

❒ Use Property Get when you access the contents of the property.

The syntax (the stub) for the Property Procedure is similar to a Sub or Function Procedure:

```
Property Let MyName (ReceivedVariables)
    (your programming goes here)
End Property
```

Then, when you invoke a Property Procedure, you use a unique syntax (unlike a Sub or Function call). You put the passed argument to the right of an equal sign, as in

```
MyName = "Stan"
```

or

```
N$ = "Stan"
MyName = N$
```

If you are sending more than a single argument to a Property Procedure, you enclose all arguments in parentheses, *except for the final argument,* which goes on the other side of an equal sign:

```
    MyName (FirstSentArg, SecondSentArg) = ThirdSentArg
```

**Example**

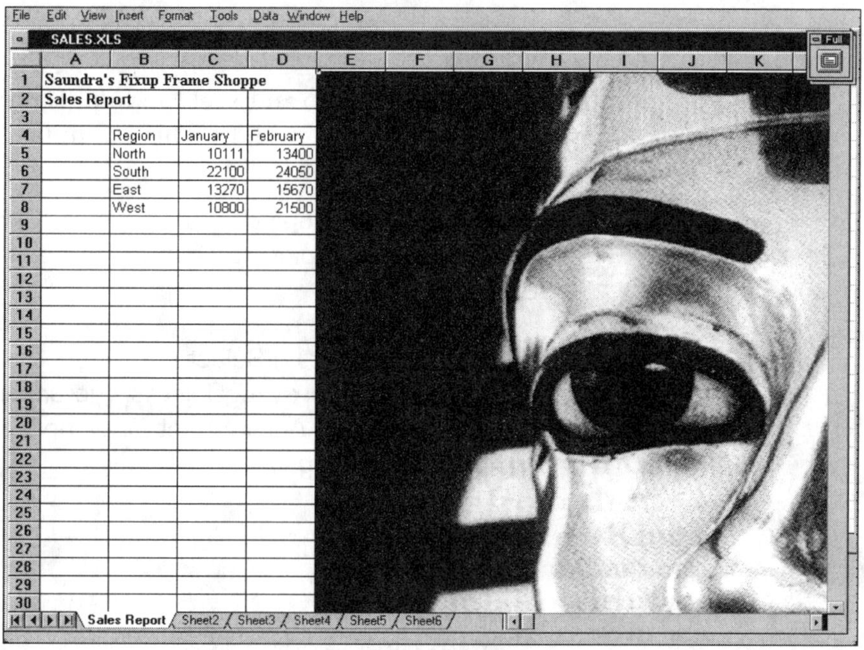


Figure 11-53: We can use a Property Procedure to reduce this graphic.

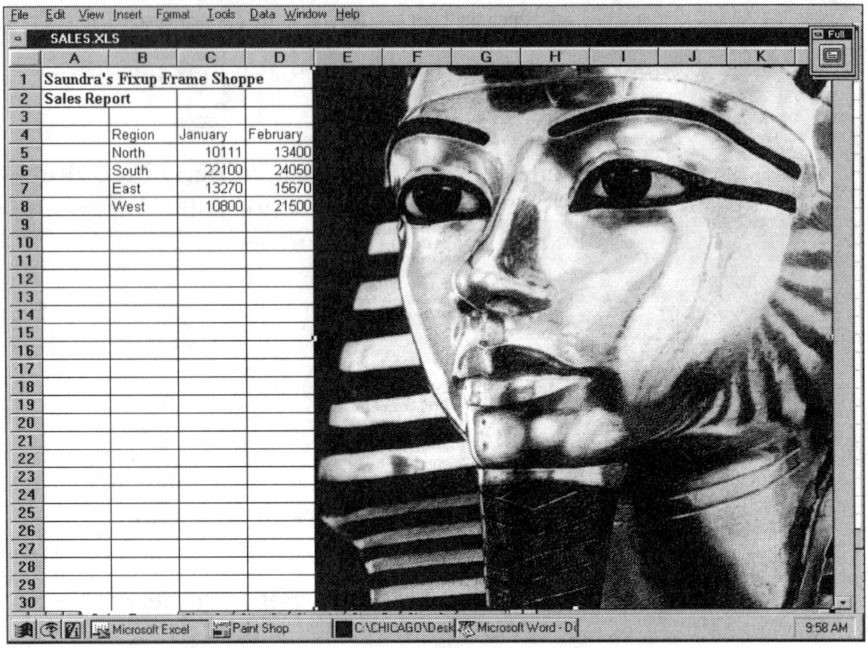


Figure 11-54: Now it fits precisely where it should.

Type the following into an Excel Module. Then insert a picture into Sheet1 in Excel (press Alt+I, P). This example uses a Property Procedure named UpDown to adjust the picture.

```
Dim TheOne As Object
    'Enlarges the picture
Sub adjustUp( )
    Dim v As Variant
    Sheets("Sheet1").Select
    ActiveSheet.DrawingObjects("Picture 1").Select
    Set TheOne = ActiveSheet.DrawingObjects("Picture 1")
    UpDown = "Big"
End Sub

'Reduces the picture
Sub adjustDown( )
    Dim v As Variant
    Sheets("Sheet1").Select
    ActiveSheet.DrawingObjects("Picture 1").Select
    Set TheOne = ActiveSheet.DrawingObjects("Picture 1")
    UpDown = "Small"
End Sub
```

```
Property Let UpDown(Size As String)
    If Size = "Big" Then
    TheOne.Height = 1200
    TheOne.Width = 1200
    Else
    TheOne.Height = 400
    TheOne.Width = 400
    End If
End Property
```

# PUBLIC (AKA "GLOBAL") **statement**

**Description**

This Statement used to be called *Global,* but now you can use either *Public* or *Global.* The Public command defines a Variable (or Constant or Procedure) that will be available to all parts of your program. In the case of a macro-oriented application like Excel, the Variable will be available to *all* Modules. Public can be used only at the top of a VBA Module (prior to any Procedures in that Module) or in the General Declarations section of a Visual Basic program.

If you don't declare a Variable as Public, it will by default be available for use only within a single Procedure. (There are two other options: Dim and Private make a Variable available Module-wide, but not in other Modules. Dim can also be used within a single Procedure.)

Variables can have different zones of influence. They can differ in how widely throughout the program the Variable can be read (to find out what it contains, its value) or written to (to change its value).

A Variable declared (using ReDim) within a single Procedure (a Subroutine or Function) can be read or written to only within that Procedure. Unless it is an Array (described earlier), you don't even have to officially declare a Variable with ReDim; you can just use it.

A Variable declared (using Dim) within the General Declarations section of a VB Form or at the top of a VBA Module is available to all the Subs or Functions in that Form or Module. But a Variable declared using Public is available to every section of your entire program.

The range of a Variable's influence is called its *scope*. You determine scope by the location where you declare a Variable. And where you declare it governs which of the three Variable declaration commands you can use: Public (Global), Private (Dim) or ReDim. (Static is a fourth way of declaring Variables and Arrays, and it is a special case. Static preserves the contents of the Variables in the Procedure where it's used.)

Also note that scope applies to Procedures as well. Although not explicitly needed, because Procedures are Public by default, some programmers find it useful to declare a Procedure Private. That Procedure then cannot be called from other Modules. To make a Procedure Private, do this:

```
Private Sub MySubroutine ( )
    (your programming goes here)
End Sub
```

**Used With** Variables, Arrays and Procedures.

**Variables** You can do any of the following:

- ❒ Provide the Variable's name with no specification about its Variable type. The Variable defaults to a Variant type:

```
Public Update
```

- ❒ Declare a Variable type other than the default by stating the type as a word, with the As command:

```
Public Reminder As String
```

- ❒ Declare a Variable type other than the default, by attaching the type's symbol to the Variable name. This Variable becomes a Text String Variable because $ is the text symbol:

```
Public Reminder$
```

- ❒ Declare an Array. An Array is a cluster of Variables of the same type. An Array uses index numbers to distinguish the different items within the Array because all the items share the same name.
- ❒ Create Arrays for related pieces of information, such as a list of the names and addresses of all your telephone contacts. Names(4) is a different Variable than Names(41). Arrays are useful because you can use them in loops and keep changing the

Variable by simply changing the index—an index is subject to mathematical manipulation, where text names are not. This Array can contain 51 names, because we "dimension" it to 50 (the index numbers range from 0 to 50):

```
Public Names$(50)
```

- ❒ Declare an Array, the index numbers of which range from 1 to 50:

```
Public Names (1 To 50) As String
```

- ❒ Declare a fixed-length String (Text) Variable. Unless you specifically declare a string as fixed, all String Variables are dynamic and adjust in size to accommodate the text you store in them. Certain special situations require fixed-length strings. (See the Get command.)

  Notice that the Public Declarations involving strings above created space for strings (Text Variables) of varying size (in other words, "dynamic Variables" that can resize themselves while a program runs). Public Names (1 To 50) would allow you to put the name William P. Sanderson III into a single one of the 50 "cells" we created in the preceding example Array.

  However, when you declare a fixed-length string, you are defining the number of characters that this Variable can hold, not the number of Variable-length text items. Fixed-length strings are a special type of Variable and are not true Arrays at all. This example creates a string 75 characters in length:

```
Public WelshForHelp As String * 75
```

- ❒ Declare a multidimensional Array—one having 12 rows and 3 columns. This is a way to link related information, such as 12 names, each with an address and phone number Variable. VBA allows you to create as many as 60 dimensions for a single Array! It has been reported, however, that the one programmer who did try to use 60 dimensions ended up quitting programming and moving to Quebec to sell greeting cards in a mall. Be warned.

  A two-dimensional Array is like a graph, a crossword puzzle or a spreadsheet. Cells of information are related in an X-Y coordinate system. A three-dimensional Array is like a honeycomb—it has not only width and height, but also depth.

You would read a two-dimensional Array like this: X$ = Names (6,2). For example, this is how you would the address of the sixth person in this Array:

```
Public Names$ (1 To 12, 1 To 3)
```

(We're storing the addresses in the second dimension.)

- ❒ Define a dynamic Array. These are handy because they conserve memory. Dynamic Arrays come into existence in your program when they are needed, but go away as soon as you leave the Sub or Function where they reside. The ReDim Statement is used within a Sub or Function to bring a dynamic Array to life, but you can optionally declare a dynamic Array using Public with empty parentheses:

```
Public Ages ( ) As Integer
```

Or you can combine several declarations on one line following a Public Statement:

```
Public A, B( ), Counter as Integer, X$, L (12 To 4)
```

**Uses** Use Public to make the contents of a Variable (or Array or Constant) available to your entire program (you can also declare an entire Procedure, Subroutine, Event or Function to be Public, and all the Variables within it then become Public in scope):

```
Public MySubroutine
```

Public Variables are accessible from any location in your program. Any instructions in any Module, Form, Function or Subroutine can find out or change the Variable's value.

**Cautions** Most versions of Basic allow you to implicitly create an Array by just using it, like this:

```
Sub FormClick( )
    For i = 1 To 8
    a(i) = i
Next
```

This is not permitted in VBA. VBA requires that you formally declare all Arrays using Public or Dim (in a Module) or ReDim or Dim (in Subs or Functions):

```
Public a(1 To 12) As Integer
    Sub FormClick( )
```

```
        For i = 1 To 8
        a(i) = i
        Next
        For Each n In a
        Debug.Print n
        Next
    End Sub
```

However, ordinary non-Array Variables can be implicitly declared by simply using them.

You can use Public with the special Type Variable structure.

There are limits to Arrays, but the limits go way beyond what you'll ever need. Indices can be negative (Public History (–3000 To 1992)), but an Array's size (the number of items in it, its index range) can at best range only between –32,768 and 32,767. Most Variable types cannot have indices this large.

How large a given index can be depends on the Variable type because Variables take up differing amounts of memory. For example, a Variable such as an Integer (with no fractions or decimal points involved) takes up two bytes of computer memory. You can use an index of up to 16,383 with Integers (Public Maximum Integer (16383)).

Overflow can be a problem if you use too many indices. Variable types such as floating point (decimals involved) obviously take up more memory, and Arrays of floating-point numbers cannot have as many items as can Integer Arrays. If you get too ambitious with indices, VBA will offer an error message such as "Overflow" or "Subscript Out Of Range." But in normal life, these large indices are seldom needed. You could always create two Arrays, or a multidimensional Array, if you need to work with more items than a single Array can contain.

You can't use Public inside or between Procedures. You can use it only at the top of a Module (or in VB, in the General Declarations section).

Don't overuse Public Variables. Sure, it's convenient to have a Variable that's available to all Events, Subs and Functions. If you like to build programs from a personal toolkit of Subroutines, you don't want to have to check for duplicated Variable names every time you add a Public Variable. It's best to be conservative. Or use very strange names, such as adding *P* to the end of each Public Variable name: NameP$, for instance, to identify the Variable as Public. Microsoft Consulting Services (MCS) has set up a standard that uses prefixes, in lowercase, to identify all kinds of variables. For example, they use *g* for global and *i* for integer. So to identify a global integer variable, you could name it "giBuildHouse." Be aware that you can create havoc if you import Subroutines that share Variable names with Public Variables.

**See Also** Private, Dim, ReDim, Static

## QUIT

**method**

**Description** Closes the application. If you have macros designed to be triggered when the user closes the application, *they will not be triggered*. However, if the user has changed data, the typical "Do you want to save?" message boxes will appear before the application shuts down. In VB, see the End command.

You can prevent even these warning message boxes by setting the DisplayAlerts Property to False:

```
Application.DisplayAlerts = False
```

**Example** This is the only syntax:

```
Application.Quit
```

**See Also** The Close command (as it applies to windows and workbooks)

## RANGE

**method/object**

**Description** Allows you to manipulate ranges in an Excel workbook. In Excel, a *range* is a group of contiguous spreadsheet cells (or a single cell).

The Range Method/Object is one of a large number of paired entities (a Method and an Object) that share the same name. Other examples are menus, worksheets, toolbars, Modules and dozens of others. For more on Method/Objects, see "Modules."

**Variables**

Cells are the primary container for data in a spreadsheet. Thus it is predictable that the Excel version of VBA provides considerable flexibility for manipulating ranges. Defining a range permits you to collectively query or manipulate its cells—change their appearance and size, copy them to a different location and so on. Here is an overview of various ways to address ranges in Excel VBA:

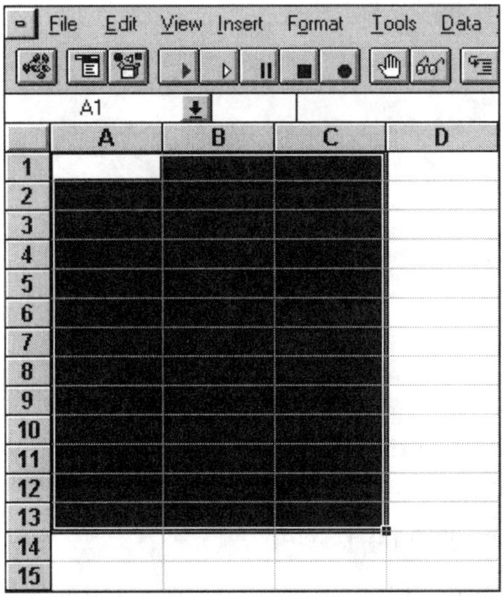


Figure 11-55: A range from cell A1 to C13, selected.

This syntax describes the upper-left, then lower-right, dimensions of the range:

```
Sheets("Sheet1").Select
    ActiveSheet.Range("A1:C13").Select
```

And this syntax selects a single cell:

```
ActiveSheet.Range("A14").Select
```

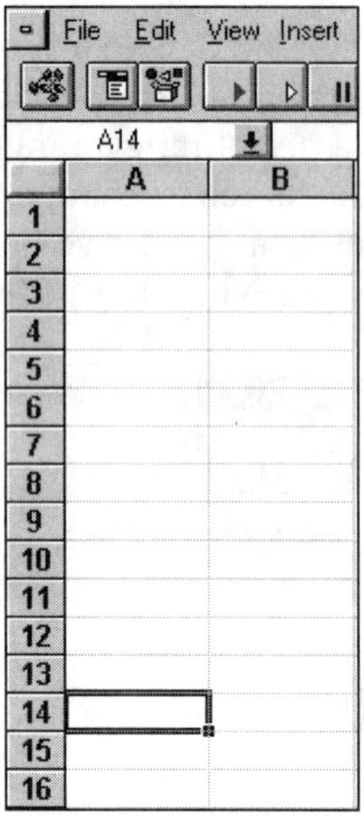

Figure 11-56: A single-celled range, selected.

If you mean to refer to the current worksheet, you can leave out ActiveSheet and use this shortcut:

```
Range("A14").Select
```

This works only if the current sheet is actually a worksheet, and not a Module.

If you want to adjust the contents of a range of cells, you must first establish the range, adding the Cells command. See the example below.

**Example** To make changes to the contents of a range, use the Cells command:

```
Sub DoRange( )
    Sheets("Sheet1").Select
    Range(Cells(3, 3), Cells(6, 6)).Value = "SEE!"
End Sub
```

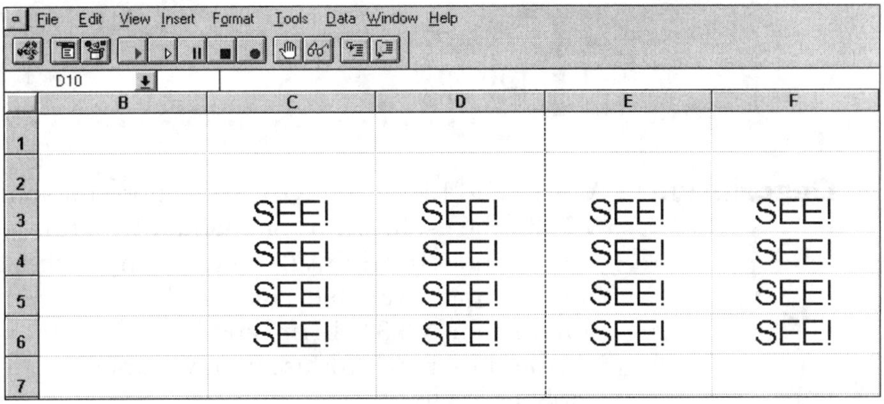


Figure 11-57: To fill all the cells, combine the Cells command with the Range command.

**See Also** Cells

# SendToBack (see "BringToFront")

# ToolbarButtons, Toolbars (see "CopyFace")

# TRIM

**function**

**Description**

VB has had LTrim and RTrim Functions for some time. Now VBA and VB add the useful Trim command. LTrim (these commands are called LTrim$ and RTrim$ in VB) removes any spaces from the left side of a Text ("String") Variable. (Technically, there are two versions of this command in VB 3.0, LTrim and LTrim$. LTrim is for use with Variants, and LTrim$ is for use with variable-length strings.) When you apply LTrim to

```
        Andy Doodie
```

the result is:

```
Andy Doodie
```

RTrim removes extraneous spaces from the right side of a Text Variable. *Trim* is a combination of the two, stripping off extra spaces from both sides of a piece of text.

**Used With**

Text ("String") Variables

**Variables**

```
A$ = "  Nobody home. Eat your fish!                 "
Debug.Print Trim$(A$)
```

**Results in**

Nobody home. Eat your fish!
You can assign the results to a Text Variable, like this

```
X$ = Trim(A$)
    Debug.Print X$
```

**Results in**

Nobody home. Eat your fish!

**Uses**

- ❒ Clean up user input. You can never tell what the user might do. When typing in a lot of data, the user might accidentally hit the Tab key or enter some extra spaces. If your program is going to alphabetize a list and one of the items has a space as its first character, that item will appear before the A's. To prevent this, you want to clean up any items you are about to alphabetize (or compare, such as If A$ < B$). So use Trim to make sure that you are comparing apples to apples and not dealing with some accidental leading or trailing spaces in a piece of text. And while you're at it, eliminate random capitalization with the LCase$ Function, too. (For an alternative to LCase$, see "StrComp.")

- Clean up numbers translated by Str$. You can transform a number into a Text ("String") Variable (into printable digits rather than a pure number) by using Str$(X). However, Str$ inserts an extra space in front of a number to provide room for a minus sign. Trim is a way of getting rid of this extra space. (See the example below.)
- When reading text files, you can remove paragraph indentations, centering or other formatting that involves using space characters to achieve a visual effect.

**Cautions** Trim works the same with either variable-length or fixed-length Text ("String") Variables.

**Example** When you use the Str$ command to transform a number (a Numeric Variable) into a Text ("String") Variable, Basic inserts an extra space to allow for a possible minus (–) sign. This has mystified programmers for a generation, but that's what happens. The space is inserted so that a column of numbers would line up when displayed if you added a space to positive numbers and left negative numbers with their minus (–) sign intact.

However, contemporary computers no longer format columns by counting character spaces. This is a holdover from the hoary DOS method of displaying text characters in equally spaced "cells" onscreen. The characters in Windows are much lovelier, much more the way you see things professionally printed in books. Windows characters are *proportional* (the characters vary in width), so it is useless to use character-cell-spacing as a way of formatting or lining up columns of displayed text.

Nonetheless, Str$ still adds a space character to the left of a positive number. Trim gets rid of the space. Here's an example:

```
Sub FixIt( )
    x = 144
        Debug.Print x
    y$ = Str$(x)
        Debug.Print y$
        Debug.Print Trim(y$)
    x = 144
        Debug.Print x
    y$ = Str$(x)
        Debug.Print y$
        Debug.Print Trim(y$)
```

```
      x = -12
          Debug.Print Trim(x)
  End Sub
```

**Results in**

```
144
 144
144
 144
 144
144
-12
```

Note that Trim does not remove symbols like the minus sign. Note also that you can forget all about Str$ Variable conversions if you use the Variant Variable type.

**See Also** LSet, RSet

## TYPE

**statement**

**Description**

The Type command is used in a Module to declare custom, user-defined Variable types. This is not a new command to Basic. However, the Type structure in VBA can contain Objects as well as dynamic Arrays. This was not permitted in previous versions of Basic.

The Type command can be used to organize related information (in a database-like format) to store and retrieve it efficiently in a disk file. Some programmers also use it to clarify relationships between associated Variables, or create clusters of kindred Variables.

First we'll look at the disk-file use. You generally use the Type Statement to create a customized cluster of Variables for use with the random access file technique (see the Open command). A random access file stores pieces of information of fixed sizes, within *records* of a fixed size (and records are themselves subdivided into *fields* of fixed sizes). You decide what amount of information these subdivisions will contain—how many characters in each piece of text, for example. However, you must then make all the records and fields that same size.

Ordinarily, you cluster the Variables used with a random access file into a group of related information, like a mini-database:

- ❒ Name
- ❒ Address
- ❒ Telephone number

When used with a random access file, the smallest unit of data (each Variable)—such as the name, address or phone number—is called a field. Together, for a single entry, these fields are called a record. Not coincidentally, this is the same terminology that is used to describe the subdivisions of a table in a database. The easiest way to manipulate these records is to put the fields together into a user-defined Variable with the Type command.

Because Text Variables ("strings") by default can be of varying length, you can fix their length by using the * N technique. (Using: Dim Mytext As String * 30 is one approach. The Type command can also create fixed-length strings.)

You can use the Type command only in a Module, and not within a Sub or Function.

In a sense, the Type command enables you to create a special kind of Array (see "Arrays"). A normal Array is a collection of Variables, which must all be of the same type. (However, the new Variant Variable type allows you to get around this rule.) However, using the Type command you can create a custom grouping of mixed Variables called a *user-defined data type*. In Visual Basic 3.0, the one kind of Variable that cannot be used as part of a Type structure is the Object type; however, this is permitted in VBA and now in VB 4.0.

**Used With**

- ❒ Random access files.
- ❒ To create a specialized custom data structure to help the programmer group information into related items with meaningful Variable names.

**Variables**

You can use the Type command only within a Module and outside of a Procedure.

```
Type AddressBook
    Nam As String * 50
    Address As String * 200
    Phone As String * 12
    Age As Integer
End Type
```

To create and use a Type Variable structure, follow these three steps:

1. Define the general Type structure in a Module as illustrated above.
2. Create a particular Variable of that type (Dim NewVar As AddressBook, for example).
3. Manipulate the Variable as if it were an ordinary Variable (add, change or examine the data). The only difference between this and ordinary Variables is that the *NewVar* we created has four interior Variables. You manipulate them using the name NewVar, separated by a period (.) from the name of an interior Variables, such as

```
NewVar.Name = "Rusty Wheels"
```

or

```
Print NewVar.Age.
```

Let's define a particular Variable as being of the "AddressBook" type. Once the general type has been defined, you must name a particular Variable that will be of that type.

You can use four "Variable defining" commands to make a particular Variable a type:

- The Public or Global command (used in a Module).
- The Dim command (used in a Module or a Procedure). You can also use ReDim (described earlier) within a Procedure. Dim limits the scope of the Variable to the current Module or the current Procedure.)
- The Private command (used outside of a Procedure only; limits the scope of the Variable to the current Module).
- The Static command (used within an individual Subroutine or Function).

Any of these creates a Variable and defines its structure as being of the custom type. In other words, this new Variable has the interior Variables Name, Address, Phone and Age.

Only after you have declared this new Variable can you use the custom structure. You cannot use the name of the type (AddressBook) directly within commands that save, retrieve, print or otherwise manipulate data. The type is a structure that you define; then later you can define other Variables as being "of that type." The word AddressBook is used only when you are defining a new Variable to be of the "AddressBook" type.

In other words, you establish a type by describing the kinds of Variables it contains, and the order in which they reside within the structure. You define a structure in a Module:

```
Type AddressBook
    Nam As String * 50
    Address As String * 200
    Phone As String * 12
    Age As Integer
End Type
```

Then, in a Subroutine, Function or the Module itself, you announce that a Variable is of that already-defined structural type.

To complete this example, we'll announce that a Variable called PersonnelRecords is to be constructed like the AddressBook structure (which we have already defined as containing Name, Address, Phone and Age). PersonnelRecords will, therefore, follow the pattern defined as the "addressbook type of Variable." PersonnelRecords will be a structure with four interior Variables of an already-described Variable type and length:

```
Dim PersonnelRecords As AddressBook
```

PersonnelRecords has now become a Variable structure. How do you manipulate the interior Variables in this structure? You use a period (.) to separate the name of the structure from the name of one of its subsidiary Variables. PersonnelRecords can now be used in the following fashion. This example puts literal information into the structure:

```
PersonnelRecords.Nam = "Alice Dragonnette"
    PersonnelRecords.Address = "2455 West Circle Drive"
    PersonnelRecords.Phone = "929-4549-9090"
    PersonnelRecords.Age = 45
```

This one uses Variables to put information in the structure:

```
N$ = "Sal Lee"
PersonnelRecords.Nam = N$
```

To get information from the structure, do this:

```
Telephone$ = PersonnelRecords.Phone
```

Or if you are really attracted to Type Variables as a concept, you can make a more complex structure—an Array of a user-defined Type Variable:

```
Dim PersonnelRecords(1 To 30) As AddressBook
```

After that, you would have an Array of structures, with all the usual benefits of Arrays:

```
PersonnelRecords(12).Age = 45
```

You can also put Arrays inside a Type structure. In a Module, define the type:

```
Type CDCollection
    Jazz (300) As String
    Classical (1 to 600) as Variant
    Rock (400,400) As String
End Type
```

Then, define a Variable to be of that type:

```
Dim cds As CDCollection
```

Then, to use one of the internal Arrays:

```
Sub FillOne ( )
    cds.jazz(3) = "Miles Davis"
End Sub
```

Notice that to reference an item in an internal Array within a Type structure, you put the index in parentheses after the internal name of the Array:

```
cds.jazz(3)
```

By contrast, if you're using an Array of Type structure, you put the parentheses after the structure name, but before the interior Variable name:

```
PersonnelRecords(12).Age = 45.
```

**Uses** The Type command can be used to create fixed data structures, similar to Arrays, which are then used with random access files.

One significant advantage of a Type Variable structure is that you can manipulate the entire structure with one command. You can copy or save an entire structure without specifying each of its internal Variables. For instance, if you are storing the following structure in a random access file, you don't go through and store each separate element of the structure:

```
Put #1, PersonnelRecords.Nam
Put #1, PersonnelRecords.Address
Put #1, PersonnelRecords.Phone
Put #1, PersonnelRecords.Age
```

Instead, you simply save the entire structure as a single item:

```
Put #1, PersonnelRecords
```

Likewise, you can copy the cluster Variable, PersonnelRecords, into another Variable of the same type. (You must have previously defined some other Variable as being of the AddressBook type—Dim Backup As AddressBook, for example). Then, to copy all the information stored in the interior Variables of PersonnelRecords into the parallel structure of the Variable Backup, you use the LSet command:

```
LSet Backup = PersonnelRecords
```

(Technically, Backup and PersonnelRecords need not be of the same type to use LSet, but they must both be either user-defined types or strings. If they are user-defined, they need not be of the same user-defined type.)

Random access files aren't the only way to use this handy technique. Some programmers like to use Type Variable structures in other ways. If you like to organize your data in this quasi-Array fashion, you might use the Type command often. If you want to define custom groupings of Variables for some special purpose, use Type. However, ordinary Variables and Arrays are usually simpler to manipulate. The structures of Variables created by the Type command are similar to the "records" used in databases in the Pascal programming language or to "structures" in C.

Type structures are also used in some situations to pass structures to the API (see Chapter 8). Bitmap API Routines, for instance, such as GetDIBits, require structures as arguments when you "call" the API Function.

Type structures can pass a group of Variables to a Subroutine.

**Cautions** You can create Type structures that include variable-length Text ("String") Variables (just leave off the * 25 in Newname As String * 25). However, you cannot then use such a structure with random access files.

You *can* build complicated, almost paradoxical, structures by using one Type structure as a Variable within another (in a Module, for instance):

```
Type Directions
    North As String * 10
    South As String * 10
    East As String * 10
    West As String * 10
End Type
Type Mileage
    Car As Integer
    Bus As Integer
    Trailer As Integer
    Distance As Directions 'this is a Type structure
End Type
```

We put this Type-within-Type technique under Cautions rather than Uses because this structure-within-structure could get too complex to be easily visualized, and could become a source of programming errors.

You can use "Static" Arrays within a Type structure.

**Note** You can use Constants, but you cannot define the dimensions of a static Array within a Type structure by using Variables.

This, for example, won't work:

```
Children (Start To Total)
```

You cannot use Line Labels or line numbers inside a Type structure definition.

However, you can now use Object Variables and dynamic Arrays within a Type structure.

**Example** In a Module, enter the following:

```
Type InvoiceType
    Date as String * 10
    InvNumber as Integer
    PastDue as Integer
End Type

Sub Testing ( )

Static Billthem As InvoiceType
Date$ = "07-19-1992"
```

```
Billthem.Date = Date$
Billthem.InvNumber = 1552
Billthem.PastDue = 30
Debug.Print Billthem.Date
Debug.Print Billthem.InvNumber
Debug.Print Billthem.PastDue

End Sub
```

**Results in**

```
07-19-1992
1552
30
```

# TypeName

**function**

**Description**

At first glance, this seems to be an odd one. It returns a Text ("String") description of a Variable's type. If you don't know a Variable's type, you can use the IsNumeric or other "Is" commands (described elsewhere in this section). You can also use the VarType command, which provides one of 15 code numbers to identify the type. However, the benefit of TypeName is that it can be more specific than the current code numbers permit. VB4 has the TypeName function (also see the VarType function).

For instance, Windows has many objects now and will shortly have many more. These objects are not, strictly speaking, Variable "types" (they are all of the "Object" type). However, in some situations you'll want your program to know specifically what *kind* of Object is being described by a Variable. There are "Range" Objects and "cells" Objects and on and on. At this point, the limited codes provided by VarType may not offer the information you want.

TypeName provides a *text* description. Computers work most often with numbers; humans work most often with text. So readability is an additional virtue of the text description offered by TypeName. When you're looking through the programming, the word "integer" is more descriptive than the code for integer (2). There is a trend now toward forcing computers to use text. One example is the new "named parameters" where arguments are labeled:

```
ChartWizard Source:=Range("A1:E2"), Gallery:=xl3DPie,_
Format:=4
```

Note that the parameters here that describe this Chart have labels: Source, Gallery and Format. In Basic before VBA, this human-friendly approach did not exist. Instead, the computer (and the programmer) understood the purpose of each parameter based on its position in the list. So only the parameters were given; no labels identified them. It would look like this:

```
ChartWizard ("A1:E2", xl3DPie, 4)
```

In this same spirit of *describing things in human terms*, the computer can provide a text description (rather than a type-code number) of the kind of Variable that's being used.

Here is an Excel macro example you can try that illustrates the difference in specificity between VarType and TypeName:

```
Sub Display( )
    Dim x As Range
    Worksheets(1).Range("a1").Value = 1
    Set x = Worksheets(1).Range("a1")
    MsgBox VarType(x)
    MsgBox TypeName(x)
End Sub
```

The VarType message box displays 5 (the code for double-precision floating point number). The TypeName box says "Range." Far more useful, don't you think?

**Used With** Variables.

**Uses** The primary value of TypeName is that it provides highly specific information about an Object Variable, the particular kind of Object represented by that Variable. TypeName can be used instead of VarType to report on the nature of an Object Variable's contents: If TypeName(Variablename)="Range" Then . . .

As a secondary benefit, TypeName makes your programs more readable. You can use it, for instance, in a Select...Case structure (rather than using the VarType command that returns a code number instead of an English word). See the example below.

TypeName can also be used when your program needs to discover the *type* being held in a Variant Variable so that it can manipulate the data. (You have to approach text differently than, for example, numbers. It makes no sense to divide two pieces of text; "tree" cannot be divided by "glass.")

**Cautions** If you are using a command that is case-sensitive (that distinguishes between uppercase and lowercase letters), beware that the TypeName command returns initial caps, as in *String* or *Integer.* The example below would fail to detect *String* if we used Case "string" or Case "STRING" because TypeName returns the string with an initial cap:

**Example**

```
Dim ThisVar as String

Select Case TypeName(ThisVar)

Case "Integer"
    Debug.Print "It's an integer variable"
Case "String"
    Debug.Print "It's a string variable"
End Select
```

**Results in** It's a string variable

**See Also** VarType, IsNumeric, IsDate and the other Is... commands

# UNGROUP (SEE "COLLECTION")

# WAIT

**method**

**Description** Unlike Visual Basic, VBA doesn't yet have the highly useful Timer Controls. Timers allow you to set precise delays, cause something to happen at a particular date/time, cause something to repeat at intervals, and accomplish other valuable tasks. Until VBA includes Timers, all you can do is use the Wait command. Unlike a Timer, the Wait command freezes the computer. Excel cannot perform other tasks, nor can the user.

For most uses, you should avoid the Wait command; instead, use the VBA command OnTime.

**Variables** To pause until 1:20 PM, use this:

```
Application.Wait "13:20"
```

# WINDOWS

**method/object**

**Description** In the Windows operating system, a *window* is the main unit of communication: it is usually filled with a document in a word processor, a picture in a photo-retouching program, a spreadsheet in a spreadsheet program, and so on. To the programmer, a window is the primary unit of organization (the Form in Visual Basic, for instance). You use the VBA command Windows to access Window Objects and to affect several qualities of these Objects.

The Windows commands allow you to access and manipulate windows in a VBA-capable application. The Windows Method is one of a large number of paired entities (paired into a Method and an Object) that share the same name. Other examples are menus, worksheets, toolbars, Modules and dozens of others that are building blocks of Excel. When VBA is included in Word, Access and other applications, the elements of each of these applications will also be provided to you, the programmer, in this same way: as a Method or as an Object. Among these Method/Objects will, certainly, be the one called *Windows*. Word won't, of course, have a "WorkSheets" Method/Object, but it surely will have a ToolBars and a Windows command.

When you use one of these Method/Objects, the distinction between *Method* and *Object* becomes somewhat blurry. Everything can happen on a single line in your program. In other words, you don't use the term *Windows* separately as a Method and then, later, as an Object. For more on this, see "Modules."

The Windows Object has the following Properties: Application, Count, Parent. The Windows Object has the following Methods: Arrange, Item.

**Variables** This line lets you work with a single window:

```
Application.Windows(index)
```

The index can be an index number or the name of the window you are after. For example, to make the second window (in the Windows Object collection) invisible:

```
Application.Windows(2).Visible = False
```

Or you can use the alternative syntax, providing the name of the particular window rather than its index number in the collection:

```
Application.Windows("Window3").Visible = False
```

And this accesses the entire collection of windows:

```
ActiveWorkbook.Windows.Visible = False
```

**Example** We'll create a new window (a copy of the current Excel window). First we reduce the size of the current window, in case it is maximized. Then we create the new window and resize it so that both windows are visible onscreen. Then we use the Windows Method/Object to make the second window invisible.

```
Sub Macro1( )
    ActiveWindow.WindowState = xlNormal
    ActiveWindow.NewWindow
    With ActiveWindow
        .Top = 141.25
        .Left = 229
    End With
    Application.Windows(2).Visible = True
End Sub
```

**See Also** Modules, Collection

## WITH...END WITH statement

See "Named Properties" in Section 1 of this chapter.

## MOVING ON

Now we go from the future of Basic into a house of mirrors called *recursion*. You may have heard the poem:

Roses are red
Violets are blue
I'm a split personality
And so am I!

Gird yourself for the next chapter. We've tried to make the topic clear (recursion is a procedure that makes use of *itself*). Even if you find it bewildering, recursion is worth learning. It's much the best programming solution in some situations.

# Chapter 12

# Recursive Programming

In this chapter we'll look at recursion, which in some situations is a powerful technique for implementing efficient, compact programs. Yet it isn't widely understood or widely used. It seems mysterious at first glance, paradoxical. However, it is not much more complicated than any other technique once you understand how it works.

## WHAT IS RECURSION?

So we'll get rid of the scary part right off the bat: Recursion means that something does something to itself. Now, we can all think of examples in the real world of this kind of circular behavior. The screech of a feedbacking guitar is recursive; writing your autobiography is recursive. Indeed, any word that starts with *auto* is describing a recursion. An automobile powers itself (or at least it seemed that way, in the days of the horse-drawn carriage).

You get the idea: something turns upon itself and becomes a kind of perpetual motion machine—deriving energy from itself, creating a feedback cycle where output is forced to become input.

The problem with recursion is that we don't generally think recursively. The human brain wasn't designed—or it wasn't trained—to think recursively. There are, however, examples of recursive patterns in our daily life and here is a common one:

Let's say that in reading a book you found the sentence "Cats avoid white queso," which you can't understand because you don't know what queso means. You open a dictionary and look up the definition of queso. The dictionary says: "Queso is a cheese which tastes like jack cheese." This time you don't know what jack cheese is, so you turn to another page, where you read "jack cheese is a soft, white, salty cheese." When you know what jack cheese is, you can then understand what queso is, and finally understand the very first statement.

The process of looking up a word while trying to look up another word is a recursive process. To understand a definition, you must understand the words used in it. If you don't know the meaning of a word in the first definition, you must interrupt your effort to understand the definition and look up the unknown word. Hopefully, this process will end somewhere and you can backtrack, this time understanding one definition after another like falling dominoes. This is exactly how recursion works: we interrupt an action to perform a similar action.

A primary characteristic of recursion is that *output becomes input.* Just like the sound of a feedbacking electric guitar. Normally, the sound of an electric guitar goes out to the ears of the audience and then fades away. This process is linear, not circular. But if you turn up the speakers enough, the output feeds back into the microphone which feeds to the speakers which feeds more to the mike which feeds more to the speakers. And so on until someone turns down the volume or something smoulders, and then blows up.

## Recursion Can't Go Forever

In the dictionary example above, the result (the output) of one dictionary lookup becomes the seed (the input) for the next lookup. Then the next definition becomes the next seed, and so on. By this process, we slowly approach our goal through successive repetitions until we have reached a satisfactory specificity, or depth, of recursion. We could call this *successive approximations,* since each step brings us closer to our goal. The *depth* of a recursion (the number of times we'll feed output back into our recursive process) depends on how much detail is desired. What *kind* of detail depends on the purpose of the recursion: It could be the degree of clarity of a definition, or the number of parts you want some text broken down into, and so on.

However, recursion always requires that you provide some end point. You must specify, within the recursive process itself, when the recursion will end. You must check for some condition that satisfies the goal you're trying to achieve. The definition lookups in the previous example can't go on forever. This process will stop as soon as we run into a definition we can understand.

## RECURSION IN PROGRAMMING

A recursive Function, or Subroutine, is a Function that calls itself. Here is the structure of a recursive Function:

```
Function Recurse( ) As Integer
    {VB commands}
    n = Recurse( )              'THE FUNCTION CALLS ITSELF
    {more VB commands}
End Function
```

A Function can call any other Function in your program, even itself!

You can provide an argument or arguments to a recursive procedure, just like any ordinary procedure. Likewise, you can write a recursive procedure that doesn't accept an argument. Normal Functions might call on the services of other Functions (or Subroutines), but they don't call on *themselves*. But a recursive Function is different. To complete its task, it resorts to itself.

Let's say you are creating a Function to perform a task. Midway, you find out that you need to repeat the same process all over. In other words, you have to perform a subtask that is identical to the original task. When the subtask completes, the program continues working on the original task. This is what the Recurse( ) Function above does. In the middle of its execution, it calls itself, and when the last-called Recurse( ) Function completes its execution, the original Function continues with the section {*more VB commands*}.

Since recursive programming is a new concept for many readers, we will approach this chapter in a different manner. We will introduce the topic of recursion with some simple examples, then progress to more complex examples. The first few examples can be implemented nonrecursively just as easily (if not more easily) as they can be implemented recursively.

Toward the end of the chapter you will find two interesting examples that cannot be effectively implemented without recursion. Have you ever wanted to provide a feature that searches all subdirectories for a particular file or piece of text? Recursion, as this example will demonstrate, is by far the best and most straightforward technique.

## Recursion Is Useful & Practical

Take a look at Figure 12-1. What you see is a simple application that locates files on your disk. The files at the bottom of the screen are those with a specific date. Notice that there are many more. DOC files in the directory C:\WINWORD, but only the ones created (or updated) on 12/10/93 are displayed. This application is the heart of the Windows File Manager or the Explorer application under Windows 95. It scans your hard disk for specific files and displays them. In its simplest form, it's a File Search utility. But with our utility you can set any type of restrictions (file names, date, time, size, etc.) and manipulate the files on your disk in ways that are not possible with the File Manager.

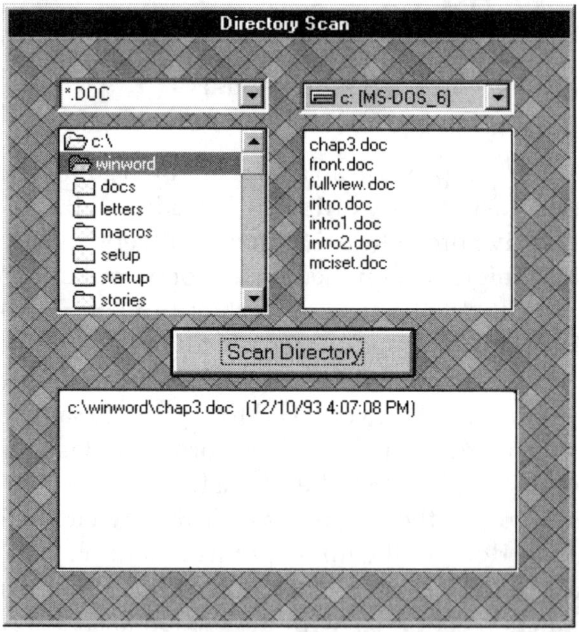


Figure 12-1: You know you were editing some documents last night, but you just can't remember where they were. If this sounds familiar, then DirScan is a "must have" tool.

Sometimes, you just have to use recursion.

What the figure doesn't show is the logic behind this application. Let's stop for a moment and think about the implementation of this program. You will soon conclude that there is no simple way to code it. However, once you are familiar with recursive programming, you will be surprised how easy it is to put together a utility like this.

The Directory Scan utility is a very useful and practical example, but before we get to it, we must explain a few basic concepts about recursion and start with simpler examples.

## Parsing Path Names

Often we need a simple Function to parse a path name and extract each subdirectory's name. Let's say you have the full name of a file stored in a string, as C:\VB\SAMPLES\FILE.FRM. The components of the path name are separated with the backslash character. To isolate and extract them from the path name, we must locate the first occurrence of the backslash character in the string, and then remove everything from that point to the left. Once we have extracted the first component of the full file name, which is the drive name, we are left with the rest of the filename (VB\SAMPLES\FILE.FRM). We continue until we have extracted all the components. Most programmers would "parse" (separate text into component parts) a path like this, using a While...Wend loop like the following:

```
Function NameParse(path$) As Integer
' path$ is a string containing a file name,
' such as C:\VB\SAMPLES\FILE.FRM
    X = InStr(path$, "\")
    While X > 0
        L = Len(path$)
        SubDir$ = Mid$(path$, 1, X - 1)
        path$ = Mid$(path$, X + 1, L - X)
        X = InStr(path$, "\")
        Debug.Print SubDir$
    Wend
End Function
```

This Function, which prints the components of a file name in the Debug window, is easy to understand, and most Visual Basic programmers would come up with a similar Function for isolating the subdirectory names of a full file name. However, if done recursively, parsing can be a little cleaner, can even seem more "natural."

### Example: Parsing File Names

Let's call our recursive Function NameParse( ). We will call NameParse( ) again and again (from within itself), each time feeding it the increasingly shorter path name, until all components of the path name are extracted.

```
Function NameParse (path$) As Integer

    X = InStr(path$, "\")
    If X = 0 Then
        NameParse = 1
```

```
            Exit Function
        Else
            L = Len(path$)
            Subdir$ = Left$(path$, X)
            path$ = Right$(path$, L - X)
            NameParse = NameParse(path$) + 1
        End If

    End Function
```

The NameParse( ) Function scans the path$ string from left to right and isolates each subdirectory name, using the backslash character as a guide. Each time it locates a new backslash, it removes everything to the left of it from the string and then it parses the rest of the string, by calling itself.

Despite its reputation, recursion is a natural way of coding.

How would you describe this Function in English? NameParse( ) extracts the first component of the path name from the left of the string and then calls itself to do the same thing with a shorter argument and so on until there are no more slashes in the string. As long as there are slashes in the string, there is more than one component in the string, and the parsing process continues.

### Tracing the Steps of Recursion

Let's see the steps involved in parsing the string C:\VB\SAMPLES\FILE.FRM. The first time NameParse( ) is called, it locates the first slash in the file name. The If clause is skipped, and execution continues with the lines of the Else clause, which extract the drive name from the path$ string. The last statement calls the same Function. What's happening now? For one thing, the NameParse( ) Function hasn't ended. When a Function calls another Function (or Subroutine), it suspends its own execution until the called Function returns.

The computer will execute the same Function, just like it did before, this time with a different argument. After extracting the drive name and the first slash from NameParse( ), the path$ argument becomes "VB\SAMPLES\FILE.FRM" and is passed to the NameParse( ) Function. The first invocation of NameParse( ) remains in memory and waits for the completion of the Function it just called. In the meantime the computer loads another copy of the Function in memory and executes it as it would execute any other Function. (We've simplified this process a bit for clarity. We'll explain it more fully below.)

The code locates the first backslash in the string, extracts the name of the first subdirectory (which is VB) and calls the NameParse( ) Function again, only this time with the argument "SAMPLES\FILE.FRM". The second invocation of the Function doesn't end. It will wait, too, for the completion of the Function it just called. The third invocation of the NameParse( ) Function extracts the directory name "SAMPLES" and calls itself with the argument "FILE.FRM".

This time, at last, there is no backslash in the path name, and the If clause is executed, ending the most recent invocation of the NameParse( ) Function. The control of the program returns to the calling Function, which increases the return value of the last call to the NameParse( ) Function and ends right there—there are no more lines to be executed. The same process continues until all pending Functions terminate as well. Each of the interrupted Functions accepts the return value of a recursive call of the NameParse( ) Function, increases it by one and returns it as its result. The very first call of the NameParse( ) Function will return the value 4.

## How Recursion Works

What happens when a Function (or Subroutine) calls itself? As far as the computer and the operating system are concerned, it doesn't make any difference whether a Function calls itself or another Function. What happens when a Function calls another one? The calling Function suspends its execution for a while, until the called Function returns its result. At that point, the first Function accepts the result and continues its execution where it was interrupted.

Every time a Function is called, it's executed from start to end. The same is true with recursive Functions. Do not attempt to trace the execution of the newly called Function from the point where the previous one was interrupted (the line NameParse=NameParse(path$)+1 in the previous Function).

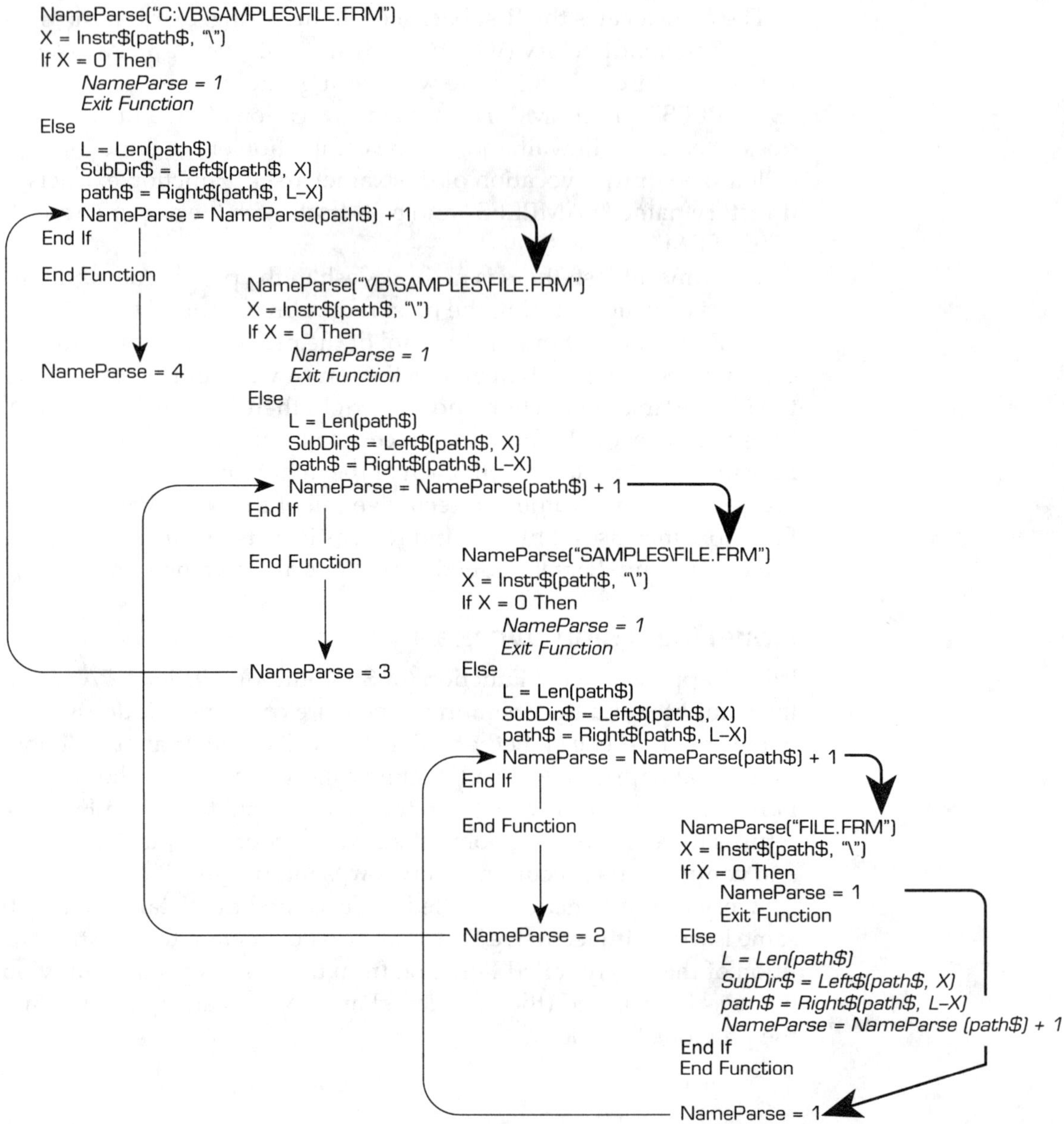


Figure 12-2: The process of parsing the string "C:\VB\SAMPLES\FILE.FRM" with the NameParse( ) Function. The lines that are not executed are shown in italics. Thick lines show the direction of the recursive calls. Thin lines show the propagation of the result through the recursively called Functions.

The stack is a First-In-First-Out structure.

Recursion may be easier to understand if you think that the operating system makes up new Functions and calls them one after the other. NameParse calls NameParse1( ), NameParse1( ) calls NameParse2( ) and so on. When it's done, it discards all these "imaginary" Functions and you never see them. This picture may help you follow the code of a recursive Function, but to fully understand recursion you must be aware of a mechanism called *stack*.

## The Stack Mechanism

Recall that, every time a new Function is called, the current Function's status must be stored somewhere in the memory, so that it can later resume its execution. The memory area where the Function's status is stored is the called *stack*. The stack is a protected area of the system's memory, where the operating system stores all the information needed to return from a Function (or Subroutine) call.

You can guess what would happen if your applications had access to this memory area. The stack is an extremely important mechanism for the proper operation not only of the applications, but of the operating system as well, and that's why it is handled by the operating system exclusively. There are ways to rearrange the contents of the stack, and this technique is used frequently in assembly language programming. But every mistake we make there causes the computer to crash. High-level languages, such as Visual Basic, don't allow the programmer to fool around with the stack.

The stack handles recursive functions just like ordinary ones because it doesn't know which function calls which.

Why is this area of memory called stack? Each new item is stacked on the top of the stack, and we can only remove the topmost item. It is also called a Last-In-First-Out structure. The first item to be removed is the last one we placed there, in the same way we pile plates on top of the stack and always remove the top plate. This mechanism is extremely useful, because it maintains the order of the items. Every time a new Function is called, the operating system places on the stack the address from which the Function was called. This address is called the *return address* because this is where the newly called Function must return within the program. If this Function calls another one, the new return address is placed on the stack too. As each Function terminates, the operating system knows where to return, because the return address is always on the top of the stack. (The return address is the location in memory of the next command to be executed—in our example, this is the location of the line NameParse=NameParse(path$)+1.)

### The Stack Is Also Used to Pass Arguments

The stack performs another important Function as well. It is used for passing arguments and results back and forth between Functions. When a Function is called, the calling Function places the arguments on the stack, in the order they appear in the Function's argument list. The called Function retrieves the arguments from the stack in the same order and uses them in the calculations. When done, the called Function places its result on the stack where the calling Function can find it. The arguments passed with the help of the stack are called *positional arguments* because they are detected by their placement on the stack. That's why it is so important that the arguments are of the same type and used in the same order as declared. If not, the stack will be corrupted and your system will crash.

This will not happen because Visual Basic protects you against such errors. However, there are cases in which Visual Basic has no way of checking the arguments, and an application can corrupt the stack. The corruption of the stack has a predictable result: your system's crash. We will return to the topic of the stack's integrity in the discussion of Dynamic Link Libraries (Chapter 15).

The same process takes place when a Function calls itself. The computer places the arguments on the stack along with the status of the Function which is about to be interrupted. Then it "loads" and executes another copy of the called Function. Think about it: Would the computer read each line of the new Function and compare it against the lines of the previous Function? Of course not. It simply initializes the local variables of the new Function and executes the code. The local variables are in essence the status of the program.

At this point, we should clarify something we said earlier. In order to simplify our explanation of the mechanics of recursion, we said that each time a recursive procedure calls itself, the operating system loads another *copy* of the procedure in the memory and executes it. In reality, no new copies of the procedure are loaded in memory. This would very quickly deplete all the available memory.

The procedure is already in memory, and can be executed again and again. However, every time it's executed, it starts with *a new set of local variables.* The local variables of our example were x, l, and SubDir$. Because its variables are initialized every time, it appears as if a separate copy of the procedure is loaded and executed every time. In reality, the same code remains in memory, but the procedure acts on a different set of variables every time.

When thinking about recursion, however, it is probably unwise to worry about how the computer handles it. As far as your programs are concerned, you can consider that recursive Functions are loaded in memory as many times as needed without any memory penalty. The variables X and L of the NameParse Function retain their values. As each new call to NameParse is made, the operating system creates two new variables X and L which belong to the newly called Function. The variables X and L of the interrupted Function are local, and will have their original values when execution of the interrupted Function resumes.

The values of the local variables of the interrupted Function are stored in the computer's memory and will be recalled from there when the newly called Function returns. In Figures 12-3 and 12-4 you see a simplified picture of the stack as NameParse( ) parses the string "C:\VB\SAMPLES\FILE.FRM". Figure 12-3 is read from left to right. Each time a new item is placed on the stack, the size of the stack increases. Figure 12-4 is read from right to left. Every time an interrupted Function can resume its calculations, it removes the topmost item from the stack. When NameParse( ) returns, the stack is left in its original state.

| | | | |
|---|---|---|---|
| | | | NP("FILE.FRM")+1 |
| | | NP("SAMPLES\FILE.FRM")+1 | NP("SAMPLES\FILE.FRM")+1 |
| | NP("VB\SAMPLES\FILE.FRM")+1 | NP("VB\SAMPLES\FILE.FRM")+1 | NP("VB\SAMPLES\FILE.FRM")+1 |
| NP("C:\VB\SAMPLES\FILE.FRM")+1 | NP("C:\VB\SAMPLES\FILE.FRM")+1 | NP("C:\VB\SAMPLES\FILE.FRM")+1 | NP("C:\VB\SAMPLES\FILE.FRM")+1 |
| {other data} | {other data} | {other data} | {other data} |

Figure 12-3: Each time the Function NameParse( )—abbreviated here as "NP"—cannot complete its execution, it leaves a copy of the unfinished calculations on the stack and calls itself with a shorter argument. The stack size increases with each recursive call.

| | | | |
|---|---|---|---|
| | | | NP=1 |
| | | NP=2 | NP= NP("SAMPLES\FILE.FRM")+1 |
| | NP=3 | NP= NP("VB\SAMPLES\FILE.FRM"+1) | NP= NP("VB\SAMPLES\FILE.FRM")+1 |
| NP=4 | NP= NP("C:\VB\SAMPLES\FILE.FRM")+1 | NP= NP("C:\VB\SAMPLES\FILE.FRM")+1 | NP= NP("C:\VB\SAMPLES\FILE.FRM")+1 |
| {other data} | {other data} | {other data} | {other data} |

Figure 12-4: As soon as the last recursive call of NameParse( ) returns its result, the suspended calculations resume from right to left. After the calculation of NameParse("C:\VB\SAMPLES\ FILE.FRM") is complete, the stack is restored to its original status. (NameParse is abbreviated here as "NP.")

The pictures of the stack in Figures 12-3 and 12-4 are simplified and are intended to illustrate the role of the stack while a recursive Function calls itself. In reality, there is more complexity to the stack, but from a high-level language's point of view, you can ignore it.

Next we'll present another recursive algorithm, somewhat more complicated and more practical than the previous one. This Function can be implemented nonrecursively as well, but it demonstrates better the recursive nature of certain algorithms—something that wasn't quite obvious in the NameParse example.

### Example: Binary Search

Let's return to the Binary Search algorithm, which we have implemented nonrecursively in Chapter 2. As you will see, the Binary Search algorithm is recursive in nature, and we can implement it with a recursive Function.

We will start with a detailed explanation of the Binary Search algorithm and then we will convert the verbal description to code. Remember that the Binary Search algorithm assumes an array's (or List's) elements are sorted.

Suppose we have an array of strings, *sdata*, and we are looking for the index of the element *value*. Here's what we do:

1. First we establish whether the desired element is in the first or second half of the array, by comparing *value* to the middle element of the array. If the indices of the first and last element of the array are *First* and *Last*, the index of the middle element is (*First*+*Last*)/2. After comparing *value* to the middle element,

*sdata*( (*First*+*Last*)/2 ), we know whether *value* is in the first or second half of the array.

2. Next we halve the range of the array we are going to search by changing the value of the *First* or *Last* variable, depending on the outcome of the comparison. If *value* is in the first half of the array, we leave the *First* variable as is and set the *Last* variable equal to the middle index, in effect limiting the range of the array to be searched. Conversely, if the value we are looking for is in the second half of the array, we leave the *Last* variable as is and make the *First* variable equal to the index of the middle element.
3. After setting the two variables, we call the same Function (let's call it BSearch), which repeats the same steps, until we are left with a single element in the array. If the value of this element is not *value,* then we know that the string we are looking for is not in the array.

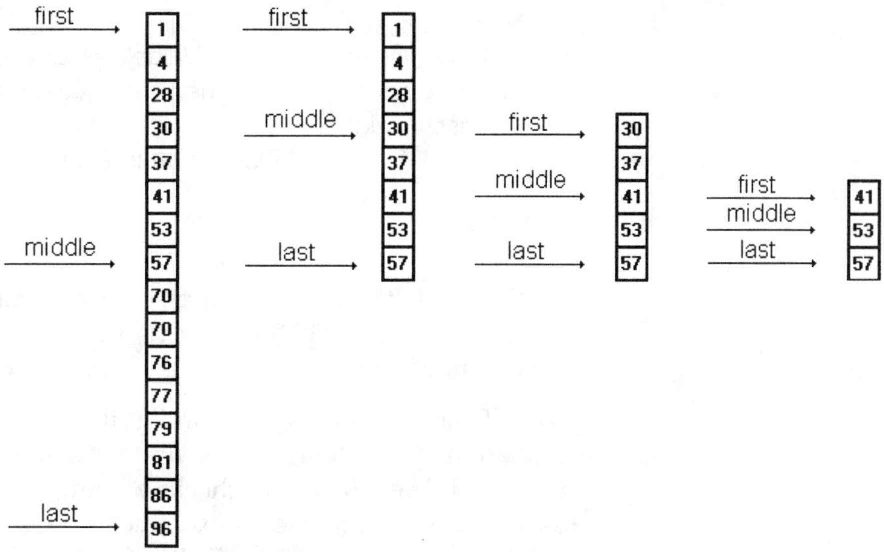


Figure 12-5 shows the steps involved in locating the number 53 in a sorted array of 10 elements.

This algorithm calls for a recursive Function, because it is described in terms of itself. Here is the code of the BSearch( ) Function:

```
Function BSearch (First As Integer, Last As Integer, Value  →
As String) As Integer
Dim middle As Integer
' Is the middle element the desired one ?
middle = (First + Last) / 2
If sdata(middle) = Value Then  ' If middle element is the  →
desired one
    BSearch = middle  ' assign value to Function
    Exit Function     ' and exit
End If

' If only one element in the List, exit Function
If middle = First Or middle = Last Then
    BSearch = -1      ' value not found in the array
    Exit Function
End If

' Must look further.
' Half the list according to Value's position in it
If Value < sdata(middle) Then  ' If Value in the 1st half
    Last = middle
Else                    ' Else Value in 2nd half
    First = middle + 1
End If

' Search in the proper half and assign result to Function
BSearch = BSearch(First, Last, Value)
End Function
```

The BSearch( ) Function is a straightforward coding of the verbal explanation of the algorithm. At first it calculates the index of the array's middle element and checks whether it is the desired element or not. If so, it assigns the index value to the Function and exits. If not, it halves the array and calls itself again. The Function ends unsuccessfully if the array has a single element, in which case the value –1 is returned.

If you use recursion to describe an algorithm, it's best to implement it with a recursive Function.

## And Now for Some Real Recursion

You have seen two recursive algorithms that, can be implemented nonrecursively just as easily. Why bother with recursion, then? There are two reasons. As you will soon see, there are algorithms—such as the one in our next example— that cannot be implemented nonrecursively. The second reason for using recursion is the simplicity of the implementation of a recursive algorithm. If you use recursion to explain an algorithm, then it is best to implement it with a recursive Function.

### Example: Scanning Directories

Our next example demonstrates the real benefits of recursion. We are going to implement an application that cries out for recursion—an application that's hard to implement without recursion. We assume that you are familiar with the Windows File Manager or Windows 95 Explorer. Both programs allow you to scan the directory structure of your disks and locate files, copy them, move them around, or delete them. ScanDir, shown in Figure 12-6, is a simple application that scans an entire directory or disk and locates any given file(s). The ScanDir application can be found in the 12\APPS\SCANDIR subdirectory of the CD.

CD-ROM

#### How ScanDir Works

Our goal is to design an application that will scan a directory (including its subdirectories) to locate a given file or group of files. Let's assume we start at the root directory (C:\, in most cases) and we are looking for EXE files. The root directory probably contains a few easily located EXE files, and a number of subdirectories. We must visit each subdirectory and repeat the same operation—locating the EXE files and scanning the subdirectories. Some of the root's directories may have their own subdirectories, which we must visit too. Obviously, we are talking about a recursive routine. The Scan procedure, implemented as a Subroutine, will scan the subdirectories of the current directory by calling itself.

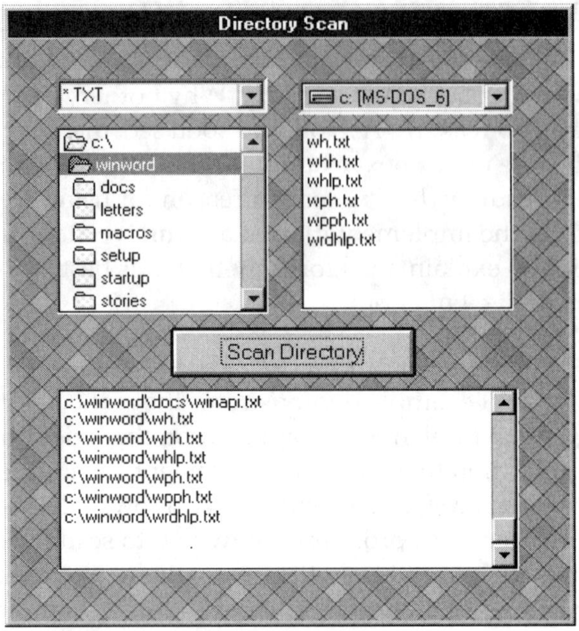


Figure 12-6: The ScanDir application is a very useful desktop utility for locating files on the hard disk.

Here the implementation of the Scan Subroutine in pseudocode:

```
Sub Scan
sd = number of subdirectories
if sd > 0 then
    for i=1 to sd
        change directory to subdirectory #i
        Scan
    next
    count (or process) current subdirectory's files
    return to parent directory
else
    count (or process) current subdirectory's files
    return to parent directory
endif
End Sub
```

This Subroutine keeps calling itself as long as there are subdirectories. After it has scanned the current directory's subdirectories, it counts (or processes) the files. When it reaches a directory without subdirectories, it simply looks for specific files and counts them (you can just as easily copy, move or delete them, look for the specific string in each file, and so on).

### Tracing Scan( )

Let's see how Scan( ) works on a typical disk. The E: drive, whose directory structure is shown in Figure 12-7, contains a single subdirectory, \win. It in turn contains two subdirectories, \win\system and \win\vb. The first contains no subdirectories, while the second contains the subdirectories \win\vb\images and \win\vb\sounds. Each subdirectory contains a number of files, which our application will simply count.

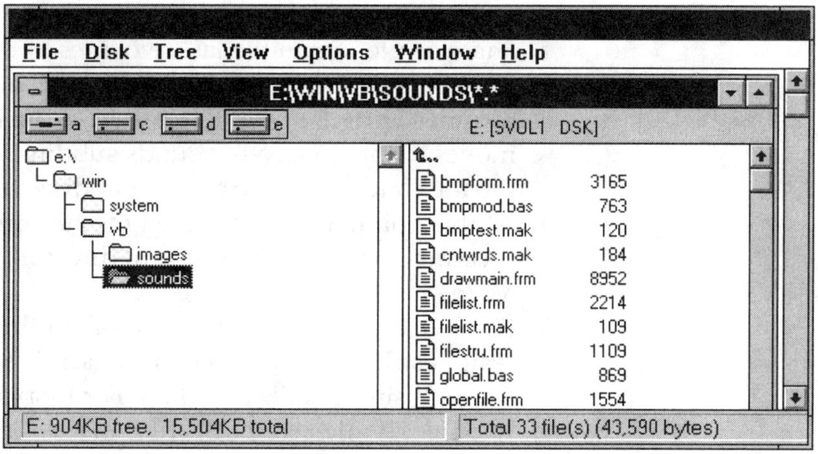


Figure 12-7: The subdirectories of the E:disk.

The Scan Subroutine will scan the disk E: in the following order:

- The root directory has a single subdirectory (sd=1). So, the For loop is executed once, and the application switches to the subdirectory \win, where it calls itself.
- This time sd becomes 2, and the application switches to the first subdirectory (\win\system), where it calls itself again.
- At this point there are no subdirectories, and the entire If clause is skipped.

- The program executes the last two lines of the pseudocode (counts the files in \win\system) and moves one directory up (from \win\system to \win). The most recently called Scan Subroutine terminates here because there are no more subdirectories, and therefore no more calls to the Scan Subroutine, in this branch of the directory structure.
- Program execution resumes with the second iteration of the most recently interrupted For loop. The current directory is \win and we are ready to move to the second subdirectory, \win\vb.
- Once there, the program calls the Scan Subroutine again.
- This time, there are two more subdirectories (sd=2) and the For loop will be executed twice again. The first time, the program moves to \win\vb\images. It finds no subdirectories there and executes again the last two lines of the pseudocode. The Scan Subroutine terminates again, and the interrupted one resumes with the second iteration of the For loop. Now it moves to the \win\vb\sounds subdirectory, where it counts the files and returns to the parent directory (\win\vb).
- At this point, it has exhausted the subdirectories of \win\vb. It counts the files of the current directory and moves up to \win.
- Finally, the For loop of the first call of the Scan Subroutine resumes. The loop counter is already 1, and it is not repeated again. It simply falls out of the For loop and executes the next two lines, which count the files in the root directory. Then the program ends. The whole process is depicted in Figure 12-8.

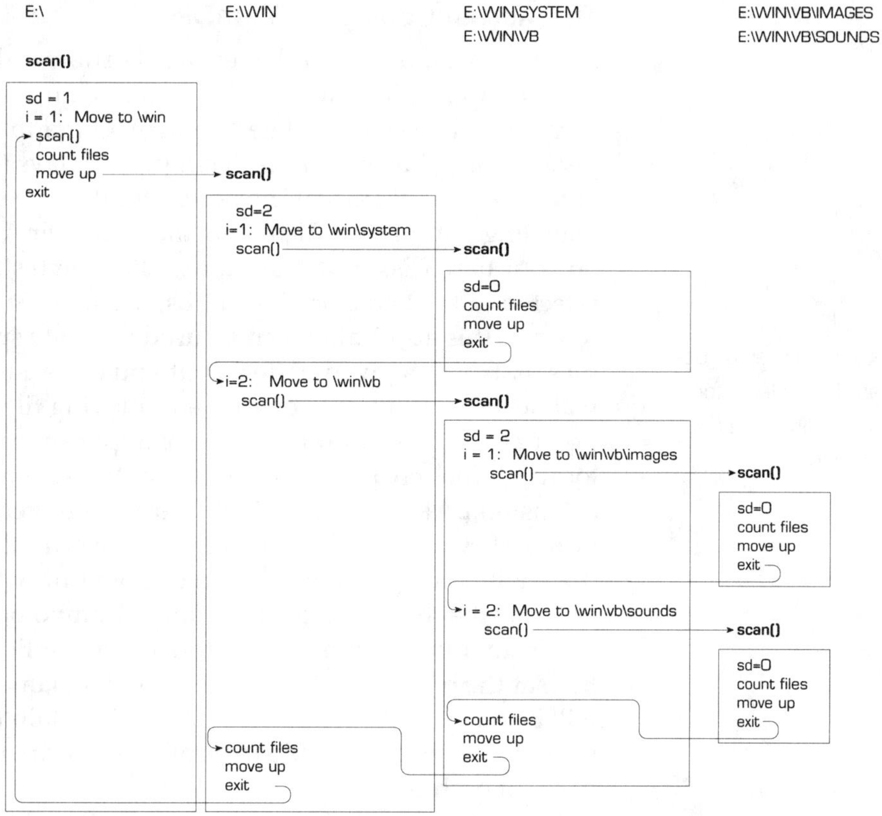


Figure 12-8: In the figure's upper portion you see the subdirectories of the E: drive. The successive calls of the Scan Subroutine are depicted in the lower portion. Each box depicts a single invocation of the scan( ) Subroutine. The lines pointing to the right show every new call of the Subroutine, while those pointing left show where each Function returns. As you can see, the deepest level of recursion is 3—from E:\, to E:\WIN, to E:\WIN\VB to E:\WIN\VB\IMAGES and E:\WIN\VB\SOUNDS. In the frames are the commands of the pseudocode commands that are executed in each call of the Scan Function, in the order they were executed.

One last detail. Two lines of the pseudocode are repeated. Couldn't we avoid this repetition? We could (and probably should), but the way the code is written is simpler to follow and even simpler to explain.

### The Actual Coding of ScanDir

Now we're ready to build a real application with real code. The ScanDir application, which is shown in Figure 12-6, is a simplified version of the Windows File Manager. Our application doesn't perform any file operations. It simply displays the files that match a given pattern in a List at the bottom of the screen. If you set the file matching pattern to a file name, then ScanDir will locate all the files on your hard disk with this name. The search starts at the directory selected in the Directory List and spans all its subdirectories.

ScanDir can be used as the skeleton for many disk-wide file operations.

As is, this application can be used to locate specific files and count files matching a given pattern, but you can easily adapt it to create a real desktop utility for copying and moving files around. Or, you can use it as the basis for other types of applications (for example, to locate all files created between two dates, remove all files with extension BAK, or locate a file's most recent version). The Explorer utility of Windows 95 is much more powerful than File Manager, but there will always be a need for a custom utility like ScanDir.

Draw the three File Controls and a Combo Box on the upper half of the Form. Put a Command Button and a List Box (or a multiline Text Box) at the bottom of the Form, where the names of the selected files will be displayed. The Combo Box will contain the file patterns you wish to match. In the code that follows, we are using the default name of each control.

First add the code for connecting the File Controls to each other. The code is very simple, but we will list it here:

```
Sub Drive1_Change ( )

    ChDrive Drive1.Drive
    Dir1.Path = Drive1.Drive

End Sub

Sub Dir1_Change ( )

    ChDir Dir1.Path
    File1.Path = Dir1.Path

End Sub
```

Every time the user changes the value of the Combo Box, the File List Control must be updated accordingly. Changes made to a Combo Box are reported with two different events: the Click Event, which occurs every time the user selects different entry, and the Change Event, which occurs every time a new character is typed in the Box.

Here is the code for both events:

```
Sub Combo1_Change ( )
    File1.Pattern = Combo1.Text
End Sub
```

and

```
Sub Combo1_Click ( )
    Call Combo1_Change
End Sub
```

It would have been just as easy to insert the line

```
File1.Pattern=Combo1.Text
```

in both Subroutines, but remember: eventually you would change this line in one Subroutine and forget to modify the other one accordingly.

The most common file extensions are added to the Combo Box when the program starts:

```
Sub Form_Load ( )
    Combo1.AddItem "*.TXT"
    Combo1.AddItem "*.DOC"
    Combo1.AddItem "*.PCX"
    Combo1.AddItem "*.TIF"
    Combo1.AddItem "*.BMP;*.DIB"
    Combo1.AddItem "*.GIF"
    Combo1.AddItem "*.*"

    Combo1.ListIndex = 0
    File1.Pattern = Combo1.Text
End Sub
```

The Scan Subroutine is contained in the Command Button's Click Event. It is the equivalent of the description (pseudocode) we presented earlier, but it contains many more lines. In a real application we must take care of numerous details, such as updating the File Controls and setting their properties. That's why we used the pseudocode to explain the bare bones of the application. Now let's focus on the details of the application.

The code of the Click Event of the Scan Directory button is

```
Sub Command1_Click ( )

    Screen.MousePointer = 11     ' HOURGLASS cursor
    List1.Clear
    startingDir = CurDir
    Call Scan
    Screen.MousePointer = 0      ' Default cursor shape

End Sub
```

startingDir is a string variable declared in the Form's Declarations section. This string variable is initialized to the current directory's name and will be used in the Scan Subroutine. All the work is done by the Scan Subroutine, whose implementation is shown here:

```
Sub Scan ()
Dim sd As Integer

    sd = Dir1.ListCount
    If sd > 0 Then
        For i = 0 To sd - 1
            ChDir Dir1.List(i)
            Dir1.Path = Dir1.List(i)
            File1.Path = Dir1.List(i)
            Call RefreshLists
        Call Scan
        Next
        File1.Path = Dir1.Path
        Call AddFileNames
        Call MoveParentDir
    Else
        File1.Path = Dir1.Path
        Call AddFileNames
        Call MoveParentDir
    End If

End Sub
```

The Directory List (Dir1) keeps track of the subdirectories. Each time we move to a new directory, we update the Directory List's contents. That's how we know if there are subdirectories and how many. At the same time, we update the File List (File1) so that our application sees only the files that match the pattern. For this scheme to work, we must set the File List's Pattern property to the proper value every time the user selects, or types, a new file matching pattern (using the Click and Change Events of the Combo Box).

The AddFileNames Subroutine adds the selected file names (the ones displayed in the File List) to the List Box. Here is its implementation:

```
 Sub AddFileNames ( )
' Copy all filenames from FILE LIST to the list
' with the search results

    On Error Resume Next
' Add slash in filename unless we are at the root directory
    Path$ = Dir1.Path
    If Right$(Path$, 1) <> "\" Then Path$ = Path$ + "\"
' For each entry in File List to the List Box
    For j = 1 To File1.ListCount
        fname$ = Path$ + File1.List(j - 1)
        List1.AddItem fname$
    Next
    List1.Refresh       ' Refresh List Box to see new data
    total = total + File1.ListCount

End Sub
```

The AddFileNames Subroutine is the one you should modify to perform any kind of operation you wish on the selected files.

Finally, here is the code of the MoveParentDir, which switches to the parent directory:

```
Sub MoveParentDir()
' DO NOT ATTEMPT TO MOVE UP FROM ORIGINAL DIRECTORY

   If UCase$(Dir1.List(-1)) <> UCase$(startingDir) Then
      ChDir Dir1.List(-2)
      Dir1.Path = Dir1.List(-2)
   End If

End Sub
```

The current directory in the Directory List is the one with index –1. Its subdirectories have positive indices starting with 0, while its parent directory has an index of –2. To move to the parent directory we must use the expression Dir1.List(–2), unless we are already at the root directory, which has no parent directory.

One last Subroutine used in the Scan Subroutine is RefreshLists, which causes the contents of the Directory and File Lists to be redrawn every time we switch to another directory:

```
Sub RefreshLists ( )

    Dir1.Refresh
    File1.Refresh

End Sub
```

In your application you probably won't want to display every new directory and its files during execution. We chose to update the Lists so that you can see the progress of the recursive algorithm. If you add some delay in the RefreshLists Subroutine, you can slow down the program and watch how it scans the subdirectories of your disk. In situations where you don't want to display the contents of the File Controls, make them invisible.

### Test-Driving the Application

Run this application and see how the Scan Subroutine scans your entire hard disk—watch the names of the subdirectories and corresponding files displayed in the Directory and File Lists. If you have to, you can single-step the application and follow the execution of the program on a piece of paper.

To display the files with a given date, as we did in the introduction of this chapter, replace the line with the AddItem method of the AddFileNames routine with the appropriate If structure. Here is the modified AddFileNames Subroutine, which looks for files created (or updated) on a specific date:

```
Sub AddFileNames ( )
' Modified to copy to the List Box
' only the files with a given creation date
Path$ = Dir1.Path
If Right$(Path$, 1) <> "\" Then Path$ = Path$ + "\"
' For each entry in File List
For j = 1 To File1.ListCount
    fname$ = Path$ + File1.List(j - 1)      ' Form full name,
    fdate$ = FileDateTime(fname$)           ' get file's date
    If Left$(fdate$, 10) = "12/10/1993" Then  ' & filter it
        List1.AddItem fname$ + " (" + fdate$ + ")"
    End If
```

```
Next
List1.Refresh
total = total + File1.ListCount

End Sub
```

By properly modifying the AddFileNames routine, you can select files based on any number of criteria, even perform basic operations on them. (The value of the date depends on your system's settings, too. Make sure it is defined correctly.)

## QuickSort: The Ultimate Sorting Routine

The Binary Search algorithm is the fastest searching algorithm, but there is a catch: the array's elements must be already sorted for this algorithm to work. We must therefore add to our collection of useful tools a few good data sorting routines. Chapter 2 presented the ShellSort algorithm, a simple, very efficient sorting algorithm. In this chapter we present the ultimate sorting algorithm, the QuickSort algorithm. Invented by C. A. R. Hoare in 1960, QuickSort is an excellent example of recursive programming. The very fact that the fastest known sorting algorithm is recursive should be enough to justify the techniques covered in this chapter.

Like the Binary Search algorithm, QuickSort halves the array at each step and ends up sorting very small arrays.

Like Binary Search, QuickSort partitions the array to be sorted in two subarrays, and continues with each one separately. It partitions each subarray again and again until all subarrays contain a single element. The partitioning is done so that one subarray contains all the elements that are less than some value and the other one contains all the elements that are greater than, or equal to, the same value. The value used to partition the array is called *pivot*, and it is usually the value of the array's middle element. After the array's partition, we have two subarrays that can be sorted separately, because each element of the first subarray is less than any of the second subarray's elements, and no elements of one subarray need be moved to the other one. Then we call the same routine twice, once for each subarray. This process continues until we are left with subarrays containing a single element. This is clearly another recursive algorithm.

### How the QuickSort Algorithm Works

The basic operation of the QuickSort algorithm is the partition of the array, which is performed as follows: We start with two pointers at the two ends of the array, which move toward the middle. Every time we locate two out-of-order elements, we swap them and continue. This process stops when the two pointers meet or cross each other. At this point we have partitioned the array in two subarrays and we must call the same Function twice, one time for the first subarray and another one for the second.

In Figure 12-9 you see how the elements of the initial array are rearranged so that the ones to the left of the pivot element are smaller, while the ones to its right are greater. The process of partitioning the entire array is depicted in Figure 12-10.

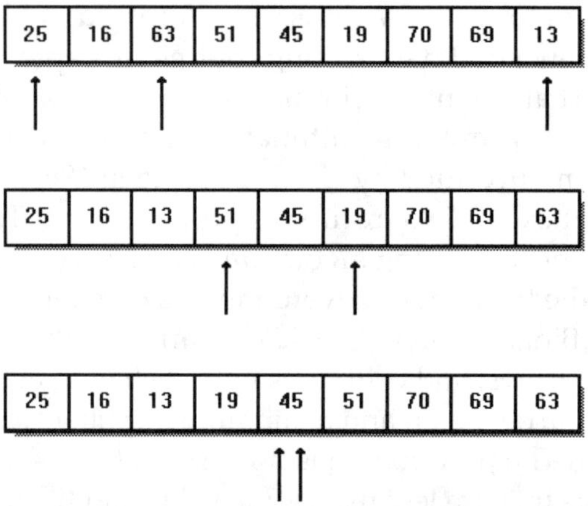


Figure 12-9: The process of rearranging the elements of an array to the left and right of the pivot. The two arrows represent the position of the pointers when out-of-order elements are found and swapped. The low pointer starts at 25 and moves to 63, the first element greater than 45. The high pointer remains at 13, which is smaller than 45. The next two elements to be swapped are 51 and 19. The rearrangement of the elements stops when the two pointers meet or cross each other.

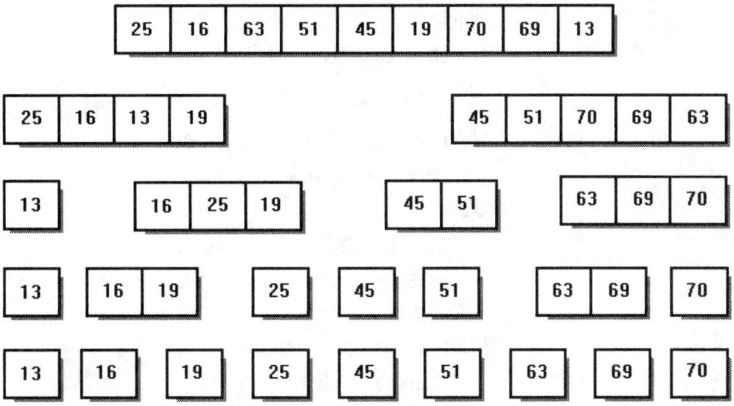


Figure 12-10: The process of partitioning an array according to the QuickSort algorithm. By the time the array is partitioned in single elements, it is sorted.

We will now implement a Subroutine called QSort, which will sort the elements of the array ddata( ) of doubles. QSort will accept two arguments, which are the indices of the original array that delimit the subarray to be sorted. The first time it must be called with the indices of the first and last element of the array. After that, the Subroutine will be called recursively, with the limits of each subarray as its arguments.

The first step is to select the pivot (the middle element) and rearrange the elements so that the ones smaller than the pivot are moved to its left, and the ones greater than (or equal to) the pivot are moved to its right. This is accomplished with the help of two pointers, which start at the two ends of the array and move toward each other. Every time we locate two out-of-order elements, we swap them and continue until the pointers cross. An out-of-order element is one that is to the left of the pivot and is greater than the pivot, or one that is to the right of the pivot and is smaller.

Once the array has been partitioned in two subarrays, we must call the QSort Subroutine for each one, provided that the corresponding subarray has two or more elements. Here is the complete code:

```
Sub QSort (lower As Long, upper As Long)
Dim pivot As Double
Dim first As Long, last As Long, middle As Long

' Locate pivot
    first = lower    ' lower pointer
    last = upper     ' upper pointer
```

```
    middle = (first + last) / 2
    pivot = ddata(middle)
    Do          ' move pointers against each other
    While ddata(first) < pivot
        first = first + 1
    Wend
    While ddata(last) > pivot
        last = last - 1
    Wend
    If first <= last Then
        temp = ddata(first)
        ddata(first) = ddata(last)
        ddata(last) = temp
        first = first + 1
        last = last - 1
    End If
    Loop Until first > last
    If lower < last Then
        Call QSort(lower, last)
    End If
    If first < upper Then
        Call QSort(first, upper)
    End If
End Sub
```

Do you see the purpose of the two If clauses at the end of the listing? If they weren't there, the QSort Subroutine would call itself even for subarrays with a single element and it would never end. A recursive routine *must exit explicitly*.

CD-ROM

Figure 12-11 shows the QuickSrt application, which sorts an array of double-precision floating-point variables (12\APPS\QUICKSRT on the CD). The size of the array is specified with the help of the scroll bar, and its elements contain random data, generated by the program. The time required to sort the array is reported with accuracy of milliseconds. It takes approximately 9 seconds to sort an array of 30,000 doubles with the QuickSort algorithm on a 486/66 system (approximately three times faster than the ShellSort algorithm in Chapter 2).

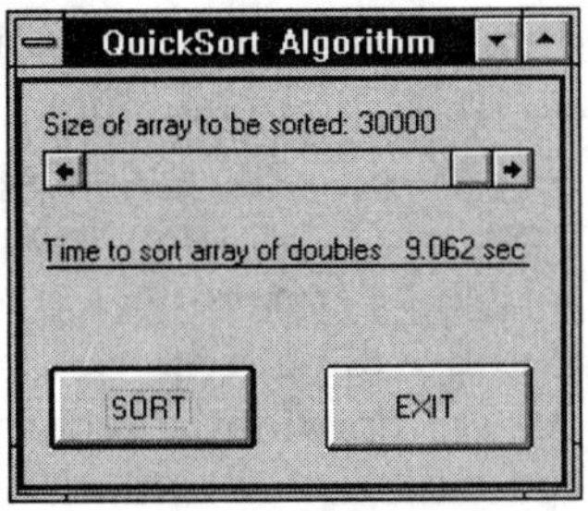


Figure 12-11: The QuickSrt application measures the time that it takes the QuickSort algorithm to sort various-sized arrays of doubles.

### QuickSort's Flaw

The QSort Subroutine is extremely fast, but it has a serious drawback. Can you guess what will happen if you attempt to sort an array whose elements are *already sorted?* If, for example, the first element of the array is already in place, then the original array will be split into two subarrays of sizes 1 and N–1 respectively (N is the number of elements of the array). The first subarray is already sorted, but the second one will be split into two subarrays of sizes 1 and (N–2), and so on. It's easy to see that the QuickSort algorithm would work better if the subarrays to be sorted at each step are of equal size (or nearly equal size). Their sizes would be halved at each step and very quickly we would have a large number of very small arrays to sort. The QuickSort algorithm has the absurd property that it works best for unordered arrays and worst for arrays that are completely sorted.

## To Recurse, or to Iterate?

Recursive programming may not be the bread and butter of the application programmer, but in the few cases where you will have to implement a recursive algorithm, you will find it extremely useful. The difficulty with recursive programming is not the implementation of a recursive routine, but simply recognizing that your programming goal is best achieved through recursion.

Recursion is so close to iteration, and yet so different.

Recursion bears some resemblance to iterative loops, such as For and While loops, but it is not quite the same. The difference between a recursive routine and a loop is that the recursive routine repeats itself (calls itself) before it is completed. On the other hand, a loop's body must finish before it is repeated.

Say you are trying to implement an algorithm with For or While loops. If you see yourself trying to break out of the loop prematurely (Exit For or Exit While), or your code is getting too messy (too many IF...THENs, or, even worse, GOTOs), chances are you are wrestling with a problem better solved by recursion. Once you recognize that recursion is called for, you'll will be surprised how neatly and compactly it can be coded. Most important, a recursive solution is more understandable, more readable, more *natural*, than the complexities of multiple IF...THENs or early exits from a loop.

It is worthwhile to see why our first two examples can be implemented nonrecursively, while the last two can't. The Scan( ) and QSort( ) routines are called again before the end of the code, and we don't know in advance how many times they will be called. The BSearch( ) Function is called at the very last line of the code, and it is possible to determine how many times it will be called. Therefore, it can be implemented with a loop. The same is true for the NameParse( ) Function.

### Still Scared?

A recursive routine is one that calls itself and does not differ from any other routine, except for one detail. A recursive routine's code must *exit explicitly*. In the first example, the Function NameParse would keep calling itself forever if it weren't for the If clause. You must code the recursive routine so that it ends at some point (in other words there must be a "way out" of the sequence of recursive calls).

Recursive programming is simple, but *thinking* recursively is not. The difficulty with recursive programming is to identify the recursive nature of a problem and then implement a recursive algorithm. If you are still uncomfortable with the idea of recursion, remember that your computer doesn't handle recursive routines any differently than ordinary procedures. The computer doesn't know that the called Function (or Subroutine) is calling itself. If it's that simple for your computer to handle recursion, why should it be more complicated for you? Try a few more examples. Soon you will get the hang of it, and recursion will become an important addition to your programming arsenal.

## Depth of Recursion

If you write a never-ending recursive routine, your program will not run forever. Sooner or later (rather sooner than later), your computer's stack memory will be exhausted and you will see the message "Out of Stack Space" on your screen. Each time a routine is called recursively, some space is used on the stack to tell the computer where to return to, as well as for storing the arguments. This space is released when the routine returns. If the routine is called recursively too many times, your computer runs out of stack memory and the application terminates.

Visual Basic sets aside 20k for the stack, which is enough space to permit a few hundred recursive calls. The exact number of recursive calls, or *depth of recursion*, depends on the number and type of arguments you are using (which also must be stored on the stack). The exact depth of recursion is not extremely important, since you cannot limit these calls in your applications. In most cases you will not even come close to this limit. Consider the DirScan application, for example, which cannot possibly run out of memory; how many levels of subdirectories can a user create on the hard disk? It is much more likely to exceed the List Box's limits, if you specify a very general pattern, such as *.*.

Since it's possible to exhaust the system's stack memory with a recursive routine, your application should be prepared to handle this situation. When Visual Basic runs out of stack memory, it generates the error code 28, which corresponds to the error message "Out of Stack Space." Be sure to include the code to trap this error. Of course, there is nothing you can do to remedy this situation, but you can at least display your own error message and give the user a chance to save any open files and terminate the application in an orderly fashion.

### Helping QuickSort in its Worst Cases

We have explained how QuickSort slows down when the array is already sorted. This strange property has another unpleasant side effect. If the array is completely sorted, the QSort Subroutine must be called recursively N–1 times. In other words, it is very likely that the QSort Subroutine will run out of stack memory! There are ways to cope with this problem, but first you must examine the nature (or source) of your data. In most cases, the raw data are unordered. If you have reason to believe that the data are already sorted (or partially sorted), you can first scramble a few elements to unsort the original data. Then the QSort Subroutine will work fine.

### Example: A Math Parser

The last example of this section deals with math expressions. It can be used in a variety of applications, from really simple ones to the most complicated.

You may skip it if you hate math. However, we believe that quite a few people use Visual Basic in scientific calculations, and they will be interested in seeing how a math parser works. Moreover, we will show you how to plot any math Function with an application very similar to VBPlot, which we explored in Chapter 5.

CD-ROM

If you would like to include the Functionality of the math parser in your own applications, look at the application VBParse in the directory 12\APPS\VBPARSE of the CD. It contains a single Function, parse( ), which can evaluate any valid math expression. Just copy it to your project along with the definition of four Form-wide variables.

*Parsing* means scanning text and extracting information or performing certain calculations based on the components of the text. Visual Basic can calculate all kinds of math expressions embedded in your code or entered into the Debug Window. But there is no simple way to evaluate a mathematical expression typed in by the user while a program is running.

Evaluating user-input math expressions in your code isn't as simple as typing them in the Debug Window.

A parser does exactly that. It scans a piece of text containing a math expression, and calculates its value (for example, it might accept a string like "5+4*3^2"). The VBParse application is shown in Figure 12-12. The user can type any valid expression in the large Text Box, click on the Command Button with the equals sign and see the result in the smaller Text Box. The expression may contain any of Visual Basic's math Functions, or even an independent variable, X. Moreover, the variable X may have a single value, or vary in a range of values, similar to a For...Next loop. In the latter case, the results are displayed one after the other in the smaller Text Box. But you can modify the code to redirect the consecutive numbers to a Grid, or even plot them with the VBPlot application (see the FNCPlot application, explained later). The Equals Button is the default one on this Form, so you must press Ctrl+Enter to change lines in the Expression Text Box.

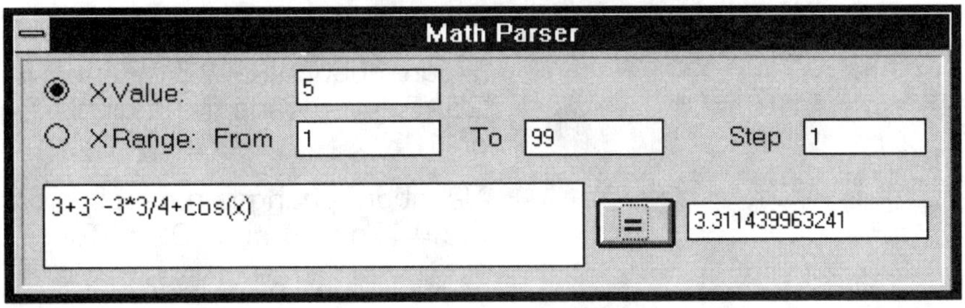


Figure 12-12: The VBParse application can evaluate any valid math expression, just like Visual Basic.

## Parsing Math Expressions

The computer doesn't perform any magic steps when it calculates math expressions. It does exactly what you would do with paper and pencil. Here's how to do it:

We start from left side of the text and perform the operations in the order we find the operators and operands. From time to time, though, we must suspend a calculation to perform one with higher precedence.

The meaning of a math expression is ambiguous unless its operations are organized into some order of precedence. For example, 5+3/2 results in 4 if you add 5+3 to get 8, and then divide 8 by 2. But it results in 6.5 if, as is the case, division "has precedence over" addition and should be carried out first. Following the established rules of precedence, we must first divide 3 by 2, getting 1.5, and then add this to 5, getting 6.5.

Let's see how the expression 3+4*5 is calculated, from left to right. We can't perform the addition before we have the result of the multiplication, because multiplication has a higher precedence than addition. (Note that precedence can be overridden by the user when typing in a math expression. Anything enclosed within parentheses is carried out first, regardless of precedence—in 3*(4+5), the addition would be done first.)

So the overall task in parsing a math expression is to perform operations from left to right, suspending them temporarily every time we encounter an operation with higher precedence or parenthetic expressions which must be evaluated on their own, regardless of precedence. Table 12-1 shows the order of precedence (from higher to lower) of the usual math operators.

| Symbol | Description |
|---|---|
| ^ | Exponentiation (5 ^ 2 means five times itself, or 25. 5 ^ 3 means five multiplied by itself three times, or 125). |
| – | Negation (changes a negative number's sign, like 44 to –44 and –22 to 22). |
| *, / | Multiplication or division. |
| \ | Integer division (division resulting in no remainder, no fraction. 8 \ 6 is 1). |
| Mod | Modulo arithmetic (the remainder after division. 23 Mod 12 is 11). |
| +, – | Addition or subtraction. |

Table 12-1: Order of precedence of math operators.

### The Math Parser Application

CD-ROM

The entire parser is contained in a single Form. The project is called VBPARSE.MAK and you can find it in the 12\APPS\VBPARSE subdirectory of the CD. Since the global variables are defined in the Form's Declarations section, you can add this Form to any of your applications that calls for a math parser and the variables will not interfere with other variables used by your application. The application makes use of four Form-wide variables, which are defined as follows:

```
Dim Expression As String        ' The expression to be parsed
Dim Token As String             ' The current token
Dim TypeOfToken                 ' The type of the current token
Dim ParserError As Integer      ' Indicates an error condition
```

*Expression* is a string that holds the expression. A math expression is made up of *tokens*, which are the smallest individual elements, the *atoms* of the expression. Tokens are numbers, operators, parentheses and Function names. The name of a built-in Function, such as ABS or EXP, is a token because it can't be broken down into smaller pieces. The expression 30.3+4^–2, consists of the following tokens:

- 30.3 (number)
- \+ (operator)
- 4 (number)
- ^ (operator)
- – (operator)
- 2 (number)

To handle the tokens properly, our parser must be able to recognize each token and its type. Each time a new token is extracted from the expression, it's stored in the Token variable, and a special word describing its type is assigned to the TypeOfToken variable. The parser recognizes the following types of tokens:

- Numbers, which are indicated with the keyword "num".
- Function names, which are indicated with the keyword "Function".
- Single-character tokens , like parentheses, and math operators, which are denoted by the value of the Token variable. (*Note:* The only math operator that isn't a single character token is the Mod operator and must be handled differently.)

Error can occur anywhere in the process, and there is no recovery procedure. The evaluation must end right there.

The ParserError variable is a flag, that can be set to True throughout the program, should an error be detected. It doesn't really matter where the error was detected, since the parsing process can't continue. As you will see, the evaluation of an expression terminates as soon as an error is detected.

## A Very Simple Parser

Because the application's complete implementation is not very easy to follow, we'll start with the simplest form of a math parser: a Function that evaluates simple expressions made up of numbers and the basic math operators, such as 3+3*2, or 13–4^2. (In other words, we'll ignore for now the precedence of the operators and the possibility of parentheses.)

The first step in implementing a parser is a routine that extracts the individual tokens from any given expression. You will see its implementation shortly, but first let's describe its operation. GetNextToken( ) scans the expression from left to right, extracts the first token from the expression and sets two global variables: TypeOfToken (which is a string indicating the type of token ) and Token (which is the actual value of the token). GetNextToken is implemented as a Subroutine that accepts no arguments and returns no result, because it operates on global variables.

```
Sub GetNextToken ()
Dim c As String

    TypeOfToken = ""
    Token = ""
```

```
' skip all white spaces (spaces, LFs, CRs, TABs)
    Do
        c = Left$(expression, 1)
        expression = Mid$(expression, 2)
    Loop While c = " " Or c = Chr$(10) Or c = Chr$(13) Or  →
    c = Chr$(9)

    Select Case LCase$(c)
' Can handle decimal numbers, but not scientific notation
    Case "0" To "9", "."
        TypeOfToken = "num"
        Do
            Token = Token + c
            c = Left$(expression, 1)
            expression = Mid$(expression, 2)
        Loop While (c >= "0" And c <= "9") Or c = "."
        expression = c + expression
' Any string is treated as a Function name
    Case "a" To "z"
        TypeOfToken = "Function"
        Do
            Token = Token + c
            c = LCase$(Left$(expression, 1))
            expression = Mid$(expression, 2)
        Loop While (c >= "a" And c <= "z")
        expression = c + expression

    Case Else
        TypeOfToken = c
    End Select

' Is it a valid number ?
    If TypeOfToken = "num" Then
        If Not IsNumeric(Token) Then
            If Not ParserError Then MsgBox "Invalid number"
            ParserError = True
            Exit Sub
        End If
    End If
```

```
    If Token = "" Then          ' takes care of operators  →
    and parens
       Token = TypeOfToken
    End If

End Sub
```

GetNextToken is another useful tool you can use in your math applications as is.

The GetNextToken( ) Subroutine is straightforward. It extracts the first token from the left side of the expression and assigns it to the Token variable. It also recognizes the type of each token so that the rest of the code can handle different types of tokens differently. Table 12-2 lists the three types of tokens:

| | |
|---|---|
| Numbers: | integers, reals |
| Symbols: | math operators: ^, *, /, \, +, –, mod<br>parentheses<br>unary minus |
| Function names: | (abs, log, etc) |

Table 12-2: Types of tokens.

The core of this application is the parse( ) Function, which processes the expression. Here is the implementation of the simple parse( ) Function:

```
Function Parse () As Double
Dim n As Double

   Call GetNextToken
   If TypeOfToken = "num" Then
      n = Val(Token)
      Call GetNextToken
   Else
      ParserError = True
   End If

   Do While Not ParserError
      Select Case Token
         Case "^": n = n ^ Parse(): GoTo NextSymbol
         Case "*": n = n * Parse(): GoTo NextSymbol
         Case "/": n = n / Parse(): GoTo NextSymbol
         Case "\": n = n \ Parse(): GoTo NextSymbol
```

```
            Case "+": n = n + Parse(): GoTo NextSymbol
            Case "-": n = n - Parse(): GoTo NextSymbol
        End Select
        Exit Do
NextSymbol:
    Loop
    Parse = n

End Function
```

The parse( ) Function gets the first token, which should be a number, and assigns its value to the variable *n*. It then reads the next token, which should be a math operator. Based on the value of the last token, parse( ) performs the appropriate operation between n and the value returned by another call to parse( ). If the first token is not a number, or the second token is not a valid math operator, then the parse( ) Function ends and returns the current value of n.

### Following the Evaluation of a Simple Expression

Let's follow the steps involved in calculating 3+4*5.

1. The first time parse( ) is called, it extracts the first token ("3") from the expression, and n becomes 3. The token is also removed from Expression, which now becomes "+4*5".
2. Then it calls GetNextToken( ) again and examines the TypeOfToken variable. The next token is the addition symbol, and parse( ) is ready to add 3 to the next operand (n=3+parse( )).
3. The next operand is not a single number, but another operation. parse( ) suspends the execution of the addition and calls itself again.
4. After the second call of GetNextToken( ), the expression string becomes "4*5". The second invocation of the parse( ) Function will return the value to be added to 3.
5. parse( ) starts its execution by calling the GetNextToken Subroutine. This time the GetNextToken returns an operand (4), and the next token, which is the multiplication symbol. parse( ) is now ready to perform a multiplication: n=4*parse( ).
6. The multiplication is suspended again, and parse( ) calls itself for a second time. This time n becomes 5, and there is no other token left in the expression.

Computers excel in math because they are so tediously methodical.

7. The execution of the parse( ) Function falls to the parse=n line (none of the Cases is satisfied), and returns the value 5.
8. This value is used in the most recently interrupted multiplication, n=4*5, and n becomes 20. The execution of the second most recently interrupted Function continues with the line parse=n, and this time the value 20 is returned.
9. The value 20 is used as the second operand in the very first interrupted operation, which can now complete: n=3+20 (=23). This is the value returned by the parse( ) Function.

What if we rearrange the terms of the expression this time, and use parse( ) to calculate 4*5+3? The first operand is 4 and the next token is the symbol of multiplication. parse( ) is called again with the line n=4*parse( ), and this time it retrieves the next operand (5) and the symbol of addition. The last time parse( ) is called, it returns the result 5+3, which in turn is multiplied by 4 to produce the incorrect result 32.

What happened this time? The parse( ) Function calculated the expression from left to right, without taking into account the operator precedence. You are so accustomed to performing simple calculations like 4*5+3 that you automatically perform the multiplication first, and then add the last operand. Our parse( ) Function, however, hasn't been told that the multiplication has a higher precedence than addition. We must therefore modify our Function, so that it can account for operator precedence.

Notice also that this version of parse( ) doesn't do any error checking. It simply returns an incorrect result. Our aim is to explain how to build a math parser, starting with the simplest case. Later on, we will add all the necessary error-trapping code. The code of our first version of the parser is implemented in the application PARSE1 (subdirectory 12\APPS\VBPARSE\VBPARSE1 on the CD). If you need additional help in understanding the previous discussion, run the PARSE1 application and see how it evaluates simple expressions. If you get an incorrect result, you can trace the program's steps to see why the incorrect result was produced. Notice that the PARSE1 application contains no error-checking code, and it may crash on you. The error-checking code would have added significant complexity to our code at this point. The final version of our math parser contains all the necessary error-checking code.

CD-ROM

### Forcing Operator Precedence With Parentheses

One solution to the problem of operator precedence is to enforce the proper operator precedence using parentheses. This isn't the optimal solution, but since our parser should be able to handle parentheses anyway, why not implement this feature now?

We'll add a few lines before the Else clause to handle the special case of the opening parenthesis. Every time the parse( ) Function sees an opening parenthesis, it must calculate its contents up to the matching closing parenthesis, and use this value as the next operand. And what's a better way to calculate a subexpression in parentheses than calling parse( ) again? Next, you see the modified parse( ) Function with a few extra lines of code, properly marked:

```
Function Parse () As Double
Dim n As Double

   Call GetNextToken
   If TypeOfToken = "num" Then
      n = Val(Token)
      Call GetNextToken
   ElseIf TypeOfToken = "(" Then
      n = Parse()
      If TypeOfToken <> ")" Then ParserError = True
      Call GetNextToken
   Else
      ParserError = True
   End If

   Do While Not ParserError
      Select Case Token
         Case "^": n = n ^ Parse(): GoTo NextSymbol
         Case "*": n = n * Parse(): GoTo NextSymbol
         Case "/": n = n / Parse(): GoTo NextSymbol
         Case "\": n = n \ Parse(): GoTo NextSymbol
         Case "+": n = n + Parse(): GoTo NextSymbol
         Case "-": n = n - Parse(): GoTo NextSymbol
   End Select
   Exit Do
NextSymbol:
   Loop
   Parse = n

End Function
```

Notice that because of the recursive nature of the parse() Function, these few lines can handle any number of nested parentheses.

The opening parenthesis appears always in the place of an operand. If the parse( ) Function finds the opening parenthesis when an operand was expected, it calls itself again. Then it calculates the entire subexpression between the opening and the matching closing parenthesis before it continues with the current calculation. The extra four lines of code can handle nested parentheses, too. Not only that, but they check for the matching closing parenthesis and set an error flag to terminate all pending instances of parse( ) if the matching parenthesis was not found.

If you rewrite the last expression as (3*4)+5, the new parse( ) Function will evaluate it correctly. You can also test it with expressions containing nested parentheses, such as (3*(4+5)+(6^2))+2.

So far, our parse( ) Function can evaluate all kinds of arithmetic expressions, as long as you use parentheses to enforce the proper operator precedence.

### Handling Function Calls & the Unary Minus

Before we turn our attention to operator precedence, we will add the code for handling two more special cases, the unary minus and Function calls, such as log( ) or abs( ). These cases are also handled by two Else If clauses, as shown in the next listing:

```
Function Parse () As Double
Dim n As Double
Dim fname As String

    Call GetNextToken
    If TypeOfToken = "num" Then
        n = Val(Token)
        Call GetNextToken
    ElseIf TypeOfToken = "(" Then
        n = Parse()
        If TypeOfToken <> ")" Then ParserError = True
        Call GetNextToken
    ElseIf TypeOfToken = "-" Then
        n = -Parse()
    ElseIf TypeOfToken = "Function" Then
        fname = Token
        Call GetNextToken
        If TypeOfToken <> "(" Then ParserError = True
        n = Parse()
        If TypeOfToken <> ")" Then ParserError = True
```

```
            Call GetNextToken
            n = FunctionEvaluate(fname, n)
        Else
            ParserError = True
            MsgBox "Error during evaluation"
            Exit Function
        End If

        Do While Not ParserError
            Select Case Token
                Case "^": n = n ^ Parse(): GoTo NextSymbol
                Case "*": n = n * Parse(): GoTo NextSymbol
                Case "/": n = n / Parse(): GoTo NextSymbol
                Case "\": n = n \ Parse(): GoTo NextSymbol
                Case "+": n = n + Parse(): GoTo NextSymbol
                Case "-": n = n - Parse(): GoTo NextSymbol
            End Select
            Exit Do
    NextSymbol:
        Loop
        Parse = n

    End Function
```

(This Function contains some error-trapping code.)

Although it uses the minus sign, unary minus is not a subtraction.

The unary minus is a special operator that must be handled differently than the regular minus sign. You know what the minus sign does in a math expression: it subtracts the trailing number from the number in front of it. The minus sign is an operator that needs two operands. The unary minus appears in front of a single operand and inverts its sign, as in –3+2 or 3^–2. Most programmers put the unary minus in a pair of parentheses, to make their expressions easier to read: (–3)+2 or 3^(–2). The minus sign in the previous expressions doesn't indicate a subtraction. Instead, it inverts the sign of the following number. The unary minus can be used with parentheses. too. The expression –(–3) is the number 3, and so is the expression –(2–5).

The unary minus is easy to handle. We simply invert the sign of the number or subexpression that follows. Notice that the unary minus cannot be mistaken for the subtraction symbol, because, like the opening parenthesis, it appears always in the place of an operand. The other minus (the sign of subtraction) is handled by the body of If statements. Check out the operation of the Math Parser with an expression that contains both minus signs, such as: 7–(–4+2)^2, or 16^(–1/2), which is the square root of 16.

### Function Evaluation

Our next step is the handling of regular Functions. If GetNextToken( ) extracts a string from the expression (by assigning the keyword "Function" to the TypeOfToken variable), we assume it is a Function name and attempt to calculate its value. First we make sure that there is an opening parenthesis right after the Function name. Then we call parse( ) to evaluate the expression in the parentheses following the Function name and check for the matching closing parenthesis. Finally, we call the FunctionEvaluate( ) Function to evaluate the Function call with the argument returned by the last call to parse( ).

The FunctionEvaluate( ) Function accepts two arguments, which are a string with the Visual Basic Function name and a double. Here is its implementation:

```
Function FunctionEvaluate (FunctionName$, arg As Double) →
Dim fvalue As Double

On Error GoTo DispErrorMssg

Select Case LCase$(FunctionName$)
    Case "abs": fvalue = Abs(arg)
    Case "atn": fvalue = Atn(arg)
    Case "cos": fvalue = Cos(arg)
    Case "exp": fvalue = Exp(arg)
    Case "fix": fvalue = Fix(arg)
    Case "int": fvalue = Int(arg)
    Case "log": fvalue = Log(arg)
    Case "rnd": fvalue = Rnd(arg)
    Case "sgn": fvalue = Sgn(arg)
    Case "sin": fvalue = Sin(arg)
    Case "sqr": fvalue = Sqr(arg)
    Case "tan": fvalue = Tan(arg)
    Case "x": fvalue = x
    ' The following cases are some derived math Functions
    ' You must also update the ValidSymbols variable in the
    ' GetNextToken Subroutine
    ' Case "sec": fvalue = 1 / Cos(arg)
```

```
        ' Case "cosec": fvalue = 1 / Sin(arg)
        ' Case "cotan": fvalue = 1 / Tan(arg), etc, etc

        Case Else
            Errormsg$ = "Can't evaluate Function " + FunctionName$
            MsgBox Errormsg$
            ParserError = True
            Exit Function
        End Select
        FunctionEvaluate = fvalue
        Exit Function
    DispErrorMssg:
        Errormsg$ = Error$ + Chr$(10) + "in evaluating " +
    UCase$(FunctionName$)
        If Not ParserError Then MsgBox Errormsg$
        ParserError = True
        Exit Function
        Resume Next

    End Function
```

The FunctionEvaluate( ) Function is straightforward. The only point worth discussing here is the error handling. There are two possible sources of errors: calling FunctionEvaluate( ) with a nonexistent Function name (ATAN instead of ATN, for example) or calling it with a bad argument, such as sqr(-4). The two cases are handled differently, but they both terminate the calculations by setting ParserError to True.

The section of the parse( ) Function that handles parentheses can handle nested parentheses, too, so any Function may be followed by any subexpression in parentheses. In other words, the parse( ) Function can manage Function calls like log(3+4*(5-2)), or even exp(1+sin(log(33.3)))—should you ever desire to evaluate totally meaningless Functions! This version of our math parser can be found in the 12\APPS\VBPARSE\VBPARSE2 subdirectory of the CD.

CD-ROM

## Proper Precedence, Too

Operator precedence will help us avoid numerous nested parentheses.

Let's come back to the issue of operator precedence. We left this topic for last because it can't be handled with just a few extra lines. To force operator precedence, we must modify the parse( ) Function so that it knows when to interrupt an operation to perform another one, and when not to. For example, parse( ) must not interrupt a multiplication to perform an addition, but it must interrupt either multiplication or addition to raise a number to a power. To calculate 3*4+5, the parse( ) Function must complete the multiplication 3*4 before performing the addition. To calculate 3*4^2, however, it must interrupt the multiplication to calculate the quantity 4^2.

To force the operator precedence, we must be able to call parse( ) with an argument, which is the precedence level of the current operator. We will assign a precedence level to each operator and take this level into consideration in interrupting the current calculation. The precedence level is an integer that is larger for operators with higher precedence. Table 12-3 shows the precedence levels for all Visual Basic operators, from the highest to the lowest. The precedence levels are numbered arbitrarily, as long as operators with higher precedence are assigned higher numbers than operators with lower precedence.

| Operator | Precedence Level |
|---|---|
| ^ | 5 |
| * | 4 |
| / | 4 |
| \ | 3 |
| mod | 2 |
| + | 1 |
| – | 1 |

Table 12-3: The operator precedence levels used in the parse( ) Function.

Notice that some operators have the same precedence. Successive operators on the same precedence level are executed from left to right, unless the default precedence is overridden with parentheses.

Here is the final version of the parse( ) Function, which takes into account the operator precedence (it also contains quite a few lines for error checking):

```
Function Parse (p As Integer) As Double
Dim n As Double
Dim FunctionName As String

    Call GetNextToken
    If ParserError Then Exit Function
    If TypeOfToken = "num" Then
        n = Val(Token)
```

```
            Call GetNextToken
            If ParserError Then Exit Function
        ElseIf TypeOfToken = "-" Then
            n = -Parse(5)
        ElseIf TypeOfToken = "(" Then
            n = Parse(1)
            If TypeOfToken <> ")" Then
                If Not ParserError Then
                    Call SelectError
                    MsgBox "Unbalanced Parens"
                End If
                ParserError = -1
                Exit Function
            End If
            Call GetNextToken
            If ParserError Then Exit Function
    ' It's either a Function name, or a variable name
        ElseIf TypeOfToken = "Function" Then    ' Function names...
            FunctionName = Token
            If LCase$(Token) <> "x" Then
                FunctionName = Token
                Call GetNextToken
                If TypeOfToken <> "(" Then          ' ...MUST be    →
                followed by opening paren
                    If Not ParserError Then
                        Call SelectError
                        MsgBox "Function name not followed by Parens"
                    End If
                    ParserError = -1
                    Exit Function
                End If
                n = Parse(1)            ' Evaluate Function's arguments
                If TypeOfToken <> ")" Then          ' closing paren ?
                    If Not ParserError Then
                        Call SelectError
                        MsgBox "Unbalanced Parens"
                    End If
                    ParserError = -1
                    Exit Function
                End If
            End If
            Call GetNextToken
```

```
            If ParserError Then Exit Function
            n = FunctionEvaluate(FunctionName, n)
        Else
            If Not ParserError Then
                Call SelectError
                MsgBox "Unexpected Symbol Encountered"
            End If
            ParserError = -1
            Exit Function
        End If

    ' Here is the main loop. It handles the basic structure:
    '       number <Operator> number
    '.repeatedly, until it runs out of (valid) tokens
    On Error GoTo OpError
        Do While Not ParserError
            Select Case TypeOfToken
            Case "^":
                If p <= 5 Then n = n ^ Parse(6): GoTo NextSymbol
            Case "*":
                If p <= 4 Then n = n * Parse(5): GoTo NextSymbol
            Case "/":
                If p <= 4 Then n = n / Parse(5): GoTo NextSymbol
            Case "\":
                If p <= 3 Then n = n \ Parse(4): GoTo NextSymbol
            Case "mod":
                If p <= 2 Then n = n Mod Parse(3): GoTo NextSymbol
            Case "+":
                If p <= 1 Then n = n + Parse(2): GoTo NextSymbol
            Case "-":
                If p <= 1 Then n = n - Parse(2): GoTo NextSymbol
            End Select
            Exit Do

    NextSymbol:
        Loop
        Parse = n
        Exit Function

    OpError:                    ' invalid operation
        If Not ParserError Then
```

```
            Call SelectError
            Errormsg$ = "Illegal Operand" + Chr$(10) + Error$
            MsgBox Errormsg$
        End If
        ParserError = -1
        Exit Function
        Resume

    End Function
```

Notice that this Function contains quite a few lines for error trapping (we'll discuss them shortly). The last implementation of the parse( ) Function includes an argument: the precedence level. The argument of our parse( ) Function does the trick very simply. As you can see, parse( ) is called with a precedence level. Before performing a math operation, it looks at the current precedence level and doesn't interrupt it to calculate one with lower precedence. To make sure that all operations will be performed, we must supply the argument 1 (parse(1)) the very first time we call parse( ).

This version of parse( ) doesn't need parentheses to force operator precedence. You can type expressions like 4*2^3/5 or 2*3^–4, and the parse( ) Function will evaluate them correctly.

### Adding a Variable to the Expression

The last step is to include the code for handling the variable X. As you have seen in Figure 12-12, the VBPARSE application lets you specify a variable (X) and calculates the expression for a specific value of X, or a range of values. GetNextToken will think that X is a Function name and will classify it as "Function." The parse( ) Function, therefore, must handle it as a special case of a Function. If the TypeOfToken is "x", the FunctionEvaluate( ) Function simply returns the value of the variable x. This feature was implemented in the last version of parse( ).

### Error Checking

The final version of the parse( ) Function does a lot of error checking. A potential problem with recursive Functions is that an error may occur at any level. Once an error has been detected, you can't just exit and return to the main program. All suspended Functions must exit as well. When parse( ) detects an error, it sets the ParserError variable to True, displays a Message Box with the appropriate error message and exits. This error, however, will propagate upward through every suspended instance of the parse( ) Function, to the very first call to parse( ). As each of the interrupted Function sees that ParserError is True, it displays the same error message.

To avoid this situation, we always check the value of ParserError. If it's True, it means that an error message has already been displayed, and we don't display it again. That's why you see the following structure so often in the parse( ) Function.

```
If Not ParserError Then
    Call SelectError
    MsgBox Error_Message
End If
```

(Error_Message is the appropriate error message for each case). The SelectError Subroutine selects (highlights) the token that caused the problem in the Text Box, to help the user correct it. Sometimes, however, the actual error may be the result of previous calculations, and the selected token will be the place where the parse( ) Function detected it, and not the actual token that caused the problem.

CD-ROM

To help you experiment with the math parser and better understand its operation, we have included three different applications in the 12\APPS\VBPARSE subdirectory of the CD. VBPARSE1 is the simplest parser, which can handle numbers and math operators only; this was our first implementation of parse( ). VBPARSE2 is identical to VBPARSE1, but it can handle parentheses and the unary minus. VBPARSE is the complete application, which can evaluate all the valid math expressions that Visual Basic can.

---

Do you see the recursive nature of the parse( ) algorithm? You have realized by now that the parse( ) Function must be interrupted every time it encounters a subexpression, or an operator with a higher precedence, to calculate an intermediate result before it completes the current calculation. Try to think of a nonrecursive way to implement a parser, and you will soon be lost in a maze of IFs, ELSEIFs and GOTOs.

---

Parsers are one of the most difficult topics in programming, yet you couldn't do much without them. The Visual Basic compiler itself is a parser, and you can imagine how much more complicated it is than our math parser. A compiler must handle not only math expressions, but commands, too. So next time you discover a small bug in your favorite language, be a little understanding.

### Using the Parser

In Chapter 5 we presented the VBPlot application for plotting Functions and data sets. The drawback of this application was that it couldn't plot user-supplied Functions. In other words, you had to insert the expression to be plotted in the code.

CD-ROM

The FNCPLOT application we include in the 12\APPS\FNCPLOT subdirectory of the CD allows you to specify your own Function and plot it. Figure 12-13 illustrates the Parameters Form of the application, where you can enter your Function and the range of X values to be plotted. Figure 12-14 shows the FNCPLOT application in action. The expression plotted is the one entered in the Parameters Form. The code of the application is a combination of VBPlot and VBPARSE. If you like, load the application in Visual Basic's editor and look at it.

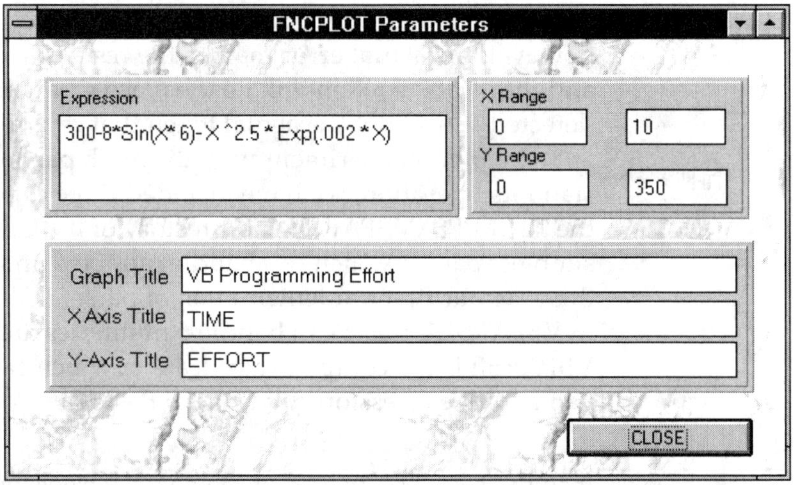


Figure 12-13: FNCPLOT: Specifying the expression to be plotted.

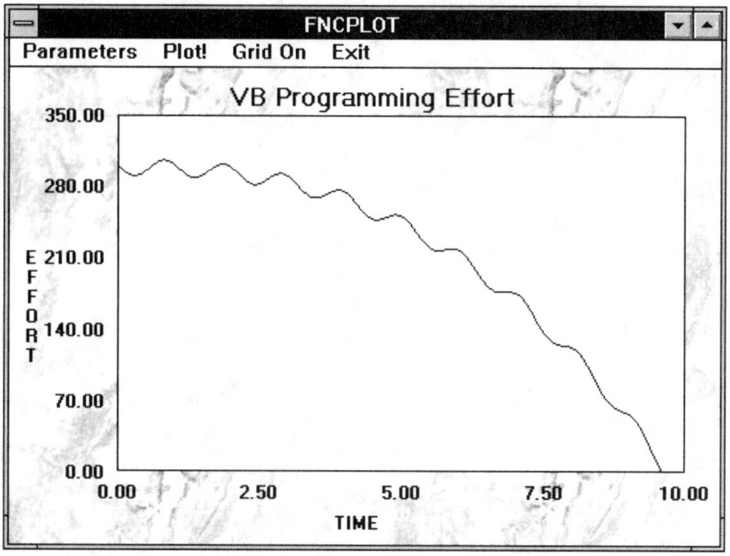


Figure 12-14: FNCPLOT: The plot of the expression of Figure 12-13.

## MOVING ON

In the next chapter we are going to tackle a new and totally different topic: the role of Visual Basic in the workgroup. Visual Basic can be used for the development of stand-alone as well as network applications. As the network increasingly becomes part of everyday life with computers, workgroup applications are emerging. These are applications that not only integrate with other applications, but also provide communication between users and applications.

If you are working in a networked environment, chances are you are using Windows for Workgroups instead of Windows 3.1. You are probably making use of applications like electronic mail to communicate with the other users in the network. If so, you'll be interested in how Visual Basic can help you automate the flow of information in your working environment. You will learn how to send electronic messages from within your applications, extract your messages from Mail's Inbox with simple Visual Basic commands, and write applications that talk to each other.

These new applications are called *mail-aware* and *mail-enabled*, and you'll will be seeing many of them in the near future. If you plan to use Visual Basic in the workgoup environment, the next chapter contains plenty of information to get you started.

# Chapter 13

# Workgroup Networking

Visual Basic works as well in the network environment of Windows for Workgroups as it does in Windows. In this chapter we'll see how to use VB to accomplish some unique things in a network environment.

To implement the examples of this chapter, we used a Windows for Workgroups network with several Windows 95 workstations. The Windows for Workgroup environment is used extensively in small network installations and will remain in use for a while. Windows 95 includes all of the functionality of Windows for Workgroups and will gradually replace both Windows 3.11 and Windows for Workgroups. The same examples will work under Windows for Workgroups and Windows 95, as well as under Windows 3.11 equipped with Microsoft's Mail System. In the rest of the chapter, we will refer to any of the aforementioned Windows configurations as "Windows." Our examples will also work on any Windows workstation with messaging capabilities.

## WHAT IS A WORKGROUP?

Windows is not just an operating system: it is Microsoft's proposal for the future of personal computers and workstations. As such it includes network support. As we move toward "global computing," networked environments will play an increasingly important role in personal computing.

Windows for Workgroups extends the Windows operating system to the *workgroup*, a small team with common needs, means and goals. The people working in a small company may form a single workgroup. In a larger company, each department could be a separate workgroup. Employees working on a project could be a workgroup, since they share common goals, and some may belong to more than one workgroup.

A workgroup, therefore, is not a physical network, but a way of organizing a work environment on a network. Windows for Workgroups is not a network operating system. Rather, it is a set of tools for interconnecting a number of users, based on their needs and requirements rather than their physical locations. However, it provides all the basic requirements of a network, such as sharing of files and printers, electronic mail and so on. Moreover, it can be incorporated into different networks, such as Novell or LAN Manager.

Although each computer on a network may be equipped with the best software available, there are few tools for integrating the work environment. Personal computer networks allow users to share files and printers. Networks also offer client-server capabilities. However, they do very little by themselves to automate users' work flow.

Workgroup software is the latest trend in software development. Many analysts predict that the workgroup market will grow rapidly through the '90s. Until recently, software developers have focused on individual productivity. Software has became more powerful, faster and easier to learn and use. We have reached a point where we cannot significantly increase the individual productivity by making the same software faster or more powerful, at least not as easily as a few years ago.

Workgroup software focuses on the needs of the workgroup, and not the needs of individual users.

To increase the productivity of the work environment, developers have switched their attention to service the needs of groups, rather than individuals. Workgroup applications increase productivity by improving communication and coordination between workgroup members and, to some extent, by automating the processes that require coordination among members. Applications are customized to suit the needs of the workgroup, making the members more efficient—no work is duplicated, meetings can be arranged electronically or even take place over the network, and members can access common files, even a common clipboard.

Whether workgroup computing will live up to expectations will become evident in the near future. But all indications are in favor of this new generation of software. Many companies are designing workgroup solutions under Windows for Workgroups and Windows 95. Microsoft is adding many workgroup features to its Office 95 suite of applications.

We've selected what we consider to be the single most important component of Microsoft's workgroup environment to demonstrate how to develop applications for the workgroup. This component is the *messaging subsystem*.

This chapter goes beyond electronic mail. You will find out how to incorporate messaging capabilities in your applications and how to let the applications themselves exchange messages. These capabilities will add a new dimension to your applications.

## THE MESSAGING SUBSYSTEM

The messaging subsystem is the basic mechanism for information exchange among users or applications. The Mail application that comes with Windows takes advantage of the messaging subsystem. One of the sample programs that comes with Visual Basic shows you how to write an application like MS Mail in Visual Basic. We will present the capabilities of the Windows messaging subsystem from Visual Basic's point of view. And we'll show how to write applications that exploit the communication capabilities of the operating system. Our examples, however, will go further than just demonstrating how to write a customized Mail application.

MAPI is a set of routines that gives applications access to the Windows messaging mechanism.

From an application's point of view, the messaging subsystem is a set of API Functions, called MAPI. MAPI stands for Messaging Application Programming Interface. This set of routines runs on top of the Windows messaging subsystem and gives your applications access to the messaging subsystem. The messaging subsystem works like the print subsystem of the Windows operating system. All applications access a lower-level, common interface within Windows that provides the appropriate printer-specific behaviors through a simple dialog box (the Print dialog box). In this way, neither the application nor the programmer needs to know the specifics of any given printer.

Similarly, the exchange of electronic messages in the Windows environment passes through the lower-level messaging subsystem, which provides a simple message create-and-send dialog box. With the help of this dialog box, shown in Figure 13-1, you can easily integrate basic messaging capabilities with your applications.

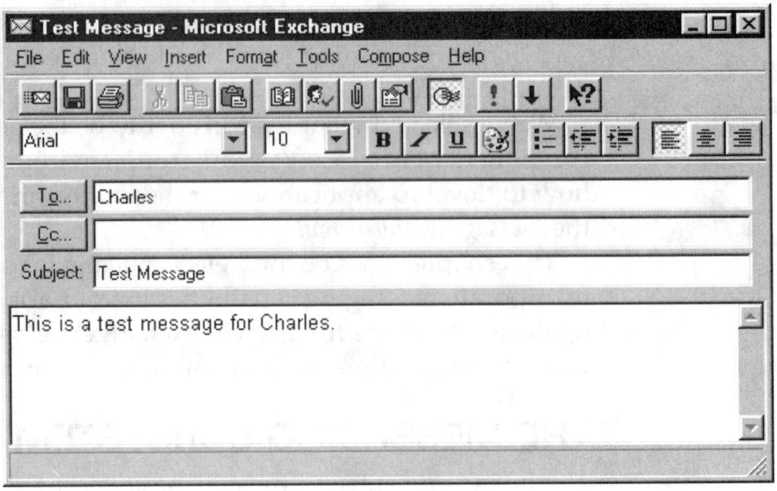


Figure 13-1: With this dialog box, you can create and send messages to any other member of the workgroup, and beyond. Notice that messages can have attachments (Attach Button) and be addressed to more than one recipient (Cc: field).

Built into Windows for Workgroups is an ambitious messaging subsystem, providing all the messaging services applications may need. MAPI is the interface to the messaging subsystem, a way for applications to tap into this system and take advantage of its capabilities. Visual Basic makes use of the so-called Simple MAPI, a subset of the complete MAPI. The Simple MAPI is itself quite full-featured, and you can use it to build powerful custom messaging applications. The Professional Edition of Visual Basic provides the basic messaging capabilities of the Simple MAPI with its two MAPI Controls: MAPI Session and MAPI Messages. Let's look at these Controls and see how you can use them to develop workgroup applications.

## VISUAL BASIC'S MAPI CONTROLS

MAPI Session and MAPI Messages are collectively called MAPI Controls. These Controls are placed on the Form to give the application access to the messaging subsystem, but they are invisible at run time, like the Common Dialog Control or a Timer. Moreover, the two MAPI Controls have Properties and Methods but no Events. (*Note:* The MAPI Controls of Visual Basic 3.0 have Properties only. By setting their values, you can control the underlying messaging subsystem and incorporate many of its functions in your application. For example, to send a message, you set the Action Property to 2. With Visual Basic 4.0, you can either set the Action Property or call the Send Method.)

Why two separate VB messaging Controls? Messaging involves two distinct actions. From the programmer's point of view, the MAPI Session Control is the simpler of the two: it merely connects to or disconnects from the Mail Server. It's like picking up, or hanging up, the phone. MAPI Messages does all the rest: creating, addressing and displaying messages and handling such tasks as message deletion and forwarding

Visual Basic lets you incorporate messaging functions in your applications through two specialized Controls: MAPI Session and MAPI Messages.

The Properties of the MAPI Controls fall into three categories: *connectivity*, *addressing* and *message handling*. Connectivity includes the Properties that allow you to establish a mail session and communicate with the Mail Server. Once connected, you have access to all services of the messaging subsystem, just as if you were in the Mail application of Windows. In reality, both the MAPI Controls and the Mail application are serviced by the same engine, which is the Windows messaging subsystem. The second category, addressing, relates to the circulation of the messages (addressing and forwarding messages, for example). Message handling lets you create and delete messages, attach information to them and so on. All the actions that relate to message addressing and handling are performed by the MAPI Messages Control.

Each connection between an application and the messaging subsystem is called a *session*. The MAPI Session Control provides the connectivity Properties. You can log in to the Mail Server (that is, establish a session), download your messages and disconnect when you are done. The actual exchange of messages takes place through the Properties of the MAPI Messages Control.

## Logging In (MAPI Session Control)

When Windows for Workgroups (or Windows 95) is installed, one person is designated as the "mail administrator." That person assigns a user name and a mailbox name (a "mailbox," as it's called) to each user. All messages addressed to a specific user (in other words to his or her user name) are stored in the mailbox and remain there until the user reads and deletes them.

To log in to the Mail System, the user must provide his or her user name and password. The password is there for security reasons. The user name, though, determines which mailbox will be used. The Messaging System maintains a separate mailbox for each user, which must be a unique name. The user name is an alias for the actual mailbox name, and the mailbox name may not even sound like the user name. A small workgroup environment may someday become part of a large network, with users all over the country. Making up unique user names or mailbox names in a distributed environment is, of course, out of the question. But if you concatenate the name of the workgroup and the name of the workstation with the user's mailbox name, you end up with a unique name. This name is the *electronic address* of the user who owns the specific mailbox.

User names are "aliases." The messaging subsystem itself uses longer "electronic addresses": the name of the workgroup, the name of the workstation and the user's name.

One of the computers we used in preparing this book belongs to a workgroup called TOOLKIT, and the workstation name is CHRONOS. The mailbox for user Charles is called CWBOX. You can read a user's mailbox name in the Address Book (shown in Figure 13-2). The complete address for user Charles is MS:TOOLKIT/CHRONOS/CWBOX.

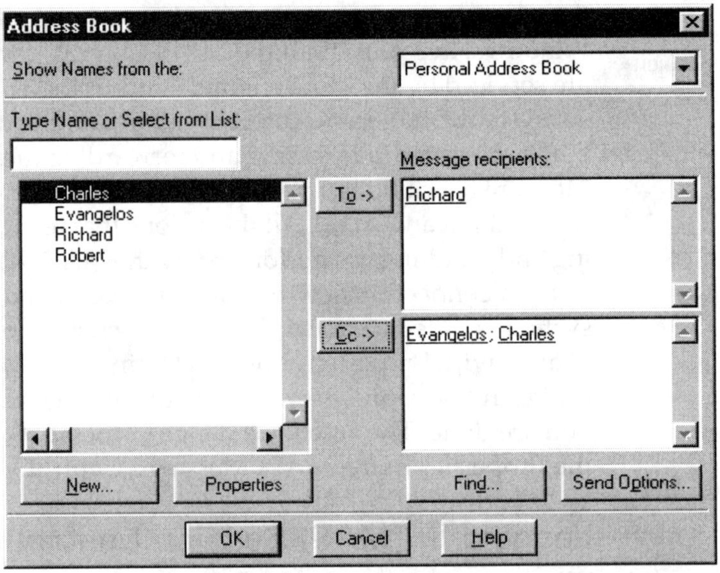


Figure 13-2: The Address Book, as it appears when a new message is sent. The To and Cc Command Buttons allow the user to add message recipients.

Because mailbox names are lengthy and confusing, we use aliases. "Charles" might be the alias, the user name, that shows up in the Address Book. However, when someone uses the Address Book to address a message to "Charles," the mail system sends the message to his *complete* electronic address: MS:TOOLKIT/CHRONOS/CWBOX.

Fortunately, a user never has to worry about complete electronic addresses. A programmer, though, may have to deal with the full electronic addresses on the network. To find out the full electronic address of a user on the network, you must know the name of the workgroup, the name of the workstation on the workgroup and the user's mailbox.

## Establishing a Mail Session

Let's design an application to connect to and disconnect from the Mail Server. This is the simplest thing you can do with the MAPI Session Control.

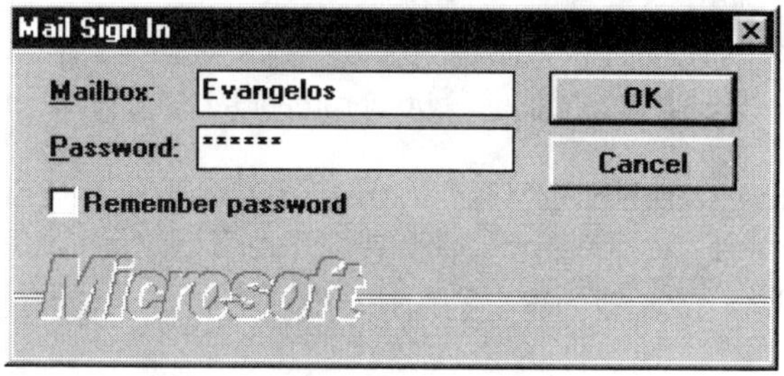


Figure 13-3: The Mail login window.

When someone starts Microsoft's Mail application, the window in Figure 13-3 is displayed on the screen, prompting for a user name and password. The same happens if one of your VB applications starts a mail session with the MAPI Session Control.

### Example: Starting a Mail Session

To start a mail session, place a MAPI Session Control on a new Form and create two Command Buttons, Login and Logout, as shown in Figure 13-4. Although the MAPI Session Control will not be visible at run time, it is necessary. Then enter the following lines in each of the Command Buttons:

```
Private SignOnButton_Click( )
    MAPISession1.Action = SESSION_SIGNON  ' =1
End Sub
Private SignOffButton_Click( )
    MAPISession1.Action = SESSION_SIGNOFF  ' =2
End Sub
```

If you are using Visual Basic 4.0, you can call the SignOn and SignOff Methods respectively. The VB4 statement

```
MAPISession1.SignOn
```

is equivalent to the following VB3 statement:

```
MAPISession1.Action = 1
```

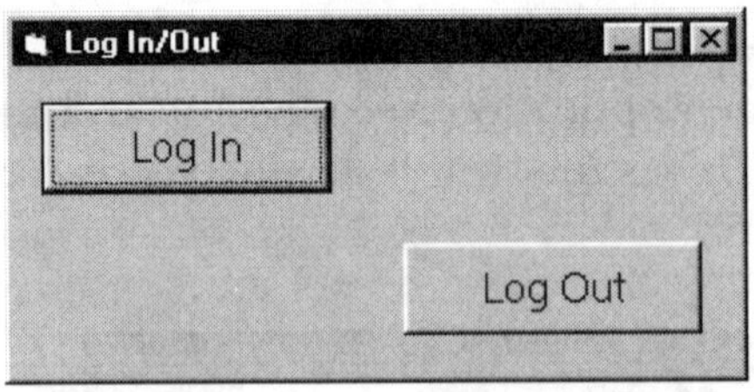


Figure 13-4: It takes just two commands to log in to and out of the Mail Server.

To establish (or terminate) a session, just set the Control's Action Property to the appropriate value. The Action Property may take on two values, as shown in Table 13-1:

| Value | Constant | Description |
|---|---|---|
| 1 | (SESSION_SIGNON) | Establishes a session. |
| 2 | (SESSION_SIGNOFF) | Terminates a session. |

Table 13-1: Possible values of the MAPI Session's Action Property.

Once logged in, the program disables the LOGIN Command Button and enables the LOGOUT Button. When the session is broken, it enables the LOGIN Button and disables the LOGOUT Button. When you write a messaging application, make sure that all messaging functions are disabled before a session is established. After the user has logged in successfully, enable the messaging functions.

When you establish a mail session (or MAPI session), it is not always a new session. If another program has established a connection to the Mail Server, each new application that requires messaging services will be attached to the same session. If the Mail application was running already, you are actually riding piggyback on top of the existing session. You can, however, request a new session by setting the value of the NewSession Property to True (it defaults to False). The messaging subsystem requires that a user is connected to it before messages can be exchanged. The same user need not connect more than once to the messaging subsystem. The same user, however, can launch multiple applications that use the messaging subsystem.

The MAPI Session Control doesn't create a new session if one already exists.

To run the previous simple application and establish a (new) mail session, click on the LOGIN Command Button. Then switch back to Program Manager, start Mail and notice that you are not asked for your name and password. The computer knows that your workstation is connected to the Mail Server already and doesn't start a new session.

Now switch to your application and terminate the session with the LOGOUT Command Button. If you switch back to the MS Mail application, you'll see that it is still running. This means that as long as some application remains connected to the Mail Server, the session stays alive. To terminate the session, terminate the MS Mail application. If you use the LOGIN application to log in to the Mail Server, this time you will be prompted to enter your password again.

### Automating the Login Process

To facilitate the login process, you can supply the user name and password of the user who is executing the application. The Properties UserName and Password allow you to supply the parameters required to establish a new session. Add the following lines to the Command1_Click( ) subroutine:

```
Sub Command1_Click( )
    MAPISession1.UserName = "Charlie" ' your user name
    MAPISession1.Password = "******"' your password
    MAPISession1.Action = SESSION_SIGNON    ' =1
End Sub
```

But be careful how you set the three Properties that govern the Mail Login Window—LogonUI (which is explained in the next paragraph), UserName and Password. You might be tempted to avoid having the user log in each time your application runs (by, for instance, storing the user name and password in your application's INI file). However, there are the usual drawbacks to this sort of thing: what if someone else reads the INI file entry, or what if the user changes his or her password?

If possible, don't automate the login procedure by supplying the user's password.

If you do want your VB application to log in for the user automatically (not displaying the usual login window), you *can* set the LogonUI Property to False (its default is True). LogonUI determines whether or not the Login window will appear. You must also then assign values to the UserName and Password Properties.

The last Property of the MAPI Session Control is DownloadMail, which specifies whether new messages will be downloaded from the Server (we will see later where the messages are stored). The default is True, which means that every time you establish a session, all unread messages are downloaded from the Mail Server.

Now the session is established. Next, the Mail System assigns a value to the Control's SessionID Property. This value is the handle (the ID) of the session and must be used to identify the session in subsequent commands to the Server. It cannot be changed by your application.

## Handling Messages (MAPI Messages Control)

The second MAPI Control is the workhorse of any Visual Basic application that wants to interface with the messaging subsystem. It handles the actual message exchange and allows your application to retrieve and manage incoming messages (forward, delete, etc.) and create and send new ones.

The MAPI Messages Control incorporates all the functionality of the Mail System. You can display the dialog that lets the user enter the message (including attachments), address it and send it. Once you are logged in to the Mail Server, this dialog box can be displayed with a single line of programming, as you will see in the next example.

The first thing you must do is identify the session to the to the MAPI Session Control. To do this, the Control's SessionID Property must be set to the value that the messaging subsystem returned when the session was established. This value is stored in the MAPI Session's SessionID Property, and so the first thing you must do when logging into the Mail Server is to assign this value to the SessionID property of the MAPI Messages Control. Here is a typical segment of code that establishes a new session:

```
On Error Goto ErrDisp
MAPISession1.SignOn
MAPIMessages1.SessionID = MAPISession1.SessionID
...
Exit Sub

ErrDisp:
    MsgBox Err$
    Exit Sub

End Sub
```

If you are using VB3, replace the SignOn Method with the Action Property.

To understand what the MAPI Messages Control does and how to use it, we must first understand messages. Let's look at the structure of messages, and what you are allowed to do with them. Then we'll explore the Properties that actually handle messages.

## What's in a Message?

A message is made up of three entities: an originator, recipients and the message itself, which includes the message text and attachments. Figure 13-5 is a pictorial representation of a message.

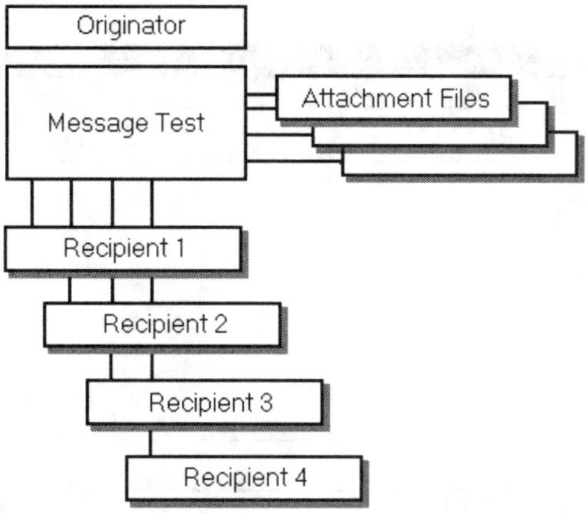


Figure 13-5: The outline of an electronic message. The attachments are optional, and so is the Message Text, but for a meaningful message you must provide one of them. A message must also have at least one recipient. The system automatically fills in the originator and can't be altered.

The message text is what you type in the Mail dialog box when you send a new message. It is the information you want to convey to the other party. The originator and the recipient(s) must be entries of the Address Book, which is displayed by Mail each time a message is sent.

You can attach any file to a mail message.

The attachments can be various files, such as Word documents (DOC), Excel spreadsheets (XLS) or even sound (WAV) or other multimedia files. When you want to send a document to a co-worker in the Windows for Workgroup environment, you don't have to include the entire document in your message. You can simply type a short message, such as "Here is the XLS file with our quarterly sales," and then attach the corresponding spreadsheet. Figures 13-6 and 13-7 show how the MS Mail application handles attachments. The sender creates the message and attaches the file SLS0794.XLS through the Insert File dialog box (Figure 13-6). The InBox application under Windows 95 uses the term "Insert File" instead of "Attach File." However, since the MAPI Controls use the term "Attachment" to describe these files, we will keep calling them attachments. When the recipient opens the message, he or she sees the window of Figure 13-7. To view the figures, the recipient double-clicks on the icon of the attached file, which launches the application that created the attachment (in this example, MS Excel).

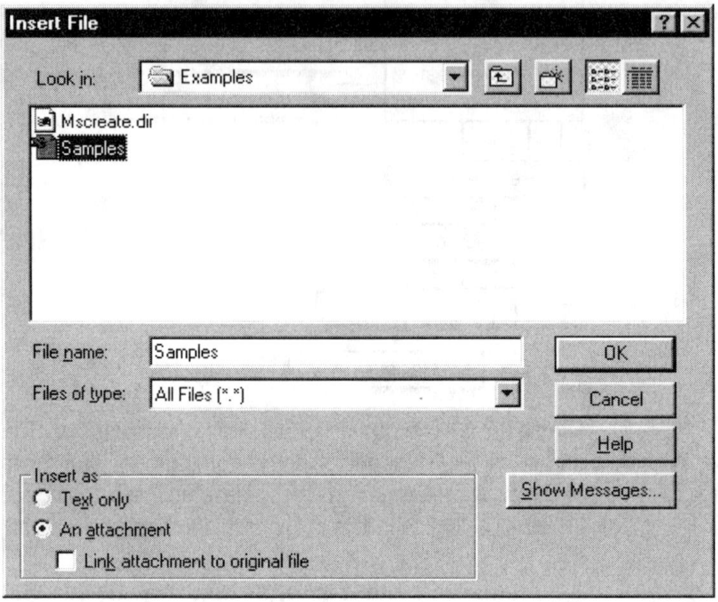


Figure 13-6: Attaching an Excel spreadsheet to a message. The Insert File dialog box is displayed by the Mail application each time you click on the Attach Command Button (see Figure 13-1).

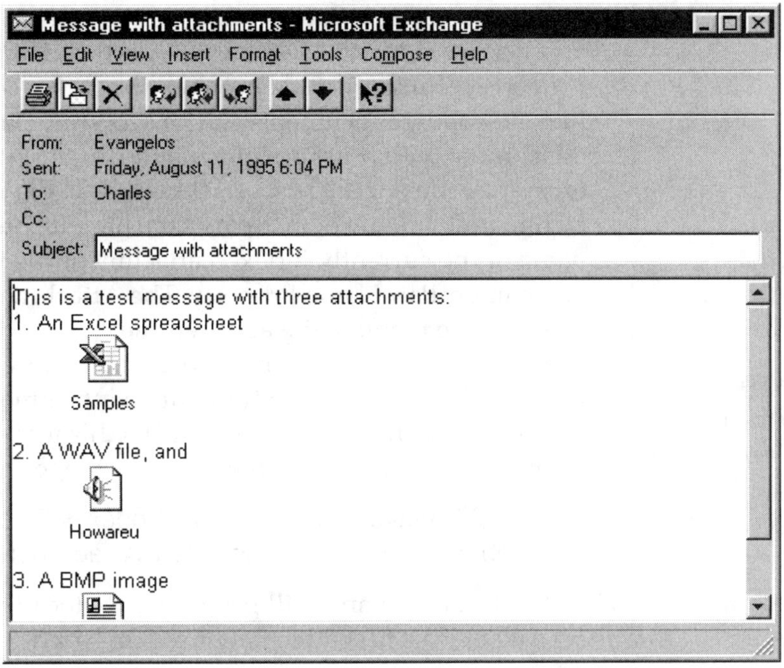


Figure 13-7: This is how the attached file looks when the recipient reads the message.

## Handling Incoming Messages

The messages live in the Post Office, and you can access them with the MsgIndex Property of the MAPI Messages Control. In other words, messages are not sent to each user's workstation. They remain in the workgroup's Post Office (there can be multiple Post Offices on the same network) and are recalled via the Mail application (or a custom application, as we will see shortly). The total number of messages is given by the MsgCount Property. To select a message, you must assign its index to the MsgIndex Property, whose valid values go from 0 to MsgCount –1. The first message has index 0, the second message has index 1, and so on.

Once you have selected a message, you can read its subject (Property MsgSubject), the electronic address of its sender (Property MsgOrigAddress), the sender's user name (Property MsgOrigDisplayName) and the message text (Property MsgNoteText). These properties are "read only"—it wouldn't make much sense to modify your incoming messages. You can set the values of these Properties only when you create a new message (as described in the next section).

If the message contains attachments, you can retrieve them with another set of MAPI Messages Properties. The AttachmentCount Property returns the total number of attachments in the message. Just like messages, attachments can be accessed via an index. To select an attachment, you must assign its index to the AttachmentIndex Property. The index of the first attachment is 0, the index of the next attachment is 1, and so on, up to AttachmentCount –1. The full path name of the currently indexed attachment file is given by the AttachmentPathName Property. The AttachmentFileName Property contains the name of the attached file.

Set the MsgIndex Property to –1 to create a new message, or to any nonnegative number to extract a message.

Since attachments can be incorporated anywhere in the message's text, we should be able to find out an attachment's position. The Property AttachmentPosition returns this information. To find out the position of the first attachment of a message, use the commands:

```
MAPIMessages1.AttachmentIndex = 0
Debug.Print MAPIMessages1.AttachmentPosition
```

The last command will print the byte location in the message's text, where the first attachment was inserted.

## Creating New Messages

To create a new message, you must call the Compose Method of Visual Basic 4.0, or create a new buffer by setting the MsgIndex Property of the MAPIMessages Control to –1 (which is what the Compose Method does). With that done, you are working with a new message and can set its Subject, Text and Recipient fields with the Properties mentioned previously. Creating a new message is fairly easy. After you have established a session and assigned the session's ID to the MAPIMessages1.SessionID Property, issue the following commands:

```
MAPIMessages1.MsgIndex = –1
MAPIMessages1.MsgSubject = "New investment opportunity"
MAPIMessages1.MsgNoteText = "BiBiSoftware is going public!"
MAPIMessages1.MsgReceiptRequested = True
' replace the value in the next line with your address
MAPIMessages1.RecipAddress = "MS:TOOLKIT/CHRONOS/ →
CWBOX"
MAPIMessages1.Action = MESSAGE_SEND   ' = 3
```

The MsgReceiptRequested Property simply requests a delivery receipt, just like registered mail (its default is False).

The value of the Action Property (3) tells the computer to send the message without displaying the standard dialog box (notice that we are providing the recipient's electronic address). If the address isn't correct, or if for some other reason the message cannot be delivered, it will be returned to its originator with the indication "Undeliverable Mail." The user can take whatever action seems appropriate. Alternatively, you can set the Action Property to 2 to display the Mail's Address Book and let the user select the recipient, or address the message with the RecipDisplayName Property.

The Action Property determines the kind of action you want the messaging subsystem to perform. Depending on the value you assign, you can forward messages, reply to messages, delete them and, in general, perform all kinds of message processing. Table 13-2 describes the possible values for this command. Our examples use only the most common ones, but you can experiment on your own with the rest. All Action Properties have an equivalent Method in Visual Basic 4.0. To send a message, for example, you can use the Send Method, whose syntax is

```
MAPIMessages1.Send [dialog As Integer]
```

where dialog can be True (the mail dialog box is displayed) or False (the mail dialog box is not displayed, and your program must provide all the information). Notice that the dialog argument is optional. If you want to skip the mail dialog box, issue the command

```
MAPIMessages1.Send
```

without the argument.

Similarly, the MESSAGE_COPY value of the Action Property can be replaced by the Copy Method, and the MESSAGE_FORWARD value with the Forward command. You can look up the syntax of the various commands in Visual Basic's Help files. In the Table 13-2 the equivalent VB4 Methods are mentioned under the Property constant name.

| Value | Constant | Description |
|---|---|---|
| 1 | MESSAGE_FETCH (Fetch) | Recalls all messages from the Inbox. You can specify the type of messages recalled with the FetchMsgType and FetchUnreadOnly properties. Specify their order with the FetchSorted Property. |
| 2 | MESSAGE_SENDDLG (Send) | Sends a message with the mail dialog box. |

| Value | Constant | Description |
|---|---|---|
| 3 | MESSAGE_SEND (Send) | Sends a message without the dialog box. The application must set all the fields, including the message's address. |
| 4 | MESSAGE_SAVEMSG (Save) | Saves the current message. This operation allows you to save the current message in the Inbox and finish (send) it at a later time. |
| 5 | MESSAGE_COPY (Copy) | Creates a new message with the information of the current message. |
| 6 | MESSAGE_COMPOSE (Compose) | Creates a new message by setting MsgIndex to –1 and clearing all fields. |
| 7 | MESSAGE_REPLY (Reply) | Replies to a message by copying the current message and adding the RE: prefix to the beginning of the subject line. |
| 8 | MESSAGE_REPLYALL (ReplyAll) | Replies to all message recipients (similar to the previous action). |
| 9 | MESSAGE_FORWARD (Forward) | Forwards a message by copying the current message and adding the FW: prefix to the beginning of the subject line. |
| 10 | MESSAGE_DELETE (Delete(0)) | Deletes the current message and decrements the total number of messages (MsgCount Property) by 1. |
| 11 | MESSAGE_SHOWADBOOK (Show(0)) | Displays the Address Book. The user can add/modify sets of recipients, but cannot select an address for message delivery. |
| 12 | MESSAGE_SHOWDETAILS (Show(1)) | Displays a dialog box with the details of the currently selected recipient. |

| Value | Constant | Description |
|---|---|---|
| 13 | MESSAGE_RESOLVENAME | Resolves the name of the current recipient. |
| 14 | RECIPIENT_DELETE (Delete(1)) | Deletes the currently indexed recipient and decrements the total number of recipients (RecipCount Property) by 1. |
| 15 | ATTACHMENT_DELETE (Delete(2)) | Deletes the currently indexed attachment and decrements the total number of attachments (AttachmentCount Property) by 1. |

Table 13-2: The possible values of the MAPI Messages Action Property and the corresponding VB4 Methods.

Be careful with message addressing. The RecipAddress field is the recipient's electronic address in the network. The RecipDisplayName Property is the recipient's name as it appears in the Address Book. The two Properties have very different values.

## Handling Recipients

The last major class of MAPI Messages Properties handles the message's recipients. The total number of recipients is given by the Property RecipCount. To select a recipient, use the RecipIndex Property, which may have any value from 0 to RecipCount –1. The RecipAddress and RecipDisplayName Properties return the electronic address and user name of the currently indexed recipient. Of course, each message has only one primary recipient. Multiple recipients are copy recipients (CC) or blind-copy recipients (BCC). To find out (or set) the type of recipient, use the Property RecipType, whose possible values are shown in Table 13-3:

| Value | Constant | Description |
|---|---|---|
| 0 | RECIPTYPE_ORIG | The message's originator. |
| 1 | RECIPTYPE_TO | The primary recipient. |
| 2 | RECIPTYPE_CC | A copy recipient. |
| 3 | RECIPTYPE_BCC | A blind-copy recipient. |

Table 13-3: Possible values of the RecipType Property.

Now that you've been introduced to the Properties of MAPI Controls, let's develop our first messaging application.

## ADDING MAIL OPTIONS TO APPLICATIONS

CD-ROM

Our first example application demonstrates the basic mechanisms of the messaging subsystem. The application is called MAILER, and you will find it in the 13\APPS\MAILER subdirectory of the CD.

### EXAMPLE: SENDING & RECEIVING MESSAGES

In the Form shown in Figure 13-8 you can enter a message in the text box and send it using the Send Text Command Button. You can also look at the unread messages in your mailbox with the List Messages Button.

You can test the application very easily, even on a stand-alone system with Windows for Workgroups, by sending messages to yourself (with the Send Text Command Button) and then recalling them in the List Box (with the List Messages Button).

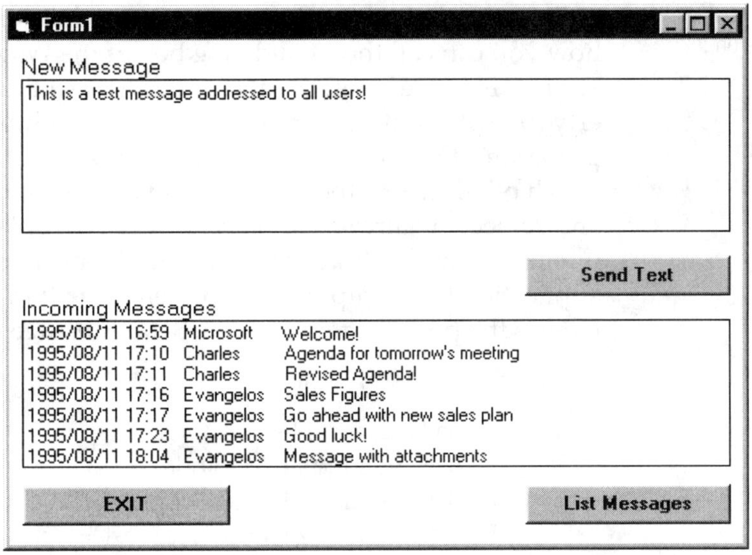


Figure 13-8: A simple but functional messaging application.

This example demonstrates the three basic operations of the message exchange process:

- Establishing a new session.
- Creating new messages.
- Reading incoming messages.

Let's start with the code for establishing a new session, which is executed as soon as the application starts:

```
Sub Form_Load ( )

On Error GoTo ExitApp
    MAPISession1.Action = SESSION_SIGNON
    MAPIMessages1.SessionID = MAPISession1.SessionID
    Exit Sub

ExitApp:
    MsgBox "Could not start a mail session"
    Exit Sub

End Sub
```

The MAPI Session and MAPI Messages Controls must be placed somewhere on the Form (they will be invisible at run time). We start a new session (or connect to an existing one) with the MAPISession1.Action Property, as explained earlier.

Once a session is established, you can display the standard Mail dialog box with a single VB command.

The code for the Send Message Command Button demonstrates how you can call the Mail dialog box of the Windows messaging subsystem. First we create a new message by setting its MsgIndex Property to –1. Then we assign values to the MsgSubject and MsgNoteText properties. Finally, we call the Mail dialog box, which lets the user attach other files to the message and address it. The message's text and subject are already in place. If we hadn't placed them there from within our application, the user would have to copy the text from the application to the clipboard and then paste it in the Mail dialog box. Here is the programming for the Send Message Command Button:

```
Sub Command1_Click ( )

On Error Resume Next
    MAPIMessages1.MsgIndex = –1
    MAPIMessages1.MsgSubject = "MAPI Tests"
    MAPIMessages1.MsgNoteText = Trim(Text1.Text)
    MAPIMessages1.Action = MESSAGE_SENDDLG       ' = 2

End Sub
```

By setting Action to 2 (or calling the Send Method), you can display the Mail dialog box. There, the user can specify all components of the message (including attachments) and then address it for delivery.

The List Messages Command Button recalls all unread messages from the Inbox and displays them on the List. This application displays only the date and time the message was received, the originator and the subject. Here is the programming for the List Messages Command Button:

```
Sub Command2_Click ( )

    MAPIMessages1.Action = MESSAGE_FETCH  ' = 1
    totMessages = MAPIMessages1.MsgCount
    If totMessages = 0 Then
        MsgBox "There are no unread messages in your Mail →
        Box"
        Exit Sub
    End If
    List1.Clear

    For i = 0 To totMessages - 1
```

```
            MAPIMessages1.MsgIndex = i
            datetime = MAPIMessages1.MsgDateReceived
            originator = MAPIMessages1.MsgOrigDisplayName
            subject = MAPIMessages1.MsgSubject
            item = datetime + " " + originator + " " + subject
            List1.AddItem item
        Next

    End Sub
```

The first line recalls all unread messages from the Inbox. We read the total number of messages and add a string for each message to the List Box. Notice that messages are not stored in an array or any other user-specified structure. The Mail System maintains a list of all messages, and your application can access them with the MsgIndex Property. The messages appear in the order they are stored in the Inbox, unless you specify a different order with the MsgFetchSorted Property. (You can also assign the value of the MsgIndex property to the ItemData property for the item you just added to the List Box, so that you can access the actual messages later.)

You can incorporate much of Microsoft's Mail functionality into your VB applications with minimal programming effort.

At any time you can work with only one message, which is specified with the MsgIndex Property. The properties MsgSubject, MsgDateReceived, and so on refer to the corresponding fields of the currently indexed message.

When you are done, terminate the session. Here is the programming of the Exit Command Button:

```
    Sub Command3_Click ( )

        MAPISession1.Action = SESSION_SIGNOFF    ' = 2
        End

    End Sub
```

Of course, this isn't the most exciting thing you can do with the MAPI Controls. And there is no reason to create your own applications to simply duplicate the functions of a full-featured application like Microsoft's Mail.

Next we'll explore how to build on the messaging subsystem, give your applications new capabilities and integrate them into a network environment.

## MESSAGING-AWARE & MESSAGING-ENABLED APPLICATIONS

Applications that take advantage of the messaging subsystem are called *messaging-aware* or *messaging-enabled*. Messaging-aware applications take advantage of the messaging subsystem if it exists, but they do not depend on it for their operation. For example, you can add a Send Mail command to a text editor built with the Text Box Control, or to a spreadsheet based on the Grid Control. The application will work fine on a stand-alone system with Windows. But it will take advantage of the messaging system in the network, letting the user send messages to other users without switching to another application. This is a messaging-aware application.

Unlike messaging-aware applications, a messaging-enabled application *relies* on the messaging subsystem in order to function at all. A scheduling application like Schedule+, which comes with Windows for Workgroups, lets users view co-workers' schedules and send (or approve) meeting requests to their calendars. This type of application is meaningless without the messaging subsystem.

Messaging-enabled applications will not work without a messaging subsystem.

Messaging-aware applications are not difficult to write, as the Mailer example above demonstrates. Actually, the few lines of programming in the Mailer example are all you need to build a messaging-aware application. Just add a few extra Command Buttons or menu options to your own application, and offer your users the capability to send messages to workgroup members. Messaging-enabled applications are capable of much more than just electronic-message exchange. But they are not much more difficult to program.

Messaging-enabled applications do not require additional commands, nor do they follow a different programming paradigm. Let's construct two practical applications that are messaging-enabled.

### EXAMPLE: INSTANT MAIL NOTIFICATION

CD-ROM

Our first messaging-enabled application is called POPMAIL; you can find it in the 13\APPS\POPMAIL subdirectory of the CD. This application remains idle most of the time and is activated everytime a new message arrives.

POPMAIL is based on the Timer Control, and alerts the user when a new message arrives. The Mail Server can notify the user upon arrival of new messages, but POPMAIL can be customized in any way you like. For example, you can write the code to read the message and display it on the monitor if it's an urgent one, or forward it to another user depending on its originator, and so on.

Normally, this application is kept minimized so that it won't interfere with the flow of work. To view the messages, the user can double-click on the icon and see the window shown in Figure 13-9. This window contains a Grid, and messages are displayed in consecutive rows. The Grid is populated with each double-click of the application's icon, or whenever the user clicks on the Refresh List Button. The user can then click on Show Message to see the message text, as shown in Figure 13-10.

If the message has attachments, he can click on Show Attachments to see the names of the attached files (Figure 13-11). The Message Attachments Form simply displays the names of the attached files, so that the user can view their names, but it will not actually open them. When done, the user can reduce the POPMAIL Form to an icon by clicking on the Minimize Button and return to any other Windows application. If new messages arrive, POPMAIL will notify you immediately and you can view them by double-clicking on its icon.

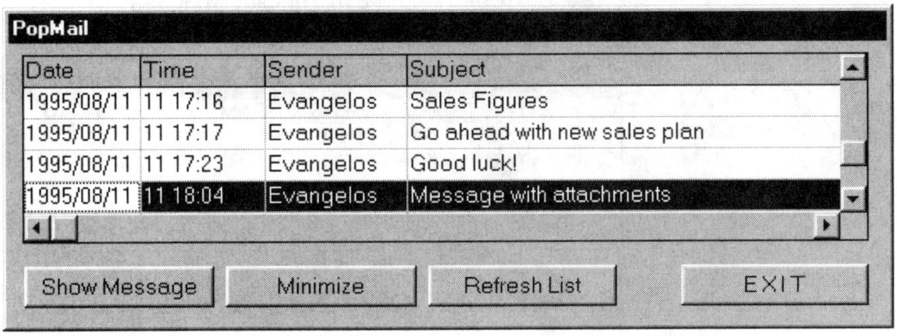


Figure 13-9: The main Form of the POPMAIL application.

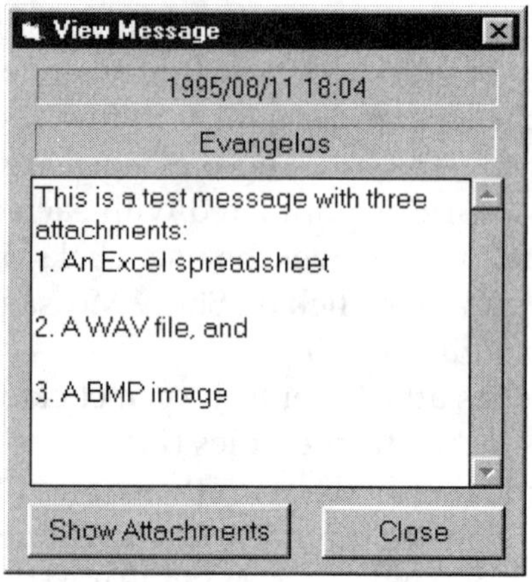


Figure 13-10: The Show Message window of the POPMAIL application. Here the user can read the text of the currently selected message of the previous Form. If the message contains attachments, the user can click on the Show Attachments Button. (You don't see the icons associated with the attachments because this is a Text Box Control and can't display images.)

Figure 13-11: The Message Attachments window of the POPMAIL application. Here the user can see the names of the attached files (but not the files themselves).

This application is meant to provide instant access to new mail messages. So to be useful, it must be simpler and faster than the Mail application. The price for this simplicity is its limited message-handling capabilities. To view the attached files, reply or forward the messages or even delete them, the user must resort to the actual Mail application (or another custom application that uses the messaging subsystem).

Our POPMAIL application provides little more than notification of new mail, but this is a handy feature for users who don't check their mail regularly or wish to be notified about new messages immediately. It gets the immediate attention of a co-worker, yet is less intrusive than the Chat application, which interrupts everything a user is doing at the time. Many users choose to disable that intrusive feature.

The POPMAIL application displays all unread messages, not only the new ones. (This makes the application less useful for people who leave their messages in the Inbox and remove them only when they start having trouble locating one.)

When the program starts, it establishes a session with the MAPI Session1 Control, as we have already discussed. The heart of the application is the Timer's Timer Event, whose code is shown next:

```
Private Sub Timer1_Timer( )

    MAPIMessages1.Action = 1
    oldMessages = totMessages
    totMessages = MAPIMessages1.MsgCount

    If totMessages > 0 Then
        If oldMessages >= totMessages Then
            Form1.Caption = Format$(totMessages, "0") +  →
            "Unread Message(s)"
        ElseIf oldMessages < totMessages Then
            Form1.Caption = "New Message!"
            For j = 1 To 3
                Beep
            Next
            Form1.WindowState = 1
        End If
    Else
        Form1.Caption = "No Unread Messages"
    End If

End Sub
```

This Subroutine is executed every 30 seconds (you can change the Timer's Interval Property to make the monitoring of new messages tighter or looser). Every 30 seconds the program recalls the number of total messages and compares it to the number of messages retrieved the last time the Timer1_Timer Event was invoked. If there are new messages, it sets the Caption of the Form (which is usually minimized) to "New Message!" and emits a long beep. You can make it more intrusive by popping up the POPMAIL window, or even playing a WAVE file, but we prefer a simple beep.

Notice that the application doesn't notify the user constantly about the arrival of new messages. If the user hasn't acknowledged a new message by reading it, chances are that he or she does not wish to be interrupted, and it would be rude on our part to keep beeping or popping up new Forms on the screen. However, it is easy to modify the behavior of the program, even connect it to another application. For example, you could enable the "New Mail" menu option of another application, should new mail arrive.

To see the new messages, the user must double-click on the icon. This brings the window shown in Figure 13-9 onscreen. Here is the Form's Load Event, which initializes the Form:

```
Sub Form_Load ( )

    MAPISession1.LogonUI = True
    MAPISession1.DownloadMail = False
    MAPISession1.Action = 1
    MAPIMessages1.SessionID = MAPISession1.SessionID

    Grid1.ColWidth(0) = TextWidth("12/12/1994")
    Grid1.ColWidth(1) = TextWidth("12:12.60 PM")
    Grid1.ColWidth(2) = TextWidth("MSG SENDER")
    Grid1.ColWidth(3) = TextWidth("TYPICAL SIZE OF A →
    MESSAGE'S SUBJECT")
    Grid1.Width = Grid1.GridLineWidth * →
    Screen.TwipsPerPixelX * 5 + Grid1.ColWidth(0) + →
    Grid1.ColWidth(1) + Grid1.ColWidth(2) + Grid1.ColWidth(3)
    Grid1.Height = 6 * Grid1.RowHeight(0) + →
    Grid1.GridLineWidth * Screen.TwipsPerPixelY * 6

    Grid1.Row = 0
    Grid1.Col = 0: Grid1.Text = "Date"
    Grid1.Col = 1: Grid1.Text = "Time"
    Grid1.Col = 2: Grid1.Text = "Sender"
    Grid1.Col = 3: Grid1.Text = "Subject"
    MAPIMessages1.Action = 1
    totMessages = MAPIMessages1.MsgCount
    oldMessages = totMessages
    Timer1.Interval = 0
    If totMessages = 0 Then
        MsgBox "There are no unread messages!"
        Form1.WindowState = 1
    End If
    DisplayMessages

End Sub
```

After setting up the Grid's titles, the program disables the Timer by setting its Interval to 0 (there's no reason to monitor the Inbox when the user can Refresh the list at will). It then displays the messages with the DisplayMessages Subroutine. Similar code is executed every time the Form is restored from its iconic state, which is signaled by the Form's Resize Event:

```
Private Sub Form_Resize ( )

    If Form1.WindowState = 1 Then   ' MINIMIZED
        Timer1.Interval = 30000
        Form1.Caption = Format$(totMessages, "0") + " Un →
            read Message(s)"
    Else
        totMessages = MAPIMessages1.MsgCount
        If totMessages = 0 Then
        Grid1.Rows = 1
            MsgBox "There are no Unread Messages"
            Form1.WindowState = 1
            Exit Sub
        End If
        oldCaption = Form1.Caption
        Form1.Caption = "POPUP"
        Timer1.Interval = 0
        DisplayMessages
    End If

End Sub
```

Notice that the same routine is also executed when the Form is minimized again. Every time the Form is restored to its original size, the program counts the unread messages and sets the Form's Caption accordingly. Every time it is reduced to an icon, it restores the value of the Timer's interval to 30000. The Minimize Button does nothing more than minimize the window by setting its WindowState Property to 1. The Refresh List Button's code is fairly straightforward: it recalls all unread messages and displays them on the Grid.

Finally, here is the code for the DisplayMessages Subroutine, which places the messages on the rows of the Grid:

```
Private Sub DisplayMessages ( )

    Grid1.Rows = 1

    If totMessages >= Grid1.Rows Then
```

```
        Grid1.Rows = totMessages + 2
        Grid1.FixedRows = 1
    End If

    For i = 0 To totMessages - 1
        MAPIMessages1.MsgIndex = i
        Grid1.Row = i + 1
        Grid1.Col = 0
        Grid1.Text = Left$(MAPIMessages1.MsgDateReceived, →
            10)
        Grid1.Col = 1
        Grid1.Text =Right$(MAPIMessages1.MsgDateReceived, →
            8)
        Grid1.Col = 2
    Grid1.Text = MAPIMessages1.MsgOrigDisplayName
    Grid1.Col = 3
    Grid1.Text = MAPIMessages1.MsgSubject
    Next

End Sub
```

This code is similar to the code of the MAILER application, which displayed the messages in a list box. (We could have used a List in POPMAIL too, but the Grid Control allows the user to change the size of each field. For example, he may choose to make the Time and Date columns very narrow, so that he can see more of the subject field.)

### Example: Customizing Mail Messages

Now we'll create an example application, TelNotes, that allows applications to communicate with one another. Unlike DDE (Dynamic Data Exchange, which uses VB's various Link commands), TelNotes will use the messaging subsystem to allow communication among applications on different computers. TelNotes can be found in the 13\APPS\TELNOTES subdirectory of the CD.

CD-ROM

When large numbers of streamlined messages are exchanged over the workgroup, consider adding customized software to handle them.

Another way that TelNotes with messaging is superior to DDE: with TelNotes only the sender application need be running for the message to be distributed. If the recipient application isn't running, the message will be held in the Post Office until the recipient application is started up. TelNotes allows a telephone operator to take telephone messages and relay the information to other members of the workgroup by computer rather than by filling out pink message forms and delivering them in person. (If you are familiar with DDE, you'll notice that the messaging-enabled applications have a wider scope than DDE applications, and that the messaging subsystem is a more general-purpose tool than DDE.)

The TelNotes application is made up of two programs, the SENDER and RECVR. The sender application is controlled by the telephone operator, who creates and dispatches the messages. Any other member of the workgroup can start the receiving application on another workstation and read telephone messages on a simple, easy-to-read Form. Figures 13-12 and 13-13 show the two programs in action.

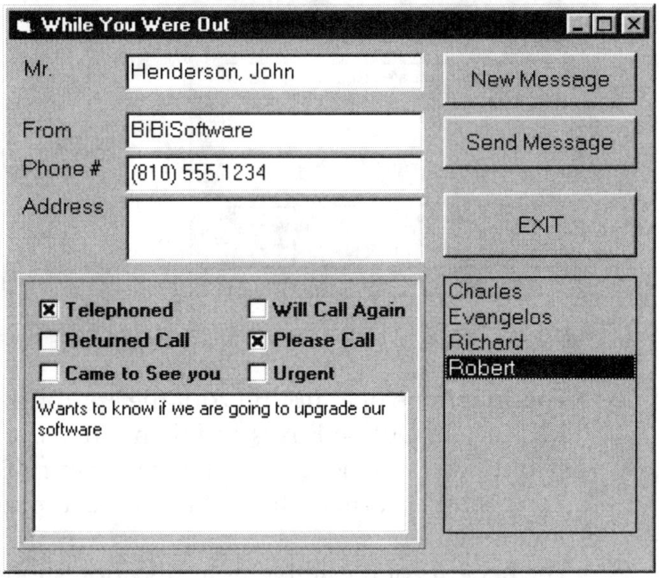


Figure 13-12: SENDER, the sending program of the TelNotes application.

Figure 13-13: RECVR, the receiving program of the TelNotes application.

The telephone operator fills out the appropriate fields on the Form, checks certain Option Boxes and then sends the electronic "while you were out" slip to a member of the workgroup. The receiver sees the slip on a similar form on his or her own computer and takes the appropriate action.

The benefits of the TelNotes application should be obvious to anyone who has worked in a fast-paced business environment. The electronic slips are never lost or misplaced, and they are never delivered too late (unless, of course, the receiving party doesn't check his or her mail). With some extra effort, they can be filed for future reference and the information they contain can be easily transferred to other applications with a simple copy-and-paste operation. The electronic slip is not only easier to distribute, it's also easier to distribute to multiple persons.

## Interpersonal or Interprocess Messages?

This application also demonstrates another important aspect of the Windows messaging subsystem—*interprocess* messages. You would expect to find the electronic slips among the regular messages you receive in your mail box. Unlike the interpersonal messages (the

Interprocess messages are handled just like interpersonal messages, but they don't clutter the users' Inboxes.

regular messages we've been working with so far), interprocess messages are meant to be exchanged among applications, and they never appear in your Inbox. However, they will appear in the Sent Items folder of the InBox application (with the IPC Type Message indication). This means that the user of the SENDER application must clear the Sent Items folder frequently—you can also write a simple application to delete them. The code will be similar to that of the MAILER application, only instead of fetching unread messages, it will be fetching IPC type messages and, rather than displaying them on the Grid, it will delete them. Interprocess messages let you design workgroup applications that run on the messaging subsystem but do not interfere with the user's Inbox. Only the application that was designed to handle them can see them. Interprocess messages are also called *custom message types*.

The new elements in this example are the FetchMsgType and the MsgType Properties of the MAPI Messages Control. The MsgType sets (or reads) the type of message. The FetchMsgType Property specifies the type of messages to be fetched. The message type is made up of three strings separated by periods, as in

```
IPC.Toolkit.TelNotes
```

which is the custom message type we are going to use in the TelNotes application. The first component is a three-character string that can have a value of IPM (for interpersonal messages) or IPC (for interprocess, or custom type, messages). The second component is the name of the application vendor (actually, it can be any name), and the third is the type of the custom message (can be any name, too). The only limitations are that the total length of the string not exceed 64 characters and the first component be IPC or IPM.

If you develop a messaging-enabled application that uses interprocess messages to exchange voice messages, you could name it "IPC.BiBiSoftware.VoiceMail." The FetchMsgType and MsgType properties are case-sensitive; that is, you cannot recall the last custom message type as "IPC.BIBISoftware.VoiceMail" or "IPC.Bibisoftware.Voicemail."

The MsgType sets the type of the current outgoing message. So far, we haven't had to set this because the default is the interpersonal message (IPM). To specify an IPM type of message, you can set this Property to an empty string (or leave the MsgType Property untouched).

### Creating the Slips (SENDER)

The first program of TelNotes creates the messages by concatenating the fields of the slip entry Form into a large string. This large string becomes the message's text. The first character of the message indicates whether the person is addressed as Mr. (value 1) or Ms. (value 2). If you click on the Label "Mr.," its caption becomes "Ms." Click again, and its caption is restored to the previous value. The next six characters of the message indicate the status of the six Option Boxes of the Form (they are "0" for unchecked and "1" for checked Option Boxes).

Following the status of the Option Boxes are the strings representing the date and time the slip was sent. These two values are determined by the system—that's why there are no corresponding fields in the slip's entry Form. Next, we store the name and company of the person who made the call, the phone number and address and, finally, the contents of the Text Box with any possible instructions, remarks or explanations. Successive fields are separated by a carriage return/line feed combination; this simplifies the unpacking of fields at the recipient's end.

You'll notice that we are not using the Address Book to address the messages. Clicking a name on a list is much faster, and speed is what this application is all about. The TelNotes application is supposed to make the telephone operator's job easier, and not to force the operator to open and close windows with every message. To make our application still faster and simpler to use, we add the names of the workgroup's users to a list so that they are always visible.

By placing all users' electronic addresses in a list, we speed up the recipient selection process.

They can be the actual user names, or any names the telephone operator would rather use. The names are added to the List when the program starts, and at the same time, we store in an array the actual user names, or their electronic addresses. The VB3 version of the application uses the actual addresses (and the RecipAddress Property to send them), while in the VB4 version of SENDER we use user names (and the RecipDisplayName Property to send them).

Here is the Form's Load Event for the Visual Basic 4.0 version of the application:

```
Private Sub Form_Load( )

  On Error GoTo ExitApp
  MAPISession1.LogonUI = True
  MAPISession1.DownloadMail = False
  MAPISession1.Action = 1
```

```
    MAPIMessages1.SessionID = MAPISession1.SessionID

    ' The following lines will not work on your computer
    ' replace them with your workgroup's users
    List1.AddItem "Charles"
    RecipientAddress(0) = "Charles"
    List1.AddItem "Evangelos"
    RecipientAddress(1) = "Evangelos"
    List1.AddItem "Richard"
    RecipientAddress(2) = "richard"
    List1.AddItem "Robert"
    RecipientAddress(3) = "Robert"

    ' add more user names
    MrMrsLabel.Caption = "Mr."
    Exit Sub

ExitApp:
    MsgBox "Couldn't start a Mail Session. Please try again →
    with the correct User Name/Password"
    End
End Sub
```

Entering each and every address manually is a significant burden to the programmer. Unfortunately, the Simple MAPI provides no means of extracting all names or their addresses from the Mail Server. The "user-friendly" approach would be to display the Address Book, but this would slow down the program too much for this type of application. The TelNotes application is used to send simple messages to one recipient at a time. Our goal is to design the fastest possible application, and displaying the Address Book wouldn't help. It is much easier and faster for the user to click on a name in the List Box. Besides, we would have no use for any additional functionality provided by the Address Book (telephone messages have no attachments or copy recipients).

You may find it helpful to send a message to all users from your workstation and then look up the list of recipients. Write down the addresses of the recipients (as given by the RecipAddress Property of the MAPIMessages1 Control) and then assign them to the elements of the RecipientAddress array. This also means that you cannot test this application as is. You must enter the appropriate user names and addresses in the Form's Load Event to be able to send slips and then use the receiving application to read them.

Here is the code for the Send Button, which creates the message from the Form's fields and sends it to the recipient selected in the List Box:

```
Private Sub SendButton_Click( )
Dim Address As String * 40

   If List1.TEXT = "" Then
      MsgBox "Select a Recipient from the Recipients' List "
      Exit Sub
   End If
   Screen.MousePointer = HOURGLASS     ' = 11
   MAPIMessages1.SessionID = MAPISession1.SessionID
   MAPIMessages1.MsgIndex = -1
   MAPIMessages1.MsgType = MssgID
   MAPIMessages1.MsgSubject = "Telephone Note - IPC  →
   Type Message"
   MAPIMessages1.RecipDisplayName =  →
   RecipientAddress(List1.ListIndex)
   MAPIMessages1.RecipType = 1

   If MrMrsLabel.Caption = "Mr." Then
      bstring = "1"
   Else
      bstring = "2"
   End If

   For i = 1 To 6
      If MsgOption(i).VALUE = True Then
         bstring = bstring + "1"
      Else
         bstring = bstring + "0"
      End If
   Next

   cr = Chr$(13) + Chr$(10)
   Txt$ = bstring + cr
   Txt$ = Txt$ + Str$(Date) + cr + Str$(Time) + cr
   Txt$ = Txt$ + Trim(NameText.TEXT) + cr +  →
   Trim(FromText.TEXT) + cr
```

```
    Txt$ = Txt$ + Trim(PhoneText.TEXT) + cr
    LSet Address = Trim(AddressText.TEXT)
    Txt$ = Txt$ + Address
    Txt$ = Txt$ + Trim(MessageText.TEXT)
    MAPIMessages1.MsgNoteText = Txt$

    On Error GoTo DispError
    MAPIMessages1.Send              ' Action = 3
    Screen.MousePointer = DEFAULT   ' = 0
Exit Sub

DispError:
    Print Err
    Print Error$
    Screen.MousePointer = DEFAULT   ' = 0
    Exit Sub

End Sub
```

MsgID is a global variable that contains the message type (IPC.Toolkit.TelNotes) so that we won't have to type it again (and risk breaking the connection between the two applications because of a typing mistake—the MsgType Property is case-sensitive).

In our example, we don't allow multiple selections because most slips are sent to a single recipient. To send the same slip to multiple recipients, you can just select another user name and click on the Send Command Button again without changing the contents of the fields. (Of course, you can always modify the application to accommodate multiple recipients.)

Most of the lines simply form the body of the message by appending all the Form's fields to the string Txt$. Txt$ then becomes the message's text and is delivered to its destination.

### Reading the Slips (RECVR)

You have seen how to read electronic messages, you know the structure of the incoming messages, and you could easily write a program that reads the incoming messages. Figure 13-13 shows the window of the RECVR part of the application, which displays the telephone slips. The two arrows allow you to move to the previous or next message, and with the two buttons between them you can delete the current message or copy it to the Clipboard. This last capability was

Treat custom messages differently from regular mail messages.

added to show how you can export messages and process them with other applications.

When the program starts, it establishes a connection and downloads the messages of its custom type. If there are messages, it displays the first one with the DispMessage subroutine. This subroutine does the reverse of the Send Command Button of the SENDER application: it unpacks the fields from the message text and sets the corresponding fields on the Form. The code is fairly straightforward, and you can examine it in RECVR.FRM.

The Previous and Next Buttons increase and decrease the index of the current message by 1 respectively and display the new message.

Here is the Delete Button's programming:

```
Private Sub Command3D3_Click ( )

    On Error GoTo NoDelete
    MAPIMessages1.Action = MESSAGE_DELETE' = 10
    TotalMessages = MAPIMessages1.MsgCount
    UnreadCaption.Caption = "Unread Notes: " + →
    Format$(TotalMessages, "0")
    If TotalMessages >= 1 Then
        currentMessage = MAPIMessages1.MsgIndex
        DispMessage
    Else
        Command3D1.Enabled = False
        Command3D2.Enabled = False
        Command3D3.Enabled = False
        Command3D4.Enabled = False
        DateLabel.Caption = ""
        TimeLabel.Caption = ""
        Text1.Text = ""
        Text2.Text = ""
        Text3.Text = ""
        Text4.Text = ""
        Text5.Text = ""
    End If

NoDelete:
    Exit Sub
End Sub
```

The last Notepad Command Button copies the contents of the current slip onto the Clipboard, after formatting the contents in some way. Figure 13-14 is a snapshot of the Clipboard after two telephone messages have been copied there. The formatting is very simple, but suitable for printing the slips.

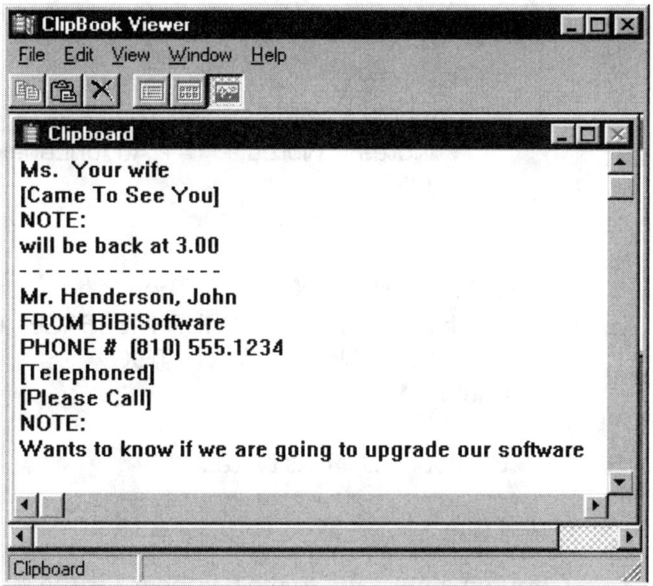


Figure 13-14: Copying the telephone slips to the Clipboard.

Here is the code of the Command Button that formats and transfers the contents of the current slip to the Clipboard:

```
Private Sub CopyButton_Click( )

    cr = Chr$(13) + Chr$(10)
    Notes = Clipboard.GetText(1)
    Clipboard.Clear
    Notes = Notes + String$(60, "-")
    Notes = Notes + cr

    Notes = Notes + "Mr.      " + Text2.TEXT + cr
    If Trim(Text3.TEXT) <> "" Then
        Notes = Notes + "FROM      " + Text3.TEXT + cr
    End If
```

```
        If Trim(Text4.TEXT) <> "" Then
            Notes = Notes + "PHONE # " + Trim(Text4.TEXT) + cr
        End If

        If Trim(Text5.TEXT) <> "" Then
            Notes = Notes + "ADDRESS " + Trim(Text5.TEXT) + cr
        End If

        For i = 1 To 6
            If ActionLabel(i).Enabled Then
                Notes = Notes + "[" + ActionLabel(i).Caption + "]" + cr
            End If
        Next

        If Trim(Text1.TEXT) <> "" Then
            Notes = Notes + "YOUR MESSAGE" + cr
            Notes = Notes + Text1.TEXT
        End If

        Clipboard.SetText Notes, 1

    End Sub
```

Copying a message to the Clipboard is the simplest form of message processing, but it is a good starting point. Each message is appended to previous messages in the Clipboard. You could next insert code into TelNotes that would permit printing or filing of the slips directly by the application. This application can be a starting point for more advanced applications, such as expense reports. For example, workgroup members could submit expenses (or time sheets, or supply order forms, for that matter) on an electronic form. Managers could view and approve (or reject) them and file the approved expenses with a simple mouse-click.

Once telephone slips are in the computer, they can be used like any other type of information.

The TelNotes application may not be of particular use to every workgroup. But it should suggest all kinds of applications that you could write in VB to automate a workgroup's work flow. The Windows messaging subsystem, made highly efficient for the programmer via the simplicity of Visual Basic's MAPI Controls, can help you develop simple workgroup applications that could considerably improve the effectiveness of almost any workgroup.

For example, a message routing application could send messages to a number of different recipients, one after the other. Each recipient would have the option to add information to the message, modify certain fields, add more recipients and so on. (This is the kind of functionality already built into Microsoft's Office 95 suite of applications.)

### Other Useful Tools

If you are serious about developing workgroup applications with Visual Basic, look into two new Microsoft products, Electronic Form Designer and Templates for Workgroups.

Electronic Form Designer is based on Visual Basic and allows you to create customized Forms for use with the Mail System.

Templates for Workgroups is a collection of template programs that demonstrate how you can automate communication between applications such as Excel, Access, Word and Schedule+, but always with the help of Visual Basic. Nevertheless, there is no need to rush to add these extra layers of API calls to your messaging applications. There's a lot you can do in with messaging right now, using Visual Basic, as the examples in this chapter demonstrate.

## MOVING ON

Next up: fractals. These complex and often stunningly beautiful images are quite addictive. In the next chapter you'll learn not only how they can be successfully generated in VB, but also the bases of their creation—the fascinating "imaginary" numbers and strange geometry on which fractals are built.

Chapter 14 has been written to be understandable to anyone with no more background than eighth grade math. You'll also get all the tools you need to experiment with fractal-generating algorithms in VB, and not just a black box that creates these mysterious images. You can zoom down into them to your heart's content, discovering the always-changing shapes and startling colors that hide within what is, in fact, an infinite world.

Also, as a worthwhile byproduct of generating fractals in VB, we'll have a chance to touch on several general topics concerning graphics (such as defining and using your own palettes, using True Color, and so on). These tips should be useful in any graphics application.

# Chapter 14

# Fractals: Infinity Made Visible

People who start playing around with fractals sometimes get hooked. Fractals are like alien worlds—obviously different from things we see in nature, yet also somehow familiar.

You can zoom into a fractal endlessly, producing fascinating variations of color, texture and shape. And what you see as you take this tour somehow looks both natural, like a cabbage or a tree, but also mysterious enough to earn fractals their reputation as the most complex objects in all math.

In this chapter we're going to demonstrate how you can generate fractals in VB. Beyond that, we'll also attempt to explain to nonmathematicians the strange numbers and odd dimensions that produce fractals. Along the way, we'll look at how VB handles 256-color palettes and True Color, as well as some general techniques for working with all types of graphics.

Mathematicians like fractals because they produce images of often startling beauty. Most mathematical formulae, when plotted, result in wave-like lines, arcs and other simple, really rather visually boring, geometric designs. Fractals, by contrast, yield extremely complex, lacy colorful patterns which hover just beyond symmetry. You never really see the same thing twice, though at first you might think so. Fractals are also often "natural" looking—that is, they imitate the patterns produced when a coastline erodes, or when an octopus grows a tentacle.

Fractals are equally appealing to mathematicians and lay people.

In this chapter, we'll provide the (surprisingly simple) programming that you can use to produce and explore fractals in VB. But we'll go beyond what most books do. We'll offer more than just another black box that produces pretty pictures. We will attempt to fully explain the interesting underlying structures that give rise to images of such startling realism and beauty.

If you are only interested in adding fractal textures or designs to your VB applications, then please ignore the descriptions in this chapter of the mathematics which produces them. However, we think that even the mathematically challenged will find the explanations entertaining and understandable.

The fractal-generating algorithms in this chapter are self-contained. We have isolated the programming that produces the actual images from the Functions that do the math. Therefore, if you wish, you can practically ignore the part of the program that does the dirty work and conduct your own experiments by merely adjusting some ordinary, easily understood parameters. Before you begin exploring the nature of fractals, you may wish to look at the images in the \FRACTALS subdirectory of the CD. All fractal images were produced with this book's applications.

CD-ROM

## WHAT IS A FRACTAL?

One way of describing a fractal is "the adventures of a small number on the complex plane." A fractal is a peculiar and very dense "graph" generated by a mathematical process. Although the resulting images are literally infinitely complex, the underlying algorithms are short and rather simple.

When you want to *see* relationships between numbers—to *see* mathematical expressions—you can put them into a kind of grid called a *plot*. The coordinates of this space are arbitrary—that is, you can set up the marks (the Scalemode, in VB terms) to be large enough to embrace whatever expression you are trying to make visual.

Let's see how plotting works in practice. Say we want to display a visual representation of the expression, "it takes longer to drive somewhere if you go slower." There are three qualities here: distance, time and speed. The formula that describes their relationship is: distance = time * velocity. If you *plot* this relationship, you can display increase in time horizontally and increase in distance vertically. In Figure 14-1, you can see a plot which shows what happens when traveling at 40 and 50 miles per hour. By going along the Time line, you can move up to the diagonal line to discover the resulting distance traveled at that particular time (and vice versa, translating distance into time).

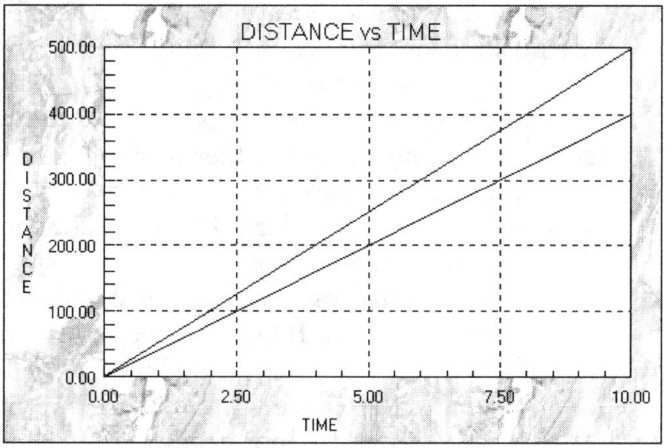


Figure 14-1: A plot is just another kind of chart or graph.

One virtue of plotting, of translating a mathematical expression or equation into a visual analog, is that you can see relationships you might not notice by merely reading the numbers. At a glance you often see a larger, overall view of the entire relationship or structure that for most of us is not so clear in an equation.

For instance, if you want to know how long it will take you to drive to L.A. from San Diego, you could draw diagonal lines representing different speeds as shown in Figure 14-1. At a glance, you could see the way that 50 MPH differs from 40 MHP.

However, not all numbers used by mathematicians are those familiar normal (or "real") numbers that we use every day, like 120 miles or 3 hours. For example, to translate waveforms into audio frequencies, or to anaylze an FM radio signal, or, indeed, to generate fractals, it is necessary for a mathematician to use "imaginary" numbers.

## Real & Imaginary Numbers

In the 16th century, mathematicians began trying to describe a pretty odd duck, the square root of minus one. When you multiply a number by itself, you *square* it; 4 * 4 is 16. And you can also describe this relationship between 4 and 16 the other way: 4 is the *square root* of 16. It seems obvious that there is a square root for any number. With 4, the square root is 2, and so on. Squares and roots had been used for thousands of years, but finally attention was focused on –1 which, though paradoxical in some ways, eventually proved quite useful.

What is the square root of –1? It's unusual, to say the least. For one thing, it's neither positive nor negative. When you square a positive number, you always get another positive number (a positive multiplied by a positive yields a positive). But when you multiply a negative number by a negative number, *you also get a positive.* So the thing that you could multiply by itself to get –1 is neither positive, nor negative (and of course not zero). In other words, it's not a real number.

Descartes called the square root of minus one an "imaginary" number, and the name stuck. This distinguishes it from "real" numbers like 2, or the square root of 25, or –12 or .55, which all seem somehow more natural. After all, we can find things around us of which there are two or five, or somebody removed a dozen bagels from the kitchen, or an oil can is half full. We *experience* these "real" numbers. But where have you ever seen a number that is simultaneously neither positive nor negative?

The square root of –1 is the imaginary unit and is denoted as *i* (sometimes *j*). With the introduction of the imaginary unit, it was possible to calculate the square root of any negative number. What's the square root of –4? If you attempt to calculate it wih Visual Basic's Sqr( ) Function, as

```
Print Sqr(-4)
```

you'll get the error message Invalid Function Call (which is a major understatement). Visual Basic can't calculate square roots of negative numbers because it can handle only real numbers.

Let's start by writing –4 as –1*4. The square root of this quantity is the square root of –1 (which is the imaginary unit i) times the square root of 4 (which is 2). The square root of –4, therefore, is 2*i, where i is the imaginary unit.

We can easily verify the previous result because the square of 2*i must be –4. Let's calculate the quantity:

```
(2*i)*(2*i) = 4*i*i
```

We know that i is the square root of –1, and therefore the quantity i*i is –1. Thus the term 4*i*i is –4. The imaginary number 2*i is indeed the square root of –4.

We have seen that there are two kinds of numbers: real ones (like the speed of a car or the distance to the moon) and imaginary ones (like the square root of a negative number). It is possible to combine real and imaginary numbers to produce *complex* numbers. When you combine real with imaginary numbers, you get points on a grid, as shown in Figure 14-2. Real numbers on this grid describe the horizontal distances, and imaginary numbers describe the vertical distances. The resulting complex numbers are denoted as 4+i*7 or 6+i*5.

Notice that this isn't really an addition. The plus sign says that the real and imaginary numbers are tied together to form a complex number. It's like describing a point on a city map by using two coordinates, such as A-13.

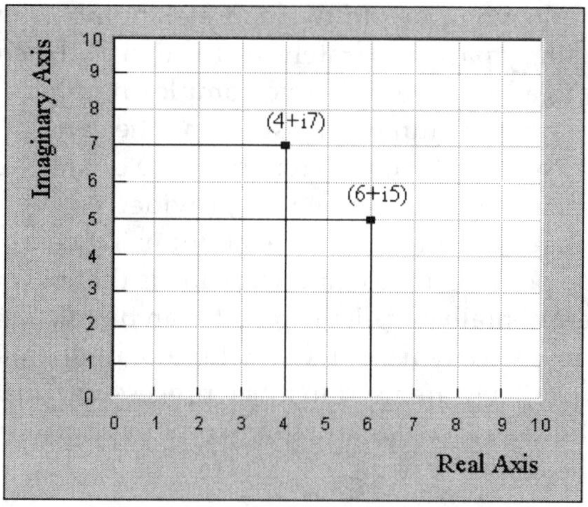


Figure 14-2: A number on the complex plane is described like a location on city map: by its horizontal and vertical coordinates. The horizontal coordinate is a real number, and the vertical coordinate is an imaginary number. Together, they form a complex number.

Sometimes we don't even use the symbol of addition to indicate a complex number. Instead, we can write the previous complex numbers as (4,i*7) or (6, i*5). You can even drop the i, if you keep in mind that the first number is the real one, and the second number is the imaginary one.

One last remark about real and imaginary numbers. We mentioned that there are two kinds of numbers—the familiar real numbers and the imaginary ones. Both, however, are complex numbers. A complex number without imaginary part is a real number. Similarly, a complex number without a real part is an imaginary number. The real numbers we are all familiar with are therefore a special case of complex numbers.

The two components of a complex number are quite distinct. The number (4+i*7) is a complex number and not an addition. The component 4 corresponds to a point on the horizontal axis (which would be the time in the example of Figure 14-1), and the number 7 corresponds to the vertical axis (which would be distance in the same example). It doesn't make any more sense to add the two components of a complex number than it does to add time and distance. The real part of a complex number is the letter in the map metaphor (A), and the imaginary part is the number (13).

It is possible, however, to manipulate complex numbers. For example, you can add two complex numbers by adding their real and imaginary parts separately. At the end of the chapter we'll describe how to add or multiply two complex numbers. If you aren't familiar with complex numbers, just follow the general description of the algorithms and worry later about the details—or don't worry at all, and just use the functions we provide.

What's useful and special about using complex numbers to describe points on the complex plane is that new and important real, experimentally verifiable results can be calculated. Complex numbers are now widely used in every field of mathematics and applied science. They are used in voice processing, image compression, radar, earthquake analysis and many other applications. Fractals, too, live on the complex plane.

### Transformations

A fractal is the graphical representation of an iterative process (like an ordinary For...Next loop), which is based on multiplying a complex number by itself. This process is called a *transformation* because each time we multiply a number by itself, we transform it to another number.

Three things can happen when you repeatedly multiply a number by itself. If it is a real number bigger than 1, it will grow towards an infinitely large number (2 * 2 becomes 4; then 4 * 4 becomes 16, 16 * 16 becomes 256 and so on quickly off to infinity).

If our starting number is less than one (a fraction), it will shrink towards an infinitely small number close to zero. For example, multiply 1/2 by 1/2 and you get 1/4, then 1/4 by 1/4 becomes 1/16, and so on down to a very little piece of a pie.

However, there is a third possible result. On the fence between the numbers that grow huge and the fractions that shrink is the number one. The number one, and the number one alone, is completely stable and cannot balloon or shrink, cannot move in either direction towards infinity.

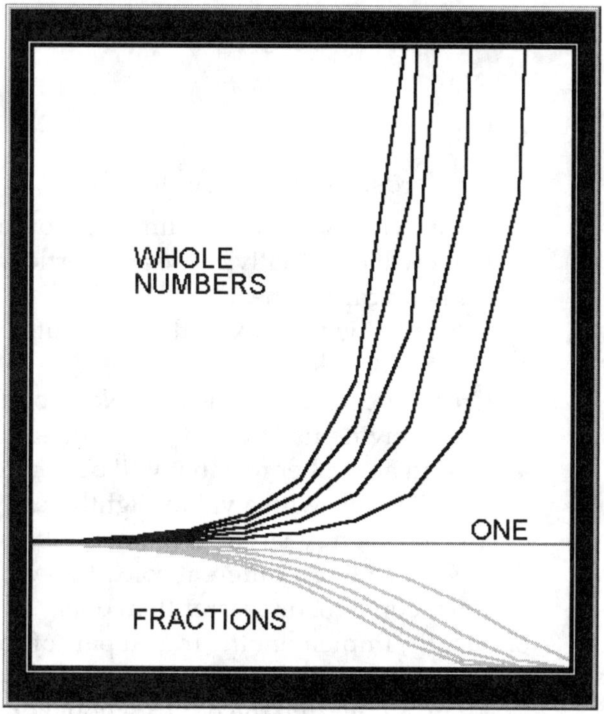


Figure 14-3: Numbers greater than one escape to infinity off the top, and fractions drop to zero at the bottom. The number one is the only number that remains stable, traveling cleanly across the grid.

Figure 14-3 illustrates how numbers above 1 will rapidly shoot off the scale and numbers below 1 will somewhat less rapidly decay to 0. Here is the program that produced these effects:

```
Private Sub Form_Load( )
Show
On Error Resume Next
    Picture1.Scale (15, 5)-(25, 0)
    For j = 0 To 20 Step 2
        a = 0.9999998 + j * 0.00000002
        If a < 1 Then Picture1.ForeColor = QBColor(7)
        If a = 1 Then Picture1.ForeColor = QBColor(8)
        If a > 1 Then Picture1.ForeColor = QBColor(0)
```

```
            For i = 0 To 50
                a = a * a
                Picture1.Line (XOld, YOld)-(i, a)
                XOld = i
                YOld = a
            Next
        Next

    End Sub
```

In other words, we take these steps:

1. Begin with On Error Resume Next because these transformations will eventually cause an overflow (going past VB's numeric capabilities).
2. Scale the Picture Box so that the plot will be displayed within its boundaries.
3. Create the iteration (the For...Next loop), which will run 11 times, giving us 11 events to witness.
4. Assign a number to *a* that will be very close to the number one. We start with a value slightly less than one and end with a value slightly larger than one.
5. Give each line a different color, based on whether it is lower than, equal to, or greater than one.
6. Finally, implement the fractal part of this whole process: the 0 to 50 loop multiplies *a* by itself.
7. Draw a line from the old (previous) point to the new point to represent the change in *a* when it is squared.
8. Store the new point so we can draw the next line.

As you can see, numbers even extremely close to one will rapidly diverge towards zero or infinity, depending on which side of one they are. This divergence is the basis for drawing fractal images. You have heard the word *attractors*. For any given transformation, attractors are numbers that draw other numbers towards them. Zero and infinity are the attractors in our example above—they "attract" the initial numbers toward themselves like magnets. (The value one is not an attractor, but a "stable" point of the transformation. Nothing changes when we multiply one by itself.)

All fractals are built upon the competing magnetism of two attractors. And between these two attractors there is always a border (in our previous example, this border is the number one). If you start an iteration with a = 1, the result will always be one, since one is the only number which, when squared (or otherwise multiplied by itself) remains unaffected, remains one. However, a fractal such as the Mandelbrot Set is a more complicated border—it is a visual depiction of an iteration involving imaginary and complex numbers, not the number one.

### Complex Numbers Produce Exceptionally Rich Shapes

Our example above is a simple transformation. We merely squared a number, then squared the result, and again and again. But watch what happens when we mix in a complex number.

Let's write an iteration that involves squaring, but adds a complex number into the mix. This will not be a radical change. (We will put in a complex number, but we'll use zero for the imaginary component when we start the iterations. Therefore, in this case, the imaginary component will have no effect on the outcome.) We're going to use this rather "mild" complex number, with its imaginary part neutered, because we want to approach these ideas one step at a time. Neutering the imaginary number provides us with a simpler, more easily understood example. So, say our starting point is z = (0,0) and the constant c = (1,0). (From now on we'll use the notation *z*, rather than *a*, to represent the points we generate to create our plots. *z* is just a convention to remind us that we're no longer using real numbers, but instead are now using complex numbers. Also, the constant c, like a constant in VB, remains unchanged—a static value throughout all the iterations.)

If we repeat the operation z = z^2+c a few times, we will get the numbers:

0^2+1 = 1
1^2+1 = 2
2^2+1 = 5
5^2+1 = 26

As you can see, the results get larger and larger, as before, and in a small number of iterations they escape to infinity, also as before. However, because of the additional constant, the pattern (2...5...26) is becoming a slightly less ordinary sequence than our simpler example, 2...4...16. The constant is slightly disturbing the simple squaring as the transformation heads away from 1.

Let's now go a step further and produce a more intricate result. If we change the constant c from 1 to –1, we see a very interesting effect: rather than fly off the top of the grid to infinity or sink down to zero, the line flutters between zero and minus one. This transformation results in an oscillation. If c = –1, the results are

(-1)^2 - 1 = 0
0 - 1 = –1
(-1)^2 –1 = 0
...and so on.

This elementary transformation offers another possibility. Some numbers will neither inflate to infinity, nor shrink to zero. They oscillate between two values.

Let's follow the same transformation with c=(0+i*1):

0^2 + (0 + i) = i
i^2 +(0 + i)= (-1 + i)
(-1 + i)^2+(0 + i) = i
i^2+(0 + i)=(-1 + i)

This is another example of a complex number that oscillates, this time between the values i and (–1 + i). Don't be alarmed if you aren't familiar with complex numbers and can't follow these numeric examples. The important thing to keep in mind is that some numbers will escape to infinity, while others will remain bounded. And this distinction gives rise to the most magnificent computer-generated images.

Finally, what if c = (0, 0) and z = (0.5, 0)? If you apply the same transformation, z (which represents our current position on the grid) gets smaller and smaller and practically vanishes after a number of iterations. This transformation has the same two attractors, but the boundary between them is no longer a simple circle (the number one). Figures 14-4 and 14-5 show the trajectories of two points on the complex plane—as you can see, we're not dealing with simple, stable, familiar geometric shapes here.

At the heart of every fractal image is a very simple transformation—a trivial transformation, like squaring a number over and over again. If this transformation is disturbed with the introduction of an imaginary number, there arises the beautiful and elaborate filigree that we all recognize as fractal images. The word *fractal* comes from the Latin root that also produced *fracture* and *fraction*.

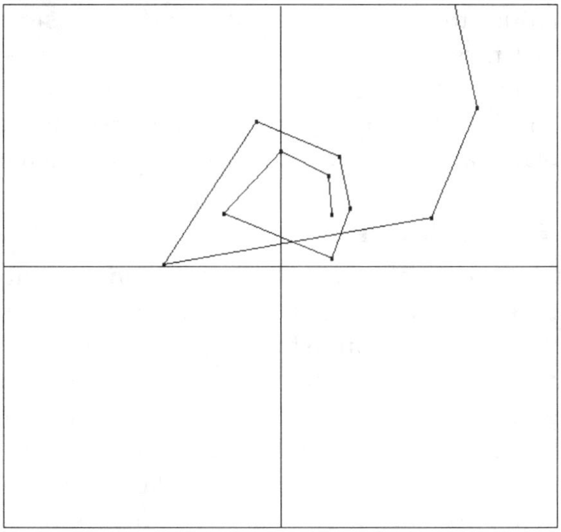

Figure 14-4: This is the trajectory of a point that's in the process of flying off into infinity. This point, an "escapee," will be displayed as a dot outside the boundary of the Mandelbrot Set.

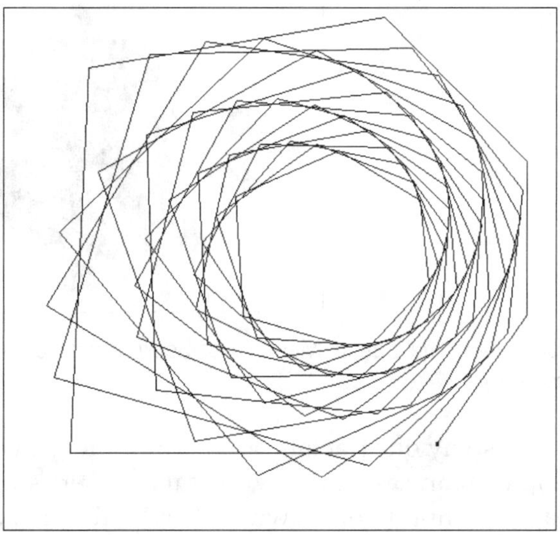

Figure 14-5: This trajectory reveals that this point will remain a "prisoner." It cannot puncture the boundaries and will eventually fall to zero. Notice how it approaches zero in an aperture-like, symmetric path.

Notice that now our results are not that simple horizontal line between zero and infinity that we got before (see Figure 14-3). *z* is a complex number, so the boundary between the two attractors (zero and infinity) is no longer a single number like one. It's a shape of indescribable complexity and beauty, as we will shortly see.

## The Mandelbrot Set

A *set* is a group of items that share some quality or another. All numbers that are negative are described as the "set" of negative numbers. "The Mandelbrot Set" is the group of numbers that, when plugged into the formula $z = z^2 + c$, remain "bounded" (don't escape to infinity). Technically, this set is the portion of the complex plane that is attracted to zero. A number will either fly off towards infinity (and therefore not be part of the Mandelbrot Set) or it will go towards zero (or, possibly, oscillate). The numbers going toward zero or oscillating, when all painted in, create the classic Mandelbrot shape as shown in Figure 14-6.

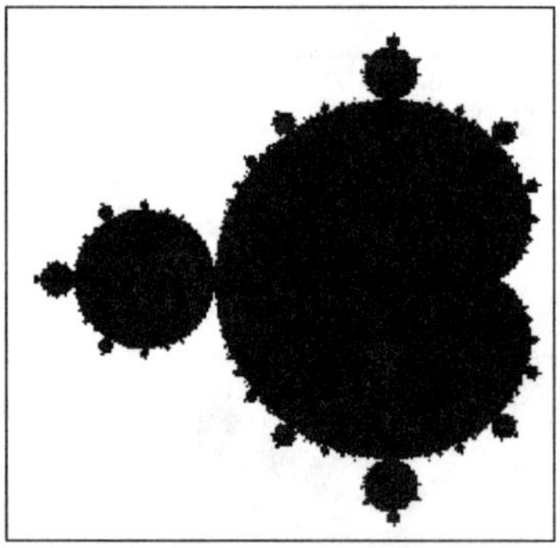

Figure 14-6: The classic Mandelbrot Set is revealed here as a somewhat lumpy symmetry.

To display our fractals on the computer screen, we can think of the complex plane as a grid, with real numbers shown horizontally and imaginary numbers shown vertically. To calculate the Mandelbrot Set in VB, we'll first arbitrarily choose a zone within the grid to paint in. For each point in this area, we assign the corresponding complex number to c (corresponding to this particular position on the grid) and, starting with $z = 0$, we repeat the transformation against this value enough times to discover whether or not this particular position will escape to infinity. If it will, we color it white to show it is outside of the Mandelbrot Set. If it won't escape, we color it black to show that it is part of the set. In other words, we calculate the square of z, add the constant c and, once again, put the result into z. This process is repeated again and again until we are reasonably confident that we know whether this one is an escapee or not. For a black-and-white fractal, 32 times is enough; for highly detailed fractals, we may check a pixel thousands of times before we're are reasonably sure it remains bound.

The result is an intricate shape known as the Mandelbrot Set. The irregular "line" between the black and white areas is the boundary between the two attractors (zero and infinity).

### Escapees & Prisoners

Points that remain bounded within a fractal set's boundaries are called *prisoners*, while those that escape to infinity are called *escapees*.

How do we find out if one of our points succeeds in escaping to infinity? Obviously, we shouldn't have to wait for an overflow condition. It can be mathematically proven that if either the real or the imaginary part of z is larger than 2 or smaller than –2, it will inevitably escape to infinity. However, if the result remains in the range (–2,2) after a large number of iterations, then the point is bounded. So, we could just run it through the iterations enough times to satisfy ourselves that it is or isn't escaping by going beyond 2 in either direction. However, we're going to use a slightly different approach.

Another way to test for escapees is to compare the result of each iteration against a very large number, like 100,000. If our result (either its real, or its imaginary, part) is larger than 100,000, we know that this point escapes to infinity. As we'll soon see, we want to know more about each point that simply whether or not it escapes—so we'll use this compare-to-huge-number technique.

One last detail before we get to the actual VB programming that produces fractals. We mentioned that the operation must be repeated for every point in our grid. Because a computer screen has a limited number of pixels, we need to calculate the values of only those points we can plot on the screen (in other words, the pixels, the dots that are visible to the user). If the area of our grid is from –1 to +1 in both axes, and the Picture Box we will use to display the Mandelbrot Set has a resolution of 256 by 256 pixels, we must find only the points of the grid that correspond to pixels. The increment between two successive points must be 2/255, and therefore the points we will use are –1, –1+(2/255), –1+2*(2/255) and so on, up to –1+255*(2/255). The last point is 1, the other endpoint.

In Figure 14-7 you see how the complex plane is mapped to screen coordinates by overlaying a Picture Box on the complex plane. The grid is the Picture Box where the fractal will be displayed, and the grid's intersections are pixels. We must calculate the fractal only at the points that correspond to pixels. The pixel (1,2), for example, corresponds to a point on the complex plane with coordinates (0.5,1).

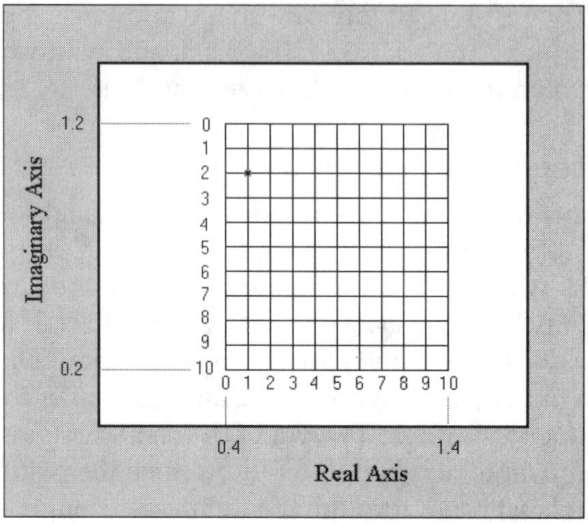


Figure 14-7: Mapping the complex plane to pixel coordinates. The pixel (1, 2) corresponds to the point (0.5, 1) on the complex plane.

## Programming the Mandelbrot Set

Now for the VB programming that opens the door to what many people find a hypnotic and even addictive world. Because fractals are the visual analog of the most complex object in all mathematics, we should be grateful that we amateurs and even nonmathematicians are privileged to see with our computers what even the math geniuses who discovered fractals couldn't visualize.

### Example: Calculating the Mandelbrot Set

CD-ROM

The main Form of our first fractal application, VBFRACT, is shown in Figure 14-8. VBFRACT can be found in the 14\APPS\VBFRACT of the CD. This application can generate black-and-white, as well as colored Mandelbrot Sets. (The Julia Set is another kind of fractal image, and we'll get to it shortly.) The Picture Box has dimensions (256 X 256) pixels.

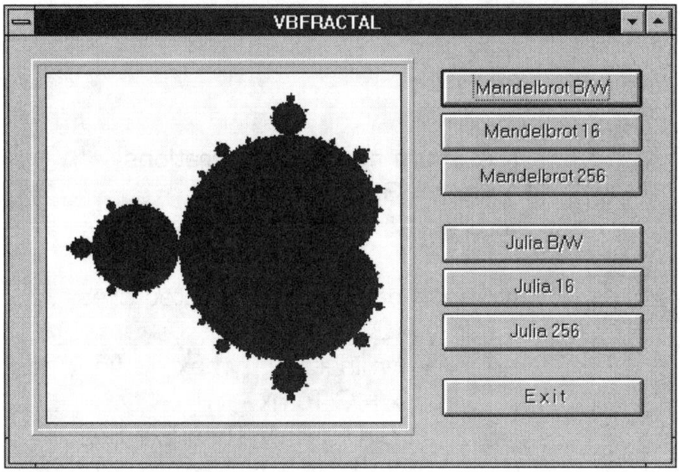


Figure 14-8: A multipurpose VB fractal generator.

Let's start with the black-and-white Mandelbrot Set. The only parameters to define are

- ❒ The area of the complex plane we wish to map (Xmin, Xmax, Ymin, YMax).
- ❒ The resolution of the Picture Box (nx, ny).
- ❒ The maximum number of iterations required to establish that a given point remains bounded (maxiter).

Thirty-two iterations is a good starting point for the black-and-white Mandelbrot Set. Larger values, like 500 iterations, yield more accurate sets, but of course require longer calculation times. So, let's plunge in. Here's the programming that results in Figure 14-6:

```
Sub MandelBWButton_Click ( )
Dim X As Double, Y As Double
Dim ix As Integer, iy As Integer
Dim nx As Integer, ny As Integer
Dim MaxIter As Integer
Dim xmin As Double, ymin As Double, xmax As Double, →
ymax As Double

STOPNOW = False
' Define picture resolution
nx = 256
ny = 256
' Select area of the complex plane to map on the screen
```

```
xmin = –1.5
xmax = .5
ymin = –1
ymax = 1
' Maximum number of iterations
MaxIter = 32
Picture1.Cls

' for each point in the selected area  ...
   For iy = 0 To ny - 1
      Y = (ymin + iy * (ymax - ymin) / (ny - 1))
      For ix = 0 To nx - 1
         If STOPNOW Then Exit Sub
         X = (xmin + ix * (xmax - xmin) / (nx - 1))
' ... check whether it escapes to infinity or not
         M = VBMandel(X, Y, MaxIter)
         If M = MaxIter Then
            Picture1.PSet (ix, iy), BLACK
         Else
            Picture1.PSet (ix, iy), LTGRAY
         End If
      Next
      DoEvents
   Next
   STOPNOW = True
End Sub
```

BLACK and LTGRAY are constants. The STOPNOW global variable lets the program know when to stop the drawing of the current fractal because the user has requested the drawing of another fractal, by clicking on one of the other Command Buttons.

Above, X and Y are the grid coordinates of each pixel on the complex plane. In other words, they are the grid coordinates that correspond to the pixels of our display. (Remember that we are calculating the Mandelbrot Set for points on the complex plane that correspond to grid intersections, pixels, on our display.) Since our Picture Box dimensions are 256 X 256 pixels, we must repeat the transformation 256 X 256 times. If a point escapes quickly to infinity, the calculations may need to be repeated just a few times. For points that persist in remaining bounded, the transformation must be repeated MaxIter times. The two loops scan all grid points that correspond to the pixels inside the Picture Box, and the same basic transformation is repeated for each pixel. The lines that assign values to the variables x and y map the display's pixels (ix, iy) to the grid's coordinates.

### The Actual Mandelbrot Generating Function

The essential calculation that discovers whether or not our pixel is an escapee takes place in the VBMandel( ) Function:

```
Function VBMandel (cx As Double, cy As Double, MaxIter →
As Integer) As Integer
Dim x2 As Double, y2 As Double
Dim temp As Double
Dim X As Double, Y As Double

    X = 0
    Y = 0
    x2 = 0
    y2 = 0
    iter = 0
    While ((iter < MaxIter) And ((Abs(x2) + Abs(y2)) < 100000))
        temp = x2 - y2 + cx
        Y = 2 * X * Y + cy
        X = temp
        x2 = X * X
        y2 = Y * Y
        iter = iter + 1
    Wend
    VBMandel = iter

End Function
```

VBMandel( ) tells us the number of iterations executed. If VBMandel( ) has managed to repeat its calculations MaxIter times, the point is bounded; it is colored black. The first five lines of the While loop multiply a complex number by itself and add the constant c, as we described earlier in the chapter. (For those who really want to know the gory details, multiplication and addition of complex numbers will be explained at the end of this chapter.) If the point escapes quickly to infinity (which happens when the sum of the absolute values of its real and imaginary parts exceed the number 100,000) we exit the loop before reaching the maximum number of iterations.

## Julia Sets

We will now temporarily leave the Mandelbrot Set to describe how to generate a different type of fractal image, known as *Julia Sets*. This is a second major style of fractal. A Julia Set (see Figure 14-9) is generated by the same process as a Mandelbrot Set, only here the function $z=z^2+c$ is defined differently. In a Julia Set, the variable z takes on *every* value of the grid, and c remains the same throughout the entire process. The constant c can have any value, as long as both its parts (the real and the imaginary part) are between –2 and 2. In other words, c is added to each point in the complex plane, and the same transformation is repeated over and over.

Despite the different shape, Julia Sets are based on the same transformation as Mandelbrot Sets.

Unlike the Mandelbrot Set, whose shape is always the same, a Julia Set can be many different designs, depending on the value of the constant c. Different values of c result in quite different images. However every one of those images can, like any other fractal, be zoomed into. And the zooming will reveal, variously, shapes and designs that resemble (but are not quite identical to) the original. This is why fractal geometry is sometimes referred to as *self-similar*.

Unfortunately, not all c values yield interesting Julia Sets, and it's not always easy to come up with a good value for the parameter c. The value used most often to produce the "classic" Julia Set is –0.74543 + i0.11301. (We'll suggest a few other good c values later in this chapter.)

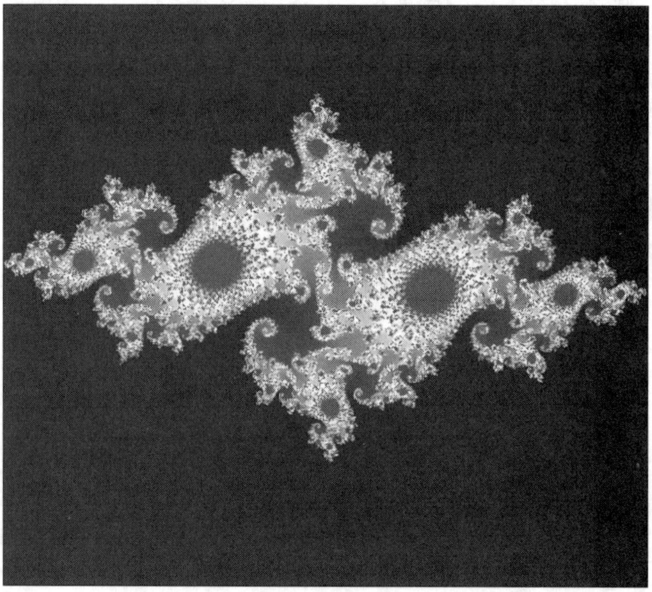

Figure 14-9: This is the "classic" Julia Set shape, but Julia Sets beget many different shapes depending on what numbers you feed them.

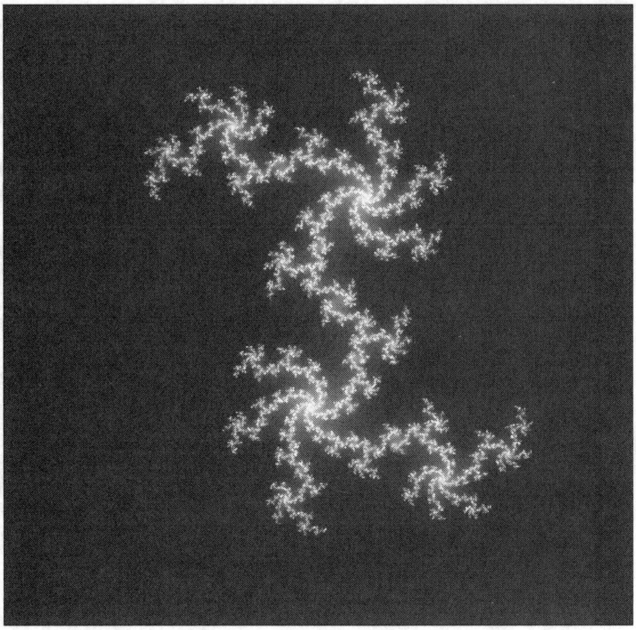

Figure 14-10: Here's another Julia Set, quite distinct from Figure 14-9.

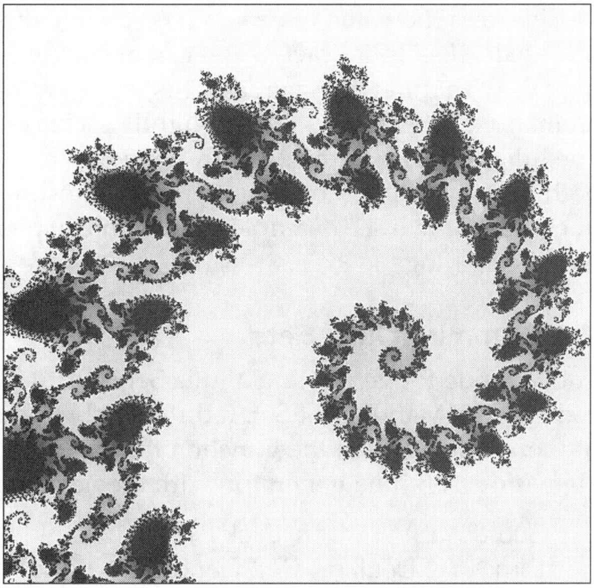

Figure 14-11: And yet another Julia Set.

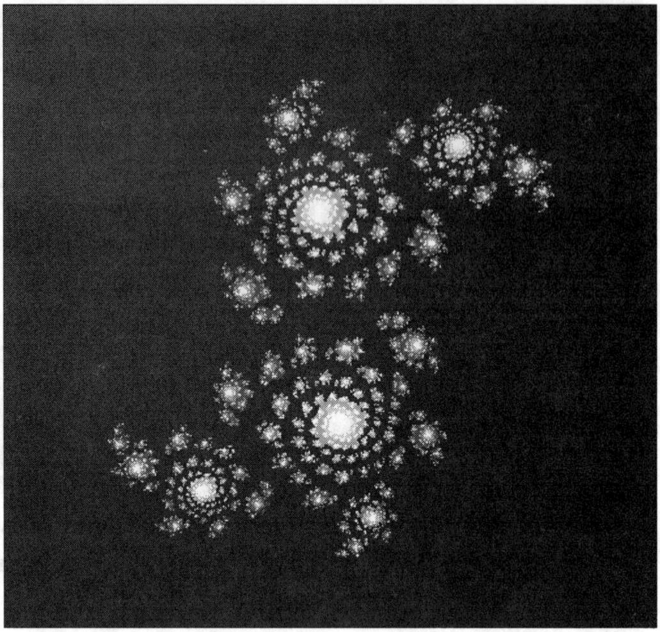

Figure 14-12: A variation on the classic Julia Set.

Although the value of c remains the same throughout the drawing of an *individual* Julia fractal, you can of course create successive fractals with different c values. This is one way to make an interesting animation. For instance, if you slightly increase the value of c from one Julia drawing to the next (by changing the real, the imaginary, or both parts) you'll discover extremely interesting animation sequences. We will see examples of this in Chapter 9, "Multimedia: The New Technology."

### Programming Julia Sets

The VB code for generating a Julia Set is virtually identical to the code for the Mandelbrot Set. It differs only in that it assigns a value to the constant c, and in the Function that does the escapee analysis. Here is our VB Julia generator, with the new lines underlined:

```
Sub JuliaBWButton_Click ( )
Dim X As Double, Y As Double
Dim cx As Double, cy As Double
Dim MaxIter As Integer
Dim ix As Integer, iy As Integer
Dim nx As Integer, ny As Integer
```

```
Dim xmin As Double, ymin As Double, xmax As Double,  →
ymax As Double

STOPNOW = False
nx = 256
ny = 256
' The value of the c parameter
cx = -.74543
cy = .11301
' Center fractal around (cx, cy) value
xmin = -1.5 - cx
xmax = 1.5 - cx
ymin = -1.5 - cy
ymax = 1.5 - cy

MaxIter = 64
Picture1.Cls

For iy = 0 To ny - 1
   Y = ymin + iy * (ymax - ymin) / (ny - 1)
   For ix = 0 To nx - 1
      If STOPNOW Then Exit Sub
      X = xmin + ix * (xmax - xmin) / (nx - 1)
      Color = VBJulia(cx, cy, X, Y, MaxIter)
      If Color = MaxIter Then
         Picture1.PSet (ix, iy), BLACK
      Else
         Picture1.PSet (ix, iy), LTGRAY
      End If
   Next
   DoEvents
Next
STOPNOW = True

End Sub
```

cx and cy are the real and imaginary parts, respectively, of the complex constant c. In the last four underlined lines, we adjust the minimum and maximum values of the area we are painting, to center the Julia Set within our Picture Box. Also notice that we are using a larger value for the MaxIter variable (we iterate more, to add more detail to our Julia Set).

The actual escapee calculations take place in the VBJulia( ) Function, which accepts two more arguments than the comparable Mandelbrot VBMandel( ) Function. The first two arguments are the real and imaginary parts of the complex constant c. X and Y are the coordinates of each point on the grid while we are working on it, as in the Mandelbrot subroutine.

```
Function VBJulia (cx As Double, cy As Double, X As Double,  →
Y As Double, MaxIter As Integer) As Integer
Dim iter As Integer
Dim x2 As Double, y2 As Double
Dim xtemp As Double, ytemp As Double

    iter = 0
    x2 = X + cx
    y2 = Y + cy
    While ((iter < MaxIter) And ((Abs(x2) + Abs(y2)) < 100000))
        xtemp = x2 * x2 - y2 * y2 + cx
        ytemp = 2 * x2 * y2 + cy
        x2 = xtemp
        y2 = ytemp
        iter = iter + 1
    Wend
    VBJulia = iter

End Function
```

Just like the VBMandel( ) Function, the VBJulia( ) Function returns the number of repetitions required for the point to escape to infinity. Again, if the point under consideration remained bounded up to the maximum number of iterations, it is considered bounded and we color it black. If not, the point escapes to infinity and we color it white.

## COLORED FRACTALS

Black-and-white fractals can be elegant and intriguing, but colored fractals are often breathtaking. Where does the color come from? What does it represent within the deep structure of this most puzzling mathematical object?

Different colors represent different escape velocities. As you know, when we test some points in the Picture Box, they rocket off into infinity rather quickly (the VBMandel( ) or VBJulia( ) Functions have reported a low number of iterations in the *iter* variable). Others take longer, and some points never do escape (*iter* = *MaxIter*). Points that escape to infinity with different velocities are colored differently. So, although you could assign any colors you want to represent the various speeds of escape or entrapment of each point, there must nonetheless be a consistent pattern of color created within any single Julia or Mandelbrot Set. In other words, red could indicate only the fastest escapees or could mean only the bound points or some other in-between escape velocity. So what red means in general is up to you. But all points colored the same shade of red within a given fractal image share the same velocity.

Color adds another important dimension to a fractal image.

These mysterious variations of escape velocity (and the resulting patterns of position and color) give fractals their beauty and complexity. We mentioned earlier that once the absolute value of the real or imaginary part of the point under consideration becomes larger than 2, the point will eventually escape. We could have used this well-known fact to end our calculations sooner and make our programs slightly faster, but when drawing colored fractals we are also interested in the *velocity* of escape, not in the mere fact that a point will eventually escape. So, we permit iterations to go on longer than strictly necessary because this provides us with the information about velocity which is what we use to determine the color of each point. (By gathering more information about velocity, we can increase the color detail within our fractal.)

Here we must make a distinction between what can be done on computers capable of displaying 16 or 256 colors. On a 16-color VGA system, the mapping of the number of iterations to colors is simple (and inflexible). On 256-color systems, you are free to define colors and can try numerous color combinations.

Let's first consider how to display fractals of only 16 colors. As you will see, colored fractals are generated in much the same way as black-and-white fractals, which means that we do not have to rewrite our basic algorithms.

## 16-Color Fractals

Recall that the VBMandel( ) and VBJulia( ) Functions return the number of times a point was tested before (or if) it escaped. To generate 16 colors representing 16 different speeds of escape, all we have to do is replace the statements that assigned black and white to the points with the following lines, which assign one of the basic 16 colors:

```
If Color = MaxIter Then
    Picture1.PSet (ix, iy), BLACK
Else
    Picture1.PSet (ix, iy), QBColor( Color Mod 16 )
End If
```

The points that remain bounded are still colored black. The remaining points are colored according to how quickly they escape. The Mod operator makes sure that QBColor is always given a valid color number. (QBColor only accepts numbers between 0 and 15, so by getting the result, the remainder, after Color is divided by 15, we ensure that we are feeding QBColor a number it can digest. We are leaving bounded points with a constant color, BLACK.)

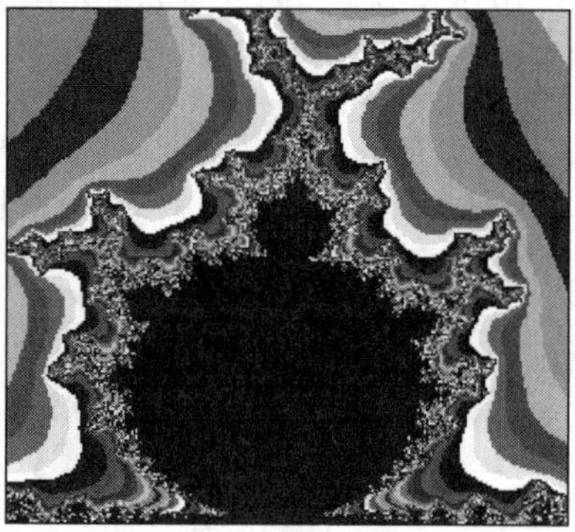

Figure 14-13: The "Folded Range" is one of many ways that a fractal can generate color patterns.

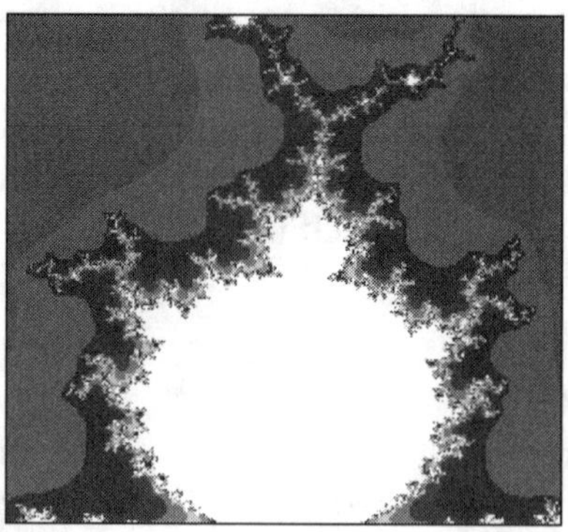

Figure 14-14: Another coloration results when you use a "banded range" approach.

There are, of course, many ways you could decide to represent the various escape velocities of these points with colors. Using the Mod operator causes a "folding" of the range of velocities. In other words, the same color is given to any point that escapes at the 1th, 16th or 32nd iteration, and so on along the entire range of iterations you have allowed.

To avoid this folding, you could replace the Mod approach with one that divides the range into 16 zones. It assigns the first QBColor to any point within the first 16th of the range, and so on. In this case, points represent "bands" of the range. To see the difference in these two approaches, look at Figures 14-13 and 14-14.

To use the "banding" technique displayed in Figure 14-14, replace

```
QBColor( Color Mod 15 )
```

with

```
QBColor(Color * 15 / MaxIter)
```

(Color here is the number of repetitions returned by the Functions VBMandel or VBJulia.) As you can see, points that escape very quickly are mapped to QBColor(0) or QBColor(1). Points that escape slowly are mapped to higher colors. When color=MaxIter, the argument of the QBColor( ) Function is 15 (the maximum value accepted by QBColor( ), which corresponds to white). The rest of the programming to generate 16-color fractals is identical to the programming for black-and-white fractals.

Of course, you can experiment with your own approaches for color mapping.

## 256-Color Fractals

The standard VGA palette has only 16 colors, so the transitions between successive colors are not smooth. This is why the fractals in Figures 14-13 and 14-14 are not very impressive. With a 256-color palette, however, we can create fractals with smooth transitions between successive colors. The shapes and backgrounds can look as smooth as burnished brass.

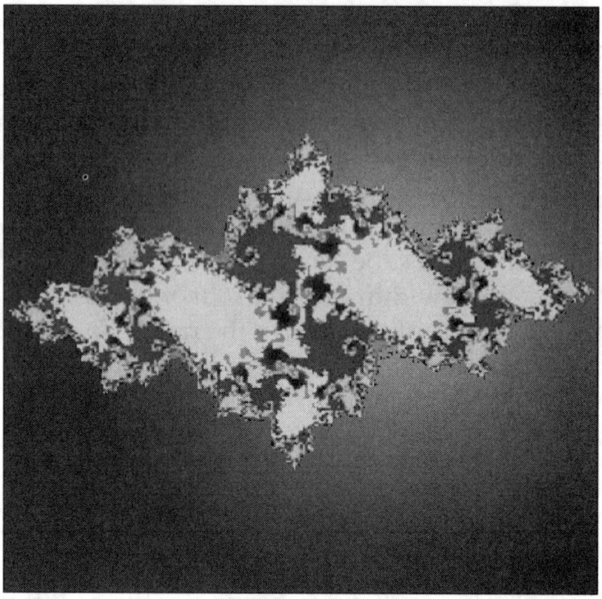

Figure 14-15: The results of various palettes differ considerably (compare this to Figure 14-13).

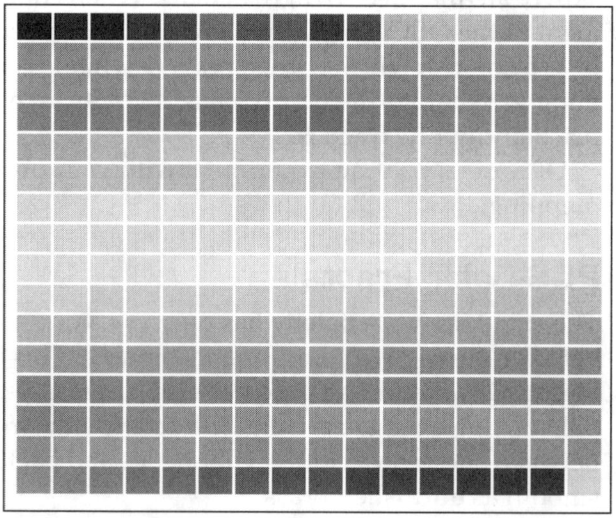

Figure 14-16: This is the palette used in Figure 14-15. Note the general smoothness of transitions between shades of color.

Figure 14-17: Here we used a palette with more abrupt transitions between color bands than those in Figure 14-15.

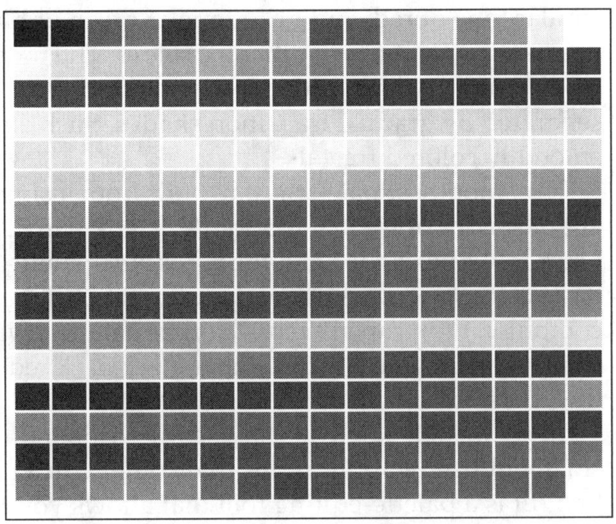

Figure 14-18:This is the palette used in Figure 14-17. A number of transitions are abrupt, and some ranges are quite random in their shading, producing more grain in the fractal.

### Defining Your Palette

In a 256-color system we not only have more colors, but also the freedom to define *which* 256 colors will be used. That's very handy, but if you think about it, you'll realize it's not easy to come up with a color set for a fractal. Fractals are unpredictable by nature, and there is no way to predict which colors will do best in any particular complex image. Should we color red the points that escape immediately to infinity, or those that take longer? And how many basic colors should we use in the palette? And often of supreme importance to the look of the final picture—how will the palette be organized? Do we want a gradual shift from one shade at the start, to a comparable shade at the end, such as light to dark blue? Or perhaps a rainbow effect with all colors included?

The fractal algorithms won't help us, so we'll follow a different approach. We will attempt to design a 256-color palette that satisfies two basic requirements. First, transitions among colors must be as smooth as possible. Let's say we have a point that escapes to infinity after 100 iterations, and it is colored red. It's likely that some of its neighboring points will escape to infinity after 101 or 99 iterations. Often a better-looking image results if these points are colored with a similar tone of red, and not a tone of green or blue. Second, we don't necessarily want many different colors. The most pleasing effects can result from a palette with a few basic colors, widely spaced apart and separated by gradual transition shades. Such a palette yields the most smoothly colored fractals.

The smoothest palette is one built from a single color, just a gradient of shades of the same color. A palette with 256 tones of gray, from black to white, is the smoothest possible palette. It contains only two basic colors and as many of their transition tones as you can get on a computer. (You can also create other palettes, which contain smooth transitions between, for example, very dark red and white, with all the pinks between.)

To create palettes, you can use Microsoft's BitEdit and PalEdit, two small but useful applications that come with Video for Windows. PalEdit is a palette-editing tool that allows you to load an image and change its palette, cycle the palette colors, merge two palettes and even sort them in various orders.

To manipulate a palette, run BitEdit and load a picture whose colors you like. Then click on Options/Show Palette. You can now double-click on any color displayed and edit it. You can also rearrange the colors, or create entirely new palettes. However, it's always easier to start with an existing palette that contains most of the color ranges you are interested in.

Here's how to create a new DIB palette (a single-pixel image with the desired palette, as discussed in Chapter 6) with the PalEdit application. First create a new image with dimensions 1 X 1 (this is a single pixel). Then choose Apply Palette and select the name of the image (a BMP or DIB file) with the desired palette. Once the palette has been applied, save the single-pixel image under a new file name.

Another excellent computer art program is Electronic Arts' Deluxe Paint, which provides powerful tools for manipulating palettes. Deluxe Paint is a DOS-based application, but we found it very useful in creating palettes for fractal images.

There aren't many different fractal algorithms. To create great fractal images, you must experiment with colors and palettes.

Once you have decided what palette to use, you must decide the number of iterations. Obviously, the maximum number of iterations must now be 256 or larger, or we will not make optimal use of a 256-color palette. A good value is, in fact, 256, and the mapping function is quite simple. The number of iterations it takes for a point to escape to infinity becomes a direct index into the color palette itself.

(With a grayscale palette, small numbers of iterations—points that escape to infinity quickly—are colored with dark gray tones. Large numbers of iterations, which correspond to points that escape to infinity slowly, are colored with light gray tones.)

To access a palette's colors from within Visual Basic, you must first load the DIB (or BMP) file with the palette on the corresponding Picture Box and then read the palette's entries from the file and store them in an array. The DIB file must be a single-pixel image with the palette information, as discussed in Chapter 6. The array that contains the RGB descriptions of the colors is defined as

```
Dim Palette(256) As RGBTriplet
```

where RGBTriplet is a user-defined Type:

```
Type RGBTriplet
    Red As Byte
    Green As Byte
    Blue As Byte
End Type
```

Of course, in the VB3 version of the programs, the fields of the RGBTriplet type are dimensioned as Integers.

Each color entry is stored in one row of the Palette( ) array. Unfortunately, Visual Basic doesn't provide a Function equivalent to QBColor( ) for 256-color palettes, so we must specify the colors in terms of their RGB components. If a point escapes to infinity after 99 iterations, it will be colored with the 99th entry of the palette. The definition of this color is:

```
RGB(Palette(99).Red, Palette(99).Green, Palette(99).Blue)
```

CD-ROM

On the CD are several palettes that can be used with the VBFRACT application. These palettes are duplicated in all subdirectories containing applications that use them, such as VBFRACT. You will also find them in the PALETTES subdirectory.

SMOOTH.DIB is the smoothest color palette and contains many shades of a few basic colors. (DIB means Device Independent Bitmap, and these files are interchangeable with BMP files.) You can take a look at this palette with the PAL256 application in Chapter 6. Microsoft recommends loading a palette by creating a single-pixel DIB file, then importing it (for more on how to create these DIB files, see Chapter 6, "Color & Imaging").

Palette handling is covered extensively in Chapter 6.

RAINBOW.DIB, PASTEL.DIB and MONO.DIB are the palettes that come with Visual Basic, and they can be used to color fractals fairly well.

### Coloring Fractals With Palettes

Here are the steps involved in creating a 256-color fractal:

1. We select a palette and load it onto the Picture Box where the fractal will be displayed (by loading a DIB file with the desired palette). This is done by the following command:

   ```
   Picture1.LoadPicture PALETTEFILE
   ```

   where PALETTEFILE is a string variable containing the name of the file with the palette. (Change the value of the PALETTEFILE variable to try out different palettes.) This line loads the palette onto the Picture Box. The purpose here is to prepare the Picture Box to display the correct colors for this palette. An alternative method would be to load a DIB or BMP file into the Picture Property of the Picture Box during program design. However, this method is clumsy for several reasons, and should be avoided.

2. Then extract the palette from the .DIB file and store the color values in an array. Here's the LoadPalette( ) Subroutine that does just that (you can find a similar subroutine in Chapter 6, where we discussed the structure of DIB files):

```
Sub LoadPalette ( )
Dim file As BITMAPFILEHEADER
Dim info As BITMAPINFOHEADER
Dim r As Byte, g As Byte, b As Byte, a As Byte

    Open PALETTEFILE For Binary As #1
    Get #1, , file
    Get #1, , info
    If info.biBitCount <> 8 Then
        i = MsgBox("Not an 8-bit palette", 32)
        Exit Sub
    Else
    NColors = 256
    For i = 1 To NColors
        Get #1, , b: Get #1, , g
        Get #1, , r: Get #1, , a
        Palette(i, 1)=r
        Palette(i, 2)=g
        Palette(i, 3)=b
    Next
End If
Close #1
End Sub
```

In the VB3 version of the program, the 1-byte variables r, g, b are defined as String*1.

3. Now we are ready to proceed with the calculations. The functions for calculating 256-color fractals are no different than the ones we used for black & white or 16-color fractals. We have to change only the lines that assign the color of the current pixel. So to transform the 16-color version of VBMandel to a 256-color version, change

```
If Color = MaxIter Then
    Picture1.PSet (ix, iy), BLACK
Else
    Picture1.PSet (ix, iy), QBColor( Color Mod 15 )
End If
```

to this:

```
CIndex = Color mod 256
Picture1.PSet(ix, iy), RGB(Palette(Cindex).Red,   →
Palette(Cindex).Green, Palette(Cindex).Blue)
```

Above, Color is the number of repetitions required for a point to escape to infinity, and it is used as an index to the color palette. Of course, the number of maximum iterations (MaxIter) must be at least 256. The Mod command makes sure that no matter how large the maximum number of iterations is, the color index always has a value between 0 and 255.

CD-ROM

The procedures we described so far are implemented in the VBFRACT application on the CD (subdirectory 14\APPS). The complete application contains a few extra lines of code that we didn't put here in the book. Leaving them out helps to simplify the explanation of the programs. If you are not interested in looking more at complex number manipulation, use the VBMandel( ) and VBJulia( ) Functions as "black boxes." They do all the work, but you don't have to know how they work. However, you might want to adjust some of the VB code to experiment with various palettes and color assignment techniques. You can also increase the maximum number of iterations (the variable *maxiter*) to add more detail to the fractals.

## THE REAL MAGIC OF FRACTALS

Up to now, we've been variously limited by ranges of color, organization of the palette, and seeing only the outermost view of the generated fractal. We now introduce an application that surmounts these limitations. MDIFract employs True Color (more than 16 million potential colors). True Color permits smooth transitions between adjacent colors, as well as absolute freedom in defining colors. Consequently, we will be able to display fractals of the highest quality.

### EXAMPLE: A FRACTAL GENERATOR

MDIFract, shown in Figure 14-19, also allows you to zoom in on a given fractal so that you can see how colors and shapes emerge and vary, the further into a fractal you move. (Generally, the first, outermost view of a fractal contains less variety of color. Often, the real beauty of a fractal is hidden among the filaments. To really explore a fractal, move repeatedly down through the filaments within.) You can also zoom in at various "speeds," depending on which Zoom option you select in the Parameters window. And you can click on the icons for either Julia or Mandelbrot, as well as specify the size of the resulting image.

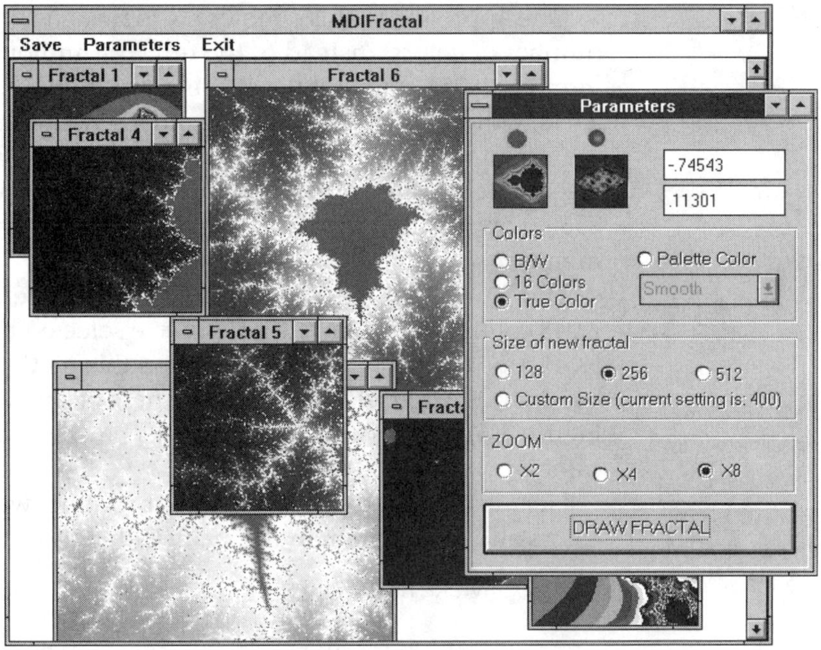


Figure 14-19: The MDIFract application permits zooming and True Color images.

Again, the basic algorithms for calculating the Mandelbrot and Julia Sets need not be changed from our previous application, VBFRACT. For this new application, we use a larger number of iterations (a larger value for MaxIter, the maximum number of iterations). The difference between 256-color and True Color fractals is that with True Color, we need not load a palette. We simply set the color of each pixel with VB's RGB( ) Function, which can describe all 16 million plus colors. (You will be able to use True Color technique only if your display supports True Color. The application, however, works on all systems.)

MDIFract is not the ultimate fractal generator, but it is a short Visual Basic application that can serve as a vehicle for your own exploration of the world of fractals.

## "True Color Palettes," Too

True Color allows more flexibility in setting a fractal's colors, but how do we decide a method of assigning colors to particular "velocities of escape?" This is the same problem we had with fewer colors: the number of iterations is *just a number*, and isn't mapped to a pixel color until we devise some way of correlating iterations to colors.

One approach to this problem is to design a palette with a limited number of colors, instead of the full 16.7 million. We'll use many more than 256 colors, but a still-limited number, perhaps 1,024, or 4,096, will do the trick. Even the most intricate fractal shapes don't require more than a few thousand colors to get fluid gradients and elegant detail. However, the results will be no improvement over a 256-color palette if displayed on anything less than a True Color monitor.

CD-ROM

True Color offers far better possibilities for colored fractals, but it requires some special handling, just like 256 color palettes.

The True Color fractals on the CD were generated with a palette of 2,048 colors. To design the palette, we selected basic colors using the RGB cube (see Chapter 6 for more on this method of organizing a spectrum). After selecting eight corners of the RGB cube (shown in Figure 5-3), we created all 256 shades between successive corners and came up with a 2,048-color palette.

Here is the MakeTrueColors( ) Subroutine, which generates the colors and stores them in the array Colors( ):

```
Sub MakeTrueColors ( )

    For i = 0 To 255            ' Black to Red
        Colors(k).Red = i
        Colors(k).Green = 0
        Colors(k).Blue = 0
        k = k + 1
    Next

    For i = 0 To 255            ' Red to Yellow
        Colors(k).Red = 255
        Colors(k).Green = i
        Colors(k).Blue = 0
        k = k + 1
    Next

    For i = 0 To 255            ' Yellow to White
        Colors(k).Red = 255
        Colors(k).Green = 255
        Colors(k).Blue = i
        k = k + 1
    Next

    For i = 255 To 0 Step -1    ' White to Magenta
        Colors(k).Red = 255
```

```
        Colors(k).Green = i
        Colors(k).Blue = 255
        k = k + 1
    Next

    For i = 255 To 0 Step -1     ' Magenta to Blue
        Colors(k).Red = i
        Colors(k).Green = 0
        Colors(k).Blue = 255
        k = k + 1
    Next

    For i = 0 To 255             ' Blue to Cyan
        Colors(k).Red = 0
        Colors(k).Green = i
        Colors(k).Blue = 255
        k = k + 1
    Next

    For i = 255 To 0 Step -1     ' Cyan to Green
        Colors(k).Red = 0
        Colors(k).Green = 255
        Colors(k).Blue = i
        k = k + 1
    Next

    For i = 255 To 0 Step -1     ' Green to Black
        Colors(k).Red = 0
        Colors(k).Green = i
        Colors(k).Blue = 0
        k = k + 1
    Next

End Sub
```

You can easily design different True Color palettes by changing the order of the corners of the RGB Cube. You can come up with a totally new way to scan the corners and (why not) the interior of the RGB cube.

True Color palettes are not regular Windows palettes.

You probably realize that our Colors( ) palette is not a palette in the Windows sense. For example, we don't load it into a Picture Box to see the colors (as is the case with the Windows-style 256-color palettes). We don't even have to store the color definitions in an array; it merely simplifies our programming to do so. Without the array, we would have to process several commands for coloring each pixel. By storing the color definitions in an array, we can paint each pixel with a single command, such as

```
Picture1.PSet (ix, iy) RGB(Colors(color).Red,  →
Colors(color).Green, Colors (color).Blue
```

where color is the number of iterations performed before the point at coordinates (ix, iy) escaped to infinity.

CD-ROM

For more information on coloring fractals and adjusting a fractal's colors, please read the file README.TXT in the subdirectory 14\GOODFRCT of the CD.

## The MDIFract Application

Our application uses an MDI Form and each new fractal is displayed in its own child Form. This way the user can compare various zooms of a fractal image. Click on Parameters to display the Parameters window. From here you can specify the basic parameters of a fractal (size and colors). The size options—128, 256, 512 and Custom—are the dimensions of the child window where the new fractal will be displayed. The Custom option allows you to define the desired resolution with the help of a standard dialog box. The minimum dimensions the application allows for a child window are 64 x 64 pixels, while the is upper limit is 9,999. Use the size 128 to quickly locate the area of the fractal you wish to view on your screen. When you are satisfied, you can create a fractal with larger dimensions.

CD-ROM

Click on the Palette Option Box to select a palette from the Combo Box underneath it. The MDIFRACT application you will find on the CD (subdirectory 14\APPS\MDIFRACT) provides a variety of palettes. Each new fractal (or new zoom) window can have its own palette. However, on 256-color systems you should not combine multiple palettes (for best results, stick with a single palette while you are zooming into a fractal).

To zoom into the detail of an existing fractal, press the left mouse button, and a selection square will appear. Drag the square to the zone you want blown up and release the button. (At any time, you can change the zoom factor or image size using the Parameters window.) When you are done, click on the Draw Fractal Command Button to generate a new fractal.

We didn't use the more common approach of selecting the zoom area with a mouse-dragging operation for a very simple reason: we wanted to keep track of the total magnification. If you set the Zooming Factor to 4, the first time you zoom into a fractal image, you magnify 16 times. The second time you magnify 16*16, or 256 times, and so on.

MDIFract is an MDI application, in which each new fractal is displayed in a new MDI window (or child window). All fractals already on the screen are available to the user and can either be zoomed into or saved to disk.

## Zooming Into a Fractal

MDIFract is a rather lengthy application to present in its entirety here. The core of the application is based on the VBFract application's functions, which we have explored in detail already.

The bulk of the code deals with the manipulation of the MDI child Forms, loading palettes, and other issues that have been covered in earlier sections. You can load the MDIFract application to Visual Basic's editor and examine the code. There is only one section of the code we would like to discuss here, to show how the program lets the user zoom into a given fractal. It's not a simple process because the user can choose any of the existing fractals to zoom into. Moreover, the coordinates specified when the mouse is dragged over a child Form are specified in pixels.

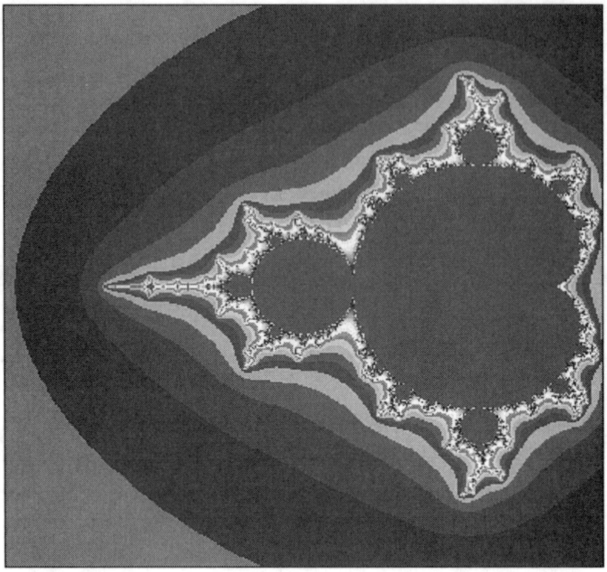

Figure 14-20: You can zoom into a fractal. In there somewhere you often find the most beautiful images of all. Here we are at 1X.

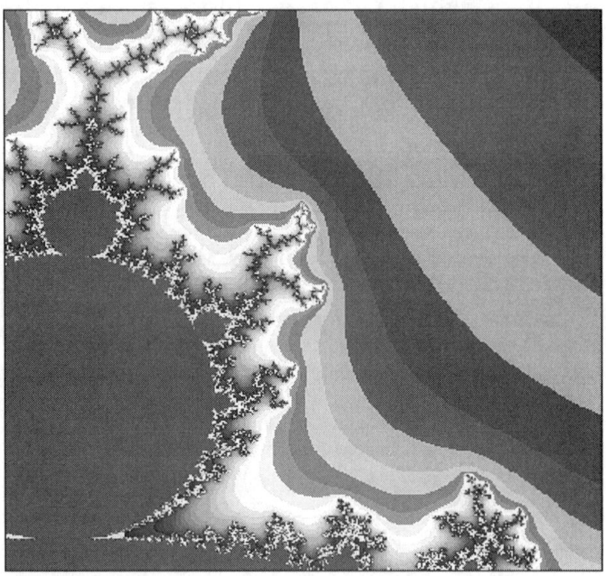

Figure 14-21: Now, in further at 8X, we see details of the large outer circle on top of the previous figure.

Figure 14-22: Down a factor of two this time (16X, relative to Figure 14-20). Branching patterns begin to dominate the spherical patterns.

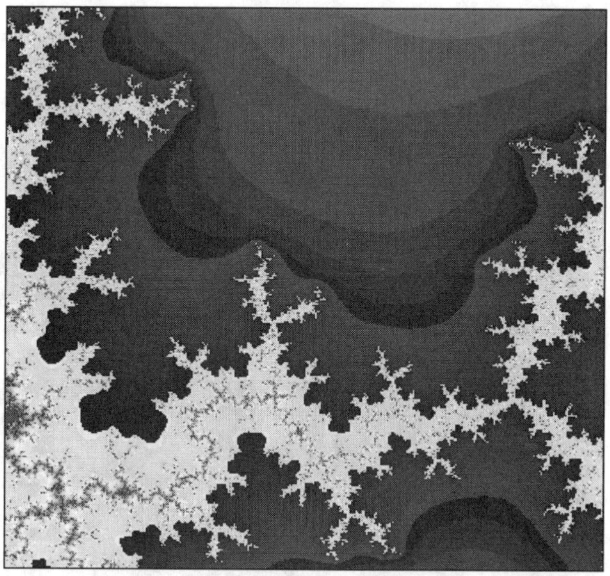

Figure 14-23: Moving down by a factor of 8 again (128X), the original spherical shapes are gone. The famous "fractal coastline" effect is clear (fractals are used in some computer games to create artificial background scenery).

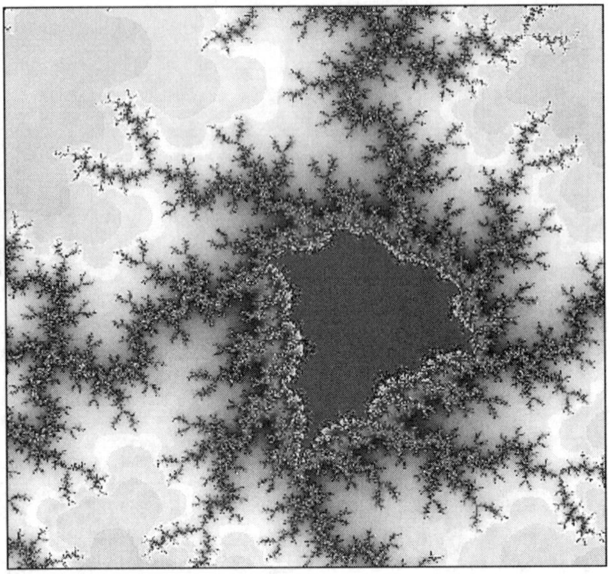

CD-ROM

Figure 14-24: Down now to 1,024X, and a whole new, roughly triangular shape pops out in livid red against a neon, blue-green background (see the image in color on the CD). This triangle is a severe distortion of the original shape.

Figure 14-25: Now the lower tip of the red triangle reveals a "flood plain" at 8,192X.

Figure 14-26: Further into the flood plain at 32,768X.

Figure 14-27: At 262,144 times the original fractal, strange new paramecium-shaped objects show up. If you go down far enough, the original shapes start to reappear as well, but slightly altered. Figure 14-27 shows a piece of Figure 14-20 that is several orders of magnitude smaller—a tiny fraction of a pixel in the original.

The variables XMin, XMax, YMin and YMax are the X and Y limits of the current fractal, and they are defined by the user (our program uses both the mouse-selection box drawn on screen, as well as the chosen zooming factor). Because the user can use any fractal already on the screen to specify the new X and Y ranges, our program must know the limits of the fractal in each child window to determine the new area. These limits are stored in the array FractalXY( ). The first row contains the four limits of the fractal of the first child window, the second row the limits of the second child window and so on.

We use mouse events to let the user select an area of an existing fractal to zoom into. This selection is implemented in the MouseDown, MouseMove and MouseUp Events whenever the mouse is being dragged over a child Form. In the MouseDown Event, we draw a square according to the zooming factor selected from the Zoom menu:

```
Sub Form_MouseDown (Button As Integer, Shift As Integer, →
X As Single, Y As Single)

    If NOWDRAWING Then
        Beep
        Exit Sub
    End If
    If Button And 1 Then
        Me.DrawMode = 7   'XOR PEN
' The next few lines center the box at (X, Y)
        XSide = Me.ScaleWidth / ZoomFactor
        YSide = Me.ScaleHeight / ZoomFactor
        Line (X - .5 * XSide, Y - .5 * YSide)-(X + .5 * XSide, →
        Y + .5 * YSide), , B
        XOld = X
        YOld = Y
    End If

End Sub
```

Likewise, we want to prevent the user from attempting to zoom into a Form that is currently active and drawing a fractal. So we set CancelDraw to True here to stop the drawing of the current fractal.

Here's the programming for the MouseMove Event, which slides the selection box over the fractal window:

```
Sub Form_MouseMove (Button As Integer, Shift As Integer, →
X As Single, Y As Single)

    If NOWDRAWING Or Me.DrawMode <> 7 Then
        Exit Sub
    End If

    If Button And 1 Then
        XSide = Me.ScaleWidth / ZoomFactor
        YSide = Me.ScaleHeight / ZoomFactor
        Line (XOld - .5 * XSide, YOld - .5 * YSide)-(XOld + →
        .5 * (Me.ScaleWidth / ZoomFactor), YOld + .5 * →
        (Me.ScaleHeight / ZoomFactor)), , B
        Line (X - .5 * (Me.ScaleWidth / ZoomFactor), Y - →
        .5 * (Me.ScaleHeight / ZoomFactor))-(X + .5 * →
        (Me.ScaleWidth / ZoomFactor), Y + .5 * →
        (Me.ScaleHeight / ZoomFactor)), , B
        XOld = X
        YOld = Y
    End If

End Sub
```

The box drawn at the previous coordinates is redrawn (XOR will toggle the bits back to their pre-box state—see the explanation of the XOR mode in Chapter 5). Then the new box, at the new position, is drawn.

In the MouseUp Event, we erase the last drawn selection box by drawing another one in XOR mode and convert the box's coordinates from pixels into coordinates of the complex plane:

```
Sub Form_MouseUp (Button As Integer, Shift As Integer, X As
Single, Y As Single)
Dim DeltaX As Double, DeltaY As Double

    If NOWDRAWING Or Me.DrawMode <> 7 Then
        Exit Sub
    End If
    XSide = Me.ScaleWidth / ZoomFactor
    YSide = Me.ScaleHeight / ZoomFactor

    Line (X - .5 * XSide, Y - .5 * YSide)-(X + .5 * XSide, →
    Y + .5 * YSide), , B
```

```
        Me.DrawMode = 13

        DeltaX = FractalXY(Me.Tag, 2) - FractalXY(Me.Tag, 1)
        DeltaY = FractalXY(Me.Tag, 4) - FractalXY(Me.Tag, 3)

        XMin = FractalXY(Me.Tag, 1) + X * DeltaX /  →
        Me.ScaleWidth - (DeltaX / ZoomFactor) / 2
        YMin = FractalXY(Me.Tag, 3) + Y * DeltaY /  →
        Me.ScaleHeight - (DeltaY / ZoomFactor) / 2
        XMax = FractalXY(Me.Tag, 1) + X * DeltaX /  →
        Me.ScaleWidth + (DeltaX / ZoomFactor) / 2
        YMax = FractalXY(Me.Tag, 3) + Y * DeltaY /  →
        Me.ScaleHeight + (DeltaY / ZoomFactor) / 2
        CancelDraw = False

    End Sub
```

When the user releases the mouse button, we know which coordinates he or she wishes to zoom into (the Zoom factor must be taken into consideration as well). So we translate these pixel values into the equivalent grid coordinates. The limits of the next fractal to be drawn are Xmin, Ymin, Xmax and YMax.

In an application like MDIFract, you must set the AutoRedraw Property to True.

Each new child window opened on the MDI Form can potentially cover one or more of the existing windows. Also, the user may wish to close some windows in order to view underlying ones. For these things to happen, the AutoRedraw Property of each child window must be True. Another compelling reason for setting the child Form's AutoRedraw to True, is because we want to be able to save the images to files. However, when the AutoRedraw Property is True, the user can't watch the drawing's progress onscreen. We don't want to ask the user to wait until the completion of the image before it is made visible.

To make it possible to have AutoRedraw active and to display the fractal activity dynamically, we use a simple trick. We force VB to display the emerging fractal by refreshing the contents of the window (with the Refresh command). How often? For this application, refreshing the Form after each line of pixels is calculated works very well:

```
    Fractals(CurrentFractal).Refresh
```

This is exactly what we did in the VBImage application of Chapter 6, to display each new row of pixels as they were processed.

### Fractal Resolution & Self-Similarity

Figures 14-20 through 14-27 illustrate the unique nature of fractals. Fractal images do not have "resolution." They never run out of shapes or colors, no matter how deep you zoom into them. Think of the zoom operation as an electronic microscope that probes the deep fractal space. There are limits to how deep you can probe, but these limits are due to the instrument, not the object you are examining. The power of your electronic microscope goes as far deep as double-precision numbers can take it. Keep zooming and you will keep discovering new patterns, until you reach the smallest number Visual Basic can represent. This is where your microscope's resolution, but not the fractal space, ends.

Fractal pictures exhibit another unique property. Successive magnifications of a fractal image look more like different sections of the same image, rather than drastically different magnifications of the same image. This property of some shapes, in which successive magnifications look like the original, is called *self-similarity* and is the most obvious characteristic of a fractal image. Although unreal, they look familiar and remind you of anything from trees to galaxies.

## Helping Visual Basic

Because there are many calculations involved in creating complex fractals, we have helped VB out a little with our MDIFract application. If you look at the code, you will see that this time we are not using the VBMandel( ) and VBJulia( ) Functions. We added a dynamic link library (DLL), created in Delphi (VB cannot create DLLs). The DLL contains two Functions, one for creating Mandelbrot, and another for creating Julia, fractals. They are declared in the MDIFract application like this:

```
Declare Function TPWMandel Lib "MANDEL.DLL" (ByVal cx →
As Double, ByVal cy As Double, ByVal maxiter As Integer) →
As Integer

Declare Function TPWJulia Lib "JULIA.DLL" (ByVal X As →
Double, ByVal Y As Double, ByVal x1 As Double, ByVal y1 →
As Double, ByVal i As Integer) As Integer
```

The DLL functions execute much faster than their equivalent Visual Basic functions. Other than that, they are identical and perform the exact same calculations. (From VB's point of view, these DLLs are just two functions, so you can explore the MDIFract application without knowing how the DLLs work. For details on how to create DLLs to improve VB's performance in speed-critical sections of your programs, see Chapter 15. (If you don't want to write your own DLLs, you can just use the ones we've supplied as if they were normal VB Functions.) When this book was published, Delphi could not yet produce 32-bit DLLs. That's why the VB4 version of the MDIFract application is not a 32-bit program.

## Some Great Julias

At upper right in the MDIFract Parameters window, there are two boxes where you can type in your own numbers for the complex constant of the Julia Set (the real and imaginary numbers respectively). Here is a list of numbers you can try that produce interesting Julia Sets. (Note, however, that most numbers you enter randomly will produce uninteresting fractals, and that your numbers must be between –2 and +2).

Also remember that often the most elegant pictures result from zooming into the initial Julia fractal six or eight times (also try setting the Zoom Factor to 8 right off the bat).

1. Cx=-0.754 Cy=0.049
2. Cx=-0.744 Cy=0.097
3. Cx=-0.736 Cy=0.097
4. Cx=-0.756 Cy=0.097
5. Cx=-0.743 Cy=0.097
6. Cx=-0.766227 Cy=0.096990
7. Cx=-0.9 Cy=0.12
8. Cx=-0.745429 Cy=0.113008
9. Cx=-1.0300 Cy=-0.9200
10. Cx=0.320 Cy=0.043
11. Cx=0.3080 Cy=0.46
12. Cx=-1.330 Cy=0.043
13. Cx=-0.16 Cy=1.32
14. Cx=-1.8 Cy=-1.67

### Beyond the Mandelbrot & Julia Sets

In this chapter we have explored two types of fractal images: the Mandelbrot and Julia Sets. They are both based on the same transformation: $z = z^2 + c$. Each point on the complex plane is transformed repeatedly by the previous function until it either escapes to infinity or sinks toward zero.

For the Mandelbrot Set, z starts at zero and c is the value of each point on the complex plane (which is a complex number). For the Julia Set, z is the value of the point on the complex plane under consideration, and c is a complex number you specify. That's why there are many different Julia Sets. Recall that the value of the constant c must remain constant throughout the process of calculating a Julia Set.

There are other ways to create fractal images, based on different functions. One such function is

```
z=λ*cos(z)
```

where λ is a complex constant (like c) and z is the value of the current point of the complex plane. Calculating the cosine of a complex number is fairly complicated, and we chose to avoid this type of fractal here (Visual Basic's Cos( ) Function works with real numbers only). However, because this type of fractal is well suited for animation, we are exploring it in Chapter 9, where we show you how to create fractal animation on your PC.

## Animated Fractals

The Julia Set depends on a constant, c, which may take on any user-specified value. If you run MDIFract and create several Julia Sets with similar but not identical Cx and Cy values, you will notice that the resulting Julia Sets beget slightly different shapes. Depending on how large, or small, the differences in the Cx and Cy values are, the transformation of the Julia shape can be drastic or subtle. It is therefore possible to create very interesting animation sequences of fractal images by varying the values of the Cx and Cy parameters.

Another possibility for fractal animation is to slowly zoom into a specific area of the fractal image we are interested in. Since the real beauty of a fractal image is hidden deeply within its filaments, we can create fractal animation by slowly descending into the uncharted coastlines of any fractal image.

## COMPLEX NUMBER OPERATIONS

Most readers are not likely interested in the details about addition and multiplication of complex numbers. So, we left this discussion for the end of the chapter.

For the intrepid, here are the three basic complex number operations: addition, subtraction and multiplication. Complex numbers are actually pairs of numbers (the real and imaginary parts) that are handled separately. The sum of two complex numbers is another complex number, whose real number is the sum of the real parts and whose imaginary part is the sum of the imaginary parts of the operands.

### Adding & Subtracting Complex Numbers

Here are the formulae for adding and subtracting complex numbers:

$$(a + ib) + (c + id) = (a + c) + i(b + d)$$
$$(a + ib) - (c + id) = (a - c) + i(b - d)$$

or

$$(a, b) + (c, d) = (a + c, b + d)$$
$$(a, b) - (c, d) = (a - c, b - d)$$

And here are some examples of addition and subtraction of complex numbers:

$$(3 + i7) + (-2 + i2) = (1 + i9) \text{ also: } (3, 7) + (-2, 2) = (1, 9)$$
$$(3 + i7) - (-2 + i2) = (5 + i5) \text{ also: } (3, 7) - (-2, 2) = (5, 5)$$

### Multiplying Complex Numbers

To multiply two complex numbers, we form all four products:

$$(a + ib) * (c + id) = a*c + ib*c + ia*d + ib*id$$

Since i is the square root of –1, the square of i is –1. The term ib*id, therefore, is reduced to –bd.

Then, we separate the real and imaginary parts, to form the new complex number:

$$a*c + ib*c + ia*d + ib*id = a*c + i(b*c + a*d) - b*d =$$
$$(a*c - b*d + i(b*c + a*d)), \text{ or } (a*c - b*d, b*c + a*d)$$

Here's an example of complex number multiplication:

$$(3, i7) * (-2, i4) = (3*(-2) - (7*4), 7*(-2) + 3*4) = (-34, -2)$$

### The Transformation $z=z^2+c$

Let's follow the lines of the VBMandel( ) and VBJulia( ) Functions that implement the transformation $z=z^2+c$. *z* is a point on the complex plane, defined by two numbers: the real and imaginary part. Let's call these parts x and y. Similarly, *c* is another complex number whose real part is Cx and imaginary part is Cy. The previous transformation can now be written as

$$z = (x + iy)^2 + (Cx + iCy)$$

The square of a complex number is calculated as follows (it's a direct application of the multiplication formula given earlier):

$$(x + iy)^2 = (x + iy)*(x + iy) = x^2 - y^2 + i2xy$$

The result is another complex number, whose real part is $(x^2 - y^2)$ and imaginary part is 2xy. It can also be written as $(x^2 - y^2 + i2xy)$.

Then we add the constant C to the result. The new number z becomes:

$$((x^2 - y^2) + i2xy) + (Cx + iCy) =$$
$$(x^2 - y^2 + Cx) + i(2xy + Cy)$$

The result of the operation $z^2 + c$ is another complex number, whose real part is $(x^2-y^2+Cx)$ and imaginary part is $(2xy+Cy)$. This number becomes the new value of the variable z, and the process continues. Look at the VBMandel( ) Function to see that this is how it implements the basic transformation $z = z^2 + c$. The variables X2 and Y2 hold the values $x^2$ and $y^2$ respectively.

Let's explain this further with a numeric example. We will apply the transformation to the point (0.2 + i0.5) of the complex plane. We start with z = (0 + i0), square it and add the constant (0.2 + i0.5):

$$z = z^2 + c = (0 + i0)^2 + (0.2 + i0.5) = (0.2 + i0.5)$$

This is the value of z for next transformation:

$$z = z^2 + c = (0.2 + i0.5)^2 + (0.2 + i0.5) = -0.01 + i0.7$$

This value is assigned to z, and the same transformation is repeated over and over again, until either the result exceeds a very large value, or the maximum number of iterations is exhausted.

## MOVING ON

As you may have noticed, the MDIFRACT application is much faster than the VBFRACT application. The reason for this improvement in speed is the inclusion of the MANDEL.DLL (which contains the TPWMandel( ) Function for generating the Mandelbrot Set) and JULIA.DLL (which contains the TPWJulia( ) Function). The functions in these DLLs were implemented in Delphi, a truly compiled language that produces executable code that runs faster than Visual Basic, especially when computing with double-precision numbers.

In the next chapter, we'll demonstrate how to write your own custom DLLs to speed up your Visual Basic applications. You'll also find the implementation of the fractal-generating functions in Delphi.

# Chapter 15

# Create Your Own DLLs

In Chapter 14 we explored how to generate fractals in Visual Basic. However, because fractals place an enormous computational burden on any language, we employed a Dynamic Link Library (DLL) to speed up the calculations in our final application, MDIFract. The application itself didn't get any more complicated; instead of calling a VB function, we simply called an external function. But FRACTAL.DLL made our programs run up to three times faster.

So what's the secret about DLLs? What can they do that Visual Basic can't? DLLs run faster than VB programs. And in some applications, especially ones involving noninteger numbers, DLLs can improve the execution speed of your VB program by 200 to 300 percent or more.

The speed improvements noted here are based on examples in this chapter. Your DLL functions may result in greater or less improvement, depending on the types of programs for which you write them. However, by writing a DLL you can almost always expect swifter calculations when floating-point numbers are involved. Visual Basic isn't slow overall. But handling floating-point numbers isn't what it does best.

In this chapter we'll see what DLLs can do. You can't write DLLs in Visual Basic. But we will show you how easy it is to write one in Turbo Pascal for Windows (TPW) or Delphi, even if you don't have any experience with Pascal.

If you thought you couldn't make your own DLLs without understanding subclassing, etc., etc.—that is, without resorting to C—read on.

# QUEST FOR SPEED

A decade ago, when people wanted to speed up a Basic program, they wrote brief, key sections of the program in assembly language and just "called" this swift assembly language routine. You "called" it essentially the same way you call any normal subroutine, by typing in the name of the subroutine and "passing" any variables it needs to do its job. This same approach, and a similar benefit in speed, is available to the VB programmer by calling DLLs.

Visual Basic is a very efficient programming tool under Windows. In certain cases, however, it can use some help.

You don't want to abandon VB programming just because you sometimes need more speed than VB can provide. Visual Basic is addictive and so very easy on the programmer. It is the perfect tool for mastering the elements of the Windows interface. VB applications are not slow overall, but sorting procedures, for example, could stand improvement. Or a fractal drawing application can go on repeatedly executing the same few lines of code. Replace those few lines with a DLL. Create an external, fast piece of executable code that can be called from Visual Basic, and the application will become faster.

## Compiled Versus Interpreted Languages

DLLs are faster than native Visual Basic code because they are produced by a compiler. Delphi, Turbo Pascal and Visual C++ are compiled languages. To run a Delphi program, you must first compile it, and then execute it. The compiler is a program that translates the program you wrote (the *source code*) to a form that the machine can understand. The product of a compiler is an *executable* program, sometimes called *binary code* (a file with extension EXE).

The executable file contains code that your machine can understand and execute, but it is quite unintelligible to humans—with rare exceptions, of course. Some people still program in machine language and can understand it, but most of us are moving away from this level. To most everyone's relief, we can now work with graphical, intelligent user interfaces like VB, which simplify our communication with the machine.

But sometimes you want the fastest possible execution time, and compilation is the way to achieve it. Compilers are optimized for the hardware on which they run. The Delphi or Visual C++ compiler, for example, can produce the most efficient executable program for the 80X86 processors. They produce optimum sequences of commands for the processor that will execute the program.

The distinction between "compiled" and "interpreted" languages is not hard and fast. It's like the difference between Texan and Mexican cooking—overlapping in places, blended together sometimes. However, to simplify the following definitions, we'll temporarily assume that there is a polarity between compiled and interpreted languages. And this polarity divides languages into two camps: those which are easier for the human to program (interpreted) and those which are easier for the computer to translate into action (compiled).

Compiled languages are faster than interpreted languages, but not as convenient to work with.

In a nutshell, compiled languages produce executable code that speaks more directly to the computer, so the computer runs such code more quickly. Interpreted languages generally feature a more English-like syntax, so they make it easier for people to write programs and express their ideas in ways familiar to humans. What's more, a section of programming written in an interpreted language can be immediately and conveniently tested while the program is being written.

Languages like Pascal and C++ are called "compiled," because they rely on a compiler to execute. Visual Basic is an interpreted language, as were most earlier versions of BASIC. VB interprets your commands to the processor, one at a time, *while your program executes.* In this respect, it is like a human interpreter translating a speech while it's being delivered. Even if the translator talks fast, the process involves two steps and is inevitably slower than one person delivering a speech without translation.

Compilers on the other hand, pre-translate a program (to stretch our analogy, the entire speech has already been translated, so it can be delivered directly, without "interpretation"). And because compilers don't have to translate on the spot in real time, they can provide the information more quickly.

Speed of execution is not always the most important criterion in selecting a language. Compiled languages are not as simple and easy to use as interpreted languages, nor are they as convenient for the programmer. If you wanted to use Pascal or C, you'd have to give up many of the facilities Visual Basic provides. You would give up the Immediate Execution (Debug) window, for example. Without it, you wouldn't be able to interrupt a program to correct mistakes and then resume running it for further testing. These and other reasons explain the great and increasing popularity of VB. It isn't the fastest language, but it is surely the most convenient and efficient for the programmer.

You can create executable, runnable Windows programs using the Make Exe option in Visual Basic's File menu. Make Exe doesn't generate fully compiled code. It produces so-called P-code. P-code *is* closer to machine language than native Visual Basic commands, but it must still be interpreted when the .EXE program is run; it can't be executed as is by the computer's microprocessor.

Speed tests show that when you make an executable of a VB program, it runs no faster than the same program started by pressing F5 to run it in VB's design window. Either way, the Functions we're exploring in this chapter run only half or a third as fast in native VB as they do after being translated into a TPW-generated DLL.

For this reason, there are times when you may want to write a DLL—a highly optimized little contrivance that will replace some lines in your VB program with a rocket engine, a blast of speed when you need it.

## Why Pascal?

After looking around at the alternatives, we have concluded that Pascal was the answer. Pascal is a simple, forthcoming language, in many ways similar to Basic. As you will see in the examples of this chapter, the conversion of Visual Basic code to Pascal is straightforward too. There are currently two popular Pascal compilers, Turbo Pascal for Windows and Delphi. They are both from Borland, the company that has been building the best Pascal compilers for years.

Turbo Pascal for Windows was the evolution of the legendary Turbo Pascal, the most popular programming environment under DOS. Recently, Turbo Pascal for Windows was replaced by Delphi, which is an integrated development environment based on the Pascal programming language, yet very similar to Visual Basic's environment. It could have been called Visual Pascal because that's what it is. Delphi is compatible with Turbo Pascal for Windows, and the code we are going to present here can be compiled with either product. By the time this book had gone to print, Delphi couldn't produce 32-bit code, so all the applications of this chapter can be used with the VB3 and VB4 16-bit versions only. Shortly after the release of Windows 95, Borland plans to upgrade Delphi to produce 32-bit code as well. To create the 32-bit versions of the DLLs presented in this chapter, you need only recompile the projects with the new version of Delphi.

There's been a concern among VB programmers since Delphi hit the market, as to whether they should switch to the new environment. It is faster than Visual Basic, yet there are many similarities that would ease the transition. Our suggestion is that you don't give up Visual Basic. Just combine the best of both environments. In the rest of the chapter you'll find out how to convert the critical sections of your VB application to DLLs to improve its execution speed.

Pascal is close to Visual Basic, and Delphi has an easy user interface.

But why not go to C to create DLLs? C is very different from Visual Basic and will throw off many VB programmers. Some people find C's syntax alien and counterintuitive.

Another reason we chose Pascal over C is the fact that Pascal programs are easier to read. C has been criticized for its convoluted "sentence structure." It has even been called a "write-only language." Also, there are miles of Turbo Pascal source code out there in dozens of books, which can be converted to DLLs in seconds.

If you already know C, you will probably be able to write your own DLLs. If you know only Visual Basic, however, and you need only a few fast procedures in DLL form, you are better off with Delphi.

When you want to speed up a computation-intensive Function or Sub in your VB program, consider writing a DLL in Pascal. In the following examples, we'll first write some lines of code in VB. Then we'll translate them to Pascal.

It's easy to translate one of your VB Functions into Pascal. Creating a DLL in Pascal doesn't require knowledge of any underlying Windows mechanisms. You can just type in a few lines of code, and the Pascal compiler seems to know what to do. Like VB, Delphi (or TPW) will take it from there and do a lot of the tedious clerical work for you. So when you need speed, write a little DLL in Pascal. As you'll see in the examples below, doing this is well within the reach of the typical Visual Basic programmer.

## WRITING YOUR OWN DLLS

A DLL is a fundamental Windows mechanism for calling procedures that reside outside your project. These procedures are on the disk drive, waiting to be used. But they're not embedded within your VB like a typical VB Function or Sub that you write while programming.

In the Windows environment, you can create Functions or Subs and then compile them into a special container called a DLL (Dynamic Link Library). These new procedures are then stored in executable form in their own files on disk, and can be called from any language, without being explicitly "linked" to an application prior to runtime. As the name *DLL* implies, they are linked (attached) to your application dynamically, at run time.

One typical group of DLLs comprises the files that contain the Windows API procedures (GDI.EXE, which contains the procedures for graphics operations, USER.EXE, etc.). Microsoft has implemented the API procedures as DLLs so that they can be available to any program written in any language.

A DLL is a collection of procedures that can be available to any program on demand.

Another benefit of DLLs is that once they are loaded in memory, they can service many applications. In other words, more than one application can call the functions of a DLL while the DLL sits there in the computer's memory. The DLL itself need not be reloaded. Some common programming tasks, like spell checking, for example, have been implemented in DLL form, so that multiple applications (Word, Excel, Mail) can call on their services. Excel will not load its spell checking programs in memory if Word is already running. It will use the same DLLs as Word and thereby conserve the user's RAM memory. The Microsoft Graph applet is another utility that can be called from many programs because it too is implemented as a DLL.

To Visual Basic, a DLL procedure is no different than any other procedure, even those built into the Windows API. All you have to do is specify the location of the procedure (Declare it in your VB program by specifying its name and arguments) and provide any arguments (details such as pointers or variables) that the procedure needs.

## Declaring DLL Functions

The declaration of external procedures must be made in the declarations section of a Module or Form. If you don't have a Module in your VB program (only Forms), press Alt+F, M. All variables or declarations that you want to be *global* in VB (allowing program-wide access to the procedure or variable declared Global) must be put into a Module. The declaration of a DLL function has the following form:

```
Declare Function function_name Lib library_name (arguments)→
As Function_type
```

function_name is the name of the Function, as it appears in the DLL's source code. The library_name is the name of the DLL file in which the Function is implemented. In the parentheses you type the arguments expected by the Function. Finally, following the *As* keyword, you specify the variable type of the Function itself (the nature of the variable returned by the Function, such as Integer, Long and so on).

Similarly, you can declare Subroutines:

```
Declare Sub subroutine_name Lib library_name (arguments)
```

A subroutine does not return a value, so it doesn't have a variable type (there is no *As* keyword). However, we won't use subroutines (they are far less commonly used in DLLs than Functions). We will only concern ourselves with Functions.

## The Argument-Passing Mechanism

The most important part of the declaration is the list of arguments, which is similar to that of any VB procedure. However, there is a fundamental difference between Visual Basic and most other languages in this respect. Visual Basic provides two mechanisms for passing arguments: *by reference* (the default mechanism), which passes to the called procedure the address of the variable, and *by value*, which merely passes a *copy* of the variable.

ByVal passes a copy of a variable to the procedure. ByRef passes the address of the variables.

When passing arguments by reference, the procedure changes the variable itself because the procedure has the variable's actual address. The address is the location in memory that holds the contents of the variable, so if the DLL procedure knows the address, it can directly modify the value by changing the corresponding bytes in memory. By contrast, when passing arguments by value, Visual Basic makes a copy of the variable and passes it to the procedure. So any changes made to the variable by the procedure are local, and upon return to the calling program, the variable retains its original value.

By default, most programming languages pass arguments by value. But Visual Basic by default passes them by reference. To work with most DLLs we must explicitly tell Visual Basic that an argument has to be passed by value (we must use the ByVal command).

Note that arrays and strings are always passed by reference, and these are the only cases where we need not include the ByVal keyword. This difference between numeric variables and string (or array) variables originates in the first dialects of BASIC, which used the reference mechanism exclusively.

The reason arrays are not passed by value is obvious when you think about it: if you had a thousand-element array, it could really slow things down to transmit the entire contents of the array whenever you pass it as an argument to a Function. Instead, Visual Basic passes the address of the first element of the array. In the following paragraphs, we will include examples of both mechanisms.

When using DLLs, you must get used to declaring variables "ByVal," just as with most API calls.

To specify whether an argument will be passed by value or by reference, you use the keywords ByVal and ByRef, respectively. Which argument passing mechanism will be used is determined by the DLL, and not by the declaration itself. ByVal and ByRef simply tell VB how to send the arguments. You must not pass an argument by reference when the DLL expects it by value, and vice versa. (For more discussion of ByVal and ByRef, see Chapter 8.) Of course, you can have both types of arguments in the same declaration, such as in the following statement:

```
Declare Function PixelRGB Lib "\MYDLLS\GRAPHDLL.DLL" →
(ByVal X As Integer, ByVal Y As Integer, R As Integer, G As →
Integer, B As Integer) As Integer
```

This PixelRGB Function accepts two integer arguments by value and three more integers by reference. The first two arguments specify the location of a pixel, and the procedure doesn't need to change them (so we can just send a copy of this information, ByVal). The next three arguments are used for storing the values of the RGB representation of the pixel's color. Since the procedure calculates and returns these three values, the corresponding arguments must be passed by reference so that the procedure can actually have an effect on these variables. Notice that the keyword ByRef can be (and is in this example) omitted.

### Example: Calculating the Mandelbrot Set

A simple Pascal DLL can speed up the fractal-generating functions by nearly 300%.

Here is a quite interesting example. In Chapter 14 we discussed the fractal-generating algorithms, and we made use of a DLL to speed up the calculations. Here, we are going to implement that DLL.

The Mandelbrot Set is calculated with a simple iterative algorithm. It's simple to type in, but takes the computer a long time to execute. The algorithm that generates fractals is explained in Chapter 14. As you know, if you tried running the applications in that chapter, their implementation in pure Visual Basic isn't extremely fast.

Let's start by looking again at the heart of the VB code in our VBFractal application, the section of code that produces the Mandelbrot Set. The basic algorithm scans each point of the plane and calculates whether it is bounded (is a prisoner) or it escapes to infinity (is an escapee). All this work is done by the Function Mandel( ), which returns the number of iterations it performed to the VB program that actually displays the results. This number is used to color the corresponding point. Here is the original VB Function:

```
Function Mandel (cx As Double, cy As Double, maxiter As→
Integer) As Integer
Dim x As Double, y As Double
Dim x2 As Double, y2 As Double
Dim iter As Integer

x = 0
y = 0
x2 = 0
y2 = 0
iter = 0

While (iter < maxiter) And (abs(x2 + y2) < 100000)
    temp = x2 - y2 + cx
    y = 2 * x * y + cy
    x = temp
    x2 = x * x
    y2 = y * y
    iter = iter + 1
Wend

Mandel = iter

End Function
```

Simple functions that iterate many times are ideal candidates for conversion to DLLs.

The Mandel( ) Function is a straightforward algorithm, which may be repeated up to *maxiter* times for each pixel. (The more times you repeat, it the more detail will show up in your fractal.) The implementation of the algorithm in VB is very slow—painfully slow in systems without a math coprocessor.

Clearly it is highly desirable to make this section of the application run faster. Let's rewrite in Pascal the key loop—the place where VB spends most of its time when this program executes.

## Converting the Mandel Function to Turbo Pascal

Now we'll convert (translate) this function into Pascal as a DLL function.

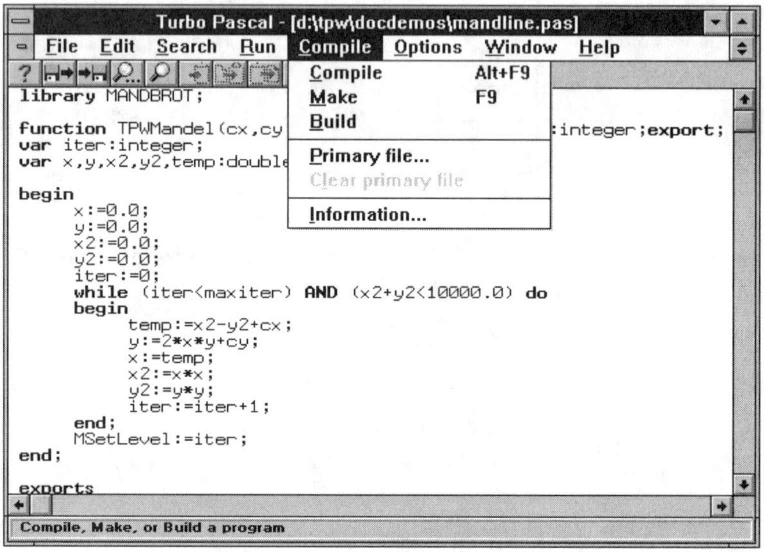

Figure 15-1: The Turbo Pascal for Windows programming environment is easy for VB programmers to use.

CD-ROM

If you are using Turbo Pascal for Windows, open the MANDEL.PAS project in the subdirectory 15\TPW of the CD. The default extension for Turbo Pascal projects is PAS. The default project extension for Delphi is DPR, but it understands PAS projects as well. When you open the MANDEL project (or any others of the supplied projects) in Delphi, you'll see the warning, "Error in module JULIA: USES clause missing or incorrect." Click on OK and continue. This is a minor bug in the compiler, which will be fixed in the future versions. Delphi expects to see an executable application, not just a single function, and that's why it produces this message.

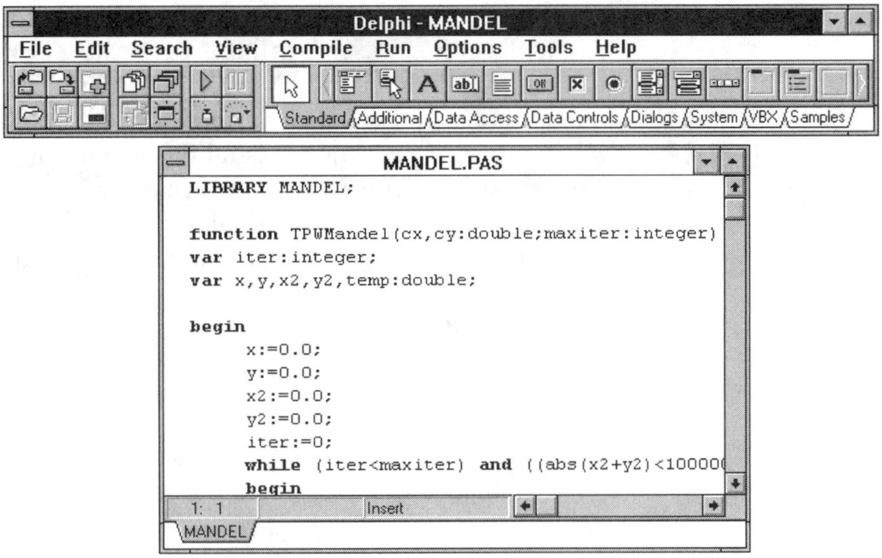


Figure 15-2: The same project in Delphi's editor.

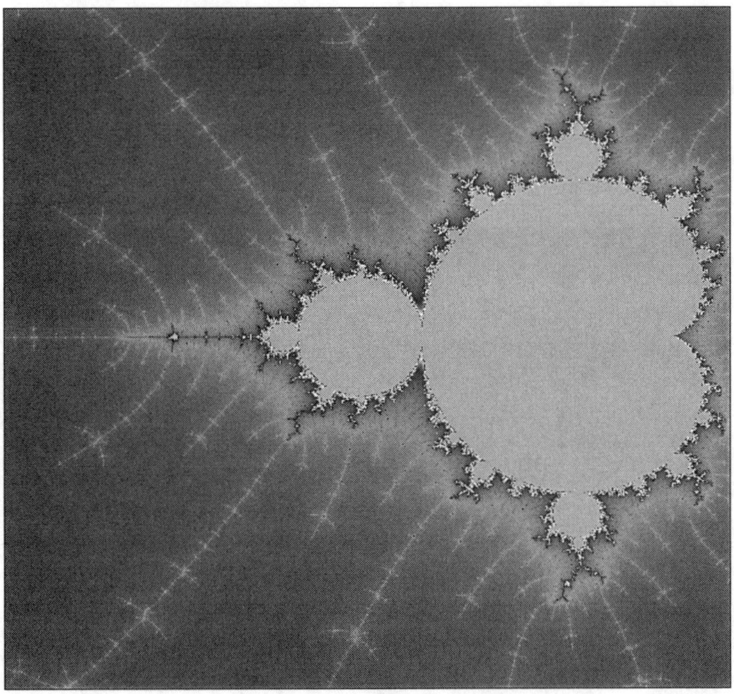

Figure 15-3: A typical Mandelbrot fractal, highly detailed. With our DLL, you can produce fractals in high resolution without having to wait forever.

The DLL will contain merely the single Function for calculating the Mandelbrot Set. We will call this procedure TPWMandel, and the source file will be named MANDEL.PAS (in the 15\APPS\TPWDLLS subdirectory of the CD). The contents of the MANDEL.PAS file are shown next. If you know Visual Basic, you can certainly understand this translation into TPW by just reading it.

CD-ROM

Compared to the VB original, you can see that the TPW version has a few more lines. These extra lines direct the compiler to generate the proper DLL. Here's TPW, doing the same thing as our VB Function Mandel( ):

```
LIBRARY MANDEL;

function
TPWMandel(cx,cy:double;maxiter:integer):integer;export;
var iter:integer;
var x,y,x2,y2,temp:double;

begin
    x:=0.0;
    y:=0.0;
    x2:=0.0;
    y2:=0.0;
    iter:=0;
    while (iter<maxiter) and ((abs(x2+y2)<100000) ) do
    begin
        temp:=x2-y2+cx;
        y:=2*x*y+cy;
        x:=temp;
        x2:=x*x;
        y2:=y*y;
        iter:=iter+1;
    end;
    TPWMandel:=iter;
end;

exports
    TPWMandel index 1;

begin
end.
```

The code of the TPWMandel Function is identical in both Turbo Pascal for Windows and Delphi. The warning you saw when you loaded the project in Delphi has no further consequences.

The first line above is there for the compiler (we must tell the compiler that we intend to create a DLL, and that it is called MANDEL.DLL). Next, we implement the procedure TPWMandel, starting with its declaration, as we did in VB:

```
procedure TPWMandel (cx, cy: double; maxiter: integer): →
integer; export;
```

As you can see, declaring a Pascal Function's arguments is very similar to a VB declaration. Instead of the keyword *As* we use a colon, and the various arguments are separated by a semicolon.

Notice too that in Pascal, multiple arguments of the same type are declared together, with a comma between them. (By the way, this syntax would simplify Dim statements in Visual Basic, but it hasn't been implemented yet. Wouldn't it be simpler to write Dim i, j As Integer, instead of Dim i As Integer, j As Integer?)

## Creating the DLL

Unlike Visual Basic, Pascal requires that all variables be declared—even the loops' counters.

The keyword *export* tells the compiler to create a DLL, whose procedures can be called by any other Windows application. In reality, the compiler doesn't know where the exported procedure will be called from. It exports it to Windows, and any other application that may need it can then call it through the Windows mechanisms. (If this Function were to be used only internally by other procedures in the same file, we wouldn't have to export it.)

Next we declare the local variables. Each line begins with the *var* keyword, followed by a list of variables of the same type and ending with the type of the variables. Table 15-1 lists the data types of both languages.

| Visual Basic | Pascal | Length (bytes) |
|---|---|---|
| String * 1 | char | 1 (0 to 255) |
| String * 1 | shortint | 1 (-128 to 127) |
| Integer | integer | 2 |
| Long Integer | longint | 4 |
| Single | single | 4 |
| Double | double | 8 |
| Currency | comp | 8 |

Table 15-1: The basic data types of Visual Basic and Pascal. Pascal provides some data types that have no counterparts in Visual Basic. What Pascal lacks (and so do most other languages) is the Variant data type, which gives you so much freedom in programming. You can also use the char and shortint data types of Pascal, as long as you dimension the corresponding variables as String * 1 in your Visual Basic code.

## The Actual Code of the Function

Finally, we are ready to proceed with the translation of the Function itself, from the VB original into Pascal. The keywords Begin and End have no counterpart in Visual Basic, but they are used in Pascal to delimit sections of code. For example, in VB a For ... Next, or a While ... Wend loop is delimited by the keywords themselves. VB knows that *For* signals the start, and *Next* the end, of the loop. VB uses *paired keywords* in these situations.

Pascal uses the first keyword only (For or While), and the body of the statements is enclosed within the Begin...End keywords. The first Begin denotes the beginning of the function, and the corresponding End denotes the end of it. In Visual Basic you use the keywords Function, End Function or Sub, End Sub to enclose the statements within a function or subroutine. In Pascal you use the keyword Function and the pair Begin...End.

The implementation of the procedure is straightforward. Each line of the Mandel Function is translated from VB to Pascal almost as is. In Pascal, the assignment operator is := rather than VB's =. Pascal uses a semicolon at the end of each statement. Notice that the semicolon declares the end of a statement and not the end of a line.

The equals sign is a relational operator: it compares the values on its sides. If you wanted to test the value of a variable against a numeric value, such as 10, you would use a statement like this:

```
If variable_name = 10 Then
```

If you are familiar with C syntax, you will recall that the equals sign is an assignment operator, and the relational operator is two equals signs (==).

Each program line in Pascal must end with a semicolon.

You can type multiple statements on the same line, as long as they are separated by a semicolon (in VB, you use a colon). In Pascal, however, the use of the semicolon is mandatory. Notice also that only the keyword Begin or flow control structures (the For loop, for example) are not followed by semicolons. If you have no prior experience with Pascal, the compiler will help you pinpoint your errors with descriptive error messages. But the rules we've outlined are the primary syntactical differences between VB and Pascal.

The line below the *exports* heading tells the compiler the order of the exported procedures:

```
exports
    TPWMandel index 1;
```

Here we only have a single Function, and it has the index 1. In a later example, we will see a DLL that includes more than one Function (multiple Functions are listed at the end of the source file with consecutive indices, as you will see).

The last two lines are the main program:

```
begin
end.
```

In Pascal you first write all the Functions and then the main program. Our DLL is a collection of procedures without a main program. That's exactly what the last pair of Begin/End statements does: it tells the compiler that there is no main program, just one or more procedures that must be compiled into a DLL file. The last command in the file, End, must be followed by a period. The compiler will ignore everything that follows.

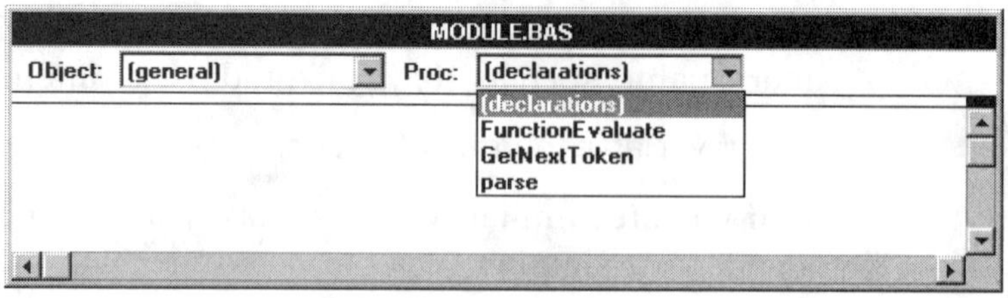


Figure 15-4: Like this Module in VB, our DLLs contain one or more procedures, but no main program.

To create the DLL under TPW, save the file under a file name (MANDEL.PAS). Then build the DLL file by selecting Make from the TPW Compile menu, or by pressing the F9 key. TPW will create the MANDEL.DLL file in the same directory where you stored the source file. From there you can move it to the subdirectory with your VB project. On the CD, the DLLs are stored in the same subdirectory with the .PAS files, under 15\APPS\TPWDLLS. They are also included in the subdirectories of the projects that use them.

If you want to create a new project in Delphi, use the File/New Project command. Like Visual Basic, Delphi will automatically create a new Form and a Unit (equivalent to Visual Basic's Module), as shown in Figure 15-5. Notice the similarities between the Delphi and Visual Basic environments.

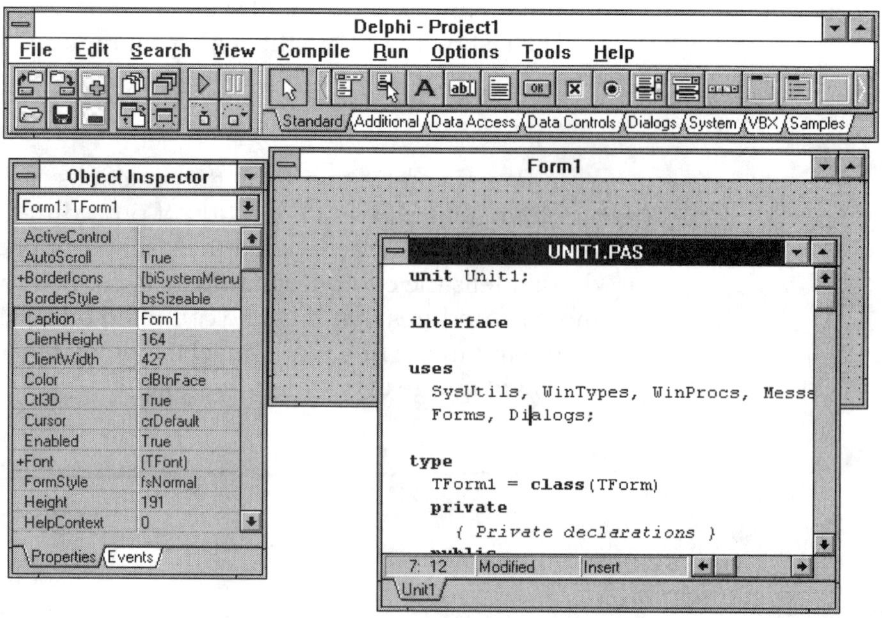


Figure 15-5: The Delphi environment is very similar to that of Visual Basic.

Our goal is not to write a complete application in Delphi. All we want to do is convert certain routines from VB to Pascal and compile them as DLLs. So you must close the Form and enter your Pascal code in the Unit's window. When you are done, save the Unit with the File/Save File As command. Use the same file name as the library you want to create and the extension PAS. If you attempt to compile the Module at this stage, you will receive the error message: "Error in module Unit1: Module header is missing or incorrect." After you have saved the file with the PAS extension, open it again, this time as a project. You will get the same warning when Delphi loads the project, but this time you'll be able to compile it.

Once a function has been implemented in TPW or Delphi, you can call it just like any API function from within your application.

Now return to your VB project and replace the line that calls the Mandel procedure with a call to the TPWMandel procedure. Calling a procedure in a DLL is just as simple as calling another VB procedure, as long as the procedure and its arguments have been declared in the declarations section of the VB Form or a .BAS file (a Module). To declare this external procedure, open a Module and type the following declaration *on a single line*:

```
Declare Procedure TPWMandel Lib "MANDEL.DLL" (ByVal X →
as Double, Byval Y as Double, ByVal Max As Integer) As Integer
```

Just make sure that the name of the library (MANDEL.DLL) matches the location of the DLL function on your disk (or move the MANDEL.DLL file to your WINDOWS\SYSTEM directory).

## Converting the Julia( ) Function

Converting the Julia( ) Function to Pascal is very similar. The Julia( ) Function is used in the VBFRACT application to create the Julia set. Both the source code, JULIA.PAS, and the resulting DLL, JULIA.DLL, can be found in the 15\APPS\TPWDLLS subdirectory of the CD. In the 15\APPS\FRACTAL subdirectory is the VBFRACT application presented in Chapter 9 and an adaptation of it called TPWFRACT. TPWFRACT is identical to VBFRACT, except that it uses the TPWMandel( ) and TPWJulia( ) Functions to create the Mandelbrot and Julia sets accordingly. Just run both programs and see what difference the TPWMandel( ) and TPWJulia( ) Functions can make on your computer. The two DLL functions are declared in the application's module as

```
Declare Function TPWMandel Lib "MANDEL.DLL" (ByVal cx →
As Double, ByVal cy As Double, ByVal maxiter As Integer) As →
Integer
```

```
Declare Function TPWJulia Lib "JULIA.DLL" (ByVal x As →
Double, ByVal y As Double, ByVal x1 As Double, ByVal y1 As →
Double, ByVal maxiter As Integer) As Integer
```

Notice that these DLLs can't be used with the 32-bit version of Visual Basic under Windows 95. When you obtain the Windows 95 version of Delphi, just recompile the projects and you will be able to use the DLLs with the 32-bit version of Visual Basic 4.0.

## How Much Pascal, How Much VB?

Use as much Pascal as absolutely necessary, no more.

Why not also do the graphics, displaying the pixels from within this (or another) Pascal Function? We could write a DLL that accepts as arguments the limits of the Mandelbrot Set and displays it. However, this would complicate our translation from Visual Basic to Pascal, and require that we learn how TPW (or Delphi) handles windows and displays graphics.

If we were to go that far with Pascal, why bother with Visual Basic in the first place? Visual Basic is superior for most programming tasks, particularly for developing a user interface. So why not just combine the best of both environments? You can do this by using Delphi only to speed up some time-consuming calculations.

# MORE ABOUT ARGUMENTS

Passing integers or floating-point numbers between VB and a DLL Function is as simple as passing them to a Function within VB itself. You need only use the keyword ByVal, which forces VB to pass a copy of the argument rather than the argument itself.

For more demanding calculations, you may need to pass a large amount of data, such as an array. Some typical mathematical calculations you may wish to perform with TPW procedures are matrix inversion and Fast Fourier Transform (FFT). Both algorithms require the exchange of considerable chunks of data between the calling application and the DLL Functions. These data are stored in arrays that you must pass back and forth between VB and the DLL.

Any improvement in your sorting routines should be welcome.

Sorting is another potentially dicey situation in any programming language. Sorting large arrays is an inherently slow process, and since the algorithms cannot be made any better, the best we can do is to implement them in a faster executable file. Let's examine some DLL Functions that accept arrays as arguments and return the results in the same arrays. It's not hard, as you will see.

**EXAMPLE:** SORTING DATA

To demonstrate the exchange of arrays between Visual Basic and Pascal, we will use the Shell sorting algorithm, an efficient, yet simple, sorting technique. The algorithm was presented in Chapter 2, so we repeat here the Visual Basic code:

```
Private Function SHELSORT(N As Integer) As Integer
Dim gap As Integer, i As Integer, j As Integer
Dim temp As Double

On Error GoTo FAILED
    gap = N / 2
    While (gap > 0)
        For i = gap To N - 1
            j = i - gap
            Do While ((j >= 0))
                If ddata(j) < ddata(j + gap) Then Exit Do
                temp = ddata(j)
                ddata(j) = ddata(j + gap)
                ddata(j + gap) = temp
                j = j - gap
            Loop
        Next
        gap = gap / 2
    Wend
    SHELSORT = 1
    Exit Function
FAILED:
    SHELSORT = -1
    Exit Function

End Function
```

Table 15-2 shows the time it took on a 386SX system to sort an array of 1,000, 2,000, 5,000 and 8,000 doubles. The second row of the same table shows the corresponding times when the same procedure is implemented in TPW.

As you see, the VB+DLL approach sorts the data significantly faster than VB. The benefits of sorting doubles in Pascal make this DLL attractive for sorting large arrays of doubles, especially on not-so-fast systems. This same ratio of improvement in speed is maintained even on machines with math coprocessors.

| | | | | |
|---|---|---|---|---|
| Array Size | 1,000 | 2,000 | 5000 | 8,000 |
| Visual Basic | 11 | 23 | 71 | 135 |
| DLL | 6 | 13 | 48 | 74 |

Table 15-2: Sorting arrays of doubles with pure Visual Basic vs. employing a DLL on a 386SX system. Times are given in seconds.

The ShelSort Function wants an integer argument that specifies the number of elements to be sorted. There is also an implied argument, the name of the array to be sorted. In VB, the name of the array—ddata( )—is used in the function without declaration because it is a global variable. But when we convert this procedure to Pascal, we must pass the name of the array as an argument.

Being able to pass arrays between VB and DLL functions allows you to process large quantities of data with fast DLL functions.

To test the procedure, you can write a simple application that assigns random values to the elements of the array *ddata* and then calls the procedure. The array must be declared as a global variable, and its dimension should be determined by the needs of your application. (Notice that you may choose to sort only a section of the array, by making *N* smaller than the array's declared dimension. It is best, however, to redimension the array according to the number of elements you wish to sort.) The only requirement here is that you make sure the Pascal Function doesn't try to access any nonexistent elements. To do this, use VB's UBound Function before you call the Pascal TPWShelSort( ). Ubound tells you the number of elements in any array. Also, the Pascal procedure is designed to sort an array no larger than 8,000 elements.

To create the new DLL, start a new project in TPW, type the following lines and save the file under the name SHELSORT.PAS:

```
library SHELSORT;

TYPE
arraydbl=array[0 .. 8000] of double;

Function TPWShelSort(var b:arraydbl;n:integer):integer;export;
var gap,i,j: integer;
var temp:double;

begin
    gap:=n DIV 2;
    while (gap>0) do
    begin
```

```
            for i:=gap to n-1 do
            begin
                j:=i-gap;
                while ((j>=0) AND (b[j]>b[j+gap])) do
                    begin
                        temp:=b[j]; b[j]:=b[j+gap]; b[j+gap]:=temp;
                        j:=j-gap;
                    end;
                end;
            gap:=gap DIV 2;
        end;
        TPWShelSort:=1;
    end;

    exports
        TPWShelSort index 1;
    begin

    end.
```

As you can guess, you could cut the original VB code, paste it into the Delphi editor and then merely change a little punctuation. There's not much difference at all between these languages. Of course, Pascal has a touch of the petty bureaucrat: Unlike VB, Pascal *requires* that you declare all variables. Those who prefer not to declare variables might feel as if you are going through customs inspection when writing in Pascal.

## Declaring Arrays in Pascal

Notice that the array of doubles is declared as a new TYPE, (TYPE arraydbl=array[0 .. 8000] of double;), and in the procedure declaration we use a variable of the same type:

```
Function TPWShelSort(var b:arraydbl; n:integer):integer;→
export;
```

Pascal's TYPE keyword is functionally no different than the equivalent VB keyword. They differ only in syntax.

```
var i,j,k:integer;
var index1, index2:integer;
var t: arraydbl;
var Temp:double;

begin
```

Figure 15-6: Pascal requires the "Var" in a variable declaration.

The first major difference between the VB and Pascal versions of this Function is the Pascal keyword Var in the declaration of the arguments. The reason is that the array will not be passed to the procedure by value. The keyword Var simply tells the compiler that the first argument of the Function is an array of doubles, and that the Function should use the array passed to it by the calling procedure as if it were a local array. In other words, it shouldn't create a new array.

Pascal's data structures, like arrays, can't exceed the 64k boundary.

Why did we declare an array of 8,000 elements? We could define a different size array; it simply must be large enough to hold the data passed from VB. The maximum size of any data structure in Pascal cannot exceed 64k, which means 64k/8 bytes = 8k double reals, or 64k/4 bytes = 16k long integers, or 64k/2 bytes = 32k integers. Since 64k isn't much memory to use up, you should declare an array of the maximum number of elements (8k double reals, for example). Calling this procedure with a smaller VB array than we declared in the Pascal Function causes no problems, since our function will not attempt to access any elements beyond the array's actual size.

However, a serious problem will arise if you try to process an array that exceeds this limit. If you pass to the TPWShelSort procedure an array of 20,000 doubles, your application will crash. To avoid this, make sure the second argument (*b*, in our example) is always less than 8,000.

What if we wanted to preserve the original, unsorted array? Could we pass the array by value? The answer is no, because Functions cannot return arrays. Even if you could pass the array by value, the procedure could not return its results. If you have to preserve the original data, you must make a copy of the array in VB before calling the DLL.

Next we declare the local variables, and the body of the procedure starts with the first Begin keyword. The body of our DLL barely differs from the body of the VB Function. A Pascal array is no different than a VB array. The VB notation A(4) is translated in Pascal to

A[4]. In both cases we have data of the same type stored in sequential memory locations, and the name of the array is the address of the first element. So the only thing you have to worry about is the differing punctuation—changing VB's parentheses to Pascal's brackets.

Now create the DLL with the Compile command. The DLL file will be created in the same subdirectory where the source file was saved. To be able to use it, you must move it either to the subdirectory with your Visual Basic application or to the WINDOWS\SYSTEM subdirectory. Most people place the DLLs in the WINDOWS\SYSTEM subdirectory so that applications will locate them no matter what the application path. When more than one application is using the same DLL, it makes sense to place it in the SYSTEM subdirectory so that you will not have to copy it into the subdirectory for each application that uses it. (If you want to put DLLs in a separate directory, yet have them available to all applications, just add the directory to your PATH setting in AUTOEXEC.BAT.)

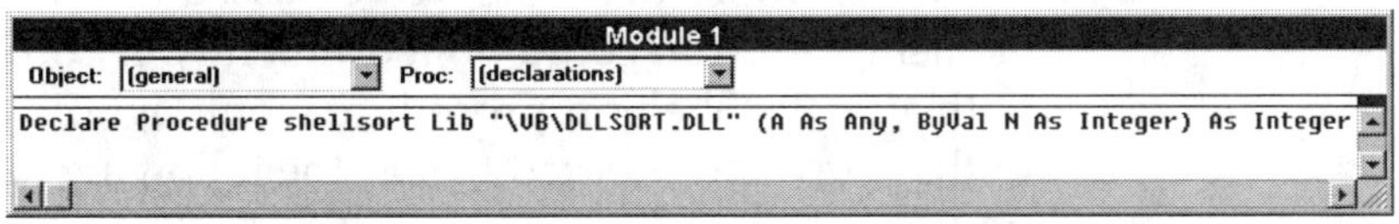


Figure 15-7: If you put your declaration of the Pascal DLL Function in a Module, any Form in your program can access it.

## Passing Arrays as Arguments From VB

Now let's fire it up and test it. Recall that to be able to use the new DLL Function in our VB application, we must first declare it. If you don't have a Module in your VB program (only Forms), press Alt+F, M. All Global declarations must be put into a Module. Type this into the General Declarations section of your Module. It must all be on a *single line*:

```
Declare Procedure TPWShelsort Lib "SHELSORT.DLL" (A As→
Any, ByVal N As Integer) As Integer
```

*As Any* means that you, the programmer, must make sure that the data you pass to the function match the data expected by the function.

Note the phrase *As Any*. The main difference between passing simple individual variables and array variables is that arrays need not be declared as a particular *type* in the DLL procedure's argument list. (A single variable would be declared As Integer or As String, and so on). Instead, for an array we can use the keyword Any, which removes any constraint on the type of the data. *Any* means any data type, and Visual Basic simply passes the data to the procedure without checking its type. This relaxation, however, makes the programmer responsible for passing the proper type of variables for the corresponding DLL procedure.

## Test-Driving the Sorting Function

We have declared the function TPWShelSort and compiled it as a DLL. It's on disk, waiting to be called upon from within VB. Here's what you'd do to make use of this DLL Function from within VB, assuming you already have an array named a( ) filled with 400 double-precision floating-point numbers:

```
N = 400
a% = TPWShelSort(a(0), N)
```

N is the number of elements in the array. It can also be the number of elements within a larger array that you are interested in sorting at this time. Notice that here we've passed the array by means of its first element, a(0). You could do it differently. If you called TPWShelSort with a(5), the ShelSort procedure would ignore the first five elements of the array and proceed to sort the following N elements, working up from element 5.

One point worth repeating is that array indices start at zero by default. The first element of an array is always item zero. For example, if you declare an array such as Dim a(5 To 10) As Double, VB doesn't waste any memory to store the nonexistent elements (0 To 4). It simply adjusts the indices so that when your code asks for element a(5), VB retrieves the very first element of the array. This same approach is used in Pascal. In the examples, we've included the VB statement *Option Base 0* to simplify things. You can modify the examples to use any other indexing scheme, but is it worth it? For straightforward math calculations like those in our examples, strange indexing would be both perplexing and of dubious value.

CD-ROM

In the 15\APPS\SHELSORT subdirectory of the CD you will find an application called SHELSORT. This application sorts an array with both the VB and the Pascal implementations of the ShelSort algorithm, and displays the time required in each case. The Form of the application is shown in Figure 15-8. Use the scroll bar to define the number of elements in the array (up to 8,000 elements). The array's elements are assigned random numbers every time the user clicks on the SORT Button. Then the array is sorted, first by ShelSort( ) and then by TPWShelSort( ), and the results are displayed.

Even on very fast machines, the TPW DLL will make a difference in your program's speed.

If you run this application on a 486/66 system, the times will drop down to just a few seconds. An array with 100 elements can be sorted in less than a second, even with Visual Basic. But an array of 8,000 elements will be sorted nearly two times as fast with the TPWShelSort( ) Function (2.5 seconds vs. 5 seconds). Notice that most of the delay you experience with SHELSORT originates in loading the array's elements with random numbers, and not sorting the data. This time, however, is not included in the timing of the two routines.

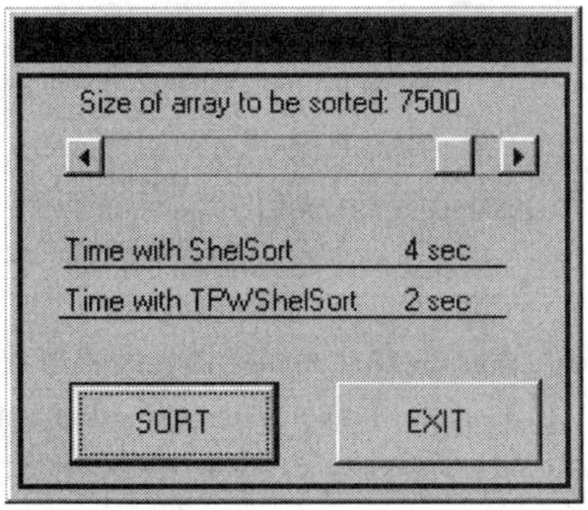


Figure 15-8: The SHELSORT program lets you compare the time to sort the same array with the ShelSort algorithm in plain VB and with the help of a DLL.

Here is the code behind the SORT Command Button. Notice that most lines deal with keeping track of time. The actual sorting is handled by a single line.

```
Sub Command1_Click ( )
Dim i As Integer

    totElements% = HScroll1.Value
    For i = 0 To totElements% - 1
        ddata(i) = Rnd(2) * 1000
        b(i) = ddata(i)   ' keep copy for TPWShelSort
    Next

    Screen.MousePointer = 11

    T1# = GetCurrentTime( )
    success% = shelsort(totElements%)
    T2# = GetCurrentTime( )

    srtTime# = (T2# - T1#) / 1000
    If success% Then
```

```
            Label4.Caption = Format(srtTime#, "0.000") & " sec"
        Else
            MsgBox "Sorting algorithm failed..."
        End If

        T1# = GetCurrentTime( )
        success% = TPWShelSort(b(0), totElements%)
        T2# = GetCurrentTime( )

        srtTime# = (T2# - T1#) / 1000
        If success% Then
            Label5.Caption = Format(srtTime#, "0.000") & " sec"
        Else
            MsgBox "Sorting algorithm failed..."
        End If

        Screen.MousePointer = 0

    End Sub
```

If you have an eye for detail, you have probably noticed that the lines of the ShelSort( ) and TPWShelSort( ) Functions are not identical. The Visual Basic ShelSort( ) Function contains an extra statement, which makes the time comparisons not quite fair. In the Pascal program we use the line:

```
while ((j>=0) AND (b[j]>b[j+gap])) do
```

But in Visual Basic we use the lines:

```
Do While j >= 0
    If a(j) < a(j + gap) Then Exit Do
```

Why didn't we use a line like the following in the VB program?

```
While ( j >= 0 and a(j) > a(j + gap))
```

The reason is that we want this loop to execute if *both* conditions are True: Both (j >= 0) and ( a(j) > a(j+gap) ). Visual Basic will evaluate both conditions, and then it will execute the loop if they are both True. However, because j may become negative, VB will eventually attempt to access an array element with a negative index and stop with an error message.

The Pascal compiler handles this situation somewhat differently. As soon as it discovers that j is negative, it exits the loop. It really doesn't make any difference whether the second condition is True or not. As soon as the first condition fails the test, then we know that there is no way they can be both True, and therefore it doesn't make sense to evaluate the second condition— it can't alter the result. This is called evaluation "short-circuit" and can be very important in programs that iterate a lot.

By the way, this is an illustration of the superiority of compiled, versus interpreted, languages. The Delphi (or Turbo Pascal) compiler has the time to search for expressions that can be short-circuited (or other areas of the code that can be optimized) because this takes place during compilation, not at run time. An interpreted language, however, can't afford to completely optimize the code at run time.

## HIGHER DIMENSIONS

The rest of this chapter is for the truly adventurous. We'll show you how to put more than one Function into a single DLL and how to pass arrays of multiple dimensions to a DLL.

What if we wanted to process an array that was two- or three-dimensional? As you doubtless know, arrays need not be a simple row of cells. For example, Arrayname (10) has 10 elements, ordered one next to the other in a single row. They can also be two-dimensional, like a crossword puzzle or a honeycomb: Arrayname (10,20) has ten rows, each made up of 20 cells (a total of 200 elements). Or they can even be given additional dimensions like stacked honeycombs, as in Arrayname (10, 20, 30). This array is equivalent to 30 of the previous arrays, one on top of the other (a total of 6,000 elements).

It is possible to pass arrays with multiple dimensions between VB and Pascal DLLs.

It is possible to pass arrays of higher dimensions between Visual Basic and Pascal. However, the two references to the array (the one we declare in our application and the one in the DLL procedure) must be declared the same, or their elements will not match. In other words, you cannot declare a simple one-dimensional array in your Pascal procedure and pass a two-dimensional array to it from VB. This would result in a havoc of information. All elements would be there, but Turbo Pascal wouldn't know their structure.

But what if you want your DLL to be multipurpose, to be flexible enough to service arrays of different dimensions? Must we change the declaration of the array in our DLL and recompile it if we want to pass it an array of different dimensions?

### Faking Multidimensional Arrays

There is a way around this problem. *Array elements are stored in sequential memory locations.* A two-dimensional array is made up of rows and columns. The elements of the first row are stored in sequential memory locations, starting with the first element of the row, then the second element, and so on. After the last element of the first row, you'll find the first element of the second row and so on, up to the last element of the array. When you declare a two-dimensional array, you define the rows and columns like this:

```
Dim Arrayname (rows, columns) As Double
```

So to access, for example, the element on the fourth row, fifth column, you would say: Print Arrayname (3,4) (assuming that indexing starts at zero).

Remember that the idea of "dimensions" is a convenience for us humans—a way to visualize the shape and features of an array, or the information stored in it. We could store the words of a crossword puzzle in a one-dimensional array, but it helps us visualize our data more easily if they are stored in a two-dimensional array. The computer doesn't know anything about dimensions. All it knows is the location of the first element of the array.

Multidimensional arrays were designed for the programmer's convenience and not for the language.

Suppose we ask Visual Basic to give us the data in element A(3,5) of an array that was declared with the statement Dim A(10,10) As Double. VB would go down to the 280th byte from the first item in the array. VB calculates the distance (offset) of the desired element from the first element in this array. VB then tells the computer to read this memory location. In our example, VB would determine the offset for the element A(3,5) like this: 3*10+5=35 elements. Because each element is a *double* variable, and it takes 8 bytes to store each double, the computer will read the number stored 35*8 (or 280) bytes away from the address of the array's first element.

If you've followed this, you can see that however we visualize an array, VB and the computer ultimately relate to it as if it were a long, segmented tapeworm. To VB, an array, of however many dimensions, is always just a list that starts somewhere in memory and proceeds in a linear way up into memory as far as necessary.

We can imitate VB's way of thinking: we can access an array of two or more dimensions as if it were one-dimensional. To do so, we must convert the two indices to a single offset. Here's how an array looks when stored in computer memory. This one is declared with the command Dim Arrayname (1,2):

```
Memory Addresses ——>
[0,0] [0,1] [0,2] [1,0] [1,1] [1,2]
```

An array with a different indexing scheme would also be stored in this linear fashion, but the indexes would refer to different locations.

**Memory addresses⟶**

[0,0] [0,1] [0,2] [0,3] [1,0] [1,1] [1,2] [1,3] [2,0] [2,1] [2,2] [2,3] [3,0] [3,1] [3,2] [3,3]

[0,0] [0,1] [0,2] [0,3] [0,4] [0,5] [0,6] [0,7] [1,0] [1,1] [1,2] [1,3] [1,4] [1,5] [1,6] [1,7]

↑

**index of element [2, 3] = 2 * 4 + 3 = 11**

**index of element [1, 3] = 1 * 8 + 3 = 11**

Figure 15-9: The elements of multidimensional arrays are stored in consecutive memory locations and can be accessed in more than one way. The array on top here has dimensions 4 X 4; the bottom array has dimensions 8 X 2.

Therefore, we can declare a two-dimensional array in VB and a one-dimensional array in our DLL procedure. The element (i, j) in the VB array is the element with index i*D+j in the one-dimensional array. *D* is the number of elements per row of the array, the "rows" in the declaration: Dim Arrayname (rows, columns).

This simple technique will allow us to use a one-dimensional array in our DLL Function, which can nevertheless accommodate any two-dimensional array we pass to the DLL from our VB application. Of course, our DLL must accept two additional arguments: the dimensions of the array being passed. This same technique can also be extended for arrays of three, four or more dimensions.

## Example: Adding & Subtracting Arrays

The MatrixAdd and MatrixSubtract Functions listed next accept two arrays, a and b, and their dimensions, N1 (number of rows) and N2 (number of columns). Then the Functions replace the elements of the first array with the sum and differences of the corresponding elements of the two arrays. Of course, these operations are meaningful only if the two arrays to be operated upon have the same dimensions.

The MATRIX DLL can serve as the starting point for writing a general matrix manipulation DLL in Pascal.

The main purpose of this example is to show how to pass various multidimensional arrays to a one-dimensional DLL. The example also illustrates how to create a DLL that contains more than one Function.

To be blunt about it, writing a Pascal DLL to add or subtract two arrays is not actually useful. VB can execute these operations just as quickly as can a compiled Pascal DLL. A matrix *inversion* (division) Function would demonstrate a speed improvement. However, we want to keep the programming simple in this example. Our point is to demonstrate passing multidimensional arrays between VB and Pascal, and how to make a DLL that contains more than one Function. (If you can write a matrix inversion Function in Visual Basic, you can certainly convert it to Pascal without our help.)

Once again, we will start with the Visual Basic implementation of the algorithm. At first, dimension two arrays of doubles with the statement:

```
Dim a(20, 20) As Double, b(20, 20) As Double
```

Then enter the following code in a Subroutine:

```
Sub ArrayAdd(N1 As Integer, N2 As Integer)
' Adds two arrays. They must have dimensions (N1 X N2)
For i = 0 To N1 - 1
    For j = 0 To N2 - 1
        a(i, j) = a(i, j) + b(i, j)
    Next
Next

End Sub
```

And enter this code in another Subroutine:

```
Sub ArraysSubtract(N1 As Integer, N2 As Integer)
' Subtracts two arrays. They must have dimensions (N1 X N2)
For i = 0 To N1 - 1
    For j = 0 To N2 - 1
        a(i, j) = a(i, j) - b(i, j)
    Next
Next

End Sub
```

These Subroutines add (or subtract) the equivalent array elements, and the result is stored in the first array a( ).

Here are the equivalent functions in Turbo Pascal (create a new project and call it MATRIX.PAS, and then enter the following lines):

```
Library MATRIX;

TYPE
 arraydbl=array[0..8000] of double;

Function TPWArrayAdd(var a1 : arraydbl; var a2 : arraydbl;→
D1, D2:integer):integer; export;
var i,j, N:integer;

begin
    for i:=0 to D1-1 do
    begin
        for j:=0 to D2-1 do
        begin
            N:=i*D1+j;
            a1[N]:=a1[N]+a2[N];
        end;
    end;
    TPWArrayAdd:=1;
end;
Function TPWArraySubtract(var a1: arraydbl; var a2: arraydbl;→
D1, D2:integer):integer; export;
var i,j, N:integer;

begin
    for i:=0 to D1-1 do
    begin
        for j:=0 to D2-1 do
        begin
            N:=i*D1+j;
            a1[N]:=a1[N]-a2[N];
        end;
    end;
    TPWArraySubtract:=1;

end;

exports
    arrayadd        index 1,
    arraysubtract   index 2;
begin

end.
```

Compile the project to create the MATRIX.DLL file and copy it either to the subdirectory with your VB application or to the Windows\System subdirectory, as we explained above.

Then, into the general declarations section of a VB Module, type these two declarations. Be sure that each declaration is typed *on a single line* (no carriage return until you've finished typing the ending *As Integer*):

```
Declare Procedure MatrixAdd Lib "MATRIX.DLL" (A As Any, B→
As Any, ByVal N1 As Integer, ByVal N2 As Integer) As Integer
Declare Procedure MatrixSubtract Lib "MATRIX.DLL" (A As→
Any, B As Any, ByVal N1 As Integer, ByVal N2 As Integer) As
Integer
```

When you pass multidimensional arrays as arguments, you must also supply their dimensions.

To call them from your VB application, pass the arrays by means of their first element:

```
a% = MatrixAdd( Data1(0, 0), Data2(0, 0), N1, N2)
```

Above, N1 and N2 are the dimensions of the arrays used in their declarations. Here is how you can make use of the TPWArrayAdd( ) and TPWArraySubtract( ) Functions in your VB projects:

First, dimension the arrays in the Declarations Section of the Form or a Module:

```
Dim a(10, 10) As Double, b(10, 10) As Double
```

Then, assign values to their elements and add or subtract them as follows:

```
Dim N1 As Integer
N1 = 10
Dim N2 As Integer
N2 = 10

r% = TPWArrayAdd(a(0, 0), b(0, 0), N1, N2)
```

The result will returned in the array a( ). In general, you must always check the return value, r%, to make sure the operation has been completed successfully. (The TPWArrayAdd( ) Function returns no error codes, but most functions should.)

When using DLLs, always check the return code of the function.

The file MATRIX.PAS has the same structure as the previous examples of Pascal files in this chapter, except that it contains two procedures, and their names appear in the exports list. The procedures themselves are straightforward and not really more complicated than the equivalent VB procedures. You can use this file as your starting point for developing a DLL that can perform all matrix operations.

The MATRIX application (subdirectory 15\APPS\MATRIX of the CD) shows how to use the MATRIX DLL. It adds, or subtracts, two square (50 X 50) matrices using the TPWArrayAdd( ) and TPWArraySubtract( ) Functions. Its main Form is shown in Figure 15-10. Only the first few rows and columns of the matrices are displayed on the screen so that you can verify the results. Load the MATRIX project in VB's editor to look at the declarations of the functions and the way they are called.

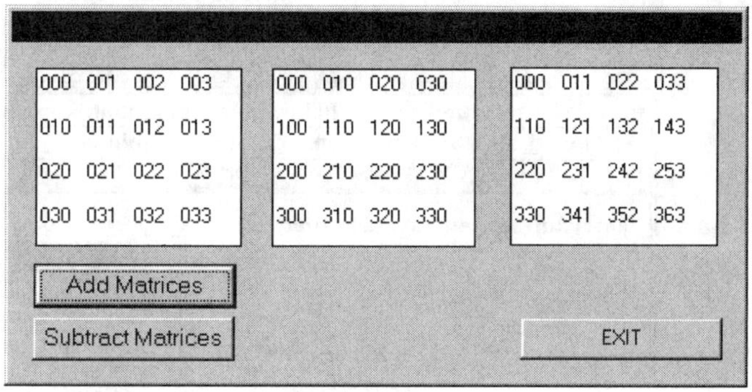


Figure 15-10: The MATRIX program uses two DLL functions to add and subtract matrices.

## A Few Words of Caution

Here are a few cautionary notes to consider when you create DLLs. First, always save your project before you run it. The arguments are passed through the stack. The stack is an extremely important mechanism. If it gets fouled up, this will not only destabilize your application, it may derange Windows itself. (In Chapter 12, "Recursive Programming," we discuss the role of the stack in detail.)

If there is a mismatch between the arguments your application passes to the DLL and the arguments the DLL expects, then the DLL procedure may attempt to access data that don't belong to it. Windows will detect this condition, but can't do anything about it. You will simply be informed that your application has caused a memory violation, and your application will be closed. A memory violation error is almost sure to result if you try to access nonexistent array elements. You will experience the same error if you pass an argument by value when the DLL expects it to be passed by reference.

Visual Basic will check your arguments before using an external procedure, to make sure they are used as declared in the procedure declaration. This is a great help, but keep in mind that Visual Basic has no way of knowing for sure what the arguments of the DLL procedure really are. It simply takes for granted that you meant what you said when you typed in the procedure's declaration. VB simply checks the actual arguments against the original declaration.

When calling DLL procedures, VB tests the actual arguments against the function declarations, but it doesn't know how the arguments were defined in the DLL itself.

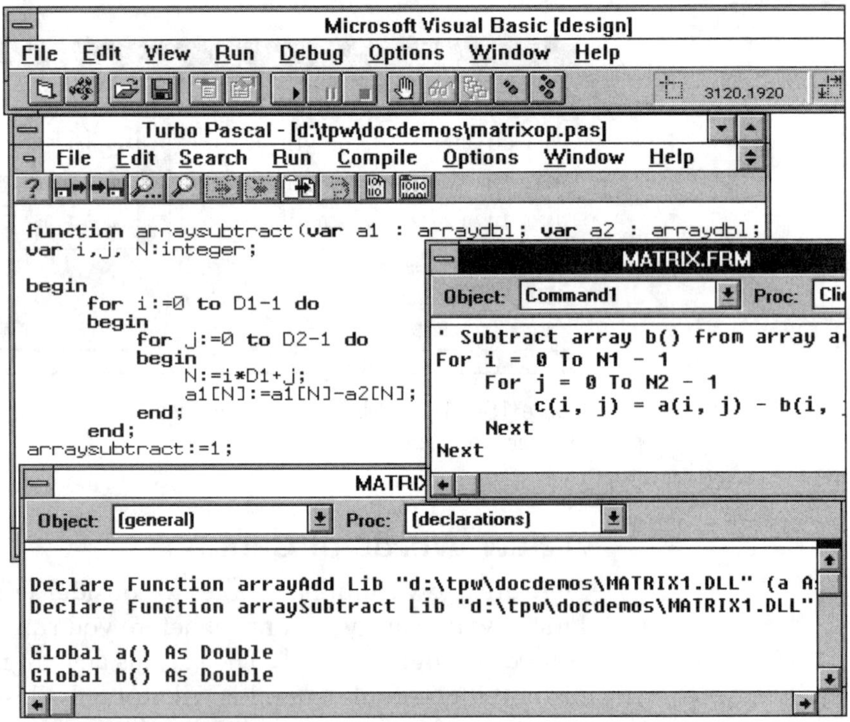


Figure 15-11: It's convenient to have both Turbo Pascal and Visual Basic open at the same time, and move back and forth between them.

You might find it very convenient to open both the Visual Basic and Delphi (or TPW) windows at the same time, and go back and forth. However, this practice requires that you ensure that your VB program is accessing the most recently compiled DLL. Every time your VB application needs a DLL procedure, it loads the appropriate

DLL in memory, and it does not unload it unless it needs that memory. So if you simply stop your VB application, switch to TPW to make a change and then rebuild (compile) the DLL, *you could still be contacting the old DLL when you return to test your VB project*. Make sure you *Restart* your VB project (not simply *Continue* to run it from a "break"). Even Restarting doesn't always force VB to reload the DLL in memory. If you want to be completely sure things are up-to-date, close Visual Basic itself, and start it again.

## Why Learn Pascal?

As you've seen, the techniques we've discussed in this chapter do not require knowledge of Delphi or Turbo Pascal for Windows. Implementing a function in Pascal is not difficult, because it is so easy to convert a Visual Basic function (or subroutine) into a Pascal function.

Pascal is an easy language, especially if you're just translating a few simple Functions into it. And once you have learned the basic argument-passing mechanisms, you can consult the many books on Turbo Pascal that contain Functions that are already written for you.

Are we implying that you can make use of a language without mastering it? How many users can claim that they have mastered all the capabilities of Word for Windows, or Excel? Yet they use it and get what they want from it.

Combine the best features of each language to create your own mixed-language environment.

The real advantage of this approach is that you need not learn the Windows interface from another language's point of view. You can still use Visual Basic's unequalled efficiency to design elaborate Forms and implement all Windows operations in VB, your favorite environment. Then, if an application would benefit from a little turbo-charging, locate the place in your VB program that's retarding execution a bit too much, and make a DLL with Turbo Pascal to speed things up. And this was demonstrated best in our FRACTAL.DLL, which contains Finctions for calculating the Mandelbrot and Julia Sets.

## MOVING ON

In Chapter 16 we are going to tackle an interesting and practical topic: encryption. People have tried to disguise information for thousands of years. Sometimes it's a matter of protecting financial or proprietary business data. Other times, it's a matter of life and death. However, computers have fundamentally changed the way cryptography is practiced today.

Cryptology is divided into two disciplines: *cryptanalysis* (breaking a coded message and translating it back into the original) and *cryptography* (distorting a message into a code). In the next chapter we'll explore both of these techniques. We'll also look at an encryption algorithm written in VB that we believe is secure enough to safeguard your messages against most hackers. And we'll give you a chance to win $1,000 by cracking the coded message found at the end of Chapter 16, according to the contest rules also provided there.

# Chapter 16

# Encryption

Chapter 16 has been deleted from the international edition of the *Visual Basic 4.0 Power Toolkit* in accordance with United States law.

# Appendix A

# About the Online Companion

The *Visual Basic Online Companion* is your one-stop location for Visual Basic resources on the Internet. It serves as an informative tool as well as an annotated software library aiding in your exploration of the Visual Basic programming environment.

The online companion links you to available Visual Basic newsgroups, Web pages and e-mail discussion groups. So you can just click on the reference name and jump directly to the resource you are interested in.

Perhaps one of the most valuable features of the online companion is its Software Archive. Here, you'll find and be able to download the lastest demos, coding examples and valuable utilities that are freely available on the Internet.

The online companion also links you to the Ventana Library, where you'll find useful press and jacket information on a variety of Ventana Press offerings. Plus, you have access to a wide selection of exciting new releases and coming attractions. And Ventana's Online Library lets you order the books you want.

The *Visual Basic Online Companion* represents Ventana Online's ongoing commitment to offering the most dynamic and exciting products possible. And soon Ventana Online will be adding more services, including more multimedia supplements, searchable indexes and sections of the book reproduced and hyperlinked to the Internet resources they reference.

To access, connect via the World Wide Web to **http://www.vmedia.com/vbasic.html**

# Appendix B

# About the Companion CD-ROM

We wrote this book with the goal of taking Visual Basic to the edge, to show how the VB programmer can do anything, can accomplish incomparable feats in record time, and above all, to make things clear and understandable. Bundled on the CD are all the information, tools, samples and demos we could think of or get permission to include that you would need to unlock the most advanced capabilities of Visual Basic and Windows.

## INSTALLING THE CD-ROM

1. **In Windows 95,** place the CD-ROM into the appropriate drive. Click Start. Choose Run and click OK. Be sure to verify the drive selection in the Run program window.

   **In Windows 3.1,** place the CD-ROM into the appropriate drive. In the Program Manager window, select File/Run.
2. Type **D:\SETUP** (where D: is your CD-ROM drive) in the Command Line box and press Enter. The setup routine will create a program item called Visual Basic 4.0 Power Toolkit.
3. Double-click the Visual Basic 4.0 Power Toolkit program item.
4. From the menu screen that appears, click on the appropriate items to explore the CD-ROM. For a summary description of the CD's contents, click Overview.

## USING THE CD-ROM

To make the best use of the CD, look at the corresponding chapter for additional instructions before running its applications and example programs. Each chapter's applications are stored in the subdirectory *X*\APPS, where *X* is the chapter number (for example, 6\APPS contains the applications and examples of Chapter 6).

Each APPS subdirectory has two subdirectories, VB3 and VB4, where the two versions of the applications are stored. Chapter 6, for example, has three applications called IMGSHOW, PALET256 and VBIMAGE:

- ❒ VB3 users will find them in the subdirectories 6\APPS\VB3\IMGSHOW, 6\APPS\VB3\PALET256 and 6\APPS\VB3\VBIMAGE.
- ❒ VB4 users will find the VB4 versions of the same applications in the following subdirectories: 6\APPS\VB4\IMGSHOW, 6\APPS\VB4\PALET256 and 6\APPS\VB4\VBIMAGE.
- ❒ In the chapter's text, we refer to the location of the VBImage application as 6\APPS\VBIMAGE. Depending on the version of Visual Basic you are using, you should open the project in the VB3 or VB4 subdirectory.

Also be sure to copy the necessary files from the CD to your hard drive. For example, copy the DLLs for examples in Chapter 15 from subdirectory 15\APPS on the CD to your WINDOWS\SYSTEM directory (or otherwise locate them in your path).

Files copied from the CD on the hard disk will have their read-only and archive attributes set, since they came from a read-only medium. To be able to modify and save on disk any of the book's projects, you must first clear the read-only attribute of the files making up each project, as follows:

1. Start the Windows 3.1 File Manager, or the Windows 95 Explorer.
2. Select the files and look at their Properties. If you are using Windows 3.1, select the files, then select the File/Properties command from the main menu. If you are using Windows 95, right-click on the file's icon and, from the popup menu, select Properties. If the read-only box is marked, clear it by clicking on it with the mouse.

## LICENSE, DISCLAIMER & LIMITATION OF LIABILITY

The *Visual Basic 4.0 Power Toolkit* CD-ROM is offered without support other than the ReadMe file on the CD-ROM and the information in the *Visual Basic 4.0 Power Toolkit* book. The publisher and authors assume no responsibility for the suitability of the files and programs contained on the disk. Programs on the disk are intended only for your personal use and may not be duplicated or used for resale.



Thank you for your purchase of the *Visual Basic 4.0 Power Toolkit.* The files on the CD-ROM will save you hours of time typing the programs found in the book.

## HOW DO I GET IN TOUCH WITH VENTANA?

Ventana Communications Group, Inc. and the authors welcome your comments and questions about the *Visual Basic 4.0 Power Toolkit* (or any of our other books). If you'd like to contact Ventana, use your pen or pencil, phone or fax to reach us at:

Managing Editor
Ventana Communications Group, Inc.
PO Box 13964
Research Triangle Park, NC 27709-3964
Fax: (919) 544-9472

Technical Support is available for installation-related problems only. Phone (919) 544-9404, extension 81, or via the Internet at help@vmedia.com. Fax back service is also available by dialing (919) 544-9404, extension 2000.

# Index

## A

# B



# C

# D

# E

# F



# G

# H



# I

## J



## K



## L

# M

## N



## O



## P

# Q

# T

# U



# V

# W

# X



# Z

## The Visual Guide to Visual Basic 4.0 for Windows

*$34.95, 1456 pages, illustrated*

The definitive reference for Visual Basic is completely revised for Visual Basic 4.0—packed with useful, easy-to-understand examples, more than 600 illustrations and thorough explanations of every Visual Basic command and feature.

## The Visual Guide to Visual C++

*$29.95, 888 pages, illustrated*

A uniquely visual reference for Microsoft's next-generation programming language. Written for both new and experienced programmers, it features a complete overview of tools and features in each class of the "Visual C++ Foundation Class Library"—including names and prototypes, descriptions, parameters, return values, notes and examples. Ideal for day-to-day reference! The companion disk contains code examples, including programs and subroutines from the book.

## The Visual Guide to Paradox for Windows

*$29.95, 692 pages, illustrated*

A pictorial approach to Paradox! Hundreds of examples and illustrations show how to achieve complex database development with simple drag-and-drop techniques. Users learn how to access and modify database files, use Form and Report Designers and Experts, program with ObjectPAL and more—all with icons, buttons, graphics and OLE. The companion disk contains sample macros, forms, reports, tables, queries and a ready-to-use database.

**Books marked with this logo include a free Internet *Online Companion*™, featuring archives of free utilities plus a software archive and links to other Internet resources.**